HANDBOOK
of
NEW MEDIA

HANDBOOK
of
NEW MEDIA

Social Shaping
and Consequences of ICTs

Edited by
LEAH A. LIEVROUW
and SONIA LIVINGSTONE

SAGE Publications
London • Thousand Oaks • New Delhi

General Introduction © Leah A. Lieverouw and Sonia Livingstone, 2002
Part One Introduction © Sonia Livingstone, 2002
Chapter 1 © Frank Webster, 2002
Chapter 2 © Nicholas W. Jankowski, 2002
Chapter 3 © Sara Bentivegna, 2002
Chapter 4 © Nancy K. Baym, 2002
Chapter 5 © David Buckingham, 2002
Chapter 6 © Douglas Kellner, 2002
Chapter 7 © Ronald E. Rice, 2002
Part Two Introduction © Leah A. Lieverouw, 2002
Chapter 8 © Patrice Flichy, 2002
Chapter 9 © Susan Leigh Star and Geoffrey C. Bowker, 2002
Chapter 10 © Sally J. McMillan, 2002
Chapter 11 © Leah A. Lieverouw, 2002
Part Three Introduction © Noshir S. Contractor, 2002
Chapter 12 © Kathleen M. Carley, 2002
Chapter 13 © Andrea B. Hollingshead and Noshir S. Contractor, 2002
Chapter 14 © Michèle H. Jackson, Marshall Scott Poole and Tim Kukn, 2002
Chapter 15 © Fançois Bar with Caroline Simard, 2002

Part Four Introduction © John Ure, 2002
Chapter 16 © Pablo J. Boczkowski, 2002
Chapter 17 © Philip Cooke, 2002
Chapter 18 © Terry Flew and Stephen McElhinney, 2002
Chapter 19 © Anders Henten and Eric Skouby, 2002
Chapter 20 © Don Lamberton, 2002
Chapter 21 © Peter Lovelock and John Ure, 2002
Chapter 22 © Heather E. Hudson, 2002
Part Five Introduction © Bella Mooy, Harry Trebing and Laura Stein, 2002
Chapter 23 © Dwayne Winseck, 2002
Chapter 24 © Laura Stein and Nikhil Sinha, 2002
Chapter 25 © Stefaan G. Verhulst, 2002
Chapter 26 © Oscar H. Grandy, Jr., 2002
Chapter 27 © Gwen Urey, 2002
Part Six Introduction © Mark Poster, 2002
Chapter 28 © Jennifer Daryl Slack and J. Macgregor Wise, 2002
Chapter 29 © Michael R. Curry, 2002
Chapter 30 © Timothy W. Luke, 2002
Chapter 31 © Don Slater, 2002

First published 2002

SAGE Publications Ltd
6 Bonhill Street
London EC2A 4PU

SAGE Publications Inc
2455 Teller Road
Thousand Oaks, California 91320

SAGE Publications India Pvt Ltd
32, M-Block Market
Greater Kailash - I
New Delhi 110 048

British Library Cataloguing in Publication data

A catalogue record for this book is available from the British Library

ISBN 0 7619 6510 6

Library of Congress Control Number available

Typeset by SIVA Math Setters, Chennai, India
Printed in Great Britain by The Cromwell Press Ltd, Trowbridge, Wiltshire

Contents

The Editors

Leah A. Lievrouw is Professor, Department of Information Studies, in the Graduate School of Education and Information Studies at the University of California, Los Angeles. She is also affiliated with UCLA's Communication Studies Program. Her research and writing focus on the social and cultural changes associated with information and communication technologies and the relationship between new technologies and knowledge. Her articles have appeared in *Communication Research, Critical Studies in Mass Communication, The Information Society, International Journal of Technology Management, Journal of the American Society for Information Science, Knowledge: Creation, Diffusion, Utilization, Knowledge in Society,* and *Telecommunications Policy,* among other journals. Her books include *Mediation, Information and Communication: Information and Behavior*, vol. 3 (co-edited with Brent Ruben; Transaction, 1990) and *Competing Visions, Complex Realities: Social Aspects of the Information Society* (co-edited with Jorge Reina Schement; Ablex, 1987). She is also co-editor of the journal *New Media & Society* (London: Sage). Professor Lievrouw received a Ph.D. in communication theory and research in 1986 from the Annenberg School for Communication at the University of Southern California. She was formerly a member of the faculties of the Department of Telecommunication and Film at the University of Alabama and the Department of Communication at Rutgers University.

Sonia Livingstone has published widely in the fields of social psychology, mass communication and new media research, focusing on audiences' interpretative engagement with different media forms and genres and, more recently, the social contexts for the use of new information and communication technologies. She is author of *Making Sense of Television* (2nd edition, Routledge, 1998), *Mass Consumption and Personal Identity* (with Peter Lunt; Open University, 1992), *Talk on Television* (with Peter Lunt; Routledge, 1994), and *Young People and New Media* (Sage, forthcoming), and co-editor of *Children and their Changing Media Environment* (with Moira Bovill; Lawrence Erlbaum Associates, 2001). She has held visiting professor positions at the Universities of Copenhagen, Stockholm, and Illinois at Urbana-Champaign, and is on the editorial board of several leading journals in the field, including *New Media & Society, The Communication Review, Journal of Communication, Journal of Broadcasting and Electronic Media* and *European Journal of Communication*. Her current research concerns children's use of the internet at home and school. Professor Livingstone is Head of the Social Psychology Department and a member of media@lse, an interdepartmental graduate programme at the London School of Economics and Political Science.

The Contributors

François Bar is Assistant Professor in Stanford University's Department of Communication. He served as Director of Network Research at the Stanford Computer Industry Project (SCIP) and is a member of the Berkeley Roundtable on the International Economy (BRIE), at UC Berkeley. He received his Ph.D. from the UC Berkeley (1990) and holds a Diplôme d'Ingénieur from the École Nationale des Ponts et Chaussées (ENPC), Paris, France. His research interests include comparative telecommunication policy, as well as economic, strategic and social dimensions of computer networking, new media and the Internet. His research has been published in books of collected studies and in journals including *The Information Society, Telecommunication Policy, Infrastructure Economics and Policy, Communications & Strategie*s, *Réseaux*, and the *International Journal of Technology Management*. He serves on the advisory board of Stanford's Science, Technology and Society Program, and has held visiting faculty appointments at the University of Toronto, the University of Paris-XIII, Theseus, and Eurecom.

Nancy K. Baym (PhD Speech Communication, University of Illinois, 1994) is an Assistant Professor of Communication Studies at the University of Kansas, where she teaches communication on the Internet, interpersonal communication, nonverbal communication, and qualitative methods. Her ethnographic research into online community and television fandom appears in the book *Tune In, Log On: Soaps, Fandom, and Online Community* (Sage) and in several articles in journals and edited collections. More recently, she has been studying how the social life that takes place on the Internet is woven into the full fabric of mediated and unmediated interpersonal communication. As Vice President of the Association of Internet Researchers, Baym coordinated that association's first annual conference, 'Internet Research 1.0: The State of the Interdiscipline' in 2000. She serves on the editorial boards of *New Media & Society, The Information Society, Critical Studies in Media Communication*, and *Research on Language and Social Interaction*.

Sara Bentivegna is Professor of Theories of Mass Communication at the University of Rome 'La Sapienza'. Her interests are in the field of political communication, and her recent works are about the relation between politics and the net. Her publications include *Talking Politics on the Net* (1998), published by The Joan Shorenstein Center on the Press, Politics and Public Policy at Harvard University, and *La Politica Nella Rete* (Rome: Meltemi, 1999).

Pablo J. Boczkowski is Assistant Professor of Organization Studies at the Massachusetts Institute of Technology's Sloan School of Management. His research looks at technological and organizational innovation in the new media industry. He holds a PhD in Science and Technology Studies from Cornell University, and was previously Mellon Fellow in the Department of Sociology at Columbia University. His work has appeared in publications such as *Journal of Communication* and *New Media & Society*, and received awards from the American Sociological Association, the International Communication Association, and the Central States Communication Association.

Geoffrey C. Bowker is Professor in the Department of Communication, University from California, San Diego. His PhD is in History and Philosophy of Science at Melbourne University. He studies social and organizational aspects of the development of very large-scale infrastructures. His first book (*Science on the Run*, Cambridge, MA: MIT Press) discussed the development of information practices in the oil industry. He has recently completed with Leigh Star a book on the history and sociology of medical classifications (*Sorting Things Out: Classification and its Concequences* – published by MIT Press in September 1999) and has co-edited a volume on computer support cooperative work (*Social Science, Technical Systems and Cooperative Work: Beyond the Great Divide*, LEA Press, 1997). He is currently working on an NSF funded project to examine the mobility of knowledge in distributed scientific collaborations using high end collaborative software. He is also writing a book entitled *Memory Practices in the Sciences* about archival practices in the sciences over the past 200 years. He is on the steering committee of the University of California Digital Cultures project.

David Buckingham is Professor of Education at the Institute of Education, London University, where he has recently established the Centre for the Study of Children, Youth and Media. He has directed several major research projects on media education, and on children's interactions with television and other electronic media. He is the author, co-author or editor of numerous books, including *Children Talking Television* (Falmer, 1993), *Moving Images* (Manchester University Press, 1996), *The Making of Citizens* (Routledge, 2000) and *After the Death of Childhood* (Polity, 2000). He is currently directing research projects on parents' and children's uses of educational media in the home; young people's interpretations of sexual representations on television; and the uses of digital media by migrant/refugee children across Europe.

Kathleen M. Carley received her PhD from Harvard and is a Professor of Sociology and Organizations at Carnegie Mellon University. Her research spans the areas of computational organization theory, social and organizational adaptation and evolution, social network analysis and evolution, computational text analysis, knowledge management, information security, and the impact of telecommunication technologies on communication, information diffusion, and e-commerce. Her research combines multi-agent models with social networks and cognitive science. She has written over 60 papers and is the co-author of two books using computational models and associated empirical evidence to explore the impact on group and organizational processes of individual learning, interaction, and response to changing conditions such as turnover, mobility, new technology, and discovery. Currently, she directs the center for Computational Analysis of Social and Organizational Systems at CMU, and with Al Wallace is the founding co-editor of the journal *Computational Organization Theory*.

Noshir S. Contractor is Associate Professor of Speech Communication and Psychology at the University of Illinois at Urbana-Champaign. His research interests include applications of systems theories of complexity to communication, the role of emergent networks in organizations, and collaboration technologies in the workplace. He is currently investigating factors that lead to formation, maintenance, and dissolution of dynamically linked knowledge networks in work communities. He is the Principal Investigator on a major three-year grant from the National Science Foundation's Knowledge and Distributed Intelligence Initiative to study the co-evolution of knowledge networks and twenty-first-century organizational forms. Professor Contractor has published or presented over 75 research papers dealing with communication. His papers have received top-paper awards from both the International Communication Association and the National Communication (formerly Speech) Association. In 2000 he was awarded the Outstanding Member Award by the Organizational Communication Division of the International Communication Association. He currently serves on the editorial boards of *Management Communication Quarterly, Journal of Applied Communication Research, Human Communication Research* and the *World Wide Web Electronic Journal of Computer-Mediated Communication*.

Philip Cooke is Professor of Regional Development and Director of the Centre for Advanced Studies at the University of Wales, Cardiff. He specializes in research on innovation systems, industry clustering and the role of venture capital in the knowledge economy. He has produced ten books, the most recent being *Knowledge Economies* (Routledge, 2001), *The Governance of Innovation in Europe* (with P. Boekholt and F. Toedtling, Pinter, 2000) *Regional Innovation Systems* (edited with H. Braczyk and M. Heidenreich, UCL Press, 1998) and *The Associational Economy* (with K. Morgan, Oxford University Press, 1998). In 1999 he was appointed to the UK Minister of Science's Biotechnology Clusters Task Force and in 2000–01 to the UK Department of Trade and Industry's Cluster Policy Steering Group charged with steering investment to new economy clusters such as new media, internet games and biotechnology, and old ones such as ceramics and marine engineering.

Michael R. Curry is a Professor in the Department of Geography at the University of California, Los Angeles. He holds degrees in liberal arts, philosophy, and geography. He is the author of two books, *The Work in the World: Geographical Practice and the Written Word* (Minnesota Press, 1996) and *Digital Places: Living with Geographic Information Technologies* (Routledge, 1998), and a number of articles and book chapters on the history of geographic ideas and their relationship to changes in information and other technologies. His work concerns a set of common claims – that because of technology the world is getting smaller, that places are becoming more and more alike, and that human identity is less and less tied to places, but rather to something else, such as ethnicity, religion, or consumer preference. He is currently working on a book on the history of the interrelationship between the ideas of place and of privacy. In addition, he is working on a number of other projects on the nature of privacy (including a collaborative project on the privacy implications of certain geographical technologies, such as emergency response systems and intelligent transportation systems) and on the history of the ideas of space and place.

Dr Terry Flew is a Senior Lecturer in Media Communication in the Creative Industries Faculty, Queensland University of Technology, Brisbane, Australia. He is the author of *New Media Technologies: An Introduction* (Oxford, 2002 (forthcoming)).

Patrice Flichy is Professor in the Department of Sociology at the University of Marne la Vallée in France, and editor of *Réseaux,* a French journal on communication studies. His research and writing focus on innovation and uses in ICT, in the past and today. His books include *L'imaginaire d'Internet* (La Découverte, Paris, 2001); *Dynamics of Modern Communication. The Shaping and Impact of New Communication Technologies* (Sage, London, 1995). *L'innovation technique* (La Découverte, Paris, 1995); *European Telematics: The Emerging Economy of Words* (co-edited with Paul Beaud and Josiane Jouët, Elsevier, Amsterdam, 1991).

Professor Flichy received a PhD in sociology in 1971 from the University of Paris-I. He also holds a degree in business management from the Ecole des Hautes Etudes Commerciales. He was formerly head of the Laboratory of Sociology of France Telecom Research Development.

Oscar H. Gandy, Jr holds the Herbert I. Schiller Information and Society Term Chair at the Annenberg School for Communication at the University of Pennsylvania. He is author of *The Panoptic Sort* and *Beyond Agenda Setting*, two books that explore issues of information and public policy. His most recent book, *Communication and Race*, explores the structure of media and society, as well as the cognitive structures that reflect and are reproduced through media use. He is a co-editor of *Framing Public Life*, a volume that explores the status of framing theory and research. A book in progress, *If it Weren't for Bad Luck*, explores the ways in which probability and its representation affect the lives of different groups in society. He was awarded the Dallas Smythe Award from the Union for Democratic Communication, and the Wayne Danielson Award from the University of Texas at Austin.

Anders Henten is Associate Professor at the Center for Tele-Information (CTI) at the Technical University of Denmark. He is a graduate in communications and international development studies from Roskilde University in Denmark and holds a PhD from the Technical University of Denmark. His main areas of research are socioeconomic implications of information and communication technologies including e-commerce and business models, internationalization of services, and regulations of communications. He teaches courses in 'e-commerce – markets and business models', 'standardization in telecommunications', and 'regulation of telecommunications'. Anders Henten has worked professionally in the areas of communications economy and policy for more than a decade. He has published nationally and internationally – more than 100 academic publications in international journals, books, anthologies, and conference proceedings.

Andrea B. Hollingshead is Associate Professor of Speech Communication and Psychology at the University of Illinois at Urbana-Champaign. Her research investigates transactive memory, knowledge management, and information processing in groups and organizations. She also studies the impacts of technology and the Internet on the ways that groups communicate, collaborate, and create community. Professor Hollingshead is co-author of *Groups Interacting with Technology* with Joseph McGrath. Recent articles have appeared in the *Journal of Personality and Social Psychology*, *Journal of Experimental Social Psychology*, *Organizational Behavior and Human Decision Processes*, *Small Group Research*, *Group Processes and Intergroup Relations*, and *Human Communication Research*.

Heather E. Hudson is Director of the Telecommunications Management and Policy Program in the School of Business and Management at the University of San Francisco. Dr Hudson has planned and evaluated communication projects in northern Canada, Alaska, and more than 50 developing countries in Africa, Asia and the Pacific, the Middle East, and Latin America. She has also consulted for government agencies, consumer and native organizations, foreign governments, telecommunications companies, and international organizations including the World Bank, the ITU, UNDP, UNESCO, USAID, CIDA, International Development Research Centre (IDRC), and the Commonwealth of Learning.

Dr. Hudson received an Honours BA in English from the University of British Columbia, MA and PhD in Communication Research from Stanford University and JD from the University of Texas at Austin. She is the author of several books including *Global Connections: International Telecommunications Infrastructure and Policy; Communication Satellites: Their Development and Impact; When Telephones Reach the Village,* and co-author of *Rural America in the Information Age* and *Electronic Byways: State Policies for Rural Development through Telecommunications*. Dr Hudson has also published more than 100 articles and book chapters, and presented numerous conference papers, as well as providing expert testimony on telecommunications applications and domestic and international policy issues such as universal service, information infrastructure, and telecommunications planning for socioeconomic development.

Michèle H. Jackson (PhD, University of Minnesota), teaches, consults, and conducts research in the area of computer-based technologies and their relationship to small-group communication and to organizations. Her research has appeared in *Information, Communication, and Society*, the *Proceedings of the Academy of Management, Communication Yearbook*, and the *Journal of Computer Mediated Communication*. She is a past Tomash Fellow for the History of Information Processing at the Charles Babbage Institute, and a past research fellow for the Poynter Institute for Media Studies. She has consulted recently for the University of Colorado and the State of Colorado, and until recently served on the faculty of an engineering-focused interdisciplinary telecommunications program. Dr Jackson currently is assistant professor in the Department of Communication at the University of Colorado at Boulder.

Nicholas W. Jankowski is Associate Professor in the Department of Communication, University of Nijmegen. He has been involved in the investigation of community media and other small-scale communication facilities since the mid-1970s. His publications include: *The People's Voice: Local Radio and Television in Europe*; *The Contours of Multimedia; Community Media in the Information Age;* and *A Handbook of Qualitative Methodologies for Mass Communication Research.* He is preparing a methodology textbook on new media research. One of his current research interests involves the study of initiatives designed to contribute to public discourse through Internet-based discussions. Jankowski is co-editor of the journal *New Media & Society* and associate editor of *Communications: The European Journal of Communication Research.*

Douglas Kellner is George Kneller Chair in the Philosophy of Education at the University of California, Los Angeles. He is author of many books on social theory, politics, history and culture, including *Camera Politica: The Politics and Ideology of Contemporary Hollywood Film*, co-authored with Michael Ryan; *Critical Theory, Marxism, and Modernity*; *Jean Baudrillard: From Marxism to Postmodernism and Beyond*; *Postmodern Theory: Critical Interrogations* (with Steven Best); *Television and the Crisis of Democracy*; *The Persian Gulf TV War*; *Media Culture*; and *The Postmodern Turn* (with Steven Best). Forthcoming are a book on the 2000 US presidential election, *The Postmodern Adventure* (co-authored with Steven Best), and *Media Spectacle.*

Tim Kuhn (Ph.D., Arizona State University) is an Assistant Professor in the Communication Department at the University of Colorado at Boulder. His scholarly interests are in examining the ways in which communication is both a creator and mediator of organizational knowledge, learning and planned change. This guiding interest has led to the creation of a constructionist model depicting the interaction of individual and collective knowledge, communication networks, and information/ communication technologies that explains the accomplishment of coordinated activities. He is also interested in theorizing and studying organizations as complex discursive systems, and has been involved in developing computer-aided techniques that allow the investigation of large bodies of organizational discourse. His recent work on these topics can be found in *Human Communication Research* and *Communication Quarterly.*

Don Lamberton is Visiting Fellow, Graduate Program in Public Policy, Asia Pacific School of Economics and Management, Australian National University, and Adjunct Professor in Communication, University of Canberra. He edits two journals: *Information Economics and Policy* and *Prometheus,* and is a member of other editorial boards. His recent books are: *The Economics of Communication and Information* (1996), *The New Frontiers of Communications Policy* (1997), *Communication and Trade* (1998), *Managing the Global: Globalization, Employment and Quality of Life* (forthcoming), and *The Economics of Language* (forthcoming). He received his BEc degree from the University of Sydney and his D.Phil. from Oxford University. He has held permanent or visiting appointments at many universities and research centres, including eleven Australian universities and universities in the US and UK. He served as a member of Australian Government committees of inquiry (public libraries, industrial property, and marine industries science and technology) and as a consultant to OECD, UNESCO, ITU, UNCTC, Australian Bureau of Statistics, Australia Post, and Prices Surveillance Authority.

Peter Lovelock is the Director of MFC Insight, an IT Research Consultancy headquartered in Beijing. Under Dr Lovelock's tutelage Insight has built the premier IT consulting and research unit on the Chinese mainland, providing strategic guidance to clients such as Ericsson, Vodafone, Xinde and Vivendi. He is also Deputy Director of the Telecommunications Research Project at the University of Hong Kong.

Dr Lovelock has worked extensively on Asian IT regulatory assessment, implementation and execution projects, as well as due diligence and market entry strategic guidance over the years as part of teams for finance, legal, and management consulting companies, as well as for the Telecommunications Research Project.

During 1997 and 1998 Dr Lovelock worked as a policy analyst at the United Nation's International Telecommunication Union (ITU) in Geneva. During this period he was a contributing author to a range of the ITU's major research publications, including *World Telecommunications Development Report 1998*, *Challenges to the Network*, and *Worldwide Telecommunications Regulatory Trends* (6 volumes).

Dr Lovelock has been writing on both the telecommunications and media industries in Asia for over ten years, including chapters in *Telecommunications in Asia*, and the IEC's *Annual Review of Communications*, along with contributions to *Telecommunications Policy* and *Politique Internationale,* among others.

Timothy W. Luke is University Distinguished Professor of Political Science and co-director of the Center for Digital Discourse and Culture at Virginia Polytechnic Institute and State University in Blacksburg, Virginia. His research interests are tied to the politics of information societies, international affairs, and ecological criticism. He has just completed a new critical study of ideological politics at a number of major museums in the United States, which is entitled *Museum Pieces: Probing the Powerplays at Culture, History, Nature, and Technology Museums* (University of Minnesota Press, forthcoming). His most recent books are *Capitalism, Democracy, and Ecology: Departing from Marx* (University of Illinois Press, 1999), and *Ecocritique: Contesting the Politics of Nature, Economy, and Culture* (University of Minnesota Press, 1997). He is also the author of *Shows of Force: Politics, Power and Ideology in Art Exhibitions* (Duke University Press, 1992).

Stephen McElhinney teaches in the postgraduate program of the Centre for International Communication at Macquarie University in Sydney, Australia. He has research and policy interests in globalization, intellectual property and audio-visual industries.

Sally J. McMillan is an Assistant Professor in the Advertising Department at the University of Tennessee-Knoxville. Her research focuses on definitions and history of new media and the impacts of communication technology on organizations and society. She has a particular interest in the nature and role of interactivity in computer-mediated environments. She has also published several articles related to methodologies for online research. Her research has been published in journals such as *Journalism and Mass Communication Quarterly*, the *Journal of Computer Mediated Communication*, *New Media & Society*, and the *Journal of Advertising Research*. Prior to earning her PhD in Communication and Society at the University of Oregon, McMillan worked for 15 years in communication-related roles in book publishing, newspaper reporting, public relations consulting, non-profit management, and executive-level marketing and management for computer technology firms. She teaches graduate and undergraduate courses in interactive advertising, advertising research, and advertising management.

Bella Mody is Professor in the Department of Telecommunication at Michigan State University. She is co-editor of *The Handbook on International and Intercultural Communication* (Sage, 2001) and *Telecommunication Politics: Ownership and Control of the Information Highway in Developing Countries* (Lawrence Erlbaum, 1995). She is author of *Designing Messages for Development Communication* (Sage, 1991) and journal articles on international communication, international development communication, and audience research for development communication campaign design. Her special interests are technology, labour, class, and gender. She has edited/co-edited special issues of the *Journal of International Communication*, *Gazette*, and *Communication Theory*. She is a consultant to international agencies and non-governmental organizations on media applications for development communication. Mody has been Chair of the Intercultural and Development Communication Division of the International Communication Association (1999–2001). She was formerly a social scientist with the Satellite Instructional TV Experiment in the Government of India's space agency and a faculty member at Stanford University and San Francisco State University.

Marshall Scott Poole (PhD, University of Wisconsin) is Professor of Speech Communication at Texas A&M University. He has conducted research and published extensively on the topics of group and organizational communication, computer-mediated communication systems, conflict management, and organizational innovation. He has co-authored or edited seven books including *Communication and Group Decision-Making*, *Research on the Management of Innovation*, and *Organizational Change and Innovation Processes: Theory and Methods for Research*. He has published in a number of journals, including *Management Science*, *MIS Quarterly*, *Human Communication Research*, *Academy of Management Journal*, and *Communication Monographs*. He is currently a senior editor of *Information Systems Research* and *Organization Science*.

Mark Poster is Director of the Film Studies Program at the University of California, Irvine, and a member of the History Department. He has a courtesy appointment in the Department of Information and Computer Science. He is a member of the Critical Theory Institute. His recent and forthcoming books are: *What's the Matter with the Internet?: A Critical Theory of Cyberspace* (University of Minnesota Press, 2001); *The Information Subject* in Critical Voices Series (New York: Gordon and Breach Arts International, 2001); *Cultural History and Postmodernity* (New York: Columbia University Press, 1997); *The Second Media Age* (London: Polity and New York: Blackwell, 1995); and *The Mode of Information* (London: Blackwell and Chicago: University of Chicago Press, 1990).

Ronald E. Rice (PhD, MA, Stanford University, 1982) is Professor and Chair of the Department of Communication at the School of Communication, Information and Library Studies, Rutgers University. He has co-authored or co-edited *Public Communication Campaigns* (3rd edn, 2000), *The Internet and Health Communication* (2000); *The New Media: Communication, Research and Technology* (1984), *Managing Organizational Innovation* (1987) and *Research Methods and the New Media* (1989). He has conducted research and published widely in communication science, public communication campaigns, computer-mediated communication systems, methodology, organizational and management theory, information systems, information science and bibliometrics, and social networks. His publications have won awards as best dissertation from the American Society for Information Science, and as best paper from the International Communication Association and the Academy of Management. Dr Rice has been elected divisional officer in both the ICA and the Academy of Management. He has served as associate editor for *MIS Quarterly*, and for *Human Communication Research*. He is on the editorial board of *Communication Monographs, Journal of the American Society for Information Science; Journal of Communication; Communication Theory; Management Communication Quarterly; Journal of Business Communication; New Media and Society; Journal of Management Information Systems*; and *Journal of Business Communication,* and is a series editor for Hampton Press.

Caroline Simard (BSc, Université de Montréal, MA, Rutgers University) is a doctoral student at Stanford University's Department of Communication. Her research interests include new media and economic relationships, networks of economic relationships in Silicon Valley, knowledge networks and knowledge management, social network analysis, and the impact of information technology on organizations.

Nikhil Sinha is Executive Vice President, eFunds Corporation. Previously he was Associate Professor in the Department of Radio-Television-Film and Associate Director of the Telecommunications and Information Policy Institute at the University of Texas at Austin. He has also worked in the Information and Broadcasting Ministry of the Government of India and as a consultant to the Informatics and Telecommunications Division for the World Bank, and as an advisor to the Indian Telecommunications Commission and the Indian Planning Commission. He has published numerous articles and book chapters on international regulatory and policy issues on telecommunications and information technology.

Knud Erik Skouby (MSc Economics, University of Copenhagen), has worked as a consultant and university teacher since 1972. His areas of interest include planning technological development and technology assessment, particularly within telecommunications. He is the founding Director of the Center for Tele-Information (CTI) and Deputy Director, COM Center, at the Technical University of Denmark. Knud Erik Skouby has participated as a project manager and partner in a number of international, European and Danish research projects. He has also served as a member of organizing boards and evaluation committees, and as invited speaker to a number of international conferences, published a number of Danish and international articles, books and conference proceedings in the areas of telecommunications regulation, technology assessment (information technology and telecommunications), demand forecasting and political economy.

Jennifer Daryl Slack is Associate Professor of Communication and Cultural Studies at Michigan Technological University Department of Humanities. Her work on culture and technology is based on over 20 years of teaching and study. Notably, she has taught courses on culture and technology since 1981 and tracked the changes in her students' sense of the role and importance of technology. She is author of *Communication Technologies and Society* (Ablex, 1984), co-editor of *The Ideology of the Information Age* (Ablex, 1987), and author of numerous articles on culture and technology. *Culture and Technology: A Primer*, co-authored with J. Macgregor Wise, is forthcoming from Peter Lang.

Don Slater is a Reader in Sociology at the London School of Economics and Political Science. He has written extensively on Internet and new media, from an ethnographic perspective. Most recently he conducted a study of the use of the Internet in Trinidad, with Daniel Miller, published as *The Internet: An Ethnographic Approach* (Oxford: Berg, 2000). An earlier online ethnography of pornography trading was published in *Body and Society* 4(4), 1998. He also writes extensively on the relation between culture and economy. His recent work includes *Consumer Culture and Modernity* (Cambridge: Polity Press, 1997) and (with Fran Tonkiss) *Market Society: Markets and Modern Social Thought* (Cambridge: Polity Press, 2001).

Susan Leigh Star is Professor of Communication at the University of California, San Diego. She writes about the social and historical aspects of science, information and technology, particularly on the values embedded in information technologies. With Geoffrey Bowker, she is the author of *Sorting Things Out: Classification and Its Consequences* (MIT Press, 1999), and has edited a number of other volumes, including *Ecologies of Knowledge* (SUNY, 1995). Her training was in the symbolic interactionist/pragmatist tradition in American sociology, which has grounded her research in the study of work, identity and meaning. She has also written on feminist theory, and is a poet.

Laura Stein is an Assistant Professor in the Department of Communication at the University of Massachusetts at Amherst. She researches and writes about communication law and policy, political communication, speech rights, and new technologies. Her articles have appeared in numerous collections and journals, including *Communication Law and Policy*, *Javnost / The Public*, and *Peace Review*. She has also worked in the management, production, and distribution of public and educational media.

Harry M. Trebing is Professor of Economics Emeritus and Senior Fellow at the Institute of Public Utilities, Michigan State University, and Adjunct Professor (Economics), New Mexico State University. He is founder and director of the Institute of Public Utilities, MSU (1966–91) and former Chief Economist for the US Postal Rate Commission and the US Federal Communications Commission. He has been a member of advisory panels for government agencies and the Congressional Office of Technology Assessment, and has received a two-year National Science Foundation grant to study regulatory reform in energy utilities. Currently he serves as a member of the editorial boards of three professional journals, and as a member of the Michigan Utility Consumer Participation Board (by appointment of the Governor in 1991). He is the recipient of distinguished service awards from the National Association of State Utility Consumer Advocates, the National Association of Regulatory Utility Commissioners, five universities, and the Government of Guam. He is the author of numerous publications dealing with public utility regulation. He holds BA and MA degrees from the University of Maryland, and a PhD from the University of Wisconsin.

John Ure is a specialist in the economics, policy and regulation of telecommunications and related areas of information technology, new media and electronic commerce. As director of the Telecommunications Research Project (TRP) at the University of Hong Kong his output of papers, articles and conference presentations has been prolific. His book *Telecommunications in Asia: Policy, Planning and Development* (Hong Kong University Press, 1995, 1997, of which he was editor and principal author) rapidly became a standard reference for the region. He serves on numerous public bodies in Hong Kong, advises the consumer councils in Hong Kong and Macao, is a consultant for both the World Bank and the International Telecommunications Union (ITU) in the Asia–Pacific region. He runs training courses for the telecommunications regulators and for the private sector. He also supervises postgraduate students at doctorate and master levels, and serves on the editorial boards of *Info* and *Telecommunications Policy*.

Gwen Urey is an Associate Professor and department chair in Urban and Regional Planning at California State Polytechnic University, Pomona. Her research and teaching interests include planning for and issues surrounding ownership and control over infrastructure of all types in US cities and in developing countries. She is also interested in the use of technology in teaching and learning both in school and community settings.

Stefaan G. Verhulst has been the director of the Programme in Comparative Media Law and Policy at Oxford University since its inception in 1996. Prior to that, he was a lecturer on communications law and policy issues in Belgium before becoming founder and co-director of the International Media and

Information-Communications Policy and Law studies programme at the School of Law, University of Glasgow. He has served in, and is currently a consultant and researcher for, numerous organizations including the Council of Europe, European Commission and UNESCO. In the fall of 2000, he was a Scholar in Residence at the John and Mary R. Markle Foundation. Together with Monroe Price, he shares the UNESCO Chair in Communications. He is the editor of the *International Journal of Communications Law and Policy* and the *Communications Law in Transition Newsletter* and is the UK legal correspondent for the European Audiovisual Observatory.

Frank Webster was educated at the University of Durham (BA, MA) and the London School of Economics (PhD) and is currently Professor of Sociology and Head of the Department of Cultural Studies and Sociology at the University of Birmingham, UK. He is the author of many books, including: *The New Photography: Responsibility in Visual Communication* (1980); *Information Technology: A Luddite Analysis* (with Kevin Robins) (1986); *The Technical Fix: Computers, Industry and Education* (with Kevin Robins) (1989); *Theories of the Information Society* (1995); *The Postmodern University? Contested Visions of Higher Education* (with A. Smith) (1997); *Times of the Technoculture: from the Information Society to the Virtual Life* (with Kevin Robins) (1999); *Understanding Contemporary Society: Theories of the Present* (with G. Browning and A. Halcli) (2000); and *Politics and Culture in the Information Age: A New Politics?* (2001). He is currently preparing *The Virtual University* (with Kevin Robins) for Oxford University Press.

Dwayne Winseck is Associate Professor at the School of Journalism and Communication, Carleton University, Ottawa, Canada. Before arriving in Ottawa in 1998, he lived and taught in Britain, the People's Republic of China, the Turkish Republic of Northern Cyprus and the United States. His research focuses on the political economy of communication, media history, communication policy, theories of democracy and global communication. He has authored and co-edited three books on these topics: *Reconvergence: A Political Economy of Telecommunications in Canada* (Hampton Press, 1998); *Democratizing Communication: Comparative Perspectives on Information and Power* (Hampton Press, 1997); and *Media in Global Context* (Edward Arnold, 1997). He has also published numerous book chapters as well as journal articles in the *Canadian Journal of Communication, Gazette, Javnost/the Public, New Media and Society, European Journal of Communication, Media, Culture and Society*, and elsewhere.

J. Macgregor Wise (PhD, University of Illinois at Urbana-Champaign) is Assistant Professor of Communication Studies at Arizona State University West. His work is situated at the intersection of cultural studies, media studies, and the sociology and philosophy of technology. He is the author of *Exploring Technology and Social Space* (Sage, 1997) and co-author with Jennifer Daryl Slack of the forthcoming *Culture and Technology: A Primer* (Peter Lang).

Acknowledgements

Putting together a volume of this size draws on the ideas, efforts and enthusiasm of many people, and we would like to thank all those involved for contributing to the final publication of the *Handbook*. The section editors and the individual chapter authors have worked hard through several rounds of discussion and revisions over the last couple of years, and we are extremely grateful for their care and efforts, which have made the *Handbook* as good as we could have hoped for.

Our International Advisory Board supported the project strongly from the outset, and we thank them for their advice and continuing interest in the project – especially the months of reviewing and careful commentary that they provided on the chapter proposals and initial drafts. The diversity of their experience, perspectives and expertise was a crucial asset throughout the editorial process.

In particular, we want to acknowledge International Advisory Board member Rohan Samarajiva, who originated the idea for the *Handbook*, recruited one of the present editors (Lievrouw) to co-edit the volume, and initiated our outstanding relationship with Sage Publications. Rohan had to withdraw from direct oversight of the project when he was appointed Director General of Telecommunications for Sri Lanka; he has since moved to the Delft University of Technology. But without his enormous drive and creativity the *Handbook* might never have gotten off the ground in the first place.

In addition, the review and revision process could not have been completed without the additional help of a long list of 'anonymous reviewers', who themselves comprise a 'who's who' of new media researchers. Their wide-ranging interests, and the variety of disciplinary and professional backgrounds they represent, allowed them to provide commentary and suggestions that enlarged the scope and significance of the entire volume. While the list is long we think it is essential that they be recognized here: Phil Agre, Patricia Aufderheide, Sandra Braman, Donald Case, Stephen Coleman, Dianne Cornell, William Drake, Mike Featherstone, Anne Friedberg, Les Gasser, Tim Kelly, Stephen Kline, Martin Lea, Harmeet Sawhney, Sid Shniad, Diane Sonnenwald, Gerald Sussman, Damian Tambini, Janet Wasko, and Rolf Wigand.

We should also mention that some of our contributing authors also served as reviewers for other chapters in the book.

We could not have completed the *Handbook* without significant institutional support, in terms of both time and resources. We would therefore like to thank our colleagues at both UCLA and LSE, who provided administrative and intellectual support (as well as the occasional airfare).

Our commissioning editor at Sage, Julia Hall, has been the classic tower of strength, encouraging us every step of the way from the first glimmerings in 1996, to the start of 'real work' in 1998, through the process of recruiting contributors and Board members, to the review process in 1999 and early 2000, and right through shaping up the final manuscript. It was in fact her idea to ask Sonia Livingstone to step in as co-editor when Rohan Samarajiva left the project. Julia has been patient, strict, cheerful, resolute, reasonable, funny, and much else as needed. We owe her a very great debt. We also thank other key members of Sage staff for their help with promotion and production – they have made sure that the *Handbook* will be an important resource and will find the right audience.

Finally, on a more personal note, we would like to thank our partners, Dan Danzig and Peter Lunt, for putting up with so many hours, months, indeed years spent reading chapters, dealing with authors, working through contracts, traveling to conferences, and even a couple of cross-Atlantic shuttles. It has been exhausting, but also a great deal of fun sustaining so fruitful a collaboration, debating with so many people the shape and future of our field, and learning so much ourselves in the process.

We hope that you, the reader, find this *Handbook* as useful and inspiring as we have tried to make it.

Leah Lievrouw
University of California, Los Angeles

Sonia Livingstone
London School of Economics and Political Science

Introduction

The Social Shaping and Consequences of ICTs

LEAH A. LIEVROUW

and

SONIA LIVINGSTONE

As this is being written, 'new media' is a buzzword, shorthand for a volatile cultural and technology industry that includes multimedia, entertainment and e-commerce. However, in social research the term has a long history, having been used since the 1960s and 1970s by investigators studying the forms, uses and implications of information and communication technologies (ICTs) (e.g. Parker, 1970a; 1973b; Parker and Dunn, 1972). As our contributor and International Advisory Board member Ron Rice pointed out in his foundational collection, *The New Media* (1984), behind the usual meaning of gadgets and trends lie multilayered relationships among economic, political, behavioural, cultural and institutional as well as technological phenomena. Social researchers, critics, historians and designers have all sought to understand them.

A quick visit to a bookstore (online or 'live') immediately reveals the scatter of new-media-related research and scholarship across what are often Balkanized literatures. Any new research front, especially one that is 'transdisciplinary', undergoes an initial period of exploration and expansion. Scholars ask new questions, gather data that is often hard to characterize or manage, and borrow or invent all sorts of frameworks and models in attempts to speak meaningfully about what they find. The sheer diversity and proliferation can be exhilarating and liberating – and difficult to comprehend. Eventually, the pendulum swings back toward synthesis and efforts are made to find common threads or themes.

The present volume was conceived as a move in this direction for new media studies. However, our goal is not to create fixed boundaries for the area, to dictate a canonical literature, or even to argue for a single coherent speciality. Rather, we believe that the continuing openness of new media research, after decades of growth and diversity, continues to be one of its most compelling and productive strengths. Its transdisciplinary goals and structure are entirely appropriate at this moment in Western intellectual history, though they may pose challenges to institutional and disciplinary conventions that are closer to the nineteenth century than the twenty-first.

In this volume, we have attempted to identify major research areas where substantial or influential work has already been done, and to suggest parallel themes or concerns that have surfaced within and among them. Our aim is to deal with the scatter by encouraging, for example, economists of information or technology to consider identity and gender as they are understood in cultural studies; by asking cultural historians to look at the psychology of media use; by persuading sociologists of social change to think about regulatory regimes; and by leading system designers to think about human geography.

Of course, to some extent this strategy only highlights a familiar fact of life for new media scholars: regardless of their disciplinary training or affiliations (ours happen to be in communication and information studies and in social psychology, respectively), we must read and engage across multiple disciplines, whether scientific or humanist, interpretive or empirical. It is difficult, but essential, to be able to look across terminologies, descriptive and explanatory tools, illustrative cases, even assumptions about everyday life. (Happily, an outstanding synthesis like Castells' *Information Age* trilogy or Luhmann's *Social Systems* does occasionally arrive.) The task can be particularly fearsome for students or colleagues who are new to the area, and we have tried to keep these readers in mind as we organized the *Handbook*.

Given the pervasiveness and significance of media and communication technologies in contemporary society it may be surprising that no single volume has yet attempted to draw together the principal strands of research and scholarship that comprise the best current understanding of the relationship between new media and society. Certainly, the chapters and reference lists in this book testify that a huge body of relevant work has been published, particularly over the last 20 years. In the last five years alone perhaps a dozen new scholarly journals on the topic have been launched as venues for publishing research from many disciplines. And by the late 1990s, new media programmes and faculty could be found throughout the world.

Though the speciality dates back several decades, only in the 1990s was there a major impetus for dramatic expansion in the field. In many ways the recent growth of new media studies has coincided with that of the Internet, though of course it is by no means the only significant new media technology. Since the 1970s, when the first 'personal computers' were introduced and the ARPANET was built as an elite channel for technical communication, the Internet has become a platform for commerce, sociality and popular culture. At the same time, new media research has expanded from a handful of specialists in telecommunications regulation and policy, small-group processes, social network analysis, the social psychology of computing and media, organizational communication and 'man–machine studies' to become a major focus of research and scholarship in its own right. Only lately have large numbers of scholars been drawn to the field, creating the need for a collection like this one which draws together so many diverse developments and identifies key themes and challenges for future research.

Therefore, in this introductory chapter we do several things to help frame contemporary social research and scholarship on new media as it is represented in the following chapters. First, we trace the research projects, problems and intellectual traditions that informed and set the stage for the beginnings of new media research. Second, we propose a definition for new media that acknowledges these early influences as well as the evolution of the field over the last couple of decades. Third, we identify and discuss several important characteristics that distinguish the 'social shaping and consequences' of new media. And fourth, we review

some continuing issues and new developments in the methodology of new media research. Obviously, our approach cannot be exhaustive or definitive; instead, we offer observations that suggest the range of possible ways ahead. We end with some observations on the contents and organization of this volume.

EARLY INFLUENCES ON NEW MEDIA RESEARCH

There is, inevitably, some arbitrariness in setting a starting point for any historical review. For new media studies, the problem is compounded because the area has always been multidisciplinary and international, so different fields and specialities have entered the scene at different times in different places.[1] Its early influences include research projects and initiatives that developed outside the mainstream of, or at the intersection among, the major disciplines. Each had its distinct concerns or problematics, or examined particular social phenomena or contexts, so collectively this early body of work tended to be a somewhat scattered response to the innovative information and communication technologies of that era. Nonetheless, many of these projects and studies have had a guiding influence on more recent research, and several of their authors are contributors to, or members of the International Advisory Board for, the present volume. They continue to be cited and would be included in any 'core' bibliography of new media studies (for a more extensive overview, see Lievrouw et al., 2001).

For example, in economics, *Handbook* contributor and Board member Don Lamberton (1971), Kenneth Arrow (1979; 1984), Charles Jonscher (1983) and others worked out important conceptualizations of the economics of information. Their insights about information as an economic good or commodity laid the foundation for new understandings of intellectual property and of the value and significance of 'information work'. Fritz Machlup (1962) and Marc Porat (Porat and Rubin, 1977) conducted some of the first studies that identified and described the extent and significance of information work in the US. In 1978, Simon Nora and Alain Minc, *inspecteurs de finances* for the French government, issued their internationally cited report on the economic significance and challenge of *télématique* for French society (Nora and Minc, 1981 [1978]). Joseph Schumpeter's (1939) theories of 'long waves' of economic development were an important influence on information society theories (Shields and Samarajiva, 1993). *Handbook* Board member Youichi Ito and his collaborators at Keio University based their analysis of *johoka shakai*, or informationalized society, on measurements of the stocks and flows of information in Japan during the 1960s. Their *johoka* index incorporated the amount of information produced per year, the distribution of communication media, the quality of information activities, and a ratio of information expenditures as a proportion of total expenditures (Ito, 1981). This approach has continued to dominate information society analyses in Japan (Kurisaki and Yanagimachi, 1992).

In sociology, Daniel Bell's (1973) theory of 'post-industrial society' quickly became a point of departure for studies of information technologies and social change, though it was also widely criticized (for example, see Webster in this volume). Anthony Giddens (another of our Board members) analysed the changing perceptions of space and time associated with information technology, and later, media as instruments of social surveillance and control in modern societies (Giddens, 1979; 1984). In an extensive historical study, James Beniger (1986) described the 'control revolution' facilitated by communication technologies from the nineteenth-century industrial era onward.

Social psychology provided many early insights into the uses of ICTs. In the UK, Short et al. (1976) proposed that teleconferencing systems could be evaluated in terms of their 'social presence'. Similarly, Robert Johansen and his colleagues (1979) at the Institute for the Future (near Stanford University) formulated the concept of 'telepresence' based on their studies of meetings conducted via video conferencing technology. At the New Jersey Institute of Technology, Roxanne Hiltz and Murray Turoff (1993 [1978]) conducted one of the earliest studies of interaction among geographically dispersed work groups of scientists and engineers via computer-mediated communication. Lee Sproull, Sara Kiesler and their students and colleagues at Carnegie-Mellon University were among the first to note the effects of the anonymity and 'reduced social context cues' of computer-based messaging, which, they argued, contribute to disinhibited communication and 'flaming' (Kiesler et al., 1984; Sproull and Kiesler, 1991). At the Massachusetts Institute of Technology, Sherry Turkle observed both children and computer science students and faculty learning to program. Her seminal essay, 'Computer as Rorschach' (1980), and her subsequent book, *The Second Self* (1984), introduced the idea that computers are 'projective devices' that allow users to control many aspects of their self-presentation and interaction.

Important work was done by scholars in many other fields, including the political scientist Ithiel de Sola Pool (1977; 1983), telecommunications engineer Colin Cherry (1978 [1957]; 1985) and management expert Thomas J. Allen (1977). However, at the same time, while these other fields and disciplines responded to changes in modes of communication and information technology that they had previously taken for granted, communication research was also developing, constituting a central plank of new media studies. Indeed, the moment when the mass communication research literature developed an identifiable interest in 'new media' coincided with the breakup of mass media in the 1970s, as broadcasting converged with digital telecommunications, information systems and computing (e.g. Parker, 1973a). Therefore, interest in new media, especially within the communication discipline, was inextricably tied up with the transformation of 'old' mass media from the outset. These transformations were thought to be associated with the evolution of mass society into a service-based 'information society', or alternatively a more differentiated, perhaps fragmented, perhaps more heterarchical, network society.

In this context, some mass media researchers began to redirect their attention to newer technologies and channels that did not fit the conventional 'mass' framework. Such channels, including the telephone, videotex, audio and video teleconferencing, photocopying, facsimile, and computer-mediated communication (CMC) via the fledgling ARPANET and other systems, had been neglected because they did not fit easily into either the mass media or interpersonal/speech communication specialities within communication research (Rogers, 1999). They also lay outside the main theoretical and methodological concerns of other social science and humanities disciplines. Of these technologies, only the telephone had a major presence in the home; researchers often had to study others within the settings of the universities, government agencies or other large organizations where they were used.

Therefore, and doubtless for reasons to do with the availability of research funding and the 'applied' or 'administrative' nature of the questions being asked (Lazarsfeld, 1941; Melody and Mansell, 1983), many early studies of new media technologies within communication research took a somewhat traditional approach, considering the 'impacts' of new technologies on attitudes, behaviour, organizations, policy and so on. They focused on workers' perceptions of new technologies, the features and functions of different systems, the types of communication or information services that the systems supported, and their 'effects' on work performance and productivity. Policy studies considered the implications of new media for different industry structures and regulatory options, or described changes in employment and occupational structures attributable to the rise of new technologies and 'information industries'. They examined the prospects for extending established frameworks for universal service obligations, cross-subsidies, rate regulation, and decency and privacy laws to new media systems. In short, a broadly administrative response to technological innovation, modelled primarily after the mass communication 'effects' tradition, came to dominate the field of new media research at an early stage, particularly in the US.

At Stanford University, for example, Edwin Parker and his associates explored the uses of computing for information retrieval and 'information utilities' (Parker 1970b; 1973b). They also studied the effects of new technologies (such as slow-scan television, direct broadcast satellites and telephone systems) on what was then termed 'development communication' (Parker, 1978). Parker, *Handbook* Board member Everett Rogers, and others examined the role of new media technologies in social and economic development, applying diffusion of innovations theory to the provision of social and information services to rural or underserved areas and nations (Parker and Hudson, 1975; Parker and Mohammadi, 1977; Rogers, 1995; see also Heather Hudson's chapter in this volume). In Canada, government initiatives on computer-mediated communication and videotex in the 1970s produced clusters of new media researchers in Quebec and elsewhere. By the early 1980s, the Annenberg School for Communication at the University of Southern California in Los Angeles had become a centre for new media research grounded in the social psychology of telecommunications, organizational communication, and communication law and policy.

The European tradition of new media research took a rather different direction in the beginning, emphasizing a cultural/critical studies approach to media content and industries, on the one hand, and a broadly Marxist political economy of media, on the other.[2] Just as the different theoretical, philosophical, methodological and political commitments of administrative and critical (or, variously, 'positivist' and 'relativist', or 'quantitative' and 'qualitative') research were being explicitly debated in media and communication research more generally (see e.g. Ferment in the Field, 1983), new media research underwent a similar divergence of its own. Eschewing the preference for middle-range theory that characterized administrative research (Boudon, 1991), European scholars on the whole became more critical of new media than their US counterparts (with some exceptions, noted below). They drew upon a variety of social theories, ranging from Bourdieu's analysis of the relation between economy and culture (Bourdieu, 1977 [1972]; 1980) to Foucault's linking of technology to the administrative imperatives, standardization processes and procedures of bureaucratic organization (Foucault, 1970 [1966]; 1980). Social theories of modernity and social change, including Bell's post-industrial society, Habermas' theory of the public sphere and Giddens' theory of structuration, also inspired new theoretical approaches that connected new media technologies to the co-determination of social structure and action.

British media studies, for example, took an explicitly cultural/critical approach to new media,

as they had to mass media previously. Raymond Williams (1974) was a key figure in this tradition, not only in establishing a critical approach to the mass media, contextualizing them in relation to both political economy and cultural analysis, but also in developing the relation between studies of mass communication and the study of technology and technological innovation. This perspective carried over into early studies of new media content and industry structure in the UK and Europe and has, more recently, also stimulated the study of the social and cultural contexts of ICT consumption and use (Silverstone and Hirsch, 1992; Jouet, 1994; Miller and Slater, 2000).

The political economy of media was another significant influence in European (and later, in North American) new media studies, especially during the 1980s as critics mounted a response to post-industrialism and the popular vision of the 'information society' promulgated by industry and government. As argued by *Handbook* contributor Frank Webster and Kevin Robins (Robins and Webster, 1985; Webster, 1995; Webster and Robins, 1986; 1989) and Nicholas Garnham (1986; 1990; 1994), among others, new media systems and services tend to reinforce the economic and political power of existing systems and institutions. In effect, they argued, the information society is the latest stage of industrial capitalism, not a radical departure from the past.

This critique of the cultural, economic and political power of mass media was advanced forcefully by a number of European scholars, including *Handbook* Board members Armand Mattelart in France, and Cees Hamelink, Tapio Varis and Osmo Wiio in Finland. It was also well represented in North America by the late Herb Schiller and his colleagues at the University of California, San Diego (Schiller, 1981), George Gerbner at the University of Pennsylvania's Annenberg School for Communication, and Dallas Smythe and his research group at Simon Fraser University in Canada. Their colleagues and students (including several of the contributors to this volume) carried the critical perspective forward to studies of new media content, ownership structures and technology development (see e.g. Mosco, 1982; 1996; D. Schiller, 1982; Slack and Fejes, 1987; Gandy, 1993).

These and related perspectives provided the key framework for the development of new media research in the UK. Central to this development was the decision, in 1985, of the Economic and Social Research Council to provide ten years of funding for the first coordinated research Programme on Information and Communication Technologies (PICT) (which was succeeded by the Virtual Society? Programme headed by *Handbook* Board member Steve Woolgar at Brunel University). This multimillion-pound research programme not only served to make visible the various strands of research on new media already developed in the UK, but also drew on a wide array of academic disciplines to establish what has become a burgeoning tradition of new media research in the UK. Combining critical and empirical approaches, the PICT legacy in particular is that of an active, policy-oriented research community committed to a broadly 'social shaping' position, concerned to understand and critique how governments, regions, organizations and households are shaping as well as being shaped by technological developments in the field of new media (for an overview of PICT-related research, see the edited volume by our Board member Bill Dutton, 1996).

While some observers have asked how far mass communication theory can be extended to the new media (e.g. McQuail, 1986; Morris and Ogan, 1996), the effects-type approach is still found in new media research in many countries (e.g. Lea, 1992; Reeves and Nass, 1996). Today, however, it is balanced by more complex levels of analysis and a more critical perspective that locate the changing perceptions and practices surrounding new media within a broader institutional, economic and cultural context.

Nonetheless, there are some 'blind spots'. For example, international and comparative studies are still relatively scarce. The new media research traditions of non-Western countries remain less familiar to, and so less influential for, the largely English-language scholars and literature we have traced here. It is fair to say that, until very recently, rather more comparative literature has been produced concerning traditional mass media (e.g. Blumler et al., 1992; Chaffee and Chu, 1992; Lull, 1988) than new media, though there are notable exceptions (such as George Barnett's world-systems theory approach to international telephone uses and networks: Barnett and Choi, 1995; Barnett and Salisbury, 1996). Several major international bodies, such as UNESCO, OECD and the European Commission, collate national- and regional-level data that are used in comparative studies (UNESCO, 2000; see also Urey in this volume).

In part, this limited 'internationalization' of the field reflects the flows and connections among research communities cross-nationally. It demonstrates that new media themselves have developed and diffused according to different time-scales in different places, which is largely though not exclusively a matter of economics. Only recently, for instance, since 'Europe' expanded its borders after 1989, has there been research on new media within the context of ex-Soviet countries (Lengel, 2000). Within Europe in particular, however, pan-European work has burgeoned, stimulated by the increasingly unified European economic and policy community (e.g. McQuail et al., 1986; Tydeman and Kelm, 1986; Becker and Schoenbach, 1989; Robins and Morley, 1989; Schultz, 1992; Livingstone and Bovill, 2001). This policy-oriented research, which is informed by Habermas' theory of the public sphere in particular, reflects a formative trend in new media research at both the national and pan-European level, and contrasts with a great deal of US policy research. It has arisen in response to a growing sense that the strong public service tradition in European media is being undermined by changes within the European media environment (Ferguson, 1986; Burgelman, 1997; Calabrese and Burgelman, 1999).

As new media research has progressed from its early efforts to its recent proliferation in the 1990s, it has become more specialized; some of that variety is illustrated by the diverse chapters that follow. However, today this drift toward specialization is being challenged by broader developments in social theory. For example, as sociologists, political scientists, economists and others debate phenomena like globalization (e.g. Beck, Giddens, Luhmann), they often assume but rarely focus on or theorize the central role of ICTs in these hotly contested, incompletely global transformations in politics, economics and culture. Today, new media researchers face the new and important challenge of making their concepts, arguments and findings count, and having their theories and methods taken seriously, in this wider playing field.

WHAT IS / ARE NEW MEDIA?

The thumbnail history outlined above provides a sense of just how many points of entry there have been to new media research, and the many ways in which new media might be defined. The field needs a definition that is abstract enough to accommodate the range of systems, contents, issues and settings that researchers consider essential, yet not so broad that new media cannot be distinguished from other established areas within communication research and other disciplines.

At the risk of oversimplification, we can say that researchers concerned with technological, economic, or behavioural issues have tended to define new media in terms of system features and services, industry structures and ownership, or the psychology of media users, respectively. Critical/cultural scholars, following the media studies tradition, have drawn more on definitions based on new media content and its forms.

Undoubtedly, most definitions of new media and ICTs to date have focused on their technological features. Wilbur Schramm (1977) classified communication media on the basis of channel characteristics that parallel human sensory perception, such as motion versus still visuals, sound versus silent, text versus picture, or one-way (simplex) versus two-way (duplex) transmission.

He distinguished between inexpensive, small-scale 'little media' and 'big media' with large, complex, expensive infrastructures and organizational arrangements. Ithiel de Sola Pool, a political scientist and pioneer of new media research, defined *new communications technologies* as 'shorthand for about 25 main devices', which he duly listed (Pool, 1990: 19). Other definitions of new media technology have taken a similar classificatory approach (Durlak, 1987; Steuer, 1995).

Ron Rice stressed the two-way capabilities of computing and telecommunications, and defined new media as 'those communication technologies, typically involving computer capabilities (microprocessor or mainframe), that allow or facilitate interactivity among users or between users and information' (Rice and Associates, 1984: 35). The demassified, time-shifting features of new media have been contrasted with the one-to-many, one-way message flows of traditional mass media (Rogers, 1986). More recently, writers have emphasized the convergence of computing and telecommunications technologies (Baldwin et al., 1996). Studies of human–computer interaction and interface design focus on system features that affect the perceptions and cognitive 'human factors' of technology users (Reeves and Nass, 1996).

Consistent with this orientation toward system features, user perceptions and the mass media effects tradition in US communication research (especially the Shannon–Weaver linear model of communication that includes channel as a variable in the communication process), early studies of new media tended toward technological determinism. They emphasized the effects or 'impacts' of ICTs *on* users, organizations and societies. Technological determinism – the belief that technologies have an overwhelming and inevitable power to drive human actions and social change – is often taken for granted in technologically advanced societies. The opposing 'social shaping of technology' approach (see Lievrouw in this volume) contends that technologies are continuously remade by the things users do with them. Some technologies certainly constrain action, but people can always make choices about using them.

While many new media scholars today have developed a view of technology that is closer to the social shaping perspective, and despite the somewhat relentless critique of technological determinism over the last two decades, the language of 'impacts' persists (Smith and Marx, 1994; MacKenzie and Wajcman, 1999; Kling, 1999). For example, an article in the 1992 *Annual Review of Information Science and Technology* was entitled 'The impact of information technology on the individual' (Palmquist, 1992). A forthcoming special issue of the *Journal of Broadcasting and Electronic Media* is planned on new media 'impacts' in broadcasting. Yet, as Raymond Williams (1974)

forcefully pointed out, the link between technological determinism and narratives of progress (or, less commonly, narratives of decline) – narratives which cast science (typically allied to commercial imperatives) as the driver of not only technological innovation but also social change, with 'improvements' in technology becoming readily aligned with 'progress' in society – can be misleading or even dangerous.

For example, as several of our contributors point out, the Internet is popularly portrayed as a single medium which sprung fully formed into our lives less than a decade ago. However, this is misleading in two senses. First, 'the Internet' is shorthand for a bundle of different media and modalities – e-mail, websites, newsgroups, e-commerce and so forth – that make it perhaps the most complex and plural of the electronic media yet invented. Second, these different modes have their own communication characteristics, are subject to differing economic and social conditions of use and, significantly, have different histories stretching back over several decades. Clearly, these differences must be accounted for; they undermine any possibility of identifying singular impacts or effects because the (plural) meanings and consequences of the Internet are contingent on a wide range of specific historical and cultural conditions.

The dangers of defining communication media in terms of system features or 'impacts' are also illustrated by recent debates in American media law and regulation. Traditionally, media systems have been regulated in the US according to their technological configurations or infrastructures. Speech and publishing are largely unregulated (that is, their content cannot be censored) because historically those forms of communication are protected under the First Amendment of the US Constitution (though exceptions include pornography, libel and defamation, and speech that incites violence). First Amendment protection has been extended to other recording media as well, such as photography, film, audio and video, on the grounds that they too constitute 'speech'.

The American telephone system (essentially AT&T and a few smaller operators), in contrast, was regulated under the Communications Act of 1934 as a 'common carrier', a concept borrowed from transportation law. The common carrier metaphor suggested that because the telephone system was a natural monopoly, AT&T should be required to serve any customers who were willing to pay, without regard for the content of their messages. Broadcasting was also regulated under the 1936 Act because the 'airwaves' (like water, perhaps) were a scarce resource that should be rationed because there were fewer radio (and later, television) frequencies available than broadcasters who wanted to use them. Broadcast licences were awarded to owners of radio and television stations whose programmes would serve the 'public interest, convenience and necessity' – and could be revoked if licensees aired material that did not meet this deliberately vague requirement.

Today technological convergence has blurred these channel-based metaphors – speech, transportation, airwaves – with serious consequences for the regulatory schemes that invoke them (First Amendment, common carriage, licensing). For example, though American Internet users often assume that they have First Amendment speech rights online, or expect the same level of privacy that they have for telephone calls, Internet service providers insist that they are entitled to intercept, read and censor any messages that pass through their systems because they may be held financially and legally liable for those communications. Employees who might reasonably assume that their books, papers and other print materials are safe from 'unreasonable search and seizure' find that similar privacy protections do not always extend to computer disks or hard drives. 'Content providers' like newspaper and book publishers, movie studios, and record companies, on the other hand, maintain that they should have the same rights of expression (and property rights) online as they do in print or on film. In response to recent technological developments and pressures from the media industries, the US Telecommunications Act of 1996 rolled back or weakened many of the rules of the 1934 Act. These include restrictions on cross-ownership of broadcast and publishing media, and the number of outlets that a single owner may have in a given market. While the 1996 Act does not solve all of the regulatory or equity problems of new media, the current regulatory climate shows that it is obviously becoming more difficult to distinguish among media, or to regulate them, on the basis of system features or technology alone.

Beyond Features

No wonder, then, that contemporary discussions of new media have begun to incorporate more than technological characteristics. For the inaugural issue of the journal *New Media & Society* (What's New about New Media?, 1999), editors asked several scholars (including one of the present authors) to respond to the question: what is 'new' about new media? What distinguishes them from other media, either technologically or socially? Some contributors mentioned channel characteristics or features like those reviewed above, or commented on the historical problem of labelling any technology as 'new' by definition. But others pointed out that new technologies give users an unprecedented ability to modify and redistribute content – contributing to what *Handbook* Part Six editor Mark Poster called the 'underdetermination' of new media in comparison with traditional media. Rakow suggested that media research has not yet come

to terms with the fact that new media allow any user to 'speak', an issue echoed by Sonia Livingstone's call for a reconceptualization of the notion of audience.

Kevin Robins, reviewing the recent work of Pierre Lévy, agreed that new media have produced a new kind of 'knowledge space' or 'communication space' that is 'de-referentialized', that is, disconnected from local, situated knowledge and experience. But unlike Lévy, who sees this development as an emancipatory break from older forms of knowledge that were linear, hierarchical and rigid, Robins argued that the new 'relation to knowledge' serves to further global corporate capitalism and the interests of a relatively small elite. In this environment, information and communication are valued not for their substance or meaning, but for their capacity to be processed, circulated, or connected for their own sake: 'contemporary knowledge culture is regarded as essentially about the acquisition of generic information skills and competencies' (1999: 20). In the same issue, Bill Melody proposed that new media are 'more influenced by economic factors' and more central to the new information economy than traditional media have been. The high degree of interconnectedness, and the volume of communication and information moving through networks, has created greater economic instability.

Insights like these bring us closer to a framework that more fully captures the rich interweaving of media technology, human action and social structure. While a single definition can hardly capture the variety of ways that the term is used today – or even in this book – we can still propose a framework for thinking about new media that goes beyond simple classification of systems and features. Therefore, by *new media* we mean information and communication technologies and their associated social contexts, incorporating:

- the artifacts or devices that enable and extend our abilities to communicate;
- the communication activities or practices we engage in to develop and use these devices; and
- the social arrangements or organizations that form around the devices and practices.

Together, we can think of the three aspects of media technology as an 'ensemble', in Michel Callon's phrase, or as infrastructure in the sense that Susan Leigh Star and Geof Bowker define it in this volume. The three elements are inextricable and mutually determining.

Clearly, from the viewpoint of this definition, many technologies are infrastructural, in that they combine elements of technology, practice and social organization. So what can we say distinguishes new media as a particular focus of study? Many apparently novel traits of new media have been described, including hyperreality, virtuality, anonymity, interactivity and so on. However, we believe that new media can be characterized more usefully in terms of, first, the particular ways that they are both the instrument and the product of social shaping, and second, their particular social consequences.

A number of the chapters here make the point that new media technologies both shape, and are shaped by, their social, economic and cultural contexts. More specifically for new media, however, such shaping is *recombinant*. That is, new media systems are products of a continuous hybridization of both existing technologies and innovations in interconnected technical and institutional networks. The recombinant/hybrid metaphor suggests that while ICTs are influenced by the existing technological context, and may have unintended consequences, to a great extent they are the result of human actions and decisions. They are not determined by an independent, inevitable causality or evolutionary process unique to technology itself; rather, designers, users, regulators and others can take advantage of the current state of technical knowledge, and recombine technologies and new knowledge to achieve their particular goals or purposes.

The metaphor also suggests the essentially continuous nature of new media development. Even technologies that are perceived as being unprecedented are found upon closer analysis to have been designed, built and implemented around existing technologies and practices. Change, then, comes in waves or cycles; occasionally, a wave may be of such magnitude that it appears to be a 'revolution' or a complete break with the past, but from a longer perspective it is still part of an ongoing process.

Certainly, some media technologies may work so well, or be adopted so broadly, that they become very stable and resistant to change (for example, the NTSC television broadcast standard in the US). But in the last few decades, the social, political and economic premium placed on innovation, as well as the digitization of different media systems, have tended to push new media technologies toward instability. In this context, hybridization has created an unstable sociotechnical landscape and has compelled researchers to treat systems and their uses as moving targets (for example, the rapid coevolution of technologies and social groups that share audio and video over the Internet). This characteristic was first seen in the technological convergence of traditional media with computing and telecommunications that prompted the early studies within communication research and other fields in the 1960s and 1970s. It also accounts for the persistent sense of 'newness' that has been associated with media systems ever since.

Another specific aspect of social shaping associated with new media is that the point-to-point 'network' has become accepted as the archetypal form of contemporary social and technical organization. Today, the *network metaphor* applies not just to new media technologies, but also to the patterns of social relations and organizing and the institutional formations associated with them. It can be argued that more traditional mass media technologies, as well as the organizations that employed them and the institutions that governed them, embodied industrial-era notions of social and work organization. For example, though broadcasting was often organized into systems called 'networks', such systems were usually hierarchical. This type of configuration supported the large-scale production and distribution of messages directed from a few media centres (ordinarily, major cities or cultural capitals) to 'mass' audiences. It ensured the smooth and rapid diffusion of information from the 'top' or 'centre' of the hierarchy to the bottom or periphery – and provided little or no capacity for messages going the other way, so-called feedback. As it is understood today, however, the term 'network' denotes a broad, multiplex interconnection in which many points or 'nodes' (persons, groups, machines, collections of information, organizations) are embedded. Links among nodes may be created or abandoned on an as-needed basis at any location in the system, and any node can be either a sender or a receiver of messages – or both.

Certainly, high-tech firms, including new media services, tend to congregate in particular geographic places (the 'clusters' discussed by Cooke in this volume), and the network topographies of telecommunications, computing and media are far from evenly distributed around the world, or even across regions. But these hubs and regions do not necessarily dominate new media content as a few major cities and cultural centres did for mass media. New kinds of 'spaces and places' for sociality and culture have been created (see Curry in this volume), as systems like the Internet have been designed specifically to allow any node to connect to any other with network access. This architecture was introduced with the telephone system (and to a lesser extent, by the telegraph system before that), and it is both physically and qualitatively different from the 'networks' of broadcasting and print. Indeed, economists and others first recognized that the positive 'network externalities' associated with the telephone system were different in kind from the economies of scale of broadcasting or print. The larger the network, the more valuable it becomes to every additional new user, as each user gains the advantage of links to more potential respondents and sources of information.

Not only are new media shaped in characteristic ways; they also have distinctive social consequences. Perhaps the most obvious, one that that has been commented on since the days of McLuhan, is the *ubiquity* of new media. Though not every individual in a society may use (or indeed have access to) new media technologies, we can say they are ubiquitous because they affect everyone in the societies where they are employed. The reach of

ICTs extends far beyond the obvious arenas of entertainment and the workplace. Banking systems, utilities, education, law enforcement, military defence, health care and politics, for example, are all dependent on extensive ICT systems for record-keeping, monitoring and transmitting information – activities that affect anyone who deals with these services or activities.

The sense of ubiquity underlies several major issues that are discussed in the chapters that follow. For example, though ubiquity might be assumed, new technologies and the resources to use them are not distributed evenly or fairly, as evidenced by the flurry of research and news coverage about the 'digital divide' in the late 1990s (see Gandy, and Hudson, in this volume). By the same token, any system with pervasive reach and influence prompts questions about the control of the system and the power and cultural influence it affords those who are in control; new media systems are no exception. And while the relationship among media messages, public opinion and political participation has been studied extensively, the Internet and other new media technologies have presented new arenas for discourse that challenge the definition and understanding of the public sphere and what constitutes political action (see Bentivegna, and Luke, in this volume).

Another consequence of new media is the sense of *interactivity* that they convey to users. Interactivity is the main topic of the chapter by Sally McMillan in this volume, and is discussed in the introduction to Part Two. Briefly, however, we can say that because switching is a pivotal part of new media systems, they afford users more selectivity in their choices of information sources and interactions with other people. Communication researchers have known for decades that mass media audiences attend to, perceive and retain information selectively. Yet new media also give users the means to generate, seek and share content selectively, and to interact with other individuals and groups, on a scale that was impractical with traditional mass media. This selectivity accounts for much of the sense of interactivity or social presence associated with new media, as well as their 'demassified', or individualized, targeted quality. In turn, the sheer proliferation and diversity of content and sources now available have raised concerns about the quality of the content (for example, its authenticity or reliability), as well as questions about the nature of online experience and interaction (for example, about anonymity or identity of participants in online interaction).

NEW MEDIA, NEW METHODS?

Because the *Handbook* is organized around major substantive areas of research and scholarship, we have not dedicated a chapter specifically to the methodology of new media research. However, new media studies pose a number of empirical and analytical challenges that merit a brief discussion here.

The chapters in this volume represent a significant collation of past and current empirical research, as well as conceptual frameworks for analysing new media in relation to their social shaping and social consequences. While the field abounds with new and pressing research questions, only recently has attention been paid to the methods by which these are being addressed. Beyond the challenges posed by the multidisciplinary nature of the field, which results in often conflicting conventions underpinning the conduct and evaluation of empirical research, *Handbook* readers may discern two broad methodological issues. First, do new media require new methods to observe and study them? Second, how does empirical research contribute to the shaping and consequences of the new media being studied?

In response to the first issue, and as is evident from the recent bounty of books and articles addressing the conduct of empirical media research, and new media research in particular, two positions have emerged. The first presumes, at least implicitly, that media research rests on the same, well-established methods as any other area of social science (or humanities). In relation to the new media, therefore, the use of surveys, interviews, case studies, observation, textual analysis and so forth is considered to be 'business as usual'. Those adopting this position would argue that in new media research as elsewhere (perhaps even more so here, given the rush to produce findings before they go out of date), traditional standards of reliability, validity, generalizability and so forth are crucial to the evaluation of good research (e.g. Webster in this volume). This is perhaps the most common perspective, and is clearly laid out in the well-used textbook by Williams et al. (1988). Similarly, Deacon et al. (1999) deal with the Internet solely as a new source of information for media and communication researchers. They offer guidelines to its effective use as a knowledge resource, but say little about it as a subject of empirical research in its own right.

The contrasting position tends to draw primarily on a qualitative or ethnographic tradition (e.g. Hine, 2000), arguing that traditional methods must be changed both conceptually and procedurally. To the extent that new media generally, and virtual environments in particular, challenge key concepts of media research – authority and power, production and consumption, community and identity, and so forth – then research must frame and operationalize its questions (and answers) in different ways (Lyman and Wakeford, 1999). So too, again particularly for virtual environments, many guidelines, practices and evaluative criteria regarding, for example, research ethics, the nature of naturalistic/ unobtrusive versus participant observation, or criteria for survey sampling and evaluating response rates, must be reformulated (Mann and Stewart, 2000).

The second broad methodological consideration concerns the social uses of new media research. It will be apparent in many of the chapters that follow that a major research strategy is to track what are, in effect, real-world experiments, in which new communication infrastructures and changing social phenomena are observed. From these experiments, we can infer early indications of the likely future 'impacts' of these new media and see the social shaping of technology itself, occurring through a path-dependent process of technological change in which contingent histories of adoption matter (see Lievrouw in this volume).

However, because the media being observed are often new or provisional, the research itself may affect the course of its design, implementation or use more than it might for older media, which are more stable and where a critical or neutral distance is more readily sustainable. MacKenzie and Wajcman observe that 'the very process of adoption tends to improve the performance of those technologies that are adopted' (1999: 19); by the same token, researchers must also acknowledge that studies of this adoption feed back into the design process itself. In other words, in so far as new media technologies are shaped not only in the rarefied world of design and innovation but also through their early history of adoption and everyday use, such experiments, and the research that accompanies and assesses them, play a role in the social shaping and social consequences of new media.

Researchers vary in their response to this situation. For many, 'it would be an unforgivable dereliction of the responsibilities of intellectuals if the potentials offered by current developments were not fully explored, and a concerted effort made to shape their direction to bring about at least some of the much talked about utopian visions of communication in the electronic age' (Kress, 1998: 79; see also Biocca, 1993). For others, a critical distance between the researcher and the new media phenomena being researched is crucial to the independence of the research findings.

The very pace of change – both technological and social – poses a challenge to new media research. In other words, the field is in flux, not so much because it is new (indeed, it is at least 20 years old) but because the object of study itself and its social contexts have never been – nor are they likely to become – stable. Researchers working in the area must tolerate ambiguity and be comfortable with the study of moving targets. At the same time, anticipating the future significance of the new media is hazardous in the extreme. Boddy (1985) notes some of the widespread misconceptions, within both public

and industry circles, that existed at the time of television's arrival as a mass medium. Many observers failed to anticipate the success of television in dominating culture, information, lifestyles and, more arguably perhaps, public and political life in the second half of the twentieth century. Interestingly, in his highly influential book *Television: Technology and Cultural Form*, Raymond Williams (1974) had similar difficulties with prediction. He conceptualized new technologies primarily in terms of the transformation of television; despite his considerable percipience, he did not anticipate the convergence between broadcasting, telecommunication and, especially, information technology.

We might end this section with a note on terminology. In researching new media, some of the terms from mass media research still apply – production, media institution, design – though they are undoubtedly more complex and less fixed than hitherto. Other terms, however, apply less well. *Text* is one, as new media exploit the intertextual or transtextual (Drotner, 1992), as the meanings conveyed by new media result from an interactive engagement between producers and consumers, and as the texts are mutable, transformed through processes of relocation, transmission, and recombination.

Even more problematically perhaps, there is an uncertainty over how to label people in terms of their relationship with new media. The term *audience*, which was and to some extent still is satisfactory for mass media research, fits poorly within the domain of new media. In a number of important ways, audiences are becoming 'users'. Analytically, audiences are being relocated away from the screen, their activities contextualized into the everyday lifeworld. They are also becoming users because they are grappling with the meaning of new and unfamiliar media objects (i.e. as technologies, or consumer goods), and this not only in their homes but also in schools and workplaces. Further, they are becoming users because new media and information technologies open up new, more active modes of engagement with media – *playing* computer games, *surfing* the web, *searching* databases, *responding* to e-mail, *visiting* a chat room, *shopping* online and so on. Etymologically, the term 'audience' only satisfactorily covers the activities of listening and watching (though even this has been expanded to include the activities which contextualize listening and viewing). But the term 'user', despite its problematic histories (e.g. in uses and gratifications research, or its instrumental connotations in technology-driven studies of information retrieval, interface design and 'human factors', which suggest that users of media technologies differ little from users of washing machines or cars), better covers this variety of modes of engagement.

What is significant about people's uses of new media remains, in many ways, what was also significant about audiences for traditional media: that is, the extent to which media engagement is necessary for a common culture, for shared community values or, conversely, the extent to which media engagement undermines, fragments, manipulates or exploits people collectively (as publics, markets, nations and so on). In this sense, the term 'audience' is still appropriate. But grammatically it is awkward, as are 'communicators', 'consumers' or 'users'. One can only conclude, as do the authors of the chapters included here, that no one term can be expected to cover the variety of significant relationships which now exist between people and the media. Perhaps most important is that we use the array of available terms with care, and not lose sight of the observation that has become a consensus among audience researchers (Livingstone, 1999), that the nature of the relationship, rather than the artificial creation of a reified entity (audience, user, consumer), is most central to the analysis of new media and their social consequences. To focus on the relationship also serves to locate this relationship in a social context, for people are, first and foremost, workers, business people, parents, teachers, friends – thoroughly embedded social roles which precede their status as 'users' or 'audiences'.

OVERVIEW OF THIS VOLUME

In putting together this book, we have stressed research on socially situated technologies, and on studies that document circumstances where strong cultural concerns or social norms have developed around ICTs. As its subtitle suggests, the social contexts and uses of new media are as important as the technologies themselves. 'Social shaping' and 'consequences' suggest the evolving, dynamic nature of the systems and their related issues, as well as major approaches to research in the area. On the one hand, there is a concern with agency and action; on the other, a concern with social effects, structure and impacts. While the *Handbook* attempts to cover the field as comprehensively as is practical, no single approach can be said to characterize the whole work, though certain sections may illustrate widely held perspectives.

Overall, one principal purpose of this volume is to lay out the present boundaries of new media research so as to allow a clear view of the current state of the art. We agree that 'as new fields evolve, there are periodic attempts to take stock of what's happened so far, how things are going, and what still needs to be done' (Johansen, 1984). Consequently, the emphasis throughout the chapters that follow is on documenting the most significant social research findings and insights in areas where a substantial amount of work has already been accomplished, rather than on speculations about

future technological directions or scenarios. Thus, one ambition of the *Handbook*, prosaically but perhaps most usefully, is that it sets out to draw together in a single place the key resources and trends among the rapidly diversifying variety of new media research. The goal is to make visible and readily accessible work which has already been conducted but which may not be familiar to specialists in particular disciplines. In some domains, the stress is on consolidating and building on significant contributions already made within the field, while in others it seems more important to incorporate key ideas and approaches from outside, given the interdisciplinary nature of new media research.

Although the field of new media studies generally is highly multidisciplinary, undoubtedly different specializations draw particularly on some disciplinary literatures, as the book parts demonstrate. Hence, Part One, concerned with locating new media within the changing social landscape, draws mainly on sociological, social psychological and political science traditions. In Part Two, science and technology studies, information science and communication research come to the fore. Part Three integrates organization studies, management and organizational communication in its analysis of how new media fit into, or transform, organizations. By contrast, Part Four, centred on the fast-moving and often nationally specific field of new media policy and regulation, makes use of legal perspectives as well as those of political economy. The latter perspective is important also in the more economically oriented Part Five, which is concerned with new media industries and markets. Finally, Part Six draws perhaps most broadly on developments in social theory, philosophy, sociology and the humanities in its aim of mapping a cultural approach to the new media.

A more ambitious aim than that of collating new media research is that of facilitating the identification of key themes and debates which have thus far framed the major contours of new media research, in order to support both critical perspectives on research and the development of future research projects. Hence we have invited chapter authors to identify not only major trends but also problematic claims or assumptions, remaining gaps in the research record, and new domains to be explored. In such future developments it is our hope that researchers from different disciplines and perspectives will not only converge productively on the problematics of new media shaping and consequences, but also take back these perspectives into their home disciplines. For it seems that, at least until very recently, little new-media- or ICT-related research has found its way into the most prestigious, core or mainstream journals in communication research, sociology, social psychology, education, law, economics or political science.

New media research spans not only multiple disciplines but also many countries. Yet, as already noted, it has proved more challenging than anticipated, and perhaps we have been less successful than we had hoped in achieving a multinational coverage of new media research. Research communities tend to be national in orientation, addressing national policy developments, responsive to national funding sources in particular economic and cultural contexts, and networked within distinct linguistic and intellectual traditions. While we are aware of the advantages of learning from comparative research, to some extent, the challenges of developing a comparative overview in the field of new media remain for the future.

Therefore, we offer the *Handbook of New Media* as one in what we hope will be a series of useful surveys and syntheses of new media studies, as more questions are asked, as more comprehensive and creative answers are found, and as the field and its influence continue to grow.

NOTES

1 For a longer historical perspective, bearing in mind that all media were once 'new' and gave rise to various hopes and anxieties, readers are encouraged to review the opening chapter of Rice and Associates (1984) as well as several histories of media technologies that have informed the field, including books by Jim Beniger (1986), James Carey (1989), Claude Fischer (1992), Patrice Flichy, (1995 [1991]), Carolyn Marvin (1988) and, more recently, Brian Winston (1996), as well as the edited collection by Chandler and Cortada (2000).

2 This dichotomy is well summarized in the introduction to a collection of key articles from the journal *Media, Culture & Society* (Collins et al., 1986).

REFERENCES

Allen, T.J. (1977) *Managing the Flow of Technology: Technology Transfer and the Dissemination of Technological Innovation within the R&D Organization.* Cambridge, MA: MIT Press.

Arrow, K. (1979) 'The economics of information', in M.L. Dertouzos and J. Moses (eds), *The Computer Age: a Twenty-Year View.* Cambridge, MA: MIT Press. pp. 306–17.

Arrow, K. (1984) *Collected Papers.* Vol. 4: *The Economics of Information.* Oxford: Blackwell.

Baldwin, T.F., McVoy, D.S. and Steinfield, C. (eds) (1996) *Convergence: Integrating Media, Information and Communication.* Thousand Oaks, CA: Sage.

Barnett, G.A. and Choi, Y. (1995) 'Physical distance and language as determinants of the international telecommunications network', *International Political Science Review*, 16: 249–65.

Barnett, G.A. and Salisbury, J.G.T. (1996) 'Communication and globalization: a longitudinal analysis of the international telecommunication network', *Journal of World System Research*, 2 (16): 1–17.

Becker, L.B. and Schoenbach, K. (eds) (1989) *Audience Responses to Media Diversification: Coping with Plenty.* Hillsdale, NJ: Erlbaum.

Bell, D. (1973) *The Coming of Post-Industrial Society: a Venture in Social Forecasting.* New York: Basic.

Beniger, J.R. (1986) *The Control Revolution: Technological and Economic Origins of the Information Society.* Cambridge, MA: Harvard University Press.

Biocca, F. (1993) 'Communication research in the design of communication interfaces and systems', *Journal of Communication*, 43 (4): 59–68.

Blumler, J., McLeod, J.M. and Rosengren, K.E. (eds) (1992) *Communication and Culture across Space and Time: Prospects of Comparative Analysis.* Newbury Park, CA: Sage.

Boddy, W. (1985) '"The shining centre of the home": ontologies of television in the "Golden Age"', in P. Drummond and R. Paterson (eds), *Television in Transition.* London: British Film Institute.

Boudon, R. (1991) 'What middle-range theories are', *Contemporary Social Psychology*, 20 (4): 519–24.

Bourdieu, P. (1977 [1972]) *Outline of a Theory of Practice*, trans. R. Nice. Cambridge: Cambridge University Press.

Bourdieu, P. (1980) 'The production of belief: contribution to a theory of symbolic goods', *Media, Culture & Society*, 2 (3): 261–93.

Burgelman, J.-C. (1997) 'Issues and assumptions in communications policy and research in Western Europe: a critical analysis', in J. Corner, P. Schlesinger and R. Silverstone (eds), *International Media Research: a Critical Survey.* London: Routledge.

Calabrese, A. and Burgelman, J.-C. (eds) (1999) *Communication, Citizenship, and Social Policy: Rethinking the Limits of the Welfare State.* Lanham, MD and Oxford: Rowman & Littlefield.

Carey, J.W. (1989) *Communication as Culture: Essays on Media and Society.* Boston and London: Unwin Hyman.

Chaffee, S.H. and Chu, G. (1992) 'Communication and cultural change in China', in J. Blumler, J.M. McLeod and K.E. Rosengren (eds), *Communication and Culture across Space and Time: Prospects of Comparative Analysis.* Newbury Park, CA: Sage. pp. 209–37.

Chandler, A.D. Jr and Cortada, J.W. (eds) (2000) *A Nation Transformed by Information: How Information Has Shaped the United States from Colonial Times to the Present.* Oxford and New York: Oxford University Press.

Cherry, E.C. (1978 [1957]) *On Human Communication*, 3rd edn. Cambridge, MA: MIT Press.

Cherry, E.C. (1985) *The Age of Access: Information Technology and Social Revolution. The Posthumous Papers of Colin Cherry*, compiled and edited by W. Edmondson. London: Croom Helm.

Collins, R., Curran, J., Garnham, N., Scannell, P., Schlesinger, P. and Sparks, C. (eds) (1986) *Media, Culture and Society: a Critical Reader.* London: Sage.

Deacon, D., Pickering, M., Golding, P. and Murdock, G. (1999). *Researching Communications: a Practical Guide to Methods in Media and Cultural Analysis*. London: Arnold.

Drotner, K. (1992) 'Modernity and media panics', in M. Skovmand and K.C. Schroder (eds), *Media Cultures: Reappraising Transnational Media*. London: Routledge.

Durlak, J.T. (1987) 'A typology for interactive media', in M.L. McLaughlin (ed.), *Communication Yearbook 10*. Newbury Park, CA: Sage. pp. 743–56.

Dutton, W.H. (ed.) (1996) *Information and Communication Technologies: Visions and Realities*. Oxford: Oxford University Press.

Ferguson, M. (ed.) (1986) *New Communication Technologies and the Public Interest*. London: Sage.

Ferment in the Field (1983) Special issue of *Journal of Communication*, 33 (3), summer.

Fischer, C.S. (1992) *America Calling: a Social History of the Telephone to 1940*. Berkeley and Los Angeles: University of California Press.

Flichy, P. (1995 [1991]) *Dynamics of Modern Communication: the Shaping and Impact of New Communication Technologies*, trans. L. Libbrecht. London: Sage.

Foucault, M. (1970 [1966]) *The Order of Things: an Archaeology of the Human Sciences*, trans. A. Sheridan. New York: Pantheon.

Foucault, M. (1980) *Power/Knowledge: Selected Interviews and Other Writings 1972–1977*, trans. C. Gordon et al. New York: Pantheon.

Gandy, O.H. Jr (1993) *The Panoptic Sort: a Political Economy of Personal Information*. Boulder, CO: Westview.

Garnham, N. (1986) 'Contribution to a political economy of mass-communication', in R. Collins, J. Curran, N. Garnham, P. Scannell, P. Schlesinger and C. Sparks (eds), *Media, Culture and Society: a Critical Reader*. London: Sage. pp. 9–32.

Garnham, N. (1990) *Capitalism and Communication: Global Culture and the Economics of Information*. London: Sage.

Garnham, N. (1994) 'Whatever happened to the information society?', in R.E. Mansell (ed.), *The Management of Information and Communication Technologies: Emerging Patterns of Control*. London: Aslib, The Association for Information Management. pp. 42–51.

Giddens, A. (1979) *Central Problems in Social Theory*. Berkeley and Los Angeles: University of California Press.

Giddens, A. (1984) *The Constitution of Society: Outline of the Theory of Structuration*. Cambridge: Polity.

Hiltz, S.R. and Turoff, M. (1993 [1978]) *The Network Nation: Human Communication via Computer*, rev. edn. Cambridge: MIT Press.

Hine, C. (2000) *Virtual Ethnography*. London: Sage.

Ito, Y. (1981) 'The *johoka shakai* approach to the study of communication in Japan', in C. Wilhoit and H. deBock (eds), *Mass Communication Review Yearbook*, vol. 2. Beverly Hills, CA: Sage. pp. 671–98.

Johansen, R. (1984) 'Foreword', in R.E. Rice and Associates (eds), *The New Media: Communication, Research and Technology*. Beverly Hills, CA: Sage. pp. 7–8.

Johansen, R., Vallee, J. and Spangler, K. (1979) *Electronic Meetings: Technical Alternatives and Social Choice*. Reading, MA: Addison-Wesley.

Jonscher, C. (1983) 'Information resources and economic productivity', *Information Economics and Policy*, 1: 13–35.

Jouet, J. (1994) 'Communication and mediation', *Réseaux*, 2 (1): 73–90.

Kiesler, S.B., Siegel, J. and McGuire, T.W. (1984) 'Social psychological aspects of computer-mediated communication', *American Psychologist*, 39, 1123–34.

Kling, R. (1999) 'What is social informatics and why does it matter?', *D-Lib Magazine* (online), 5 (1). URL: http://www.dlib.org/dlib/january99/kling/01kling.html.

Kress, G. (1998) 'Visual and verbal models of representation in electronically mediated communication: the potentials of new forms of text', in I. Snyder (ed.), *Page to Screen: Taking Literacy into the Electronic Era*. London and New York: Routledge. pp. 53–79.

Kurisaki, Y. and Yanagimachi, H. (1992) 'The impact of information on the economic development of sub-regional centres: a trial application of an "information activity" index to the 43 cities in Japan', in C. Antonelli (ed.), *The Economics of Information Networks*. Amsterdam and London: North-Holland. pp. 71–89.

Lamberton, D.M. (ed.) (1971) *The Economics of Information and Knowledge*. Harmondsworth: Penguin.

Lazarsfeld, P.F. (1941) 'Remarks on administrative and critical communications research', *Studies in Philosophy and Science*, 9: 3–16.

Lea, M. (ed.) (1992) *Contexts of Computer-Mediated Communication*. New York: Harvester Wheatsheaf.

Lengel, L. (ed.) (2000) *Culture and Technology in the New Europe: Civic Discourse in Transformation in Post-Communist Nations*. Stamford, CT: Ablex.

Lievrouw, L.A., Bucy, E.P., Finn, T.A., Frindte, W., Gershon, R.A., Haythornthwaite, C., Köhler, T., Metz, JM and Sundar, S.S. (2001) 'Bridging the sub-disciplines: an overview of communication and technology research', in W.B. Gudykunst (ed.), *Communication Yearbook 24*. Thousand Oaks, CA: Sage, for the International Communication Association. pp. 271–95.

Livingstone, S. (1999) 'New media, new audiences', *New Media & Society*, 1 (1): 59–66.

Livingstone, S. and M. Bovill, M. (eds) (2001) *Children and their Changing Media Environment: a European Comparative Study*. Mahwah, NJ: Erlbaum.

Lull, J. (ed.) (1988) *World Families Watch Television*. Newbury Park, CA: Sage.

Lyman, P. and Wakeford, N. (1999) 'Going into the (virtual) field', *American Behavioral Scientist*, 43 (3): 359–76.

Machlup, F. (1962) *The Production and Distribution of Knowledge in the United States*. Princeton, NJ: Princeton University Press.

MacKenzie, D. and Wajcman, J. (eds) (1999) *The Social Shaping of Technology*, 2nd edn. Buckingham: Open University Press.

Mann, C. and Stewart, F. (2000) *Internet Communication and Qualitative Research: a Handbook for Researching Online*. London: Sage.

Marvin, C. (1988) *When Old Technologies Were New: Thinking about Electric Communication in the Late Nineteenth Century*. New York and Oxford: Oxford University Press.

McQuail, D. (1986) 'Is media theory adequate to the challenge of new communications technologies?', in M. Ferguson (ed.), *New Communication Technologies and the Public Interest: Comparative Perspectives on Policy and Research*. London: Sage.

McQuail, D., Siune, K. and Euromedia Research Group (eds) (1986) *New Media Politics: Comparative Perspectives in Western Europe*. London: Sage.

Melody, W.H. and Mansell, R.E. (1983) 'The debate over critical vs. administrative research: circularity or challenge', *Journal of Communication* 33 (3): 103–16.

Miller, D. and Slater, D. (2000) *The Internet: an Ethnographic Approach*. London: Berg.

Morris, M. and Ogan, C. (1996) 'The Internet as mass medium', *Journal of Communication*, 46 (1): 39–51.

Mosco, V. (1982) *Pushbutton Fantasies: Critical Perspectives on Videotex and Information Technology*. Norwood, NJ: Ablex.

Mosco, V. (1996) *The Political Economy of Communication: Rethinking and Renewal*. London: Sage.

Nora, S. and Minc, A. (1981 [1978]) *The Computerization of Society: a Report to the President of France*. Cambridge, MA: MIT Press.

Palmquist, R.A. (1992) 'The impact of information technology on the individual', *Annual Review of Information Science and Technology*, 27: 3–42.

Parker, E. (1970a) 'The new communication media', in C.S. Wallia (ed.), *Toward Century 21: Technology, Society and Human Values*. New York: Basic. pp. 97–106.

Parker, E. (1970b) 'Information utilities and mass communication', in H. Sackman and N. Nie (eds), *The Information Utility and Social Choice*. Montvale, NJ: AFIPS. pp. 51–70.

Parker, E. (1973a) 'Technological change and the mass media', in I. Pool, W. Schramm, F. Frey, N. Maccoby and E. Parker (eds), *Handbook of Communication*. Chicago: Rand McNally. pp. 619–45.

Parker, E. (1973b) 'Implications of new information technology', *Public Opinion Quarterly*, 37 (4): 590–600.

Parker, E. (1978) 'Communication satellites for rural development', *Telecommunications Policy*, 2 (4): 309–15.

Parker, E. and Dunn, D. (1972) 'Information technology: its social potential', *Science*, 176: 1392–9.

Parker, E. and Hudson, H. (1975) 'Telecommunication planning for rural development', *IEEE Transactions on Communications*, 23 (10): 1177–85.

Parker, E. and Mohammadi, A. (1977) 'National development support communication', in M. Teheranian, F. Hakiszadeh and M. Vidale (eds), *Communications Policy for National Development: a Comparative Perspective*. London: Routledge & Kegan Paul. pp. 167–201.

Pool, I. de S. (ed.) (1977) *The Social Impact of the Telephone*. Cambridge, MA: MIT Press.

Pool, I. de S. (1983) *Technologies of Freedom*. Cambridge, MA: Harvard University Press.

Pool, I. de S. (1990) *Technologies of Boundaries: on Telecommunications in a Global Age*, edited by Eli M. Noam. Cambridge, MA: Harvard University Press.

Porat, M.U. and Rubin, M.R. (1977) *The Information Economy*. OT Special Publication 77-12, 9 vols. Washington, DC: US Department of Commerce, Office of Telecommunications.

Reeves, B. and Nass, C. (1996) *The Media Equation: How People Treat Computers, Television and New Media Like Real People and Places*. Stanford, CA: CSLI and Cambridge: Cambridge University Press.

Rice, R.E. and Associates (eds) (1984) *The New Media: Communication, Research and Technology*. Beverly Hills, CA: Sage.

Robins, K. and Morley, D. (1989) 'Spaces of identity: communications technologies and the reconfiguration of Europe', *Screen*, 30 (4): 11–34.

Robins, K. and Webster, F. (1985) ' "The revolution of the fixed wheel": information, technology and social Taylorism', in P. Drummond and R. Paterson (eds), *Television in Transition*. London: British Film Institute. pp. 36–63.

Rogers, E.M. (1986) *Communication Technology: the New Media in Society*. New York: Free Press.

Rogers, E.M. (1995) *Diffusion of Innovations*, 4th edn. New York: Free Press.

Rogers, E.M. (1999) 'Anatomy of the two subdisciplines of communication study', *Human Communication Research*, 25: 618–31.

Schiller, D. (1982) *Telematics and Government*. Norwood, NJ: Ablex.

Schiller, H.I. (1981) *Who Knows: Information in the Age of the Fortune 500*. Norwood, NJ: Ablex.

Schramm, W. (1977) *Big Media, Little Media: Tools and Technologies for Instruction*. Beverly Hills, CA: Sage.

Schultz, W. (1992) 'European media systems in transition: general trends and modifying conditions. The case of the Federal Republic of Germany', *Gazette*, 49: 23–40.

Schumpeter, J. (1939) *Business Cycles: a Theoretical, Historical and Statistical Analysis of the Capitalist Process*. New York: McGraw-Hill.

Shields, P. and Samarajiva, R. (1993) 'Competing frameworks for research on information-communication technologies and society: toward a synthesis', in S.A. Deetz (ed.), *Communication Yearbook 16*. Newbury Park, CA: Sage. pp. 349–80.

Short, J., Williams, E. and Christie, B. (1976) *The Social Psychology of Telecommunications*. New York: Wiley.

Silverstone, R. and Hirsch, E. (eds) (1992) *Consuming Technologies: Media and Information in Domestic Spaces*. London and New York: Routledge.

Slack, J.D. and Fejes, F. (eds) (1987) *The Ideology of the Information Age*. Norwood, NJ: Ablex.

Smith, M.R. and Marx, L. (eds) (1994) *Does Technology Drive History? The Dilemma of Technological Determinism*. Cambridge, MA: MIT Press.

Sproull, L. and Kiesler, S. (1991) *Connections: New Ways of Working in the Networked Organization*. Cambridge, MA: MIT Press.

Steuer, J. (1995) 'Defining virtual reality: dimensions determining telepresence', in F. Biocca and M.R. Levy (eds), *Communication in the Age of Virtual Reality*. Mahwah, NJ: Erlbaum. pp. 33–56.

Turkle, S. (1980) 'Computer as Rorschach', *Society/ Transaction*, January/February: 15–24.

Turkle, S. (1984) *The Second Self: Computers and the Human Spirit*. New York: Simon & Schuster.

Tydeman, J. and Kelm, E.J. (1986) *New Media in Europe: Satellites, Cable, VCRs and Videotex*. London: McGraw-Hill.

UNESCO (2000) *World Communication and Information Report, 1999–2000*. Paris: UNESCO.

Webster, F. (1995) *Theories of the Information Society*. London: Routledge.

Webster, F. and Robins, K. (1986) *Information Technology: a Luddite Analysis*. Norwood, NJ: Ablex.

Webster, F. and Robins, K. (1989) 'Plan and control: towards a cultural history of the information society', *Theory and Society*, 18: 323–51.

What's New about New Media? (1999) Special themed section of *New Media & Society*, 1 (1): 10–82.

Williams, F., Rice, R.E. and Rogers, E.M. (1988) *Research Methods and the New Media*. New York: Free Press.

Williams, R. (1974) *Television: Technology and Cultural Form*. London: Fontana.

Winston, B. (1996) *Media Technology and Society: a History. From the Telegraph to the Internet*. London and New York: Routledge.

PART ONE: THE CHANGING SOCIAL LANDSCAPE

Introduction

SONIA LIVINGSTONE

PUTTING NEW MEDIA INTO CONTEXT

Rather than beginning with an account of the latest media technologies, as often seems tempting, and then attempting to unravel their consequences, this part of the *Handbook* sets the scene by starting with questions of society, social problems and social change. The metaphor of the 'landscape' which underpins this part was chosen for its breadth and openness in guiding the identification of where and why certain questions arise regarding the social shaping and social consequences of new media across a variety of disciplines or research domains. It argues that media are always embedded in a social landscape, which precedes, shapes, contextualizes and continues after any specific technological innovation. While the social shaping argument is addressed more directly in Part Two of this volume, this first part asks less how the technologies came to be as they are and more how they are used in different conditions, often by well-established social institutional forms. Indeed, a consensus is emerging within the maturing field of new media studies that it is imperative to put new media into context, to locate them within the social landscape, and to map the changing media environment in relation to the human activities which, in turn, structure that environment. Such an analysis, through its stress on a multiplicity of contextualizing processes, is intended effectively to undermine any simple account of the supposed impacts of technology on society.

In this introduction, I draw out some of the assumptions and debates which underpin the different positions jostling – productively, I believe – for attention on the subject of new media and the changing social landscape. One must first note that any mapping of 'the social landscape' is inevitably partial. The seven chapters included here were selected so as to represent both the disciplinary diversity (communication studies, sociology, political science, social psychology, education, cultural studies, etc.) and the multiple levels of analysis (from macro-level theories of the information society through meso-level accounts of community to the micro-level analysis of interpersonal communication) with which the changing social landscape is currently being researched. Across the chapters, a variety of conceptions of the relation between technological and social change are evident, ranging from what might be termed a cultural determinism to a qualified or soft technological determinism, and from those which identify a dramatic change in the social landscape to those which are highly cautious about any evidence for social change. The authors in this part agree, however, that technologies must be contextualized within the historical and culturally specific conditions of their development, diffusion and use, and so each tends to take the terms of their analysis from the social landscape rather than from features of the new media themselves.

The social 'landscape' is, however, itself a far from neutral metaphor. In recent cultural geography, the tendency to conceive of landscape itself as natural and given has been strongly challenged, for landscapes are themselves culturally constituted through a set of historically specific material and discursive practices (Barnes and Duncan, 1992). Thus, the landscape metaphor draws us forever back to society in seeking an account of new media. For landscapes containing new media are busy, contested, peopled landscapes, drawing new media into the contestation of the major contours, the navigable paths and the beneficial and harmful directions to be taken. Appadurai (1996: 33–6) usefully unpacks the landscape metaphor into five dimensions of global cultural flows which together construct the imagined worlds in which we live. These he identifies as ethnoscape (the shifting landscape of persons, identities, diaspora), technoscape (the fluid, networked configuration of technologies), financescapes (the disposition of global capital), mediascapes (the distribution of information, images and audiences) and ideoscapes (the ideologies and counter-ideologies which link images and ideas to the power of states). His purpose is to highlight the disjunctures between economy, culture and politics that arise from the interaction among these flows. This focus on interaction means that, for our present purposes, addressing social, cultural and economic questions about the new media cannot be restricted to the mediascape or technoscape, but must encompass all these and doubtless yet other flows, according to a dynamic rather than a static conception of the social landscape.

This contextual orientation is both stimulating and yet somewhat problematic in practice; indeed its very attractions also pinpoint its disadvantages. First, the key terms – landscape, context, ecology, environment – are both open and vague, broad-ranging yet without limit. Hence, while we invited authors of this and other parts to map the history and geography of 'their' segment of the social landscape, each has in practice found it necessary to limit this perhaps impractical brief in accordance with the balance of research in the published literature. Second, while these key terms serve to put the media in their place, avoiding an excessive 'media-centrism' which fails to recognize the constructive processes which shape both the nature and the uses of new media, yet one risks losing sight altogether of media and their particular technological, semiotic or other characteristics when grappling with the complexity of the many interlocking and conflicting social processes which in turn define and shape the landscape. Third, in so far as new media are becoming recognized as significant within and so increasingly researched by many traditionally distinct academic disciplines, sustaining a focus on the new media requires an interdisciplinarity that challenges the typically discipline-based expertise of researchers as well as encouraging them in new, boundary-crossing work.

RELATING TECHNOLOGICAL AND SOCIAL CHANGE

Underlying the metaphor of the social landscape, or the stress on social context, in new media studies is a debate over how technological innovation is related to social change. As many have observed, no aspect of society at the start of the twenty-first century – from work to family life, from politics to entertainment, from religion to sexuality – is untouched by innovations in information and communication technologies. Yet, such observations can all too easily lend themselves to the kind of technological determinism that social science now widely critiques. As Raymond Williams noted, 'in *technological determinism*, research and development have been assumed as self-generating. The new technologies are invented as it were in an independent sphere, and then create new societies or new human conditions' (1974: 13). Rather than researching questions which cast technological innovation as the cause and society as the effect, social science has developed the counter-view that 'the technological, instead of being a sphere separate from social life, is part of what makes society possible – in other words, it is constitutive of society' (MacKenzie and Wajcman, 1999: 23). Thus, before and indeed after any new medium is introduced there is a lengthy process of development and design, of the identification of a market and the construction of a 'need', all of these being fundamentally social activities rather than purely technical ones.

Although this alternative to technological determinism is widely endorsed, interestingly it seems in continual need of restatement, as will be apparent throughout this volume. For despite a range of critiques, technological determinism remains alive and well and, whether in academic, public or policy forums, significant social changes are being attributed to technological innovation which are more properly attributable to preceding or concomitant social, political or economic changes. Such discourses are readily exemplified by concerns over children, tending to construe childhood as a fixed and idealized essence vulnerable to the external and undesirable intrusion of new media. In countering this naive technological determinism, Buckingham shows how the expectations and fears commonly associated with new media instead derive from long-standing social and moral concerns regarding childhood, tensions which historians have traced back several centuries to the origin of the Western conception of childhood itself (Luke, 1989). A similar argument can be made for other aspects of the social landscape.

Nonetheless, just how new media are 'part of' society remains subject to theoretical dispute. The critique of technological determinism is most assertively posed by those who implicitly or explicitly develop the alternative case for cultural determinism. In support of this view, one may note that when discussions over social contexts and consequences of new media become most lively or contentious, it is generally because people are discussing not technology but society – how is society changing, what are the key drivers of change, and which changes are for the better or the worse? Instead of regarding ICT as, for example, a panacea for the ills of modern society (loss of political participation, of community belonging, of childhood innocence), the cultural approach instead seeks to understand the social relations that brought these about in the first place. ICT may mediate these, but the social relations – whether of democracy, or culture, or social exclusion – remain primary. Consequently, by questioning the popular view that the new media somehow constitute a new realm which raises entirely new questions and demands new analytic concepts, the authors in this part prefer to analyse human activities within well-established frameworks, taking as their starting point questions of democracy, childhood, community and so forth.

There appears to be a contingent, though not necessary, link between the stress on the cultural (or economic) origins of new-media-related phenomena and a critical response to the question of social change. Particularly in so far as social institutions, processes and distinctions reproduce traditional power relations just as much through the new media as elsewhere, the cultural approach tends to respond to the hype surrounding new media by asserting 'no change' or 'there is nothing new under the sun' (Livingstone, 1999a). For part of the research community, this also represents a response to the particular pressures that the widespread interest in new media is placing on the academy. Thus increasingly, it seems expected that academics are able to predict, and so intervene in, events which shape the future; notably, a considerable wariness about engaging in futurology characterizes the essays in this part (see also Silverstone, 1997). Even though to counter technological determinism as an explanation for social change need not demand that one argue against social change *per se*, this wariness regarding new media's relation to social change has its advantages. Particularly, as some of the chapters in this part illustrate, research most effectively begins with what is known, evading the hype, learning the lessons of history rather than 'reinventing the wheel', and moving only cautiously in the direction of what may, perhaps, be new.

Curiously, in avoiding a technologically determinist approach, it may seem that some researchers of new media readily bracket off the 'black box' of the technologies involved, being primarily interested in exploring new or distinctive patterns of interaction among people in their uses of new media. Such an approach – advocated in extreme terms by none of our authors – neutralizes new

media, undermining attention to their specific characteristics, histories and potentials. However, in attempting to move beyond both a simple cultural and a hard technological determinism, it remains a challenge to encompass both the breadth of the social landscape and the detailed technological or semiotic specificities of the new media. Here MacKenzie and Wajcman's (1999) distinction between technological determinism as a theory of technology and as a theory of society proves useful. As the former, technological determinism clearly fails: technological innovation is a thoroughly social process, from conception, design, production, marketing, diffusion, appropriation, use and consequences. But as a theory of society and social change, one may agree with MacKenzie and Wajcman (1999: 3) that technological determinism contains 'a partial truth'. In other words, provided it is firmly understood that, as argued in Part Two of the *Handbook*, technologies are social products which embed human relations in their very constitution, we may – for convenience in our arguments and discussion – cast them in the role of actors, along with other kinds of actor, when explaining social processes, whether education, political life, childhood, labour and so forth. But this is only a shorthand, for 'precisely because technological determinism is partly right as a theory of society (technology matters not just physically and biologically, but also to our human relations to each other), its deficiency as a theory of technology impoverishes the political life of our societies' (1999: 5).

A focus on the 'theory of society' is of course highly abstract, particularly unmanageable when faced with the concrete particularities of new media, and for this reason ways of conceptualizing the scope and flows of the social landscape are essential. More pragmatically, however, we may also learn here from past 'new' media. If we shift our focus for a moment from new media to research on the social uses of now older media, especially television, the argument for context (or landscape) has been thoroughly stated (e.g. Radway, 1988). Indeed, the research corpus on the social, institutional and political nature of both media production and media reception or consumption in everyday life is well known. In new media studies, however, where media forms and contents are much less familiar, and where little research as yet exists on either production or use, it is easy to find new media technologies intrinsically fascinating objects, losing sight of the particular social contexts, located within particular cultural flows, which render them meaningful (Livingstone, 1999b). Thus in new media research, one may find that the overwhelming perception that technology is making a difference to society leads some researchers to assert the rhetorical rejection of technological determinism expected of right-thinking social scientists but then to endorse implicitly a more qualified and contextualized 'soft' determinism (as a partial explanation of society, as argued above). Such a soft determinism is interestingly developed by drawing on the theoretical continuities between research on 'old' and 'new' media, specifically through the analogy of technology as text. While avoiding a simple determinism, this analogy invites the identification of how technologies, like texts, are designed and interpreted – both within particular social contexts – so as to facilitate certain social options and close off others. Thus, several of the authors in this part are interested in pursuing the ways in which the social processes of new media design and use in turn shape communication in specific realms (politics, community, etc.) and through engagement with relevant public and policy forums so as to open up, or close down, certain social possibilities (see the chapters by Jankowski, Bentivegna and Kellner).

This softer, more constructionist position is to some degree consistent with the dominant public conception of new media. This is both useful and dangerous, for among both the general public and the specific publics for academic research (such as policy-makers and research funding bodies), the assumption that new technologies are somehow introduced into society and then 'bring about' social change serves as the trope which mobilizes interest in academic research. The danger is that such assumptions easily shift from soft to hard technological determinism, and from a theory of society to one of technology, while all the while such lay beliefs are themselves constitutive of the social contexts which frame new technology development, appropriation and, indeed, research. Undermining or qualifying these assumptions, particularly when they are seen to draw on a widespread moral anxiety sufficient to stifle complex, careful or contingent responses on the part of a policy community, becomes in turn a key strategy for some social scientists in the field when disseminating their research (see the chapters by Webster and Buckingham).

RESEARCHING THE NEW MEDIA

While the relation between technological and social change represents the key debate underlying this part of the *Handbook*, the differing positions adopted by the authors on other aspects of new media research illustrate further debates current in the field. First, it is clear that varying assessments of the pace, urgency even, of both social and technological change frame new media debates. While, as already noted, the widespread hype surrounding new media appears in and of itself sufficient to generate a sceptical response from the academy, there are indeed genuine difficulties in measuring social change. This in turn has implications for the role of new media research in either critiquing or intervening in the political and economic management of new media. Thus Webster opens this first part by reminding us not to bypass conventional standards of intellectual and empirical rigour in making sense of the new media, noting that these standards are easily swept aside in the rush to research a supposedly fast-changing world. On the other hand, Kellner, later in this part, warns that the academy may itself be bypassed should it fail to address the questions asked regarding new media as and when these rise to the top of public and policy agendas.

This is not simply a matter of trading academic standards against timely intervention in policy, but also reflects the long-standing debate within media and communications between so-called administrative and critical traditions of research (Levy and Gurevitch, 1994; see also Ferment in the Field, 1983). Is it the responsibility of research actively to shape technological change or to evaluate the process of social shaping from a position of independence and distance? Should communication research produce knowledge in order to inform or to critique the strategic activities of the establishment, and when is either approach in the public interest? Compromise positions are often favoured, although it remains problematic that the former requires knowledge to be produced according to an external timetable, while the latter is generally best furthered with the benefit of hindsight. Interestingly too, it would appear that a soft form of technological determinism is more often endorsed by those concerned to intervene in policies regarding new media design and appropriation in order to further prosocial goals, though such a link is far from necessary. Of the chapters in this part, Bentivegna, Jankowski, Rice and Kellner appear more interested in rethinking technologies in terms of their potential benefits to the cultural and political life of our societies, while Webster, Buckingham and Baym are to varying degrees more critical of the grand claims made for new media.

More generally, one may ask, in what terms should the study of new media pursue its project? For the authors in this part, as already noted, the key analytic terms derive primarily from the social landscape. Thus, rather than identifying a radical break between past and future, they take a broadly evolutionary approach which tends to view technological innovation through the lens of well-established social and political conceptual frameworks. Thus while they explore, to varying degrees, how new technologically mediated possibilities for communication, participation and relationship may open up new visions of society, they root their accounts in the slow-to-change social landscape, stressing the complexity and the diversity of the economic, political, social and cultural processes which contextualize new media. For example, Bentivegna addresses the relation of politics and new media by beginning with the difficulties faced by Western democracies, identifying how, by drawing on the theory of the public sphere, these can be construed as problems of access, communication and social relations. In so far as new media implement new models of communication, they may contribute to the conditions that bring about change in democratic participation and citizenship. Similarly, Baym grounds her account of computer-mediated communication within the social psychological analysis of interpersonal relations, noting how new forms of electronic communication have been analysed in relation to the standards for diversity and interactivity set by the age-old model of face-to-face communication (and found wanting, in these terms). And Buckingham relates children's use of electronic entertainment back to another age-old social activity, that of play, while Webster critiques the grand claims regarding the transformation of society into an 'information society', grounding his critique in the longer-term continuities in work, communication, economy, etc.

Thus, it is the thrust of this part that the social landscape – its character, its problems, its concepts and debates – precedes, and remains more significant than, any particular technological innovation. Another way of putting this is to say that in so far as the social landscape is undergoing change, it is social and cultural rather than technological boundaries which are centrally at issue. In the domain of politics, the key boundary is that of state institutions versus the public sphere in providing a forum for citizen deliberation. In the domain of childhood, the key boundary is that of child and adult, often mapped onto innocent and corrupt, or ignorant and knowledgeable, or safe and dangerous. In the realm of education, new media are seen to pose a fundamental challenge to a long-endorsed pedagogic tradition based on authoritative, elite forms of knowledge and a valorization of print over visual literacy. And so forth. Indeed, it is the tensions over these boundaries which shape, discursively and materially, the design, diffusion and appropriation of new media technologies.

I have noted here just some of the debates evident in the attempt to contextualize new media within 'the bigger picture'. Like the physical landscape, the social landscape is both as old as the hills and yet the setting for, and so constitutive of, present and future action. Within this landscape, the authors of this part advocate a broad and multifaceted approach to identifying the key factors which shape the emerging place of new media in social life, while also advocating considerable caution in announcing the sighting of wholly original forms of social life, particularly those attributable to new media. For through the complex interplay between the social landscape and the human activity that it shapes and is shaped by, we are witnessing a process of evolutionary change in which, in terms of both process and consequences, new media play a still hotly contested part.

REFERENCES

Appadurai, A. (1996) *Modernity at Large: Cultural Dimensions of Globalization.* Minneapolis: University of Minnesota Press.

Barnes, T.J. and Duncan, J.S. (eds) (1992) *Writing Worlds: Discourse, Text and Metaphor in the Representation of Landscape.* London: Routledge.

Ferment in the Field (1983) Special issue of *Journal of Communication*, 33 (3), summer.

Levy, M.R. and Gurevitch, M. (eds) (1994) *Defining Media Studies: Reflections on the Future of the Field.* New York: Oxford University Press.

Livingstone, S. (1999a) 'New media, new audiences', *New Media & Society*, 1 (1): 59–66.

Livingstone, S. (1999b) 'From audiences to users? Doing audience research in a new media age', in G. Bechelloni and M. Buonanno (eds), *Audiences: Multiple Voices.* Firenze: Edizioni Fondazione Hypercampo.

Luke, C. (1989) *Pedagogy, Printing and Protestantism: the Discourse on Childhood.* Albany, NY: State University of New York Press.

MacKenzie, D. and Wajcman, J. (eds) (1999) *The Social Shaping of Technology*, 2nd edn. Buckingham: Open University Press.

Radway, J. (1988) 'Reception study: ethnography and the problems of dispersed audiences and nomadic subjects', *Cultural Studies*, 2 (3): 359–76.

Silverstone, R.S. (1997) 'New media in European households', in U.T. Lange and K. Goldhammer (eds), *Exploring the Limits: Europe's Changing Communication Environment.* Berlin: Springer. pp. 113–34.

Williams, R. (1974) *Television: Technology and Cultural Form.* London: Fontana.

1

The Information Society Revisited

FRANK WEBSTER

The term 'information society' is widely used both inside academia and in the wider society. One has but to pick up the newspapers or turn on the television to encounter references to a new information age, or to browse the shelves of bookshops to come across titles displaying the words. There are several reasons why this should be so, but most prominent amongst them is surely the prevalence of information itself in the present era. There is simply a very great deal more information about than hitherto: perhaps most obviously in an explosion of media and media products (from cable TV channels to compact disk records, from mobile telephones to the Internet), but also importantly in the rapid and accelerating permeation of computerized technologies throughout society, in the increased provision and take-up of education in most social systems, and in the growth of occupations that deal, for the most part, with information (clerks, professionals, instructors and so on). Experiencing such developments, it is not surprising that many observers have come to describe our age in terms of one of its most palpable features: hence, logically, the information society.

In 1995 I published a book, *Theories of the Information Society*, that brought together a range of social theories which attempted to account for the significance of information over recent decades. The presumption was that in this chapter the book's arguments would be updated to take account of new thinking that has come from debate on and consideration of the development of more recent phenomena such as cyberspace and cyborgs. It is certain that the rapid development of these new technologies as well as of digital television and mobile telecommunications, and the take-up of personal computers, e-mail and e-commerce, have further stimulated talk of an information age having come

upon us. Again, the fact that there is now a great deal more information around than even a decade ago, and that this is demonstrable from everyday experiences (from watching television round the clock, through electronic banking services, to a significant increase in the information intensity of a good deal of modern-day work), has encouraged commentators to declare, more confidently than ever, that we inhabit an information society.

It is in this context that this chapter reviews and evaluates the concept of an information society. However, it would be less than honest if I did not, at the outset, state plainly my own view on the salience of the term. My conclusion is that the concept 'information society' is of little use to social scientists, and still less to the wider public's understanding of transformations in the world today. The term perhaps has some heuristic value for the social scientist (Lyon, 1988: 8), in so far as it encourages scholars to focus attention on an indisputably important feature of the world today – information. But as a means of understanding and explaining that world I find the conception of information society of limited use. In this I share the view of Manuel Castells when he declares that 'we should abandon the notion of "information society"' (2000: 10).

I shall reveal why I have come to this conclusion in the course of this chapter, but the major reasons are as follows. I find the concept of information society unsatisfactory because of:

- inconsistencies and lack of clarity as regards criteria used to distinguish an information society;
- imprecise use of the term 'information';
- the unsupportable supposition of information society theorists that quantitative increases in information lead to qualitative social changes.

These objections do not mean that I find information unworthy of study. On the contrary, there seem to me good reasons for close analysis of informational trends. The chief difficulty, however, is with the argument that informational developments signal the emergence of a new type of social system, an information society. It is a proposition which rests on faulty logic and inadequate evidence.

DEFINITIONS OF AN INFORMATION SOCIETY

It is possible to identify six ways of distinguishing an information society. Five of these focus on measures of one or other of the following phenomena:

- technological innovation and diffusion;
- occupational change;
- economic value;
- information flows;
- the expansion of symbols and signs.

These are not mutually exclusive, though scholars place different emphases on each dimension. All of these conceptions rely on a quantitative assessment of a particular phenomenon to argue that its expansion has brought about a qualitatively different form of social organization. In this way each theorization adopts a form of reasoning which is *ex post facto*: there is evidence of there being more information in society today, therefore we have an information society. As we shall see, there are serious difficulties with this form of argument. Nonetheless, it is undeniable that it has an immediate, even commonsensical, appeal, and it is a familiar form of reasoning. For example, it is frequently suggested that, just as a decline in the numbers of farm workers and a rise in factory employment signalled the end of agricultural society and the emergence of industrialism, so too are quantitative changes in information indicative of the coming of an information society. I criticize this form of argument below.

The sixth definition of an information society is singular in that it refers, not to the fact of there being more information, but to changes in the ways in which life is now conducted because of information. The argument offered here, that theoretical information/knowledge is the fulcrum of contemporary life, suggests a distinct conception of the information society. In my view, this is the most persuasive (if the least commonly mooted) argument for the applicability of the concept of information society.

I propose now to examine each of the first five definitions in turn. I then consider the questions of quantity and quality, and the nature of information, before examining the sixth definition.

Technology

Technological conceptions centre on an array of innovations that have appeared over the past 20 years or so. New technologies are one of the most visible indicators of new times, and accordingly are frequently taken to signal the coming of an information society. These include cable and satellite television, computer-to-computer communications, PCs, new office technologies – notably online information services and word processors – and CD-ROM facilities. The suggestion is, simply, that such a volume of technological innovations must lead to a reconstitution of the social world because its impact is so profound.

During the late 1970s and early 1980s commentators got excited about the 'mighty micro's' capacity to revolutionize our way of life (McHale, 1976; Martin, 1978; Evans, 1979), and none more so than the world's leading futurist, Alvin Toffler (1980). His suggestion, in a memorable metaphor, is that, over time, the world has been decisively shaped by three waves of technological innovation, each as unstoppable as the mightiest tidal force. The first was the agricultural revolution and the second the industrial revolution. The third is the information revolution that is engulfing us now and which presages a new way of living (which, attests Toffler, will turn out fine if only we ride with the wave).

More recently, futurism's enthusiasms have been boosted by computing's capacity to transform telecommunications, to in effect merge the two technologies (Toffler, 1990). It is this spread of computer communications technologies (e-mail, data and text communications, online information exchange, etc.) that currently inspires most speculation about a new society in the making (Gates, 1995; Negroponte, 1995; Dertouzos, 1997). The rapid growth of the Internet especially, with its capacities for simultaneously promoting economic success, education and the democratic process, has stimulated much commentary. Media regularly feature accounts of the arrival of an information 'superhighway' on which the populace must become adept at driving. Authoritative voices are raised to announce that 'a new order ... is being forced upon an unsuspecting world by advances in telecommunications. The future is being born in the so-called *Information Superhighways* ... [and] anyone bypassed by these highways faces ruin' (Angell, 1995: 10).

More soberly, the spread of national, international and genuinely global information exchanges between and within banks, corporations, governments, universities and voluntary bodies indicates a similar trend towards the establishment of a technological infrastructure that allows instant computer communications at any time of day in any place that is suitably equipped (Connors, 1993).

Most academic analysts, while avoiding the exaggerated language of futurists and politicians, have nonetheless adopted what is at root a similar approach (Feather, 1998). For instance, from Japan there have been attempts to measure the growth of *joho shakai* (information society) since the 1960s (Duff et al., 1996). The Japanese Ministry of Posts and Telecommunications (MPT) commenced a census in 1975 which endeavours to track changes in the volume (e.g. numbers of telephone messages) and vehicles (e.g. penetration of telecommunications equipment) of information using sophisticated techniques (Ito, 1991; 1994). In Britain, a much respected school of thought has devised a neo-Schumpeterian approach to change. Combining Schumpeter's argument that major technological innovations bring about 'creative destruction' with Kondratieff's theme of 'long waves' of economic development, these researchers contend that information and communications technologies represent the establishment of a new epoch (Freeman, 1987) which will be uncomfortable during its earlier phases, but over the longer term will be economically beneficial. This new 'technoeconomic paradigm' constitutes the 'information age' which is set to mature early in this new century (cf. Hall and Preston, 1988).

Occupational Change

This is the approach most favoured by sociologists. It is also one closely associated, with good reason, with the work of Daniel Bell (1973) who is the most important theorist of 'post-industrial society' (a term virtually synonymous with information society, and used as such in much of Bell's own writing). Here the occupational structure is examined over time and patterns of change are observed. The suggestion is that we have achieved an information society when the preponderance of occupations is found in information work. The decline of manufacturing employment and the rise of service sector employment is interpreted as the loss of manual jobs and its replacement with white-collar work. Since the raw material of non-manual labour is information (as opposed to the brawn and dexterity plus machinery characteristic of manual labour), substantial increases in such informational work can be said to announce the arrival of an information society.

There is *prima facie* evidence for this: in Western European and North American nations over 70 per cent of the workforce is now found in the service sector of the economy, and white-collar occupations are now a majority. On these grounds alone it would seem plausible to argue that we inhabit an information society since the 'predominant group (of occupations) consists of information workers' (Bell, 1979: 183).

An emphasis on occupational change as the marker of an information society has displaced once dominant concerns with technology in recent years. It should also be understood that this conception of the 'information society' is quite different from that which suggests it is information and communications *technologies* which distinguish the new age. A focus on occupational change is one which stresses the transformative power of information itself rather than the influence of information technologies, information being what is drawn upon and generated in occupations or embodied in people through education and experiences. Charles Leadbetter (1999) titled a book to highlight the insight that it is information which is foundational in the present epoch. 'Living on thin air' was once a familiar admonition by the worldly-wise to those reluctant to earn a living by the sweat of their brows. But all such advice is now outdated, Leadbetter arguing that this is exactly how to make one's livelihood in the information age. *Living on Thin Air* proclaims that 'thinking smart', being 'inventive', and having the capacity to develop and exploit 'networks' are actually the key to the new 'weightless' economy (Coyne, 1997; Dertouzos, 1997), since wealth production comes, not from physical effort, but from 'ideas, knowledge, skills, talent and creativity' (Leadbetter, 1999: 18). His book highlights examples of such successes: designers, deal-makers, image-creators, musicians, biotechnologists, genetic engineers and niche-finders abound.

Leadbetter puts into popular parlance what many thinkers now argue as a matter of course. A range of influential writers, from Robert Reich (1992) and Peter Drucker (1993) to Manuel Castells (1996–8), suggest that the economy today is led and energized by people whose major characteristic is the capacity to manipulate information. Preferred terms vary between authors, from 'symbolic analysts' and 'knowledge experts' to 'informational labour', but in all one message is constant: today's movers and shakers are those whose work involves creating and using information. Twenty per cent (and expanding) of the US workforce (Reich, 1992: 179) is constituted by this group which manages, designs, creates and refines information, this being the raw material of our globalized and fast-changing world.

All analysts agree that information operatives vary enormously in what they actually do. For instance, many manage corporate affairs in various capacities, some handle financial networks, others work in a burgeoning media sector, or in the law, or higher education, or accounting, or public relations, or local government, while still others are in design where they are occupied with adding value to mundane materials. Despite such diversity, all share a propensity to reskill themselves as a matter of routine. In this way they are at one with the flexible world economy which demands constant change on all sides. This commitment to what others have called 'lifelong learning' ensures that informational labour keeps ahead of the game, capable of building a portfolio of experience on various projects while ever ready to adapt positively to novel situations.

A corollary of this is that informational labour, whatever particular differences are in evidence, shares talents most commonly nurtured in higher education. Specific skills learned in universities do matter, but they quickly date and the graduate must constantly retrain to keep abreast of things. Much more important then is the 'human capital' nurtured in the experience of higher education, something which expresses itself in a heightened capacity to communicate effectively, to analyse situations dispassionately, to come up with a strategy for advance, to broker deals with other actors, to identify strengths and weaknesses in a given milieu, and so on (Reich, 1992: 178–9). The inculcation of such qualities places an especial premium on higher education and, in this light, it is scarcely surprising that the calibre and capabilities of a nation's education system have become central to government policy (Brown and Lauder, 1995). The *leitmotiv* of Blair's UK administration is 'education, education, education', a litany repeated in all advanced nations which intend to see their citizenry capture a high proportion of 'symbolic analysis' jobs in the future (Seltzer and Bentley, 1999). Not surprisingly, then, a system of mass higher education is taken to be an indicator of an information society.

Economy

This approach charts the growth in economic worth of informational activities. If one is able to plot an increase in the proportion of gross national product (GNP) accounted for by the information business then logically there comes a point at which one may declare the achievement of an information economy. Once the greater part of economic activity is taken up by information activity rather than say subsistence agriculture or industrial manufacture, then it follows that we may speak of an information society (Jonscher, 1999).

In principle straightforward, but in practice an extraordinarily complex econometric exercise, much of the pioneering work was done by Fritz Machlup (1902–83) of Princeton University (Machlup, 1962). His identification of information industries such as education, law, publishing, media and computer manufacture, and his attempt to estimate their changing economic worth, have been refined by Marc Porat (1977a; 1977b).

Porat distinguished the primary and secondary information sectors of the economy, the former being susceptible to ready economic valuation since it had an ascribable market price, the latter being harder to price but nonetheless essential to all modern-day organizations, involving informational activities within companies and state institutions

(for example, the personnel wings of a company, the research and development sections of a business). In this way Porat is able to distinguish the two informational sectors, then to consolidate them, to separate out the non-informational elements of the economy and, by reaggregrating national economic statistics, to conclude that, with almost half the US's GNP accounted for by these combined informational sectors, 'the United States is now an information-based economy'. As such it is an 'information society [where] the major arenas of economic activity are the information goods and service producers, and the public and private (secondary information sector) bureaucracies' (Porat, 1978: 32).

Space

This conception of the information society, while it does draw on economics and sociology, has at its core the geographer's distinctive stress on space. Here the major emphasis is on information networks which connect locations and in consequence can have profound effects on the organization of time and space. It has become an especially popular index of the information society throughout the 1990s as information networks have become increasingly prominent features of social organization.

It is usual to stress the centrality of information networks that may link together different locations within and between an office, a town, a region, a continent and indeed the entire world. As the electricity grid runs through an entire country to be accessed at will by individuals with the appropriate connections, so too may we imagine now a 'wired society' operating at the national, international and global level to provide an 'information ring main' (Barron and Curnow, 1979) to each home, shop, university and office – and even to the mobile individual who has his laptop and modem in his briefcase.

Increasingly we are all connected to networks of one sort or another – and they themselves are expanding their reach and capabilities in an exponential manner (Urry, 2000). We come across them personally at many levels: in electronic point of sale terminals in shops and restaurants, in accessing data across continents, in e-mailing colleagues, or in exchanging information on the Internet. We may not personally have experienced this realm of 'cyberspace', but the information ring main functions still more frantically at the level of international banks, intergovernmental agencies and corporate relationships.

A popular idea here is that the electronic highways result in a new emphasis on the flow of information (Castells, 1996–8), something which leads to a radical revision of time/space relations. In a 'network society' constraints of the clock and of distance have been radically relieved, the corporations and even the individual being capable of managing their affairs effectively on a global scale. The academic researcher no longer needs to travel from the university to consult the Library of Congress since she can interrogate it on the Internet; the business corporation no longer needs to fly out its managers to find out what is happening in their Far East outlets because computer communications enable routine and systematic surveillance from afar. The suggestion of many is that this heralds a major transformation of our social order (Mulgan, 1991), sufficient to mark even a revolutionary change.

Culture

The final conception of an information society is easily acknowledged. Each of us is aware from our everyday lives that there has been an extraordinary increase in the information in social circulation. For instance, television programming is round-the-clock. There are also several broadcast channels available, and the TV receiver has been enhanced to incorporate video technologies, cable and satellite, and even computerized information services. More recently, an avalanche of computerized games has become attached to PCs and 'virtual reality' products have begun to enter the home. There is very much more radio output available now than even a decade ago, at local, national and international level. And radios are no longer fixed in the front room, but spread through the home, in the car, in the office and, with the walkman, everywhere. Movies have long been an important part of people's information environment. Though over the years attendances at cinemas have declined, movies are today very much more prevalent than ever: available still at cinema outlets, broadcast on television, readily borrowed from video rental shops, cheaply purchased from the shelves of chain stores. Walk along any street and it is almost impossible to miss the advertising hoardings, the billboards, the window displays in shops. Visit any railway or bus station and one cannot but be struck by the widespread availability of paperback books and inexpensive magazines. In addition, audiotape, compact disk and radio all offer more, and more readily available, music, poetry, drama, humour and education to the general public. Newspapers are extensively available and a good many new titles fall on our doorsteps as free sheets. Junk mail is delivered daily. And so forth.

The informational features of our world are more thoroughly penetrative than a short list of television, radio and other media systems suggests. This sort of listing implies that new media surround us, presenting us with messages to which we may or may not respond. In truth the informational environment is a great deal more intimate, more constitutive of us, than this suggests. One may consider, for example, the informational dimensions of the clothes we wear, the styling of our hair and faces, the very ways in which nowadays we work at our image (from body shape to speech, people are intensely aware of the messages they may be projecting and how they feel about themselves in certain clothes, with a particular hairstyle, etc.). Reflection on the complexities of fashion, the intricacy of the ways in which we design ourselves for everyday presentation, makes one well aware that social intercourse nowadays involves a greater degree of informational content than previously.

Contemporary culture is manifestly more heavily information laden than any of its predecessors. We exist in a media-saturated environment which means that life is quintessentially about symbolization, about exchanging and receiving – or trying to exchange and resisting reception of – messages about ourselves and others. It is in acknowledgement of this explosion of signification that many writers conceive of our having entered an information society, one where everything that we see and do is simulated (Poster, 1990; 1995).

FROM QUANTITY TO QUALITY?

Critiques of information society scenarios revolve around a discontent with quantitative measures when they are used to designate profound, systemic change. The central criticism is that quantitative indices of the spread of information and information technologies cannot be interpreted as evidence of really deep-seated social change. On the contrary, they can be regarded as the consolidation and extension of established patterns of interest and control (Beniger, 1986; Webster and Robins, 1986).

Definitions of the information society offer a quantitative measure (numbers of white-collar workers, percentage of GNP devoted to information, etc.) and assume that, at some unspecified point, we enter an information society when this begins to predominate. But there are no clear grounds for designating as a new type of society one in which all we witness is greater quantities of information in circulation and storage. If there is just more information then it is hard to understand why anyone should suggest that we have before us something radically new. This is a point made well by Anthony Giddens (1985: 178) when he observes that all societies, as soon as they are formed into nation-states, are information societies in so far as routine gathering, storage and control of information about population and resources are essential to their operation. On this axis all that differentiates the present era from, say, seventeenth-century England, is much greater quantities of information that are amassed, dissembled and processed. If what we are experiencing in the informational realm today is but an extrapolation and intensification of trends established long ago, then it is hard to see on what basis it can be alleged that these developments are bringing about a new sort of society.

Furthermore, it is at least intellectually possible to imagine a radically different sort of society coming into being, one that may even merit the title 'information society', though this transformation may be manifested in only small quantitative increases of information. That is, it may be feasible to describe as a new sort of society one in which it is possible to locate information of a qualitatively different order, though the information changes appear quantitatively minor. This does not require that we discover that a majority of the workforce is engaged in information occupations or that the economy generates a specified sum from informational activity. For example, it is theoretically possible to imagine an information society where only a small minority of information experts hold decisive power. On a quantitative measure, say of occupational patterns, this would not qualify for information society status, but we could feel impelled to so designate it because of the decisive role of information/knowledge in the power structure and direction of social change.

Bluntly, quantitative measures – simply more information – cannot of themselves identify a break with previous systems, while it is at least theoretically possible to regard small but decisive qualitative changes as marking a system break. Further, it is especially odd that so many of those who identify an information society as a new type of society do so by presuming that this qualitative change can be defined simply by calculating how much information is in circulation, how many people work in information jobs and so on. What we have here is the assumption that quantitative increases transform – in unspecified ways – into qualitative changes in the social system. But to argue that a plethora of personal computers or a preponderance of white-collar occupations means we have an information society is tautologous. We have been presented with no argument as to why more information should result in the coming of a new era; we have had only the unfounded assertion that more information defines a new society.

Moreover, quantitative measures tend to homogenize highly disparate activities. For example, in totalling the value of information activities in the economy and arriving at a given sum, information society theorists arguably overlook crucial qualitative differences within information. For instance, sales of a single tabloid newspaper in Britain are vastly greater than those of all the quality broadsheets combined. But who would suggest that these newspapers can be lumped together in the same category? The crucial issue to most observers is the quality of the information, of news, reportage and opinion, that these newspapers

contain. Indeed, so crucial is the issue of quality here that it is possible to present a credible argument that contends that a mass circulation tabloid or entertainment-dominated television represents the very antithesis of an information society, with a 'dumbed down' audience being swamped by garbage information (Postman, 1985; Washburn and Thornton, 1996).

This example alerts us to a related matter, the tendency for quantitative measures to overlook strategic issues. For instance, a raw count of information occupations is blind to the differences between groups, equating, say, social workers and stock exchange dealers, schoolteachers and corporate executives, clerks and lawyers. All are, of course, information workers, and hence equal in terms of the statistician's categories, but some of them clearly are very much more equal than others. In a cognate manner, postmodernist Jean Baudrillard's (1983) willingness to announce the 'implosion' of meaning in the realm of the sign in effect puts light entertainment, news and documentary programming on the same plane – all artifacts that can be experienced by audiences in any way they feel disposed.

There are a good many criticisms to be made of the methods used to measure an information society. All return to the issue that, while finished statistics may appear precise and firm, behind them lies a great deal of subjectivity and variable interpretation. For instance, discriminating between informational and non-informational occupations is a difficult task, involving distinctions of degree rather than of kind. Thus a photocopier repair person is deemed to be an information worker by virtue of working with advanced technologies, while the farmhand is seen as merely manual, though it is likely that a good deal of information will be required in the performance of their duties. The point is, we need to be sceptical of apparently conclusive figures which are the outcomes of researchers' perceptions of where occupations are to be most appropriately categorized.

There are related complaints to be made about technological measures of the information society. At first sight technologies seem to be especially robust measures, but what is to count as a relevant technology? PCs, computer-to-computer facilities, video, telephone exchanges, cable, camcorders, satellites, Gameboy toys, Exocet missiles, CD players – as soon as one begins the list, problems arise. Again, which of the long list of potential technologies might take priority over others? Networked systems over free-standing PCs? Further, how is one to count computers: by processing power, by use (machines in larger offices are likely to be much more exactly used than those in the home), or by cost? And how can one assess the role of software packages in the expansion of information technology?

Finally, but by no means least, even when one is alert to the difficulties that come with trying to establish what technologies are to be counted and how they are to be weighted against one another, there looms the vexing question: how much technology must there be in place to enable commentators to describe something as an information society? It is not frivolous to ask whether an information society is one in which everyone has a PC in the home, or whether it is more appropriate to designate this as three-quarters of the way towards a mature information society compared with those that have an established information network in place (but then again, when is a network a network?).

A connected and familiar criticism of technological conceptions of an information society is that they are determinist (Dickson, 1974). First, they assume that technology is the major force in social change – hence arguments which refer to the 'world the steam engine made', 'the atomic age', the 'computer society'. A moment's reflection reveals that history is much more complicated. For example, it is clearly the case that climate, mineralogical deposits, economics, education, war and a host of other factors have contributed to social change, some of these being, at the least, powerful forces influencing technological innovation itself (consider, for example, the influence of war and defence pressures on the development of high technology). Second, technological determinists work with a model which holds to a clear separation of technology and society, the former being in some way apart from social influence yet destined to have the most profound social effects. Technology here is at once sealed from the social world yet capable of shattering established social relations. Perhaps for this reason, technological development is frequently presented as an unworldly thing, led by eccentric inventors or possessed boffins, which yet impacts society dramatically when it is launched on the unsuspecting public. Again, however, it is not difficult to appreciate that technology is a part of society, subject to social shaping by factors such as investment priorities from corporate and government bodies, market opportunities and value commitments. Accepting this position casts doubt on those thinkers who would have it that technological innovations are such as to define a new type of information society (MacKenzie, 1996).

WHAT IS INFORMATION?

When one first encounters statistical series which chart increases in information, it might appear that we are using a term that is precise and widely understood. Initially at least it does seem unproblematical to observe that information increase is identifiable in, say, growth in numbers of magazine titles available, in book issues from public libraries, in the volume of telephone traffic, in enrolment on advanced education courses, in television sales, in hits on websites, in the scale of exchange rate flows, in the expansion of online databases, in take-up of PCs and so forth.

However, a difficulty here is the profligate way in which the term 'information' is used. When bundled in this manner, different definitions of the word are collapsed. The closer one looks at what is meant by 'information', the more awkward does it seem to find a precise and unambiguous definition. Commentators write as if the meaning of the term is self-evident, but in this they are mistaken. Indeed, Norman Stevens concludes that 'so diverse are the definitions of information today … that it is impossible to reconcile them', and, he continues, 'there is little consistency in the way in which the term information is used … resulting in an assumption, probably incorrect, that there is a broad underlying definition of information that encompasses all uses of the term in all fields that is commonly and directly understood' (1986: 5).

Amongst the diversity of definitions of information in play, Zhang Yuexiao (1988: 400) reports that there have been identified some 400 conceptions of information presented by researchers in various fields and cultures. Most significant is the divide between those approaches which conceive of information in non-semantic ways and those which insist in its being something that has meaning. The latter is the most widely understood lay definition, information being regarded as data and ideas that are identifiable, organized in some way, often communicated, stored in various forms (books, television, etc.) and used in a meaningful way (Stevens, 1986: 9). However, it is important to appreciate that this is not the engineer's understanding of information, which is a matter of measuring signals (Shannon and Weaver, 1964 [1949]). Thus measures of information increase that concern themselves with the processing power of computers or the acceleration of transmission rates by telecommunications exchanges invoke one definition of the term, that of the technologist which evacuates content. Commentators who define information in semantic terms, and perhaps look to the extension of signs and symbols in advertising and on television, are operationalizing a quite different conception of information. Elsewhere, those who take the growth in economic import of information – say, the expansion of the publishing business or trading in video materials – adopt a conception of the subject that is amenable to assessment by price, but which is a definition that elides questions of semantics. Again, one of the most common ways of identifying an information society is by counting the number of information workers in employment, a definition of information which centres on a process rather than a product, focusing on what people do rather than on what is produced. This may be intrinsically interesting, but it is a quite different notion of information from one which would emphasize its expression in artifacts such as books and computers.

This lack of precision, and the habit of aggregating highly diverse conceptions into the single category, ought to encourage closer scrutiny of a blanket term that has been used rather promiscuously in recent years. That said, Theodore Roszak's (1986: x) observation that it is the 'very emptiness' of the word 'information' which paradoxically has allowed it 'to be filled with mesmerizing glamour' merits serious consideration. Indeed, when one encounters writers who insist that more information makes for an information society, it is as well to query just what it is they are counting as information here. Michel Foucault (1980) urged scholars to scrutinize ways in which things get talked about, arguing that examination of the construction of 'discourses' can be illuminating as well as somewhat subversive. A Foucauldian account of the genealogy of 'information', one which looks attentively at variable ways in which the term is conceived and applied by information theorists, computer scientists, semiologists, librarians, sociologists and economists, would make for an instructive read. Not least, it would lead one to hesitate before making sweeping statements along the lines that 'information' is transforming the very foundations of life as we know it.

THEORETICAL KNOWLEDGE

There is another suggestion, intriguing if imprecise, which contends that we are on the point of entry into a distinctly novel information society, yet without a need to reflect on the meanings of the information so developed. This proposition has it that we no longer need to seek quantitative measures of information expansion (information employees, tradeable information, etc.), because a decisive qualitative change has taken place as regards the ways in which information is used. This marks such a break with the past that we may legitimately refer to the coming of an information society.

From this point of view an information society is regarded as one in which theoretical knowledge takes on a pre-eminence which it has hitherto lacked. The theme which unites what is in fact rather a disparate range of thinkers is that, in this information society (though frequently 'knowledge society' is preferred, for the obvious reason that it conjures much more than agglomerated bits of information), affairs are organized and arranged in such a way as to prioritize theory.

It is worth noting that Daniel Bell presents this as an 'axial principle' of post-industrial society and

that, although the weight of his analysis leans towards quantitative increases in service (i.e. information) occupations as indicators of post-industrialism, he is emphatic that 'what is radically new today is the codification of theoretical knowledge and its centrality for innovation' (1979: 189).

It is easy enough to understand what Bell means by this when we contrast today's post-industrialism with its predecessor industrial society. In the past, it is argued, innovations were made, on the whole, by 'inspired and talented tinkerers who were indifferent to science and the fundamental laws underlying their investigations' (Bell, 1973: 20). In contrast to this decidedly practical and problem-solving orientation, it is suggested by Bell that nowadays innovations start from theoretical premises. That is, now that we have arrived at a situation in which it is possible to codify known scientific principles, our knowledge of these becomes the starting point of action. In this way, what was once dismissed as useless – as just 'theory' – has becomes the axis of practical innovations.

Again, it is not difficult to find illustrations of this 'change in the character of knowledge itself' (1973: 20). For instance, Alan Turing's paper 'On computable numbers', published in 1937, set out mathematical principles which underpin later applications in computer science; the development of integrated circuits that enabled the 'microelectronics revolution' to get under way in the late 1970s was founded on known principles of solid-state physics; and innovations in areas as diverse as compact disk technology, lasers and nuclear energy were reliant on breakthroughs in theoretical physics which were regarded, initially as least, as being without practical consequence. In fact, it is rather difficult to think of technological applications nowadays which do not hinge on theoretical knowledge, whether it is calculating the needs of households for supply of potable water, constructing aircraft, building bridges or generating energy. Not surprisingly, perhaps, we find historian Eric Hobsbawm confirming Bell's perception, concluding that during this century 'the theorists [have been] in the driving seat ... telling the practitioners what they were to look for and should find in the light of their theories' (1994: 534–5).

Bell takes his argument for what he terms the 'primacy of theoretical knowledge' considerably further, to suggest that it is pre-eminent not only in the realm of technological innovation, but even in social and political affairs. For instance, governments today introduce policies based on theoretical models of the economy. These are variable – Keynesian, monetarist, supply side, *laissez-faire*, collectivist – but each underpins the day-to-day decisions that ministers may make in response to practical exigencies. Alternatively, it is salutary to reflect on contemporary policies oriented towards resolving environmental problems. It quickly becomes evident that these are not merely responses to particularly pressing problems (an oil spillage at sea, desertification). They do involve such contingencies, of course, but they are also proposals developed on the basis of theoretical models of the ecosystem's sustainability. Thus, for instance, environmental debates are routinely informed by theoretical projections on matters such as population growth, fish stocks and the condition of the ozone layer. Practical policies are only imaginable on the basis of these sorts of theoretical model: for example, appropriate reactions to a noticeably dry or warmer summer in the UK are comprehensible only in a context of theoretical models of the long-term likelihood of and consequences of global warming. To be sure, such models are at present inchoate and unrefined, but they and other instances help us to appreciate that, while theoretical knowledge does not have to be 'true' in any absolute sense, it does play a decisive part in our lives.

Theoretical knowledge is undeniably an arresting idea, one which *prima facie* defines a new type of society which hinges on the generation and use of information/knowledge. If theory is at the point of initiation of developments, in contrast to one-time practical demands, then such knowledge could be said to herald a new sort of society. Moreover, we are talking here not merely of more white-collar workers or more bits of information being produced, but of a new foundational principle of social life.

Nonetheless, a major difficulty with this notion is defining with any precision what is meant by theoretical knowledge (Kumar, 1978: 219–30). Theory evokes abstract and generalizable rules, laws and procedures and, with this, there can be agreement that advances, especially in scientific knowledge, have resulted in their codification in texts which are learned by would-be practitioners and which in turn become integrated into their practical work. This principle can reasonably be thought to be at the heart of research and development projects at the forefront of innovations, but it is clearly in evidence too in a large range of professions such as architecture, building, handling of food and even the design of much clothing.

However, there are those who would extend the notion of theoretical knowledge to encompass a much vaster range, all of which could be cited as evidence of a knowledge-based society. Here, for example, one might include the training of many white-collar employees in law, social services, accountancy, etc. as evidence of the primacy of knowledge in the contemporary world. Indeed, one might argue that the whole of higher education, at the least, is concerned with transmitting theoretical knowledge. After all, it is a common refrain, in Britain at least, that the rapid transition to mass higher education (with about 30 per cent of the age group attending universities) has been required by the need to equip appropriately large numbers

of people to operate successfully in the 'knowledge society' (Webster, 2000). Such knowledge as is transmitted is undoubtedly codified and generally abstracted from practical applications, and it is even generalizable, though it is surely of a different order of magnitude to the theoretical knowledge expounded in sciences such as chemistry and physics.

Nico Stehr (1994), proposing that we now inhabit a 'knowledge society', does extend the definition of theory in such a way, arguing that nowadays knowledge has come to be constitutive of the way that we live. Recourse to theoretical knowledge is now central to virtually everything that we do, from designing new technologies and producing everyday artifacts to making sense of our own lives when we draw upon large repositories of knowledge to help us better understand our own location.

Here we are extending the idea of theoretical knowledge a very great deal, but it is helpful in so far as Stehr echoes themes in the work of social theorist Anthony Giddens that merit comment. Stehr proposes a threefold typology of the development of knowledge: *meaningful*, that is the Enlightenment ideal of knowledge for better understanding; *productive*, that is knowledge applied to industry; and *action*, where knowledge is intimately connected to production with, for example, the inclusion of intelligent devices, and where it influences the performance of one's everyday activities. This last form of knowledge appears close to Giddens' emphasis on what he refers to as the *intensified reflexivity* of 'late modern' existence. What Giddens highlights here is that, increasingly, modernity has been a story of people's release from the strictures of nature and certain forms of community, where it appeared that one had to do what one did as it was a matter of 'fate', towards individuals and groups making choices about their own and collective destinies in circumstances of 'manufactured uncertainty'. That is, the world increasingly is not bounded by fixed and unchangeable limits, but is rather recognized as malleable and the outcome of human decisions. A requisite of this is heightened self and collective interrogation, otherwise reflexivity, though this is not to be perceived as some trend towards self-absorption. Quite the contrary, it is premised on openness to ideas, information and theories from very diverse realms, which are examined and incorporated as circumstances and people so decide.

A key point here is that a 'post-traditional' (Giddens, 1994) society which is characterized by intensified reflexivity of actors and institutions hinges on information/knowledge. Of course, some of this is local and particular (one's biography reflected upon, a company carefully scrutinizing its sales and stock records), but a great deal is also abstract, emanating especially from electronic media and from other, notably educational, institutions.

If one accepts Giddens' argument that we do inhabit a world of 'high modernity' in which reflexivity is much more pronounced than hitherto, then it is feasible to conceive of this as heightening the import of information and knowledge in contemporary life. A world of choices, for both organizations and individuals, is reliant on the availability and generation of detailed and rich information. If one follows Giddens' contention that ours is an era of intensified reflexivity on the basis of which we forge our material as well as social conditions, then it follows that this will sustain and will demand a complex and deep information environment. It is perhaps not quite the same sort of theoretical knowledge as that which Daniel Bell has proposed, but in so far as it is abstract and codified then it could find inclusion in a suitably widened category.

Nevertheless, there are reasons why we should hesitate to depict any novel information society in these terms. Not least is that Anthony Giddens himself is reluctant to do so. While he does emphasize that a 'world of intensified reflexivity is a world of *clever people*' (1994: 7), he appears unwilling to present this as other than an extension of long-term trends. Life today is certainly more information intensive, but this is not sufficient to justify projections that it represents a new sort of society.

In addition, Giddens has also raised doubts about the novelty of theoretical knowledge. Several years ago he observed that 'there is nothing which is specifically new in the application of "theoretical knowledge"… Indeed … rationality of technique … is the primary factor which from the beginning has distinguished industrialism from all preceding forms of social order' (1981: 262). This being so, we return to the problem of designating as novel today's society in which theoretical knowledge is prevalent.

Giddens' objection also begs the key question: just what do commentators mean by theoretical knowledge? It is clear, from the quotation above, that Giddens feels that the classical sociologist Max Weber's conception of formal rationality which underpins purposive action (most famously manifested in the growth of bureaucratic structures) might apply on one definition. After all, it involves abstract and codifiable principles, rules and regulations (the entire bureaucratic machine), as well as requiring from participants the command of abstract knowledge (how the system works). Theoretical knowledge, in these terms, is not much more than learning the rules and procedures of how bureaucracies function. If so, then one is forced also to ask what is especially new about this.

This leads us to the wider complaint about the imprecision of the term 'theoretical knowledge'. If, for instance, the 'primacy of theoretical knowledge' is taken to refer to known scientific principles (the boiling point of water, the conductivity of elements etc.) which are codified in texts, then this is one matter. However, if theoretical knowledge is taken to include hypothetical models such as the relation between inflation and unemployment, poverty and life chances, or social class and educational opportunity, then this surely is another matter. It may be that such theoretical knowledge is distinguishable from laws of physics only by degree, but this remains an important difference nonetheless. If theoretical knowledge is perceived as the prominence in modern life of expert systems that operate services such as water and sewerage, air traffic control and the telephone networks, through the systematic monitoring of activities which are (re)organized on the basis of established principles (of toxicity, safety of margins and so forth), then this too is another thing. Alternatively, if theoretical knowledge is to be understood as a trend towards very much more intensified reflexivity amongst individuals as well as institutions, on the basis of which they then shape their future courses of action, then this is another thing again. Finally, if the rise of theoretical knowledge is to be chartered by the spread of educational certification – a common strategy – then this is to introduce still another significantly different definition. Such imprecisions must lead one to be wary of theoretical knowledge as a sound means of distinguishing an information society, albeit that a shift towards the primacy of theory does appear to be a marked feature of recent history.

CONCLUSION

This chapter has examined six analytically separable conceptions of the information society. It has argued that all are suspect to a greater or lesser degree, so much so that the idea of an information society cannot be sustained. In each case defining criteria are imprecise and vague. Moreover, the claim that the information society marks a profound transformation in our ways of life cannot be supported on the basis of the quantitative indices that are typically advanced. There can be no doubt that, in advanced nations, information and communication technologies are now pervasive and that information has grown in economic significance, as the substance of much work, and in amounts of symbolic output. But the idea that all such might signal the shift towards a new society, an information society, is mistaken. Indeed, what is most striking are the continuities of the present age with previous social and economic arrangements, informational developments being heavily influenced by familiar constraints and priorities (H. Schiller, 1981; 1984; 1996; D. Schiller, 1999). As Krishan Kumar has concluded, the information explosion 'has not produced a radical shift in the way industrial societies are organized, or in the direction in which they have been moving. The imperatives of profit, power and control seem as predominant now as they have ever been in the history of capitalist industrialism. The difference lies in the greater range and intensity of their applications ... not in any change in the principles themselves' (1995: 154). It is ironic that the most persuasive conception of an information society, that which centres on the role of theoretical knowledge, is the least commonly suggested by information society adherents.

References

Angell, Ian (1995) 'Winners and losers in the information age', *LSE Magazine*, 7 (1): 10–12.

Barron, Iann and Curnow, Ray (1979) *The Future with Microelectronics: Forecasting the Effects of Information Technology*. London: Pinter.

Baudrillard, Jean (1983) *In the Shadow of the Silent Majorities*. New York: Semiotext(e).

Bell, Daniel (1973) *The Coming of Post-Industrial Society: a Venture in Social Forecasting*. Harmondsworth: Penguin.

Bell, Daniel (1979) 'The social framework of the information society', in Michael L. Dertouzos and Joel Moses (eds), *The Computer Age: a Twenty-Year View*. Cambridge, MA: MIT Press. pp. 163–211.

Beniger, James R. (1986) *The Control Revolution: Technological and Economic Origins of the Information Society*. Cambridge, MA: Harvard University Press.

Brown, Phillip and Lauder, Hugh (1995) 'Post-Fordist possibilities: education, training, and national development', in L. Bash and A. Green (eds), *World Yearbook of Education 1995: Youth, Education and Work*, vol. 2. London: Kogan Page. pp. 19–32.

Castells, Manuel (1996–8) *The Information Age*, 3 vols. Vol. 1: *The Rise of the Network Society* (1996). Vol. 2: *The Power of Identity* (1997). Vol. 3: *End of Millennium* (1998). Oxford: Blackwell.

Castells, Manuel (2000) 'Materials for an explanatory theory of the network society', *British Journal of Sociology*, 51 (1): 5–24.

Connors, Michael (1993) *The Race to the Intelligent State*. Oxford: Blackwell.

Coyne, Diane (1997) *The Weightless Economy*. Oxford: Capstone.

Dertouzos, Michael (1997) *What Will Be: How the New World of Information Will Change Our Lives*. London: Piatkus.

Dickson, David (1974) *Alternative Technology and the Politics of Technical Change*. London: Fontana.

Drucker, Peter (1993) *Post-Capitalist Society*. New York: Harper Collins.

Duff, Alistair, Craig, D. and McNeill, D.A. (1996) 'A note on the origins of the information society', *Journal of Information Science*, 22 (2): 117–22.

Evans, Christopher (1979) *The Mighty Micro: the Impact of the Micro-Chip Revolution*. London: Gollancz.

Feather, John (1998) *The Information Society: a Study of Continuity and Change*, 2nd edn. London: Library Association.

Foucault, Michel (1980) 'Two lectures', in *Power/Knowledge*. Brighton: Harvester.

Freeman, Christopher (1987) *Technology Policy and Economic Performance*. London: Pinter.

Gates, Bill (1995) *The Road Ahead*. Harmondsworth: Penguin.

Giddens, Anthony (1981) *The Class Structure of the Advanced Societies*, 2nd edn. London: Hutchinson.

Giddens, Anthony (1985) *The Nation State and Violence: Volume Two of a Contemporary Critique of Historical Materialism*. Cambridge: Polity.

Giddens, Anthony (1994) *Beyond Left and Right*. Cambridge: Polity.

Hall, Peter and Preston, Paschal (1988) *The Carrier Wave: New Information Technology and the Geography of Innovation, 1846–2003*. London: Unwin Hyman.

Hobsbawm, Eric (1994) *Age of Extremes: the Short Twentieth Century*. London: Joseph.

Ito, Y. (1991) 'Birth of *joho shakia* and *johaka* concepts in Japan and their diffusion outside Japan', *KEIO Communication Review*, 13: 3–12.

Ito, Youichi (1994) 'Japan', in Georgette Wang (ed.), *Treading Different Paths: Informatization in Asian Nations*. Norwood, NJ: Ablex. pp. 68–98.

Jonscher, Charles (1999) *Wired Life*. New York: Bantam.

Kumar, Krishan (1978) *Prophecy and Progress: the Sociology of Industrial and Post-Industrial Society*. London: Allen Lane.

Kumar, Krishan (1995) *From Post-Industrial to Postmodern Society*. Oxford: Blackwell.

Leadbetter, Charles (1999) *Living on Thin Air: the New Economy*. London: Hodder & Stoughton.

Lyon, David (1988) *The Information Society: Issues and Illusions*. Cambridge: Polity.

Machlup, Fritz (1962) *The Production and Distribution of Knowledge in the United States*. Princeton, NJ: Princeton University Press.

MacKenzie, Donald (1996) *Knowing Machines: Essays on Technical Change*. Cambridge, MA: MIT Press.

Martin, James (1978) *The Wired Society*. Englewood Cliffs, NJ: Prentice-Hall.

McHale, John (1976) *The Changing Information Environment*. London: Elek.

Mulgan, Geoff J. (1991) *Communication and Control: Networks and the New Economies of Communication*. Cambridge: Polity.

Negroponte, Nicholas (1995) *Being Digital*. London: Hodder & Stoughton.

Porat, Marc Uri (1977a) *The Information Economy: Definition and Measurement* (executive summary and major findings). OT Special Publication 77-12 (1). Washington, DC: US Department of Commerce, Office of Telecommunications.

Porat, Marc Uri (1977b) *The Information Economy: Sources and Methods for Measuring the Primary Information Sector* (detailed industry reports). OT Special Publication 77-12 (2). Washington, DC: US Department of Commerce, Office of Telecommunications.

Porat, Marc Uri (1978) 'Communication policy in an information society', in G.O. Robinson (ed.), *Communications for Tomorrow*. New York: Praeger. pp. 3–60.

Poster, Mark (1990) *The Mode of Information: Poststructuralism and Social Context*. Cambridge: Polity.

Poster, Mark (1995) *The Second Media Age*. Cambridge: Polity.

Postman, Neil (1985) *Amusing Ourselves to Death: Public Discourse in the Age of Show Business*. New York: Penguin.

Reich, R. (1992) *The Work of Nations: Preparing Ourselves for 21st Century Capitalism*. New York: Vintage.

Roszak, Theodore (1986) *The Cult of Information: the Folklore of Computers and the True Art of Thinking*. Cambridge: Lutterworth.

Schiller, Dan (1999) *Digital Capitalism: Networking the Global Market System*. Cambridge, MA: MIT Press.

Schiller, Herbert I. (1981) *Who Knows: Information in the Age of the Fortune 500*. Norwood, NJ: Ablex.

Schiller, Herbert I. (1984) *Information and the Crisis Economy*. Norwood, NJ: Ablex.

Schiller, Herbert I. (1996) *Information Inequality*. New York: Routledge.

Seltzer, Kimberley and Bentley, Tom (1999) *The Creative Age: Knowledge and Skills for the New Economy*. London: Demos.

Shannon, C. and Weaver, W. (1964 [1949]) *The Mathematical Theory of Communication*. Urbana, IL: University of Illinois Press.

Stehr, Nico (1994) *Knowledge Societies*. London: Sage.

Stevens, Norman (1986) 'The history of information', *Advances in Librarianship*, 14: 1–48.

Toffler, Alvin (1980) *The Third Wave*. New York: Morrow.

Toffler, Alvin (1990) *Powershift: Knowledge, Wealth, and Violence at the Edge of the 21st Century*. New York: Bantam.

Urry, John (2000) *Sociology beyond Societies: Mobilities for the 21st Century*. London: Routledge.

Washburn, Katherine and Thornton, John (eds) (1996) *Dumbing Down: Essays on the Strip-Mining of American Culture*. New York: Norton.

Webster, Frank (1995) *Theories of the Information Society*. London: Routledge.

Webster, Frank (2000) 'Higher education', in G. Browning, A. Halcli and F. Webster (eds), *Understanding Contemporary Society: Theories of the Present*. London: Sage. pp. 312–27.

Webster, Frank and Robins, Kevin (1986) *Information Technology: a Luddite Analysis*. Norwood, NJ: Ablex.

Zhang, Yuexiao (1988) 'Definitions and sciences of information', *Information Processing and Management*, 24 (4): 479–91.

2

Creating Community with Media: History, Theories and Scientific Investigations

NICHOLAS W. JANKOWSKI

Of all the promises and prognoses made about old and new media, perhaps the most compelling has been the possibility of regenerating community through mediated forms of communication. This theme found expression during the development of radio in the 1920s and 1930s and later with television in the 1950s. It was particularly prominent during the introduction of community radio and television in the 1970s; it has reached extraordinary proportions with the more recent emergence of 'virtual communities' on Internet-based services.

This chapter traces the relationship between (new) media and community. The first section sketches three historical periods when the relation between community and media has been central. A brief description of new media is also provided here. The second section explores the transformation of the concept of community from early locality-oriented sociological studies to those conducted from a multidisciplinary examination of Internet-based communication facilities where a geographical 'place' is absent. The third section provides illustrations of three types of studies relating community and media: small-scale electronic media, community information networks, and public discussions and debates via electronic networks. The fourth and last section examines the main methodological approaches and suggests the contours of a research agenda oriented towards further exploration of the interface between community and new media.

COMMUNITY AND MEDIA: AN ONGOING AFFAIR

An abundance of claims, optimistic and pessimistic, have been made regarding what impact the media – and most recently the Internet – may have on society in general and community in particular. It seems as if each generation has been represented by its pundits on the contribution media may have on the human condition. During the Golden Age of radio, for example, that medium was promised to bring culture into every living room; later, television was destined to transform education (see e.g. Czitrom, 1982; Douglas, 1997; Head, 1972). Both of these media were equally feared as potential tools for political propaganda; television and movies, moreover, were suspected of being able to undermine the very fabric of society, deforming young minds and debasing cultural heritage. Most of such claims, initially, had little grounding in evidence, and when systematic and extensive studies were eventually conducted the results were, at best, mixed.[1]

Similar claims also accompanied the introduction of the Internet. This new communication technology, it is said, will eradicate the inequalities and evils in society. Education will improve exponentially; citizens will become concerned and active; commerce, under the stewardship of the 'new economy', will thrive. Some, such as the co-founder of the Electronic Frontier Foundation, envision the

Internet as nothing less than 'the most transforming technological event since the capture of fire' (Barlow et al., 1995: 40). Rheingold (1993a; 1993b; 2000) is well known for his position that the Internet can help rediscover or reinvigorate community. In his widely cited book *The Virtual Community* (cited, once again, later in this chapter), he voices the general belief that the loss of traditional community values can be regained through communication via the Internet.

Such claims, as Fernback (1999) and others have observed, are more polemical expressions than considered assessments based on empirical evidence. Similarly, Wellman and Gulia (1999: 169) criticize such accounts as 'presentist and unscholarly' and historically uninformed. Most of these claims, they point out, fail to acknowledge the long-standing concern of sociologists regarding the impact of various facets of modernization – industrialization, urbanization, transportation – on society.

This section considers the special and ongoing relationship between communication and media across time. Primary attention is given to 'new media', and for that reason it is important to dwell, at least briefly, on what is meant by that term. First of all, it must be acknowledged that 'newness' is a relative notion with regard to both time and place. What is new today is old tomorrow, and what is new in one cultural context may be unknown or outmoded in another. This relativistic feature of the term has prompted some scholars (e.g. Fauconnier, 1973; Hamelink, 1980) to suggest other identifiers: telematics, and information and communication technologies, are two such rivals. Other unique features of new media have also been addressed, coming to something of a climax in the series of essays published in the maiden issue of *New Media & Society* in 1999. There, 'what's new about new media' was considered by ten leading communications scholars. Although – understandably – no consensus was achieved, it is interesting to note that much of the newness addressed had to do with transformations in the ways individuals are able to relate to media and to determine the place and functions of these media in their everyday lives. New media are, to a large degree, socially constructed phenomena and often deviate substantially from the designer's original intent.

For the purposes of this chapter, the characteristics of new media outlined by McQuail (1994: 20–6) serve as a useful delineation of the term. New media, he suggests, generally involve decentralization of channels for the distribution of messages; an increase in the capacity available for transferral of messages thanks to satellites, cable and computer networks; an increase in the options available for audience members to become involved in the communication process, often entailing an interactive form of communication; and an increase in the degree of flexibility for determining the form and content through digitization of messages. Negroponte (1995) considers this last aspect the most fundamental feature, and digitization for him essentially means that the content of one medium can be interchanged with another.

The developments usually associated with new media are many and include such technologies as CD-I and CD-ROM; cable television and computer networks; various computer-mediated communication (CMC) developments such as e-mail, newsgroups and discussion lists, and real-time chat services; and Internet-based news services provided by traditional newspapers and broadcasters. Many of these examples are technological in substance and have, by themselves, little to do with the communication process as embedded within specific historical, societal or personal contexts. New media, as considered in this chapter, are seen as developments in communication grounded within such contexts. For this reason, there is value in examining the relation of media, new for their time and place, with concern for community. Although the argument could be made that such examination might legitimately begin as far back as Gutenberg's invention of movable type or, even further, the Egyptian development of parchment, preference is given to sketching the special relationship between community and media evident since the early 1900s when community studies developed as a serious academic enterprise. The second 'wave' of studies concerned with community and media can be traced to the late 1960s and 1970s when small-scale electronic community media emerged on the scene. The third and last period to be sketched is the era of the Internet. Only a few of the striking highlights are mentioned here; more detailed illustrations of studies concerned with community and new media are reserved for the following section.

First Wave of Community and Media Studies

A concerted effort to investigate possible relations between media and community occurred under the auspices of the Chicago School in the 1920s and 1930s. In particular, Park (1922) was interested in the role of the community press regarding identity formation among immigrant groups. In a subsequent study he observed that newspaper reading was more a characteristic among residents in cities than in rural areas (Park, 1929). Also, Park found that different kinds of news were read in the city than in the country: in the city readers had more interest in news from outside the region and in the country readers preferred local news.

Merton (1949) followed up on this distinction in his study of 'Rovere' and identified two groups of residents: localites and cosmopolitans. Localites were oriented toward the local community, engaged in locally based social activities and primarily attended to the local newspaper as a source for local news. Cosmopolitans, in contrast, had a broader orientation and range of social activities, and consumed media from outside the locality. Merton was suggesting, in other words, that media use and community participation were reflections of individual traits.

Janowitz (1952) took a different approach to the topic of community and media, and stressed the role of community structure with regard to local newspaper use. Like Park, Janowitz was concerned about the role of newspapers in integrating individuals into a community. He felt local newspapers could contribute to consensus within a local community, and he investigated the role of family, social cohesion and community participation on community newspaper readership. Janowitz found that community integration and community involvement are related to greater attention to local newspapers.

These and other contributions to the relation between media and community are reviewed by Stamm (1985) in his study of newspaper use and community ties. On the basis of this review, Stamm develops a model whereby community ties can be seen as either antecedents to or consequences of community media use. He suggests that an individual's tie to place (e.g. length of residence), to structure (e.g. membership of local organizations) and to process (e.g. participation in local activities) are associated with an individual's newspaper readership. Stamm's (1985: 8) model describes newspaper use across time and he postulates that at different points in time community newspaper readership contributes to establishing community ties, and at other times the opposite occurs: community ties contribute to newspaper use. This line of research has recently been extended by Westerik (2001) through construction and testing of a causal model involving these and other variables.

Second Wave: Electronic Community Media

With development of portable video recording technology and cable television distribution systems in the late 1960s and early 1970s, a new thrust of interest developed for geographically defined as well as spatially dispersed groups to employ these communication technologies for community initiatives and actions. Use of these electronic tools of communication was in many ways an extension of print technologies – the stencil machine and offset press technology – introduced a decade earlier

during the 1960s when counter-culture and political groups established their own newspapers, known as the underground or alternative press (Denis and Rivers, 1974).

The media in these contexts were also coined 'community media', and this term referred to a diverse range of mediated forms of communication: electronic media such as radio and television, print media such as newspapers and magazines, and later electronic network initiatives embracing characteristics of both traditional print and electronic media. The manner in which community television is defined is typical of these small-scale initiatives: 'made by local people as distinct from professional broadcasters' (Lewis, 1976: 61). Members of the community, often in alliance with professional station staff, are meant to be responsible for the ideas and production of the resulting programming. Community members are generally involved in all facets of station activities and exercise control over day-to-day and long-range policy matters.

New media such as community radio and television were the focus of studies across Western Europe (e.g. Halloran, 1977; Jankowski, 1988) and North America (e.g. Widlok, 1992). Several reviews sketch how groups utilized such small-scale electronic media for political and cultural purposes (e.g. Downing, 1984; 2000; Girard, 1992; Jallov, 1997). European studies of this 'people's voice', undertaken during the 1970s and 1980s, were collected in an anthology documenting its development and impact (Jankowski et al., 1992). In the introduction to this volume the editors express their affinity with the goals of the *then* new media:

> We were ... taken by the dreams of developing or rebuilding a sense of community within new housing estates and aging neighborhoods, and applying these new media to that task. Sometimes these new community oriented media were meant to simply inform their audiences of events. Sometimes they went a step further and attempted to mobilize citizens in efforts to bring about change and improvement. Sometimes emancipatory objectives were embedded in station programming. (1992: 1)

In an assessment of those goals, Prehn (1992) points out that the initiators of community media frequently overestimated the need of people to express themselves via the media. This miscalculation often increased the difficulty of maintaining the necessary level of programming production for an established broadcasting schedule. And this problem led to the formation of a professional organizational structure antithetical to the original community-oriented objectives.

The legacy of this wave of activity relating community and media is mixed. Certainly the aspirations have remained intact, as will be demonstrated in the next section, but the results of the multitude of initiatives to achieve alternative voices reaching intended audiences are unclear. In an overall assessment of a national experiment with community electronic media in the Netherlands, the researchers suggest that the contribution of community media to community-building processes worked best in those situations where a sense of community was already well established (Hollander, 1982; Stappers et al., 1992). In residential areas short on social capital, it seems as if community media can do little to 'make things better' (see also Jankowski et al., 2001).

Third Wave: Era of the Internet

It is often difficult to pinpoint precisely when a new epoch has begun, but serious academic concern for the Internet can be traced to publication of a joint theme issue prepared by the *Journal of Communication* and the electronic upstart *Journal of Computer-Mediated Communication* (JCMC) in 1996. Another indication of the significance and importance of this third wave was the formation of the Association of Internet Researchers and the holding of its first international conference in September 2000. And, almost simultaneously across North America, Europe and Asia, new academic departments and research centres have been and are being established, all claiming niches in this new academic frontier. Some of these initiatives have taken virtual or online communities as objects of study.[2]

In terms of publishing, this new frontier has been no less than a gold rush and, for some, a lucrative gold mine. Major academic journals have recently been launched and others are on the drawing board.[3] The book publications regarding the Internet and aspects of community have quite literally exploded since publication of Benedikt's (1991) *Cyberspace: First Steps*. The series of volumes edited by Jones (1995a; 1997; 1998a; 1999) on cybersociety, virtual culture and Internet research rank as core contributions, as does a recent volume entitled *Communities in Cyberspace* (Smith and Kollock, 1999). The claim to key literature is also merited by a range of other studies on identity formation and the Internet (e.g. Stone, 1991; Turkle, 1995).

Yet another niche of literature in this area is concerned with the employment of electronic or computer networks in geographically based communities. Sometimes called public education networks (PENs), community information networks or community informatics, the literature around these developments is accumulating rapidly. Several PhD dissertations have been or are nearing completion (e.g. Hampton, 2001; Malina, 2001; Prell, 2001; Silver, 2000). Conferences have been held and books recently released on this facet of community and new media (e.g. Gurstein, 2000; Loader and Keeble, 2001).

In conclusion, much is in flux, and such movement impairs vision and reflection. Still, it seems fair to say that academic concern for community, particularly within Internet environments, is alive and well. Whether such robustness will continue may depend largely on the degree to which conceptual refinement is achieved during the coming years. How far that refinement has yet to go is sketched in the next section.

Community has been called many things. Nisbet (1966: 47) considers it one of the 'most fundamental and far-reaching' concepts of sociology. Fundamental though it may be, sociologists have not succeeded in achieving consensus on what is exactly meant by the term. In an inventory taken during the heyday of sociological concern, Hillery (1955) collected 94 distinct definitions of the concept. This plethora of meanings has led some to doubt its scientific utility. In the entry in an authoritative dictionary of sociology, for example, the authors introduce the concept as 'one of the more elusive and vague in sociology and is by now largely without specific meaning' (Abercrombie et al., 1994: 75).

Community as a popular concept has proven strikingly resilient to such attacks, however, and has gained a new life in academic discourse since discussion of the various forms of virtual communities allegedly emerging in cyberspace. It has caught, once again, the collective imagination, so much so that some Internet scholars lament the 'use and overuse of "community" in the popular and scholarly press' (Dyson, cited in Cherny, 1999: 247). It is safe to say that the concept of community is as central to present-day studies of the Internet as it was during the earlier years of sociology. The main difference seems to be redirection of emphasis from geographic place to a feeling or sense of collectivity.

This section of the chapter traces the development and change of the main formulations of community from the early period of sociology through the decades of the Chicago School and subsequent follow-up studies. More recent theoretical and methodological reorientation, with emphasis on social ties, is considered thereafter. Finally, the discussions and efforts to define community within the context of the Internet are dealt with at some length, and new formulations of community within this environment are highlighted.

Early Sociological Conceptualizations of Community

Discussions of community within the discipline of sociology frequently begin with the contributions of

Tönnies (1887/1957), particularly his formulations of *Gemeinschaft* and *Gesellschaft. Gemeinschaft*, usually translated as 'community', refers to relationships that are 'intimate, enduring and based upon a clear understanding of where each person stands in society' (Bell and Newby, 1972: 24). Found in pre-industrial societies, these relations were felt to be culturally homogeneous and strongly influenced by institutions such as the church and the family. The core of *Gemeinschaft* involves 'sentimental attachment to the conventions and mores of a beloved place enshrined in a tradition which was handed down over the generations from family to family' (Newby, 1980: 15).

Tönnies' term *Gesellschaft* is generally translated as 'society' or 'association', and refers to 'large-scale, impersonal, calculative and contractual relationships' (Newby, 1980: 15) believed to be increasing during the period of industrialization at the turn of the nineteenth century. Actions are taken in light of their potential benefit for the individual. Relations are contractual and functionally specific. Because of the individual orientation, *Gesellschaft* is characterized by a continual state of tension.

These constructions should be seen as ideal types, as Tönnies intended. Further, it is important to realize that, for Tönnies, locality was but one of the factors of community. His term also involved consideration of a relationship meant to characterize the whole of society, of 'communion' as well as 'community' (Newby, 1980: 16). Nevertheless, emphasis in subsequent sociological studies stressed the locality dimension, as did Wirth's (1938) exposition on urban life and Redfield's (1947) elaboration of Tönnies' duality into a so-called rural–urban continuum. Wirth, for example, is noted for emphasizing that *where* we live has a profound influence upon *how* we live (Newby, 1980: 18). This idea – the centrality of locality – came under increasing challenge thanks to more recent research findings. Gans (1962), for example, took issue much later with the fundamental premise in the work of Wirth and Redfield, and argued that lifestyles are determined not by locality but by other variables, particularly social class and stage in the life cycle (Newby, 1980: 28).

Social Ties as Indicators of Community

The debate around community has, for some, the characteristics of a dead end. Stacey (1974), for example, feels sociologists should discard the concept of community altogether because of its normative lading and because of the substantial definitional disagreements. Her proposal is to concentrate on the role of institutions within specific localities.

Other proposals have also been made, and one of the most enticing is the argument made regarding social ties in understanding many of the issues previously assembled under the concept of community. The central approach being taken here is network analysis – examination of the relationships (ties) established between individuals, groups or institutions (nodes). This approach allows researchers to avoid the value-laden term 'community'. Equally important, the approach opens up investigation across localities: the rural with the urban, the suburban with the metropolitan.

Social network analysis has become the *cause célèbre* in much of the work of Wellman and colleagues (Garton et al., 1999; Wellman, 1997; 1999; Wellman and Berkowitz, 1988; 1997), and most recently in their investigation of the utilization of electronic networks within residential areas (e.g. Wellman and Hampton, 1999; Hampton and Wellman, 2000). In a discussion of what he calls the 'community question', Wellman (1999) explains the features and value of social network analysis. The network approach, he asserts, avoids individual-level research perspectives, focusing instead on the relations between the nodes or units of a network. This approach provides an opportunity to consider such features as the density and 'tightness' of relations, the degree of heterogeneity among units within a network, and the impact that connections and positions within a network may have on individual or collective action.

Virtual Community

As already mentioned, Rheingold is perhaps more responsible than anyone else for generating interest in and enthusiasm for virtual communities. His book *The Virtual Community: Homesteading on the Electronic Frontier* (2000) gives a personal glimpse of what life is like in the nether world of cyberspace. Drawing on many years of personal experience in one of the first virtual communities, the WELL (Whole Earth 'Lectronic Link), Rheingold elaborates on the range of activities participants engage in while in that virtual environment, a range about as broad as is conceivable:

> People in virtual communities use words on screens to exchange pleasantries and argue, engage in intellectual discourse, conduct commerce, exchange knowledge, share emotional support, make plans, brainstorm, gossip, feud, fall in love, find friends and lose them, play games, flirt, create a little high art and a lot of idle talk. People in virtual communities do just about everything people do in real life, but we leave our bodies behind. You can't kiss anybody and nobody can punch you in the nose, but a lot can happen within those boundaries. (1993b: 3)

Rheingold has been frequently criticized for taking an excessively euphoric and uncritical stance regarding virtual communities (e.g. Fernback and Thompson, 1995b) and for lacking theoretical sophistication in his approach. Both criticisms have a degree of truth, but both are at the same time misleading and misplaced. Although Rheingold is certainly hopeful about the contribution that virtual communities may make to enriching collective life, he is at the same time uncertain about whether the efforts will succeed and poses questions in this direction. For example, he speculates, 'fragmentation, hierarchization, rigidifying social boundaries, and single-niche colonies of people who share intolerances could become prevalent in the future' (Rheingold, 1993b: 207).

Such foreboding has not impeded interest, however, and Jones has perhaps done more to place the study of online community on the academic agenda than any other individual. Largely through the two edited volumes on what he calls 'cybersociety' (Jones, 1995a; 1998a), but also through his collections on virtual culture (Jones, 1997) and Internet research (Jones, 1999), he has brought together a critical mass of scholars concerned with community in cyberspace.

Jones sets the stage in his introductory essays in the two volumes on cybersociety (Jones, 1995b; 1998b) for the remainder of the contributions. He discusses and problematizes the possibility of community that is based on forms of computer-mediated communication, and critiques the often unquestioned position taken by community sociologists who automatically associate community with locality, with geographic place. Jones, like Bender (1978) and others before him, contends such identification robs the concept of community of its essence and mistakenly gives priority to organizational ease. Jones also draws from the conceptualization of communication as a form of ritual, citing his mentor James Carey: 'Communication under a transmission view is the extension of messages across geography for the purposes of control, the ... case under a ritual view is the sacred ceremony that draws persons together in fellowship and commonality' (Carey, 1989: 18; cited in Jones, 1995b: 12).

There is an overwhelming feeling that new communities are being created, along with new forms of communities. The 'new form' these virtual communities may be taking is aptly expressed for Jones in a definition suggested by Stone (1991: 85): 'incontrovertibly social spaces in which people still meet face-to-face, but under new definitions of both "meet" and "face"... [V]irtual communities [are] passage points for collections of common beliefs and practices that united people who were physically separated' (cited in Jones, 1995b: 19).

A series of theoretical contributions about community in the Jones volumes has been prepared by Fernback (1997; 1999; see also Fernback and Thompson, 1995a; 1995b). Fernback addresses contributions from the early sociologists Tönnies and Simmel, but she also reviews contributions

from Dewey and more recent literature from the 'new communitarians' Etzioni (1993) and Bellah et al. (1985). Unlike some earlier descriptions of community, she stresses the dynamic nature of the concept: 'as society evolves the notion of community evolves concomitantly' (Fernback, 1997). A current strain of the concept is known as virtual community which she defines as 'social relationship forged in cyberspace through repeated contact within a specified boundary or place (e.g. a conference or chat line) that is symbolically delineated by topic of interest' (Fernback and Thompson, 1995b).

One of the striking and problematic features of virtual communities, according to Fernback and Thompson (1995b), is the fluidity of association individuals may have with such communities. Individuals can become active and prominent quickly, and just as quickly disappear altogether: 'Leaving a virtual community might be as easy as changing the channel on a television set.' Such fluidity may have consequences, they point out, for the stability of virtual communities to a greater degree than is the case for 'real-life' or offline communities. For this reason they are pessimistic about the potential of online communities to contribute to 'the already fragmented landscape of the public sphere'.

In a subsequent work Fernback compares characteristics of virtual communities and American culture. The principles of free speech, individualism, equality and open access are associated with virtual communities, she claims, and are 'the same symbolic interests that define the character of American democracy' (Fernback, 1997: 39). It remains to be demonstrated that the above characteristics attributed to virtual communities are universal, but even should that be the case it remains particularly ethnocentric to identify them with American cultural icons. Such parochialism seems out of place in a discussion of a form of community that, by definition, is not constrained by the geographical boundaries or the cultural manifestations of a particular nation-state.

Van Dijk (1998) takes a different approach to the topic of virtual communities from both Jones and Fernback. He sets, first of all, the task of determining whether such social constructions can compensate for the general sense of loss of community prevailing in society. He then provides a working definition of virtual communities similar to other formulations, noting that they 'are communities which are not tied to a particular place or time, but which still serve common interests in social, cultural and mental reality ranging from general to special interests or activities' (1998: 40). On the basis of a review of some of the available literature on communities, van Dijk distils four characteristics he says are common to all communities: having members, a social organization, language and patterns of interaction, and a culture and common

Table 2.1   *Ideal types of organic and virtual communities*

Characteristic	Organic	Virtual
Composition and activity	Tight group (age)	Loose affiliation
	Several activities	Special activities
Social organization	Tied to place and time	Not tied to place and time
Language and interaction	Verbal and non-verbal	Verbal and paralanguage
Culture and identity	Total singular	Partial plural
	Homogeneous	Heterogeneous

Source: van Dijk, 1998: 45

identity. These characteristics are then used to compare virtual communities with real-life or what he prefers to call 'organic' communities. This exercise leads to a typology of ideal types wherein virtual communities are described as those with relatively loose relations, which are unconcerned with considerations of time and place, which contain a well-developed paralanguage, and which are pluralistic and heterogeneous in composition (see Table 2.1). As is the case with most efforts to construct ideal types, this profile of virtual communities falls short of adequately describing actual cases. Many virtual communities can be characterized by the strong ties among their members, are grounded in time and place, and reflect a homogeneous membership.

With this typology in hand, van Dijk formulates the central question of his study: 'To what extent can virtual communities replace organic communities and provide forces to countervail the present social processes of fragmentation and individualization?' (1998: 48). Reviewing conclusions based on early CMC research, he asserts that electronic groups will come to resemble their organic counterparts regarding their structure and rules. His overall conclusion is that virtual communities cannot reclaim 'lost' community in society, largely because the cultures and identities created are 'too partial, heterogeneous and fluid to create a strong sense of membership and belonging' (1998: 59). He contends that the quality of discourse is 'poor' and genuine dialogue is missing. At best, virtual communities may supplement organic communities, but are unable to replace them, according to van Dijk.

The above assertions might serve as hypotheses, but it is much too premature to claim them as conclusions. The empirical studies necessary to substantiate such claims have not been conducted. In a review by one of the few persons to have undertaken on extended ethnographic fieldwork of an online community, Baym supports this criticism: 'we do not have the empirical grounds on which to assess how (or if) online community affects offline community' (1998: 38).

Baym (1995; 1998; 1999), in addition to providing rich insight into a Usenet newsgroup devoted to discussion of television soap operas, also elaborates on a theoretical model of online community. She is concerned with understanding how such communities develop and manifest themselves, and what occurs during the process of being online that leads participants to experience these virtual phenomena as communities. Baym develops what she calls an 'emergent model of online community' (1998: 38). She argues that five already existing features influence the character of an online community: external context, temporal structure, system infrastructure, group purposes and the characteristics of participants. These features impinge on the development of an online community regarding 'group-specific forms of expression, identities, relationships and normative conventions' (1998: 38).

The model Baym develops for online community can be represented schematically as illustrated in Table 2.2. Here, some of her original terms have been renamed, and the categories of temporal and system infrastructure have been combined. The cells within the table could contain summary data of a particular online community, such as the television soap opera newsgroup r.a.t.s. in the case of Baym's study. The model, once applied to a number of online communities, provides opportunity for comparative analysis. Baym notes that the overall purpose of her model is not to be predictive in nature, but to provide a framework for understanding how online communities develop. Although each community may be unique, as she argues, the model nevertheless provides guidelines for comparing online communities.

Another elaboration of the meaning of virtual community comes from the field of linguistics. In a case study of a multi-user dungeon (MUD), Cherny (1999) reviews definitions for speech communities, discourse communities and communities of practice. Following Hymes (1972), Cherny (1999: 13) suggests that a speech community involves sharing rules for speaking and interpreting communicative performance. Members of a speech community use language to delineate the boundaries of the community, to unify its members and to exclude others.

'Discourse community', as elaborated by Gurak (1997: 11), is concerned with the 'use of discourse for purposeful social action in a public arena'. This form of community resembles the 'interpretive community' to which language composition scholars allude. Finally, 'community of practice' refers to relations maintained by persons across time who

Table 2.2 *A model for online communities: characteristics and influences*

Characteristics	Influences			
	Communication	Identity	Relationships	Norms
Content				
Structure				
Objectives				
Participants				

Source: adapted from Baym, 1995; 1998

are involved in a collective set of activities. The 'academic community' could be considered an illustration of such a community of practice. One of the important features of this form of community is that it provides the overall conditions and basis for interpreting and making sense of events and activities. Participants share a general understanding of their activities and of the meaning ascribed to them. Although the distinctions between these terms is not always clear, they collectively suggest new avenues for understanding community from a perspective where use of language is central. The linguistics perspective seems particularly appropriate for computer-mediated communication because of its focus on forms of language and discourse.

Another current development is infusion of the concept 'social capital' into discussions and investigations of virtual communities (e.g. Blanchard and Horan, 1998). Coined by Putnam (1993; 1995; 2000), social capital can be seen as a recent variant of the older tradition of community development, community work and community action initiatives prominent in the United States in the 1960s. Riedel et al. (1998) examined the presence of social capital in a community network in a rural town in Minnesota, focusing on three components: interpersonal trust, social norms and association membership. These components of social capital were also used in another study of a digital community network in The Hague (Jankowski et al., 2001).

ILLUSTRATIVE STUDIES OF NEW MEDIA AND COMMUNITY

The various formulations of community presented in the previous section have found reflection in many empirical studies of the media. Here, illustrations are provided for three areas of research: small-scale electronic media, physically based online communities, and public discussion and debate on the Internet. Although research from other areas could have been chosen (e.g. community development and design,[4] culture and language, identity formation[5] and commercially oriented virtual communities[6]), the studies presented here illustrate some of the current work being conducted around community and (new) media.

Small-Scale Electronic Media

A recent compilation of community media research (Jankowski, 2001) contains a section of four chapters devoted to issues and illustrations of the public sphere as related to community radio and television. There, Mitchell (2001) explores how women's community radio may serve as a tool for women's empowerment. With empirical data from women's radio stations and projects across Europe, Mitchell examines how radio can be used to develop a feminist public sphere. Coleman (2001) provides an analysis of phone-in radio programmes in the Irish Republic and considers how these programmes may contribute towards better exchange between disparate groups in that society. He argues that this form of discourse provides opportunity for communication that would otherwise be unlikely or difficult. A contribution by Stein (2001) assesses the role of public access television in political communication in the United States. She examines the political uses of access television within radical media projects and argues that such media host a range of democratic speech absent from the traditional media industries. Finally, Barlow (2001) examines the policies and practices of three community radio stations in Australia regarding key features of that sector of broadcasting. While all of the stations seem to pay homage to the principles of access and participation, he finds that these three stations differ substantially in their practices. Moreover, all of the stations are subject to the strain caused by the concerns of professionalization, popularization and commercialization of community radio.

Physically Based Virtual Communities

There are basically two categories of virtual communities: those with a distinct relation to a geographical locality and those having no such binding with a particular space. Freenets, PENs, community information networks and digital cities are some of the types of physically based virtual communities. Preference is given to the term 'digital community network' to describe virtual communities in this category. Two recent studies of these virtual communities serve as illustrations of the research being conducted in this area.

The first investigation, conducted by Silver (2000), provides a comparative analysis of Blacksburg Electronic Village (BEV) in Virginia with the Seattle Community Network in the state of Washington. Silver is concerned with differences in the development, design and use of these two digital community networks. Regarding development, Silver notes that the Blacksburg Electronic Village is essentially a prototype of a 'top-down' approach whereby large amounts of capital were invested to construct a state-of-the-art facility. Silver suggests that a small group of actors – persons from local industry, government and the university situated in the town – conceived the initiative, financed it and brought it to operational level. Involvement of community organizations, groups and individual citizens during this process was minimal. Involvement by Blackburg residents after site construction came to resemble the behaviour of consumers rather than of community members. According to Silver, the 'most common use of the BEV was for commercial purposes: to download coupons, check movie times, or purchase goods online' (2000: 282).

The Seattle Community Network, in contrast, was conceived by a broad assemblage of community organizations and groups from an early phase in its development. These community units engaged in what Silver calls participatory design, and they determined overall policy and structure for the community network. In this respect, the network reflected a 'bottom-up' initiative and was intended to serve as a tool for community development. The Seattle Community Network was promoted through workshops and outreach programmes, was made accessible through public facilities such as libraries and was provided free of charge to Seattle area residents. This community network, according to Silver, came to offer 'a culturally rich, civic-based online platform of resources, materials, and discussion forums with and within which residents of Seattle can share ideas, interact with one another, and build communities' (2000: 294).

The second investigation of digital community networks to be presented here involves 'Netville', a wired suburb located on the outskirts of Toronto. Netville is a complex of approximately 120 homes designed and built in the mid 1990s. A special feature of this suburb, distinguishing it from most others in North America, is that it was equipped from the beginning with a local electronic network capable of providing high-speed Internet access; a computer videophone facility; a variety of music, health and entertainment services; and neighbourhood discussion forums. These features were widely promoted during the early sale of homes in the estate and a special research consortium was established to monitor technical and social developments.

The social science fieldwork was conducted by Hampton (2001) whose concern was to determine the influence such a state-of-the-art communication infrastrucuture might have on the social relations that residents maintain with neighbours, friends, relatives and colleagues – within and outside Netville, online and offline.[7] The study was based on a long-standing premise developed and frequently argued by the 'Toronto School' of community studies (e.g. Wellman, 1979; 1999), suggesting that community is not of necessity locality-bound. This position argues that social ties constitute the central feature of community and not locality, and that these ties – be they weak or strong – should be the focus of empirical study of community. It is, in the words of Hampton and Wellman, 'the sociable, supportive, and identity-giving interactions that define community, and not the local space in which they might take place' (2000: 195).

Netville provided opportunity for an extended field study of this premise, linked to the new 'variable' of an electronic network infrastructure with accompanying communication services. As part of this study, Hampton resided in Netville for a period of two years and integrated into the social life of the neighbourhood. He participated in both online and offline activities, the discussion lists and the barbecues, and conducted what Hampton and Wellman (1999) describe as a classical community ethnography. In addition, Hampton and Wellman conducted a survey of the residents regarding their network of social ties.

Findings from this survey suggest that the electronic network supported both weak and strong social ties ranging from those purely functional in nature to those grounded in social and personal issues. In probing for the breadth of social ties among residents, Hampton and Wellman (2000) report that those residents connected to the electronic network significantly differed from residents not connected: they knew more of their neighbours' names, they talked to and visited with them more often. The wired residents, in other words, maintained a broader ranger of social contacts than their non-wired counterparts. Hampton and Wellman suggest this may have had to do with the presence of the electronic network and particularly because of the neighbourhood e-mail list maintained on the network for residents. The network seemed to have been particularly valuable during periods of social action, i.e. during conflicts with the housing developer and especially during a conflict about an unexpected discontinuance of the network.

Internet and Public Discussion

The place of public discussion and debate has been a central feature of community media initiatives for decades, and this feature is equally central to many Internet-based facilities. Newsgroups, discussion lists, and specially constructed sites for debating social, political and cultural issues abound on the Internet. Empirical research is beginning to emerge around these phenomena, particularly from the perspective of the concept of public sphere. One of the most extensive studies to date has been carried out by Schneider (1996; 1997) around a Usenet discussion group concerned with abortion. During the period of a year, Schneider collected 46,000 messages posted on the site and examined them along four dimensions considered central to Habermas' (1989) notion of public sphere: *equality* of access to the arena of debate, *diversity* of opinions and topics relevant to a particular debate, *reciprocity* or degree of interaction between persons involved in a debate, and the *quality* or degree to which participants contribute information relevant to the topic.

Schneider operationalized each of these dimensions so that a quantitative analysis could be conducted on the entire number of postings during the period of study.[8] He found, overall, that contributions to the newsgroup were diverse in substance and that participants exhibited an acceptable degree of reciprocity. Although access to the discussion was theoretically open, actual involvement in the debate – a feature also relevant for the equality dimension of public sphere in this study – was strikingly low. Of the nearly 3000 contributors to the discussion during the year period, fewer than 0.5 per cent were responsible for more than 40 per cent of all postings. Put differently, some 5 per cent of the participants posted almost 80 per cent of the contributions. Finally, regarding the dimension quality, Schneider found that the most frequent contributors to the discussion were the least likely to post messages 'on topic', i.e. related to the issue of abortion. This feature, he suggests, exacerbated the inequality reflected in the discussion.

The findings from this study pose serious concerns regarding the contribution of Internet-based discussions to public debate. Although the potential of such discussions may be great, as Schneider and others (e.g. Jankowski and van Selm, 2000) continue to repeat, the actual degree of involvement is minuscule, and much of what is contributed is not relevant to the topic.

RESEARCHING NEW MEDIA AND COMMUNITY: METHODS AND QUESTIONS

No one research methodology or agenda of questions dominates work currently being undertaken around new media and community. As illustrated in the previous section, investigations are emerging from a variety of disciplines employing diverse tools of study and directed at different areas of concern. As pluralist as the field is, some overriding preferences for methods and questions can be discerned and are elaborated in this section.

Research Methods

Regarding research methods, about a decade ago an overview of the place of qualitative methods in studying community media was prepared (Jankowski, 1991). Then it appeared as if this approach was increasing in importance within the field of mass communication studies in general and within the more specialized concern of small-scale media in particular. The 'qualitative turn', it seemed, had arrived.

Now, looking at studies concerned with new media and community, it appears, once again, that qualitative or interpretive studies are prominent. Several of the empirical studies mentioned or presented earlier in this chapter feature characteristics of classical community study fieldwork (e.g. Baym, 1999; Malina, 2001; Silver, 2000). Others (e.g. Cherny, 1999; Jankowski and van Selm, 2000) develop a form of textual or discourse analysis. Yet others (Harrison and Stephen, 1999; Harrison et al., 2001) integrate the conventional concerns of academic research with those regarding design and development of community information networks.

Quantitative approaches are also represented in current work. Schneider's (1997) study of public debate on a Usenet newsgroup represents a sophisticated quantitative analysis of a very large body of messages. Hampton (2001) employs survey research and network analysis within the context of a sociological field study. More generally, the degree of interest in online survey research is substantial. The first major text on this method has appeared (Dillman, 2000) and there has been a range of journal articles (e.g. Coomber, 1997; Mehta and Sivadas, 1995; Swoboda et al., 1997). It is only a matter of time before these data collection tools become applied to studies of new media and community.

Innovations in methods and methodologies are also being developed. For example, an ongoing study (Ahern et al., 2000) combines an experimental design with structured and open interview instrumentation to explore the nature of public discussion and debate on the Internet. In another study, this one of Campaign 2000 in the United States, innovative software and new strategies for website analysis are being developed (Schneider and Larsen, 2000).[9]

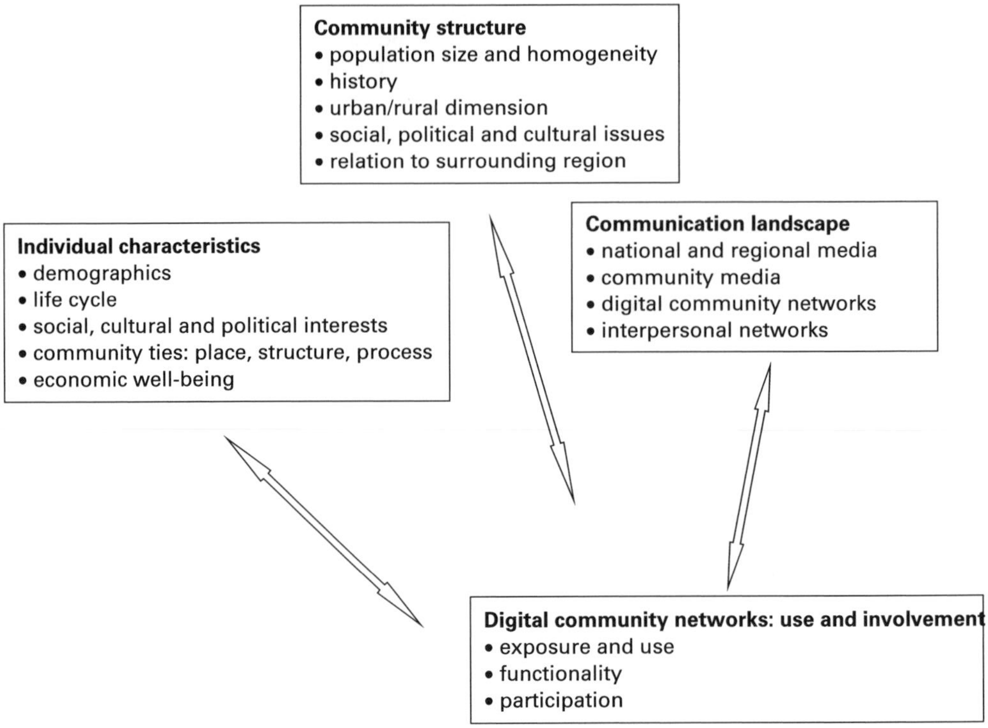

Community structure
- population size and homogeneity
- history
- urban/rural dimension
- social, political and cultural issues
- relation to surrounding region

Individual characteristics
- demographics
- life cycle
- social, cultural and political interests
- community ties: place, structure, process
- economic well-being

Communication landscape
- national and regional media
- community media
- digital community networks
- interpersonal networks

Digital community networks: use and involvement
- exposure and use
- functionality
- participation

Figure 2.1   *Components of community communication and digital community networks (Jankowski et al., 2001)*

Many of the current and proposed investigations are constructed as case studies (e.g. Jankowski et al., 2001). This type of study has been subjected to severe criticism. In discussing community study as a method of research (similar to the case study method) Bell and Newby (1972: 17) summarize some of the commonly voiced reservations: excessive reliance on a single observer, lack of systematic data collection, insufficient distinction between researcher and object of study. Baym (1999: 18–21) eschews much of what presently passes for ethnography, but for different reasons. Following criticisms of ethnography developed by Nightingale (1996) and Press (1996), Baym notes that much of what passes for this form of inquiry in the study of audiences is limited to brief forays in the field coupled with individual and group interviews. She suggests, as a minimum standard, that multiple forms of data collection be undertaken during an extensive period of fieldwork.

In addition to Baym's suggestions, it should be mentioned that much refinement has been achieved in both qualitative data collection and analysis procedures since Bell and Newby itemized the above reservations. For example, the systematic analysis procedures elaborated by Miles and Huberman (1994) and the utilization of computer programs to aid qualitative analysis and development of grounded theory (e.g. Hijmans and Peeters, 2000) are illustrative of these advances. These can be – but still all too seldom are – applied to community media studies. Even with such technical perfections, it remains essential to do more than simply increase the number of case studies. Core questions formulated within a theoretical framework are also necessary, as argued below.

Research Agenda

In addition to developments in methods, advances are also being made in determining the key questions for community and media. For example, an overview is provided of the proposed research concerns shared by contributors to a recent volume on community media (Jankowski, 2001). For one specific area a model has been constructed within which research questions can be addressed. Hollander (2000) draws on the earlier work of Stamm (1985) and proposes a causal relation between community structure, characteristics of individual community residents, the media landscape and community media use. He suggests that different causal relations may be dominant for different configurations of the variables related to each of the above factors. The model by Hollander has been further modified for application to investigations of digital community networks and thereby proposes a framework for formulation of a range of research interests (see Figure 2.1). The overriding research question for this model is: *to what degree and in what manner do aspects of community structure, individual characteristics and media landscape relate to the use of and involvement in digital community networks by local residents?*

Although not embedded within a model, the research questions formulated by Wellman and Gulia (1999) represent the most extensive agenda prepared to date on virtual communities. They pose seven clusters of questions regarding the nature of online relationships and their relation to offline relationships and to community involvement.

A more compact list of questions has been formulated by Baym (1999: 210–16) in the conclusion of her study of an online community of television soap fans, discussed earlier. She suggests four central questions for further research:

- What forces shape online identities?
- How do online communities evolve over time?
- How does online participation connect to offline life?
- How do online communities influence offline communities?

The questions are similar to those posed by Wellman and Gulia, but include concern for the evolution of online communities across time. But, like Wellman and Gulia, Baym does not extend this formulation of questions to the level of a model integrating findings from each of the separate questions and thereby lending direction for further empirical study.

As Wellman and Gulia observe: 'It is time to replace anecdote with evidence ... The answers have not yet been found. Indeed, the questions are just starting to be formulated' (1999: 185). In addition to formulating relevant questions as initiated by these scholars, the time has also come to generate theoretically based models similar to those constructed for emerging online communities (Baym, 1995; 1998) and for digital community networks (Jankowski et al., 2001) that are relevant to other realms of new media and community. Research questions embedded within such models will then provide the needed direction and grounding missing from much of the current wave of case studies concerned with community and new media.

NOTES

I wish to thank my colleagues, at home and abroad, who contributed comments and suggestions during the preparation of this chapter, in alphabetical order: Nancy Baym, Hans Beentjes, Ed Hollander, Steve Jones, Sonia Livingstone, Martine van Selm, Barry Wellman and Henk Westerik. Margot van der Goot, graduate student assistant, helped put the references into proper shape. Finally, special thanks are due to colleague David Silver who graciously shared his treasure chest of knowledge on cyberculture. Responsibility for the limitations inherent in this review rest, of course, with me.

1 See e.g. Gunter and Harrison (1998) for an overview of media violence studies.

2 Examples include the Center for the Study of Online Community at the University of California at Los Angeles, the Centre for Urban and Community Studies at the University of Toronto, and the Electronic Learning Communities research programme at Georgia Institute of Technology. See also the Resource Center for Cyberculture Studies, presently located at the University of Maryland (http://otal.umd.edu/~rccs/).

3 An incomplete list of academic journals concerned with new media includes: *The Information Society; Information, Communication & Society; New Media & Society; Television and New Media; Journal of Computer-Mediated Communication; and Journal of Online Behavior.*

4 A primer for issues related to the construction of community information networks is Schuler's (1996) practically oriented volume. Harrison et al. (2001) explore design and research interventionist strategies for development of digital community networks.

5 Space does not permit consideration of studies about multi-user dungeons (MUDs) and their contribution to collective and individual identity. The literature in this area is substantial, but the following authors provide a good introduction to this genre: Bromberg (1996), Cherny (1999), Dibbell (1993), Donath (1999), Reid (1994; 1999), Stone (1991), and – especially – Turkle (1995).

6 Many e-commerce operations (e.g. Amazon.com, Participate.com) and Internet service providers (e.g. AOL) have latched onto the notion of community building in order to enhance consumerism and commercial gain. This development is also not addressed in this chapter. Cherny (1999: 253–4) considers it briefly and authors (e.g. Hagel and Armstrong, 1997) affiliated with business schools have noted some aspects of this interface.

7 A number of draft manuscripts, journal articles and book chapters have appeared on the Netville project (Hampton, 2000; Hampton and Wellman, 1999; 2000; Wellman and Hampton, 1999). The most complete publication is Hampton's (2001) PhD dissertation.

8 The theoretical perspective and method of analysis is described in detail by Schneider (1997) in his dissertation, available online: http://www.sunyit.edu/~steve/. A brief review of the four dimensions of public sphere and Schneider's findings may be found in Jankowski and van Selm (2000).

9 For further information on the research project focusing on Campaign 2000, see http://www.NetElection.org.

REFERENCES

Abercrombie, N., Hill, S. and Turner, B.S (1994) *The Penguin Dictionary of Sociology*, 3rd edn (1st edn 1984). London: Penguin.

Ahern, R.K., Stromer-Galley, J. and Neuman, W.R. (2000) 'When voters can interact and compare candidates online: experimentally investigating political web effects'. Paper presented at the International Communication Association Conference, Acapulco, Mexico.

Barlow, D. (2001) 'Conceptions of access and participation in Australian community radio stations', in N.W. Jankowski (with O. Prehn) (ed.), *Community Media in the Information Age: Perspectives and Prospects*. Cresskill, NJ: Hampton.

Barlow, J.P., Birkets, S., Kelly, K. and Slouka, M. (1995) 'What are we doing on-line?', *Harper's*, August: 35–46.

Baym, N.K. (1995) 'The emergence of community in computer-mediated communication', in S.G. Jones (ed.), *Cybersociety: Computer-Mediated Communication and Community*. Thousand Oaks, CA: Sage. pp. 138–63.

Baym, N.K. (1998) 'The emergence of on-line community', in S. Jones (ed.), *Cybersociety 2.0: Revisiting Computer-Mediated Communication and Community*. Thousand Oaks, CA: Sage. pp. 35–67.

Baym, N.K. (1999) *Tune in, Log on: Soaps, Fandom, and Online Community*. Thousand Oaks, CA: Sage.

Bell, C. and Newby, H. (1972) *Community Studies: An Introduction to the Sociology of the Local Community*. New York: Praeger.

Bellah, R., Madsen, R., Sullivan, W., Swidler, A. and Tipton, S. (1985) *Habits of the Heart: Individualism and Commitment in American Life*. Berkeley, CA: University of California Press.

Bender, T. (1978) *Community and Social Change in America*. New Brunswick, NJ: Rutgers University Press.

Benedikt, M. (1991) *Cyberspace: First Steps*. Cambridge, MA: MIT Press.

Blanchard, A. and Horan, T. (1998) 'Virtual communities and social capital', *Social Science Computer Review*, 16 (3): 293–307.

Bromberg, H. (1996) 'Are MUDs communities? Identity, belongings and consciousness in virtual worlds', in R. Shields (ed.), *Cultures of Internet: Virtual Spaces, Real Histories, Living Bodies*. London: Sage. pp. 143–52.

Carey, J. (1989) *Communication as Culture*. Boston, MA: Unwin-Hyman.

Cherny, L. (1999) *Conversation and Community: Chat in a Virtual World*. Chicago: University of Chicago Press.

Coleman, S. (2001) 'BBC Radio Ulster's talkback phone-in: public feedback in a divided public space', in N.W. Jankowski (with O. Prehn) (ed.), *Community Media in the Information Age: Perspectives and Prospects*. Cresskill, NJ: Hampton.

Coomber, R. (1997) 'Using the Internet for survey research', *Sociological Research Online*, 2 (2). Available online: http://www.socresonline.org.uk/socresonline/2/2/2.html.

Czitrom, D.J. (1982) *Media and the American Mind: from Morse to McLuhan*. Chapel Hill, NC: University of North Carolina Press.

Denis, E.E. and Rivers, W.L. (1974) *The Other Voices: New Journalism in America*. San Francisco: Canfield.

Dibbell, J. (1993) 'Rape in cyberspace', *The Village Voice*, 21 December: 38.

Dillman, D.A. (2000) *Mail and Internet Surveys: the Tailored Design Method*. New York: Wiley.

Donath, J.S. (1999) 'Identity and deception in the virtual community', in M.A. Smith and P. Kollock (eds), *Communities in Cyberspace*. London: Routledge. pp. 29–59.

Douglas, S.J. (1997) *Inventing American Broadcasting 1899–1922*. Baltimore, MD: Johns Hopkins University Press.

Downing, J. (1984) *Radical Media: the Political Experience of Alternative Communication*. Boston, MA: South End.

Downing, J. (2000) *Radical Media: Rebellious Communication and Social Movements*. Thousand Oaks, CA: Sage.

Etzioni, A. (1993) *The Spirit of Community: Rights, Responsibilities, and the Communitarian Agenda*. New York: Crown.

Fauconnier, G. (1973) *Massamedia en Samenleving: inleiding tot de wetenschappelijke studie van de massa communicatie* (Mass Media and Society: Introduction to the Scientific Study of Mass Communication). Antwerp: De Nederlandsche Boekhandel.

Fernback, J. (1997) 'The individual within the collective: virtual ideology and the realization of collective principles', in S.G. Jones (ed.), *Virtual Culture: Identity and Communication in Cybersociety*. London: Sage. pp. 36–54.

Fernback, J. (1999) 'There is there there: notes toward a definition of cybercommunity', in S. Jones (ed.), *Doing Internet Research*. London: Sage. pp. 203–20.

Fernback, J. and Thompson, B. (1995a) 'Computer-mediated communication and the American collectivity: the dimensions of community within cyberspace'. Paper presented at the International Communication Association, Albuquerque, NM.

Fernback, J. and Thompson, B. (1995b) 'Virtual communities: abort, retry, failure?' Unpublished paper. Available online: http://www.well.com/user/hlr/texts/VCcivil.

Gans, H. (1962) *The Urban Villagers: Group and Class in the Life of Italian-Americans*. New York: Free Press.

Garton, L., Haythornthwaite, C. and Wellman, B. (1999) 'Studying on-line social networks', in S. Jones (ed.), *Doing Internet Research: Critical Issues and Methods for Examining the Net*. Thousand Oaks, CA: Sage. pp. 75–105.

Girard, B. (1992) *A Passion for Radio: Radio Waves and Community*. Montreal: Black Rose.

Gunter, B. and Harrison, J. (1998) *Violence on Television: an Analysis of Amount, Nature, Location and Origin of Violence in British Programmes*. London: Routledge.

Gurak, L. (1997) *Persuasion and Privacy in Cyberspace: the Online Protests over Lotis Marketplace and the Clipper Chip*. New Haven, CT: Yale University Press.

Gurstein, M. (2000) *Community Informatics: Enabling Communities with Information and Communication Technologies*. Hershey, PA: Idea Group.

Habermas, J. (1989) *The Structural Transformation of the Public Sphere: An Inquiry into a Category of Bourgeois Society*. Oxford: Polity.

Hagel, J. and Armstrong, A. (1997) *Net Gain: Expanding Markets through Virtual Communities*. Boston: Harvard Business School Press.

Halloran, J. (1977) 'Communication and community: the evaluation of an experiment'. Report. Strasburg: Council of Europe.

Hamelink, C. (1980) *De Computer Samenleving (The Computer Society)*. Baarn, the Netherlands: In den Toren.

Hampton, K. (2000) 'Grieving for a lost network: collective action in a wired suburb'. Unpublished manuscript. Available online: www.mysocialnetwork.net.

Hampton, K. (2001) 'Living the wired life in the wired suburb: Netville, globalization and civic society'. PhD dissertation, University of Toronto.

Hampton, K. and Wellman, B. (1999) 'Netville on-line and off-line: observing and surveying a wired suburb', *American Behavioral Scientist*, 43 (3): 475–92.

Hampton, K. and Wellman, B. (2000) 'Examining community in the digital neighborhood: early results from Canada's wired suburb', in T. Ishida and K. Isbister (eds), *Digital Cities: Technologies, Experiences, and Future Perspectives*. Berlin: Springer. pp. 475–92.

Harrison, T. and Stephen, T. (1999) 'Researching and creating community networks', in S. Jones (ed.), *Doing Internet Research: Critical Issues and Methods for Examining the Net*. London: Sage. pp. 221–41.

Harrison, T., Zappen, J.P. and Prell, C. (2001) 'Transforming new communication technologies into community media', in N.W. Jankowski (with O. Prehn) (ed.), *Community Media in the Information Age: Perspectives and Prospects*. Cresskill, NJ: Hampton.

Head, S.W. (1972) *Broadcasting in America: a Survey of Television and Radio*, 2nd edn (1st edn 1956). Boston: Houghton Mifflin.

Hijmans, E. and Peters, V. (2000) 'Grounded theory in media research and the use of the computer', *Communications: the European Journal of Communication Research*, 25 (4): 407–32.

Hillery, G. (1955) 'Definitions of community: areas of agreement', *Rural Sociology*, 20: 111–23.

Hollander, E. (1982) *Kleinschalige Massacommunictie: Lokale Omroepvormen in West Europa (Small-scale Mass Communication: Forms of Local Broadcasting in West Europe)*. The Hague: State.

Hollander, E. (2000) 'Online communities as community media: a theoretical and analytical framework for the study of digital community networks', *Communications: the European Journal of Communication Research*, 25 (4): 371–86.

Hymes, D. (1972) 'Models of the interaction of language and social life', in J. Gumperz and D. Hymes (eds), *Directions in Sociolinguistics*. New York: Holt, Rinehart, & Winston. pp. 35–71.

Jallov, B. (1997) 'Women's voices crossing frontiers: 1996 European directory of women's community radio stations and women's radio production collectives'. Report. Sheffield: AMARC–Europe Women's Network.

Janowitz, M. (1952) *The Community Press in an Urban Setting*. Glencoe, IL: Free Press.

Jankowski, N.W. (1988) 'Community television in Amsterdam: access to, participation in and use of the "Lokale Omroep Bijlmermeer"'. PhD dissertation, University of Amsterdam.

Jankowski, N.W. (1991) 'Qualitative research and community media', in K.B. Jensen and N.W. Jankowski (eds), *A Handbook of Qualitative Methodologies for Mass Communication Research*. London: Routledge. pp. 163–74.

Jankowski, N.W. (with Prehn, O.) (ed.) (2001) *Community Media in the Information Age: Perspectives and Prospects*. Cresskill, NJ: Hampton.

Jankowski, N. and van Selm, M. (2000) 'The promise and practice of public debate in cyberspace', in K.L. Hacker and J. van Dijk (eds), *Digital Democracy: Issues of Theory and Practice*. London: Sage. pp. 149–65.

Jankowski, N., Prehn, O. and Stappers, J. (eds) (1992) *The People's Voice: Local Radio and Television in Europe*. London: Libbey.

Jankowski, N., van Selm, M. and Hollander, E. (2001) 'On crafting a study of digital community networks: theoretical and methodological considerations', in B. Loader and L. Keeble (eds), *Community Informatics: Shaping Computer-Mediated Social Networks*. London: Taylor.

Jones, S.G. (ed.) (1995a) *Cybersociety: Computer-Mediated Communication and Community*. Thousand Oaks, CA: Sage.

Jones, S.G. (1995b) 'Understanding community in the information age', in S.G. Jones (ed.), *Cybersociety: Computer-Mediated Communication and Community*. Thousand Oaks, CA: Sage. pp. 10–34.

Jones, S. (ed.) (1997) *Virtual Culture: Identity and Communication in Cybersociety*. London: Sage.

Jones, S. (ed.) (1998a) *Cybersociety 2.0: Revisiting Computer-Mediated Communication and Community*. Thousand Oaks, CA: Sage.

Jones, S. (1998b) 'Information, Internet, and community: notes toward an understanding of community in the information age', in S. Jones (ed.), *Cybersociety 2.0: Revisiting Computer-Mediated Communication and Community*. Thousand Oaks, CA: Sage. pp. 1–33.

Jones, S. (ed.) (1999) *Doing Internet Research: Critical Issues and Methods for Examining the Net*. Thousand Oaks, CA: Sage.

Lewis, P. (1976) *Bristol Channel and Community Television*. London: IBA.

Loader, B. and Keeble, L. (eds) (2001) *Community Informatics: Shaping Computer-Mediated Social Networks*. London: Taylor.

McQuail, D. (1994) *Mass Communication Theory: an Introduction*, 3rd edn (1st edn 1983). London: Sage.

Malina, A. (2001) 'Community building in cyberspace: a case study of a community network'. PhD dissertation, Queen Margaret College, Edinburgh, Scotland.

Mehta, R. and Sivadas, E. (1995) 'Comparing response rates and response content in mail versus electronic mail surveys', *Journal of the Market Research Society*, 37 (4): 429–39.

Merton, R.K. (1949) 'Patterns of influence: a study of interpersonal influence and communications behavior in a local community', in P.F. Lazarsfeld and F.N. Stanton (eds), *Communication Research 1948–49*. New York: Arno. pp. 180–219.

Miles, M.B. and Huberman, M. (1994) *Qualitative Data Analysis: an Expanded Sourcebook*. Thousand Oaks, CA: Sage.

Mitchell, C. (2001) 'On air/off air: defining women's radio space in European women's community radio', in N.W. Jankowski (with O. Prehn) (ed.), *Community Media in the Information Age: Perspectives and Prospects*. Cresskill, NJ: Hampton.

Negroponte, N. (1995) *Being Digital*. New York: Knopf.

Newby, H. (1980) *An Introduction to Sociology. Block 3: Comparison and Change: Community*. Milton Keynes: Open University Press.

Nightingale, V. (1996) *Studying Audiences: the Shock of the Real*. London: Routledge.

Nisbet, R. (1966) *The Sociological Tradition*. London: Heinemann.

Park, R.E. (1922) *The Immigrant Press and its Control*. New York: Harper & Row.

Park, R. (1929) 'Urbanization as measured by newspaper circulation', *American Journal of Sociology*, 34: 60–79.

Prehn, O. (1992) 'From small scale utopianism to large scale pragmatism', in N. Jankowski, O. Prehn and J. Stappers (eds), *The People's Voice: Local Radio and Television in Europe*. London: Libbey. pp. 247–68.

Prell, C.L. (2001) 'The design and diffusion of a community network and its effect on social capital'. PhD dissertation, Rensselaer Polytechnic Institute, Troy, NY.

Press, A.L. (1996) 'Towards a qualitative methodology of audience study: using ethnography to study the popular culture audience', in J.H.L. Grossberg and E. Wartella (eds), *The Audience and its Landscape*. Boulder, CO: Westview. pp. 113–30.

Putnam, R.D. (with Leonardi, R. and Nanetti, R.Y.) (1993) *Making Democracy Work: Civic Traditions in Modern Italy*. Princeton, NJ: Princeton University Press.

Putnam, R.D. (1995) 'Bowling alone: America's declining social capital', *Journal of Democracy*, 6 (1): 65–78.

Putnam, R.D. (2000) *Bowling Alone: the Collapse and Revival of American Community*. New York: Simon & Schuster.

Redfield, R. (1947) 'The folk society', *American Journal of Sociology*, 52: 293.

Reid, E.M. (1994) 'Cultural formations in text-based virtual reality'. Master's thesis, University of Melbourne. Available online: ftp://ftp.lambda.moo.mud.org/pub/MOO/papers/CulturalFormations.txt.

Reid, E. (1999) 'Hierarchy and power: social control in cyberspace', in M.A. Smith and P. Kollock (eds), *Communities in Cyberspace*. London: Routledge. pp. 107–33.

Rheingold, H. (1993a) 'A slice of life in my virtual community', in L.M. Harasim (ed.), *Global Networks*. Cambridge: MIT Press. pp. 57–80. Draft version available at: http://home.ntt.com/eegtti/eeg_260html.

Rheingold, H. (1993b) *The Virtual Community: Homesteading on the Electronic Frontier*. Reading, MA: Addison-Wesley. Available online: http://www.rheingold.com/vc/book/.

Rheingold, H. (2000) *The Virtual Community: Homesteading on the Electronic Frontier*, rev edn. Cambridge, MA: MIT Press.

Riedel, E., Dresel, L., Wagoner, M.J., Sullivan, J.L. and Borgida, E. (1998) 'Electric communities: assessing equality of accesss in a rural Minnesota community', *Social Science Computer Review*, 15 (4): 370–90.

Schneider, S. (1996) 'A case study of abortion conversation on the Internet', *Social Science Computer Review*, 14 (4): 373–93.

Schneider, S. (1997) 'Expanding the public sphere through computer-mediated communication: political discussion about abortion in a Usenet newsgroup'. PhD dissertation, Massachusetts Institute of Technology, Cambridge, MA. Available: online: http://www.sunyit.edu/~steve/.

Schneider, S. and Larsen, E. (2000) 'The 2000 Presidential Primary candidates: the view from the Web'. Paper presented at the International Communication Association Conference, Acapulco, Mexico.

Schuler, D. (1996) *New Community Networks: Wired for Change*. New York: ACM Press.

Silver, D. (2000) 'Cyberspace under construction: design, discourse, and diversity in the Blacksburg Electronic Village and the Seattle Community Network'. PhD dissertation, University of Maryland.

Smith, M. and Kollock, P. (eds) (1999) *Communities in Cyberspace*. London: Routledge.

Stacey, M. (1974) 'The myth of community studies', in C. Bell and H. Newby (eds), *The Sociology of Community*. London: Cass. pp. 13–26.

Stamm, K.R. (1985) *Newspaper Use and Community Ties: toward a Dynamic Theory*. Norwood, NJ: Ablex.

Stappers, J., Olderaan, F. and Wit, P. de (1992) 'The Netherlands: emergence of a new medium', in N. Jankowski, O. Prehn and J. Stappers (eds), *The People's Voice: Local Radio and Television in Europe*. London: Libbey. pp. 90–103.

Stein, L. (2001) 'Democratic "talk", access television and participatory political communication', in N.W. Jankowski (with O. Prehn) (ed.), *Community Media in the Information Age: Perspectives and Prospects*. Cresskill, NJ: Hampton.

Stone, A.R. (1991) 'Will the real body please stand up: boundary stories about virtual cultures', in M. Benedikt (ed.), *Cyberspace: First Steps*. Cambridge, MA: MIT Press. pp. 81–118.

Swoboda, W.J., Mühlberger, N., Weikunat, R. and Schneeweiss, S. (1997) 'Internet surveys by direct mailing: an innovative way of collecting data', *Social Science Computer Review*, 15 (3): 242–55.

Tönnies, F. (1887/1957) *Community and Society*. New York: Harper Torchback.

Turkle, S. (1995) *Life on the Screen: Identity in the Age of the Internet*. New York: Simon & Schuster.

Van Dijk, J. (1998) 'The reality of virtual communities', *Trends in Communication*, 1 (1): 39–63.

Wellman, B. (1979) 'The community question: the intimate networks of East Yorkers', *American Journal of Sociology*, 84: 1201–31.

Wellman, B. (1997) 'An electronic group is virtually a social network', in S. Kiesler (ed.), *Culture of the Internet*. Mahwah, NJ: Lawrence Erlbaum. pp. 179–205.

Wellman, B. (ed.) (1999) *Networks in the Global Village*. Boulder, CO: Westview.

Wellman, B. and Berkowitz, S.D. (eds) (1988) *Social Structures: a Network Approach*. Cambridge: Cambridge University Press.

Wellman, B. and Berkowitz, S.D. (eds) (1997) *Social Structures: a Network Approach*, updated edn. Greenwich, CT: JAI Press.

Wellman, B. and Gulia, M. (1999) 'Net surfers don't ride alone: virtual communities as communities', in P. Kollock and M. Smith (eds), *Communities in Cyberspace*. Berkeley, CA: University of California Press. pp. 167–94.

Wellman, B. and Hampton, K. (1999) 'Living networked in a wired world', *Contemporary Sociology*, 28 (6): 648–54.

Westerik, H. (2001) 'De verklaring van het gebruik van lokale media' (Explanation of the use of local media). PhD dissertation, University of Nijmegen, the Netherlands.

Widlok, P. (1992) 'Der andere Hörfunk: community Radios in den USA' (The other form of broadcasting: community radio in the USA). PhD dissertation, University of Münster.

Wirth, L. (1938) 'Urbanism as a way of life', *American Journal of Sociology*, 44: 1–24.

3

Politics and New Media

S A R A   B E N T I V E G N A

Recent developments in the 2000 United States presidential campaigns, including the first application of electronic voting in the Arizona Democratic primaries and the success of fundraising via the Internet, have relaunched the issue of new media's role in the political decision-making process. The key question confronting political leaders, commentators and scholars is once again the democratic character widely attributed to the new communication technologies, in so far as these are believed capable of modifying long-established systems and balances. It has been said, with varying degrees of conviction, that the diffusion of the new media,[1] especially the Internet, can transform the now devitalized relationship between political bodies and the citizenry they represent and govern. A transformation of this relationship would result from, first, the fact that communication processes have finally been freed from the arbitration of journalism exercised in traditional media circles and, second, innovative forms of direct interaction. In communication terms we are witnessing a shift from a broadcasting model typical of the old media and traditional political organizations to a netcasting model without a centre sustained by its dual role as sender and receiver at the disposal of its users. In political terms, the creation of an arena made possible by the Internet, where every one has a voice, together with the possibility of activating direct relations between politicians and citizens, leads to the development of an electronic marketplace. This would manifest itself as a modern version of the public sphere as formulated by Habermas, and would also lead to the eradication of the gap dividing political life from the daily life of citizens.

Such a momentous transformation in the relationship between the political realm and the citizenry has yet to occur. However, we do not concur with Margolis and Resnick's pessimistic conclusion that 'cyberspace has not become the locus of a new politics that spills out of the computer screen and revitalizes citizenship and democracy. If anything, ordinary politics in all its complexity and vitality has invaded and captured cyberspace' (2000: 2). Instead, we feel that politics in cyberspace is attempting to redefine itself in light of the profound changes affecting the social system in the past decades by exploiting the Internet's intrinsic potential. However, before welcoming a new model of democracy, a digital democracy, it would be necessary to promote a political culture that includes not only better information to citizens, electronic town halls and electronic plebiscites but also 'the reform of state power and the restructuring of civil society' (Held, 1996: 316). Otherwise, the Internet – and other new technologies – 'rather than acting as a revolutionary tool rearranging political power and instigating direct democracy [are] destined to become dominated by the same actors who currently utilize other mediums' (Davis, 1999: 5).

THE INTERNET BETWEEN DEMOCRACY AND CONTROL

Among the various positions adopted following the introduction of computer-mediated communication (CMC) in the political field during the early 1990s, we can now single out two opposing currents. These currents have underscored both those political innovations considered capable of 'challenging the monopoly of the political hierarchy' (Rheingold, 1993: 14) and those risks associated with the widening gap between the 'haves' and 'have nots', namely the exercise of dominion and manipulation of the citizenry. The development and consolidation of cyberspace in the last few years have effectively negated both positions while leaving open many of the questions raised.

Those who lean toward a positive interpretation of the new media hold that new technologies can be used to promote citizen participation in debates regarding matters of concern to the public. This assumes special significance in light of the progressive disenchantment toward politics fermenting in all democratic systems in the past few decades. This disenchantment alarms the political citizens themselves because of a conceivable loss of legitimacy in the exercise of power. The possible theoretical turn-around created by the affirmation of an innovative model of communication that allows the citizenry to assume the dual role of receiver and sender has made a significant contribution to this positive interpretation of the desired revitalization of politics. In part, this optimistic interpretation is also an outgrowth of the incredible expansion of the information supply now accessible to citizens. 'Surfing the web' not only makes it possible to read all the periodicals one wishes but also permits access to the unabridged text of a statement made by a specific institution or individual on a specific occasion. One can view the images and hear the speaker live, consult the latest legislation passed and obtain information on virtually every public institution. This information expansion is of high democratic value in its own right because it permits the monitoring of a government's exercise of power and its activities by those it governs. It also possesses an added value in the multiplication of opportunities to speak out by those wishing to communicate with others, giving substance to those technologies of freedom referred to by de Sola Pool (1983). This augments not only the information available but also the opportunities for citizens, who have lacked space in traditional media, to express themselves. This underscores the opportunity to invent new forms of community, albeit virtual, within a public sphere where citizens can debate politically significant subjects (see Jankowski in this volume).

On the other hand, those inclined toward a negative interpretation identify a risk of creating a form of technological dominion over individuals, capable of controlling and manipulating opinions, decisions and behaviour to an extent never before possible. They also cite the risk of the progressive transformation of representative democracy, for such a democracy would be based on the constant consultation of citizens and open to virtually any topic on which the opinion of subjects was sought. In short, this transmuted democracy could call citizens, possibly on a daily basis, to express their opinion on questions at the heart of the political debate. With keen insight and pessimism Rodotà mused that 'as innervated as technology is, will democracy be able to elude one of the possible outcomes of technological innovation: reinforcement of the current trends marking a shift toward populism and plebiscites? Or will it be possible to direct it along the path of a "strong democracy" whose "strength" resides in the strength of active citizens capable of effective participation in decision-making processes?' (1997: 5).

Reflections on the democratic potential of the new media and on the risks connected to their diffusion bring to mind an image of a two-headed technology, like the ancient god Janus, with one face representing the technologies of freedom, the other the technologies of control. However, the uses of CMC have up to now disproved both interpretations, creating only an additional space for communication in which processes and mechanisms proper to the social context have been relaunched. Some assert that the Internet encloses 'an organizational structure of political life present in the real world' (Resnick, 1998: 49). They maintain that cyberspace has undergone a process of 'normalization' which reproduces structures previously identifiable in reality. The virtue of this interpretation is that it has helped clear the field of superficial optimism and catastrophic predictions, bringing analysis and interpretation back to the terrain of the tangible applications of the new media. In fact, to fully grasp the role of the new media within the broader communication process involving political citizens, we must put into context their use within a specific type of society to allow us to identify and analyse feasible applications and developments (Arterton, 1987). We must equally abandon illusions about the miraculous power of the Internet on behalf of the renaissance of a country's political life in the absence of other profound transformations, as some have been inclined to do (Dertouzos, 1991; Ess, 1996). The social and political implications of the use of new technologies cannot be assessed without an account of the values, behaviour and expectations proper to the citizenry in a given historical and political moment. In short, realizing the democratic potential of new media's increased supply of information and direct channels of communication depends on the social context. This context should circulate a real request for information not fully satisfied by the traditional media and in which the direct relationship between the governors and the governed is perceived as fundamental to the functioning of democratic institutions. The work of contextualizing is actually related to the need to study the 'real' application of the new technologies as discussed by Sclove (1995) several years ago. Only by starting from this approach will we be able to identify the true potential and true risks accompanying the adoption of the new media in contemporary societies.

THE PUBLIC SPHERE IN CYBERSPACE

The electronic marketplace that provides citizens with an environment in which they can meet through surfing the web has been considered by many experts to be a modern translation of the concept of the public sphere conceived by Habermas (1962/1991). In other words, new media are seen to permit 'the sphere of private people [to] come together as a public to engage them[selves] in a debate over general rules' (1991: 27). Ever since this concept was formulated, discussion of the evolution of democratic processes has consistently adopted it as a key reference point. The ongoing interest in the public sphere is the result of its adoption as an indicator of a society's democratic character. In short, its presence is a sign of the existence of occasions for exchange and debate among individuals on matters of public concern. This interest is the result of its assumption as an 'analytical category, a conceptual device which, while pointing to a specific social phenomenon, can also aid us in analysing and researching the phenomenon' (Dahlgren and Sparks, 1991: 2). By virtue of this double characterization – indicator of democracy or analytical category – the concept of the public sphere has been and continues to be assiduously employed to study phenomena ranging from the creation of a 'television marketspace' (Phelan, 1991) to the diffusion of the new technologies.

The public sphere may be represented figuratively as the Greek *agora*, the ancient meeting place for private citizens in which public debates and discussions took place. Over time it has assumed the guise of the *coffeehouse* or *pub*, in which meetings and discussions among individuals took place and in which the 'public voice' was expressed. Analysing the evolution of the public sphere, Habermas identified in the process of the affirmation of the independence of the British press the birth of a forum for rational debate free from ideological pressures, spurred by the profit motive characteristic of modern enterprises (1991: 184). So the public sphere comes to be defined in relation to the mass media, because the mass media permit the circulation of opinions and offer the conditions in which the forum can function.

Habermas considered that the progressive interweaving of state and society that was consolidated at the end of the nineteenth century would bring about the end of the bourgeois public sphere. He also believed that this would bring about the transformation of the media for,

'in comparison with the press of the liberal era, the mass media have on the one hand attained an incomparably greater range and effectiveness – the sphere of the public realm itself has expanded correspondingly. On the other hand they have been moved ever further out of this sphere and re-entered the once private sphere of commodity exchange. The more their effectiveness in terms of publicity increased, the more they became accessible to the pressure of certain private interests' (1991: 188).

In short, rather than representing a forum for rational debate, the public sphere has become a venue in which contrasting interests compete, completely excluding the citizens. Thus, the public sphere has progressively ceased to be a space 'open' to the members of a society and has acquired, instead, the features of a place in which different organizations represent interests and attempt to achieve a consensus among themselves and the representatives of government. In this context, it is no longer possible for citizens to participate in a rational debate on questions of public concern.

Habermas' portrayal of the crisis and transformation of the public sphere, indeed his very concept of public sphere, has been bombarded by criticism. Fraser affirmed that equality among individuals as avowed in Habermas' reconstruction is groundless and that 'we can no longer assume that the bourgeois conception of the public sphere was simply an unrealized utopian ideal; it was also a masculine ideological notion that functioned to legitimate an emergent form of class rule' (1993: 8). Students of the media system have criticized the inadequacy of an approach that ignores the audience's active role (Curran, 1991; Golding, 1997) and the changes introduced by an increasingly broad and diversified supply (Dahlgren, 1995). More specifically, Dahlgren and Spaks argue that 'the media's centrality here has not just to do with its journalism and current affairs output, but with their overall logic and strategy. Journalism is embedded in and largely contextualized by the other media output with which it appears' (1991: 16–17).

Given the renewed attention to the components of 'choice' and 'formation' of consumption by citizens, and given awareness of the transformations affecting the social system and the media system, scholars have revised the concept of public sphere, now asking the question 'of how and to what extent can the mass media, especially in their journalistic role, help citizens learn about the world, debate their responses to it and reach informed decisions about what courses of action to adopt' (1991: 1). This approach argues that the mass media continue to perform a key role, by making available the tools necessary to read and interpret the world around us. The new communication technologies offer additional opportunities in so far as they allow the range of supply to expand, on the one hand, and activate occasions for discussion among citizens, on the other. The expansion of supply and of the opportunities for citizens to speak out is the key to the enthusiasm with which the new, modern version of the public sphere launched by the Internet has been greeted. Dertouzos (1991) believes that citizens 'are capable of expressing their ideas, of communicating their apprehensions and requests openly', while Rheingold sees in the opportunities offered by the Internet 'a road to revitalize an open and thorough debate among citizens who wish to nourish the roots of a democratic society' (1993: 279). It is certainly true that, in many respects, the virtual marketplace being created on the Internet may be considered Habermas' Athenian *agora* when he affirmed that 'in the discussion among citizens issues were made topical and took on shape' and that 'citizens indeed interacted as equals with equals' (1991: 4). Thus in newsgroups, bulletin boards and the other computer networks created through the Internet, citizens interact 'as equals among equals' and create discussions of public concern, starting with their personal experience (Knapp, 1997) and with the frames of reference offered by the media as a whole. Of course, this no longer takes place through a form of face-to-face communication but, as Poster observed, 'the age of the public sphere as face-to-face talk is clearly over: the question of democracy must henceforth take into account new forms of electronically mediated discourse' (1997: 209).

In the new version of the public sphere being delineated on the Internet, the most interesting aspects are the introduction of equality among the members engaged in a discussion, the reference to personal experience in interpreting the topics debated and, last, the use of the information offered by the entire media system to construct the frames of reference within which topics are introduced. The element of equality characterizing the discussions among citizens has its first discernible indicator in the absence of preconceived positions of 'power' in the management of the communication exchange. Except for discussion groups, which require the regulatory presence of a host, in none of the others is there an institutional figure who leads the debate, nor is it possible to single out the figure of the 'expert', the possessor of knowledge extraneous to the other members. As in radio and television talk shows, we are witnessing the affirmation of knowledge deriving from common-sense experience. This affirmation also seems to exclude references to data and information not shared by all the participants: 'it is in the nature of the show to discourage the use of data or theories that are not immediately explicable and plausible. The talk show rejects the arrogance of a discourse that defines itself on the basis of its difference from common sense' (Carpignano et al., 1993: 117).

Adopting common sense as the foundation of Internet discourse makes an implicit reference to the personal experiences of those involved. This is the second element characterizing the conversation within newsgroups created on the Internet. Participants draw on everyday experience as their constant reference universe in identifying the topics of discussion and in using the information their

experience offers. Everyday experience shapes the character of a discussion when, for example, the difficulties of finding a job are illustrated in relation to one's personal experience, and also when it permits the identification of subjects worthy of discussion. In other words, everyday experience has become the privileged element of mediation in political discussion. Lastly, the media system itself has a great impact on the construction of the frames of reference adopted to initiate or participate in discussions. The media system determines the public agenda (Bentivegna, 1994) since it proposes the arguments around which discussion grows according to the classic scheme formulated by McCombs and Shaw (1972). At the same time it furnishes the material needed to develop confrontation among citizens. Thus, the media system takes the form of both a 'source' and a 'tool' that allows interactive communication.

Equality among members, the reference to personal experience and the relationship with the media are, therefore, three distinctive elements of the technological version of the public sphere offered by the Internet. The success of Internet discussion groups testifies to the effective capacity of these groups to represent an occasion of exchange among citizens, based solely on sharing an interest in the arguments proposed (Bentivegna, 1998). In other words the birth of a discussion group represents nothing else than the interest of a certain number of people in a topic, taken up and developed among individuals interacting as 'equals among equals' in the virtual marketplace they have created.

We must partially amend this view of free participation among equals when we consider the characteristics of the pool of users who have gained access to the Internet. The still limited diffusion of Internet connections requires a basic distinction between those countries in which it may be possible to create an electronic public sphere and those in which it is impossible both now and in the near future. The periodic international surveys conducted by research groups still register significant gaps not only between the United States and other countries but also among the various countries of Europe. With regard to the characteristics of the pool of users we should point out that in all countries in which empirical surveys have been performed the profile of the surfer is usually male, with a high educational level and an equally high income level. Without exploring other significant variables in the definition of the Internet user profile, we may affirm that the electronic public sphere constructed through the use of the new technologies is only 'apparently' open to all citizens interested in discussing questions of public interest. By virtue of this structural limitation, as well as the accusation levelled at cyberspace of being dominated by the profit logic, McChesney (1996) has termed it a 'partial public sphere'.

The work of Golding (1997) shows a similar scepticism. After analysing the current state of mass communication practice and policy in Great Britain in relation to the threat to public service broadcasting, the decline of a diverse national press, the continuing advance of a centripetal state, and the growth of unequal access to communications, Golding affirms that 'the public sphere is a domain inhabited by those comfortably ensconced within J.K. Galbraith's culture of contentment, while excluding significant and populous sections of the community' (1997: 10). Even more drastic is the view of Wilhelm, who asserts that 'new information and communication technologies, as currently designed and used, pose formidable obstacles to achieving a more just and human social order in the digital age' (2000: 6).

Given the rapid diffusion of connections across diverse countries, as well as the awareness of the opportunity to spread Internet culture among citizens, it is probable that in the future the social, economic and cultural gaps between those who do and do not have access to the Internet will be reduced. But until this occurs the Internet is still a new and complementary resource for citizens who are already engaged in public affairs. Bimber (1998) calls this phenomenon the 'democratization of elites' and emphasizes the risk connected with a process that may enlarge the gap between the politically active and inactive in society.

THE DEMOCRATIC POTENTIALS
OF THE INTERNET

While the new communication technologies offer a range of applications, the Internet is seen to possess what may be broadly termed 'democratic' potentials untraceable in the traditional media. So we can say that these potentials constitute a watershed between the old and the new media. In effect, this watershed is a rather peculiar one since, as McLuhan observed, 'the advent of a new medium often reveals the traits and premises, if there were any, of an old medium' (1960: 567). In this case, too, numerous potentials attributed to the Internet can be found in other media, particularly in television. Nonetheless, taken together, all these potentials make the Internet unlike any previous communication medium. In a nutshell, the potentials attributed to the Internet are:

- interactivity;
- co-presence of vertical and horizontal communication;
- disintermediation in the communication process;
- convenient costs;
- speed of communication;
- the absence of boundaries.

Interactivity

The analysis of interactivity (see McMillan, in this volume) in the present context should be distinguished from developments in television, video on demand and so on. The type of interactivity discussed here concerns the relationship of the user with the communication supply and the relationships among the users themselves. The user exploits the Internet's interactivity when, starting from one site, she/he constructs, for example, an individual itinerary when gathering information on a specific issue. The user continues to be interactive when she/he participates in a forum, communicating opinions and viewpoints, or when participating in a discussion group on a topic in which she/he is interested. Thus, the citizen assumes the double role of sender and receiver in the communication flow. In short, by providing opportunities for both information and participation, the Internet may be seen as putting the user in a position to exercise a form of control over public life and government decisions. It also puts users in a position to exert a form of pressure when they have the opportunity to communicate dissent on decisions and measures by activating organized forms of protest either on the Internet or through traditional means. In this way, the Internet could prove highly significant for a country's democratic life. Thus, interactivity enables citizens to assume an 'active' position by participating in the conduct of institutions and citizens through the gathering and processing of information, organizing forms of pressure or protesting against decisions deemed unjust or harmful to society as a whole. This creates virtual communities constructed through the sharing of particular visions of the world and specific political projects (Bentivegna, 1999). These democratic processes of formation and expression of political consensus are situated in cyberspace, creating a sort of superposition of the real and the virtual world. This does not automatically bring about an improvement in the relationship between citizens and the political realm, as numerous empirical research projects on this aspect have shown (Markle Foundation, 1997). All the same, the opportunity to exercise these forms of control and intervention is crucial to the functioning of a country's democratic processes. As Hacker (1996) notes, the significant advantages presented by the new technologies are that they grant to the public the opportunity to interact directly with the government, reflecting a theory of democracy based upon the premise that government works best when there is an active and continual interaction between those who govern and those who are governed.

Co-presence

The co-presence of horizontal and vertical communication has an effect similar to that of the new relationship linking the receivers and senders of communication. Vertical communication is in many respects similar to that identifiable in the traditional media and exists when the sender (here, typically a government agency) constructs a communication flow to the receiver (the citizen or subject) in order to communicate initiatives, statements and viewpoints or even to solicit forms of support and mobilization. Another form of vertical communication absent in the traditional media, except in the guise of audience interventions in talk shows, involves the citizen, originally in the role of receiver, now in the role of sender, constructing a communication flow directed at the political leader, now in the role of receiver. Communication becomes horizontal when all citizens are in a relationship of equality. This can be identified in discussion groups and in the various occasions of organizing initiatives and mobilization. In this case, the element of interactivity joins with horizontal communication to create a relationship exclusive to the Internet.

Disintermediation

Disintermediation in the communication flow, as activated by the Internet, refers to the emergence of a new communication model based on the disappearance of, or at least a significant reduction in, the role of the storyteller (Bonchek, 1997). Hitherto, the storyteller has been responsible for providing the narrative thread used to follow a text. Suppression of the storytelling function may be seen as an intrinsic effect in the very model of the Internet, since it places the user in a position to conduct research and formulate an underlying interpretive current necessary to navigate the web. Surfing, which certain experts consider a distinctive trait of the Internet culture (Porter, 1997), translates, in the relationship between the political realm and citizens, into a diminished role for the journalists, in particular, whose 'storytelling' role has in many ways become 'superfluous' because of the possibility of accessing documents, declarations, reports, laws, etc. once inaccessible to the vast audience of television viewers and newspaper readers. The online availability of this material becomes even more precious and 'welcome' to citizens given the trend, consolidated in recent years, of a style of journalistic coverage of politics

based less and less on the words of political leaders and more and more on the journalist's commentary (Patterson, 1996). In fact, the political universe filtered down to citizens through the traditional media is increasingly mediated by circumscribing politics to the flash fragment of the television soundbite. The process of disintermediation activated by the Internet has a clear impact on redesigning the complex of relations between the media system, the political system and citizens, to the clear advantage of the last, who are in a position to access information once available only to the small circle of journalists.

Cost

The cost-effectiveness of a presence on the Internet has had a major influence on the expansion of the range of supply available to citizens. The low costs permit even small groups and movements to acquire a visible Internet presence that in the traditional media would be unaffordable, thus interrupting the dominion of the big parties (Bonchek, 1997; Mann, 1995; McGookin, 1995; Phillips, 1995; Rheingold, 1993). Despite this reduced dominion of the major political parties, unequal economic means still result in inequalities (Mann, 1995; Margolis, 1996). Greater economic resources inevitably allow construction and management of a site more interesting to users. Furthermore, advertising costs penalize economically weaker subjects. All the same, the limited investment required to open and manage a site allows a presence that would be impossible to acquire in the traditional media.

Speed

Concomitant with the Internet's cost-effectiveness is the immense speed of communication processes. Both synchronous and asynchronous communications permit the diffusion of texts and messages at a speed never before possible in the traditional media. The Internet appears to offer the best available opportunity for the consultation of texts and the gathering of consensus for initiatives – in other words, for the mobilization of subjects sharing the same concerns. The speed of the Internet has no parallel in some of the traditional media (the press, for example), and the same holds true for the diversification of the messages addressed to different segments of users.

Boundaries

The absence of boundaries of the Internet not only contributes to the diffusion of arguments of

potential interest to everyone but, contemporane-
ously, also permits the circulation of the experiences, opinions and proposals by all interested
parties.

On the whole, the potentials attributed to the
Internet can certainly be considered fundamental
to a country's democratic development. Undeniably, the possibility of establishing direct relationships among governments and citizens, to activate
communication flows among individuals, to have
direct access to information, to disseminate
opinions and ideas at a low cost, to circulate information 'packages' in real time or to activate conversations anywhere on the planet, all expedite the
functioning of participation and control mechanisms in a democracy. It is worth noting that the
attribution of these capabilities to the Internet does
not automatically bring about an overall improvement in political life. All we have done here is
identify the potential for political communication
opened up on the Internet. On the other hand, a
parallel set of elements contributes to annulling
these positive influences, significantly reducing
the Internet's contribution to democratic development and delaying the emergence of an electronic
democracy.

THE LIMITS OF THE INTERNET

Despite the potentials and opportunities we have
described, the arrival of politics on the Internet has
not brought about the sweeping transformations
expected by some. The gap between the political
realm and citizens has apparently not been reduced,
participation in political life has remained substantially stable, and exchanges and confrontations
among citizens are as intense now as in the past.
How can we explain this 'failure' to transform and
improve democratic processes? Beyond an analysis
of the contexts in which electronic politics are situated, we must also discuss how the very aspects of
the Internet that generate its democratic potential
are also those capable of simultaneous transformation into their exact opposite. Apparently paradoxical, an account of how potentially positive elements
of CMC could become negative may explain the
failure to improve political communication in its
broadest sense.

The increased information supply, for example,
hailed by all as a positive 'mark' of the impact
of the new communication technologies on a
country's democratic life, can be transformed into
its antithesis, an information glut that increases the
distance and disinterest of citizens. Numerous scholars have pointed to the problem of an 'information
glut' as a problem for societies of the future, characterized by increasingly sophisticated technological

applications. Specifically, the notion of an information glut refers to two closely connected sets of
problems: the existence of an underlying interpretive thread that permits navigation, and the availability of tools to verify the truthfulness of the
information acquired.

The presence of an underlying thread is indispensable in organizing and making sense of
the numerous items of information gathered
through consultation of the sites of political parties,
institutions, movements, groups and traditional
media (television and press), with their continuous
supply of information. Starting with the site of a
daily paper, one could initiate navigation to acquire
other information on an argument of particular
interest. Reading an article on the enactment of a tax
initiative could be the starting point for navigation
to the sites of the institutional bodies responsible for
introducing and overseeing the initiative, by
the average citizen, the parties opposing it or the
consumer groups assessing it This excursion, of
variable duration, is undertaken by the citizen without the aid of an external guide (for example, the
journalist playing the role of storyteller) to reconstruct the dynamics underlying the new law and its
consequences. Although, the fulfilment of the
storytelling function is to some degree implicit in
the very structure of the Internet site in the organization of its pages and the activation of links
(Jacques and Ratzan, 1997), a profound difference
remains between the terms and costs of acquiring
information through the traditional media and
through the Internet: simple and reduced in the first
case, complex and elevated in the second. In other
words, obtaining information through the Internet is
an elaborate and costly operation in terms of time
and engagement for the citizen, who must be highly
motivated and capable of constructing a research
itinerary. Furthermore, we must bear in mind that
'the capacity of the human brain to reprocess information is limited, as is the time possible to devote
to this operation and the individual inclination to
perform it. Average individuals are unable to
absorb all the information at their disposal, even if
they concern areas of knowledge of special interest
to them' (Graber, 1996b: 38).

Internet users must also be in a position to recognize the so-called 'fake information' disseminated on the Internet. The likelihood of acquiring
inaccurate or false information is extremely high,
given that the possibility of hiding behind fictitious
names and codes is known by all and used by some.
In the light of the complexity of acquiring information encountered by citizens using the Internet, the
authors of the Markle Foundation (1997) review
maintain that, 'at worst, the Internet produces a
web of deceptive information, at best it offers a
flow of decontextualized information that is hard to
decipher and utilize'. In short, making use of the

overwhelming supply of information that the Internet makes possible can become a challenging activity that not all individuals are able or willing to undertake. In today's society the cost of acquiring political information has been restricted, by a significant share of citizens, to a very low level that shows no signs of rising following the increase in supply. A greater availability of information does not translate automatically into improved control and participation mechanisms. In effect, those best positioned to exploit the information potential offered by the Internet are those users characterized by an already strong interest in political life and its functioning. As is true of other new media, the Internet does not stimulate new interests in uninterested citizens but reinforces the interest of those already engaged (Graber, 1996a).

A further limitation of the Internet is its potential to create virtual communities so successful as to take the place of offline ones. Although it is a benefit of the Internet that it permits communicative exchanges among individuals, this raises the risk that these can become a substitute for real life (see Baym, and Slater, in this volume). Faced with the difficulty of reconstituting real communities based on shared experiences and needs, the virtual communities may be seen as occasions that facilitate relationships with others in light of the protection of anonymity and the negation of physical distance. The main flaw in this type of community, according to some scholars, is its characterization in terms of 'lifestyle enclaves flourishing where individual needs depend on others only in the search for companionship in the space of leisure time' (Doheney-Farina, 1996: 50). In short it is argued that these virtual communities cannot replace the 'civic community' that Putnam (1993) has portrayed. On the contrary, they diminish even further the need for individuals to come together and provide only a pale substitute. While accounts of the experiences of virtual communities themselves partially refute the pessimistic conclusions of some scholars (Cozic, 1996; Doheney-Farina, 1996; McLaughlin et al., 1995), the scant impact of virtual communities on strengthening and developing political life gives rise to the legitimate view that 'virtual' is progressively being transformed into 'vicarious'.

The opportunity to speak out available to all citizens who feel they have something to say may represent the peak of the application of the 'freedom technologies'. It can also become a serious obstacle to the development of democracy when it creates an incomprehensible jumble of voices that cannot come to the aid of the citizen. The mechanism of inclusivity activated and guaranteed by the Internet may produce a confusing situation that annihilates any progress in achieving greater consensus in political life. The result of a continuous

self-expression can be transformed 'into a cacophony of voices impeding any serious discussion. The online debates on important issues are frequently polarized by messages assuming extreme positions. [The Internet] is a great medium for hobbies, but it is not the place for reasonable and pondered judgments' (Stoll, 1995: 32). In sum, for a multitude of reasons, both external and internal, we have not witnessed thus far any significant improvement in certain aspects of political life following the arrival of the Internet. The external reasons are tied to the broader sociopolitical context. The internal reasons have to do with the Internet itself. This chapter has analysed the latter, emphasizing how what may be considered an obstacle to the transformation of the relationship between politics and citizens is actually the flipside of what has been hailed a momentous positive innovation. The oscillation between the two poles has produced simultaneous clashing and divergent interpretations on the nature of the Internet, postponing the advent of an electronic democracy.

THE INTERNET AND DEMOCRACY: A DEVELOPING RELATIONSHIP

The ways in which the Internet's democratic potential may be transformed into obstacles to democracy represent the key feature of this new communication medium. Its most important innovation resides precisely in its multiplicity of uses, and this is what invites further analysis. The absence of a centre and of well-established pathways (albeit such as to require still rarely available cultural competencies) permits the formulation of personalized navigation strategies tailored to specific needs. This diversity of use inevitably leads to profound differences among users, possessors of competencies sometimes impossible to compare. Nonetheless, these differences cannot be imputed to a negative effect arising out of the diffusion of CMC. Diversified uses of the television medium have been widely accepted and even cultivated by segments of the public. Similarly, diversified uses of the new communication technologies must also be accepted.

Accusations of progressive commercialization and emphasis on the entertainment aspects cannot be used to explain the presumed failure of the Internet to improve democratic processes. In fact, the growing commercialization of the Internet and its accent on entertainment testify, first, to the consolidated presence of organized subjects that transfer into the virtual world activities and products from the real world and, second, to the consumption trends conceived in these terms. From this standpoint Resnick (1998) is right on the money when he affirms that the Internet has been normalized, as is McChesney (1996), who sees in cyberspace the progressive affirmation of the business world. Nevertheless, it must be remembered that the citizens who 'consume' this supply have a positive answer to a cyberspace structured in these terms.

The commercialization of the Internet is a product of the sweeping changes in the market and the needs of the subjects operating in it. The diffusion of forms of entertainment is a response to a demand evidently not satisfied elsewhere. The 'strong' presence of these dimensions in virtual space cannot be employed to accuse the Internet of not having contributed to improving democracy in contemporary societies. In fact, the model of the Internet without a centre and without hierarchies permits the coexistence of different dimensions, from entertainment to politics, impeding the formation of monopolies.

Considerations of the relationship between the Internet and democracy must, therefore, be tackled by exploring other questions. First of all, one must query the model of democracy that is, all too often implicitly, assumed. The model of participatory democracy has been seen as the closest approximation to direct democracy, with its expectation of involving citizens in decision-making processes. Modelled after the Athenian ideal, it differs considerably from the model of representative democracy. To the extent that participatory democracy is based upon the premise that citizens want to be involved in political processes, one may argue that with new technologies they can now do this: they can interact directly with both national and local government, conduct political transactions (such as voter registration), and connect with those who share a similar political stance. The model assumes that all citizens have access to the new technologies and that there is a willingness to take advantage of the new tools to become more informed and more involved in civic life. But to what extent is this scenario real?

First and foremost, there is a question of access. Data for the month of March 2000 published by Nua Internet Surveys reveal that Internet users number 304 million, 136 million of whom are concentrated in the United States and Canada, 83 million in Europe, 69 million in Asia/Pacific, 11 million in South America, 3 million in Africa and some 2 million in the Middle East. While the number of users is sky-rocketing, strong imbalances persist between strong and weak countries, and the sharp profile of users persists as well: in all countries the average user is male, between 30 and 45 years of age, with a university education and an elevated socioeconomic status.

The diffusion of the Internet among the young age brackets is lowering the median age of Internet users. The profile continues to be marked by a high educational level, good economic resources and what Wilhelm calls 'antecedent resources' or 'the skills and capacities that a person brings to the table to achieve a certain (political) functioning' (2000: 32). The differences between 'haves' and 'have nots' remain and continue to determine inequalities in the possibilities of using the Internet. The need to guarantee equal opportunities to all subjects in accessing the new communication technologies has been written into the agendas of the countries where the Internet is most developed (the United States and the UK), testifying to the need for 'political' intervention to correct the actual situation. Whether one surfs the Internet to consult the latest Disney site or to consult the summary of a political debate, the conditions to do so must be in place.

Another question concerns the difficulties experienced by citizens in using the Internet. The unexpected availability of an additional and, in a sense, alternative space has found citizens unequipped to exploit this new potential. Attracted to or obliged to be in cyberspace, traditional political players have sometimes created just a 'showcase' presence that is wholly marginal in their overall communication strategies. Being on the Internet has become, in certain cases, a sort of status symbol, an indicator of modernity but one that is difficult to use. For this reason, in past years many sites have been constructed on the exclusive supply of information on party structures, on party leadership, on current initiatives, and on the candidates in election campaigns, but with almost nothing on the true potential of the Internet for direct contact with citizens.

In the United States, where politics has been online for many years, the Internet's potentials are still only partially exploited. A survey by the Markle Foundation (1997) of several sites devoted to the major political parties and to organizations dedicated to the improvement of the political and cultural participation of citizens reveals an almost exclusive offer of information that fails to exploit interactivity. While the highly democratic value of information is recognized, the use of the Internet is 'limited' to only a partial exploitation of its available potential. Studies of the recent primary campaigns for the 2000 United States presidential campaign allow us to identify a shrewder use of the Internet by candidates and political institutions. This use included but was not limited to: fundraising, organization of cyber volunteering, activation of town halls, and requests for citizen collaboration in drafting the party's political platform (Democratic National Committee). We cannot yet assess the true impact of these innovations on the processes of citizen participation and on the real capacity of political actors to recover the ability to listen to the demands and needs expressed by citizens.

The difficulty in exploiting the potential of the Internet by those who have the greatest interest in doing so allows us to explain the relatively marginal position of CMC until now in the transformation of the relationship between citizens and politics. Nonetheless, the use of the Internet by citizens to reactivate relations with the political domain must be noted. Even though it has not led to the rebirth of the Athenian *agora*, it has certainly helped create the coordinates for a meeting space without controls and external restrictions. The existence of numerous discussion groups, and the speed with which they are springing up daily, testify to the need to have independently managed meeting points. The birth of 'netiquette' and the mechanisms enacted to ensure that it is respected represent a form of maturity and civility worthy of respect.

The key question regarding these initiatives lies in the characteristics of the subjects activating or taking part in them. In fact, these subjects are very well informed and concerned with the functioning of public life and the mechanisms of democratic control. Sometimes, as Hill and Hughes (1998) have maintained, participants in the newsgroups relaunch modes of relating and objectives proper to political groups: recruiting new subjects and shunning those who do not share the group's political line. Rather than becoming an arena where contact between the political sphere and distant citizens is reinforced, the discussion groups activated on the Internet reproduce externally identifiable dynamics that are designed to reinforce pre-existing relationships. The contribution of the discussion groups to improving the relationship between citizens and politics has been rather limited, except in the case of certain subjects who exploit through discussion groups the opportunity to activate occasions for exchange and debate. As Davis notes, 'the most likely Internet users will continue to be the affluent, the most common users of Internet political information will be the already politically interested, and those who will use Internet for political activity will be primarily those who are already politically active' (1999: 168).

The accusations aimed at the Internet of failing to reactivate new, direct relations between the political world and citizens are based on an underlying equivocation created by a transposition of elements starting with the possible sharing of a model characterized by the absence of a locus. These accusations strive to show that the Internet is not a tool of democracy, and any value it holds for democracy is marginal. Instead, the Internet offers a new model of democracy, a democracy with no reference to a centre, no longer equivalent to the form of the nation-state and no longer equivalent to the global form of decision-making. Rethinking the notion of democracy may derive from a prototype invention that in turn derives from the model of the Internet,

but it will not be the mechanical consequence of a quantitative diffusion of the Internet (Berardi, 1996: 116). So the Internet and democracy may coexist and nourish each other, but there is nothing automatic in their affirmation and mutual development. The sharing of a model – consolidated in the case of the Internet and in competition with others in the case of democracy – does not involve the attribution of other connotations either in the current situation or in the future one.

Seen in these terms, recognition of the democratic nature of the Internet once again becomes the object of analysis conducted on the tangible applications identified up to now. So it is no longer a tool of democracy *tout court* but a tool both flexible and open to multiple uses and purposes, not least of which is the creation of a new 'locus' of encounter between political subjects and citizens. This is a locus without a centre and without vertical control that can also host 'a *free* and *influential* public space, a sphere of social action not separate but fully linked to and a protagonist in conflicts and antagonisms' (Carlini, 1996: 21). Creation of this venue is the fruit not only of the application of the new technologies but also of the contribution of all those who must guarantee an active presence toward this end. The Internet will be a tool of democracy only when all those navigating it will allow it to be so. Until then, the Internet will continue to be whatever we want it to be: a fascinating tool with multiple uses ranging from business to escape, from the acquisition of information to discussion on a vast range of topics.

NOTE

1 I use the term 'new media' here to describe very broadly the Internet and the system of private and commercial networks that are connected to it. I include the web, e-mail and other aspects of these networks.

REFERENCES

Arterton, F.C. (1987) *Teledemocracy: Can Technology Protect Democracy?* Newbury Park, CA: Sage.

Bentivegna, S. (ed.) (1994) *Mediare la realtà: mass media, sistema politico e opinione pubblica*. Milano: Angeli.

Bentivegna, S. (1998) 'Talking politics on the Net'. Paper presented at the Joan Shorenstein Center on the Press, Politics and Public Policy, John Kennedy School of Government, Harvard University.

Bentivegna, S. (1999) *La politica in rete*. Roma: Meltemi.

Berardi, F. (ed.) (1996) *La rete come paradigma e la reinvenzione della democrazia*. Roma: Castelvecchi.

Bimber, B. (1998) 'Toward an empirical mapping of political participation on the Internet'. Paper presented at the American Political Science Association Annual Meeting, Boston, MA.

Bonchek, M. (1997) 'From broadcast to netcast: the Internet and the flow of political information'. Available at: http://www.ai.mit.edu/people/msb/thesis.

Carlini, F. (1996) *Internet, Pinocchio e il Gendarme: le prospettive della democrazia in rete*. Roma: Manifestolibri.

Carpignano, P., Andersen, R., Aronowitz, S. and Di Fazio, W. (1993) 'Chatter in the age of electronic reproduction: talk, television and the "Public Mind"', in B. Robbins (ed.), *The Phantom Public Sphere*. Minneapolis: University of Minnesota Press.

Cozic, C.P. (ed.) (1996) *The Information Highway*. San Diego: Greenhaven.

Curran, J. (1991) 'Rethinking the media as a public sphere', in P. Dahlgren and C. Sparks (eds), *Communication and Citizenship*. London: Routledge.

Dahlgren, P. (1995) *Television and the Public Sphere*. London: Sage.

Dahlgren, P. and Sparks, C. (eds) (1991) *Communication and Citizenship*. London: Routledge.

Davis, R. (1999) *The Web of Politics: the Internet's Impact on the American Political System*. Oxford: Oxford University Press.

Dertouzos, M.L. (1991) 'Communication, computers and networks', *Scientific American*, 265 (3): 74–80.

Doheney-Farina, S. (1996) *The Wired Neighborhood*. New Haven, CT: Yale University Press.

Ess, C. (ed.) (1996) *Philosophical Perspectives on Computer-Mediated Communication*. Albany, NY: State University of New York Press.

Fraser, N. (1993) 'Rethinking the public sphere: a contribution to the critique of actually existing democracy', in B. Robbins (ed.), *The Phantom Public Sphere*. Minneapolis: University of Minnesota Press.

Golding, P. (1997) 'The mass media and the public sphere'. Paper presented at the Joan Shorenstein Center on the Press, Politics and Public Policy, John Kennedy School of Government, Harvard University.

Graber, D. (1996a) 'Disparity of information resources: the widening gap between the rich and poor'. Paper presented at the American Political Science Association Annual Meeting, San Francisco.

Graber, D. (1996b) 'I nuovi media e gli elettori: vero amore o passione passeggera?', in S. Bentivegna (ed.), *Comunicare politica nel sistema dei media*. Genova: Costa & Nolan.

Habermas, J. (1962) *Strukturwandel der Offentlicheit*. Darmstadt and Newwied: Hermann Luchterhand. Also published as *The Structural Transformation of the Public Sphere*. Cambridge, MA: MIT Press, 1991.

Hacker, K.L. (1996) 'Missing links: the evolution of electronic democratization', *Media, Culture & Society*, 18. pp. 213–32.

Held, D. (1996) *Models of Democracy*, 2nd edn. Cambridge: Polity.

Hill, K.A. and Hughes, J.E. (1998) *Cyberpolitics: Citizen Activism in the Age of the Internet*. Lanham, MD: Rowman & Littlefield.

Jacques, W.W. and Ratzan, S.C. (1997) 'The Internet's World Wide Web and political accountability', *American Behavioral Scientist*, 40: 1226–7.

Knapp, J.A. (1997) 'Internet newsgroups as an electronic public sphere', in D. Porter (ed.), *Internet Culture*. New York and London: Routledge.

Mann, B. (1995) *Politics on the Net*. Indianapolis: Que Corporation.

Margolis, M. (1996) 'Electioneering in cyberspace: parties, candidates, and interest groups and the 1996 presidential race in the Internet'. Paper presented at the American Political Science Association Annual Meeting, San Francisco.

Margolis, M. and Resnick, D. (2000) *Politics as Usual: the Cyberspace 'Revolution'*. Thousand Oaks, CA: Sage.

Markle Foundation (1997) *The State of 'Electronically Enhanced Democracy': a Survey of the Internet*. October.

McChesney, R.W. (1996) 'The Internet and US communication policy-making in historical and critical perspective', *Journal of Communication*, 46: 98–124.

McCombs, M.E. and Shaw, D.L. (1972) 'The agenda-setting function of mass media', *Public Opinion Quarterly*, 36: 176–87.

McGookin, S. (1995) 'Internet may give stimulus to democracy', *Financial Times*, December 17.

McLaughlin, M.L., Osborne, K.K. and Smith, C.B. (1995) 'Standards of conduct on Usenet', in S.J. Jones (ed.), *Cybersociety: Computer-Mediated Communication and Community*. Thousand Oaks, CA: Sage.

McLuhan, M. (1960) 'Effects of the improvements of communication media', *Journal of Economic History*, 20: 566–75.

Patterson, T. (1996) 'La logica dei media: la critica come tema della copertura giornalistica', in S. Bentivegna (ed.), *Comunicare politica nel sistema dei media*. Genova: Costa & Nolan.

Phelan, J.M. (1991) 'Selling consent: the public sphere as televisual market place', in P. Dahlgren and C. Sparks (eds), *Communication and Citizenship*. London: Routledge.

Phillips, K. (1995) 'Virtual Washington', *Time*, 145.

Pool, I. de Sola (1983) *Technologies of Freedom*. Cambridge, MA: Belknap.

Porter, D. (ed.) (1997) *Internet Culture*. New York and London: Routledge.

Poster, M. (1997) 'Cyberdemocracy: Internet and the public sphere', in D. Porter (ed.), *Internet Culture*. New York and London: Routledge.

Putnam, R.D. (1993) *Making Democracy Work: Civic Traditions in Modern Italy*. Princeton, NJ: Princeton University Press.

Resnick, D. (1998) 'Politics on the Internet: the normalization of cyberspace', in C. Toulouse and T.W. Luke (eds), *The Politics of Cyberspace*. New York and London: Routledge.

Rheingold, H. (1993) *The Virtual Community: Homesteading on the Electronic Frontier*. Reading, MA: Addison-Wesley.

Rodotà, S. (1997) *Tecnopolitica: la democrazia e le nuove tecnologie della comunicazione*. Bari: Laterza.

Sclove, R.E. (1995) *Democracy and Technology*. New York: Guilford.

Stoll, C. (1995) *Silicon Snake Oil: Second Thoughts on the Information*. New York: Doubleday.

Wilhelm, A.G. (2000) *Democracy in the Digital Age*. New York: Routledge.

4

Interpersonal Life Online

NANCY K. BAYM

In concluding her 1984 analysis of experimental research on computer-mediated communication, linguist Naomi Baron wrote that 'computer mediated communication – at least as currently used – is ill suited for such "social" uses of language' (1984: 136). Fourteen years later, in a move indicative of the shift in this line of research, she argued that 'e-mail is, in many respects, an ideal tool for building or maintaining social relationships' (1998: 157). Although computer-mediated communication was not invented with interpersonal interaction in mind, the rise of the Internet has clarified that this technology is fundamentally social (Parks and Roberts, 1998; Sproull and Faraj, 1997). E-mail, used primarily for person-to-person contact, is the Internet's 'killer app' and the best predictor of whether new users will stay online (Kraut et al., in press). Even aspects of the Internet that do not seem particularly social, such as business sites, online magazines and information services, have integrated social opportunities such as chat spaces and bulletin boards into their sites (Parks and Roberts, 1998). The early failure of its inventors and scholars to grasp the social implications of this medium is typical of the history of many new media. As Kraut et al. (in press) have pointed out, the interpersonal implications of the telephone were also not apparent to its innovators or early analysts. This chapter examines the Internet, and computer-mediated communication (hereafter CMC) more broadly, arguing that CMC's interpersonal opportunities are among its most important.

Research into CMC began in the 1970s, as networked computer systems were being installed in large organizational contexts and as maverick computer enthusiasts were creating interactive dial-in bulletin board systems. At the time, organizational computing systems which allowed multiple users to interact consisted primarily of local area networks that offered e-mail, group decision-making software and computer conferencing. Despite the early presence of recreational CMC, its use in organizational contexts set the research agenda through the 1980s. Today's forms of CMC include asynchronous media such as mailing lists (discussion forums organized by topic and distributed to subscribers through e-mail), newsgroups (publicly accessible discussion forums organized by topic which are similar in form to e-mail but do not require e-mail subscriptions), and message boards on the World Wide Web. Synchronous computer-mediated forms of communication include chat (multi-user 'channels' or 'rooms' in which people gather in small numbers to discuss topics both general and specific), MUDs and MOOs (multi-user 'places' elaborately constructed through text for purposes of role-playing games, social interaction and education), instant messages (a more targeted form of chat, in which users keep 'buddy' lists and can keep tabs on whether or not their friends are online and available to receive messages), and graphic user worlds (akin to MUDs and MOOs but graphical). A sense of the popularity of these media (at least in the United States) can be gained from a Pew Internet and American Life Project poll in the spring of 2000. They found that each day 91 per cent of American net users (an estimated 84 million people) send e-mail, 45 per cent (primarily young people) send instant messages, and 28 per cent participate in chat rooms or online discussions.

Although organizations are far from the only context for CMC use, early organizational research codified core assumptions and comparisons to which much interpersonal CMC scholarship still reacts. I begin by elaborating this backdrop. I then explore contemporary thought about the characteristics of

CMC. Having laid out these two frameworks for CMC research, the remainder of the chapter focuses on four areas of interpersonal meaning that have received the most attention: online language use, identity, personal relationships and social groups.

MEDIA CHARACTERISTICS

The Cues-Filtered-Out Perspective

Most early efforts at analysing CMC were based on the premise that media characteristics have consistent effects on communication. Drawing largely on small-group research from social psychology, in particular the work of Bales (1950), this research had practical goals. Early applications and studies (e.g. Martino, 1972; Price, 1975) were generally concerned with efficiency and effectiveness (Kiesler et al., 1984). This research agenda essentially asked what happened when face-to-face work groups meet via computer instead. Questions included how CMC affected the quality of group decisions, leadership, participation and time to decision (Rice and Love, 1987). Given this concern, the basis of comparison was (and often remains) face-to-face communication, the key features of which were taken to be the ongoing provision of feedback and the clarity of participants' relative social status. Social presence theory (Short et al., 1976) and later media richness theory (Daft and Lengel, 1984), both of which argued that media differ in the information they can provide and therefore in the extent to which they are appropriate for different communication tasks, were combined into what Culnan and Marcus (1987) called the 'cues-filtered-out' approach. This work is summarized and critiqued at length elsewhere (e.g. Lea and Spears, 1995; Walther et al., 1994) so I hit only the highlights here.

Cues-filtered-out took the defining features of CMC to be the absence of regulating feedback and reduced status and position cues. This was taken to result in anonymity and deindividuation, with a variety of communicative consequences (e.g. Hiltz and Turoff, 1978; Kiesler et al., 1984). In experiments where small face-to-face groups were compared with small computer-mediated groups, researchers found that the latter took longer to complete tasks, single leaders were less likely to emerge, participation became more equal, and there was more uninhibited behaviour (e.g. Hiltz and Turoff, 1978; Siegel et al., 1986). Most famous of the 'uninhibited' behaviours is flaming, which Walther et al. (1994) in a meta-analysis defined operationally as name calling, swearing, insults, impolite statements, threats and put-downs, crude flirtations of a demeaning or sexually explicit nature, and attacks on groups or individuals.

The task-oriented claims made from this approach have held up reasonably well, but the interpersonal implications of the cues-filtered-out approach have been roundly criticazed, and this deterministic perspective has for the most part been dropped (although, as I will discuss below, the issue of limited non-verbal cues remains central). The criticisms were methodological, empirical and conceptual. Methodologically, most of the lab studies brought together unrealistically small, zero-history groups for a median time period of 30 minutes (Rafaeli and Sudweeks, 1997; Walther et al., 1994; Weisband and Atwater, 1999). Among differences in research designs were group characteristics and members, communication system infrastructures, functions or tasks around which the groups were organized, and groups' temporal structures (Hollingshead and McGrath, 1995; Walther, 1992; Walther and Burgoon, 1992). However, these variations were rarely addressed within the work, confounding experimental designs with findings (Hollingshead and McGrath, 1995).

Empirically, the laboratory evidence for differences between face-to-face and computer-mediated communication was statistically significant, but the magnitude of difference was small (Walther et al., 1994). More importantly, research using a different methodological approach – the field study – turned up evidence that socioemotional communication not only existed in computer-mediated groups, but was more likely to be prosocial than antisocial. Hiltz and Turoff (1978) reported that users compensated for the coldness of the medium with extra efforts to be friendly, warm and personal. Social cues reported in early CMC field studies included ASCII art, salutations, degree of formality of language, paralanguage, communication styles and message headers (Hiltz and Turoff, 1978; Lea et al., 1992). In a content analysis of transcripts from a professionally oriented CompuServe forum, Rice and Love (1987) found that socioemotional content (defined as showing solidarity, tension relief, agreement, antagonism, tension and disagreement) constituted around 30 per cent of messages. Only 0.4 per cent of the content was negative, and 18 per cent showed solidarity. In their critique of the notion that flaming is rampant in computer-mediated systems, Lea et al. (1992) concluded that there was no comparative evidence that flaming is more common in CMC than in other media or face-to-face. The richer portrait of CMC revealed by field research has since led to more sophisticated conceptualizations of variables in experimental research.

Most conceptual criticisms of the cues-filtered-out perspective revolved around definitions of socioemotional communication and disinhibition. As Lea (1991) pointed out, Bale's category system, which was often used to code messages, has very restrictive definitions of socioemotional. It also requires that messages be identified as either socioemotional or task-oriented, whereas messages are usually multifunctional and can be both. Thus, even studies such as Rice and Love's, which found considerable socioemotional communication, may have underestimated its prevalence. Regarding disinhibition, many studies included positive as well as negative comments as uninhibited behaviour (Lea et al., 1992), so that most socioemotional or off-task communication was seen as disinhibited. Empirical evidence also showed that even flaming, which seemed to be the most clearly disinhibited behaviour, sometimes took inhibited forms (for instance, punctuation marks substituted for letters in swear words). Furthermore, flaming was shown to be context-dependent, occurring at different levels across computer-mediated groups (Lea et al., 1992). If the cues-filtered-out perspective was right that media characteristics have consistent effects, there was no way to account for the development of norms regarding the appropriateness of flaming, or the fact that over time groups came to sanction inappropriate behaviours (Hiltz and Turoff, 1978; Lea et al., 1992). I return to the issues of context and norm development throughout what follows.

Communication-Relevant Qualities of Computer Media

Despite the criticisms, the experimental findings of cues-filtered-out research cannot simply be dismissed (Walther, 1992; Walther et al., 1994). Most CMC researchers have continued to rely on media characteristics to think through key questions. However, rather than positing limited cues as the primary independent variable, or assuming that limited cues invariably produce particular results, the challenge now is to explain the roles that media characteristics can play in shaping communication and to clarify the variables that produce differing results in varying contexts. This has led to more sophisticated methodological and conceptual analyses. The media qualities with the greatest interpersonal implications fall into roughly three categories: those having to do with spatiotemporal issues, with the participants, and with the electronic and (usually) written nature of the medium. I focus on the Internet in what follows, though most of the discussion can be generalized to other forms of CMC such as local area networks.

In terms of time and space, as long as one is in a country or region that has access, the Internet makes physical location largely irrelevant (e.g. Baron, 1998; Lea and Spears, 1995; McKenna and Bargh, 2000; Sproull and Faraj, 1997). Interaction between two people in the same building is indistinguishable from interaction between people half a world apart. This creates a kind of spaceless proximity that did not exist to this extent before, a sense enhanced by the speed of transmission and immateriality of time, especially in synchronous CMC (Baron, 1998; Carnevale and Probst, 1997; McKenna and Bargh, 2000). In asynchronous CMC, the fact that one can read and respond to messages in one's own time has been taken to expand the potential for interpersonal engagement and thus to be a critical feature of the medium. In a real break from earlier technologies such as the telephone, CMC dramatically reduces the costs associated with communication across distance (Baron, 1998; Pew, 2000; Sproull and Faraj, 1997). This explains in part why many people report that e-mail is good for keeping in touch with friends and family far away and also that they make fewer long-distance phone calls after going online (Dimmick et al., 2000; Pew, 2000).

A second characteristic of CMC is the limited information available regarding participants. The notion of reduced social cues remains central. However, the effort has shifted from asking simply what effect this has, to more nuanced efforts to understand the variety of possible consequences, the contexts which give rise to different options, and the creative ways in which communicators make use of, or compensate for, this media characteristic. The reduction of physical appearance cues, along with the evidence of status and attractiveness they bear, creates a kind of invisibility or anonymity (Carnevale and Probst, 1997; McKenna and Bargh, 2000; Sproull and Faraj, 1997; Turkle, 1996), which opens the potential for multiplicity of identities (Stone, 1995; Turkle, 1996), a high degree of privacy (Baron, 1998), and a lower sense of social risk (Curtis, 1997) or accountability (Stone, 1995), among other possibilities (topics I return to in the discussion of identity).

In addition to obscuring information about participants as individuals, CMC can also hide information regarding the participant structure of interactions. The net blurs the boundary between interpersonal and mass media (Baym, 1996; Lea and Spears, 1995; Morris and Ogan, 1996; Rafaeli and Sudweeks, 1997). E-mail and instant messaging are usually clearly interpersonal given their specific addressees, but other forms of CMC are harder to categorize. As Culnan and Marcus (1987) argued, addressivity in CMC is fundamentally different from face-to-face communication, as there is usually no need to specify identity and location of recipient in the latter. Furthermore, in many forms of CMC, such as newsgroups and mailing lists, it can be difficult if not impossible to judge the size of one's audience (Carnevale and Probst, 1997). Finally, just as a producer loses control over who watches a television show once it is aired, there is usually little, if any, control over access to and participation in computer-mediated groups (Galegher et al., 1998). Interactions between two individuals can thus have consequences for social formations larger than pairs. Just as the mail, telegraph and telephone bridged time and space before the net, anonymity and unclear participant structures occurred in pre-Internet days, but not on anything like their current scale.

Finally, computer-mediated messages can be stored in memory, replicated, retrieved at later dates, and edited prior to sending, which has also been taken to have interpersonal consequences (Carnevale and Probst, 1997; Cherny, 1999; Culnan and Marcus, 1987; Walther, 1996). Some (e.g. Hiltz and Turoff, 1978; Walther, 1996) suggest that the additional visual channel of written discourse combined with the ability to edit leads to better organized and better thought out statements than occur face-to-face. Again, all of the consequences of these media characteristics were possible before computers, but the Internet combines them in such a way and on such a scale as to represent a qualitative shift in mediated communication. These characteristics together form a backdrop for the discussion that follows.

Media Comparisons

In casting the characteristics of CMC in terms of space, time, visual and auditory cues, participant structure and storage capabilities, the basis of comparison is usually face-to-face communication, a fact that follows both from the early agenda of CMC research and from the tendency of CMC users to think of the medium as conversational. However, as suggested by those who view CMC as a cross between interpersonal and mass media, and those who have compared it to the telephone, face-to-face conversation is by no means the only basis for comparison. Discourse analysts, in particular, have paid a good deal of detailed attention to language forms in CMC, often comparing CMC to writing. Rather than drawing on social psychology, these scholars were more likely to be guided by linguistic anthropologists (e.g. Bauman and Sherzer, 1974; Gumperz and Hymes, 1972). While the former tradition often focuses on identifying variables through the decontextualized space of the laboratory, the latter seeks to describe language forms in naturally occurring contexts, and to explain these forms in terms of those contexts. Discourse analysts have rarely looked at organizations, focusing instead on classroom and recreational groups.

Early on, Baron (1984) noted the need to distinguish between the use of CMC to replace writing and its use to replace speech. In the time since, many (e.g. Baron, 1998; Ferrara et al., 1991; Wilkins, 1991) have explored the extent to which CMC compares to writing, usually concluding that CMC represents 'a hybrid language variety displaying characteristics of both oral and written language' (Ferrara et al., 1991: 10). Like writing, CMC

involves participants who are often temporally separated and do not share physical co-presence. Communicators in CMC must make explicit much of the information that would be carried by the voice, gestures or other non-verbal cues in face-to-face conversation. Like speech, much CMC is direct, contextualized and interactive (e.g. Baym, 1996; Galegher et al., 1998). Writers can assume that their readers will share many referents, will be reading within a few days and will be able to respond. Messages are often open to reformulation.

These analyses of online interaction recognized that media characteristics influence linguistic forms. For instance, in synchronous CMC one sees many language features that can be attributed to the desire to increase speed by typing less (and, for heavy users, to minimize carpal tunnel syndrome). In Internet relay chat and MOOs, people use abbreviations, acronyms, shortened words, the deletion of subject pronouns, and contractions in response to the medium (Cherny, 1999; Werry, 1996), much as they did with the telegraph. However, participants in many CMC media also actively strive to make their language seem conversational (Werry, 1996), indicating that the medium is only one influence on language. Wilkins points to lexical repetition, which 'made it possible for the participants to follow the conversational sequence, to integrate entries with the appropriate preceding ones, and thus to experience the discourse as conversation' (1991: 63). Werry (1996) and Galegher et al., (1998) point to the informal style of much CMC. 'The discourse,' concluded Galegher et al., 'does not depart discernibly from oral and written patterns of conversation' (1998: 524). That CMC appears more similar to speech and writing than different also points to the limits of conceptualizing the medium as a core causal variable. Most of this research has been conducted in English-speaking groups, owing largely to the (now changing) historical predominance of the English language on the Internet and of the location of so many CMC researchers in the United States, Australia and England. Werry's work, however, examined both English- and French-speaking groups and found these phenomena in both languages. Non-English CMC is an area ripe for research, and one which has begun to receive increased attention.

As is the case with flaming, language forms online are highly normative and vary across and within CMC contexts. These norms, argued Ferrara et al. (1991), are acquired through interactions with other users. As the technology evolves, the usership grows and the varieties of CMC evolve, it becomes increasingly difficult to differentiate claims about the medium from claims about participants or stage of normative development (Baron, 1998). Baron (1998) argued that e-mail should be considered a 'creole' language, in that it is a still emerging hybrid of other language varieties. I would argue this is true of all CMC. That the nature of Internet discourse is still emerging further suggests the limited causal power of the medium and the futility of making simple generalizations about online interaction.

Users' perceptions of CMC and their desires regarding these media are central to the forms computer-mediated discourse takes. As Lea (1991) showed, even perceptions of a single computer medium like e-mail are complex and varied. In his effort to explore users' perceptions of the similarities and differences between e-mail and other media, Lea used the repertory grid method in which subjects construct categories of meaning as bases for comparison. He found that e-mail was seen as written, asynchronous, spontaneous, informal, and slightly impoverished and impersonal. Perceptions varied as to whether e-mail was seen as consequential or inconsequential, or direct or indirect. Lea concluded that e-mail was in some ways more like note and letter writing, and in other ways more like face-to-face communication and telephoning. In a blow to what he termed 'rationalist' models that assume reduced cues will make CMC more efficient and businesslike, Lea's subjects didn't construe CMC as particularly information efficient or inefficient relative to other media.

Ultimately, computer media should not be understood as deficient versions of face-to-face communication (Culnan and Marcus, 1987), or as peculiar versions of the telephone, the television or the written word. Instead, theoretical approaches need to consider CMC's unique and varied qualities, and understand how users draw on their existing communicative competencies in multiple media to actively construct social meaning within the challenges and opportunities posed by this medium. The next section examines four primary areas of interpersonal social meanings: language use, identity, relationships and social groups.

Interpersonal Issues in CMC

Computer-Mediated Language Use

Rationalist conceptions of CMC assumed that cue deprivation would create discourse that was more serious and information-oriented than face-to-face communication (Lea, 1991; Rice and Love, 1987). Aside from the fact that sometimes people turned more nasty than reasonable, this idea has also been undermined by a wide variety of field studies that explored recreational CMC from qualitative linguistic, sociological, communication and anthropological perspectives and consistently found that language use online is often remarkably playful. In what may have been the first pair of studies along these lines, Myers (1987a; 1987b) studied role-playing game systems using participant observation and interviewing. Looking at the discourse, he concluded that there was a tremendous amount of play with punctuation and spelling (Myers, 1987b). He argued this resulted from a desire for spontaneity. Danet et al. (1995; 1997), Werry (1996) and Cherny (1999) are among those who have shown similar play with phonetic and visual qualities of language use in synchronous computer media. Danet et al. (1997) argued that the computer medium is inherently playful because of its 'ephemerality, speed, interactivity, and freedom from the tyranny of materials'.

The most common variety of playful language activity online is probably humour, which seems to be more common online than off. In a large project (see Sudweeks et al., 1998) in which dozens of researchers from several countries and universities conducted a quantitative content analysis of thousands of messages from international Usenet newsgroups, BITNET lists and CompuServe, Rafaeli and Sudweeks (1997) found that more than 20 per cent of the messages contained humour. In my analysis of a Usenet newsgroup that discussed American soap operas (Baym, 1995), I found that 27 per cent of messages addressing a dark and troubling storyline were humorous. The forms of humour included clever nicknames for characters (e.g. Natalie, also called Nat, was dubbed 'Not' when a new actress took over the role, and became 'Splat' when the character was killed in a car accident), plot parodies, and many others. Surveys revealed that humour made both messages and participants stand out as especially likeable.

Language play is a form of performance. Bauman (1975) and Hymes (1975) described performance as communication that is marked as open for evaluation by an audience. As Danet et al. (1997) argued, online performance draws attention to the language and the medium, turning the lack of other cues into a communicative asset. Communicative performances serve a variety of social functions, among them displaying competence (often in the service of self-enhancement), entertaining an audience and facilitating group cohesion (Bauman, 1975). By making the language form and content performative and playful, participants in CMC enhance the appeal of the discourse, build online identities and foster fun relationships.

Computer-Mediated Identities

Since language is so often the only form of communication in CMC, it becomes the primary means of managing and forming impressions of our own and others' selves. Perhaps no aspect of online social life has received as much attention as identity, in both (often conflated) senses of personal individuality and category membership. O'Brien

(1999: 95) points to two 'conceptual clusters' that characterize online identity formation as well as the interests of scholars studying the phenomenon. Most analytic attention (scholarly and popular) has focused on the cluster of 'disembodied/multiplicity/fantasy', while most online identities are along the lines of 'embodied/authenticity/reality'. In a prescient essay titled 'Anonymity is part of the magic' (a quote drawn from an interview), Myers (1987a) drew attention to how reduced cues opened up the potential for identity play. The users he interviewed took this to be one of the medium's primary appeals. Reid (1991) explored the postmodern nature of this phenomenon in Internet relay chat in an essay that was among the first to describe online gender swapping. As evidenced by Turkle (1996) and Stone (1995), the postmodern implications of anonymity and identity play can be theoretically intoxicating. By divorcing our selves from our bodies, from time and from space, the computer opens a realm in which the multiplicity of identity that is taken to characterize contemporary life (e.g. Gergen, 1991) reaches an apex. We can be multiple people simultaneously, with no one of these selves necessarily more valid than any other. These varied identities can have varied degrees of relation to the embodied 'self'. Organizational research, guided by its practical agenda, conceptualized anonymity as problematic. The research outlined here, guided by a postmodern theoretical agenda, conceptualizes anonymity as indicative of a broad cultural shift. Though popular media often view online anonymity as dangerous, Turkle (1997: 151) examined how some of the MUD users she interviewed used the Internet as a way to grapple with psychological issues such as parental relationships, and argued that MUDs are 'privileged spaces for thinking through and working through issues of personal identity'.

One possible outcome of these experiments in identity is the resolution of identity issues offline. Turkle (1996; 1997) wrote of the potential to work on identity issues involving control and mastery. Myers (1987a) argued that his subjects gained a sense of efficacy or power through the self-creation process. McKenna and Bargh (2000) proposed that constructing a new identity which is successful within a new peer group can allow for role changes that create real changes in self-concept. Some (e.g. Haraway, 1991) have suggested that this may ultimately go beyond individual effects to redefine identity categories such as gender in offline life. This argument is disputed by others (e.g. Donath, 1999) who point out that people tend not to erase or redefine gender online but to exaggerate it, so that men who pretend to be women usually portray themselves as exceptionally sexually attractive in highly stereotypical ways. This has also been found amongst adolescent women who misrepresent their appearance online (Clark, 1998). At this point, we are still a long way from knowing the offline consequences of online identity (McKenna and Bargh, 2000).

Most attention given to computer-mediated identity play has centred on MUDs. In this regard, it is instructive to remember the Pew finding that only 28 per cent of American Internet users participate in any kind of online discussion groups, and a minuscule percentage of such groups are MUDs. In comparison with the 91 per cent of people who use e-mail and the 45 per cent who use instant messaging (which do not lend themselves to the same kind of anonymity), MUDs hardly represent typical online interaction. According to Curtis (1997), creator of the LambdaMOO, the most popular social MUD and site of much MUD research, even in MUDs, role playing and gender swapping are uncommon. Parks and Roberts (1998) argued that there are no data to indicate identity deception is either widespread or more common online. To the contrary, some research suggests that anonymity, and its associated lessening of social risk, may allow people to be more honest and take greater risks in their self-disclosures than they would offline (McKenna and Bargh, 2000). The Pew poll, for instance, found that Americans feel they can be more honest in e-mail with loved ones and friends than they can be in conversation. Rather than making us less like our embodied selves, CMC's reduced cues sometimes allow us to be more true to our embodied selves than we can be in the flesh.

honesty

Online identities are also made to correspond to embodied identities through contextualization. In an analysis of (woefully understudied) personal web home pages, Wynn and Katz found that people 'pull together a cohesive presentation of self across eclectic social contexts in which individuals participate' (1998: 324). Rather than being multiple or anonymous, the online identities constructed through home pages were richly contextualized in offline social contexts and groups through self-descriptions, implied audiences, and links to websites of other people and groups. Wellman made a similar point in a review essay when he wrote that too many scholars and pundits 'treat life online as an isolated social phenomenon…They usually ignore the fact that people bring to their online interactions such baggage as their gender, stage in the life cycle, cultural milieu, socioeconomic status, and off line connections with others' (1997b: 446). In short, the focus on disembodied identity reflects theoretical interests and the lure of the exotic rather than an effort to understand the typical.

A different approach to identity has been taken by Lea and Spears (e.g. 1995), who seek a theoretical explanation for the variation in online identity. Their SIDE (social individuation and deindividuation) model is based on self-categorization theory (Tajfel and Turner, 1986; Turner et al., 1987) which conceptualizes self as a range of self-categories including both personal and social identities. SIDE theory tries to identify situational conditions that will invoke particular self-categories and make the behaviour normative to that self-category possible and appropriate (Lea and Spears, 1995). From this perspective, some online contexts will do little to make the self-categories associated with offline selves relevant, and these will be most likely to result in identity play, deception and other behaviours divorced from social contexts. Other contexts will make those categories more relevant, and will invoke self-representations and behaviour consistent with embodied versions of the self. Consistent with this theory, Myers (1987a) and Baym (2000) have argued that the selves constructed in online groups are dependent on the norms of the groups within which they are constructed, so that what is an appropriate identity in one context may not be in another. 'The process of self-creation,' wrote Myers, 'depends very heavily on continuous group negotiation within previously negotiated interaction contexts' (1987a: 259).

To summarize: to the extent that it exists in CMC, anonymity is used in varying ways in different contexts. In some cases, it offers the chance to explore untried identities or to falsify the self. In other cases, it offers the freedom to be more open and honest than one would otherwise be. In still other cases, anonymity is an obstacle to be overcome through various forms of self-disclosure. It is too often forgotten that in much – perhaps even most – CMC, however, anonymity is not an issue, as people are corresponding with people they also know offline and building online selves that are richly contextualized in their offline social networks.

Computer-Mediated Relationships

The same forces that can affect identity online also offer new possibilities for developing and sustaining interpersonal relationships in this medium. Just as studies of online identity have gravitated toward novel identities, most of the attention regarding interpersonal relationships in CMC has explored the formation of new relationships, with particular attention to friendship and, to a lesser extent, romance. In their excellent review of relational theory and its implications for CMC, Lea and Spears (1995) argued that theories of personal relationships are biased toward face-to-face communication, and often define relationships in terms of face-to-face qualities, leaving them unable to explain relational development in CMC. They fault traditional theories such as Altman and Taylor's (1973) canonical social penetration model for their 'emphasis on physical proximity, face-to-face interaction, and nonverbal communication and talk as the essential processes of relating, and a general

tendency to use physical and spatial metaphors in describing and accounting for relationships' (1995: 212). Lea and Spears also fault these theories for their tendency to ignore relationships that cross boundaries, don't lead to marriage or are negative. On the other side of the coin, they point out that perspectives on CMC that focus on disembodiment, such as those discussed in the previous section, also raise doubts about the possibility of forming genuine personal relationships through mediated means.

One of the wonderful things about CMC is that it gives us an opportunity to rethink theories of communication. In this case, despite the implications of many interpersonal and postmodern theories that people can't or won't form personal relationships through CMC, people do, and do so often and fairly successfully. CMC, and the Internet, offer new opportunities for creating relationships. The Internet's discussion groups broaden the field of potential relational partners beyond those physically proximate (Lea and Spears, 1995). Kraut et al.'s (in press) interviews suggest that online groups are the main way in which people start online relationships. Parks and Floyd (1996) conducted a survey of Usenet participants in which they found that almost a third had formed friendships through Usenet. In a follow-up study of MOOs, Parks and Roberts (1998) found that such a high percentage of their respondents had formed personal relationships through MOOs that they were statistically unable to compare them with those who had not. I documented many interpersonal friendships and occasional romances that had emerged through a Usenet group (Baym, 2000). Indeed, the people I studied often described the group as 'a bunch of close friends'. Relational opportunities online are also increased by the aforementioned reduction of social risk, which makes some people more willing to strike up conversations with strangers (Curtis, 1997). Furthermore, liking and attraction face-to-face are often based in the early stages on physical appearance (e.g. Duck, 1977). In CMC, people are more likely to be brought together by shared interests, giving them the chance to discover similarity in values and interests, and to focus on one another's conversational style without attending to appearance (McKenna and Bargh, 2000). This is a devastating reversal for stage models of relational development such as social penetration which so often rely on physical attraction to explain the early stages of relational development (Lea and Spears, 1995). Computer-mediated relationships often follow a predictable developmental trajectory (Baker, 1998; Parks and Floyd, 1996), moving from public discussion, to e-mail, to the telephone and then to face-to-face meetings. Of the friendship pairs in Parks and Floyd's (1996) study, 98 per cent had spoken on the telephone and a third had met face-to-face. Eventually, CMC becomes just one way that relational partners interact (Wellman and Gulia, 1999).

Walther has conducted a line of research which seeks to explain relational development in the face of reduced cues. His social information processing theory proposes that, regardless of medium, people experience the need to reduce uncertainty and increase affinity. As a result, CMC users 'adapt their linguistic and textual behaviors to the solicitation and presentation of socially revealing, relational behavior' such as personal self-disclosures (Walther et al., 1994: 465). Walther and Burgoon (1992) showed that, over time, CMC becomes more similar to face-to-face communication in terms of socioemotional conversation and impression formation. In zero-history groups, Walther (1994) found that the expectation of future interaction increased the likelihood of the expression of immediacy and affection, similarity and depth, trust and composure. The differences between interpersonal information revelation and processing in CMC and face-to-face are issues not of quality, he argued, but of rate.

Some dismiss relationships formed via CMC as inferior to those formed face-to-face, raising the issue of relational quality. Wellman and Gulia (1999) argued that most relationships formed through the net are specialized weak ties, encouraged by the lack of status and situational cues. However, Wellman and Gulia also argue that strong ties emerge online and, as is the case offline, these ties encourage frequent, companionable contact; they are voluntary, mutually reciprocal and supportive of partners' needs; and they create long-term contact. Lea and Spears (1995) argued for understanding CMC relationships through the eyes of those who have them, claiming that a lack of face-to-face meeting does not render relationships less real or significant to those involved. Parks and Floyd (1996) used scales that measure commitment in face-to-face relationships, and found that Usenet relationships were moderately committed, generally exceeding the scales' midpoints. Parks and Roberts (1998) did this too, and also asked people to make specific comparisons with an offline relationship. They found that MOO relationships were stronger than those formed through Usenet (a finding they attributed to the sense of co-presence created by synchronous communication) and as a whole showed moderate to high levels of development. Parks and Roberts (1998) did find some differences between MOO relationships and face-to-face ones. Offline relationships were slightly more developed, but there were no differences in depth and breadth of interaction; cross-sex friendships were more common in MOOs than in newsgroups or offline; and respondents spent significantly more hours per week with their offline relational partners than their online counterparts. The differences between Usenet and MOOs point again

to the importance of context in understanding interpersonal dynamics in online environments.

At times, relationships formed online may be more appealing than those formed face-to-face, a phenomenon Walther (1996) labelled 'hyperpersonal interaction'. In hyperpersonal communication, users overestimate the attractiveness of their online relational partners, relative to people they know offline, making CMC more socially desirable than face-to-face communication. Walther (1996) offers several explanations for this, including the freedom to idealize that the lack of visual cues provides, the ability for communicators to choose which aspects of the self to disclose and when to disclose them, the increased ability to devote attention to message formation, and the likelihood that these factors will combine such that computer-mediated messages show more self-awareness and introspection. To this list might be added Lea and Spears' (1995) point that when one meets in a group linked by common interest, it is easy to assume that the other is similar to the self in other ways as well. In an experiment, McKenna and Bargh (2000) found that people who met online once, then met face-to-face, liked each other more than people who met face-to-face both times. Like online language and identity, relationships formed online do not seem to differ radically from those formed face-to-face. Indeed, they often evolve into face-to-face relationships. They can be weak or strong, specialized or broad, committed or casual, idealized or well grounded.

The Internet also serves as a means for people with existing ties to maintain their relationships, a phenomenon which has only recently gained any academic attention and remains underexplored. In a study comparing Internet and telephone use, Stafford et al. (1999) found that e-mail was used to support and maintain meaningful relationships. This was especially true of long-distance relationships, and those which people didn't have the time to keep up with face-to-face (Dimmick et al., 2000; Pew, 2000; Wellman and Gulia, 1999). The Pew (2000) poll found that e-mail increases contact with family and friends for significant majorities of online Americans, and that siblings who have e-mail use it more than they use the telephone to contact one another. Though the maintenance of existing relationships is less exotic a topic than the creation of entirely new ones, a more balanced understanding of the interpersonal implications of CMC will have to devote considerably more attention to this more common dimension of online life.

Computer-Mediated Social Groups

From the earliest research into CMC, there has been a strong interest in groups. The organizational research, as we have seen, begins with the assumption that CMC groups are different from others, and examines the effect of computer mediation on small-group processes. A second strain of research explores voluntary social groups, often focusing on issues of community. The term 'community' has become almost synonymous with 'online group', especially when the term is advantageous for site developers. This implies that any group involved in social discussion is necessarily a community. However, as is the case in offline groups, online groups vary widely. Though 'community' may apply to some, it is forced with others. Rafaeli and Sudweeks (1997) argued that groups differ in terms of their interactivity, or the extent on a continuum to which sequences of messages relate to each other. Interactivity functions as a mechanism that makes people want to become involved in and stay with Internet groups.

A complete review of the literature on online social groups is beyond the scope of this chapter. In keeping with my focus on interpersonal issues, I focus on three common and consistent findings in analyses of online groups: they are normatively regulated, hierarchical and often very supportive. As with language, identities and relationships, work on online social groups reveals that 'everything old is new again'. In many ways computer-mediated groups are not very different from other kinds of groups. I close this section with a glance at the ongoing debate concerning the label 'community'.

Many studies of online communities have described how groups develop norms for their interaction. The term 'ways of speaking' is used in the ethnography of communication to describe how group values, beliefs and social structures are embodied in a culture's language form and use. Emergent ways of speaking online range from the use of particular words, phrases or other routines to standards of appropriate and inappropriate conduct and means for handling behavioural violations. Lea et al. (1992) argued that norms in CMC are locally defined, created by the group rather than the medium. There are norms that run across groups; however, it is questionable whether any behavioural standards apply to all computer-mediated groups. McLaughlin et al. (1995), for example, conducted a study of messages from several Usenet groups which chastised others' behaviour, and were able to derive 'a taxonomy of reproachable conduct' that applies across Usenet. Werry (1996) points to a general code of conduct for Internet relay chat. I have discussed Baron's (1998) claim that norms for e-mail use are still emerging, a claim true of other modes of CMC as well. I have argued that community in CMC is an emergent process (Baym, 1998), in which the pre-existing factors of system infrastructure, temporal structure, participant characteristics and external contexts are appropriated in unpredictable ways by users. The outcome is a set of social meanings that allow participants to experience the group as community. These social meanings include identities and relationships, as well as group-specific forms of expression and behavioural standards. Tepper (1997) has written about a Usenet group which uses the practice of asking stupid questions as a way to distinguish insiders (who know better than to answer them) from outsiders (who plunge in with earnest responses). Cherny (1999) offers a rich description of many ways MOO participants developed unique ways of interacting and making jokes. All of these can be considered normative, in that they become normal within the group, while remaining unfamiliar (and often incomprehensible) to outsiders. Knowing the inner discourse of a group, with its codes, in-jokes, vocabulary and routines, can offer a sense of belonging that many find appealing. Other norms for appropriate behaviour within groups include those that regulate the appropriateness of flaming (Baym, 1993; Lea et al., 1992) and the use and misuse of anonymity (Baym, 2000). Galegher et al. (1998) showed differences in how one establishes legitimacy and authority depending on whether a group is recreational or explicitly supportive.

Online groups also take social form through the emergence of social hierarchies, a finding which runs counter to the experimental finding that computer mediation creates equality, but which is completely consistent with offline groups. In one-shot situations, it may be rare for single leaders to emerge and participation may be fairly evenly distributed in CMC. Over time, however, groups develop patterns of participation which are radically unequal. At the simplest level, one can distinguish heavy users, light users and lurkers. Baym (1993), Galegher et al. (1998) and others have shown patterns of participation in which the majority of participants write only once or never, while a tiny minority write the majority of the messages. Participants may gain status through a variety of means other than loquacity, including skilled use of the software (Myers, 1987a), shared expertise (Kollock, 1999) and clever performance (Baym, 1993), forms of social capital at play offline as well. Some computer-mediated groups have hierarchies built into their design, pointing again to the importance of context. MUDs, for instance, partition users into levels with differing degrees of control over the system. At one extreme are those who can delete other users; at the other are guests with no abilities to create lasting change (Reid, 1999). MUDs also develop emergent hierarchical structures; in adventure-based MUDs these are based on competition and strength, while in social MUDs they are based on contributions to the group (Reid, 1999).

Another finding from field research into voluntary groups which runs counter to the findings from short-term experimental groups is that online groups tend to be interpersonally supportive, even when they are not designed to be (Wellman and Gulia, 1999). Some groups are explicitly supportive, providing camaraderie and advice on fields such as medical conditions, addiction and abuse recovery. Other groups, while ostensibly organized to discuss hobbies or other lighter-weight topics, may nonetheless provide social support. In a content analysis comparing levels of empathy in online patient and emotional support groups with other sorts of online groups, Preece and Ghozati (1998) found that empathy is more prevalent in patient and emotional support groups, but that most groups use empathic communication. Kollock (1999) pointed out that online groups are notable for the provision of expert and informational support. Adapting social exchange theory (e.g. Ekeh, 1974; Roloff, 1981) to the Internet, he argued that the features of online interaction (specifically that gifts of information and advice are given to unknown recipients one might never encounter again and that one can't expect immediate reciprocation) change the costs and benefits of social action such that even a response to a single person becomes a public good. In addition to the potential of such offerings to increase one's own status within a group, Kollock (1999) located the motivations for contributing in this environment to anticipated future reciprocity and the sense of efficacy that can come from being able to help.

Wellman and Gulia (1999) have argued that there is something distinctive about the provision of support, information, affiliation and sense of belonging to a group of people one hardly knows. These qualities (among others) have led many to label these groups 'communities', a label much debated in both popular and scholarly discourse. Some are highly enthusiastic about such communities because they overcome barriers of time and space and offer access to others with a shared interest, that may not be available locally (e.g. Rheingold, 1993). Others express concern that in an increasingly fragmented offline world, online groups substitute for 'real' (i.e. geographically local) community, falling short in several ways. Lockard, for instance, argued that 'to accept only communication in place of a community's manifold functions is to sell our common faith in community vastly short' (1997: 225). The most serious charges against calling online groups communities are their homogeneity and lack of moral commitment. Because participants can leave with a mere click, online communities 'do not oblige their participants to deal with diversity' (Healy, 1997: 63).

There have been several reviews of the concept of community and its applicability to CMC (e.g. Fernback, 1999; Komito, 1998), most of which point out that debates over the definition of 'community' far predate the Internet. Komito (1998), in an interesting analysis of different kinds of community, argued that many online groups are best likened to foraging communities. Foraging communities are aggregations of individuals, membership is temporary and voluntary, people move and groups are redefined based on ecological or personal factors, and they are typically egalitarian. Ultimately, however, Komito concludes that 'the most useful means of looking at Net communities may be to treat "community" as background, and focus instead on how individuals and groups cope with continuously changing sets of resources and constraints and how individuals make regular adjustments in their rules for social interaction' (1998: 104–5).

INTERPERSONAL CONSEQUENCES OF THE INTERNET

This review of interpersonal issues in online life just scratches the surface of a broad range of research that comes from many disciplines and makes use of multiple methods. I have focused on what happens in the online context, arguing that much of what happens there is highly sociable, and that this interpersonal interaction is among the greatest appeals of CMC. The simple picture of CMC and its effects painted by early experimental research has given way to a far more varied and complex portrait – or set of portraits – as the use of CMC has grown and people have found new ways to make use of it. Far from being impersonal, CMC is often playful and creative. People use it as a means to assert their own identities and to explore new means of self-presentation. New relationships ranging from weak acquaintanceships to deep romantic bonds are formed, and relationships with people formed offline are perpetuated through CMC. Social groups form that offer a sense of belonging, information, empathy and social status, among other rewards. All of these phenomena offer powerful incentives for people to become involved with CMC and to stay online once there.

However, as the controversy surrounding the use of the term 'community' indicates, there is concern from many quarters that our increased use of the Internet will have deleterious consequences for the rest of our lives. This concern has been bolstered by Kraut et al.'s (1998) unexpected finding that first-year users of the Internet became more socially isolated and depressed the more they went online, and by Nie and Erbring (2000) whose subjects reported becoming more socially isolated the more they used the Internet. These studies have both been attacked on methodological grounds. Kraut et al. (1998) have been criticized for their atypical sample, and for describing the Internet as causing depression when the users who showed increased symptoms of depression did not seem to meet clinical definitions of depression (Rierdan, 1999). Nie and Erbring's study has been challenged for its leading questions, for offering no assessment of the magnitude of reported reductions in social contact, and for assuming all online activities are 'non-social'. A questionnaire study of students at the University of Texas (Scherer, 1997) puts the issue into sharper perspective. Scherer found that 13 per cent of Internet users reported some signs of dependency on the Internet, specifically that it interfered with academic work, professional performance or social life. Those reporting such 'Internet addiction' were significantly more likely to be male. This suggests that it may be a relatively small percentage of net users for whom the Internet has negative consequences. A serious problem with all of these studies is their retreat to determinism; the Internet is conceptualized as a single entity, as though it makes no difference with whom one communicates online and as though all online contexts are identical.

Critics of the notion that online life lessens the quality of offline life argue that community and sociability are not 'zero-sum games' (Orleans and Laney, 2000; Wellman and Gulia, 1999). Wellman (1997a; 1997b Wellman and Gulia, 1999) has been among the most vociferous proponents of the notion that use of the Internet is integrated into the rest of life. Wellman and Gulia (1999) argued that the problems with conceptualizing the net as something that will divorce people from face-to-face life include the facts that online ties are strong and important, that the comparison between electronic communities and face-to-face ones is false given the overlap in online and offline contacts, and that people manage relationships in multiple media. Wellman wrote: 'community ties are already geographically dispersed, sparsely knit, specialized in content, and connected heavily by telecommunications (phone and fax). Although virtual communities may carry these trends a bit further, they also sustain in person encounters between community members' (1997a: 198). In organizational contexts, people who communicate heavily in one modality tend to communicate heavily in others; heavier users of CMC are also more likely to use the telephone and to have face-to-face conversations (Kraut and Attewell, 1997).

There is also evidence that people who use the Internet are as socially and culturally involved as those who do not. Robinson and Kestnbaum found that 'computer users are at least as active as, if not more active than, nonusers in most arts-related activities' (1999: 215). In terms of interpersonal relationships, an observational study of children's home use of the computer determined that 'online communication was usually not a substitute for interpersonal communication; rather, both often occurred simultaneously' (Orleans and Laney, 2000: 65). The online world was a topic for children's conversation, children surfed the net

together to find commonly valued items, they used the Internet for shared social experimentation, and the Internet gave them the chance to show off esteemed knowledge and skills for one another. The Pew (2000) study found that Internet users were more active socially than non-users: 61 per cent of non-users reported visiting family or friends the day before, whereas 72 per cent of Internet users had done so. This included heavy and long-time Internet users. Even the Internet-dependent students in Scherer's (1997) study had more relationships face-to-face than they had online, although they were more likely to have a larger proportion of their relationships online. It may very well be that for some people the Internet has damaging personal and interpersonal consequences. For others, an online social life extends and complements the sociability they maintain offline. As a whole, however, we must conclude that, as McKenna and Bargh put it, 'there is no simple main effect of the Internet on the average person' (2000: 59). The questions that have yet to be asked will explore which individual variables combine with the many variable of Internet use and contexts and with what range of impacts.

SUMMARY AND FUTURE DIRECTIONS

Research into the interpersonal dynamics of CMC began with the naive assumption that media characteristics would have determining effects on interaction. There are numerous ways in which media characteristics contribute to interpersonal social processes. Language takes on enhanced roles and hybrid forms as a result of the limited non-verbal cues and the written yet speedy nature of the medium. Identity play, self-revelation and the creation of new relationships are enabled by the cue and participant structures. Social group formation is encouraged by the spatiotemporal and inexpensive nature of the net, qualities which also enable offline groups to move online and which let relationships that developed offline be perpetuated online. However, there are many other contributors to online interpersonal dynamics, including contexts, users and the choices those users make. The computer medium is far more complex and diverse than first imagined.

The shift from simplistic thinking to a recognition of the range of computer-mediated communication is in part a shift in methods and approach. Early research was characterized by a narrow and practical agenda which generally relied on laboratory experiments. These experiments often failed to recognize confounding variables, leading to the sense that any effects found must result from 'the computer'. Field research explored a broader range of CMC contexts, examining organizations, but also looking at role playing and social groups in bulletin boards, IRC, Usenet and other recreational forms of CMC. This work in natural contexts revealed both the variables that had been confounded in experimental work, and the wealth of alternative scenarios for CMC. The diversity revealed by fieldwork has played back into laboratory work, so that more recent experimental work has been oriented toward discerning the range of variables that can cause a range of outcomes in a range of CMC contexts. The lesson is not that one method is better than another, but that regardless of method, researchers need to recognize the breadth of CMC contexts and the significant (and often unpredictable) inputs of users.

If we look at context, it is clear that what happens in a decision-making organizational group with zero history (e.g. levelling of status, anonymity, rudeness) is quite different from what happens in a recreational MOO with a built-in power structure and a long history, where one will find a status hierarchy, well-known participants (who are likely to have met offline), well-developed friendships, and standards for appropriate interaction. What happens in a social MOO differs from what happens in a social Usenet group; indeed MOOs differ from each other. E-mail between friends or family may not resemble any of these. The infrastructure of different kinds of computer-mediated interaction (e.g. one-to-one, one-to-many, many-to-many, real-time versus asynchronous, built-in power structure or not) also provides context that shapes what occurs within. There are also a variety of reasons for interacting via computers – among them work, play, relational maintenance, the seeking of social support – each of which gives rise to differing sets of expectations, brings different realms of background knowledge to bear, and otherwise shapes the basic context in which interaction takes place. Many contexts from offline life are imported into online interaction, an area about which we still know far too little. Any assessment of the interpersonal import of CMC requires a complex understanding of how the use of CMC fits into the overall distribution and conduct of people's interpersonal interactions.

Users must be considered for at least two reasons: they have critical individual differences and they are creative. Far from being monolithic, people differ in their perceptions of the Internet, in what they want online, and in what they find online. Some find support and friendships that enhance their lives, others find their lives diminished by their time online. Nearly all of the research into CMC has been conducted at the level of the group, or averaged across individuals; we know too little about the individual differences that made a difference in computer-mediated experience.

Users are also creative, and they shape online contexts in ways that may not be predictable even from rich understandings of contexts and media. People who want their interaction to resemble conversation may create groups with a good deal of abbreviation and language play, while those who want their interaction to resemble writing may create spaces that look like formal letters. Rather than resigning themselves to 'cuelessness', people rose to the occasion and found alternative ways to express themselves. Though they will always have their place, predictive theories of CMC will always fall short.

There are no simple questions to ask about CMC, as there is no single thing that is CMC, any more than there is a single thing called 'telephone-mediated communication', or 'television-mediated communication'. Discussions about the quality of CMC, which are surely worth having, must be predicated on this more complicated and messy reality. The studies to be done should look at the varieties and dimensions of contexts, and the varieties, perceptions and creativity of users, and should explore both the predictable and the unpredictable social meanings that emerge from the many combinations of these variables. CMC's uses and implications must be contextualized in the offline worlds in which they are embedded. In short, we must remember that the computer may be new, but like the many new media that came before, it is only a medium.

REFERENCES

Altman, I. and Taylor, D.A. (1973) *Social Penetration: the Development of Interpersonal Relationships*. New York: Holt, Rinehart & Winston.

Baker, A. (1998) 'Cyberspace couples finding romance online then meeting for the first time in real life', *Computer Mediated Communication Magazine*, http://www.december.com/cmc/mag/1998/jul/baker.html.

Bales, R.F. (1950) *Interaction Process Analysis: a Method for the Study of Small Groups*. Reading, MA: Addison-Wesley.

Baron, N.S. (1984) 'Computer mediated communication as a force in language change', *Visible Language*, 18 (2): 118–41.

Baron, N.S. (1998) 'Letters by phone or speech by other means: the linguistics of e-mail', *Language and Communication*, 18: 133–70.

Bauman, R. (1975) 'Verbal art as performance', *American Anthropologist*, 77 (2): 290–311.

Bauman, R. and Sherzer, J. (1974) *Explorations in the Ethnography of Speaking*. London: Cambridge University Press.

Baym, N. (1993) 'Interpreting soap operas and creating community: inside a computer-mediated fan culture', *Journal of Folklore Research*, 30 (2/3): 143–76.

Baym, N. (1995) 'The performance of humor in computer-mediated communication', *Journal of Computer-Mediated Communication*, 1 (2), http://www.ascusc.org/jcmc/vol1/issue2/baym.html.

Baym, N. (1996) 'Agreement and disagreement in a computer-mediated group', *Research on Language and Social Interaction*, 29: 315–46.

Baym, N. (1998) 'The emergence of online community', in S. Jones (ed.), *Cybersociety 2.0: Revisiting Computer-Mediated Communication and Community.* Thousand Oaks, CA: Sage. pp. 35–68.

Baym, N. (2000) *Tune In, Log On: Soaps, Fandom, and Online Community.* Thousand Oaks, CA: Sage.

Carnevale, P. and Probst, T.M. (1997) 'Conflict on the Internet', in S. Kiesler (ed.), *Culture of the Internet.* Mahwah, NJ: Erlbaum. pp. 233–55.

Cherny, L. (1999) *Conversation and Community: Chat in a Virtual World.* Stanford, CA: CSLI.

Clark, L.S. (1998) 'Dating on the net: teens and the rise of "pure" relationships', in S. Jones (ed.), *Cybersociety 2.0: Revisiting Computer-Mediated Communication and Community.* Thousand Oaks, CA: Sage. pp. 159–83.

Culnan, M.J. and Markus, M.L. (1987) 'Information technologies', in F.M. Jablin, L.L. Putnam, K.H. Roberts and L.W. Porter (eds), *Handbook of Organizational Computing: An Interdisciplinary Perspective.* Newbury Park, CA: Sage. pp. 420–43.

Curtis, P. (1997) 'Mudding: social phenomena in text-based virtual realities', in S. Kiesler (ed.), *Culture of the Internet.* Mahwah, NJ: Erlbaum. pp. 121–42.

Daft, R.L. and Lengel, R.H. (1984) 'Information richness: a new approach to managerial behaviour and organizational design', *Research in Organizational Behaviour*, 6: 191–233.

Danet, B., Wachenhauser, T., Cividalli, A., Bechar-Israeli, H. and Rosenbaum-Tamari, Y. (1995) 'Curtain time 20:00 GMT: experiments in virtual theater on Internet relay chat', *Journal of Computer-Mediated Communication*, 1 (2), http://www.ascusc.org/jcmc/vol1/issue2/contents.html.

Danet, B., Ruedenberg-Wright, L. and Rosenbaum-Tamari, Y. (1997) '"HMMM ... WHERE'S THAT SMOKE COMING FROM?": writing, play and performance on internet relay chat', *Journal of Computer-Mediated Communication*, 2 (4), http://www.ascusc.org/jcmc/vol2/issue4/danet.html.

Dimmick, J., Kline, S.L. and Stafford, L. (2000) 'The gratification niches of personal e-mail and the telephone: competition, displacement, and complementarity', *Communication Research*, 27 (2): 227–48.

Donath, J. (1999) 'Identity and deception in the virtual community', in M. Smith and P. Kollock (eds), *Communities in Cyberspace.* New York: Routledge. pp. 29–59.

Duck, S.W. (1977) *The Study of Acquaintance.* Farnborough, Hants: Teakfield–Saxon House.

Ekeh, P.P. (1974) *Social Exchange Theory: the Two Traditions.* Cambridge, MA: Harvard University Press.

Fernback, J. (1999) 'There is a there there: notes toward a definition of cybercommunity', in S.G. Jones (ed.), *Doing Internet Research: Critical Issues and Methods for Examining the Net.* Thousand Oaks, CA: Sage. pp. 203–20.

Ferrara, K., Brunner, H. and Whittemore, G. (1991) 'Interactive written discourse as an emergent register', *Written Communication*, 8 (1): 8–34.

Galegher, J., Sproull, L. and Kiesler, S. (1998) 'Legitimacy, authority, and community in electronic support groups', *Written Communication*, 15 (4): 493–530.

Gergen, K. (1991) *The Saturated Self: Dilemmas of Identity in Contemporary Life.* New York: Basic.

Gumperz, J.J. and Hymes, D. (1972) *Directions in Sociolinguistics: the Ethnography of Communication.* New York: Holt, Rinehart & Winston.

Haraway, D.J. (1991) *Simians, Cyborgs, and Women: the Reinvention of Nature.* London: Free Association.

Healy, D. (1997) 'Cyberspace and place: the internet as middle landscape on the electronic frontier', in D. Porter (ed.), *Internet Culture.* New York: Routledge. pp. 55–71.

Hiltz, S.R. and Turoff, M. (1978) *The Network Nation: Human Communication via Computer.* Reading, MA: Addison-Wesley.

Hollingshead, A.B. and McGrath, J.E. (1995) 'The whole is less than the sum of its parts: a critical review of research on computer-assisted groups', in R. Guzzo and E. Salas (eds), *Team Effectiveness and Decision Making in Organizations.* San Francisco, CA: Jossey-Bass. pp. 46–78.

Hymes, D. (1975) 'Folklore's nature and the sun's myth', *Journal of American Folklore*, 88: 345–69.

Kiesler, S., Siegel, J. and McGuire, T.W. (1984) 'Social psychological aspect of computer-mediated communication', *American Psychologist*, 39 (10): 1123–34.

Kollock, P. (1999) 'The economies of online cooperation: gifts and public goods in cyberspace', in M. Smith and P. Kollock (eds), *Communities in Cyberspace.* New York: Routledge. pp. 220–42.

Komito, L. (1998) 'The net as a foraging society', *The Information Society*, 14 (2): 97–106.

Kraut, R.E. and Attewell, P. (1997) 'Media use in a global corporation: electronic mail and organizational knowledge', in S. Kiesler (ed.), *Culture of the Internet*, Mahwah, NJ: Erlbaum. pp. 323–42.

Kraut, R., Mukhopadhyay, T., Szczypula, J., Kiesler, S. and Scherlis, B. (2000) 'Information and communication: alternative uses of the Internet in households', *Information Systems Research*, 10: 287–303.

Kraut, R., Patterson, M., Lundmark, V., Kiesler, S., Mukhopadhyay, T. and Scherlis, W. (1998) 'Internet paradox: a social technology that reduces social involvement and psychological well-being?', *American Psychologist*, 53 (9): 1017–31.

Lea, M. (1991) 'Rationalist assumptions in cross-media comparisons of computer-mediated communication', *Behaviour & Information Technology*, 10 (2): 153–72.

Lea, M. and Spears, R. (1995) 'Love at first byte?', in J. Wood and S. Duck (eds), *Understudied Relationships: Off the Beaten Track.* Thousand Oaks, CA: Sage. pp. 197–240.

Lea, M., O'Shea, T., Fung, P. and Spears, R. (1992) '"Flaming" in computer-mediated communication:

observations, explanations, implications', in M. Lea (ed.), *Contexts of Computer-Mediated Communication*. London: Harvester Wheatsheaf. pp. 89–112.

Lockard, J. (1997) 'Progressive politics, electronic individualism and the myth of virtual community', in D. Porter (ed.), *Internet Culture*. New York: Routledge. pp. 219–32.

Martino, J.P. (1972) *Technological Forecasting for Decisionmaking*. New York: American Elsevier.

McKenna, K.Y.A. and Bargh, J.A. (2000) 'Plan 9 from cyberspace: the implications of the Internet for personality and social psychology', *Personality and Social Psychology Review*, 4 (1): 57–75.

McLaughlin, M.L., Osborne, K.K. and Smith, C.B. (1995) 'Standards of conduct on Usenet', in Steve Jones (ed.), *Cybersociety: Computer-Mediated Communication and Community*. Thousand Oaks, CA: Sage. pp. 90–111.

Morris, M. and Ogan, C. (1996) 'The internet as mass medium', *Journal of Communication*, 46 (1): 39–50.

Myers, D. (1987a) '"Anonymity is part of the magic": individual manipulation of computer-mediated communication contexts', *Qualitative Sociology*, 19 (3): 251–66.

Myers, D. (1987b) 'A new environment for communication play: online play', in G.A. Fine (ed.), *Meaningful Play, Playful Meaning*. Champaign, IL: Human Kinetics. pp. 231–45.

Nie, N.H. and Erbring, L. (2000) *Internet and Society: a Preliminary Report*. Palo Alto, CA: Stanford Institute for the Quantitative Study of Society. Available at: http://www.stanford.edu/group/siqss/.

O'Brien, J. (1999) 'Writing in the body: gender (re)production in online interaction', in M. Smith and P. Kollock (eds), *Communities in Cyberspace*. New York: Routledge. pp. 76–106.

Orleans, M. and Laney, M.C. (2000) 'Children's computer use in the home: isolation or sociation?', *Social Science Computer Review*, 18 (1): 56–72.

Parks, M.R. and Floyd, K. (1996) 'Making friends in cyberspace', *Journal of Communication*, 46 (1): 80–97.

Parks, M.R. and Roberts, L.D. (1998) '"Making MOOsic": the development of personal relationships online and a comparison to their offline counterparts', *Journal of Social and Personal Relationships*, 15 (4): 517–37.

Pew (2000) *Tracking Online Life: How Women Use the Internet to Cultivate Relationships with Family and Friends*. Washington, DC: Pew Internet and American Life Project. Available at: www.pewinternet.org.

Preece, J. and Ghozati, K. (1988) 'In search of empathy online: a review of 100 online communities', in *Proceedings of the 1998 Association for Information Systems Americas Conference*. pp. 92–4.

Price, C.R. (1975) 'Conferencing via computer: cost effective communication for the era of forced choice', in H.A. Linstone and M. Turoff (eds), *The Delphi Method: Techniques and Applications*. Reading, MA: Addison-Wesley. pp. 497–516.

Rafaeli, S. and Sudweeks, F. (1997) 'Networked interactivity', *Journal of Computer-Mediated Communication*, 2 (4), http://www.ascusc.org/jcmc/vol2/issue4/rafaeli.sudweeks.html.

Reid, E.M. (1991) 'Electropolis: communication and community on Internet relay chat'. Masters Thesis, University of Melbourne, Australia.

Reid, E. (1999) 'Hierarchy and power: social control in cyberspace', in M. Smith and P. Kollock (eds), *Communities in Cyberspace*. New York: Routledge. pp. 107–33.

Rheingold, H. (1993) *The Virtual Community*. Reading, MA: Addison-Wesley.

Rice, R.E. and Love, G. (1987) 'Electronic emotion: socioemotional content in a computer-mediated communication network', *Communication Research*, 14 (1): 85–108.

Rierdan, J. (1999) 'Internet–depression link?', *American Psychologist*, 54 (9): 781–2.

Robinson, J.P. and Kestnbaum, M. (1999) 'The personal computer, culture, and other uses of free time', *Social Science Computer Review*, 17 (2): 209–16.

Roloff, M.E. (1981) *Interpersonal Communication: the Social Exchange Approach*. Beverly Hills, CA: Sage.

Scherer, K. (1997) 'College life online: healthy and unhealthy Internet use', *Journal of College Student Development*, 38 (6): 655–65.

Short, J., Williams, E. and Christie, B. (1976) *The Social Psychology of Telecommunications*. Chichester: Wiley.

Siegel, J., Dubrovsky, V., Kiesler, S. and McGuire, T.W. (1986) 'Group processes in computer-mediated communication', *Organizational Behavior and Human Decision Processes*, 37: 157–87.

Sproull, L. and Faraj, S. (1997) 'Atheism, sex, and databases: the net as a social technology', in S. Kiesler (ed.), *Culture of the Internet*. Mahwah, NJ: Lawrence Erlbaum. pp. 35–52.

Stafford, L., Kline, S.L. and Dimmick, J. (1999) 'Home e-mail: relational maintenance and gratification opportunities', *Journal of Broadcasting & Electronic Media*, 43 (4): 659–69.

Stone, A.R. (1995) *The War of Desire and Technology at the Close of the Mechanical Age*. Cambridge, MA: MIT Press.

Sudweeks, F., McLaughlin, M. and Rafaeli, S. (1998) *Networks and Netplay: Virtual Groups on the Internet*. Cambridge, MA: MIT Press.

Tajfel, H. and Turner, J.C. (1986) 'The social identity theory of intergroup behavior', in S. Worchel and W.G. Austin (eds), *Psychology of Intergroup Relations*. Chicago: Nelson-Hall.

Tepper, M. (1997) 'Usenet communities and the cultural politics of information', in D. Porter (ed.), *Internet Culture*. New York: Routledge. pp. 39–54.

Turkle, S. (1996) *Life on the Screen: Identity in the Age of the Internet*. New York: Simon & Schuster.

Turkle, S. (1997) 'Constructions and reconstructions of self in virtual reality: playing in the MUDs', in S. Kiesler (ed.), *Culture of the Internet*. Mahwah, NJ: Lawrence Erlbaum. pp. 143–55.

Turner, J.C., Hogg, M.A., Oakes, P.J., Reicher, S.D. and Wetherell, M.S. (1987) *Rediscovering the*

Social Group: a Self Categorization Theory. Oxford: Blackwell.

Walther, J.B. (1992) 'Interpersonal effects in computer-mediated interaction', *Communication Research*, 19 (1): 52–90.

Walther, J. (1994) 'Anticipated ongoing interaction versus channel effects on relational communication in computer-mediated interaction', *Human Communication Research*, 20 (4): 473–501.

Walther, J. (1996) 'Computer-mediated communication: impersonal, interpersonal and hyperpersonal interaction', *Communication Research*, 23 (1): 3–43.

Walther, J.B. and Burgoon, J.K. (1992) 'Relational communication in computer-mediated interaction', *Human Communication Research*, 18 (1): 50–88.

Walther, J.B., Anderson, J.F. and Park, D. (1994) 'Interpersonal effects in computer-mediated interaction: a meta-analysis of social and anti-social communication', *Communication Research*, 21(4): 460–87.

Weisband, S. and Atwater, L. (1999) 'Evaluating self and others in electronic and face-to-face groups', *Journal of Applied Psychology*, 84 (4): 632–9.

Wellman, B. (1997a) 'An electronic group is virtually a social network', in S. Kiesler (ed.), *Culture of the Internet*. Mahwah, NJ: Lawrence Erlbaum. pp. 179–208.

Wellman, B. (1997b) 'The road to utopia and dystopia on the information highway', *Contemporary Sociology*, 26 (4): 445–9.

Wellman, B. and Gulia, M. (1999) 'Virtual communities as communities: net surfers don't ride alone', in M. Smith and P. Kollock (eds), *Communities in Cyberspace*. New York: Routledge. pp. 167–94.

Werry, C.C. (1996) 'Linguistic and interactional features of Internet relay chat', in S. Herring (ed.), *Computer-Mediated Communication: Linguistic, Social, and Cross-Cultural Perspectives*. Amsterdam: Benjamins. pp. 47–63.

Wilkins, H. (1991) 'Computer talk: long-distance conversations by computer', *Written Communication*, 8 (1): 56–78.

Wynn, E. and Katz, J.E. (1998) 'Hyperbole over cyberspace: self-presentation and social boundaries in Internet home pages and discourse', *The Information Society*, 13 (4): 297–328.

5

The Electronic Generation?
Children and New Media

DAVID BUCKINGHAM

Some grand claims have been made about the impact of new media on children's lives. Like the idea of childhood itself, new technology is often invested with our most intense fantasies and fears. It holds out the promise of a better future, while simultaneously provoking anxieties about a fundamental break with the past. In this scenario, children are perceived both as the avant-garde of media users and as the ones who are most at risk from new developments. Childhood therefore provides a revealing lens through which many broader aspects of new media can be more clearly seen.

This chapter focuses on children's uses of new media (particularly computers) in the context of leisure time, in the home and in the peer group. The chapter begins by considering recent popular debates on these issues, drawing on material aimed at a general readership. Challenging generalized notions of 'childhood', it then moves on to consider the diverse social uses of new media among different groups of children. This is followed by a discussion of children's experiences of new media, focusing primarily upon computer games and 'online culture'; and a consideration of the 'educational' uses of new media by parents and children in the home. The chapter concludes with a brief discussion of implications for cultural and educational policy.

NIGHTMARES AND UTOPIAS

The advent of new cultural forms is often greeted by sharply divergent responses. This has been particularly true of digital media. On the one hand, these new media are seen to have enormous positive potential, particularly for learning; while on the other, they are frequently seen to be harmful to those perceived to be most at risk. In both cases, it is children – or more accurately, the *idea* of childhood – which is the vehicle for many of these aspirations and concerns.

Similar tensions were apparent in the early years of television. Amid current fears about the impact of television violence, it is interesting to recall that television was initially promoted to parents as an *educational* medium (Melody, 1973). Likewise, in the 1950s and 1960s, television and other new electronic technologies were widely seen to embody the future of education (Cuban, 1986). Yet even here, hopes of a utopian future were often balanced against fears of loss and cultural decline. Television was seen both as a new way of bringing the family together, and as something which would undermine natural family interaction. The medium was extolled as a way of nurturing children's educational development, and simultaneously condemned for taking them away from more wholesome activities (Spigel, 1992).

Contemporary responses to new media are similarly polarized. On the one hand, there is a form of visionary utopianism, particularly among educationists. Seymour Papert (1993), for example, argues that computers bring about new forms of learning, which transcend the limitations of older linear methods such as print and television. It is children who are seen to be most responsive to these new approaches: the computer somehow releases their natural creativity and desire to learn, which are blocked and frustrated by old-fashioned methods. Others have argued that computers empower children to communicate with each other, to express themselves and to participate in public life in ways that were previously impossible. Jon Katz (1996), for instance, regards the Internet as a means of children's liberation: it provides children with opportunities to escape from adult control, and to create their own cultures and communities. 'For the first time,' he argues, 'children can reach past the suffocating boundaries of social convention, past their elders' rigid notions of what is good for them' (1996: 122). Likewise, Don Tapscott (1997) argues that the Internet is creating an 'electronic generation' that is more democratic, more imaginative, more socially responsible and better informed than preceding generations. Digital technology, he argues, will eventually bring about a 'generational explosion', a 'social awakening' that will overthrow traditional hierarchies of knowledge and power. This kind of generational rhetoric is also powerfully reflected in advertising for computers. Children are typically seen to possess a natural wisdom in their relationships with technology that the majority of adults are seen to lack. Ads for Apple Macs or Microsoft focus not on the scientific specifications but on the magical promise of the technology: the computer is represented here as a window onto new worlds, a way of developing children's intuitive sense of wonder and thirst for knowledge (Nixon, 1998).

On the other hand, there is a much more negative account of the impact of these new media on children's lives. This account focuses not so much on their *educational* potential, but on their role as a means of *entertainment* – and it depends upon making an absolute distinction between the two. Some of the anxieties that are regularly rehearsed in relation to television have now been carried over to these new media. Thus, digital media are frequently seen to be a bad influence on children's behaviour – and particularly to cause imitative violence. Events like the shootings at Columbine High School in Colorado, USA in 1999 are frequently blamed on violent computer games or on children's access to 'hate sites' on the World Wide Web. The more 'realistic' graphic effects become, it is argued, the more likely they are to encourage 'copycat' behaviour (Provenzo, 1991). These new media are also seen to be bad for the brain – and indeed for the body. Thus, there have been numerous clinical studies of phenomena such as 'Nintendo elbow' and epileptic fits allegedly caused by computer games, through to research on computer 'addiction' and its negative effects on children's imagination and academic achievement (Griffiths, 1996). Meanwhile, new media are accused of making children antisocial, and of destroying normal human interaction and family life. The phenomenon of the 'Otaku-Zoku' or 'stay-at-home tribe' in Japan is seen as emblematic of the ways in which young people are coming to prefer the distance and anonymity of virtual communication to the reality of face-to-face interaction (Tobin, 1998). These media are also seen to have negative moral and ideological effects on children. Thus, games playing is seen to be a highly gendered activity, which reinforces traditional stereotypes and negative role models, and encourages male violence towards women. Meanwhile, there is increasing anxiety about the accessibility of pornography on the Internet, and about the dangers of children being seduced by online paedophiles. And finally, there is growing concern about the practice of online marketing to children, both through direct selling and through the gathering of market research data (Center for Media Education, 1997).

These arguments, like those about the effects of television, often involve a form of scapegoating. Like television, the computer becomes a convenient bad object, onto which we can displace a whole range of worries and frustrations. This often leads to calls for children's access to the medium to be restricted – whether through tighter regulation (such as ratings systems for computer games) or by means of a 'technological fix' (such as blocking software for the Internet). The effectiveness of such moves is debatable, but they undoubtedly enable legislators to show that they are 'doing something' about seemingly intractable social problems (Shuker, 1996). Meanwhile, there are renewed calls for educational intervention by parents and teachers – although such intervention often appears to be seen as a surrogate form of censorship, and hence may be something that children are inclined to resist (Buckingham and Sefton-Green, 1997).

As with debates around television, both the positive and the negative arguments here draw upon more general beliefs about childhood. On the one hand, children are seen to possess a natural, spontaneous creativity, which is somehow (perhaps paradoxically) released by the machine; while on the other, children are seen as vulnerable, innocent and in need of protection. These mythological constructions of childhood are in turn aligned with parallel mythologies about technology. Both positions are characterized by a powerful technological determinism – that is, a belief that technology will bring about social changes in and of itself (see Williams, 1974). Whether we see these changes as good or bad, they are seen to follow inexorably from the implementation or availability of the technology. Thus, computers are believed to produce 'fundamental shifts in the way we create and experience human identity' (Turkle, 1995). Through their encounters with new media, it is argued, contemporary children have become 'aliens': they represent a 'postmodern generation' whose subjectivity has been formed through the all-encompassing electronic habitat in which they live (Green and Bigum, 1993).

However overstated they may appear, these contrasting perspectives pose complex dilemmas for parents and others concerned with children's welfare. On the one hand, many parents feel that they should be exercising greater control, in order to protect their children from harm; although, on the other hand, they are keen to exploit the educational potential of the technology. So to what extent can children be seen as technologically literate 'cyberkids' – or merely as victims seduced by the deceptions of the electronic screen? Can the broadly 'educational' benefits of these media be distinguished from their role as 'entertainment', and on what basis? And what should be the role of parents or teachers – or indeed the state – in regulating children's access to these new media?

Beyond Mythology and Determinism

As yet, we know very little about how children perceive, interpret and use new media. As in the case of television, much of the research has been preoccupied with the search for evidence of negative effects; and much of it has been based on implicitly behaviourist assumptions (Barker and Petley, 2001). There has been very little attention to the social contexts in which the technology is used, or to the social relationships of which it forms a part.

Children are one of the most significant target markets for new media. Even taking account of other social differences, households with children are much more likely to possess a multimedia computer or computer games console than those without children (Office for National Statistics, 1999). Likewise, many of the new cultural forms made possible by these technologies are primarily identified with the young; and while this is most obviously the case with computer games, it is increasingly true of the Internet as well. Children's use of the WWW is increasing dramatically: according to a 1999 NOP survey in Britain, over 50 per cent of children now surf the web at home or at school (www.nop.co.uk); while in the US, 45 per cent have Internet access in the home (Rideout et al., 1999).

Nevertheless, we need to be aware of differences *within* the apparently homogeneous category of 'children'. There are significant inequalities in access between different social groups; and as other contributors to this volume indicate, these are particularly apparent in terms of social class and gender. In the UK, for example, research conducted in the late 1990s found that fewer than half as many working-class children had access to a PC at home, compared with middle-class children; while the percentage with Internet links was one-tenth of the

figure for middle-class children (van der Voort et al., 1998). As with many other new technologies (not least television in the 1950s), those with greater disposable income are almost always the 'early adopters': they have newer and more powerful equipment, and more opportunities to develop the skills that are needed to use it.

Likewise, researchers have consistently found that girls have less access to computers, are less interested in them and spend less time using them than boys (Cupitt and Stockbridge, 1996; Funk and Buchman, 1996; Kubey and Larson, 1990; Livingstone and Bovill, 1999). Both boys and girls are inclined to agree that computers are primarily 'for boys' (Bannert and Arbinger, 1996; Durndell et al., 1995). Even within comparatively 'media-rich' homes, girls are less likely than boys to own PCs or games consoles or have access to them in their bedrooms (Livingstone and Bovill, 1999). These differences are not only to do with *access*, but also to do with *purpose* and *content*: girls are more inclined than boys to use new media for the purpose of communication (Livingstone and Bovill, 1999), and their tastes in software are also quite different from those of boys (see below).

However, as Livingstone and Bovill (1999) point out, physical *access* to technology should not necessarily be equated with levels of *use*. Children who live in 'media-rich' homes do not necessarily have greater individualized access to media in their own bedrooms. These authors prefer to distinguish between different 'media use styles' – such as 'traditionalists', 'screen entertainment fans' and 'PC fans' – defined by clusters of age, class and gender variables. These different use styles reflect and in turn reproduce particular sets of tastes and values, and particular philosophies of child-rearing. Children from different social groups possess not only different levels of access to technology, but also different attitudes and orientations towards it – or, in effect, different forms of 'cultural capital' (cf. Bourdieu, 1984). Research in the US suggests that this may also be related to ethnicity, as minority children may perceive computing to be a 'white' activity and hence avoid it (Straubhaar, 2000). Some commentators argue that these gaps between the 'technology rich' and the 'technology poor' will eventually disappear as an inevitable consequence of the diffusion of new media; while others fear a growing polarization, and the emergence of a 'media underclass' in which children will be disproportionately represented (Buckingham, 2000).

While this kind of research draws attention to social differences in the uses of technology, it tends to essentialize the differences between media. 'Computer games' or 'the Internet' are implicitly assumed to represent the same thing to all who use them. In this respect, broad demographic analyses need to be complemented by an understanding of how media and technologies are mediated through existing social relationships (Silverstone and Hirsch, 1992). Thus, we need to know more about how technology enters into the peer group and the family, how children gain access to it, how they learn about it, and how its use is regulated and controlled (for instance by parents). It is through such processes that technology comes to be defined as (for example) 'masculine' or 'feminine', 'educational' or 'entertaining', in ways which systematically favour access among particular social groups.

For example, research strongly refutes the popular idea that computer games playing is an antisocial activity (Buckingham, 1993; Jenkins, 1993; Jessen, 1999; Livingstone and Bovill, 1999). While the actual playing of games is sometimes an individual, isolated pursuit, it is also often collaborative, and the focus of a great deal of talk and interaction. Furthermore, the culture surrounding games is an important means of establishing and sustaining interpersonal relationships – from the swapping of games, advice and 'cheats', through to participation in the more public culture of games shops, arcades, magazines and TV shows. The culture of games playing involves an ongoing construction of an 'interpretive community' (cf. Radway, 1984) – and in this respect, as Jessen (1999) argues, it may be better suited to the pattern of children's play than older media such as books, which one is alone in consuming. However, this social process is mediated by the operations of the market. Much of the discussion is about what you can buy, what you have bought, or what you are going to buy – and this is a discussion in which children are not equal. Furthermore, this surrounding culture is an arena for the 'border-work' that characterizes children's gender relationships (Thorne, 1993): it frequently serves to mark the boundaries between boys and girls, and thereby to prevent girls gaining access to technology or to the knowledge that is required to use it (Orr Vered, 1998). Through such processes, children are actively constructing and defining themselves, both as consumers and as gendered subjects. This kind of analysis potentially moves beyond the either/or dichotomy sketched above – the view of children either as passive recipients of adults' attempts at socialization, or alternatively as a sophisticated, 'media-literate' audience.

However, research about children's access to media says very little about the nature of their *experiences* of these media. In moving on to address this issue, the following sections focus on two contrasting aspects of children's relationships with new media: computer games and 'online culture'.

ALL IN THE GAME?

Computer games now represent the fastest-growing sector of the global media and entertainment industries (see Herz, 1997; Sheff, 1993). Games based in public arcades date back to the early 1970s, but it was the advent of home computer games in the late 1970s that resulted in a period of rapid expansion, led by manufacturers such as Atari. Following a collapse in the market around 1984, a 'second wave' of computer gaming, dominated by the Japanese companies Nintendo, Sega and Sony, followed in the second half of the 1980s (Haddon, 1988). Growth in the market has been fairly inexorable since that time. The revenues from computer games now outstrip those of the Hollywood film industry; and Nintendo is currently Japan's most profitable company.

Children are by no means the only market for computer games – adults (over 18) account for between one-third and two-fifths of sales – although they are undeniably the most significant one (Shuker, 1996). The market penetration of games consoles is approaching saturation, at least among boys; although the regular succession of more powerful 'new generation' machines – combined with the rapid turnover of the younger market – means that hardware rapidly becomes obsolescent. Game software is comparatively highly priced, and since software platforms are incompatible (both between different systems and between successive 'generations' of machines), the profitability of the more popular games is extremely high.

Games have increasingly been integrated within what Marsha Kinder (1991) calls the 'transmedia intertextuality' of contemporary children's culture. Many of the most popular games use characters and scenarios from movies, while others have subsequently generated feature films and television shows in their own right. The success of Nintendo's 'Pokémon' illustrates how such integrated marketing has become a key strategy for the 'digital empires' that increasingly dominate children's culture: simultaneously a computer game, a television series, a feature film and a card game, 'Pokémon' has also generated an extensive range of books, comics, toys and other merchandise. As Kinder suggests, media-based commodities of this kind have become a crucial factor in the social construction of children's peer group cultures. Meanwhile, educationalists such as Papert (1993) point out that games are now children's primary means of access to the world of computers; and that, rather than reinforcing distinctions between 'education' and 'entertainment', software designers need to capitalize on the educational potential of game play (Johnson-Eilola, 1998).

However, academic research in this field has been extremely limited. This is partly a result of the difficulty of keeping pace with change. Yet it may also reflect the fact that, unlike television, games do not immediately reveal themselves to the outside observer. The experience of game playing requires a great investment of time, and no small amount of expertise. As a result, many academics who have written about computer games have done so from a considerable distance. They have been inclined to generalize, without making fundamental distinctions between different genres or discussing particular games in any detail; they have concentrated on relatively superficial visual characteristics of games, without discussing the experience of game play; and they have imported conceptual and methodological approaches from studies of older media such as film and television without paying sufficient attention to the unique characteristics of the new medium.

THE LIMITS OF EFFECTS

Interestingly, much of the early research in this field – roughly coinciding with the 'first wave' of domestic computer games – focused on their positive effects. (A useful 'state-of-the-art' survey of this early work can be found in *Video Games and Human Behavior: a Research Agenda for the 80s*, 1983.) Patricia Greenfield (1984), for example, argues that game playing involves a whole range of cognitive skills – not merely hand–eye coordination, but also problem-solving, memory, inductive thinking, parallel processing, spatial awareness and so on. The notion that game playing is simply a 'mindless' activity is effectively refuted here; although the evidence on whether it actually *develops* these skills is rather more questionable.

However, research in this field has been increasingly dominated by anxieties about the negative psychological, moral and behavioural effects of computer games. Thus, research studies have attempted to assess the impact of playing computer games on aggressive behaviour; on psychological variables such as self-esteem; on educational achievement; and on the development of stereotyped attitudes. Researchers have typically used survey methods, although there have been some more experimental studies of short-term effects. As some recent reviews have suggested (Durkin, 1995; Gunter, 1998), the findings of these studies have been uneven and inconsistent; and even less critical reviews (Funk et al., 1997; Griffiths, 1996) have been fairly equivocal in their conclusions.

In many respects, the limitations of the research reflect those of parallel research on the effects of television. These would include:

1 *A crude approach to categorizing games 'texts'* Research studies rarely go further than superficial distinctions based on content. For example, distinctions are frequently made between 'violent' and 'non-violent' games, between 'educational' and 'non-educational' games, or between games that are judged to be more or less 'realistic'; but these distinctions are not based on subjects' own judgements, and are often inadequately defined.

2 *Inconsistent and/or unexplained findings* Experimental studies of the effects of 'violent' games conducted in the late 1980s, for example, failed to generate consistent findings (e.g. Graybill et al., 1985; 1987); some only found effects among girls (Cooper and Mackie, 1986); while others simply failed to establish causal relationships at all (Winkel et al., 1987). Survey-based studies frequently establish correlations between game playing and 'negative' qualities such as poor self-esteem, although reliable evidence about the direction and significance of any *causal* relationship is rarely provided (e.g. Funk and Buchman, 1996).

3 *Untested and inadequately theorized notions of the mechanisms by which effects are assumed to be caused* As in television research, key terms such as 'addiction' (Griffiths, 1994), 'arousal' (Kubey and Larson, 1990), 'identification' (Funk et al., 1997) and 'modelling' (Funk and Buchman, 1996) are often loosely defined and measured. They are frequently offered as *post hoc* explanations, rather than hypotheses that are empirically tested by the research.

4 *A neglect of the social context of games playing, and of research itself* Few effects studies pay attention to the social interaction that characterizes most game playing: they are solely concerned with the interaction between mind and screen. As in much media effects research, college students are frequently used as research subjects; yet the ability of students to recognize and respond to the 'demand characteristics' of research significantly limits the capacity for generalization.

Close attention to particular studies reveals more specific weaknesses. A recent paper by Funk and Buchman (1996) illustrates some of these. The study is concerned with the relationships between 'violent' games and adolescents' 'self-concept'. Apart from the many questions that one might raise about the methods used to measure these two variables, the authors themselves are bound to admit several crucial limitations to their analysis. Some of these, such as the unreliability of self-reports of media use and the fact that correlation does not establish proof of causality, are widely recognized in the field. In this instance, the analysis also throws up some apparently incongruous findings that the authors struggle to explain; and in fact only a small amount of the variance is accounted for by the key independent variables, and then only among girls. In effect, the authors fail to find what they are looking for – which is confirmation of the negative effects of violence in games, a finding which they regard as having been incontrovertibly established by research on television. And so, in their conclusion, they fall back on an entirely hypothetical construct, that of the 'high-risk player' (who is, interestingly, male), even while admitting that their methods have been insufficiently sensitive to prove that he exists.

A rather different – though equally familiar – problem is raised by Eugene Provenzo's (1991) study. Provenzo's chosen method is content analysis; although in fact he analyses only the covers of the games rather than the actual games themselves – an approach which, as Jenkins (1993) points out, can be highly misleading. Here again, the categories used in the content analysis (such as 'violence') are inadequately defined and inconsistently applied; and the descriptions of particular games are very superficial. In comparing games with 'great literature', Provenzo persistently invokes received judgements of taste that he fails to justify. However, the most telling limitation of this study is its use of data about *texts* to support very powerful assertions about their *effects*. Provenzo asserts that games are 'powerful teaching machines and instruments of cultural transmission'; they 'socialize women to be dependent [and] men to assume dominant gender roles'; they are 'instruments of a larger social, political and cultural hegemony'; and they are ultimately 'dehumanizing'. These are all explicit claims about the *effectiveness* of texts; yet no evidence whatsoever is provided to support them.

GAME BOYS, GAME GIRLS

Much of the emphasis here has been on the role of games in gender socialization. Computer games are frequently defined, both by researchers and by children themselves, as 'boys' toys' (Jessen, 1999). Surveys consistently suggest that girls have less access to computer games, and play less often. Critics argue that this situation may be disadvantaging girls in their educational encounters with computers, and in their subsequent employment prospects, as high-status jobs increasingly require computing skills (Cassell and Jenkins, 1998a).

The causes and consequences of this situation have been interpreted in various ways, however. While the games industry is seeking to broaden its market, the majority of games still appear to be designed primarily with boys in mind. Provenzo's (1991) findings here largely remain true: there are few 'positive images' of women, and females often feature only as 'damsels in distress', awaiting rescue by the male adventurer. More recent research (Subrahmanyam and Greenfield, 1998) suggests that girls generally do not favour the qualities that are characteristic of many computer games, such as an emphasis on 'action', contests between good and evil, fantasy settings and teams of characters (see also Cupitt and Stockbridge, 1996; Funk and Buchman, 1996; Kafai, 1998). Some studies find that boys are more 'aroused' than girls by the experience of new media, particularly when in the company of other boys (Kubey and Larson, 1990); although others have found the opposite (Cooper and Mackie, 1986).

However, such arguments can reinforce the essentialist notions of gender that they are outwardly concerned to challenge. Such research is often based on a fairly crude form of socialization theory, accompanied by a tendency to pathologize masculinity. Turkle (1984), for example, implicitly stigmatizes the rule-bound, 'hard' approach to computing which she defines as characteristic of boys, particularly during puberty. Alloway and Gilbert (1998) condemn computer game culture as a whole as 'masculinist, aggressive and violent', arguing that it simply reproduces oppressive forms of male subjectivity. Such arguments are reinforced by several of the researchers mentioned above (e.g. Funk and Buchman, 1996; Kubey and Larson, 1990; Provenzo, 1991). Here again, however, it is implicitly assumed that the 'messages' contained within the games are swallowed whole by their users. As Gailey (1993) suggests, this approach regards children as empty receptacles, and neglects the diverse ways in which the games are interpreted and used.

Both theoretically and empirically, some of these concerns are also beginning to appear rather outdated. The market in games is certainly skewed towards boys, but it is by no means exclusively confined to them: estimates in the late 1990s suggest that girls account for around 25 per cent of the market, and that this figure is steadily growing. Indeed, the move of games culture from the male-dominated public space of the arcades (Braun and Giroux, 1989; Panelas, 1983) to the domestic space of the living room or the child's bedroom has increased the potential access for girls (Cunningham, 1995). As the games industry has increasingly reached out to girls, female characters have featured more strongly; although whether a character like Lara Croft (in 'Tomb Raider') would qualify as a 'positive image' is certainly open to debate. Games are also becoming more diverse, and some of the newer role-playing games are less obviously targeted at boys, at least in terms of the characteristics identified above. Meanwhile, computers themselves have become easier to operate, which may mean that they are less likely to be perceived as intimidatingly 'technological' and hence as 'masculine'.

Cassell and Jenkins (1998b) offer an intriguing analysis of one attempt to change this situation, in the form of the 'girl games movement' of the late 1990s. This movement resulted from a particular combination of feminist academics, young women players and those within the industry who were attempting to reach out to a female audience. This new form of 'entrepreneurial feminism' had to walk a difficult line between the attempt to satisfy the existing girls' market and the attempt to change gender relations. On the one hand, there was an effort to create and sustain a positive space for girls, albeit in a way which may appear to sustain gender stereotypes; while on the other, there was an attempt to make that space more 'empowering' for girls, thereby running the risk of alienating them. As Cassell and Jenkins explain, these dilemmas were manifested in many areas of games design, from the construction of narratives to the colour coding of the packaging.

The obvious 'absent presence' in Cassell and Jenkins' book, however, is that of boys (Sefton-Green, 1999a). Jenkins' (1998) own contribution is alone in attempting to address the pleasures of masculinity, and to consider how these might be addressed by the games. He argues that games should be seen as virtual 'play spaces' that compensate for the growing lack of such spaces in the real world, as children (and especially boys) have been increasingly confined to the home. According to Jenkins, the games (and the peer group culture that surrounds them) offer the same pleasures that used to be afforded to earlier generations of boys in outdoor play: the exploration and mastery of space, goal-driven activity, self-control rather than parental control, and male bonding. Rather than seeing these qualities as a kind of early training in 'masculinist violence', Jenkins attempts to understand them in their own terms.

Despite its fairly narrow focus, Cassell and Jenkins' book points towards the kind of multifaceted analysis of the games phenomenon that needs to be developed in future research. What remains lacking from their account, however, is an indication of how *effective* the 'girl games movement' actually was in reaching and engaging girl players. As this implies, investigations of industry strategies need to be combined with accounts of the experiences of games playing, and with much more detailed analyses of games 'texts' themselves.

GAMES AS TEXTS

As I have noted, analyses of children's relationships with computer games tend to rely on generalized assertions about games, or reductive categorizations of content. Analyses of games themselves have been few and far between. Some academics have used forms of literary and cultural theory to account for the nature of games, although in many cases at a high level of generality. Klein (1984), for example, argues that early games like 'Pac-Man' reflect oral sadomasochistic fantasies of

engulfment; Kestenbaum and Weinstein (1984) see them as 'transitional objects'; while Skirrow (1986) regards them as a form of fantasy resolution for male performance anxiety. In more overtly political terms, Stallybrass (1992) uses the work of Adorno and Benjamin to develop a theory of game playing as a form of infantile regression promoted by capitalist consumer culture; while Fiske (1989) attempts to explain the appeal of games using an equally generalized account of popular culture as a form of 'ideological resistance'. Such arguments rarely make basic distinctions between different types of games, let alone refer to particular games in any detail.

By contrast, a series of studies by David Myers (1990; 1991; 1992a; 1992b) points to the level of analysis that is urgently required here. Myers uses poststructuralist, 'reader-oriented' literary theory to account for the organization of game worlds and narratives. Significantly, he accounts for the texts precisely as *games*, setting his analyses in the context of debates from play theory, for example about the nature of rules, the tensions between order and disorder, the experience of time and the recursive nature of play. This leads Myers to categorize the games in very different ways: rather than focusing on immediately observable content (such as the presence or absence of 'violence'), his emphasis is on the different styles of interactivity (or what players call 'game play') offered by different games.

As Jenkins (1993) has argued, simply importing concepts and methodologies from studies of 'older' media to the analysis of new media such as computer games can be positively misleading. Notions of 'identification' (e.g. Turkle, 1984) and 'representation' taken from film studies may be inappropriate when it comes to characters who are simply devices to insert the player into the game. An emphasis on goal-driven narratives, and on the significance of narrative closure, may lead to a neglect of the pleasures of spectacle; and focusing on the experience of time in games may lead one to neglect the significance of space, and the metaphors of exploration and conquest around which they are organized (Fuller and Jenkins, 1995). The ideological effectivity of games may lie not so much in their provision of 'role models' as in the exploratory processes they establish. Myers' (1990) analysis, for example, seriously challenges the assertion made by authors such as Provenzo (1991) that game playing is simply a matter of following rules, and that it therefore encourages a kind of ideological conformity.

While it is important to learn from research on 'older' media (cf. Chen, 1984; Reeves and Wartella, 1985), it is also necessary to develop new methods of analysis that account for the specificities of new media and the social contexts in which they are used. This kind of analysis is all the more significant as the games (and the cultures that surround them) continue to develop. As Provenzo (1991) and other critics have feared, the games are indeed becoming more 'realistic' and 'graphic'; but they are also becoming significantly more complex and multilayered. To compare early games like 'Pong' or 'Space Invaders' with current successes like 'Pokémon' or 'Final Fantasy 8' is to recognize the extraordinarily rapid evolution of the form. Technological developments will also offer new challenges here: the growing importance of multi-player games and gaming over the Internet reinforces the need for studies that pay much closer attention to the social context of games playing, and the culture that surrounds it.

CHILDREN'S ONLINE CULTURE

By contrast with the moral panics that have characterized discussion of computer games, debates about the potential of the Internet for young people have been significantly more positive. Rather than considering the Internet merely as a distribution medium, researchers have focused on the potential uses of chat groups, electronic mail and web pages as forms of autonomous creative expression. These are arenas in which, it is argued, children and young people are no longer constrained by the limitations of their parents' cultures (Tapscott, 1997).

Analyses of WWW home pages produced by children have seen them as instances of 'identity construction' analogous to the decoration of bedroom walls (Chandler and Roberts-Young, 1998). The home page is seen here as a hybrid form that combines aspects of public communication (such as broadcasting or publishing) with those of private communication (such as the personal diary or the letter). This hybridity is particularly reflected in the combination of written and spoken forms that characterizes these new media (Abbott, 1998). For some, the constant changes that characterize children's home pages are symptomatic of a 'post-modern' fluidity of identity (cf. Turkle, 1995); although others argue that the net is a place where young people feel they can be 'truly themselves' (Tobin, 1998). Susannah Stern (1999) provides an account of three different types of home pages produced by teenage girls that begins to indicate the diverse styles and purposes of children's online culture. In Stern's categorization, 'spirited' sites convey buoyancy and cheerfulness, and are used as a form of 'self-glorification'; 'sombre' sites are disillusioned, angry and introspective, serving as 'an asylum from a difficult and hostile world'; while 'self-conscious' sites oscillate between the two, reflecting the authors' lack of confidence about sharing too much online. Like other researchers in this field, however, Stern appears uncertain about whether to view the sites as vehicles for

'self-construction' or (more straightforwardly) as 'self-expression' – and hence as a safe space in which girls can 'speak their experience'.

Similar issues arise in the analysis of Internet relay chat (IRC), although the possibility that children may 'pass' as adults, or adults as children, makes it very difficult to assess the reliability of data. Just as some have claimed that the anonymity of chat rooms can provide opportunities for play with gender identities, so the same may be true in relation to age (Smith and Curtin, 1998; Turkle, 1995). Serious ethical dilemmas inevitably arise in this kind of research, particularly given the ease with which one can eavesdrop on apparently 'private' communications (see Baym, 1998); and these may be particularly acute in relation to children. Nevertheless, some researchers have argued that children and young people may be particularly empowered by these online communities. Tobin (1998), for example, argues that online communication may provide a means for boys to share 'personal' concerns and problems that is denied to them in other social encounters; while Abbott (1998) suggests that the use of oral linguistic forms in this context displays 'a striving for immediacy, response and dialogue, a sense of communion' which is only partially satisfied elsewhere.

A related theme here is that of *pedagogy*. Tobin (1998) argues that online communication produces 'learning communities' that cross boundaries of age and geography, and that are more democratic and collaborative than traditional educational institutions. As in more general assertions about online communities (e.g. Rheingold, 1993), such arguments tend to neglect the occasionally *un*democratic and exclusionary nature of online communication; although the opportunities these media present for group interaction, when compared with equivalent older technologies such as the telephone, cannot be denied. Combined with assertions about the more self-managed, participatory learning *styles* developed by computers – by games as much as by 'educational' software – these arguments lead towards a notion of a 'deschooled' society that comes close to that proposed by Ivan Illich 30 years ago (Illich, 1971; Snyder, 1998).

If research about computer games has been somewhat constrained by the 'carryover' of ideas from older media, work on children's online culture has only just begun to develop appropriate hypotheses and methods. Much of the research, for example on electronic fanzines (Leonard, 1998) or 'multi-user domains' (Turkle, 1995), is in fact concerned with young people aged over 18. Such studies are almost bound to focus on unrepresentative cases, although some appear unduly preoccupied with the more avant-garde manifestations of 'cyberculture' (e.g. Turkle, 1995). As with games, researchers are dealing with forms of children's culture to which it is very difficult to gain access – and which, in many respects, seem almost deliberately designed to exclude them. Most of the studies mentioned here are highly descriptive, and some carry an almost colonialist air, as though they were reports from strange and distant lands. Future research will need to be much more detailed and sustained. Researchers will need to triangulate between the analysis of texts (such as home pages and IRC sessions) and interviews with their producers and users; analyse the evolution of particular pages and sites over time; consider the place of such activities in the context of 'real-life' relationships in the family and the peer group; and consider how participants in online culture may be representative of broader social categories.

EDUCATION AND ENTERTAINMENT

As I have noted, much of the positive potential of new media for children has been seen to rest in their *educational* role. Longer-term fantasies of a deschooled, 'wired' society are perhaps the most utopian aspect of this; although claims about the educational value of home computing have long been a central aspect of the industry's marketing strategies (Buckingham et al., 2001; Nixon, 1998). Advertising for these media often represents them as a way of investing in children's future; and indeed as a means of compensating for what are seen to be the inadequacies of contemporary schooling. Thus, it is claimed that computer software will 'make learning fun' by using imagery and modes of address drawn from children's popular culture, and by employing what purport to be 'interactive' approaches. These new forms of 'edutainment' are offered both as an acceptable leisure-time pursuit, and as a glamorous alternative to the apparent tedium of much school work.

There have been some contrasting assessments of the educational value of these new media, however. Seymour Papert (1996), for example, waxes lyrical about children's 'love affair' with computers, arguing that they provide a more creative and spontaneous form of learning that can dramatically improve family relationships. By contrast, sceptics such as Jane Healy (1998) argue that much of the learning that computers provide is superficial and trivial, and that claims about their educational potential are highly overstated. Despite these differences between them, however, such authors agree on the importance of high-quality software, support from parents and strong connections between home and school if this potential is to be realized.

In a substantial empirical study, Giacquinta et al. (1993) conclude that the educational 'promise' of this technology has been largely unfulfilled. While parents are likely to invest in computers and software with educational benefits in mind, and while they often have access to good quality educational programs, they are rarely used. In general, children prefer to use home computers for playing games, and resist overtly 'educational' activities; and this is reinforced by the dominant view of the computer as a toy or plaything. Parents also lack the time and expertise to support their children's use of computers; furthermore the uses of computers in schools are frequently limited, and there is little dialogue between parents and teachers on the issue. Finally, males are generally the major users and decision-makers in relation to home computing, while females (particularly mothers) are often defined as incompetent; and since mothers are generally the primary care-givers, this further reduces the potential for parental support. According to these authors, the benefits of technology will only be realized if we pay attention to the 'social envelope' – that is, to the sets of expectations, contexts and social practices – that surrounds it. Thus, for example, they suggest that schools can play a significant role as 'linking agents' to encourage educational computing in the home; but this will in turn require broader changes in the relationships between parents and teachers.

The Giacquinta et al. (1993) study was undertaken in the mid 1980s, before the advent of multimedia home computers and the Internet – although there is little reason to believe that their conclusions no longer apply. In a more recent study involving the present author, Sefton-Green and Buckingham (1996) are similarly sceptical about the 'creative' potential of home computing. While children were certainly aware of the potential of the technology, they were rarely in a position to use it. They understood in principle what their *computers* could do – for example in digital animation, design, sound and video editing, and 'multimedia authoring' – but they rarely engaged in such activities themselves. Some of the reasons for this were essentially 'technical'; and in this respect, the machines (or the advertisements for them) seemed to promise more than they were capable of delivering. However, there were also some important social reasons why the technology was not living up to its creative potential. Very few parents knew how to support their children in using the computer in this way; although children in middle-class families, whose parents or relatives were often more familiar with technology, were in a better position. For most children, however, using computers seemed to be a way of filling in time when they were bored. This sense of disconnectedness was also reflected in the lack of an *audience* for this material. Children described how they would show their work to their mum or stick it on their bedroom wall, but otherwise nobody ever saw or knew about it – a striking contrast with the intensely sociable culture of computer gaming.

There remains a need for further research on the *pedagogy* of computer use in the home – for example, how (and by whom) children are introduced to computers, and how parents encourage or regulate their use. We need to know more about how both groups perceive and balance out the 'educational' and 'entertainment' aspects of these new media. While parents are encouraged to invest in computers for broadly 'educational' purposes, children are much more inclined to use them for 'entertainment' (Cupitt and Stockbridge, 1996; Downes, 1999; Giacquinta et al., 1993). Over the past decade, these competing views have often been manifested in parents' decisions about whether to buy a PC or a games console; yet with the advent of games consoles that allow Internet access (such as the Sega Dreamcast), these distinctions may prove more difficult to sustain. Meanwhile, the growing availability of the Internet may provide many more outlets for young people's creative work (Sefton-Green, 1999b); but it remains to be seen how far these 'virtual audiences' can substitute for real audiences of family and peers.

Towards New Policies

Many of the issues discussed in this chapter have significant implications for cultural and educational policy. The dangers of a polarization between the information rich and the information poor, and the various forms of 'social exclusion' that it might encourage, have been recognized since the early days of new media research (e.g. Chen and Paisley, 1985) and are now widely acknowledged by policymakers. Governments have increasingly recognized that the diffusion of technology cannot be left to market forces, and that regulation and intervention are required in order to ensure that all homes and schools are 'wired' to electronic networks.

At the time of writing, much of the impetus here is focused on questions of physical *access*. However, access is not simply a matter of technology. It is also a question of the skills and competencies – the cultural and educational capital – that are required to use technology creatively and effectively. These forms of capital are also unevenly distributed: different social groups are positioned in very different ways in relation to public discourses about education, and in relation to the institution of the school. New technology is becoming a crucial part of many people's working lives, but it is doing so in very different ways for different groups of workers; and, in the process, new gaps of knowledge and skill may be opening up. Meanwhile, cutting across these moves are more familiar concerns about children's relationships with media. Growing anxieties about pornography on the Internet or online marketing to children have led to debates about the need for content regulation and parental control (Oswell, 1999; Price, 1998). Yet it is far from clear how we can prevent children gaining access to 'harmful' content, while simultaneously encouraging them to make the most of the educational and cultural potential of these new media.

As this implies, policy-makers need to take much fuller account of the social contexts in which children encounter new media, and the kinds of support which are necessary in order to use them most effectively. This may require a fairly radical rethinking of the institutional contexts (such as schools) in which technologies are made available to children; and of the relationships between schools, homes and other sites of educational and cultural activity (Schon et al., 1999). Simply providing children with 'information' is not enough: we have to enable them to develop the intellectual and cultural competencies that are required to select, interpret and utilize it. Despite the optimism of some advocates, children do not automatically know how to use new media technology, let alone evaluate what it provides. Technology alone will not transform them into the autonomous 'cyberkids' of the popular imagination. We need to pay much closer attention to what is taking place in their interactions with these new media, and to the forms of support and education they need in order to make those interactions as productive as they promise to be.

References

Abbott, C. (1998) 'Making connections: young people and the internet', in J. Sefton-Green (ed.), *Digital Diversions: Youth Culture in the Age of Multimedia*. London: UCL Press. pp. 84–105.

Alloway, N. and Gilbert, P. (1998) 'Video game culture: playing with masculinity, violence and pleasure', in S. Howard (ed.), *Wired-Up: Young People and Electronic Media*. London: UCL Press. pp. 95–114.

Bannert, M. and Arbinger, P.R. (1996) 'Gender-related differences in exposure to and use of computers: results of a survey of secondary school students', *European Journal of Psychology of Education*, 11 (3): 269–82.

Barker, M. and Petley, J. (eds) (2001) *Ill Effects: the Media Effects Debate*, 2nd edn. London: Routledge.

Baym, N. (1998) 'The emergence of on-line community', in S. Jones (ed.), *Cybersociety 2.0: Revisiting Computer-Mediated Communication and Community*. Thousand Oaks, CA: Sage. pp. 35–68.

Bourdieu, P. (1984) *Distinction: a Social Critique of the Judgement of Taste*. London: Routledge & Kegan Paul.

Braun, C. and Giroux, J. (1989) 'Arcade video games: proxemic, cognitive and content analyses', *Journal of Leisure Research*, 21 (2): 92–105.

Buckingham, D. (1993) 'Just playing games', *English and Media Magazine*, 28: 21–5.

Buckingham, D. (2000) *After the Death of Childhood: Growing Up in the Age of Electronic Media*. Cambridge: Polity.

Buckingham, D. and Sefton-Green, J. (1997) 'From regulation to education', *English and Media Magazine*, 36: 28–32.

Buckingham, D., Scanlon, M. and Sefton-Green, J. (2001) 'Selling the digital dream: marketing educational technology to teachers and parents', in A. Loveless and V. Ellis (eds), *ICT, Pedagogy and the Curriculum: Subject to Change*. London: Routledge. pp. 20–40.

Cassell, J. and Jenkins, H. (eds) (1998a) 'Chess for girls? Feminism and computer games', in J. Cassell and H. Jenkins (eds), *From Barbie to Mortal Kombat: Gender and Computer Games*. Cambridge, MA: MIT Press. pp. 2–45.

Cassell, J. and Jenkins, H. (eds) (1998b) *From Barbie to Mortal Kombat: Gender and Computer Games*. Cambridge, MA: MIT Press.

Center for Media Education (1997) *Webs of Deception*. Washington, DC.

Chandler, D. and Roberts-Young, D. (1998) 'The construction of identity in the personal homepages of adolescents', URL: http://www.aber.ac.uk/~dgc/strasbourg.html.

Chen, M. (1984) 'Computers in the lives of our children: looking back on a generation of television research', in R.E. Rice (ed.), *The New Media: Communication, Research and Technology*. Beverly Hills, CA: Sage. pp. 269–86.

Chen, M. and Paisley, W. (eds) (1985) *Children and Microcomputers: Research on the Newest Medium*. Beverly Hills, CA: Sage.

Cooper, J. and Mackie, D. (1986) 'Video games and aggression in children', *Journal of Applied Social Psychology*, 16 (8): 726–44.

Cuban, L. (1986) *Teachers and Machines: the Classroom Use of Technology since 1920*. New York: Teachers' College Press.

Cunningham, H. (1995) 'Moral kombat and computer game-girls', in C. Bazalgette and D. Buckingham (eds), *In Front of the Children: Screen Entertainment and Young Audiences*. London: British Film Institute. pp. 188–200.

Cupitt, M. and Stockbridge, S. (1996) *Families and Electronic Entertainment*. Sydney: Australian Broadcasting Corporation/Office of Film and Literature Classification.

Downes, T. (1999) 'Children's and parents' discourses about computers in the home and school', *Convergence*, 5 (2): 104–11.

Durkin, K. (1995) *Computer Games: their Effects on Young People. A Review*. Sydney: Office of Film and Literature Classification.

Durndell, A., Glissov, P. and Siann, G. (1995) 'Gender and computing: persisting differences', *Educational Research*, 37 (3): 219–27.

Fiske, J. (1989) *Reading the Popular*. London: Unwin Hyman.

Fuller, M. and Jenkins, H. (1995) 'Nintendo and new world travel writing: a dialogue', in S. Jones (ed.), *Cybersociety: Computer-Mediated Communication and Community*. London: Sage. pp. 57–72.

Funk, J. and Buchman, D. (1996) 'Playing violent video and computer games and adolescent self-concept', *Journal of Communication*, 46 (1): 19–32.

Funk, J., Germann, J. and Buchman, D. (1997) 'Children and electronic games in the United States', *Trends in Communication*, 2: 111–26.

Gailey, C.W. (1993) 'Mediated messages: gender, class and cosmos in home video games', *Journal of Popular Culture*, 27 (1): 81–97.

Giacquinta, J.B., Bauer, J. and Levin, J.E. (1993) *Beyond Technology's Promise: an Examination of Children's Educational Computing at Home*. Cambridge: Cambridge University Press.

Graybill, D., Strawniak, M., Hunter, T. and O'Leary, M. (1985) 'Effects of playing violent versus nonviolent video games on the aggressive ideation of aggressive and nonaggressive children', *Child Study Journal*, 15 (3): 199–205.

Graybill, D. Strawniak, M., Hunter, T. and O'Leary, M. (1987) 'Effects of playing versus observing violent versus nonviolent video games on children's aggression', *Psychology*, 24 (3): 1–8.

Green, B. and Bigum, C. (1993) 'Aliens in the classroom', *Australian Journal of Education*, 37 (2): 119–41.

Greenfield, P.M. (1984) *Mind and Media: the Effects of Television, Computers and Video Games*. London: Fontana.

Griffiths, M. (1994) 'Computer games: harmless or addictive?', *Education and Health*, 12 (2): 28–30.

Griffiths, M. (1996) 'Computer game playing in children and adolescents: a review of the literature', in T. Gill (ed.), *Electronic Children: How Children Are Responding to the Information Revolution*. London: National Children's Bureau.

Gunter, B. (1998) *The Effects of Video Games on Children: the Myth Unmasked*. Sheffield: Sheffield Academic Press.

Haddon, L. (1988) 'Electronic and computer games: the history of an interactive medium', *Screen*, 29 (2): 52–73.

Healy, J. (1998) *Failure to Connect: How Computers Affect our Children's Minds – for Better and Worse*. New York: Simon & Schuster.

Herz, J.C. (1997) *Joystick Nation: How Videogames Gobbled our Money, Won our Hearts and Rewired our Minds*. London: Abacus.

Illich, I. (1971) *Deschooling Society*. New York: Harper & Row.

Jenkins, H. (1993) '"x logic": repositioning Nintendo in children's lives', *Quarterly Review of Film and Video*, 14 (4): 55–70.

Jenkins, H. (1998) '"Complete freedom of movement": video games as gendered play spaces', in J. Cassell and H. Jenkins (eds), *From Barbie to Mortal Kombat: Gender and Computer Games*. Cambridge, MA: MIT Press. pp. 262–97.

Jessen, C. (1999) *Children's Computer Culture: Three Essays on Children and Computers*. Odense, Denmark: Odense University.

Johnson-Eilola, J. (1998) 'Living on the surface: learning in the age of global communication networks', in I. Snyder (ed.), *Page to Screen: Taking Literacy into the Electronic Era*. London: Routledge. pp. 185–210.

Kafai, Y.B. (1998) 'Video game designs by girls and boys: variability and consistency of gender differences', in J. Cassell and H. Jenkins (eds), *From Barbie to Mortal Kombat: Gender and Computer Games*. Cambridge, MA: MIT Press. pp. 90–114.

Katz, J. (1996) 'The rights of kids in the digital age', *Wired*, 4.07: 120–3, 166–70.

Kestenbaum, G. and Weinstein, L. (1984) 'Personality, psychopathology and developmental issues in male adolescent game use', *Journal of the American Academy of Child Psychiatry*, 24 (3): 329–37.

Kinder, M. (1991) *Playing with Power in Movies, Television and Video Games*. Berkeley, CA: University of California Press.

Klein, M. (1984) 'The bite of Pac-Man', *Journal of Psychohistory*, 2 (3): 395–401.

Kubey, R. and Larson, R. (1990) 'The use and experience of the new video media among children and young adolescents', *Communication Research*, 17 (1): 107–30.

Leonard, M. (1998) 'Paper places: travelling the new grrll geographies', in T. Skelton and G. Valentine (eds), *Cool Places: Geographies of Youth Cultures*. London: Routledge.

Livingstone, S. and Bovill, M. (1999) *Young People, New Media*. Report of the Research Project 'Children, Young People and the Changing Media Environment'. London: London School of Economics and Political Science. http://psych.lse.ac.uk/young_people.

Melody, W. (1973) *Children's Television: the Economics of Exploitation*. New Haven, CT: Yale University Press.

Myers, D. (1990) 'Computer game genres', *Play and Culture*, 3 (2): 286–301.

Myers, D. (1991) 'Computer game semiotics', *Play and Culture*, 4 (3): 334–45.

Myers, D. (1992a) 'Simulating the self', *Play and Culture*, 5 (4): 420–40.

Myers, D. (1992b) 'Time, symbol transformations, and computer games', *Play and Culture*, 5 (4): 441–57.

Nixon, H. (1998) 'Fun and games are serious business', in J. Sefton-Green (ed.), *Digital Diversions: Youth Culture in the Age of Multimedia*. London: UCL Press. pp. 21–42.

Office for National Statistics (1999) *General Household Survey 1998*. London: Office for National Statistics.

Orr Vered, K. (1998) 'Blue group boys play *Incredible Machine*, girls play hopscotch: social discourse and gendered play at the computer', in J. Sefton-Green (ed.), *Digital Diversions: Youth Culture in the Age of Multimedia*. London: UCL Press. pp. 43–61.

Oswell, D. (1999) 'The dark side of cyberspace: internet content regulation and child protection', *Convergence*, 5 (2): 42–62.

Panelas, T. (1983) 'Adolescents and video games: consumption of leisure and the social construction of the peer group', *Youth and Society*, 15 (1): 51–65.

Papert, S. (1993) *The Children's Machine: Rethinking School in the Age of the Computer*. New York: Basic.

Papert, S. (1996) *The Connected Family*. Atlanta, GA: Longstreet.

Price, M. (ed.) (1998) *The V-Chip Debate: Content Filtering from Television to the Internet*. Mahwah, NJ: Erlbaum.

Provenzo, E.F. (1991) *Video Kids: Making Sense of Nintendo*. Cambridge, MA: Harvard University Press.

Radway, J. (1984) *Reading the Romance*. Chapel Hill, NC: University of North Carolina Press.

Reeves, B. and Wartella, E. (1985) 'Historical trends in research on children and the media, 1900–1960', *Journal of Communication*, 35 (2): 118–33.

Rheingold, H. (1993) *The Virtual Community: Homesteading on the Electronic Frontier*. Reading, MA: Addison-Wesley.

Rideout, V.J., Foehr, U.G., Roberts, D.F. and Brodie, M. (1999) *Kids & Media @ the New Millennium*. Menlo Park, CA: Henry J. Kaiser Family Foundation.

Schon, D., Sanyal, B. and Mitchell, W. (eds) (1999) *High Technology and Low-Income Communities*. Cambridge, MA: MIT Press.

Sefton-Green, J. (1999a) 'Playing the game: the critical study of computer games', *Convergence*, 5 (2): 114–20.

Sefton-Green, J. (ed.) (1999b) *Young People, Creativity and New Technologies: the Challenge of Digital Arts*. London: Routledge.

Sefton-Green, J. and Buckingham, D. (1996) 'Digital visions: children's "creative" uses of multimedia technologies', *Convergence*, 2 (2): 47–79.

Sheff, D. (1993) *Game Over: Nintendo's Battle to Dominate an Industry*. London: Hodder & Stoughton.

Shuker, R. (1996) 'Video games: serious fun', *Continuum*, 9 (2): 125–45.

Silverstone, R. and Hirsch, E. (eds) (1992) *Consuming Technologies: Media and Information in Domestic Spaces*. London: Routledge.

Skirrow, G. (1986) 'Hellivision: an analysis of video games', in C. MacCabe (ed.), *High Theory/Low Culture*. Manchester: Manchester University Press. pp. 115–42.

Smith, R. and Curtin, P. (1998) 'Children, computers and life online: education in a cyber-world', in I. Snyder (ed.), *Page to Screen: Taking Literacy into the Electronic Era*. London: Routledge. pp. 211–33.

Snyder, I. (ed.) (1998) *Page to Screen: Taking Literacy into the Electronic Era*. London: Routledge

Spigel, L. (1992) *Make Room for TV*. Chicago: Chicago University Press.

Stallybrass, J. (1992) 'Just gaming: allegory and economy in computer games', *New Left Review*, 198: 83–106.

Stern, S. (1999) 'Adolescent girls' expression on WWW home pages: spirited, sombre and self-conscious sites', *Convergence*, 5 (2): 22–41.

Straubhaar, T. (2000) 'Digital divide in East Austin', URL: ftp://uts.cc.utexas.edu/coc/rtf/digitaldivide/UT DigitalDivide.html

Subrahmanyam, K. and Greenfield, P.M. (1998) 'Computer games for girls: what makes them play?', in J. Cassell and H. Jenkins (eds), *From Barbie to Mortal Kombat: Gender and Computer Games*. Cambridge, MA: MIT Press. pp. 46–71.

Tapscott, D. (1997) *Growing up Digital: the Rise of the Net Generation*. New York: McGraw-Hill.

Thorne, B. (1993) *Gender Play: Girls and Boys at School*. New Brunswick, NJ: Rutgers University Press.

Tobin, J. (1998) 'An American Otaku (or, a boy's virtual life on the Net)', in J. Sefton-Green (ed.), *Digital Diversions: Youth Culture in the Age of Multimedia*. London: UCL Press. pp. 106–27.

Turkle, S. (1984) *The Second Self: Computers and the Human Spirit*. New York: Simon & Schuster.

Turkle, S. (1995) *Life on Screen: Identity in the Age of the Internet*. New York: Simon & Schuster.

Van der Voort, T., Beentjes, J., Bovill, M., Gaskell, G., Koolstra, C., Livingstone, S. and Marseille, N. (1998) 'Young people's ownership of new and old forms of media in Britain and the Netherlands', *European Journal of Communication*, 13 (4): 457–77.

Video Games and Human Behavior: a Research Agenda for the 80s (1983) Papers and proceedings of a symposium at the Harvard Graduate School of Education. Cambridge, MA: Monroe C. Gutman Library and Harvard Graduate School of Education.

Williams, R. (1974) *Television: Technology and Cultural Form*. Glasgow: Fontana.

Winkel, M., Novak, D.M. and Hopson, H. (1987) 'Personality factors, subject gender and the effects of aggressive video games on aggression in adolescence', *Journal of Research in Personality*, 21: 211–23.

6

New Media and New Literacies: Reconstructing Education for the New Millennium

DOUGLAS KELLNER

As we enter a new millennium, most people are by now aware that we are in the midst of one of the most dramatic technological revolutions in history which is changing everything about the ways that we work, communicate and spend our leisure time. The technological revolution centres on computer, information, communication and multimedia technologies, is often interpreted as the beginnings of a knowledge or information society, and therefore ascribes education a central role in every aspect of life. This great transformation poses tremendous challenges to educators to rethink their basic tenets, to deploy the media in creative and productive ways, and to restructure schooling to respond constructively and progressively to the technological and social changes that we are now experiencing.

At the same time that we are undergoing technological revolution, important demographic and sociopolitical changes are occurring in the United States and throughout the world. Emigration patterns have brought an explosion of new peoples into the US in recent decades and the country is now more racially and ethnically diverse, more multicultural, than ever before. This creates the challenge of providing people from diverse races, classes and backgrounds with the tools and competencies to enable them to succeed and participate in an ever more complex and changing world.[1]

In this chapter, I argue that we need multiple literacies for our multicultural society, that we need to develop new literacies to meet the challenge of new media and technologies, and that literacies of diverse sorts – including a more fundamental importance for print literacy – are of crucial importance in restructuring education for a high-tech and multicultural society and global culture. My argument is that in a period of dramatic technological and social change, education needs to cultivate a variety of new types of literacies to make it relevant to the demands of a new millennium. My assumptions are that media are altering every aspect of our society and culture, and that we need to comprehend and make use of them both to understand and to transform our worlds. My goal would be to introduce new literacies to empower individuals and groups traditionally excluded and thus to reconstruct education to make it more responsive to the challenges of a democratic and multicultural society.

TECHNOLOGY AND THE RESTRUCTURING OF EDUCATION

To dramatize the issues at stake, we should seriously consider the claim that we are now undergoing one of the most significant technological revolutions for education since the progression from oral to print- and book-based teaching.[2] Just as the transition to print literacy and book culture involved a dramatic transformation of education, as Marshall McLuhan (1962; 1964), Walter Ong (1988) and others have argued, so too does the current technological revolution demand a major restructuring of education today with new curricula, pedagogy, literacies, practices and goals. Furthermore, the technological revolution of the present era makes possible the radical reconstruction and restructuring of education and society argued for in the progressive era by Dewey and in the 1960s and 1970s by Ivan Illich, Paolo Freire and others who sought radical educational and social reform.[3]

Put in historical perspective, it is now possible to see modern education as preparation for industrial civilization and minimal citizenship in a passive representative democracy. The demands of the new global economy, culture and polity require a more informed, participatory and active citizenship, and thus increased roles and challenges for education. Modern education, in short, emphasizes submission to authority, rote memorization and what Freire called the 'banking concept' of education in which learned teachers deposit knowledge into passive students, inculcating conformity, subordination and normalization. These traits are becoming obsolete in a global post-industrial and networked society with its demands for new skills for the workplace, participation in new social and political environment, and interaction within novel forms of culture and everyday life.

In short, I wish to argue that the technological revolution renders necessary the sort of thorough restructuring of education that radicals demanded during the last century, indeed back to the Enlightenment if one includes Rousseau and Wollstonecraft who saw the enlightened restructuring of education as the key to democracy. Today, however, intense pressures for change now come directly from technology and the economy and not ideology or educational reformist ideas, with a new global economy and new technologies demanding new skills, competencies, literacies and practices. While this technological revolution has highly ambiguous effects – that I'll note in this study – it provides educational reformers with the challenge of whether education will be restructured to promote democracy and human needs, or whether education will be transformed primarily to serve the needs of business and the global economy.

It is therefore a burning question what sort of restructuring will take place, in whose interests, and for what ends. Indeed, more than ever we need philosophical reflection on the ends and purposes of education, on what we are doing and trying to achieve in our educational practices and institutions. In this situation, it may be instructive to return to Dewey and see the connections between education and democracy, the need for the reconstruction of education and society, and the value of experimental pedagogy to seek solutions to the problems of education in the present day. Hence, a progressive reconstruction of education will urge that it be done in the interests of democratization, ensuring access to new media and technologies for all, helping to overcome the so-called digital divide and divisions of the haves and have nots, so that education is placed *à la* Dewey (1997 [1916]) and

Freire (1972; 1998) in the service of democracy and social justice.

Yet we should be more aware than Dewey of the obduracy of divisions of class, gender and race, and work self-consciously for multicultural democracy and education. This task suggests that we valorize difference and cultural specificity, as well as equality and shared universal Deweyan proper values such as freedom, equality, individualism and participation. Theorizing a democratic and multicultural reconstruction of education thus forces us to confront the digital divide: that there are divisions between information and technology have and have nots, just as there are class, gender and race divisions in every sphere of the existing constellations of society and culture. The latest surveys of the digital divide, however, indicate that the key indicators are class and education and not race and gender: hence the often circulated argument that new media and technologies merely reinforce the hegemony of upper-class white males must be questioned.[4]

With the proper resources, policies, pedagogies and practices, we can, I believe, work to reduce the (unfortunately growing) gap between haves and have nots, although I want to make clear that I do not believe that technology alone will suffice to democratize and adequately reconstruct education. That is, technology itself does not necessarily improve teaching and learning, and will certainly not of itself overcome acute socioeconomic divisions. Indeed, without proper resources, pedagogy and educational practices, technology might be an obstacle or burden to genuine learning and will probably increase rather than overcome existing divisions of power, cultural capital and wealth.

Studies of the implementation of technology in schools reveal that without adequate teaching training and technology policy, the results of introducing computers and new media into education are highly ambiguous.[5] During the rest of this chapter, I want to focus on the role of computers and information technology in contemporary education and the need for new pedagogies and an expanded concept of literacy to respond to the importance of new media and technologies in every aspect of life. My goal will be to propose some ways that new media and new literacies can serve as efficacious learning tools which will contribute to producing a more democratic and egalitarian society and not just providing skills and tools to privileged individuals and groups that will improve their cultural capital and social power at the expense of others. How, indeed, are we going to restructure education to provide individuals and groups with the tools, the competencies, the literacies to overcome the class, gender and racial divides that bifurcate our society and, at least in terms of economic indicators, seem to be growing rather than diminishing?

Before taking on this challenge we must address the technophobic argument against new media and technologies *per se*. I have been developing what I call a critical theory of technology which criticizes uses or types of technology as tools of domination; rejects the hype and pretensions of new media and technologies; sees the limitations of pedagogy and educational proposals based primarily on technology without adequate emphasis on pedagogy and on teacher and student empowerment; insists on developing educational reform and restructuring to promote multicultural democracy; and calls for appropriate restructuring of technology to democratize education and society. Yet a critical theory of media and technology also sees how they can be used, and perhaps redesigned and restructured, for positive purposes such as enhancing education and democracy and overcoming the divide between haves and have nots, while enabling individuals to democratically and creatively participate in a new economy, society and culture.[6]

Hence, a critical theory of technology avoids both technophobia and technophilia. It rejects technological determinism, and is critical of the limitations, biases and downsides of new media and technologies, but wants to use and redesign these tools in the interests of education for democracy and social reconstruction in the promotion of social justice. It is also, in the Deweyan spirit, pragmatic and experimental, recognizing that there is no agreed way to deploy new technologies for enhancing education and democratization. Thus, we must be prepared to accept that some of the attempts to use technology for education may well fail, as have no doubt many of our own attempts to use new media and technologies for education. A critical theory of technology is aware that media and technologies have unforeseen consequences and that good intentions and seemingly good projects may have results that were neither desired nor positive. However, such is life, and it is now a time to be daring and innovative and not conservative and stodgy in our rethinking of education and the use of new media and technologies in educational practices and pedagogies.

Consequently, the question is not whether computers are good or bad in the classroom or more broadly for education. Rather, it is a question of what to do with them: what useful purposes can computers serve, what sort of skills do students and teachers need to effectively deploy new media, computers and information technology, what sort of effects might they have on learning, and what new literacies, views of education and social relations do we need to democratize and improve education today?[7]

EDUCATION AND LITERACY

Both traditionalists and reformists would probably agree that education and literacy are intimately connected. 'Literacy' in my conception comprises gaining competencies in effectively using socially constructed forms of communication and representation. Learning literacies involves attaining competencies in practices in contexts that are governed by rules and conventions. Literacies are socially constructed in educational and cultural practices and involved in various institutional discourses and practices. Literacies evolve and shift in response to social and cultural change and to the interests of the elites who control hegemonic institutions.

Literacy thus involves gaining the skills and knowledge to read and interpret the text of the world and to successfully navigate and negotiate its challenges, conflicts and crises. Literacy is thus a necessary condition to equip people to participate in the local, national and global economy, culture and polity. As Dewey (1997 [1916]) argued, education is necessary to enable people to participate in democracy, and thus, without an educated, informed and literate citizenry, a robust democracy is impossible. Moreover, there are crucial links between literacy, democracy, empowerment and participation, and without developing adequate literacies the differences between haves and have nots cannot be overcome and individuals and groups will be left out of the emerging economy, networked society and culture.

To accompany reading, writing and traditional print literacies, one could argue that in an era of technological revolution and new media we need to develop new forms of media literacy, computer literacy and multimedia literacies that I and others call by the covering concept of 'multiliteracies' or 'multiple literacies'.[8] New media and cultural forms demand novel skills and competencies, and if education is to be relevant to the problems and challenges of contemporary life it must expand the concept of literacy and develop new curricula and pedagogies.

I would resist, however, extreme claims that the era of the book and print literacy are over. Although there are discontinuities and novelties in the current constellation, there are also important continuities. Indeed, one could argue that in the new information-communication technology environment, traditional print literacy takes on increasing importance in the computer mediated cyberworld precisely because one needs to critically scrutinize and scroll tremendous amounts of information, putting new emphasis on developing reading and writing abilities. For instance, Internet discussion groups, chat rooms, e-mail and various forums require writing skills in which a new emphasis on the importance of clarity and precision is emerging as communications proliferate. In this context of information saturation, it becomes an ethical imperative not to contribute to cultural and information overload, and to communicate concisely one's thoughts and feelings.

MEDIA LITERACY: AN
UNFULFILLED CHALLENGE

In the new multimedia environment, media literacy is arguably more important than ever. Cultural studies and critical pedagogy have begun to teach us to recognize the ubiquity of media culture in contemporary society, the growing trends toward multicultural education, and the need for media literacy that addresses the issue of multicultural and social difference.[9] There is expanding recognition that media representations help construct our images and understanding of the world and that education must meet the dual challenges of teaching media literacy in a multicultural society and sensitizing students and publics to the inequities and injustices of a society based on gender, race and class inequalities and discrimination. Recent critical studies see the role of mainstream media in exacerbating or diminishing these inequalities and the ways that media education and the production of alternative media can help create a healthy multiculturalism of diversity and more robust democracy. They thus confront some of the most serious difficulties and problems that face us as educators and citizens at the beginning of the twenty-first century.

Yet despite the ubiquity of media culture in contemporary society and everyday life, although it is widely recognized that the media themselves are a form of pedagogy, and despite copious criticisms of the distorted values, ideals and representations of the world in media culture, media education in K–12 schooling has never really been established and developed. The current technological revolution, however, brings to the fore more than ever the role of media such as television, popular music, film and advertising, as the Internet rapidly absorbs these cultural forms and creates new cyberspaces and forms of culture and pedagogy. It is highly irresponsible in the face of saturation by Internet and media culture to ignore these forms of socialization and education; consequently a critical reconstruction of education should produce pedagogies that provide media literacy and enable students, teachers and citizens to discern the nature and effects of media culture.

Media culture teaches proper and improper behaviour, gender roles, values and knowledge of the world. One is often not aware that one is being educated and constructed by media culture; thus its pedagogy is often invisible and subliminal, calling for critical approaches that make us aware of how media construct meanings, influence and educate audiences, and impose their messages and values. A media-literate person is skilful in analysing media codes and conventions, able to criticize stereotypes, values and ideologies, and competent to interpret the multiple meanings and messages generated by media texts. Media literacy thus helps people to use media intelligently, to discriminate and evaluate media content, to dissect media forms critically, and to investigate media effects and uses (see Kellner, 1995a; 1995b).

Yet within educational circles, there is a debate over what constitutes the field of media pedagogy, with different agendas and programmes. A traditional 'protectionist' approach would attempt to 'inoculate' young people against the effects of media addiction and manipulation by cultivating a taste for book literacy, high culture and the values of truth, beauty and justice, and by denigrating all forms of media and computer culture. Neil Postman in his books *Amusing Ourselves to Death* (1985) and *Technopolis* (1992) exemplifies this approach. A 'media literacy' movement, by contrast, attempts to teach students to read, analyse and decode media texts, in a fashion parallel to the advancement of print literacy. Media arts education in turn teaches students to appreciate the aesthetic qualities of media and to use various media technologies as instruments of self-expression and creation. Critical media literacy, in my conception, builds on these approaches, analysing media culture as products of social production and struggle, and teaching students to be critical of media representations and discourses, but also stressing the importance of learning to use the media as modes of self-expression and social activism.

Developing critical media literacy and pedagogy also involves perceiving how media such as film or video can be used positively to teach a wide range of topics, like multicultural understanding and education. If, for example, multicultural education is to champion genuine diversity and expand the curriculum, it is important both for groups excluded from mainstream education to learn about their own heritage and for dominant groups to explore the experiences and voices of minority and excluded groups. Thus, media literacy can promote multicultural literacy, conceived as understanding and engaging the heterogeneity of cultures and subcultures that constitute an increasingly global and multicultural world.[10]

Critical media literacy not only teaches students to learn from media, to resist media manipulation, and to use media materials in constructive ways, but is also concerned with developing skills that will help create good citizens and that will make them more motivated and competent participants in social life. Critical media literacy is thus tied to the project of radical democracy and concerned to develop skills that will enhance democratization and participation. Critical media literacy takes a comprehensive approach that would teach critical skills and how to use media as instruments of social communication and change. The technologies of communication are becoming more and more accessible to young people and average citizens, and can be used to promote education, democratic self-expression and social progress. Thus, technologies that could help produce the end of participatory democracy, by transforming politics into media spectacles and the battle of images, and by turning spectators into cultural zombies, could also be used to help invigorate democratic debate and participation (Kellner, 1990; 1998; 2000).

Indeed, teaching critical media literacy could be a participatory, collaborative project. Watching television shows or films together could promote productive discussions between teachers and students (or parents and children), with emphasis on eliciting students' views, producing a variety of interpretations of media texts and teaching basic principles of hermeneutics and criticism. Students and youth are often more media savvy, knowledgeable and immersed in media culture than their teachers, and thus can contribute to the educational process through sharing their ideas, perceptions and insights. On the other hand, critical discussion, debate and analysis ought to be encouraged, with teachers bringing to bear their critical perspectives on student readings of media material. Since media culture is often part and parcel of students' identity and most powerful cultural experience, teachers must be sensitive in criticizing artifacts and perceptions that students hold dear; yet an atmosphere of critical respect for difference *and* inquiry into the nature and effects of media culture should be promoted.

Media literacy thus involves developing conceptions of interpretation and criticism. Engaging in assessment and evaluation of media texts is particularly challenging and entails careful discussion of specific moral, pedagogical, political or aesthetic criteria of critique. That is, one can, *à la* British cultural studies, engage the politics of representation in discussing the specific images of gender, class, race, ethnicity, sexual preference or other identity categories in media texts (Kellner, 1995a). Or one could discuss the moral values and behaviour represented, what specific messages or representations of social experience are presented, how they are interpreted by audiences, and potential pedagogical effects. One can also attempt to determine criteria for aesthetic evaluation, discussing what constitutes a good or bad media text.

In developing media literacy, one needs to develop sensitivity to visual imagery, sound and discourse, as well as to narrative structure and textual meaning and effects. Thus, one draws upon the aesthetics developed in literary, film and video, and art studies, combining such material in addressing the specificities of the particular text or artifact in question. Media studies is exciting and challenging in that it can embrace artifacts ranging from familiar film and television programmes, to popular music, to buildings and cities.

A major challenge in developing critical media literacy, however, results from the fact that it is not a pedagogy in the traditional sense with firmly established principles, a canon of texts and tried-and-true teaching procedures. Critical media pedagogy is in its infancy: it is just beginning to produce results, and is thus more open and experimental than established print-oriented pedagogy. Moreover, the material of media culture is so polymorphous, multivalent and polysemic that it necessitates sensitivity to different readings, interpretations and perceptions of the complex images, scenes, narratives, meanings and messages of media culture which in its own ways is as complex and challenging to decipher critically as book culture.

It is also highly instructive to teach students at all levels to explore critically *popular* media materials, including the most familiar film, television, music and other forms of media culture. Yet, here one needs to avoid an uncritical media populism, of the sort that is emerging within certain sectors of British and North American cultural studies. In a review of *Rethinking Media Literacy* (McLaren et al., 1995), for instance, Jon Lewis attacked what he saw as the overly critical postures of the contributors to that volume, arguing: 'If the point of a critical media literacy is to meet students halfway – to begin to take seriously what *they* take seriously, to read what *they* read, to watch what *they* watch – teachers *must* learn to love pop culture' (1996: 26). Note the authoritarian injunction that 'teachers *must* learn to love pop culture' (italics are Lewis's), followed by an attack on more critical approaches to media literacy.

Teaching critical media literacy, however, involves occupation of a site above the dichotomy of fandom and censor. One can teach how media culture provides significant statements or insights about the social world, empowering visions of gender, race and class, or complex aesthetic structures and practices, thus putting a positive spin on how it can provide significant contributions to education. Yet one ought to indicate also how media culture can advance sexism, racism, ethnocentrism, homophobia and other forms of prejudice, as well as misinformation, problematic ideologies and questionable values, thus promoting a dialectical approach to the media.

Furthermore, critical media literacy teaching should engage students' interests and concerns, and involve a collaborative approach between teachers and students since students are deeply absorbed in media culture and may know more about some of its artifacts and domains than their teachers. Consequently, students should be encouraged to speak, discuss and intervene in the teaching/learning process. This is not to say that media literacy training should romanticize student views that may be superficial, mistaken, uninformed and full of various problematical biases. Yet exercises in media literacy can often productively involve intense student participation in a mutual learning process where teachers and students together learn media literacy skills and competencies.

It is also probably a mistake to attempt to institute a top-down program of media literacy, with fixed texts, curricula and prescribed materials. Diverse teachers and students will have very different interests and concerns, and will naturally emphasize varying subject matter and choose examples relevant to their own and their students' interests. Courses in critical media literacy could thus be flexible enough to enable teachers and students to constitute their own curricula to address material and topics of current concern, and to engage their own interests. Moreover, and crucially, educators should discern that we are in the midst of one of the most intense technological revolutions in history and must learn to adapt new computer technologies to education and to develop new literacies.

COMPUTER LITERACY: AN EXPANDED CONCEPT

In this section, which is looking toward education in the new millennium, I want to argue that students should learn new forms of computer literacy. This involves learning how to use computer technologies to do research and gather information, as well as to perceive computer culture as a terrain which contains texts, spectacles, games and interactive multimedia which call for new literacies. Moreover, computer culture is a discursive and political matrix in which students, teachers and citizens can all intervene, engaging in discussion groups and collaborative research projects, creating their websites, producing innovative multimedia for cultural dissemination, and engaging in novel modes of social interaction and learning. Computer culture enables individuals to participate actively in the production of culture, ranging from discussion of public issues to creation of their own cultural forms. However, to take part in this culture not only requires enhancing skills of print literacy, which are often restricted to the growing elite of students who are privileged to attend adequate and superior public and private schools, but also demands new forms of literacy, thus posing significant challenges to education.

It is a defining fact of the present age that computer culture is proliferating and transforming every dimension of life from work to education. Thus to respond intelligently to the dramatic technological revolution of our time we need to begin teaching computer literacy from an early age. 'Computer literacy', however, itself needs to be theorized. Often the term is synonymous with technical ability to use computers, to master existing programs, and maybe undertake some programming oneself. I suggest expanding the conception of computer literacy from using computer programs and hardware to a broader concept of information and multimedia literacy. This necessitates promoting more sophisticated abilities in traditional reading and writing, as well as the capability to critically dissect cultural forms taught as part of critical media literacy and multimedia pedagogy.

In my expanded conception, computer literacy thus involves learning how to use computers, access information and educational material, use e-mail and list servers, and construct websites. Computer literacy comprises the accessing and processing of diverse sorts of information proliferating in the so-called 'information society' (for critiques of this concept see Webster, 1995). It encompasses learning to find sources of information ranging from traditional sites like libraries and print media to new Internet websites and search engines. Computer information literacy involves learning where information is found, how to access it, and how to organize, interpret and evaluate it.

One exciting development in the current technological revolution is that library materials and information are accessible from the entire world. To some extent, the Internet is potentially the all-encompassing library, imperfectly constructed in Alexandria, Egypt, that would contain the great books of the world. Yet while a mind-boggling number of the classics are found on the Internet, we still need the local library to access and collect books, journals and print material not found on the Internet, as well as the essential texts of various disciplines and the culture as a whole. Information literacy, however, and the new tasks for librarians, thus also involve knowing what one can and cannot find on the Internet, how to access it, and where the most reliable and useful information is at hand for specific tasks and projects.

But computer and information literacies also involve learning how to read hypertexts, to traverse the ever-changing fields of cyberculture, and to participate in a digital and interactive multimedia culture that encompasses work, education, politics, culture and everyday life. There are two major domains of hypertext: one that is primarily literary and involves avant-garde literary/writing strategies and practices (see Joyce, 1995), and one that is more multimedia, multisemiotic and multimodal and that mushroomed into the World Wide Web. Hypertext was initially seen as an innovative and exciting new mode of writing which increased the potential for writers to explore novel modes of textuality and expression (Landow, 1992; 1997). As multimedia hypertext developed on the Internet, it was soon theorized as a multisemiotic and multimodal form of culture. This mode is now increasingly seen as the dominant form of a new hyperlinked, interactive and multimedia cyberculture (see Burbules and

Callister, 1996; 2000; Snyder 1996; and the articles in Snyder, 1997).[11]

Hence, on this conception, genuine computer literacy involves not just technical knowledge and skills, but refined reading, writing, research and communicating ability that involves heightened capacities for critically accessing, analysing, interpreting, processing and storing both print-based and multimedia material. In a new information/ entertainment society, immersed in transformative multimedia technology, knowledge and information come not merely in the form of print and words, but through images, sounds and multimedia material as well. Computer literacy thus also involves the ability to discover and access information, as well as the intensified ability to read, to scan texts and computer databases and websites, and to access information and images in a variety of forms, ranging from graphics, to visual images, to audio and video materials, to good old print media. The creation of new multimedia websites, databases and texts requires accessing, downloading and organizing the digitized verbal, imagistic, and audio and video materials that are the new building blocks of multimedia culture.

Within multimedia computerized culture, visual literacy takes on increased importance. On the whole, computer screens are more graphic, visual and interactive than conventional print fields. This disconcerted many of us when first confronted with the new environments. Icons, windows, mouses and the various clicking, linking and interaction functions involved in computer-mediated hypertext dictate new competencies and a dramatic expansion of literacy. Visuality is obviously crucial, compelling one to quickly scan visual fields, perceive and interact with icons and graphics, and use technical devices such as a mouse to access the desired material and field. But tactility is also important, as one must learn the navigational skills of how to proceed from one field and screen to another, how to negotiate hypertexts and links, and how to move from one program to another if one operates, as most now do, in a window-based computer environment.

Thus, in my expanded conception, computer literacy involves technical abilities concerning developing basic typing skills, mastering computer programs, accessing information, and using computer technologies for a variety of purposes ranging from interpersonal communication to artistic expression to political debate. There are ever more hybridizations between media and computer culture as audio and video material becomes part of the Internet, as CD-ROM and multimedia develop, and as new media and technologies become part and parcel of the home, school and workplace. Therefore, the skills of decoding images, sounds and spectacle learned in critical media literacy training can also be valuable as part of computer literacy as well.

MULTIMEDIA AND MULTIPLE LITERACIES: THE NEW FRONTIER

The new multimedia environments thus necessitate a diversity of types of multisemiotic and multi-modal interaction, involving interfacing with words and print material and often images, graphics, and audio and video material. As technological convergence develops apace, one needs to combine the skills of critical media literacy with traditional print literacy and new forms of multiple literacies to access and master the new multimedia hypertext environments. Literacy in this conception involves the abilities to engage effectively in socially constructed forms of communication and representation. Thus, while reading and interpreting print was the appropriate mode of literacy for books, critical media literacy entails reading and interpreting discourse, images, spectacle, narratives and the forms and genres of media culture. Forms of multimedia communication involve print, speech, visuality and audio, in a hybrid field which combines these forms, all of which involve skills of interpreting and critique.

The term 'multiple literacies' thus points to the many different kinds of literacies needed to access, interpret, criticize and participate in the emergent new forms of culture and society.[12] Obviously, the key notions here is the multiple, the proliferation of media and forms that demands a multiplicity of competencies and skills and abilities to access, interact and help construct a new semiotic terrain. Multiple literacies involve reading across varied and hybrid semiotic fields and being able to critically and hermeneutically process print, graphics and representations, as well as moving images and sounds. The term 'hybridity' suggests the combination and interaction of diverse media and the need to synthesize the various forms in an active process of the construction of meaning. Reading a music video, for instance, involves processing images, music, spectacle and sometimes narrative in a multisemiotic activity that simultaneously draws on diverse aesthetic forms. Interacting with a website or CD-ROM often involves scanning text, graphics and moving images, and clicking onto the fields that one seeks to peruse and explore, looking for appropriate material. This might lead one to draw upon a multiplicity of materials in new interactive learning or entertainment environments, whereby one must simultaneously read and interpret images, graphics, animation and text.

While traditional literacies concern practices in contexts that are governed by rules and conventions, multiliteracies are currently evolving so that their pedagogies comprise a new, although bustling and competitive field. Multimedia sites are not entirely new, however. Multisemiotic textuality was first evident in newspapers (consider the difference between *The New York Times* and *USA Today* in terms of image, text, colour graphics, design and content) and is now evident in textbooks that are much more visual, graphic and multimodal than the previously linear and discursive texts of old. But it is CD-ROMs, websites and new multimedia that are the most distinctively multimodal and multisemiotic forms. These sites are the new frontier of learning and literacy, the great challenge to education for the millennium. As we move further into the twenty-first century, we need to theorize the literacies necessary to interact in these emergent multimedia environments and to gain the skills that will enable individuals to learn, work and create in emergent cultural spaces and domains.

Cultivating new literacies and reconstructing education for democratization will also involve constructing new pedagogies and social relations. New multimedia technologies enable group projects for students and more of a problem-solving pedagogy *à la* Dewey and Freire than traditional top-down teaching models.[13] If students are to access information, engage in cultural communication and production, and gain the skills necessary to succeed in the new economy and culture, they are compelled to acquire enhanced literacies, to work cooperatively with others, and to navigate new cultural and social terrains. Such group activity may generate more egalitarian relations between teachers and students and more democratic and cooperative social relations. Of course, it also demands reconsideration of grading and testing procedures, rethinking the roles of teacher and student, and constructing projects and pedagogies appropriate to the new cultural and social environments.

Moreover, we are soon going to have to rethink standard assessment tests and other instruments in relation to the new media and technologies; having the literacy and skills to successfully access material sought after, communicate, work and create within computer and multimedia culture is quite different from reading and writing in the mode of print literacy. While traditional skills of reading and writing continue to be of the utmost importance in cyberculture, they are sublated within multiliteracy, so eventually an entirely different sort of test is going to need to be devised in order to register individuals' multiliteracy competencies and to predict success in a new technological and educational environment. In this new environment, it becomes increasingly irrational to focus education on producing higher test scores on exams that themselves are becoming obsolete and outdated by the changes in the economy, society and culture.[14]

Critical pedagogies of the future must also confront the problem of online education, of how the emergent cultural terrain of cyberspace produces new sites of information, education and culture, as well as novel online forms of interaction between students and teacher. In addition, possibilities of students developing their own spaces, cultural forms, and modes of interaction and communication should be promoted. The challenge will also arise of how to balance classroom instruction with online instruction, as well as sorting out the strengths and limitations of print versus online multimedia material.[15] Indeed, the new media and cultural spaces require us to rethink education in its entirety, ranging from the role of the teacher, through teacher–student relations, classroom instruction, grading and testing, and the value and limitations of books, multimedia and other teaching material, to the goals of education itself.

Online education and virtual learning also confront us with novel problems such as copyright and ownership of educational materials; collaborations between computer programmers, artists and designers, and teachers and students in the construction of teaching material and sites; and the respective role of federal and local government, the community, corporations and private organizations in financing education and providing the skills and tools necessary for a new world economy and global culture. Furthermore, the technological revolution of our time forces a rethinking of philosophical problems of knowledge, truth, identity and reality in virtual environments. Hence, both philosophy and the philosophy of education most be reconstructed to meet the challenges of democracy and a new high-tech economy.

The technological revolution thus forces us to radically rethink and reconstruct education. The terrain and goals of education must be reconsidered and the conception of literacy expanded. Questions of the digital divide must be confronted and the ways that education can promote democratization and social justice should be discussed and developed. While there are certainly dangers that the technological revolution will increase divisions between haves and have nots, it is possible that old gender, race and class divisions can be overcome in a society that rewards new literacies and provides opportunities for those who have developed competencies in the new media and culture. In this context, it is especially important that appropriate resources, training and pedagogies be constructed to help those groups and communities who were disadvantaged and marginalized during the past epoch of industrialization and modernity.

In addition, individuals should be given the capacities to understand, critique and transform the social and cultural conditions in which they live, gaining capacities to be creative and transformative subjects and not just objects of domination and manipulation. This necessitates developing critical thinking, reflection, and the ability to engage in discourse, cultural creation, and political action and movements. Active and engaged subjects are produced in social interaction with others, as well as with tools and techniques, so social skills and individual capacities for communication, creativity and action must be part of the multiple literacies that a radical reconstruction of education seeks and cultivates.

Crucially, multiliteracies and new pedagogies must become reflective and critical, aware of the educational, social and political assumptions involved in the restructuring of education and society that we are now undergoing. In response to the excessive hype concerning new technologies and education, it is necessary to maintain the critical dimension and to reflect upon the nature and effects of new media and the pedagogies developed as a response to their challenge. Many advocates of new media and technologies, however, eschew critique for a purely affirmative agenda. For instance, after an excellent discussion of new modes of literacy and the need to rethink education, Gunther Kress (1997) argues that we must move from critique to design, beyond a negative deconstruction to more positive construction.

But rather than following such modern logic of either/or, we need to pursue the logic of both/and, perceiving design and critique, deconstruction and reconstruction, as complementary and supplementary rather than as antithetical choices. Certainly, we need to design alternative technologies, pedagogies and curricula for the future, and should attempt to design new social and pedagogical relations as well, but we need to criticize misuse, inappropriate use, overinflated claims, and exclusions and oppressions involved in the introduction of new media into education. The critical dimension is needed more than ever as we attempt to develop improved teaching strategies and pedagogy, and design new pedagogies and curricula. In this process, we must be constantly critical, practising critique and self-criticism, questioning our assumptions, discourses and practices, as we experimentally develop novel and alternative literacies and pedagogy.

In all educational and other experiments, critique is indeed of fundamental importance. From the Deweyan perspective, progressive education involves trial and error, design and criticism. The experimental method itself comprises critique of limitations, failures and flawed design. In discussing new media and multiple literacies, one also needs to constantly raise the question of whose interests these new media and pedagogies serve. Are they serving all social groups and individuals? If not, who is being excluded and why? We also need to raise the question of the extent to which new media and literacies are preparing students and citizens for the present and future and producing conditions for a more vibrant democratic society, or simply reproducing existing inequalities and injustice.

Finally, creating multiple literacies must be contextual, engaging the lifeworld of the students and teachers participating in the new adventures of education. Learning involves developing abilities to interact intelligently with one's environment and fellow humans, and calls for vibrant social and conversational environments. Education requires doing and can be gained from practice and social interaction. One can obviously spend too much time with technologies and fail to develop basic social skills and competencies. As Rousseau, Wollstonecraft and Dewey argued, education involves developing proficiencies that enable individuals to develop successfully within their concrete environments, to learn from practice, and to be able to interact, work and create in their own societies and cultures. In contemporary US culture, for instance, multiple literacies necessitate multicultural literacies – being able to understand and work with a heterogeneity of cultural groups and forms, acquiring literacies in a multiplicity of media, and gaining the competencies to participate in a democratic culture and society (see Courts, 1998; Weil, 1998).

RECONSTRUCTING EDUCATION

From the policy perspective, it seems clear that it is the duty of the federal, state and local government, as well as other interested parties, to provide the necessary equipment and tools to teachers, students and schools in order to make it possible for education to cultivate the skills necessary for participation in the new global economy, networked society and cyberculture. Second, it is necessary that teachers have proper training to make use of the technology in their classrooms and that there are labs with training or support people who have the proper skills and can ensure that teachers and students can effectively deploy the new media and technologies.[16] Recent studies have indicated that without proper teacher training the technology itself will not do the teaching and may be a source of frustration, thus blocking the educational goals desired (see Rawls, 2000; Zimmerman, 2000). Consequently, teacher training and intelligent computer lab design and use, as well as development of more intelligent and user-friendly software, are necessary to improve education in the information age.

But, as I have argued in this chapter, teachers and students need to develop new pedagogies and modes of learning in the new information and multimedia environment. This could involve a democratization and restructuring of education such as was envisaged by John Dewey and Paolo Friere in which education is seen as a dialogical, democraticizing and experimental practice. New information technologies encourage the sort of experimental and collaborative projects proposed by Dewey (1997 [1916]) as important for progressive education. This could also involve the more dialogical relations between student and teachers envisaged by Paolo Freire (1972; 1998) in which teachers learn from students and promote collaborative, dialogical and non-authoritarian teaching methods.

This re-visioning of education involves the recognition that teachers can learn from students and that often students are ahead of teachers in various technological literacies and technical abilities. Many of us (and this is true of myself) have learned much of what we know of computers and new media and technologies from students. We should also recognize the extent to which young people helped invent the Internet and have grown up in a cyberculture in which they may have cultivated technological skills from an early age.[17] Peer-to-peer communication among young people is highly sophisticated and developed, and democratic pedagogies should build upon and enhance these resources and practices.

One of the challenges of contemporary education is to overcome the disconnection between students' experiences, subjectivities and interests rooted in the new multimedia cyberculture, and those found in the classroom situation and grounded in print culture and traditional learning and disciplines (see Luke and Luke, 2001). As early as the 1960s, Marshall McLuhan (1964) had pointed to the disconnection experienced by students raised on radio, television and popular culture when confronted with print materials. Today, the disconnection is even more striking in the contrast between an interactive and multimedia cyberculture and traditional forms of authoritarian lecturing and problematic print materials, thus suggesting a generational divide as well as a digital divide.

The disconnection and divides can be overcome, however, by more actively and collaboratively bringing students into interactive classrooms or learning situations in which they are able to transmit their skills and knowledge to fellow students and teachers alike. Such a democratic and interactive reconstruction of education thus provides the resources for progressive social reconstruction, as well as cultivating the new skills and literacies needed for the emergent global economy and cyberculture. So far, arguments for restructuring education mostly come from the high-tech and corporate sector who are primarily interested in new media and literacies and the reconstruction of education for the workforce and economy. But restructuring can serve the interests of democratization as well as the global economy. Following Dewey, we should accordingly press for education that is aimed at producing better democratic citizens, as well as players in the new economy.

Further, to cultivate new literacies for democratizing education and society in the new millennium, we need the Deweyan experimental method of trying out and testing ideas in how computers and new information technology can aid reading, research and the teaching of traditional material. This involves trial and error, attempting to discern what works and what does not in using new media to democratize and enhance education. Thus, like Dewey, we need to perceive the interconnection of science, technology, education and democracy in the present conjuncture. To have an enlivened democracy, we must have educated and informed citizens who require training in science and technology, and in the acquisition of new multiple literacies. Cultivating multiple literacies involves the scientific method of trial and error, seeking collaborative solutions to problems, and working together to reconstruct education and society democratically. As Dewey noted, this experimental and collaborative method is also the ethos of democracy, which involves dialogue, cooperation and working together, as well as designing and properly using voting machines. (I am, of course, ironically pointing to the non-results of the 2000 US presidential election, and suggesting a massive disconnection between the high-tech economy and cyberculture, and traditional voting machines and practices.)

It appears that technology will certainly drive the reconstruction of education, but we should make sure that it works to enhance democracy and empower individuals and not just corporations and a privileged technoelite. Producing democratic citizens and empowering the next generation for democracy as well as a new economy should be a major goal of the reconstruction of education in the new millennium. Moreover, as Freire (1972; 1998) reminds us, critical pedagogy comprises the skills of both reading the word and reading the world. Hence, multiple literacies include not only media and computer literacies, but a diverse range of social and cultural literacies, ranging from ecoliteracy (e.g. understanding the body and environment), to economic and financial literacy, to a variety of other competencies that enable us to live well in our social worlds. Education, at its best, provides the symbolic and cultural capital that empowers people to survive and prosper in an increasingly complex and changing world and the resources to produce a more cooperative, democratic, egalitarian and just society. Thus, with Plato, Rousseau, Wollstonecraft, Dewey, Freire and others, I see philosophy of education as reflecting on the good life and the good society and the ways that education can contribute to creating a better world. But as the world changes, so too must education, which will be part of the problem or part of the solution as we enter a new millennium.

The project of transforming education will take different forms in different contexts. In the over-developed countries, individuals must be empowered to work and act in a high-tech information economy, and thus must learn skills of media and computer literacy, in order to survive in the new social environment. Traditional skills of knowledge and critique must also be enhanced, so that students can name the system, describe and grasp the changes occurring and the defining features of the new global order, and learn to engage in critical and oppositional practice in the interests of democratization and progressive transformation. This process challenges us to develop a vision of how life can be, of alternatives to the present order, and of the necessity of struggle and political organization to realize progressive goals. Languages of knowledge and critique must thus be supplemented by the discourse of hope and praxis.

In much of the world, the struggle for daily existence is paramount and meeting unmet human and social needs is a high priority. Yet everywhere education can provide the competencies and skills to improve one's life, to create a better society, and to fashion a more civilized and developed world. Moreover, as the entire world becomes part of a global and networked society, gaining the multiple literacies discussed in this chapter is important everywhere as media and cyberculture become more ubiquitous and the world economy demands ever more sophisticated technical skills.

This is a time of challenge and a time for experiment. It is time to put existing pedagogies, practices and educational philosophies in question and to construct new ones. It is a time for new pedagogical experiments to see what works and what doesn't work in the new millennium. It is a time to reflect on our goals and to discern what we want to achieve with education and how we can achieve it. Ironically, it is a time to return to the classical philosophy of education which situates reflections on education within reflections on the good life and society, at the same time as we consider how we can transform education to become relevant to a high-tech society. It is time to return to John Dewey, to rethink that intimate connection between education and democracy at the same time as we address the multicultural challenges that Dewey – in the midst of a still vital melting-pot ideology and liberal progressivist optimism – did not address.

Most saliently, it is time to take up the Deweyan attitude of pragmatic experimentation to see what it is that the new media and technologies can and cannot do in order to see how they can enhance education. But we should also resist the hype, maintain a critical attitude and pedagogy, and continue to combine print literacy and classical materials with new literacies and materials. It is a mistake to advance an either/or logic of print literacy versus computer literacy, or to privilege books over new media, for both can enhance education and life and require different literacies. In the current turbulent situation of the global restructuring of capitalism and worldwide struggles for democratization, I believe that we have for the first time in decades a chance to reconstruct education and society. In this conjuncture, technology is a revolutionizing force, whereby all political parties and candidates pay lip service to education, to overcoming the digital divide, and to expanding literacy.[18] Hence, the time is ripe to take up the

challenge and to move to reconstruct education and society so that groups and individuals excluded from the benefits of the economy, culture and society may more fully participate and receive opportunities not possible in earlier social constellations.

NOTES

An earlier and different version of this study appeared in *Educational Theory* (Kellner, 1998) and I am grateful to its editor Nicholas Burbules for discussion that helped develop my ideas. A later version was published in a Routledge volume on multiculturalism (Kellner, 1999b), edited by George Katsiaficas and Teodros Kiros, and I am thankful to the editors for discussions which helped with clarification of my position on multiculturalism and education. Yet another version was presented at UCLA on 26 February 1998 at my Kneller Chair Inaugural Lecture, and I am grateful to members of the audience for discussion of the issues that I am engaging with. The chapter was also presented at the Philosophy of Education Society Convention in Toronto on 1 April 2000, and I am grateful to this audience for vigorous polemic and to commentator Nicholas Burbules for constructive critique and supplementation, which helped in the production of this text. Finally, I was able to refine ideas in this chapter at the October 2000 PacBell/UCLA Conference on informational literacy and at the California Association for the Philosophy of Education (CAPE) meetings at UCLA the same month, and am also thankful to audiences at these events for constructive commentary and discussion, especially Aimee Dorr and Howard Besser who organized the PacBell/UCLA conference and participated in CAPE discussions. For ongoing discussions of the issues in this chapter I am especially grateful to Rhonda Hammer and Allan and Carmen Luke.

1 Studies reveal that women, minorities and immigrants now constitute roughly 85 per cent of the growth in the labour force, while these groups represent about 60 per cent of all workers (see Duderstadt, 1999–2000: 38). In the past decade, the number of Hispanics in the United States increased by 35 per cent and Asians by more than 40 per cent. Since 1991, California has had no single, dominant ethnic or racial minority and almost half of the high school students in the state are African-American or Latino. Meanwhile, a 'tidal wave' of children of baby boomers are about to enter college (see Atkinson, 1999–2000: 49–50). Obviously, I am writing this study from a US perspective, but would suggest that my arguments have broader reference in an increasingly globalized society marked by a networked economy, increasing migration and multiculturalism, and a proliferating Internet-based cyberculture.

2 There is by now a tremendous number of books and articles on the new economy, technological revolution, emergent cybercultural spaces and the implications for every aspect of life from education to war. See, for example, the monumental studies by Castells (1996; 1997;

1998) and the analyses of the restructuring of capital, technological revolution and the postmodern turn in Best and Kellner (2001).

3 For materials pertaining to the educational reform proposed by Dewey and Freire and the broader conceptions of relating education to creation of the good life and good society advanced by Plato, Rousseau, Wollstonecraft and others which inform this chapter, see my philosophy of education website, my education and technology website which contains materials pertinent to this study. www.gseis.ucla.edu/faculty/kellner/kellner.html.

4 The 'digital divide' has emerged as the buzzword for perceived divisions between information technology haves and have nots in the current economy and society. A US Department of Commerce report released in July 1999 claimed that the digital divide in relation to race is dramatically escalating and the Clinton administration and media picked up on this theme (see the report 'Americans in the information age: falling through the net' at http://www.ntia.doc.gov/ntiahome/digitaldivide/). A critique of the data involved in the report emerged, claiming that they were outdated; more recent studies by Stanford University, Cheskin Research, A.C. Nielson, and the Forester Institute claim that education and class are more significant factors than race in constructing the divide (see http:cyberatlas.internet.com/bigpicture/demographics for a collection of reports and statistics on the divide). In any case, it is clear that there is a gaping division between information technology haves and have nots, that this is a major challenge to developing an egalitarian and democratic society, and that something needs to be done about the problem. My contribution involves the argument that empowering the have nots requires the dissemination of new literacies, thus empowering groups and individuals previously excluded from economic opportunities and sociopolitical participation.

5 See the recent PhD dissertations by two of my UCLA students, Jennifer Janofsky Rawls (2000) and Roy Zimmermann (2000). See also Bernard Warner, 'Computers for youth: spreading the net', *The Standard*, 27 March 2000, which reports: 'A study conducted recently by Denver-based Quality Education Data showed school districts across the country spent $6.7 billion on technology in the 1998–1999 school year, up almost 25 per cent from the previous year. But the same study revealed that an equally crucial funding component – computer training for teachers – was startlingly low, rising just 5.2 per cent over the same period.' In June 2000, however, President Bill Clinton argued for increased funding for teacher training to use new technologies, so it appears that there is growing recognition of the problem.

6 On the need for a critical theory of technology to overcome technophobia and technophilia, see Kellner (1999a) and Best and Kellner (2001). For arguments on the need to reconstruct technology to meet the needs of democratization, see Feenberg (1991; 1995; 1999).

7 I am occasionally attacked for 'optimism' when I make proposals advocating the use of media and information technologies for democratization and social reconstruction. I would argue, however, that we need to go beyond the dichotomies of optimism and pessimism, that a gloomy pessimism gets us nowhere, and that while there are plenty of troubling phenomena to criticize, Gramsci's 'pessimism of the intellect, optimism of the will' is the most productive way to engage the problems and dangers of the contemporary era, rather than pessimistic 'critique' that is devoid of positive proposals for reconstruction and change. I am thus aware that there are serious challenges to democracy and causes for grave concern in regard to the development of the global economy and the technological revolution, but in this study I am concentrating on a positive reconstructive agenda. For more critical concerns regarding these issues, see Best and Kellner (2001).

8 The New London Group (Cazden et al., 1996) has produced the concept of 'multiliteracy' to describe the types of literacy required to engage new multimedia technology, while Semali and Watts Pailliotet (1999) and their collaborators propose the concept 'intermediality' to call attention to the need to generate literacies that allow interaction between various media and new multimedia, and that promote interdisciplinary and interactive education in an attempt to create education that facilitates democratic social change. I develop a concept of multiple literacies in the pages that follow.

9 For an earlier and expanded discussion of media literacy, see Kellner (1998). Carson and Friedman (1995) contains studies discussing the use of media to deal with multicultural education. Examples of teaching media literacy which I draw on include Masterman (1989 [1985]), Kellner and Ryan (1988), Schwoch et al. (1992), Fleming (1993), Giroux (1992; 1993; 1994; 1996), Giroux and McLaren (1994), Sholle and Densky (1994), McLaren et al. (1995), Kellner (1995a; 1995b), Luke (1996; 1997a; 1997b), Giroux and Shannon (1997) and Semali and Watts Pailliotet (1999). See also the work of Barry Duncan and the Canadian Association for Media Literacy (website: http://www.nald.ca/province/que/litcent/media.htm) and the Los Angeles based Center for Media Literacy (www.medialit.org). It is a scandal that there are not more efforts to promote media literacy throughout the school system of K–12 and into the university. Perhaps the ubiquity of computer and multimedia culture will awaken educators and citizens to the importance of developing media literacy to create individuals empowered to intelligently access, read, interpret and criticize contemporary media and cyberculture.

10 On multicultural literacy, see Courts (1998) and Weil (1998).

11 Yet some early advocates of hypertext attacked the emergence of the World Wide Web as a debased medium which regressed to the field of earlier media, like television, forcing the word to renegotiate its power against the image and spectacles of sight and sound, once again decentring the written word: see, for instance, Joyce (1995) and the discussion in Landow (1992; 1997). As the Internet becomes a multimedia hypertext, however, it is clear that contemporary education must teach reading a multimodal hypertext as a basic skill and mode of literacy.

12 For other recent conceptions of multimedia literacy that I draw upon here, see the discussions of literacies needed for reading hypertext in Burbules and Callister (1996; 2000); the concept of multiliteracy in the New London Group (Cazden et al., 1996) and Luke (1997a; 1997b); and the papers in Snyder (1997) and Semali and Watts Pailliotet (1999).

13 Since some people associated with critical pedagogy are technophobes, it is interesting that Freire was positive toward media and new technologies, seeing technologies as potential tools for empowering citizens, as well as instruments of domination in the hands of ruling elites. Freire wrote that: 'Technical and scientific training need not be inimical to humanistic education as long as science and technology in the revolutionary society are at the service of permanent liberation, of humanization' (1972: 157). Freire also stated that: 'It is not the media themselves which I criticize, but the way they are used' (1972: 136). Moreover, he argued for the importance of teaching media literacy to empower individuals against manipulation and oppression, and of using the most appropriate media to help teach the subject matter in question (1972: 114–16).

14 On the centrality of preparation for exams in contemporary education and the role of standardized tests in the US educational and social system, see Lemann (1999). While I have not myself researched the policy literature on this issue, in the many discussions of SATs and their biases which I have read, I have not encountered critiques that indicate the obsolescence of many standardized tests in a new technological environment and the need to come up with new testing procedures based on the new cultural and social fields that we are increasingly immersed in. I would predict that proposals for devising such tests will emerge and that this issue will be hotly debated and contested in the future.

15 For sensible critiques of online education see Feenberg (1999).

16 It is encouraging that computers and new technologies are getting into the schools in the US at an impressive rate. The 25 September 2000 US News & World Report notes that in 1994 when Present Clinton vowed to connect every school to the information superhighway, only one in three schools, and just 3 per cent of the classrooms, were wired to the Internet. But by 1999, according to the National Center for Education Statistics, 95 per cent of schools and 63 per cent of classrooms had Internet access. The 2000 News and World Report showed that 76 per cent of the public polled believed that the US government should support efforts to train teachers to use new technologies in their classrooms, and that those surveyed said that they saw new technologies and gaining necessary literacies and skills as essential to their own professional and personal advancement; that 71 per cent thought that the Internet could enhance their own educational level; while 86 per cent thought that the net could help their children learn more and that 71 per cent claimed that they had gone online for educational reasons – up from 36 per cent when the same group was polled in 1999.

17 For instance, Mosaic, Netscape and the first browsers were invented by young computer users, as were many of the first websites, list servers, chat rooms and so on. A hacker culture emerged that was initially conceptualized as a reconfiguring and improving of computer systems, and was related to design, system and use, before the term became synonymous with theft and mischief, such as setting loose worms and viruses.

18 Openings for addressing the problems of the digital divide are widespread. See the articles on efforts by the UN, US governmental agencies, the G8 countries, corporations and local groups to address the challenge in the 3 April 2000 yahoo.com website. They include a 3 April 2000 Reuters report that the UN 'sets ambitious goals for the new millennium to overcome the digital divide'; a 2 April AFP report that 'G8 powers vow to bridge the "digital divide"'; a 29 March AP report that 'Lawmakers Mull Rural Web Services'; a 28 March BBC report on Britain's digital divide and efforts to overcome it; a 27 March Industry Standard report on local efforts to provide computer access to minority youth; and a 24 March BBC report that 'Clinton warns of cyber divide' (http://fullcoverage.yahoo.com/Full-Coverage/Tech/Digital-Divide/). I am arguing, however, that without promotion of a broader conception of computer and multimedia literacy, efforts to address the divide will be limited and flawed. Hence, educators and citizens of the future will either be part of the solution in working to solve the intractable problems of social justice by helping to empower groups and individuals on the have-not side of the divide, or part of the problem in continuing business as usual while divides between the haves and the have nots perhaps widen and intensify. For my reflections on how new technologies are being used by new social movements to promote progressive social change, see Kellner (1999a; 2000).

REFERENCES

Atkinson, Richard C. (1999–2000) 'The future arrives first in California', Issues in Science and Technology (Winter): 43–51.

Best, Steven and Kellner, Douglas (2001) The Postmodern Adventure. New York: Guilford.

Burbules, Nicholas C. and Callister, Thomas (1996) 'Knowledge at the crossroads: some alternative futures of hypertext learning environments', Educational Theory, 46 (1): 23–50.

Burbules, Nicholas C. and Callister, Thomas (2000) Watch IT: the Risks and Promises of Information Technology. Boulder, CO: Westview.

Carson, Diane and Friedman, Lester D. (1995) Shared Differences: Multicultural Media and Practical Pedagogy. Urbana and Chicago: University of Illinois Press.

Castells, Manuel (1996) The Rise of the Network Society. Oxford: Blackwell.

Castells, Manuel (1997) The Power of Identity. Oxford: Blackwell.

Castells, Manuel (1998) End of Millennium. Oxford: Blackwell.

Cazden, Courtney, Cope, Bill, Fairclough, Norman, Gee, James, Kalantzis, Mary, Kress, Gunter, Luke, Allan, Luke, Carmen, Michaels, Sarah and Nakata, Martin (1996) 'A pedagogy of multiliteracies: designing social futures', *Harvard Educational Review*, 66: 60–92.

Courts, Patrick L. (1998) *Multicultural Literacies: Dialect, Discourses, and Diversity*. New York: Lang.

Dewey, John (1997 [1916]) *Democracy and Education*. New York: Free Press.

Duderstadt, James J. (1999–2000) 'New roles for the 21st century university', *Issues in Science and Technology* (Winter): 37–44.

Feenberg, Andrew (1991) *Critical Theory of Technology*. New York: Oxford University Press.

Feenberg, Andrew (1995) *Alternative Modernity*. Berkeley, CA: University of California Press.

Feenberg, Andrew (1999) *Questioning Technology*. New York and London: Routledge.

Fleming, Dan (1993) *Media Teaching*. Oxford: Blackwell.

Freire, Paulo (1972) *Pedagogy of the Oppressed*. New York: Herder & Herder.

Freire, Paulo (1998) *A Paulo Freire Reader*. New York: Herder & Herder.

Giroux, Henry (1992) *Border Crossing*. New York: Routledge.

Giroux, Henry (1993) *Living Dangerously: Multiculturalism and the Politics of Difference*. New York: Lang.

Giroux, Henry (1994) *Disturbing Pleasures*. New York: Routledge.

Giroux, Henry (1996) *Fugitive Cultures: Race, Violence, and Youth*. New York: Routledge.

Giroux, Henry and McLaren, Peter (eds) (1994) *Between Borders. Pedagogy and the Politics of Cultural Studies*. New York: Routledge.

Giroux, Henry and Shannon, Patrick (1997) *Education and Cultural Studies*. London and New York: Routledge.

Joyce, Michael (1995) *Of Two Minds: Hypertext Pedagogy and Politics*. Ann Arbor, MI: University of Michigan Press.

Kellner, Douglas (1990) *Television and the Crisis of Democracy*. Boulder, CO: Westview.

Kellner, Douglas (1995a) *Media Culture*. London and New York: Routledge.

Kellner, Douglas (1995b) 'Cultural studies, multiculturalism, and media culture', in Gail Dines and Jean Humez (eds), *Gender, Race, and Class in Media*. Thousand Oaks, CA and London: Sage. pp. 5–17.

Kellner, Douglas (1998) 'Multiple literacies and critical pedagogy in a multicultural society', *Educational Theory*, 48 (1): 103–22.

Kellner, Douglas (1999a) 'New technologies, the welfare state, and the prospects for democratization', in Andrew Calabrese and Jean-Claude Burgelman (eds), *Communication, Citizenship, and Social Policy*. Lanham, MD: Rowman & Littlefield. pp. 239–56.

Kellner, Douglas (1999b) 'Multiple literacies and critical pedagogy in a multicultural society', in George Katsiaficas and Teodros Kiros (eds), *The Promise of Multiculturalism*. New York: Routledge. pp. 211–36.

Kellner, Douglas (2000) 'Globalization and new social movements: lessons for critical theory and pedagogy', in Nicholas Burbules and Carlos Torres (eds), *Globalization and Education*. New York: Routledge.

Kellner, Douglas and Ryan, Michael (1988) *Camera Politica: the Politics and Ideology of Contemporary Hollywood Film*. Bloomington, IN: Indiana University Press.

Kress, Gunther (1997) 'Visual and verbal modes of representation in electronically mediated communication: the potentials of new forms of text', in Ilana Snyder (ed.), *Page to Screen: Taking Literacy into the Electronic Era*. New South Wales: Allen & Unwin. pp. 53–79.

Landow, George (1992) *Hypertext: the Convergence of Contemporary Critical Theory and Technology*. Baltimore, MD: Johns Hopkins University Press.

Landow, George (1997) *Hypertext 2.0*, 2nd edn. Baltimore, MD: Johns Hopkins University Press.

Lemann, Nicholas (1999) *The Big Test: the Secret History of the American Meritocracy*. New York: Farrar, Straus & Giroux.

Lewis, Jon (1996) 'Practice what you preach', *Afterimage* (Summer): 25–6.

Luke, Allan and Luke, Carmen (2001) 'Adolescence lost/childhood regained: on early intervention and the emergence of the techno-subject', *Journal of Literacy in Early Childhood*.

Luke, Carmen (1996) 'Reading gender and culture in media discourses and texts', in G. Bull and M. Anstey (eds), *The Literacy Lexicon*. New York and Sydney: Prentice-Hall.

Luke, Carmen (1997a) *Technological Literacy*. Melbourne: National Languages and Literacy Institute, Adult Literacy Network.

Luke, Carmen (1997b) 'Media literacy and cultural studies', in Sandy Muspratt, Allan Luke and Peter Freebody (eds), *Constructing Critical Literacies*. Cresskill, NY: Hampton. pp. 19–50.

Masterman, Len (1989 [1985]) *Teaching the Media*. London and New York: Routledge.

McLaren, Peter, Hammer, Rhonda, Sholle, David and Reilly, Susan (1995) *Rethinking Media Literacy: a Critical Pedagogy of Representation*. New York: Lang.

McLuhan, Marshall (1962) *The Gutenberg Galaxy*. New York: Signet.

McLuhan, Marshall (1964) *Understanding Media: the Extensions of Man*. New York: Signet.

Ong, Walter (1988) *Orality and Literacy: the Technologizing of the Word*. London and New York: Routledge.

Postman, Neil (1985) *Amusing Ourselves to Death*. New York: Viking-Penguin.

Postman, Neil (1992) *Technopolis: the Surrender of Culture to Technology*. New York: Random House.

Rawls, Jennifer Janofsky (2000) 'The role of micropolitics in school-site technology efforts: a case study of the relationship between Teachers and the technology movement at their school'. PhD dissertation, UCLA.

Schwoch, James, White, Mimi and Reilly, Susan (1992) *Media Knowledge*. Albany, NY: State University of New York Press.

Semali, Ladislau and Watts Pailliotet, Ann (1999) *Intermediality*. Boulder, CO: Westview.

Sholle, David and Densky, Stan (1994) *Media Education and the (Re)Production of Culture*. Westport, CT: Bergin & Garvey.

Snyder, Ilana (1996) *Hypertext: the Electronic Labyrinth*. Melbourne and New York: Melbourne University Press and New York University Press.

Snyder, Ilana (ed.) (1997) *Page to Screen: Taking Literacy into the Electronic Era*. New South Wales: Allen & Unwin.

Webster, Frank (1995) *Theories of the Information Society*. London and New York: Routledge.

Weil, Danny K. (1998) *Toward a Critical Multicultural Literacy*. New York: Lang.

Zimmerman, Roy (2000) 'The intersection of technology and teachers: challenges and problems'. PhD dissertation, UCLA.

7

Primary Issues in Internet Use: Access, Civic and Community Involvement, and Social Interaction and Expression

RONALD E. RICE

The Internet is being used by large numbers of the US population, and that usage is growing quickly. The Internet took seven years to achieve the same level of diffusion into US households – 30 per cent – that it took the telephone 38 years and the television 17 years to accomplish. The mid 2000 AOL national survey (based on a representative national telephone survey of those 18 or older who have online access in their homes) found that 76 million people (39 per cent of the US population) used the Internet, up from 45 million in 1998 (AOL, 2000). A study by UCLA in November 2000 reported that 66.9 per cent of Americans used the Internet; in the first quarter of 2000, approximately 55,000 people each day became new Internet users (UCLA, 2000). In December 2000, a Pew Institute report indicated that 56 per cent of the US population over 18, or 104 million, had access to the Internet (Yahoo!News, 2001). About 75 per cent of students older than 12, and 29 per cent of those under 12, had access to the Internet; 56 per cent of all users went online every day. Just a few months later, a Nielsen/NetRatings (2001) report found 60 per cent of US citizens, or a total of 168 million, used the Internet from home, work or both.

This rapid adoption of a new way to seek and distribute information, communicate with others, and sell goods and services naturally raises a vast range of enduring as well as new social and policy issues. This chapter reviews relevant research on three primary issues: (1) access, (2) civic, political and community involvement, and (3) social interaction and forms of expression. Rheingold (1993) identified three main consequences of the Internet and online communities similar to the second and third main issues: supporting citizen activity in politics and power, increased interactivity with diverse others, and a new vocabulary and form of communication. The following sections review these three research issues by grouping arguments and results into pessimistic and optimistic perspectives.

ACCESS

The first fundamental concern is access, including: who has or does not have access to the Internet; what motivates people to use the Internet; what barriers there are to usage; and what characterizes those who stop using the Internet (Katz and Aspden, 1997a; 1997b; 1997c). New technologies in general may bridge gaps between rich and poor, powerful and powerless, haves and have nots (for example, Downing, 1989; ECRL, 1999; Freire, 1969; Furlong, 1989; Greenberger and Puffer, 1989; NTIA, 1999; Pfaffenberger, 1990; Schon et al., 1999). New technologies may enhance or hinder access to information in a democracy (Deetz, 1989a; 1989b; Dervin, 1980; Dervin and Shields, 1990; Lievrouw, 1994; Murdock and Golding, 1989), in the workplace (Deetz, 1990;

Garson, 1988; Kraut, 1989; US Congress, 1987; Zuboff, 1988) or in broader social or cultural contexts (Bourque and Warren, 1987; Dervin and Shields, 1990; Krendl et al., 1989; Larose and Mettler, 1989; Mulgan, 1991; Pool, 1983; US Congress, 1990; Weinberg, 1987). While new communication technologies can provide new ways of participating and interacting, they may also widen existing gaps, further blocking access to those already without access (Gillespie and Robins, 1989; Hudson, 1988; Jansen, 1989; Rubinyi, 1989; Schiller, 1996; Wresch, 1996).

Access is the major public policy area for those who see the Internet as a universal service and a significant influence on political and economic equity (McCreadie and Rice, 1999a; 1999b; Rice et al., 2001). The usual term for this differential access to and use of the Internet according to gender, income, race and location is 'the digital divide' (Cooper and Kimmelman, 1999; Hoffman and Novak, 1998; Hoffman et al., 1996; McConnaughey and Lader, 1998).

While on the one hand the Internet and other communication and information technologies can increase human capital by providing better access to education and training, on the other hand those who do not have sufficient resources or experience will be further excluded from human and social capital (McNutt, 1998). Information labour markets will prefer individuals who have both current and prior access to, experience with, and skills necessary for communication networks. New applications, software and technologies require a good understanding of the Internet and existing communication protocols that are already in place, so even if those currently without access become users, they will still be disadvantaged (Carrier, 1998). Long-term disadvantages stemming from having no or delayed access accrue in less obvious ways, too. Bikson and Panis (1999: 156) discovered that employees who used computers in their jobs are paid 10 to 15 per cent more than non-computer users who hold similar positions. Besides economic benefits, communication technologies have greatly increased participation in communication activities such as decision-making and discussions at the workplace (Carrier, 1998). Individuals with communication and information access are generally better informed about their employers. They are aware of corporate decisions, and are usually more prepared to participate in decision-making processes. So there are major social and economic rationales for investing in increased access to all citizens, such as through community networks (McNutt, 1998). For example, Neu et al. (1999) provide examples of how e-mail can provide access and general citizen information to the elderly and governmental information to social security beneficiaries.

Pessimistic Perspective

Access to Computers and the Internet

Many studies show that minorities such as blacks and non-white Hispanics are much less likely to possess home computers and have less access to networks than whites and Asians and therefore miss the opportunity to participate in Internet activities (Neu et al., 1999). For example, Bikson and Panis (1999) summarize results from the 'Current Population Survey' conducted by the Bureau of the Census in 1993 (143, 129 respondents) and 1997 (123, 249 respondents). Concerning network services, in 1997, 7 per cent of individuals over age 60 and 11 per cent under age 20 used them, compared with 33 per cent between ages 20 and 59, all higher than in 1993. When socioeconomic variables were controlled, the gap between the under-20 users and 20–59 users decreased significantly. Controlling for other characteristics, the two younger groups have quite similar usage levels, but usage levels of older adults are still significantly lower. Usage of network services by those in the lowest income quartile (around $20,000) rose from 3 per cent in 1993 to 7 per cent in 1997, while usage by those in the highest quartile (above $60,000 per year) rose from 23 per cent to 45 per cent. Thus the gap associated with income *rose* over those four years, even after controlling for other variables, representing approximately a two-year time lag in adoption of online services between the bottom and top quartiles (1999: 12). Gaps in use of network services by educational level also rose, with usage in 1993 by 1 per cent of those without high school diplomas and 34 per cent by college graduates, rising to 5 per cent and 56 per cent in 1997 (these differences are statistically significant even after controlling for other factors). Concerning differences by race/ethnicity, usage by whites (13 per cent to 28 per cent) and Asians (10 per cent to 25 per cent) jumped between 1993 and 1997, while the growth rate for blacks, Hispanics and native Americans was fairly steady, again showing a widening gap, again controlling for other variables. Differences in network access by gender were very slight (approximately 2.5 per cent more by men) yet still remain after statistically controlling for other influences. Finally, 15 per cent of rural people and 25 per cent of urban people used network services in 1997, up from approximately 7 per cent and 12 per cent in 1993, representing a growing gap. These differences were significant even when socioeconomic variables were controlled.

A recently started, ambitious study by the UCLA Center for Community Policy (UCLA, 2000) is analysing a panel of 2096 representative households across time, comparing Internet users with non-users and with non-users who become users later on. It is part of a group of similar projects in other countries. The study found that while only 31.2 per cent of those who had not graduated from high school used the Internet in the fall of 2000, 86.3 per cent of those with at least a college degree did; 53.1 per cent of high school graduates and 70.2 per cent of those with some college used the Internet. At the youngest ages (12–15), use of the Internet is nearly universal (91.6 per cent) among American females; the only other age range where they exceed male use is 46–55 years (74.3 per cent compared to 66.1 per cent). After that, the gender gap widens considerably (at 66 +, rates are 18.4 per cent for females and 40.4 per cent for males).

A study published by the non-profit Consumer Federation of America (Cooper, 2000) collected responses from a single statistically balanced panel (n = 1902) measured at two time periods (February 1999 and June 2000) drawn from respondents agreeing to participate in a large-scale 'Life Styles Study'. The overall conclusion is that 'the disconnected are, in fact, disadvantaged and disenfranchised' (2000: 1). In particular, they compare the *fully* connected (36 per cent of the population, with Internet service providers or high-speed Internet access at home), the *partially* connected (17 per cent, with basic Internet or e-mail service at home), the *potentially* connected (21 per cent, no home Internet service, but do have home computer or cell phone), and the *disconnected* (26 per cent, without Internet service, computer or cell phone). The disconnected earn less than half the income of the fully connected ($25, 500 versus $45, 200), are much less likely to have a college degree (13 versus 46 per cent), and are more likely to be black (12 versus 7 per cent), be older (53 versus 44 years) and have smaller households (2.1 versus 2.8). Each of these significantly predicts differences across the four levels of connectedness, with income being the most powerful predictor. Overall, the study concludes that there is about a three- to five-year lag in penetration between those with above-median and below-median incomes. Cooper (2000: 1) agrees with the argument held by Castells and others that such differential timing in access to power and information – even if the later adopters catch up after several years – is itself a significant source of social inequality and unequal participation.

Moreover, 40 per cent of those who are disconnected or partially connected do not expect to be connected four years hence; of the current disconnected about 92 per cent feel this way. The UCLA (2000) study also notes that 58.6 per cent of current non-users (32.1 per cent) are somewhat likely or very likely to not gain access within a year, and this worsens for older respondents. Further, it also reports that in mid 2000, 10.3 per cent of non-users are actually Internet dropouts (formerly used the Internet at least once a month, but no longer); Katz et al. (2001) report that this 10 per cent figure is fairly consistent in surveys they conducted in 1995, 1996, 1997 and 2000. So widespread, full connection is unlikely any time soon. Here, income, age and education predict intentions to connect in the future, while race does not. There are few differences between the partially and fully connected in percentage of respondents indicating they have engaged in various activities online (consuming, gathering information, visiting government or politician websites, sending e-mails to a newspaper or discussing politics online), but there are significant dropoffs for potentially connected and even more so for the disconnected. That is, simply having access, independent of the quality or speed of the connection, is the crucial distinction.

Barriers, Influences and Consequences

Clearly, there are many physical and socioeconomic barriers to equal access. Barriers to using the Internet reported by the UCLA (2000) study respondents include: no computer or terminal available (37.7 per cent), no interest (33.3 per cent), do not know how to use (18.9 per cent), too expensive (9.1 per cent) (and then various other factors). Within the United States in 1997, '65 per cent of public schools had access to the Internet, but schools with richer student populations were still 25 per cent more likely to be connected than schools with poorer student populations' (Tapscott, 1997: 260). And even within those schools, 'more than 74 per cent of schools have computers, but only 10 per cent of students say they have used a computer at school in the past week' (1997: 266). Van Dijk (1999) identifies four general obstacles that appear to prevent people from using new media: (1) people, especially the elderly and unskilled, are intimidated by new technology or had a bad first experience with it, (2) no or difficult access to computers or networks, (3) lack of user friendliness and unattractive usage style, and (4) lack of significant usage opportunities. A perhaps more pervasive and less tangible obstacle is the growing primacy of commercial motivations for the Internet over access *per se*: 'Calling the Internet the Great Equalizer helps to sell more computers. The metaphor masquerades as a quick fix to social inequality while ignoring the factors that lead to inequality' (Wolf, 1998: 26).

Neu et al. (1999) report that the network use gap between whites and Hispanics and blacks of similar socioeconomic status widened from 1993 to 1997, implying that some of the digital divide may be due to differences in interests and priorities. A more invisible factor in this digital divide may be embedded distinctions: 'the design of new media techniques carries the imprint of the social-cultural characteristics of its producers; predominantly male, well-educated, English speaking, and members of the ethnic majority in a particular country' (van Dijk, 1999: 152). This style does not appeal to most women, less educated people and ethnic minorities. There is also a 'usage gap in which well-educated people use computers for work, private business, education and other reasons whereas those with less education and the young use computers for entertainment and/or computer games followed by education' (1999: 153). The learning process, as well as resistance to change, may be dominating factors in minimal Internet access by older age groups (Neu et al., 1999: Chapter 6). Further, differences in access become more pronounced for some variables when comparing having general access with having online access from the home (Corrado, 2000: 5). Home access is associated with using the Internet regularly by whites with higher education and incomes. Thus, in reality, there is no simple two-tiered digital divide: 'A better representation would be a continuum or spectrum of differentiated positions across the population with the "information elite" at the top and a group of "excluded people" at the bottom' (van Dijk, 1999: 155).

Indeed, cultural, rather than strict economic, educational and racial differences are receiving increased attention, from both government and commercial studies. The Cultural Access Group (2001) conducted an online marketing survey of 2205 users (766 African-Americans, 1439 Hispanics) of ethnic websites, and 1294 general market respondents, via a online banner that connected interested users to an online survey. Clearly, this is an extremely biased sample: African-Americans who responded to this survey were more highly educated (83 per cent had some college) and more female (76 per cent) than the general market respondents (79 per cent and 35 per cent, respectively). African-Americans and Hispanics in this sample have lower in-home access than the general market respondents, indicate that cost was the major deterrent to in-home access, have been online for fewer years, and spend less time online than the general market. African-Americans were, however, more likely to use the Internet for getting information on family/relationship issues (34, 25, 13 per cent), getting information on health issues (44, 40, 31 per cent) and chatting online (26, 26, 12 per cent) than Hispanics or the general market. Curiously, Hispanics were more likely than African-Americans or the general market to agree that the Internet has improved society overall (73, 50, 55 per cent), created opportunities for all people (80, 69, 70 per cent), broken down racial barriers (60, 27, 33 per cent) or broken down economic barriers (48, 29, 29 per cent). This may be partially explained by the fact that African-Americans, compared with Hispanics and the general market, agree that people of colour have unique

needs on the Internet (52, 16, 14 per cent), but only 37 per cent of African-American, compared with 64 per cent of Hispanic, respondents felt that there was adequate Internet content for their ethnic group.

Rojas et al. (in press) go further in identifying other factors contributing to the digital divide, such as the interrelations among economic capital, cultural capital, ethnicity, gender and age. Their in-depth study of 12 families in Austin, Texas identified a variety of dispositions toward computer technology, influenced by 'practices [such as family histories of technology and media use and habits], perceptions and attitudes, technical education, awareness of technology [especially relating to economic mobility], desires for information, job requirements, social relations with community members and community organizations, and geographical location'. Often, particular individuals reside in a crossfire of competing and contrasting influences (such as family and peers, cultural and social capital, educational and consumer motivations, and early gender roles) on computer and online technology. Similarly, Haddon (2001) argues that 'social exclusion' is context-dependent (neither necessarily economically based nor equivalent across all domains of a person's life), involves not only political and civic involvement but also people's ability to occupy social roles, and may also involve rejection of or lack of interest in new technologies. So, for example, his ethnographic study of 20 single-parent and 20 elderly households, using time-budget diaries and interviews, found a wide variety of influences on interest in such new media: economic constraints, need to keep in touch with children, limited conceptualizations of how these media could be used (because of the respondents' experiences of surviving in low-income situations), low priorities compared with pressing issues such as day care, smaller or less available social networks (and thus less reason to use communication media) because of not working, lowered symbolic value of used or cheaper technologies, greater resistance by the elderly to innovations or to consumerism in general, little exposure by the now elderly to new technologies in their former workplaces, a greater awareness by the elderly of how they were spending their money owing to their earlier experience of austere economic times, and simply greater familiarity with more traditional media such as the telephone and the television.

Other Divides

The digital divide occurs at the international level as well. 'Young and well educated people with a high income living in rich Western countries and regions have increased their lead on elderly people, less educated people, and people with lower income and from poorer countries and regions ... There is only one exception to this increase in relative differences in access to computers and networks: the gap between males and females is decreasing though this is happening much faster in Northern America than in Europe' (van Dijk, 1999: 150). However, he points out that this is a familiar pattern in the adoption of new media, similar to that of the telephone, the radio, the television and the VCR. Nonetheless, 'the information gap between have and have-not countries is growing. According to Jupiter Communications, of the 23.4 million households connected to the Net in 1996, 66 per cent were in North America, 16 per cent in Europe, and 14 per cent in the Asian Pacific. The gap is not just one of developed countries versus under-developed countries' (Wellman, 2000); see http://www.nua.ie/surveys/how_many_online/index.html for statistics on the geographic distribution of users. However, mobile/wireless communication will likely help developing areas that currently have no or inadequate telephone infrastructure to gain faster and more pervasive access to the Internet.

There are other aspects of access than just equal distribution across demographic and national boundaries. People who have hearing, sight, movement and other disabilities may also be disadvantaged by limitations on their ability to access information, contacts and opportunities for expression on the Internet.

Optimistic Perspective

Recent studies (ECRL, 1999; Katz et al., 2001) have been finding that at least racial and gender differences in Internet access disappear after other variables are taken into account statistically. It is possible that as the CPS research was conducted before the WWW and browser-based Internet usage had diffused widely, the 'network services' referred to in 1993 and 1997 did truly require exceptional technical resources and skills. Once browsers, modems, bandwidth, popular and commercial Internet resources, and connectivity became more user-friendly and widespread, various digital divides could then diminish. A Pew Institute study (Yahoo!News, 2001) found that by the end of 2000, 58 per cent of men and 54 per cent of women were Internet users; figures for Hispanics were 47 per cent and for blacks 43 per cent. However, while 82 per cent of those with incomes greater than $75,000 had access, only 3 per cent of those with annual incomes less than $30,000 did so; and while 75 per cent of those 18–29 years of age had access, only 15 per cent of those older than 75 did. According to the AOL (2000) survey, more women (53 per cent) started Internet use in 2000 than did men; overall, 49 per cent of Internet users were women. The proportion of men grew as users had been online for more years; Katz et al. (2001) found similar trends. The AOL survey found that 33 per cent of those

starting Internet use in 2000 had high school education (overall US 51 per cent) compared with 22 per cent in 1999. Of starters, 24 per cent had household incomes of less than $35,000 (overall US 34 per cent) compared with 11 per cent in 1999. Education and income were noticeably greater as users had more years online. Also, the more years online, the more days and hours spent online per week.

There are efforts to overcome some of the limitations on access that are due to disabilities. In 1990, the government searched for a way to provide universal service and include persons with disabilities. In 1990, Title IV of the Americans with Disabilities Act addressed disability issues by requiring all service carriers to provide communication access for hearing-impaired American citizens (Borchert, 1998: 56). And 'Section 255 of the Telecommunications Act requires that telecommunication services and equipment providers make their goods and services accessible to individuals with disabilities' (1998: 60) A good example of this is the recent Windows operating systems, which offer program and application shortcuts for people with disabilities. Through communication networks which offer full duplex voice, data transmission, graphics and video communication, there is the potential for people with disabilities to overcome these limitations.

CIVIC AND COMMUNITY
IINVOLVEMENT

The second fundamental issue is whether the Internet will decrease or increase political participation and community involvement, fostering more diverse and better informed citizens, and mediated communities with greater social capital.

Civic and Political Involvement

Pessimistic Perspective

Even if the Internet represents the potential for greater political involvement, the unequal access to Internet resources by various groups in society, relative to traditional outlets such as newspapers, radio and TV, should paradoxically narrow the basis of political participation and government legitimacy (White, 1997; see also Bentivegna, this volume). Hill and Hughes report that 'Internet users and activists (those who use it for political reasons) are considerably younger than the general public, with Internet activists averaging a very young 32.8 years' (1998: 29). This age may be even lower, as the survey only counted those over age 18. Males were the majority of Internet users and activists (72 per cent). There actually seems to be a higher percentage of non-white Internet activists, so 'there is no great "ethnic gap" in Internet activism'. However, Internet users and activists do have much more education than the general public, with 53 per cent and 56 per cent, respectively, having college degrees. Internet activists 'are not more partisan but they are more Democratic than the general public' (1998: 33). These users are more involved in information gathering and more knowledgeable about current political events than is the general public (1998: 35). On Usenet's political newsgroups 'most threads are neutral but with clear right-wing anti-government overtones', possibly because right-wing people may not feel represented by the media – but they also might just be more active in posting to newsgroups (1998: 73). Chat rooms are heavily right-wing owing to greater activity by those members, and not because of a greater number of right-wing participants *per se* (1998: 128). Hill and Hughes find about an equal amount of left-wing and right-wing websites, but conservative sites are more in-depth and have 'higher production values'.

Others argue that the Internet could weaken the legitimacy of the governing process, by encouraging the spread of small, 'net-savvy' special interest communities who could pursue their own narrow agenda at the cost of the public commonweal (Starobin, 1996). The quality and validity of material reported on the Internet are also increasingly problematical, leading to concerns about the corruption or debasement of elections, and a consequent reduction in political participation. There has been concern about a possible reduction in the objectivity of traditional media if these media were to lose their status and impact as a result of the growth of Internet usage (Symposium, 1995; van Alstyne, 1995). Some theorists have argued that the Internet is destroying community groups and voluntary associations that are necessary for the democratic process to succeed (Putnam, 1996; Turkle, 1996). Other critics fear that the Internet will absorb and dissipate the energy of the citizenry away from traditional political processes (Carpini, 1996; Rash, 1997). Van Dijk locates a central tension: 'Some would argue that *freedom*, for example the freedom of choice for consumers, will increase because of the interactivity offered by this technology. Others paint a more pessimistic picture, and predict that freedom will be endangered by a decrease in privacy for the individual as a registered citizen, a "transparent" employee and a consumer screened for every personal characteristic, and by the growing opportunities for central control' (1999: 2).

According to Hill and Hughes (1998), pessimists believe that electronic voting is problematic, because it doesn't involve debating or discussion and allows a voter to be more passive. Van Dijk (1999) believes that there will be so much information

on the Internet that it would be hard to figure out what was valid, and thus will lead to faulty decision-making. The Internet also often removes one layer of filtering of political information – that done by gatekeepers of the mainstream media. Democracy can be strengthened when citizens become politically more informed and involved in government through the Internet, but increasingly the Internet 'is susceptible to control from above' (1999: 2). Further, self-selection plays a large role: those who were previously politically interested are those who make up the population of Internet users who utilize the web for political reasons (1999: 183).

Free speech can be both promoted and inhibited by the Internet. Theoretically, anyone can design a website and post any opinion on it. However, Shapiro and Leone (1999) suggest that free speech may actually suffer with the development of the Internet, because of both exposure and access issues. First, people may have a hard time finding an audience to reach because others may not be willing to listen. People will not feel like responding to solicitations describing the opinions of others or they may filter their information so they only receive what directly interests them. Filtering and personalization of news via software agents can lead to narrow-mindedness and social fragmentation. Therefore, views that contradict or question any particular person's opinions may never reach that person, allowing that individual to remain ignorant of opposing perspectives. Second, not everyone will have the resources to pay for advertising one's opinions – in addition to the by now familiar access constraints such as technology and technological knowledge – thus limiting some people's right to free speech.

Overall, Hill and Hughes find little evidence supporting the claim that the 'Internet changes people's minds politically ... Rather, reading Web pages seems to be an act of self-selection; people go on-line to find out more information about a subject, not to be transformed' (1998: 183). Indeed, the UCLA (2000) study shows that while 45.6 per cent of Internet users (versus 28.1 per cent of non-users) feel that the Internet helps people to better understand politics, only 29.3 per cent of users and 16.8 per cent of non-users feel that Internet use leads to people having greater political power. 'Likewise, debate and information-based discussion in the Usenet newsgroups and political chat rooms serves to reinforce pre-existing ideological positions, not to change them.' They also conclude that the Internet won't necessarily bring worldwide tolerance. 'Simply because people can talk to each other regardless of distance does not mean they will cooperate.' For example, alt.politics.french is a newsgroup which often includes 'insults hurled back and forth across the English Channel between people in Britain and France.' Rash (1997) and others note that the Internet easily supports hate groups and conspiracy theorists in the political process.

Fallows (2000) argues that most of the predicted impacts of the Internet on politics have not (yet) appeared: bypassing mass media and other gate-keeping intermediaries (Morris, 2000), circumventing centralized authority, freeing politicians from having to constantly raise money, facilitating new and diverse candidates, fostering virtual issues constituencies and reducing the influence of particular states or political blocs. However, two changes are already significant. The first is a reduced time for shifts in prevailing opinion and media narratives. The second is that the network economy has stimulated more and more concentrated media conglomerates using convergent bandwidth, as multinationals attempt to gain control over delivery channels of multimedia content. Fallows (2000), Hundt (2000) and McChesney (2000) all argue that this concentration of media reduces diversity in perspectives and opinions, and reinforces particular kinds of coverage and programming, leading to a much more powerful effect on political knowledge, participation and voting than any supposed consequence of extended Internet use by individuals and groups. And the inherent structural and power constraints of the political system are likely to limit the possibilities of the Internet for extensive political change (Margolis and Resnick, 2000).

Optimistic Perspective

Others strongly argue that the Internet may very well foster political involvement: 'Life in cyberspace seems to be shaping up exactly like Thomas Jefferson would have wanted: founded on the primacy of individual liberty and a commitment to pluralism, diversity, and community' (Kapor, 1993: 53). Users are not necessarily social isolates, unaware of civic and political issues: in mid 2000, the online users in the AOL survey were particularly politically involved, as 84 per cent were registered to vote and 45 per cent intended to go online to get presidential candidate information (and 39 per cent for state candidate, 32 per cent for local candidate). Of the young people (between 9 and 17 years of age) in the companion AOL youth study (based on 505 young people in homes with online access), 41 per cent reported a greater interest in current events owing to being online (55 per cent reporting no difference). And they clearly feel that being online has had a much more positive influence on them than has television (57 versus 39 per cent).

Hill and Hughes (1998) summarize the perspectives of some optimists concerning the role of the Internet in citizen activism. Rheingold (1993) believes people will become more involved in the democratic process, such as through increased online debate, and Rash (1997) states that the Internet will open up the opportunity for new parties and ideas to develop. Shapiro and Leone (1999) associate the Internet with 'the control revolution', whereby control is being transferred from large institutions to individuals. This is due to six core features of the Internet that can enhance individual control. The first four already exist: (1) many-to-many interactivity, (2) digital content, making communication flexible 'in terms of how it can be stored, used, and manipulated' (1999: 16), (3) the design of the Internet as a distributed, packet-based network, and (4) the interoperability of the Internet, so that information can flow freely throughout a network without bottlenecks or barriers. The next two must be achieved in order to foster individual control: (5) broadband capacity and (6) universal access.

Certainly the Internet has already become a powerful political tool for political parties, non-governmental organizations, congressional campaigns and local activist groups (Browning and Weitzner, 1996; Corrado, 2000; Davis, 1999; Rash, 1997). It allows political actors to monitor voting records, assess campaign contributions and financing, conduct online focus groups, increase voter access, keep up with recent and distant news, obtain campaign donations more quickly and efficiently (such as through online credit card payment), file contribution disclosure reports online, create and support mailing lists, get voters to the polling place, and more. Rash (1997), in particular, suggests that the impact of the Internet in the 1996 US presidential election was comparable to the role of television in the 1960 election.

The Consumer Federation of America study (Cooper, 2000) emphasizes that comparing non-online civic activities (reading newspaper, reading news magazine, contacting local public official, writing letter to editor, circulating a petition, attending a political rally), their categories of 'disconnected' and 'potentially connected' (defined earlier in the 'access' section) are fairly similar to 'partially' and 'fully connected'. This implies that non-users are fairly equal to users in their connections in physical space, but that users have the additional advantage of online activities and access. That is, 'the problem is not that the disconnected do not participate in physical space, it is that they cannot participate in cyberspace' (2000: 17). Further, those currently connected and those planning to gain access within four years have very similar attitudes about the importance of technology and computers. However, those not planning to gain access have considerably less positive attitudes about the importance of computers and Internet access. Cooper (2000) reported that while non-users are more likely to attend rallies, Internet users are more likely to engage a bit more (an additional 5 to 25 per cent) in civic, political and media activities than non-users. Internet users in the UCLA (2000) study, compared with non-users, were slightly more likely to exercise and to participate in clubs/organizations, were slightly less likely to socialize with household members or to know neighbours by name, and had the same levels of socializing with friends, time spent sleeping, and number of friends outside their households. Further, users held fairly similar attitudes about various personal values, having slightly higher preference for visiting with friends, but slightly lower preference for attending religious services and for contributing to efforts to protect the environment. Non-users reported slightly higher levels of life dissatisfaction, interaction anxiety, powerlessness and loneliness (all about 0.2 to 0.3 difference on a 1–5 scale). Users in the Katz et al. (2001) study were more likely to participate in community and leisure organizations, but not religious organizations.

However, Davis (1999) concludes that citizens will not take significant advantage of the potential, and that dominant political actors will be the primary beneficiaries, supporting the status quo. For example, even though governmental representatives do receive e-mail from those who wish to 'express views on topics of current interest … e-mail is rarely the medium through which individuals carry out personalized transactions with government agencies'. People 'may express personal opinions regarding public issues in e-mail to their congressmen, but electronic queries or filings regarding their own personal circumstances, needs, or activities are still rare' (Neu et al., 1999: 3). However, there is tremendous potential for this form of citizen–government communication, for many of the usual reasons such as decreased costs, errors and delays. While this form of communication is growing, several obstacles still have to be overcome, such as security (using a trusted intermediary and electronic signatures) and privacy issues, as well as technology implementation and personnel training. Because the Internet is becoming transparently integrated into existing cultural forms, and provides potentially easy access to information, it can increase the democratic franchise (Sobchack, 1996). However, a major problem lies with knowing how to use the computer properly and being able to access specific information.

To some extent, the question of whether the Internet can foster political activism and knowledge of governance is somewhat simplistic, considering that the Internet itself involves considerable political, governmental, regulatory and economic institutions, and requires complex governance and even debates over what kinds of governance are appropriate and possible (Loader, 1997; Margolis and Resnick, 2000).

Community Involvement

Pessimistic Perspective

Simply put, some argue that cyberspace cannot be a source of real community and/or detracts from meaningful real-world communities (Baudrillard, 1983; Beniger, 1988; Gergen, 1991; Kiesler et al., 1984; Numes, 1995; Stoll, 1995; Turkle, 1996; see also Jankowski, and Baym, this volume). Schement distinguishes two key elements of communities: primary and secondary relationships. Internet communities 'are really made up of secondary relationships' in which people only know each other in 'a single, or only a few, dimensions' in contrast to primary relationships in which people know each other in multiple dimensions (reported in Bollier, 1995: 10). John Seely Brown believes that 'it is not always clear where accountability and responsibility reside in virtual communities' because the lack of primary relationships may induce 'careless, irresponsible, and even anti-social' behaviour (Bollier, 1995: 12). The use of online systems to communicate with more distant others may reduce the vitality and integration of physical communities (Calhoun, 1986). Somewhat more grandiosely, virtual communities may become 'a counter-hegemonic movement in which socially or politically marginalized groups find expressive space on the Internet in which to locate like-minded others, speak freely, and forge solidarity' (Lindlof and Shatzer, 1998: 174).

Shapiro and Leone warn that careless use of the Internet may lead to three fundamental problems: (1) overpersonalization, that is the use of information about users to target messages, products and control, and the use of filters and focused discussion groups to keep us from being exposed to diverse perspectives; (2) disintermediation, which may get out of hand as we forget the value of liaisons and gatekeepers in not only selecting but also verifying news, commerce and politics; and (3) the danger that 'we may rely too much on market based solutions to problems such as protecting privacy' (1999: 104). 'With fewer shared experiences and information sources, citizens may feel less of a connection with, and less of an obligation toward, one another' (1999: 120). Both Shapiro and Leone (1999) and Rice (1987a) point out that online ties are likely to be more ephemeral, less sustainable and more easily exitable compared with physical community relations. Along with the increased choice that online media provide comes an increased ability to 'disengage with little or no consequence' (Jones, 1999: 220).

Computer-mediated communication (CMC) 'may yet be the clearest evidence of Beniger's (1988) "pseudo-community", part of the "reversal" of a centuries-old trend from organic community based on interpersonal relationships to impersonal association integrated by mass means' (Jones, 1999: 369). 'The new mass media have an especially characteristic ability to create an illusion of apparently intimate face-to-face communication between a presenter and an individual viewer', thus creating what other researchers have called 'parasocial interaction' (Jensen, 1999). Further, differential access to and knowledge of these technologies create powerful boundaries between potential community members, and reinforce certain kinds of roles, statuses and social networks.

There's a subtle paradox involved in this issue of shared interests in online communities. What van Dijk (1999) calls an 'organic community' (comprising face-to-face interactions) is made up of a relatively homogeneous group of people because they have several interests in common, whereas a virtual community is relatively heterogeneous since only one interest links them. Therefore, an organic community has a better chance of building and maintaining its own culture and identity than a virtual community. Virtual communities can't replace organic communities since they are limited, but perhaps they can supplement and strengthen organic communities.

More community-oriented issues include just exactly how identity can be formed, maintained and accessed by others when the individuals cannot be seen, and may be constantly changing; what social processes are available for organizing, coordinating and controlling online (especially deviant) behaviours in ways that promote the community; how online communities change over time and what's necessary to maintain them; and how online communities might support collective action and social capital (Smith and Kollock, 1998; Surratt, 1998).

The Nature of 'Real' Community

One interesting response to this position that current, richly human physical communities are threatened by new media such as the Internet is to question the very nature of communities (see Jankowski in this volume). Wellman (2000) emphasizes that traditional communities were controlled by social class, management of labour power, access to resources, fixed capital, limited mobility and a few powerful gatekeepers, all embedded in a primary network. Revolutionary challenges to these community networks were associated with changes in media and transportation: horses, railroads, automobiles and airplanes, books, telegraph, telephone, radio and television. The 'huge increase in speed [associated first with the telegraph] has made door-to-door communications residual, and made most communications place-to-place or person-to-person. The length of the message is a more salient limiting factor than the distance that the message has to travel' (Wellman, 2001).

Thus, paradoxically, because media have allowed community to move inside the home or the office by means of the telephone or other media, most North Americans have little interpersonal connection with their neighbourhood or the social control of a neighbourhood group. 'Most of the major innovations of the past hundred years have made it progressively easier to avoid contact – and particularly conversation – with people who aren't colleagues, or family, or friends' (Johnson, 1997: 69); the cinema, car, telephone and television are particularly implicated.

> 'For example, the percentage of Americans regularly socializing with neighbours has been steadily declining for at least 25 years. In 1999, only 20 per cent spent a social evening with neighbours several times per week as compared with 30 per cent in 1974. Similarly regularly socializing in pubs has declined from 11 per cent to 8 per cent' (Smith, 1999; cited in Wellman, 2000).

Putnam (1995; 2000) argues that community has been significantly declining in the United States, and Skocpol (2000) shows that interest groups with local constituencies and interaction have declined in general in the US, creating a vacuum filled by disconnected people committed to little more than commercialism. Putnam (2000) documents that while membership in community organizations has not really declined so much, active involvement and participation have. Further, many new voluntary organizations are lobbying and direct-mail offices with no real membership activity. People entertain less frequently in their homes, donations in terms of constant dollars have declined, voting and trust in government are low, and church attendance continues its drop.

Further, rather than finding community in tightly interconnected groups, 'Most people operate in multiple, thinly-connected, partial communities as they deal with networks of kin, neighbours, friends, workmates and organizational ties. Rather than fitting into the same group as those around them, each person has his/her own "personal community"' (Wellman, 2000). In a seminar reported by Bollier (1995: 7), Firestone notes that 'A lot of people have very superficial relationships with their geographic neighbors even though they see them all the time, yet have very close relationships with professional colleagues who they may only see occasionally.'

Optimistic Perspective

Considering these alternative views of community, it can be argued that because of new communication possibilities, people are no longer forced to interact with specific, physically proximate others in order to participate in community. People now tend to choose physical neighbourhoods for reasons of safety, schooling and medical services (Dear et al., 1996). A related consequence is that actual network ties leap over physically linked areas, so that the overall social geography corresponds much less to physical geography. We may best think of

Internet communities as a supplement to physical communities rather than as complete substitutes. Cerulo (1997), somewhat rejecting Beniger's (1988) critique of the pseudo-community created by digital mass media, argues that we need to reconceptualize community owing to the rise of new communication technologies, based on evidence about social interaction and social bonding (see also Rice, 1987a). First, pervasive examples of parasocial interaction with mediated personalities, call-in radio shows, and emotional support in online discussion groups argue for a wider concept of social interaction that does not presume that mediated relations are necessarily fleeting, impersonal or deceptive. Second, while there are many concerns about the superficiality or isolation associated with online relations, new media are perhaps better characterized as 'changing the nature and character of social bonds' (Cerulo, 1997: 53).

A more forceful optimistic argument is that cyberspace involvement can create alternative communities that are as valuable and useful as our familiar, physically located communities (Pool, 1983; Rheingold, 1993). Network ties may exist in cyberspace but they still represent places where people connect concerning shared interests, support, sociability and identity (Wellman, 2000). This potential is largely due to a combination of several factors: increased bandwidth, continuous access, wireless portability, globalized connectivity and personalization (such as collaborative filtering and content associated by shared users, individual e-mail profiles and web portals, and online communities of interests). People may use online communities to bypass constraints and inequity in unmediated interactions (Stone, 1991). Rather than being seen as disconnected from a group or a locale, these communities transcend these constraints, shifting from door-to-door relations to person-to-person and role-to-role interactions.

CMC 'brings us a form of efficient social contact'; it is a 'technology, medium, and engine of social relations', allowing us to move in terms of 'status, class, social role[s], and character' (Jones, 1999: 224–5). The vastly increased ability to share information is a crucial factor in community formation. Jones emphasizes that new media facilitate increased choice: the 'information highway' will allow us to 'forge our own places from among the many that exist, not by creating new places but by simply choosing from the menu of those available' (1999: 220). Johnson echoes this argument: 'Instead of being a medium for shut-ins and introverts, the digital computer turns out to be the first major technology of the twentieth century that brings strangers closer together, rather than pushing them farther apart' (1997: 69). For example, the soc.culture hierarchy on Usenet includes over 150 newsgroups whose memberships include nearly all of the ethnic and national cultural communities in

the world. The Cultural Access Group's (2001) study of ethnic differences among online users reported that 59 per cent of their African-American and 73 per cent of their Hispanic respondents said that the Internet keeps them connected to their ethnic community, and that the content on African-American (79 per cent) or Hispanic (69 per cent) websites is meaningful to them.

Turkle disputes the argument that Internet communities promote only secondary relationships, as suggested by Schement and Bollier (reported in Bollier, 1995: 10–12). She gives the example of one SeniorNet member who received dozens of calls and cards from her cyberfriends as she lay dying in the hospital. Further, Turkle claims that MOOs and MUDs 'honor people's desires to connect and not to be lonely, and to form community' (Bollier, 1995: 27). Paradoxically, the rapid growth of the Internet may be the single strongest indicator of people's desire for a 'more connected way of living', a greater affiliation among fellow humans (Shapiro and Leone, 1999: 208).

Shapiro and Leone also reject the notion of 'cyberspace … as elsewhere': 'our actions online have … a real impact on the lives of other human beings' (1999: 38). Shapiro and Leone provide a good example of how the Internet helps connect those with similar political interests, activities and goals. Htun Aung Gyaw is a Burmese dissident fighting the military government that rules his homeland Myanmar; he is currently a student at Cornell University but uses the Internet to communicate with other Burmese democracy activists around the world. Stacey Horn's (1998) account of ECHO, the New-York-based virtual salon, reinforces the idea that online behaviours, relations and concerns are essentially the same as those of physical communities. This case shows how online communities can reinforce and complement, even create and foster, physical communities and interest in local culture. As with the WELL in Berkeley, ECHO participants get together at different New York settings for social gatherings, and conversation and relations blend together their online and offline lives. Cherny's (1999) study of a MUD also reinforces the notion that online communities can develop cohesion, unity, shared history and close relationships using only appropriately varied forms of online, text-based language.

Other research shows that people interact happily and fruitfully online (for the most part) and in ways similar to face-to-face contact (Wellman and Gulia, 1999b). Further, it is misleading to represent online relationships as mutually exclusive with offline ones; they often support and complement each other. Wellman (2000) concludes that 'The shift to a personalized, wireless world affords truly *personal communities* that supply support, sociability, information and a sense of belonging separately to each individual.' For example, Hampton and Wellman (2000) found, in their study of a leading-edge, broadband wired suburb near Toronto called 'Netville', that online users are more active neighbours (knowing about 25 neighbours) than are non-users (about eight), and they range more widely throughout the neighbourhood. They also found that once the learning curve was overcome, family members helped each other with the computers and shared their online discoveries, rather than watching television. Hampton (2000) found increased social network, social capital and local community involvement associated with the Netville online infrastructure. Nearly two-thirds of the 109 homes were connected. The study compared those who bought homes and were planning to move into Netville, those 45 not connected, and those who were connected. After the service provider established a neighbourhood e-mail list (NET-L), residents quickly used it for neighbourhood interaction, organizing activities, online introductions, and increased knowledge of local events, service and opinions; it provided common conversational topics and personalized initial interactions. The density of the social network based on the ability to recognize other community members by name was 31 per cent among wired households but only 7 per cent among non-wired ones. The stronger criterion of 'talk with on a regular basis' revealed a density of 11 per cent in the wired households and only 3 per cent in the non-wired households. From a community action perspective, the system allowed Netville members to react to the local housing developer about housing problems, through faster organizing and a greater number of active members. This allowed them to achieve greater concessions from the developer and blocked a second development.

Shapiro and Leone (1999) describe the effectiveness of a supplemental community network in Blacksburg, Virginia, where over 60 per cent of the citizens participate. Parents and teachers communicate online and citizens participate in surveys regarding municipal government. They also describe the development of a community network in a London neighbourhood in which neighbours were given computers and Internet access. Those neighbours participated in debates over local parking rules and came to know each other better. One participant said, 'I used to know maybe 5 or 6 people on the street, now I know at least 40 per cent of them quite well and some very closely' (1999: 211). Other studies of community networks point out a variety of advantages, challenges and developments (Gurstein, 2000; Kahin and Keller, 1995; Schon et al., 1999; Schuler, 1996; Tsagarousianou et al., 1998). While much attention is paid to the exotic and social aspects of online communities, they also represent consequential social policy issues, such as supporting neighbourhood and community relations, local school systems, and public access to government services and information (Doheny-Farina, 1998), especially health information and services (Rice and Katz, 2001).

Rheingold says:

> My direct observations of online behavior around the world over the past ten years have led me to conclude that whenever CMC technology becomes available to people anywhere, they inevitably build virtual communities with it, just as microorganisms inevitably create colonies ... I suspect that one of the explanations for this phenomenon is the hunger for community that grows in the breasts of people around the world as more and more informal public spaces disappear from our real lives. I also suspect that these new media attract colonies of enthusiasts because CMC enables people to do things with each other in new ways, and to do altogether new kinds of things – just as the telegraph, telephone, and television did. (1993: 6)

Indeed, he concludes that the Internet, Usenet and e-mail allow for people to access and transmit information that may not be allowed to surface in other communities. Johnson agrees: 'If the depth of shared experience is the yardstick by which you ultimately measure your community ... then I must admit that I have a hard time imagining a better platform for community building than the traditional, text-based bulletin board system utilized by ECHO and the Well (along with many Web sites)' (1997: 70). For example, Slack and Williams (2000) studied the Craigmillar Community Information Service (CCIS), developed for a town outside Edinburgh where many citizens are poor and underemployed. Countering positions that argue that online networks will foster isolated, inequitable and ahistorical societies, they argue that 'The growth and uptake of ICTs provides a point of contact at which the local and global intersect, wherein there is a potential for each to influence the other' (2000: 321). Before the CCIS, Craigmillar exhibited no sense of community feeling, showed no motivation to socialize, and offered no social or cultural activities. By means of the CCIS, however, 'Craigmillar has ... developed a strategy of self-presentation that counters external representations and which works by being grounded in the highly spatialized notion of a tightly knit community' (2000: 322).

A Broader Question of Impacts

Some are skeptical that the Internet represents major change in political and community involvement at all (Davis, 1999; Jonscher, 1999; Stoll, 1999; Valovic, 2000; Webster, 1995), protesting that the concept of the information society, and the Internet, are overhyped by wildly optimistic claims fostered by media, corporate and techie beneficiaries, and that computers can only support pre-existing human needs for social relations, not replace them.

Fischer (1997) concludes that the effects of new communication technologies in general on community (networks of social relations) are modest, varying across technologies, and complex, indirect and contradictory. He notes that even with the telephone, a truly discontinuous technology, only a few truly notable changes can be identified (greater ability to organize, conduct and maintain social relations over distances, especially by women – essentially, being able to conduct normal social relations more effectively). He notes that concerns about threats to community were also raised for the telephone, automobile, radio and television. Further, he shows that residential mobility has generally declined since World War II, that local news has become increasingly more important, and that telecommuting has so far had limited effects.

With respect to variations across media technologies, Fischer distinguishes between point-to-point and broadcast media, and the associated difference in a public or private setting. After the diffusion of cinema, there was much greater sociability before, during and after going to the movies (especially among children and women): 'It appears that movies enabled considerable social interaction, and attendance reinforced social ties' (1997: 115). However, there was probably an opposite effect for television, after the social novelty wore off, as evidenced by declines in movie attendance, social visiting and physical activity. Finally, effects are often contradictory: the use of a particular technology – simultaneously by the same user, or in opposite ways by different users – may cancel out large-scale changes. For example, during the initial stages, the automobile increased sociability (especially for women and even more so for farm women), while the more modern period associates the automobile with the rise of suburban sprawl and increased distances between homes (and thus female homemakers). There are many recent examples of other technology triggers, such as canals, railroads, automobiles, highways, aviation, telegraph, telephone, radio, television and satellites (Stefik, 1999). 'Technologies of connection' represent boundaries and points of resistance, often creating 'conflict between global and local values' (1999: 3). Legal and economic systems are not ready initially, the effects are not usually evident initially, and the form and application of the technology are not initially fixed. For example, one of the early uses of phonographs was to play recorded political speeches in public auditoriums, introducing voters to the voices of politicians. Initial goals for technologies both 'limit and shape their opportunities' (1999: 19).

Fischer (1997) argues that the primary source of major changes in community may be other social factors, such as family size, increased age of solitary seniors, later marriage, cross-ethnic marriages, sexual relations before marriage, social

security, longevity, etc. And, while indeed homes are more widely scattered, and professions involve interaction with others across greater distances, transportation, culturalties and telecommunications facilitate increased communication across these obstacles. He concludes that, in general, we should think about 'these technologies as tools people use to pursue their social ends [rather] than as forces that control people's actions' (1997: 115).

Winner (1999) also argues that we have continually transformed ourselves as a society as technology has changed. He proposes six questions to ask to see if these new technologies are creating 'conditions that sustain selfhood and civic culture':

'(1) Around these instruments, what kinds of bonds, attachments, and obligations are in the making? (2) To whom or to what are people connected or dependent upon? (3) Do ordinary people see themselves as having a crucial role in what is taking shape? (4) Do people see themselves as competent, able to make decisions? (5) Do they feel that their voices matter in making decisions that will affect family, workplace, community, nation? And (6) Do they feel themselves to be fairly treated?' (1999: 208). Unlike Fischer, Winner is not sanguine about the consequences.

Not only because 'power over the most important decisions about how technologies were introduced was far from evenly distributed' (1999: 211) but also because 'during the middle decades of the 20th century, virtues appropriate to the development of machines – productive order, efficiency, control, forward looking dynamics – became prevailing social virtues as well'. He sees a shift from those prior values to 'mobility, flexibility, entrepreneurialism, expendability, and a willingness to dissolve social bonds in the pursuit of material gain'.

SOCIAL INTERACTION AND EXPRESSION

Although the actual architecture, and initial intention, of the Internet is to connect computers, one of its major social uses and consequences is as a complex medium of communication, neither completely interpersonal nor a mass medium. Thus the third issue is whether the Internet will hinder or foster social interaction, expression and new forms of identity (Baron, 1984; Gergen, 1991; Hiltz and Turoff, 1995; Parks and Floyd, 1996; Turkle, 1996; Wynn and Katz, 1997; see Baym, this volume). Can online social activity and creativity translate into meaningful friendships and relationships? There are of course many different domains of involvement and expression. Jordan (1999), for example, proposes that power on and with the Internet occurs at the individual level (even at the simple level of reinforcing our sense of identity each time we log on), the community level (determined to some extent by the capabilities and constraints of technology and virtual communities) and the collective imagination level (contrasting, for example, online immortality or constant surveillance, and different applications of virtual reality).

Pessimistic Perspective

This perspective holds that CMC technology is too inherently antithetical to the nature of human life, and too limited technologically for meaningful relationships to form (Stoll, 1995). Thus, cyberspace cannot be a source of meaningful friendships (Baudrillard, 1983; Beniger, 1988; Numes, 1995). Many have argued for the socially isolating and psychologically depressing effect of (at least extreme) Internet use (Heim, 1993; Kraut et al., 1998; Kroker and Weinstein, 1994; Nie and Erbring, 2000; Stoll, 1995; Turkle, reported in Bollier, 1995). Online relationships may involve lower interdependence, commitment and permanence (Parks and Roberts, 1998; Rice, 1987a). Computer-mediated communication can foster 'experimentation' (such as lying to others who cannot immediately know what the truth is) about one's identity and qualities. Such an atmosphere can be dominated by trickery, lechery, manipulation, emotional swindles. So much posturing, 'gender switching' and faking of identities can take place that it is extremely difficult for any real relationships to be created and maintained (Turkle, 1996). For example, online chat room discussions often remind Johnson of graffiti of the worst kind: 'isolated declarations of selfhood, failed conversations, slogans, and tag lines. You don't see a community in these exchanges; you see a group of individuals all talking past one another, and talking in an abbreviated, almost unintelligible code' (1997: 70).

Kraut et al.'s (1998) 'HomeNet' study analysed 73 households during their first one to two years online. They used a panel design to improve the validity of causal claims, and included reliable measures of psychological states and social involvement (social network, social support, loneliness, stress, depression), as well as objective system usage data (average hours per week spent online, number of e-mail messages, and WWW sites accessed per week). Greater social extroversion and more extended social networks predicted less Internet use in the following year or two; conversely, greater Internet use predicted decreased local and distant social networks. Neither social support nor stress was unrelated to Internet use. However, while neither loneliness nor depression predicted greater subsequent Internet use, greater use did predict increased loneliness and depression. Kraut et al. (1998) concluded that Internet users experienced reduced communication among household members, reduced personal network size, and increased depression and loneliness. They suggest that the best

explanation for these results is that online activity replaces strong social ties in the unmediated world with weak online ties, which cannot resolve loneliness and depression as well, as they are not as physically available and may not understand the contexts of particular situations. They do note that, while the research design allows them to make causal claims, this sample may not be representative, so the results may not be generalizable.

Indeed, Shapiro and Leone feel that 'the more time we spend online, the less time we will have to interact directly with our families, our neighbors, and other community members' (1999: 118). For example, Nie and Erbring (2000) found that web TV users spent less unmediated time with others. They argue that Internet use focuses on the individual, whereas watching TV may at least provide 'some sort of shared experience' (2000: 118). We may develop relationships online but may let our relationships with those around us suffer. The same tremendous ease with which users can 'personalize' the presentation, results and use of the Internet also facilitates a narrowing of focus and exposure to diverse perspectives. Further, it helps advertisers and other information providers in targeting their services, products and opinions to users identified by their online preferences and usage patterns (Schroeder and Ledger, 1998; Shapiro and Leone, 1999).

One's freedom of expression on the Internet is another's predation and indecency, especially when the users are children (Schroeder and Ledger, 1998). Tapscott (1997) identifies some possible disadvantages of the increased individuality and interactivity provided to young users by the Internet, such as disconnection from formal institutions, misleading and dangerous representations of information and identities, flaming, overload, lack of evaluation by informed gatekeepers, and emphasis on the short term. A few critics of virtual communities reviewed by Bollier (1995) feel that virtual communities and other Internet communications allow users to make superficial types of friendships instead of developing multidimensional relationships with those around them. Issues of the digital divide and expression intermingle, such as the online representation of racial identity and the offline representations of the racial makeup of cyberspace (Kolko et al., 1999; Smith and Kollock, 1998).

Optimistic Perspective

Increased frequency and diversity of Interactions

The optimistic perspective increasingly sees the Internet as a medium for social interaction (Rice, 1987a). Numerous case studies of CMC have shown that 'the social' is an important glue that binds together the task-oriented aspects of CMC, and in some cases even supplants them (Rice, 1987b). This work has been complemented by research on the functioning of medical discussion lists and newsgroups, health and psychological support groups, Internet relay chats, multi-user dungeons, object-oriented MUDS, and even online dating services, all of which are essentially social- and affect-oriented as opposed to task-oriented (Rice, 2001). A good proportion of those searching and participating in health information sites and discussion groups do so as 'third-party' intermediaries, seeking information and support for their significant others, for themselves to help them deal with illnesses of significant others, or to bring information from the Internet to stimulate, challenge or engage their health care providers (Aspden and Katz, 2001). The growth and persistence of web-based chat rooms and 'instant messaging' offering 'community' would seem to provide additional evidence refuting the 'non-social' nature of CMC.

Baym summarizes a decade of research as revealing that 'the ways in which people have appropriated the commercial and non-commercial networks demonstrate that CMC not only lends itself to social uses but is, in fact, a site for an unusual amount of social creativity' (1995: 160). Rice (1987a) argued that fundamental aspects of social groups and communities may well be supported, even extended, through online communities, though the boundaries and permanence of such groups might be quite different. Turkle (1997) wrote a classic ethnographic study of the inhabitants of the computer community, online, at work and at home. Porter's (1997) edited book provides a variety of additional perspectives, including the problem of interacting with virtual bodies.

Van Dijk (1999: 201–12, 239–40) summarizes some of the benefits of CMC: people can compensate for missing cues in images, sounds, texts and data by using available textual cues; people can focus more on the content of the text by reading e-mails; people can engage in more informal conversations and settings; and electronic group conversations often encourage normally quiet people and women to participate more. Walther (1996) shows that mediated interaction is usually personal, especially when participants have time and interest, and mediated interaction may even be 'hyperpersonal', managing interaction and impressions more than is possible face-to-face. Straus (1997) similarly found that CMC is not necessarily less personalized than face-to-face communication. Further, unmediated communication is highly constrained by the need for geographic and temporal proximity, limited processing and storage potential; it does, however, tend to foster greater communication quality and more explicit sequencing of contributions (Rice, 1987b; van Dijk, 1999).

Hamman's (1999) ethnographic study concluded that Internet communication complements real-world relations, and Wellman and Gulia's (1999a) review of research on Internet communities argued that offline relationships may be strengthened as well as weakened. Surveys by Parks and colleagues found evidence of intimate and well-developed online relationships, often leading to real-world interactions, even though the frequency and duration of online relationships tend to be shorter (Parks and Roberts, 1998), and involve issues extending beyond the Internet communities (Parks and Floyd, 1996). Scherer's (1997) survey of college students showed no difference in sociability between those who exhibited Internet dependencies and regular users, even though they use Internet communication more and had fewer face-to-face social interactions. A Pew Research Center (2000) poll reported that Internet users indicated that e-mail had improved their social and kinship connections, and more so for those who had used the Internet longer and more frequently. Indeed, there were fewer social isolates among users than non-users, and users had a greater number of recent social contacts and greater access to social support. Riphagen and Kanfer (1997) showed that e-mail users and non-users had similar numbers of relationships, but users had more distant relationships, suggesting that e-mail reduced local interactions. Katz et al. (2001) found similar results, except that users had more offline relationships in general.

Survey results show diverse, extensive and growing use of the Internet for social interaction. In 2000, those online activities reported by the greatest percentage of the AOL (2000) respondents were doing research (91 per cent), communicating with friends and family (90 per cent), getting information about products to buy (80 per cent), getting news (76 per cent) and getting health information (70 per cent), and then there were many others (less than 60 per cent). The percentages reporting these activities, especially for doing research and getting health information, were higher for those online for more years. Of 12 new activities mentioned by the AOL (2000) respondents, the greatest interest was for sending/receiving pictures to and from family/friends (92 per cent). Of the AOL respondents, 44 per cent reported that they were more in touch with brothers/sisters, 40 per cent more in touch with aunts/uncles/cousins, 23 per cent more in touch with parents, 12 per cent more in touch with grandparents, and 38 per cent more in touch with other relatives, because of being online. Amazingly, 41 per cent reported that they had reconnected with people they had lost touch with – for an average of 12 years! And 48 per cent reported using instant messaging, especially to connect with friends (82 per cent) but also with family and relatives. And these percentages were somewhat greater for those who had been online for more years. Women were more likely to include family members on their instant messaging contact list (for siblings, 40 per cent compared with 26 per cent for men, and for parents, 35 per cent compared with 24 per cent). People also spent time together online: 80 per cent with their children, and 68 per cent with their spouse. In the AOL survey, overall, people still preferred the telephone to online for communicating with friends (57 versus 35 per cent) and family (71 versus 24 per cent), but these differences decrease for those people who have been online more years.

The online activities most frequently mentioned by those 9 to 17 years of age in the AOL youth study were: write letters/notes to friends and relatives (61 per cent), use instant messages (55 per cent) and play games (53 per cent) (another dozen activities were reported by fewer than 40 per cent of respondents). The activities reported noticeably more by young women were writing letters/notes, using instant messaging, getting information about rock stars or music groups, visiting chat rooms and writing to a penpal in another state or country. Young users had an average of 35 people on their instant messaging contact list, with those 15–17 years old reporting an average of 43.3 others. These contacts were primarily friends but also included various relatives, and 3 per cent reported that people they met online were on their instant messaging contact lists. Initial results from a study of survey responses to the National Geographic Society's website in the fall of 1998, from 35,000 Americans, 5000 Canadians and 15,000 others, showed that (1) high e-mail contact does not reduce other forms of interaction, (2) younger people used e-mail more for friends, near and far, (3) older people used e-mail more for kin, near and far, (4) women used e-mail more with kin at a distance, but (5) overall, communication frequencies for men and women were basically the same for all media.

The Internet at Home and in School

Tapscott (1997) discusses more than just access by, or representation of, different demographic groups on the Internet. He describes the very generation that is growing up with the Internet, what he calls N-Gen (the net generation, consisting of those aged 2 to 27 in 1997). This generation watches less TV, and is able to communicate through e-mail, develop web pages and start businesses. He emphasizes that these young users take advantage of the Internet to play, explore their world, try out different identities, express themselves through personal web pages, develop relationships with friends and family and become socialized. These activities are centred in interactive use of the medium and communication with others, as opposed to the more passive use of traditional mass media, and are (still) centred in a text-based medium, which promotes written literacy (see also Cherny, 1999; and Kellner, this volume).

Lacking facial expression, body language, tone of voice, clothing, physical surroundings, and other contextual information, the N-Gen has had to innovate within the limitations of the ASCII keyboard. As a result of this, a new script is emerging with new contextual information, subtleties, and to ... Almost all of the adults we encountered who work with N-Geners commented on how articulate they are as a group, and that the youngsters had views on subjects that seemed advanced for their age. While this is to be expected from the Net-savvy elite demographic group, we can expect that the interactive environment will strengthen verbal ability and the expression of ideas in every group. (Tapscott, 1997: 64, 70)

Tapscott gives as just one example the rise of youth e-zines, which 'provide a portrait of the culture of interaction – the antithesis of broadcast culture' (1997: 84). He suggests that early online communication will foster greater value for collaborative skills, based on 'peer-oriented relationships rather than hierarchies within families and companies' (1997: 212).

Tapscott summarizes one teacher's experience when she ran a community computing centre in New Haven, Connecticut. The class with the computer-savvy teacher became more computer literate than the other classes who had teachers who knew little about computers. The teacher would bring in people who worked in New Haven to talk to the kids about their job. The kids would send e-mails to these visiting guests. 'It broke down the power dynamic that exists between a kid and an adult' (1997: 149). A third of the respondents in the AOL (2000) youth study felt that going online had made them a better student, 31 per cent said it had improved their language skills, and 56 per cent preferred going online for help with their homework, compared with 27 per cent for the library and other resources. Critics argue as to whether familial relationships are affected by increased Internet use.

Tapscott argues that families may become closer as a result of Internet use in the household: 'The new media hold the promise of strengthening the family by moving many family activities [such as working, learning, shopping] dispersed by industrial society back into the home' (1997: 252). Since children today quite frequently know more about computers than their parents, the children often rise in the family hierarchy. 'Open families adopt the interactive model ... The traditional authoritarian model is changing due to the generational gap in that, for the first time, children know more than their parents about something really important' (1997: 251). For example, in the AOL (2000) youth survey, 61 per cent reported going online at least once with their parents, 44 per cent (52 per cent for those 15–17 years old) said they had some influence in getting their parents or family members to go online, and 66 per cent said that they had helped their parents get online or use the Internet (see also Buckingham, this volume).

Respondents to the UCLA (2000) study indicate that their use of the Internet helps to create and maintain friendships as well as communicate with the family. Indeed, the two most popular Internet activities reported by users were web surfing/browsing (81.7 per cent) and using e-mail (81.6 per cent) – that is, general information seeking and communicating with others. Concerning the attributes of the Internet, respondents were most satisfied with their 'ability to communicate with other people' – more so than with relevant information, goods and services, ease of finding information, and connection speed. Most (89.0 per cent) of the parents in the study reported that their children spent about the same time with their friends since they started using the Internet; 4.0 per cent indicated more time, and 7.0 per cent less time. While 27.5 per cent reported spending no time on the Internet together with other household members, 47.1 per cent reported doing so at least some time each week. Indeed, more people reported feeling ignored because of others' television use (36.5 per cent) than Internet use (24.7 per cent). Overall, 91.8 per cent indicate no change in the time members of the household spend together since becoming connected to the Internet. On average, Internet users feel that the Internet has slightly increased (3.3 on a scale of 1 [greatly decreased] to 5 [greatly increased]) the number of people regularly contacted, and extent of communicating with family and friends; 26.2 per cent reported having online friends (on average, almost 13 friends) that they have never met, and 12.4 per cent have met in person someone they first met online (on average 5.6 such new friendships).

Tapscott claims that children sacrifice TV time, not social time, to use their family's computer. He also maintains that video games are often intended for multiple users. The 'average AOL home spends almost 15 per cent less time watching TV than the US average ... More than 40 per cent of respondents in a recent survey conducted by Jupiter Communications and the KidsCom Company said that they watch less TV because of their internet use ... In a study conducted by Odyssey, respondents were asked, "What activities are you typically taking time from to go online?" The number one answer, at 30 per cent, was television' (1997: 30). Kids who are part of this generation are not wasting time on the net. 'Time spent on the Net is not passive time, it's active time' (1997: 8–10): they read, investigate, learn how to solve problems and compose their thoughts. Of the respondents to the AOL (2000) youth survey, 62 per cent (but 73 per cent of young men) reported they would rather go online than watch television, though young women (54 per cent) would prefer the telephone.

Indeed, Tapscott states that, for the first time

ever, children are taking control of critical elements of a technological revolution:

> Net based communications usually starts around 11 for girls and 13 for boys – basically during adolescence. At these ages, children seek autonomy and the creation of an identity. The Net seems to provide a vehicle to explore the self and for children to establish themselves as independent, self-governing individuals ... Of the potential 28 per cent of American children who had potential Net access at the end of 1997, between 6.7 and 7 million individual N-Geners are characterized as active users; 85 per cent–90 per cent of this population ... were participating in live chat on a regular basis. (1997: 56)

On the one hand these media foster increased openness, but on the other they reduce the consequences or judgements associated with unmediated interactions. Tapscott reports some beneficial aspects of what are usually seen as harmful uses of the Internet. For example, youth see cybersex as safe, experimental and mutual; they 'can always disconnect if disinterested or harassed ... They seem more interested in developing both the emotional and the physical side of real relationships, with the Internet as just one more "safe" mode of communication' (1997: 172–3).

Associations with Other Media Use

Kayany and Yelsma (2000) argue that households comprise both social and technological dimensions; so the addition of new elements such as online media affects the organization of roles, relationships and functions. Their study of 185 people in 84 households showed that online use affects time spent mostly in TV viewing, some in telephone use, some in newspaper reading, and a small amount in family conversations, with greater declines reported by children. Both informational and entertainment functions of media were rated as more important by more frequent online users. The authors concluded that online media seem to be displacing informational functions for TV, but not entertainment functions for either TV or newspaper.

James et al. (1995) studied home-based media via an online questionnaire, finding that computer bulletin board use reduced time spent using TV, books, telephone, and letters. Robinson et al. (1997), analysing data from a national probability telephone survey (1994, 1995), found that print media and CMC use seem to reinforce the use of each other, but there was no relationship to radio or TV use. Thus, displacement effects are most likely among functionally equivalent media, and among media that depend on the same limited resources, as well as provide similar resources, uses and gratifications.

Other studies find that use of computer and Internet decreases some other media use. Reagan (1987) reported that young computer users are less likely to use radio, newspapers, local and network TV. The Pew Research Center (1997) found that online news consumers viewed TV news less, and the GVU (1997) online surveys reported that web surfing replaces weekly TV viewing. Coffey and Stipp (1997) analysed home media diaries, finding only a very small percentage of respondents use their computers during prime time; few people have a computer in the same room as television (Media Metrix, 1997); heavy computer users are not heavy TV viewers (Crispell, 1997); and greater computer use is associated with greater use of print media (Perse and Dunn, 1998). A European survey reported that from 50 per cent to 60 per cent of British, German, Swedish and French Internet users said they were watching less television since going online, and 29 per cent reported reading fewer magazines and newspapers. However, 90 per cent indicated that online usage did not interfere with their normal social life (Internetnews, 2000). Jessel (1995) and Miller and Clemente (1997) also show that nearly a third of online users reported spending less time watching television than before their online usage. AOL's (2000) representative national Internet users' survey also found declines in other media use, but less so than the European study. Users reported watching less television (24 per cent compared with 16 per cent in 1999), reading fewer print newspapers (19 versus 13 per cent) and reading fewer print magazines (18 versus 11 per cent), and those percentages generally increase the more users have been online.

Internet users report that they use more media overall than non-users (UCLA, 2000), especially books, video games, recorded music and radio. However, users report watching about 28 per cent less television per week than do non-users. More (67.3 per cent) also rate the Internet as an 'important' or 'extremely important' information source, compared with 53.1 per cent for television and 46.8 per cent for radio.

One study applying the uses and gratifications approach (Ferguson and Perse, 2000) analysed data from an online survey and a three-day media-use diary from over 200 college students at two universities that had extensive Internet access. Entertainment was the most salient motivation for web use, after required school activities; after search engines, the most frequently visited sites were entertainment and sports. Thus, the play component of the web may displace TV viewing, as entertainment is a primary gratification from TV. However, little web surfing seems motivated by the need to pass time. The second most important motivation for watching TV is for relaxation, but web use was not much motivated by this,

probably because it requires active choice and cognition. Finally, companionship motivations were not salient for web use: 'There was little evidence that the World Wide Web can substitute for personal interaction' (2000: 170), or even much parasocial interaction, but this may change with greater bandwidth, which would allow for streaming video and responsive Internet telephony.

Applying a uses and gratifications perspective to survey responses from 279 students, Papacharissi and Rubin (2000) found that the Internet was used as a 'functional alternative to face-to-face communication for those who are anxious about face-to-face communication and who did not find face-to-face communication to be rewarding' (2000: 188). Those who rated the Internet as providing more social presence were more likely to say they used the Internet to help pass time, for convenience and for entertainment. They note that interpersonal utilities and information seeking are distinct types of uses; for those with satisfying interpersonal relations, the Internet was used more for information seeking; for those with unrewarding or anxiety-inducing interpersonal relations, the Internet was used as an alternative medium for social interaction, and such users had a greater affinity for the Internet. This set of results reverses the causality of the Kraut et al. (1998) study: in this interpretation, the Internet provides greater freedom of expression, fewer visible requirements for interaction, and fewer stressful personal interactions. 'These findings highlight the potential of the Internet as a social medium that can augment our socializing capabilities' (Papacharissi and Rubin, 2000: 193).

LaRose et al. (2000) also challenge Kraut et al.'s (1998; 1999) results, which indicated that Internet use by new adopters was associated with increased loneliness, depression and stress over a one- to two-year period. LaRose et al. argue that one factor possibly explaining these differences is experience with the Internet: many of the studies finding a negative association between sociability and Internet use involved novice users. Experienced users would tend to have greater facility in managing social cues online, would have less stress about learning the technology, and may have been less likely to have recently moved which would reduce their access to social networks. Also, the Homenet respondents studied by Kraut et al. reported overall low levels of depression, so they may have not had as great a need for social support.

As Kraut et al.'s results might have been specific to novice Internet users, LaRose and his colleagues analysed a new set of respondents, 171 students. What did they find? Internet use influenced depression through two paths. Prior Internet experience and Internet usage increased self-efficacy, which reduced online stress, which, as part of general life hassles, increased depression. Second, Internet use leads to more e-mail sent to known others, which increased social support, which decreased depression. However, Internet use also created Internet stress, leading to more depression, which could be mediated by Internet self-efficacy. Also, they found reduced depression in Internet users among these college students, as 'they may have used the Internet to obtain social support rather than to replace it' (LaRose et al., 2000: 12). There was, essentially, no relation between Internet use and depression, but general stress (hassles) and Internet stress *were* significantly related to depression. Thus, novice users may not have enough expertise to develop the self-efficacy necessary to moderate the new Internet stresses. So, while the central point in the Kraut et al. studies is that Internet usage displaces strong (face-to-face) social ties with weak (online) ties, it may be more accurate to say that some people turn to the Internet to obtain strong social support, especially when they can't find that in their unmediated situation, and do so because of online advantages (such as anonymity for sensitive topics, specialized expertise, group norms, etc.).

Franzen (2000) also critiques the Kraut et al. (1998) results, by analysing differences between responses to an online survey from 15,842 Internet users (20 per cent response) and a mailed survey to a control group of 1196 non-users (50 per cent response). He points out that the Homenet study used no control group, so could not test for maturation or local history effects (such as participants concentrating on Internet use early on in the study because of the novelty). Franzen's study found few differences in network size (in fact non-users reported 10 while users reported 12) or time spent with friends between users and non-users (though users had 23 per cent more friends), controlling for a variety of demographic, social and media factors. There was no effect of the number of months since first starting to use the Internet on network size. Consequentially, however, he shows that the number of people contacted online via e-mail increased the number of close friends, but longer or more intensive time spent on the Internet did not affect that number, or time spent socializing with others, though it did slightly reduce overall network size. So it is the ability to contact others via the Internet that leads to the associated increase in social networks. Respondents also reported many positive effects of e-mail usage on social networks. He concludes that 'Internet users are, on average, not socially isolated but quite to the contrary a relatively socially active group', and also suggests that larger social networks lead to greater e-mail contacts which in turn generates larger networks.

Increasing Diversity of Voices

The Internet can be a great communication tool for those who have a hard time meeting new friends owing to physical handicaps, diseases or even poor social skills (Wallace, 1999). These people can easily find others like them throughout the country and around the world, providing support and a chance to decrease loneliness or low self-esteem. Jones (1997) emphasizes that online communities can especially support otherwise marginalized cultures – both those discriminated against, and those acting as sources of discrimination against others. For example, the 7800 older SeniorNet members from the US and Canada say the network helps them ease their loneliness: 'It hosts welcoming events, celebrates anniversary parties, and mourns when one of its members dies' (Bollier, 1995: 3). The WELL is another example of an Internet community; WELL members live in the San Francisco Bay Area and often meet face-to-face (Rheingold, 1993). Other online communities include health support groups for people with illnesses that are not frequent enough to foster local physical communities (Rice, 2001).

Certainly the Internet has provided possibilities for viable communicative spaces for feminist networking and interaction (see Harcourt, 1999; Terry and Calvert, 1997). Harcourt in particular consider how the Internet might be used to support women's empowerment in developing countries, to bridge cultures, both local and global, and to coordinate women's issues at international conferences and working groups.

Internet users may increase their tolerance for a greater diversity of views, because the content of the message, not the physical appearance of the messenger/writer, is emphasized. However, as Hill and Hughes (1998: 184) point out, just because people have the opportunity to build friendships does not mean that they will be amiable. New forms of online expression also include virtual sex, alternate cyber identities and electronic stalking (Civin, 1999; Odzer, 1997). Odzer, in particular, argues that while the interaction occurs in virtual and fantasy environments, the psychological and emotional relations are real in both experience and consequence. Indeed, she puts forth online eroticism as a valid form of emotional relationship and self-growth. Others, however, analyse online sex as one manifestation of loneliness, isolation and depression.

At the other extreme of social relations, Cobb (1998) discusses how online technology and spirituality are reinforcing and convergent. Indeed, the transcendent transformations in technology can be seen as ongoing God-inspired creation. Consider, for instance, that the experience of cyberspace is in some ways the antithesis of materialism, being largely non-material itself, and an untapped manifestation of the human collectivity. And what might it mean about human nature when artificial intelligence does satisfactorily mirror human actions, intentions and communication? Certainly there are many online religious communities and websites (from the most orthodox to the most fantastic), all supporting humans' needs for and expressions of spirituality. On the other hand, as with critiques of online communities in general, it may be difficult to avoid overemphasizing the individual's own experience, at the cost of real, personal religious relations with other humans, and with the inherent self-submerging nature of great religions.

Potential Transformations

More extravagantly, Levy (1997) suggests a transformation not only from a material economy to an information economy, but farther into a 'social economy', or a collective intelligence mediated through cyberspace, where interactions, relationships and communication become the central resource and social infrastructure, fostered by information and communication technology. This is precisely the argument of social capital, where the value-added and positive network externalities (or public goods) aspects of shared knowledge, collaboration and social networks cannot be captured, processed and mass produced. This rise of the role of social interactions, now unimpeded by physical, cultural, language and temporal boundaries, will bring great challenges to traditional notions of countries, nationalities and economies.

Others, such as Robertson (1998), argue that because scientific theory or our analytic ability, now augmented and even superseded in some cases by computing power, can generate cumulative as well as discontinuous change, the current transformation is clearly revolutionary. Indeed, he argues that the computer and information revolution will be more transcendent than language, writing and printing, in terms of consequences for knowledge, culture, education, entertainment and ordinary life. Johnson (1997) makes a somewhat similar claim, equating the rise of various computer interfaces (the hardware, software and usage patterns) with the development of literacy. One of the ways he constructs this argument is to reject the dichotomy between technology and art, so as to be able to consider artifacts such as Gothic cathedrals and hypertext both as instances of interfaces.

Levy (1998) goes further in conceptualizing the possibilities of online identity. Rather than oppose 'virtual' with 'real', he places both in a larger typology that also includes 'possibility' and 'actuality'. Virtualization has been occurring in many social domains, from contacts to intelligence as well as to identity – indeed it is an inherent aspect of the human mind, because cognition and action are both

social processes. He feels that this virtualization does not replace or destroy personal identity, but rather augments and transforms it.

Conclusion

This chapter has reviewed research literature and results concerning three primary social issues surrounding the increased use of the Internet: access, civic and community involvement, and social interaction and new forms of expression.

While some evidence indicates that the digital divide is decreasing or even disappearing with respect to gender and race, differences in income and education are still great, and in some studies increasing. The general lag in access and use may create enduring and subsequential negative social consequences, persisting even after later adopters achieve full access. There are many barriers, obstacles and challenges to more equitable access, and some of those may be deeply embedded in social and cultural contexts and differences.

Many critics are quite pessimistic about the impact of Internet use on civic, political and community involvement. People may use a less diverse range of media, individuals' actions may be less private, online activists may be more extreme, users may have difficulty assessing the vast amounts of information available, people may basically reinforce their prior beliefs by participating only in selected interest groups, and the greatest current threat may be the growing concentration across media industries. Some conceptualizations of the attributes of the Internet and communities reject the notion that organic communities can thrive in mediated, online form, as they constitute secondary and distant relationships. Further, individual privacy is threatened, especially by commercial interests, and online communities typically are bound only by a single shared interest. More fundamentally, the nature of current 'real' communities can be debated, as some evidence (especially by Putnam) shows that various forms of social involvement have been declining for many years in the US, and that very few people actually interact densely with physically proximate neighbours; rather, they participate in thin local communities and dispersed family and work networks.

On the other hand, recent studies and surveys find that Internet users tend to be more interested in current events; campaigns and political activists have already started using the Internet for a variety of purposes; users are more involved in civic and political activities than non-users; and many government offices provide e-mail and web access. Nonetheless, real online dialogue among different interest groups is rare, and government access is typically one-way. However, many communities are strengthened through online interaction, if only because of the lower obstacles, such as time, distance and need to initially know others personally before communicating. It's probably more appropriate to think of online interaction as complementing physical communities. Nonetheless, there are many vibrant and long-lived mediated communities, ranging from health support groups to dispersed cultural and ethnic groups. The very growth and intensity of online communities may well speak to the perceived decline in real communities, as humans seek out social support and interaction. Indeed, many aspects of relationships, emotions and identities are experienced as just as real through the Internet as they are over other media (such as the telephone) or face-to-face. There are several case studies showing that small communities have been reinvigorated through online systems. Researchers taking a more historical approach warn that there are likely few really revolutionary changes associated with new technologies, and people embed these new media within familiar social contexts.

Finally, concerning social interaction and expression, pessimistic perspectives claim that not only does mediated communication impoverish the nature of interactions, but online interactions can be deceiving, simplistic, hateful and transient. Some conclude that high or extended Internet use leads to isolation and depression, as weak mediated relations replace strong unmediated ones, and narrowly focused relations replace more diverse ones. However, both survey and ethnographic studies show that rich, fertile, diverse and expanded interactions are possible through the Internet. There are many online groups with impassioned members providing emotional and other resources to each other, and users regularly rate communicating with others – family, friends and new people they have met online – as their most favourite and important activity. Some studies show that interactive Internet usage replaces passive television watching, but that overall Internet users are greater media participants. The net generation may well be more literate, creative and socially skilled because of their early familiarity with the Internet, including trying out various aspects of their developing identity online. Interacting with teachers and other students is easier when supported by the Internet, and both students and patients are more likely to talk about sensitive issues online, possibly because of the protection of anonymity. A noticeable percentage of users meet new people they come to call friends online, and go on to meet these people in person. Several studies have specifically countered some prior research linking Internet use with isolation or depression, showing indeed that experienced Internet users may find greater support online, become more satisfied with their interactions and communication, and generate new relationships

through the ability to contact others more easily. Indeed, some speculate that the Internet can also foster greater tolerance through exposure to a wider diversity of voices, and even support transcendent and spiritual growth. All these possibilities may lead to major growth in our concepts of identity, groups and society.

While the uses and effects of many major communication technologies (such as the pen, telegraph, telephone, photocopier, memo), have been studied retrospectively, if at all the recent rapid growth of the Internet affords communication researchers a unique opportunity to describe, assess, predict and evaluate short-term changes as well as long-term developments. If the current speculation and research seem to indicate diverse, contradictory and simultaneous consequences, at several levels of analysis, this may be because that is fundamentally the nature of social change. However, it is far better to ground this understanding of the complexity of this major phenomenon in research than in speculation and assertion.

NOTE

I thank Drs James Katz and Philip Aspden for inviting me to be part of their Syntopia project on studies of the Internet, and helping me to articulate the three primary themes of this chapter.

REFERENCES

AOL (2000) *American Online/Roper Starch Cyberstudy 2000*. Roper CNT375.

Aspden, P. and Katz, J. (2001) 'Assessments of quality of health care information and referrals to physicians: a nationwide survey', in R.E. Rice and J. Katz (eds), *The Internet and Health Communication*. Thousand Oaks, CA: Sage. pp. 107–19.

Baron, N.S. (1984) Computer-mediated communication as a force in language change. *Visible Language*, 18 (2): 118–41.

Baudrillard, J. (1983) *Simulations*, trans. P. Foss, P. Patton and P. Beitchman. New York: Semiotext(e).

Baym, N.K. (1995) 'The emergence of community in computer-mediated communication', in S.G. Jones (ed.), *Cybersociety: Computer-Mediated Communication and Community*. Thousand Oaks, CA: Sage. pp. 138–63.

Beniger, J. (1988) 'The personalization of mass media and the growth of pseudo-community', *Communication Research*, 14 (3): 352–71.

Bikson, T. and Panis, C. (1999) *Citizens, Computers, and Connectivity*. Santa Monica, CA: RAND.

Bollier, D. (ed.) (1995) *The Future of Community and Personal Identity in the Coming Electronic Culture*. Washington, DC: Aspen Institute.

Borchert, M. (1998) 'The challenge of cyberspace: Internet access and persons with disabilities', in B. Ebo (ed.), *Cyberghetto or Cybertopia: Race, Class, and Gender on the Internet*. New York: Praeger. pp. 45–64.

Bourque, S.C. and Warren, K.B. (1987) 'Technology, gender, and development', *Daedalus*, 116 (4): 173–98.

Browning, G. and Weitzner, D. (1996) *Electronic Democracy: Using the Internet to Influence American Politics*. White Plains, NY: Information Today, Inc.

Calhoun, C. (1986) 'Computer technology, large-scale societal integration and the local community', *Urban Affairs Quarterly*, 22: 329–49.

Carpini, M.X.D. (1996) 'Voters, candidates, and campaigns in the new information age: an overview and assessment', *Harvard International Journal of Press/Politics*, 1: 36–56.

Carrier, R. (1998) 'Training the information-poor in an age of unequal access', in B. Ebo (ed.), *Cyberghetto or Cybertopia: Race, Class, and Gender on the Internet*. New York: Praeger.

Cerulo, K. (1997) 'Reframing sociological concepts for a brave new (virtual?) world', *Sociological Inquiry*, 67 (1): 48–58.

Cherny, L. (1999) *Conversation and Community: Discourse in a Social MUD*. Chicago: Chicago University Press.

Civin, M. (1999) *Male, Female, Email: the Struggle for Relatedness in a Paranoid Society*. New York: Other Press.

Cobb, J. (1998) *Cybergrace: the search for God in Cyberspace*. New York: Crown.

Coffey, S. and Stipp, H. (1997) 'The interactions between computer and television usage', *Journal of Advertising Research*, 37 (2): 61–7.

Cooper, M. (2000) *Disconnected, Disadvantaged, and Disenfranchised: Explorations in the Digital Divide*. New York: Consumer Federation of America.

Cooper, M. and Kimmelman, G. (1999) *The Digital Divide Confronts the Telecommunications Act of 1996: Economic Reality versus Public Policy*. Washington, DC: Consumer Union. Available at: http://www.consunion.org/other/telecom2-0299.htm.

Corrado, A. (2000) *Campaigns in Cyberspace: toward a New Regulatory Approach*. Queenstown, MD: Aspen Institute.

Crispell, D. (1997) 'The Internet on TV', *American Demographics*, 19 (5): 32–3.

Cultural Access Group (2001) *Ethnicity in the Electronic Age: Looking at the Internet through Multicultural Lens*. Los Angeles, CA: Access Worldwide Communications, Inc.

Davis, R. (1999) *The Web of Politics: the Internet's Impact on the American Political System*. New York: Oxford University Press.

Dear, M.J., Schockman, H. and Hise, G. (eds) (1996) *Rethinking Los Angeles*. Thousand Oaks, CA: Sage.

Deetz, S. (1989a) 'Communication technology policy and interest representation: Habermas' theory of communicative action'. Paper presented to the International Communication Association Meeting, San Francisco, 30 May.

Deetz, S. (1989b) 'Representation of interests and communication technologies: issues in democracy and policy', in S. Deetz (ed.), *Introduction to Communication*, 2nd edn. Needham Heights, MA: Ginn. pp. 128–45. Reprinted from S. Deetz, *Communication and the Culture of Technology*. Washington State University Press, 1980.

Deetz, S. (1990) 'Suppressed conflict, consent, and inequitable interest representation'. Paper presented at the annual meeting of the International Communication Association, Dublin, Ireland, June.

Dervin, B. (1980) 'Communication gaps and inequities: moving toward a reconceptualization', in B. Dervin and M.J. Voigt (eds), *Progress in Communication Sciences*, vol. 2. Norwood, NJ: Ablex. pp. 73–112.

Dervin, B. and Shields, P. (1990) 'Users: the missing link in technology research'. Paper presented at the Communication Technology Section Meeting, International Association for Mass Communication Research, Lake Bled, Yugoslavia, August.

Doheny-Farina, S. (1998) *The Wired Neighborhood*. New Haven, CT: Yale University Press.

Downing, J.D.H. (1989) 'Computers for political change: PeaceNet and public data access', *Journal of Communication*, 39 (3): 154–62.

ECRL (1999) 'The evolution of the digital divide: examining the relationship of race to Internet access and usage over time'. Electronic Commerce Research Laboratory. Tennessee: Vanderbilt University, Owen Graduate School of Management. Available at: http://www.ecommerce.vanderbilt.edu.

Fallows, J. (2000) 'Internet illusions', *New York Times Book Review*, 16 November: 28–31.

Ferguson, D. and Perse, E. (2000) 'The World Wide Web as a functional alternative to television', *Journal of Broadcasting & Electronic Media*, 44 (2): 155–74.

Fischer, C. (1997) 'Technology and community: historical complexities', *Sociological Inquiry*, 67 (1): 113–18.

Franzen, A. (2000) 'Does the Internet make us lonely?', *European Sociological Review*, 16(4): 427–38.

Freire, P. (1969) *Pedagogy of the Oppressed*. New York: Continuum.

Furlong, M.S. (1989) 'An electronic community for older adults: the SeniorNet network', *Journal of Communication*, 39 (3): 145–53.

Garson, B. (1988) *The Electronic Sweatshop: How Computers are Transforming the Office of the Future into the Factory of the Past*. New York: Simon & Schuster.

Gergen, K. (1991) *The Saturated Self: Dilemmas of Identity in Contemporary Life*. New York: HarperCollins.

Gillespie, A. and Robins, K. (1989) 'Geographical inequalities: the spatial bias of the new communications technologies', *Journal of Communication*, 39 (3): 7–19.

Greenberger, M. and Puffer, J.C. (1989) 'Telemedicine: toward better health care for the elderly', *Journal of Communication*, 39 (3): 137–44.

Gurstein, M. (ed.) (2000) *Community Informatics: Enabling Communities with Information and Communications Technologies*. Hershey, PA: Idea Group.

GVU (1997) *GVU's 7th WWW User Survey*. Graphics, Visualization and Usabilities Center. Available at:

http:// www.guv.gatech.edu/user_surveys/survey-1997-04.

Haddon, L. (2001) 'Social exclusion and information and communication technologies', *New Media & Society*, 2 (4): 387–406.

Hamman, R. (1999) 'Computer networks linking communities: a study of the effects of computer network use upon pre-existing communities', in U. Thiedke (ed.), *Virtual Groups: Characteristics and Problematic Dimensions* (in German). Wiesbaden, Germany: Westdeutscher. Available at: http://www.socio.demon.co.uk/mphil/short.html.

Hampton, K. (2000) 'Grieving for a lost network: collective action in a wired suburb'. Cambridge, MA: MIT Department of Urban Studies and Planning, October.

Hampton, K. and Wellman, B. (2000) 'Examining community in the digital neighborhood: early results from Canada's wired suburb', in T. Ishida and K. Isbister (eds), *Digital Cities*. Heidelberg: Springer. pp. 475–92.

Harcourt, W. (1999) *Women@Internet: Creating New Cultures in Cyberspace*. New York: Zed.

Heim, M. (1993) *The Metaphysics of Virtual Reality*. Oxford: Oxford University Press.

Hill, K.A. and Hughes, J. (1998) *Cyperpolitics: Citizen Activism in the Age of the Internet*. New York: Rowman & Littlefield.

Hiltz, S.R. and Turoff, M. (1995) *Network Nation*, rev. edn. Cambridge, MA: MIT Press.

Hoffman, D. and Novak, T. (1998) 'Information access: bridging the racial divide on the Internet', *Science*, 280 (5362): 390–1.

Hoffman, D., Kalsbeek, W. and Novak, T. (1996) 'Internet and Web use in the U.S.', *Communications of the ACM*, 39 (12): 36–46.

Horn, S. (1998) *Cyberville: Clicks, Culture, and the Creation of an Online Town*. New York: Warner.

Hudson, H.E. (1988) 'Ending the tyranny of distance: the impact of new communications technologies in rural North America', in J.R. Schement and L.A. Lievrouw (eds), *Competing Visions, Complex Realities: Social Aspects of the Information Society*. Norwood, NJ: Ablex. pp. 91–104.

Hundt, R. (2000) *You Say You Want a Revolution:a Story of Information Age Politics*. New Haven, CT: Yale University Press.

Internetnews (2000) 'Internet is gaining ground on tv watching', October, http://www.internews.com/intl-news/article/0,6_450071,00.html.

James, M., Wotring, C. and Forrest, E. (1995) 'An exploratory study of the perceived benefits of electronic bulletin board use and their impact on other communication activities', *Journal of Broadcasting & Electronic Media*, 39: 30–50.

Jansen, S.C. (1989) 'Gender and the information society: a socially structured silence', *Journal of Communication*, 39 (3): 196–215.

Jensen, J. (1999) 'Interactivity', in P. Mayer (ed.), *Computer Media and Communication*. New York: Oxford University Press. pp. 160–87.

Jessel, M. (1995) 'Internet begins to cut into TV viewing', *Broadcasting and Cable*, 40: 318–30.

Johnson, S. (1997) *Interface Culture: How New Technology Transforms the Way we Create and Communicate*. New York: Harper Edge.

Jones, S. (ed.) (1997) *Virtual Culture: Identity and Communication in Cybersociety*. Thousand Oaks, CA: Sage.

Jones, S. (1999) 'Understanding community in the information age', in P. Mayer (ed.), *Computer Media and Communication*. New York: Oxford University Press. pp. 219–40.

Jonscher, C. (1999) *The Evolution of Wired Life: from the Alphabet to the Soul-Catcher Chip – How Information Technologies Change Our World*. New York: Wiley.

Jordan, T. (1999) *Cyberpower: the Culture and Politics of Cyberspace and the Internet*. New York: Routledge.

Kahin, B. and Keller, J. (eds) (1995) *Public Access to the Internet*. Cambridge, MA: MIT Press.

Kapor, M. (1993) 'Where is the digital highway really heading?', *Wired*, July/August: 53–9, 94.

Katz, J. and Aspden, P. (1997a) 'Motives, hurdles, and dropouts: who is on and off the Internet and why', *Communications of the ACM*, 40 (4): 97–102.

Katz, J. and Aspden, P. (1997b) 'A nation of strangers', *Communications of the ACM*, 40 (12): 81–6.

Katz, J. and Aspden, P. (1997c) 'Motivations for and barriers to Internet usage: results of a national public opinion survey', *Internet Research: Electronic Networking Applications and Policy*, 7 (3): 170–88.

Katz, J., Rice, R.E. and Aspden, P. (2001) 'The Internet, 1995–2000: access, civic involvement, and social interaction', *American Behavioral Scientist*, 45(3): 404–19.

Kayany, J. and Yelsma, P. (2000) 'Displacement effects of online media in the socio-technical contexts of households', *Journal of Broadcasting & Electronic Media*, 44 (2): 215–29.

Kiesler, S., Siegel, H. and McGuire, T.W. (1984) 'Social psychological aspects of computer-mediated communication', *American Psychologist*, 39 (10): 1123–34.

Kolko, B., Nakamura, L. and Rodman, G. (eds) (1999) *Race in Cyberspace*. New York: Routledge.

Kraut, R.E. (1989) 'Telecommuting: the trade-offs of home work', *Journal of Communication*, 39 (3): 19–47.

Kraut, R., Lundmark, V., Patterson, M., Kiesler, S., Mukopadhyay, T. and Scherlis, M. (1998) 'Internet paradox: a social technology that reduces social involvement and psychological well-being?', *American Psychologist*, 53 (9): 1017–31.

Kraut, R., Mukhopadhyay, T., Szczypula, J., Kiesler, S. and Sherlis, B. (1999) 'Information and communication: alternative uses of the Internet in households', *Information Systems Research*, 10: 287–303.

Krendl, K.A., Broihier, M.C. and Fleetwood, C. (1989) 'Children and computers: do sex-related differences persist?', *Journal of Communication*, 39 (3): 85–93.

Kroker, A. and Weinstein, M. (1994) *Data Trash: the Theory of the Virtual Class*. New York: St Martin's.

LaRose, R. and Mettler, J. (1989) 'Who uses information technologies in rural America?', *Journal of Communication*, 39 (3): 48–60.

LaRose, R., Eastin, M. and Gregg, J. (2001) 'Reformulating the Internet paradox: social cognitive explanations of Internet use and depression', *Journal of Online Behavior*, submitted.

Levy, P. (1997) *Collective Intelligence: Mankind's Emerging World in Cyberspace*, trans. R. Bononno. New York: Plenum.

Levy, P. (1998) *Becoming Virtual: Reality in the Digital Age*, trans. R. Bononno. New York: Plenum.

Lievrouw, L.A. (1994) 'Information resources and democracy: understanding the paradox', *Journal of the American Society for Information Science*, 45 (6): 350–7.

Lindlof, T. and Shatzer, M. (1998) 'Media ethnography in virtual space: strategies, limits and possibilities', *Journal of Broadcasting Electronic Media*, 42 (2): 170–89.

Loader, B. (ed.) (1997) *The Governance of Cyberspace: Politics, Technology and Global Restructuring*. New York: Routledge.

Margolis, M. and Resnick, D. (2000) *Politics as Usual: the Cyberspace 'Revolution'*. Thousand Oaks, CA: Sage.

McChesney, R. (2000) *Rich Media, Poor Democracy: Communication Politics in Dubious Times*, rev. edn. New York: New Press.

McConnaughey, J. and Lader, W. (1998) *Falling through the Net II: New Data on the Digital Divide*. Washington, DC: US Department of Commerce. Available at http://www.ntia.doc.gov/ntiahome/net2/ falling.html.

McCreadie, M. and Rice, R.E. (1999a) 'Trends in analysing access to information. Part I: Cross-disciplinary conceptualizations', *Information Processing and Management*, 35 (1): 45–76.

McCreadie, M. and Rice, R.E. (1999b) 'Trends in analysing access to information. Part II: Unique and integrating conceptualizations', *Information Processing and Management*, 35 (1): 77–99.

McNutt, J. (1998) 'Ensuring social justice for the new underclass: community interventions to meet the needs of the new poor', in B. Ebo (ed.), *Cyberghetto or Cybertopia; Race, Class, and Gender on the Internet*. New York: Praeger. pp. 33–44.

Media Metrix (1997) Online press release, http://www. mediametric.com/pcmpr33.htm.

Miller, T. and Clemente, P. (1997) *1997 American Internet User Survey*. New York: FIND/SVP Emerging Technologies Research Group. Available at: http://etrg.findsvp.com/internet/findf.html.

Morris, D. (2000) *Vote.com*. Los Angeles: Renaissance.

Mulgan, G.J. (1991) *Communication and Control: Networks and the New Economies of Communication*. New York: Guilford.

Murdock, G. and Golding, P. (1989) 'Information poverty and political inequality: citizenship in the age of privatized communications', *Journal of Communication*, 39 (3): 180–95.

Neu, C.R., Anderson, R.H. and Bikson, T.K. (1999) *Sending your Government a Message: E-mail Communication between Citizens and Government*. Santa Monica, CA: RAND.

Nie, N. and Erbring, L. (2000) 'Internet and society', http://www.stanford.edu/group/siqss/Press_Release/ Preliminary_Report.pdf.

Nielsen/NetRatings (2001) 'Three out of five Americans on the web', http://news.excite.com/news/r/010214/14/ net-interaccess-dc.

NTIA (1999) *Falling through the Net: A Report on Telecommunications and the Information Technology Gap in America*. Washington, DC.: NTIA. Available at: http://www.ntia.doc.gov/ntiahome/digitaldivide.

Numes, M. (1995) 'Jean Baudrillard in cyberspace: Internet, virtuality, and postmodernity', *Style*, 29 (2): 21–7.

Odzer, C. (1997) *Virtual Spaces: Sex and the Cyber Citizen*. New York: Berkley.

Papacharissi, Z. and Rubin, A. (2000) 'Predictors of Internet use', *Journal of Broadcasting & Electronic Media*, 44 (2): 175–96.

Parks, M.R. and Floyd, K. (1996) 'Making friends in cyberspace', *Journal of Communication*, 46 (1): 80–97.

Parks, M.R. and Roberts, L.D. (1998) '"Making MOOsic": the development of personal relationships online and a comparison to their offline counterparts', *Journal of Social and Personal Relationships*, 15 (4): 517–37.

Perse, E. and Dunn, D. (1998) 'The utility of home computers: implications of multimedia and connectivity', *Journal of Broadcasting & Electronic Media*, 42: 435–56.

Pew Research Center (1997) 'TV news viewership declines'. http://www.peoplepress.org/mediaque.htm.

Pew Research Center (2000) 'Tracking online life: how women use the Internet to cultivate relationships with family and friends', http://www.pewinternet.org/ reports/toc.asp?Report=11.

Pfaffenberger, B. (1990) *Democratizing Information: Online Databases and the Rise of End-User Searching*. Boston: Hall.

Pool, I. de Sola (1983) *Technologies of Freedom*. Cambridge, MA: Belknap.

Porter, D. (ed.) (1997) *Internet Culture*. New York: Routledge.

Putnam, R. (1995) 'Bowling alone: America's declining social capital', *Journal of Democracy*, 6 (1): 65–78.

Putnam, R. (1996) 'The strange disappearance of civic life in America', *The American Prospect*, 24: 34–46.

Putnam, R. (2000) *Bowling Alone: the Collapse and Revival of American Community*. New York: Simon & Schuster.

Rash, W. (1997) *Politics on the Nets: Wiring the Political Process*. New York: Freeman.

Reagan, J. (1987) 'Classifying adopters and nonadopters of four technologies using political activity, media use and demographic variables', *Telematics and Informatics*, 4: 3–16.

Rheingold, H. (1993) *The Virtual Community: Homesteading on the Electronic Frontier*. Reading, MA: Addison-Wesley.

Rice, R.E. (1987a) 'New patterns of social structure in an information society', in J. Schement and L. Lievrouw (eds), *Competing Visions, Complex Realities: Social Aspects of the Information Society*. Norwood, NJ: Ablex. pp. 107–20.

Rice, R.E. (1987b) 'Computer-mediated communication and organizational innovation', *Journal of Communication*, 37: 65–94.

Rice, R.E. (2001) 'The Internet and health communication: a framework of experiences', in R.E. Rice and J.E. Katz (eds), *The Internet and Health Communication: Experiences and Expectations*. Thousand Oaks, CA: Sage. pp. 5–46.

Rice, R.E. and Katz, J.E. (eds) (2001) *The Internet and Health Communication: Experiences and Expectations*. Thousand Oaks, CA: Sage.

Rice, R.E., McCreadie, M. and Chang, S.-J. (2001) *Accessing and Browsing Information and Communication: a Multidisciplinary Approach*. Cambridge, MA: MIT Press.

Riphagen, J. and Kanfer, A. (1997) 'How does e-mail affect our lives?' National Center for Supercomputing Applications. Available at: http://www.ncsa.uiuc.edu/edu/trg/e-mail/index.html.

Robertson, D. (1998) *The New Renaissance: Computers and the Next Level of Civilization*. New York: Oxford University Press.

Robinson, J., Barth, K. and Kohut, A. (1997) 'Social impact research: personal computers, mass media and use of time', *Social Science Computer Review*, 15 (1): 65–82.

Rojas, V., Roychowdhury, D., Okur, O., Straubhaar, J. and Estrada-Ortiz, Y. (in press) 'Beyond access: cultural capital and the roots of the digital divide', in E. Bucy and J. Newhagen (eds), *Media Access: Social and Psychological Dimensions of New Technology Use*. Hillsdale, NJ: Erlbaum.

Rubinyi, R.M. (1989) 'Computers and community: the organizational impact', *Journal of Communication*, 39 (3): 110–23.

Scherer, K. (1997) 'College life on-line: healthy and unhealthy Internet use', *Journal of College Student Development*, 38: 655–65.

Schiller, H. (1996) *Information Inequality: the Deepening Social Crisis in America*. London: Routledge.

Schon, D., Sanyal, B. and Mitchell, W. (eds) (1999) *High Technology and Low-Income Communities*. Cambridge, MA: MIT Press.

Schroeder, K. and Ledger, J. (1998) *Life and Death on the Internet*. Menasha, WI: Supple.

Schuler, D. (1996) *New Community Networks: Wired for Change*. New York: ACM.

Shapiro, A. and Leone, R. (1999) *The Control Revolution: How the Internet is Putting Individuals in Charge and Changing the World We Know*. New York: Public Affairs Century Foundation.

Skocpol, T. (2000) *The Missing Middle: Working Families and the Future of American Social Policy*. New York: Norton.

Slack, R.S. and Williams, R.A. (2000) 'The dialectics of place and space: on community in the "information age"', *New Media & Society*, 2 (3): 313–34.

Smith, M. and Kollock, P. (eds) (1998) *Communities in Cyberspace*. New York: Routledge.

Smith, T. (1999) *The Emerging 21st Century American Family*. Report to National Opinion Research Center, Chicago.

Sobchack, V. (1996) 'Democratic franchise and the electronic frontier', in Z. Sardar and J. Ravetz (eds), *Cyberfutures: Culture and Politics on the Information Superhighway*. New York: New York University Press.

Starobin, P. (1996) 'On the square', *National Journal*, 25 June: 1145–9.

Stefik, M. (1999) *The Internet Edge: Social, Legal, and Technological Challenges for a Networked World*. Cambridge, MA: MIT Press.

Stoll, C. (1995) *Silicon Snake Oil: Second Thoughts on the Information Highway*. New York: Doubleday.

Stoll, C. (1999) *High Tech Heretic*. New York: Doubleday.

Stone, A. (1991) 'Will the real body please stand up? Boundary stories about virtual cultures', in M. Benedikt (ed.), *Cyberspace: First Steps*. Cambridge, MA: MIT Press. pp. 81–119.

Straus, S. (1997) 'Technology, group processes, and group outcomes: testing the connections in performance in computer-mediated and face-to-face groups', *Human–Computer Interaction*, 12: 227–66.

Surratt, C. (1998) *Netlife: Internet Citizens and their Communities*. Commack, NY: Nova Science.

Symposium (1995) 'Emerging media technology and the First Amendment', *Yale Law Journal*, 104: 1613–850.

Tapscott, D. (1997) *Growing up Digital: The Rise of the Net Generation*. New York: McGraw-Hill.

Terry, J. and Calvert, M. (eds) (1997) *Processed Lives: Gender and Technology in Everyday Life*. New York: Routledge.

Tsagarousianou, R., Tambini, D. and Bryan, C. (eds) (1998) *Cyberdemocracy: Technology, Cities and Civic Networks*. New York: Routledge.

Turkle, S. (1996) 'Virtuality and its discontents: searching for community in cyberspace', *The American Prospect*, 24: 50–7.

Turkle, S. (1997) *Life on the Screen: Identity in the Age of the Internet*. New York: Simon & Schuster. Also: New York: Touchstone, 1995.

UCLA (2000) *The UCLA Internet Report: Surveying the Digital Future*. UCLA Center for Communication Policy. Available at: http://www.ccp.ucal.edu.

US Congress (1987) *The Electronic Supervisor: New Technology, New Tensions*. Office of Technology Assessment OTA-CIT-333. Washington, DC: US Government Printing Office.

US Congress (1990) *Critical Connections: Communication for the Future*. Office of Technology Assessment. OTA-CIT-407. Washington, DC: US Government Printing Office.

Valovic, T. (2000) *Digital Mythologies: the Hidden Complexities of the Internet*. New Brunswick, NJ: Rutgers University Press.

Van Alstyne, W.W. (1995) *First Amendment: Cases and Materials*, 2nd edn. Westbury, NY: Foundation.

Van Dijk, J. (1999) *The Network Society: Social Aspects of New Media*, trans. L. Spoorenberg. Thousand Oaks, CA: Sage.

Wallace, P. (1999) *The Psychology of the Internet.* New York: Cambridge University Press.

Walther, J. (1996) 'Computer-mediated communication: impersonal, interpersonal, and hyperpersonal interaction', *Communication Research*, 23 (1): 3–43.

Webster, F. (1995) *Theories of the Information Society.* New York: Routledge.

Weinberg, S. (1987) 'Expanding access to technology: computer equity for women', in B.D. Wright, M.M. Ferree, G.O. Mellow, L.H. Lewis, M.-L.D. Samper, R. Asher and K. Claspell (eds), *Women, Work, and Technology: Transformations.* Ann Arbor, MI: University of Michigan Press. pp. 281–90.

Wellman, B. (2000) 'Physical place and cyberspace: the rise of networked individualism', *International Journal of Urban and Regional Research*, December.

Wellman, B. and Gulia, M. (1999a) 'Virtual communities as communities: net surfers don't ride alone', in M.A. Smith and P. Kollock (eds), *Communities in Cyberspace.* New York: Routledge. pp. 167–94.

Wellman, B. and Gulia, M. (1999b) 'Net surfers don't ride alone', in B. Wellman (ed.), *Networks in the Global Village.* Boulder, CO: Westview. pp. 331–66.

White, C.S. (1997) 'Citizen participation and the Internet: prospects for civic deliberation in the information age', *Social Studies*, 88: 23–8.

Winner, L. (1999) 'Who will be in cyberspace?', in P. Mayer (ed.), *Computer Media and Communication.* New York: Oxford University Press. pp. 207–18.

Wolf, A. (1998) 'Exposing the great equalizer: demythologizing Internet equity', in B. Ebo (ed.), *Cyberghetto or Cybertopia: Race, Class, and Gender on the Internet.* New York: Praeger. pp. 15–31.

Wresch, W. (1996) *Disconnected: Haves and Have-Nots in the Information Age.* New Brunswick, NJ: Rutgers University Press.

Wynn, E. and Katz, J. (1997) 'Hyperbole over cyberspace: self-presentation and social boundaries in Internet home pages and discourse', *The Information Society*, 13 (4): 297–329.

Yahoo!News (2001) 'Hispanics, blacks and women surfing the Internet in greater numbers', 19 February, http://dailynews.hayoo.com/h/ll/20010219/co/hispanics_blacks_and_women_surfing_the_internet_ingreater_numbers.

Zuboff, S. (1988) *In the Age of the Smart Machine: the Future of Work and Power.* New York: Basic.

PART TWO: TECHNOLOGY DESIGN AND DEVELOPMENT

Introduction

LEAH A. LIEVROUW

In this part of the *Handbook*, the contributors consider the design and development of new media as technologies *per se*. In terms of the definition of new media given in the Introduction to the volume, all three aspects of media technology – artifacts or devices, communication activities or practices, and social arrangements or organizations – are implicated, but in this part we place a bit more emphasis on the first aspect, the built systems. The authors range widely across frameworks for understanding new media design, development and use; in some cases, they build on these existing frameworks to propose new frameworks of their own.

Four main streams or lines of research and scholarship underpin most current understandings of new media design and development. The first is historical, reaching back to early histories of electric, and then electronic, media that emphasized stories of inventors and their inventions. For example, the familiar stories about Alexander Graham Bell (and Elisha Gray) and the telephone; Samuel Morse and the telegraph; Thomas Edison and the phonograph; Guglielmo Marconi and wireless radio; and Philo Farnsworth and Vladimir Zworykin and television, are part of many introductory media textbooks (e.g. Sterling and Kittross, 1990; Crowley and Heyer, 1995; Straubhaar and LaRose, 2000). Such accounts, which accord most of the credit for technological innovation and change to certain extraordinary individuals (so-called 'great-man history'), persist today in some popular histories of the Internet (Segaller, 1998).

In the last few decades, however, scholarship in the history of technology has shifted more toward the perspective of cultural or social history, and has attempted to incorporate cultural, economic and political contexts more fully into the stories of technological change. Patrice Flichy's chapter in this part, and his book *Dynamics of Modern Communication* (1995 [1991]), exemplify this approach. For example, most early histories of the American telephone system were funded by AT&T, and so tended to stress the primary role of Bell, and later the discoveries and inventions generated at Bell Laboratories. However, in the 1960s and 1970s scholars without ties to AT&T began to take a more disinterested approach. They published histories that explored the economic power of the company, the management decisions and regulatory compromises that fostered system growth, as well as the social changes and expectations in American society that affected how telephones were used (Brooks, 1975; Fischer, 1992). Describing the example of *Telefon Hirmondó* in Hungary, Carolyn Marvin (1988) showed that in its early days the telephone was perceived and used in many places as a broadcast news-type medium for elites, and thus did not 'naturally' or automatically lend itself to use as a medium for interpersonal conversation. Similarly, recent histories of computing and the Internet (Edwards, 1996; Ceruzzi, 1998; Abbate, 1999) demonstrate that from the outset these technologies were not simply the products of successive generations of technical inventions and improvements. They were also the outcome of changing organizational structures, growing demands for data and information, the rapid growth and research initiatives of elite American universities, and the military discourse and popular fears associated with the Cold War.

Another important thread in studies of new media design and development can be thought of as broadly cognitive and behavioural, that is, its focus is on how people understand and use media. Again, this thread reaches back many decades, to psychological studies of media conducted during the 1920s, 1930s and thereafter. These included the Payne Fund studies of the 'effects' of motion pictures on young people's attitudes and behaviour (Jowett et al., 1996), and later the work of Paul Lazarsfeld and his colleagues at Columbia University, and of Carl Hovland's research group at Yale University, on persuasion and propaganda, particularly via motion pictures and radio. This approach carried over into numerous subsequent studies of the effects of television (see Rogers, 1994; Schramm, 1997). Studies of 'effects' took the content of mediated communications into account, but they were perhaps even more focused on the potential influence of the medium itself. This strong view of the effects of communication technology *per se* has been called the *technology as source* approach. It asks 'whether the technologies themselves generate psychological effects in, and elicit social and behavioral responses from, users' and whether 'specific technological features may affect users' reception of different types of content' (Lievrouw et al., 2001: 283). This approach, together with concepts drawn from 'man–machine studies', human factors engineering and human–computer interaction (see Greenbaum and Kyng, 1991; Shneiderman, 1998), has been carried forward into studies of new media, particularly computing. For example, the *media equation* thesis advanced by Byron Reeves and Clifford Nass (1996) argues that the particular features of computer interfaces induce people to treat computers just as they do other people, by anthropomorphizing or attributing human knowledge, motives and personalities to the machines.

A weaker version of this psychological perspective can be characterized as the *technology as channel* view (Lievrouw et al., 2001). This approach, which has been particularly influential in studies of organizational communication, considers how well media technologies support or facilitate interpersonal and small-group interaction, especially as compared with face-to-face interaction. Seminal studies in this area include those by Short et al. (1976), Johansen et al. (1979), Hiltz and Turoff (1993 [1978]), Sproull and Kiesler (1991) and Sherry Turkle (1984), which are discussed in the introductory chapter to this volume. More recently, Joseph Walther (1992; 1996) has proposed that computer-mediated communication is not inherently any less 'personal' or involving than face-to-face interaction, and that close personal relationships can be started and nurtured online. Other scholars have examined the influence of CMC on power relations (Lea and Spears, 1991; Spears and Lea, 1994) and the concept of interactivity (Rafaeli, 1988). The latter topic is summarized and elaborated in the chapter by Sally McMillan in this part.

A third line of research influencing current ideas about new media development is grounded in ethnography and micro-sociological studies of technology. This *social shaping of technology* approach is generally concerned with the everyday uses of technologies, including media, with a particular focus on the ways that people modify, avoid, reinvent or otherwise adapt technologies to their particular purposes and circumstances. This perspective is covered in some detail in the chapters by Lievrouw and by Star and Bowker in this part, as well as in Part Three by Jackson, Poole and Kuhn, so the main points need not be reiterated here. However, one important hallmark of this approach is empirical: these studies typically use ethnographic techniques to observe the uses of technologies that are already well integrated into social settings such as workplaces (e.g. Suchman, 1987; Star, 1995; Kling, 1996; Viller and Sommerville, 1999) or homes (Silverstone and Hirsch, 1992; Livingstone and Bovill, 2001).

An important related body of research studies how technologies are conceived and developed by engineers and designers (e.g. Bucciarelli, 1994). For example, studies of *participatory design* (Sonnenwald, 1993; Clement, 1994) examine how technologies evolve in processes of negotiation among engineers, designers, users, managers and others. Another area, *computer-supported cooperative work* (CSCW), links computer interface design to processes of interaction in small groups, rather than assuming that computers are used exclusively by lone individuals (Winograd and Flores, 1987; Orlikowski, 1993; Dix et al., 1998).

The fourth strand of research dealing with new media development is more macro-sociological and economic. It considers how new technologies or other new ideas are introduced and spread in society. This perspective is exemplified by *diffusion of innovations* theory (Rogers, 1995). It is discussed at length in the chapter here by Lievrouw, but as a general matter it has been widely influential in studies of national development, marketing and large-scale studies of social structure and networks.

These four strands – we might call them the historical, psychological, micro-sociological/ethnographic and macro-sociological/economic – have to some extent converged in contemporary accounts of how new media technologies 'happen'. Elements from all four can be found in the chapters in this part.

Nonetheless, despite the variety and depth of the relevant research to date, the particular features and functions of media systems are so various, and continue to develop so quickly, that they remain difficult to summarize neatly, even in several chapters. As the Introduction to this volume points out, the recombinant nature of information and communication technology in the late twentieth and early twenty-first centuries confounds conventional classifications of either systems (for example, 'television', 'telephone', 'printing press', 'computer', 'audio recording', 'photography') or content ('feature film', 'conversation', 'database', 'fax', 'network news', 'novel'). This characteristic is in large part responsible for the persistent sense of novelty that is popularly associated with new media systems. Moreover, from a marketing standpoint, firms that design, manufacture and sell these technologies have a stake in playing up this sense of newness, so as to promote steady rates of consumption. Courts and regulators, in turn, reinforce the sense of ahistoricity by formulating and enforcing technology-related policies in a piecemeal fashion, reacting to the latest controversy or industry demand instead of long-term trends in technological development or social and cultural continuities.

So, for the purposes of this brief introduction, it is useful to point out a few main characteristics identified in these chapters that make information and communication technologies significant objects of study from the perspective of social (and especially communication) research. The first is that they are infrastructural. That is, drawing on the definition offered by Star and Bowker, they are fully embedded into social arrangements, other technologies and everyday practices; their reach extends across space and/or time; and they are taken for granted and perceived as transparent by those who use them.

As with other contemporary technical infrastructures (for example, transportation or power systems), media systems require enormous investments in built facilities and equipment, as well as ongoing maintenance and support services. As they grow, new organizational and regulatory structures develop along with them, to help distribute the costs and benefits of the system. People learn to use the systems and to rely on them. In time, the system becomes commonplace, almost invisible. (In the case of media systems that employ wireless technologies, or wired networks are hidden in walls or under the ground, parts of the system are literally 'invisible'.) Users only become aware of the system when it breaks down, when the service that is always there suddenly isn't, or runs so poorly that it interrupts or intrudes on other activities. Indeed, the brief accounts of the development of electronic mail and videotex included in Lievrouw's chapter demonstrate that the success or failure of these media depended in large part on building a reasonably reliable and usable technical system that was appropriate to its social context, with enough institutional support to ensure its survival and maintenance.

Of course, every form of communication in some sense has an 'infrastructure'. Even face-to-face interaction requires that communicators share some sort of symbolic system (language, non-verbal cues), and an understanding of the surrounding social and physical context, in order to share meaning. Language, behaviour and context thus constitute a sort of 'platform' that permits interpersonal communication. A parallel might be drawn with the roles of users, documents (content) and systems in interactivity, outlined by McMillan in her chapter. But what seems to distinguish media systems generally, and new media systems in particular, is the complexity and extensiveness of the material structure involved, and the corresponding degree of social commitment that members of a society or community must make to using the systems and adapting their patterns of communication and practice to these systems.

The second key characteristic of new media systems is often noted, especially by communication researchers: interactivity. In her chapter Sally McMillan ably traces the various definitions of interactivity across many literatures, and proposes a three-part framework for studying interactivity. Perhaps what has made interactivity so compelling in new media studies is that today's ICTs make it possible for mediated communication to resemble interpersonal interaction more closely than previous media technologies have done. Indeed, new media have given rise to entirely new forms of mediated interpersonal interaction, such as MUDs, chat rooms, teleconferences and of course electronic mail. Older electronic media were principally transmission technologies, well suited for sending general-interest messages from a few major information sources to large, more or less heterogeneous audiences. However, the pivotal technical feature of new media systems is switching, that is, the capacity to handle many point-to-point or 'n-way' messages, so that every user of the system is a potential generator as well as a receiver of messages and other content. This pattern was established with the telegraph; the telephone extended it into virtually every American household and workplace; and the Internet and wireless technologies have extended it even further to individuals wherever they are located. Essentially, new media technologies have enhanced the responsiveness of communication systems, ranging from simple request-and-delivery or query-and-response services (which might more accurately be called *transactional*) to the more complex patterns of interpersonal expression and sociality that we think of as truly interactive.

Every author in this part reminds us how important it is to remember that the technologies have not simply arrived fully formed, to be taken up and implemented by users exactly as their designers intended. In every case the original visions for particular technologies have proven naive, incomplete or mistaken. People's expectations of and demands for interactivity have been an important driver in this respect. As Lievrouw argues, the engineers and military planners who built the ARPANET were principally concerned with getting the most use out of the system's terminal equipment – the computer nodes of the network. ARPANET was intended to support file sharing and distributed data processing on these exotic and expensive machines. Instead, engineers, reseearchers and administrators were surprised to find that colleagues with ARPANET access almost immediately started using it for interpersonal messaging, which quickly became a major component of network traffic. Electronic mail fitted well into the everyday collaborative practices of scientists and engineers, and soon spread beyond computing to the rest of academia. Universities and research facilities entered an unprecedented phase of investment in computing and telecommunications systems to support faculty and student research and interaction, building a network that later became the original Internet 'backbone'. Interpersonal interaction may not have been the only motive behind these developments, but it was certainly a powerful one that became the Internet's enduring 'killer app'.

The third characteristic of new media technologies is interrelated with the others: ICTs are historically situated. The ARPANET example above makes this point, as does the discussion of new media technologies in the workplace and the home by Patrice Flichy, and the many examples given in the chapter by Leigh Star and Geof Bowker. As with any other human enterprise, new media technologies change over time, within the context of evolving social worlds and settings. They tend to fit prevailing beliefs and attitudes about communication, whether it is the 'mass society' associated with high modernism of the mid twentieth century, or the America 'broken up' by marketing and niche media in the 1990s (Turow, 1997). In periods when socialization and assimilation have been concerns, media have been sources of essential common knowledge and mainstream culture. When difference and individuality have been ascendant, media have provided avenues for self-expression and the cultivation of particular interests. In times marked by urbanization and a mobile population, the telephone has helped people to maintain ties with distant families and friends. By the same token, direct broadcast satellites and the Internet have given users the means to get away to 'electronic cottages' where they can select just what content and which people they wish to engage with.

Together, then, the chapters in this part summarize some of the characteristics that have made new media technologies both so pervasive and so adaptable across social contexts. Borrowing Sherry Turkle's phrase about computers, new media are indeed 'projective devices' for our interests, affiliations and desires, and not just conduits for delivering the information commodity. Individuals and small social groups have much more of a 'voice' (and a 'face', for that matter) via new media systems than was ever possible through centrally or hierarchically organized, and rigorously edited or 'gated', mass media. Though the major corporate owners and regulators of converging media systems attempt to exert technical and legal control over their use,[1] it is becoming ever more difficult to talk about 'the media' as clearly demarcated or monolithic industries with end-to-end control over their systems. The many uses and users of new media technologies have been remarkably nimble and creative in response to institutional and technical constraints (for example, standardization or intellectual property claims). There is every indication that this pattern, in which institutional control is balanced by creative workarounds, sabotage or new uses, will continue to be a defining trait of new media design and development.

NOTE

1 For example, content producers, such as book publishers and the music recording industry, are attempting to hold on to familiar formats and distribution systems by extending traditional intellectual property protections into new technical formats rather than rethinking the basis for those formats in the first place. As a recent piece in *The Economist* put it, this is probably because their 'chief concern is protecting [their] business model, not preventing piracy' (2001: 19).

REFERENCES

Abbate, J. (1999) *Inventing the Internet*. Cambridge, MA: MIT Press.

Brooks, J. (1975) *Telephone: the First Hundred Years*. New York: Harper & Row.

Bucciarelli, L.L. (1994) *Designing Engineers*. Cambridge, MA: MIT Press.

Ceruzzi, P.E. (1998) *A History of Modern Computing*. Cambridge, MA: MIT Press.

Clement, A. (1994) 'Computing at work: empowering action by low-level users', *Communications of the ACM*, 37 (1): 52–65.

Crowley, D. and Heyer, P. (1995) *Communication in History: Technology, Culture, Society*, 2nd edn. White Plains, NY: Longman.

Dix, A.J., Finlay, J.E., Abowd, G.D. and Beale, R. (1998) *Human–Computer Interaction*. London: Prentice-Hall.

Edwards, P.N. (1996) *The Closed World: Computers and the Politics of Discourse in Cold War America*. Cambridge, MA: MIT Press.

Fischer, C.S. (1992) *America Calling: a Social History of the Telephone to 1940*. Berkeley and Los Angeles: University of California Press.

Flichy, P. (1995 [1991]) *Dynamics of Modern Communication: the Shaping and Impact of New Communication Technologies*, trans. L. Libbrecht. London: Sage.

Greenbaum, J. and Kyng, M. (eds) (1991) *Design at Work: Cooperative Design of Computer Systems*. Hillsdale, NJ: Erlbaum.

Hiltz, S.R. and Turoff, M. (1993 [1978]) *The Network Nation: Human Communication via Computer*, rev. edn. Cambridge, MA: MIT Press.

Johansen, R., Vallee, J. and Spangler, K. (1979) *Electronic Meetings: Technical Alternatives and Social Choice*. Reading, MA: Addison-Wesley.

Jowett, G.S., Jarvie, I.C. and Fuller, K.H. (1996) *Children and the Movies: Media Influence and the Payne Fund Controversy*. New York: Cambridge University Press.

Kling, R. (ed.) (1996) *Computerization and Controversy: Value Conflicts and Social Choices*. San Diego, CA: Academic.

Lea, M. and Spears, R. (1991) 'Computer-mediated communication, de-individuation and group decision making', *International Journal of Man–Machine Studies*, 34: 283–301.

Lievrouw, L.A., Bucy, E.P., Finn, T.A., Frindte, W., Gershon, R.A., Haythornthwaite, C., Köhler, T., Metz, JM and Sundar, S.S. (2001) 'Bridging the subdisciplines: an overview of communication and technology research', in W.B. Gudykunst (ed.), *Communication Yearbook 24*. Thousand Oaks, CA: Sage, for the International Communication Association. pp. 271–95.

Livingstone, S. and Bovill, M. (eds) (2001) *Children and their Changing Media Environment: a European Comparative Study*. Mahwah, NJ: Erlbaum.

Marvin, C. (1988) *When Old Technologies Were New: Thinking about Electric Communication in the Late Nineteenth Century*. New York and Oxford: Oxford University Press.

Orlikowski, W.J. (1993) 'Learning from Notes: organizational issues in groupware implementation', *Information Systems Research*, 9 (3): 237–50.

Rafaeli, S. (1988) 'Interactivity: from new media to communication', in R. Hawkins, J.M. Wiemann and S. Pingree (eds), *Advancing Communication Science: Merging Mass and Interpersonal Processes*. Newbury Park, CA: Sage. pp. 124–81.

Reeves, B. and Nass, C. (1996) *The Media Equation: How People Treat Computers, Television and New Media Like Real People and Places*. Stanford, CA: CSLI, and Cambridge: Cambridge University Press.

Rogers, E.M. (1994) *A History of Communication Study: a Biographical Approach*. New York: Free Press.

Rogers, E.M. (1995) *Diffusion of Innovations*, 4th edn. New York: Free Press.

Schramm, W. (1997) *The Beginnings of Communication Study in America: a Personal Memoir*, edited by S.H. Chaffee and E.M. Rogers. Thousand Oaks, CA: Sage.

Segaller, S. (1998) *Nerds 2.0.1: a Brief History of the Internet*. New York: TV Books, for Oregon Public Television.

Shneiderman, B. (1998) *Designing the User Interface: Strategies for Effective Human–Computer Interaction*. Reading, MA: Addison-Wesley.

Short, J., Williams, E. and Christie, B. (1976) *The Social Psychology of Telecommunications*. New York: Wiley.

Silverstone, R. and Hirsch, E. (eds) (1992) *Consuming Technologies: Media and Information in Domestic Spaces*. London: Routledge.

Sonnenwald, D.H. (1993) 'Communication in design'. Unpublished PhD dissertation, Rutgers University, New Brunswick, NJ.

Spears, R. and Lea, M. (1994) 'Panacea or panopticon? The hidden power in computer-mediated communication', *Communication Research*, 21, 427–59.

Sproull, L. and Kiesler, S. (1991) *Connections: New Ways of Working in the Networked Organization*. Cambridge, MA: MIT Press.

Star, S.L. (ed.) (1995) *The Cultures of Computing*. London: Blackwell/The Sociological Review.

Sterling, C.H. and Kittross, J.M. (1990) *Stay Tuned: a Concise History of American Broadcasting*, 2nd edn. Belmont, CA: Wadsworth.

Straubhaar, J. and LaRose, R. (2000) *Media Now: Communications Media in the Information Age*, 2nd edn. Belmont, CA: Wadsworth/Thomson Learning.

Suchman, L. (1987) *Plans and Situated Actions: the Problem of Machine–Human Communication*. Cambridge: Cambridge University Press.

The Economist (2001) 'The same old song', February: 19–20.

Turkle, S. (1984) *The second self: Computers and the human spirit*. New York: Simon and Schuster.

Turow, J. (1997) *Breaking Up America: Advertisers and the New Media World*. Chicago, IL: University of Chicago Press.

Viller, S. and Sommerville, I. (1999) 'Coherence: an approach to representing ethnographic analyses in systems design', *Human–Computer Interaction*, 14: 9–41.

Walther, J.B. (1992) 'Interpersonal effects in computer-mediated interaction: a relational perspective', *Communication Research*, 19: 52–90.

Walther, J.B. (1996) 'Computer-mediated communication: impersonal, interpersonal, and hyperpersonal interaction', *Communication Research*, 23: 3–43.

Winograd, T. and Flores, F. (1987) *Understanding Computers and Cognition: a New Foundation for Design*. Reading, MA: Addison-Wesley.

8

New Media History

PATRICE FLICHY

Many histories of information and communication could be written: the history of institutions and firms, the history of programmes and creative works, the history of techniques, and the history of practices and uses which, in turn, can be related to that of work and leisure but also to that of the public sphere. All these histories are related to very different fields of social science, and the information and communication sector is far too vast to present all these perspectives here. I have chosen to take as the main theme of this chapter the question of relations between ICTs and society. With this point of view we are at the heart of a number of debates: debate on the effects of communication, which for a long time mobilized sociologists of the media; extensive debate on determinism among historians of techniques; and debate around the sociotechnical perspective which has now been adopted by most sociologists of science and technology.

We shall focus on three points in particular: the launching and development of ICTs, their uses in a professional context and, lastly, their uses in a leisure context.

INNOVATION IN ICTS

Does Technology Drive History?

In many histories of computing the transistor, then the microprocessor, are considered to be the determining elements. Behind this very common theory lies the idea that technical progress is inevitable and globally linear. Electronic components and basic technologies such as digitization are seen as determining the form of the technical devices we use.

Similarly, these new machines have been expected to determine the organization of work (Friedmann, 1978), our leisure activities and, more broadly, our ways of thinking (McLuhan, 1964) or even society at large (Ellul, 1964).

By contrast, other researchers such as the historian David Noble (1984) clearly show, through the case of automatically controlled machine tools, that there is no one best way, and that the effect of a technique cannot be understood without simultaneously studying its use and the choices made by its designers. After the Second World War two alternatives were explored to automate production: record–playback (automatic analogue) machines and numerical control machines. The former recorded the design of a part drawn by a human operator and then automatically produced copies. The numeric machine, by contrast, did not need to memorize human knowhow; it was capable of programming design and production. If the numeric option triumphed, it was not because it was more reliable or easier to implement, but because it corresponded to the representations that designers and corporate managers (future buyers) had of automated industrial production.

Numerical control was always more than a technology for cutting metals, especially in the eyes of its MIT designers who knew little about metal cutting: it was a symbol of the computer age, of mathematical elegance, of power, order and predictability, of continuous flow, of remote control, of the automatic factory. Record–playback, on the other hand, however much it represented a significant advance on manual methods, retained a vestige of traditional human skills; as such, in the eyes of the future (and engineers always confuse the present and the future) it was obsolete. (Noble, 1979: 29–30)

Studying Successes and Failures

One conclusion can be drawn from Noble's study: there is never a single technical solution; as a rule, several solutions are studied in parallel. The historian has to study these different solutions and analyse both successes and failures (Bijker et al., 1987). The RCA videodisk is a good example of failure. Margaret Graham (1986) showed that the television corporation RCA had everything it needed to launch its new product successfully one of the best US research laboratories, positive market research, support from the media and, lastly, access to a very large programme catalogue. Despite all these assets, RCA sold no more than 500,000 copies of its videodisk player in three years. Another technical system, the VCR, developed in Japan, was to dominate the market with a resulting loss for RCA of $600 million. The company that had launched television in the US was eventually bought out by General Electric and then by the French company Thomson. Thus, as many computer manufacturers were to discover, a company can pay very dearly for a failure. The main lesson that Graham draws from this case is that technical or commercial competencies are not enough if they are not properly coordinated. That was the underlying cause of the videodisk's failure. As sociologists of technology have shown: 'rather than rational decision-making, it is necessary to talk of an aggregation of interests that can or cannot be produced. Innovation is the art of involving a growing number of allies who are made stronger and stronger' (Akrich et al., 1988: 17; see also Latow, 1987). This strategy of alliances was what enabled France Télécom to successfully launch its videotex (the minitel) in the early 1980s. A few months before the new medium was launched, this telematic project collided with a virulent combination of media and political opposition. In fact, France Télécom, which at the time was still the French Post Office (PTT), wanted to create and run the whole system on its own. It hoped not only to provide the network and terminals but also to install all the information to be offered to the public on its own servers. Other European post and telecommunications authorities had opted for the same schema. However, faced with intense opposition France Télécom backed down and decided to move from a closed to an open system in which any firm could become a service provider. France Télécom simply transported the information and took care of the billing (with a share of the revenue paid back to the supplier). Owing to partnerships with service providers and especially with the press, 20 per cent of French households adopted the new service (Flichy, 1991).[1]

Boundary Objects

Behind the questions of coordination of designers within a company or of partnerships with the outside, lies the question of the mobilization of the different parties concerned by innovation: R&D engineers, marketing specialists, salespeople, repairers, partner companies (manufacturers of components, content providers, etc.) but also users. In an interactionist approach, sociologists have used the notion of boundary objects. These are objects situated at the intersection of several social worlds, which meet the needs of all worlds simultaneously. 'They are objects which are both plastic enough to adapt to local needs and the constraints of the several parties employing them, yet robust enough to maintain a common identity' (Star and Griesemer, 1989: 393). A boundary object is the result of complex interaction between the different actors concerned. This is the exact opposite of the naive idea of innovation spawned ready-made by the inventor's mind. The history of Macintosh clearly illustrates this point. Two computers using the principle of graphic windows were produced concurrently at Apple: Lisa, a failure, and Macintosh, the Californian company's leading machine. Lisa was designed in a rather cumbersome organizational frame, with a strict division of tasks between teams. Macintosh, by contrast, was developed by a small, tightly knit team in which choices made by individuals were always discussed collectively. The software developers gave their opinions on the hardware and vice versa. Moreover, the people in charge of building the factory and of marketing and finance were also included in these discussions. This continuous negotiation caused the project to be amended more than once. A computer that was originally designed for the general public was eventually substituted for Lisa as an office machine. The simplicity of its use, imagined from the outset, was one of this computer's most attractive features (Guterl, 1984). The Macintosh is a computer situated on the boundary between hardware and software, between the computer specialist and the layperson.[2]

Path Dependency

While the perspective of boundary objects is very useful for the study of specific cases, other perspectives are needed to analyse more long-term phenomena. The path-dependency concept devised by economist and historian Paul David is particularly illuminating. Through the paradigmatic example of the typewriter keyboard which has not evolved since its invention, David (1985) builds a model that compares dynamic growth to a tree. At each branch the actors face a choice. This choice may sometimes be linked to a minor element, but once a solution has been chosen by a large number of actors it becomes relatively stable. The outcome of initial choices is relatively unpredictable but a time comes when a technique or an industrial mode of organization is imposed, with a resulting phenomenon of lock-in.

IBM's entry into the PC market is an interesting example of path dependency. Big Blue was aware that this was an entirely new market and that it needed to find a specific mode of organization to produce a fundamentally different computer. A task force was set up to produce and market this microcomputer, independently of the rest of the company. Unlike Apple and in the true IBM tradition, it chose an open architecture not protected by patents. This meant that users could buy peripherals and software from other companies. The task force also decided to break away from IBM's traditional vertical integration. The central processing unit would thus be bought from Intel and the operating system from a startup, Microsoft. There were two main reasons for this policy: the desire to be reactive and to short-circuit the usual functioning; and the desire to show the Department of Justice that IBM had stopped its monopolistic behaviour. The strategy was a success. In 1982, the first full year of production, IBM's microcomputer revenues totalled £500 million and in 1985 £5.5 billion, 'a record of revenue growth unsurpassed in industrial history' (Chandler, 2000: 33). But it also had a whole series of unexpected effects. While the appearance of rivals (producers of clones and specialized software) was part of the game, the key position that this afforded Intel and, to an even greater extent, Microsoft (Cusumano, 1995) was far less predictable. These two companies rapidly became the two main players in the microcomputing industry, at IBM's expense.

The Internet is another case of a path-dependent history. It has sometimes been said that ARPANET, the ancestor of the network of networks, was built so that the US Army could maintain communication links in case of a Soviet attack. In fact, this network had a far more modest aim: it was to link the computing departments of universities working for ARPA, the US Defense Department's advanced research agency (Hafner and Lyon, 1996: 41, 77). Telecommunication companies and especially AT&T refused to build this new data network. It was therefore designed by computer specialists who had a new view of computing, suited to communication between machines with the same status. This computer-mediated communication was profoundly different from IBM's centralized and hierarchized computing system or from a telephone network.

From the outset ARPANET was a highly decentralized network which stopped at the university entrance. This technical architecture left a large degree of leeway to each computing site which could organize itself as it wished as regards hardware and software and could create its own local area network. The only constraint was the need to be able to connect to an interface. These technical choices in favour of decentralization were also to be found in the organization of work needed to develop the network. Construction of the network was entrusted to a small company closely linked to MIT. This company dealt with no technical problems posed by data exchange beyond the interface, considering that they were the universities' responsibility. Unlike the time-sharing system developed by IBM, in particular, where the central computer is in a master–slave position to the terminals, in ARPANET host computers were on an equal footing with terminals.

Whereas ARPANET was launched and coordinated by ARPA, Usenet, which constituted another branch of what was to become Internet, was developed cooperatively by research centres not linked to ARPANET. Usenet did not have its own financing. The administrators of the system were computer scientists who participated on a voluntary basis, making space on their hard disks to record news and transmitting it by telephone.

The Internet was designed in the second half of the 1970s as an 'internetwork architecture', that is, a metaprotocol for interaction between networks built on different principles. The idea of an open architecture leaves total autonomy to each network. Since the metaprotocol manages only interaction between networks, each individual network can maintain its own mode of functioning. Furthermore, the Internet has no central authority. The Internet society is only an associative coordination structure. Applications proposed on the ARPANET or Internet (e-mail, newsgroups, database sharing and, later, the World Wide Web) were proposed by different designers and can be used by anyone who wants to (Norberg and O'Neill, 1996; Abbate, 1999).

The two main principles of decentralization and free access in which the Internet is grounded stem essentially from the academic functioning of its founders. When the Internet subsequently became a system of communication for the general public, these two principles were perpetuated to a large extent. The network is still not managed by a single operator, and a large amount of software, especially browsers, circulates freely on the web, at least in its most basic form.

Engineers' Representations

The initial choices that will profoundly influence the trajectory of a technology are related not only to contingent decisions but also to the representations of the designers. Thus, the founding fathers of the Internet, such as Licklider or Engelbart, thought that computing was not only a calculation tool but also a means of communication. Hiltz and Turoff considered that once computer-mediated communication was widespread 'we will become the Network Nation, exchanging vast amounts of both information and social-emotional communications with colleagues, friends and strangers who share similar interests, who are spread out all over the nation'(1978: xxvii–xxiv). This theme of the creation of collective intelligence through networking was to mobilize many computer specialists in the 1970s and 1980s, and to appeal strongly to users. The Californian bulletin board the WELL, for example, functioned around that idea (Rheingold, 1994).

We similarly find a common project among hackers, those young computer enthusiasts who were to play an essential part in the design of the first microcomputers (Freiberger and Swaine, 1984). They shared the same principles:

- access to computers should be unlimited and total
- all information should be free
- mistrust authority, promote decentralization
- hackers should be judged by their hacking, not bogus criteria such as degrees, age, race or position
- you can create art and beauty on a computer
- computers can change your life for the better. (Levy, 1985: 40–5)

They considered that computing was a device to be made available to all, which would help to build a new society.

Technological imagination is a key component of the development of technology. Without the myths produced by the American counter-culture in the early 1970s, the microcomputer would probably have remained a mere curiosity. The ideology of computing for all, in a decentralized form, suddenly lent a whole new dimension to hackers' tinkering in their garages. However, we can talk of the influence of the counter-culture on the microcomputing project only if we consider that there were hackers who chose to associate the values of the counter-culture with their passion for computing. They defined the problems that they chose to grapple with. The community ideology alone did not create the microcomputer; at best, it produced a mythical frame of use. The basis of hackers' activity was immersion both in the counter-culture and in the world of computer tinkering; these two components were not only juxtaposed but also very closely linked. The ties needed for the establishment of a permanent sociotechnological frame were built by the actors; the technological or social dreams thus had no power other than supplying resources for the action.

This type of study of the representations of designers of information tools has also been made by Simon Schaffer (1995) on Babbage's calculating engine, generally considered to be the computer's mechanical ancestor. Babbage, a Victorian mathematician, also conducted research on the division of labour observed in factories and at the Greenwich Royal Observatory where dozens of employees did calculations from morning till night to prepare mathematical tables. To make the production of goods and calculations more efficient, it was necessary to automate the factory system. Just as Jacquard had mechanized weaving with his famous loom, so too Babbage wanted to mechanize the production of numeric tables. He hoped to speed up the production of tables which were perfectly accurate and rid of all human error. But Schaffer does more than point out the analogy between Babbage's machine and the factory system. He draws a map of the places and networks in which the credibility of Babbage's machine was regularly evaluated. Although the machine was never totally operational, it was exhibited often enough to contribute towards the production of a need that it could not entirely fulfil.

Representations of the Media

Representations of techniques are interesting to observe, not only in inventors but also in the first users. Susan Douglas studied enthusiasts of the wireless, whose passion for this new technology was to popularize Marconi's invention and attract the attention of the press. A short story from 1912 is a good example of these representations of the new medium. In it Francis Collins describes the practices of new users of the wireless:

> imagine a gigantic spider's web with innumerable threads radiating from New York more than a thousand miles over land and sea in all directions. In his station, our operator may be compared to the spider, sleepless, vigilant, ever watching for the faintest tremor from the farthest corner of his invisible fabric ... These operators, thousands of miles apart, talk and joke with one another as though they were in the same room. (Douglas, 1987: 199)

This is clearly a new imaginary type of communication that Collins is proposing. But this utopian discourse, which not only described potential users but also indicated everything that the wireless could do for society and individuals, was becoming a reality. Everyone could communicate instantly and independently with persons very far away, whenever they wanted to. Communication was free in that it did not depend on telegraph or telephone operators and therefore did not have to be paid for. As Susan Douglas says: 'The ether was an exciting new frontier in which men and boys could congregate, compete, test their mettle, and be privy to a range of new information. Social order and social control were defied' (1987: 214).

After the First World War a new 'wireless mania' appeared. This time it concerned wireless telephony, soon to become radio broadcasting. This new device was also to create a new community feeling. Douglas, in 'The social destiny of radio' wrote: 'How fine is the texture of the web that radio is even now spinning! It is achieving the task of making us feel together, think together, live together' (Douglas, 1987: 306).

Internet utopias, which in a sense are related to those of radio, also changed when the new technology left the world of designers in universities and groups of hackers (Flichy, forthcoming). For example, the first manuals for the public at large gave a fairly coherent representation of the net that combined characteristics of scientific communities and those of communities of electronics enthusiasts. One of these guides considered that internauts 'freed from physical limitations ... are developing new types of cohesive and effective communities – ones which are defined more by common interest and purpose than by an accident of geography, ones on which what really counts is what you say and think and feel, not how you look' (Gaffin and Kapor, 1991: 8–9). Rheingold considers that virtual communities bring together individuals from all corners of the globe who exchange information or expertise. More broadly, they build ties of cooperation and develop conversations that are as intellectually and emotionally rich as those of real life. It is a world of balanced interaction between equals. In short, the net can make it possible not only to work collectively but also to re-establish a social link that is slackening, and to breathe life into public debate and democratic life (Rheingold, 1994).

Later the press started to write extensively about the Internet. In 1995 an editorial in *Time* noted that:

> most conventional computer systems are hierarchical and proprietary; they run on copyrighted software in a pyramid structure that gives dictatorial powers to the system operators to sit on top. The Internet, by contrast, is open (non-proprietary) and rabidly democratic. No one owns it. No single organization controls it. It is run like a commune with 4.8 million fiercely independent members (called hosts). It crosses national boundaries and answers to no sovereign. It is literally lawless ... Stripped of the external trappings of wealth, power, beauty and social status, people tend to be judged in the cyberspace of Internet only by their ideas. (*Time*, special issue, March 1995: 9)

Newsweek made 1995 Internet Year. It opened its year-end issue with the following phrase stretched across four pages: 'this changes ... everything' (*Newsweek*, special double issue, 2 January 1996). The editorial noted that the Internet is 'the medium that will change the way we communicate, shop, publish and (so the cybersmut cops warned) be damned'.

Thus, with the Internet, like the wireless, we find two examples of the 'rhetoric of the sublime technology' that Leo Marx (1964) already referred to regarding the steam engine. This rhetoric nevertheless takes on a specific form with communication systems, for it concerns not only a particular domain of productive activity but also social links and, more generally, the way society is constituted. The communication utopias of wireless and Internet are therefore fairly similar. They successively refer to interpersonal communication, group communication and, later, mass communication. In so far as both technologies soon acquired an international dimension, so that they could cover the entire planet, the utopias also granted much importance to the feeling of ubiquity found less strongly in other electric or electronic media. Finally, these utopias emphasized the principles of liberty and free access that characterize the development of these two technologies. They were defined in contrast to the two main technical systems of the time: telegraph and telephone in the case of wireless technology; and the absence of compatibility between computing systems, along with the centralized and hierarchical view of data networks that IBM incarnated, in the case of the Internet.

ICTs IN THE PROFESSIONAL SPHERE

Historical comparisons between the nineteenth and twentieth centuries are equally enlightening as regards the role of ICTs in economic activity. James Beniger shows that the industrial revolution was accompanied by what he calls 'the control revolution'. Changes in the scale of productive activity necessitated new modes of organization, for example the bureaucratic organization developed by railways, the organization of material processing established in industries, telecommunications used by distribution, and mass media used by marketing. For him, information is at the centre of this control revolution which continued developing in the second half of the twentieth century. 'Microprocessing and computing technology, contrary to currently fashionable opinion, do not represent a new force only recently unleashed on an unprepared society but merely the most recent instalment in the continuing development of the Control Revolution' (Beniger, 1986: 435).

The First Generation of Office Machines

Let us consider in more detail these nineteenth-century information and communication tools that were to facilitate the organization of business and markets. The telegraph was a decisive element in the organization of markets, first of all the stock market. In Europe the transmission of stock market information was the first use to which the telegraph was put, in the 1850s, and it facilitated the unification of values (Flichy, 1995: 46–50). In the United States the telegraph, in conjunction with the railroad, made it possible to unify regional markets and to create a large national market from east coast to west (DuBoff, 1983). It also facilitated the creation of large-scale business enterprises which made huge economies of scale and scope possible. The telegraph and railway companies were the prototype of such enterprises. Circulating messages or goods from one end of the North American continent to the other demanded complex coordination and could not be organized by the market alone. It necessitated the creation of large multisite corporations that decentralized responsibilities and simultaneously created functional coordination in finance and technical research (Chandler, 1977). The railway companies that used the telegraph to control traffic processed these data and thus developed the first management methods subsequently applied in other industrial sectors. With the increase in the size of firms the coordination of work was profoundly modified. In small pre-industrial firms the owner and a few skilled artisans organized the work verbally. Writing was reserved for communication with the outside. By contrast, in large industrial firms writing was to be used extensively in internal coordination. Managers were thus to standardize production processes through handbooks or circular letters. Sales manuals were given to sales agents in order to standardize prices and the sale process itself. The development of accounting, which made it possible to calculate costs precisely and to better determine prices, also used writing (Yates, 1989). In industrial work, this use of the written document was to be systematized, at the end of the century, in Taylorism. The existence of written instructions given by the methods department to each worker was one of the basic elements of the scientific organization of work (Taylor, 1911). Office work also increased substantially. In the US the number of clerical workers rose from 74,000 in 1870 to 2.8 million in 1920 (Yates, 2000: 112).

To produce and manage this paper, various tools appeared: the typewriter, the roneo machine, the calculator, but also furniture to file and store documents, etc. All these devices were, in a sense, the first generation of data processing machines. We thus witness several parallel evolutions: growth in the size of firms, increase in the number of written documents, and appearance of new machines. But Joanne Yates (1994) has clearly shown that these evolutions would not necessarily have been articulated to one another without a locus of mediation and incentives to change. The managerial literature that developed at the time, as well as the first business schools, were to propose management methods and recommend the use of new office machines. For this new managerial ideology, writing was the most appropriate procedure to set up efficient coordination between the different actors in the firm. This systematic management also proposed management tools.

Mainframe and Centralized Organization

Computing, designed to meet scientists' and the defence force's needs (Campbell-Kelly and Aspray, 1996), did not immediately find its place in managerial activity. Ten years after the advent of computing, a pioneer such as Howard Aiken could still write: 'if it should ever turn out that the basic logics of a machine designed for the numerical solution of differential equations coincide with the logics of a machine intended to make bills for a department store, I would regard this as the most amazing coincidence that I have ever encountered' (quoted by Ceruzzi, 1987: 197). The shift from calculating machines to management machines was made by companies that already had extensive technical and commercial experience in punch card tabulating technology, such as NCR, Burroughs and of course IBM (Cortada, 1993).

So, when IBM built the first mainframe computers it knew business organization so well that it could conceive a structure well adapted to the dominant form of organization: the multidivisional functional hierarchy. A database system like IMS (Information Management System) clearly reflected this organizational hierarchy (Nolan, 2000: 220).

This parallel between technical and organizational structures was also observed by French sociologists of labour who noted that, despite the utopian discourse of computer specialists on the structuring effects of computers in the processing and circulation of information, computing introduced no change in the firm; on the contrary, it reproduced the existing order (Ballé and Peaucelle, 1972). To understand this, we need to examine in detail the work of computer specialists in firms. To rationalize the circulation and processing of information they started by drawing up computer guidelines. They first analysed the existing functioning but, since few of them had any particular skills regarding the best modes of organization, they simply formalized written rules. When there were no such rules they had them formulated by the hierarchy. The computer program was thus to incorporate all these rules into an automatic data processing and circulation system. The bending of rules that characterizes any bureaucracy thus became more difficult. In this way computerization rigidified procedures rather than renewing them. We can consider, like Colette Hoffsaes, that:

faced with the inability to know the rules of functioning of organizations, the past was repeated ... Computer specialists had a project for change but they were not in a position to change the aims that were known by and embodied in the operatives. Rather, they were to help them to do better what they already did. They thus intervened at the process level, the stability of which they tended to increase. (1978: 307)

Computing did nevertheless bring some changes. The role of those that Peter Drucker (1974) calls 'knowledge workers' or 'professional managers' increased. Their new mission in the firm was no longer to control others; on the contrary, they defined themselves by their own work. Moreover, executive tasks became more routine and less qualified. The division of labour was accentuated and a Taylorization of tertiary work emerged. While data were codified by the departments that produced them (pay, accounting, etc.), they were then captured in large centralized workshops where card punchers and then controllers processed them. Punch cards were then processed by keyboard operators in large computer rooms. Lastly, the data were returned to the service that had produced them.

Data telecommunications and the use of 'dumb terminals' were to modify the process a little. They made it possible to integrate on a single machine the codification and keying in of data as well as their updating. Big computing workshops were consequently fragmented and data capture activities, which in the meantime had become more qualified, moved closer to the data production services or in some instances even became part of them. In parallel, the number of junior management posts were sharply reduced. The division of work and its control were henceforth done by the computing system rather than by the hierarchy. Yet corporate organization changed little. Those first computing networks were extremely hierarchized and the new device had been designed and organized centrally by the data processing division.

From the managers' point of view, the situation was somewhat different. Owing to the possibilities afforded by management computing, each manager, at corporate management level and in the divisions and even the departments, had a financial statement at regular intervals. With quasi-immediate access to this information, the US corporate model, in which each manager is responsible for the revenue generated by his/her unit, was able to function efficiently (Nolan, 2000: 229).

Microcomputing and the Temptation to Decentralize

While mainframe computing was initialized and developed by managers in order to automate routine data processing tasks, microcomputing was adopted at grassroots level. Another current of French sociology of labour, which studies not phenomena of reproduction but elements of transformation, facts which impact on the future, closely studied the diffusion of microcomputing. These sociologists have shown that it was often employees who had a fair amount of autonomy in the organization of their work (personal secretaries, archivists, etc.) who grasped this new tool and proposed small applications adapted to their immediate environment: management of leave, monitoring budgets, bibliographic database, etc. (Alter, 1991).

These innovative people later became experts in microcomputing and thus acquired a new legitimacy and a little more power. In a new technical world which was particularly uncertain because users received no support from the data processing divisions, which were opposed to PCs at the time, these first users soon became resource persons who not only mastered the new technology but were also capable of using it to improve their own productivity. This situation corresponds to an innovation model studied by von Hippel (1988). He considers that end users are often essential innovators. They do not need much technical expertise to find new uses. Their strength derives from close contact with daily problems that the new devices have to solve. This model of uncontrolled diffusion was to spread particularly fast because investments in microcomputers were sufficiently small to enable many departments to take decisions in this respect on their own. Thus, contact was made directly between sellers and users, along the lines of a model resembling a market for the public at large rather than a business market.

Yet these innovators did encounter a good deal of opposition. Apart from the data processing divisions which saw the PC as a technological alternative which they did not control, middle management also saw it as a potential challenge to the organization, with greater autonomy for employees. By contrast, top management saw microcomputers as an opportunity to create a counter-power *vis-à-vis* the data processing division. It therefore left local initiatives to develop, as an experiment. Initially it accepted a diversity of models of computerization in the various services.

While this fragmented innovation model made it possible to mobilize multiple initiatives, it was potentially also a source of disorder and inefficiency. Thus, in a second stage top management took over the reins, in collaboration with the data processing divisions who were forced to include the PC in their plan. The project was to replace partial computerization in islands of the organization by a totally integrated information system (Cerruti and Reiser, 1993). The setting up of such a system posed not only technical but also organizational problems, for these new machines allowed for automation but also for a different way of thinking and managing. Zuboff (1988) has clearly shown that informating and automating are the two faces of computers in firms.

Digital Network and Interactive Deployment

While we can roughly say that mainframe computing developed in a centralized way, while micro-computing started off being decentralized, intranet and network data communications correspond to a more interactive mode in the development of computing. Bar et al. (2000) have thus constructed a cyclical model of the development of digital networks. Initially, intranet was used to automate existing work processes, for example to organize the circulation of documents in a firm. It was a way of enhancing efficiency and improving productivity. Once the network was available it could be used for other purposes, such as information searches on request or simple administrative procedures, for example ordering supplies, requests for leave, etc. Through this experimental phase, new communication technologies fitted into the organization better. The third phase could then begin, in which the firm was to be reorganized and to modify its digital network simultaneously.

Research on French firms has reached similar conclusions (Benghozi et al., 2000). These authors also note development in phases, although computerization was initiated either by local experimentation or by a decision by top management. Yet the network expanded fully only if there was articulation between the two phases. The idea was to construct a learning device in a context of controlled disorder. If we now review the setting up of digital networks, we note that effects on organization were diverse. Within a single business sector, such as the press, diametrically opposed organizational choices have been observed. At a newspaper in the west of France, local editorial staff devote as little time as possible to computing which is left to employees previously responsible for setting the newspaper. This is a case where computerized workflow has not undermined the division of work. By contrast, at a newspaper in the north, the introduction of an integrated computing system radically modified the organization of work. In local offices the same person does investigative work and typesetting (Ruellan and Thierry, 1998). These two contrasting models clearly show that in these cases the introduction of network computing does not, in itself, induce a new organization. Thus, even if there is no technical determinism, is there organizational determinism? It would appear so, given that in many cases the setting up of intranet or of co-operative devices in smaller businesses is related to substantial organizational change. In reality,

such reorganization is actually an opportunity to introduce these new tools.

The various studies cited, both in the US and in France, are thus grounded in a conception where technology coevolves with the organization and its members (Leonard-Barton, 1988; Orlikowski, 1992). They therefore contrast with current discourse on the revolution in the organization of work generated by digital networks.

ICTs and Private Life

The Gradual Slide from Public to Private Sphere

The history of information technology in the private sphere, as in the business world, originates in the nineteenth century. Public life changed profoundly during that period. Richard Sennett (1977) considers that it lost its character of conviviality and interaction, to become a space in which people mix together in silence. With regard to this 'public private life' he talks of 'daydreaming', referring to the same phenomenon as did Edgar Allan Poe in 'The man of the crowd' (1971) or Baudelaire (1978) in his study of the stroller. In that work Baudelaire presented an individual who is both out of his home and at home everywhere. This articulation between public and private is also characteristic of the theatre. For a good part of the century, the theatre was above all a place for social interaction. The box was a sort of drawing room where people could converse, observe others and watch the show. Gradually, it became more usual to switch off the lights in the hall and to focus on the stage. Audiences had to listen in silence. New theatres were designed to enable audiences to see the stage, above all. Theatres thus received a solitary crowd; the public was an entity in which individuals experienced their emotions separately (see Flichy, 1995: 152–5).

We also find this dialectic between public and private spheres with the beginnings of photography. In the mid nineteenth century the photo portrait, a private image, became the main use of the new medium. But photographers who took these pictures set themselves up in the most frequented urban places. Their studios became veritable urban attractions. Inside, they were decorated like parlours; outside, collections of portraits several metres high were displayed on the pavement. In their windows copies of diverse portraits were exhibited, for example, crowned heads, artists, individuals who by nature have to show themselves, but also portraits of ordinary people (Mary, 1993: 83–4). Thus, if the man in the street had his portrait taken to give to his family, his picture also became public.

This play between public and private images appeared in several respects. Ordinary people were photographed in stereotyped poses; they chose the décor from a catalogue and the photographer often touched up the picture to make it closer to current standards of beauty. Important people, on the other hand, displayed details of their private lives in addition to their official poses. Furthermore, with the multiplication of copies photography was no longer used only for private souvenirs; it became a medium. People usually had between 10 and 100 copies of their 'portrait card' or 'photo visiting card' printed, but in some cases tens of thousands of copies were made. These photo portraits were put into albums with not only photographs of family and friends but also portraits of celebrities bought from specialized publishers. The binding of the albums played on the secret/representation ambiguity; they were often beautifully decorated and sometimes had a lock to protect the owner's privacy.

The debate between private and collective media also appeared with the beginnings of the cinema. Edison thought his kinetoscope would be installed in public places, to be used by individuals (Clark, 1977). The success of the projector proposed by Lumière and other inventors was, by contrast, partly owing to the fact that it fitted into a tradition of collective shows. The content proposed, like that of the other visual media, turned around the dual attraction of daily life and fantasy. The idea was to show something that surprised by both its familiarity and its strangeness. Lumière focused more on the former, with scenes from daily life in both the private sphere ('Le déjeuner de bébé', 'La dispute de bébé', etc.) and in public ('La sortie des usines Lumière', 'L'arrivée du train en gare de la Ciotat', etc.). Lumière's first projectionists were also cameramen. They filmed scenes in the towns in which they were and showed them the same evening to an audience that was likely to recognize itself in the film.

This fairground cinema made people familiar with the new medium but it eventually bored them. The real success of the cinema appeared when it started telling stories, that is, when it became a narrative medium. The success of narrative filmmakers such as William Paul in England and Charles Pathé in France was based on their entry into an industrial economy. The French industrialist soon discovered that it was in his interests to make a large number of copies and to distribute them throughout the world. He developed a system of industrial production similar to that of the press, in which he produced one film per week and later several (Abel, 1995).

Going to the cinema soon became a regular habit. Audiences behaved as they did at café concerts. For example, in 1912 a Venetian journalist wrote:

the most beautiful cinema is that of Sant Margeria, where working class women go ... Oh! How they applaud in certain scenes. Hordes of children sometimes go to see series of landscapes and discover vulgar scenes: 'one doesn't kiss on the mouth' and the public answers 'si' ('yes one does'); 'no one touches my lips' and the public again choruses 'si'. (Turnaturi, 1995)

In the United States the new entertainment medium attracted a large immigrant population in particular (Sklar, 1975). The narrative cinema was to become a big consumer of scenarios, sometimes found in legitimate literature. That was how the cultured classes were to become interested in this new medium that gradually became the seventh art. As the Italian historian Gabriella Turnaturi (1995) notes, on the eve of the First World War 'a slow and difficult process of unification of customs, culture and traditions took place through the learning of a common language in the obscurity of cinema halls'.

While the cinema was part of the emergence of collective urban entertainment, the late nineteenth century also saw the advent of entertainment at home. Withdrawal into the home, pointed out by historians of private life, was reflected mainly in the appearance of private musical life which adopted the piano as the main instrument. The piano became an emblematic element of the middle classes' furniture. It was to bring public music into the domestic sphere, a transformation achieved through a very specific activity in the writing of music: reduction. Composers arranged scores written for an orchestra into pieces for piano. This same phenomenon of adaptation can be found at the beginning of jazz in the United States, where publishers simplified the rhythmic complexity of ragtime. In the tradition of the Frankfurt School, this activity of adaptation and reduction was often denounced: the capitalist market was killing art. Can we not consider, on the contrary, that these score sheets were the instrument of mediation between public and private music?

But music for amateur pianists was not only scholarly music. A very large market developed for sheet music for songs. In some cases over a million copies of the so-called 'royalty songs' were printed. Singing these songs, accompanied by the piano, was an important feature in the domestic entertainment of the upper and middle classes. It is estimated that by 1914 one quarter of English homes had a piano (Ehrlich, 1976).

It was in this context that the phonograph appeared. This device soon found a place in the domestic sphere. In the United States 3 per cent of all homes had one by 1900, 15 per cent by 1910 and 50 per cent by 1920. At first the catalogue consisted of songs, popular ballads or a few well-known symphonies. A second catalogue was later created, consisting of major operatic arias (Gelatt, 1965). While some singers were starting to be very popular, phonographic recordings were to enable people to remember tunes and popular songs they had already heard. As Walter Benjamin said, 'the art of collecting is a practical form of re-remembering' (1989: 222). This taste for collection concerned not only records but also photographs and postcards. The latter were used to send pictures of historical buildings to those who did not travel. The same applied to records which found a public among those who could not go to the opera and could thus listen to 'the most enchanting selection of the world's greatest singers'[3] at home.

Thus the phonograph, like the piano, was not only the instrument that allowed a private musical activity to be substituted for a public one. It was also owing to this device that music for shows was arranged for music at home (see Flichy, 1995: 67–75).

Radio and Television, Family Media

Between the two wars, radio was to replace records to a large extent. The new medium was presented as a tool enabling people to listen to plays or to music at home. Advertisements often presented the radio set as a theatre in the living room. Sets were 'designed to fit into all contexts of family life and the privacy of the home'.[4] Of the receiver it was said that 'all the waves in the world come to nest in it'.[5] We thus witness a privatization of the public sphere of entertainment. As many documents of the time show, reception was a family activity (Isola, 1990), a sort of ritual. It was often the father who tuned the radio and silence was demanded to listen to it. C.A. Lewis (1942), the first programme manager at the BBC, considered that:

> broadcasting means the rediscovery of the home. In these days when house and hearth have been largely given up in favour of a multitude of other interests and activities outside, with the consequent disintegration of family ties and affections, it appears that this new persuasion may to some extent reinstate the parental roof in its old accustomed place.

This family medium was considerably successful. In the US in 1927, five years after the first broadcasts were launched, 24 per cent of all households had a wireless. In 1932, despite the economic crisis, this number had risen to 60 per cent. In the UK, 73 per cent of all households had a set on the eve of World War II, and listened to radio on average four hours a day (Briggs, 1965: 253).

From the end of the 1940s television entered the domestic sphere. Yet its introduction into the home took place differently to that of the phonograph and radio. Whereas in the Victorian world there was a profound break between the public and private spheres, and the home was designed to

be a closed space, the domestic space of post-war North American suburbs was built on a complex interaction between public and private. According to Lynn Spigel, 'in paradoxical terms, privacy was something which could be enjoyed only in the company of others'. Middle-class suburbs described in magazines at the time 'suggested the new form of social cohesion which allowed people to be alone and together at the same time' (1992: 6).

A typical feature of the model home of that period was the large open living room and 'American kitchen'. Rooms opened onto the outside, giving the impression that public space was a continuation of domestic space. It was this new conception of space articulating public and private that prevailed at the birth of television. In 1946 Thomas Hutchinson published an introduction to this new medium, called *Here is Television: Your Window on the World* for the general public. Four years later, in another book for the general public, called *Radio, Television and Society*, Charles Siepmann wrote: 'television provides a maximum extension of the perceived environment with a minimum of effort … It is bringing the world to people's door' (Spigel, 1992: 7).

This theme can also be found in advertisements from that period. While adverts for the phonograph focused on the decorative aspect of the machine as a part of the furnishings of a room,[6] those for radio emphasized the same point but added the idea that the set brought sounds of the world into the home ('all the world's roads lie before you, it's a beautiful, splendid adventure … right in your armchair!'[7]). Advertisements for television showed the world. Photographs of a TV set featured the Eiffel Tower, Big Ben or the Statue of Liberty, for example. One advertisement showed a baseball field with an armchair and a TV set on it, with a baseball player on the screen.

This association of the domestic sphere with historical buildings or famous cities is also found in the first television series. In 'Make Room for Daddy', the hero's apartment has a splendid view of the New York skyline. One of the key characters in 'I Love Lucy' sees the hills of Hollywood from his bedroom window. These characters thus act against a backdrop of prestigious sites (Spigel, 1992: 10). Another theme runs through advertising during that period: the dramatization of the domestic sphere. Certain advertisements referred to television as a 'family', 'chairside' or 'living room' theatre (1992: 12). Some showed a woman in a black evening gown watching television at home. But it was also the great ritual events of our societies that television brought into the home: national celebrations, coronations and major sports events (Dayan and Katz, 1992).

The association between daily life and the entertainment world was furthermore found in new ways in which the American middle classes decorated their homes. What in Europe is called an American kitchen enabled the housewife to prepare meals while watching television. Very popular TV programmes in the 1950s also show the wish to include the entertainment world in daily life. In certain episodes of 'I Love Lucy' famous Hollywood actors are invited to dinner in ordinary homes (Mann, 1992: 44).

By contrast, television in the 1980s no longer tried to mix the two or to orchestrate major societal rituals. Instead, small family rituals were organized. In this new form that Italian sociologists have called 'neo-television' (Eco, 1985; Casetti and Odin, 1990), the content of interaction or the personality of the participants is of little consequence; the only thing that matters is their presence. Television displays daily life but also becomes a reference to serve as a standard for daily life. We thus witness a constant play in which television and society mirror each other.

Live Together Separately

As the family gathered together around television to watch it collectively (Meyrowitz, 1985), it abandoned radio which became an individual medium. Owing to the portability and low cost of transistor radios, everybody could listen alone in their bedroom while doing something else. This new family could 'live together separately' (Flichy, 1995: 158). It was probably with rock music, which appeared at that time, that use of the transistor and the related medium, the record player, appeared in full force. Whereas in the 1950s collective listening around the jukebox was decisive, listening was subsequently done at home, especially by teenage girls whose culture became a 'culture of the bedroom, the place where girls meet, listen to music and teach each other make-up skills, practise their dancing' (Frith, 1978: 64). Rock music listened to on a transistor radio or record player gave teenagers the opportunity to control their own space. This behaviour was part of the 'juxtaposed home'; it allowed teenagers to remove themselves from adult supervision while still living with their parents (Flichy, 1995: 160–5). This shift in listening from the living room to the bedroom was therefore far more than a new mode of listening, it was a way of asserting oneself, of creating a peer subculture. Was this individualization of listening to become generalized and affect television? In the mid 1980s that was far from being the case. David Morley's ethnographic study shows the family television to be a perpetual source of tension within the family between men, women, parents and children (Morley, 1986). As families acquired more and more sets, living room wars (Ang, 1996) were expected to disappear. Yet the TV set did not, as in the case of the transistor radio,

disappear from the living room. It has remained the main set around which the family gathers, while sets in bedrooms are used less.[8]

What about the mobile telephone, the PC and the Internet? Research in these areas is still limited and final conclusions can hardly be drawn. The current literature nevertheless allows us to make some hypotheses. In Europe the mobile phone seems to be the communication device that has developed fastest.[9] Like radio in the 1950s, it has spread rapidly among the youth. Once again, this device has enabled them to become more autonomous as regards the family cell, to live in it but to be elsewhere. Yet the cell phone, which is above all an individual communication device, does not seem to be causing the disappearance of the fixed phone which remains the family phone (Heurtin, 1998).

Despite discourse on the information society revolution, one has to agree that the microcomputer followed by its connection to the Internet have not spread as fast in homes as radio and television.[10] In the US, for example, it took about 20 years before households were equipped with at least one computer (more than one in the home remains rare). It seems that in many cases one member of the family tends to appropriate the set. A French study shows that in wealthy families it is often the father and that in working-class families it is, by contrast, a child and often the oldest son. In this case the set is installed in his bedroom (Jouët and Pasquier, 1999: 41). Yet, contrary to widespread belief, the computer does not isolate its user from others. It is characterized by a high level of sociability within peer groups. Young people exchange software and various tips for more efficient use of hardware and software. Video games are often played collectively. Alongside these horizontal social networks, Kirsten Drotner sees the emergence of vertical networks that function between generations: skills are passed on no longer from oldest to youngest but from teenagers to adults (1999: 103–4).

Virtual Communication

Although computing and the Internet, unlike radio and television and like the mobile phone, are personal tools, they are nevertheless characterized by complex social relations in peer groups and between generations. Sociability among internauts also has another degree of complexity: the fact that the individual can communicate anonymously behind a pseudonym and simultaneously have several pseudonyms and therefore several personalities. French sociologists had already noticed the phenomenon with the minitel. Users of minitel forums wanted not only to give themselves a new identity but also to take advantage of their mask to have different social behaviour, to reveal other facets of themselves and thus to better display their true identity (Jouët, 1991; Toussaint, 1991). Sherry Turkle studied the question of multiple identities on the Internet and especially in MUDs. One of her interviewees declared: 'I'm not one thing, I'm many things. Each part gets to be more fully expressed in MUDs than in the real world. So even though I play more than one self on MUDs, I feel more like "myself" when I'm MUDding' (Turkle, 1997: 185). These different lives can be lived out simultaneously in different windows of the same computer screen. 'I split my mind, say another player, I can see myself as being two or three or more. And I just turn on one part of my mind and then another when I go from window to window' (Turkle, 1996: 194). Are we heading for an identity crisis? Or can we consider, like Turkle, that this coexistence of different identities is one of the characteristics of our postmodern age?

CONCLUSION

Today the Internet constitutes the last phase in the history of information and communication technologies. But the network of networks is also a particularly interesting case since it enables us to recap most of the points considered in this chapter. This is simply one of the possible versions of digital networks. It is the result of a long history that started in the late 1960s. While IBM and AT&T had the competencies to launch a digital network, it was the collaboration of academics and hackers, with military funding, that spawned this network. The initial choices were profoundly marked by the representations of these actors who dreamed of a communicating, free, universal and non-hierarchized network. It was this same utopia that was spread by the media in the early 1990s. By contrast, the diffusion of the new technology in the corporate world combines a centralized model from mainframe computing and an open model launched by microcomputing. At home, the Internet combines the characteristics of several means of information and communication. It is a tool for interpersonal interaction and collective communication in virtual groups, but also a new medium with multiple sources of information. But this multiform information and communication tool also tends to undermine the separation between the professional and private spheres. It makes it easy to work from home and sometimes to attend to personal things at work. Unlike radio and television on the one hand and the telephone on the other, which were quickly standardized around an economic model and a media format, the Internet is fundamentally heterogeneous. This diversity is a key asset. As a result, use of the Internet cannot be unified around an economic model or a communicational format. It is not a medium but a system which is tending to become as complex as the society of which it is claimed to be a virtual copy.

NOTES

1 By contrast, in the 1990s the minitel stagnated. The France Télécom monopoly impeded all development of the system. This device soon seemed obsolete compared with the Internet.

2 On the history of Macintosh see also Levy (1994), and more broadly on the history of Apple see Carlton (1997).

3 Advertising slogan for the red label launched by the Gramophone Company in 1902.

4 'Le 12ème salon de la TSF', *L'Illustration*, 12 October 1935, Supplement: xx.

5 *L'Illustration*, 7 September 1935, Annonces: viii.

6 See the catalogue *Archeofon* (1989), Milano, Electra.

7 'Le 12ème salon de la TSF', *L'Illustration*, 12 October 1935, Supplement: xxi.

8 Sonia Livingstone (1999: 81) contests this thesis and is surprised that I have not seen the similarity between the evolution of radio and that of television. Although habits changed a great deal in the 1990s, the fact remains that the individualization of TV viewing has been only partial, unlike that of radio listening.

9 Historical comparisons are difficult in this domain. In the audiovisual media the number of sets per household are counted, and in telecommunications the number of sets per 100 inhabitants. This ratio does not distinguish business equipment from domestic equipment, and for mobile phones one has to take into account that the purchase is more often individual than collective.

10 Many authors defend the opposite point of view. See the table by the Morgan Stanley Research Group which classifies speed of penetration of the main communication technologies, cited in 'State of the Internet: USIC's report on use and threats in 1999', http://www.usic.org/usic99. This difference of evaluation stems from the fact that these authors take the invention of the technique, and not the beginning of its distribution in society at large, as the starting point of that diffusion.

REFERENCES

Abbate, Janet (1999) *Inventing the Internet*. Cambridge, MA: MIT Press.

Abel, Richard (1995) 'The perils of Pathé or the Americanization of the American cinema', in Leo Charney and Vanessa Schwartz (eds), *Cinema and the*

Invention of Modern Life. Berkeley, CA: University of California Press.

Akrich, Madeleine, Callon, Michel and Latour, Bruno (1988) 'A quoi tient le succès des innovations?', *Annale des Mines. Gérer et comprendre*, (11).

Alter, Norbert (1991) *La Gestion du désordre en entreprise*. Paris: L'Harmattan.

Ang, Ien (ed.) (1996) *Living Room Wars: Rethinking Media Audiences for a Postmodern World*. London: Routledge.

Ballé, Catherine and Peaucelle, Jean-Louis (1972) *Le Pouvoir informatique dans l'entreprise*. Paris: Les Editions d'Organisation.

Bar, François, Kane, Neil and Simard, Caroline (2000) 'Digital networks and organizational change: the evolutionary deployment of corporate information infrastructure'. Paper presented at the International Sunbelt Social Network Conference, Vancouver, 13–16 April 2000.

Baudelaire, Charles (1978) *The Painter of Modern Life and Other Essays*. New York: Garland.

Benghozi, Pierre-Jean, Flichy, Patrice and d'Iribarne, Alain (2000) 'Le développement d'intranet dans les entreprises françaises. Premiers constats', *Réseaux*, (104).

Beniger, James (1986) *The Control Revolution: Technological and Economic Origins of the Information Society*. Cambridge, MA: Harvard University Press.

Benjamin, Walter (1989) *Paris, capitale du XIXè siècle*. Paris: Le Cerf.

Bijker, Wiebe, Hughes, Thomas and Pinch, Trevor (1987) *The Social Construction of Technological Systems: New Directions in the Sociology and History of Technology*. Cambridge, MA: MIT Press.

Briggs, Asa (1965) *The History of Broadcasting in the United Kingdom*. Vol. 2: *The Golden Age of Wireless*. London: Oxford University Press.

Campbell-Kelly, Martin and Aspray, William (1996) *Computer: a History of the Information Machine*. New York: Basic.

Carlton, Jim (1997) *Apple: the Inside Story of Intrigue, Egomania, and Business Blunders*. New York: Times Business/Random House.

Casetti, Francesco and Odin, Roger (1990) 'De la paléo à la néo-télévision. Approche sémio-pragmatique', *Communications*, 51.

Cerruti, G. and Reiser, V. (1993) 'Information systems, computer systems and new strategies of rationalization', in Martin Heidenreich (ed.), *Computers and Culture in Organizations: the Introduction and Use of Production Control Systems in French, Italian, and German*. Berlin: Edition Sigma.

Ceruzzi, Paul (1987) 'An unforeseen revolution: computers and expectations, 1935–1985', in Joseph Corn (ed.), *Imagining Tomorrow: History, Technology and the American Future*. Cambridge, MA: MIT Press.

Chandler, Alfred, Jr (1977) *The Visible Hand: the Managerial Revolution in American Business*. Cambridge, MA: Harvard University Press.

Chandler, Alfred, Jr (2000) 'The information age in historical perspective', in Alfred Chandler Jr and James Cortada (eds), *A Nation Transformed by Information*. New York: Oxford University Press. pp. 3–37.

Clark, Ronald (1977) *Edison: the Man Who Made the Future*. New York: Putnam.

Cortada, James (1993) *The Computer in the United States: from Laboratory to Market, 1930 to 1960*. Armonk, NY: Sharpe.

Cusumano, Michael (1995) *Microsoft Secrets: How the World's Most Powerful Software Company Creates Technology, Shapes Markets, and Manages People*. New York: Free Press.

David, Paul (1985) 'Clio and the Economics of QWERTY', *American Economic Review*, 75 (2): 332–7.

Dayan, Daniel and Katz, Elihu (1992) *Media Events: the Live Broadcasting of History*. Cambridge, MA: Harvard University Press.

Douglas, Susan (1987) *Inventing American Broadcasting (1899–1922)*. Baltimore, MD: Johns Hopkins University Press.

Drotner, Kirsten (1999) 'Netsurfers and game navigators: new media and youthful leisure cultures in Denmark', *Réseaux*, 7 (1): 83–108.

Drucker, Peter (1974) *Management: Tasks, Responsibilities, Practices*. New York: Harper & Row.

DuBoff, Richard (1983) 'The telegraph and the structure of markets in the United States, 1845–1900', *Research in Economic History*, 8: 253–77.

Eco, Umberto (1985) 'TV la transparence perdue', in Umberto Eco, *La Guerre du faux*. Paris: Grasset.

Ehrlich, Cyril (1976) *The Piano: a History*. London: Dent.

Ellul, Jacques (1964) *The Technological Society*. New York: Knopf.

Flichy, Patrice (1991) 'The losers win. A comparative history of two innovations: videotext and the videodisc', in Josiane Jouët, Patrice Flichy and Paul Beaud (eds), *European Telematics: the Emerging Economy of Words*. Amsterdam: North-Holland. pp. 73–86.

Flichy, Patrice *(1995) Dynamics of Modern Communication: the Shaping and Impact of New Communication Technologies*. London: Sage.

Flichy, Patrice (forthcoming) *L'Imaginaire d'Internet*. Paris: La Découverte.

Freiberger, Paul and Swaine, Michael (1984) *Fire in the Valley: the Making of the Personal Computer*. Berkeley, CA: McGraw-Hill.

Friedmann, Georges (1978) *The Anatomy of Work: Labor, Leisure and the Implications of Automation*. Westport, CT: Greenwood.

Frith, Simon (1978) *The Sociology of Rock*. London: Constable.

Gaffin, Adam and Kapor, Mitchell (1991) *Big Dummy's Guide to the Internet*. Available at: http://www.thegulf.com/InternetGuide.html.

Gelatt, Roland (1965) *The Fabulous Phonograph: from Edison to Stereo*. New York: Appleton-Century.

Graham, Margaret (1986) *RCA and the VideoDisc: the Business of Research*. New York: Cambridge University Press.

Guterl, Fred (1984) 'Design case history: Apple's Macintosh', *IEEE Spectrum*, December: 34–43.

Hafner, Katie and Lyon, Mathew (1996) *Where Wizards Stay Up Late: the Origins of the Internet*. New York: Simon & Schuster.

Heurtin, Jean-Philippe (1998) 'Le téléphone mobile, une communication itinérante ou individuelle? Premiers éléments d'une analyse des usages en France', *Réseaux*, (90): 37–50.

Hiltz, Starr and Turoff, Murray (1978) *The Network Nation: Human Communication via Computer*. Cambridge, MA: MIT Press.

Hoffsaes, Colette (1978) 'L'informatique dans l'organisation: changement ou stabilité?', *Sociologie du travail*, (3).

Isola, Gianni (1990) *Abbassa la tua radio, per favore: storia dell'ascolto radiofonico nell'Italia fascista*. Firenze: La nuova Italia.

Jouët, Josiane (1991) 'A telematic community: the Axiens', in Josiane Jouët, Patrice Flichy and Paul Beaud (eds), *European Telematics: the Emerging Economy of Words*. Amsterdam: North-Holland. pp. 181–202.

Jouët, Josiane and Pasquier, Dominique (1999) 'Youth and screen culture', *Réseaux*, 7 (1): 31–58.

Latour, Bruno (1987) *Science in Action: How to Follow Scientists and Engineers through Society*. Cambridge, MA: Harvard University Press.

Leonard-Barton, Dorothy (1988) 'Implementation as mutual adaptation of technology and organization', *Research Policy*, 17 (5): 251–67.

Levy, Steven (1985) *Hackers, Heroes of the Computer Revolution*. New York: Dell.

Levy, Steven (1994) *Insanely Great: the Life and Times of Macintosh, the Computer that Changed Everything*. New York: Viking.

Lewis, C.A. (1942) *Broadcasting from Within*. London: Newnes.

Livingstone, Sonia (1999) 'Young people and the new media: on learning lessons from TV to apply to the PC', *Réseaux*, 7 (1): 59–81.

Mann, Denise (1992) 'The spectacularization of everyday life: recycling hollywood stars and fans in early variety shows', in Lynn Spigel and Denise Mann (eds), *Private Screenings: Television and the Female Consumer*. Minneapolis: University of Minnesota Press.

Marx, Leo (1964) *The Machine in the Garden: Technology and the Pastoral Ideal in America*. New York: Oxford University Press.

Mary, Bertrand (1993) *La Photo sw la cheminée: naissance d'un culte moderne*. Paris: Métailié.

McLuhan, Marshall (1964) *Understanding Media: the Extensions of Man*. New York: McGraw-Hill.

Meyrowitz, Joshua (1985) *No Sense of Place: the Impact of Electronic Media on Social Behavior*. New York: Oxford University Press.

Morley, David (1986) *Family Television: Cultural Power and Domestic Leisure*. London: Comedia.

Noble, David (1979) 'Social choice in machine design: the case of automatically controlled machine tools', in Andrew Zimbalist (ed.), *Case Studies on the Labor Process*. New York: Monthly Review Press.

Noble, David (1984) *Forces of Production: a Social History of Industrial Automation*. New York: Knopf.

Nolan, Richard (2000) 'Information technology management', in Alfred Chandler and James Cortada Jr (eds), *A Nation Transformed by Information*. New York: Oxford University Press.

Norberg, Arthur and O'Neill, Judy (1996) *Transforming Computer Technology: Information Processing for the Pentagon (1962–1986)*. Baltimore: Johns Hopkins University Press.

Orlikowski, Wanda (1992) 'The duality of technology: rethinking the concept of technology in organizations', *Organization Science*, 3 (3): 398–427.

Poe, Edgar Allan (1971) 'The man of the crowd', in Edgar Allan Poe, *Tales of Mystery and Imagination*. New York: Everyman.

Rheingold, Howard (1993) *The Virtual Community: Homesteading on the Electronic Frontier*. New York: HarperCollins.

Ruellan, Denis and Thierry, Daniel (1998) *Journal local et réseaux informatiques: travail coopératif, décentralisation et identité des journalistes*. Paris: L'Harmattan.

Schaffer, Simon (1995) *Babbage's Intelligence: Calculating Engines and the Factory System*. Available at: http://www.wmin.ac.uk/media/schaffer/schaffer01.html.

Sennett, Richard (1977) *The Fall of Public Man*. New York: Knopf.

Sklar, Robert (1975) *Movie-Made America: a Cultural History of American Movies*. New York: Random House.

Spigel, Lynn (1992) 'Installing the television and domestic space 1948–1955', in Lynn Spigel and Denise Mann (eds), *Private Screenings: Television and the Female Consumer*. Minneapolis: University of Minnesota Press.

Star, Susan and Griesemer, James (1989) 'Institutional ecology, translations and boundary objects: amateurs and professionals in Berkeley's Museum of Vertebrate Zoology (1907–1939)', *Social Studies of Science*, 19: 387–420.

Taylor, Frederick (1911) *The Principles of Scientific Management*. New York: Harper.

Toussaint, Yves (1991) 'Concealment and dissimulation on the messageries', in Josiane Jouët, Patrice Flichy and Paul Beaud (eds), *European Telematics: the Emerging Economy of Words*. Amsterdam: North-Holland. pp. 229–49.

Turkle, Sherry (1996) 'Who am we?', *Wired*, January.

Turkle, Sherry (1997) *Life on the Screen*. New York: Touchstone.

Turnaturi, Gabriella (1995) 'Les métamorphoses du divertissement citadin', in Alain Corbin (ed.), *L'Avènement des loisirs 1860–1960*. Paris: Aubier.

Von Hippel, Eric (1988) *The Sources of Innovation*. New York: Oxford University Press.

Yates, JoAnne (1989) *Control through Communication: the Rise of System in American Management*. Baltimore: Johns Hopkins University Press.

Yates, JoAnne (1994) 'Evolving information use in firms, 1850–1920: ideology and information techniques and technologies', in Lisa Bud-Frierman (ed.), *Information Acumen: the Understanding and Use of Knowledge in Modern Business*. London: Routledge.

Yates, JoAnne (2000) 'Business use of information and technology during the industrial age', in Alfred Chandler Jr and James Cortada (eds), *A Nation Transformed by Information*. New York: Oxford University Press. pp. 107–35.

Zuboff, Shoshana (1988) *In the Age of the Smart Machine: the Future of Work and Power*. New York: Basic Books.

9

How to Infrastructure

SUSAN LEIGH STAR
and
GEOFFREY C. BOWKER

Resources appear, too, as shared visions of the possible and acceptable dreams of the innovative, as techniques, knowledge, know-how, and the institutions for learning these things. Infrastructure in these terms is a dense interwoven fabric that is, at the same time, dynamic, thoroughly ecological, even fragile.

(Bucciarelli, 1994: 131)

The central topic of this chapter is the infrastructure that subtends new media: overwhelmingly for our purposes this means the Internet in all its guises. We seek to explore the development and design of infrastructure; our main argument will be that a social and theoretical understanding of infrastructure is key to the design of new media applications in our highly networked, information convergent society.

When we think of infrastructure in a common-sense way, infrastructure is that which runs 'underneath' actual structures – railroad tracks, city plumbing and sewage, electricity, roads and highways, cable wires that connect to the broadcast grid and bring pictures to our TVs. It is that upon which something else rides, or works, a platform of sorts. This common-sense definition begins to unravel when we populate the picture, and begin to look at multiple, overlapping and perhaps contradictory infrastructural arrangements. For the railroad engineer, the rails are only infrastructure when she or he is a passenger. Almost anyone can flip an electric switch, for a variety of purposes. When the switch fails, we are forced to look more deeply into the cause: first check the light bulb, then the other appliances on the same circuit, then look at the circuit breaker box, then look down the block to see if it is a power outage in the neighbourhood or city, and

lastly, depending on one's home repair skills, consider calling an electrician. Finally, increasingly many of us are faced with infrastructures, designed by one group, that may not work for us. For instance, someone in a wheelchair appreciates the tiny (and not so tiny) barriers that are considered 'wheelchair accessible' by the able-bodied. Four steps can be a mountain if the specific conditions of usability are overlooked. So we have three separate themes here:

1 the moving target of infrastructure, from easy-to-use black box to active topic of work and research;
2 the breakdown of infrastructure that opens the taken-for-granted;
3 the relative usefulness of infrastructure for different populations.

One thing that unites each of these strands is the notion that infrastructure is not absolute, but relative to working conditions. It never stands apart from the people who design, maintain and use it. Its designers try to make it as invisible as possible, while leaving pointers to make it visible when it needs to be repaired or remapped. It is tricky to study for this reason.

Perhaps for these reasons, infrastructure is an often neglected aspect of communication studies, except in areas such as the specific regulation of an infrastructure, or the history of one type (such as the telephone, the automobile or the Internet). Both such kinds of studies are invaluable, and certainly central to the discipline of communication. Communication infrastructures include printing, telegraph, radio, fax, television, the Internet and the web, and movie production and distribution. Under some circumstances the human body becomes infrastructure, such as in the study of face-to-face conversations.

Interestingly, for example in the study of body language, human emotions and situations are the infrastructure, and the targets of study are facial and body muscles, posture and proximity. This chapter outlines several facets of importance to theory and research on the design, development and use of infrastructure. We will also refer to some policy articles for purely policy-related infrastructure issues, such as the regulation of telecommunications or the standards setting process for the Internet. See Part V.

Given the above qualifications, what then are we left with that is infrastructure? Can it be anything? Like many concepts in communication, the relational quality of infrastructure talks about that which is between – between people, mediated by tools, and emergent (Jewett and Kling, 1991). Like the term 'communication' itself, and others such as 'meaning', 'audience', 'free speech', or 'regulation', the exact sense of the term 'infrastructure' and its 'betweenness' are both theoretical and empirical questions.

We will work from Star and Ruhleder's (1996) definition of the salient features of infrastructure in order to bound and clarify the term.

- *Embeddedness*   Infrastructure is sunk into, inside of, other structures, social arrangements and technologies.
- *Transparency*   Infrastructure is transparent to use, in the sense that it does not have to be reinvented each time or assembled for each task, but invisibly supports those tasks.
- *Reach or scope*   This may be either spatial or temporal: infrastructure has reach beyond a single event or one-site practice.
- *Learned as part of membership*   The taken-for-grantedness of artifacts and organizational arrangements is a *sine qua non* of membership in a community of practice (Lave and Wenger, 1991; Star and Ruhleder, 1996). Strangers and outsiders encounter infrastructure as a target object to be learned about. New participants acquire a naturalized familiarity with its objects as they become members.
- *Links with conventions of practice*   Infrastructure both shapes and is shaped by the conventions of a community of practice, e.g. the ways that cycles of day–night work are affected by and affect electrical power rates and needs. Generations of typists have learned the QWERTY keyboard; its limitations are inherited by the computer keyboard and thence by the design of today's computer furniture (Becker, 1982).
- *Embodiment of standards*   Modified by scope and often by conflicting conventions, infrastructure takes on transparency by plugging into other infrastructures and tools in a standardized fashion.
- *Built on an installed base*   Infrastructure does not grow *de novo*; it wrestles with the inertia of the installed base and inherits strengths and limitations from that base. Optical fibres run along old railroad lines; new systems are designed for backward compatibility; and failing to account for these constraints may be fatal or distorting to new development processes (Monteiro and Hanseth, 1996).
- *Becomes visible upon breakdown*   The normally invisible quality of working infrastructure becomes visible when it breaks: the server is down, the bridge washes out, there is a power blackout. Even when there are back-up mechanisms or procedures, their existence further highlights the now visible infrastructure.

Something that was once an object of development and design becomes sunk into infrastructure over time. Therefore a historical, archaeological approach to the development of an infrastructure like the Internet needs complementary sociological, regulatory and technical studies.

SOCIOHISTORICAL ANALYSES
OF INFRASTRUCTURE

Much current work in the sociohistorical analysis of infrastructure has derived from the field of science and technology studies (STS). Latour and Woolgar's *Laboratory Life* (1979) helped open a window to a more qualitative, intensively observational set of studies of scientific work and practice. The authors drew particular attention to the role of the scientists' information infrastructure (articles, graphs, pieces of paper) in their work. By the 1990s, STS researchers began to turn their attention to the design and use of computing and information technologies (see e.g. Star, 1995). Woolgar has called this the 'technical turn' in STS. Using many of the same techniques as had laboratory studies of science, these researchers studied (and in some cases, worked in partnership with) the design, use, manufacture and distribution of information technology (Henderson, 1999; Downey and Lucena, 1994; Collins and Kusch, 1998; to name just a few)[1].

The combination of the technical turn and studies of materials brought infrastructure to the fore in STS (see e.g. Star and Ruhleder, 1996; Latour and Hernant, 1999). The ethnographic eye that helped reveal the inner workings of science or technology research and development was helpful in interpreting infrastructure. Arguments about standardization, selection and maintenance of tools, and the right materials for the job of knowledge production have slowly come into centre stage via this synthesis (Clarke and Fujimura, 1992). Along with this has come a rediscovery of some of the tools germane to cognate disciplines which had previously analysed material culture and the built environment.

These have included, *inter alia*, fields such as architecture (where scholars sometimes read the built environment as a kind of text), literary theory (especially those aspects of literary theory that help surface hidden assumptions and narrative structure), social geography (where the values and biases inherent in such tools as maps are a lively topic of inquiry) and information science (Bowker and Star, 1999; *Library Trends*, 1998).

Thomas Hughes (1983), in his historical discussion of the rise of electricity networks in Europe and the United States, developed a suite of tools for analysing the development and design of infrastructure. He drew attention to the importance of *reverse salients* – technological, social or political sticking points which can slow the development of an infrastructure. Crucially, he argued that the solution to a reverse salient does not have to be from the same register as the problem: there might be a political solution to a technical problem and so forth (cf. Latour, 1996). Thus, for example, the technical problem of low-bandwidth communications in e-mail was partially solved by the social solution of using a complex set of 'emoticons' to provide a layering of the flat ASCII text. The design implication here is that there is no possible *a priori* assignation of different tasks to different bodies of specialists in the design of communication infrastructures for new media: the emergent infrastructure itself represents one of a number of possible distributions of tasks and properties between hardware, software and people (see Tanenbaum, 1996 for a full discussion of the variety of possible representations of the Internet, with different distributions between them).

Hughes further pointed out that the early electricity networks drew off skills developed in the design of gas networks before them and canals before that: each generation of engineers imports solutions from one infrastructure to the next. This trend has continued with the current design of the web. This has both positive and negative consequences. On the positive side, it points to the fact that skills can be usefully transferred from one medium to the next. However, the negative side is that this can lead to a lack of imagination. Paul David (1995; cf. Landauer, 1995) has written about the 'productivity paradox' that saw productivity decline with the introduction of the electric dynamo in factories in the nineteenth century and with the introduction of the computer in organizations in the twentieth. He makes the strong point that it was not until ways of thinking through the new technology emerged that improvements occurred: the dynamo made a bad steam engine, the computer a bad typewriter, and so on. This draws attention to the importance of the metaphors that we use to think through technology: Mark Stefik (1996) speaks of a set of 'archetypes' that have been used to drive design on the Internet. It is important to recognize that these archetypes might also be traps.

David's argument works because infrastructures don't just exist by themselves – they are embedded in organizations of many kinds. Bowker (1994b) has developed the concept of infrastructural inversion to describe the fact that historical changes frequently ascribed to some spectacular product of an age are frequently more a feature of an infrastructure permitting the development of that product. Thus the rise of computing machinery in the late nineteenth century was consequent on (not causative of) changes in office organization; the twin rise of life expectancy and the medical profession at the same time was consequent on (not causative of) the development of water and sanitation infrastructures. Operating this inversion is a struggle against the tendency of infrastructure to disappear (except when breaking down). It means learning to look closely at technologies and arrangements which, by design and by habit, tend to fade into the woodwork (sometimes literally!). Infrastructural inversion foregrounds these normally invisible Lilliputian threads, and furthermore gives them causal prominence in many areas normally attributed to heroic actors, social movements or cultural mores. The inversion is similar to the argument made by Becker in his book *Art Worlds* (1982). Most history and social analysis of art has neglected the details of infrastructure within which communities of artistic practice emerge, instead focusing on aesthetics as devoid from these issues. Becker's inversion examines the conventions and constraints of the material artistic infrastructure, and its ramifications. For example, the convention of musical concerts lasting about two hours ramifies throughout the producing organization. Parking attendants, unions, ticket takers and theatre rentals are arranged in cascading dependence on this interval of time. An eight-hour musical piece, which is occasionally written, means rearranging all of these expectations – which in turn is so expensive that such productions are rare. Or paintings are about the size, usually, that will hang comfortably on a wall. They are also the size that fits rolls of canvas, the skills of framers, and the very doorways of museums and galleries. These constraints are mutable only at great cost, and artists must always consider them before violating them. The infrastructure designer must always be aware of the multiple sets of contexts her work impinges on. Frequently a technical innovation must be accompanied by an organizational innovation in order to work: the design of sociotechnical systems engages both the technologist and the organization theorist.

Common to a set of key texts (Bud-Frierman, 1994; Clarke and Fujimura, 1992; Fischer, 1992; Friedlander, 1995; Rosenberg, 1982), analysing infrastructure is a problematizing of this relationship between background and foreground. A given infrastructure may have become transparent, but a number of significant political, ethical and social choices have without doubt been folded into its development – and this background needs to be understood if we are to produce thoughtful analyses of the nature of infrastructural work. For example, a road network may be designed politically to prevent access by the poor to a given facility (Davis, 1997 makes this point about SeaWorld in San Diego; Winner, 1986 about beach access in New York). Equally, a highly standardized instrument like the census form folds in strong claims about the nature and importance of a particular set of ethnic categories (Bowker and Star, 1999). Web designers frequently wrap choices about the kind of visitor they want into their website (few sites are designed with access for the blind, say, since HTML is written in such a way that it does not force designers to produce alternative text for every image they produce); and complex sites often require a high-speed connection, so the less wealthy user with a slow modem will be excluded by her own understandable impatience.

How Infrastructure Happens

Both standardization and classification are essential to the development of working infrastructures. Work done on standards committees and in setting up classification schemes is frequently overlooked in social and political analyses of infrastructure, and yet it is of crucial importance. In this section, we will review work that explores these issues.

There is no question that in the development of large-scale information infrastructures, we need standards. In a sense this is a trivial observation: strings of bits travelling along wires are meaningless unless there is a shared set of handshakes among the various media they pass through. An e-mail message is typically broken up into regular size chunks, and then wrapped in various 'envelopes', each of which represents a different layer of the infrastructure. A given message might be encoded using the MIME (multipurpose Internet mail extensions protocol): this will allow various other mail programs to read it. It might then be chunked into smaller parts, each of which is wrapped in an envelope designating its ultimate address and its order in the message. This envelope will be further wrapped in an envelope telling it how to enter the Internet. It will then quite possibly be wrapped in further envelopes telling it how to change from a configuration of electrons on a wire to a radio message beamed to a satellite and back down again (Tanenbaum, 1996; Hurley and Keller, 1999). Each envelope is progressively opened at the end, and the original message reassembled from its contingent parts then appears 'transparently' on your desktop. It is the standards that let this happen.

One observation that we can make at once is that it is standard all the way down: each layer of infrastructure requires its own set of standards. We might also say that it is standard all the way up. There is no simple break point at which one can say that communication protocols stop and technical standards start. As a thought experiment, let us take the example of a scientific paper. I write a paper about palaeoecology for the journal *Science*. I know that my immediate audience will not be leading-edge palaeoecologists, but a wider community who know only a little about Devonian plant communities. So I wrap the kernel in an introduction and conclusion that discuss in general terms the nature and significance of my findings. A journalist might well write a more popular piece for the 'Perspectives' section which will point to my paper. If this is my first paper for *Science* then I will probably go through quite a complex set of negotiations through the peer review process in order to ensure the correct 'handshake' between my message and its audience: is it written at the right level, have I used the right tone of authority, and so forth. Yates (1989) has written about similar sets of standards/protocols that arose with the development of office memoranda in the nineteenth century; she and Orlikowski have observed similar effects in the development of e-mail genres (Orlikowski et al., 1993). I then need to be sure that the right set of economic agreements has been put into place so that my paper can be found on the web by anyone at any time (Kahin and Keller, 1997).

This common vision of disciplinary, economic and network protocols serves the purpose of highlighting a central fact about infrastructures. It is not just the bits and bytes that get hustled into standard form in order for the technical infrastructure to work. People's discursive and work practices get hustled into standard form as well. Working infrastructures standardize both people and machines. A further example will clarify this point. In order for the large-scale states of the nineteenth century to operate efficiently and effectively, the new science of statistics (of the same etymological root as the word 'state') was developed. People were sorted into categories, and a series of information technologies was put into place to provide an infrastructure to government work (regular ten-year censuses; special tables and printers; by the end of the nineteenth century, punch card machines for faster processing of results). These standardized categories (male, African-American, professional, etc.) thus spawned their own set of technical standards (80-column sheets – later transferred to 80-column punch cards and computer screens). They also spawned their own set of standardized people. As Alain Desrosières and Laurent Thévenot (1988) note, different categories for professional works in the French, German and British censuses led to the creation of very different social structures and government programmes around them. Early in the nineteenth century, the differences between professionals in one country or the other was minimal. By the end of the century these differences had become entrenched and reified: unions had formed around them, informal dress codes had been adopted and so forth.

At both the technical and the social level, there is no guarantee that the best set of standards will win.[2] The process of the creation of standards for infrastructures is a long, tortuous, contingent one. The best known stories here are the adoption of the QWERTY keyboard (good for its time in preventing keys jamming in manual typewriters; counterproductive now for most in that it puts most of the work onto the left hand, a hardship for many, but one appreciated by the southpaws (left-handers) amongst us; but so entrenched that there is no end in sight for it: David, 1986); the victory of the VHS standard over the technically superior Betamax standard; the victory of DOS and its successors over superior operating systems.

So why does the best standard not always win? In an infrastructure you are never alone: no node is an island. Suppose there are 500 users of DOS to every one user of a Macintosh. A software developer has less motivation to write software for Macs, which have a much smaller potential user base. So the strong get stronger. Going down one level into the infrastructure, companies are more likely to write APIs (application program interfaces – to allow communication between one program and another) for interoperation between a new program and an industry standard one than a rarely used one. More generally put, a new kind of economic logic has developed around the network infrastructures that have been created over the past 200 years – the logic of 'network externalities' (David, 1986; David and Greenstein, 1990; David and Rothwell, 1994). The logic runs as follows. If a person buys a telephone for $50 and there are only five people on the network, then owning a telephone is not worth very much, even if the five are fast friends. If 5000 more people buy telephones then the first five have not had to lay out another cent, but their phones are suddenly much more valuable. This situation describes positive externalities. *De facto* standards (such as DOS, QWERTY, etc.) gain and hold on to their position largely through the development of positive externalities. The design lesson here is that integration with existing programs is key to the success of new infrastructural tools.

Arguably some of the most far-reaching decisions of the past 50 years have been taken by standards setting bodies – although one does not find a 'standards' section of the bookshop alongside 'history' and 'new age'. Consider, for example, the political and social implications of the 'open source' movement. This movement has a long history, running deep into the origin of the Internet, proclaiming the democratic and liberatory value of freely sharing software code. The Internet, indeed, was cobbled together out of a set of freely distributed software standards. The open source movement has been seen as running counter to the dominance of large centralized industries: the argument goes that it puts power over the media back into the hands of the people in a way that might truly transform capitalist society (Poster, 1995). This promise of cyberdemocracy is integrally social, political and technical. While there is much talk of an 'information revolution' (though be it noted there has been fairly regular talk of the same since the 1830s: Bowker, 1994a), there is not enough of the ways in which people and communities are in part constituted by the new infrastructure. One important example here is the development of patient support groups on the Internet – allowing sufferers of a rare illness to share moral support, information about new drugs and medical trials and folk treatments. Such patient communities would have been impossible in the past in the case of very rare diseases; certainly, even for more common diseases, they permit patients from rural areas access to the dense information networks of the city. Groups such as these frequently organize face-to-face meetings after they have 'met' on the Internet (Baym, 2000).

There are many models for information infrastructures. The Internet itself can be cut up conceptually a number of different ways. There is over time and between models a distribution of properties between hardware, software and people. Thus one can get two computers 'talking' to each other by running a dedicated line between them or by pre-empting a given physical circuit (hardware solutions) or by creating a 'virtual circuit' (software solution) which runs over multiple different physical circuits. Or finally you can still (and this is the fastest way of getting terabits of data from San Francisco to LA) put a hard disk in a truck and drive it down (Tanenbaum, 1996). Each kind of circuit is made up of a different stable configuration of wires, bits and people; but they are all (as far as the infrastructure itself is concerned) interchangeable. One can think of standards in the infrastructure as the tools for stabilizing these configurations. There is a continuum of strategies for standards setting. At the one end of the spectrum is the strategy of one standard fits all. This can be imposed by government fiat (for example the Navy's failed attempt to impose ADA as the sole programming language for their applications) or can take the form of an emergent monopoly (for example, Microsoft Windows/NT). At the other end of the spectrum is the 'let a thousand standards bloom' model. In such a case, one concentrates on producing interfaces such as APIs between programs and on such standards as the ANSI/NISO Z39.50 information retrieval protocol. Z39.50 is a standard that has been developed for being able to make a single enquiry over multiple databases: it has been very widely adopted in the library world. You can use whatever database program you wish to make your bibliographic database with, provided that the program itself subscribes to the standard. This means in essence that certain key fields like 'author', 'title' and 'keyword' will be defined in the database. Now, instead of having to load up multiple different database programs in order to search over many databases (a challenge of significance well beyond the library community, as large-scale heterogeneous datasets are coming into centre stage in a number of scientific and cultural fields) one can frame a single query using the Z39.50 standard and have your results returned seamlessly from many different sources. One metaphor about these two extremes is that the former is the 'colonial' model of infrastructure development where the latter is the 'democratic' model. There is some truth to the implied claim that one's political philosophy will determine one's choice; and there is some solace for democrats in the observation that with the development of the Internet the latter has almost invariably won out: most Internet standards have been cobbled together in such a way that they permit maximal flexibility and heterogeneity. Thus, for example, if one tracks the emergence and deployment of collaborative computing, one finds that large-scale stand-alone programs have done much worse than less powerful programs that permit easy integration with one's other programs and with the Internet (Star and Ruhleder, 1996).

There are utopian visions that when we get all the standards in place, there will be seamless access to the world's store of information from any place on the planet. The World Brain project (http://www. imagination-engines.com/world.htm), for example, claims that it is developing 'not a mere kitten brain, not an on-line library, but a true synthetic genius that will deliver us from war, poverty, and suffering'; compare also the utopian vision of the Principia Cybernetica (http://pespmc1.vub.ac.be/). Gregory (2000) has called such efforts 'incomplete utopian projects'. It is the incompleteness that we must turn to here: they always remain incomplete; they are always outnumbered, always outgunned by the forces against them. The World Brain, for example, echoes H.G. Wells' long-forgotten project of the same name, announced just as optimistically some 60 years earlier: 'An immense, an ever-increasing wealth of knowledge is scattered about the world today, a wealth of knowledge and suggestion that – systematically ordered and generally disseminated – would probably give this giant vision and direction and suffice to solve all the mighty difficulties of our age' (1938: 66–7, cited in Rayward, 1999).

The reason for pointing to these persistent failures is that they reflect some key features of infrastructures. They show that infrastructural development and maintenance require work, a relatively stable technology and communication. The work side is frequently overlooked. Consider the claim in the 1920s that with the advent of microfiche, the end of the book was nigh: everyone would have their own personal libraries; we would no longer need to waste vast amounts of natural resources on producing paper; all the largest library would need would be a few rooms and a set of microfiche readers (Abbott, 1988). A possible vision, and one that we should not discount just because it did not happen; MacKenzie (1990) reminds us that technological roads not taken can appear futile – for example, anyone who has used a microfiche reader will attest that it's a most uncomfortable experience – whereas if the same resources had gone into the failure as into the successful technology, it probably could have been a winner. However, the microfiche dream, like the universal digital library, runs up against the problem that someone has to sit there and do the necessary photography/scanning; and this takes a huge amount of time and resources. It is easy enough to develop a potentially revolutionary technology; it is extremely hard to implement it.

Further, one needs a relatively stable technology. If one thinks of some of the great infrastructural technologies of the past (gas, electric, sewage and so forth) one can see that once the infrastructure is put into place it tends to have a long life. Electrical wiring from before World War II is still in use in many households; in major cities there is frequently no good map of sewage pipes, since their origin goes too far back in time. The Internet is only virtually stable – through the mediation of a set of relatively stable protocols: for this reason, Edwards (1998) suggests that we call it an internetwork technology rather than a Hughesian (Hughes, 1983) network technology such as the electricity network. However, there is nothing to guarantee the stability of vast datasets. At the turn of the twentieth century, Otlet developed a scheme for a universal library which would work by providing automatic electro-mechanical access to extremely well-catalogued microfiches, which could link between each other (Rayward, 1975). All the world's knowledge would be put onto these fiches; his vision was a precursor to today's hypertext. He made huge strides in developing this system (though he only had the person power to achieve a minuscule fraction of his goal). However, within 40 years, with the development of computer memory, his whole enterprise was effectively doomed to languish as it does today in boxes in a basement. Why retrieve information electromechanically using levers and gears when you can call it up at the speed of light from a computer? Much the same can be said of Bush's never realized but inspirational vision of the Memex – an electromechanical precursor to the workstation

(Bush et al., 1991). Large databases from the early days of the computer revolution are now completely lost. Who now reads punch cards – a technology whose first major use in this country was to deal with the massive datasets of the 1890 census, and which dominated information storage and handling for some 70 years? Closer to the present day, the 'electronic medical record' has been announced every few years since the 1960s – and yet it has not been globally attained. Changes in database architecture, storage capabilities of computers and ingrained organizational practices have rendered it a chimera. The development of stable standards together with due attention being paid to backwards compatibility provide in principle a fix to these problems. It can all unravel very easily, though. The bottom line is that no storage medium is permanent (CDs will not last anywhere near as long as books printed on acid-free paper) – so that our emergent information infrastructure will require a continued maintenance effort to keep data accessible and usable as it passes from one storage medium to another and is analysed by one generation of database technology to the next.

Finally, in order to really build an information infrastructure, you need to pay close attention to issues of communication. We can parse this partly as the problem of reliable metadata. Metadata ('data about data': Michener et al., 1997) is the technical term for all the information that a single piece of data out there on the Internet can carry with it in order to provide sufficient context for another user to be able to first locate it and then use it. The most widespread metadata standards are the Dublin Core, developed for library applications; and the Federal Geographic Data Committee (FGDC: http://www.fgdc.gov/) standard developed for geographical information systems. If everyone can agree to standard names for certain kinds of data, then one can easily search for, say, authors over multiple databases. We have already seen this. Philosophically, however, metadata open up into some far deeper problems. Take the example of biodiversity science. It is generally agreed that if we want to preserve a decent proportion of animal and floral life from the current great extinction event (one of six since the origin of life on this planet) then policy-makers need the best possible information about the current species size and distribution, as well as the ability to model the effect of potential and current environmental changes. In order to do this, you need to be able to bring together data from many different scientific disciplines using many different information technologies (from paper to supercomputer). Now imagine that I am measuring lake water acidity in the Midwest in order to see if there are any effects from recent acid rain. I might be lucky and come across a very large dataset going back 80 or 100 years and giving lake water acidity levels at one-year intervals. However, this might

well not be enough for me to actually use the data. It makes quite a difference if the measurement was taken immediately at the lake or later, when the samples were brought back to the laboratory: there will be different amounts of dissolved carbon dioxide in the sample. And as it happens, it makes a difference which technology of measurement I use: a new technology can provide a consistent jump in values for the same sample (see Bowker, 2000 for a detailed discussion of this and related cases of metadata problems). Now to make matters worse, I as a scientist am no expert in measuring lake water; I am an expert modeller, and I just want some data to plug into my model. But the point is that there is no such thing as pure data. You always have to know some context. And as you develop metadata standards you always need to think about how much information you need to give in order to make your information maximally useful over time. And here we circle back to the first difficulty with developing an information infrastructure: the more information that you provide in order to make the data useful to the widest community and over the longest time, the more work you have to do. Yet empirical studies have shown time and again that people will not see it as a good use of their time to preserve information about their data beyond what is necessary to guarantee its immediate usefulness. Thus Fagot-Largeault (1989) describes the medical culture of producing quick and easy diagnoses on death certificates in order to meet the administrative need and free time to get onto the next (live) patient.

So standards are necessary – from social protocols down to wiring size. Indeed, when you foreground the infrastructure of your lives, you will see that you encounter thousands of standards in a single day. However, as we have aleady seen, the development and maintenance of standards are complex ethical and philosophical problems: ethical since decisions taken at the stage of development standards can have enormous implications for user communities; and philosophical since standards frequently deal with very basic ways of splitting up the world (the base categories of Z39.50 sketch out an interestingly restricted ontology of 'authorship', for example). Further, standards implementation requires a vast amount of resources. Standards undergird our potential for action in the world, both political and scientific; they make the infrastructure possible.

Representation in a database can be a key means for a group or profession to gain recognition – yet there are frequently costs involved. For instance, a group of nurses in Iowa developed a Nursing Interventions Classification in order to carve out a place in hospital information systems for nursing work. However, they recognized while doing this that the scheme put them in danger both of being stripped of some of their work ('it doesn't take a skilled professional to do this') and of losing some of the essence of their contribution in the scheme (it is hard to code for 'humour', for example) (Bowker and Star, 1999). Such cases have proliferated with the development of interlocking large-scale information infrastructures.[3]

The installed base of a particular infrastructure carries huge inertia. And yet infrastructures do change over time, sometimes transforming remarkably rapidly, sometimes apparently discontinuously (a country going from postal communication to cellular phones without passing through landlines, for example). This is made more complicated by the ways in which the built environment (libraries, schools, offices, homes, traffic lights, airports, hospitals) is increasingly imbricated with information technologies of every sort (Taylor and van Every, 1993; 2000). These include sensors, databases, digital cameras, networked PCs and all forms of display units. A deeper sense of this comes with the realization that these forms of information technology are increasingly *integrated* (they can share information via protocols and standards) and *convergent* (they are delivered through a single point, such as web pages embedded in a cellular telephone, where one's plane schedule for a connecting flight may be checked while on board the current flight). In some cases, this may result in serious privacy and ethical boundaries. An example of this would be the sale of a hospital to a pharmaceutical company, along with its records; the pharmaceutical company might use the list of patients and their illnesses to direct mail niche markets based on, for example, a chronic condition.[4]

ACCESS AND USABILITY ISSUES

One of the places where the relational aspects of infrastructure appear most strongly is in the barriers presented to the poor or those with no access to hardware or training; those with disabilities; and the institutional racism and sexism that form barriers to usability. As aspects of the latter are covered in other chapters, we shall confine these remarks to resources and issues touching on infrastructure.

The sense that new networked media will create a two-class society – the 'information rich' and the 'information poor' – seems to be coming true. Access to training, hardware and maintenance is in general much more difficult, if not impossible, for the poor. Attempts to remedy this on the part of community and non-profit organizations, NGOs and governments have used a variety of means to mitigate this phenomenon. As with development work, many of the early efforts neglected local infrastructural considerations, such as availability of telephones for dialup access, costs of maintenance and supplies,

and security. A typical scenario would be that large companies would donate slightly outmoded computers to a 'needy' classroom, not recognizing that these classrooms lacked a telephone, and that the teachers, while dedicated, were so overloaded that they had no time to catch up on their own computer skills. More recent work has begun to take these considerations into account. An important part of this is working locally, cooperatively designing solutions that work *in situ*.[5]

A cognate community organizing effort has come through the freenet and community networks social movements. Freenets are local-efforts, usually voluntary or via a public library, to provide at least basic Internet access on a democratic basis.[6] One way to view these efforts is as a direct organizing attempt to address gaps in current local infrastructure. People living in low-income communities have a keen sense of the failures of imposed solutions that do not take account of their circumstances or their lack of infrastructural resources (or their often rich resources that are not formally taken into account in requirements analysis, such as support from churches, existing reform movements, or the social networks through which information travels: Bishop, 2001).[7]

There has been much hope expressed that, in the developing world, the new information infrastructure will provide the potential for a narrowing of the knowledge gaps between countries. Thus an effective global digital library would allow Third World researchers access to the latest journals. Distributed computing environments (such as the Grid[8]) would permit supercomputer grade access to computing to scientists throughout the world. The example of the use of cell phone technology to provide a jump in technology in countries without landlines has opened the possibility of great leaps being made into the information future. As powerful as these visions are, they need to be tempered with some real concerns. The first is that an information infrastructure like the Internet functions like a Greek democracy of old: everyone who has access may be an equal citizen, but those without access are left further and further out of the picture. Further, as noted above with respect to the school environment, access is never really equal: the fastest connections and computers (needed for running the latest software) tend to be concentrated in the First World. Third, governments in the developing world have indicated real doubts about the usefulness of opening their data resources out onto the Internet. Just as in the nineteenth century the *laissez-faire* economics of free trade was advocated by developed countries with most to gain (because they had organizations in place ready to take advantage of emerging possibilities), so in our age the greatest advocates of the free and open exchange of information are developed countries with robust computing infrastructures. Some in developing countries see this as a second wave of colonialism: the first pillaged material resources and the second will pillage information. All of these concerns can be met through the development of careful information policies. Works such as Mansell and Wehn's (1998) both point to the extent of work that needs to be done and open up the very real possibilities that are emerging.

Much has been written on the social barriers for all women, and men of colour, in feeling comfortable in computing environments, including the web. Since before the web, feminists have analysed the 'chilly climate' for girls and women learning computing, as well as the glass ceiling in the information technology industries. Holeton (1998) has several excellent chapters devoted to gender issues; the series *Women, Work and Computing*, hosted by IFIPS Special Interest Group 8.1 and issued every four years for more than a decade, provides critiques of identity, design, employment and epistemology in the world of gender and computing (see for example Eriksson et al., 1991). The infrastructural aspects of this stretch in many directions, beginning with the early mathematics and physics (traditionally male- and white-dominated fields) orientation of much of computer science, forming a complex *a priori* barrier to advancement for women and for men of colour. Other issues have included sexism and racism in the content of websites and online conversations.[9]

The Internet has proven a good resource for community organizing on the basis of ecological racism, and for organizing indigenous peoples[10] (who are often scattered and unable to meet face-to-face on a regular basis). Within this movement, there are attempts to put dying or very remote indigenous languages (such as that of the Suomi people in Lapland) online, so that they may be remembered and spread. These are good examples of social movements and ethnic groups taking over the infrastructure for their own purposes.[11] An overlapping but distinct set of issues can also be found in the infrastructural barriers faced by people with disabilities. Blind people now have available (if they can afford it, or if a social service agency can provide it) Braille terminals (that translate text to a Braille keyboard); fast text readers with optical character recognition that transform text into speech; and on some websites, alternative 'text-only' pages with short descriptions of the graphics involved. It is, however, an ongoing difficulty to convince web page designers consistently to make this option available. For those living with an inability to move or to work a keyboard or voice recognition systems, a number of augmenting devices have been developed over the years. These include mice that can be operated by tongues, eye movements, toes or minor head movements. The impact of rapidly improving voice recognition systems on these communities is yet to be fully

realized, especially for those living on restricted incomes, as is often true of disabled people. In addition, the basic communication processes carried by e-mail and the web make self-employment and new kinds of networks and social participation available for many of these people.[12]

CONCLUSION: DESIGN IMPLICATIONS

In 1994, Stewart Brand wrote a wonderful book entitled *How Buildings Learn: What Happens after They Are Built*. He pointed out that we tend to view the architect as the designer of a given building, and as a result we overlook the massive modifications that any building undergoes in the course of its life. Much the same point can be made about designing infrastructures. The work of design is in many ways secondary to the work of modification. A good information infrastructure is one that is stable enough to allow information to be able to persist in time (word processor programs, for this reason, are generally 'backwards compatible' – meaning that the newer version of a program can open files created with an earlier version). However, it should also be modifiable – at the individual level in terms of 'tailorability' (allowing a user to modify it for their own purposes: see Nardi, 1993), and at the social level in terms of being able to respond to emergent social needs (web standards have developed quickly to cater for image and video manipulation on the web).

Designing for flexibility is not an easy task. In general, the required flexibility is emergent. It is clear that you do not need a single great architect for an infrastructure. Eric Raymond's classic, though flawed, article 'The cathedral and the bazaar' (1999) says that unlike in the old days when a set of master blueprints was needed to build a cathedral, now we can see very large-scale infrastructures (he is talking of the Linux operating system) being designed in more of an evolutionary, distributed process. The flaw we are referring to is that his history is wrong: cathedrals themselves often did not have master planners (Turnbull, 1993) but were built in just such an *ad hoc* fashion. Raymond does, however, make the very strong point that complex, interoperating systems (and, we would add, cathedrals) can be built in a distributed fashion, providing you have a good set of protocols in place for receiving and vetting changes. These social arrangements (the protocols) are best developed and maintained by standards bodies containing representatives of all major stakeholders.

We have argued throughout this chapter that there are significant ethical and political concerns in the design of infrastructures. The Scandinavian school of 'participatory design' has successfully responded to this challenge. It developed in part in response to union demands for an input into the design of information technologies that would be implanted in the workplace. A key feature in its design process has been the use of ethnographers of work practice to analyse the ways in which work is carried on in order to anticipate and design for social and cultural effects as well as to produce a technically efficient design (see Bowker et al., 1997: Introduction). This design process has been adopted by some major 'infrastructure' companies such as Intel, Hewlett Packard and Apple. This movement suggests a complementary way of reading the design implications of our analysis of infrastructure in this chapter. This is that the most important thing is for the user of the infrastructure to first become aware of the social and political work that the infrastructure is doing and then seek ways to modify it (locally or globally) as need be. Infrastructures subtend complex ecologies: their design process should always be tentative, flexible and open.

NOTES

1 In addition, several detailed studies of the material culture of scientific work began to appear, many of which began to pick upon aspects of infrastructure (see e.g. Clarke, 1998).

2 See Callon (1992) for a fine general discussion of the development of technoeconomic networks; compare Grindley (1995) and Abbate and Kahin (1995).

3 See Suchman and Lynch (1990) for a good overview.

4 Graham and Marvin (1996) provide a comprehensive set of richly theoretical readings on the relationship between the built urban environment and the information/telecommunications infrastructure, ranging from the home and surveillance to city maps, teleshopping, manufacturing and the city itself as a node in an informatic network. From the socio-informatic-regional perspective, Kling et al. (1991) do a detailed analysis of the information economy of Orange County, California. Neumann et al. (2001) suggest some methodological challenges and approaches for the 'ethnography of infrastructure', beginning with the built environment and its classifications and standards.

5 Much good work along these lines can be found at the Participatory Design Conferences (PDCS) held in tandem with the computer-supported cooperative work (CSCW) annual conferences. More information about this can be found at the site for Computer Professionals for Social Responsibility (CPSR): http://www.cpsr.org/. This is also a good site for reviewing privacy and free speech issues. See also the foundational textbook by Greenbaum and Kyng (1991), the book by Namioka and Schuler (1993), and the report by the European Commission (1998) on the issues of globalizing and localizing information and communication technology.

6 A good overview can be found in Schuler (1996). A listing of specific freenets can be found at http://www.lights.com/freenet/. This listing is fairly international for the North and for Australia. *Bytes for All* is an e-zine (electronic magazine) devoted to universal access to IT, and can be found at http://www.bytesforall.org/. A specific example of federated projects in the city of Chicago gives links of several neighbourhood organizations and their emerging community-driven infrastructures: http://www.uic.edu/~schorsch/.

7 Schön et al. (1999) present a variety of compelling chapters about community organizing efforts, public policy and social empowerment, including many detailed case studies and theoretical foundations.

8 The term refers to a 'grid' of high-performance research networks. The web-based Grid portal helps computer scientists, scientists and engineers by simplifying and consolidating access to advanced computing systems. It is one of a number of initiatives allowing distributed scientific collaboration.

9 See for example Kalí Tal on 'The unbearable whiteness of being: African American critical theory and cyberculture', http://www.kalital.com/Text/Writing/Whitenes. html; Lisa Nakamura on 'Race in/for cyberspace', http://www.iup.edu/en/workdays/Nakamura.html, which addresses racism in MUDs and MOOs; and the University of Iowa's Communication Department resource page on 'Race and gender in cyberspace', http://www.uiowa. edu/%7 Ecommstud/resources/ GenderMedia/cyber.html). Kolko et al. (2000) review some interesting and wide-ranging cases.

10 A good link to Indigenous people's Internet resources (mostly US, Canada and Australia) is found at: http://www.uiowa.edu/%7Ecommstud/resources/ GenderMedia/native.html.

11 See Summerton (1994) for a good overview of case studies of social movements aimed at changing large-scale infrastructure.

12 A comprehensive home page sponsored by WGBH, US public television, gives advice and links for access for people with several types of disabilities (and some international links): http://www.wgbh.org/wgbh/pages/ncam/.

REFERENCES

Abbate, Janet (1999) *Inventing the Internet*. Cambridge, MA: MIT Press.

Abbate, J. and Kahin, B. (eds) (1995) *Standards Policy for Information Infrastructure*. Cambridge, MA: MIT Press.

Abbott, Andrew (1988) *The System of Professions: an Essay on the Division of Expert Labor*. Chicago: University of Chicago Press.

Baym, Nancy K. (2000) *Tune In, Log On: Soaps, Fandom, and Online Community*. Thousand Oaks, CA: Sage.

Becker, Howard S. (1982) *Art Worlds*. Berkeley, CA: University of California Press.

Bishop, A.P. (ed.) (2001) *Digital Library Use: Social Practice in Design and Evaluation*, Cambridge, MA: MIT Press.

Bowker, Geoffrey C. (1994a) 'Information mythology: the world of/as information', in Lisa Bud-Frierman (ed.), *Information Acumen: the Understanding and Use of Knowledge in Modern Business*. London: Routledge. pp. 231–47.

Bowker, Geoffrey C. (1994b) *Science on the Run: Information Management and Industrial Geophysics at Schlumberger, 1920–1940*. Cambridge, MA: MIT Press.

Bowker, Geoffrey C. (2000) 'Mapping biodiversity', *International Journal of GIS*, 14 (8): 739–54.

Bowker, Geoffrey C. and Star, Susan Leigh (1999) *Sorting Things Out: Classification and its Consequences*. Cambridge, MA: MIT Press.

Bowker, Geoffrey, Star, Susan Leigh, Turner, William and Gasser, Les (eds) (1997) *Social Science, Technical Systems, and Cooperative Work: beyond the Great Divide*. Mahwah, NJ: Erlbaum.

Brand, Stewart (1994) *How Buildings Learn: What Happens after They Are Built*. New York: Viking.

Bucciarelli, L.L. (1994) *Designing Engineers*. Cambridge, MA: MIT Press.

Bud-Frierman, Lisa (ed.) (1994) *Information Acumen: the Understanding and Use of Knowledge in Modern Business*. London: Routledge.

Bush, Vannevar, Nyce, James M. and Kahn, Paul (1991) *From Memex to Hypertext: Vannevar Bush and the Mind's Machine*. Boston: Academic.

Callon, Michel (1992) 'The dynamics of techno-economic networks', in Rod Coombs, Paolo Saviotti and Vivien Walsh (eds), *Technological Change and Company Strategies: Economic and Sociological Perspectives*. London: Harcourt Brace Jovanovich. pp. 72–102.

Clarke, Adele (1998) *Disciplining Reproduction: Modernity, American Life Sciences, and 'The Problems of Sex'*, Berkeley, CA: University of California Press.

Clarke, Adele E. and Fujimura, Joan H. (eds) (1992) *The Right Tools for the Job: at Work in Twentieth-Century Life Sciences*. Princeton, NJ: Princeton University Press.

Collins, Harry M. and Kusch, Martin (1998) *The Shape of Actions: What Humans and Machines Can Do*. Cambridge, MA: MIT Press.

David, Paul, A. (1986) 'Understanding the economics of QWERTY: the necessity of history', in W.N. Parker (ed.), *Economic History and the Modern Economist*. Oxford: Basil Blackwell.

David, Paul A. (1995) 'The dynamo and the computer: an historical perspective on the modern productivity paradox', *American Economic Review*, 80 (May): 355.

David, Paul A. and Greenstein, Shane (1990) 'The economics of compatibility standards: an introduction to recent research', in *Economics of Innovation and New Technology*, vol. 1. pp. 3–41.

David, Paul and Rothwell, Geoffrey S. (1994) *Standardization, Diversity and Learning: Strategies for the Coevolution of Technology and Industrial Capacity*. Stanford, CA: Center for Economic Policy Research, Stanford University.

Davis, Susan G. (1997) *Spectacular Nature: Corporate Culture and the SeaWorld Experience*. Berkeley, CA: University of California Press.

Desrosières, Alain and Thévenot, Laurent (1988) *Les Catégories socio-professionnelles*. Paris: Découverte.

Downey, Gary and Lucena, Juan (1994) 'Engineering studies', in S. Jasanoff, G. Markle, J. Petersen and T. Pinch (eds), *Handbook of Science, Technology, and Society*. Newbury Park, CA: Sage.

Edwards, Paul N. (1998) 'Y2K: millennial reflections on computers as infrastructure', *History and Technology*, 15: 7–29.

Eriksson, I., Kitchenham, B. and Tijdens, K. (eds) (1991) *Women, Work and Computerization: Understanding and Overcoming Bias in Work and Education*. Amsterdam: North Holland.

European Commission (1998) *Domesticating the World Wide Webs of Information and Communication Technology*, ed. Per Hetland and Hans-Peter Meyer-Dallach. Report COSTA4. Vol. 7 of 'Making the Global Village Local?' series. Brussels: European Commission.

Fagot-Largeault, Anne (1989) *Causes de la Mort: Histoire Naturelle et Facteurs de Risque*. Paris: Librairie Philosophique J. Vrin.

Fischer, Claude S. (1992) *America Calling: a Social History of the Telephone to 1940*. Berkeley, CA: University of California Press.

Friedlander, Amy (1995) *Emerging Infrastructure: the Growth of Railroads*. Reston, VA: Corporation for National Research Initiatives.

Graham, Stephen and Marvin, Simon (1996) *Telecommunications and the City*. London: Routledge.

Greenbaum, Joan and Kyng, Morten (1991) *Design at Work: Cooperative Design of Computer Systems*. Hillsdale, NJ: Erlbaum.

Gregory, Judith (2000) 'Sorcerer's apprentice: creating the electronic health record, re-inventing medical records and patient care'. PhD thesis, University of California at San Diego.

Grindley, Peter (1995) *Standards, Strategy, and Policy: Cases and Stories*. Oxford and New York: Oxford University Press.

Henderson, Kathryn (1999) *On Line and on Paper: Visual Representations, Visual Culture, and Computer Graphics in Design Engineering*. Cambridge, MA: MIT Press.

Holeton, Richard (ed.) (1998) *Composing Cyberspace: Identity, Community, and Knowledge in the Electronic Age*. Boston: McGraw-Hill.

Hughes, Thomas P. (1983) *Networks of Power: Electrification in Western Society, 1880–1930*. Baltimore: Johns Hopkins University Press.

Hurley, Deborah and Keller, James (1999) *The first 100 Feet: Options for Internet and Broadband Access*. Cambridge, MA: MIT Press.

Jewett, Tom and Kling, Rob (1991) 'The dynamics of computerization in a social science research team: a case study of infrastructure, strategies, and skills', *Social Science Computer Review*, 9: 246–75.

Kahin, Brian and Keller, James (1997) *Coordinating the Internet*. Cambridge, MA: MIT Press.

Kling, Rob, Olin, Spencer and Poster, Mark (eds) (1991) *Postsuburban California: the Transformation of Orange County since World War II*. Berkeley, CA: University of California Press.

Kolko, Beth, Nakamura, Lisa and Rodman, Gilbert (eds) (2000) *Race in Cyberspace*. New York: Routledge.

Landauer, Thomas K. (1995) *The Trouble with Computers: Usefulness, Usability, and Productivity*. Cambridge, MA: MIT Press.

Latour, Bruno (1996) *Aramis or the Love of Technology*. Cambridge, MA: Harvard University Press.

Latour, Bruno and Hernant, Emilie (1999) *Paris: Ville Invisible*. Paris: Découverte.

Library Trends (1998) Special issue on 'How Classifications Work: Problems and Challenges in an Electronic Age', 47 (2): 185–340.

Latour, Bruno and Woolgar, Steve (1979) *Laboratory Life: the Construction of Scientific Facts*. Thousand Oaks, CA: Sage.

Lave, Jean and Wenger, Etienne (1991) *Situated Learning: Legitimate Peripheral Participation*. Cambridge: Cambridge University Press.

MacKenzie, Donald A. (1990) *Inventing Accuracy: an Historical Sociology of Nuclear Missile Guidance*. Cambridge, MA: MIT Press.

Mansell, Robin and Wehn, Uta (1998) *Knowledge Societies: Information Technology for Sustainable Development*. United Nations Commission on Science and Technology for Development. Oxford and New York: Oxford University Press for and on behalf of the United Nations.

Michener, William K., Brunt, James W, Helly, John J., Kirchner, Thomas B. and Stafford, Susan G. (1997) 'Nongeospatial metadata for the ecological sciences', *Ecological Applications*, 7: 330–42.

Monteiro, Eric and Hanseth, Ole (1996) 'Social shaping of information infrastructure: on being specific about the technology', in Wanda J. Orlikowski, Geoff Walsham, Matthew R. Jones and Janice I. DeGross (eds), *Proceedings of the IFIP WG8.2 Working Conference on Information Technology and Changes in Organizational Work*, December 1995. London: Chapman and Hall. pp. 325–43.

Namioka, A. and Schuler, D. (1993) *Participatory Design: Principles and Practice*. Hillsdale, NJ: Erlbaum.

Nardi, Bonnie A. (1993) *A Small Matter of Programming: Perspectives on End User Computing*. Cambridge, MA: MIT Press.

Neumann, Laura, Bowker, Geoffrey C. and Star, Susan Leigh (2001) 'Transparency beyond the individual level of scale: convergence between information artifacts and communities of practice', in A.P. Bishop (ed.), *Digital Library Use: Social Practice in Design and Evaluation*. Cambridge, MA: MIT Press.

Orlikowski, Wanda, Yates, JoAnne, Okamura, Kazuo and Fujimoto, Masayo (1993) 'Shaping electronic communication: the structuring and metastructuring of technology in the context of use', *Organization Science*, 6 (4): 423–44.

Poster, Mark (1995) 'Cyberdemocracy', http://www.hnet.uci.edu/mposter/writings/democ.html.

Raymond, Eric S. (1999) *The Cathedral and the Bazaar: Musings on Linux and Open Source by an Accidental Revolutionary*, foreword by Bob Young. Beijing and Cambridge, MA: O'Reilly.

Rayward, W. Boyd (1975) *The Universe of Information: the Work of Paul Otlet for Documentation and International Organisation*. Moscow: All-Union Institute for Scientific and Technical Information (VINITI) for International Federation for Documentation (FID).

Rayward, Boyd (1999) 'H.G. Wells's idea of a world brain: a critical re-assessment', *Journal of the American Society for Information Science*, 50 (15 May): 557–73.

Rosenberg, Nathan (1982) *Inside the Black Box: Technology and Economics*. Cambridge: Cambridge University Press.

Schön, Donald A., Sanyal, Bish and Mitchell, William J. (1999) *High Technology and Low-Income Communities: Prospects for the Positive Use of Advanced Information Technology*. Cambridge, MA: MIT Press.

Schuler, Douglas (1996) *New Community Networks: Wired for Change*. New York: ACM.

Star, Susan Leigh (ed.) (1995) *The Cultures of Computing*. Oxford: Basil Blackwell.

Star, Susan Leigh and Ruhleder, Karen (1996) 'Steps toward an ecology of infrastructure: design and access for large information spaces', *Information Systems Research*, 7: 111–34.

Stefik, Mark (1996) *Internet Dreams: Archetypes, Myths, and Metaphors*. Cambridge, MA: MIT Press.

Suchman, Lucy and Lynch, Michael (eds) (1990) *Representation in Scientific Practice*. Cambridge, MA: MIT Press.

Summerton, Jane (ed.) (1994) *Changing Large Technical Systems*. Boulder, CO: Westview.

Tanenbaum, Andrew S. (1996) *Computer Networks*. Upper Saddle River, NJ: Prentice-Hall.

Taylor, James R. and van Every, Elizabeth J. (1993) *The Vulnerable Fortress: Bureaucratic Organization and Management in the Information Age*. Toronto: University of Toronto Press.

Taylor, James R. and van Every, Elizabeth J. (2000) *The Emergent Organization: Communication as its Site and Surface*. Mahwah, NJ: Erlbaum.

Turnbull, David (1993) 'The *ad hoc* collective work of building Gothic cathedrals with templates, string, and geometry', *Science, Technology & Human Values*, 18: 315–43.

Wells, H.G. (1938) *World Brain*. London: Methuen.

Winner, Langdon (1986) 'Do artifacts have politics?', in Judy Wacjman and Donald MacKenzie (eds), *The Social Shaping of Technology: How the Refrigerator Got its Hum*. Milton Keynes: Open University Press.

Yates, JoAnne (1989) *Control through Communication: the Rise of System in American Management*. Baltimore: Johns Hopkins University Press.

10

Exploring Models of Interactivity from Multiple Research Traditions: Users, Documents, and Systems

SALLY J. McMILLAN

Interactivity. We 'know it when we see it', but what is it? When asked to define the term, many individuals – even scholars of new media – may feel stumped. Rafaeli noted some of the common conceptions about interactivity in the mid 1980s:

> Interactivity is generally assumed to be a natural attribute of face-to-face conversation, but it has been proposed to occur in mediated communication settings as well. For example, interactivity is also one of the defining characteristics of two-way cable systems, electronic text systems, and some programming work as in interactive video games. Interactivity is present in the operation of traditional media, too. The phenomena of letters to the editor, talk shows on radio and television, listener participation in programs, and in programming are all characterized by interactivity. (1988: 110)

In the early 1990s, use of the term 'interactivity' exploded in the popular, trade and scholarly press (McMillan, 1999). Researchers are actively engaged in scholarship that explores how people interact through media, the nature of interactive content, and how individuals interface with the computers and telecommunications tools that host interactive communication.

Interactivity is generally considered to be a central characteristic of new media. But it is not enough to say that new media are interactive. It is important to understand what makes them interactive. It is also important to realize that interactivity means different things to different people in different contexts. Understanding interactivity can

help practitioners create environments that facilitate interaction. Individuals who use new media can more effectively utilize interactivity if they understand it. And for scholars, understanding interactivity is central to developing theory and research about new media.

This chapter begins with a brief overview of new media and basic definitions of interactivity in new media environments. Three traditions of interactivity research are identified: human-to-human interaction, human-to-documents interaction and human-to-system interaction. Within each of these traditions, definitions of interactivity both before and after the evolution of new media are examined. Central characteristics of interactivity as identified in each of these three traditions are used to develop models that illustrate multiple types of interactivity. Finally, some suggestions are made for future study of interactivity.

NEW MEDIA AND INTERACTIVITY

Interactivity is not unique to new media. This chapter will illustrate ways in which the concept of interactivity has emerged from multiple long-standing research traditions. But new media do facilitate interactivity in new environments. And, it is in the context of new media that the concept of interactivity has become a widely recognized subject of exploration. Thus, it is important to have a basic understanding of new media and key concepts related to interactivity in the context of these new media before examining interactivity in more depth.

New Media

Many observers tend to write about 'new media' such as networked computing and telecommunications as if they had been recently discovered in their fully developed state. Huhtamo wrote that: 'One of the most common features of many technocultural discourses is their lack of historical consciousness' (1999: 97). These new media are not completely new phenomena. They have been growing out of 'old media' for some time. Furthermore, the concept of new technology is not unique to the current digital revolution. Marvin wrote that: '*New technologies* is a historically relative term. We are not the first generation to wonder at the rapid and extraordinary shifts in the dimensions of the world and human relationships it contains as a result of new forms of communication' (1988: 3).

Some researchers have consciously attempted to make historical linkages between new media and old. For example, Leonhirth et al. (1997) explored metaphors for the concept of the online mailing list, comparing it to the telegraph, the round table and the bonfire. But other authors have suggested that terms used to define new media are too dependent on old media forms. For example, Murray (1997) argued that the term 'multimedia', which most authors use to mean the 'digital integration of media types within a single technological system' (Jankowski and Hanssen, 1996: 4), is a word with little descriptive power. Murray compared the word 'multimedia' as a descriptor of new technology to the term 'photo-play' which was used to describe early films. She suggested that such additive, catchall phrases are evidence that a medium is 'in an early stage of development and is still depending on formats derived from earlier technologies instead of exploiting its own expressive power' (1997: 67).

Williams et al. (1994) defined new media as applications of microelectronics, computers and telecommunications that offer new services or enhancement of old ones. Marvin (1988) also focused on the interplay between new and old purposes in new media. She suggested the tension created by the coexistence of the old and new becomes a focus of interest because it is novel.

Other authors have identified specific characteristics of new media. For example, Negroponte (1995) suggested that one of the things that differentiates new media from old is that new media are based on the transmission of digital bits rather than physical atoms. Pavlik (1998) indicated that for the media consumer, the major differences between old media and new are greater user choice and control.

Williams et al. (1988) identified three characteristics of new media: interactivity, demassification and asynchronicity. New media not only demassify, but they also 'create a continuum between formerly discrete categories of interpersonal and massmediated communication' (Rice and Williams, 1984: 57). Chaffee (1972) suggested that most new communication technologies, with the exception of the telephone, have advanced the art of mass communication. However, he indicated that the latest batch of new technologies seems to be shifting the balance toward interpersonal communication. Cathcart and Gumpert (1983) also identified ways in which new technologies facilitate 'mediated interpersonal communication'.

While much of the current analysis of new media focuses on technologies such as the World Wide Web and collaborative decision-making systems, relatively recent research has focused on other forms of new media technologies such as video telephones (Carey, 1989), electronic bulletin board systems (Rafaeli, 1986; Rafaeli and LaRose, 1993), videotex, and teletext and other forms of interactive television (Bretz, 1983; Feenberg, 1992; Paisley, 1983; Pavlik, 1998). However, much of the literature on new media reflects Murray's optimism about the networked computer, in which: 'All the major representational formats of the previous five thousand years of history have now been translated into digital form' (1997: 27). Nevertheless, this new digital technology, despite its synthetic capabilities, does not yet seem to be eliminating other media. Rather, a recent study reported that many individuals actually use their computers concurrently with other older media such as television (Coffee and Stipp, 1997).

Many scholars have observed that the term 'interactivity', while frequently used in conjunction with the discussion of new media, is often either undefined or underdefined (Hanssen et al., 1996; Heeter, 1989; 2000; Huhtamo, 1999; Miller et al., 1997; Rafaeli, 1988; Schultz, 2000; Simms, 1997; Smethers, 1998). But there is a growing body of literature that attempts to remedy this situation. Researchers have begun to seek definitions of interactivity by examining various characteristics of the new media environment.

Interactive Features

Some of the earliest research on interactivity in new media focused on the properties and/or features of the message and/or the medium. For example, consensus derived from an international symposium in 1980 resulted in a definition of interactivity as 'a style of control and interactive systems that exhibit that style' (Guedj et al., 1980: 69). Other definitions of interactivity in this tradition include Markus' (1990) suggestion that interactivity is a characteristic of technologies that enable multidirectional communication.

Other definitions that embed interactivity in the features of the message/medium include conceptions of interactivity as being based in functionality such as user control and participation (Jensen, 1998; Latchem et al., 1993b; Lieb, 1998; Morrison, 1998; Murray, 1997; Street and Rimal, 1997). Some studies have begun the process of operationalizing specific features that can be identified and categorized as interactive (Ahren et al., 2000; Ha and James, 1998; Massey and Levy, 1999; McMillan, 2000b; Schultz, 1999; 2000). Others have associated these interactive features with specific strategies such as mass customization, virtual stores and collaborative learning (Blattberg and Deighton, 1991; Day, 1998; Landow, 1992).

Perceived Interactivity

In contrast to scholars who seek to identify 'features' of interactivity, others have suggested that interactivity may be 'in the eye of the beholder' (Lee, 2000; McMillan, 2000a; McMillan and Downes, 2000; Morrison, 1998; Newhagen et al., 1996). Heeter (2000) proposed that orientation to interactivity is a personality characteristic and Kiousis (1999) also suggested that interactivity resides, at least in part, in individuals' perceptions.

A recent study (Burgoon et al., 2000) suggested that one way to conceptualize interactivity is based on the qualitative experiences that users equate with interactivity. Morrison (1998) noted that it is important to understand how individuals perceive interactivity in order to grasp the influence of newer media technologies in their lives. Newhagen and his colleagues have insisted that the individual and individual perceptions must take conceptual centre stage in studies of new media (Newhagen, 1998; Newhagen et al., 1996). Wu (1999) and McMillan (2000a; 2000b) found that users' attitude toward websites is positively related to their perceived interactivity of the website. Reeves and Nass (1996) suggested that, in general, perceptions are far more influential than reality in terms of individuals' interactions with computers. Lee (2000) suggested that the most important thing to be examined in measuring the level of interactivity is not the provision of technological features, but rather how users perceive and/or experience those features.

Interactive Exchange

Rafaeli, one of the most cited scholars on the subject of interactivity, identified interactivity as being located in the relatedness of information exchange among participants rather than in either features or perceptions. He defined interactivity as going beyond simple one-way 'action' or two-way 'reaction' that may not be truly responsive. He wrote: 'Interactivity is an expression of the extent that in a given series of communication exchanges, any third (or later) transmission (or message) is related to the degree to which previous exchanges referred to even earlier transmissions' (1988: 111).

Other authors have also focused on the exchanges among participants in interactive media (Haeckel, 1998; Rice and Williams, 1984). Ha and James defined interactivity as 'the extent to which the communicator and the audience respond to, or are willing to facilitate, each other's communication needs' (1998: 461). A subset to this literature addresses the idea that interactive exchanges make sender and receiver roles interchangeable (Bretz, 1983; Rice, 1984). Additionally, literature that focuses on interactivity as exchange often focuses on the importance of reducing the time lag between exchanges (Bretz, 1983).

Mahood et al. (2000) identified two kinds of interactive exchange: the dialogue view and the message-based view. They suggested that the dialogue view, based in literature on role exchange and mutual discourse, focuses primarily on conversational-style exchanges. In contrast, the message-based view deals more with the relationships between messages sent previously and how those messages relate to those that precede them. However, it seems that both the dialogue view and the message-based view of interactivity focus primarily on communication exchanges.

Multidimensional Perspectives

Several scholars have suggested that interactivity cannot be neatly defined based on features, perceptions or exchanges. Instead, they define interactivity as a multidimensional construct. Heeter (1989) provided an early attempt to conceptualize multiple dimensions of interactivity in new media. She suggested a six-dimensional choice based on: complexity of user choice, effort users must exert, responsiveness to the user, monitoring information use, ease of adding information, and facilitation of interpersonal communication. Attempts to operationalize her conceptual definition have met with limited success (Massey and Levy, 1999; McMillan, 1998b). Masey and Levy suggested that one reason that they had to adapt Heeter's conceptual definition was that they found two broad meanings for interactivity in online journalism. One dimension they identified as interpersonal interactivity, or the extent to which audiences can have computer-mediated conversations in the 'spaces' created for them by journalists. The other dimension they defined as content interactivity in which journalists technologically empower consumers over content. Schultz (2000) also indicated that two types of interactivity characterize journalistic websites: reader-to-reader and journalist-to-reader.

This dual approach to interactivity is reflected in other areas of new media research. For example, Lee (2000) indicated that two broad types of interactivity are interacting with people and interacting with technology. Hoffman and Novak (1996) described person interactivity and machine interactivity. Stromer-Galley (2000) identified human-to-human and human-to-media interaction. Carey defined interactive media as: 'Technologies that provide person-to-person communications … and person-to-machine interactions' (1989: 328).

Other researchers have suggested more dimensions are needed to explore different ways of interacting with new media. For example, Szuprowicz (1995) identified three levels of interactivity: user-to-user, user-to-documents and user-to-computer (or user-to-system). Others have identified similar three-dimensional constructs (Barker and Tucker, 1990; Haeckel, 1998; Jensen, 1998). Kayany et al. (1996) suggested that within these three types of interactivity users exert three types of control: relational (or interpersonal), content (or document-based) and process/sequence (or interface-based) controls. Additional interactivity dimensions have been identified that are setting-specific. For example, Stromer-Galley and Foot (2000) identified 'citizen–campaign interaction' in political websites and Chesebro and Bonsall (1989) added dimensions for program-dominated interaction and artificial intelligence.

However, the three-dimensional construct of user-to-user, user-to-documents and user-to-system interactivity seems to encompass the primary literature on interactivity in new media. Furthermore, this three-part construct parallels historical developments in the concept of interactivity that predated new media. The following section will examine these three types of interactivity as they have evolved both before and after the advent of new media.

THREE TRADITIONS OF INTERACTIVITY

The user-to-user, user-to-documents and user-to-system traditions of interactivity have been evolving for decades. However, in many ways distinctions among these traditions are arbitrary. For example, the user-to-user tradition focuses on human communication, but subjects such as how readers respond to newspaper editors, while clearly part of the human communication tradition, also cross over into the user-to-documents literature that addresses how people interact with content and content creators. Yet, despite the relatively arbitrary nature of the distinctions, these three research traditions do provide a basic framework for investigation of the past, present and future of interactivity.

While each tradition is treated separately, areas of overlap among the traditions will also be probed. In particular, the three models designed to illustrate the nature of interactivity in these three traditions clearly show some commonalities such as the importance of the concept of 'control'.

User-to-User Interaction

User-to-user interaction focuses on ways that individuals interact with each other. This tradition is based in human communication research. User-to-user interaction clearly predates new media and extends back to the earliest communication between sentient beings. Among many users of new media, the concept of interactivity is closely tied to the discovery of new tools for facilitating old techniques of human communication. Several research traditions related to user-to-user communication both before and after the advent of new media are briefly reviewed below.

Interpersonal Interaction

Goffman's (1967) analysis of the 'interaction ritual' placed human interaction at the forefront of communication research. Goffman wrote that 'the proper study of interaction is not the individual and his psychology, but rather the syntactic relations among the acts of different persons mutually present to one another' (1967: 2). Co-presence was central to Goffman's work that examined glances, gestures and other verbal and non-verbal elements that influence communication. Argyle's (1969) work also examined the visible, audible, intentional and unintentional signals which are central to co-present interpersonal communication.

Berger (1979) identified various stages for dealing with uncertainty in interpersonal relationships. These begin with passive strategies, then move to active strategies, and then go on to interactive strategies. Among the interactive strategies that he identified were verbal interrogation, self-disclosure, and detection of deception in the communication exchange. He also noted that anticipated future interaction might impact on the strategy that an individual selects for addressing uncertainty in interpersonal interactions. Other researchers also examined dimensions of interpersonal interaction (see, for example, Wish et al., 1976).

Symbolic Interaction

Goffman's (1967) work also led to the development of the field of symbolic interaction. Blumer (1969) identified three premises that underlie the concept of symbolic interaction. First, human beings act toward things on the basis of the meanings that those things have for them. Second, the meanings of such things are derived from, or arise out of, the social interaction that an individual has with others. And finally, those meanings are modified through an interpretive process used by individuals in dealing with the things they encounter.

Blumer suggested that in non-symbolic interaction, individuals respond directly to one another's gestures or actions; in symbolic interaction, they interpret each other's gestures and act on the basis of the meaning yielded by that interpretation. He further noted that mutual role taking is central to symbolic interaction. The symbolic interaction approach served as the foundation for a body of literature that examined webs of interaction in non-technology environments (see, for example, Miller et al., 1997; Ruben, 1975).

Social Interaction

Bales' (1950) work on categorizing small-group interaction underlies much of the subsequent literature on interaction in groups and organizations. Bales identified stages in group interaction. Later research built on Bales' work on social interaction by examining communication rules for cooperation or competition in groups (Shimanoff, 1988), relationships between task and interaction (Poole, 1985), and the impact of time limits and task quality on group interaction and group performance (Kelly and McGrath, 1985; McGrath, 1990; 1991; Straus and McGrath, 1994).

By the late 1980s, scholars who studied social interaction in face-to-face group settings had begun to equate the terms 'interaction' and 'communication'. For example, Hirokawa (1988) wrote that 'interaction profiles' were a common technique used by researchers to examine who tends to interact with whom – in other words, who communicates directly with whom in a group setting.

But it is important to recognize that face-to-face communication does not necessarily lead to social interaction. Schudson (1978) pointed out that many communication scholars hold an 'ideal of conversation' which assumes that face-to-face interpersonal communication is characterized by continuous feedback and egalitarian norms which make mass media seem inferior to conversation. However, he argued that most conversations don't match this ideal and, in some cases, mass media have actually helped to improve standards of interpersonal communication. Thus, Schudson suggested that social interaction can be facilitated by mediated communication. Lievrouw and Finn (1990) also pointed out that all communication is mediated: even face-to-face communication is mediated through one or more of the five senses.

Interaction as Feedback

Another long-standing research tradition examines interaction between individuals who are often characterized by their roles as either source or receiver. This form of interaction is often explored within the limited framework of the 'feedback' that receivers give to the senders of professionally prepared communication vehicles such as newspapers. Clearly this tradition is related to both user-to-user interaction and user-to-documents interaction. It is briefly reviewed here because the primary focus is not on mass communication but rather on the ways that individuals have limited capability to interact with the individuals who create content.

Even before Wiener (1948) developed cybernetic theory which led to increased interest in media 'feedback' tools, some communication scholars had begun to explore the ways in which members of the audience can interact with content creators through letters to the editor. For example, Sayre (1939) examined the contents of fan mail sent to a radio station. Other researchers later conducted more in-depth analysis of radio fan mail (Bierig and Dimmick, 1979; Turow, 1974; 1977), letters to editors of print media such as newspapers (Davis and Rarick, 1964; Forsythe, 1950; Grey and Brown, 1970; Lander, 1972; Rafaeli, 1990), and letters to television news providers (Gans, 1977; McGuire and Leroy, 1977).

In general, the authors suggested that letters to media content providers can fulfil some needs for audience interaction and can also provide feedback to content creators. However, the studies tend to suggest that opinions expressed in the letters are not generally representative of the larger audience and such opinions rarely change editorial positions or actions. Thus, 'feedback' would seem to be similar to the 'reaction' stage which Rafaeli (1988) identified as the middle step in the action/reaction/ interaction process.

User-to-User Interaction in New Media

Unquestionably, new media bring change to human communications. Fundamentally, media such as computer networks and telecommunication systems add a layer of technology between communicating partners (Chilcoat and DeWine, 1985). Walther (1996) noted that the impulse to interpersonal communication seems inherently human, yet may be more easily enacted via technology. Among the new media that enable social uses are: electronic mail, networked electronic bulletin boards, chat and electronic shopping (Chesebro and Bonsall, 1989). However, as Lievrouw and Finn (1990) pointed out, communication behaviours rather than communication technologies drive the evolution of meaning in communication systems.

Much of the literature on human interaction can serve as a foundation for examination of user-to-user interaction, which is also widely known as computer-mediated communication (CMC). Hesse et al. asserted that CMC 'provides us with a medium in which to test, modify, and expand our understanding of human social interaction' (1988: 162). Reeves and Nass suggested that as individuals interact through new media they expect those media to obey 'social and natural rules. All these rules come from the world of interpersonal interaction, and from studies about how people interact with the real world. But all of them apply equally well to media' (1996: 5).

As Danowski (1982) noted, many of the research techniques used for evaluating human communication in CMC are similar to those techniques used for evaluating other human communication. Among the effects that have been explored are the impacts of CMC on ability to form impressions of communicators in the absence of non-verbal cues (Lea and Spears, 1992; Rafaeli and Sudweeks, 1997; Walther, 1995), idea generation and group participation (Bikson et al., 1989; DeVries, 1996; Fredin, 1983; Romiszowski, 1993; Shaw et al., 1993; Siegel et al., 1986; Valacich et al., 1993; Walther, 1996), personal identity and decision-making (Bezjian-Avery et al., 1998; Cooley, 1999; Garramone et al., 1986; Sherblom, 1988; Yom, 1996), and sociability and engagement (Ha and James, 1998; Kiesler, 1986; Rafaeli and Sudweeks, 1997).

Direction of Communication

Within the CMC tradition, a fundamental assumption is that the medium serves primarily as a conduit for communication that flows back and forth among communication participants. Pavlik wrote that 'interactivity means two-way communication between source and receiver, or, more broadly multidirectional communication between any number of sources and receivers' (1998: 137). Many other authors have echoed this view (Beniger, 1987; Bretz, 1983; Chesebro, 1985; Duncan, 1989; Durlak, 1987; Garramone et al., 1986; Kirsh, 1997; Rafaeli and Sudweeks, 1997; Zack, 1993).

Within some of the literature, two-way communication is characterized by an egalitarian notion of mutual discourse and mutual role taking (Ball-Rokeach and Reardon, 1988; Burgoon et al., 2000; Hanssen et al., 1996; Williams et al., 1988). For example, Hanssen and his colleagues wrote: 'new communication technologies make possible creation of virtual environments in which the traditional roles of senders and receivers no longer apply' (1996: 61).

Among other scholars, the multidirectional capabilities of new media serve more for providing feedback than for truly mutual discourse. Ha and James asserted that: 'despite its importance, discussions of interactivity have been filled with a restrictive assumption that requires reexamination. This assumption is that reciprocal, two-way communication is a common desire of both the communicator and the audience' (1998: 460). Other scholars who consider CMC from the marketer's perspective tend to focus on feedback from consumers to marketers (see, for example, Duncan and Moriarty, 1998), but even though this form of feedback may not be egalitarian it is still often viewed as empowering. Day wrote that 'the essence of interactive marketing is the use of information *from* the customer rather than *about* the customer' (1998: 47). Newhagen et al. (1996) provided evidence that the feedback function corresponds to self-efficacy among individuals who send e-mail to a news site. However, Nielsen (2000) warned that site designers should not build in feedback tools unless they are willing to respond to messages – an effort that can require substantial resources.

Within the CMC tradition, direction of communication has been shown to play a unique role in the diffusion of interactive technologies. Mahler and Rogers wrote: 'because the main purpose of an interactive telecommunications innovation is to connect the potential adopter with others who have adopted the innovation, the innovation has little perceived utility for an individual until others with whom the individual wishes to communicate have adopted' (1999: 724). Thus, the concept of critical mass becomes very important in diffusion of technologies that allow for multidirectional communication (Allen, 1988; Mahler and Rogers, 1999; Markus, 1990; Williams et al., 1988; 1994).

Control

New media also provide new tools that enable communicators to have more control over their communication experience. Beniger (1986) suggested that the industrial revolution spawned a 'control revolution' in which systems were put into place for managing increases in production and changes in distribution. New media also provide new kinds of controls. Many scholars have noted that a key benefit of computer-mediated communication is that it allows participants to communicate without being bound by constraints of time or geography (Ball-Rokeach and Reardon, 1988; Bikson et al., 1989; Burgoon et al., 2000; Cathcart and Gumpert, 1983; Danowski, 1982; Hesse et al., 1988; Hiltz and Turoff, 1993; Hoffman and Novak, 1996; McGrath, 1990; Shaw et al., 1993; Walther, 1994; 1996; Walther and Burgoon, 1992; Walther et al., 1994). For example, Cathcart and Gumpert wrote that 'interpersonal mediated communication refers to any person-to-person interaction where a medium has been interposed to transcend the limitations of time and space' (1983: 271).

CMC can also shift patterns of control among communication participants. Kiesler noted that 'to some degree all communication technologies weaken the controls over information distribution that people have in dealing with each other face to face' (1986: 48). She further observed that CMC tends to break down hierarchies and cut across

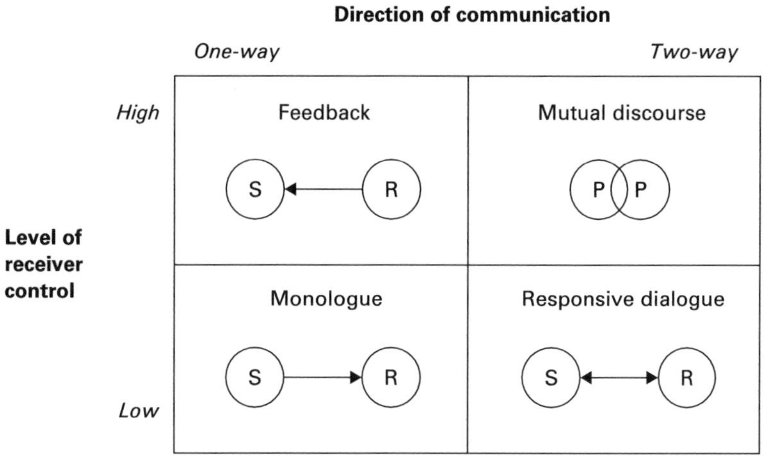

Direction of communication

One-way   Two-way

Figure 10.1   *Four models of user-to-user interactivity*
S = sender, R = receiver, P = participant (sender/receiver roles are interchangeable)

organizational boundaries. McGrath (1990) also observed flattened hierarchies in CMC-based communication. Landow (1992) noted that CMC results in power shifts in the educational environment as well, and suggested that these shifts have the potential to transform roles of teacher and pupil.

A Proposed Model for User-to-User Interactivity

Directionality of communication and level of control over the communication environment are, as noted above, central to interactivity in CMC environments. Figure 10.1 proposes four models of user-to-user interactivity based on the juxtaposition of those two dimensions.

The monologue model, which utilized primarily one-way, sender-controlled communication, can be witnessed in some marketing communications and political communications environments that focus primarily on 'getting the word out'. Feedback is often added to such sites when the communicator wants to add 'interactivity' to the environment. However, while feedback tools such as e-mail links might theoretically open two-way communication channels, such tools often provide the person who is giving the feedback with relatively little control over the communication exchange.

Responsive dialogue meets the criteria set forth in Rafaeli's (1988) popular definition in that each message reflects awareness of all earlier messages. However, in the responsive dialogue model, the message sender still retains primary control. This model might be found at websites that provide customer service or e-commerce. Mutual dialogue is responsive, but it also gives more egalitarian control to all participants so that sender and receiver roles

become indistinguishable. Chat rooms and instant messaging tools often facilitate mutual discourse.

User-to-Documents Interactivity

People interact with each other, but they also interact with documents and the creators of those documents. This user-to-documents interactivity can be seen in the ways that active audiences interpret and use mass media messages. New forms of interaction with documents are also emerging in new media as evidenced in areas such as active navigation of websites and active participation in creation of interactive fiction. As illustrated in the following sections, user-to-documents interactivity applies to both old media and new media and involves both perceived interaction with content creators and actual creation of content.

Parasocial Interaction

Parasocial interaction illustrates ways in which limited forms of interaction with content creators can be achieved even when actual mechanisms for interactivity are limited. Horton and Wohl suggested that radio, television and film can give the illusion of face-to-face relationships with the performer:

> The conditions of response to the performer are analogous to those in a primary group. The most remote and illustrious men are met *as if* they were in the circle of one's peers; the same is true of a character in a story who comes to life in these media in an especially vivid and arresting way. We propose to call this seeming face-to-face relationship between spectator and performer a *para-social relationship*. (1956: 215)

Again, the distinctions between research traditions are blurred. Clearly, parasocial interaction is a form of user-to-user interaction (or at least it simulates that kind of interpersonal interaction). But it is reviewed here because it is in the context of mass media, which focus predominantly on user-to-documents interaction, that the concept of parasocial interaction has primarily been applied.

Levy (1979) suggested that the parasocial relationship requires time to develop and is based on the perceived 'shared' experiences with media personalities. Beniger (1987) suggested that feelings of 'intimacy' can be developed between individuals who are associated with the media and members of their audience. Houlberg (1984) found evidence of such parasocial relationships between viewing audiences and local television newscasters. Norlund (1978) suggested that parasocial interaction depends on the development of media personalities for the audience to 'interact' with. He suggested that media have varying levels of interaction potential based on: the extent to which the medium is able to approximate reality, whether the content is characterized by the presence of dominating characters, and whether the content is characterized by individuals who appear regularly.

Rafaeli (1990) identified some concerns that may arise in parasocial interaction. He suggested that the attempt to form a bond of emotional intimacy between television celebrities and members of the audience was a type of manipulation designed primarily to result in a larger, more loyal audience. Beniger (1987) also warned that the personalization of mass media might lead to the development of a sense of 'pseudo-community' in which parasocial interactions substitute for 'real' interactions.

Norlund also warned of potential negative side effects of parasocial interaction: 'It seems that media interaction can lead to greater dependency on mass media as well as a tendency to use the mass media (rather than for instance interacting with people) in certain situations of stress and loneliness' (1978: 171–2). Williams et al. (1994) also noted the potential for individuals to depend on media for fulfilling social interaction needs. They suggested links between such media use and media dependency theory (Ball-Rokeach et al., 1984), which states that the power of the media is a function of dependencies of individuals, groups, organizations and systems on the scarce information resources that are controlled by the media.

Creating Content

In addition to parasocial interaction with content creators, other forms of user-to-documents interactivity have also emerged in traditional media. In particular, some forms of user-to-documents interactivity actually rely on the active audience members to supply the content of traditional media.

Telephone calls to radio stations allow for audience participation in the creation of content. The call-in show has a substantial history as a subset of radio programming (Crittenden, 1971). Some researchers (Bierig and Dimmick, 1979) suggest that such shows function as a substitute for face-to-face communication, and others (Turow, 1974) suggest that calls to 'talk stations' are rooted in the need for personal communication with the 'outside world'. However, there is also evidence that radio (Crittenden, 1971) and television (Newhagen, 1994) talk shows are related to self-efficacy, or the sense of being able to cope with the political system.

Some forms of mediated communication actually require participation. For example, citizen's band radio would be devoid of content were it not for the individuals who broadcast their messages. Citizen's Band (CB) communication is built on a unique form of interpersonal discourse (Powell and Ary, 1977) and CB radio has faced a unique history of regulation (Marvin and Schultze, 1977) that is based in part on its unique interactive nature. Dannefer and Poushinsky (1977) defined interactivity in CB radio as 'step reflexivity' because it permits two-way communication, but only one person can talk at a time.

Interacting with Old Media

Some media, such as newspapers, seem to have limited capacity for parasocial interaction or interaction through participation. However, other older media forms do have interactive potential. For example Standage (1998) suggested that the telegraph, with its two-way wired communication, was a precursor to the Internet. Researchers have also identified strong parallels between the development of the radio and development of the Internet in terms of cultural history (Douglas, 1987; Lappin, 1995) and market evolution (McMillan, 1998a; Smulyan, 1994). The interactive potential and early interactive uses of radio are noted in much of this work.

Before the radio, the invention of the telephone heralded a new age in mediated interactive communication. Bretz (1983) noted that despite its availability to a great mass of people, few individuals today think of the telephone as a mass medium. He suggests that the primary reason for this perception is that radio is distributed in only one direction, thus lending it to 'broadcast' and mass communication. By contrast the telephone requires two wires that facilitate a kind of back-and-forth communication that seems more appropriate to interpersonal interactions. However, this distinction between radio as broadcast and telephone as interpersonal was by no means self-evident in the early developmental stages of these media. Experiments existed in telephone broadcasts (Marvin, 1988), and when telephone was introduced many managers envisioned it as a device for transmitting orders and information to their employees (Kiesler, 1986). Nevertheless, the telephone has evolved primarily as an interpersonal communication tool upon which individuals rely for feelings of connectedness and control over their environments (Wurtzel and Turner, 1977).

Interacting with New Media

Research on new media has further explored interactivity with both the content and the creators of content in those new media environments. Rafaeli and LaRose noted that: 'Collaborative mass media systems, in which the audience is the primary source of media content as well as its receiver, represent a new and significant departure from mass media forms. They expand the very definition of mass media from "one-to-many" to "many-to-many" communication' (1993: 277).

A key theme that emerges in literature that examines interaction with content and content creators is that the 'audience' is not a passive receiver of information, but rather an active co-creator. A key characteristic of the active audience is that individuals have control over both presentation and content (Barak and Fisher, 1997; Bezjian-Avery et al., 1998; Chesebro and Bonsall, 1989; Fredin, 1989; Hanssen et al., 1996; Latchem et al., 1993a; Looms, 1993; Miles, 1992; Morrison, 1998; Steuer, 1992; Street and Rimal, 1997; Tucker, 1990; Williams et al., 1988).

In many cases, the literature suggests that the individual's control of content extends beyond simply navigating through a standard set of options. Researchers have suggested that interactive content should dynamically respond to individual actions. Straubhaar and LaRose wrote that interactivity should be used to 'refer to situations where real-time feedback is collected from the receivers of a communications channel and is used by the source to continually modify the message as it is being delivered to the receiver' (1996: 12). Similar concepts have been explored in applied fields such as education (Barker and Tucker, 1990; Hester, 1999) and marketing (Blattberg and Deighton, 1991; Xie, 2000).

Despite the role of the active audience, the role of professional content creators has not been eliminated. Communication professionals create content for online newspapers, educational CD-ROMs and interactive fiction.

Mass communication researchers who have begun to examine interactive journalism have found that journalists seem to be providing few opportunities for audiences to be either active or interactive (Newhagen et al., 1996; Schultz, 1999; see also Chapter 16). Media such as 'interactive television' offer little more than a menu of choices for services such as movies on demand (Pavlik, 1998), and news-on-demand systems often offer little opportunity for interchange between the audience and the content creators (Mayburry, 2000). However, some research has looked at issues such as ways that e-mail is being used as a tool for communication between content creators and the audience (Newhagen et al., 1996). Journalists must recognize that new media tools such as the Internet can be a mass medium (Morris and Ogan, 1996), but they must also recognize that new media tools must offer some substantial improvements over existing media if they are to change relationships between audience and content creators (Fredin, 1989). Interactive journalism must address issues such as the 24-hour news cycle (Borden and Harvey, 1998), but such studies should more directly address interactivity at multiple levels.

Interactive fiction has also attracted comment and observation as an emerging form of interactive content. Landow suggested that interactive fiction, which allows readers to have some level of control over the outcome of a story, 'blurs the boundaries between reader and writer' (1992: 5). Scholars have also examined other issues related to interactive fiction such as the role of playfulness in content (Bolter, 1991), linearity and structure (Fredin, 1997; Hunt, 2000; Iser, 1989; Murray, 1995; 1997; 1999).

A Proposed Model for User-to-Documents Interactivity

The dimensions of communication direction and participant control that were identified in the earlier section on user-to-user interactivity can also be applied in conceptualizing user-to-documents interactivity. The active audience is central to the concept of communication direction and content creators tend to either retain or relinquish control of content. Figure 10.2 proposes four models of interactivity based on the juxtaposition of those two dimensions.

The packaged content model grows out of the mass media tradition in which content creators package content and deliver it to relatively passive audiences. This limited form of user-to-system interactivity can be found at many online newspapers and magazines. The content-on-demand model assumes a more active audience. But the audience is not a creator of content. Rather, individual members of the audience customize the content to meet their individual needs. This model is reflected in some of the information science literature and is also implemented in customized web pages that deliver news, weather, sports and other content as specified by individual preferences.

Content exchange assumes that all participants can be either senders or receivers of content. Bulletin boards are an example of this type of information exchange that often occurs asynchronously. Co-created content assumes that all participants share in the creation of content. Group decision

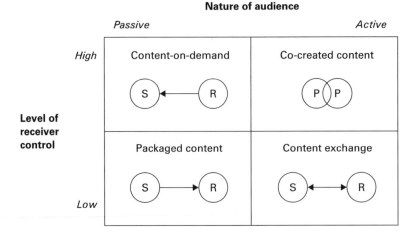

Figure 10.2   *Four models of user-to-documents interactivity*
S = sender, R = receiver, P = participant (sender/receiver roles are interchangeable)

support systems are designed to create this kind of environment. Interactive fiction, MUDs and MOOs might provide other examples of situations in which multiple active individuals create the content that provides the building blocks for an interactive environment.

User-to-System Interactivity

Individuals interact with each other through new media; they interact with documents and document creators, too. But a third form of interactivity is also central to new media – the interaction between people and the computer (or other type of new media system) itself. The study of human interaction with computers is not new and this section provides an overview of that history. Additionally, some key theories related to uses of new media systems are briefly explored and the balance of control in the human–computer relationship is considered.

Early Explorations of Human–Technology Interfaces

In the mid 1900s computer scientists began using the term 'interactivity' to describe a new form of interface that was different from, and more user-friendly than, batch processing (Alter, 1977; Miles, 1992; Zeltzer, 1992). The ability to issue commands to the computer directly was viewed as more 'conversational' and 'interactive' and more supportive of management decision-making (Vasarhelyi, 1977).

However, even before interactive processing replaced batch processing of commands, scholars had begun to think about how humans might interact with machines. Turing's (1956) often cited test of computer intelligence proposed that a computer and a human being are equally intelligent if other human beings are unable to distinguish between the responses of a computer and those of a human being. Ten years after Turing proposed his test of computer–human interaction, MIT professor Joseph Weizenbaum developed a computer program that he named ELIZA. The program was able to carry on a 'conversation' by replaying sentences typed into it. While users of the system were not likely to confuse the machine with a person, its natural-language responses often resembled the 'conversation' that a patient might have with a Jungian psychologist (Murray, 1997).

The study of user-to-system interactivity grows out of the field of human factors research which studies the ways that humans respond to information presented to them by a computer (Guedj et al., 1980). Biocca wrote that: 'the words *human factors* refer to important aspects of human performance, behavior, and desire that must be considered in the design of any machine, hardware, program, or information system' (1993: 63).

Much of the human factors literature focuses on design of the experience that users will have when they interact with the computer system. Kay suggested that 'the dawn of user interface design first happened when computer designers finally noticed, not just that end users had functioning minds, but that a better understanding of how those minds worked would completely shift the paradigm of interaction' (1990: 192). Design of the user interface is often considered to be both an art and a science (Guedj et al., 1980; Kirsh, 1997; Salzman and Rosenthal, 1994; Simms, 1997) and is central to the future of interactive processes.

In the 1970s, as computer scientists began to explore not only the design but also the consequences of interactive versus batch processing, they noted the importance of understanding human interaction as a way of improving human–computer interaction (Chapanis et al., 1972). And some researchers began to apply Bales' (1950) work on symbolic interaction to human–computer interactions (Alter, 1977).

Media Richness and Social Presence

Symbolic interaction also provided the basis for a body of literature that began to develop in the late 1980s that examined how a dynamic web of communications could impact on the content richness of media, symbolic cues provided by the medium, and situational determinants of media choice such as time and distance (Daft et al., 1987; Trevino and Webster, 1992; Trevino et al., 1987; 1990). For example, Trevino et al. (1987) found that managers tended to select face-to-face communication for content and symbolic reasons, whereas electronic mail and the telephone were more often chosen because of situational constraints such as time or geography.

The richness of the medium can sometimes reduce the sense of distance between communicators. Closely related to media richness is the study of social presence that explores the ways that the communication systems enable individuals to feel as if they are co-present even when they are not physically in the same place or time. Social presence research grows out of the telecommunications tradition and explores the use of long-standing technologies (such as the telephone) that enable mediated interpersonal communication. Short et al. (1976) used the principles of social psychology to develop the field of social presence research. They indicated that: 'the capacity to transmit information about facial expression, direction of looking, posture, dress and non-verbal vocal cues, all contribute to the Social Presence of a communication medium' (1976: 65).

Researchers used the concept of social presence to further examine mediated interpersonal communication (see, for example, Burke et al., 1999; Rice and Williams, 1984) and issues such as relationships between social presence, anticipated future interaction and group performance (Berger, 1979). This work provided the basis for additional research on media richness and telepresence in the late 1980s and the 1990s (Daft et al., 1987; Fulk and Boyd, 1991; Fulk et al., 1991; Lea and Spears, 1992; Schmitz and Fulk, 1991; Steuer, 1992; Trevino et al., 1987; 1990; Walther, 1992; 1994; Walther and Burgoon, 1992; Walther et al., 1994; Zack, 1993).

Social presence theory has also been applied to computer-mediated communication in ways that illustrate shifting patterns of control in CMC (Chesebro, 1985; d'Ambra and Rice, 1994; Fulk et al., 1992; Hiltz et al., 1989; Kiesler et al., 1984; Lea and Spears, 1992; Schmitz and Fulk, 1991; Sherblom, 1988; Sproull and Kiesler, 1986; Straus and McGrath, 1994; Trevino et al., 1990; Walther, 1992; Zack, 1993). For example, Schmitz and Fulk (1991) conducted a study that investigated the effects of perceived social influences from organizational colleagues on the uses and assessments of electronic mail. They found that 'an explicit consideration of social influences aids in understanding how individuals perceive and use information technology' (1991: 487). In other words, social influence provides controls that help individuals adapt to new technologies.

The Human–Computer Equation

Within the field of human factors or human–computer interaction (HCI) research, definitions of interactivity tend to focus on the ways that the human communicates directly with computers and other new media systems (Burgoon et al., 2000; Hanssen et al., 1996; Huhtamo, 1999; Milheim, 1996; Murray, 1997; Paisley, 1983; Preece, 1993; Reardon and Rogers, 1988; Tan and Nguyen, 1993; Trevino and Webster, 1992). Typically, research in this tradition defines the interaction between a single human and a single computer as the most elemental form of interactivity (Shaw et al., 1993). Crawford (1990) depicted the communication between human and computer as a kind of 'interactive circuit' through which the user and computer are in continuous communication. In briefly tracing the history of HCI studies, Laurel wrote:

> When the concept of the interface first began to emerge, it was commonly understood as the hardware and software through which a human and computer could communicate. As it has evolved, the concept has come to include the cognitive and emotional aspects of the user's experience as well. (1990a: xi)

Reeves and Nass noted that, in the study of human–computer interaction, 'one of the two words surrounding the hyphen usually leads' (2000: 65). Some studies focus more on human perception, others more on computer design.

Among the studies that focus on the human side are those that examine how individuals interpret computer personality (Moon and Nass, 1996), the level of agency that individuals perceive they have in working with the computer (Huhtamo, 1999; Murray, 1997), individual decision styles (Vasarhelyi, 1977), and goals that the individual brings to the system (Belkin et al., 1993; Xie, 2000).

A subset of the literature that focuses on the human side of the HCI equation addresses the concept of flow (Csikszentmihalyi, 1975), which 'represents the user's perception of the interaction

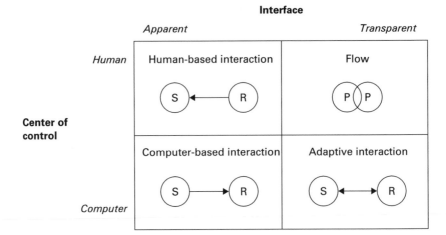

Figure 10.3　*Four models of user-to-system interactivity*
S = sender, R = receiver, P = participant (sender/receiver roles are interchangeable)

with the medium as playful and exploratory' (Trevino and Webster, 1992: 540). Ghani and Deshpande wrote:

> Flow, which is characterized by intense concentration and enjoyment, was found to be significantly linked with exploratory use behavior, which in turn was linked to extent of computer use. Flow was itself determined by the individual's sense of being in control and the level of challenge perceived in using computers. (1994: 381)

Scholars have suggested that increased flow can lead to positive outcomes such as improved attitude (Trevino and Webster, 1992), more depth of interchange with computer systems (Hesse et al., 1988), heightened creativity and reduced anxiety (Webster and Martocchio, 1992), enhanced marketing opportunities (Hoffman and Novak, 1996), and insights into problem-solving skills (Ord, 1989).

Studies that focus more on the computer side of the human–computer equation tend to examine issues such as interfaces and input devices (Baecker, 1980; Biocca, 1993; Laurel, 1990b; Naimark, 1990; Nielsen, 2000; Schneiderman, 1998; Simms, 1997), navigation tools (Heeter, 2000; Nielsen, 2000), interactive features that allow for user choice and input (Belkin et al., 1993; Daft et al., 1987; Durlak, 1987; Hanssen et al., 1996; Looms, 1993; Mahood et al., 2000; Steuer, 1992; Zeltzer, 1992), and system activity (Milheim, 1996; Valacich et al., 1993).

A subset of this literature focuses specifically on hypertextuality and the ways in which linked text can be used to manage non-linear communication (Belkin et al., 1993; Klein, 2000; Landow, 1992; Mayhew, 1998; Schaffer and Hannafin, 1986; Sundar et al., 1998; 1999). Hypertext is generally

defined as blocks of text and the electronic links that join them. The concept of hypertext was developed by Theodor H. Nelson in the 1960s and has earlier roots in Vannevar Bush's (1945) article on mechanically linked information retrieval systems (Landow, 1992). The primary advantage of hypertext is the control that it gives to the user who navigates through a computer-based system.

A Proposed Model for User-to-System Interactivity

The dimensions that were incorporated into Figures 10.1 and 10.2 can also be adapted and applied to user-to-system interaction. The control dimension, which was central to both Figures 10.1 and 10.2, remains central in this model as well. However, the issue changes slightly. The question becomes: who is in control, the computer or the human(s) interacting with it? The second dimension parallels the direction of communication dimension in Figure 10.1 and the nature of audience dimension in Figure 10.2. In HCI the second key issue is the interface. How much is the interface apparent enough to require user attention versus becoming a transparent part of the user's experience? Figure 10.3 proposes four models of interactivity based on the juxtaposition of those two dimensions.

Computer-controlled interaction assumes that the computer will 'present' information to learners who will respond to that information. Users are very aware that they are sitting in front of a computer. Much computer-based instruction uses this kind of interactivity. Filling in web-based forms is another example. By contrast, human-controlled interaction assumes a much more active individual who uses interface tools provided by programmers and designers to manipulate the computer and obtain information. For example, this form of interactivity would occur when individuals use tools such as databases, spreadsheets and word processors to manipulate and organize data so that the data are more useful to them and their colleagues.

Adaptive communication assumes that the computer is still in command of the interaction, but that it is more responsive to individual needs. For example, advanced gaming and educational systems are able to adapt to changes in the individual's skill level. The state of flow is generally assumed to be characterized by a state of high user activity in which the computer becomes virtually transparent as individuals 'lose themselves' in the computer environment. Virtual reality systems seek this level, but it may also be characteristic of gaming environments and other situations in which the user interfaces seamlessly with the computer.

FUTURE DIRECTIONS

The proposed models presented in Figures 10.1, 10.2 and 10.3 offer a way of organizing and making sense of the many different perspectives and definitions of interactivity. If 'interactivity' is to move beyond its current status as a widely used but poorly conceptualized term, we must recognize that there are three fundamentally different types of interactivity. Scholars and others who use the term should indicate whether they are focusing on user-to-user, user-to-documents or user-to-system interactivity, or some combination of the three.

Within each of these types of interactivity, an important factor to consider is the locus of control. As control shifts among senders and receivers and between humans and computer systems, the nature of interactivity shifts. Studies that focus on user-to-user interactivity should also carefully consider the direction of communication between and among senders and receivers who interact in computer-based environments. Studies that focus on user-to-documents interactivity should carefully consider the audience: how active do members of the audience wish to be? And studies that focus on user-to-system interactivity should focus on the human–computer interface: how transparent can and should that interface be?

These models may provide direction for scholars who seek to explore specific aspects of interactive communication. For example, studies of role taking in interactive environments are probably most appropriately based in the user-to-user literature, while studies of interactive fiction are probably centred in user-to-documents literature, and studies involving virtual reality centre on user-to-system issues. However, these classifications should not be viewed as either mutually exclusive or all-inclusive.

For example, virtual reality studies need to incorporate human communication factors from the user-to-user model, and content creators who are considering how users interact with documents also need to address interface issues from the user-to-system model. And some forms of interactivity and new media may not fit into any of these categories at all.

In sum, when approaching interactivity at the surface level we may be able to 'know it when we see it'. But we can understand it better if we recognize that it is a multifaceted concept that resides in the users, the documents and the systems that facilitate interactive communication.

NOTE

The author thanks Kyoungtae Nam for his research assistance on this chapter.

REFERENCES

Ahren, R. Kirkland, Stromer-Galley, Jennifer and Neuman, W. Russell (2000) 'Interactivity and structured issue comparisons on the political web: an experimental study of the 2000 New Hampshire presidential primary'. Paper presented at the International Communication Association Annual Conference, Acapulco, 1–5 June.

Allen, David (1988) 'New telecommunications services: network externalities and critical mass', *Telecommunication Policy*, 12 (3): 257–71.

Alter, Steven (1977) 'Why is man–computer interaction important for decision support systems?', *Interfaces*, 7 (2): 109–15.

Argyle, Michael (1969) *Social Interaction*. New York: Atherton.

Baecker, Ronald (1980) 'Towards an effective characterization of graphical interaction', in R.A. Guedj, P.J.W. ten Hagen, F.R. Hopgood, H.A. Tucker and D.A. Duce (eds), *Methodology of Interaction*. Amsterdam: North Holland. pp. 127–47.

Bales, R.F. (1950) 'A set of categories for the analysis of small group interaction', *American Sociological Review*, 15: 257–63.

Ball-Rokeach, Sandra J. and Reardon, Kathleen (1988) 'Monologue, dialogue, and telelog: comparing an emergent form of communication with traditional forms', in R.P. Hawkins, J.M. Wiemann and S. Pingree (eds), *Advancing Communication Science: Merging Mass and Interpersonal Process*. Newbury Park, CA: Sage. pp. 135–61.

Ball-Rokeach, Sandra J., Rokeach, M. and Grube, J.W. (1984) *The Great American Values Test: Influencing Behavior and Belief through Television*. New York: Free Press.

Barak, Azy and Fisher, William A. (1997) 'Effects of interactive computer erotica on men's attitudes and behavior toward women: an experimental study', *Computers in Human Behavior*, 13 (3): 353–69.

Barker, John and Tucker, Richard N. (1990) *The Interactive Learning Revolution: Multimedia in Education and Training*. London: Kogan Page.

Belkin, N.J., Marchetti, P.G. and Cool, C. (1993) 'Braque: design of an interface to support users' interaction in information retrieval', *Information Processing & Management*, 29 (3): 325–44.

Beniger, James R. (1986) *The Control Revolution: Technological and Economic Origins of the Information Society*. Cambridge, MA: Harvard University Press.

Beniger, James R. (1987) 'Personalization of mass media and the growth of pseudo-community', *Communication Research*, 14 (3): 352–71.

Berger, Charles R. (1979) 'Beyond initial interaction: uncertainty, understanding, and the development of interpersonal relationships', in H. Giles and R.N. St Clair (eds), *Language and Social Psychology*. Oxford: Basil Blackwell. pp. 122–44.

Bezjian-Avery, Alexa, Calder, Bobby and Iacobucci, Dawn (1998) 'New media interactive advertising vs. traditional advertising', *Journal of Advertising Research*, 38 (4): 23–32.

Bierig, Jeffrey and Dimmick, John (1979) 'The late night radio talk show as interpersonal communication', *Journalism Quarterly*, 56 (1): 92–6.

Bikson, Tora K., Eveland, J.D. and Guetek, Barbara A. (1989) 'Flexible interactive technologies and multi-person tasks: current problems and future prospects', in M.H. Olson (ed.), *Technological Support for Work Group Collaboration*. Hillsdale, NJ: Erlbaum. pp. 89–112.

Biocca, Frank (1993) 'Communication research in the design of communication interfaces and systems', *Journal of Communication*, 43 (4): 59–68.

Blattberg, Robert C. and Deighton, John (1991) 'Interactive marketing: exploiting the age of addressability', *Sloan Management Review*, 32 (1): 5–14.

Blumer, Herbert (1969) *Symbolic Interactionism: Perspective and Method*. Englewood Cliffs, NJ: Prentice-Hall.

Bolter, Jay David (1991) *Writing Space: the Computer, Hypertext, and the History of Writing*. Hillsdale, NJ: Erlbaum.

Borden, Diane L. and Harvey, Kerrick (1998) *The Electronic Grapevine: Rumor, Reputation, and Reporting in the New Online Environment*. Mahwah, NJ: Erlbaum.

Bretz, R. (1983) *Media for Interactive Communication*. Beverly Hills, CA: Sage.

Burgoon, Judee K., Bonito, Joseph A., Bengtsson, Bjorn, Ramirez, Artemio Jr, Dunbar, Norah E. and Miczo, Nathan (2000) 'Testing the interactivity model: communication processes, partner assessments, and the quality of collaborative work', *Journal of Management Information Systems*, 16 (3): 33–56.

Burke, Kelly, Aytes, Kregg, Chidambaram, Laku and Johnson, Jeffrey J. (1999) 'A study of partially distributed work groups: the impact of media, location, and time on perceptions and performance', *Small Group Research*, 30 (4): 453–90.

Bush, V. (1945) 'As we may think', *Atlantic Monthly*, 176 (July): 101–8.

Carey, John (1989) 'Interactive media', in *International Encyclopedia of Communications*. New York: Oxford University Press. pp. 328–30.

Cathcart, Robert and Gumpert, Gary (1983) 'Mediated interpersonal communication: toward a new typology', *Quarterly Journal of Speech*, 69 (3): 267–77.

Chaffee, Steven. H (1972) 'The interpersonal context of mass communication', in F.G. Kline and P.J. Tichenor (eds), *Current Perspectives in Mass Communication Research*. Beverly Hills, CA: Sage. pp. 95–120.

Chapanis, Alphonse, Ochsman, Robert B., Parrish, Robert N. and Weeks, Gerald D. (1972) 'Studies in interactive communication. I: The effects of four communication modes on the behavior of teams during cooperative problem-solving', *Human Factors*, 14 (6): 487–509.

Chesebro, James W. (1985) 'Computer mediated interpersonal communication', in B.D. Ruben (ed.), *Information and Behavior*, vol. 1. New Brunswick, NJ: Transaction. pp. 202–22.

Chesebro, James W. and Bonsall, Donald G. (1989) *Computer Mediated Communication: Human Relationships in a Computerized World*. Tuscaloosa, AL: University of Alabama Press.

Chilcoat, Yvonne, and DeWine, Sue (1985) 'Teleconferencing and interpersonal communication perception', *Journal of Applied Communication Research*, 13 (1): 14–32.

Coffee, Steve and Stipp, Horst (1997) 'The interactions between computer and television usage', *Journal of Advertising Research*, 37 (2): 61–6.

Cooley, Tracy (1999) 'Interactive communication – public relations on the web', *Public Relations Quarterly*, 144 (2): 41–2.

Crawford, Chris (1990) 'Lessons from computer game design', in B. Laurel (ed.), *The Art of Human–Computer Interface Design*. Reading, MA: Addison-Wesley. pp. 103–11.

Crittenden, John (1971) 'Democratic functions of the open mike forum', *Public Opinion Quarterly*, 35: 200–10.

Csikszentmihalyi, M (1975) *Beyond Boredom and Anxiety*. San Francisco: Jossey-Bass.

Daft, Richard L., Lengel, Robert H. and Trevino, Linda Klebe (1987) 'Message equivocality, media selection, and manager performance: implications for information systems', *MIS Quarterly*, 12 (3): 355–66.

d'Ambra, John and Rice, Ronald E. (1994) 'Multimedia approaches for the study of computer-mediated communication, equivocality, and media selection', *IEEE Transactions on Professional Communication*, 37 (4): 231–9.

Dannefer, W. Dale and Poushinsky, Nicholas (1977) 'CB in perspective: language and community', *Journal of Communication*, 27 (3): 122–6.

Danowski, James A. (1982) 'Computer mediated communication: a network-based analysis using a CBBS conference', in M. Burgoon (ed.), *Communication Yearbook 6*. Beverly Hills, CA: Sage. pp. 905–24.

Davis, Hal and Rarick, Galen (1964) 'Functions of editorials and letters to the editor', *Journalism Quarterly*, 41 (1): 108–9.

Day, George S. (1998) 'Organizing for interactivity', *Journal of Interactive Marketing*, 12 (1): 47–53.

DeVries, Yousri Eldin (1996) 'The interactive component of distance learning implemented in the art studio course', *Education*, 117 (2): 180–4.

Douglas, Susan J. (1987) *Inventing American Broadcasting: 1899–1922*. Baltimore: Johns Hopkins University Press.

Duncan, Starkey Jr (1989) 'Interaction, face-to-face', in *International Encyclopedia of Communications*. New York: Oxford University Press. pp. 325–7.

Duncan, Tom and Moriarty, Sandra E. (1998) 'A communication-based marketing model for managing relationships', *Journal of Marketing*, 62: 1–13.

Durlak, Jerome T. (1987) 'A typology for interactive media', in M.L. McLaughlin (ed.), *Communication Yearbook 10*. Newbury Park, CA: Sage. pp. 743–57.

Feenberg, Andrew (1992) 'From information to communication: the French experience with videotex', in M. Lea (ed.), *Contexts of Computer-Mediated Communication*. New York: Harvester-Wheatsheaf. pp. 168–87.

Forsythe, Sidney A. (1950) 'An exploratory study of letters to the editor and their contributors', *Public Opinion Quarterly*, 14 (1): 143–4.

Fredin, Eric S. (1983) 'The context of communication: interactive telecommunication, interpersonal communication, and their effects on ideas', *Communication Research*, 10 (4): 553–81.

Fredin, Eric S. (1989) 'Interactive communication systems, values, and the requirement of self-reflection', in J.A. Anderson (ed.), *Communication Yearbook 12*. Newbury Park, CA: Sage. pp. 533–46.

Fredin, Eric S. (1997) *Rethinking the News Story for the Internet: Hyperstory Prototypes and a Model of the User*. Columbia, SC: AEJMC.

Fulk, Janet and Boyd, Brian (1991) 'Emerging theories of communication and organizations', *Journal of Management*, 17 (2): 407–46.

Fulk, Janet, Schmitz, Joseph and Steinfeld, Charles W. (1991) 'A social influence model of technology use', in J. Fulk and C.W. Steinfeld (eds), *Organization and Communication Technology*. Newbury Park, CA: Sage. pp. 117–40.

Fulk, Janet, Schmitz, Joseph A. and Schwarz, Deanna (1992) 'The dynamics of context–behavior interactions in computer-mediated communication', in M. Lea (ed.), *Contexts of Computer-Mediated Communication*. New York: Harvester-Wheatsheaf. pp. 7–29.

Gans, Herbert J. (1977) 'Audience mail: letters to an anchorman', *Journal of Communication*, 27 (3): 86–91.

Garramone, Gina M., Harris, Allen C. and Anderson, Ronald (1986) 'Uses of political computer bulletin boards', *Journal of Broadcasting and Electronic Media*, 30 (3): 325–39.

Ghani, Jawaid A. and Deshpande, Satish P. (1994) 'Task characteristics and the experience of optimal flow in human–computer interaction', *Journal of Psychology*, 128 (4): 381–91.

Goffman, Erving (1967) *Interaction Ritual: Essays on Face-to-Face Behavior*. Chicago: Aldine.

Grey, David L. and Brown, Trevor R. (1970) 'Letters to the editor: hazy reflections of public opinion', *Journalism Quarterly*, 47 (1): 450–6, 71.

Guedj, Richard A., ten Hagen, Paul J.W., Hopgood, F. Robert, Tucker, Hugh A. and Duce, David A. (1980) *Methodology of Interaction*. Amsterdam: North-Holland.

Ha, Louisa and James, Lincoln (1998) 'Interactivity re-examined: a baseline analysis of early business web sites', *Journal of Broadcasting & Electronic Media*, 42 (4): 457–74.

Haeckel, Stephan H. (1998) 'About the nature and future of interactive marketing', *Journal of Interactive Marketing*, 12 (1): 63–71.

Hanssen, Lucien, Jankowski, Nicholas W. and Etienne, Reinier (1996) 'Interactivity from the perspective of communication studies', in N.W. Jankowski and L. Hanssen (eds), *Contours of Multimedia: Recent Technological, Theoretical, and Empirical Developments*. Luton: University of Luton Press. pp. 61–73.

Heeter, Carrie (1989) 'Implications of new interactive technologies for conceptualizing communication', in J.L. Salvaggio and J. Bryant (eds), *Media Use in the Information Age: Emerging Patterns of Adoption and Computer Use*. Hillsdale, NJ: Erlbaum. pp. 217–35.

Heeter, Carrie (2000) 'Interactivity in the context of designed experiences', *Journal of Interactive Advertising*, 1 (1). Available online: http://www.jiad.org.

Hesse, Bradford W., Werner, Carol M. and Altman, Irwin (1988) 'Temporal aspects of computer-mediated communication', *Computers in Human Behavior*, 4: 147–65.

Hester, Joe Bob (1999) 'Using a web-based interactive test as a learning tool', *Journalism and Mass Communication Educator*, 54 (1): 35–41.

Hiltz, Starr Roxanne and Turoff, Murray (1993) *The Network Nation: Human Communication via Computer*, rev. edn. Cambridge, MA: MIT Press.

Hiltz, Starr Roxanne, Turoff, Murray and Johnson, Kenneth (1989) 'Experiments in group decision making. 3: Disinhibition, deindividuation and group processes in pen name and real name computer conferences', *Decision Support Systems*, 5: 217–32.

Hirokawa, Randy Y. (1988) 'Group communication research: considerations for the use of interaction analysis', in C.H. Tardy (ed.), *A Handbook for the Study of Human Communication: Methods and Instruments for Observing, Measuring, and Assessing Communication Processes*. Norwood, NJ: Ablex. pp. 229–45.

Hoffman, Donna L. and Novak, Thomas P. (1996) 'Marketing in hypermedia computer-mediated environments: conceptual foundations', *Journal of Marketing*, 60: 50–68.

Horton, Donald and Wohl, R. Richard (1956) 'Mass communication and para-social interaction: observations on intimacy at a distance', *Psychiatry*, 19: 215–29.

Houlberg, Rick (1984) 'Local television news audience and the para-social interaction', *Journal of Broadcasting*, 28 (4): 423–9.

Huhtamo, Erkki (1999) 'From cybernation to interaction: a contribution to an archaeology of interactivity', in P. Lunenfeld (ed.), *The Digital Dialectic: New Essays on New Media*. Cambridge, MA: MIT Press. pp. 96–110.

Hunt, Peter (2000) 'Futures for children's literature: evolution or radical break', *Cambridge Journal of Education*, 30 (1): 111–19.

Iser, Wolfgang (1989) 'Interaction between text and reader', in J. Corner and J. Hawthorn (eds), *Communication Studies: an Introductory Reader*. London: Arnold. pp. 160–4.

Jankowski, Nicholas W. and Hanssen, Lucien (1996) 'Introduction: multimedia comes of age', in N.W. Jankowski and L. Hanssen (eds), *The Contours of Multimedia: Recent Technological, Theoretical, and Empirical Developments*. Luton: University of Luton Press. pp. 1–21.

Jensen, Jens F. (1998) 'Interactivity: tracing a new concept in media and communication studies', *Nordicom Review*, 19 (1): 185–204.

Kay, Alan (1990) 'User interface: a personal view', in B. Laurel (ed.), *The Art of Human–Computer Interface Design*. Reading, MA: Addison-Wesley. pp. 191–207.

Kayany, Joseph M., Wotring, C. Edward and Forrest, Edward J. (1996) 'Relational control and interactive media choice in technology-mediated communication situations', *Human Communication Research*, 22 (3): 399–421.

Kelly, Janice R. and McGrath, Joseph E. (1985) 'Effects of time limits and task types on task performance and Interaction of four-person groups', *Journal of Personality and Social Psychology*, 49 (2): 395–407.

Kiesler, Sara (1986) 'Thinking ahead: the hidden messages in computer networks', *Harvard Business Review*, 27 (3): 46–60.

Kiesler, Sara, Siegel, Jane and McGuire, Timothy W. (1984) 'Social-psychological aspects of computer-mediated communication', *American Psychologist*, 39 (10): 1123–34.

Kiousis, S. (1999) 'Broadening the boundaries of interactivity: a concept explication'. Paper presented at the Association for Education in Journalism and Mass Communication Annual Conference, New Orleans, LA, August.

Kirsh, David (1997) 'Interactivity and multimedia interfaces', *Instructional Science*, 25: 79–96.

Klein, Leo R. (2000) 'The joys of interactivity', *Library Journal*, 12 (5): 20–2.

Lander, Byron G. (1972) 'Functions of letters to the editor: a reexamination', *Journalism Quarterly*, 49 (1): 142–3.

Landow, George P. (1992) *Hypertext: the Convergence of Contemporary Critical Theory and Technology*. Baltimore, MD: Johns Hopkins University Press.

Lappin, Todd (1995) 'Deja vu all over again', *Wired*, May: 174–7, 218–22.

Latchem, Colin, Williamson, John and Henderson-Lancett, Lexie (1993a) 'IMM: an overview', in C. Latchem, J. Williamson and L. Henderson-Lancett (eds), *Interactive Multimedia: Practice and Purpose*. London: Kogan Page. pp. 19–38.

Latchem, Colin, Williamson, John and Henderson-Lancett, Lexie (1993b) *Interactive Multimedia: Practice and Purpose*. London: Kogan Page.

Laurel, Brenda (1990a) 'Introduction', in B. Laurel (ed.), *The Art of Human–Computer Interface Design*. Reading, MA: Addison-Wesley. pp. xi–xvi.

Laurel, Brenda (1990b) 'Users and contexts', in B. Laurel (ed.), *The Art of Human–Computer Interface Design*. Reading, MA: Addison-Wesley. pp. 91–3.

Lea, Martin and Spears, Russell (1992) 'Paralanguage and social perception in computer-mediated communication', *Journal of Organizational Computing*, 2 (3, 4): 321–41.

Lee, Jae-Shin (2000) 'Interactivity: a new approach', Paper presented at the Association for Education in Journalism and Mass Communication, Phoenix, AZ.

Leonhirth, William J., Mindich, David T.Z. and Straumanis, Andris (1997) 'Wanted … a metaphor of history: using past information systems to explain internet mailing lists', *Electronic Journal of Communication*, 7 (4). Available online: http://sss.cios/org/getfile/LEONHIRT_V7N497.

Levy, Mark R. (1979) 'Watching TV news as para-social interaction', *Journal of Broadcasting*, 23 (1): 67–89.

Lieb, Thom (1998) 'Inactivity on interactivity', *Journal of Electronic Publishing*, 3 (3). Available online: http://www.press.umich.edu/jep/03-3/lieb0303.html.

Lievrouw, Leah A. and Finn, T. Andrew (1990) 'Identifying the common dimensions of communication: the communication systems model', in B.D. Ruben and L.A. Lievrouw (eds), *Mediation, Information and Communication: Information and Behavior*, vol. 3. New Brunswick, NJ: Transaction. pp. 37–65.

Looms, Peter Olaf (1993) 'Interactive multimedia in education', in C. Latchem, J. Williamson and L. Henderson-Lancett (eds), *Interactive Multimedia: Practice and Purpose*. London: Kogan Page. pp. 115–34.

Mahler, Alwin and Rogers, Everett M. (1999) 'The diffusion of interactive communication innovations and the critical mass: the adoption of telecommunication services by German banks', *Telecommunications Policy*, 23 (10/11): 719–40.

Mahood, Chad, Kalyanaraman, Sriram and Sundar, S. Shyam (2000) 'The effects of erotica and dehumanizing pornography in an online interactive environment'. Paper presented at the Association for Education in Journalism and Mass Communication, Phoenix, AZ, 9–12 August.

Markus, M. Lynne (1990) 'Toward a "critical mass" theory of interactive media', in J. Fulk and C. Steinfeld (eds), *Organization and Communication Technology*. Newbury Park, CA: Sage. pp. 194–218.

Marvin, Carolyn (1988) *When Old Technologies Were New: Thinking about Electric Communication in the Late Nineteenth Century*. New York: Oxford University Press.

Marvin, Carolyn and Schultze, Quentin J. (1977) 'CB in perspective: the first thirty years', *Journal of Communication*, 27 (3): 104–17.

Massey, Brian L. and Levy, Mark R. (1999) 'Interactivity, online journalism, and English-language web newspapers in Asia', *Journalism & Mass Communication Quarterly*, 76 (1): 138–51.

Mayburry, Mark (2000) 'News on demand', *Communications of the ACM*, 43 (2): 33–4.

Mayhew, Deborah J. (1998) 'Introduction', in C. Forsythe, E. Grose and J. Ratner (eds), *Human Factors and Web Development*. Mahwah, NJ: Erlbaum. pp. 1–13.

McGrath, Joseph E. (1990) 'Time matters in groups', in J. Galegher, R.E. Kraut and C. Egido (eds), *Intellectual Teamwork: Social and Technical Foundations of Cooperative Work*. Hillsdale, NJ: Erlbaum. pp. 23–61.

McGrath, Joseph E. (1991) 'Time, interaction, and performance (TIP): a theory of groups', *Small Group Research*, 22 (2): 147–74.

McGuire, Bernadette and Leroy, David J. (1977) 'Audience mail: letters to the broadcaster', *Journal of Communication*, 27: 79–85.

McMillan, Sally J. (1998a) 'The role of advertising in new media: a historical analysis of radio with comparisons to computer-mediated communication', in D.D. Muehling (ed.), *Proceedings of the 1998 Conference of the American Academy of Advertising*. Pullman, WA: Washington State University. pp. 157–66.

McMillan, Sally J. (1998b) 'Who pays for content? Funding in interactive media', *Journal of Computer Mediated Communication*, 4 (1). Available online: http://www.ascusc.org/jcmc/vol4/issue1/mcmillan.html.

McMillan, Sally J. (1999) 'Advertising age and interactivity: tracing media evolution through the advertising trade press', in M. Roberts (ed.), *Proceedings of the 1999 Conference of the American Academy of Advertising*. Gainesville, FL: University of Florida. pp. 107–14.

McMillan, Sally J. (2000a) 'Interactivity is in the eye of the beholder: function, perception, involvement, and attitude toward the web site', in M.A. Shaver (ed.), *Proceedings of the 2000 Conference of the American Academy of Advertising*. East Lansing, MI: Michigan State University. pp. 71–8.

McMillan, Sally J. (2000b) 'What Is Interactivity and what does it do?'. Paper presented at the Association of Education in Journalism and Mass Communication Conference, Phoenix, AZ, August.

McMillan, Sally J. and Downes, Edward J. (2000) 'Defining interactivity: a qualitative identification of key dimensions', *New Media and Society*, 2 (2): 157–79.

Miles, Ian (1992) 'When mediation is the message: how suppliers envisage new markets', in M. Lea (ed.), *Contexts of Computer-Mediated Communication*. New York: Harvester-Wheatsheaf. pp. 145–67.

Milheim, William D. (1996) 'Interactivity and computer-based instruction', *Journal of Educational Technology Systems*, 24 (3): 225–33.

Miller, Dan E., Katovich, Michael A. and Saxton, Stanley L. (1997) *Constructing Complexity: Symbolic Interaction and Social Forms*, vol. 3. Greenwich, CT: JAI.

Moon, Youngme and Nass, Clifford (1996) 'How "real" are computer personalities? Psychological responses to personality types in human–computer interaction', *Communication Research*, 23 (6): 651–74.

Morris, Merrill and Ogan, Christine (1996) 'The Internet as mass medium', *Journal of Computer Mediated Communication*, 1 (4). Available online: http://www.ascusc.org/jcmc/vol1/issue4/morris.html.

Morrison, Margaret (1998) 'A look at interactivity from a consumer perspective', in J.B. Ford and E.J.D. Honeycutt (eds), *Developments in Marketing Science*, vol. 21. Norfolk, VA: Academy of Marketing Science. pp. 149–54.

Murray, Janet H. (1995) 'The pedagogy of cyberfiction: teaching a course on reading and writing interactive narrative', in E. Barrett and M. Redmond (eds), *Contextual Media: Multimedia and Interpretation*. Cambridge, MA: MIT Press. pp. 129–62.

Murray, Janet H. (1997) *Hamlet on the Holodeck: the Future of Narrative in Cyberspace*. New York: Free Press.

Murray, Janet H. (1999) 'Interactive design: a profession in search of professional education', *The Chronicle of Higher Education*, 23 April: B4–5.

Naimark, Michael (1990) 'Realness and interactivity', in B. Laurel (ed.), *The Art of Human–Computer Interface Design*. Menlo Park, CA: Addison-Wesley. pp. 455–9.

Negroponte, Nicholas (1995) *Being Digital*. New York: Knopf.

Newhagen, John E. (1994) 'Self efficacy and call-in political television show use', *Communication Research*, 21 (3): 366–79.

Newhagen, John E. (1998) 'Hitting the agenda reset button for the Internet: the problem of matching research with development'. Paper presented at the International Communication Association Annual Conference, Jerusalem, July.

Newhagen, John E., Cordes, John W. and Levy, Mark R. (1996) 'Nightly@NBC.Com: audience scope and the perception of interactivity in viewer mail on the Internet', *Journal of Communication*, 45 (3): 164–75.

Nielsen, Jakob (2000) *Designing Web Usability*. Indianapolis: New Riders.

Norlund, Jan-Erik (1978) 'Media interaction', *Communication Research*, 5 (2): 150–75.

Ord, Jacqueline G. (1989) 'Who's joking? The information system at play', *Interacting with Computers*, 1 (1): 118–28.

Paisley, William (1983) 'Computerizing information: lessons of a videotext trial', *Journal of Communication*, 33 (1): 153–61.

Pavlik, John V. (1998) *New Media Technology: Cultural and Commercial Perspectives*, 2nd edn. Boston: Allyn and Bacon.

Poole, Marshall Scott (1985) 'Task and interaction sequences: a theory of coherence in group decision-making interaction', in R.L. Street and J.N. Capella (eds), *Sequence and Pattern in Communicative Behaviour*. London: Arnold. pp. 206–24.

Powell, Jon T. and Ary, Donald (1977) 'CB in perspective: communication without commitment', *Journal of Communication*, 27 (3): 118–21.

Preece, Jenny (1993) 'Hypermedia, multimedia and human factors', in C. Latchem, J. Williamson and L. Henderson-Lancett (eds), *Interactive Multimedia: Practice and Purpose*. London: Kogan Page. pp. 135–50.

Rafaeli, Sheizaf (1986) 'The electronic bulletin board: a computer driven mass medium', *Computers and the Social Sciences*, 2 (3): 123–36.

Rafaeli, Sheizaf (1988) 'Interactivity: from new media to communication', in R.P. Hawkins, J.M. Wiemann and S. Pingree (eds), *Advancing Communication Science: Merging Mass and Interpersonal Process*. Newbury Park, CA: Sage. pp. 110–34.

Rafaeli, Sheizaf (1990) 'Interacting with media: parasocial interaction and real interaction', in B.D. Ruben and L.A. Lievrouw (eds), *Mediation, Information and Communication: Information and Behavior*, vol. 3. New Brunswick, NJ: Transaction. pp. 125–81.

Rafaeli, Sheizaf and LaRose, Robert J. (1993) 'Electronic bulletin boards and "public goods" explanations of collaborative mass media', *Communication Research*, 20 (2): 277–97.

Rafaeli, Sheizaf and Sudweeks, Fay (1997) 'Networked interactivity', *Journal of Computer Mediated Communication*, 2 (4). Available online: http://www.usc.edu/dept/annenberg/vol2/issue4/rafaeli.sudweeks.html.

Reardon, Kathleen K. and Rogers, Everett M. (1988) 'Interpersonal versus mass media communication: a false dichotomy', *Human Communication Research*, 15 (2): 284–303.

Reeves, Byron and Nass, Clifford (1996) *The Media Equation: How People Treat Computers, Television, and New Media Like Real People and Places*. New York: Cambridge University Press/CSLI.

Reeves, Byron and Nass, Clifford (2000) 'Perceptual bandwidth', *Communications of the ACM*, 43 (3): 65–70.

Rice, Ronald E. (1984) 'New media technology: growth and integration', in R.E. Rice (ed.), *The New Media: Communication, Research, and Technology*. Beverly Hills, CA: Sage. pp. 33–54.

Rice, Ronald E. and Williams, Frederick (1984) 'Theories old and new: the study of new media', in R.E. Rice (ed.), *The New Media: Communication, Research, and Technology*. Beverly Hills, CA: Sage. pp. 55–80.

Romiszowski, Alexander J. (1993) 'Developing interactive multimedia courseware and networks: some current issues', in C. Latchem, J. Williamson and L. Henderson-Lancett (eds), *Interactive Multimedia: Practice and Purpose* London: Kogan Page. pp. 57–78.

Ruben, B.D. (1975) 'Intrapersonal, interpersonal, and mass communication processes in individual and multi-person systems', in B.D. Ruben and J.Y. Kim (eds), *General Systems Theory and Human Communication*. Rochelle Park, NY: Hayden. pp. 164–90.

Salzman, Harold and Rosenthal, Stephen R. (1994) *Software by Design: Shaping Technology and the Workplace*. New York: Oxford University Press.

Sayre, Jeanette (1939) 'Progress in radio fan-mail analysis', *Public Opinion Quarterly*, 3 (2): 272–8.

Schaffer, Lemuel C. and Hannafin, Michael J. (1986) 'The effects of progressive interactivity in learning from interactive video', *Educational Communication and Technology*, 34 (2): 89–96.

Schmitz, Joseph and Fulk, Janet (1991) 'Organizational colleagues, media richness, and electronic mail: a test of the social influence model of technology use', *Communication Research*, 18 (4): 487–523.

Schneiderman, Ben (1998) *Designing the User Interface: Strategies for Effective Human–Computer Interaction*, 3rd edn. Reading, MA: Addison-Wesley.

Schudson, Michael (1978) 'The ideal of conversation in the study of mass media', *Communication Research*, 5 (3): 320–9.

Schultz, Tanjev (1999) 'Interactive options in online journalism: a content analysis of 100 US newspapers', *Journal of Computer Mediated Communication*, 5 (1). Available online: http://www.ascusc.org/jcmc/vol5/issue1/schultz.html.

Schultz, Tanjev (2000) 'Mass media and the concept of interactivity: an exploratory study of online forums and reader e-mail', *Media, Culture & Society*, 22 (2): 205–21.

Shaw, Thomas, Aranson, Karl and Belardo, Salvatore (1993) 'The effects of computer mediated interactivity on idea generation: an experimental investigation', *IEEE Transactions on Systems, Man and Cybernetics*, 23 (3): 737–45.

Sherblom, John (1988) 'Direction, function, and signature in electronic mail', *Journal of Business Communication*, 25 (4): 39–54.

Shimanoff, Susan B. (1988) 'Group interaction via communication rules', in R.S. Cathcart and L.A. Samover (eds), *Small Group Communication: A Reader*, 5th edn. Dubuque, IA: Brown. pp. 50–64.

Short, John, Williams, Ederyn and Christie, Bruce (1976) *The Social Psychology of Telecommunications*. London: Wiley.

Siegel, Jane, Dubrovsky, Vitaly, Kiesler, Sara and McGuire, Timothy W. (1986) 'Group processes in computer-mediated communication', *Organizational Behavior and Human Decision Processes*, 37: 157–87.

Simms, R. (1997) 'Interactivity: a forgotten art?', *Computers in Human Behavior*, 13: 157–80.

Smethers, Steven (1998) 'Cyberspace in the curricula: new legal and ethical issues', *Journalism & Mass Communication Educator*, 53 (4): 15–23.

Smulyan, Susan (1994) *Selling Radio: the Commercialization of American Broadcasting, 1920–1934*. Washington, DC: Smithsonian Institution Press.

Sproull, Lee and Kiesler, Sara (1986) 'Reducing social context cues: electronic mail in organizational communication', *Management Science*, 32 (11): 1492–512.

Standage, Tom (1998) *The Victorian Internet*. New York: Walker.

Steuer, Jonathan (1992) 'Defining virtual reality: dimensions determining telepresence', *Journal of Communication*, 42 (4): 73–93.

Straubhaar, Joseph and LaRose, Robert (1996) *Communications Media in the Information Society*. Belmont, CA: Wadsworth.

Straus, Susan G. and McGrath, Joseph E. (1994) 'Does the medium matter? The interaction of task type and technology on group performance and member reactions', *Journal of Applied Psychology*, 79 (1): 87–97.

Street, Richard L. Jr and Rimal, Rajiv N. (1997) 'Health promotion and interactive technology: a conceptual foundation', in R.L. Street, W.R. Gold and T. Manning (eds), *Health Promotion and Interactive Technology*. Mahwah, NJ: Erlbaum. pp. 1–18.

Stromer-Galley, Jennifer (2000) 'Online interaction and why candidates avoid it', *Journal of Communication*, 50 (4): 111–32.

Stromer-Galley, Jennifer and Foot, Kirsten A. (2000) 'Citizens, campaigns, and online interactivity', Paper presented at the International Communication Association Annual Conference, Acapulco, Mexico, 1–5 June.

Sundar, S. Shyam, Narayan, Sunetra, Obregon, Rafael and Uppal, Charu (1998) 'Does web advertising work? memory for print vs. online media', *Journalism & Mass Communication Quarterly*, 75 (4): 822–35.

Sundar, S. Shyam, Brown, Justin and Kalyanaraman, Sriam (1999) 'Reactivity vs. interactivity: impression formation effects of message contingency in political websites'. Paper presented at the International Communication Association Annual Conference, San Francisco, CA, 27–31 May.

Szuprowicz, Bohdan O. (1995) *Multimedia Networking*. New York: McGraw-Hill.

Tan, William and Nguyen, Ann (1993) 'Lifecycle costing models for interactive multimedia systems', in C. Latchem, J. Williamson and L. Henderson-Lancett (eds), *Interactive Multimedia: Practice and Purpose*. London: Kogan Page. pp. 151–64.

Trevino, Linda Klebe and Webster, Jane (1992) 'Flow in computer-mediated communication: electronic mail and voice mail evaluation and impacts', *Communication Research*, 19 (5): 539–73.

Trevino, Linda Klebe, Lengel, Robert H. and Daft, Richard L. (1987) 'Media symbolism, media richness, and media choice in organizations: a symbolic interactionist perspective', *Communication Research*, 14 (5): 553–74.

Trevino, Linda Klebe, Daft, Richard L. and Lengel, Robert H. (1990) 'Understanding managers' media choices: a symbolic interactionist perspective', in J. Fulk and C. Steinfeld (eds), *Organizations and Communication Technology*. Newbury Park, CA: Sage. pp. 71–94.

Tucker, Richard N. (1990) 'Transitions in European education', in R.N. Tucker (ed.), *The Interactive Learning Revolution: Multimedia in Education and Training*. London: Kogan Page. pp. 34–45.

Turing, A.M. (1956) 'Can a machine think?', in J.R. Newman (ed.), *Machines, Music, and Puzzles*. New York: Simon & Schuster. pp. 2099–123.

Turow, Joseph (1974) 'Talk show radio as interpersonal communication', *Journal of Broadcasting*, 18 (2): 171–9.

Turow, Joseph (1977) 'Another view of "citizen feedback" to the mass media', *Public Opinion Quarterly*, 41 (4): 534–43.

Valacich, Joseph S., Paranka, David, George, Joey F. and Nunamaker, J.F. Jr (1993) 'Communication concurrency and the new media: a new dimension for media richness', *Communication Research*, 20 (2): 249–76.

Vasarhelyi, Miklos Antal (1977) 'Man–machine planning systems: a cognitive style examination of interactive decision making', *Journal of Accounting Research*, 15 (1): 138–53.

Walther, Joseph B. (1992) 'Interpersonal effects in computer-mediated interaction: a relational perspective', *Communication Research*, 19 (1): 52–90.

Walther, Joseph B. (1994) 'Anticipated ongoing interaction versus channel effects on relational communication in computer-mediated interaction', *Human Communication Research*, 20 (4): 473–501.

Walther, Joseph B. (1995) 'Relational aspects of computer-mediated communication: experimental observations over time in computer-mediated interaction', *Organization Science*, 6 (2): 186–203.

Walther, Joseph B. (1996) 'Computer-mediated communication: impersonal, interpersonal, and hyperpersonal interaction', *Communication Research*, 23 (1): 3–43.

Walther, Joseph B. and Burgoon, Judee K. (1992) 'Relational communication in computer-mediated interaction', *Human Communication Research*, 19 (1): 50–88.

Walther, Joseph B., Anderson, Jeffrey F. and Park, David W. (1994) 'Interpersonal effects in computer-mediated interaction: a meta-analysis of social and antisocial communication', *Communication Research*, 21 (4): 460–87.

Webster, Jane and Martocchio, Joseph J. (1992) 'Microcomputer playfulness: development of a measure with workplace implications', *MIS Quarterly*, 16 (2): 201–26.

Wiener, Norbert (1948) *Cybernetics: or Control and Communication in the Animal and the Machine*. Cambridge, MA: Technology Press.

Williams, Frederick, Rice, Ronald E. and Rogers, Everett M. (1988) *Research Methods and the New Media*. New York: Free Press.

Williams, Frederick, Strover, Sharon and Grant, August E. (1994) 'Social aspects of new media technologies', in J. Bryant and D. Zillman (eds), *Media Effects: Advances in Theory and Research*. Hillsdale, NJ: Erlbaum. pp. 463–82.

Wish, Myron, Deutsch, Morton and Kaplan, Susan J. (1976) 'Perceived dimensions of interpersonal relations', *Journal of Personality and Social Psychology*, 33 (4): 409–20.

Wu, Guohua (1999) 'Perceived interactivity and attitude toward website', Paper presented at the American Academy of Advertising Annual Conference, Albuquerque, NM, March.

Wurtzel, Alan H. and Turner, Colin (1977) 'What missing the telephone means', *Journal of Communication*, 27 (2): 48–57.

Xie, Hong (2000) 'Shifts of interactive intentions and information-seeking strategies in interactive information retrieval', *Journal of the American Society for Information Science*, 51 (9): 841–57.

Yom, Sue Son (1996) 'The Internet and the future of minority health', *Journal of the American Medical Association*, 275 (9): 735.

Zack, Michael H. (1993) 'Interactivity and communication mode choice in ongoing management groups', *Information Systems Research*, 4 (3): 207–39.

Zeltzer, David (1992) 'Autonomy, interaction, and presence', *Teleoperators and Virtual Environments*, 1 (1): 127–32.

11

Determination and Contingency in New Media Development: Diffusion of Innovations and Social Shaping of Technology Perspectives

LEAH A. LIEVROUW

Across many literatures technologies are described as having trajectories, stages, cycles and growth curves; they diffuse, transfer, are 'pushed' and 'pulled', and evolve. Many current observers agree that 'technology' includes not only the built devices themselves, but also the practices and knowledge related to them and the social arrangements that form around those devices, practices and knowledge (Mackenzie and Wacjman, 1999; Dierkes and Hoffmann, 1992; see also the Introduction to this volume). Thought of this way, technology is dynamic, even fluid: 'The interaction between material and nonmaterial components and coupling of technical and social components can be captured in the concept of technology as a project' (Rammert, 1992: 63). New media technologies are no exception. They develop in dynamic environments where users, designers, manufacturers, investors, regulators, distributors and others work out their interrelated and competing interests, cultural assumptions, desires and visions.

This chapter has two main purposes. The first is to review and compare two major bodies of research on technology and society that have been particularly influential in new media research. *Diffusion of innovations theory* (Rogers, 1995) and the *social shaping of technology* (SST) perspective (Mackay and Gillespie, 1992; MacKenzie and Wajcman, 1999; Williams and Edge, 1996) are sometimes characterized as competing or even antithetical approaches to technological change. They might also be classified as 'mediated impact' and 'mutual shaping' explanations of technological development, respectively (Boczkowski, 1999). While the two perspectives differ in important respects, they also share common concerns and theoretical grounding.

The comparison of diffusion and SST is illustrated by two examples. Electronic mail and videotex originated at about the same time in the 1960s and 1970s; e-mail was eventually adopted in universities, workplaces and homes, while videotex never found a 'niche' in the US and encountered considerable consumer resistance elsewhere. Both cases have been studied extensively, and the present discussion draws on those studies to show how diffusion and SST would frame the cases differently.

Based on the comparison of SST and diffusion and the two case studies, the second purpose is to characterize the development and use of new media technologies as a process that involves a constant tension between *determination* and *contingency*, that is, between the imposition of order and uncertainty. It is argued that determination and contingency are interdependent and iterative, and that this relationship can be seen at several key junctures or 'moments' in new media development and use. The chapter closes with a discussion of determination and contingency as common threads in both theoretical traditions.

THE DEVELOPMENT OF NEW MEDIA
TECHNOLOGIES

As with other technologies, new media development is not just a matter of engineering or optimal solutions to technical problems; it can be characterized as a *sociotechnical* phenomenon (Bijker, 1995; Bijker and Law, 1992; Suchman, 1996). It brings together engineering specifications (such as interoperability, ergonomics, human factors, interface design, navigation, system implementation) and media production values (such as visual or sound quality, post-production techniques or style) in the changing social, institutional, economic, cultural and policy context of everyday reception and use.

It is often tempting to focus on the origins of technology, on design, invention or innovation, and to give designers or inventors priority in the process. But this can be a misleading approach because 'Technologies are created not by lone inventors or geniuses working in a social vacuum, but by a combination of social forces and processes' (Mackay and Gillespie, 1992: 688; see also McMillan, and Flichy, in this volume). Bucciarelli explains that technology design is a fundamentally communicative process that brings objects, actions and social relationships together: 'design is best seen as a social process of negotiation and consensus, a consensus somewhat awkwardly expressed in the final product' (1994: 20–1).

Moreover, some observers argue that technology design continues in use (Suchman, 1987; Suchman and Jordan, 1997). 'Design and use mutually shape one another in iterative, social processes' (Brown and Duguid, 1994: 29). Technology design has been said to lie somewhere between a technology-driven, science-influenced 'one best solution' approach, and claims that design simply responds to human 'needs' or markets (Bucciarelli, 1994). For new media, the idea of design-in-use suggests that development encompasses both channels and content. As formerly distinct forms and genres of content based on particular media technologies (for example, feature films, personal letters, pop music albums, radio programmes, printed books) have converged into a single digital bit stream that can be retrieved via different types of terminal equipment (wireless phones, PDAs, satellite-based multichannel systems), artists, designers and consumers alike have devised new ways to create, manipulate and capture those content streams.[1]

New information and communication technologies may be designed and intended from the outset to fulfil particular needs or purposes. However, we need only consider the histories of the telephone (Fischer, 1992; Umble, 1992), radio (Aitken, 1985; Slotten, 1995), computing (Abbate, 1999; Ceruzzi, 1998; Edwards, 1996; MacKenzie, 1991) or the typewriter (David, 1985; Knie, 1992) to find that some are likely to have open and unanticipated uses or consequences, while others become firmly – perhaps prematurely – entrenched. Other apparently good inventions never succeed.

COMPARING DIFFUSION AND SST

Two seminal social science research perspectives have sought to capture the complexity of the relationship between society and technology, including media technology. *Diffusion of innovations* theory and the *social shaping of technology* perspective have enjoyed widespread influence in studies of technology and social change. Both SST and diffusion study the origins and uses of new technologies. Both address the evolution and rate of technological development. Though they differ in emphasis, both contextualize technology relative to human action, social relationships and culture. Both examine the choices people make about technologies and, to differing degrees, both are concerned with the consequences of technology adoption and use. They also focus on information flows and communication relationships that foster new ideas and ways of doing things.

SST and diffusion also share theoretical roots in nineteenth-century European social thought and the interactionist tradition associated with the Chicago School of sociology.[2] Along with its close relative, structural or network analysis, diffusion traces its foundations to the work of Georg Simmel. He conceptualized society as a fundamentally interactive and intersubjective 'web of affiliations' rather than a static, separate superstructure overshadowing human action (Emirbayer and Goodwin, 1994; Rogers, 1995; Rogers and Kincaid, 1981). Simmel's theories were a major influence among Chicago School sociologists in the 1920s and 1930s, particularly for Robert Park and Charles Cooley (Hamilton, 1996), who taught succeeding generations of social network researchers (for example, Fischer, 1982). Mitchell notes that the social network approach, given its focus on communication among network members and the meanings they attribute to their relationships, 'converges with that of the symbolic interactionists' (1975: 20, note 2). And Wellman (1988: 25) notes the 'Simmelian sensibility' that characterizes network or structural analysis, the premise that the structure of social relations determines the content of those relations, including norms and values.

In the SST tradition, too, scholars have been influenced by concepts and methods from Chicago School sociology. The social construction of technology perspective, discussed below, reflects many of the assumptions and empirical orientations of social interactionism and ethnomethodology. Simmel's 'pioneering sociology of consumption' (Holton, 1996: 45), which examined the effects of the emotional and aesthetic aspects of life on a society's popular culture, resonates with the SST emphasis on the 'consumption' or shaping of technology by its users (Mackay and Gillespie, 1992).

Despite these common influences and concerns, however, SST and diffusion have divergent histories, disciplinary roots, theoretical assumptions and methodologies. Their differences have given them windows with distinct views of technology and society.

Social Shaping of Technology

Several areas of theory and research coexist under the umbrella of social shaping of technology, but they all share a basic theoretical commitment: that technological determinism is an inadequate description or explanation of technological innovation and development, or of social change more generally (MacKenzie and Wacjman, 1999; Williams and Edge, 1996). Technological determinism has been a prominent theme in accounts of modernity and social progress; the idea is neatly captured in the motto of the 1933 Chicago World's Fair: 'Science Finds – Industry Applies – Man Conforms' (Rydell, 1993: 98–9). In contrast, SST emphasizes the importance of human choices and action in technological change, rather than seeing technology as politically and ethically neutral, an independent force with its own inevitable logic and motives, or as a mysterious black box that cannot be analysed socially. From the SST point of view, to talk about the 'impacts' of technology on society, as though technology is the hammer and society the nail, is to accept implicitly the basic premise of technological determinism.

In the 1960s several prominent critics began to question the prevailing assumption that technology drives social change (McDermott, 1969; Mumford, 1964; 1970). More recent critiques have also helped to discredit the deterministic view (for example, Winner, 1977; 1986). Despite nearly 30 years of SST research, however, deterministic assumptions and language continue to dominate popular culture in technologically advanced societies, to the distress of some observers (MacKenzie and Wacjman, 1999). Still, the critique of technological determinism has been a powerful influence in social science research about technology, and indeed in engineering. Many prestigious American engineering schools (including MIT, Georgia Tech, Virginia Tech, Cornell and the Rochester Polytechnic Institute), as well as prominent departments at Amsterdam, Delft, Paris, Sussex and Edinburgh, have courses and degree programmes in science, technology and society that incorporate the SST perspective.

SST takes a particular philosophical view of the nature of knowledge and its manifestations in society, specifically that knowledge and its products (including science and technology) are essentially social phenomena. The *sociology of scientific knowledge* or SSK has identified critical points of contingency in the process of scientific research when events (such as data collection, explanations, discoveries) could have gone differently, that is, when the people involved showed 'interpretive flexibility'. By conducting historical studies and ethnographic fieldwork, many sociologists of knowledge have concluded that scientists' own beliefs, opportunities and relationships are as important in the establishment of scientific facts or truths as the natural phenomena that they study (Knorr, 1981; Latour and Woolgar, 1986).

Despite the intense anxiety of some scientists who object to science and technological innovation themselves being treated as objects of study (Gross and Levitt, 1994), anti-determinist and constructivist researchers in SST do not seek to deny or undermine the benefits of science and technology. Rather, the stated aim of SST is to formulate policies to guide technology development so that its benefits are more 'human-centred', usable, equitable, appropriate and responsive to everyday culture and practice (Williams and Edge, 1996).

The *strong programme* of SSK has provoked some of the greatest worries among scientist critics of SST. The strong programme is often identified with historian and philosopher David Bloor and his colleagues at the University of Edinburgh (Bloor, 1991). He proposes that the creation and acceptance of *all* knowledge claims (including those of SSK) must be explained 'in social terms, rather than by reference to the natural world' (Williams and Edge, 1996: 869). Furthermore, its proponents say, this method should be applied equally both to knowledge that is considered factual and that which is considered biased, mistaken or fraudulent. The *weak programme* of SSK, on the other hand, examines only the social conditions of knowledge growth or the sources of biased or distorted knowledge, and not the 'rational acts of apprehending inferences and evidence' as facts, truths or errors (Bloor, 1992: 494).

Both the strong and weak programmes of SSK have influenced social studies of technology. Notably, the *social construction of technology* (SCOT) approach (Bijker et al., 1987; Bijker and Law, 1992; see also the chapter by Jackson, Poole and Kuhn, in this volume) has borrowed the idea of interpretive flexibility to examine the choices available to designers, developers and users in the course of technological development. Given their focus on the social context of innovation and change, SCOT analyses have much in common with the weak programme of SSK.

The SCOT framework has produced several research fronts. For example, studies of *large technical systems* (LTS) (Hughes, 1987; LaPorte, 1991; Mayntz and Hughes, 1988; Summerton, 1994) have applied SCOT principles to the analysis of extensive, complex technologies such as electrical power grids (Hughes, 1983), supercomputing (MacKenzie, 1991) and videotex and telephone systems (Galambos, 1988; Mayntz and Schneider, 1988; Schneider, 1991; 1994; 2000). Also, the growing field of *social informatics* (Kling, 1996; 1999) has combined a broad SCOT approach with methods from industrial and organizational sociology to study the evolution of information systems and computing (see Kling and Scacchi, 1982; Star, 1995; Star and Ruhleder, 1986; Suchman, 1996). Leigh Star has elaborated a particular aspect of interpretive flexibility to argue that a given technology, for example computers, may be understood and used very differently by different social groups. They become 'boundary objects' whose forms and uses are negotiated among groups (Star and Griesemer, 1989; see the chapter by Flichy in this volume).

By emphasizing the influence of society on technology, rather than the reverse, SST has attempted to understand the complex society–technology relationship. Researchers have tried to transcend 'one-way' or linear accounts of technology and society that imply that progress is irreversible. However, in recent years SST's adherents have recognized that while they might have reversed the direction of causality, the hypothesis that society shapes technology remains an essentially linear explanation (MacKenzie and Wacjman, 1999).

One of the most compelling bodies of SST research, *actor-network theory* or ANT (Callon, 1986; Latour, 1993; Law and Hassard, 1999), is grounded in SCOT but attempts to overcome the problem of linear causality. ANT rejects both strong technological determinism, on the one hand, and the strong social constructivist argument, on the other. Its proponents (including Bruno Latour, Michel Callon and their colleagues at the Centre de Sociologie de l'Innovation of the École Supérieure des Mines in Paris) consider people, technologies and institutions alike as 'actants' that have equal potential to influence technological development (Callon et al., 1986; Hughes, 1986). Neither technology 'push' nor market 'pull' can fully account for the shaping of technology, they argue; technologies and people alike should be thought of as inter-related nodes in constantly changing sociotechnical networks, which constitute the forms and uses of technology differently in different times and places for different groups. Furthermore, according to ANT, technologies are not infinitely flexible or negotiable; they tend to become embedded and stabilize within institutional and social structures and influence or even determine subsequent technological choices.

Diffusion of Innovations

As its name suggests, diffusion of innovations theory describes how new ideas or practices are introduced and adopted in a social system, with a special focus on the communication relations and information flows that promote adoption (Rogers, 1995). Diffusion is a specialization of communication research that combines theories of personal influence and persuasion with the analytical techniques and theories of social structural or network analysis in sociology (Blau, 1982; Wellman and Berkowitz, 1988). Diffusion of innovations is also a key construct in the economics of information and technology transfer (Antonelli, 1991a; 1991b; Dosi et al., 1988; Griliches, 1988). Though diffusion processes are studied in many social contexts and disciplines (Valente, 1995), the diffusion of new ICTs has been studied most extensively in sociology, communication research and economics. Sociological/communication studies tend to emphasize social relations and interaction in the diffusion process, while economic studies stress industry and market structures and economic motives for adoption, such as profitability.

Diffusion theory models the dynamics of technology adoption, including the rate of adoption and the eventual spread of the innovation in a social system. A new technology (or other innovation) is introduced in a social group (community, organization, nation, market, industry), often by a change agent with an interest in promoting it (private firm, public agency or influential individual). Typically, a few actors are the first or early adopters; the success of the innovation often depends on their social status or influence. Other members of the group, who are either directly acquainted with or share similar interests with the early adopters, may be persuaded to adopt the innovation, and they in turn influence others. Successive waves of adoption continue until the innovation reaches a saturation point or *ceiling* that varies depending on the characteristics of the innovation and the social system. Important concepts in diffusion include the adoption *threshold*, the number of adopters necessary to induce one more actor to adopt an innovation (Valente, 1995), and *critical mass*, the point at which enough actors have adopted an innovation for it to succeed, based on the rate or momentum of adoption (Allen, 1983; Mahler and Rogers, 1999; Markus, 1987; Rogers, 1995).

The sociological/communication and economic traditions of diffusion research frame technology somewhat differently. Sociology and communication have a long-standing interest in the development and use of technology in particular social contexts (Rogers, 1995). On the other hand, in neoclassical economics technology has usually been treated as an exogenous factor, like 'manna from heaven' in Christopher Freeman's phrase

(1991: 303; see also Antonelli, 1991; Dosi et al., 1988). Economists have tended to view technology as a 'black box' that could be an economic input or output, but not a component of the economy itself (Rosenberg, 1982).

However, difficulties arose with neoclassical analysis as economies shifted toward services and information technology in the 1960s and 1970s. Technologies were no longer ancillary to the 'real' productivity of the manufacturing and extractive sectors, but had become the very centrepiece of developed economies. Critics argued that mainstream economics could not meet the analytical challenge (see Lamberton in this volume). In the 1970s and 1980s, Freeman and his associates, influenced by the early work of Joseph Schumpeter, called for a new economic approach to understanding technological innovation and development (Dosi et al., 1988; Henten and Skouby in this volume). They argued that, analogously to the paradigm shifts in science described by Thomas Kuhn, societies may undergo shifts in *sociotechnical paradigms* that have profound economic consequences.

Economic and sociological/communication diffusion studies share a fundamental theoretical and analytic focus on network structures and dynamics. In sociological network analysis, this emphasis has been called the 'anti-categorical imperative' (Emirbayer and Goodwin, 1994). That is, network analysts, including diffusion researchers, assume that the relationships or links among social actors explain more about their actions than does the conventional procedure of classifying actors according to their individual traits or characteristics, and then predicting action based on that classification. Action, network scholars say, must be considered within the context of complex and changing social relations that are directly observable, and not as the result of individual values, motivations or other psychological states that are difficult or impossible to observe.

Network analysis and diffusion studies have a generally holistic, inclusive orientation. Wellman and Berkowitz (1988) argue that the network approach is consistent with a late-twentieth-century intellectual shift in the sciences and social sciences away from atomistic, reductionist and cumulative explanations, and toward explanations of complexity in which parts are defined by their interactions. Likewise, economists of information and technological change contend that by definition networks have a high degree of complementarity, compatibility and strong interdependence among network elements (people, innovations, firms, etc.).

Another key concept is *network externalities* (see also the chapter by Star and Bowker in this volume). Sometimes called a 'snowball effect' (Bodet et al., 1991: 310), the idea is that the value of a network to a given member increases with the size of the network. Katz and Shapiro (1986: 146) have pointed out that 'This effect has long been recognized in the context of communications networks such as the telephone and telex ... the more subscribers there are on a given communications network, the greater are the services provided by that network' (quoted in Antonelli, 1991: 18, note 15). Ironically, analysts say, early adopters of a technology receive less of a benefit than later adopters do; in fact to some extent they subsidize the benefits of later adopters.

A basic axiom of network analysis and diffusion is that 'Networks structure competitive and collaborative activities to secure scarce resources' (Wellman, 1988: 46). Large, stable networks (those with greater externalities, to use the economic term) tend to maintain the resource or value status quo, and can actually impede the introduction and diffusion of innovations and create barriers to entry of new ideas or techniques. Technological development, especially in telecommunications, tends to have 'high levels of lock-in effects' (Antonelli, 1991: 12). Antonelli argues that since network externalities can inhibit technological change, network economics must balance competition and cooperation, in contrast to the exclusive focus on markets and competition in neoclassical economics (see also Flichy in this volume).

Both sociological and economic diffusion research have been criticized, often for similar reasons. Critics charge that diffusion theory is technologically deterministic because it treats innovations as given and focuses more on the effects or impact of innovations in social systems. Rogers (1995) calls these diffusions 'pro-innovation bias'. The perceived pro-innovation bias has led critics to question the impartiality of diffusion research because it seems to ally the interests of researchers with those of change agents or technology proponents. In economic diffusion research, the determinist tendency arises in its treatment of technology as exogenous, though this has been modified somewhat by the growing emphasis on sociotechnical paradigms. Economists have also called for greater attention to the creation and development of the innovations themselves, along the lines of some SST studies (Dierkes and Hoffmann, 1992). However, most accounts of diffusion continue to depict the process as linear, for example by using the classic S-shaped diffusion curve to illustrate the rate of adoption or by describing technology use in terms of industry 'push' versus market 'pull'.

Diffusion is also criticized on the grounds that it assumes that technologies and other innovations are unitary, stable phenomena throughout the diffusion process. However, most sociologists, communication researchers and economists acknowledge that technological innovations are rarely singular inventions. Rather, they are constellations or 'clusters' of interrelated or complementary innovations (Perez and Soete, 1988; Freeman, 1991). Rice and Rogers (1980) have proposed that technologies are *reinvented* as they diffuse, creating a kind of punctuated equilibrium alternating between rapid growth and plateaus in the rate of diffusion, rather than a single S-curve. Koontz (1976) has characterized innovations as either tightly or loosely bound bundles of subinnovations. Tight bundles may diffuse more slowly, while loose bundles diffuse quickly because they allow users to adapt their components more flexibly. Freeman (1991) has distinguished between radical and incremental innovations, which produce different diffusion patterns. As Perez and Soete put it: 'There are plenty of reasons for expecting both the innovation and its surrounding economic environment to change as diffusion proceeds' (1988: 462). Freeman concurs: '"diffusion" is seldom if ever a simple process of replication by unimaginative imitators' (1991: 305).

To recap some of the main points about SST and diffusion, SST is based in constructivist epistemology and rejects technological determinism. Diffusion derives from theories of social influence and persuasion and asserts that networks of relationships and shared meaning shape social action, including the adoption of technology (Rogers and Kincaid, 1981). Both struggle to transcend linear models of causality, with varying success. Diffusion is frequently associated with institutions that sponsor innovations and promote technological development; SST emphasizes the consumption side and the everyday use of technology. Diffusion research analyses adoption patterns of successful and unsuccessful innovations to formulate models that allow the prediction of future trends. SST advocates intervention in the development of technologies before they are 'pushed' into society.

Two Cases: E-mail and Videotex

Two brief case studies are offered here to illustrate the similarities and differences between SST and diffusion. Electronic mail and videotex are 'telematic' technologies, that is, they merge data processing/computation with telecommunications systems. Originally, e-mail required an expensive and esoteric technical infrastructure and served a very small community of highly specialized scientists and engineers. Today, however, e-mail has been adopted widely throughout the world. Videotex, on the other hand, merged computerized information databases with widely available broadcast and telephone systems, and provided broad-based news and community information for general audiences. Nonetheless, it never really found a niche in American households or business, and was adopted very slowly elsewhere. Even in France, where it has been most successful, videotex use is now declining

and faces competition from similar services available through the Internet.

Electronic Mail

By most accounts electronic mail arose accidentally as a byproduct of the US Defense Advanced Research Projects Agency's ARPANET. The ARPANET project began in the late 1960s as a means to share data processing facilities at universities, military bases and other DARPA-funded research sites, via satellite and telecommunications networks. The system allowed researchers to move data files among sites and gave them access to remote computing facilities when local systems were unavailable or insufficient to handle a given job. The centrepiece of the system was the sabotage-resistant technique of packet switching, which divided files or data processing jobs into small chunks called packets. Packets were sent separately through any available network links, and reassembled into their original form at the destination computer. Packets could be moved through any open route among networked computers, even if some links or nodes in the network were damaged or unavailable. The ARPANET grew rapidly, from 11 nodes in 1970 to almost 90 in 1985; each node connected many computers to the network (Abbate, 1999; Ceruzzi, 1998; Jennings et al., 1986; Newell and Sproull, 1982).

Once the ARPANET was running in the 1970s, researchers at member sites quickly realized that they could use the system to exchange messages with colleagues at other sites as well as to exchange files or data processing jobs. E-mail 'emerged soon after the first few nodes were working' (Ceruzzi, 1998: 298). Specialized software was developed that performed most of the e-mail functions still used today, such as saving or responding to messages, or sending a message to a list of recipients. Soon, messaging overtook other uses, and computer scientists took note of what was perhaps the first 'killer app':

> The value of electronic mail came as a surprise to the developers of the ARPANET, who expected the network to be used principally for computer-to-computer communication for resource sharing but found instead that the dominant use was mail. (Newell and Sproull, 1982: 848)

> ARPANET was used less as a tool for sharing remote computational resources than it was for sharing information. The major lesson from the ARPANET experience is that information sharing is a key benefit of computer networking. (Jennings et al., 1986: 945)

However, network access was distributed unevenly from the outset; technical and administrative barriers slowed the spread of electronic mail for nearly

20 years. Given the esoteric nature of the research and the security constraints of defence projects, the designers of the ARPANET had always intended the system to link a relatively small, elite group of scientists and engineers. Therefore,

> ARPANET also had the negative effect of creating a have–have not situation in experimental computer research. Scientists and engineers carrying out such research at institutions other than the twenty or so ARPANET sites were at a clear disadvantage in accessing pertinent technical information and in attracting faculty and students. (1986: 945–6)

Other observers 'sensed a growing split in the community between those with ARPANET access and those without it' (Comer, 1983: 747–8), which included access to resources, facilities and scholarly interaction with colleagues at other institutions. To help alleviate the widening gaps, the National Science Foundation established NSFnet, which linked researchers at many US campuses to NSF supercomputer centres through the ARPANET (Comer, 1983; Jennings et al., 1986). A confederation of non-ARPANET computer science departments created CSNET in the early 1980s to connect with their colleagues at ARPANET sites (Comer, 1983).

As networked computing grew other barriers arose, particularly between scientists and engineers and other university-based scholars and researchers who recognized the potential benefits of high-speed asynchronous messaging for their own specialities, but did not have access to the network. 'In general, the existing ARPANET connections are in departments of computer science and electrical engineering and are not readily accessible by other researchers' (Jennings et al., 1986: 946). With the help of IBM, a consortium of non-ARPANET colleges and universities using IBM mainframes established BITNET (Because It's There Net) in 1981, with the first link between the City University of New York and Yale University (Abbate, 1999: 202; Ceruzzi, 1998). By 1985 BITNET connected about 600 computers in 175 institutions: 'It is not limited to specific academic disciplines, and may be used for any academic or administrative purposes' (Jennings et al., 1986: 947).

Abbate (1999) gives a detailed account of the transformation of the ARPANET into an NSF-supported 'backbone' that became the core of the Internet, and how separate networks like BITNET eventually were connected to the Internet. However, for a time interconnection between Internet and BITNET sites was often awkward; some scholars and researchers maintained both Internet and BITNET e-mail addresses to reach colleagues in different disciplines or institutions. There was also a persistent sense of a two-class system associated with BITNET, with Internet addresses (major government and research institutions with plenty of extramural funding) having more cachet than their BITNET counterparts. (Network address status distinctions resurfaced in the 1990s with the .edu, .org, .gov, .mil and .com domains of US Internet addresses, and continues in ICANN debates about the allocation of domain names.) Nonetheless, BITNET opened e-mail access to an unprecedented number of researchers and students, and established electronic mail, bulletin boards and discussion lists as a routine mode of communication throughout American academia.

At about the same time in the 1970s and 1980s, public data networks were being developed in Europe, Canada and the US for clients prohibited from using the non-profit research networks. These networks, such as Telenet in the US, were expensive; they conveyed files and data via dedicated transmission lines, much like a long-distance telephone call. Instead of the TCP/IP networking protocol used in the ARPANET, which connected many diverse computer networks, public data networks employed the X.25 protocol developed by national postal, telegraph and telephone ministries (PTTs) and adopted by the Consultative Committee on International Telegraphy and Telephony (CCITT) (Abbate, 1994). The framers of the X.25 protocol assumed that a uniform standard for computer networks would eventually emerge, such as the reliable, high-speed Ethernet local area network developed at XeroxPARC (Abbate, 1994; Ceruzzi, 1998).

Therefore another barrier was created, this time between the (mainly American) non-profit research- and university-based Internet on the one hand and (US and international) public data networks and private sector organizational 'intranets' on the other. This barrier endured until the late 1980s, when moves began to privatize the Internet and so open it to commercial and entertainment uses (Abbate, 1999). The distinction virtually disappeared in the mid 1990s, when the hypertext transfer protocol (HTTP) for the World Wide Web, combined with the client–server network configurations that had originally been designed for Xerox's Ethernet, effectively bridged the TCP/IP and X.25 standards (Abbate, 1994).

As networked computing and the use of electronic mail spread from high-level, DARPA-funded research sites to computer science and engineering more generally, then throughout academia, and finally to the private sector, e-mail and the Internet became increasingly taken for granted as communication media, with all the social expectations and difficulties of other media. For example, users found that the style of interaction among computer scientists and engineers was not always appropriate in other contexts. Early ARPANET users – often students, using UNIX-based research workstations – had created news or discussion groups in which members posted messages and expressed their opinions on a wide range of topics. Writing in 1982, two prominent computer scientists observed that electronic mail has come to be used in an informal way ... messages have the informality of speech, perhaps because the sender views the message as an alternative to a telephone call' (Newell and Sproull, 1982: 848). E-mail and bulletin board discussions often became heated and lengthy, in part because members would use aliases to avoid being identified as the source or target of an often brutal, *ad hominem* style of criticism called 'flaming'. Flaming and aliases were understood and accepted within the relatively small, closed world of computing research, but were foreign to newcomers from other disciplines.

As computer networks proliferated, the Internet shifted to the private sector, and e-mail attracted more diverse users, social scientists had more opportunities to study the uses of e-mail and other computer-mediated communication (CMC) technologies (Garton and Wellman, 1995; Rice, 1980; Steinfield, 1986). E-mail users began to develop and enforce consensual rules of 'netiquette'. They cultivated a more civil style of interaction to limit the rhetorical excesses of the engineers' 'flame wars'.

Today, it can be argued that e-mail development has entered a new phase of consolidation and control. E-mail users must often adapt their work and communication patterns to established systems, and are prohibited from modifying systems to suit their own needs. While the technology has been adopted widely in private sector work settings, managers routinely control e-mail content as well as access. E-mail records are routinely subpoenaed in US legal actions. The original 'acceptable use policy' imposed by DARPA and the NSF, which restricted uses of the ARPANET and Internet to non-profit research and teaching activities, has given way to a flurry of organizational use policies that can severely restrict what users may or may not say about their workplaces, corporate sponsors or other private firms, or even about the provider of the Internet service being used. Voluntary 'netiquette' has given way in many organizations to strictly enforced, top-down controls on expression and the surveillance of employee messages by management. A recent study by the UCLA Center for Communication Policy (2000) reported that in 2000, almost half of respondents to a survey said that their e-mail use was monitored by employers, and over half said that employers monitored what websites they visited. Today, e-mail is a routine, and perhaps the most routinely monitored and sanctioned, form of interpersonal communication in the US and elsewhere.

Videotex

Though unfamiliar to most Americans, videotex information systems are common in other parts of the world, including Canada, Japan, Europe and the UK. Videotex systems link users' television sets or a specially dedicated terminal (or in more current systems, their PCs) to computerized information databases via telephone or cable lines. (A similar system, teletext, provides the same type of information over the air as part of the television broadcast signal.) Subscribers use a keypad device, such as a specially modified remote control channel changer or keyboard, to call up 'pages' of information that are displayed on the television screen. Pages incorporate text and very simple graphics; content ranges from news, sports scores and weather reports to telephone directory information, want ads, rail and airline schedules, stock prices and gardening tips. Early systems connected subscribers to a single centralized database; later systems incorporated networked computers and distributed databases. In some ways videotex can be seen as a precursor to today's World Wide Web, where users call up web pages from any one of millions of databases on demand.[3]

The first videotex system, Prestel, was introduced in the UK in 1979 by a division of the British Post Office (now British Telecom). By the mid 1980s the Bundespost in the Federal Republic of Germany had started the Bildschirmtext system, based on Prestel technology; the Canadian government had launched its Telidon project; and in the UK Prestel was joined by the BBC's teletext service, Ceefax. The French Télétel service, based on a hybrid videotex/teletext platform called Antiope, was developed by the Direction Générale des Télécommunications section (DGT) of the French PTT ministry (now France Télécom). Télétel was distinctive because it displayed pages of text on small, specially designed terminals called minitels instead of television sets. The developers of all these systems envisioned them as 'information utilities' and anticipated rapid, widespread adoption in households and workplaces.

However, videotex got off to a slow start. In Britain, Prestel never grew as quickly as planners predicted. At its most extensive, the system attracted fewer than 100,000 subscribers; these numbers were soon surpassed by the BBC's Ceefax. The German Bildschirmtext system experienced similarly slow growth until Deutsche Telekom (the successor to the telecommunications branch of the state Bundespost) modified the system in the 1990s to be PC accessible via the Internet. Facing early consumer resistance, the operators of both Prestel and Bildschirmtext shifted their focus from households to business and professional users. In Canada, Telidon offered a technically superior system with better graphics, but the system never attracted enough subscribers to get past the trial stage.

In France, Télétel was the only real videotex success, owing partly to the free distribution of millions of minitel terminals to households and business telephone customers between 1983 and 1990 (Schneider, 2000). The French public was slow to adopt PCs in the 1980s, and minitels gave them access to basic French-language information and messaging services similar to those available in English over the Internet. Originally, the system provided only telephone directory assistance, but it was soon expanded to include personal messaging and bulletin-board-type services, for example 'erotic "conversation" groups' (Schneider, 2000: 320) called *messageries roses*. Students even used minitel messaging to organize nationwide protests in the 1980s. Since the mid 1990s, however, minitel use has declined as PC adoption and Internet use have grown in France.

In the US, videotex encountered even bigger problems during the 1980s. Information services similar to those offered on videotex systems were available online to subscribers with PCs and modems, including H&R Block's CompuServe, the Dow Jones Information Service, The Source from Reader's Digest, and later, IBM and Sears' Prodigy system and America Online (AOL). Several major media firms conducted videotex trials in selected US markets in the 1980s using Canadian, British and French technologies (Case, 1994; Mosco, 1982; Rogers, 1986). Knight-Ridder introduced the Viewtron system in Miami/Coral Gables, FL; the Times-Mirror Company built the Gateway system in Orange County, CA; IBM, Sears and CBS joined forces in the Trintex project; CBS and AT&T ran an experimental system in New Jersey; and Time/Life planned a trial as well. Besides these firms, a number of others were involved in the design and development of terminal equipment, information services and system infrastructures (Mosco, 1982).

Despite millions of dollars spent on the various American trials, however, sponsors soon abandoned videotex systems because they attracted so few subscribers. Though media companies were involved in many of the trials, critics charged that they were never really interested in developing services that would rival their existing operations in publishing, broadcasting or online services. The trials, it was alleged, were virtually designed to fail, offering general-interest content that was readily available elsewhere and charging high prices for terminal equipment and connection time. Because most trials were conducted in affluent suburban neighbourhoods, there were doubts about the general appeal of the services. By the late 1980s hopes for American videotex services delivered to television sets or dedicated terminals had faded, though several providers (including online newspapers) migrated their services to be available online via personal computers.

Most accounts of videotex history cite several reasons for its difficulties in the US and elsewhere.

First, videotex was a top-down phenomenon, depending more on industry and government push than on consumer pull. It tended to be most successful where state agencies and national telecommunications monopolies sponsored and built systems along the lines of other telecommunications services such as the telephone. In the late 1970s, national monopolies were searching for new uses for their rapidly expanding bandwidth, and state industrial policies promoted national champions (e.g. British Telecom, French Télécom, Deutsche Telekom) in international markets for telecommunications and computing equipment and services. Videotex systems were promising on both counts. It is notable, for example, that many American videotex trials employed foreign technologies. Though a consortium of US players developed the North American Presentation Level Protocol Syntax (NAPLPS) protocol in the early 1980s, AT&T lobbied the FCC to accept a modified version of Canadian Telidon technology as the US standard, while CBS advocated the French Antiope system. However, where no state or monopoly interest was willing to underwrite the startup and maintenance costs of such large distributed systems – as in the US – videotex stalled.

Others cite problems with the technology itself, particularly the cost, complexity and relatively unsophisticated display capabilities of specially adapted television sets or dedicated videotex terminals. In a sense, these platforms were 'closed' in that they did not give subscribers access to content or services beyond the provider's system. Videotex adapters could add hundreds of dollars to the price of a TV; keypad codes could be arcane and difficult to remember; and (with the exception of the Telidon system) page displays were often limited to a few lines of ragged text and crudely rendered graphics. As more users called up pages, the slower page retrievals became. And many systems that made large initial capital investments got 'locked in' to early technical standards and could not afford to upgrade later.

Furthermore, videotex was introduced in the US at about the same time as personal computers and modems, which provided access to similar rival information services like CompuServe. PCs and modems had the advantage of being a more 'open' platform: users could subscribe to whatever services they chose, and were not restricted to one provider or source of information. Furthermore, almost any computer screen could produce better graphics and more readable text than videotex, even before graphical user interfaces like the Macintosh desktop or its derivative, Windows, became common. Videotex-adapted television sets could hardly compete with PCs in terms of speed, flexibility and power. To some extent, then, videotex enjoyed greater popularity where markets for personal computing had not yet developed. Once PCs and the

Internet became widely available, existing videotex systems had to go online to survive, or be replaced by Internet-based services and eventually the World Wide Web.

Another reason for videotex's poor showing may be ideological (Case, 1994). Videotex evolved during a period dominated by expansive new visions and rhetoric heralding the emerging 'information society', in which information would be the new commodity and communication the new market. This faith in the new technologies may have created unrealistic or premature expectations among key players for videotex and similar services. Many believed that the new hybrid technological infrastructure, which combined computing and telecommunications (and gave rise to awkward neologisms like 'compunications' and *télématique*, or 'telematics' in English) would break down institutional and national boundaries, reduce or eliminate the costs of labour, materials and transportation, and deliver information and services to consumers instantly and transparently at a fraction of the previous cost. These new 'information utilities', including videotex, would create new markets in information and, indeed, in bandwidth itself (Dordick et al., 1981). Industries were particularly interested in the potential for transaction-based services such as home shopping, banking and financial transactions, electronic document delivery, and other on-demand, so-called 'interactive' services (Greenberger, 1985; Institute for the Future, 1970; Tydeman et al., 1982). Such transaction-based services promised new sources of profit for the private sector and a revival for stagnating national economies (Nora and Minc, 1981; Sigel, 1980).

With the benefit of hindsight it seems clear that while videotex delivered via television sets or dedicated terminals may have failed as a particular technological platform, the essentially commodified and transactional vision of telematics and information utilities lives on in recent market enthusiasms for e-commerce, electronic publishing, online trading and auctions, and 'end user information services' (Case, 1994). Still, information delivery and commercial transactions have never been as compelling to consumers as the opportunity for interpersonal interaction online. Many surveys show that people use the Internet far more frequently for electronic mail and related services like real-time messaging or chat rooms than for shopping, banking or document retrieval (for example, Nie and Erbring, 2000; Pew Internet and American Life Project, 2000). Indeed, 'new economy' analysts now routinely distinguish between 'content' uses of new media where every mouse click represents potential revenue (such as shopping; music, video or electronic book downloads; web browsing; travel booking), and 'community' uses (e-mail, chat, instant messaging) which tend to be less lucrative. The early vision of telematics, focused on information delivery and commercial transactions, was the primary influence on videotex design and implementation. But users seem to have expected more.

DETERMINATION AND CONTINGENCY

The preceding cases illustrate that the new media development process entails design and use, negotiation and consensus, engineering specifications and market demands, channels and content, the material and the social. More generally, these dualities can be recast as a dynamic relationship between determination and contingency. *Determination* is the effort to specify conditions or 'impose coherence' in a situation with the intent of achieving some desired outcome (Schön, 1988; 1990). *Contingency* is the existence of many possible conditions in an uncertain situation. Complete certainty is never fully achieved, so in a sense there is no final design 'solution' for a given technological problem.[4] Rather, designers contend with contingency by making choices from among existing conditions or by creating new ones. In turn, these choices create new conditions and uncertainties that prompt further specifications or choices, and so on. Technology design and development can therefore be relatively 'loose' or 'tight' depending on the prevailing tendency at any given point toward contingency or determination, respectively.

Diffusion and SST can be thought of as having differing profiles in terms of the determination/contingency framework. For example, diffusion might be said to tend more toward determination *vis-à-vis* the origin of technologies, the actors involved, and dynamics and distributive mechanisms, though it leans more toward contingency regarding choice and consequences. SST, on the other hand, seems to align more with contingency on almost all counts, though some scholars (especially actor-network theorists) also recognize that technological change often leads to closure and irreversibility when innovations are widely adopted. Interestingly, frameworks like actor-network theory and sociotechnical paradigms could both be placed near the middle in terms of determination and contingency. They both emphasize the networked interrelationships among individuals, technologies and institutions, and the barriers to innovation brought about by technological 'embeddedness', standardization, network externalities, or prevailing technological regimes ('paradigms').

Moments of Technology Development

Furthermore, the e-mail and videotex cases suggest that determination and contingency are played out at several critical points or 'moments' in development.

Table 11.1 *Determination versus contingency in moments of new media development*

Moments	Determination ⟷	Contingency
Origin	Institutional sources of innovation Innovation pre-defined by R&D process	Innovation is open, reflexive
Actors	A few controlling interests Human or organizational actors	Many players, no single interest Institutions, technologies and people can all act, have influence

Dynamics	Slow, stable, organized, linear
	Dominant groups create barriers
	  to entry
	Externalities, irreversibility
		Rapid, volatile, reversible, disorganized
		  or self-organizing systems

Choice	Few choices	Many choices
Formal properties	Established styles, forms, genres Existing forms constrain new ones	Experimental, recombinant, temporary forms

Distributive
  mechanisms
	Centralized, restricted access,
	  few channels
		Decentralized, open access,
		  multiple channels

Consequences	Closure, stability, standardization,
	  barriers to entry, monopoly
		Lack of standards, 'churn',
		  proliferating forms and uses,
		  competition

Moments in this context are not specific points in time, but rather notable or conspicuous elements having the potential to move development in one direction or another. They do not necessarily follow in the linear order that the following list suggests; moments can and frequently do overlap or relate in other ways. Table 11.1 gives examples of how the moments can vary depending on the prevailing tendency toward determination or contingency.

Origin

In the first moment of the development process new ideas are generated and tried out. Origins may be responses to specific problems or situations, or may arise more spontaneously, when an idea is proposed just because it is possible or interesting. Origin is principally a creative moment; it can be intensely active or may take the form of a simple conceptualization. Origins may involve whole teams of people sharing and negotiating ideas, or individuals trying to solve problems in a new way. In the economics of technology, Schumpeter distinguishes between 'invention' and 'innovation' (Freeman, 1991): invention corresponds to the generation of a new concept, while innovation involves its communication or transfer beyond the originator(s).

Actors

The second moment is the *actors* involved in new media development. Actors include anyone who makes choices that affect the subsequent uses or forms of the technology, including professionally trained specialists. Sonnenwald (1993) argues that there are many types of actors involved in design, each with different (sometimes conflicting) interests, requirements and expectations.

Dynamics

The third moment is complex and extends throughout the development process. Dynamics involves the movement and momentum of a new technological idea, its expression, and its adoption and use. Development dynamics may be volatile or stable, fast or slow, may move ahead easily or be impeded or encounter resistance, or even be reversed. Technologies may become standardized (that is, undergo closure), or standards may break down. Dynamics is illustrated by the concept of critical mass in diffusion theory, technological trajectories in the economics of technological change (Dosi, 1982; Nelson and Winter, 1977; 1982), and momentum in SST (Hughes, 1987).

Choice

The fourth moment is closely related to dynamics, and also operates more or less constantly throughout the development process. Contingency is characterized by a wide variety of choices, while determination forecloses or limits choice. More 'durable' technologies constrain subsequent choices (Latour, 1991).

Formal Properties

Expressions or physical forms of a technology emerge as it develops. Form may be influenced by ergonomic or aesthetic considerations or by the usability of the technology. In diffusion theory, the formal properties of an innovation make it observable by potential adopters. Style or production values can be important aspects of form.

Distributive Mechanisms

The sixth moment involves the means by which new ideas, things or practices spread. Distributive mechanisms include interpersonal networks, existing media technologies, markets, and organizational or institutional structures. Fairness or equity of distribution is an important consideration (for example, as governed by universal service regulations for telephone service). Distribution is often highly politicized because different actors may have relatively more or less power to influence or benefit from distribution. Access to technology is one outcome of particular patterns of distribution.

Consequences

The final moment involves the effects, 'impacts' or other outcomes of a technology, whether intended or unanticipated. Consequences may emerge early in the development process and 'feed forward' to affect later phases, or may not become apparent until the technology is widespread. Consequences affect subsequent development; for example, a successful technology is likely to generate a whole group of imitators or similar works (perhaps creating a genre with particular formal properties). An unsuccessful technology may discourage further experimentation or creative uses of related ideas.

Determination and Contingency in E-mail and Videotex

In retrospect, though e-mail succeeded and the original videotex platform did not, both demonstrate the interrelationship between determination and contingency in the moments of media development. Videotex seems to have been the more determined technology, especially at the outset. Fewer actors were involved, typically in alliances between PTTs and national monopolies, or among corporate media firms. Technical standards were established early, which had the effect of locking in relatively unsophisticated graphics and interfaces, at least in some systems. The first operators had clearly defined markets in mind, though their subscription projections were generally overoptimistic. Consumer resistance slowed the initial momentum of videotex development; operators tried to rekindle interest by reorienting the services from household to business customers, but this strategy was not much more successful. In France, videotex was more flexible, offering messaging and chat as well as information services, and the state/PTT alliance made much larger initial investments and subsidized the service heavily for nearly a decade. The system was inexpensive for consumers and the number of subscribers grew steadily. But as more information services went online and more households and businesses adopted PCs and modems, videotex lost much of its appeal in France, as it had elsewhere.

E-mail also began as a highly constrained system. The underlying ARPANET infrastructure, including packet switching, was institutionally commissioned, paid for and controlled by ARPA. As with videotex, very few actors were involved at the outset and access to the system was strictly limited, but unlike the sponsors of videotex ARPA provided little institutional 'push' that would move the technology beyond its original base in federally funded computer science research.

In fact, e-mail itself – an unanticipated use of the system that demonstrated users' 'interpretive flexibility' – shifted the dynamic of networked computing toward proliferation and contingency. The ARPANET was transformed by 'user activism' that began with electronic mail (Abbate, 1999: 90). E-mail opened up collaborative possibilities far beyond the file sharing and distributed data processing originally envisioned by ARPA project directors. Perhaps unwittingly, computer scientists with ARPANET access played the role of 'early adopters' in the diffusion sense, modelling the benefits of e-mail for colleagues in computer science and eventually throughout academia. E-mail had immediate intuitive appeal; user 'pull' rather than industry push helped accelerate the trend toward networked computing and 'internetworking' among major institutions. Eventually the same model was reproduced all the way to the desktop with the Internet, PCs, modems and local area networks.

Certainly, technical and administrative barriers to networking and e-mail arose at each step in its development and diffusion. It took about 25 years for e-mail to move from DARPA researchers, to computer science at large, to other disciplines in major research universities and large corporate organizations, to smaller universities and colleges, and finally to most American businesses and households. But along the way, networked computing as a medium, including e-mail, transformed expectations about interpersonal communication, written discourse, privacy, workplace life, organizational forms and hierarchies, as well as the access to information and entertainment that videotex was supposed to provide. Today, e-mail is virtually ubiquitous in education, business and government in developed nations, and use is rising around the world.

From an SST perspective, we might say that videotex developers misunderstood potential users and their everyday needs for information. Systems were complex and expensive, and offered information and services that could readily be obtained elsewhere. System sponsors seemed to have a deterministic, 'build it and they will come' faith that the availability of the technology itself would compel subscribers to change their information seeking habits – and pay for the privilege. There was little opportunity for subscribers to modify or adapt the system for their own purposes, except in France, where impromptu bulletin boards and chat groups developed. The transaction-based platform precluded real interpersonal interaction in most systems. For e-mail, on the other hand, the developers themselves were the original users, and had some latitude to design the system according to their needs and preferences. The system was also 'free' to most individual users in the early stages, in the sense that it was subsidized by large research grants, and later underwritten by the research universities, government and private firms. (Users would later assume more of the costs of connect time, software and hardware.) A system originally intended for file sharing and distributed data processing (transactions) was adapted to permit interpersonal communication. In the process it became, and still is, the 'killer app' of networked computing.

From the diffusion perspective, the roles of system designers and innovators, the influence of opinion leaders on later adopters, the social ties and persuasive interactions among system users, the presence or absence of critical mass, adaptation or reinvention, and the network effects or externalities of system growth are all clear in both cases. The diffusion curve of most videotex systems never achieved critical mass or 'takeoff', while the curve for e-mail has something of a punctuated equilibrium shape, with alternating phases of growth and stability. Videotex was a relatively stable innovation, while e-mail's features evolved as new groups of users adopted it. For example, the simple text format of e-mail messages remained more or less unchanged until business users added features like document attachments and links to calendars and spreadsheets and a friendlier graphical interface.

Conclusion

To conclude, in this chapter I have attempted to provide a general conceptual overview of the development of new media technologies. It is a complex, multilayered process that involves many different groups and their interests, but one way to understand it is to consider shifts between determination and contingency at different moments or steps in the development process. I have focused on two important perspectives on technology and social change that have been widely influential in new media research, to show how they incorporate determination and contingency in their analyses. Diffusion of innovations and social shaping of technology have different disciplinary and philosophical foundations and different orientations toward technology and action. Yet both provide useful tools for observing and describing the technology development process.

I reviewed the development of two media technologies, videotex and electronic mail, to identify instances of determination and contingency in each case. I also briefly compared the two technologies from the viewpoints of diffusion and SST, to demonstrate how the two perspectives might analyse them differently while still incorporating moments of determination and contingency. The cases presented here are necessarily brief; more extensive historical analysis might reveal important details or themes that have been overlooked here. Similarly, the descriptions of diffusion theory and SST would benefit from a more comprehensive literature review highlighting significant theoretical refinements and empirical studies. Readers are encouraged to review the main works cited here for additional background.

However, despite this limited treatment the determination–contingency framework, organized around the moments of technology development, may offer a means for future studies to compare and triangulate theoretical approaches as well as the media technologies themselves.

Notes

I would like to acknowledge the research and editorial assistance of Marjorie Rauen with this chapter. Pablo Boczkowski also provided invaluable comments and suggestions, particularly regarding the section on videotex.

1 With worrisome consequences for content regulation and intellectual property rights, as Verhulst points out in the present volume.

2 I thank Don Case for this insight.

3 For more background about the development and history of videotex, see Case (1994), Mayntz and Schneider (1988), Mosco (1982), Rogers (1986), Schneider (2000), Schneider et al. (1991), and Tydeman et al. (1982). This section draws primarily from these works. Also, see Boczkowski (2001) and his chapter in the present volume.

4 Though as Latour (1993; 1996) emphasizes, some solutions – we might think of books or broadcast television – may become so durable that they powerfully constrain any subsequent developments

References

Abbate, J. (1994) 'The Internet challenge: conflict and compromise in computer networking', in J. Summerton (ed.), *Changing Large Technical Systems*. Boulder, CO: Westview. pp. 193–210.

Abbate, J. (1999) *Inventing the Internet*. Cambridge, MA: MIT Press.

Aitken, H.G.J. (1985) *The Continuous Wave: Technology and American Radio, 1900–1932*. Princeton, NJ: Princeton University Press.

Allen, D. (1983) 'New telecommunications services: network externalities and critical mass', *Telecommunications Policy*, 12 (3): 257–71.

Antonelli, C. (1991a) 'The economic theory of information networks', in C. Antonelli (ed.), *The Economics of Information Networks*. Amsterdam: North-Holland. pp. 5–27.

Antonelli, C. (ed.) (1991b) *The Economics of Information Networks*. Amsterdam: North-Holland.

Bijker, W.E. (1995) *Of Bicycles, Bakelites and Bulbs: toward a Theory of Sociotechnical Change*. Cambridge, MA: MIT Press.

Bijker, W.E. and Law, J. (eds) (1992) *Shaping Technology/Building Society: Studies in Sociotechnical Change*. Cambridge, MA: MIT Press.

Bijker, W.E., Hughes, T.P. and Pinch, T. (1987) *The Social Construction of Technological Systems*. Cambridge, MA: MIT Press.

Blau, P. (1982) 'Structural sociology and network analysis: an overview', in P.V. Marsden and N. Lin (eds), *Social Structure and Network Analysis*. Beverly Hills, CA: Sage. pp. 273–9.

Bloor, D. (1991) *Knowledge and Social Imagery*, 2nd edn. Chicago, IL: University of Chicago Press.

Bloor, D. (1992) 'Strong programme', in J. Dancy and E. Sosa (eds), *A Companion to Epistemology*, London: Blackwell. p. 494.

Boczkowski, P.J. (1999) 'Mutual shaping of users and technologies in a national virtual community', *Journal of Communication*, 49 (2): 86–108.

Boczkowski, P.J. (2001) 'Affording flexibility: transforming information practices in online newspapers'. Unpublished doctoral dissertation, Cornell University, Ithaca, NY.

Bodet, C., Joram, D. and Lamarche, T. (1991) 'Savoir-faire and telecommunication market structure: cooperation, domination and competition', in C. Antonelli (ed), *The Economics of Information Networks*. Amsterdam: North-Holland. pp. 301–24.

Brown, J.S. and Duguid, P. (1994) 'Borderline issues: social and material aspects of design', *Human–Computer Interaction*, 9: 3–36.

Bucciarelli, L.L. (1994) *Designing Engineers*. Cambridge, MA: MIT Press.

Callon, M. (1986) 'The sociology of an actor-network: the case of the electric vehicle', in M. Callon, J. Law and A. Rip (eds), *Mapping the Dynamics of Science and Technology: Sociology of Science in the Real World*. London: Macmillan. pp. 19–34.

Callon, M., Law, J. and Rip, A. (eds) (1986) *Mapping the Dynamics of Science and Technology: Sociology of Science in the Real World*. London: Macmillan.

Case, D.O. (1994) 'The social shaping of videotex: how information services for the public have evolved', *Journal of the American Society for Information Science*, 45 (7): 483–97.

Ceruzzi, P.E. (1998) *A History of Modern Computing*. Cambridge, MA: MIT Press.

Comer, D. (1983) 'The computer science research network CSNET: a history and status report', *Communications of the ACM*, 26 (10): 747–53

David, P.A. (1985) 'Clio and the economics of QWERTY', *American Economic Review*, 75 (2): 332–7.

Dierkes, M. and Hoffmann, U. (eds) (1992) *New Technology at the Outset: Social Forces in the Shaping of Technological Innovations*. Frankfurt and New York: Campus.

Dordick, H., Bradley, H. and Nanus, B. (1981) *The Emerging Network Marketplace*. Norwood, NJ: Ablex.

Dosi, G. (1982) 'Technical paradigms and technological trajectories: a suggested interpretation of the determinants and directions of technological change', *Research Policy*, 11: 147.

Dosi, G., Freeman, C., Nelson, R., Silverberg, G. and Soete, L. (eds) (1988) *Technical Change and Economic Theory*. London: Pinter.

Edwards, P.N. (1996) *The Closed World: Computers and the Politics of Discourse in Cold War America*. Cambridge, MA: MIT Press.

Emirbayer, M. and Goodwin, J. (1994) 'Network analysis, culture and the problem of agency', *American Journal of Sociology*, 99 (6): 1411–54.

Fischer, C.S. (1982) *To Dwell Among Friends: Personal Networks in Town and City*. Chicago and London: University of Chicago Press.

Fischer, C.S. (1992) *America Calling: a Social History of the Telephone to 1940*. Berkeley, CA: University of California Press.

Freeman, C. (1991) 'The nature of innovation and the evolution of the productive system', in *Technology and Productivity: the Challenge for Economic Policy*. Proceedings of a conference sponsored by the Technology/Economy Programme, OECD. Paris: Organization for Economic Cooperation and Development. pp. 303–14.

Galambos, L. (1988) 'Looking for the boundaries of technological determinism: a brief history of the US telephone system', in R. Mayntz and T.P. Hughes (eds), *The Development of Large Technical Systems*. Frankfurt and Boulder, CO: Campus and Westview. pp. 135–53.

Garton, L. and Wellman, B. (1995) 'Social impacts of electronic mail in organizations: a review of the research literature', in B.R. Burleson (ed.), *Communication Yearbook 18*. Thousand Oaks, CA: Sage. pp. 434–53.

Greenberger, M. (ed.) (1985). *Electronic Publishing Plus*. White Plains, NY: Knowledge Industry.

Griliches, Z. (1988) *Technology, Education and Productivity*. New York: Basil Blackwell.

Gross, P.R. and Levitt, N. (1994) *Higher Superstition: the Academic Left and its Quarrels with Science*. Baltimore, MD: Johns Hopkins University Press.

Hamilton, P. (1996) 'Systems theory', in B.S. Turner (ed.), *The Blackwell Companion to Social Theory*. London: Blackwell. pp. 143–70.

Holton, R.J. (1996) 'Classical social theory', in B.S. Turner (ed.), *The Blackwell Companion to Social Theory*. London: Blackwell. pp. 25–52.

Hughes, T.P. (1983) *Networks of Power: Electrification in Western Society, 1880–1930*. Baltimore, MD: Johns Hopkins University Press.

Hughes, T.P. (1986) 'The seamless web: technology science, etcetera, etcetera', *Social Studies of Science*, 16: 281–92.

Hughes, T.P. (1987) 'The evolution of large technical systems', in W.E. Bijker, T.P. Hughes and T. Pinch (eds), *The Social Construction of Technological Systems*. Cambridge, MA: MIT Press. pp. 51–82.

Institute for the Future (1970) *Potential Demand for Two-Way Information Services to the Home 1970–1990*. Menlo Park, CA: Institute for the Future.

Jennings, D.M., Landweber, L.H., Fuchs, I.H., Farber, D.J. and Adrion, W.R. (1986) 'Computer networking for scientists', *Science*, 231 (28 February): 943–50.

Katz, M.L. and Shapiro, C. (1986) 'Product compatibility choice in a market with technological progress', *Oxford Economic Papers*, November (supplement): 146–65.

Kling, R. (ed.) (1996) *Computerization and Controversy: Value Conflicts and Social Choices*, 2nd edn. San Diego, CA: Academic.

Kling, R. (1999) 'What is social informatics and why does it matter?', *D-Lib Magazine*, 5(1). URL (consulted 7 August 2000): http://www.dlib-org:80/dlib/january99/kling/01kling.html.

Kling, R. and Scacchi, W. (1982) 'The web of computing: computer technology as social organization', *Advances in Computers*, 21: 1–90.

Knie, A. (1992) Yesterday's decisions determine tomorrow's options: the case of the mechanical typewriter', in M. Dierkes and U. Hoffmann (eds), *New Technology at the Outset: Social Forces in the Shaping of Technological Innovations*. Frankfurt and New York: Campus. pp. 161–72.

Knorr, K. (1981) *The Manufacture of Knowledge: an Essay on the Constructivist and Contextual Nature of Science*. Oxford: Pergamon.

Koontz, V. (1976) 'Determinants of individuals' knowledge, attitudes and decisions regarding a health innovation in Maine'. Unpublished doctoral dissertation, University of Michigan, Ann Arbor, MI.

LaPorte, T.R. (ed.) (1991) *Social Responses to Large Technical Systems: Control or Anticipation*. Dordrecht and Boston: Kluwer.

Latour, B. (1991) 'Technology is society made durable', in J. Law (ed.), *A Sociology of Monsters: Essays on Power, Technology and Domination*. London: Routledge. pp. 103–31.

Latour, B. (1993) *We Have Never Been Modern*. New York: Harvester Wheatsheaf.

Latour, B. (1996) *Aramis, or the Love of Technology*. Cambridge, MA: Harvard University Press.

Latour, B. and Woolgar, S. (1986) *Laboratory Life: the Construction of Scientific Facts*, 2nd edn. Princeton, NJ: Princeton University Press.

Law, J. and Hassard, J. (eds) (1999) *Actor-Network Theory and After*. Oxford: Blackwell.

Mackay, H. and Gillespie, G. (1992) 'Extending the social shaping of technology approach: ideology and appropriation', *Social Studies of Science*, 22: 685–716.

MacKenzie, D. (1991) 'Notes toward a sociology of supercomputing', in T.R. LaPorte (ed.), *Social Responses to Large Technical Systems*. Dordrecht: Kluwer. pp. 159–75.

MacKenzie, D. and Wajcman, J. (eds) (1999) *The Social Shaping of Technology*, 2nd edn. Philadelphia, PA and London: Open University Press and Taylor & Francis.

Mahler, A. and Rogers, E.M. (1999) 'The diffusion of interactive communication innovations and the critical mass: the adoption of telecommunications services by German banks', *Telecommunications Policy*, 23 (10–11): 719–40.

Markus, M.L. (1987) 'Toward a "critical mass" theory of interactive media: universal access, interdependence and diffusion', *Communication Research*, 14: 491–511.

Mayntz, R. and Hughes, T.P. (eds) (1988) *The Development of Large Technical Systems*. Boulder, CO: Westview.

Mayntz, R. and Schneider, V. (1988) 'The dynamics of system development in a comparative perspective: interactive videotex in Germany, France and Britain', in R. Mayntz and T.P. Hughes (eds), *The Development of Large Technical Systems*. Boulder, CO: Westview Press. pp. 263–98.

McDermott, J. (1969) 'Technology: the opiate of the masses', *New York Review of Books*, 31 July.

Mitchell, J.C. (1975) 'The concept and use of social networks' (1969), in J.C. Mitchell (ed.), *Social Networks in Urban Situations: Analyses of Personal Relationships in Central African Towns*. Manchester: Manchester University Press, for the Institute for African Studies, University of Zambia. pp. 1–50.

Mosco, V. (1982) *Pushbutton Fantasies: Critical Perspectives on Videotex and Information Technology*. Norwood, NJ: Ablex.

Mumford, L. (1964) *The Myth of the Machine*. Vol. 1: *Technics and Human Development*. New York: Harcourt Brace Jovanovich.

Mumford, L. (1970) *The Myth of the Machine*. Vol. 2: *The Pentagon of Power*. New York: Harcourt Brace Jovanovich.

Nelson, R. and Winter, S. (1977) 'In search of a useful theory of innovation', *Research Policy*, 6 (1): 36–75.

Nelson, R. and Winter, S. (1982) *An Evolutionary Theory of Economic Change*. Cambridge, MA: Harvard University Press.

Newell, A. and Sproull, R.F. (1982) 'Computer networks: Prospects for scientists', *Science*, 215 (12 February): 843–52.

Nie, N.H. and Erbring, L. (2000) *Internet and Society: a Preliminary Report*. Stanford, CA: Stanford Institute for the Quantitative Study of Society, Stanford University. URL (consulted March 2001): http://www.stanford.edu/group/siqss/.

Nora, S. and Minc, A. (1981) *The Computerization of Society*. Cambridge, MA: MIT Press.

Perez, C. and Soete, L. (1988) 'Catching up in technology: entry barriers and windows of opportunity', in G. Dosi, C. Freeman, R. Nelson, G. Silverberg and L. Soete (eds), *Technical Change and Economic Theory*. London and New York: Pinter. pp. 458–79.

Pew Internet and American Life Project (2000) *Tracking Online Life: How Women Use the Internet to Cultivate Relationships with Family and Friends*. Washington, DC: Pew Internet and American Life Project. URL (consulted March 2001): http://www.pewinternet.org.

Rammert, W. (1992) 'Research on the generation and development of technology: the state of the art in Germany', in M. Dierkes and U. Hoffmann (eds), *New Technology at the Outset: Social Forces in the Shaping of Technological Innovations*. Frankfurt and New York: Campus. pp. 62–89.

Rice, R.E. (1980) 'The impacts of computer-mediated organizational and interpersonal communication', *Annual Review of Information Science and Technology*, 15: 221–49.

Rice, R.E. and Rogers, E.M. (1980) 'Reinvention in the innovation process', *Knowledge: Creation, Diffusion, Utilization*, 1(4): 499–514.

Rogers, E.M. (1986) *Communication Technology: the New Media in Society*. New York: Free Press.

Rogers, E.M. (1995) *Diffusion of Innovations*, 4th edn. New York: Free Press.

Rogers, E.M. and Kincaid, D.L. (1981) *Communication Networks: toward a New Paradigm for Research*. New York: Free Press.

Rosenberg, N. (1982) *Inside the Black Box: Technology and Economics*. New York and Cambridge: Cambridge University Press.

Rydell, R.W. (1993) *World of Fairs*. Chicago, IL: University of Chicago Press.

Schneider, V. (1991) 'The governance of large technical systems: the case of telecommunications', in T.R. LaPorte (ed.), *Responding to Large Technical Systems: Control or Anticipation*. Dordrecht and Boston: Kluwer. pp. 19–42.

Schneider, V. (1994) 'Multinationals in transition: global technical integration and the role of corporate telecommunication networks', in J. Summerton (ed.), *Changing Large Technical Systems*. Boulder, CO: Westview. pp. 71–91.

Schneider, V. (2000) 'Evolution in cyberspace: the adaptation of national videotext systems to the Internet', *The Information Society*, 16 (4): 319–28.

Schneider, V., Charon, T., Graham, J.M., Miles, I. and Vedel, T. (1991) 'The dynamics of videotex development in Britain, France and Germany: a cross-national comparison', *European Journal of Communication*, 6: 187–212.

Schön, D.A. (1988) 'Designing: rules, types and worlds', *Design Studies*, 9 (3): 181–90.

Schön, D.A. (1990) 'The design process', in V.A. Howard (ed.), *Varieties of Thinking: Essays from Harvard's Philosophy of Education Research Center*. New York: Routledge. pp. 110–41.

Sigel, E. (ed.) (1980) *Videotext: the Coming Revolution in Home/Office Information Retrieval*. White Plains, NY: Knowledge Industry.

Slotten, H.R. (1995) 'Radio engineers, the Federal Radio Commission, and the social shaping of broadcast technology: creating "Radio Paradise"', *Technology and Culture*, 36 (4): 950–86.

Sonnenwald, D.H. (1993) 'Communication in design', Unpublished PhD dissertation, Rutgers University, New Brunswick, NJ.

Star, S.L. (ed.) (1995) *The Cultures of Computing*. Oxford: Blackwell.

Star, S.L. and Griesemer, J.R. (1989) 'Institutional ecology, translations and boundary objects: amateurs and professionals in Berkeley's Museum of Vertebrate Zoology, 1907–1939', *Social Studies of Science*, 19: 387–420.

Star, S.L. and Ruhleder, K. (1996) 'Steps towards an ecology of infrastructure: design and access for large information spaces', *Information Systems Research*, 7 (1): 111–34.

Steinfield, C. (1986) 'Computer-mediated communication systems', *Annual Review of Information Science and Technology*, 21: 167–202.

Suchman, L. (1987) *Plans and Situated Actions: the Problem of Machine–Human Communication*. Cambridge: Cambridge University Press.

Suchman, L. (1996) 'Supporting articulation work', in R. Kling (ed.), *Computerization and Controversy: Value Conflicts and Social Choices*, 2nd edn. San Diego, CA: Academic. pp. 407–23.

Suchman, L. and Jordan, B. (1997) 'Computerization and women's knowledge', in P.E. Agre and D. Schuler (eds), *Reinventing Technology, Rediscovering Community*. Greenwich, CT: Ablex. pp. 97–105.

Summerton, J. (1994) *Changing Large Technical Systems*. Boulder, CO: Westview.

Tydeman, J., Lipinski, H., Adler, R., Nyhan, M. and Zwimpfer, L. (1982) *Teletext and Videotex in the United States: Market Potential, Technology, Policy Issues*. New York: McGraw-Hill.

UCLA Center for Communication Policy (2000) *The UCLA Internet Report: Surveying the Digital Future*. Los Angeles, CA: UCLA Center for Communication Policy. URL (consulted March 2001): http://www.ccp.ucla.edu.

Umble, D.Z. (1992) 'The Amish and the telephone: resistance and reconstruction', in R. Silverstone and E. Hirsch (eds), *Consuming Technologies: Media and Information in Domestic Spaces*. London: Routledge. pp. 183–94.

Valente, T. (1995) *Network Models of the Diffusion of Innovations*. Cresskill, NJ: Hampton.

Wellman, B. (1988) 'Structural analysis: from method and metaphor to theory and substance', in B. Wellman and S.D. Berkowitz (eds), *Social Structures: a Network*

Approach. Cambridge: Cambridge University Press. pp. 19–61.

Wellman, B. and Berkowitz, S.D. (1988) 'Introduction: studying social structures', in B. Wellman and S.D. Berkowitz (eds), *Social Structures: a Network Approach*. Cambridge: Cambridge University Press. pp. 1–13.

Williams, R. and Edge, D. (1996) 'The social shaping of technology', *Research Policy*, 25: 865–99.

Winner, L. (1977) *Autonomous Technology: Technics-out-of-Control as a Theme in Political Thought*. Cambridge, MA: MIT Press.

Winner, L. (1986) 'Do artifacts have politics?', *in The Whale and the Reactor: a Search for Limits in an Age of High Technology*. Chicago, IL: University of Chicago Press. pp. 19–39.

PART THREE: NEW MEDIA AND ORGANIZING

Introduction

NOSHIR S. CONTRACTOR

As we enter the twenty-first century, new media are fundamentally challenging conventional wisdom about organizations and organizing. However, well before the term 'new media' first gained currency almost three decades ago, scholars have been interested in questions concerning the relationship between emerging communication technologies and contemporary forms of organizing. At the turn of the twentieth century, the inventions of telephony, telegraphy and electro-mechanical typesetting (Beniger, 1986; Yates, 1989) played a key role in supporting the dominant organizational forms that sustained the industrial revolution: bureaucracy (Weber, 1947; 1978) and its elaboration, the multi-divisional form (Chandler, 1977). These organizational forms relied heavily on the new media of the time to facilitate the flow of information up the hierarchy as well as the downward flow of orders.

Today, recent inventions, spawned by the conversion and convergence of all media into the common currency of digital bits and bytes, are once again accompanied by a discourse about fundamentally new forms of organizing. In this post-industrial era (Bell, 1973) there is general consensus that new forms of organizing, which are likely to be knowledge intensive (Badaracco, 1991) and agile (Goldman et al., 1995), will supplant the vertical hierarchies of their bureaucratic predecessors. Using as an example the software industry, Raymond (1999) argues that the 'bazaar' (the chaotic marketplace exemplified by Linux and the Open Source Movement) will eclipse the 'cathedral' (exemplified by hierarchical organizations like Microsoft) as the preferred mode of organizing. In a more tempered vein some, such as Williamson (1996), have argued that these new forms of organizing will instead represent hybrids of hierarchies and markets. Others posit the emergence of network forms (Castells 1996; Jarvenpaa and Ives, 1994; Monge and Fulk, 1999; Powell, 1990), spherical forms (Miles and Snow, 1995), cellular forms (Miles et al., 1997), Moebius-strip forms (Sabel, 1990), virtual forms (Nohria and Berkley, 1994) and heterarchies (Hedlund, 1986; Stark, 1999). Still others argue that these more enduring organizational forms will be replaced by the rise of a more ephemeral e-lance (electronic freelance) economy (Malone and Laubacher, 1998).

The relationship between new media and these new forms of organizing is a focal point of considerable interest and debate among organizational scholars. It is also the central concern of each of the chapters in this part on 'New Media and Organizing'. The contributions to this part review, critique and extend the theories we need for understanding the complex interrelationships between new media and new forms of organizing and discuss the analytic tools we need for investigating them. The theoretical and empirical reviews offered by the chapters in this part examine the role of new media in organizing at different levels: individual agents, groups, organizational and interorganizational levels. In addition they bring to bear different intellectual perspectives (agent-based modelling, social constructionist and network perspectives). This introductory essay overviews some of the central themes that are amplified in the chapters included in this part of the *Handbook*.

From a Technological Imperative to an Emergent Perspective

One can argue that many of the new forms of organizing can only be conceived in light of recent technological developments. Indeed, many of these new forms rely on the potential of digital technologies to help realize coordination-intensive, fluid and flexible structures while holding the line on coordination costs (Malone and Rockart, 1991). However, some scholars (DiMaggio et al., 2001; Powell, 2001) note that many of the structures associated with these new organizational forms preceded the advent of technologies that were alleged to have caused them.

This debate illustrates an enduring and fundamental intellectual tension between, what at two extremes, constitute the 'technological imperative' and the 'organizational imperative' (Markus and Robey, 1988). Research from a technological imperative seeks to find changes in organizations resulting from changes in the technology. Scholarship from an organizational imperative seeks to explain changes in the use of technology based on organizational constraints. As the chapters in this part describe, prior research on new media and organizing has been predominantly from the technological imperative. Throughout history, the introduction of new communication technologies has prompted proponents of the 'technological imperative' (or, in its more extreme form, 'technological determinism') to investigate the effects of these technologies on the processes of organizing. The advent of the telephone, for instance, prompted many to examine whether it would result in increased centralization or decentralization in the workplace. As Pool (1981) documents extensively, the introduction of the telephone facilitated an increase in centralization (the development of offices in high-rise buildings downtown) and an increase in decentralization (the development of suburban offices). Pool termed this phenomenon the 'dual-effects' hypothesis: technologies have opposite effects at the same time and in spite of each other. The likelihood that one effect is more prominent depends less on the technology and more on other social and organizational contingencies.

More recently in the 1980s, undaunted by the lessons learned from the introduction of the telephone, the introduction of e-mail in organizations prompted similar research questions about its impact on centralization in organizations. After a decade of active research, the results mirrored the dual effects found in the case of the telephone

(Rice, 1994). The advent of the Internet and the web has unleashed a new spate of research in the same tradition and it is arriving at similar inconclusive results. For instance, contrary to conventional wisdom that the new network forms of organizing should be less centralized, Ahuja and Carley (1999) found that these forms of organizing often exhibited very high levels of centralization and hierarchy in the communication network. In fact, in a recent review, O'Mahoney and Barley (1999: 143–5) note that the empirical research is inconclusive on 'whether information technologies further centralization or decentralization', which appears to depend on management contingencies. The recurrence of studies from a technological imperative perspective with each new cycle of technological innovation suggests an abiding, albeit perhaps naive, desire to seek simple, univalent and unidirectional organizational effects of new media.

Alongside the substantial amount of research based on a technological imperative, and partly in response to it, there is a growing body of theorizing and research that embraces the 'emergent' perspective. The emergent perspective seeks to strike a balance by acknowledging the role of technologies in triggering organizational impacts but also explicitly incorporating the organizational imperatives that might moderate the influence of the technology. Theories based on an emergent perspective, such as adaptive structuration theory (DeSanctis and Poole, 1994), seek to understand the recursive and often unanticipated patterns that emerge by examining the interrelationships between the use of new media and the organizational structures and norms that influence, and are in turn influenced by, their use.

Many of the chapters in this part lament the preponderance of prior research on new media and organizing from a technological imperative perspective. They describe how the inconclusive results of this research have prompted scholars to challenge the assumptions of technological determinism. The chapters discuss different theoretical and methodological strategies that may help researchers migrate to a more emergent perspective. Some advocate the study of this emergence from a complex systems perspective.

From New Media as Conduit to New Media as Agent

While the emergent perspective embodies a more sophisticated understanding of how any, perhaps even older, technology is used in organizing processes, there are some unprecedented characteristics of new media that add additional layers of complexity. As discussed in several chapters in this part, new media do more than simply serve as a conduit for individuals, groups and organizations to communicate with one another. In many cases, the

Table III.1   *New media and networks of human and non-human agents*

	Human agents (individuals or aggregates)	Non-human agents (webbots, avatars, etc.)
Human agents (individuals or aggregates)	Traditional organizational networks	Publish, retrieve/access
Non-human agents (webbots, avatars, etc.)	Push technology applications (e.g. Infogate)	P2P technology applications (e.g. avatars, Napster, Gnutella, SETI, the Grid)

new media are themselves important 'nodes' acting as agents or associates within the network (Jones and Jasek, 1997). These non-human (also referred to in various chapters in this part as 'intelligent', 'smart' or 'artificial') agents carry out many of the organizational tasks traditionally associated only with human agents. Some of these agents, called 'avatars', serve as digital incarnations of human agents. They are designed by human agents to act as semi-autonomous agents interacting with other agents, be they human, knowledge repositories or others' avatars. Based on the personal information invested in them by their human agents, they can schedule meetings, continually monitor or search for specific information, carry out trades, and bid on auctions. While avatars are agents that have human counterparts, other agents such as 'know-bots' (knowledge robots) have their own independent identity. They are programmed to repeat structured tasks, such as continually searching the web for topics of interest. Knowbots serve as active knowledge repositories continually retrieving information on specific topics from other human or non-human agents and proactively 'pushing' this information to other agents when they may have a need for it. Still other agents facilitate collaboration among human agents by offering information or 'gisted' summaries relevant to the current discussion or managing floor control by inviting contributions from participants who have not contributed.

Clearly new media, serving in their newfound capacity as non-human agents, are going to play an increasingly important role in twenty-first-century forms of organizing. It is therefore critical for researchers to better understand their contributions and limitations and incorporate these into theoretical and empirical investigations. Several chapters in this part offer innovative approaches that will advance our theoretical and methodological ability to understand the role of new media as agents of organizing.

FROM NETWORKS IN ORGANIZATIONS TO NETWORK AS ORGANIZATION

In his classic book *Images of Organization*, Morgan (1986) recounts how metaphors shape the ways in which we conceptualize and understand the organizations we investigate. They shape the research questions we ask and the methods we use to answer those questions. They privilege certain issues while concealing others. In the industrial era, the machine served as a dominant metaphor shaping our conceptualization of organizations. Reflecting changes in contemporary societal values, the dominance of the organization-as-machine metaphor was replaced in succession by organization-as-living systems in the 1970s, organization-as-cultures in the 1980s, and organization-as-computers in the 1990s. With the explosion of the Internet and the web, there is little argument that the dominant metaphor today is organization-as-networks. While there has been considerable scholarship on networks in organizations over the past three decades (for reviews see Krackhardt and Brass, 1994; Monge and Contractor, 2001; Monge and Eisenberg, 1987), embracing the metaphor of organization-as-network has led to a unprecedented focus on the ways in which characteristics of the network influence, and are in turn influenced by, the process of organizing. Considering organizations-as-networks invites a reconceptualization of perennial organizational issues such as information, resources, trust, cultural values, in terms of relations and flows. The metaphor prompts researchers to focus attention on why we as individuals, groups and organizations create, maintain and dissolve our various network relations. Consistent with this shift, many of the chapters in this part not only focus attention on the network infrastructure supported by the new media but also characterize the process of organizing as networks and flows. Particularly noteworthy is the attention in several chapters to the the role of knowledge management in organizing. The concept of knowledge management (Nonaka and Takeuchi, 1995) was popularized in the 1990s at a time when organizations-as-computers was the dominant metaphor. Consistent with that metaphor, knowledge management was conceptualized as a stand-alone repository for capturing organizational expertise. As some of the chapters discuss, this notion of knowledge management is problematized at a time when the intelligence is seen as residing in the network rather than in the nodes that may be connected to the network.

Prior research on networks has focused almost exclusively on relations between humans or aggregates of humans (such as groups and organizations). Table III.1 describes how this represents only the top left cell when we expand our notion of the network to include the non-human agents discussed earlier. Extending the network into the remaining three cells provides an opportunity to examine how new media influence the organizing process by providing network links from human to non-human agents (for instance, individuals publishing and retrieving information from databases), from non-human to human agents (for instance, knowbots 'pushing' information to individuals) and from non-human to non-human agents (for instance, an individual's avatar coordinating schedules with another individual's avatar). Two of the chapters in this part identify this conceptualization of the network as influential in shaping the future research agenda on new media and organizing.

In conclusion, the chapters in this part offer a thoughtful review and critique of the ways in which we have attempted to understand the relationship between new media and organizing. They draw upon theories and research from a wide variety of disciplines including anthropology, communication, computer science, decisions sciences, economics, management, psychology and sociology as well as several interdisciplinary endeavours such as the area of computer-supported cooperative work. While they generally agree on the limitations of prior research they offer distinct and, in some cases, disparate visions on the future conduct of inquiry. Taken together, these chapters capture the intellectual excitement, the breadth of theoretical frameworks, and the methodological diversity we will need to advance our understanding of the interrelationships between new media and organizing.

REFERENCES

Ahuja, M.K. and Carley, K.M. (1999) 'Network structure in virtual organizations', *Organization Science*, 10: 741–57.

Badaracco, J.L. Jr (1991) *The Knowledge Link: How Firms Compete through Strategic Alliances*. Boston, MA: Harvard University Press.

Bell, D. (1973) *The Coming of Post-Industrial Society*. New York: Basic.

Beniger, J.R. (1986) *The Control Revolution: Technological and Economic Origins of the Information Society*. Cambridge, MA: Harvard University Press.

Castells, M. (1996) *The Rise of the Network Society*. Vol. 1 of *The Information Age: Economy, Society and Culture*. Oxford: Blackwell.

Chandler, A.D. (1977) *The Visible Hand*. Cambridge, MA: Harvard University Press.

DeSanctis, G. and Poole, M.S. (1997) 'Traditions in teamwork in new organizational forms', in *Advances in Group Processes*, vol. 14. Greenwich, CT: JAI. pp. 157–76.

DiMaggio, P., Hargittai, E., Neuman, W.R. and Robinson, J.P. (2001) 'Social implications of the internet', *American Review of Sociology*, 27: 307–36.

Goldman, S.L., Nagel, R.N. and Preiss, K. (1995) *Agile Competitors and Virtual Organizations: Strategies for Enriching the Customer*. New York: Van Nostrand Reinhold.

Hedlund, G. (1986) 'The hypermodern MNC – a heterarchy?', *Human Resource Management*, 25: 9–35.

Jarvenpaa, S. and Ives, B. (1994) 'The global network organization of the future: information management opportunities and challenges', *Journal of MIS*, 10: 25–57.

Jones, P.M. and Jasek, C.A. (1997) 'Intelligent support for activity management (ISAM): an architecture to support distributed supervisory control', *IEEE Transactions on Systems, Man, and Cybernetics,* special issue on 'Human Interaction in Complex Systems', 27 (3): 274–88.

Krackhardt, D. and Brass, D.J. (1994) 'Intra-organizational networks: the micro side', in S. Wasserman and J. Galaskiewicz (eds), *Advances in Social Network Analysis: Research in the Social and Behavioral Sciences*. Thousand Oaks, CA: Sage. pp. 207–29.

Malone, T.W. and Laubacher, R.J. (1998) 'The dawn of the e-lance economy', *Harvard Business Review*, September–October: 145–52.

Malone, T.W. and Rockart, J.F. (1991) 'Computers, networks, and the corporation', *Scientific American*, 265: 128–36.

Markus, M.L. and Robey, D. (1988) 'Information technology and organizational change: causal structure in theory and research', *Management Science*, 34 (5): 583–98.

Miles, R.E., Snow, C.C., Mathews, J.A, Miles, G. and Coleman, H.J. Jr (1997) 'Organizing in the knowledge age: anticipating the cellular form', *Academy of Management Executive*, 11 (4): 7–24.

Monge, P.R. and Contractor, N.S. (2001) 'Emergence of communication networks', in F.M. Jablin and L.L. Putnam (eds), *New Handbook of Organizational Communication*. Newbury Park, CA: Sage. pp. 440–502.

Monge, P.R. and Eisenberg, E.M. (1987) 'Emergent communication networks', in F.M. Jablin, L.L. Putnam, K.H. Roberts and L.W. Porter (eds), *Handbook of Organizational Communication*. Newbury Park, CA: Sage. pp. 304–42.

Monge, P.R. and Fulk, J. (1999) 'Communication technology for global network organizations', in G. DeSanctis and J. Fulk (eds), *Shaping Organizational Form: Communication, Connection, and Community*. Thousand Oaks, CA: Sage.

Morgan, G. (1986) *Images of Organization*. Newbury Park, CA: Sage.

Nohria, N. and Berkley, J.D. (1994) 'The virtual organization: bureaucracy, technology, and the implosion of control', in C. Heckscher and A. Donnellon (eds), *The Post-Bureaucratic Organization: New Perspectives on Organizational Change*. Thousand Oaks, CA: Sage. pp. 108–28.

Nonaka, I. and Takeuchi, H. (1995) *The Knowledge-Creating Company: How Japanese Companies Create the Dynamics of Innovation*. New York: Oxford University Press.

O'Mahony, S. and Barley, S.R. (1999) 'Do digital telecommunications affect work and organization? The state of our knowledge', in *Research in Organizational Behavior*, vol. 21. Greenwich, CT: JAI. pp. 125–61.

Pool, I. de S., Decker, C., et al. (1981) 'Foresight and hindsight: the case of the telephone', in I. de S. Pool (ed.), *Social Impacts of the Telephone*. Cambridge, MA: MIT Press. pp. 127–57.

Powell, W.W. (1990) 'Neither market nor hierarchy: network forms of organization', in B. Staw (ed.), *Research in Organizational Behavior*, vol. 12. Greenwich, CT: JAI Press. pp. 295–36.

Raymond, E.S. (1999) *The Cathedral and the Bazaar: Musings on Linux and Open Source by an Accidental Revolutionary*. Sebastopol, CA: O'Reilly.

Rice, R.E. (1994). 'Network analysis and computer-mediated communication systems', *Advances in Social Network Analysis*. Newbury Park, CA: Sage. pp. 167–203.

Sabel, C.F. (1990) 'Moebius-strip organizations and open labor markets: some consequences of the reintegration of conception and execution in a volatile economy', in P. Bourdieu and J. Coleman (eds), *Social Theory for a Changing Society*. Boulder, CO and New York: Westview and Russell Sage Foundation.

Weber, M. (1947) *The Theory of Economic Organization*. New York: Free Press.

Weber, M. (1978) *Economy and Society*. Berkeley, CA: University of California Press.

Williamson, O.E. (1996) 'Economic organization: the case for candor', *Academy of Management Review*, 21: 48–57.

Yates, J. (1989) *Control through Communication: the Rise of System in American Management*. Baltimore: Johns Hopkins University Press.

12

Smart Agents and Organizations of the Future

KATHLEEN M. CARLEY

As we move to the twenty-first century, technologists point to the rapid changes in social and organizational activity that are expected to result from advances in computational technology. There can be little doubt that technology is altering organizations. Artificial agents such as webbots, robots and electronic shoppers are joining humans and organizations in the ranks of the smart agents that 'work' in and among organizations. Computers are coming to control, or are involved in the operation of, everything from the office and home environment to routine purchases to strategic organizational decisions. As computers become embedded in every device, from pens to microwaves to walls, the spaces around us become intelligent (Nixon et al., 1999; Thomas and Gellersen, 2000). Intelligent spaces are characterized by the potential for ubiquitous access to and provision of information among potentially unbounded networks of agents (Kurzweil, 1988). Yet, we have little understanding of how to coordinate organizations in which humans and artificial agents work side-by-side, let alone how they work in these intelligent spaces.

The industrial revolution enabled organizations to increase in size, number of divisions (Etzioni, 1964; Fligstein, 1985), level of bureaucracy (Weber, 1947) and level of hierarchy (Blau and Scott, 1962). Information processing became key. Increasingly communication became organized so that orders and performance reports flowed down and information, decisions and exceptions flowed up (March and Simon, 1958). Individual opportunity became based on networks of connections among jobs rather than patronage or nepotism (White, 1970; Yamaagata et al., 1997). New technologies, both at the manufacturing and at the communication level, enabled certain organizational designs and affected what was adopted (Beniger, 1986; Aldrich and Mueller, 1982).

Today, information processing, communication and knowledge management became key. Changes in computational power, telecommunications and information processing are affecting when, where and how work is done (Di Martino and Wirth, 1990; Sproull and Kiesler, 1991). Further changes in agriculture, manufacturing, transportation and technology are leading to the emergence of an increasingly mobile population and knowledge-intensive organizations. New organizational designs are emerging such as network organizations (Nohria and Eccles, 1992; Miles and Snow, 1995) and virtual organizations (Lipnack and Stamps, 1997). In these new organizations, even though information processing is key (Tushman and Nadler, 1978), communication is not constrained to be vertical (Contractor and Eisenberg, 1990). Organizational design becomes a strategic exercise in establishing and managing these relations (Burton and Obel, 1998). Rather, the network of connections within and among organizations acts to constrain and enable the flow of goods, services, agents and information.

Advances in engineering and computer science suggest further changes will be forthcoming in organizations as the population of smart agents in organizations expands and the space becomes intelligent (Carley, 1999a). This chapter explores the potential effect of such changes on organizations. We begin by exploring the nature of smart agents and organizations as computational systems. The argument is set forward that the space which organizations occupy will become intelligent and individuals' infospheres will expand. Within this space, search is likely to become the dominant task. Within this environment, the ecology of networks will constrain and enable all behaviour. The ultimate question that social and organizational theorists will need to address is what happens to these networks, to organizational performance and to organizational design when artificial smart agents begin to populate these networks.

At least four paradigms in organization science speak to the potential impact of smart agents on new organizational form: structuralism, contingency theory, information processing theory and social networks. Work on organizational design suggests that different architectures influence performance and there is no one right organizational design for all tasks (Mintzberg, 1983; Burton and Obel, 1984). However, independent of the task, the organizational form can be characterized in terms of networks (Nohria and Eccles, 1992) such that the linkages among agents influence both agent behaviour (Krackhardt and Kilduff, 1994) and organizational performance (Baum and Oliver, 1991). Further, changing technology results in alterations of traditional structures by altering the networks to produce new organizational forms (Powell, 1990). Work on information processing (Cyert and March, 1963) demonstrates that it is the limits to agents' information processing capabilities that affect organizational outcomes and that taking such limitations into account leads to more accurate prediction of organizational performance (March and Simon, 1958). This work also demonstrates that there is an interaction between knowledge (e.g. training, what agents know, and their information processing capabilities) and structure in effecting organizational performance (Masuch and LaPotin, 1989; Carley et al., 1998). However, little of this work speaks directly to the role of artificial smart agents. An exception here is some of the work on transactive memory which suggests that storing individual knowledge about who knows what in databases may have the same performance enhancing effects as when known directly by humans (Moreland et al., 1996). Another exception is the work on information flow which suggests that artificial smart agents change the topology of the underlying networks, speed the diffusion of information, and yet may maintain or exacerbate information inequalities (Kaufer and Carley, 1993; Carley, 1996). Collectively, this work leads to the conclusion that networks, cognition and the interaction among the two affect organizational performance. While this suggests that smart agents will also affect performance, it provides little guidance for the nature of those effects.

For example, key work on organizational learning has looked at the issue of search but ignored the fact that the underlying network within and among organizations constrains that search. Organizational researchers have long recognized the importance of

search as a strategic tool for organizational adaptation (Levinthal and March, 1981; March, 1996). Search is typically characterized as unconstrained and as taking resources from knowledge utilization in that agents are cognitively limited and so can do only one of the two information processing actions at a time. Hence strong organizational performance is seen to require both such search-based exploration and the utilization of known information (exploitation) (March, 1996). In contrast, the social network tradition argues that networks in which agents are embedded both constrain and enable their search (Contractor and Eisenberg, 1990; Carley, 1999b). The examination of smart agents requires that the information processing and the network views be melded into a view in which not only are agents boundedly rational (cognitively and structurally) but also their ability to search is a function of their position in the social network and the knowledge network, and of their information processing capabilities. As such, search is not traded for knowledge utilization. Further, in intelligent spaces search is being conducted by smart agents, some of whom are artificial, who themselves are able to learn and where the direction of that search is enabled and constrained by the underlying networks. A consequence is that as the density of these networks changes and as different types of agents populate these networks, the time scarcity and competition among ideas begin to determine organizational outcomes. As the networks expand in both agents and ideas, search effectively slows and organizational outcomes become a function more of order of learning.

Organizational design is a complex system in which a large number of factors interact in non-linear ways to affect performance. Moreover, it is a dynamic system, changing as humans learn, as goals change, and so on. The presence of artificial smart agents in organizations adds further complexity by enabling greater quantities of information to be stored, meta-knowledge to be created, artificial agents to act on behalf of humans, more knowledge to be created, and so on. The effects of these changes are again non-linear.

A valuable approach for studying such complex non-linear dynamic systems is computational modelling. Within organization theory, a new perspective has emerged which blends the information processing tradition and the social network tradition with a more veridical approach to cognition than bounded rationality. This perspective is known as computational organization theory (Samuelson, 2000).

Computational organization science is a new perspective on organizations and groups that has emerged in the past decade in response to the need to understand, predict and manage organizational change, including change, that is motivated by changing technology (Carley and Gasser, 1999). In this chapter, a computational organization theory perspective has been taken to explore the impact of artificial agents and intelligent spaces on organizational change. Agent-based models are used to enable theory building (Epstein and Axtell, 1997). In an agent-based model, each actor is modelled as an independent information processing agent with a set of knowledge and potential actions. In this chapter the agents have the ability to learn and to interact, and so to realize a dynamic social network. The dynamic worlds that can be explored using this approach enable the researcher to address fundamental social science and organizational questions. As experimental testbeds these models provide an environment in which researchers can explore and learn the effects of complex relations (Lant, 1994) and generate hypotheses that can be tested in other settings (Carley, 1999c).

Thus, in this chapter, initial insights into the potential impact of smart agents on organizations will be provided by doing a computational analysis. Using a computational model inspired by a network-based approach to understanding organizations, a series of illustrative virtual experiments are run. These virtual experiments are directed at exploring the impact of moving into an intelligent space on performance. The results provide us with better insight into the ways in which organizations might behave in intelligent spaces.

SMART AGENTS

Agents are intelligent if, in order to respond to a stimulus, they must engage in cognitive activity acting upon a body of information. One characteristic of cognitive activity is that it takes longer than programmed reflexes (Newell, 1990). Agents are adaptive if they change their behaviour in response to changes in information. Agents are computational if they have the ability to do any of the following: acquire, process, store, interpret or communicate information and make the connections among pieces of information. Smart agents are agents that are intelligent, adaptive and computational. Human beings are the canonical smart agents. However, many other smart agents exist that differ from humans in the degree and/or type of intelligence, adaptivity and computation they exhibit (Kaufer and Carley, 1993; Carley, 1999a). These smart agents are both natural, such as dolphins, and artificial, such as electronic personal shoppers, automated e-mail answering and sorting systems, webbots, robots and avatars.

Such artificial smart agents exist, at least in demo versions, today. Recent work in a number of areas, including that on robots (Thrun, 1996), avatars (Benford et al., 1997) and intelligent agents (Weiss, 1999) demonstrates the viability of artificial smart agents as an entire new class of organizational agents. Artificial smart agents are capable of working and communicating within and among

organizations, on their own or with modest human intervention. As these agents take their place in organizations, new forms of coordination and new organizational designs are likely to arise.

Simulation-based decision aids such as the Virtual Design Team (Jin and Levitt, 1996; Levitt et al., 1994) and ORGAHEAD (Carley and Svoboda, 1996; Carley and Lee, 1998) employ smart agents to create more realistic environments for examining group and organizational behaviour. Such multi-agent simulations enable the comparison of existing and new forms of organizing for collections of smart agents – both human and artificial.

The similarities between humans and artificial agents suggest that the difference among types of smart agents is often a matter of degree, both quantitative (the amount of knowledge of the environment and the number of capabilities) and qualitative (the aspects of the environment that the agent attends to and the types of capabilities). Carley and Newell (1994) define a knowledge/capability space for characterizing the features of agents. As agents increase in the amount and type of knowledge that they attend to, increasingly considering real-time situations, multiple agents, multiple goals and historical situations, the variety and type of responses available to them widen. As agents move from cognitively completely capable, the omniscient agent, to increasingly constrained agents, i.e. from the rational actor, to the boundedly rational actor, to the cognitive actor and to the emotional cognitive actor, they increase in their need for diverse actions. The omniscient agent has no need to collect information as it knows everything. As we move in this classification scheme from the omniscient agent in an environment without space, time, social, historical or cultural constraints to the emotional cognitive agent in the everyday space we are accustomed to, the agents become increasingly human-like, until the model social agent is reached. Using this scheme, various types of agents can be classified and compared in terms of their capabilities and every behaviour can be related to the minimally capable agent needed to generate that action. Further, every position in this space can be operationalized as a computational model of an agent. An implication of this view is that computational models can be used to examine the relative impact of different types of agents (human and artificial) on organizational behaviour. Another implication is that recognizably different social and organizational behaviours will emerge from the model as the agent characteristics change.

THE NATURE OF ORGANIZATIONS

Organizations, like human agents or simple artificial agents such as avatars, are computational systems. As noted by Carley (1999b): 'Any entity

Table 12.1 *Networks of agents, knowledge, tasks and organizations*

	Agents	Knowledge	Tasks	Organizations
Agents	Interaction network *Who knows who* Structure	Knowledge network *Who knows what* Culture	Assignment network *Who is assigned to what* Jobs	Employment network *Who works where* Demography
Knowledge		Information network *What informs what* Data	Requirements network *What is needed to do what* Needs	Competency network *What knowledge is where* Culture
Tasks			Precedence network *What needs to be done before what* Operations	Industrial network *What tasks are done where* Niche
Organizations				Interorganizational network *Which organizations work with which* Alliances

composed of intelligent, adaptive, and computational agents is also an intelligent, adaptive, and computational agent.' Thus organizations are also smart agents; but, unlike the individual agents we have been discussing, they are synthetic. A synthetic agent is an agent synthesized out of multiple subagents connected by a plethora of networks. Organizations exist within, and are defined by, an ecology of networks. As we move into the future, the behaviour of the organization as an entity as well as the behaviour of the agents within it will be affected by the movement to more intelligent spaces. As will be seen, the effect of intelligent spaces will be to alter the size and complexity of the underlying networks – interaction, knowledge and information. This is true whether those networks are among agents at the organizational or the individual level.

An Ecology of Networks

A variety of networks exist within and among organizations. The four key corporate entities – agents, knowledge, tasks and organizations – define a set of networks (see Table 12.1). The focus here is on three of these – the interaction network, the knowledge network and the information network.[1] Various aspects of organizations can be characterized in terms of these networks. For example, structure (such as the authority structure or the communication structure) is defined in terms of the interaction network, culture in terms of the

knowledge network, and potential data in terms of the information network. Properties of the organization can be measured in terms of any one of these networks or the collection of them.

For humans, as boundedly rational (Simon, 1955; 1956) or cognitive agents (Carley and Newell, 1994; Carley and Prietula, 1994), their decision-making ability, actions and performance hinges on their extant knowledge, social position and procedures and their abilities to manage and traverse these networks. Network management involves being able to search for relevant people and knowledge, dynamically generate and evaluate the value/capability of groups of people and/or knowledge that are networked together to achieve some goal, and assess the vulnerability of the system to various types of dysfunctionalities (such as loss of personnel or knowledge) and to manage change in these networks. For humans, the networks that people operate on, and in, serve to constrain and enable further action and affect the efficiencies of such actions (Burt, 1992). Similarly, for artificial agents, being able to traverse the digitized version of these networks enables machine comprehension (Bookman, 1994). For example, webbots that serve as personal shoppers are more intelligent if they are more able to navigate through the links between sites on the web.

A change in any one of these three networks can potentially result in a cascade of changes in the others. For example, when individuals learn something new (by interacting with someone in their interaction network), that evokes a change in the knowledge network which can result in a change in the interaction network (Carley, 1991). As another example, when new personnel are hired they may bring new knowledge with them. As current personnel leave, the available knowledge may be depleted.

Managing these changes is the key to knowledge management. Information technology has the potential to affect this metanetwork in several ways. First, it can affect the number and types of nodes in these networks, i.e., with the advent of new technology comes new agents, new knowledge and new connections among knowledge. Second, information technology has the potential to alter the way changes occur and their impact. For example, some suggest that holding data in databases, and using knowledge systems like Lotus Notes, provide organizations with the means to decouple personnel turnover and change in the knowledge network.

What is an Intelligent Space?

Intelligent spaces are physical spaces where access to other agents (human and artificial) is ubiquitous, the scale in terms of number of agents and amount of information is large, cognition is distributed, and computers are often invisible. The physical world in which people work and go about their daily activities is becoming increasingly intelligent. An increasing number of the objects that surround us (such as microwaves, VCRs, computers, answering machines, personal digital assistants, cell phones and security systems) have some level of intelligence, i.e. these devices are able to communicate, access, store, provide and/or process information.

Ubiquitous access means that technology will exist to enable all agents to access or provide information wherever, whenever and to whomever it is useful, thus remotely enabling other agents to act. Whether agents can exercise this ability will depend on the norms, incentives, privacy regulations and security measures adopted by the group, organization or society. In terms of scale, huge quantities of information will be automatically collected, stored and processed by a potentially ever increasing number of agents. Information, access to information, and information processing and communication capabilities (i.e. intelligence and cognition) will be distributed across agents, time, space, physical devices and communication media (Hutchins, 1991; 1995). As computers are miniaturized, made more reliable, and increased in power and storage capability, we can expect more devices to become intelligent. This increases the number of agents, but it also starts making computers invisible. A further aspect of invisibility is that the interface between the digital world and the analogue world will become seamless. For example, speech recognition and synthesis software, automatic transcription software, face recognition software, all enable a more seamless interface between the digital and analogue world.

As spaces become intelligent there will be unprecedented increases in the size and complexity of the interaction and knowledge networks in which people (and other agents) are embedded and the size and mobility of their infospheres. The term infosphere refers to the collection of remote instruments, appliances and computational resources (all of which may be artificial agents), as well as to the agents (human and artificial) and information made accessible to a person by these systems from a person's working environment, such as the desk and office or the bridge of a ship. All agents have an infosphere; however, the size of that sphere may vary as the agents change physical location. The knowledge available in these infospheres includes what agents know, who they know, and what they know how to access. For humans, the size of their infosphere is largely determined by the type of immediately accessible technology. Thus, your infosphere generally becomes smaller as you move from your office, to your car, to the hallway, to a remote mountaintop.

As spaces become intelligent, we expect two things to happen. First, infospheres will become larger. Indeed, there may be an increase in the complexity in individuals' infospheres and the associated interaction, knowledge and information networks well beyond people's ability to manage and monitor this space. Second, infospheres will become mobile. Thus, as the agents move from office to mountaintop, infospheres will degrade by choice rather than by access to technology. Moreover, technological change may lead to non-linear rates of change in these networks. For example, when one-to-one communication exists, even if every agent learns something new each time, the maximum number of new links in the knowledge network each time is N – the number of agents. In contrast, technologies which enable simultaneous many-to-many communication make it possible for the maximum number of new links in the knowledge network to grow by $N(N-1)$. Technological change also may lead to fundamentally different structures (Barley, 1990; Kaufer and Carley, 1993). For example, databases enable teams to reach consensus by interacting with the database and so sharing knowledge offline rather than reaching a shared understanding through direct interaction. Most organizational theory does not consider the effect of infospheres on organizational performance. In contrast, work on technology suggests that new technologies, by altering the infospheres, will enable more outwork, more use of temporary employees, potentially better decisions, but mixed effects on culture (Harris, 1994; Kiesler, 1996; Worthington, 1997).

As intelligent spaces alter the infospheres, the networks in which people are embedded, and those to which they have access, are likely to respond dynamically and become potentially unbounded. The theory of bounded rationality suggests that limitations on humans determine the level of performance the organization can achieve. As these boundaries are eliminated then performance should improve. It is important to recognize that technology does not eliminate boundaries but moves them, i.e., in intelligent spaces cognitive, social and institutional barriers will still exist. Simon noted that the agent makes decisions using knowledge, which includes simplifications of reality that 'may depend not only on the characteristics – sensory, neural, and other – of the organism, but equally upon the structure of the environment' (1956: 130). Artificial smart agents are not going to obviate such limitations in the human, for all that they may provide external access to information and agents. Moreover, these artificial agents themselves will also be limited both 'cognitively' in their information processing capabilities and 'structurally' by their position in the social network. Further, it is reasonably safe to assume that coordination and communication will still centre on knowing who knows whom (the interaction network) and who knows what (the knowledge network). Agents will still act as gatekeepers. However, rather than affecting who can link to whom, they will limit who does link to whom by the way in which information is located and provided. As a trivial example, currently on the web, which site a user accesses is affected by which search engine is used and the way that engine prioritizes the located sites.

How Might Smart Agents Affect Organizations?

Stories about the impact of technology on organizations abound. Artificial smart agents are expected to have a number of interesting characteristics. Three such characteristics that are important in the organizational setting are: boundary breaking, communication extension, and storage (Sproull and Kiesler, 1991). These three impacts are critical as they affect the fundamental information processing capabilities of the organization.

Artificial Smart Agents as Boundary Breakers

Within and among organizations, boundaries exist. For many network organizations, the boundary between organizations, between what is 'internal' and what is 'external', has virtually disappeared (Sproull and Kiesler, 1991; Miles and Snow, 1995). Smart agents will break still more boundaries. In particular, they will make permeable the boundaries surrounding people, tasks and resources. For example, avatars can act on behalf of a human to schedule appointments or answer routine questions, thus making the person effectively more available than otherwise to both organizational and non-organizational members.

Smart Agents as Communicators

Smart agents can communicate. The import of this is that within a community of humans and artificial agents, these communications will affect what is learned. Thus the truth, accuracy and frequency of the communications sent by artificial agents can alter organizational performance. For example, just having a database increases the effective number of agents by one and provides greater access to information, beyond that provided by just people. If each person in the organization has a personal avatar, that increases the number of agents to twice the number of people.

Smart Agents as Storage

Smart agents store information. The import of this is that within a community of humans and artificial agents, the ability of artificial agents to store information can alter the likelihood that the stored knowledge is recommunicated. Such stored information can potentially alter the group knowledge or shared mental model. This in turn can alter organizational performance. For example, databases as repositories make information available whether or not the individual who provided the information in the first place remains with the company.

COORDINATION DATABASES

How do we coordinate organizations when both human and artificial agents are present? How will the presence of these artificial agents alter the rate of organizational change? Organizational change occurs in a number of ways, ranging from internal changes to the culture to changes that affect overall performance in the market. Three key indicators of organizational change are information diffusion (Carley, 1991), consensus (Carley, 1995) and task accuracy (Carley and Svoboda, 1996). One of the most commonly attributed effects of smart agents is that they will enable information to diffuse faster. Additionally, since more information is expected to reach more people faster, consensus is expected to occur faster. Finally, smart agents are expected to enable greater accuracy as they enable the analysis of more information.

We now examine whether smart agents can effect organizational change by altering the absolute and relative rates of information diffusion, consensus

Table 12.2   *Characteristics of agents*

Agent	Initiate	Send	Receive (learn)	Availability	Amount of knowledge
Humans	Yes	Yes	Yes	Only to one other at a time	50%
Databases	No	Yes	Yes	Only to one other at a time	5%
Avatars	Yes	Yes	No	To many at a time	10%

formation and task accuracy. Using CONSTRUCT-O (Carley, 1990; 1991; 1995; 1999b) a virtual experiment is run and the results are evaluated to explore the impact of artificial agents and intelligent spaces in effecting organizational change. Changes in the absolute and relative rates of information diffusion, consensus formation and task accuracy are examined.

Three aspects of intelligent spaces are explored: changes in boundary spanning, changes in communication, and changes in storage. How might the movement to intelligent spaces impact boundary spanning, communication and storage? First, as noted, there will be effects due to scale. That is, there will be more agents and more information to which people will have access. To capture this effect a static equilibrium analysis is used, in which the effect of access to more agents is captured by examining worlds with an increasing number of agents. Similarly, access to more information is captured by examining worlds that vary in the overall amount of knowledge available.

Second, there will be new types of agents – such as databases and avatars. These agents will differ from humans by having different information processing capabilities. One of the key capabilities of databases is that they do not forget, and can store immense amounts of information beyond the tenure or lifespan of individuals. One of the key capabilities of avatars is that unlike their human counterparts, they are always available for interaction. In this analysis, we differentiate these agents in terms of the following information processing capabilities: initiation, sending, receiving (learning), availability (number they can receive from at once) and amount of initial knowledge. The differences in these agents are summarized in Table 12.2. Since knowledge is modelled as a bit string, the amount of knowledge is just the percentage of those bits initially known by the individuals. What knowledge the individuals know initially is randomly distributed over the bit string.

Availability is of course much more complicated than as characterized in this table. Humans, even without technology, can interact one-to-many. Databases may be locked for data entry to one-to-one for concurrency control but can often be simultaneously searched by many. And so on.

However, in this virtual experiment the availability for databases and humans is limited to one-to-one. There are two reasons for this. First, this is the predominant mode of interaction for both types of agents. Second, allowing only the avatars to be one-to-many aids analysis so that the impact of that information processing feature can be clearly distinguished.

There are, of course, other characteristics of the societies populated by these agents. In any society, at any given time, there is a set of available information, i.e. the union of the information known by all agents in the society. This information is available in the sense that the information, by virtue of being known by at least one member of the society, is potentially available to all. All human agents know 50 per cent of the available information chosen randomly from the set of available information. When a database is present, that database is initially set up containing little information (5 per cent of the available information chosen randomly from the available information). However, each avatar knows 10 per cent of the information available in the society. For each avatar, its information is a subset of the information initially known by its human counterpart. Each avatar knows 10 per cent of the overall knowledge but this knowledge is one-fifth of the information known by its human counterpart. Which of the information known by its human the avatar knows is chosen randomly. One of the most fundamental findings in sociology is the tendency of individuals to interact more with those to whom they are more similar, homophily (McPherson and Smith-Lovin, 1987; Carley, 1991). The reasons for this are many, including ease of communication, shared understandings and comfort. Humans, and in this model all agents, are information seeking but, given two possible interaction partners, prefer the partner with whom they have more in common. A consequence is that all agents (humans and artificial) behave in a very boundedly rational fashion. In particular, the following human agent behaviours emerge:

1   Initially they act as though there is a small incentive to contribute to the database, i.e. they will contribute if they have no one else to interact with.

Table 12.3 *Synopsis of virtual experiment*

Variable	Description	Values
Population[a]	Number of human agents	10, 20, 50
Knowledge	Number of pieces of available information	20, 40, 100
Agents	Types of agents	Humans, humans + database, humans + avatars

Number of worlds: 27.

[a]When there is a database the total number of agents is the number of humans plus one. When there are avatars the total number of agents is twice the number of humans.

2 Experts, those with much information, will contribute to the database rather than repeating themselves to others.

3 As more individuals contribute to the database novel information, i.e. information that is not already in the database, others will follow.

One can envision a large number of other possible types of agents such as referential databases, books and personal shoppers. The agents examined (humans, databases and avatars) were chosen because they have distinct information processing capabilities, correspond to a type of agent currently existing, and are likely to continue to exist in the future. Thus, the selected agents are likely to play a role in the digital economy and in transforming current workspaces into intelligent spaces.

The simulation is run for a number of time periods until quiescence is reached, i.e. no new information is being communicated. A time period is a communication–learning–repositioning cycle in which all agents find a communication partner (that might be themselves), send and/or receive a bit of information, learn new information sent to them, and on the basis of their new total knowledge change their propensities for interacting with others.

Information diffusion is measured as the number of time periods until all human agents in the organization know a randomly selected piece of information. The higher this number, the longer it takes on average for information to diffuse to any particular individual. Consensus is measured as the number of time periods until the maximum number of people who are ever going to agree, first agree. It is possible that, given a task, not all people will agree. At some point, a maximum is reached in the number of people who agree. The time at which this maximum is reached is the time used for consensus. Two individuals are said to agree if they vote the same given the task. Since individuals learn, their propensity to agree on the same tasks changes over time. Individuals can go in and out of consensus. Task accuracy is measured as the percentage of problems in a single time period that are solved correctly by the organization. An organization solves a problem correctly if the majority of people's votes are accurate. Sustained accuracy is measured as the number of time periods until the organization's accuracy has stabilized. At some point, a maximum is reached in accuracy. The time at which this maximum is first reached is the time used for sustained accuracy.

To see how smart agents might transform the workplace in terms of performance, information diffusion and consensus, a virtual experiment was run in which the number of human agents, the amount of knowable information, and the types of agents were varied. Variations examined are summarized in Table 12.3. Three categories of each variable were utilized, resulting in 27 virtual worlds, where a virtual world is a simulated society with a specific number of agents of each type with specific levels and distributions of knowledge. Each of these worlds is then simulated ten times. The results reported are the ensemble average of these different runs. Note that, for clarity of results, worlds with all three types of agents (humans, databases and avatars) simultaneously present were not run.

As previously noted, knowledge is modelled as a bit string. Here worlds differ in the length of that bit string. Which of the bits the agents initially know is determined randomly. The percentage of the bits known is specified in Table 12.2. Humans and databases can learn, i.e. over time the number of bits that they know can increase. For humans and databases, when they interact with another human they receive a single bit of information from that source. If they do not already know this information they learn it. Humans can in a similar fashion learn from databases. In stark contrast, avatars are modelled as having a set of knowledge (a sample of what their associated human knows) and this knowledge does not change over time; thus, avatars cannot learn. Clearly this is a simplification of reality as the learning always occurs if it can and it is perfect. Future work should consider errors in this process.

The task being used is the binary classification task (Carley, 1992). Each time period the organization is faced with 25 tasks. Each task is of the form:

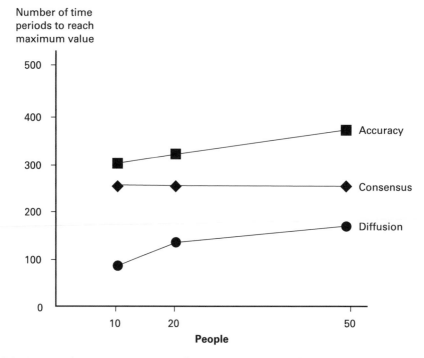

Figure 12.1   *Impact of increase in access to others' organizational performance*

decide if in this string there are more 1s or 0s. Each agent has access only to those bits of the task that correspond to information they know. Each agent decides that there are more 1s/0s if, in the set of bits that the agent is looking at (for the information they know), there are more 1s/0s. This decision can be thought of as the agent's vote.

Each of the performance metrics could be measured across all agents, rather than across just the human agents. Since not all agents can learn (e.g. avatars), these metrics would not be comparable across the various organizations examined. Therefore for this study these metrics are calculated only across the human agents.

ORGANIZATIONAL COMMUNICATION IN THE INTELLIGENT SPACE

As previously noted the basic effect of working in an intelligent space is one of scale: more agents, more information. The second effect is that the availability of information and agents is altered by the presence of artificial agents. How do these changes impact performance?

Simulation results suggest that access to more people (group size increases) will result in it taking longer for new information to reach all members of

the group and for the group to achieve high accuracy (see Figure 12.1). However, an increase in the population will have little impact on agreement. For information diffusion, there are decreasing costs to scale in population. Thus, in extremely large groups, the main impact of further increases in size will be to decrease the accuracy of decisions. Simulation suggests that access to more information will result in substantial increases in the time it takes information to diffuse, consensus to be reached, and high performance to be achieved (see Figure 12.2). The impact of information growth is much more detrimental than is the impact of population growth on the performance characteristics. These are general first-order effects due to the increase in the number of agents and the amount of information to which agents have access. This can be seen even in studies in which there are no smart agents (Carley, 1990; Kaufer and Carley, 1993).

It is typically assumed that in the digital economy everything will occur faster. It should be quicker for individuals to learn new ideas from databases or avatars than to find the person who knows the novel piece of information. Because everyone can access the same information, e.g. in the database, consensus should occur more rapidly and accuracy be improved. In contrast, the presence of artificial agents in these intelligent spaces

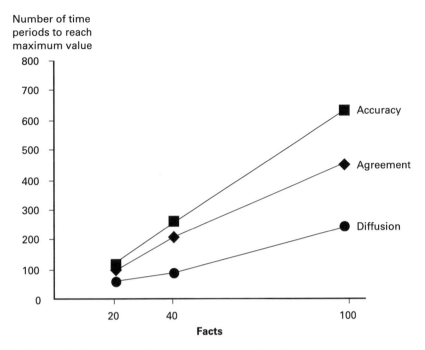

Figure 12.2   *Impact of information explosion on organizational performance*

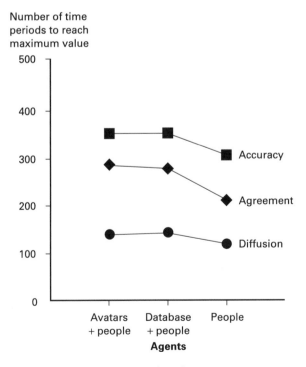

Figure 12.3   *Impact of smart agents on organizational performance*

Table 12.4   *ANOVA results*

Dependent	Degrees of freedom	Diffusion	Consensus	Accuracy
Population size	2	34.90[a]	0.25	17.20[a]
Amount of information	2	168.02[a]	910.08[a]	1091.86[a]
Type of agents present	2	3.40	41.15[a]	11.26[a]
Population size × amount of information	4	10.691[a]	0.70	5.69[a]
Population size × type of agents present	4	0.08	8.13[a]	2.60
Amount of information × type of agents present	4	0.63	16.24[a]	5.71[a]
Population size × amount of information × type of agents present	8	1.13	4.38[a]	1.20
Multiple R^2		0.658	0.893	0.905

$N = 270$, i.e. 10 runs each of 27 worlds. Values shown are F-ratios: [a] ≤ 0.001, [B] ≤ 0.005, [c] ≤ 0.01.

also serves to slow things down (see Figure 12.3). In intelligent spaces, there are now more agents for humans to interact with (databases or avatars). These interactions have little effect on the rate at which information diffuses. However, they do affect the order in which information diffuses, i.e. they affect who learns what when by increasing the number of sources for all information. As a result, they actually make it harder for agreement and high accuracy to be achieved in a timely matter. When artificial agents are not present, humans act as gatekeepers to limit both the flow of information and who gets what when. This gate-keeping facilitates building agreement in large groups, which can in turn promote higher performance. As anyone can get access to any information any time from anywhere, agreement goes down, which can reduce accuracy in performance.

Thus far only the direct effects have been examined. There are, however, some interesting interaction effects. Table 12.4 contains the results of ANOVA analyses looking at the impact of population size, amount of information, and type of agents present (just humans, humans plus database, humans plus avatars) on the performance variables. A word of caution about interpreting these statistical values. In a simulation, N can be increased arbitrarily. As N is increased, where there is an effect in the limit it becomes significant, and where there is not an effect in the limit it becomes 0. The level of statistical significance is thus used to determine the number of replications to run to achieve a robust result. The value of the coefficients and the R^2 is not in whether or not they are significant. Rather, their value is in their relative level. For example, here we see that the factors contributing to diffusion in this non-linear model are simply population size, the amount of information, and the

size of the knowledge network (population size × amount of information). Of these, the amount of information is the dominant factor.

For diffusion and accuracy the interaction between facts and population is multiplicative. For consensus, there are interesting interactions with the types of agents and people/facts. Avatars impede agreement when the population is small, whereas databases are more troublesome when the population is large. For large populations, databases and avatars increasingly impede agreement as the fact base grows; but databases are more detrimental than avatars.

CONCLUSION

Organizations are complex systems. As we move into a world of intelligent spaces, artificial smart agents should become increasingly prevalent. Understanding how these agents might alter the form of organizations is imperative. In this study, the basic characteristics of intelligent spaces were described and a combined social network information processing approach to theorizing about the likely effects of such agents was characterized. The complexity of the system was such that computational analysis was used as an aid in thinking through the possible ramifications of these changes. Computational analysis was used to build new concepts, theories and knowledge about organizations. The computational model is the embodiment of the theory of smart agents and their impact on organizations that is being developed and is in need of being tested. Since the model is a model of the underlying process it generates a large number of hypotheses (Carley, 1999c).

These hypotheses can then be tested in other settings. Let us consider some of the core hypotheses generated.

The results from the virtual experiments suggest that as we move into intelligent spaces the increase in access to people and information tends to increase the time to achieve high levels of accuracy and for any particular piece of information to diffuse. Moreover, we saw that, in these simulations, increasing the amount of available information is more devastating on performance than is increasing the number of potential communication partners. It is reasonable to expect that the amount of information people have access to will expand at a greater rate than will the number of people. A variety of factors would contribute to this being the case – increased archiving of information, digitization of old records, education leading to a decrease in population growth, etc. It is often implicitly assumed that access and use are the same, i.e. that if people have access to information they will use it. However, these results suggest that access to more information will actually slow the rate at which any particular piece of information is accessed and learned. Even in the intelligent space, people are still limited in the rate at which they can learn i.e. bounded rationality still applies. What these results suggest is that increases in competition among ideas, which occurs as the knowledge base expands, can mitigate the value of expanded access.

In these virtual experiments avatars were more helpful in large than in small organizations. An easy explanation is 'sure, that's because people would rather talk to people and in a small group you can talk to all the people'. However, that is not the causal mechanism. Rather, what is happening in these simulations is that since avatars cannot learn, their value as communicators is higher in a large organization where there are more people from whom to learn. Having agents that do not learn can actually speed communication and overall information diffusion as the same message keeps getting repeated to all interaction partners. Databases become less effective in larger populations as they keep changing and growing in their contents.

These results suggest that, for large populations, databases and avatars increasingly impede agreement as the knowledge base grows; but databases are more detrimental than avatars. This is particularly true for accuracy. The type of task used is essentially a voting task (classification and choice). High accuracy means that all of the personnel correctly identify the code and vote the same. What these results imply is that for tasks of this sort, such as budget setting, elections and setting production levels, the movement to intelligent spaces may create a sense of unease. The implication is that if

decision need to be made in the same timespan as in a non-digital economy, the level of agreement is likely to be lower and the accuracy of the decision is likely to be lower. In that way, movement to intelligent spaces may actually lead to a culture of dissent.

If these simple technologies have this effect on organizational performance, how might organizations respond to facilitate rapid diffusion, to build consensus, and to enable the organization to rapidly achieve high accuracy? This analysis provides a few clues. First, the results suggest that agents that cannot learn can speed information diffusion. One way of implementing this in the database world would be to create multiple smaller databases, on special topics, and lock them once they are full rather than allowing people to keep adding to them. Second, these results suggest that a large increase in available information can be disabling. This suggests that when consensus and rapid diffusion of new ideas are the goal, that goal can be facilitated by putting in place procedures to screen information, rate it or otherwise limit access. Third, one of the reasons that avatars and databases slow things down in these virtual worlds is that they create an effectively more densely connected interaction network. This suggests that factors that promote grouping, gatekeeping and so forth will actually facilitate information diffusion and consensus. Organizing schemes such as group distribution lists, limited web access and group-related pointers between sites, which constrain the interaction network and set boundaries, may have the ironic effect of promoting diffusion and the development of consensus within the group.

NOTES

This work was supported in part by the Office of Naval Research (ONR), United States Navy Grant no. N00014-97-1-0037, NSF IRI9633 662, NSF KDI IIS-9980109, and the Pennsylvania Infrastructure Technology Alliance, a partnership of Carnegie Mellon, Lehigh University and the Commonwealth of Pennsylvania's Department of Economic and Community Development. Additional support was provided by the Institute for Complex Engineered Systems (ICES) and the Center for Computational Analysis of Social and Organizational Systems (CASOS) at Carnegie Mellon University (http://www.ices.cmu.edu/casos). The views and conclusions contained in this document are those of the author and should not be interpreted as representing the official policies, either expressed or implied, of the Office of Naval Research, the National Science Foundation or the US government.

1 This is a reduced version of the PCANS formulation first proposed by Krackhardt and Carley (1998). They defined a metamatrix of relations among people, resources and tasks. Without loss of generality we redefine resources as knowledge and expand people to include all intelligent agents.

REFERENCES

Aldrich, H.E. and Mueller, S. (1982) 'The evolution of organizational forms: technology, coordination, and control', in B.M. Staw and L.L. Cummings (eds), *Research in Organizational Behavior*, vol. 4. Greenwich, CT: JAI. pp. 33–87.

Barley, Stephan (1990) 'The alignment of technology and structure through roles and networks', *Administrative Science Quarterly*, 61–103.

Baum, J.A.C. and Oliver, C. (1991) 'Institutional linkages and organizational mortality', *Administrative Science Quarterly*, 36: 187–218.

Benford, S., Bowers, J., Fahlen, L.E., Greenhalgh, C. and Snowdon, D. (1997) 'Embodiments, avatars, clones and agents for multi-user, multi-sensory virtual worlds', *Multimedia Systems*, 5 (2): 93–104.

Beniger, J.R. (1986) *The Control Revolution: Techno-logical and Economic Origins of the Information Society*. Cambridge, MA: Harvard University Press.

Blau, P. and Scott, W.R. (1962) *Formal Organizations*. San Francisco: Chandler.

Bookman, Lawrence A. (1994) *Trajectories through Knowledge Space: a Dynamic Framework for Machine Comprehension*. Boston: Kluwer.

Burt, Ronald S. (1992) *Structural Holes: the Social Structure of Competition*. Cambridge, MA: Harvard University Press.

Burton, R.M. and Obel, B. (1984) *Designing Efficient Organizations: Modeling and Experimentation*. Amsterdam: Elsevier Science.

Burton, Richard M. and Obel, Borge (1998) *Strategic Organizational Design: Developing Theory for Application*. Boston: Kluwer.

Carley, Kathleen (1990) 'Group stability: a socio-cognitive approach', in E. Lawler, B. Markovsky, C. Ridgeway and H. Walker (eds), *Advances in Group Processes: Theory and Research*, vol. VII. Greenwich, CT: JAI.

Carley, Kathleen (1991) 'A theory of group stability', *American Sociological Review*, 56 (3): 331–54.

Carley, Kathleen (1992) 'Organizational learning and personnel turnover', *Organization Science*, 3 (1): 20–46.

Carley, Kathleen (1995) 'Communication technologies and their effect on cultural homogeneity, consensus, and the diffusion of new ideas', *Sociological Perspectives*, 38 (4): 547–71.

Carley, Kathleen M. (1996) 'Communicating new ideas: the potential impact of information and telecommunication technology', *Technology in Society*, 18 (2): 219–30.

Carley, Kathleen M. (1998) 'Organizational adaptation', *Annals of Operations Research*, 75: 25–47.

Carley, Kathleen M. (1999a) 'Organizational change and the digital economy: a computational organization science perspective', in Erik Brynjolfsson and Brian Kahin (eds), *Understanding the Digital Economy: Data, Tools, Research*. Cambridge, MA: MIT Press.

Carley, Kathleen M. (1999b) 'On the evolution of social and organizational networks', in Steven B. Andrews and David Knoke (eds), *Research in the Sociology of Organizations*, vol. 16, special issue on 'Networks in and around Organizations'. Stamford, CT: JAI. pp. 3–30.

Carley, Kathleen M. (1999c) 'On generating hypotheses using computer simulations', *Systems Engineering*, 2 (2): 69–77.

Carley, Kathleen M. and Gasser, Les (1999) 'Computational organization theory', in Gerhard Weiss (ed.), *Distributed Artificial Intelligence*. Cambridge, MA: MIT Press. Chapter 7.

Carley, Kathleen M. and Lee, Ju-Sung (1998) 'Dynamic organizations: organizational adaptation in a changing environment', in Joel Baum (ed.), *Advances in Strategic Management*. Vol. 15: *Disciplinary Roots of Strategic Management Research*. Greenwich, CT: JAI. pp. 269–97.

Carley, Kathleen and Newell, Allen (1994) 'The nature of the social agent', *Journal of Mathematical Sociology*, 19 (4): 221–62.

Carley, Kathleen and Prietula, Michael (1994) 'ACTS theory: extending the model of bounded rationality', in Kathleen Carley and Michael Prietula (eds), *Computational Organization Theory*. Hillsdale, NJ: Earlbaum.

Carley, Kathleen M. and Svoboda, David M. (1996) 'Modeling organizational adaptation as a simulated annealing process', *Sociological Methods and Research*, 25 (1): 138–68.

Carley, Kathleen M., Prietula, Michael J. and Lin, Zhiang (1998) 'Design versus cognition: the interaction of agent cognition and organizational design on orga-nizational performance', *Journal of Artificial Societies and Social Simulation*, 1 (3): 1–19. Available 30 June 1998 at: <http://www.soc.surrey.ac.uk/JASSS/>, 1: paper 4.

Contractor, N. and Eisenberg, E. (1990) 'Com-munication networks and new media in organiza-tions', in J. Fulk and C. Steinfield (eds), *Organizations and Communication Technology*. Newbury Park, CA: Sage. pp. 145–74.

Cyert, R.M. and March, J.G. (1963) *Behavioral Theory of the Firm*. Englewood Cliffs, NJ: Prentice-Hall.

Di Martino, V. and Wirth, L. (1990) 'Telework: a new way of working and living', *International Labour Review*, 129 (5): 529–54.

Epstein, Josh and Axtell, Rob (1997) *Growing Artificial Societies*. Boston: MIT Press.

Etzioni, A. (1964) *Modern Organization*. Englewood Cliffs, NJ: Prentice-Hall.

Fligstein, Neil (1985) 'The spread of the multi-divisional form among large firms, 1919–1979', *American Sociological Review*, 50: 377–91.

Harris, D.H. (ed.) (1994) *Organizational Linkages: Understanding the Productivity Paradox*. Washington, DC: National Academy Press.

Hutchins, Edwin (1991) 'The social organization of distributed cognition', in L.B. Resnick, J.M. Levine and S.D. Teasley (eds), *Perspectives on Socially Shared Cognition*. Washington, DC: American Psychological Association.

Hutchins, Edwin (1995) *Cognition in the Wild*. Cambridge, MA: MIT Press.

Jin, Yan and Levitt, Raymond (1996) 'The virtual design team: a computational model of project organizations', *Computational and Mathematical Organization Theory*, 2 (3): 171–96.

Kaufer, David S. and Carley, Kathleen M. (1993) *Communication at a Distance: the Effect of Print on Socio-Cultural Organization and Change*. Hillsdale, NJ: Erlbaum.

Kiesler, Sara (ed.) (1996) *Culture of the Internet*. Mahwah, NJ: Erlbaum.

Krackhardt, David and Carley, Kathleen M. (1998) 'A PCANS model of structure in organization', in *Proceedings of the 1998 International Symposium on Command and Control Research and Technology*. Monterey, CA, June. pp. 113–19.

Krackhardt, David and Kilduff, Martin (1994) 'Bringing the individual back in: a structural analysis of the internal market for reputation in organizations', *Academy of Management Journal*, 37 (1): 87–108.

Kurzweil, Raymond (1988) *The Age of Intelligent Machines*. Cambridge, MA: MIT Press.

Lant, Theresa L. (1994) 'Computer simulations of organizations as experimental learning systems: implications for organization theory', in K.M. Carley and M.J. Prietula (eds), *Computational Organization Theory*. Hillsdale, NJ: LEA. pp. 195–216.

Levinthal, Daniel A. and March, James G. (1981) 'A model of adaptive organizational search', *Journal of Economic Behavior and Organization*, 2: 307–33.

Levitt, Raymond E., Cohen, Geoff P., Kunz, John C., Nass, Chris I., Christiansen, Torre and Jin, Yan (1994) 'A theoretical evaluation of measures of organizational design: interrelationship and performance predictability', in K.M. Carley and M.J. Prietula (eds), *Computational Organization Theory*. Hillsdale, NJ: Erlbaum. pp. 1–18.

Lipnack, Jessica and Stamps, Jeffrey (1997) *Virtual Teams: Reaching across Space, Time, and Organizations with Technology*. New York: Wiley.

March, James G. (1996) 'Exploration and exploitation in organizational learning', in M.D. Cohen and L.S. Sproull (eds), *Organizational Learning*. Thousand Oaks, CA: Sage.

March, James G. and Simon, H. (1958) *Organizations*. New York: Wiley.

Masuch, M. and LaPotin, P. (1989) 'Beyond garbage cans: an AI model of organizational choice', *Administrative Science Quarterly*, 34: 38–67.

McPherson, J. Miller and Smith-Lovin, Lynn (1987) 'Homophily in voluntary organizations: status distance and the composition of face-to-face groups', *American Sociological Review*, 52: 370–9.

Miles, R.E. and Snow, C.C. (1995) 'The new network firm: a spherical structure built on a human investment philosophy', *Organizational Dynamics*, 23: 5–18.

Mintzberg, H. (1983) *Structures in Five: Designing Effective Organizations*. Englewood Cliffs, NJ: Prentice-Hall.

Moreland, R.L., Argote, L. and Krishnan, R. (1996) 'Socially shared cognition at work: transactive memory and group performance', in J.L. Nye and A.M. Brower (eds), *What's Social about Social Cognition? Research on Socially Shared Cognition in Small Groups*. Thousand Oaks, CA: Sage. pp. 57–84.

Newell, A. (1990) *Unified Theories of Cognition*. Cambridge, MA: Harvard University Press.

Nixon, Paddy, Lacey, Gerard and Dobson, Simon (eds) (1999) *Managing Interactions in Smart Environments*, 1st International Workshop on Managing Interactions in Smart Environments (MANSE '99), Dublin, Ireland, December.

Nohria, Nitin and Eccles, Robert G. (eds) (1992) *Networks and Organizations: Structure, Form, and Action*. Boston, MA: Harvard Business School Press.

Powell, W.W. (1990) 'Neither markets nor hierarchy: network forms of organizations', in B.M. Staw and L.L. Cummings (eds), *Research in Organizational Behavior*, vol. 12. Greenwich, CT: JAI. pp. 295–336.

Samuelson, D. (2000) 'Designing organizations', *OR/MS Today*, December: 1–4. See also: http://www.lionhrt-pub.com/orms/orms-12-00/samuelson.html.

Simon, H. (1955) 'A behavioral model of rational choice', *Quarterly Journal of Economics*, 69: 99–118.

Simon, H. (1956) 'Rational choice and the structure of the environment', *Psychological Review*, 63: 129–38.

Sproull, L. and Kiesler, S. (1991) *Connections: New Ways of Working in the Networked Organization*. Cambridge, MA: MIT Press.

Thomas, Peter and Gellersen, Hans-W. (eds) (2000) *Proceedings of the Second International Symposium on Handheld and Ubiquitous Computing* (HUC 2000), Bristol, UK, 25–27. September.

Thrun, S. (1996) 'To know or not to know: the role of models in mobile robotics', *AI Magazine*, 18: 1.

Tushman, M.L. and Nadler, D. (1978) 'Information processing as an integrating concept in organizational design', *Academy of Management Review*, 3: 613–24.

Weber, Max (1947) *The Theory of Social and Economic Organization*, edited by A.H. Henderson and Talcott Parsons. Glencoe, IL: Free Press. pp. 329–41.

Weiss, Gerhard (ed.) (1999) *Distributed Artificial Intelligence*. Cambridge, MA: MIT Press.

White, H. (1970) *Chains of Opportunity*. Cambridge, MA: Harvard University Press.

Worthington, John (1997) *Reinventing the Workplace*. Oxford, Boston: Architectural Press.

Yamagata, H., Yeh, K.S., Stewman, S. and Dodge, H. (1997) 'Sex segregation and glass ceilings: a comparative statics model of women's career opportunities in the federal government over a quarter of a century', *American Journal of Sociology*, 103: 566–632.

13

New Media and Organizing at the Group Level

ANDREA B. HOLLINGSHEAD
and
NOSHIR S. CONTRACTOR

Traditionally, small groups have been defined by researchers as collectives ranging from a minimum of two, and in most cases three, to a maximum of 15 or so members (cf. McGrath, 1984). Members of groups have interdependent goals, are acquainted with and interact with one another and have a sense of belonging. Recent developments in digital communication technologies have brought about a radical change in our collective notion of what constitutes a group. Members of groups no longer need to be formally constituted or to be co-present (in time or place) to collaborate, share information or socialize. Instead new technologies facilitate the creation, maintenance and dissolution of groups among individuals who use different devices (such as phones, mobiles, laptops, personal digital assistants) to interact over one or more of a variety of channels (audio, video, text and graphics) offered by several forums (such as Internet newsgroups, online chat sessions via Instant Messenger, and corporate intranets). These developments have triggered a shift in conceptualizations of groups from the traditional notion of 'same time, same place' to 'any time, anywhere' and, some would argue apocryphally, 'all the time, everywhere'. In addition to the physical and temporal constraints, developments in new media have also eliminated constraints on the size of groups. In traditional face-to-face groups, the size of the group is likely to be relatively small and its membership is by definition a closed set. This is also true for some geographically distributed work teams that collaborate using communication technologies such as video and computer conferencing. However, that is not the case in many Internet-based newsgroups, where there are literally hundreds of participants (Alexander et al., in press). These participants may coalesce as a group because of a common 'practice', such as collaborating on the development of a software program, or because of a common 'interest', such as their concerns about the use of 'sweatshop' labour practices or their interest in downloading a particular genre of music. As a global community of consumers and producers we are grappling with the opportunities and challenges of these new fluid 'group forms' of organizing.

As researchers, we are challenged to redefine the theoretical and methodological apparatus to study how new media shape, and are in turn shaped by, the ways in which we organize in groups. Before the development of the World Wide Web and the Internet, research on groups with technological support was driven by three basic goals: to examine how adequately new media could permit groups to overcome time and space constraints, to evaluate the impact of technologies on the range and speed of members' access to information, and to evaluate the impact of technologies on the groups' task performance (McGrath and Hollingshead, 1994). Much of the theory and research addressed when and how the structure, interaction and performance of technologically enabled groups were similar to and different from face-to-face groups. As such, the focus of this research was on examining the ways in which new media served to substitute and enlarge communication among group members (Contractor and Bishop, 2000). With the surge in digital communication technologies, researchers started to reckon with the idea that most technologically enabled groups were inherently different from face-to-face groups, and that they were worthy of study as entities in their own right rather than simply to be bench marked against equivalent face-to-face groups. Many of the premises of existing theories were being challenged by technological developments and risked becoming less relevant at best, and obsolete at worst. Researchers are currently rethinking their definitions of groups and are developing new theories to explain and predict their behaviour, and are designing new methods to study them.

This chapter examines the role of new media at the group level of analysis. Its emphasis is on how technology shapes and is shaped by the behaviour of groups, rather than on issues relating to the design of hardware and software systems for group collaboration. The organization of this chapter reflects the evolution in theory and research on groups and new media. As we shall see, the theory and research also reflects our evolving definitions of 'new media' – starting with early experiments in teleconferencing (audio and video conferencing) in the 1970s, and continuing with proprietary computer-mediated communication systems in the 1980s, the rise of the Internet and the web as 'open' communication networks in the 1990s, and the ubiquitous, pervasive and mobile communication environment that ushers us into the twenty-first century. The chapter begins with a brief description of an early, but influential, classification of technologies that support group interaction. The second and third sections examine the theory and empirical findings of research that investigated how technologically enabled group collaborations are similar and different from face-to-face collaborations. As will become evident, most of this research was conducted, or at least premised, on conceptualizations of groups prior to recent developments in digital technologies. The fourth section presents a reconceptualization of groups that takes into account the new forms of organizing enabled by new media. This reconceptualization allows for a more fluid, dynamic and activity-based definition of groups and technology, and is drawn from a network perspective. It presents a knowledge network approach to the study of groups and technology.

A CLASSIFICATION OF TECHNOLOGIES THAT SUPPORT GROUPS

Collaboration among group members entails cognitive as well as emotional and motivational aspects of communication. Group members transmit, receive and store information of various kinds, from each other and from various other sources. These exchanges were viewed as distinct functions carried out by group members. Hence, not surprisingly, scholars conceptualized the technologies that support these functions to also be distinct. With an eye towards retrospective synthesis of research in this area, McGrath and Hollingshead (1993; 1994) presented a classification system for communication systems based on the functional role of technologies to support group collaboration. The four categories of the classification system are based on whether the technology: (1) provides within-group communication (i.e. group communication support systems or GCSS); (2) supplements information available to the group or its members by information drawn from databases (i.e. group information support systems or GISS); (3) supports communication with those outside the group (i.e. group external support systems or GXSS); and (4) structures group task performance processes and task products (i.e. group performance support systems or GPSS). The classification system was developed in the early 1990s when the World Wide Web was in its infancy. It was later updated to include communication technologies available on the Internet (Hollingshead, 2001). While the classification system was developed at a time when distinct technologies supported these different functions, it continues to be a viable framework to organize and examine contemporary technologies that typically support more than one of these four functions.

GCSS: Technologies that Mediate or Augment Within-Group Communication

The signature feature of GCSS is its ability to permit group members to communicate using new media. In some cases GCSS may mediate communication among members spatially separated from each other while they are communicating. Examples would include video conferencing, or 'texting' using short-message service (SMS). In other cases, GCSS may augment face-to-face communication by the use of overhead projectors for communicating graphics or document-sharing software over networked computers. Some GCSS support asynchronous communication for group members interacting in different time periods; others require that group members interact synchronously. As these examples illustrate, GCSS vary in the communication channels that are available to group members: visual, auditory, text and graphics.

Most research on GCSS has been based on the premise that the fewer modalities afforded by technologically mediated communication would 'filter' out some of the cues in face-to-face communication (Culnan and Markus, 1987). Based on this assumption, the research agenda sought to examine how the performance of groups using GCSS was moderated by the particular task(s) and activities in which the group was engaged, the experience of the group with the technology, and the degree to which group

Table 13.1 *A typology of group communication support systems*

Modalities available	Synchronous	Asynchronous
Visual	Video conference	Videocassette exchange
Audio	Phone conference	Voice mail
		Audiotape exchange
Text, graphics	Computer conference	E-mail
		Fax
Internet	Newsgroups	
	Chat rooms	Home pages, websites

members have a shared conceptualization of relative expertise (Hollingshead, 1998a; 1998b; Hollingshead et al., 1993). In addition to examining the performance of groups using GCSS, some research has focused on the interaction process among group members. This research (McGrath and Hollingshead, 1994) has found evidence that the sequencing, synchrony and timing of messages among group members using GCSS is moderated by the size and nature of the groups, as well as the level of ambiguity among group members.

Table 13.1 provides examples of GCSS organized by the communication channels provided by the technology (video, audio, text/graphics) and the temporal distribution of members, i.e. whether they are communicating synchronously or asynchronously. As noted at the start of this section, GCSS can support communication between members who are co-present or are geographically distributed. However, as we shall see in the review of empirical research, the preponderance of research on GCSS has been among geographically distributed groups. Culnan and Markus (1987) argue that this bias reflects an early preoccupation with the role of GCSS to mediate rather than to augment face-to-face communication. The organizing scheme also includes categories for Internet technologies, although World Wide Web browsers can support video conferencing, audio conferencing and document sharing on the Internet.

GISS: Supplementing Information Available to the Group

Group members have access to many repositories of information or knowledge besides other group members. These repositories include databases, archives and intranets. Intranets are web-based technologies that support knowledge distribution among networks of teams within organizations. The types of knowledge that are available to group members on intranets can include: (1) human resources, (2) sales and marketing activities, (3) financial information, and (4) design and manufacturing specifications and innovations (Bar et al., 1998). Other examples of GISS are information

management programs that organize schedules, files, contacts and other information on desktops to facilitate information exchange with other members. Microsoft Outlook, which comes preloaded on many PC-compatible computers, is one such information management program. More recent examples include software agents such as 'web-bots', or web-based robots, that assist group members by providing them, in some cases proactively, with relevant information scanned from digital repositories.

GXSS: Supporting External Communication

The GXSS function is a special case of both the GCSS function and the GISS function. Communication between group members and key external 'human' agents can be done with any of the GCSS systems described above. At the same time, one can consider interaction with non-human agents (such as webbots) external to the group as accessing yet another kind of information database, thus making it a special case of GISS. Organizations are increasingly able to interconnect seamlessly the human agents and non-human agents on their intranets with those of their clients, partners, suppliers or subcontractors, via secure web-based 'extranets' (Barr et al., 1998). As such, extranets serve as a unified infrastructure for GXSS that reaches beyond the traditional organizational boundary or its digital analogue, the corporate 'firewall'.

GPSS: Modifying the Group's Task Performance

For several decades, researchers have designed and evaluated strategies to structure the interaction among group members in order to enhance their effectiveness. These strategies, often under the stewardship of a facilitator or supervisor, constrain and structure the communication, the task information available, and/or the form and sequence of task responses permitted and required of the group.

Some examples of such strategies are brainstorming, the Delphi method and the nominal group technique (NGT) (for a summary, see McGrath, 1984).

More recently, technologically enabled group performance support systems (GPSS) have been deployed to assist with these strategies. An influential effort has focused specifically on technologically enabled strategies to enhance decision-making among groups. These GPSS are also called GDSS or group decision support systems (see Jessup and Valacich, 1993, for discussion). In the late 1980s and early 1990s, most GPSS were in the form of decision rooms – specially equipped computer labs supporting synchronous groups with co-located members. Most groups used these systems to augment their face-to-face decisions. These systems varied as to the type of task support provided to groups, the size of groups that could use the system, and whether a trained facilitator was necessary to augment the GPSS. Those that provided direct task support for groups usually incorporated an array of 'modules', each of which structures a different subset of a group's tasks or different portions of the group process on a given project. For example, a GPSS might include tools or modules for electronic brainstorming; for structuring various forms of evaluation and voting (rating, ranking, weighing, pick one, pick any, etc.); for identifying stakeholders and bringing their assumptions to the surface; or for exchanging anonymous or identified comments on any or all topics. Efforts are under way to develop these systems to support asynchronous and synchronous groups on the Internet. More recently, GPSS have been designed to encompass more than just decision-making. Current efforts in the area of workflow management, enterprise resource planning and computer-supported cooperative work (discussed by Star and Bowker and others elsewhere in this volume) underscore efforts to enhance group performance beyond simply decision-making.

Theoretical Perspectives

Most prior theory and research have focused primarily on how groups using technology accomplished their tasks differently from groups without access to technology. More specifically, much of the early theory relevant to the study of groups and technology addressed how the interaction and performance of groups that were separated in space and time differed from face-to-face groups. This research centred on those technologies classified as GCSS. One set of theories dealt with the topic of media choice or media selection: how people make choices about different media to use in their communication with others. Another set dealt with the topic of media effects: how technologies can impact group interaction processes and group outcomes. A third stream of theorizing explored the interrelations between technologies and group interaction by attempting to integrate the arguments offered by media choice and media effects theorists. Specifically, adaptive structuration theory (AST) examined how the structures that are imposed by technologies recursively shape and in turn are shaped by group interaction. Most of the empirical investigations of this perspective were conducted with technologies classified as GPSS. Finally, the most current theory that relates to groups and technology deals with the complexity of group processes, and suggests that technology is only one of many factors that can influence group processes and outcomes.

Media Choice

Some of the earliest theoretical work on media choice was conducted before computer use was widespread, and hence dealt with communication systems other than computers. Short et al. (1976) proposed the *social presence model* to predict which media individuals will use for certain types of interactions. Social presence refers to the degree of salience of the other person involved in the interaction, and was therefore assumed to be an 'objective' dimension that could be calibrated by a researcher independent of the users. They hypothesized that media differed in their social presence, and that individuals are aware of and agree on this difference and use it as a basis of their media choice. For instance, they argued that on an objective scale, text-based communication has a lower social presence than video conferencing, which in turn has a lower social presence than face-to-face communication. Further they argued that individuals would select a communication medium that had a social presence commensurate with the task they were trying to accomplish. Specifically, they predicted that individuals avoid a given medium for a given type of interaction if they perceive that medium as not providing a high enough degree of social presence for that type of interaction. They also predicted that communication using media low in social presence would be more appropriate for task-related communication while media high in social presence, such as face-to-face communication, were more appropriate for transacting interpersonal (or socioemotional) content.

Daft and Lengel (1986) extended the ideas embodied in the social presence model in their theory of *media richness*. They proposed that different forms of communication differ in the 'richness' of the information that they provide. Richness was defined as the ability of a medium to provide multiple cues (verbal and non-verbal), and immediate (or quick) feedback, using multiple modalities (text, video, audio and graphics). Based on these criteria they arrayed the various media from very lean (company policy manuals for rules and regulations) to lean (formal information systems) to somewhat rich (direct contact) to very rich (group meetings). Further, they argued that the various information processing tasks conducted by group members could also be objectively arrayed in terms of their equivocality and uncertainty. Some communication tasks, such as finding the latest sales figures, entailed reducing uncertainty (that is, finding the right answer to a question). Other tasks, such as crafting a sales strategy, required reducing equivocality (that is, determining what is the right question to answer). Media richness theory proposed that 'rich' media were more appropriate to reduce equivocality and 'lean' media were more appropriate to reduce uncertainty. Daft and Lengel argued that managers use (and should use) different communication methods of appropriate degrees of richness to deal with situations that differ in equivocality and uncertainty. Hence, different communication media, or structural mechanisms in their terminology, need to be used for different types of organizational tasks. The more equivocality a situation involves, the richer the information required to deal with it. They presented seven structural mechanisms ordered along an information richness continuum based on capacity for resolving equivocality versus reducing uncertainty. The seven mechanisms included: group meetings, integrators, direct contact, planning, special reports, formal information systems, and rules and regulations.

At the time media richness theory was first proposed, e-mail was not widely available in organizations; however, this theory was featured quite prominently in early empirical research that addressed predictors of e-mail usage in organizations. It was argued that managers whose choice of media reflected the equivocality or uncertainty of the task were perceived to be more competent. Some researchers (Trevino et al., 1990) found support for this argument, but many others did not (e.g. El-Shinnawy and Markus, 1997). One of the early criticisms of the model was that, like social presence theory, it assumed that media richness was considered to be an objective dimension; that is, each medium provided the same amount of richness, predetermined by the inherent attributes of the technology, regardless of who was using it (Culnan and Markus, 1997). Other scholars proposed that media richness was a subjective dimension. For example, e-mail may be perceived as a richer medium by people experienced with that technology than by those who are not. Still others noted that most tasks involved varying degrees of uncertainty and equivocality and that it was often not feasible to parse the task into subtasks that were uniformly high or low in terms of their uncertainty or equivocality. As such, for these unbundled tasks

it did not make much sense to dictate the use of lean or rich media.

Social presence theory and media richness theory were influential early attempts to understand media choice among group members. The lack of consistent empirical support for these theories was attributed to the theories' assumptions about ascribing objective attributes (social presence or media richness) to different communication technologies. As a result, alternative media selection theories were put forward that could account for these inconsistent findings.

One such theoretical formulation was the *social influence model*. Fulk et al. (1990) contended that the media richness model is more normative than descriptive of communication patterns in organizations. They argued that individual perceptions of the information richness of various media can vary, and that it was important to measure those perceptions rather than to rely solely on an objective assessment. They contended that objective features of media richness can and do influence individual perceptions of media richness, but there are other sources of such influence, such as social interaction. Drawing upon earlier research on social learning theory and social information processing theory, they argued that social interaction in the workplace shapes the creation of shared meanings, and that those shared meanings provide an important basis for shared patterns of media selection (Fulk et al., 1990; Schmitz and Fulk, 1991).

The social influence model hypothesized that media perceptions and use: (1) are subject to social influence; (2) may be subjectively or retrospectively rationalized; (3) are not necessarily aimed at maximizing efficiency; and (4) may be designed to preserve or create ambiguity to achieve strategic goals. Schmitz and Fulk (1991) found that perceived (as distinct from objectively defined) e-mail richness predicted individuals' e-mail assessments and usage and that the opinions of colleagues influenced others' media assessments. These results supported the notion that other group members can influence how individuals perceive and use technology.

The social influence model of media selection explicitly recognized the role of group members' communication networks in shaping their perception of media richness. An important implication, not addressed by the social influence theory, was how media selection in turn influenced the subsequent structure of the communication network itself (Contractor and Eisenberg, 1990). For instance, group members may be socially influenced by other members in their primarily face-to-face communication network to begin using e-mail. However, once these members begin to use e-mail, the new contacts available through this new medium may enlarge and possibly modify their pre-existing communication network. That is, it is possible that the networks that socially influence individuals' media choices may in turn occasion a restructuring in their communication network. In essence, this observation points to a 'media effect' resulting from a 'media choice'. The following section describes an influential stream of research on the effects of media use on groups.

Media choice theories may be rendered less relevant today by developments in technologies. Increasingly, the convergence to a unified multimodal (audio, video, text and graphic) forum for communication makes interest in the distinctions between media, and hence the question of media choice, obsolete. Unlike the context in which media selection theories were developed, today it is increasingly plausible – even probable – for group members to simultaneously communicate via multiple modalities through a single device. An example would be the use of the web page to simultaneously communicate via audio and video, while sharing a document, and jointly executing a graphic simulation.

Media Effects

Hiltz and Turoff (1978) were among the first to describe differences between face-to-face and computer-mediated interaction in terms of social and psychological processes, and to discuss the importance of task–media contingencies. Hiltz and Turoff argued that groups communicating via computer had access to a narrower band of communication than groups communicating face-to-face. For example, non-verbal communication and paralanguage either were not available or were substantially reduced in computer-mediated communication. In some situations, such narrowband communication allowed information to be communicated with more precision and less noise, and afforded the opportunity for rational judgement processes to operate in the group with less intrusion of non-rational considerations. In other situations, computer conferencing needed to be supplemented by other media in which non-verbal communication and paralanguage were available. They were also among the first to present empirical findings that explored the effects of computer conferencing on the distribution of participation among members, on the amount of task and social communication, and on user responses to the availability and their satisfaction with the system (Hiltz et al., 1986).

Kiesler et al. (1984) provided a theoretical rationale as to why and how groups will differ when they use computer-mediated as compared with face-to-face communication. They proposed that computer-mediated communication depersonalizes the interaction process, with several concomitant effects. Individuals tend to lose mental sight of their interaction partners. At the same time, they lose access to a variety of cues that provide feedback to members regarding the impact of their behaviour on interaction partners, their status and their individuality. Thus, computer-mediated communication removes substantial social information and eliminates much of the feedback that people ordinarily communicate to one another face-to-face. This can have both positive and negative influences on the interaction processes, task outcomes and responses of users (Sproull and Kiesler, 1991).

People feel less inhibited when interacting through a computer network as a result of the reduction in social cues that provide information regarding one's status in the group. Therefore, participants concentrate more on the messages and less on the persons involved in the communication. Individuals feel less committed to what they say, less concerned about it, and less worried about how it will be received by their communication partners. Because people communicating electronically are less aware of social differences, they feel a greater sense of anonymity and detect less individuality in others. As a consequence, individuals engaged in computer-mediated group interaction tend to:

1 feel more anonymous and detect less individuality in their communication partners;
2 participate more equally (because low-status members are less inhibited);
3 focus more on task and instrumental aspects and less on personal and social aspects of interaction (because the context is depersonalized);
4 communicate more negative and more uninhibited messages (because they are less concerned with politeness norms that tend to regulate communication in face-to-face groups); and
5 experience more difficulty in attaining group consensus (both because of elimination of much interpersonal feedback, and because of reduced concern with social norms).

All of these effects have been demonstrated empirically (for review, see Kiesler and Sproull, 1992), and will be revisited in greater detail later in this chapter.

McGrath and Hollingshead (1993; 1994), building on the work described above and applying it to work groups, maintained that group interaction and performance are greatly affected by the type and difficulty of the task that the group is performing, and that the effects of technology on group interaction and performance interact with task type. They hypothesized that the effectiveness of a group on a task will vary with the fit between the richness of the information that can be transmitted using that system's technology and the information richness requirements of the group's task. However, as groups developed more experience with a given communication technology, the richness of the information that could be transmitted effectively via that technology would increase.

McGrath and Hollingshead posited that group tasks differed in their information richness requirements. Information richness referred to how much the information contains surplus emotional, attitudinal, normative and other meanings, beyond the literal cognitive denotations of the symbols used to express it. They also posited that communication media differed in the richness of the information that they can and do convey. Face-to-face communication among interpersonally involved humans was the richest medium; communication in written form among strangers was the least rich. Computer communication among group members inexperienced with the technology is at the low-richness end of that continuum.

Drawing from McGrath's (1984) task typology, McGrath and Hollingshead hypothesized that groups working on generate tasks (e.g. simple brainstorming tasks) do not require the transmission of evaluative and emotional content. As a result, computer-supported groups may brainstorm more effectively than face-to-face groups. At the other end of the continuum, groups negotiating and resolving conflicts of views or interests may require the transmission of maximally rich information, including not only 'facts' but also values, attitudes, emotions, etc. As a result, groups interacting face-to-face should perform such tasks more effectively than groups interacting via computer. In between the two ends of the continuum are intellective tasks that have a correct answer or decision-making tasks that do not have a correct answer, which may require some intermediary level of information richness. The predictions for generate tasks and negotiation tasks received empirical support (Gallupe et al., 1991; Hollingshead et al., 1993; Valacich et al., 1994), but not those for intellective and decision-making tasks (Hollingshead et al., 1993; Straus and McGrath, 1994).

McGrath and Hollingshead (1994) also predicted that communication technologies could provide information of increasing richness over time, as groups learned how to embed additional emotional, attitudinal, normative and other meaning through continued experience.

In summary, the theoretical arguments reviewed in this section offer three related perspectives on how technologies may influence the processes and outcomes of groups. While they vary in their levels of sophistication and theoretical complexity, all three theoretical approaches to media effects are based on the premise that technological attributes of different media influence key aspects of the interaction process. These key aspects include the availability of non-verbal cues, the potential for anonymous contributions, the ability to communicate status differentials, and the information richness of the medium. These key aspects in turn helped or hindered the group's interaction process (such as amount of participation, distribution of participation

and negativity in communication on 'flaming'), as well as the group's outcomes (such as consensus, accuracy and speed of decision-making).

As such these theoretical perspectives on media effects acknowledge a modicum of technological determinism. Not unlike the media choice theories of social presence and media richness, discussed in the previous section, the theories of media effects described in this section do not privilege a socially constructed explanation for understanding media effects. The following section offers a theoretical framework that explicitly recognizes the social nature of technology and advocates an inextricable interrelatedness between media choice and media effects.

Adaptive Structuration Theory

Adaptive structuration theory (AST), proposed by Poole and DeSanctis (1990) and inspired by the influential theoretical contributions of Giddens' (1984) structuration theory, stresses the importance of group interaction processes, both in determining group outcomes and in mediating the effects of any given technology. Essentially, a social technology presents a structure of rules and operations to a group, but the group does not passively choose the technology in its pre-existing form. Rather, the group actively adapts the technology to its own ends, resulting in a restructuring of the technology as it is meshed with the group's own interaction system. Thus, a technology can be thought of as a set of social practices that emerge and evolve over time.

From this point of view, the structure of a group is not a permanent, concrete set of relations between members and their tasks. Rather, the structure is an evolving set of rules and resources available to them to produce and reproduce the apparently stable interaction systems that we observe. Thus, there is a recursive process between the structures (or the rules and resources in a group) and the systems (the interaction patterns in the groups). The rules or resources in the group shape the interactions patterns among group members. The interaction patterns among the group members, in turn, reify or subvert the rules and resources in the group. This recursive process is called adaptive structuration.

The rules and resources that groups use in the structuration process are sometimes created on the fly by the group, but more often they are *faithfully appropriated* by the group based on the social context in which it is embedded. *Appropriation* is the process by which a group selects features of a technology and socially constructs their meaning. It is through such appropriation that a group can choose to use a new technology. In some cases the group may not appropriate a technology in ways that were intended by the designers of the technology. This situation is referred to as an *ironic appropriation*. For instance, a group may have access to a group decision support system (GDSS) that provides them with an opportunity to vote on their ideas. The voting tool is intended by the designers of the technology to facilitate democratic deliberation among group members. However, in some instances members of a group may use the voting tool to prematurely close off discussion of an issue. This action would illustrate an ironic appropriation of the GDSS. By faithfully or ironically appropriating a technology, each group invests meaning in, and thereby adapts for its use, the rules and resources that it draws upon. Both technology and context affect group processes and outcomes because they affect this appropriation process.

Empirical research has shown that different, but seemingly similar, groups appropriate the same technology in different ways (DeSanctis and Poole, 1997; Poole and DeSanctis, 1992; for a review see DeSanctis and Poole, 1994). Zack and McKenney (1995) offer a recent example of work in this tradition. They examined the appropriation of the same group authoring and messaging computer system by the managing editorial groups of two morning newspapers owned by the same parent corporation. Drawing upon Poole and DeSanctis' (1990) theory of adaptive structuration, they discovered that the two groups' appropriation of the technology, as indexed by their communication networks, differed in accordance with the different contexts at the two locations. Further, they found evidence that the groups' performance outcomes for similar tasks were mediated by these interaction patterns.

Adaptive structuration theory continues to be an increasingly influential perspective to understand the socially constructed ways in which groups' choice of media and the effects of media on groups coevolve. It provides a powerful analytic framework to account for stability and change in a group's appropriation of new media. While the utility of a structurational perspective to the study of groups' use of new media is compelling, there continues to be a debate about the extent to which empirical studies offer a 'test' as opposed to an illustration of structuration theory's ability to explain the unfolding of complex processes (DeSanctis and Poole, 1994). Indeed, in a review of empirical studies from a structurational perspective, one would be hard pressed to identify a single work which failed to find support for adaptive structuration theory. Such overwhelming endorsement of a theory belies an underlying concern about the potential falsifiability of the theory. An appropriate challenge therefore would be to come up with specific predictions from the theory that, if they were not empirically validated, would plausibly represent a refutation of the premises of adaptive structuration theory. Complexity theory, discussed in the next section, offers a novel and useful approach to translate the richly evocative, but highly abbreviated, verbal explications of adaptive structuration theory into precise, falsifiable hypotheses that can be empirically validated (Poole, 1997).

Groups as Complex Systems

In the past decade there has been a plethora of scholarship calling for the extension of complexity theory – arguably a mainstay of many disciplines in the physical and life sciences – to social sciences in general, and to the study of groups in particular (Arrow et al., 2000; Contractor and Seibold, 1993; Contractor and Whitbred, 1997; Gersick, 1991; McGrath, 1991). The motivation for this call stems from a widely shared frustration with extant theories, which have proven to be inadequate at untangling with precision the complexity in group processes. The phenomena described in verbal expositions of, say, adaptive structuration theory invoke a multitude of factors that are highly interconnected, often via complex, non-linear, dynamic relationships. Lamenting the failed promise of earlier forays into systems theory, Poole notes, 'Most often, systems theory became a metaphor, rather than an instrument of analysis' (1997: 50). Two streams of research that attempt to go beyond the use of complexity theory as a metaphor (Contractor, 1999) have been developed to deal with the complexity of groups' use of new media: groups as self-organizing systems (Contractor and Seibold, 1993; Contractor and Whitbred, 1997) and groups as complex, adaptive and dynamic systems (Arrow et al., 2000).

Groups as Self-organizing Systems

In general terms, 'self-organizing systems theory (SOST) seeks to explain the emergence of patterned behaviour in systems that are initially in a state of disorganization. It offers a conceptual framework to explicitly articulate the underlying generative mechanisms and to systematically examine the processes by which these mechanisms generate, sustain and change existing structures or elaborate new structures' (Contractor and Seibold, 1993: 536).

Ilya Prigogine and his colleagues proposed the theory of self-organization. In an effort that contributed to a Nobel Prize, Prigogine and his colleagues (Glansdorff and Prigogine, 1971) mathematically proved that systems that exhibit emergence of spontaneous order must meet the following logical requirements:

1 At least one of the components in the system must exhibit autocatalysis, i.e. self-referencing.
2 At least two of the components in the system must be mutually causal.

3 The system must be open to the environment with respect to the exchange of energy and matter.

4 The system must operate in a far-from-equilibrium condition.

These four requirements offer, at a very abstract level, the conditions under which any system can self-organize. Our interests here are in applying these concepts to the study of groups using new media. Contractor and Seibold (1993) developed a self-organizing systems model for groups' use of group decision support systems (GDSS). They developed a model based on the theoretical mechanisms specified by adaptive structuration theory (Poole and DeSanctis, 1990; discussed in the previous section) about the recursive interrelationship between the structures (the rules and resources within the group) and the systems (the interaction patterns among the group members). Contractor and Seibold (1993: 537–8) specified four generative mechanisms that were consistent with the theoretical tenets of adaptive structuration theory and met the logical requirements of self-organizing systems theory:

1 Members' expertise (or resources) with the task will reinforce the content and pattern of their communication during GDSS-based discussions.

2 The content and pattern of members' communication will reinforce their perceptions of the group's norms for structuring the GDSS-based discussion.

3 Members' expertise (or resources) with GDSS will reinforce their perceptions of the group's norms for structuring the GDSS-based discussions.

4 Members' perceptions of the group's norms for structuring the GDSS-based discussion will reinforce the content and pattern of their communication.

Using simulations, they showed that based on these four theoretical mechanisms the group's use of GDSS would self-organize only under a very specific range of initial conditions. A group using GDSS was considered to have self-organized when the group's structures (that is, its members' perceptions of the rules) were stable and the group members' interaction patterns were reproducing and reinforcing (rather than subverting) these stable structures. The simulation also provided precise conditions under which the groups would *not* successfully appropriate the technology. That is, the group might initially attempt to use the technology but would then discontinue its use. These results, theoretically grounded in adaptive structuration theory and logically consistent with self-organizing systems theory, represent plausible occurrences in groups' use of new media. They also respond to one of the

criticisms levelled against adaptive structuration theory by making its explanations more amenable to falsification. In general terms, the approach illustrates how self-organizing systems theory can offer the logical conditions and the analytic framework to discover precise, empirically falsifiable hypotheses about the use (and lack thereof) of new media by groups.

Groups as Complex, Adaptive and Dynamic Systems

Arrow et al. (2000) have proposed a general theory of complex systems, which embeds technology as one aspect of the system. This theory builds on the time interaction and performance (TIP) theory proposed by McGrath (1991). TIP theory assumes that groups pursue multiple functions for multiple projects by means of complex time/activity paths. Arrow et al. (2000) extend this theory by proposing that all groups act in the service of two generic functions: (1) *to complete group projects* and (2) to *fulfil member needs*. A group's success in pursuing these two functions affects and depends on the viability and integrity of the group as a system. Thus, *maintaining system integrity* becomes a third function, instrumental to the other two. A group's system integrity in turn affects its ability to complete group projects and fulfil member needs.

Groups include three types of elements: (1) people who become group *members*; (2) goals that are embodied in group *projects*; and (3) resources that get transformed into group *technologies*. Technologies differ in how much they facilitate or constrain interpersonal activity, task activity and procedural activity; and in how effectively they support different instrumental functions (i.e. processing of information, managing of conflict and consensus, and motivation, regulation and coordination of member behaviours).

A group pursues its functions by creating and enacting a coordinated pattern of member–task–tool relations, its *coordination network*. The full coordination network includes six component networks: (1) the *member network*, or pattern of member–member relations (such as status relations); (2) the *task network*, or pattern of task–task relations (e.g. the required sequence for completion of a set of tasks); (3) the *tool network*, or pattern of tool–tool relations (e.g. the procedure by which a technology can be used most efficiently); (4) the *labour network*, or pattern of member–task relations (i.e. who is supposed to do what); (5) the *role network*, or pattern of member–tool relations (i.e. how members do their tasks); and (6) the *job network*, or pattern of task–tool relations (e.g. what piece of equipment must be used for a given task).

The life course of a group can be characterized by three logically ordered modes that are conceptually distinct but have fuzzy temporal boundaries:

formation, operation and *metamorphosis*. As a group forms, people, intentions and resources become organized into an initial coordination network of relations among members, projects and technology that demarcates that group as a bounded social entity. As a group operates over time in the service of group projects and member needs, its members elaborate, enact, monitor and modify the coordination network established during formation. Groups both learn from their own experience and adapt to events occurring in their environment. If and when a group undergoes metamorphosis, it dissolves or is transformed into a different social entity.

OVERVIEW OF MAJOR EMPIRICAL FINDINGS

A number of scholars have written literature reviews that examine communication technologies and groups (e.g. Benbasat and Lim, 1993; Hollingshead and McGrath, 1995; Kiesler and Sproull, 1992; Kraemer and Pinsonneault, 1990; McGrath and Hollingshead, 1994; McLeod, 1992; 1996; Seibold et al., 1994; Williams, 1977). Most of these reviews have compared the interaction processes and outcomes of computer-mediated groups with those of face-to-face groups. Several of those reviews have reached the same conclusions about the state of knowledge in this area: namely, that more theory-guided and programmatic research is needed (e.g. Hollingshead and McGrath, 1995; McLeod, 1992).

Interaction Patterns

Many studies have revealed that groups interacting via computers have more equal participation among members than groups interacting face-to-face (e.g. Clapper et al., 1991; Daly, 1993; Dubrovsky et al., 1991; George et al., 1990; Hiltz et al., 1986; McLeod, 1992; Rice, 1984; Siegel et al., 1986; Straus, 1996; Straus and McGrath, 1994; Zigurs et al., 1988). As described earlier, the general explanation for the effect is that people feel less inhibited when interacting through a computer network as a result of the reduction in social cues that provide information regarding one's status in the group. Because people communicating electronically are less aware of social differences, they feel a greater sense of anonymity and detect less individuality in others (Sproull and Kiesler, 1991). It is important to note some common elements across this set of studies. These studies were conducted during one experimental session with *ad hoc* groups consisting of students in a laboratory setting. However, it is also important to note that this finding was observed across a variety of communication technologies.

Many studies have also showed no evidence of the participation equalization effect in computer-mediated groups (Berdahl and Craig, 1996; Hollingshead, 1996b; Lea and Spears, 1991; McLeod and Liker, 1992; McLeod et al., 1997; Saunders et al., 1994; Spears and Lea, 1992; Watson et al., 1988; Weisband, 1992; Weisband et al., 1995). In fact, most showed that status differences among participants were displayed in their interaction in the computer-mediated setting. One explanation for the inconsistency of findings across studies is that status differences among members within the groups may have been differentially salient across studies. When members' identities were known or were available visually, the status differences in the number of contributions and the perceived influence of those contributions were maintained in the computer-mediated setting. When they were not or when members' contributions were anonymous, the participation equalization effect was more likely to occur.

It is also possible that the participation equalization may be an indication of how the medium reduces the baseline of each member's participation rather than how the medium leads to increased participation of low-status members during the group discussion (McGrath and Hollingshead, 1994; Spears and Lea, 1994). It takes more time to type a message on a computer network than it does to say that same message verbally. In the experiments cited above, the computer sessions were at least as long as those face-to-face group meetings; however, the amount and the rate of communication in the computer-mediated setting were much less. Another possible technological explanation for greater egalitarian participation patterns in computer-mediated settings is that electronic group members have the ability to participate without interruption, since turn-taking is not a norm in a computer-mediated environment (Weisband et al., 1995).

A number of studies have found that computer-mediated groups exchange less information and are less likely to repeat information in their decisions than face-to-face groups (Hollingshead, 1996a; 1996b; McLeod et al., 1997; Straus and McGrath, 1994). In some cases, this reduction can lead to poorer outcomes for newly formed groups (cf. Hollingshead, 1996a; 1996b).

Performance

Very few studies have demonstrated that groups communicating via computer perform better than groups interacting face-to-face, although many have demonstrated that computer-mediated groups perform less well than or equally well as face-to-face groups (for reviews see McGrath and Hollingshead, 1994; McLeod, 1992; 1996). Even though computer-mediated groups generate less communication and use less information in their decisions, they take longer to make them (Hollingshead, 1996a). They are also less likely to reach consensus (for reviews see Hollingshead and McGrath, 1995; Kiesler and Sproul, 1992).

As described earlier, there seems to be an interaction effect of task and technology on the quality of group performance. Computer groups produce more ideas of higher quality on idea generation tasks. Face-to-face groups tend to have higher-quality products on intellective and negotiation tasks. However, it may be the structure that is imposed by the technology rather than the technology itself that is responsible for this effect (Hollingshead and McGrath, 1995). The task structure may include: procedures that simplify the handling of complex information; procedures that explicate agenda, thus making group process more organized; and procedures that expose conflict and help the group to deal with it. Some research showed that a paper and pencil version of the task structure imposed by the technology (i.e. without electronic communication) gave higher-quality decisions than the same task structure provided by a GPSS, which in turn was higher than the no-structure face-to-face condition (Hollingshead and McGrath, 1995; Watson et al., 1988). In some cases, newly formed groups on computers may have problems with task structure that requires more complex information processing (Hollingshead, 1996a).

Longitudinal research comparing the impact of computer-mediated and face-to-face communication over time has brought into question previous findings of significant differences in performance between face-to-face and computer-mediated groups. That research has shown that computer-mediated communication hinders the interaction process and performance of groups initially, but over time, groups can adjust successfully to their mode of communication (see McGrath et al., 1993 and Arrow et al., 1996 for overviews). In addition, work on the interpersonal and relationship aspects of computer-mediated communication over time complements this finding. Walther and Burgoon (1992) showed that members of computer-mediated groups felt less connected to one another initially, but over time, members of computer-mediated groups expressed more positive feelings about one another that approximated those expressed by members of face-to-face groups. The transient effects of technology were also illustrated in a longitudinal study comparing the developments of norms in groups using GDSS with groups not using GDSS. Contractor et al. (1996) found that while members of non-GDSS groups were initially more likely than members of GDSS groups to socially influence one another's perceptions of the group's norms, this difference dissipated over time. That is, in the long term,

groups using GDSS were no more likely than groups not using GDSS to socially influence one another's perceptions of the groups' norms.

THE RECONCEPTUALIZATION OF GROUPS AND NEW MEDIA AS KNOWLEDGE NETWORKS

While it should be evident that the study of groups and new media is a vibrant area for research, we now return to the opening statements of this chapter about the theoretical and analytic challenges that confront scholars who consider the ways in which the 'new' new media of the twenty-first century will influence our ability to organize in groups. In conclusion, we offer a reconceptualization of groups' use of new media from a knowledge networks perspective.

From Knowledge Management to Knowledge Networks

Knowledge management is a critical concern for contemporary organizations, and it is expected to become increasingly important in the future (Nonaka and Takeuchi, 1995). It has long been recognized that computers could increase the range, depth and speed with which information could be acquired, processed, presented for use and shared for collaborative efforts. However, research in this area has given little attention to theoretical or conceptual issues about information acquisition, processing and integration, and even less attention to theoretical issues about the antecedents and consequences of different patterns of information distribution within work groups, and the conditions under which information can be and is easily shared among group members. Recent developments in technologies have shown their potential as knowledge management systems, although little is known about the social challenges and motivations for group members to use these systems effectively. These challenges call for a knowledge network approach (Monge and Contractor, 2001) and knowledge-based theories to understand groups' use of new media.

Groups as Knowledge Networks

The proliferation of digital technologies has dramatically changed the nature of work in groups. These technologies, as described previously, have the potential to provide many benefits to groups by linking people who have common goals and interests but are separated in time and space. They may enable organizations to develop effective teams from workers who are geographically distributed.

Today, in stark contrast to just a decade ago, virtual teams consider having employees located in time zones far removed from one another (such as California, Ireland and India) as a competitive advantage rather than a disadvantage. Members of distributed work teams can work round the clock in order to meet the competitive demands of a global marketplace. In some cases the members of these teams are 'e-lancers' (electronic freelancers) who coalesce on a short-term project and then disperse. In other cases, the technologies have the potential to enable the organization to hire and retain the best people, regardless of location (Townsend et al., 1996). These changes have led scholars to call for a reconceptualization of groups as much more fluid, dynamic, multiplex and activity based (Goodman and Wilson, 2000).

Clearly these new technologies have the potential to nurture a team by linking the members not only to one another but also to a large number of internal and external knowledge repositories. Conceptually, therefore, it is increasingly useful to consider the group and its members as a network of agents, where some of the agents are human agents while others are non-human agents (such as knowledge repositories, avatars and webbots). Human agents communicate with one another by retrieving and allocating information relevant to their collective tasks. An increasingly vexing question that group members face in this networked environment is not which medium to use (as was addressed by earlier theories of media choice), but rather which agent to use.

Groups and the media they use can be usefully reconceptualized as a *knowledge network*. A network is made up of a set of nodes and relations between these nodes. The nodes that contain the knowledge can be people, databases, computer files or other forms of repositories. The relations are the communication relations (that is, publishing, retrieving, allocating) among the nodes. The location of knowledge within this network of agents can vary along a continuum from centralized, where knowledge resides with only one agent, to distributed, where knowledge exists among many agents (Farace et al., 1977). Distributed knowledge may refer to the parts of a larger knowledge base, each possessed by separate actors within the network. In this form of distributed knowledge, actors bring relatively unique, non-redundant knowledge which enables a collective to accomplish complex tasks. Distributed knowledge occurs at many levels in the empirical world, including work groups, large-scale project teams, and interorganizational strategic alliances. Alternatively, distributed knowledge may refer to the flow or diffusion of knowledge, which increases the level of knowledge among all actors.

Communication networks, actual knowledge networks, and cognitive knowledge networks are different ways of conceptualizing the network of agents. Communication networks represent the degree to which individual agents interact with other agents in the network. Actual knowledge networks represent the actual distribution of knowledge among the network of agents. Cognitive knowledge networks represent individuals' perceptions of the distribution of knowledge in the network of agents. Knowledge networks are dynamic, in terms of both agents and linkages. Agents join or leave a knowledge network on the basis of tasks to be accomplished, and their levels of interests, resources and commitments. The links within the knowledge network are also likely to change on the basis of evolving tasks, the distribution of knowledge within the network, or changes in the agents' cognitive knowledge networks. New media, such as intranets, serve both as the infrastructure that supports the development of relations in the network and as the nodes in the network. In our own research, we have applied a knowledge network perspective to theories that investigate new media use in groups and organizations (Hollingshead et al., 2001; Monge and Contractor, 2001).

We believe there is tremendous potential for the development and extension of theories which seek to explain the development of a group's use of media as a knowledge network of human and non-human agents. The knowledge network perspective is especially well suited to test multiple theories and their contradictory or complementary influences on the evolution of the groups. Knowledge networks and their defining characteristics can be represented and analysed exceptionally well using techniques developed within the field of social network analysis (Wasserman and Faust, 1994). These techniques enable researchers to examine the dynamics of relations at multiple sites and across different levels of analysis (individual, dyads, group, organizations and industries). It is difficult to predict the types of configurations that groups with technology will take in the future. Regardless of their forms, a knowledge network perspective will allow future researchers to examine, describe and evaluate new media and organizing at the group level.

References

Alexander, S.C., Wille, J. and Hollingshead, A.B. (in press) 'Support at your keyboard: a study of on-line support groups', in L. Frey (ed.), *Group Communication in Context*, vol. 2. Hillsdale, NJ: Erlbaum.

Arrow, H., Berdahl, J.L., Bouas, K.S., Craig, K.M., Cummings, A., Lebie, L., McGrath, J.E., O'Connor, K.M., Rhoades, J.A. and Schlosser, A. (1996) 'Time, technology, and groups: an integration', *Computer Supported Cooperative Work*, 4: 253–61.

Arrow, H., McGrath, J.E. and Berdahl, J.L. (2000) *Small Groups as Complex Systems: Formation, Coordination, Development, and Adaptation*. Thousand Oaks, CA: Sage.

Bar, F., Borrus, M. and Hanson, W. (1998) 'Web portfolios: leveraging intranets, extranets, and the internet for strategic gain'. Stanford University working paper.

Benbasat, I. and Lim, L. (1993) 'The effects of group, task, context, and technology variables on the usefulness of group support systems: a meta-analysis of experimental studies', *Small Group Research*, 24: 430–62.

Berdahl, J.L. and Craig, K.L. (1996) 'Equality of participation and influence in groups: the effects of communication medium and sex composition', *Computer Supported Cooperative Work*, 4: 179–202.

Clapper, D.L., McLean, E.R. and Watson, R.T. (1991) 'An experimental investigation of the effect of group decision support on normative influence in small groups', in J.I. de Gross, I. Benbasat, G. DeSanctis and C.M. Beath (eds), *Proceedings of the Twelfth International Conference on Information Systems*. New York. pp. 273–82.

Contractor, N.S. (1999) 'Self-organizing systems research in the social sciences: reconciling the metaphors and the models', *Management Communication Quarterly*, 13: 154–66.

Contractor, N. and Bishop, A.P. (2000) 'Reconfiguring community networks: the case of PrairieKNOW', in T. Ishida (ed.), *Digital Cities: Technologies, Experiences, and Future Perspectives*. Berlin: Springer. pp. 151–64.

Contractor, N.S. and Eisenberg, E.M. (1990) 'Communication networks and new media in organizations', in J. Fulk and C.W. Steinfield (eds), *Organizations and Communication Technology*. Newbury Park, CA: Sage. pp. 145–74.

Contractor, N.S. and Seibold, D.R. (1993) 'Theoretical frameworks for the study of structuring processes in group decision support systems: adaptive structuration theory and self-organizing systems theory', *Human Communication Research*, 19: 528–63.

Contractor, N.S. and Whitbred, R. (1997) 'Decision development in work groups: a comparison of contingency and self-organizing systems perspectives', in G. Barnett and L. Thayer (eds), *Organizational Communication: Emerging Perspectives. V: The Renaissance in Systems Thinking*. Greenwich, CT: Ablex. pp. 83–104.

Contractor, N.S., Seibold, D.R. and Heller, M.A. (1996) 'Interactional influence in the structuring of media use in groups: influence of members' perceptions of group decision support system use', *Human Communication Research*, 22: 451–81.

Culnan, M.J. and Markus, M.L. (1987) 'Information technologies', in F.M. Jablin and L.L. Putnam (eds), *Handbook of Organizational Communication: an Interdisciplinary Perspective*. Newbury Park, CA: Sage. pp. 420–43.

Daft, R.L. and Lengel, R.H. (1986) 'Organizational information requirements, media richness and structural design', *Management Science*, 32: 554–71.

Daly, B. (1993) 'The influence of face-to-face versus computer-mediated communication channels on collective induction', *Accounting, Management & Information Technology*, 3 (1): 1–22.

DeSanctis, G. and Poole, M. (1994) 'Capturing the complexity in advanced technology use: adaptive structuration theory', *Organization Science*, 5: 121–47.

DeSanctis, G. and Poole, M.S. (1997) 'Transitions in teamwork in new organizational forms', in *Advances in Group Processes*, vol. 14. Greenwich, CT: JAI. pp. 157–76.

Dubrovsky, V.J., Kiesler, S. and Sethna, B.N. (1991) 'The equalization phenomenon: status effects in computer-mediated and face-to-face decision making groups', *Human–Computer Interaction*, 6: 119–46.

El-Shinnawy, M, and Markus, M.L. (1997) 'The poverty of media richness theory: explaining people's preferences for electronic mail and voice mail', *International Journal of Human Computer Studies*, 46: 443–67.

Farace, R.V., Monge, P.R. and Russell, H.M. (1977) *Communicating and Organizing*. Reading, MA: Addison-Wesley.

Fulk, J., Schmitz, J. and Steinfield, C.W. (1990) 'A social influence model of technology use', in J. Fulk and C.W. Steinfield (eds), *Organizations and Communication Technology*. Newbury Park, CA: Sage. pp. 117–40.

Gallupe, R.B., Bastianutti, L.M. and Cooper, W.H. (1991) 'Unblocking brainstorms', *Journal of Applied Psychology*, 76 (1): 137–42.

George, J., Easton, G., Nunamaker, J. and Northcraft, G. (1990) 'A study of collaborative group work with and without computer-based support', *Information Systems Research*, 1 (4): 394–415.

Gersick, C.J.G. (1991) 'Revolutionary change theories: a multilevel exploration of the punctuated equilibrium paradigm', *Academy of Management Review*, 32: 274–309.

Giddens, A. (1984) *The Constitution of Society: Outline of the Theory of Structuration*. Berkeley, CA: University of California Press.

Glansdorff, P. and Prigogine, I. (1971) *Thermodynamic Study of Structure, Stability and Fluctuations*. New York: Wiley.

Goodman, P.S. and Wilson, J.M. (2000) 'Substitutes for socialization', in M.A. Neale, E.A. Mannix and T. Griffith (eds), *Research on Managing Groups and Teams*. Vol. 3: *Technology*. Stamford, CT: JAI. pp. 53–78.

Hiltz, S.R., Johnson, K. and Turoff, M. (1986) 'Experiments in group decision making. 1: Communications process and outcome in face-to-face vs. computerized conferences', *Human Communication Research*, 13: 225–52.

Hiltz, S.R. and Turoff, M. (1978) *The Network Nation: Human Communication via Computer*. Reading, MA: Addison-Wesley.

Hollingshead, A.B. (1996a) 'Information suppression and status persistence in group decision making: the effects of communication media', *Human Communication Research*, 23: 193–219.

Hollingshead, A.B. (1996b) 'The rank order effect: decision procedure, communication technology and group decisions', *Organizational Behavior and Human Decision Processes*, 68 (3): 1–13.

Hollingshead, A.B. (1998a) 'Retrieval processes in transactive memory systems', *Journal of Personality and Social Psychology*, 74: 659–71.

Hollingshead, A.B. (1998b) 'Distributed knowledge and transactive processes in groups', in M.A. Neale, E.A. Mannix and D.H. Gruenfeld (eds), *Research on Managing Groups and Teams*, vol. 1. Greenwich, CT: JAI. pp. 103–23.

Hollingshead, A.B. (2001) 'Communication technologies, the internet, and group research', in M.A. Hogg and Scott Tindale (eds), *Blackwell Handbook of Social Psychology: Group Processes*. Malden, MA: Blackwell. pp. 557–73.

Hollingshead, A.B. and McGrath, J.E. (1995) 'Computer-assisted groups: a critical review of the empirical research', in R.A. Guzzo and E. Salas (eds), *Team Effectiveness and Decision Making in Organizations*. San Francisco: Jossey-Bass. pp. 46–78.

Hollingshead, A.B., Fulk, J. and Monge, P. (2001) 'Fostering intranet knowledge-sharing: an integration of transactive memory and public goods approaches', in P. Hinds and S. Kiesler (eds), *Distributed Work: New Research on Working across Distance Using Technology*. Cambridge, MA: MIT Press.

Hollingshead, A.B., McGrath, J.E. and O'Connor, K.M. (1993) 'Group task performance and communication technology: a longitudinal study of computer-mediated versus face-to-face work groups', *Small Group Research*, 24: 307–33.

Jessup, L.M. and Valacich, J.E. (eds) (1993) *Group Support Systems: New Perspectives*. New York: Macmillan.

Kiesler, S. and Sproull, L. (1992) 'Group decision making and technology', *Organizational Behavior and Human Decision Processes*, 52: 96–123.

Kiesler, S., Siegel, J. and McGuire, T.W. (1984) 'Social psychological aspects of computer-mediated communication', *American Psychologist*, 39: 1123–34.

Kraemer, K.L. and Pinsonneault, A. (1990) 'Technology and groups: assessments of the empirical research', in J. Galegher, R. Kraut and C. Egido (eds), *Intellectual Teamwork: Social and Technological Foundations of Cooperative Work*. Hillsdale, NJ: Erlbaum. pp. 373–404.

Lea, M. and Spears, R. (1991) 'Computer-mediated communication, de-individuation, and group decision making', *International Journal of Man–Machine Studies*, 34: 283–301.

McGrath, J.E. (1984) *Groups, Interaction, and Performance*. Englewood Cliffs, NJ: Prentice-Hall.

McGrath, J.E. (1991) 'Time, interaction, and performance (TIP): a theory of groups', *Small Group Research*, 22: 147–74.

McGrath, J.E. and Hollingshead, A.B. (1993) 'Putting the "G" back in GSS: some theoretical issues about dynamic processes in groups with technological enhancements', in L.M. Jessup and J.E. Valacich (eds), *Group Support Systems: New Perspectives*. New York: Macmillan.

McGrath, J.E. and Hollingshead, A.B. (1994) *Groups Interacting with Technology*. Newbury Park, CA: Sage.

McGrath, J.E., Arrow, H., Gruenfeld, D.H., Hollingshead, A.B. and O'Connor, K.M. (1993) 'Groups, tasks, technology, and time: an integration', *Small Group Research*, 24: 406–20.

McLeod, P.L. (1992) 'An assessment of the experimental literature on the electronic support of group work: results of a meta-analysis', *Human–Computer Interaction*, 7 (3): 257–80.

McLeod, P.L. (1996) 'New communication technologies for group research: toward an integrative framework', in R. Hirokawa and M.S. Poole (eds), *Communication and Group Decision Making*. 2nd edn. Thousand Oaks, CA: Sage. pp. 426–62.

McLeod, P.L. and Liker, J.K. (1992) 'Electronic meeting systems: evidence from a low structure environment', *Information Systems Research*, 3: 195–223.

McLeod, P.L., Baron, R.S., Marti, M.W. and Kuh, Y. (1997) 'The eyes have it: minority influence in face-to-face and computer-mediated group discussion', *Journal of Applied Psychology*, 82: 706–18.

Monge, P.R. and Contractor, N.S. (2001) 'Emergence of communication networks', in F.M. Jablin and L.L. Putnam (eds), *New Handbook of Organizational Communication*. Newbury Park, CA: Sage. pp. 440–502.

Nonaka, I. and Takeuchi, H. (1995) *The Knowledge-Creating Company: How Japanese Companies Create the Dynamics of Innovation*. New York: Oxford University Press.

Poole, M.S. (1997) 'A turn of the wheel: the case for renewal of systems inquiry in organizational communication research', in G. Barnett and L. Thayer (eds), *Organizational Communication: Emerging Perspectives. V: The Renaissance in Systems Thinking*. Greenwich, CT: Ablex. pp. 47–63.

Poole, M.S. and DeSanctis, G. (1990) 'Understanding the use of group decision support systems: the theory of adaptive structuration', in J. Fulk and C. Steinfield (eds), *Organizations and Communication Technology*. Newbury Park, CA: Sage. pp. 175–95.

Poole, M.S. and DeSanctis, G. (1992) 'Microlevel structuration in computer-supported group decision making', *Human Communication Research*, 19: 5–49.

Rice, R.E. (1984) 'Mediated group communication', in R.E. Rice & Associates (eds), *The New Media: Communication, Research, and Technology*. Beverly Hills, CA: Sage. pp. 129–54.

Saunders, C., Robey, D. and Vaverek, K. (1994) 'The persistence of status differentials in computer conferencing', *Human Communication Research*, 20: 443–72.

Schmitz, J. and Fulk, J. (1991) 'Organizational colleagues, media richness, and electronic mail: a test of the social influence model of technology use', *Communication Research*. 18: 487–523.

Seibold, D., Heller, M.A. and Contractor, N. (1994) 'Review and critique of empirical research on group decision support systems', in B. Kovacic (ed.), *Organizational Communication: New Perspectives.* Albany, NY: State University of New York Press. pp. 143–68.

Short, J.A., Williams, E. and Christie, B. (1976) *The Social Psychology of Telecommunications.* London: Wiley.

Siegel, J., Dubrovsky, V., Kiesler, S. and McGuire, T.W. (1986) 'Group processes in computer-mediated communication', *Organizational Behavior & Human Decision Processes*, 37: 157–87.

Spears, R. and Lea, M. (1992) 'Social influence and the influence of the "social" in computer-mediated communication', in M. Lea (ed.), *Contexts of Computer-Mediated Communication.* London: Harvester-Wheatsheaf. pp. 30–65.

Spears, R. and Lea, M. (1994) 'Panacea or panopticon? The hidden power in computer-mediated communication', *Communication Research*, 21: 427–59.

Sproull, L.S. and Kiesler, S. (1991) *Connections: New Ways of Working in the Networked Organization.* Cambridge, MA: MIT Press.

Straus, S. (1996) 'Getting a clue: the effects of communication media and information distribution on participation and performance in computer-mediated and face-to-face groups', *Small Group Research*, 27: 115–42.

Straus, S. and McGrath, J.E. (1994) 'Does the medium matter? The interaction of task type and technology on group performance and member reactions', *Journal of Applied Psychology*, 79: 87–97.

Townsend, A.M., DeMarie, S.M. and Hendrickson, A.R. (1996) 'Are you ready for virtual teams?', *HR Magazine*, 41: 122–6.

Trevino, L.K., Daft, R.L. and Lengel, R.H. (1990) 'Understanding managers' media choices: a symbolic interactionist perspective', in J. Fulk and C.W. Steinfield (eds), *Organizations and Communication Technology*, Newbury Park, CA: Sage. pp. 71–94.

Valacich, J.S., Paranka, D., George, J.F. and Nunamaker, J.F. (1994) 'Communication concurrency and the new media: a new dimension for media richness', *Communication Research*, 20 (2): 249–76.

Walther, J.B. and Burgoon, J.K. (1992) 'Relational communication in computer-mediated interaction', *Human Communication Research*, 19: 50–88.

Wasserman, S. and Faust, K. (1994) *Social Network Analysis: Methods and Applications.* New York: Cambridge University Press.

Watson, R., DeSanctis, G. and Poole, M.S. (1988) 'Using a GDSS to facilitate group consensus: some intended and unintended consequences', *MIS Quarterly*, 12: 463–78.

Weisband, S.P. (1992) 'Group discussion and first advocacy effects in computer-mediated and face-to-face decision making groups', *Organizational Behavior and Human Decision Processes*, 53: 352–80.

Weisband, S.P., Schneider, S.K. and Connolly, T. (1995) 'Electronic communication and social information: status salience and status differences', *Academy of Management Journal*, 38: 1124–51.

Williams, E. (1977) 'Experimental comparisons of face-to-face and mediated communication: a review', *Psychological Bulletin*, 84 (5): 963–76.

Zack, M.H. and McKenney, J.L. (1995) 'Social context and interaction in ongoing computer-supported management groups', *Organization Science*, 6: 394–422.

Zigurs, I., Poole, M.S. and DeSanctis, G. (1988) 'A study of influence in computer-mediated group decision making', *MIS Quarterly*, 12: 625–44.

14

The Social Construction of Technology in Studies of the Workplace

MICHÈLE H. JACKSON,
MARSHALL SCOTT POOLE
and
TIM KUHN

The environment of the modern organization has always been technological, but this has been understood in a number of distinct ways. For example, seen as collections of rationalized and instrumental practices, organizations themselves have been regarded as technologies in which effective information and communication processes are critical (Taylor, 1911; Thompson, 1967). Of more interest to this volume are the perspectives that have looked at information and communication technologies *within* organizations. Technologies have had profound effects on the way certain information work is done, such as actuarial work (Yates, 1993). With the expanding capabilities of digital computing, fields of study such as office automation (Johnson and Rice, 1984), operations research (Arnoff, 1957) and management information systems (Dickson, 1982) emerged to focus on the question of how computer-based information and communication technologies might be integrated into organizational processes to make organizations and organizational processes more efficient and effective or otherwise to fulfil unmet organizational needs.

Even as organizational scholars turn increasingly to considering issues of information and communication technologies (ICTs), a complementary turn is made by technology scholars who look to social and organizational issues implicated in technology design and development. Located in fields such as the sociology of technology, computer science and the anthropology of work, and typically organized under the general category of *social construction*, this research holds that technologies are and have

always been social. Our interest in this chapter is to explore the intersection between social constructionism and the study of ICTs in the workplace. We begin by identifying a set of assumptions that underlie a constructionist perspective and indicate some ways in which these assumptions appear in studies of the workplace. Fundamental to constructionism is the active effort to privilege neither social nor technical factors in constructing accounts of technology design, development, implementation or use.

In the next section we reflect on the impact constructionism has had on studies of the workplace. We observe that within these studies, scholars employ constructionism for different purposes. The first is to provide a framework for *understanding* ICTs in the workplace and the second is to provide guidance for *designing and implementing* ICTs in organizations. Our interest here is an assessment of the extent to which constructionist views are successful in each of these. Our argument will be that social constructionist views have in principle developed an understanding that privileges neither technology nor the workplace, but that their use in design and implementation have tended to tilt so as to privilege either the technology or the workplace. Using the terminology of Argyris and Schön (1978), this tilt may be seen in a contrast between the espoused theory of social constructionism (its theoretical understanding) and its theory-in-practice (its actual employment in research and in organizations). We conclude the chapter with some reflections on how scholars might address this tendency to tilt and might maintain a constructionist perspective in practical contexts.

Constructionist sensibilities tend to arise as a consequence of a move away from technological determinism. Because this move has occurred across a number of disciplines, constructionist principles come from a variety of traditions, including history, engineering and design, information studies, communication and organization studies. The perspectives historically identified with the social construction of technology typically examine periods of technology development (Jackson, 1996; see Lievrouw in this volume). Yet we find constructionism increasingly influential in studies of the use and implementation of technologies within organizations. The variety of constructionist positions makes it difficult to catalogue perspectives, but they tend to hold a number of assumptions in common.

Constructionism Denies Technological Determinism

Determinism has had a steady presence in technology studies (Marx and Smith, 1994). Generally, determinism is the position that, given a set of initial conditions, outcomes can be predicted with some amount of certainty. Underlying determinism is a logic of rationality, often referred to as technical rationality, or an assumption that the technical and social world operate according to rules that are prior to any particular situation and that predetermine the set of possible outcomes. Stronger variants of determinism hold that there exists a technological imperative, that artifacts move inexorably and in a linear fashion toward a certain end state (Edge, 1995). Within studies of technology across disciplines, determinism may be applied either to explaining the development of technologies, or to predicting the consequences of their use. All constructionist perspectives reject determinism, though at different levels. And, as a consequence, they embrace some level of indeterminacy. For example, sociologists of technology Williams and Edge point out that social shaping of technology (SST) perspectives reject the notion that technology emerges from 'a single social determinant, or through the unfolding of a predetermined technical logic' (1996: 54). In their study of technology use in organizations, Sproull and Keisler (1991) hold that the more consequential impacts of technology use cannot be anticipated.

Constructionism Recognizes the Interplay and Interdependence of Social and Technical Elements

Constructionist perspectives recognize that reference to technological elements alone can adequately explain neither technology development nor technology use (Pinch and Bijker, 1984). Instead, technical and social factors are intimately interconnected (Woolgar, 1996). It is through the interplay of these elements that technologies develop. Hughes (1986) describes this as an interactive perspective, one that provides all elements present in technological development with equal status. From an interactive perspective, technology itself is understood as a collection of dynamically related elements rather than as a static and stable entity. As Hughes (1986) makes clear, the key to the approach is the metaphor of the 'seamless web', which discourages an isolation of individual elements and encourages a recognition of the multiple determinations of technologies.

Within organizational studies, the sociotechnical systems (STS) perspective was one of the first to argue for paying attention to the interrelationship of social and technical factors. Classic STS emphasizes the importance of fit or the match between the social and the technical, in order to optimize organizational processes (Emery and Trist, 1961; Mumford, 1983). In another example, it was this commitment to both social and technical factors that helped to launch the field of computer-supported cooperative work (CSCW), which seeks to combine an understanding of the way people work with an expertise in computing technologies (Greif, 1988; Mantovani, 1996; Wilson, 1991).

Constructionism Denies that Technologies are Ever Complete

The physical nature of most technologies, including the devices that accompany information and communication technologies, means that we tend to view artifacts as able to exist apart from any context of use (Jackson, 1996). Particularly in organizational contexts, technological artifacts are easily taken for granted, with a fixed and stable nature and predetermined boundaries. Constructionism rejects this assumption and problematizes the constitution of technology, as in Bucciarelli's (1994) criticism of 'object-world' accounts of technological design. Rather than being complete or at rest, technologies continuously change and are reconstituted through their engagement in communities.

As a consequence, describing technologies becomes more complicated. Woolgar notes:

> The social researcher has no 'neutral' (that is, free of the social milieu) description of the technology around which to build a picture of 'social influences'. Instead, the 'technical character' of the technology – like what it can do and how it does it – becomes part of the phenomenon to be explained by reference to social and political factors. (1996: 88)

An important example with organizational studies is the use of structuration theory (Giddens, 1979;

Orlikowski and Robey, 1991). Structuration posits a *duality of structure*, which is the notion that human action simultaneously creates structures of social systems and is shaped by such structures. Structuration emphasizes the interaction of technology and organization in creating these systems. For example, adaptive structuration theory (AST) (Poole and DeSanctis, 1990; DeSanctis and Poole, 1994) outlines a set of appropriation processes through which a technology comes to be constituted differently by different groups of people. Similarly, the emergence perspective (Barley, 1986; Markus and Robey, 1988) demonstrates the ways in which technologies continue to be defined throughout a changing context.

Constructionism Redirects Attention from Products to Processes

Technologies in and of themselves do not receive much attention in constructionist perspectives. Instead, it is processes that are documented and analysed. The purposes of this attention vary. For actor-network theory, for example, attention to processes is the method for accomplishing the 'ruthless recursivity' essential to the theory's aim to deconstruct the 'black box' of technology (Law and Hassard, 1999). In other constructionist perspectives, attention to processes includes understanding the enrolment of actors in heterogeneous networks (Callon, 1986) and the translation of interpretations into facts (Latour, 1987). In this way, technological products come to be redefined as sets of processes.

Within studies of technology use, the attention to process helps to shift attention away from the artifact and instead to privilege work and work processes. The effect is to change what we see, making it possible to envision new or alternative modes of engagement. For example, Zuboff's (1988) classic study introduced the concept of 'informating' as a contrast to the traditional, deterministic concept of automating. Star and Bowker's (in this volume; Bowker and Star, 1999) attention to cross-disciplinary collaboration highlights the work that artifacts must do, both as boundary objects and as infrastructure. Finally, a growing body of interdisciplinary research foregrounds the activity performed within work, in particular the constant need for collaboration between social and technical factors at the level of discourse (Engestrom and Middleton, 1998; Heath and Luff, 2000; Suchman, 1987).

CONTRIBUTIONS OF SOCIAL CONSTRUCTION OF TECHNOLOGY TO UNDERSTANDING ORGANIZATIONS AND THE WORKPLACE

Social constructionist inquiries have made a number of contributions to our understanding of the process by which ICTs figure in organizations. In line with the basic assumptions just outlined, these studies have emphasized the co-construction of organization and technology: just as ICTs are fundamentally incomplete and indeterminate, so too are organizations. These studies have focused on members' interaction with technologies as artifacts, structures and contexts and on the corresponding construction of technologies as part of an organization's project and processes. These two moments are presumed to be recursive, with organization framing and being reshaped by the technology that is being constructed and reconstructed.

A major challenge for social constructionist research is maintaining a balance between ICT and organization. In principle, a thoroughgoing study would consider both ICTs and organizations as constructions, and elements of neither realm would be regarded as necessarily fixed or primary (Jackson, 1996; Poole, 1983). This is not to say that all elements of a given system under study have to be considered equally important. In some cases ICT elements play a predominant role, and in others organizational elements; and in still others particular elements of both ICTs and organizations shape the construction of all others. While some aspects of any system always have more influence than others, no *a priori* assumptions about precedence or privilege should underlie a sound analysis. Indeed, the boundaries between ICT and organization would also be problematized as a subject of inquiry.

The principles that research aspires to are, however, not always easy to realize in practice. In many studies analysts overemphasize either technology or organization, in some cases inadvertently and in others because of the orientation of their discipline or theoretical perspective. We explore the nature, extent and implications of this 'tipping' through a consideration of three insights that constructionism has brought to studies of the workplace.

Computerization of Work Requires Abstraction of this Work from its Context, Thereby Changing the Nature of the Work

A number of studies have investigated how computerization of work changes that work fundamentally by abstracting it from concrete work practices. One of the most influential, Zuboff's (1988) social ethnography of the computerization of large paper mills, describes how work that had previously been done by touch, feel and sight was transformed as the factory was automated and its work converted into a system manageable with computer controls. Under the old regime of papermaking workers developed action-centred skills which were based upon sentient information derived from physical cues. Action-centred skills, developed and enacted in physical performance, reflected tacit knowledge that was bound tightly to the context of action. Grounded in action rather than language, this knowledge was the inherent property of the individual craftsperson. Zuboff gives examples of papermakers who used the taste and feel of pulp to determine when a batch of paper was ready to roll. This type of knowledge, deeply embedded in the actions of the work itself and won slowly over years of experience, is produced and reproduced in action.

With the advent of computerization, workers had to learn new ways of thinking and new skills. These included the ability to comprehend comparatively abstract representations of work processes reflected in dials and readouts and the capacity to manipulate process controls to maintain the readings in acceptable ranges. The data workers had to use were different from the sensations they employed previously, which could not be duplicated by the system because it was restricted to information amenable to measurement through available technologies. In the computerized system knowledge was articulated and divorced from direct action and became a manipulable abstraction, independent of any particular knower.

This created a gap between conception and action, between knowledge and ability to work with the process, that workers struggled to bridge. One of the younger workers brought in under the new regime commented:

> I like to smell and feel the pulp sometimes. It can be slick, it can be slimy, it can be all different consistencies. These are the artistic aspects of making pulp that the computer doesn't know about. Some of the operators have been picking up these aspects, but there are so many numbers so readily accessible, we have to shortcut it at times and solve more problems from the office. The information is so good and rapid that we have to use it ...You have got to be able to recognize when you run things from the office and when you have to go and look. Yet, I recognize that I am not as good a pulp maker as the people who trained me, and the new operators are not as good as I am. (1988: 67)

In moving from action-centred to intellective modes of work, workers had to learn to construct meaning, something not required when action was primary. Dealing with problems of meaning construction posed particular demands on workers, including figuring out whether and how to trust the data given to them by machines and how to build adequate internal representations of their work. Successful workers learned how to construct a visualization of the process from numerical and graphical data. As the quotation illustrates, however, visualization was sometimes dependent in part upon actual physical contact with the work and not simply based on theory or mastery of the control room dials. There was an interplay between action-centred and intellective work.

Once workers developed and came to accept abstract representations and knowledge, they could move to a higher level of processing, using the data to gain insights into the 'functional relationships, states, conditions, trends, likely developments, and underlying causes of the processes they were controlling' (1988: 92). This enabled them to achieve better results and reinforced the validity of the symbolic representations of work through the information system. It also sparked a desire among workers to learn the theory behind the papermaking and the plant, because it seemed to promise faster and even better insights.

The information provided by the computer enables people to reconceptualize, restructure and improve their work. However, this improvement is only possible if managers in charge of computerization reconstruct their view of technology and use it to 'informate' work rather than merely 'automate' it. The informating view rests on managers' ability to grasp the 'smart' nature of computers and the potential they offer for enabling workers to improve operations through higher-order reasoning based on the information the computer provides about how the plant was running. A manager interested in informating work empowers employees, charging them with mastering and improving their work. Jobs are reorganized so that they are 'whole', and so that workers have a degree of control over how the work was planned and carried out. The manager serves as a coach and adviser rather than an authority. In general, workers are treated more collegially and their intellect and skills are valued. Learning and continuous improvement are valued.

While the paper plant illustrates the abstraction involved in computerization of physical work, Zuboff also shows parallel forms of abstraction in the computerization of clerical and white-collar work. Zuboff is generally neutral about the impacts of abstraction on the work itself. For Zuboff there is a difference, but the difference is neither wholly good nor wholly bad. Indeed, the positive and negative impacts of computerization stem more from whether the organization frames computerization in automating or informating terms than in the abstracting process itself.

A more evaluative view of abstraction is provided by the work of Suchman (1987) and others within the situated action perspective (Heath and Luff, 2000; Mantovani, 1996). One of the tenets of this perspective is that action cannot be represented independently of the context in which it occurs and the artifacts engaged in the action. To understand how to computerize work or any other kind of action properly requires one to grasp how this action unfolds in situations. However, there is an inherent gap between the computerization process, which requires abstraction and representation independent of the flow of behaviour, and situated action, which is the flow itself. One of the things involved in designing computer systems is development of categories that specify action types, situation types to which actions match, and other components that enable development of the system. This in itself is an artificial reification of structure from unfolding action (Bucciarelli, 1994). It is a necessary step, however, and the main thing is to minimize the inevitable distortion that occurs and attendant limitations on action. The problem with most design efforts is that their representations are artificial and idealized accounts of action as it should occur from the point of view of someone not doing the action.

The implications of this view for the design of ICTs are illustrated in the responses of Suchman and others working from the situated action perspective to the attempt by Winograd and Flores to advance a theory for design of computer systems tailored to organizational action based on speech act theory (Searle, 1979; see Winograd and Flores, 1986). Speech act theory, a formalization that addresses how language enables people to engage in actions, such as promising and asserting, was used by Winograd and Flores to derive basic categories for action in organizations. They based the design of a work group productivity system, COORDINATOR, on speech act theory, building in speech acts such as committing and rules for undertaking these actions that attempted to help organizational members coordinate their work activity.

Responding to this framework, Suchman (1994) argues that all categorizations are political in that they represent reifications from action itself. She cites critiques of speech act theory by conversational analysts:

> The argument is that speech act theory takes communi-cation as an exchange of speaker's–hearer's intent while conversation analyses underscore the irreducibly interactional structuring of talk. So, for example, con-versation analysts have documented the ways in which a speaker's intent is observably shaped by the response of hearers over the course of an utterance's (co)produc-tion...Bowers and Churcher [1988] argue that the con-sequent 'radical indeterminacy' of the unfolding course of human interaction presents a problem for any system designed automatically to track an interaction's course by projecting expected or canonically organized sequences. This, they argue, 'cannot be ignored by designers or systems for CSCW without unwittingly coercing their users.' (1994: 180)

Suchman sees such categorizations as disciplinary in nature, designed to control action, often in ways that conflict with its unfolding nature. She asks: 'Why do computer scientists go about making up all these typologies of interaction? Aren't the typolo-gies used by practitioners themselves before we go to work, as designers, good enough? And what's the matter with them if they aren't?'

Both of these approaches imply a need to view how organizations and technology fit together from a constructionist perspective. Zuboff's work indi-cates how ICTs involve the abstraction of work and a reconstruction of how work is done. This abstrac-tive process is a fertile site for understanding how work is structured by information systems. And how the restructuring is framed by management has a powerful impact on the ways in which computers figure in work, either as machines that construct work in a rigid fashion external to the workers themselves (as in traditional factories) or as 'smart machines' that give workers enhanced ability to control the construction process. The situated action approach views all interaction as constructed 'on the fly', by actors whose activity is invoked mutu-ally by their intentions and by the situation and artifacts.

Both approaches, however, tend toward one pole of the organization–ICT pair. Zuboff privileges ICT. Viewing it as the starting point of the abstrac-tive process, she tends to treat the technology as a black box that members of the organization must reconstruct their work about. Concerned not with the process of design, but rather with the reaction to the design, her perspective fastens onto the most obviously adjusting aspect, the organization. The informating–automating distinction reflects this approach as well: the technology is taken as a given, and it is the way in which management frames the use of technology that makes the difference between automating and informating strategies. In overemphasizing the sharp break in the move from action-centred to intellective work, Zuboff fore-sakes an opportunity to problematize ICT along with organization. She reports numerous instances in which organizational members reinserted them-selves into the operation of the system. For exam-ple, workers in one factory installed video cameras to help them distinguish when an ambiguous gauge indicated high pressure that might lead to an over-flow and when it indicated an actual overflow. Such 'bricolage' is one example of how the workers develop, over time, an action-centred approach to the computer system. Just as physical action toward vats and pipes developed around the old regime, so physical action toward the control board and gauges must develop in the new. There can be as much tacit knowledge associated with gauges as there is asso-ciated with open vats of paper pulp, and as much inexpressible skill around working with mental rep-resentations as there is around tasting chemicals. Ask any programmer how she/he knew to employ a particular strategy to debug a program, and the inef-fability of working with abstractive processes becomes evident.

Also missing from Zuboff's analysis is a treat-ment of how the designers of the plants adapted the ICT over time as they came online, experienced problems, got negative reactions from operators, and other common occurrences, or how the designers planned the next generation of software based on their learning in building a plant. These are the occasions where the construction of the technology would be more evident. Indeed, if we interrogated these occasions, we might find that some ICTs are designed in ways that make them more 'informatable' and others are set on trajectories that tend toward automation. Instead of defining a world of work inherently different from physical labour, had Zuboff emphasized the co-production of technology and organization, she might have be able to strip the hard shell from technology.

Suchman, the adherents of situated action, and mainstream CSCW researchers suffer the opposing tendency, and privilege the organization. The particular emphasis on situated action carries with it the presumption that the primary moment of work is action in context arranged around artifacts. Any representation external to this runs the risk of distorting the action situation. On this basis, they advocate careful study of the situation and artifacts in action, and design of ICTs so that they facilitate situated actions. However, just as COORDINATOR may have privileged the computer scientist's model of action and the control involved, so does the situated action perspective privilege the existing situation. It does not seem to consider that current practices may have evolved in oppressive, controlling organizations or in response to inadequate equipment or training. The many distortions and choices hidden in any situation or artifact are not interrogated by this approach, and as a result, they may be incorporated into any design. While use of situated action as a taking-off point may avoid imposition of awkward schemes such as speech act theory, it may also inadvertently chain the ICT to existing practices. As Hollan and Stornetta (1992) argue, ICTs need not be used as 'crutches' for existing models of communication and interaction; they could also be used to create wholly new forms that serve as 'athletic shoes' to enable people to accomplish what was not previously possible.

How might we move to a more balanced view of technology and organization? We will postpone in-depth consideration of this question until the last section of this chapter. However, at this point it is worth considering an approach that seems more successful at keeping the two terms balanced – participatory design (Schuler and Namioka, 1993). Participatory design focuses on the situation of technology use, but attempts to incorporate both the user and the developer in a collaborative system that enables action to have a voice, to critique and improve action. Suchman and other situated action researchers have advocated participatory design but an important addition is an attempt to incorporate both the user and the developer in a collaborative system. Situated action is often an important object of analysis in participative design, but it is not the

only reference point; both designer and user are free to critique current procedures and consider how computerization might improve them, or even to discard current practice altogether to generate a new application. Participative design in the hands of a creative and inquisitive user/designer sees the potential to problematize both organization and technology by questioning the grounds of both. In practice participatory design probably still leans toward the organization, because imagination is limited by what we have already experienced, but its aim is to set both user and designer free to question either or both terms in the pair. We will consider design as a type of theorizing in the final section of this chapter.

Impacts for the Organization and Organizational Theory Extend beyond the Use of the Technologies Themselves

Another intersection of constructionist perspectives and studies of the workplace is in studies of broader organizational issues. For most of the research discussed so far, the concern has been the instrumental or direct effects of ICTs, in either their intended or their unintended consequences. Yet within constructionist principles, there is no obligation to foreground the technological artifact itself. Foregrounding the organization means that researchers may dwell on the larger milieu, in which social and technical aspects interact. The main issue, then, is the way in which ICTs insinuate into organizational life.

Here the interest is less the demonstration of effects of ICTs and more the descriptions and accounts of experiences and processes within organizations. In other words, causal relationships between technology and work might not be a concern. Instead, such relationships are the background against which fundamental processes or characteristics are investigated. In this body of research, important constructionist assumptions, including the interplay of social and technical elements, guide investigation of traditional issues such as organizational culture, role hierarchies or the nature of work. What surfaces from these investigations is the insight that ICTs may have indirect impacts that come less from the use of a specific ICT than from the part the ICT plays in forming or insinuating larger organizational contexts.

One area in which social constructionism is shaping studies of the workplace is the development of theories about organizations and organizing. For Robey and Boudreau (1999), the contradictions of results presented within information technology research suggest that the organizational study of ICT may be better served by a 'logic of opposition' in contrast to a 'logic of determination'. A logic of opposition 'explains organizational change by identifying forces both promoting and impeding change' (1999: xx). They suggest that four theories could be used to guide oppositional approach: organizational politics, organizational culture, institutional theory and organizational learning.

An organizational politics perspective sees organizations as arenas where interests become aligned, misaligned, realigned. The tension from misalignment gives rise to efforts to transform the organization, and such transformations are often in opposition to the interests of other parties. Organizational members use information technology instrumentally in these political efforts.

Following Martin's (1992) perspectives on organizational culture, Robey and Boudreau consider various ways in which tensions and oppositions might surface with regard to ICT. In an integrated or unified culture, oppositions surface because the technology is at odds with the values and assumptions of the culture itself. The culture rejects the technology. For example, in an organization that has a long history of individuals becoming experts through experiencing and solving problems on their own, a technology that aims to capture that knowledge within a database, making it available to new employees, likely will be resisted. A differentiated organizational culture possesses a number of subcultures, and conflicts are likely to exist at the boundaries of those subcultures. Here members may resist an ICT because it is a tool in these conflicts. For example, a tool favoured by management for increasing control over information might be rejected by clerical workers whose culture values freedom and independent decision-making. In the third type of culture, the fragmented culture, culture is inherently ambiguous and contradictory. Oppositions are entertained simultaneously, rather than forced toward resolution. Information technology has a different importance here, one more closely aligned to constructionist principles. Here oppositions are recognized as residing within the technology itself. Robey and Boudreau note:

> Information itself is symbolic, and the technologies used to process information may produce positive social meanings such as competitiveness, modernity, status, and legitimacy, as well as negative meanings such as the restriction of personal freedom (Feldman and March 1981). Because the same artifact may simultaneously acquire different social meanings, even within the same culture, contradictory consequences resulting from information technology are easy to envision (Robey and Azevedo 1994). (1999: 176)

Institutional theory examines how organizations gain and maintain legitimacy. Oppositions arise from competing institutional forces. These forces may affect ICT development and patterns of innovation. A more interesting insight, drawing from Kling and Iacono (1989), is that technologies may take on institutional characteristics themselves, becoming traditional entities that resist modification, despite clear evidence of advantages of doing so:

> Applied to the question of information technology and organizational change, institutional theory can address conflicts among normative pressures such as efficiency, rights to privacy and autonomy, and deeply embedded notions of bureaucratic and hierarchical structure. Although systems may ostensibly be designed to advance one of these valued ideals, usually efficiency, they may inadvertently affect others. Resulting organizational forms are likely to reflect such contradictions among competing values. (1999: 177)

Finally, theories of organizational learning treat oppositions as mechanisms by which organizations adapt and improve. Robey and Boudreau note that this is an area that ICT scholars generally have not explored. However, they see potential, for example, as technology systems for capturing and managing organizational memory are created.

For Robey and Boudreau, the promise of oppositional logic in organizational theories is its potential for providing better insight for explaining information technologies in the workplace. They use theory to call for a more constructionist approach to the study of technology. In contrast to this, Chia (1995) uses perspectives from social studies of technology to call for a more constructionist understanding of the organization. Modern organizational theory, argues Chia, in privileging states and events, has an ontology of being. An alternative would be to privilege processes, and emphasize transience and emergence. Such postmodern organizational theory adopts an ontology of becoming. The resulting way of thinking is decidedly constructionist:

> Postmodern thinking thus involves a critical revision in our ontological commitments from an ontology of *being* to an ontology of *becoming*. This implies according primacy to reality as a processual, heterogeneous and emergent configuration of relations. It also implies that we may not take established social categories such as 'individuals' and 'organizations' as already given and 'out there'. Instead, these taken-for-granted categories need to be explored and explained. Consequently, it means that our theoretical focus is no longer on organizational features such as 'structures', 'cultures' and 'ethics', etc. Instead, the very idea of organization itself becomes the problematic. How does it come to acquire its apparently concrete status? What primary organizing process allows it to take on the semblance of an 'already constituted entity'? (1995: 594–5)

Chia's inspiration for this position is the scholarship in the social studies of technology, most notably the work of John Law and the notion of heterogeneous engineering. In heterogeneous engineering social, technical, conceptual and textual elements of a context are all fitted together within scientific or technological products. Such products maintain the aspect of heterogeneity even when being used. One classic example is Law's (1987) study of the Portuguese expansion into the spice trade in the thirteenth through fifteenth centuries. The various sea vessels the Portuguese used for exploration, for example, represented ongoing tensions between politics (conquest), economics (trade) and the physical world (the Atlantic). The implication of this perspective for organizational studies, Chia argues, is that rather than motivating our research by things we want to explain – outcomes, products, attributes – we start instead with the assumption that all we have are actions, interactions and orchestrations of relationships. The critical and central question for organization studies then becomes how things come to be stabilized in processes of production and reproduction, creating 'effects' such as individuals and organizations. It is micro-organizing strategies that give organizations the appearance of unity, identity and permanence.

Chia's formulation of postmodernism, thus, is very similar to constructionism. Postmodernism should eschew thinking in terms of givens or end states, and look for processes, assuming emergence and becoming. Also, it strives for analytic symmetry, an understanding that the 'distinctions in the human world are not naturally given; they are *always already* products or effects of prior organizing processes' (1995: 598). Analytic symmetry means that the research does not presume pre-existing hierarchies or orders of things. Such asymmetries are created by processes of becoming.

An important move here is to consider organiz*ing* rather than organiz*ations*. A central example of this type of thinking within organizational studies is the sense-making perspective proposed by Weick. In an overview of sense-making and action in organizations, Weick (1987) argues very strongly against the ideas that organizations cohere as ordered and rational systems, and that researchers can somehow capture what organizations are about. The costs of such a project, he says, are 'becoming clearer in the deepening irrelevance of organizational researchers for organizational participants' (1987: 10).

Weick's perspective is parallel to the social construction of technology perspectives we are considering here. It may also make an interesting contribution to studies of technologies through its emphasis on sense-making as the motivation for social action. People engage in action in order to make sense of their world and of their experiences. For Weick, it is the routines of interaction that make up sense-making. Many interactions and messages serve to assure people that things today are basically the same as they were yesterday, yet this stability is not predetermined, it is something to which people have to provide effort. Actions provide

stability in at least three ways: by evoking justifications, by displacing thinking, and by creating environments in which people are coupled with one another. Conceivably, technology studies might begin from similar assumptions regarding sense-making as a motivation for human action. An interesting question would then be the ways in which the construction of technologies function to provide some sense of stability (either for designers or users), and how that need for sense-making affects actual technological artifacts.

Taylor and his colleagues have taken some steps in this direction. Working from a rigorously communication-centred perspective, Taylor and van Every (2000) conceive of organizations as worlds of text and conversation; it is in their interaction that organizations emerge. The movement from discourse to texts and back again produces the regularity that makes organizations visible as tangible entities. In this context, technologies are the means to produce further texts, a medium to enable conversation, and they are also texts or products of conversation themselves. Taylor et al. (2001) extend this perspective to the study of organizational contexts in which computer-based technologies are used to perform work. Anchored in Giddens' (1979; 1984) theory of structuration, the authors argue explicitly for abandoning the dualism of 'technology' and 'organization', and replacing it with a perspective that attends instead to social processes and interaction. They argue for perceiving computerization as one such process. For them, the 'computerization of work' is something that happens when work is imbricated with human and non-human agents in the organizational context. This process, ongoing and continually constructed or enacted, is *computerization*:

> The enactment of a situated world is conceptualized as an ongoing 'dance of agency' or 'dialectic of resistance and accommodation' (Pickering, 1995). Out of this dance or dialectic, stable relationships of agency emerge, resulting in a division of labor and accepted rules of relationship. Patterns of agency (acting-for) emerge from the necessity of co-orientation in response to a complex environment. *Co-orientation*, it is argued, is the building block of all organizational processes and structures. *Imbrication* is the process by means of which co-orientational systems become translated into infrastructure. (Taylor et al., 2001: 26, emphasis in original)

Thus we return to the constructionist assumption of the importance of the interplay between technological and social elements – not only for the study of work or organizations, but for the very constitution of the organization as a stable social entity. Embeddedness, such an important concept to infrastructure (Star and Bowker in this volume), is a property solely of technological artifacts. In other words, it is not simply technologies that are embedded within pre-existing social contexts. Rather, each is embedded in the other. Embeddedness becomes a property sustained by processes of co-orientation and imbrication.

Learning and Knowing Are Processes that Can Be Managed by Information and Communication Technologies

An argument developing significantly over the past decade of research in organizational studies is that knowledge is the central element of an organization's distinctive competence and operational proficiency (Blackler, 1993; Foss, 1999; Grant, 1996; Kogut and Zander, 1996). Organizational knowledge, properly developed and utilized, improves products and processes and can, ultimately, help to build a 'learning organization' able to innovate and adapt to ensure its long-term viability (Daft and Huber, 1987; Senge, 1990; Weick and Ashford, 2001). Following this vision, organizations in several sectors have developed or purchased knowledge management (KM) systems.

Generally, knowledge management involves the processes of coordinating and controlling the generation, codification and transfer of knowledge (Davenport and Prusak, 1998; Osterloh and Frey, 2000). A knowledge management system is a collection of information technologies used to collect, organize, transfer and distribute knowledge among employees (Offsey, 1997: 115). In other words, KM systems are an instance of information technologies converging with information management (Myburgh, 2000). A complete KM system would provide support or techniques for each of the subprocesses of generation, codification and transfer. Most systems, however, support only one or two of these.

Knowledge generation is the creation, acquisition and synthesis of new knowledge (von Krogh et al., 2000). Operationalized within KM systems, generation is geared toward support of problem-solving. Typical applications include groupware and enhanced search capabilities such as intelligent agents. Groupware (Hollingshead and Contractor in this volume) can lead to the development of knowledge through enabling collaboration and documentation through a variety of computerized tools (Coleman, 1999; Kline and McGrath, 1999). Intelligent agents are software programs that assist users by autonomously performing tasks such as sifting through mountains of data using adaptive algorithms and neural networks (Baek et al., 1999; Corman, 1997). Research suggests that although these applications influence data management and teamwork, their contribution to innovation is unclear (Orlikowski and Hofman, 1997). Initial investigations explore contextual implications of these applications, including the degree to which designers' mental models shape KM systems

(Mandviwalla, 1996), the implication of the surrounding context for performance (Hayes and Walsham, 2000), the participation of the applications in coordinated activity (Corman, 1997), and the ways in which such applications provide rules and resources for group interactions (Ngwenyama and Lyytinen, 1997).

Knowledge codification externalizes knowledge by placing it in a standardized form, such as language. In other words, codification makes tacit knowledge explicit. Technologies employed here include visualization tools and organizational intranets. Knowledge visualization applications, such as concept mapping programs, illustrate, and therefore demonstrate, the relationships among the knowledge of individuals or of groups. Such applications help individuals perceive and understand the form and content of knowledge (Carley, 1997; Laukkanen, 1998). Organizational intranets, on the other hand, are vehicles to allow members located throughout the organization access to important information. An example might be a firm's internal yellow pages, a listing of individuals within the organization and their areas of expertise. A criticism of intranets as a system for codification is that while they may enable the assessment and display of an actor's intellectual assets, they are less likely to capture tacit knowledge, which is often seen as the key to enhanced organizational functioning (Davenport and Prusak, 1998; Nonaka and Takeuchi, 1995). Research on tacit knowledge often refers to the tight coupling between knowledge and communities of practice, a connection that can be lost upon codification and standardization (Brown and Duguid, 1991; Orr, 1990; Wenger, 1998).

Knowledge transfer packages and distributes knowledge to various organizational points of action (Wiig, 1997). Examples of applications supporting this subprocess are groupware, simulations and knowledge bases of best practices. Simulations depend on the codification of experts' knowledge, which is then taught to novices through hands-on experiences (Hutchins and Klausen, 1996; Sarter and Woods, 2000). Knowledge bases of best practices gather lessons learned from other organizational members and contexts, along with a discussion of the factors affecting their success (O'Dell and Grayson, 1998). Consistent with other KM systems, applications for transfer overcome temporal, physical and social distance, which may be beneficial to an organization. A possible problem, however, is the temptation to divorce the lessons from the context in which they were learned, conceivably leading to problems of relevance as mentioned above.

A related critique, from a constructionist perspective, is the inherent difficulty of knowledge transfer itself. If knowledge is the medium and outcome of conversation (Shotter and Gergen, 1994), then it is accurate to say that organizational knowledge is negotiated, but it is never simply conveyed from one location to another. Given this conceptualization of knowledge, the transfer-oriented concentration in much KM research often refers to the development of stocks of knowledge and their efficient distribution, rather than their intelligent deployment in particular contexts (Fahey and Prusak, 1998).

One of the contributions of the knowledge management literature has been to further unpack the shortcomings of the traditional metaphor of organization as a conduit or container for communication (Axley, 1996; Smith, 1993) in favour of seeing organization and communication – or organizing and communicating – as equivalent, or at least mutually constitutive (McPhee and Zaug, 2000; Putnam et al., 1996; Taylor et al., 1996). Communication coordinates and controls the actions of participants in the negotiation of individual and collective meanings; organization likewise coordinates and controls actors in the service of some set of goals. Such a configuration foregrounds the ongoing negotiation of knowledge. The organization, as an entity, is a portable and dynamic system through which are developed sociotechnical knowledge, skills and procedures for making sense of the world, as particular patterns of behaviour emerge and reproduce themselves in specific material and social circumstances (Reed, 1996).

The rejection of the conduit metaphor also has significant implications for how we conceptualize the processes of knowing. From an organizational learning perspective, knowledge is information made consequential through its potential to contribute to an actor's purposeful and meaningful intervention in the social setting (Davenport and Prusak, 1998; Spender, 1996). Thus, the sort of knowledge relevant in social and organizational life generally is not an object that can be simply and straightforwardly transferred between locations, but rather both medium and outcome of communicating/organizing processes, and therefore always closely tied to both the method and the context of its development.[1]

In terms of its theoretical commitments, KM reflects the assumptions of constructionism. However, in practice, KM systems tend to emphasize the individual's explicit knowledge and information at the expense of both individuals' tacit knowledge and organizations' collective knowledge, which are more difficult to access and not easily operationalized. The capabilities of existing KM systems, limited to the characterization of individuals' declarative knowledge, mean that these technologies can do little more than manipulate organizational knowledge that is stable, storable and easy to represent and manipulate.

Analysis of KM systems typically tips toward either a technical or a social perspective

(Easterby-Smith and Araujo, 1999). The *technical* view focuses on the codification and processing of knowledge and concentrates on KM products, while the *social* view examines sense-making and the knowing that occurs in communicative connections between individuals, and concentrates on knowledge processes (Lave and Wenger, 1991; Mentzas et al., 2001). In most KM literature, knowledge is viewed as an individual's possession to be extracted by the organization and shared with others, rather than an intersubjective creation. Knowledge is objective and transferable (given the correct technologies), and the inherent complexities and ambiguities involved in communicating, organizing and learning from experience (Levinthal and March, 1993; Levitt and March, 1988) are glossed or ignored. In other KM literature, more process-oriented suggestions exist, such as legitimate peripheral participation (Lave and Wenger, 1991) and communities of practice (Wenger, 1998), but technologies are rarely afforded a prominent role in these analyses.

Viewing the literature as a whole, most research clearly aligns with the technical view, concerned with information processing accuracy and efficiency, rather than the social perspective on the negotiated and indeterminate character of communal knowledge. However, some raise concerns for developing systems that are flexible (O'Leary, 1998) and that are congruent with users' needs (Davenport and Prusak, 1998). This technical focus sacrifices an understanding of the variety of knowledge types relevant in organizational life, and inadequately conceives of the connections between context and technology use. Critical concepts, including the tacitness of communal knowledge (Choo, 1998) and the ways technologies contribute to creativity, are rarely conceptualized or investigated. Further, given that knowledge exists in both explicit (declarative) and tacit (procedural) forms at both the individual and collective levels (Crossan et al., 1999; Sackmann, 1992; Spender, 1996), the degree to which KM technologies manage the full extent of organizational knowledge is unclear. Consequently, as argued by von Krogh et al., 'what the process gains in structure, logic, and speed, it loses in creativity, insights, and the forging of necessary social links' (2000: 27).

These criticisms of the present state of KM technology research are not entirely surprising. The dominant motivation of KM developers is to build applications for use, not for study and understanding. Many of the articles in this field are written by individuals who sell KM technologies and services to firms. In addition, the notion that intellectual capital is a strategic organizational asset may be foreign to many organizational members such that they do not participate fully in technology implementations, leaving these voices underreported in research reports.

In short, the ways in which the social and the technical interpenetrate is missing in existing work on KM technologies. The technologies are portrayed as active causal agents that act on the passive organizational contexts, creating change in relatively predictable ways. Some work recognizes the need to manage the context or create a learning culture into which KM technologies can be inserted (Dixon, 2000; Leonard-Barton, 1995), or the need to unlearn old technologies (Starbuck, 1996), but rarely is there recognition of the social shaping of technology. In essence, the KM literature tends to be concerned more with spanning distances between members and shaping knowledge-based activity than with supporting shared formal and informal practices.

These three examples demonstrate the extent to which the move towards a constructionist perspective has contributed to our understanding of the workplace. In return, our analysis also brings to the surface a recurring challenge to constructionist study: keeping a balance between social and technical elements in theorizing and carrying out research. As should be evident, each of the bodies of literature on which we have drawn evidences a pull toward either social or technical elements. The next section considers some causes for this 'tilting', and proposes some steps for solving the problem.

THE TENDENCY TO TILT

What accounts for this tendency toward imbalance of organization and ICT in social constructionist research and practice? In part it stems from human frailty: social constructionists, like all people, have limited information processing capacity, limited ability to deal with complexity, limited time and resources to devote to their research, and biases borne in experience and education. While these are certainly contributing factors, we do not believe they are necessary or sufficient to explain the imbalance. The history of scholarship shows clearly that advances often come when researchers find ways to rise above our human limitations. Acknowledging our limits sets the stage for finding ways to overcome them. So we will take these human limitations as necessary – but surmountable – evils, and consider possible limiting factors in social constructionist research itself. These can be counteracted, or at least used to put studies into perspective.

One factor that could introduce a slant toward ICT or organization is the nature of the organization sampled. Few constructionist studies employ large samples, and the technologies and organizations studied are generally those the researcher has access to: convenience samples rather than samples representative of a naturally occurring population of organizations or technologies.[2] In any limited sample, it is possible that accidental characteristics of the particular organization – what statisticians would call sampling error – might fix the attention of the researcher to either the organization or the technology. For instance, if the organization studied is quite stable, the construction of technology may well stand out, whereas if it is in the process of changing, the construction of the organization through the technology might become the focus. Without large, representative samples, it is not possible to determine whether a given slant is warranted or not. This is a problem that is unlikely to be overcome by current approaches to constructionist research, which are premised on the type of in-depth, intensive, close analysis that makes drawing large samples impractical and places highest value on the demonstrative case.

Another factor that could play a role is the amount of time the researcher has spent in the organization under study and the time frame of the study. The less familiar the organization is to the researcher, the more likely the researcher is to find it more fascinating than ICT and the more likely the focus on construction of the organization in terms of ICT; the more familiar the organization, the more likely the new ICT is to stand out and the more likely its construction will come to the fore. Time frame also can bias one's outlook. As Pettigrew (1985) observes, 'the more we look at present-day events, the easier it is to identify change; the longer we stay with an emergent process and the further back we go to disentangle its origins, the more likely we are to identify continuities'.

Giddens (1979) and others have noted that the opportunity to slant in one direction or the other is inherent in any social constructionist research, because researchers cannot foreground action and structure simultaneously. It is not possible to study coevolving aspects of systems simultaneously. Instead, one must first focus on either technology or organization, action or structure, and then shift to consider the other side. It takes a great deal of effort and exceptional focus to prepare a balanced analysis that acknowledges both sides of the system. In the face of the limitations due to our humanity and those due to research design and the circumstances of a study, it is important to think of ways to overcome our tendency to slant toward either technology or organization. While there is no foolproof solution, there are ways to seek balance. Some rest in how we theorize about social construction and some in the methods we use to study it.

One way to balance organization and ICT is to focus our attention on neither. Considering the organization/technology intersection as a communication system or communication environment (Mantovani, 1996) includes both organization and technology, but does not necessarily privilege either one. Focusing on communication, the process through which social construction is enacted, and searching for signs of construction of technology and/or organization would allow researchers to let the situation 'call forth' whatever emphasis it requires. Of course, effectively using communication as a guide would require researchers to think of it in ways consistent with constructionist assumptions and not to reduce it to information transfer or other simplified, linear conceptualizations.

What does it mean to think of technology and organization in terms of communication systems? For one thing, it means putting aside the tendency to regard communication as subsidiary to or shaped by social organization or by technology. One preconception in the field of communication studies is to regard communication as a 'dependent variable' that is altered or affected by other 'independent' factors. These may be factors of the technology, as in as media richness theory (Trevino et al., 1990), or of the organization, such as in a task-based approach (Nass and Mason, 1990). For the decentring move to succeed, researchers must look squarely at communication as the modality by which construction is accomplished. Second, it requires analysts to look at communication as an object of interest in itself, rather than keying only to characteristics of communication that seem derivable from organization or technology, such as the appropriation of technology (Poole and DeSanctis, 1990; DeSanctis and Poole, 1994) or the use of ICTs to control workers (Beniger, 1986). Many of the deeper layers of social construction may occur in aspects of communication that do not seem to relate to organization or technology directly, but shape or set the stage for structuring processes, such as processes of individual and organizational identity construction (Cheney and Christensen, 2001). Though it seems paradoxical, the prospect of discovering something truly new about social construction may require scholars to turn away from organization and ICT themselves, at least at the outset of their studies. One way to begin this turn would be to adopt an ethnographic stance, as do Kunda (1992) and Henderson (1998), or an autobiographical stance, as do Bucciarelli (1994) and Downey (1998).

A second option is to embrace the imbalance between organization and technology and theorize it. This would mean taking the imbalance as an empirical question and asking what factors or forces might determine whether organization is the primary mover, or whether technology was, or whether they were co-producing each other. Examples of how this might work can be seen in the various theories that have tried to enunciate the action–structure relationship (Conrad and Haynes, 2001). Some years ago, Buckley (1967) proposed that action and structure alternate in their influence in long historical cycles: at one time action would be predominant, perhaps through a revolution that

overthrew the current order and enacted new social dynamics; but over time these dynamics would generate structures that would reproduce themselves and solidify the social order, introducing a period of structural dominance that would eventually be eroded by contradictions that would usher in a new era of action, and so on in repeating cycles. A similar formulation has been advanced in punctuated equilibrium models of organizational change (Gersick, 1991). A key requirement for an effective theory of this type is identification of factors or dynamics which account for shifts from a technology-dominated process to organization-dominated processes, or vice versa. Against this 'alternating current' model, we might array the views of Giddens (1979), who advanced the concept of structuration as a duality in which structure and action mutually entail each other. This view places equal emphasis on both structure and action simultaneously producing and reproducing themselves in the enactment of social systems. Another useful approach for considering organization and ICTs together is illustrated by the coevolutionary theories of organizations that have evolved from the work of Donald Campbell (Baum and McKelvey, 1999). Other formulas could also be advanced, but these two streams of theoretical thinking illustrate the rich array of options available to those who would advance theories about the relative prominence of organization and technology. This seems to be a question in search of an answer in current research.

A third possibility for achieving balance involves articulating a type of inquiry grounded in design. As we noted above, participant design methods for system development seem to hold the possibility of bringing the user, the organization and the technology into balance. Since design is fundamental to introducing ICTs in organizations, a case can be made that design can be the basis of theories to understand how the two relate. There has been a long tradition of debate about what type of theory is best suited to communication inquiry. Debate over whether communication is best understood in terms of positivist or post-positivist explanation, interpretation, critical theory or humanistic frames has characterized discourse about communication research for decades. Craig (1989) advanced a creative and radical suggestion when he argued that communication is better understood in terms of its practical roots than as a discipline devoted to theory in the pure sense. He advanced the notion that communication should be understood as a discipline that gives rise to practical theories – theories grounded in practice, yet generalizing from it. Practical theories comprise three layers: a lower layer of advice and rules of thumb, a middle layer of pragmatic theorizing grounded in the practices that are advised, and a top layer of abstract theoretical principles drawn from the middle layer and stated in sufficiently general terms that they can be used to understand phenomena distinct from the practice at hand. Researchers who stay in this top level may conduct traditional types of research using positivist, critical or humanistic frames and never refer to practice at all. Notwithstanding, grounding in the practice of communication underlies all that they do and ultimately their work must be referred back to this, asking whether it improves or casts light on practice.

We believe that an additional aspect of the communication discipline may well provide a doorway into good theories of the construction of organizations and technology. Communication is a discipline concerned with design – design of messages, design of organizational communication systems and, in this era of burgeoning technology, design of ICT-enabled communication environments. As a design discipline, communication is concerned with creating a context for practice. This implies that theories of design should be developed to complement and frame practical theories of communication.

A theory of design, like a practical discipline, can be conceived of in terms of three layers. The lower layer is concerned with how people construct ICTs as part of organizational practices by which organizations are constructed. For example, in the area of group support systems, the lower layer might comprise various pieces of advice and schemes for how to effectively implement a GSS in organizations, such as how to adapt it to the typical meeting practices of the organization, how to use it to reform the way decisions are made in the organization, and how to tailor the agenda tool to fit the organization. (Note that this theory says little about the interface or structure of the GSS; not all design theories need to be concerned with the creation from scratch of an ICT, but instead may be concerned with adaptive design involved in fitting ICTs to situations.) The middle layer is a theory that systematizes and improves the guidelines and structures of the lower layer, for example, a theory of the functions of GSSs and the tools needed to carry out these functions (e.g. Nunamaker et al., 1993). The top layer would be a theory about how GSSs are constructed in groups, such as adaptive structuration theory (DeSanctis and Poole, 1994). An important consideration in theories of the design of ICTs would be to realize that the structure of the technology is not the design. The design aims to choreograph the action occurring within the communication space, as well as set up the space. As such, theories of design are well suited to conceive of technology and organization simultaneously.

CONCLUSION

James March, writing in 1965 about the state of what he described as the 'semi-discipline' of organization studies, noted that sessions on organizational issues appeared at the previous year's conferences for a number of disciplines, including psychology, sociology, political science, economics and management sciences. He noted that, as a group, the participants in these sessions were an 'unlikely lot', gathered from a wide range of backgrounds, but 'there is a literature of the field that is general across several of the disciplines; there is an interlocking informal society of organization theorists' (1965: xv).

A similar state exists today for the study of technology and the workplace. This chapter, far from a complete consideration of the topic, has offered research from equally as many disciplines, including communication, organizational studies, anthropology, computer science, sociology and history. March noted that he 'could not foresee the ultimate result of this development' (1965: xv). Nor can we, but it is clear that the constructionist perspective is tapping into problems and questions of enduring, interdisciplinary relevance.

We have aimed in this chapter to present a case that the social constructionist perspective on technology has provided important insights for the study of organizations. Constructionism surfaces issues that organizations – as well as organizational scholars – will need to confront in the increasingly technological workplace. First, studies of technology in the workplace point to what may be a fundamental alteration of the character of work, in that the support of work through computerization requires abstracting the work from its context. Second, the increasing interpenetration of these fields may likely bring critical changes to our underlying theories of the organization. With the broadening of technical fields through interdisciplinary efforts such as CSCW, we may see also increasing participation of organizational scholars in theorizing issues of technology. Our collective understanding can only benefit from such interdependence. Finally, we observe that ICTs' support of organizational processes has extended far beyond the original conceptualization of office automation to the point of enabling new processes, such as organizational learning.

Of course, these are only a few of the insights that have been gained. We have put aside a number of others that should be developed in a fuller treatment of the issues. One is the study of organizational culture. A number of ethnographic studies of technological organizations suggest that the requirements of technical work create distinctive organizational cultures (Kunda, 1992; Perlow, 1997) and identities (Downey, 1998). Another area that could be explored is the change to the nature of work roles and expectations. Barley and Orr point to the significance of this issue and the centrality of understanding the role of technology in this change:

Work forms the bedrock of all economic systems. When the nature and social organization of work change, so does the fabric of society ... Although it is difficult to gauge the extent to which qualitative changes are occurring in the nature of work, mounting evidence indicates that such change may be widespread. Moreover, it appears that the change points in a consistent direction, toward what might be called, for lack of a better term, the 'technization of work'. (1997: 1, 5)

A last example is the rise of new organizational forms, even 'virtual organizations', which rely heavily on ICTs for control and coordination (Fulk and DeSanctis, 1999). It is not uncommon for organizations to hope that ICTs might be vessels, or conduits, capable of bringing about radical organizational reformation (e.g. Hammer and Champy, 1993).

We have also aimed in this chapter to consider the issue of balance. Balance is critical to the constructionist perspective, for on either side of constructionism lies the return to determinacy. Our analysis of the research suggests that balance, while easy to embrace, is difficult to maintain and carry out. Most studies display some sort of 'tipping' toward either social or technological elements. We suggest that the balance required of constructionism is not simply a matter of holding to one's principles, but is instead a practical matter of some complexity. Although we advance suggestions for addressing this problem, these can only be initial steps.

Technology will continue to influence organizations – and society – in important ways. Further development of the constructionist perspective should be an important goal for organizational scholars aiming to understand and improve organizational life. Bijker argues for this attention:

Likewise, if we do not foster constructivist views of sociotechnical development, stressing the possibilities and the constraints of change and the choice in technology, a large part of the public is bound to turn their backs on the possibility of participatory decision-making, with the result that technology will really slip out of control.

Without an understanding of the interpretative flexibility of sociotechnical ensembles, the analysis of technology and society is bound to reproduce only the stabilized meanings of technical artifacts and will miss many opportunities for intervention ... A politics and a theory of sociotechnology have to meet similar requirements in this regard: a balance between malleability and obduracy in politics, and a balance between actor and structure perspectives in theory. (1995: 281)

For organizational scholars, continued reflection on the insights brought by constructionist perspectives, as well as vigilance in the face of 'tipping', can ensure we heed Bijker's call as we work against the easiness of technological determinism and deepen our understanding of organizations as sociotechnical systems.

NOTES

1 Davenport and Prusak provide several examples of what is considered knowledge in their definition: 'A fluid mix of framed experience, values, contextual information, and expert insights that provides a framework for evaluating and interpreting new experiences and information. It originates and is applied in the minds of knowers. In organizations, it often becomes embedded not only in documents or repositories, but also in organizational routines, processes, practices, and norms' (1998: 5). In reference to the definition of knowledge provided here, Davenport and Prusak argue that information is transformed into knowledge when actors have used information to engage in comparison, an analysis of the consequences of action, making connections with other information, and participating in conversations.

2 Of course, statistical sampling methods are not the only valid method for sampling in social research. Qualitative researchers often sample the extreme or the extremely typical case. However, organizations willing and able to be studied with social constructionist approaches are sufficiently difficult to find that we doubt many of them would satisfy either of these criteria.

REFERENCES

Argyris, C. and Schön, D.A. (1978) *Organizational Learning: a Theory of Action Perspective*. Reading, MA: Addison-Wesley.

Arnoff, E.L. (1957) 'Operations research at Case Institute of Technology', *Operations Research*, 289–92.

Axley, S.R. (1996) *Communication at Work: Management and the Communication-Intensive Organization*. Westport, CT: Quorum.

Baek, S., Liebowitz, J., Prasad, S.Y. and Granger, M. (1999) 'Intelligent agents for knowledge management: toward intelligent web-based collaboration within virtual teams', in J. Leibowitz (ed.), *Knowledge Management Handbook*. Boca Raton, FL: CRC. pp. 11.1–11.23.

Barley, S.R. (1986) 'Technology as an occasion for structuring: evidence from observations of CT scanners and the social order of radiology departments', *Administrative Science Quarterly*, 31 (1): 78–108.

Barley, S.R. and Orr, J.E. (1997) 'Introduction: the neglected workforce', in S.R. Barley and J.E. Orr (eds), *Between Craft and Science*. Ithaca, NY: ILR Press. pp. 1–19.

Baum, J.A.C. and McKelvey, B. (eds) (1999) *Variations in Organization Science: in Honor of Donald Campbell*. Newbury Park, CA: Sage.

Beniger, J. (1986) *The Control Revolution: Technological and Economic Origins of the Information Society.* Cambridge, MA: Harvard University Press.

Bijker, W.E. (1995) *Of Bicycles, Bakelites, and Bulbs: toward a Theory of Sociotechnical Change.* Cambridge, MA: MIT Press.

Blackler, F. (1993) 'Knowledge and the theory of organizations: organizations as activity systems and the reframing of management', *Journal of Management Studies*, 30: 863–84.

Bowers, J. and Churcher, J. (1988) 'Local and global structuring of computer-mediated communication', in *Proceedings of the ACM Conference in Computer-Supported Cooperative Work*, Portland. pp. 125–39.

Bowker, G.C. and Star, S.L. (1999) *Sorting Things Out: Classification and its Consequences.* Cambridge, MA: MIT Press.

Brown, J.S. and Duguid, P. (1991) 'Organizational learning and communities-of-practice: toward a unified view of working, learning, and innovation', *Organization Science*, 2: 40–57.

Bucciarelli, L.L. (1994) *Designing Engineers.* Cambridge, MA: MIT Press.

Buckley, W. (1967) *Sociology and Modern Systems Theory.* Englewood Cliffs, NJ: Prentice-Hall.

Callon, M. (1986) 'The sociology of an actor-network: the case of the electric vehicle', in M. Callon, J. Law and A. Rip (eds), *Mapping the Dynamics of Science and Technology: Sociology of Science in the Real World.* London: Macmillan. pp. 19–34.

Carley, K.M. (1997) 'Network text analysis: the network position of concepts', in C.W. Roberts (ed.), *Text Analysis for the Social Sciences: Methods for Drawing Statistical Inferences from Texts and Transcripts.* Mahwah, NJ: Erlbaum. pp. 79–100.

Cheney, G. and Christensen, L.T. (2001) 'Organizational identity: linkages between internal and external communication', in F. Jablin and L. Putnam (eds), *The New Handbook of Organizational Communication: Advances in Theory, Research, and Methods.* Newbury Park, CA: Sage. pp. 231–69.

Chia, R. (1995) 'From modern to postmodern organizational analysis', *Organization Studies*, 16 (4): 579–604.

Choo, C.W. (1998) *The Knowing Organization: How Organizations Use Information to Construct Meaning, Create Knowledge, and Make Decisions.* New York: Oxford University Press.

Coleman, D. (1999) 'Groupware: collaboration and knowledge sharing', in J. Liebowitz (ed.), *Knowledge Management Handbook.* Boca Raton, FL: CRC. pp. 12.1–12.15.

Conrad, C. and Haynes, J. (2001) 'Development of key constructs', in F. Jablin and L. Putnam (eds), *The New Handbook of Organizational Communication: Advances in Theory, Research, and Methods.* Newbury Park, CA: Sage. pp. 47–77.

Corman, S.R. (1997) 'The reticulation of quasi-agents in systems of organizational communication', in G.A. Barnett and L. Thayer (eds), *Organizational – Communication Emerging Perspectives. V: The Renaissance in Systems Thinking.* Greenwich, CT: Ablex. pp. 65–82.

Craig, R.T. (1989) 'Communication as a practical discipline', in B. Dervin, L. Grossberg, B.J. O'Keefe, and E. Wartella (eds), *Rethinking Communication.* Vol. 2: *Paradigm Exemplars.* Newbury Park, CA: Sage. pp. 97–122.

Crossan, M.M., Lane, H.W. and White, R.E. (1999) 'An organizational learning framework: from intuition to institution', *Academy of Management Review*, 24: 522–37.

Daft, R.L. and Huber, G.P. (1987) 'How organizations learn: a communication framework', in N. DiTomaso (ed.), *Research in the Sociology of Organizations*, vol. 5. Greenwich, CT: JAI. pp. 1–36.

Davenport, T.H. and Prusak, L. (1998) *Working Knowledge: How Organizations Manage What They Know.* Boston: Harvard Business School Press.

DeSanctis, G. and Poole, M.S. (1994) 'Capturing the complexity in advanced technology use: adaptive structuration theory', *Organization Science*, 5: 121–47.

Dickson, G.W. (1982) 'Management information systems: evolution and status'. MISRC Working Paper Series 81–02, University of Minnesota.

Dixon, N.M. (2000) *Common Knowledge: How Companies Thrive by Sharing What They Know.* Boston: Harvard Business School Press.

Downey, G.L. (1998) *The Machine in Me: an Anthropologist Sits among Computer Engineers.* New York: Routledge.

Easterby-Smith, M. and Araujo, L. (1999) 'Organizational learning: current debates and opportunities', in M. Easterby-Smith, J. Burgoyne and L. Araujo (eds), *Organizational Learning and the Learning Organization.* Thousand Oaks, CA: Sage. pp. 1–22.

Edge, D. (1995) 'The social shaping of technology', in N. Heap, R. Thomas, G. Einon, R. Mason and H. Mackay (eds), *Information Technology and Society.* London: Sage. pp. 14–32.

Emery, F.E. and Trist, E.L. (1961) 'Socio technical systems', in C.W. Churchman and M. Verhulst (eds), *Management Science, Models and Techniques*, vol. 2. Oxford: Pergamon. pp. 83–97.

Engestrom, Y. and Middleton, D. (eds) (1998) *Cognition and Communication at Work.* Cambridge: Cambridge University Press.

Fahey, L. and Prusak, L. (1998) 'The eleven deadliest sins of knowledge management', *California Management Review*, 40 (3): 265–76.

Feldman, M.S. and March, J.G. (1981) 'Information in organizations as signal and symbol', *Administrative Science Quarterly*, 26: 171–86.

Foss, N. (1999) 'Research in the strategic theory of the firm: "isolationism" and "integrationism"', *Journal of Management Studies*, 36: 725–55.

Fulk, J. and DeSanctis, G. (1999) 'Articulation of communication technology and organizational form', in G. DeSanctis and J. Fulk (eds), *Shaping Organizational Form: Communication, Connection, and Community.* Thousand Oaks, CA: Sage. pp. 3–32.

Gersick, C.G.J. (1991) 'Revolutionary change theories: a multilevel exploration of the punctuated equilibrium paradigm', *Academy of Management Review*, 16: 10–36.

Giddens, A. (1979) *Central Problems in Social Theory: Action, Structure, and Contradiction in Social Analysis*. Berkeley, CA: University of California Press.

Giddens, A. (1984) *The Constitution of Society: Outline of the Theory of Structuration*. Berkeley, CA: University of California Press.

Grant, R.M. (1996) 'Toward a knowledge-based theory of the firm', *Strategic Management Journal*, 17: 109–22.

Greif, I. (1988) 'Overview', in I. Greif (ed.), *Computer-Supported Cooperative Work: a Book of Readings*. San Mateo, CA: Morgan Kaufmann. pp. 5–12.

Hammer, M. and Champy, J. (1993) *Reengineering the Cooperation: A Manifesto for Business Revolution*. New York: Harper Business.

Hayes, N. and Walsham, G. (2000) 'Competing interpretations of computer-supported cooperative work in organizational contexts', *Organization*, 7: 49–67.

Heap, N., Thomas, R., Einon, G., Mason, R. and Mackay, H. (eds) (1995) *Information Technology and Society*. London: Sage.

Heath, C. and Luff, P. (2000) *Technology in Action*. Cambridge: Cambridge University Press.

Henderson, K. (1998) 'The aura of "high tech" in a world of messy practice', *Sociological Quarterly*, 39 (4): 645–72.

Hollan, J. and Stornetta, S. (1992) 'Beyond being there', in *CSCW, 1992*. New York: Association for Computing Machinery. pp. 842–8.

Hughes, T.P. (1986) 'The seamless web: technology, science, etcetera, etcetera', *Social Studies of Science*, 16: 281–92.

Hutchins, E. and Klausen, T. (1996) 'Distributed cognition in an airline cockpit', in Y. Engestrom and D. Middleton (eds), *Cognition and Communication at Work*. Cambridge: Cambridge University Press. pp. 69–96.

Jackson, M.H. (1996) 'The meaning of "communication technology": the technology-context scheme', in B. Burleson (ed.), *Communication Yearbook 19*. Beverly Hills, CA: Sage. pp. 229–68.

Johnson, B.M. and Rice, R.E. (1984) 'Reinvention in the innovation process: the case of word processing', in R.E. Rice et al. (eds), *The New Media: Communication, Research, and Technology*. Beverly Hills, CA: Sage. pp. 157–84.

Kline, T. and McGrath, J.-L. (1999) 'A review of the groupware literature: theories, methodologies, and a research agenda', *Canadian Psychology*, 40: 265–71.

Kling, R. and Iacono, S. (1989) 'The institutional character of computerized information systems', *Office: Technology and People*, 5: 7–28.

Kogut, B. and Zander, U. (1996) 'What firms do: co-ordination, identity, and learning', *Organization Science*, 7: 502–18.

Kunda, G. (1992) *Engineering Culture: Control and Commitment in a High-Tech Corporation*. Philadelphia: Temple University Press.

Latour, B. (1987) *Science in Action: How to Follow Scientists and Engineers through Society*. Cambridge, MA: Harvard University Press.

Laukkanen, M. (1998) 'Conducting causal mapping research: opportunities and challenges', in C. Eden and J.-C. Spender (eds), *Managerial and Organizational Cognition: Theory, Methods, and Research*. Thousand Oaks, CA: Sage. pp. 168–91.

Lave, J. and Wenger, E. (1991) *Situated Learning: Legitimate Peripheral Participation*. New York: Cambridge University Press.

Law, J. (1987) 'Technology and heterogeneous engineerings: the case of Portuguese expansion', in W.E. Bijker, T.P. Hughes and T. Pinch (eds), *The Social Construction of Technological Systems: New Directions in the Sociology and History of Technology*. Cambridge, MA: MIT Press. pp. 111–34.

Law, J. and Hassard, J. (eds) (1999) *Actor Network Theory and After*. Oxford: Blackwell.

Leonard-Barton, D. (1995) *Wellsprings of Knowledge: Building and Sustaining the Sources of Innovation*. Boston: Harvard Business School Press.

Levinthal, D.A. and March, J.G. (1993) 'The myopia of learning', *Strategic Management Journal*, 14: 95–112.

Levitt, B. and March, J.G. (1988) 'Organizational learning', in *Annual Review of Sociology*, vol. 14. Greenwich, CT: JAI. pp. 319–40.

Mandviwalla, M. (1996) 'The worldview of collaborative tools', in D.L. Day and D.K. Kovacks (eds), *Computers, Communication and Mental Models*. London: Lord & Francis. pp. 57–66.

Mantovani, G. (1996) *New Communication Environments: from Everyday to Virtual*. London: Taylor and Francis.

March, J.G. (1965) 'Introduction', in J.G. March (ed.), *Handbook of Organizations*. Chicago: Rand McNally. pp. ix–xvi.

Markus, M.L. and Robey, D. (1988) 'Information technology and oganizational change: causal structure in theory and research', *Management Science*, 34 (5): 583–98.

Martin, J. (1992) *Cultures in Organizations: Three Perspectives*. New York: Oxford University Press.

Marx, L. and Smith, M.R. (1994) 'Introduction', in M.R. Smith and L. Marx (eds), *Does Technology Drive History? The Dilemma of Technological Determinism*. Cambridge, MA: MIT Press. pp. ix–xv.

McPhee, R.D. and Zaug, P. (2000) 'The communicative constitution of organizations: a framework for explanation', *The Electronic Journal of Communication/La Revue Electronique de Communication*, 10. Available at: www.cios.org/getfile_V10n1200.

Mentzas, G., Apostoulou, D., Young, R. and Abecker, A. (2001) 'Knowledge networking: a holistic solution for leveraging corporate knowledge', *Journal of Knowledge Management*, 5: 94–106.

Mumford, E. (1983) *Designing Human Systems: the ETHICS Approach*. Manchester: Manchester Business School.

Myburgh, S. (2000) 'The convergence of information technology and information management', *Information Management Journal*, 34 (2): 4–16.

Nass, C. and Mason, L. (1990) 'On the study of technology and task: a variable-based approach', in J. Fulk and C. Steinfield (eds), *Organizations and Communication Technologies*. Newbury Park, CA: Sage. pp. 29–45.

Ngwenyama, O. and Lyytinen, K.J. (1997) 'Groupware environments as action constitutive resources: a social action framework for analyzing groupware technologies', *Computer Supported Cooperative Work*, 6: 71–93.

Nonaka, I. and Takeuchi, H. (1995) *The Knowledge-Creating Company: How Japanese Companies Create the Dynamics of Innovation*. New York: Oxford University Press.

Nunamaker, J.F., Dennis, A.R., Valacich, J.S., Vogel, D.R. and George, J.F. (1993) 'Issues in the design, development, use, and management of group support systems', in L. Jessup and J. Valacich (eds), *Group Support Systems: New Perspectives*. New York: Macmillan. pp. 123–45.

O'Dell, C. and Grayson, C.J. (1998) 'If we only knew what we know: identification and transfer of internal best practices', *California Management Review*, 40 (3): 154–74.

Offsey, S. (1997) 'Knowledge management: linking people to knowledge for bottom line results', *Journal of Knowledge Management*, 1: 113–22.

O'Leary, D.E. (1998) 'Using AI in knowledge management: knowledge bases and ontologies', *IEEE Intelligent Systems*, 13 (3): 34–9.

Orlikowski, W.J. and Hofman, J.D. (1997) 'An improvisational model for change management: the case of groupware technologies', *Sloan Management Review*, 38 (2): 11–21.

Orlikowski, W.J. and Robey, D. (1991) 'Information technology and the structuring of organizations', *Information Systems Research*, 2 (2): 143–69.

Orr, J.E. (1990) 'Sharing knowledge, celebrating identity: community memory in a service culture', in D.S. Middleton and D. Edwards (eds), *Collective Remembering: Memory in Society*. Beverly Hills, CA: Sage. pp. 169–89.

Osterloh, M. and Frey, B.S. (2000) 'Motivation, knowledge transfer, and organizational forms', *Organization Science*, 11: 538–50.

Perlow, L.A. (1997) *Finding Time: How Corporations, Individuals, and Families Can Benefit from New Work Practices*. Ithaca, NY: ILR.

Pettigrew, A.M. (1985) *The Awakening Giant: Continuity and Change in ICI*. Oxford: Basil Blackwell.

Pickering, A. (1995) *The Mangle of Practice*. Chicago: University of Chicago Press.

Pinch, T.J. and Bijker, W.E. (1984) 'The social construction of facts and artifacts: or how the sociology of science and the sociology of technology might benefit each other', *Social Studies of Science*, 14: 399–441.

Poole, M.S. (1983) 'Structural paradigms and the study of group communication', in M. Mander (ed.), *Communications in Transition: Issues and Debates in Communication Research*. New York: Praeger. pp. 186–205.

Poole, M.S. and DeSanctis, G. (1990) 'Understanding the use of group decision support systems: the theory of adaptive structuration', in J. Fulk and C. Steinfield (eds), *Organizations and Communication Technologies*. Newbury Park, CA: Sage. pp. 173–93.

Putnam, L.L., Phillips, N. and Chapman, P. (1996) 'Metaphors of communication and organization', in S.R. Clegg, C. Hardy and W.R. Nord (eds), *Handbook of Organization Studies*. Thousand Oaks, CA: Sage. pp. 375–408.

Reed, M. (1996) 'Organizational theorizing: a historically contested terrain', in S.R. Clegg, C. Hardy and W.R. Nord (eds), *Handbook of Organization Studies*. Thousand Oaks, CA: Sage. pp. 31–56.

Robey, D. and Azevedo, A. (1994) 'Cultural analysis of the organizational consequences of information technology', *Accounting, Management and Information Technologies*, 4: 23–37.

Robey, D. and Boudreau, M.-C. (1999) 'Accounting for the contradictory organizational consequences of information technology: theoretical directions and methodological implications', *Information Systems Research*, 10 (2): 167–85.

Sackmann, S.A. (1992) 'Culture and subcultures: an analysis of organizational knowledge', *Administrative Science Quarterly*, 37: 140–61.

Sarter, N.B. and Woods, D.D. (2000) 'Team play with a powerful and independent agent: a full-mission simulation study', *Human Factors*, 42: 390–402.

Schuler, D. and Namioka, A. (1993) *Participatory Design: Principles and Practices*. Hillsdale, NJ: Erlbaum.

Searle, J.R. (1979) *Expression and Meaning: Studies in the Theory of Speech Acts*. Cambridge: Cambridge University Press.

Senge, P.M. (1990) *The Fifth Discipline: the Art and Practice of the Learning Organization*. New York: Currency Doubleday.

Shotter, J. and Gergen, K.J. (1994) 'Social construction: knowledge, self, others, and continuing the conversation', in S.A. Deetz (ed.), *Communication Yearbook* 17. Newbury Park, CA: Sage. pp. 3–33.

Smith, R.C. (1993) 'Images of organizational communication: root-metaphors of the organization–communication relation'. Paper presented at the International Communication Association Conference, Washington, DC, May.

Spender, J.C. (1996) 'Organizational knowledge, learning and memory: three concepts in search of a theory', *Journal of Organizational Change Management*, 9: 63–78.

Sproull, L. and Kiesler, S. (1991) *Connections: New Ways of Working in the Networked Organization*. Cambridge, MA: MIT Press.

Starbuck, W.H. (1996) 'Unlearning ineffective or obsolete technologies', *International Journal of Technology Management*, 11: 725–37.

Suchman, L. (1987) *Plans and Situated Action*. Cambridge: Cambridge University Press.

Suchman, L. (1994) 'Do categories have politics? The language/action perspective reconsidered', *Computer Supported Cooperative Work*, 2: 177–90.

Taylor, F.W. (1911) *The Principles of Scientific Management*. New York: Harper.

Taylor, J.R. and van Every, E.J. (2000) *The Emergent Organization: Communication as its Site and Surface*. Mahwah, NJ: Erlbaum.

Taylor, J.R., Cooren, F., Giroux, N. and Robichaud, D. (1996) 'The communicational basis of organization: between the conversation and the text', *Communication Theory*, 6: 1–39.

Taylor, J.R., Groleau, C., Heaton, L. and Van Every, E. (2001) *The Computerization of Work: a Communication Perspective*. Thousand Oaks, CA: Sage.

Thompson, J.D. (1967) *Organizations in Action*. New York: McGraw-Hill.

Trevino, L.K., Daft, R.L. and Lengel, R.H. (1990) 'Understanding managers' media choices: a symbolic interactionist perspective', in J. Fulk and C. Steinfield (eds), *Organizations and Communication Technologies*. Newbury Park, CA: Sage. pp. 71–94.

Von Krogh, G., Ichijo, K. and Nonaka, I. (2000) *Enabling Knowledge Creation: How to Unlock the Mystery of Tacit Knowledge and Release the Power of Innovation*. New York: Oxford University Press.

Weick, K.E. (1987) 'Perspectives on action in organizations', in J.W. Lorsch (ed.), *Handbook of Organizational Behavior*. Englewood Cliffs, NJ: Prentice-Hall. pp. 10–28.

Weick, K.E. and Ashford, S.J. (2001) 'Learning in organizations', in F.M. Jablin and L.L. Putnam (eds), *The New Handbook of Organizational Communication: Advances in Theory, Research, and Methods*. Thousand Oaks, CA: Sage. pp. 704–31.

Wenger, E. (1998) *Communities of Practice: Learning, Meaning, and Identity*. Cambridge: Cambridge University Press.

Wiig, K.M. (1997) 'Knowledge management: introduction and perspective', *Journal of Knowledge Management*, 1: 6–14.

Williams, R. and Edge, D. (1996) 'The social shaping of technology', in W.H. Dutton and M. Peltu (eds), *Information and Communication Technologies: Visions and Realities*. Oxford: Oxford University Press. pp. 53–68.

Wilson, P. (1991) *Computer Supported Cooperative Work: An Introduction*. Oxford: Intellect.

Winograd, T. and Flores, F. (1986) *Understanding Computers and Cognition: a New Foundation for Design*. Reading, MA: Addison-Wesley.

Woolgar, S. (1996) 'Technologies as cultural artifacts', in W.H. Dutton and M. Peltu (eds), *Information and Communication Technologies: Visions and Realities*. Oxford: Oxford University Press. pp. 87–102.

Yates, J. (1993) 'Co-evolution of information-processing technology and use: interaction between the life insurance and tabulating industries', *Business History Review*, 67: 1–53.

Zuboff, S. (1988) *In the Age of the Smart Machine: the Future of Work and Power*. New York: Basic.

15

New Media Implementation and Industrial Organization

FRANÇOIS BAR with CAROLINE SIMARD

Over the past quarter-century, organizations' growing reliance upon networking technologies has brought about a deep transformation of economic activities. Information networks, once considered merely a utility like water or natural gas systems, moved centre stage during that period to become strategic infrastructures. From a technological standpoint, digital convergence was the fundamental enabler of this transition. Telecommunications and computing became more alike: networks were built upon digital technologies and increasingly served to interconnect computers, while computers relied ever more upon networks to support their basic operations. Software, at the heart of the resulting digital networks, made it possible to create new communication applications for individuals or organizations to collaborate and compete. Software also came to define network configuration – the set of rules determining who can communicate with whom, to do what and under which conditions – so that ownership of the underlying hardware alone no longer guaranteed control of the network's uses. The result was a fast-evolving, software-defined, indispensable, and increasingly capable information infrastructure: the 'new media' of much economic activity, our focus in this chapter.

While the information networks born of digital convergence spread through all economic sectors in developed countries, their deployment and implementation have taken many forms. A range of factors, such as the nature of pre-existing economic arrangements, the state of the national communication infrastructure, or national telecom policy, have influenced and shaped the deployment of intra- and interorganizational networks. As a result, while the new media share a common technological lineage, they have been put to a variety of uses in organizations, with diverse consequences. For example, digital networks have been used at times to reinforce central coordination and at others to enable decentralized power; to buttress existing organizations or to invent new ones; to strengthen long-term, stable economic partnerships or to support fluid, fast-changing virtual teams.

At the individual level, new media networks permit new work arrangements overcoming time and space constraints (Morton, 1991; Sproull and Kiesler, 1991; Wigand, 1997), allowing firms to cut costs associated with coordinating dispersed geographical facilities. These network-enabled work arrangements are said to result in increased job satisfaction and empowerment (Sproull and Kiesler, 1991), and provide access to a wider pool of potential employees, unlimited by geographical constraints (Cash et al., 1994).

At the firm level, new media networks make multiple kinds of reorganization possible. They are said to yield faster response time to market changes (Lucas, 1996), better maintenance and access to organizational memory (Morton, 1991), improved leverage of organizational knowledge (Carayannis, 1998), speedier and more efficient information flows, better coordination of group communication, greater employee participation, rapid scheduling, efficient task assignment and reporting, enhanced communication across hierarchical levels, and enhanced coordination of communication within dispersed groups (Sproull and Kiesler, 1991). They also help improve dispersed employees' organizational commitment by acting as a 'window on the corporation' and enabling better socialization of new organizational members.

In addition to improving existing organizations, the new media networks are said to permit entirely new organizational forms. First among such IT-enabled organizational forms is the networked organization where all participants are linked (Rockart and Short, 1991) and the organization flexibly reorganizes itself around each new task (Baker, 1992). Networks also play a crucial role in the establishment and maintenance of internal and external linkages, transforming hierarchies and markets. The network organization thus extends beyond the boundaries of individual firms to form a wider network of multiple organizations (Malone and Laubacher, 1998), increasing interdependence within industries (Rockart and Short, 1991). This state of increased communication between suppliers, distributors and business partners (Cash et al., 1994; Lucas, 1996) supports improved interorganizational arrangements such as strategic networks and the Japanese *keiretsu*, and timely cooperation forms such as joint ventures and consortia (Wigand, 1997). At the extreme, the network model leads to virtual organizations (Davidow and Malone, 1992), composed of a set of loosely coupled, self-organizing networked individuals in geographically dispersed locations. New media would thus usher in an 'e-lance' economy (Malone and Lanbacher, 1998), where individuals or autonomous groups come together around specific projects.

They present survey of the new media impact on industrial organization is structured in three sections. It begins with a review of the economic hopes that were pinned on the technology, in particular on its potential to increase productivity. It then examines how the impact of new media on industrial organization has been analysed, through their impact on two organizational archetypes – markets and hierarchies – and their enabling of an alternative, the network organization. The final section looks at how this analysis fits with the facts in a few emblematic case studies.

NEW MEDIA AND ECONOMIC PROMISES

The convergence of computing and telecommunications into new communication media became clear in the mid 1970s. Observers coined new terms to describe this emerging information infrastructure, such as the French *télématique* (Nora and Minc, 1978) or its less euphonic English cousin 'compunications' (Oettinger and Weinhaus, 1979). The new networks promised to create a foundation for the emerging information economy (Porat and Rubin, 1977), an economic system that would rely increasingly on information-based processes as part of production and exchange activities. In this 'post-industrial' society (Bell, 1973), agriculture and manufacturing would no longer be the basis for economic power. Instead, knowledge workers would make the greater contribution to value creation. As a result, the new media network infrastructure would become the essential backbone of economic activity and control (Beniger, 1986). It would thus usher in new ways to organize economic and social life, leading to the emergence of the information economy (Porat and Rubin, 1977) and the network society (Castells, 1998).

One crucial expectation in these formative years was that reorganizing the economy around information technology and networks would yield tremendous productivity increases, which would more than justify the investments required. Yet, throughout the early years of technology deployment, productivity gains proved elusive, prompting economist Robert Solow's (1987) quip that 'You can see the computer age everywhere but in the productivity statistics', the so-called *productivity paradox* (Brynjolfsson, 1993; David, 1990). In part, the sweeping claims inspired by information technology resulted from a propensity 'to suffer from a kind of "telescopic vision": the possible future appears both closer at hand and more vivid than the necessary intervening, temporally more proximate events on the path leading to that destination' (David, 1989: 5). Three broad categories of explanations have been offered to explain that situation: mismeasurement of real output growth, poor understanding of the true benefits of computers, and underestimation of the learning and adaptation required (David, 2000).

Brynjolfsson (1993) points out prevalent measurement errors in the formulation of the paradox. Productivity statistics do not account for the type of productivity gains which result from information technology deployment, such as increased quality, speed and responsiveness, and increased business scope. Increased scope in particular is problematic because it reduces economies of scale and often appears as a decrease in productivity despite the business's increased value to customers. Hitt and Brynjolfsson (1996) suggest that three questions should be asked: whether IT has increased productivity, whether it has improved business profitability, and whether it has created value for consumers. When separating these questions, they find that IT investment increased production output, failed to increase profitability, and significantly increased consumer value. Increased productivity leads to increased competition, which in turns leads to lower profitability.

Further, information technology alone doesn't guarantee productivity gains. Indeed, organizations can worsen their productivity if they simply deploy computer networks to automate old processes (Brynjolfsson and Hitt, 1998; David, 1990). A more realistic view of IT's benefits is to recognize that technology is just one element, not a single determinant, of the thorough business transformation required to improve productivity (Brynjolfsson and Hitt, 1998). In addition, the new media constitute a complex interrelated system. Benefits in one part of that system often require compatibility and standardization with deployments in other parts of the system as well as previous systems deployments, and the overall infrastructure is highly dependent on network externalities (David, 1990). New media systems also require the presence of complementary assets, such as trained users, to be used effectively. As a result, 'the emergence of a new techno-economic regime based on computer and communications innovations will be a protracted and historically contingent affair' (1990: 356).

As the new media networks emerged, the traditional Fordist firm and the interorganization coordination mechanisms that went along with it began reaching their limits (Cohen and Zysman, 1987). Organizations required greater flexibility, both static and dynamic, to adjust to new competitive environments (Coriat, 1994). This prompted the emergence of new organizational forms, made possible by network technologies (Piore and Sabel, 1984; Antonelli, 1992). Overall, however, the emergence of the network society is not simply driven by the deployment of a new media infrastructure. Rather, it represents a broader transformation, made possible by the development of new ways to organize production and exchange activities. In this reorganization, the new media are a critically important element, but only one element. They support change as they enable the design and implementation of new organizational forms and permit a rearticulation of production processes. They also suggest further change, as the digital network's increasing flexibility lets end users experiment directly with diverse communication configurations and the organizational arrangements they imply (Bar, 1990). In the end, the key to overcoming the productivity paradox resides in the ability to reorganize around the new media. The other chapters in this part explore this reorganization process within work groups and firms. We focus here on the broader reorganization of interactions between these entities and its implications for industrial organization.

UNDERSTANDING THE IMPACT OF NEW MEDIA ON INDUSTRIAL ORGANIZATION

An understanding of the impact of new media on the organization of economic activity starts with the fundamental theory that explores the reasons behind specific patterns of economic organization: transaction cost economics (TCE). Oliver Williamson (1975) formulated transaction cost theory, building on the work of Coase (1937), to identify the most efficient governance structure according to the varying nature of transactions between firms. He identified two extreme forms of organizations: markets and hierarchies. Markets provide a decentralized, self-governing structure within which firms can find partners and negotiate specific transactions, allowing for fluid changes in patterns of economic interaction. Hierarchies, by contrast, represent rigid, centrally governed structures within which economic actors interact in a stable and predictable fashion. According to transaction cost economics, the relative costs of setting up transactions between actors within these two extreme organizational structures leads to the choice of one over the other. Because digital networks increasingly support these interactions, they can affect the relative cost of market and hierarchical transactions, thereby resulting in changes in previous industrial organization.

Transaction cost theory is based on two key assumptions: bounded rationality and opportunism (Williamson, 1996). Actors engaged in transactions are rationally bounded and are therefore unable to process large amounts of information and consider all the alternative choices, leading to satisficing behaviour, or opting for a 'good enough' action (Simon, 1957). Applied to TCE, this means that 'all complex contracts are unavoidably incomplete' (Williamson, 1996: 37), with the risk that extra transaction costs can occur down the road because of missing information. Thus, a major purpose of organizing is the attempt to compensate for bounded rationality and to reduce opportunistic behaviour among the involved actors, establishing the relative stability necessary for long-term planning.

Hierarchies offer lower transaction costs, reduce opportunistic behaviour and mitigate the downsides of bounded rationality through a higher degree of administrative control (Williamson, 1975). Indeed, it is easier to resolve disputes internally and therefore transactions contracts can be left more incomplete than in the case of markets (Williamson, 1996). Markets by contrast, organized around spot contracts, reduce transaction costs in the case of products of a low degree of specificity, whereas hierarchies are appropriate for highly specific products (Williamson, 1975; 1996). When complexity, uncertainty and specificity increase, more information processing is needed. Hierarchies and centralized communication structures are more suited to the processing of such complex information.

Obviously, most of these transaction costs result from the acquisition, processing and transmission of information about products, production and work processes, or about the qualifications of economic partners. Therefore, because new media precisely aim at transforming information activities, they can be expected to have significant effects on these costs. Thus, transaction cost economics has been applied to understand the impacts of new media on economic organization. But if digital networks clearly have the potential to improve the functioning of both hierarchies and markets, their ultimate impact on economic organization is more controversial: will the new media result in more hierarchies, more markets, or new organizational forms?

Better Hierarchies

One effect of digital network technology on economic organization has been to promote the creation of 'electronic hierarchies' (Malone et al., 1987). Digital networks allow tighter coordination between organizations within the same value chain, leading to greater vertical integration (Clemons and Kleindorfer, 1992). This integration may be virtual (realized simply through tight interorganizational information networks), or formalized through corporate structures or cross-ownership. In either case, this leads to hierarchies where buyers work with stable, predetermined suppliers (Malone et al., 1987). Some analysts have described the electronic hierarchy as an 'electronic monopoly', reflecting the exclusive buying relationship established with a supplier (Chodhury, 1997). For example, Clemons and Row (1992) report the quasi-vertical integration enabled by network technology between Procter & Gamble and Wal-Mart. In this electronic hierarchy, P&G has electronic access to all sales data, and is able to deliver inventory to Wal-Mart as needed, enabling Wal-Mart to avoid the cost of holding inventory and order processing.

This is an example of what Malone et al. call the 'electronic integration effect' of the new media, where companies articulate tightly coupled processes around information networks. The electronic integration effect is most typically produced in electronic hierarchies (Malone et al., 1987). Indeed, it permits a level of integration that is not possible with other interorganizational networks, enabling the optimization of the integration of the total value chain (Chodhury, 1997). The supplier, through this exclusive relationship, is able to collect a significant amount of information about the buyer's needs and integrate its processes to those of the buyer to better meet those needs. However, the buyer loses the potential advantage of being able to scan the market for the better offer, which is characteristic of the market form of network governance (Chodhury, 1997).

More Perfect Markets

The same digital networks can also serve to build electronic markets. These 'e-markets' are also said to lead to the elimination of intermediaries, acting as electronic brokers that put buyers in direct communication with sellers (Malone et al., 1987). The resulting disintermediation, combined with more

intense, 'friction-free' price competition, could lead to more perfect markets (Bakos, 1996). However, as some analysts have speculated, while existing intermediaries may be eliminated or forced to adapt, new types of electronic intermediaries will emerge. Bakos (1998) foresees the emergence of intermediaries that will match buyers and sellers, provide product and customer information to interested parties, and manage physical delivery and payment functions.

Indeed, network technology has the potential to lead to an economy organized around constantly emerging electronic markets (Benjamin and Wigand, 1995; Keen, 1981; Malone et al., 1987). Malone et al. have formulated the 'electronic markets hypothesis', arguing that in addition to reducing production costs, IT will reduce coordination costs usually associated with markets. In that view, an electronic market is a multilateral interorganizational information system that, because of the scalability of the new media, can link a potentially unlimited number of buyers and suppliers (Choudhury et al., 1998). Hence, the digital network serves the function of market (Benjamin and Wigand, 1995). The network itself becomes the marketplace (Bar, 2001). This form offers price competition advantages, while offering little opportunity for electronic integration between buyer and supplier, since they engage in constantly reconfigured spot transactions rather than long-term relationships (Chodhury, 1997).

A firm will set up or join an electronic market if it assumes that the profits to be realized from a large volume of potential buyers are greater than the potential loss caused by lowering prices due to increased competition (Benjamin and Wigand, 1995). Malone et al. (1987) suggest that digital networks lead to an 'electronic brokerage effect', where electronic markets can act as brokers, resulting in an increase of possible quality alternative suppliers and buyers and a decrease in the cost of the selection process (Bakos, 1998; Benjamin and Wigand, 1995; Malone et al., 1987). This will potentially have the effect of eliminating intermediaries between the manufacturer and the buyer (disintermediation), as the information superhighway will enable direct market contact between manufacturer and consumers (Benjamin and Wigand, 1995). Besides the reduction of coordination costs, the emergence of markets will result from IT's ability to simplify complex product descriptions for highly complex products that were usually traded through hierarchies.

Beyond Hierarchies and Markets: Network Organizations

As new media transform traditional markets and hierarchies, pure examples of these two forms become more elusive. Indeed, hierarchical organizations increasingly rely on network-based, market-like processes to coordinate the work of their employees and work groups, or to conduct business with the clients, suppliers and subcontractors that constitute their extended hierarchy. Likewise, many network-based markets depend on features traditionally associated with hierarchical organizations, combining the market's arm's-length dealings with tighter longer-term relationships among market partners, including for example the pre-qualification of buyers and sellers who become part of the market's inner circle, or the establishment of a hierarchy of markets for the governance of subtasks. Confronted with such evolution, transaction cost economics tends to view these new organizational forms as hybrids of market and hierarchy.

However, others argue that we are witnessing not simply the combination of traditional markets and hierarchies, but the emergence of a distinctly new form of economic governance, the network organization (Antonelli, 1992; Jarillo, 1988). Because networks allow a distinct form of economic governance, transaction cost economics and its focus on dyadic relationships (Williamson, 1996) is ill-suited to the study of network organizations (Powell, 1990). The main distinction they identify between the new network form and the traditional markets and hierarchies is the nature of relationships between actors. In a network, independent actors cooperate on a long-term basis, and the relationship is based on trust and goodwill. In a hierarchy, relations can be long term, but a specific authority is identified as having the ability to resolve arising disputes. In a market, relationships are episodic, and last only for the duration of a specific transaction (Poldony and Page, 1998).

Network organizations existed before the emergence of the new media (such as, for example, in northern Italy's textile industry: Piore and Sabel, 1984). Digital networks however have proven essential to the more widespread adoption of new network forms of organizations. Castells suggests that digital networks favour a distinct form of organization, the network enterprise, which he defines as 'that specific form of enterprise whose system of means is constituted by the intersection of segments of autonomous systems of goals' (1998: 171). This organizational form is characterized by long-term exchange relations, but with the absence of an ultimate authority to arbitrate possible disputes (Poldony and Page, 1998). By reducing transaction costs (Ciborra, 1983; Jarillo, 1988), and more specifically coordination costs, digital networks 'can facilitate the development of stable, tightly coupled relationships among firms' (Clemons and Kleindorfer, 1992: 10). Involved in a network relationship based on long-term trust, a firm does not have to worry about opportunistic behaviour on the part of other firms in its network. The use of network technology to support the network form can further reduce transaction costs through a fast and tight coupling of the participating firm's processes.

Various strands of the literature analysing new media's impact on industrial organization tend to adopt a deterministic approach. Extrapolating from the characteristics of the new media technology they investigate, they predict corresponding characteristics of the organizations that use them. Individually, when looking at particular economic sectors or at specific organizational arrangements, these studies have assessed how the new communication technologies affect the prior balance between market and hierarchy, or promote the development of new network forms of organizations. They diverge in their assessments, some concluding that new media result in better hierarchies, some finding that new media lead to greater reliance on market processes, others showing that new media bring about entirely new organizational forms. Taken together, however, they offer a different picture. They show that new media technologies do not determine organizational form, but can in fact support a variety of different approaches to reorganization. They suggest that the resulting organizational form will be determined less by new media technology than by other characteristics of the firm's internal processes and external competitive environment. In fact, in several industries, similar communications technologies have supported different organizational outcomes in different periods, as in the cases explored below.

CASE STUDIES

This section reviews some of the classic case studies of the establishment of new media networks between economic entities and their effect on the resulting economic organization. We review some of the literature on electronic data interchange (EDI), airline computerized reservation systems, and strategic information systems. These show how similar new media systems and technologies, deployed in various circumstances or at different times, entail different organizational implications. The important variables include the competitive environment within which they are deployed, and the relative positions of the actors engaged in network-mediated interaction.

Better Hierarchies? Electronic Data Interchange

Electronic data interchange (EDI) systems were one of the earliest new media technologies aimed at enhancing interorganization interactions. First deployed in the mid 1970s, their main purpose was to facilitate the exchange of formatted information between firms (rather than free-form communication). Once two business partners agree to use a common EDI standard, they can electronically exchange highly specified messages such as parts orders, invoices or payments. The EDI standards define precise formats for data fields containing codified information including parts numbers, prices, quantities, delivery locations, shipment times or account numbers. EDI systems have made possible the automation and standardization of interorganizational communication networks (Brousseau, 1994).

The initial development of EDI standards was a laborious process, requiring painstaking definition of the information required for many diverse transactions. As a result, EDI was initially aimed at improving existing bilateral or multilateral business relationships between buyers and sellers engaged in sustained, long-term relationships. Sets of EDI standards emerged in individual industries, most notably manufacturing (principally automotive), retail and distribution (including transportation), and banking. The high specificity of interactions between members of the related value chains made them good candidates for that technology. Early EDI deployments thus aimed to rationalize existing supply chains and impose on them a coherent governance. In so doing, EDI implementations were not meant to stop at the strict automation of individual economic relationships, but intended to reorganize broad cross-firm production and exchange processes within existing supply chains. Their goal was to create an extended hierarchy that reached beyond individual firms to include their long-term business partners. A variety of EDI standards emerged in different industry sectors, each associated with the articulation of a particular electronic hierarchy.

Over time, however, a different analysis of EDI networks would emerge. EDI systems, like all communication technologies, are associated with strong network externalities (Katz and Shapiro, 1985). Therefore, companies within one industry have economic incentives to adopt common standards in order to be able to do business with each other electronically. As a result, one would expect the different EDI standards to merge, at least within industries, creating conditions for the support of a more fluid organizational structure. Common EDI standards would enable the rapid establishment of bilateral electronic dyads or their swift dissolution, where a buyer or seller uses EDI technology to sustain links with a selected number of sellers or buyers (Chodhury, 1997). Rather than supporting extended hierarchies, EDI would then enable network forms of economic organization and could even, in extreme cases, support electronic markets.

In reality, a variety of configurations emerged in different industries, in different countries and at different times. For example in the North American automotive manufacturing industry, EDI standardization was driven primarily by the large automakers. Industry-wide standardization efforts were limited as each promoted a distinct EDI implementation, partly for strategic reasons (to better control their respective supply chains) and partly for lack of traditions or policies encouraging coordination. While each auto-maker was able to force its preferred system on its parts suppliers, individual suppliers who sold to multiple auto-makers had to support multiple EDI standards and incur the related costs. The result was a series of Balkanized electronic hierarchies (Bar, 1990; 1995). By contrast in the European auto industry, a combination of policy incentives for coordination, stronger industry institutions and the greater relative strength of parts suppliers led to much greater industry-wide standardization, supporting an arrangement closer to the network form of organization (Brousseau, 1996).

These examples show how one technology, EDI, can be implemented in very different ways and lead to remarkably different organizational results. Brousseau (1994) further points out that organizational stability will also play an important role in the implementation of such technologies. In particular, EDI is unlikely to be successfully implemented in highly certain environments (because it would then be obsolete) or highly uncertain environments (because EDI implementation assumes some knowledge of what future communication needs will be) (1994: 337). In industries where the environment is uncertain and the business relationships must remain flexible, highly standardized EDI implementation could become detrimental by reducing network flexibility. In a case study of EDI implementation in Singapore, Teo et al. (1997) have shown that network technology can lead to a transformation of organizational structure, business networks, business scope and competitiveness. Hence, the real benefits of EDI systems reside not in the technology itself but in the restructuring of business processes and the establishment of new network partnerships (Gottardi and Bolisani, 1996).

Better Markets? Airline Computerized Reservation Systems

The airline industry provides another interesting illustration of the new media's consequences for the organization of economic activity. Successive waves of digital network deployment have led the organization of airline reservations from hierarchy, to biased market, to less biased market, to a network organization around Internet-based systems. With the deployment of the first computerized reservation systems (CRSs), American Airlines' SABRE in particular, airlines controlled an electronic hierarchy that extended to travel agencies. In time, that system became more open to competing airlines and other travel service providers and came to resemble more closely an electronic market, within which travel agents could access offers from all suppliers on an equal footing. The Internet promised to push the industry closer to a perfect market, where travellers would be in direct contact with airlines, negotiating for prices and conditions within a more perfect market.

A closer look at airline reservation systems shows that network technology didn't drive that transition alone. Airlines encouraged the shift from hierarchy to market, hoping for greater profits by ensuring that their reservation system offered tickets from all airlines, thus making it more attractive to the customer (Dang-Nguyen, 1996). However, research suggests that even organizations which possess significant market share can suffer profit losses when joining an electronic market. Indeed, the price reductions forced on them by competitive markets reduce their profit margins, such as has been the case for the airline carriers who joined SABRE and APOLLO (American and United's respective CRSs) (Benjamin and Wigand, 1995). Here as in other cases, however, the critical mass of other joiners leaves little choice to an organization but to join the electronic market. Even dominant players such as United and American reportedly suffered a loss as a result of having to share SABRE and APOLLO with other suppliers (Benjamin and Wigand, 1995).

Competitive incentives and the pursuit of critical mass did not alone result in the creation of a (more) open market for airline reservations. Government policy provided additional inducement, when the Department of Justice's antitrust department showed that the hierarchical airline reservation systems such as the first-generation SABRE were biased toward their owner airline company (Dang-Nguyen, 1996). Overall, this evolution suggests that networking technology, while it creates opportunities for reorganization, doesn't alone determine the economic organization of a particular activity: depending on the strategic priorities of the dominant participants, and on external factors such as antitrust policy, the application of new media can lead to tighter hierarchy as well as a more perfect market as it did in the airlines case.

American Airlines is now generating revenues by selling their system and knowhow to other companies spanning numerous industries, while still hoping to be the best at using the information strategically (Hopper, 1990). This is consistent with the proposition that in an electronic market, the profits of the market-maker will remain higher than those of other companies participating in the market (Benjamin and Wigand, 1995). SABRE is now an 'electronic travel supermarket', a 'computerized middleman' (Hopper, 1990), linking suppliers and buyers of the travel and tourism industry through network technology. Benjamin and Wigand (1995) argue that policy-makers must set guidelines to regulate electronic organizations to ensure that a market-maker refrains from creating network bias in favour of a specific supplier (as was the case with SABRE).

Strategic Use of Information Technology

An important aspect of the story becomes apparent through these various examples: when companies deploy new media infrastructure and applications, they will strive to enhance their own strategic position. In some cases, this may motivate them to sponsor a sweeping rearticulation of their supply chain or a reorganization of the marketplaces they participate in. In other cases, they may encourage the formation of alliances to foster the deployment of standardized systems. Or they may choose instead to pursue isolated, proprietary technologies precisely because such lack of interoperability creates entry barriers for their competitors. In the end, their strategic response to the particular competitive challenges they face, more than intrinsic characteristics of the new media technologies they choose to deploy, will determine the organizational consequences.

There are many examples of these strategic uses of information technologies. Companies have used information systems strategically to gain information from markets and gain a competitive advantage over other firms in the market, shifting the competitive position of organizations within industries. Cash and Konsynski (1985) give the example of an automotive manufacturer who uses network technology to scan the market for the lowest possible bid for a product, thus increasing the market position of the manufacturer by driving down prices. Clemons et al. (1996) provide several cases of dominant firms losing their most profitable customers to aggressive new entrants relying on IT. Indeed, flexible new entrants rely on IT to get information from the market, to identify and target the most profitable customers of an industry.

By providing lower costs and more effective distribution channels to customers through the use of IT, these new entrants are 'cream-skimming', attracting the most profitable customers away from established firms (Clemons et al., 1996). For example, Clemons and Weber (1994) cite the example of new entrants in the airline industry who threaten the market shares of American Airlines and United Airlines, by gathering information from the marketplace, identifying the most profitable customers, and offering them lower-cost, specific point-to-point services on the most travelled routes. Indeed, digital networks dramatically reduce the cost of capturing, storing and analysing information from the marketplace. Hence, using interorganizational networks, the Inter-Continental Hotel chain is able to target its most profitable customers by capturing very detailed information on their needs and wants and sharing it within network hotels. The Inter-Continental profitable customer will therefore obtain highly catered service, whether staying in New York or London (Clemons and Weber, 1994). Similarly, following the deregulation of the London Stock Exchange, Barclays de Zoete Wedd securities firm reacted to increased competitive pressure by using an information system named Beatrice which enabled it to identify, rank and project the growth potential of its most profitable customers. The firm was then able to target the most profitable customers and offer them new tailored services, while dropping less profitable customers (Clemons and Weber, 1990; 1994). Another possible strategy is price-discrimination, in which different customers are charged different prices (Bakos, 1998). Hence, an organization can ask more from the less profitable customer, while lowering prices for the most desirable customer, and increasing profits.

This process is not necessarily at the expense of the customer since it enables organizations to serve customers that would otherwise be priced out of the market (Bakos, 1998). This is another example of digital networks being used for competitive advantage, moving from a 'one size fits all' strategy to a tailored, market segmentation strategy (Clemons and Weber, 1994). With digital networks becoming increasingly ubiquitous, organizations are becoming less system builders than system architects, trying to gain competitive advantage from existing network structures rather than building one anew. The goal for organizations then becomes to outsmart each other in using the information network strategically (Hopper, 1990).

CONCLUSION

Our overview of the new media's impact on industrial organization shows that a diversity of outcomes can be expected. The application of digital networking technologies to economic processes of production and exchange, under different circumstances, has served to support and improve hierarchies, markets or new network forms of organization. In the effort to understand the mechanisms at work, one characteristic of new media networks is fundamental. Because the new media are built upon digital technologies, their architecture and the applications they support are defined in software. Control over their configuration is therefore flexibly separable from ownership of the underlying network infrastructure. This creates opportunities for the many actors using these networks to shape them in ways that further their competitive goals.

For the organizations involved, this ultimately boils down to an essential challenge: their ability to create relative advantage through the combination of economies of scale and economies of scope, reconciling standardized processes with rapidly changing, differentiated products and services. The resulting economic regime, which some have called 'mass variety' (Coriat, 1993), combines the search for static flexibility through adaptation to short-term market variations with the more enduring benefits stemming from dynamic flexibility. Meeting this challenge requires smart choices of technologies and work organization methods. The production systems developed around new media play an essential role in promoting better production and exchange processes, the only way to improve overall productivity, and greater flexibility in programming and reprogramming these processes.

However, new media do not dictate the outcome, nor is their implementation preordained by the technology's characteristics. Rather, they serve to suggest, supplement and support a sweeping organizational transformation of production and exchange activities, from product and service design to production methods, from marketing techniques to exchange mechanisms. For the organizations involved, this is precisely what makes the new media 'strategic'.

REFERENCES

Antonelli, C. (1992) 'Information economics and industrial organization', *Human Systems Management*, 53–60.

Baker, W.E. (1992) 'The network organization in theory and practice', in N.N.R.G. Eccles (ed.), *Networks and Organizations*. Boston, MA: Harvard Business School Press. pp. 397–429.

Bakos, Y.J. (1996) 'Reducing buyer search costs: implications for electronic marketplaces', *Management Science*, 43 (12): 1676–92.

Bakos, Y.J. (1998) 'The emerging role of electronic marketplaces on the Internet', *Communications of the ACM*, 41 (8): 35–42.

Bar, F. (1990) 'Configuring the telecommunications infrastructure for the computer age: the economics of network control'. Working Paper 43, Berkeley Roundtable on the International Economy, University of California Berkeley Institute of International Studies.

Bar, F. (1995) 'Intelligent manufacturing in the global information economy', in W. Drake (ed.), *The New Information Infrastructure: Strategies for U.S. Policy*. New York: 20th Century Fund. pp. 55–74.

Bar, F. (2001) 'The construction of marketplace architecture', in *Tracking a Transformation: E-commerce and* the Terms of Competition in Industries. The BRIE-IGCC E-conomy Project Task Force on the Internet (eds). Washington, DC: Brookings Institution Press.

Bell, D. (1973) The Coming of Post-Industrial Society; a Venture in Social Forecasting. New York: Basic.

Beniger, J.R. (1986) The Control Revolution: Technological and Economic Origins of the Information Society. Cambridge, MA: Harvard University Press.

Benjamin, R. and Wigand, R. (1995) 'Electronic markets and virtual value chains on the information superhighway', Sloan Management Review, 36 (2): 62.

Brousseau, E. (1994) 'EDI and inter-firm relationships', Information Economics & Policy, 6 (3, 4): 319–47.

Brousseau, E. (1996) 'Intermédiation par les réseaux: quelles institutions?', in E. Brousseau, P. Petit and D. Phan (eds), Mutations des télécommunications, des industries et des marches. Paris, France: Economica. pp. 171–229.

Brynjolfsson, E. (1993) 'The productivity paradox of information technology', Communications of the ACM, 36 (12): 67–77.

Brynjolfsson, E. and Hitt, L.M. (1998) 'Beyond the productivity paradox: computers are the catalyst for bigger changes', Communications of the ACM, August.

Carayannis, E.G. (1998) 'The strategic management of technological learning in project/program management: the role of extranets, intranets, and intelligent agents in knowledge generation, diffusion, and leveraging', Technovation, 18 (11): 697–703.

Cash, J.I. Jr and Kosynski, B.R. (1985) 'IS redraws competitive boundaries', Harvard Business Review, 63 (2): 134–42.

Cash, J.I. Jr, Eccles, R.G., Nohria, N. and Nolan, R. (1994) Building the Information-Age Organization: Structure, Control, and Information Technologies. Boston: Irwin.

Castells, M. (1998) The Rise of the Network Society. Cambridge, MA: Blackwell.

Chodhury, V. (1997) 'Strategic choices in the development of interorganizational information systems', Information Systems Research, 8 (1): 1–24.

Chodhury, V., Hartzel, K.S. and Kosynski, B.R. (1998) 'Uses and consequences of electronic markets: an empirical investigation in the aircraft parts industry', MIS Quarterly, 22 (4): 471–507.

Ciborra, C.U. (1983) 'Markets, bureaucracies and groups in the information society: an institutional appraisal of the impacts of information technology', Information Economics and Policy, 1: 145–60.

Clemons, E.K. and Kleindorfer, P.R. (1992) 'An economic analysis of interorganizational information technology', Decision Support Systems, 8: 431–46.

Clemons, E.K. and Row, M.C. (1992) 'Information technology and industrial cooperation: the changing economics of coordination and ownership', Journal of Management Information Systems, 9 (2): 9.

Clemons, E.K. and Weber, B.W. (1990) 'London's big bang: a case study of information technology, competitive impact, and organizational change', Journal of Management Information Systems, 6 (4): 41–59.

Clemons, E.K. and Weber, B.W. (1994) 'Segmentation, differentiation, and flexible pricing: experiences with information technology and segment-tailored strategies', Journal of Management of Information Systems, 11 (2): 9.

Clemons, E.K., Croson, D.C. and Weber, B.W. (1996) 'Market dominance as a precursor of a firm's failure: emerging technologies and the competitive advantage of new entrants', Journal of Management Information Systems, 13 (2): 59–75.

Coase, R.H. (1937) 'The nature of the firm', Economica, 4: 386–405.

Cohen, S.S. and Zysman, J. (1987) Manufacturing Matters: the Myth of the Post-Industrial Economy. New York: Basic.

Coriat, B. (1993) Globalization, Variety and Mass Production: the Metamorphosis of Mass Production in the New Competitive Age. Paris: CREI, Université Paris XIII.

Coriat, B. (1994) L'Atelier et le robot: essai sur le fordisme et la production de masse à l'âge de l'électronique. Mesnil-sur-l'Estrée: Firmin-Didot for C. Bourgeois.

Dang-Nguyen, G. (1996) 'Les systèmes de réservation aerienne et l'économie des réseaux', in E. Brousseau, P. Petit and D. Phan (eds), Mutations des télécommunications, des industries et des marches. Paris, France: Economica. pp. 231–62.

David, P.A. (1989) 'Computer and dynamo: the modern productivity paradox in a not-too-distant mirror'. CEPR Publication 172, Stanford University, Stanford, CA.

David, P.A. (1990) 'The dynamo and the computer: an historical perspective on the modern productivity paradox', The American Economic Review, Papers and Proceedings of the Annual Meeting of the American Economic Association, May, 80 (2): 355–61.

David, P.A. (2000) 'Understanding digital technology's evolutions and the path of measured productivity growth: present and future in the mirror of the past', in E. Brynjolfsson and B. Kahin (eds), Understanding the Digital Economy. Cambridge, MA: MIT Press.

Davidow, W.H. and Malone, M.S. (1992) The Virtual Corporation: Structuring and Re-vitalizing the Corporation for the 21st century. New York: HarperCollins.

Gottardi, G. and Bolisani, E. (1996) 'A critical perspective on information technology management: the case of electronic data interchange', International Journal of Technology Management, 12 (4): 369–90.

Hitt, L.M. and Brynjolfsson, E. (1996) 'Productivity, business profitability, and consumer surpluses: three different measures of information technology value', MIS Quarterly, 20 (2): 121.

Hopper, M.D. (1990) 'Rattling SABRE – new ways to compete on information', Harvard Business Review, (May–June): 118–25.

Jarillo, J.C. (1988) 'On strategic networks', Strategic Management Journal, 9: 3–41.

Katz, M.L. and Shapiro, C. (1985) 'Network externalities, competition, and compatibility', The American Economic Review, 75 (3): 424–40.

Keen, P.G.W. (1981) 'Communications in the 21st century: telecommunications and business policy', *Organizational dynamics*, 10 (2): 54–67.

Lucas, H.C. Jr (1996) *The T-form Organization*. San Francisco: Jossey-Bass.

Malone, T.W. and Laubacher, R.J. (1998) 'The dawn of the e-lance economy', *Harvard Business Review*, (Sept.–Oct.): 145–52.

Malone, T.W., Yates, J. and Benjamin, R.I. (1987) 'Electronic markets and electronic hierarchies', *Communications of the ACM*, 30 (6): 484–97.

Morton, M.S.S. (1991) 'Introduction', in M.S.S. Morton (ed.), *The Corporation of the 1990s: Information Technology and Organizational Transformation*. New York: Oxford University Press.

Nora, S. and Minc, A. (1978) *'L'Informatisation de la société: rapport à M. le Président de la République*. Paris: La Documentation française.

Oettinger, A.G. and Weinhaus, C.L. (1979) 'National stakes in the compunications revolution: jurisdictional cost separations'. Working Paper w-79-2, Harvard University Program on Information Resources Policy, Harvard University, Cambridge, MA.

Piore, M.J. and Sabel, C.F. (1984) *The Second Industrial Divide: Possibilities for Prosperity*. New York: Basic.

Poldony, J.M. and Page, K.L. (1998) 'Network forms of organization', *Annual Review of Sociology*, 24: 57–76.

Porat, M.U. and Rubin, M.R. (1977) *The Information Economy*. Washington, DC: US Government Printing Office.

Powell, W.W. (1990) 'Neither market nor hierarchy: network forms of organization', in B.M. Staw and L.L. Cummings (eds), *Research in Organizational Behavior*, vol. 12. 'Greenwich, CT: JAI. pp. 295–336.

Rockart, J.F. and Short, J.E. (1991) 'The networked organization and the management of interdependence', in M.S.S. Morton (ed.), *The Corporation of the 1990s: Information Technology and Organizational Transformation*. New York: Oxford University Press. pp. 189–219.

Simon, H. (1957) *Models of the Man*. New York: Wiley.

Solow, R.M. (1987) 'We'd better watch out', *New York Review of Books*, 12 July: 36.

Sproull, L. and Kiesler, S. (1991) *Connections: New Ways of Working in the Networked Organization*. Cambridge, MA: MIT Press.

Teo, H., Tan, B.C.Y. and Wei, K. (1997) 'Organizational transformation wing electronic data interchange: the case of TradeNet in Singapore', *Journal of Management Information Systems*, 13 (4): 139–65.

Wigand, R. (1997) 'Electronic commerce: definition, theory and context', *Information Society*, 13 (1): 1–16.

Wigand, R., Picot, A. and Reichwald, R. (1997) *Information, Organization, and Management: Expanding Markets and Corporate Boundaries*. New York: Wiley.

Williamson, O.E. (1975) *Markets and Hierarchies, Analysis and Antitrust Implications: a Study in the Economics of Internal Organization*. New York: Free Press.

Williamson, O.E. (1996) *The Mechanism of Governance*. New York: Oxford University Press.

PART FOUR: SYSTEMS, INDUSTRIES AND MARKETS

Introduction

JOHN URE

The theme of this part is political economy in its broadest sense. The chapters trace developments in a number of industries, all of which have paved the way for the growth of the new media sector. They also cover trade issues, how economists have handled the concept of information economics, and the ultimately important social question of universal access to the new information and communications technologies (ICTs).

The opening chapter from Pablo Boczkowski provides a cameo history of online newspapers, one of the earliest manifestations of new media. The faltering history of these endeavours illustrates the problems of an industry trying to anticipate both the opportunities and the threats arising from new electronic communications technologies, a history punctuated by false starts and misread opportunities. For example, early on newspaper publishers experimented with videotex and teletext, but journalistic practice was more or less confined to the massaging of 'given' news stories. Yet researchers found that adopters were interested to use the new medium to 'communicate among themselves about a wide array of issues'. Despite the fact that this was apparently a widespread practice, newspapers tended to ignore them. It was, of course, the subsequent explosion in growth of e-mail that really showed the potential for people to design their own uses for the emerging communications technology.

Although it is true that online newspapers have mostly reproduced print content in electronic form, Boczkowski points out that it is no less true that there has been a progressive growth in original material. However, studies have concentrated almost exclusively on this reproduction while over-looking original content – arguably a more fertile ground to examine changes in the technologies and practices of newspapering move 'when they from ink on paper to pixels on the screen'. Labour process studies have frequently paid visits to the production side of the newspaper industry; Boczkowski cites research on the other side of the market, on usage. Not surprisingly, research tends to confirm the view that majority adopters of online newspapers are less 'news junkies' than the early adopters and tend to be more entertainment-oriented. Research comparisons on usage are inevitably complicated by the fact that the subject is a moving target. Not only are the demographics of those online changing, but so too are their location and means of access, for example, from office to home, and from PC to handheld mobile cell phone. But, as Boczkowski suggests, recognition of this complexity perhaps offers fertile ground for scholars from a variety of disciplines to cooperate more closely in their research efforts.

As Philip Cooke points out (quoting a citation from Mansell) in his chapter on new media and new economy cluster dynamics, defining what constitutes the range of 'new media' industries is problematic since the digital economy is essentially 'devoid of shape, form, edges and geography'. Cooke therefore approaches the task through an identification of the industry's structure, or implied value chain: which we may paraphrase as content conceptualization and origination, content production and provision, service packaging and provision, distribution networks and services, and customer's premises equipment devices. This chain as 'new media' is the product of convergence at various points between 'old media' and the digital economy. The degree and speed of convergence are not constant along the chain, or at any nodal point, and, perhaps just as important for understanding the dynamics of the sector, convergence can subsequently produce divergence as a new technology or product matures and 'morphs' into its own branch of industry. Wireless access technologies are a case in point.

Cooke's primary focus is on industrial clustering, and here 'New media differ from other new economy clusters in being less likely to agglomerate around universities or research laboratories and more likely to occupy downtown fringe locations where rents may be relatively cheap because industry has vacated space, but access to large customers in film, TV, advertising and publishing is good.' From a policy perspective, knowledge of the critical success factors behind such clusters is vital, especially as governments globally seem intent on trying to create their own 'Silicon Valleys'. The news is not good. Rarely has state initiative succeeded, for the simple reason that clusters need to fulfil a function, not a policy objective. Cooke defines a cluster as 'geographically proximate firms in vertical and horizontal relationships, involving a localized enterprise support infrastructure with a shared developmental vision for business growth, based on competition and cooperation in a specific market field'. The emphasis here is on cooperation as well as competition between the companies, on non-market as well as market relations, on a shared vision or ethos based upon growth, and a large dose of interaction between firms. Governments cannot create such environments but they can facilitate them, and, among the many cases that Cooke cites, the Finnish example seems positive.

Terry Flew and Stephen McElhinney develop the theme of new media more broadly, in the context of the globalization debate. The term 'globalization' carries numerous connotations, ranging from progressive enlightenment and the values of personal or social choice, to cultural imperialism and the triumph of neoliberalism at the expense of national or ideological alternatives. Flew and McElhinney take an incisively critical look at this polarization, beginning by identifying the interrelated processes that constitute the concept. Media is central to the globalization process in three ways: as providing the technology and service delivery platforms through which international transactions take place; as a lead sector in promoting the global expansion of markets; and as providing people everywhere with information and images of distant places. Each of these three elements has its own history, so what distinguishes globalization from previous phases of international capitalism? Flew and McElhinney cite Castells, that for the first time a global economy has 'the capacity to work as a unit in real time on a planetary scale'.

The focus on work or production – and the reproduction of the social relations of capitalism – derives from Marx's conceptual framework of a social formation constituted by corresponding sets of technical and social relations. This implies an important distinction between globalization as a manifest form of unequal economic and trading relationships on the one hand, and globalization as transformation of the technical and social relations of production in all parts of the world on the other. The former implies a rather static 'exploitation' of the poor nations by the rich nations, a net deficit on the one hand, a net gain on the other, an underdevelopment on the one hand, an overdevelopment on the other. The latter implies a more complex set of possibilities, not excluding the further impoverishment of poor nations, but neither excluding the capitalistic development of them. Bearing this in mind, Flew and McElhinney make a really important observation when discussing the ubiquitous influence of United States television programming, quoting Martin-Barbero on US influence in Latin America: 'what will really affect us will be importing the US model of television'. The model, rather than the programmes, carries with it the seeds of neoliberalism in the arts, a model of enormous energy that has produced the technically most sophisticated production process in cultural history, and for that reason is the most deadly threat facing local cultural production. By contrast, local cultural consumption is perhaps more resilient; evidence certainly points to people preferring programming in their own language and reflecting points of reference to which they can easily relate.

But any well-grounded reading of political economy in developing countries amply demonstrates these national states are far from passive, neutral entities helplessly wringing their hands in the face of global override. On the contrary, they actively pursue their own agenda, and in the case of the most enlightened this agenda is a developmentalist one, which brings them into direct competition over issues of 'national interest' with the OECD economies. Flew and McElhinney discuss this in relation to national controls over the media in light of globalization, and again make an important distinction between global standardization and global domination. To participate in the global economy, developing economies are required to adopt world industry standards, although there is plenty of room for the larger economies, such as China, to develop their own versions of global standards, as China has been doing in third-generation mobile telephony. However, the adoption of world industry standards, and the increasing opportunities new media offer to convey messages, images and other content, 'are illustrative of media globalization, but not of cultural imperialism'. This distinction is important.

The term 'cultural imperialism' can easily lend itself as a defensive weapon for the local ruling elite. A senior mainland Chinese official from a state information centre in the early 1990s once informed a conference I organized in Hong Kong that, according to Deng Xiaoping, China's paramount leader who pioneered China's Open Door policy from 1978, information would be the last door to open. The contradictions between freedom of information and the promise of new media technologies to deliver it, and the obsessions of the state to manipulate national opinion through carefully orchestrated media control, are obviously not confined to authoritarian regimes in developing economies. A more productive approach is perhaps to examine the contradictions and the way they manifest themselves as clues about the dynamics of the state of the society itself. For example, in the case of China as much, if not more, can be read into the rival ambitions of different ministries and state commissions – each looking to grab a share of the new media, Internet and telecommunications markets – as can be concluded about the political and security concerns of the ruling Communist Party. Indeed these new technologies, far from taking media out of the control of the nation-state, may even offer a degree of 'reterritorialization' as Flew and McElhinney put it.

Globalization is also a theme dealt with in Henten and Skouby's chapter on information society, trade and industry, where 'formerly trade and industry policies were concentrated on regulating more closed national markets, the policies of today focus on situating the national economies as advantageously in the international economy'. The information society, especially as it is defined in the Japanese and European contexts, is accelerating the shift towards services within the more developed economies. It is also accelerating the shift towards the tradability of services as more of them become available online – in the form of either service provision or service content. Critics of the globalization thesis tend to dwell upon the former structural shift, pointing out that traditionally services constitute the least tradable sectors of an economy. Those who emphasize a new phase in the internationalization of capitalism point to the growing tradability that is closely associated with ICTs and with the new media industries.

Radical critiques of this transformation are surprisingly thin on the ground. Henten and Skouby devote sections to the regulation school, 'There is not much emphasis on the role of information or of information and communication technologies in the regulation school'; to the flexible specialization school, 'ICT is seen not as the vital technology in the development of flexible production structures,

but as one important element among others'; and to the technoeconomic paradigm, which is 'characterized by a keener concentration on technology'. Part of the problem is that 'ICT is a troublesome area for the analyst' combining, as it does, a generic issue of widely applied technology, industry-specific issues in terms of software and hardware manufacturing and supporting services, and an expanding services sector in which ICTs play a central role. The combined effects of ICTs have given rise to the ideas of 'convergence' and of the new economy, which implies new rules and a new model of accumulation but lacks definitive analysis.

We are left, therefore, with a recognition that 'social science research is still in its infancy' with regard to 'convergence', but some delineation is possible. Here Henten and Skouby return the focus towards global trends, pointing out that while neoliberalism seems to be having a field day, the dichotomy between national market regulation and freewheeling international deregulation is a false one. Rather, the drivers of the economic system are becoming global, and the strategies nation-states are adopting are exactly that, *strategies*. As they say: 'Not since the construction of the railway system has a similar common international interest and enthusiasm for a technology and its possibilities been shown.' And, for all their shortcomings, the popularity of indicative 'national plans', for developing countries in particular, reflects this strategic national thinking.

How have economists approached the analysis of information in industrial change in the media sector and beyond? This is the question addressed by Don Lamberton in his chapter on the economics of information and industrial change. Lamberton reminds us that Stigler, in 1961, 'saw information as still in "a slum dwelling in the town of economics" but with prospects of moving to a better location'. That better location was provided one year later by Fritz Machlup who occupies pride of place in modern economic theory for his path-breaking work. Not since the work of Schumpeter, heavily influenced by Marx, had an economist directed so much attention to the implications of technological change for the structure and processes of the economy; in Machlup's case specifically on the role of information and the market as the 'most effective information system in existence'. The immediate results were disappointing as mainstream 'economists rolled with the punches'. For the most part, but with notable exceptions, there has been an endeavour within the economics profession to accommodate rather than to critique the role of information and its implications for equilibrium analysis within the main body of economic theory.

Lamberton points to two problems in particular: 'the tyranny of the market' that has, until recently, made economists reluctant to investigate what goes on inside organizations, and a tendency to focus on technology as such – and a concomitant bias towards technological determinism – rather than on information. Some of the original insights of Machlup are being rediscovered by recent research, for example that while information can be reproduced at zero cost its use often requires very costly complementary resources, and this has implications for oversimple assumptions such as information as indivisible and incapable of being appropriated. The threat of market failure implied by this clearly has policy implications for a knowledge-based economy.

There are many roles that information can play in a modern socioeconomic setting, and the 'new media' industries themselves provide numerous examples such as advertising, infotainment, news and so forth. Each of these raises a question of definition as to what information is, how it is produced, distributed and used, by whom, and for what purpose and with what outcome. These are sets of questions that clearly straddle many branches of social enquiry besides economics, and in reviewing current and future research agendas Lamberton echoes Boczkowski in looking forward to approaches that reflect multidisciplined collaboration.

Peter Lovelock and John Ure leave a question mark over their chapter title: 'The new economy: Internet, telecommunications and electronic commerce?' There are a number of parallels in economic history to the spectacular dot.com bubble economy, but the question of interest is how far there is anything left of the new economy and of the new economics that supposedly was driving it, notably the phenomenon of increasing returns. Lovelock and Ure agree there have been fundamental changes associated with the diffusion of ICTs, and the new media industries have been partly a conveyance of the propaganda for the new economy and partly a part of it. Identifying the hard drive aspect of the new economy is the easy part: the combined effects of Moore's law, Metcalfe's law and Gilder's law are genuinely global waves of innovation with the United States at their epicentre. Spotting the effects in the productivity figures and other indicators of the new economy has proved more problematic, and interpreting the data as evidence one way or the other for a 'new economics' more controversial still.

It seems intuitive that network economics – well known to the telecommunications community before it was rediscovered and renamed by the IT community – plays a role in the diffusion of 'spillover effects' from ICTs, but there is no evidence that a 'new economics' has abrogated the cycles which typify the business routines of modern capitalism. There is more agreement on the long-term trends, and Lovelock and Ure illustrate this with reviews of developments in the Internet, telecommunications policy and electronic commerce. Although there seems to be consensus

as to the global dimensions of the changes in these sectors, there is less agreement about their effects. For example, is telecommunications development a cause of economic growth, a consequence, or merely a facilitator of growth? Is electronic commerce a potential equalizer, offering small and medium enterprises an equal chance to enter the world market, or is it a channel for domination by early movers and players with large resources?

One thing is for sure, and that is the world now communicates commercially and socially more and more using Internet protocol, and very many of those without access are, and will be, disadvantaged. Providing universal access to a telephone has been a twentieth-century challenge, and now at the beginning of the twenty-first century the challenge takes the form of the digital divide. Heather Hudson addresses the challenge in her chapter on universal access to the new information infrastructure.

In part answer to the question above about whether telecommunications is cause or effect of development, Hudson points out that the 'theoretical underpinning of research on the impact of information and communications technologies in general is that information is critical to the social and economic activities that comprise the development process … thus information and communication technologies (ICTs) as a means of sharing information are not simply a connection between people, but a link in the chain of the development process itself'. The term 'universal service' is increasingly giving way to the more flexible concept of 'universal access' which implies a wider variety of access technologies – such as satellite links, wireless cell phones, cable television, computers – and a wider variety of access institutions – no longer just the home, but including schools, community centres, health care centres, libraries. Technologies are enablers in this process, but policy priorities, regulatory incentives and market opportunities are equally important ingredients. For example, low-income families in rural areas may be able to afford a basic telephone service, perhaps on a shared basis, and a local service provider may be able to make a business from it, but not if long-distance connection charges levied by national telephone companies cream off all the surplus. Regulatory intervention to protect the local market from monopoly or oligopoly pricing can make the difference between an incrementally successful local service enterprise and none at all.

Advances in ICTs have rendered distance less of an obstacle to the achievement of universal access, yet income levels – including the status of ethnic groups – and states of development remain the prime determinants, within countries and between them. 'High-income countries had 22 times as many telephone lines per 100 population as low-income countries, but 96 times as many computers.' Hudson makes the important point that 'Lack of understanding of demand for telecommunications services (i.e. need for the service and ability to pay) creates problems in designing universal service policy.' Household income and population statistics may not be the best indicators, as for example in cases where community incomes can sustain a service. Environments change, such as the arrival of cable television and cybercafés, and changed environments open up avenues for imaginative policy initiatives to get service to previously unserved communities, and for paying for them.

This is a quite an optimistic note on which to conclude, particularly so when we bear in mind that the original time frame for the objective of bringing everyone 'within easy reach of a telephone' (the ITU's 1984 Maitland Commission Report: see the chapter by Lovelock and Ure) was the year 2000. But it is not rational to accept the reality that human endeavour has created the ICT revolution, yet to conclude that society is incapable of using the potential that ICTs open up to improve the welfare of humanity and the condition of the planet we share with other creatures. ICTs are the result of well-designed and well-executed research, even if it is the case that research priorities can be challenged. Similarly, policy research needs to be well designed and well executed, and the chapters in this volume contribute to that message.

16

The Development and Use of Online Newspapers: What Research Tells Us and What We Might Want to Know

PABLO J. BOCZKOWSKI

Print papers are one of the oldest, most ubiquitous and most highly standardized elements in the modern media landscape. Newspapers have changed considerably since Timotheus Ritzsch established the *Einkommende Zeitung* – 'incoming news' – in Leipzig, Germany, in 1650, which according to Smith (1979) was the first daily publication. Furthermore, these changes have been part and parcel of some of the most significant societal transformations in the past centuries from the rise of nation-states to the emergence of mass production and consumption, and from the development of large-scale communication infrastructures to the advent of modern urban life (Anderson, 1991; Blondheim, 1994; Schudson, 1978; Strasser, 1989). However, amidst these changes in format, content and production processes, one feature has remained remarkably stable: information has been delivered via ink on paper, an element intimately tied to a complex ensemble of discourses, practices and artifacts regarding the construction and appropriation of information.

Newspaper firms tinkered with various alternatives to newsprint during the twentieth century, from the *Telefon Hirmondó* phone-based newspaper in Hungary at the beginning of the century (Marvin, 1988), to the radio-based facsimile editions of the *Buffalo Evening News, Dallas Morning News, Miami Herald, New York Times* and *St Louis Post-Dispatch* in the United States in the 1930s and 1940s (Shefrin, 1949), to videotex newspapers starting in the United Kingdom in the late 1970s (Schneider et al., 1991). However, none of these endeavours moved far beyond the experimental domain until the newspaper industry appropriated the World Wide Web circa 1995 to create the first non-print alternative to achieve widespread development and use.[1] The evolution of online papers on the web has made visible taken-for-granted aspects of print's production culture, provided a window into the emergence of new regimes of content creation, and allowed the examination of broader patterns in the construction of information on the Internet.

Given the significance of this challenge to the dominance of ink on paper, it is not surprising to find an emerging but already profuse body of literature on the production and consumption of online papers. Despite such a burgeoning of scholarly activity, little has been done to assess what has been found so far, an essential element in critically planning the direction of future work. In this chapter I contribute to filling that void by offering the first comprehensive review of research on online newspapers. Whenever appropriate I will also address work concerning contemporary efforts by broadcast media to extend their news franchise in the newer information environments. Moreover, as I will discuss in the final section, since the boundaries separating print and broadcast – as well as other key categories in our understanding of media – have been very much at issue in the development of online papers, this essay also aims to contribute to work on the larger transformations currently shaping the media industries.

Despite the existence of past relevant phenomena and secondary sources, current research predominantly focusing on online newspapers has tended to overlook historical matters and possible linkages between past and present findings. To overcome this limitation, and despite the more contemporary focus of this review, in the next section I will briefly assess the results of inquiries about the most immediate antecedents to current developments – those initiatives beginning with the advent of videotex and teletext in the 1970s. Then, I will examine studies about contemporary phenomena, dividing them into three sections: production, use and interactivity.[2] I will conclude by addressing the existing literature's limitations, and suggesting directions for further research.

A caveat. Current research about online newspapers – much like the object of study in itself – is evolving rapidly and in many directions. This exacerbates the challenges of a review essay, from difficulties in locating the relevant literature to the risk that any given assessment could be inaccurate had a yet not identified piece been taken into account. However, it is my contention that more reviews like this one are needed precisely because both object and inquiry are far from being stable: the more unstable the phenomena and their analyses, the more effort should be put into mapping the territory before embarking upon any particular journey – as well as while it is taking place. A relatively low degree of cross-citation among contemporary studies, and the even less sustained discussion of the historical record, have turned a significant part of current research into a collection of monologues. My hope is that this essay will contribute to begin transforming them into a field of interconnected conversations.

Before the Popularization of the World Wide Web

The 1970s witnessed considerable activity in the creation and deployment of electronic means for dissemination of text and graphic information. Most developments focused on two technical alternatives: videotex and teletext. The first, originally generated at the British Post Office early that decade (Campbell and Thomas, 1981; Sommer, 1983; Wilkinson, 1980), consisted of 'computer-based interactive systems that electronically deliver screen text, numbers and graphics via the telephone or two-way cable for display on a television set or video monitor' (Aumente, 1987: 14). Teletext – also developed first in the United Kingdom, at the British Broadcasting Corporation (McIntyre, 1983) – was 'a one-way system for the transmission of text and graphics via over-the-air broadcasting or cable channels for display on a television set' (1987: 19).

These developments took place at a time when the 'information society' rhetoric was popular in both the press and scholarly works.[3] In a supposedly emerging era of information overload, 'the basic premise of videotex and online publishing is that the information-rich society has unmet information needs' (Neuman, 1985: 8). Thus, these new technologies became tool and symbol of an epochal change: if print had been an integral part of the industrial society, videotex and its electronic cousins were thought to be constitutive of the upcoming information society (Case, 1994). According to Sigel, 'since its commercial introduction in 1976, videotex has become a metaphor for a new world of information dissemination ... [in which] videotex stands for the future, whereas older methods of transmitting information – mainly, print on paper – represent the past' (1983a: 1).

Coupled with such an information society rhetoric there were two factors contributing to newspaper firms' exploration of electronic publishing. The first was a growing trend towards computerizing production and distribution functions across the newspaper industry since the 1960s, which meant that information was ready for electronic redeployment (Dozier and Rice, 1984; Marvin, 1980; Smith, 1980; Tydeman et al., 1982; Weaver and Wilhoit, 1986). The second was increasing concern about the long-term prospects for ink on paper as a delivery vehicle triggered by developments such as rising newsprint costs, less homogenized consumer tastes challenging mass advertising, and the growth of competitors in the markets for news and advertising (Albarran, 1996; Baer and Greenberger, 1987; Compaine, 1980; Picard and Brody, 1997; Pool, 1983; Smith, 1980; Stone, 1987).

Given these discursive, technical and socioeconomic trends, it is not surprising that newspaper firms in many industrialized nations took part in videotex and teletext efforts, especially between the mid 1970s and the mid 1980s. The most common scenario – prevalent in nations such as Canada, France, Germany and the United Kingdom – was that these firms participated in state-sponsored initiatives, providing content and editorial expertise (Charon, 1987; Desbarats, 1981; Marchand, 1987; Mayntz and Schneider, 1988; Miles, 1992; Sigel, 1983b; Tyler, 1979). In a minority of countries – most notably the United States – where the state had very limited involvement and the private sector took the front seat, several newspaper organizations were very active players in videotex and teletext endeavours, doing everything from hardware and software development to marketing and commercialization (Aumente, 1987; Baer and Greenberger, 1987; Branscomb, 1988; Criner, 1980; Davenport, 1987; Johansen et al., 1980; Mantooth, 1982; Noll, 1980; Sigel, 1980).

Regardless of the type of involvement pursued, these attempts by newspaper firms to experiment with consumer-oriented electronic publishing provide valuable information about the immediate precursors to contemporary online papers, and an important window into the dynamics of innovation in new media in general.[4] To begin, usage of news content was lower than both other types of information and what newspaper people expected. For instance, during a joint project between the Associated Press and CompuServe to publish videotex editions of a dozen print papers between 1980 and 1982 (Hecht, 1983; Laakaniemi, 1981; Mantooth, 1982; Patten, 1986), 'news accounted for less than 10 per cent of the average test family's time on CompuServe network ... [and] this usage was heavily skewed toward a few respondents; one out of ten households accounted for half of all news reading' (Blomquist, 1985: 423). Furthermore, usage dropped dramatically after a period of initial enthusiasm, suggesting that the services did not add much value to already existing counterparts: 'although electronic news may have been available sooner than its printed counterpart, it was no more comprehensive, contextualized or process-centered than any other form of news' (Ettema, 1989: 111).

This leads us directly to a third characteristic of consumer-oriented electronic publishing during the first half of the 1980s: the reproduction of print newspapers' content into the new platform. In her dissertation study of the Associated Press and CompuServe project, Mantooth found that 'the news stories were for the most part word-for-word duplicates, and aside from the headlines which had to be rewritten from the print version, the only really different face of the electronic newspapers was ... the long-term storage of such items as reviews and recipes' (1982: 90). Brown and Atwater undertook a content analysis of the three largest electronic newspaper initiatives in the United States – Knight-Ridder's Viewtron, Times-Mirror's Gateway, and Field Electronic Publishing's Keyfax – concluding that 'wire services and newspapers were the sources of news stories on all three services. No evidence of stories originating from the videotex staffs was found' (1986: 558). This was also consistent with Weaver's conclusions about developments in the European scene: 'journalists working for teletext systems in the United Kingdom and the Netherlands do almost no independent reporting. They rely primarily upon what others are writing in various wire services and newspapers' (1983: 53). According to Overduin, 'For the videotex journalist, the news of the day is "given" and the main journalistic activity is that of "massaging" or editing and rewriting that news to locate it in the database and fit it onto the screen in printed form' (1986: 231).

Another research finding was users' interest in employing videotex capabilities to communicate among themselves about a wide array of issues. The contrasting fate of two major videotex projects highlights the importance of this matter. The French government sponsored a nationwide videotex initiative, Télétel, since the late 1970s. The system was originally conceived as a way of providing users with an array of useful data; hence its initial configuration did not prominently feature one-to-one and many-to-many message flows. However, in a 1982 trial in Strasburg partly managed by a local paper, *Les Dernières Nouvelles d'Alsace*, a 'fortunate accident' happened:

> The newspaper's technical manager developed an application to correspond on line with users so as to help them or to monitor their uses. Service users quickly discovered that it was also possible to communicate in real time with each other. This application soon became so popular that it attracted users from all over France although it was only available through a local telephone number. Later it was reproduced by many other information providers. (Vedel and Charon, 1989: 101)

Analysts have suggested that the capacity to enable communication among users was key in the comparative success of the French videotex system *vis-à-vis* its contemporaneous European counterparts (Schneider et al., 1991). A different path unfolded at Viewtron, a joint venture of Knight-Ridder and AT&T in the United States between 1980 and 1986, which consisted of news, information and services such as shopping and banking, transmitted over regular phone lines to a dedicated terminal equipped with a keyboard. Viewtron afforded a multiplicity of message flows, and users showed interest in communicating among themselves. However, immersed in a media culture where one-to-many flows dominated, and unable to move away from it, Viewtron officials failed to fully exploit users' preferences.[5] For instance, a member of the Viewtron team reflected about this issue in the following terms:

> In retrospect, the interviews and usage data clearly revealed that access to databases of general news, information, and advertising was less exciting to subscribers than the ability to easily communicate with other subscribers. But that was not what anyone was prepared to hear at this time. Nearly everyone involved in the trial saw Viewtron as an advertiser-supported electronic newspaper. Its potential role as an interpersonal communication medium was considered secondary. (Fidler, 1997: 148)

Such a disregard for many-to-many information flows was widespread among American newspapers engaged in videotex efforts during this period, which let their potential be exploited by the then nascent online services – much of whose ulterior success was predicated upon user-authored content. To Aumente,

> Publishers steeped in newspaper traditions, seeking to transfer the same indexes of news, weather, sports, features, and commentary to the screen, paid dearly for a blindsided approach, while the growth of the personal

computer and telecommunications segments stressing interactivity, messaging, and innovative communication modes took root. (1987: 114)

Another feature of newspapers' videotex and teletext developments during this period was the disparity between technical and commercial performance: whereas most services functioned reasonably well, none of them achieved significant market success. This lack of commercial results was attributed to factors as diverse as ignoring users' preferences, the high cost, low speed and limited capabilities of reception devices, and the fact that the services did not add much value to existing alternatives (Cameron et al., 1996; Carveth et al., 1998; Davenport, 1987; Ettema, 1989; Greenwald, 1990; Patten, 1986). The commercial fate of these initiatives 'convinced the publishing industry that they faced no threat from electronic text' (Baldwin et al., 1996). Some analysts attributed the termination of many videotex and teletext services by the second half of the 1980s to a defensive approach that most newspaper firms took regarding the consumer-oriented electronic products: they tinkered with them more to protect their existing position in the marketplace than to conquer new ones. To Carey and Pavlik, 'many newspapers developed videotex services not as a positive step forward but out of fear that videotex might replace their core business. When it became clear that the perceived threat was illusory, they retreated quickly' (1993: 165). Thus, Ettema has argued that 'interest in the technology on the part of newspaper firms ... was probably more defensive than offensive ... The failures of videotex ventures were, then, at worst a mixed blessing for the newspaper industry' (1989: 108).

To summarize, research about consumer-oriented electronic publishing attempts by print papers during the 1970s and 1980s has shown that (1) consumers were not highly interested in the news content, (2) usage dropped considerably after the initial novelty wore off, (3) most news content available came from existing sources rather than being created originally for the new media, (4) users tended to employ interactive tools to communicate among themselves, and (5) most newspapers failed to fully exploit user-to-user information flows. Finally, some scholars have argued that online newspapers resulted from a defensive innovation approach more geared towards preserving print's status quo than building new electronic markets.

The World Wide Web Takes Centre Stage

Consumer-oriented electronic publishing efforts by newspapers decreased during the second half of the 1980s. However, the first half of the 1990s saw a resurgence of activity on this front, triggered by a host of larger societal and technical factors ranging from an increase in the adoption of personal computers at work and home, to the development of the web in 1989, and its first popular browser Mosaic four years later, to changes in telecommunications policy and infrastructure at a global scale (Abbate, 1999; Baldwin et al., 1996; Campbell-Kelly and Aspray, 1996; Castells, 1996; Ceruzzi, 1998; Mulgan, 1991). Although most resources and expectations were focused on various forms of videotex, newspapers simultaneously explored other technical alternatives such as audiotex, CD-ROM, fax and portable digital assistants[6] (Carveth et al., 1998; Dizard, 1997; Molina, 1999; Thalhimer, 1994; Willis, 1994). However, 1995 saw newspapers settling on the web as their electronic publishing environment of choice (Beamish, 1997; Carveth et al., 1998; Garrison, 1997; Martin and Hansen, 1998; Molina, 1997).[7] A count by the Newspaper Association of America showed more than 175 US dailies publishing on the web at the end of that year, a number that grew to over 750 three years later (Newspaper Association of America, 1998; *Editor and Publisher*, 1996). As Molina wrote: '*de facto*, the Web has become the prime arena for multimedia newspaper developments in the near and medium-term future' (1997: 208). In a survey of US online newspapers, Peng et al. (1999) have found that the three top reasons for publishing on the web versus other options were (1) availability of a large number of readers worldwide, 57 per cent, (2) ease of publishing, 27 per cent, and (3) superior graphical presentation, 15 per cent.

It should then come as no surprise that most research on online newspapers has also focused on the World Wide Web operations. In what follows I will review this literature by structuring it in three areas: production, use and interactivity. The last of these is the single most examined issue, and one that has blurred the boundaries that more neatly separate production and use in traditional media.[8]

Production

Some authors have called attention to how different characteristics of the web as an information environment relate to features of online journalism. In their study of a large metropolitan paper's online division, Riley et al. (1998) focused on what they considered to be a tension between the communitarian ethos of the Internet and the steps taken by this firm to exploit its online products commercially. They have argued that 'while the Web is clearly about blending boundaries between media ... the strategy of *The Paper* is clearly not of opening space but of confining it'. Thus, they described a series of steps this online newspaper took to 'colonize' the web, forming what they called a 'virtual geographic space'. Their study raised a concern that 'the commodification of information arising from the commercialization of the net and the expanding vertical market architecture is anti-community and anti-knowledge'. From a different angle, Lee and So (1999; 2000) examined transformations in the basic functions of newspapers when they move from ink on paper to pixels on the screen, concluding that some of the main changes relate to the fact that the former mediation role played by print papers is morphing into a stance of more direct participation. Regarding economic issues, this trend is manifested in the fact that for online papers 'their role of advertisement deliverer is expanded to include electronic trader' (2000: 22).

Other authors have concentrated on how the web's information architecture is intertwined with changes in the character of journalism. By contrast to print – with its high distribution costs – the expense for an online newspaper to have its content and applications being accessed by users located 1 or 10,000 miles away is the same. This potentially has the dual effect of both opening up non-local markets to local papers, and having their local dominance challenged by non-local competitors. Chyi and Sylvie (1998) have argued that – as opposed to the dual information and advertising submarkets of print papers (Lacy and Simon, 1993) – the online newspaper market is structured in four submarkets: (1) the local information market, (2) the long-distance information market, (3) the local advertising market, and (4) the long-distance advertising market. Thus, they have recommended a product differentiation and niche-oriented strategy because 'the World Wide Web offers a seemingly infinite list of choices and renders a substitution marketing fairly useless in the global market' (1998: 16). A later study by Chyi and Larosa has shown that 'most people still read the local newspaper in the ink-and-paper format, while national newspaper sites were gaining more ground online' (1999: 12). Despite this stated preference for local print news, in interviews with online news managers Chyi and Sylvie have found that 'while larger online newspapers seem to have greater ambition and more confidence in seeking business opportunities at larger geographic levels, most online newspapers operate within the geographic boundaries defined by their print counterparts' (2000: 9).

Another important research focus has been the study of how the structure of message flows on the web may affect traditional journalistic roles. According to Newhagen:

The hourglass shape of mass media architecture facilitates a power imbalance between message producers and receivers that may not exist on the Internet. In a mass media system such as television or newspapers,

journalists are in a position of power over their clientele simply because of their position at the narrowest point of the system's architecture – the point at which messages are produced. The Internet is a web of interconnected nodes; any user is equally likely to be a message receiver or sender during any given communication cycle. This architecture, then, may lend itself to more parity between communication participants. (1998: 117)

Some scholars have argued that in such an environment 'the emphasis shifts from "allocution" to "consultation"' (Bardoel, 1996: 287); thus the usual function of mediating between events and audiences is expanded to include tasks more geared to facilitating information search, creation and exchange by and among users (Kawamoto, 1998; Lee and So, 1999; Li, 1998). In particular, some researchers have called attention to the effect that these changes may have on the gatekeeping process, one of traditional journalism's paramount characteristics (Huxford, 2000; Newhagen and Levy, 1998; Singer, 1998). As Williams has put it, 'in a world where everyone can be a publisher, journalists are vulnerable to losing their franchise as gatekeepers of news' (1998: 34). In a study of a project enabling non-profits to create free websites within an online newspaper, Boczkowski (2000) has shown that the editorial function got expanded to include work processes centred upon the facilitation of content creation by a vast network of heterogeneous production agents, and coined the term 'gate-opening' to capture such a modified editorial role.

This leads us to larger issues about the organization and practice of online newsrooms. A survey taken by Jackson and Paul (1998) in 1997 has found that one of the major challenges faced by personnel in online papers was a constantly changing publishing environment and that 'the rapid pace does little to facilitate reflection or planning, but demands movement and action'. A study by Singer et al. (1999) has shown that these newsrooms are staffed by people younger and with more diverse professional and educational backgrounds than their print counterparts, and receiving financial compensation comparable to that prevalent in traditional media – 'tradepress reports of significantly higher salaries for online journalists may largely be wishful thinking' (1999: 43). These workers predominantly produce what is known as 'shovelware': taking information generated originally for a given print paper's edition, and deploying it virtually unchanged onto its website (Eriksen and Sørgaard, 1996; Martin and Hansen, 1998; Neuberger et al., 1998; Palmer and Eriksen, 1999; Ross, 1998; Tankard and Ban, 1998). This resonates with what happened in the case of videotex and teletext newspapers in the 1980s. Despite scholarly and anecdotal evidence suggesting that such content reproduction was not well received by users of those services, a decade later online newspapers on the web – at least in their first years – have been following the same path.

Several scholars have specifically looked at two sets of work relationships: between print and online newsrooms, as well as between editorial and advertising and marketing personnel within online papers. Regarding the former, in a survey by Endres (1998), editors of online publications complained about lack of cooperation from their colleagues in the print newsroom. In his examination of editorial routines at newsrooms of three online papers, Huxford has shown 'significant differences in the cultures in which the print and online journalists operate' (2000: 7). This was an issue that could have contributed to the dynamics Martin and Hansen have described in their observations of work practices at a handful of online papers:

> Coordination between the main newsroom and the online newsroom at the three sites was not ideal. While the newsprint version of a story might include a tease that led the reader to the online version for more in-depth information, there was still a dearth of contact between those reporting and writing stories for the newspaper and those working for the online service. (1998: 117)

Finally, scholars and commentators have also focused on the relationship between the editorial and marketing and advertising personnel of online newspapers (Brill, 1999; Harper, 1998; Pavlik, 1998; Williams, 1998). More specifically, they have raised concerns about the erosion of the separation between these so-called 'church and state' components of traditional media. One study that has looked at this issue in detail has been Borum's (1998) ethnographic research of an online paper. Among other findings, she has argued that:

> The content and layout decisions of the online news site were influenced in both subtle and more overt ways by financial concerns ... The most important characteristics of this process, as they relate to news content, are (1) a general organizational tone of acceptance, relative to traditional print journalism, about the profit motive's impact on shaping content, (2) the fact that the online medium itself encourages this influence, and (3) the organizational structure that fails to encourage boundaries and 'protection of editorial territory' against the invasion of advertising concerns. (1998: 91)

To summarize, research about production matters has suggested that the commodification of online papers may not be congenial with the supposedly more communitarian ethos of the Internet. It may also include playing a more direct commercial role than the usual advertising vehicle function of the press. Moreover, despite the low distribution costs of information on the web, online papers have mostly focused on local markets. In addition, because of the web's network information architecture, the dominance of traditional journalistic roles such as gatekeeping may get challenged by the emergence of an editorial function centred on gate-opening processes. Furthermore, according to one study, online newsrooms have tended to employ younger people with more diverse educational and career backgrounds than those in print, while paying them similar salaries; another study suggested that the volatile character of the web was a critical factor in the operation of online papers. Finally, these journalists have mostly produced shovelware, have not had an easy time working with their print counterparts, and have had a less stark boundary with their advertising and marketing colleagues than the more usual situation in print papers.

Use

How do people use online newspapers? Much like any other time in which a new option was added to the media repertoire, one issue that has interested researchers is the effect that usage of 'new' media has upon that of 'old' media, and vice versa. A study of the Blacksburg Electronic Village users conducted in 1994 has shown that 'more than twice as many [people] reported a decrease in television viewing time – 18 per cent – as said they spent less time reading a newspaper – 7 per cent' (Bromley and Bowles, 1995: 22). According to the authors, 'this is consistent with the notion that early adopters of interactive computer networks are avid information seekers and thus more likely to reduce media use for entertainment than for news purposes' (1995: 22). An examination of the early users' preferences in an online newspaper has also found a relationship between usage and information seeking: 'media use generally correlated positively with both the electronic preference and satisfaction variables. It should be the goal of electronic newspaper publishers to seek out heavy media users, since they represent the most lucrative initial market' (Mueller and Kamerer, 1995: 12).

A survey of Internet use of over 500 students at a US university conducted a few years after these studies has painted a different picture, since respondents used the web 'mainly as sources of entertainment and only secondarily as sources of news' (Althaus and Tewksbury, 2000: 21). However, the authors have drawn similar implications to the previous studies: 'our data suggest that while the Web supplements traditional news media, it may be in direct competition with entertainment programming on television ... entertainment rather than news content is more likely to lose audience members to the Web' (2000: 38). Although the three studies have argued that use of online news sites puts television at a 'higher risk' than print, they have explained the result employing opposed arguments, which is probably a signal of changes in who has been using these sites – and for what purposes. Research undertaken in 1998 and 1999 by Lewenstein et al. (2000) has concluded that:

> Fewer subjects appear to be news junkies in the last two years compared to four years ago. At least this seems so as judged by their other news consumption habits: often they don't subscribe to daily papers; they don't do much TV news viewing; they do still listen to radio news programs; they have cancelled some magazine subscriptions. Not many have cancelled newspaper subscriptions, but that's because some had given up subscribing before taking up online news reading. *So online news has brought them back to the news reading fold.* (emphasis in the original)

Thus, as the web has become more mainstream, the 'typical' user has switched from information seeking early adopters to entertainment-oriented latecomers. This may explain why the previous studies have different results but similar implications. Among other findings of the study by Lewenstein and her colleagues – the first scrolling-screen eyetracking investigation of its kind – were that (1) users initially look at text rather than graphics or other media,[9] (2) banner ads do catch users' attention for an average of one second, which is enough time to perceive an ad, and (3) users 'read shallow but wide, while at the same time pursuing selected topics in depth'. This last finding resonates with an earlier study by Aikat (1998) in which he examined the traffic logs of an online paper from November 1995 to May 1997. He found that users 'spent an average of fewer than 14 minutes per visit, viewing an average of seven pages each time' (1998: 94). Other interesting results include that most users accessed the site 'at their offices instead of their homes, and that introduction of new interactive features, particularly local content, may contribute to increased usage' (1998: 108).

Other studies have used experimental designs to examine specific features of site use. Tewksbury and Althaus focused on how changes in presentation formats from print to online affected reading practices, and concluded that 'as the online version presents fewer cues about the importance of events, it appears that people are more willing to use their own interests as the guiding criterion' (1999: 24). Oostendorp and Nimwegen (1998) looked at how people locate information in online newspapers, especially the influence of different navigation strategies, concluding that 'finding information for which scrolling down on a deeper hypertextual level was necessary took extra time and probably extra cognitive resources, leading to a lower recognition performance'. In a series of studies focusing on cognitive processes of online news use, Sundar and his colleagues have shown that (1) on news sites, quoted sources increased

the credibility and quality of stories (Sundar, 1998), (2) similar criteria were used to perceive print and online news (Sundar, 1999), (3) readers of print articles remembered ad material more than users of websites (Sundar et al., 1999), and (4) multimedia materials increased memory for advertising, but decreased it for story content (Sundar et al., 2000).

To sum up, research focusing on how online newspapers have been used has shown that a few years ago people looked at them mostly seeking information. However, more recently they have predominantly used them for entertainment. This change may reflect a mainstreaming in audience composition and behaviour, which initially had an important presence of early adopters. Based on these findings, current speculation is that usage of online newspapers may be affecting more television viewing than reading of print papers – a trend that, if accurate, may still take a few years to manifest more clearly. Furthermore, users have tended to concentrate on text materials, to look at banner ads long enough to perceive them, to spend little time on sites but to view several pages, and to access online papers a lot from their offices – although this may have changed since the reported Aikat study ended in 1997 owing to increased home use of the Internet. Finally, experimental studies have shown that people (1) have increasingly used their own interest to guide content appropriation in the face of fewer editorial cues provided by online papers, (2) have located information more easily the less navigating and scrolling they have to do, (3) have employed similar criteria to perceive print and online news, (4) have remembered advertising material more in print than on the web, and (5) have recalled news more and ads less in relation to multimedia.

Interactivity

This has been the single most examined issue of post-web online newspapers. A common approach has been to list a series of features that supposedly represent interactivity, then assess how interactive a given online paper is depending on the presence or absence – or varying degrees of realization – of these features. For instance, in an analysis of 135 sites conducted in February 1998, Tankard and Ban have found that most of them 'were providing e-mail addresses for the editor or webmaster and search engines for archives, but that few were providing such other means of user interactivity as discussion forums, chat rooms, surveys or polls, customized news services, and interactive games' (1998: 10). Other such studies have had similar findings (Kenney et al., 2000; Massey and Levy, 1999; Schultz, 1999; Tremayne, 1998).

Although valuable, this approach has the problem of making conclusions based on aggregate scores that lump together 'apples and oranges'. The difficulty resides in that different attributes are linked to different dimensions of interactivity: sending electronic mails to a webmaster, voting in an electronic poll, participating in a chat room, among other actions, are part of various communication experiences tied to diverse production and use dynamics.[10] This has partly resulted from the fact that:

> The concept of interactivity in relation to news is often muddled and poorly defined. In fact, the term is used to describe two essentially unrelated characteristics of online media. In one sense, 'interactivity' is used to describe the process of empowering users with additional control over the sequence in which information is presented to them. This definition relates to increased interactivity with content. But the term also is used to describe an increase in the interaction news consumers can have with news producers, a definition relating to increased feedback. (King, 1998: 26)

Those studies which have gone beyond mere 'counting' have usually focused on the second type of interactivity: users communicating with online newspapers' staff as well as with fellow users employing tools such as electronic mail, forums and chat rooms – the last two options available in one-third of the online papers surveyed by Peng et al. (1999) in February 1997. Those investigations that have examined staff–user communication have shown that journalists have not been very keen about it.[11] In their interviews at a large metropolitan paper, Riley et al. (1998) have concluded that 'most of the reporters interviewed were horrified at the idea that readers would send them e-mail about a story they wrote and might even expect an answer'. A sense of separation between staff and users resonates with what Schultz has found in his survey of *The New York Times* journalists: '12 out of 19 admitted that they do not even visit the *Times*' own online forums. Only six claimed to visit the discussion sites "from time to time". No one visited them regularly' (2000: 214).[12]

A related dimension of interactivity has to do with users' expectations of online newspapers and their personnel. In her first-person account of creating the *Washington Post*'s Digital Ink online service in the mid 1990s, McAdams (1995) has claimed that when a paper goes online its users see this process 'as evidence that the paper now wishes to have a closer relationship with its readers, and they are eager to let their opinions be known – not just in public discussions, but in personal e-mail to specific individuals'. However, in a study about how users' evaluated *The Guardian*'s website forums, Light (1999) found that their expectations of a paper's online edition were tied to their expectations of the print product. Thus, in the same way that they did not expect to interact with the print paper, they did not have that expectation online

either: 'there are major obstacles to innovative news practice on the Web, especially where there is identity with a paper product. There was a tendency for the evaluators to overlook or reject interactive elements on *The Guardian* site.'

Interactive environments such as forums and chat rooms have been often positively received by scholars since they have seemed ideal vehicles for increasing users' participation. To Pride, 'with embedded newsgroups, electronic newspapers could become a functional town square: news and views and criticism all together' (1998: 148). Along this line, Jankowski and van Selm have suggested that the role of online news sites in fostering participatory democracy should be an 'important focus of future research' (2000: 99). Moreover, to Friedland, by combining forums with non-linear narratives and archiving capabilities:

> A collection of views can be archived, reread, explored and connected in new ways that offer new models of problem solving that expand the narrative boundaries of traditional journalism. These models offer an alternative to the plebiscitary model of electronic democracy that is both deliberative and practical. (1996: 202)

So far, little empirical research has been conducted about what users actually do in these discussion contexts, what relationships they establish with online papers' staff and with fellow users, and what implications their participation may have on the character of news and on larger issues of democratic culture. One exception is Light and Rogers' (1999) study of a forum opened by *The Guardian* to discuss the British 1997 election. They have shown that people's previous experience with electronic discussion spaces influenced their participation in the forum: for instance, newcomers were 'less discursive, more likely to post in order to present opinions, and more likely to visit the forums again to read other people's contributions'. They have also found that participants and non-participants had diverse interaction styles. On the one hand, participants 'were more likely to have the view that Web culture should uphold freedom of speech'. On the other hand, non-participants 'were more likely to support the idea that postings should be edited to make them more informative, rather than lengthy, repetitive exchanges'. Another exception is Schultz's (2000) examination of participation patterns at the *New York Times*' site forums. Among other findings, he has shown that users 'not only refer to each other's postings publicly on the forum, but in addition by personal e-mail ... the more comments they sent, the more likely it was that they also got e-mail feedback' (2000: 215–16). Finally, in another empirical study of user-authored content, Boczkowski (2000) has looked at the interrelated technological, editorial and organizational processes shaping a project in which non-profits built their own publications within an online newspaper. He has argued that such a regime of content creation that he calls 'distributed construction' is characterized by:

(a) An artifact that inscribes users as active content creators and that is domesticated partly in public, (b) work processes that center the editorial function around the facilitation of content production and exchange, (c) a network of information flows in which every node can be source and destination of messages of potentially both generalized and specialized character, and (d) an organizational form based on relationships of interdependence, distributed authority, and multiple rationalities. (2000: 22–3)

In sum, research on interactivity has sometimes argued that online papers are not very interactive, although these 'scores' may not be all that useful for they have been based on homogenizing too disparate sets of communication processes, experiences and technologies. A more fruitful approach has instead looked at the practices of interactivity. Some studies have found very little staff–user interaction, something consistent with previous research on traditional media. Other investigations have concentrated on the role of expectations, yielding conflicting results: whereas one study has suggested that users of online papers expect it to be more interactive than its print counterpart, other inquiry has found users expect it to be no more so – thus potentially limiting the realization of interactive potentials. Also, experience and degree of participation have been associated with different interactive behaviours and experiences, and one examination of forum dynamics has shown the presence of a densely interconnected flow of private and public messages among users. Finally, engaging users as content co-producers has been associated with technical, editorial and organizational transformations that depart markedly from the traditional dynamics of content production in print newspapers.

THE ROAD AHEAD

The research reviewed above has told us useful and important information about how online newspapers have been produced and used, before and after the popularization of the web. However, there is still much more that remains to be known about these matters. This is partly because of limitations in the inquiries undertaken so far, and – especially in the case of events in the second half of the 1990s – partly due to the newness of the object of study. In these final paragraphs I will point to several directions for further research by analysing shortcomings in the existing literature and suggesting some important areas still unexplored, in the spirit that

such a critical examination will foster reflection about past accomplishments and design of future endeavours.

There has been a dearth of historical analyses about the evolution of online newspapers, and the relationships between past attempts and current developments. This is all the more surprising given the richness of events during the last decades and the availability of both archival material and actors who could be good candidates for oral history interviews. To Deuze (1999), recent studies 'seem to lack a contextual and historical foundation'. More work is needed with historical focus and questions. Issues that this line of inquiry could address include (1) the effect of pre-web endeavours on more recent efforts, (2) the presence or absence of longitudinal trends regarding ethnical, class and gender variations in the production and use of online newspapers, (3) the 'after life' (Simon, 1999) of artifacts, like videotex and teletext, that despite being written off as failures have continued to exist in the margins, (4) the fate of technical alternatives – like audiotex, around since the mid 1980s and in many cases commercially successful since the mid 1990s – which have not moved centre stage, (5) the career paths of actors who played important roles in both pre- and post-web projects, and (6) the influence of corporate culture and strategy upon technological change, in particular why some firms have been very active since the late 1970s, while others have remained comparatively more passive, and yet others have switched their approach over time.

There has been a methodological pattern in the inquiries undertaken so far. On the one hand, most studies focusing on production issues have been either conceptual essays or what could be called 'site analysis' – for instance, looking at what interactive features a set of sites has – or surveys. On the other hand, research looking at uses of online papers has primarily relied on experimental designs, and to a lesser extent on surveys and interviews. Although there have been a handful of examinations of production issues employing ethnographic methods (Boczkowski, 2000; Borum, 1998; Eriksen and Ihlström, 1999; Eriksen and Sørgaard, 1996; Huxford, 2000; Martin and Hansen, 1998; Molina, 1999; Riley et al., 1998), the limited breadth and depth of most of these inquiries, and the lack of such studies on usage matters, suggests that much more work remains to be done into employing the full spectrum of naturalistic methods – so crucial to understand the practice, meaning and experience of emerging media.[13] Possible issues to be addressed using these methods include (1) the routines and values of online news-making, and their relationships to those of print and broadcast journalism, (2) the construction and reconstruction of occupational identities in the new work environment, (3) the negotiations among the different occupational groups as they influence the news-making process, and (4) the relationships among all agents of production – not just editorial workers, but also design, technical, advertising and marketing personnel, users when they become co-producers, and the artifacts the different actors use – that constitute, borrowing from Becker (1982), 'the online newspaper world'.[14]

The combination of little attention to historical matters with a low use of naturalistic inquiry has probably contributed to a third type of limitation of current research: a tendency to build analysis upon a usually taken-for-granted technologically deterministic matrix.[15] When only short temporal sequences are examined, and when actors' actual practices are not observed, analysts may be more inclined to think that 'a technology enters a society from outside and "impacts" social life ... [describing] a form of cultural lag, during which adaptive problems arise' (Fischer, 1992: 12). To Bardoel, 'modern communication technology will lead to new information services and to new journalistic practices' (1996: 295). Focusing on information architecture issues, Newhagen and Levy have argued that 'data concentration is unnatural in distributed network architectures that facilitate dispersed message production. Thus, the application of canons or standards produced to deal with mass media systems may be *unnatural, unrealistic*, and *practically impossible* to apply' (1998: 16, emphasis added).

However, the history of developments in information and communication technology during the twentieth century is replete with events in which supposedly 'unnatural' or 'unrealistic' uses of new artifacts became not only 'possible' but also major commercial turning points. For instance, amateur users played a crucial role in transforming the radio from a point-to-point communication device into a broadcast medium (Douglas, 1988); residential users were key in turning the telephone from an instrumental and business device into a leisure and domestic tool (Fischer, 1988); and early adopters triggered a redefinition of the French minitel videotex system from a one-to-many service into a many-to-many communication space (Charon, 1987). Further research is needed that not only avoids technologically deterministic temptations, but also underscores the weaknesses of that kind of account. Issues particularly germane to this end could be (1) the presence of resistance to new technologies within organizations adopting them as well as among the audiences for their products, (2) the emergence of unexpected uses broadening the repertoire of activities consciously inscribed by producers in their design of media artifacts, and (3) situations in which the same technical potentials are realized in diverse ways, and different potentials are domesticated into relatively similar uses.

Other types of limitations of current research have to do with theory-building matters. When traditional media use of the web was in its infancy, Morris and Ogan urged scholars to 'rethink answers to some of the central questions of mass communication research, questions that go to the heart of the model of source–message–receiver with which the field has struggled' (1996: 39). Echoing this call, Boczkowski (1999) has suggested various ways in which computer-mediated theorizing could be exploited to study what has traditionally been the province of mass communication scholarship. Furthermore, Singer (1998) has argued that:

> The questions about online journalism have many facets, and multi-disciplinary, wide-ranging approaches may work best in attempting to answer them ... The issues raised by this new form of communication in general and journalism in particular invite us not only to make better use of what we already know but also to be open to new ways of asking those vital questions.

However, despite this and related statements, most theorizing about online newspapers has so far remained confined to the familiar landscape of notions and models such as gatekeeping, agenda-setting, uses and gratifications, and information processing – all of which have mostly been used within the field of communication and media studies. Although it is valuable to approach new technologies and their related social practices from 'tried and true' conceptual resources, it is also the case that the study of emerging media is a more fertile soil for novel theorizing than that of existing media. Thus, further research is needed that could lead to multidisciplinary theory building about online newspapers. Within communication and media studies, and given that actors have already been mixing mass and interpersonal attributes in the production and use of online papers, there seems to be a conducive environment for combining concepts and theories born out of the usually distanced camps of mass and interpersonal communication. Other fields of inquiry that could be brought to bear in a multidisciplinary theory-building effort include (1) sociology, history and economics of technical innovation, (2) sociology and anthropology of work, occupations and organizations, (3) policy studies, especially to examine the relationships between the often separate domains of media and technology policy, (4) cultural studies of technology, and (5) contextual approaches to knowing such as activity theory and distributed cognition.

As I showed above, studies looking at production matters have provided valuable knowledge about online newspapers. However, there are still some limitations common to most of them. First, although shovelware has been the dominant type of content, it is no less true that there has been a growth in original content in the last few years. Despite not constituting the majority of material available, original content may be a more appropriate ground to examine changes in the technologies and practices of newspapering as it moves from ink on paper to pixels on the screen. This relates to another shortcoming of existing research: the focus on interactivity seems to have been at the expense of looking at the appropriation of other technical features of the web, most notably multimedia. For all the talk about media convergence, there has been a dearth of studies examining the dynamics of producing multimedia content. Which leads us to a third limitation of existing research on production matters, a more conceptual one: little attention has been paid to the role of technology in the actual work practices of editorial personnel – something which is not surprising given the neglect of technology's role in most studies of news-making in print and broadcast media (Cottle, 2000; Hansen et al., 1994; Schudson, 1997; Sumpter, 2000). Reflecting upon the initial analyses of online newspapers on the web, Martin and Hansen have argued that: 'None of these studies ... has focused on the way in which computer technology and reporting norms may affect news content as it is selected from the newsroom's newsprint delivery traditions, prepared and moved to the electronic environment, and offered as online news' (1998: 108).

Further research is needed to illuminate what goes on in the creation of original content, taking advantage of the web's unique technical features – paying special attention to multimedia storytelling – and, more conceptually, examining the role of technology in news-making, a long-overdue theme in the sociology of news production. Potential issues to be addressed include (1) the differences and similarities in news-making routines for shovelware and original content, (2) the comparison between newsworthiness on the web and in traditional media, (3) the acquisition of new technical and narrative skills and their relationships to existing ones, as well as the decrease in use of existing skills, (4) the changes in gathering, processing and delivery of news content in relation to having multiple media for storing and conveying information, and (5) the presence or absence of tensions derived from the encounter of the different news-making cultures of print and broadcast journalism, as well as their relationship to computer-oriented cultures of information production.

As I described above, some studies have begun looking at how online newspapers are used. Despite the valuable information they have produced, they have been limited in various forms. The most important of these shortcomings has been the lack of naturalistic research about what people actually do with and through online newspapers. For all the useful knowledge that studies based on experimental, survey, interview and traffic log data can provide, they tend to fall short on shedding light on the habits and meanings that constitute the 'flesh and blood' of using online papers. Thus, more research is needed

that examines the discourse and practice of users. Issues that could be examined include (1) the routines and experience of using online newspapers, (2) the influence of major socioeconomic factors such as race, gender and class, (3) the relationships with the use of other media and information artifacts, (4) the similarities and differences linked to diverse contexts of use such as home, workplace, libraries, cybercafés and various transportation means, (5) the factors determining why some users become content and marketing co-producers while others remain just consumers of what others create and promote, and (6) the emergence of resistance and uses unintended by online newspapers' producers.

Beyond the specific contributions and shortcomings of the research reviewed in the preceding pages, I would like to conclude this essay by pointing out one image that comes to mind after surveying this growing area of inquiry as a whole: the emergence of a multifaceted process of boundary blurring, shaping the contours of traditional media's forays in the new information environments. Where does the division between the spheres of production and use reside when new media sites feature vast quantities of user-authored content? What is the basis for distinguishing between interpersonal and mass communication in the chat rooms and forums that not only pervade the websites of news operations, but spill over onto television programmes, radio shows and print pages? What happens to the separation between print and broadcast journalism when websites of print papers make increasing use of audio and video files, and their counterparts of television and cable operations are filled with text? What is the rationale for dividing between the immediacy of wire services and the analysis of news outlets when the websites of print and broadcast operations routinely weave these two types of content? How can we make sense of the separation between media and other information industries when software manufacturers seek to seamlessly integrate content with code, and traditional media corporations invest increasing resources in technology development? Paraphrasing Geertz's comment about the refiguration of social thought, this blurring of discursive, practical, material and organizational boundaries may represent, 'or will if it continues, a sea change in our notion not so much of what knowledge is but of what it is we want to know' (1983: 34). If that were the case, this would mean expanding the assessment of what research tells us towards a collective reflection on what we might want to know.

NOTES

Nick Jankowski, Leah Lievrouw, Denis McQuail and Sonia Livingstone provided very valuable comments on earlier versions of this chapter.

1 The World Wide Web is the part of the Internet that features multimedia sites supported through the hypertext transfer protocol. The Internet is a decentralized network linking different computer networks through a common addressing system and the TCP/IP communications protocol.

2 An issue that has begun to blur the boundaries that more neatly separate production and use in traditional media.

3 See Webster (1995) for an overview of theories of the information society.

4 Data from these initiatives remained proprietary material for the most part, so the next paragraphs are based on a combination of a few independent research projects, some first-person accounts, and some reports that appeared in trade publications.

5 A failure that commentators like Aumente (1987) and Fidler (1997) have considered a contributing factor in the system's eventual commercial demise.

6 A process which continues as I write this chapter.

7 According to Thorson et al. (1999), that same year the World Wide Web became the dominant environment for new media advertising.

8 See McMillan's chapter in this volume for an extended discussion of interactivity issues in new media.

9 This is only partly consistent with research by Mings and Harrison (2000a; 2000b), who found that while older users tend to focus almost exclusively on text information, college students looked at graphic material in a much higher proportion, thus raising the possibility of the existence of age stratification in this aspect of online papers' use.

10 See McMillan (1998) for an analysis of the relationships between different types of interactivity and funding alternatives.

11 A finding that is consistent with earlier research on newsroom practices at print and broadcast media (Darnton, 1975; Gans, 1980; Schlesinger, 1978; Sigal, 1973).

12 Newhagen et al. (1995) have described a very low response to viewers' electronic mail messages in NBC's *Nightly News*.

13 Extending the valuable tradition of sociological studies of news-making in the new media domain (Epstein, 1973; Fishman, 1980; Gans, 1980; Kaniss, 1991; Sigal, 1973; Tuchman, 1978; Warren, 1967).

14 'Art worlds consist of all the people whose activities are necessary to the production of the characteristic works which that world, and perhaps others as well, define as art. Members of art worlds coordinate the activities by which work is produced by referring to a body of conventional understandings embodied in common practice and in frequently used artifacts' (Becker, 1982: 34).

15 For discussions on the rhetoric of technological determinism in the case of information and communication artifacts see, for instance, Edwards (1995), Hamilton (1997), Kling (1994), Kling and Iacono (1988), Pfaffenberger (1989), Roscoe (1999) and Winner (1986).

REFERENCES

Abbate, J. (1999) *Inventing the Internet*. Cambridge, MA: MIT Press.

Aikat, D. (1998) 'News on the Web: usage trends of an on-line newspaper', *Convergence*, 4 (4): 94–110.

Albarran, A. (1996) *Media Economics: Understanding Markets, Industries and Concepts*. Ames, IA: Iowa State University Press.

Althaus, S. and Tewksbury, D. (2000) 'Patterns of Internet and traditional news media use in a networked community', *Political Communication*, 17: 21–45.

Anderson, B. (1991) *Imagined Communities: Reflections on the Origin and Spread of Nationalism*, 2nd edn. London: Verso.

Aumente, J. (1987) *New Electronic Pathways: Videotex, Teletext and Online Databases*. Beverly Hills, CA: Sage.

Baer, W. and Greenberger, M. (1987) 'Consumer electronic publishing in the competitive environment', *Journal of Communication*, 37: 49–63.

Baldwin, T., McVoy, S. and Steinfield, C. (1996) *Convergence: Integrating Media, Information and Communication*. Thousand Oaks, CA: Sage.

Bardoel, J. (1996) 'Beyond journalism: a profession between information society and civil society', *European Journal of Communication*, 11: 283–302.

Beamish, R. (1997) 'The local newspaper in the age of multimedia', in B. Franklin and D. Murphy (eds), *Making Local News: Local Journalism in Context*. London: Routledge. pp. 140–53.

Becker, H. (1982) *Art Worlds*. Berkeley and Los Angeles: University of California Press.

Blomquist, D. (1985) 'Videotex and American politics: the more things change …', *Information and Behavior*, 1: 406–27.

Blondheim, M. (1994) *News over the Wires: the Telegraph and the Flow of Public Information in America, 1844–1897*. Cambridge, MA: Harvard University Press.

Boczkowski, P. (1999) 'Understanding the development of online newspapers: using computer-mediated communication theorizing to study Internet publishing', *New Media & Society*, 1: 101–26.

Boczkowski, P. (2000) 'Distribute and conquer? Changing regimes of information creation in online newspapers'. Paper presented at the Annual Meeting of the International Communication Association, Acapulco, Mexico, June.

Borum, C. (1998) 'Navigating the changing landscape of news in the information age: characteristics, trends and issues of online journalism'. Unpublished master's thesis, University of Pennsylvania, Philadelphia, PA.

Branscomb, A. (1988) 'Videotex: global progress and comparative politics', *Journal of Communication*, 38: 50–9.

Brill, A. (1999) 'Online newspaper advertising: a study of format and integration with news content', in D. Schumann and E. Thorson (eds), *Advertising and the World Wide Web*. Mahwah, NJ: Erlbaum. pp. 159–73.

Bromley, R. and Bowles, D. (1995) 'Impact of Internet on use of traditional news media', *Newspaper Research Journal*, 16 (2): 14–27.

Brown, N. and Atwater, T. (1986) 'Videotex news: a content analysis of three videotex services and their companion newspapers', *Journalism Quarterly*, 63: 554–61.

Cameron, G., Curtin, P., Hollander, B., Nowak, G. and Schamp, S. (1996) 'Electronic newspapers: toward a research agenda', *Journal of Mediated Communication*, 11 (1): 3–53.

Campbell, J. and Thomas, H. (1981) 'The videotex marketplace – a theory of evolution', *Telecommunications Policy*, 5: 111–20.

Campbell-Kelly, M. and Aspray, W. (1996) *Computer: a History of the Information Machine*. New York: Basic.

Carey, J. and Pavlik, J. (1993) 'Videotex: the sword in the stone', in J. Carey and E. Dennis (eds), *Demystifying Media Technology: Readings from the Freedom Forum Center*. Mountain View, CA: Mayfield. pp. 163–8.

Carveth, R., Owers, J. and Alexander, A. (1998) 'The economics of online media', in A. Alexander, J. Owers and R. Carveth (eds), *Media Economics: Theory and Practice*, 2nd edn. Mahwah, NJ: Erlbaum. pp. 247–73.

Case, D. (1994) 'The social shaping of videotex: how information services for the public have evolved', *Journal of the American Society for Information Science*, 45: 483–97.

Castells, M. (1996) *The Rise of the Network Society*. Oxford: Blackwell.

Ceruzzi, P. (1998) *A History of Modern Computing*. Cambridge: MIT Press.

Charon, J.-M. (1987) 'Videotex: from interaction to communication', *Media, Culture & Society*, 9: 301–32.

Chyi, H. and Larosa, D. (1999) 'Access, use and preferences for online newspapers', *Newspaper Research Journal*, 20: 2–13.

Chyi, H.I. and Sylvie, G. (1998) 'Competing with whom? Where? And how? A structural analysis of the electronic newspaper market', *Journal of Media Economics*, 11 (2): 1–18.

Chyi, H. and Sylvie, G. (2000) 'Online newspaper economics: perceptions of markets, products, revenue, and competition'. Paper presented at the Annual Meeting of the International Communication Association, Acapulco, Mexico, June.

Compaine, B. (1980) *The Newspaper Industry in the 1980s: an Assessment of Economics and Technology*. White Plains, NY: Knowledge Industry.

Cottle, S. (2000) 'New(s) times: towards a "second wave" of news ethnography', *Communications: The European Journal of Communication Research*, 25: 19–41.

Criner, K. (1980) 'Teletext and videotex in North America: US videotex activities and policy concerns', *Telecommunications Policy*, 4: 3–8.

Darnton, R. (1975) 'Writing news and telling stories', *Daedalus*, 104 (Spring): 175–94.

Davenport, L. (1987) 'A coorientation analysis of newspaper editors' and readers' attitudes towards videotex, online news and databases: a study of perception and options'. Unpublished doctoral dissertation, Ohio University.

Desbarats, P. (1981) *Newspapers and Computers: an Industry in Transition*, Research Studies, vol. 8. Ottawa, Canada: Royal Commission on Newspapers.

Deuze, M. (1999) 'The WebCommunicators: issues in research into online journalism and journalists', *First Monday*, online serial, 3 (12). Available URL: http://www.firstmonday.dk/issues/issue3_12/deuze/index.html.

Dizard, W. (1997) *Old Media, New Media: Mass Communication in the Information Age*. New York: Longman.

Douglas, S. (1988) *Inventing American Broadcasting, 1899–1922*. Baltimore, MD: Johns Hopkins University Press.

Dozier, D. and Rice, R. (1984) 'Rival theories of electronic newsreading', in R. Rice (ed.), *The New Media: Communication, Research and Technology*. San Francisco: Jossey-Bass. pp. 103–28.

Editor and Publisher (1996) 'Number of papers with online edition tripled', 24 February: 39.

Edwards, P. (1995) 'From "impact" to social process: computers in society and culture', in S. Jasanoff, G. Markle, J. Petersen and T. Pinch (eds), *Handbook of Science and Technology Studies*. Thousand Oaks, CA: Sage. pp. 257–85.

Endres, K. (1998) 'Zine but not heard? Editors talk about publishing on-line'. Paper presented at the Association for Education in Journalism and Mass Communication National Convention, Baltimore, MD.

Epstein, E. (1973) *News from Nowhere: Television and the News*. New York: Random House.

Eriksen, L.B. and Ihlström, C. (1999) 'In the path of the pioneers: longitudinal study of web news genre', in *Proceedings of IRIS 22*. Department of Informatics, Gothenburg University.

Eriksen, L.B. and Sørgaard, P. (1996) 'Organisational implementation of WWW in Scandinavian newspapers: tradition based approaches dominate', in B. Dahlbom et al. (eds), *Proceedings of IRIS 19*. Goteborg Studies in Informatics Report 8, pp. 333–49. Department of Informatics, Gothenburg University.

Ettema, J. (1989) 'Interactive electronic text in the United States: can videotex ever go home again?', in J. Salvaggio and J. Bryant (eds), *Media Use in the Information Age: Emerging Patterns of Adoption and Consumer Use*. Hillsdale, NJ: Erlbaum. pp. 105–23.

Fidler, R. (1997) *Mediamorphosis: Understanding New Media*. Thousand Oaks, CA: Pine Forge Press.

Fischer, C. (1988) '"Touch someone": the telephone industry discovers sociability', *Technology & Culture*, 29: 32–61.

Fischer, C. (1992) *America Calling: A Social History of the Telephone to 1940*. Berkeley, CA: University of California Press.

Fishman, M. (1980) *Manufacturing the News*. Austin, TX: University of Texas Press.

Friedland, L. (1996) 'Electronic democracy and the new citizenship', *Media, Culture & Society*, 18: 185–212.

Gans, H. (1980) *Deciding What's News: a Study of CBS Evening News, NBC Nightly News, Newsweek and Time*. New York: Vintage.

Garrison, B. (1997) 'Online services, Internet in 1995 newsrooms', *Newspaper Research Journal*, 18 (3–4): 79–93.

Geertz, C. (1983) *Local Knowledge: Further Essays in Interpretive Anthropology*. New York: Basic.

Greenwald, M. (1990) 'The consumer videotex market: has it reached its potential?', in S. Lundstedt (ed.), *Telecommunications, Values, and the Public Interest*. Norwood, NJ: Ablex. pp. 166–81.

Hamilton, S. (1997) 'Incomplete determinism: a discourse analysis of cybernetic futurology in early cyberculture', *Journal of Communication Inquiry*, 22: 177–204.

Hansen, K., Ward, J., Conners, J. and Neuzil, M. (1994) 'Local breaking news, sources, technology and news routines', *Journalism and Mass Communication Quarterly*, 71 (3): 561–72.

Harper, C. (1998) *And That's the Way It Will Be: News and Information in a Digital World*. New York: New York University Press.

Hecht, J. (1983) 'Information services search for identity', *High Technology*, 3: 58–65.

Huxford, J. (2000) 'Cultures in collision: newspapers and the internet'. Paper presented at the Annual Meeting of the International Communication Association, Acapulco, Mexico, June.

Jackson, M. and Paul, N. (1998) *Newspaper Publishing and the World Wide Web*. St Petersburg, FL: Poynter Institute for Media Studies.

Jankowski, N. and van Selm, M. (2000) 'Traditional news media online: an examination of added values', *Communications: the European Journal of Communication Research*, 25: 85–101.

Johansen, R., Nyhan, M. and Plummer, R. (1980) 'Teletext and videotex in North America: issues and insights for the USA', *Telecommunication Policy*, 4: 31–41.

Kaniss, P. (1991) *Making Local News*. Chicago: University of Chicago Press.

Kawamoto, K. (1998) 'News and information at the crossroads: making sense of the new on-line environment in the context of traditional mass communication study', in D. Borden and K. Harvey (eds), *The Electronic Grapevine: Rumor, Reputation, and Reporting in the New On-line Environment*. Mahwah, NJ: Erlbaum. pp. 173–88.

Kenney, K., Gorelik, A. and Mwangi, S. (2000) 'Interactive features of online newspapers', *First Monday*, online serial, 5 (1). Available URL: http://www.firstmonday.dk/issues/issue5_1/kenney/index.

King, E. (1998) 'Redefining relationships: interactivity between news producers and consumers', *Convergence*, 4 (4): 26–32.

Kling, R. (1994) 'Reading "all about" computerization: how genre conventions shape nonfiction social analysis', *The Information Society*, 10: 147–72.

Kling, R. and Iacono, S. (1988) 'The mobilization of support for computerization: the role of computerization movements', *Social Problems*, 35: 226–43.

Laakaniemi, R. (1981) 'The computer connection: America's first computer-delivered newspaper', *Newspaper Research Journal*, 2 (4): 61–8.

Lacy, S. and Simon, T. (1993) *The Economics and Regulation of United States Newspapers*. Norwood, NJ: Ablex.

Lee, A. and So, C. (1999) 'Dissolving boundaries: electronic newspaper as an agent of redefining social practices'. Paper presented at the conference In Search of Boundaries: Communication, Nation-States and Cultural Identities, Hong Kong, June.

Lee, A. and So, C. (2000) 'Electronic newspaper as digital marketplaces'. Paper presented at the Annual Meeting of the International Communication Association, Acapulco, Mexico, June.

Lewenstein, M., Edwards, G., Tatar, D. and DeVigal, A. (2000) 'Stanford–Poynter project: eyetracking online news'. St Petersburg, FL: The Poynter Institute. Available URL: http://www.poynter.org/eyetrack2000/index.htm.

Li, X. (1998) 'Web page design and graphic use of three U.S. newspapers', *Journalism and Mass Communication Quarterly*, 75 (2): 353–65.

Light, A. (1999) 'Fourteen users in search of a newspaper: the effect of expectation on online behaviour'. CSRP 507. University of Sussex.

Light, A. and Rogers, Y. (1999) 'Conversation as publishing: the role of news forums on the Web', *Journal of Computer-Mediated Communication*, online serial, 4 (4). Available URL: http://www.ascusc.org/jcmc/vol4/issue4/light.html.

Mantooth, S.S. (1982) 'The electronic newspaper: its prospects and directions for future study'. Unpublished doctoral dissertation, University of Tennessee, Knoxville, TN.

Marchand, M. (1987) *La Grande Aventure du Minitel (The Great Adventure of Minitel)*. Paris: Larousse.

Martin, S. and Hansen, K. (1998) *Newspapers of Record in a Digital Age: from Hot Type to Hot Link*. Westport, CT: Praeger.

Marvin, C. (1980) 'Delivering the news of the future', *Journal of Communication*, 30: 10–20.

Marvin, C. (1988) *When Old Technologies Were New: Thinking about Electric Communication in the Late Nineteenth Century*. New York: Oxford University Press.

Massey, B. and Levy, M. (1999) 'Interactivity, online journalism, and English-language web newspapers in Asia', *Journalism & Mass Communication Quarterly*, 76: 138–51.

Mayntz, R. and Schneider, V. (1988) 'The dynamics of system development in a comparative perspective: interactive videotex in Germany, France and Britain', in R. Mayntz and T. Hughes (eds), *The Development of Large Technical Systems*. Boulder, CO: Westview. pp. 263–98.

McAdams, M. (1995) 'Inventing an online newspaper', *Interpersonal Computing and Technology: an Electronic Journal for the 21st Century*, online serial, 3 (3). Available URL: http://jan.ucc.nau.edu/~ipct-j/1995/n3/mcadams.txt.

McIntyre, C. (1983) 'Teletext in the United Kingdom', in E. Sigel (ed.), *The Future of Videotex: Worldwide Prospects for Home/Office Electronic Information Services*. White Plains, NY: Knowledge Industry. pp. 113–26.

McMillan, S. (1998) 'Who pays for content? Funding in interactive media', *Journal of Computer-Mediated Communication*, online serial, 4 (1). Available URL: http://www.ascusc.org/jcmc/vol4/issue1/mcmillan.html.

Miles, I. (1992) 'When mediation is the message: how suppliers envisage new markets', in M. Lea (ed.), *Contexts of Computer-Mediated Communication*. London: Harvester-Wheatsheaf. pp. 145–67.

Mings, S. and Harrison, T. (2000a) 'Audience use of online newspapers: a usability study'. Paper presented at the Annual Meeting of the International Communication Association, Acapulco, Mexico, June.

Mings, S. and Harrison, T. (2000b) 'Youth audience uses of online newspapers'. Unpublished manuscript.

Molina, A. (1997) 'Issues and challenges in the evolution of multimedia: the case of the newspaper', *Futures*, 29: 193–212.

Molina, A. (1999) 'Transforming visionary products into realities: constituency-building and observacting in NewsPad', *Futures*, 31: 291–332.

Morris, M. and Ogan, C. (1996) 'The Internet as mass medium', *Journal of Communication*, 46: 39–50.

Mueller, J. and Kamerer, D. (1995) 'Reader preference for electronic newspapers', *Newspaper Research Journal*, 16 (3): 2–13.

Mulgan, G. (1991) *Communication and Control: Networks and the New Economics of Communication*. Cambridge, UK: Polity.

Neuberger, C., Tonnemacher, J., Biebl, M. and Duck, A. (1998) 'Online – the future of newspapers? Germany's dailies on the World Wide Web', *Journal of Computer-Mediated Communication*, online serial, 4 (1). Available URL: http://www.ascusc.org/jcmc/vol4/issue1/neuberger.html.

Neuman, W.R. (1985) 'The media habit', in M. Greenberger (ed.), *Electronic Publishing Plus*. White Plains, NY: Knowledge Industry. pp. 5–12.

Newhagen, J. (1998) 'Hitting the agenda reset button: matching Internet research with development', *Convergence*, 4 (4): 112–19.

Newhagen, J. and Levy, M. (1998) 'The future of journalism in a distributed communication architecture', in D. Borden and K. Harvey (eds), *The Electronic Grapevine: Rumor, Reputation, and Reporting in the New On-line Environment*. Mahwah, NJ: Erlbaum. pp. 9–21.

Newhagen, J., Cordes, J. and Levy, M. (1995) 'Nightly@nbc.com: audience scope and the perception of interactivity in viewer mail on the Internet', *Journal of Communication*, 45: 164–75.

Newspaper Association of America (1998) 'Facts about newspapers 1998: a statistical summary of the newspaper industry'. Available URL: http://www.naa.org/info/facts/index.html.

Noll, A.M. (1980) 'Teletext and videotex in North America: service and system implications', *Telecommunications Policy*, 4: 25–31.

Oostendorp, H.v. and Nimwegen, C. (1998) 'Locating information in an online newspaper', *Journal of Computer-Mediated Communication*, online serial, 4 (1). Available URL: http://www.ascusc.org/jcmc/vol4/issue1/oostendorp.html.

Overduin, H. (1986) 'News judgment and the community connection in the technological limbo of videotex', *Communication*, 9: 229–46.

Palmer, J. and Eriksen, L. (1999) 'Digital newspapers explore marketing on the Internet', *Communications of the ACM*, 42 (9): 32–40.

Patten, D. (1986) *Newspapers and New Media*. White Plains, NY: Knowledge Industry.

Pavlik, J. (1998) *New Media Technology: Cultural and Commercial Perspectives*, 2nd edn. Boston: Allyn and Bacon.

Peng, F., Them, N. and Xiaoming, H. (1999) 'Trends in online newspapers: a look at the US Web', *Newspaper Research Journal*, 20 (2): 52–63.

Pfaffenberger, B. (1989) 'The social meaning of the personal computer: or, why the personal computer revolution was no revolution', *Anthropological Quarterly*, 61: 39–47.

Picard, R. and Brody, J. (1997) *The Newspaper Publishing Industry*. Boston: Allyn & Bacon.

Pool, I. de S. (1983) *Technologies of Freedom*. Cambridge, MA: Belknap/Harvard University Press.

Pride, R. (1998) 'Media critics and newsgroup-embedded newspapers: making attentive citizens attentive', in M. Salvador and P. Sias (eds), *The Public Voice in a Democracy at Risk*. Westport, CT: Praeger. pp. 127–48.

Riley, P., Keough, C., Christiansen, T., Meilich, O. and Pierson, J. (1998) 'Community or colony: the case of online newspapers and the Web', *Journal of Computer-Mediated Communication*, online serial, 4 (1). Available URL: http://www.ascusc.org/jcmc/vol4/issue1/keough.html.

Roscoe, T. (1999) 'The construction of the World Wide Web audience', *Media, Culture & Society*, 21: 673–84.

Ross, S. (1998) 'Journalists' use of on-line technology and sources', in D. Borden and K. Harvey (eds), *The Electronic Grapevine: Rumor, Reputation, and Reporting in the New On-line Environment*. Mahwah, NJ: Erlbaum. pp. 143–60.

Schlesinger, P. (1978) *Putting 'Reality' Together: BBC News*. London: Methuen.

Schneider, V., Charon, J., Miles, I., Thomas, G. and Vedel, T. (1991) 'The dynamics of videotex development in Britain, France and Germany: a cross-national comparison', *European Journal of Communication*, 6: 187–212.

Schudson, M. (1978) *Discovering the News: a Social History of American Newspapers*. New York: Basic.

Schudson, M. (1997) 'The sociology of news production revisited', in J. Curran and M. Gurevitch (eds), *Mass Media and Society*, 2nd edn. London: Arnold. pp. 141–59.

Schultz, T. (1999) 'Interactive options in online journalism: a content analysis of 100 U.S. newspapers', *Journal of Computer-Mediated Communication*, online serial, 5 (1). Available URL: http://www.ascusc.org/jcmc/vol5/issue1/schultz.html.

Schultz, T. (2000) 'Mass media and the concept of interactivity: an exploratory study of online forums and reader email', *Media, Culture & Society*, 22: 205–21.

Shefin, D. (1949) 'The radio newspaper and facsimile broadcasting'. Unpublished master's thesis, University of Missouri.

Sigal, L. (1973) *Reporters and Officials: the Organization and Politics of Newsmaking*. Lexington, MA: Heath.

Sigel, E. (1980) 'Videotext in the US' in E. Sigel (ed.), *Videotext: the Coming Revolution in Home/Office Information Retrieval*. White Plains, NY: Knowledge Industry. pp. 87–111.

Sigel, E. (1983a) 'Introduction', in E. Sigel (ed.), *The Future of Videotex: Worldwide Prospects for Home/Office Electronic Information Services*. White Plains, NY: Knowledge Industry. pp. 1–13.

Sigel, E. (1983b) 'Videotext in other countries', in E. Sigel (ed.), *The Future of Videotext: Worldwide Prospects for Home/Office Electronic Information Services*. White Plains, NY: Knowledge Industry. pp. 149–60.

Simon, B. (1999) 'Undead science: making sense of cold fusion after the (arti)fact', *Social Studies of Science*, 29: 61–85.

Singer, J. (1998) 'Online journalists: foundations for research into their changing roles', *Journal of Computer-Mediated Communication*, online serial, 4 (1). Available URL: http://www.ascusc.org/jcmc/vol4/issue1/mcmillan.html.

Singer, J., Tharp, M. and Haruta, A. (1999) 'Online staffers: superstars or second-class citizens?', *Newspaper Research Journal*, 20 (3): 29–47.

Smith, A. (1979) *The Newspaper: an International History*. London: Thames and Hudson.

Smith, A. (1980) *Goodbye Gutenberg: the Newspaper Revolution of the 1980s*. New York: Oxford University Press.

Sommer, P. (1983) 'Videotext in the United Kingdom', in E. Sigel (ed.), *The Future of Videotext: Worldwide Prospects for Home/Office Electronic Information Services*. White Plains, NY: Knowledge Industry. pp. 81–111.

Stone, G. (1987) *Examining Newspapers: What Research Reveals about America's Newspapers*. Newbury Park, CA: Sage.

Strasser, S. (1989) *Satisfaction Guaranteed: the Making of the American Mass Market*. New York: Pantheon.

Sumpter, R. (2000) 'Daily newspaper editors' audience construction routines: a case study', *Critical Studies in Media Communication*, 17: 334–46.

Sundar, S.S. (1998) 'Effect of source attribution on perception of online news stories', *Journalism and Mass Communication Quarterly*, 75 (1): 55–68.

Sundar, S.S. (1999) 'Exploring receivers' criteria for perception of print and online news', *Journalism and Mass Communication Quarterly*, 76 (2): 373–86.

Sundar, S.S., Narayan, S., Obregon, R. and Uppal, C. (1999) 'Does web advertising work? Memory for print vs. online media', *Journalism and Mass Communication Quarterly*, 75 (4): 822–35.

Sundar, S.S., Edgar, R. and Mayer, K. (2000) 'Multimedia effects on processing and perception of online news: a study of picture, audio and video downloads'. Paper presented at the Annual Meeting of the International Communication Association, Acapulco, Mexico, June.

Tankard, J. and Ban, H. (1998) 'Online newspapers: living up to their potential?' Paper presented at the Annual Convention of the Association for Journalism and Mass Communication, Baltimore, MD.

Tewksbury, D. and Althaus, S. (1999) 'Differences in knowledge acquisition among readers of the paper and online versions of a national newspaper'. Paper presented at the Annual Meeting of the International Communication Association, San Francisco, California.

Thalhimer, M. (1994) 'High tech news or just "shovelware"?', *Media Studies Journal*, (Winter): 41–52.

Thorson, E., Wells, W. and Rogers, S. (1999) 'Web advertising's birth and early childhood as viewed in the pages of *Advertising Age*', in D. Schumann and E. Thorson (eds), *Advertising and the World Wide Web*. Mahwah, NJ: Erlbaum. pp. 5–25.

Tremayne, M. (1998) 'The transforming potential of the Internet: an analysis of online news and the use of interactivity and nonlinear storytelling'. Unpublished master's thesis, University of Texas at Austin.

Tuchman, G. (1978) *Making News: a Study in the Construction of Reality*. New York: Free Press.

Tydeman, J., Lipinski, H., Adler, R., Nyhan, M. and Zwimpfer, L. (1982) *Teletext and Videotex in the United States: Market Potential, Technology and Public Policy Issues*. New York: McGraw-Hill.

Tyler, M. (1979) 'Videotex, Prestel and teletext: the economics and politics of some electronic publishing media', *Telecommunications Policy*, 3: 37–51.

Vedel, T. and Charon, J.M. (1989) 'Videotex in France: the invention of a mass-medium?', in V. Schneider, G. Thomas, T. Vedel, J.M. Charon and I. Miles (eds), *Pathways to Telematics: the Politics of Videotex in Britain, France and the Federal Republic of Germany*. pp. 83–147. Unpublished.

Warren, P. (1967) 'The metropolitan newspaper as a political institution: an organizational analysis of the New York Press'. Unpublished doctoral dissertation, Harvard University, Cambridge, MA.

Weaver, D. (1983) *Videotex Journalism: Teletext, Viewdata, and the News*. Hillsdale, NJ: Erlbaum.

Weaver, D. and Wilhoit, G.C. (1986) *The American Journalist: a Portrait of U.S. News People and their Work*. Bloomington, IN: Indiana University Press.

Webster, F. (1995) *Theories of the Information Society*. London: Routledge.

Wilkinson, M. (1980) 'Viewdata: the Prestel system', in E. Sigel (ed.), *Videotext: the Coming Revolution in Home/Office Information Retrieval*. White Plains, NY: Knowledge Industry. pp. 57–85.

Williams, W. (1998) 'The blurring of the line between advertising and journalism in the on-line environment', in D. Borden and K. Harvey (eds), *The Electronic Grapevine: Rumor, Reputation, and Reporting in the New On-line Environment*. Mahwah, NJ: Erlbaum. pp. 31–41.

Willis, J. (1994) *The Age of Multimedia and Turbonews*. Westport, CT: Praeger.

Winner, L. (1986) 'Mythinformation', in L. Winner (ed.), *The Whale and the Reactor: a Search for Limits in an Age of High Technology*. Chicago: University of Chicago Press. pp. 98–117.

17

New Media and New Economy Cluster Dynamics

PHILIP COOKE

This chapter focuses on the organizational characteristics of new media businesses. Like other new economy industries such as information and communication technologies (ICT), including varieties of software engineering, and biotechnology, such firms tend to cluster in geographical proximity. They do this for a number of reasons, but the main one seems to be to access 'spillovers'. These are external economies that come from co-location with other like-minded or complementary businesses. Opportunities for joint contracts, sharing of knowhow, and exchange of human or, more collectively, social capital are greater in such settings. New media differ from other new economy clusters in being less likely to agglomerate around universities or research laboratories and more likely to occupy downtown fringe locations where rents may be relatively cheap because industry has vacated space, but access to large customers in film, TV, advertising and publishing is good. Moreover, ambience is important too; thus fashion, funky entertainment and fusion food are likely ingredients in the general scene. But, as is reported next, important features of new media have been changing and there are good reasons for thinking that rapid transitions in forms of new media articulation have become endemic.

Thus in the 1990s the glamorous new technology was multimedia, subsequently known more widely as new media. Today, new media's public prominence has been eclipsed by interest in Internet or dot.com businesses, mobile telephony and a revived biotechnology. It is by now well appreciated that a new economy stock may well hold the public eye for a brief period, before investor hypermobility moves to the next 'new new thing' (Lewis, 2000),

but for an embryonic sector to, apparently, disappear from view is still slightly shocking. The question that drives this contribution is whether new media retain some intrinsic core identity or have already hypertransmuted into or been absorbed by the Internet and foreseeably into the convergent service delivery medium of the handheld *communicator*. This, of course, is the third-generation mobile or cell phone which in its late second-generation form, such as the Nokia Communicator, already provided telephony, Internet access, musical composition, graphic imaging and e-mail. A Palm device accessed news, music, e-mail, barcode scanning, flight schedules, language translation, expense reports and digicam functions amongst others. These are clearly varieties of multimedia device. The third generation provides TV and video services in addition to Bluetooth capabilities regarding interequipment communication, for example the refrigerator tells the mobile phone that it is running short of milk but that the fridge contents can supply ingredients for particular recipes.

Clearly, these functions are new and they are performed by media: so to repeat the question, are they new media? Unquestionably there has been 'morphing' of what, even in conference in 1997 (see for example Braczyk et al., 1999), was painfully being defined as multimedia or new media, into handheld communicator equipment by 2000. But that may not be the whole story. As industries mature, even in a few years, divergences become evident. Thus, whereas specialist banking, financial and stock market information, accessible only by PC on CD-Rom or online in 1997, was accessible on a mobile phone in 2000, advanced computer graphics of the kind now routinely deployed in films like

Star Wars were probably not. But Internet games, which *were* known as computer games, and are undoubtedly new media service products, are accessible by handheld devices and third-generation mobile or cell phones. Internet games firms are part of the dot.com revolution, as are varieties of Internet applications businesses; they have, in many cases, a high market value measured by share price and, having made an initial public offering (IPO), are often courted and acquired by the likes of Sony, Sega or Nintendo. Web page design, which was considered as the 'bottom-feeder' end of new media a few years ago, can now be performed by anyone with Microsoft Frontpage.

The texture is complex, not least because much of the nexus of businesses around new media is entrepreneurial, small or very small scale in terms of human capital, but creative and knowledge-driven with even 'virtual firms' being a pronounced feature. Classically, these businesses tend to congregate in geographical clusters, often, as we have noted, where the coffee is good and the street life is vibrant. Crossover interactions between members of social, political or economic networks focused on cultural products with design-intensive content are the lifeblood of such communities. In this sense they are rather like biotechnology firms, clustered near university campuses, that have intellectual power but crave the venture capitalists and large pharmaceutical firms to fund their next contract or milestone. But these do not cohabit spatially, unless the corporate client puts a lookout branch in the cluster. Such small-firm clusters are dynamic, productive and innovative and show remarkable new firm formation rates. The two go together: risky businesses operate in clusters because of strength in numbers, or the aforementioned spillover effects. They are an increasingly prominent organizational form as the new economy transcends the old, but as we have seen, their identity can be fleeting.

In what follows, the first section will, reasonably briefly, review the relevant literature on what multimedia and/or new media comprise. Other chapters in this book perform this function at greater length. Nevertheless, it is important to be clear about the focus of *this* contribution, since, as has been argued thus far, the sector is changing and coalescing with some technologies while diverging from others, and it is crucial to understand why and with what effects. Following that, the second section will deal with the interesting question of why industries like new media organize themselves as clusters. These are becoming widespread in new economy sectors, but they were also the spatial form that early capitalism took almost wherever it started, and as Porter (1998) shows for the US, many of those also survive and prosper. The pivotal part of this section will relate the small-firm clustering phenomenon, where creativity and innovation are pronounced,

to overall industry structure, where corporate behemoths like Time Warner in new media clumsily seek to 'get on board' by acquisition, yet lack the agility and 'absorptive capacity' (Cohen and Levinthal, 1990) to succeed, terminating with their own acquisition by a dot.com firm like America Online (AOL). There are slight resonances of this in IT where Microsoft and Intel duped IBM into losing control of a world-leading position in computing by supplying the market for IBM PC clones. It has yet to develop noticeably in biotechnology, also a highly clustered new economy sector, though UK biotech's Celltech-Chiroscience recently acquired pharmaceuticals firm Medeva and, if it wished, US biotech firm Amgen with a market capitalization of $70 billion in 2000 could probably easily afford Eli Lilly or Schering-Plough. These new-economy/old-economy dynamics are interestingly poised at the start of the millennium. Before reaching conclusions on the state of new media at the time of writing, an effort will be made to give some kind of prospective view of possible growth trajectories attending the predominant industry force that today is technological *convergence*.

NEW MEDIA IN TRANSITION

Old media were fairly easy to grasp conceptually: they were products and services that broadcast knowledge, information and entertainment in forms intermediary between the originator and the ultimate consumer of product or service. The 'Gutenberg galaxy', as Marshall McLuhan (1962) called the effect of the invention of the printing press, captures the idea perfectly. The word, hitherto accessible only to the priesthood and its interpretations of the source message, became mechanically reproducible as the book, an intermediary object capable of independent, democratic interpretation and use by its consumers. Other communication media such as newspapers, pamphlets and songsheets followed suit. Later, their electronic forms of film, radio, TV and video performed equivalent functions in wider secular fields. So what is new about new media? In one important sense nothing, since CD-ROMs, the Internet, digital databases, computer games content and advanced computer graphics that can simulate anything from tornados to *T. Rex* carry content that informs or entertains as an intermediary between creative talent and consumer. The old, new new thing, to paraphrase Lewis (2000) in respect of new media, was its convergent nature. New media involved the capability to have on disk or online a broadcast message that combined still and moving images, text, voice and music as discrete elements of a single product or service. These were made possible because of hardware advances in cabling and routing using upgraded copper or optical fibre, enabling simultaneous transmission of the multiplicity of media – hence multimedia. Clearly, all these media had been previously combinable. Once *The Jazz Singer* had appeared, moving and still images, voice and music were combined on a single medium. The line of trajectory in old media was locked into elaborations and enhancements of these basic tools. But the key to their integration was their property of supporting the *narrative* flow of the product. Coinciding with the more recent hardware enhancements in cabling and routing came the cultural turn against narrative and the rise of the *spatial* consciousness to challenge the *temporal* (Cooke, 1990). The possible and the desirable interacted in the creation of the multimedia product, a classic example of which would be Microsoft's Encarta encyclopaedia.

One of the earlier intellectual contributions to understanding the nature of new media, presented in 1995 and published as Scott (1998), argued that in California new media took the following form. Making their appearance from the mid 1980s in San Francisco, especially Silicon Valley, and Hollywood, Los Angeles, they intersected high technology and cultural industries. For Scott, the industry was organized into four hierarchical levels. At the base was machinery and hardware, notably computing, communication and associated peripherals and components. Resting on this base was programme interfacing software and systems design. Utilizing the software platform were the visual, audio and print media industries at whose intersection were found *multimedia*. Thus Scott's core definition of multimedia or new media exactly replicates ours in that they exist at the point of convergence of traditional or 'old media' and take the form of discrete combinations of voice, text and visual communication. These discrete combinations are then realized as multimedia products and services such as games and entertainment, educational products, business applications and so on. At the product and service end of this chain are two kinds of actor: developers who actually design and make titles, and publishers that market them. The latter sometimes finance the former who tend to be small–medium enterprises (SMEs). Title publishers are both large (e.g. Disney) and SME in scale. Scott concludes that new media emerged in Hollywood as an adjunct to the entertainment, film and music industries with studios such as Fox, Disney, Universal and Time Warner active as publishers and commissioners of multimedia titles. Northern California has a little of this, as with Sony Electronic Publishing and Dreamworks, but it is strongest in production of the platforms enabling multimedia titles to be produced. In addition, more business multimedia products such as financial and business-related database products (e.g. Dataquest) were developed there.

In their definitive collection on the subject, Braczyk et al. (1999) concur with the definitions discussed so far by saying that 'multimedia' has a narrow and a broader meaning. In the former case it is conceived of as a convergence of several digital media that, interestingly, contain time-sensitive (sound, motion pictures) and time-insensitive (text, graphics) elements used interactively to produce an integrated effect. This is an aspect of the novelty of new media. More broadly, rather as the opening remarks of this contribution emphasized, 'multimedia' can be said to describe the present form taken by information and communications technology (ICT). That is, convergence has almost been achieved, unifying the contributions of content developers, programme and service providers, network operators, server and router suppliers, software and computer, telephony and consumer electronics industries. This elaborates the four-level multimedia value chain identified by Scott (1998). The extent of relatively recent technological innovations that made multimedia possible is outlined by Egan and Saxenian (1999). They include: operating systems software at 32 and 64 MB for PCs, audio and video processing on PC, storage growth from CD to DVD, high-resolution and flat-panel displays, colour laser printing, software applications for desktop publishing, image processing and editing for audio and video, interface devices like touch screens, graphic scanners, digital cameras and multimedia projectors, and networking through Internet and WWW accessed through TV, PC and, recently, handheld devices.

So we are clear on the technological convergences that have made new media possible. Now it is time to look at some divergences, even though it is essential to remember that, according to Mansell (2000), the digital economy is fundamentally chaotic, 'devoid of shape, form, edges and geography', in the words of a visionary from British Telecom. Hence, among the divergences there are always coalescences caused by institutional actors such as firms and regulators. One such sphere of coalescence is Hollywood where Scott (1999) observes a 'multimedia and digital visual-effects' industry growing apace. As field leader this obviously has implications for new media and motion picture activities of all kinds. The digital visual-effects element of the couplet arose from digital enhancement through computer graphics applied to conventional media. This encompasses and unifies hitherto separate fields of multimedia, animation and special effects into a toolbox routinely used in TV and film and video programming. Scott identified, by 1997, 188 firms doing this kind of multimedia work in Los Angeles, mostly in or near Hollywood.

Another diversion is Internet games, a vast market with abiding growth opportunities. Modern games service providers rely on the fact that up to 80 per cent of games can be played in a multiplayer format on the Internet. The spectrum of providers runs from the lower end, based on a central server enabling up to 30 to be involved in a system which keeps track of the virtual game world in question, to companies supplying massive multiplayer games based in a 'server farm' capable of serving hundreds of thousands of players, British Telecom's Wireplay and recent IPO firm Gameplay being cases in point. Small startups concentrate on the former segment but are also key in designing and writing code for big games firms in the latter. Advertising to build a customer base is done online and much of the burn rate of startups is explained by the need to advertise. The more widely used games technology, the Sony Playstation 2 or Nintendo Game Boy type with sales of 80 million units, will also soon converge with the PC-based multiplayer kind. As Safer (2000) reports, Digital Bridges in early 2000 introduced Wirelessgames.com as a portal delivering multiplayer games to third-generation, wireless application protocol (WAP) enabled mobile phones. This is a step beyond the large numbers of providers who have developed games playable on the Palm handheld device.

Finally, a further divergence, which, as we have already noted, also comes back to Palms and WAP mobiles, is business information. Despite the leading-edge software to build the global financial nets that were once only the province of currency dealers, but are now routinely exploited by day-trading taxi drivers and academics *inter alia*, such systems are characterized by a combination of picosecond speed in monitoring and updating, but a rather dull passivity in service provision. The news cuttings services, while of use, are scarcely interactive and, in consequence, are incapable of supplying the kind of problem-solving advice, tailored to specific need, that is so characteristic of required enterprise support. Curiously, interactivity has been vaunted for decades, since Fowles' *French Lieutenant's Woman*, and in other narrative-oriented entertainment where there is scarcely any market for it. Recent cases in point are interactive TV and the cinematically questionable but available interactive ('choose your own plot line and ending') cine-camera developed from the personalized version so successfully deployed in *Blair Witch Project*. But on business information it has yet to surface, leaving global financial markets with relatively unimaginative services in abundance.

Underlining this, Heydebrand (1999) presents a portrait of New York's 'Silicon Alley'. First, New York is home to seven globally significant multimedia firms, amongst which Dow Jones and Co. (owners of *Wall Street Journal* and other financial titles) is the leading business information specialist. In London, Pearson Group (owners of *Financial Times* and ft.com) and, particularly, Reuters have comparable functions. Of course, New York's

dominant old/new media firms dwarf Dow Jones, particularly Time Warner, Viacom, NBC, CBS and the Hearst Corporation, and these also have new media roles in business and financial information as well as entertainment. Pavlik (1999) notes that in 1997 southern Manhattan had 1106 multimedia firms employing 23,390 while midtown and uptown together had 668 firms employing 25,378. The former, 'Silicon Alley', is, as the numbers signify, the home of the small, creative firm cluster. Most of the multimedia energy of such firms has increasingly been drawn into the dot.com surge and much of what was temporarily a sector with fleeting identity as multimedia is now better understood as having morphed in large part into that sphere.

It would be remiss not to pay some attention to the larger entertainment segment of the New York new media industry, where more skills remain in niches around computer graphics, special applications programming and content provision where small firms feed to and from corporate giants such as Time Warner (TW), now AOL–Time Warner. An insider's view of some cultural discontinuities involved in such relationships has been supplied by Wolff (1998), whose Wolff New Media (WNM) content business created *NetGuide*. In search of a possible acquisition or at least investment, WNM courted Time Warner and AOL in the 1990s. The TW New Media Group had recently appointed a new general manager of New Media to join the editor of New Media, an old media journalist who, nevertheless, occupied third position on the headed notepaper. The new appointee replaced an executive whose enthusiasm for new media was such that he announced publicly 'the death of the book', something not guaranteed to please TW shareholders. TW had an Online Steering Committee and a president of Multimedia who outranked the head of the New Media Group, but knew far less about the subject.

The TW New Media Group was responsible for the company's relationship with AOL who published *Time* on the Internet, for which AOL received free advertising in *Time*. The earnings ratio was at least 1 to 30 in AOL's favour by 1994. The Online Steering Committee was formed to solve the AOL conundrum. TW appointed WNM as a consultant to the Online Steering Group. For the editor of New Media, 'content is king' was the mission statement, to which 'technology is destiny' had recently been added. Hence, 'put *Time* on the web' became the strategy, despite the obvious evidence that AOL customers had rejected that option substantively. Pathfinder, the vehicle for this, cost TW up to $20 million per year to run on revenues of $2–4 million. Meanwhile WNM started courting AOL, only to find them a firm where the supplicant had to organize the whole corporate interaction process, the exact opposite of the rococo administrative structure of Time Warner. No result came from the interaction with AOL, whose executives gave every indication of seeking an acquirer as much as WNM, except that in early 2000 the acquired turned out to be Time Warner and the acquirer AOL. The medium had truly taken over the message.

AOL–Time Warner is the first new media conglomerate, merging all the multimedia elements of visual, print and audio media into the ISP-dominated infobahn. Sony, Bertelsmann, Viacom and the rest of the pack have to come to terms with this content and communication convergence. It may unravel because of incompatibilities, not least of management style. But if not, it will remain the exemplar of the new media paradigm and its implosion into the Internet at the outset of the new millennium. So it is important to recognize the overarching role of large and powerful units of multimedia capital such as these, who are, generally speaking, not creative except in making first moves and then aggrandizement. They may not be as intriguing to analyse as the lean and agile startups (which of course included AOL in recent time) on whom large corporate actors almost completely depend for new media content. But the creativity to achieve scale without imagination is a subject worthy of study in its own right, but regrettably perhaps, not one that is able to be pursued here. We have, rather, set the scene by exploring the transmutations of new media and defined the field in the process. The next step is to set that field in a wider context of industry organization and spatial dynamics because, despite the power of the corporate sector, there would be few, even transient, new economy industries without the exploitation, innovation and commercialization capabilities of small, dynamic new business entrants. The next section explores the settings in which such firms prosper.

THE CLUSTER IMPERATIVE IN THE NEW ECONOMY

Clustering is neither an unusual nor a new form of business organization. It was present in the beginning of the industrial age where cotton textiles firms in Britain, France and the USA concentrated in industrial districts, and handgun manufacturers famously clustered in places like Springfield, Massachusetts. They did so to access skilled labour and to pick up as free goods the knowhow that was said to be 'in the air' in such places. For much of the twentieth century the ownership of firms in such districts concentrated so that, for example, the classic auto cluster of Detroit was dominated by the big two producers, Ford and GM, with Chrysler some way behind, and now part of Daimler-Benz's global grouping. But these were once clusters of numerous independent assembly and components supplier

firms, and when Japanese competition began to bite in the 1980s the giants began to downsize and externalize production back into supply chains that were by now as much global as local. Simultaneously, new industries such as semiconductor and computer production grew as new small firms entered production in places like Silicon Valley and Boston (Rogers and Larsen, 1984; Saxenian, 1994), and while the evolutionary trajectories of even these two places have diverged, more such clusters have emerged elsewhere in the world, including the developing world (see, for example, Schmitz and Nadvi, 1999). Fired by the early success of high-technology clusters, many administrations tried to emulate Silicon Valley. Most failed dismally, but one case that stands out as successful and policy-driven is Austin, Texas (see, for instance, Henton et al., 1997) where strong private leadership involving business, government and education in association attracted blue chip firms such as Motorola and IBM as well as high-technology consortia such as Sematech and MCC. It was in the 1970s and 1980s that a soft infrastructure of investors and other knowledge-intensive service providers grew in tandem with a harder incubation infrastructure at the University of Texas, to form an establishment known as IC². From this, what had the look of a branch plant economy became more entrepreneurial as firms like Dell and its suppliers came to prominence through endogenous growth.

Clusters have now become a key mode of economic coordination and focus of government policies across the world and for a wide variety of industries. The UK IT industry's cluster prospective group Information Age Partnership definition of a cluster as a 'geographical concentration of interdependent companies and institutions connected by a system of market and non-market links' is a useful starting point, as it captures key elements of competitive *and* collaborative interaction that characterize firm relationships. It also recognizes the importance of *proximity* to those relationships and that important relationships are not limited to those between firms only. It is thus close to Michael Porter's (1998) definition, which is that: 'A cluster is a geographically proximate group of interconnected companies and associated institutions *in a particular field*, linked by commonalities and complementarities' (emphasis added). This, in turn, underpinned the definition used by the UK Minister of Science for the work of his task force on *biotechnology* clusters, as: 'geographic concentrations of interconnected companies, specialised suppliers, service providers, firms in related industries and associated institutions (for example universities, standards agencies and trade associations) in particular fields that compete but also cooperate'.

There is nothing wrong with these definitions except that they are all *static*, whereas the key feature of clusters is that they are *dynamic*. Hence we prefer the following also to be taken into account. A cluster displays a shared identity and future vision. It is characterized by 'turbulence' as firms spin off, spin out and start up from other firms or institutions. A cluster is an arena of dense and changing vertical input–output linkages, supply chains and horizontal interfirm networks. It is likely to have developed localized, third-party representative governance associations that provide common services but also lobby government for change. A cluster may have caused governments to develop policies to assist cluster development, especially where market failures are present. Over time, clusters can reveal features of emergence, dominance and decline. So we come to a preferred definition of a cluster as: 'geographically proximate firms in vertical and horizontal relationships, involving a localized enterprise support infrastructure with a shared developmental vision for business growth, based on competition and cooperation in a specific market field'.

Why are clusters more prominent now than hitherto? Why does the hierarchical firm, so pronounced a feature of the mid-twentieth-century corporate landscape, no longer act as the model for economic coordination? There are at least three key reasons for this. First, global competition, initially from Japan and South East Asia, then from the US response to it, caused large corporations to reduce in-house production and administrative overhead while increasing outsourcing and learning, for example, lean production, in order to survive. Second, innovation became a leading competitive weapon and small, knowledge-based firms, often close to universities, were further up the technological learning curve. Third, as we have seen in the case of Time-Warner and new media, the intrinsic rigidities of the hierarchical corporate organization meant rapid learning and accommodation to change could not be easily implemented.

In brief, Porter (1998) holds that a number of advantages are derived from clusters, among which are the following. First, *productivity* gains arise from access to early use of better quality and lower-cost specialized inputs from components or services suppliers in the cluster. Local sourcing can be cheaper because of minimal inventory requirements and transaction costs generally can be lower because of the existence of high-trust relations and the importance of reputation-based trading. Common purchasing can lower costs where external sourcing is necessary. Serendipitous information trading is more likely in contexts where formal or informal face-to-face contact is possible. Complementarities between firms can help joint bidding and scale benefits on contract tenders, or joint marketing of products and services. Access to public goods from research or standards bodies located in proximity can be advantageous.

Second, *innovation* gains come from *proximity* between customers and suppliers where the interaction between the two may lead to innovative specifications and responses. User-led innovation impulses are recognized as crucial to the innovation process and their discovery has led to a better understanding of the interactive rather than linear processes of innovation. Proximity to knowledge centres makes the interaction processes concerning design, testing and prototype development physically easier, especially where much of the necessary knowledge is partly or wholly tacit rather than codified. Localized benchmarking among firms on organizational as well as product and process innovation is facilitated in clusters. Qualified personnel are more easily recruited and are of key importance to knowledge transfer. Informal knowhow trading is easier in clusters than through more distant relationships.

Finally, *new businesses* are more readily formed where better information about innovative potential and market opportunities is locally available. Barriers to entry for new firms can be lower because of a clearer perception of unfulfilled needs, product or service gaps, or anticipated demand. Locally available inputs and skills further reduce barriers to entry. A cluster in itself can be an important initial market. Familiarity with local public, venture capital or business angel funding sources may speed up the investment process and minimize risk premiums for new startups and growing businesses. Clusters attract outside firms and foreign direct investors who perceive benefits from being in a specialized, leading-edge business location. These may also be a further source of corporate spinoff businesses.

Clusters work through networks between a variety of business and other appropriate actors who are familiar with each other's expertise, trustworthiness, reliability and willingness both to share relevant assets (e.g. information or lending a machine or employee if needed) and engage in normal business relationships based on market exchange. Networks can be formal or informal, soft or hard (i.e. contractual, with an agreed project and business plan). In high-technology industry, such linkages are likely to involve research organizations such as universities for knowledge, but also indirectly through spinout firms (Cooke et al., 2000). Aspects of this appear in Figure 17.1, which anatomizes key parts of the Cambridge (UK) IT cluster, showing regular cooperative as well as competitive relationships within the cluster.

A key question for policy is: can clusters be built? This refers to the role of policy on the part of different levels of government. While many correctly cast doubt on the difficulty, if not impossibility, of building clusters from zero, this has not stopped governments trying to do this in the past. Technopoles and the cognate notion of 'technopolis' are cases in point. These are large

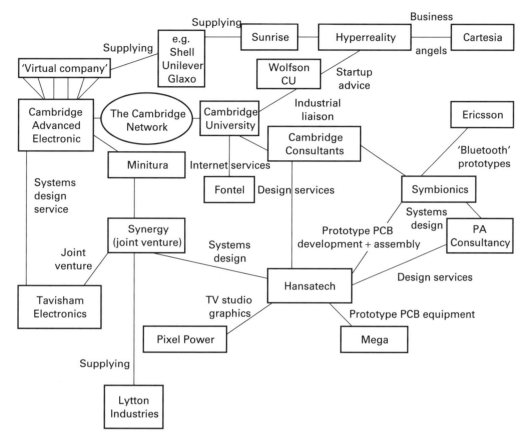

Figure 17.1 *Aspects of the Cambridge IT Cluster*

spaces, sometimes even whole towns or cities, designated by governments as locations for which incentives are available to encourage corporations or public organizations to relocate research and development (R&D) facilities. The aspiration is that these will interact with synergetic growth and innovation effects. France and Japan built 'technopoles' by attracting research branches to co-locate in special zones such as Sophia Antipolis and Tsukuba City. However, most commentators agree these are not clusters. This is because synergetic interactions scarcely occur despite proximity; most interactions persist over distance back to corporate headquarters or other corporate divisions elsewhere. Nor specifically has there been much evidence of spinoff or other kinds of new firm formation despite this also being a key aspiration. This lack of local linkage denies them the status of clusters. Hence, in North Carolina, Research Triangle Park has successfully attracted research laboratories but only recently have there been signs of some interaction with localized suppliers when implementation occurred of special new initiatives to create incubation facilities targeted at new firm

formation. Synergy effects are thus now understood to be extremely hard to create. But it is now better understood that a 'soft infrastructure' of knowledge-intensive business services ranging from investment, management, legal, patenting and technology transfer to specialist consultancies is a key presence in most successful clusters. These were typically not present in technopoles. Synergies, meaning a surplus or Gestalt effect created by fruitful interaction, can be assisted enormously by the market transactions of such private intermediaries and the supportive actions of grant-giving public ones.

However, where there is something with which to work, especially in knowledge-intensive activity, then policy may enhance cluster formation. Some examples of this include Finnish regional science and technology policy encouraging universities to set up technology parks on university campuses, with Nokia or other research labs acting as customers to multimedia software and computing services supplied by startups. The Technical University at Tampere has generated a small multimedia cluster on its Hermia Technology Park. In the US, clusters are often promoted at state level through setting up infrastructure, industry associations, grants, tax credits and R&D credits. But there still has to be a knowledge-generating source in research labs or other key firms. In Germany, there are numerous federal and state-level initiatives, most notably BioRegio which funds three biotechnology clusters at £50 million. Startups, closely linked to research labs, local (often publicly funded) venture capital and cluster management organizations, have grown from 170 to 223 during the two years since BioRegio was implemented in 1997 (Schitag et al., 1998; Giesecke, 1999).

Stimulated by the evident success of Silicon Valley, California in the 1970s and 1980s, many national and regional governments sought to encourage the formation of high-technology industry complexes by earmarking budgets and special high-tech development zones, modelled to some extent on the pattern established by the science park at Stanford University, founded in 1951 (Castells and Hall, 1994). It is well known that Frederick Terman, later Provost and Vice-President at Stanford, was the driving force behind Stanford Industrial Park, as it was officially known, and that among his student entrepreneurs were the founder of Litton Industries, and later Hewlett and Packard, preceded as tenants on the park by Varian and succeeded by Fairchild Semiconductors. Fairchild was the matrix for Intel, National Semiconductors, American Micro Devices and some 40 other US chip manufacturers from 1957, when the 'Shockley eight' began to find their feet.

The science-push emphasis of the story fitted in well with the dominant *linear* model of innovation then at the forefront of understanding of the relationship between scientific progress and the commercialization of products and processes. Clearly also, for what, with hindsight, were the truly radical innovations of semiconductors, namely integrated circuits and microprocessors, technology push was a significant impulse, at least in relation to civilian applications. Even so, the role of the Department of Defense and the National Aeronautics and Space Administration as *users* of miniaturized computers and guidance systems has perhaps been highlighted less than their role as suppliers of large-scale *funding* for the development of microcircuitry. We still know relatively little about the nature and extent of interaction between users and technologists at the early stage of the development of these new technologies, though it has been argued that 67 per cent of the functional source of innovation development for semiconductors was *users* and only 21 per cent *manufacturers* (von Hippel, 1988: 4).

To return to the efforts by policy-makers to model high-tech innovation on developments at Stanford and Silicon Valley, it is clear that most approaches have involved the idea of co-locating research centres and innovation-intensive firms in science and technology parks. In some cases this has involved designating whole cities as science cities or technopoles. Although benefits have been accrued from such plans, there is also in the literature that reviews such developments a frequent sense of disappointment that more has not been achieved. In cases drawn from France and Japan, countries that have arguably proceeded furthest with the *technopolis* policy, a certain absence of *synergies* has been observed among co-located laboratories and firms. Science parks, in themselves, have not always met the expectations of their founders and efforts have been made to learn from early mistakes. Nowadays, in response to the improvement in understanding of innovation as an interactive, possibly systemic process, more attention is paid to the factors that lead to embeddedness amongst firms and innovation support organizations (Granovetter, 1985). This anthropological idea refers to the institutional and organizational features of community and solidarity, the exercise of 'social capital' (Putnam, 1993; Cooke and Wills, 1999) and the foundations of high-trust, networked types of relationship among firms and organizations. To some extent also, there is emerging recognition that science parks are a valuable element but not the only or main objective of a localized or regionalized innovation strategy. A good deal of research has been conducted which helps understanding of the nature and range of interaction among firms and organizations engaged in innovation (see, for example, Edquist, 1997; Braczyk et al., 1998; Cooke and Morgan, 1998; de la Mothe and Paquet, 1998; Acs, 2000) and policy is moving towards a notion of the *region* as an important level at which strategic innovation support is appropriate (Cooke, 1992; Tödtling and Sedlacek, 1997; Cooke et al., 2000).

The French and Japanese examples of technopole implantation help us learn how difficult it is to plan clusters. The French were the first to experiment with the idea of technopoles at Grenoble with Meylan-ZIRST (Industrial Zone for Research in Science and Technology). This has concentrated many public and private research laboratories but produced few synergies amongst smaller or even larger firms locally. Our example is that of Sophia Antipolis, which has eventually succeeded, like Meylan-ZIRST, in attracting government research laboratories and larger private investment but is perceived still to suffer from the relative absence of interactive innovation. Even in Grenoble, Rallet and Torre (1998) noted that despite strong specialization in health technologies, research and training infrastructures were 'poorly connected' with local industry and industrial cooperation has been for a long time 'considered insufficient'. De Bernardy (1999) also suggested that, to the extent collective learning was present in Rhône-Alpes it was informal, fragile and vulnerable to market pressures.

Sophia Antipolis

Established in 1972 as a personal mission of Pierre Laffitte, co-director of the prestigious Paris École des Mines, Sophia Antipolis started slowly with little interest in the idea from business or the public sector. After 1975 a second launch was aimed at attracting R&D from US firms. Some, such as Digital, came and were joined by French firms Thomson and L'Oréal, and government pharmacological and information technology laboratories followed. By the early 1990s Sophia Antipolis had 14,000 employees with 9000 of them directly engaged in technological activities (Longhi and Quéré, 1993). Among the US firms locating development units to introduce products to the European market were Cardis, Dow and Rockwell (in addition to Digital).

In Longhi and Quéré's evaluation the following key points are made. First, innovation networks are still marginal in Sophia Antipolis, especially regarding local activities and employment. While Digital and Thomson have organized a local network, as have two pharmacological firms, interacting with production and research skills locally, few dynamic innovations have ensued and learning from local partnerships is minimal. Second, where a few linkages do exist they are almost exclusively vertical, never horizontal. This is because firms are isolated from their parent organizations and they fear 'poaching' from other co-located laboratories. Further, there is active *mistrust* between innovative large firms and local research institutions, although not between the latter and local small, innovative firms. The fear of losing proprietary knowhow is behind this mistrust. Third, there is no local labour market. There is almost no mobility between firms or organizations. In each case an internal labour market operates. The risk of information exchange is the main reason for this absence of labour market mobility. This is the single most obvious instance of the lack of an innovative network or milieu culture at Sophia Antipolis.

In terms of learning from this experience, the following points are of considerable significance. There are weak signs of innovative interaction between larger firms seeking, for example, locally available software services. Some French firms are being attracted to Sophia Antipolis by aspects of its critical mass and network potential. More new firms are, however, needed to create sufficient critical mass for synergies and creative innovation. Where external networking exists it largely remains a vertical, supply-chain relationship. The public sector policy networks are the most significant factor in potentially building up local innovative networks. So far, their main focus has been on 'selling square metres'. Thus, Longhi and Quéré (1993) conclude Sophia Antipolis is only a qualified and rather one-dimensional economic success. A more recent paper by Longhi (1999) underlines the missing preconditions for collective learning by reference to the absence of a science base, spinoff firms and weak local interactions. However, some moderation of the position occurred when the University of Nice moved its IT departments to Sophia Antipolis in 1986, helping create a local labour market supply resource. Global firms are making stronger local linkages with startups and research institutes. Elements of a localized form of systemic innovation have begun to emerge after 25 years.

Technopoles in Japan

In Japan, a major effort to build a scientific pole or cluster occurred at roughly the same time as in France. Tsukuba originated in 1958 as a satellite science city for Tokyo. Tsukuba met the criteria regarding infrastructure, location and transportation later used to judge which cities would join the technopolis programme. It was mainly government funded: the Japan Housing Corporation built housing for nearly 125,000 people and the Ministry of Construction paid for infrastructure. Laboratories and a science and technology university were relocated to the science city. Only in the 1980s did private industry show interest in the site, following construction of a motorway to service the International Science and Technology Expo of 1985. Public investment by 1990 was $1.1 billion. But many national research institutes (e.g. Inorganic Materials; Disaster Prevention; High Energy Physics; Health and Hygiene; and Environment) continue to experience difficulties in developing linkages other than the *vertical* ones typical of Japanese government agencies. Hence they do not share facilities or link to universities or private industry. There is also a lack of new spinoff firms. Tsukuba is seen as an isolated island, although in the 1990s more local conferences and information exchanges have begun to occur. But, in general, there is relatively little synergy amongst organizations.

An evaluation of the Japanese technopolis programme is reported in Castells and Hall (1994). They conclude as follows (though admitting it is quite early to judge). There has been failure to achieve the original vision. Some are dormitory or conventional new towns, not technopoles. There is a branch-plant syndrome as decentralized firms mainly conduct routine assembly work for the parent company. There has been failure to develop university–industry links; the main links are with local technical laboratories rather than universities. Notable is a lack of 'soft infrastructure' consisting of venture capital, R&D consortia and university research networks. There has been a failure to relocate R&D laboratories. These have, if anything, been relocating closer to headquarters than to factories. Problematic is a lack of interindustry linkages because of the weak R&D and strong branch-plant characteristics. There is a lack of spinoff for the same reasons as the absence of interindustry linkages and universities. In general, the conclusion made by Castells and Hall (1994) is that the Japanese technopolis programme has not yet proved itself successful in terms of interactive innovation.

Neither France nor Japan can be said to be leading players in new economy sectors, new media in particular, except for handheld electronic games by Sega and the like (though recall most of the creative work is done by startups in the UK and US). Nonaka and Reinmöller (1998) have an interesting take on this, at least for Japan. They refer to Japan's problem as 'the legacy of learning'. That is, Japan spent so much time and energy on catching up with the West by learning from its practices and seeking to improve upon them in mature sectors, that its economy became locked into old economy activities and its universities and technopoles failed to anticipate any new economy areas. Now there is a frantic effort to relearn and leapfrog as once before, but economic conditions are far less propitious for achieving this than they once were. France also suffers from an overdependence on institutional structures that are state-led and subsidized, a predeliction for mature old economy sectors and a weak base in the new economy. This could be said of the other European big-hitting economies: only the UK has a good presence in new economy business, including new media, while Germany and Italy are adrift in major ways despite strong German media corporations like Kirch and Bertelsmann.

New Media Clusters and the Industry Trajectory

We thus do not find much 'new economy' industry, particularly that relating to new media, to be satisfactorily built by public policy from scratch, with the small but interesting exception of the Finnish policy of inducing multimedia firms from technology faculties linked to a proximate and exacting user such as Nokia. More typical are the following five cases in cities varying in size from the global metropolitan to the regional business or administrative capital, where the unifying feature is the overwhelming importance for production of the kind of small firm-dominated clusters described in the preceding section, connected to large, often global customers, located not in geographic but in functional proximity. Functional proximity means 'virtual space' whereby a customer and supplier may be extremely close in their specific shared interest (in an aspect of new media, for example) but geographically poles apart. Of the two, geographic proximity is the more important from a creativity or innovation capabilities point of view, but of course without finance – especially in new media, where unlike, for instance, biotechnology there are not many huge public research grants available – there is no demand. So they are conceptually as important as one another, constituting a global capabilities relationship that is fundamental to a given new economy sector. In the largest cities, geographic and functional proximity may coincide (see, for further analysis, Rallet and Torre, 1998).

A good example of the latter case occurs in London, where small, creative new media firms are found in a cluster in Soho and numerous large corporate consumers are found in rather less funky locations in the West End. Soho is interesting in terms of industrial history, having once been London's garment district. Accordingly, comparatively large working spaces were available when these workshops and small factories were no longer viable once scale economies entered the business. The UK film industry has for long been managed and had its distribution arranged from Soho, as to some extent has the recorded music industry. But most famously Soho became one of Europe's leading adult entertainment centres with outstanding jazz and blues clubs, strip joints, and gourmet as well as more affordable restaurants and pubs with artistic clienteles. Much of this economy operated in basements, but in the 1960s into the former clothing workshops upstairs entered the UK software industry, represented by firms like Logica and Hoskyns. The large, relatively open-plan working spaces with attractive iron-frame building construction and cheap rents were ideal for such firms. So unlike SoHo, New York, where such industrial spaces were adaptively reused by artists, helping leapfrog the area into a loft-living cultural space of which one part was new media, Soho, London possessed the fine tilth of multiple cultural forms, including old media, the arts, entertainment and advertising from which multimedia could naturally grow.

As Nachum and Keeble (2000) show, London has at least 70 per cent of UK employment in media and 90 per cent in music. Of this, Soho captures about 70 per cent and, as they say, 'The entire chain of production – film production and post production, film distribution and sales agents, design, photography, music, advertising – is available in an area of about one square mile' (2000: 11). Soho is also home to foreign media firms as well as those from the UK. Hence multimedia in London has a bias towards traditional media and advertising, growing from the audio, video and print media in the neighbourhood. The main kinds of new media market served involve corporate presentation, entertainment and leisure, particularly Internet games, and advertising and marketing, notably development of Internet websites. In a study by Russ (1998) he shows that London also has subclusters in Covent Garden, Clerkenwell and Shoreditch. The first named is well known as one of Europe's leading urban cultural zones, the ambience of which was reinvigorated when the capital's fruit and vegetable market was adaptively reused for shopping and leisure activities to complement its traditional function as one of the world's leading places for opera. The other two are in London's East End, former industrial and working-class zones; Clerkenwell was once London's clockmaking quarter. These locations are selected because they are in cheap rent areas, yet the EC1 postcode is seen as valuable owing to its proximity to central London's huge financial district. Much of the market for these firms is governed by the variety of clients locally available, especially in business services. Although far smaller than the Soho clusters, firms in these mini-clusters congregate for the same reasons, notably that it is useful to be co-located as an insurance against breakdowns of equipment or for subcontracting. Trust in each other is highly valued and accessed as a normal business 'overspill'.

In Heydebrand's (1999) and Pavlik's (1999) studies of multimedia in New York, as we have seen, the entertainment and financial sectors are powerful drivers of the industry with both functional and geographic proximity being key features, albeit, as in London, the precise streetblocks occupied by the corporate giants are somewhat upscale of those of the new media firms themselves. In south Manhattan, especially around SoHo and the iconic 55 Broad Street, where was established the New York Information Technology Center, business, as elsewhere, involved entertainment software, Internet services, CD-ROM title development and website design. Surrounding them functionally and spatially are the advertising, marketing, entertainment, education, publishing and TV, film and video producers and publishers. Heydebrand (1999) sees a three-level structure to the industry with the corporate giants resting on the mass of new media businesses who themselves relate importantly to Silicon Alley's creative and innovative capability as represented particularly strongly by 55 Broad Street. Because the last named is unique to New York, it is more interesting to explore its existence as a public–private intervention than to repeat the locational lineages and rationales of the 1000 plus startups in and around SoHo. That it functions as a cluster with horizontal and vertical networks based on trust, exchange, co-bidding and competition on contracts, subcontracting and knowhow and equipment sharing as in London, is made clear by Heydebrand (1999) and Pavlik (1999) in their accounts.

The development at 55 Broad Street is different in that it is the product of the new economy governance practice of 'associationism' (Cooke and Morgan, 1998). With its first meeting in mid 1997 the New York multimedia innovation network set a mission of developing the city as the global capital of multimedia. It united mayoral and gubernatorial representation, Columbia University's NSF-backed Engineering Research Centre in multimedia, the finance and services community, venture capital, leading multimedia startups, major multimedia companies, arts and culture groups and industry associations. They met in the New York Information Technology Center, 55 Broad Street, brainchild of developer William Rudin, who invested $40 million in superwiring the building as an incubator for multimedia startups. Technologically the building offered, in 1997, turnkey multimedia transmission with satellite access, desktop fibre optics, C5 copper, video conferencing and 100 MB per second Internet bandwidth. There were 72 tenants in 1997, including International Business Machines and many startups in design, reportage, security and research amongst others. The association, like other cluster governance networks (e.g. the Massachusetts Technology Collaborative or the Massachusetts Biotechnology Council), has policies to lobby for tax, equity and rent incentives, business support programmes and expanding incubator opportunities.

We have already given some attention to Scott's (1998; 1999) studies of Californian multimedia. As we have seen, they are closely linked to the software and peripherals sectors of Silicon Valley, and business and education products, often for San Francisco clients in the north, with the Hollywood entertainment cluster in southern California being the driver of multimedia in Los Angeles. There are many smaller and startup businesses in the clusters, with many of the standard characteristics found generically elsewhere. Geographically, San Francisco's multimedia firms are strung out along Route 101 from south of San Jose to San Mateo and the main concentration in downtown San Francisco, across the Golden Gate bridge to northern Marin County. In Los Angeles, the axis is much less attenuated, concentrated on a line from Burbank through Hollywood to Santa Monica. In California, there are more developers and hardware/software technicians in the San Francisco area and more entertainment and communication companies in Los Angeles. They also overlap somewhat with pre-existing software and computing clusters, gaining externalities or 'overspills' from such co-location. Median firm size is small, converging upon nine employees, though it is supplemented with freelancers as required by specific projects; large firms tend to have a more stable labour force profile. Creative workers are rather intensively employed in the industry, at a level approximately equivalent to those employed in technical and business functions together. Firms market products globally but interact in production highly locally. Over half the value of sales is accounted for by inwardly or outwardly subcontracted activities, more than two-thirds of which is local. The San Francisco cluster is more 'associative' (Cooke and Morgan, 1998) in the sense of having developed representative organizations, but real service support is largely private rather than public in origin, except for close association with universities in the Los Angeles cluster.

A second case, of special interest because of its cluster identification and warehouse district location, is that offered by Brail and Gertler (1999) which anatomized the multimedia industry of Toronto, Canada. Underlining the functional division of the industry between developers and publishers by reference to the Canadian Interactive Multimedia Arts and Technologies (IMAT) distinction between *producers* and *publishers*, Brail and Gertler segment the market into four: corporate, education, entertainment, and information/reference. They speculate that *health* may be developing as a new segment. Interestingly, evidence is advanced of the Ontario Film Development Corporation's view that multimedia, like the film/TV industries, shows increasing *vertical* integration as producers attempt to control distribution channels. However, Brail and Gertler's research evidence suggests this is a misreading of the situation and that most Canadian multimedia firms are independent, small, creative and dualistic (full-timers and freelancers) just as in California.

The Toronto study identified some 300 firms in Ontario (from a Canadian total of some 560), of which 201 (67 per cent) are in metropolitan Toronto. The largest proportion were located near the city centre in former inner-city industrial areas. These displayed flexible workspaces, heritage buildings, proximity to other cultural industries, central business services and clients. Toronto combines two capital functions, corporate/financial and cultural (publishing, film, broadcasting) which acted as magnets for multimedia firms. Research with firms in face-to-face interviews revealed that locational preference was determined by the relational questions noted above, flexible and affordable space, and the 'downtown' ambience. Clients were mainly Toronto based but links were developing with the California clusters. Interviewees reported little interfirm information sharing, a competitive ethic, and low-trust relationships at the horizontal level, i.e. between firms of similar size and with similar or complementary assets. Informal knowhow sharing occurs between individuals rather than firms. Confidentiality clauses and secrecy on competitive bid prices are normal even though there are few competitors for contracts. Collaboration amongst firms occurs but on a strict

'need to know' basis; joint ventures are a favoured mode of collaboration. Finance is precarious, based on venture capital and involving trading of product rights in exchange for funding. High marketing and distribution costs mean firms specialize in customized products, unless they are large, generic producers. Public support for the industry is strong at national, regional and local levels, with funding of projects available from the province of Ontario.

Finally, to show the importance of the link to old media and their reregulation in the UK, first in stimulating the rise of independent TV programme producers who, second, stimulated directly through spinoff, and indirectly as a market, the formation of multimedia activity, we may look at the case of Cardiff, capital of Wales, one of the UK's four constituent countries. Here we will show both the cluster structure of the industry and the organogram of the wide variety of private and public actors that act as the enterprise support infrastructure for the cluster system, arranging scholarships and bursaries for different kinds of human capital; representing the industry at Cannes, Venice, Los Angeles and other major festivals; and pump-priming or assisting in small-firm bootstrapping to try to ensure that this small and fledgling industry, dependent mainly on a regional market but pushing to sell more widely, evolves. Cooke and Hughes (1999) provide an account of the industry derived from a survey of 300 firms in multimedia and media, animation, graphics, creative arts and services; 48 (16 per cent) were core multimedia producers (online or offline producers). Of the 145 firms responding to the questionnaire (48 per cent response rate), 28 (19 per cent) were core producers. Of these firms, 17 were specifically set up to produce online and offline products such as CDs composed of film and TV clips for entertainment; CD-interactive musical instrument tutoring; geographical information systems; financial trading CD databases and media business CD databases along with vocational training CDs. A further 11 were providers of Internet services or web page designers. Three of the first group and six of the second are currently located in Cardiff Bay.

In Figure 17.2 the degree of co-location and the known market and non-market interactions between firms are visible. Thus, for obvious reasons, editing firms and the manufacturer of editing equipment interact, but they also cross-connect to the CD-ROM and web design, computer graphics, Internet services and animation firms according to need. Not all firms are located in the main multimedia cluster district in the waterfront area, once the home to the commercial activities of the largest coal-export port in the world; many are dotted around the city of Cardiff. Nor are all firms shown, which would be graphically impossible, so this is a cut across the industry in Cardiff, rather as that of Cambridge was

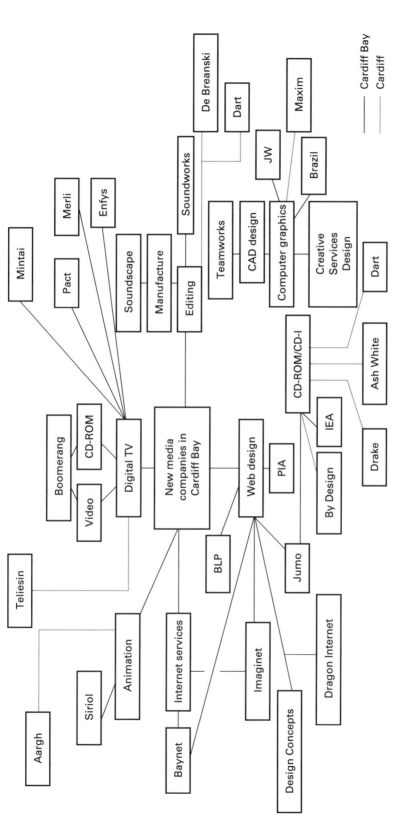

Figure 17.2 *New media companies in Cardiff and Cardiff Bay (selected)*

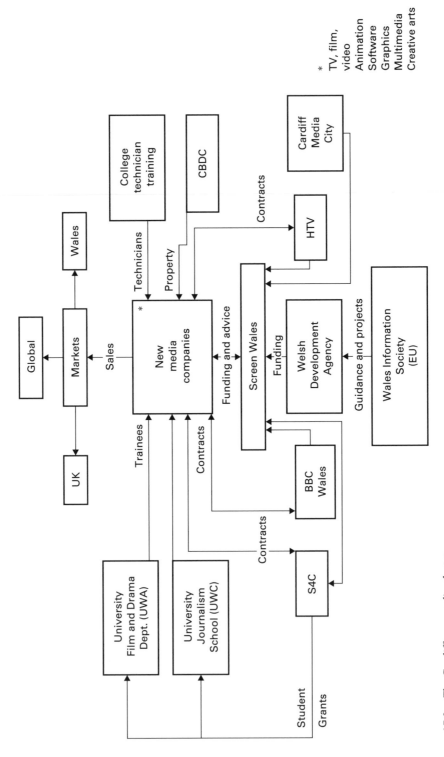

Figure 17.3 *The Cardiff new media cluster*

in the previous section. In Figure 17.3 can be seen the rather elaborate associational infrastructure and its functions that underpins the new media and old media industries in Wales.

The relative prominence of this small-scale industry is testified for by the fact that two of its film outputs, *Hedd Wyn* and *Solomon a Gaenor* (both Welsh language titles), and two cartoons received Oscar nominations in the foreign film and animation categories in the 1990s and 2000. The promotional activities of an organization like Screen Wales are of some assistance in getting these works before the appropriate assessment panels. However, of more daily importance are the contracts from the three main publishers, BBC, HTV and S4C, and to a lesser extent help in accessing EU or regional and local grants or financing through the EU Information Society and Media programmes, or special help from Cardiff's Media City or Cardiff Bay Development Corporation's support initiatives (CBDC being absorbed into Cardiff's administrative purview in April 2000). So, as in Hollywood, particularly, London, New York and Toronto, but at a smaller scale, new media in Wales are quite closely connected to old media, but developing an identity of their own to some degree before being transmuted, as elsewhere, into Internet and other means of communicating online, entertainment, business database, educational, corporate presentation and large- and smaller-scale website design and maintenance.

Concluding Remarks

Space does not allow for fuller reflection on the movements and transitions that have been registered in this account of the business and spatial dynamics of this burgeoning new industry. In drawing the discussion to a close, three key things stand out. The first of these is that there is a considerable amount of movement, coalescence and divergence but all within an overarching and strong tendency towards technological and even content convergence in new media. Before too long, all the older media that converged to form new media will be available on a WAP mobile phone. They may or may not take distinctive forms inherited from the past, like TV, radio and music channels. More likely, they will develop integrated website-like presentational forms with footer text scrolling, multiscreening for news and action presentation and music overdubs. This can be seen on some specialist TV channels at present, and will grow, but mainly for monitoring rather than 'absorptive watching' media programming. New media will join traditional media rather than replace it, just as Internet shopping will join 'going to the shops' rather than replacing that activity.

There will be more rather than less choice of media experiences.

Second, when we look at the industry dynamics and their economic geography, we find new media to be generically similar to other new economy sectors like IT and biotechnology. These are characterized by small startup firms spinning out from a creative or technologically innovative base, clustering together for reasons of mutual support, knowhow trading, trustful exchange and industry monitoring but, essentially, remaining co-located in the now classical form of the geographic cluster. This is the character of the production, or supply of value-added knowledge, side of the equation. Clusters form near knowledge centres like universities, or in new media, where street life is vibrant. Thus far, the new media businesses that have broken free of the hegemony of large old media corporate control are America Online and the more specialist businesses like Amazon.com or Yahoo! These have grown massively in scale and market capitalization at tremendous speed, without in some cases troubling the accountants to count profits, since there are none. Traditional IT is much more conservative in its business development planning than some of these new media/Internet types of firm, and perceived as less risky for obvious reasons. They too have displaced behemoths like IBM from pole position in IT, Microsoft and Intel being the key cases in point. This has yet to happen in biotechnology, but it almost certainly will because of the expert technical knowledge possessed by the entrepreneurial firms. Nevertheless, despite the present power of clusters, firms in them still require large corporations as clients and milestone project funders.

Finally, while new economy markets are dynamic, keeping first-mover advantage often reveals market failures. Supporting fledgling new media businesses and whole strands of the industry requires concerted efforts by a range of private and public actors operating associationally. This is well exemplified by the support given to the essentially private 55 Broad Street multimedia scheme, which is looking to the future of New York's position on a global basis. In Cardiff, a smaller-scale activity with roots in a relatively immature independent old media sector gains some valuable infrastructural support, human capital and global promotion from the public and private collaboration system put in place in Wales. In the final analysis, these are necessary but not sufficient to sustain businesses in swiftly changing fields like new media. Markets will dictate survival or annihilation, and markets are increasingly global, but paradoxically, as this contribution has shown, the creative spirits, innovative ideas and social interactions that make new media possible as commercial products are normally clustered in remarkably localized spaces of the new economy.

REFERENCES

Acs, Z. (ed.) (2000) *Regional Innovation, Knowledge and Global Change*. London: Pinter.

Braczyk, H., Cooke, P. and Heidenreich, M. (eds) (1998) *Regional Innovation Systems*. London: UCL Press.

Braczyk, H., Fuchs, G. and Wolf, H. (eds) (1999) *Multimedia and Regional Economic Restructuring*. London: Routledge.

Brail, S. and Gertler, M. (1999) 'The digital regional economy: emergence and evolution of Toronto's multimedia cluster', in H. Braczyk, G. Fuchs and H. Wolf (eds), *Multimedia and Regional Economic Restructuring*. London: Routledge.

Castells, M. and Hall, P. (1994) *Technopoles of the World*. London: Routledge.

Cohen, W. and Levinthal, D. (1990) 'Absorptive capacity: a new perspective on learning and innovation', *Administrative Sciences Quarterly*, 35: 128–52.

Cooke, P. (1990) *Back to the Future: Modernity, Postmodernity and Locality*. London: Unwin Hyman.

Cooke, P. (1992) 'Regional innovation systems: competitive regulation in the new Europe', *Geoforum*, 23: 365–82.

Cooke, P. and Hughes, G. (1999) 'Creating a multimedia cluster in Cardiff Bay', in H. Braczyk, G. Fuchs and H. Wolf (eds), *Multimedia and Regional Economic Restructuring*. London: Routledge.

Cooke, P. and Morgan, K. (1998) *The Associational Economy: Firms, Regions and Innovation*. Oxford: Oxford University Press.

Cooke, P. and Wills, D. (1999) 'Small firms, social capital and the enhancement of business performance through innovation programmes', *Small Business Economics*, 13: 219–34.

Cooke, P., Boekholt, P. and Tödtling, F. (2000) *The Governance of Innovation in Europe*. London: Pinter.

De Bernardy, M. (1999) 'Reactive and proactive local territory: co-operation and community in Grenoble', *Regional Studies*, 33: 343–52.

De la Mothe, J. and Paquet, G. (1998) *Local and Regional Systems of Innovation*. Dordrecht: Kluwer.

Edquist, C. (ed.) (1997) *Systems of Innovation*. London: Pinter.

Egan, E. and Saxenian, A. (1999) 'Becoming digital: sources of localization in the Bay Area multimedia cluster', in H. Braczyk, G. Fuchs and H. Wolf (eds), *Multimedia and Regional Economic Restructuring*. London: Routledge.

Giesecke, S. (1999) 'Determinants of successful S&T policy in a national system of innovation'. Unpublished paper, Economics University, Vienna.

Granovetter, M. (1985) 'Economic action and social structure: the problem of embeddedness', *American Journal of Sociology*, 91: 481–510.

Henton, D., Melville, J. and Walesh, K. (1997) *Grassroots Leaders for a New Economy*. San Francisco: Jossey-Bass.

Heydebrand, W. (1999) 'Multimedia networks, globalization and strategies of innovation: the case of Silicon Alley', in H. Braczyk, G. Fuchs and H. Wolf (eds), *Multimedia and Regional Economic Restructuring*. London: Routledge.

Lewis, A. (2000) *The New New Thing*. New York: Norton.

Longhi, C. (1999) 'Networks, collective learning and technology development in innovative high technology regions: the case of Sophia-Antipolis', *Regional Studies*, 33: 333–42.

Longhi, C. and Quéré, M. (1993) 'Innovative networks and the technopolis phenomenon: the case of Sophia-Antipolis', *Environment & Planning C: Government & Policy*, 11: 317–30.

Mansell, R. (2000) 'Knowledge and the Internet: the end of control?'. Sussex University Professorial Inaugural, Falmer, Science Policy Research Unit.

McLuhan, M. (1962) *The Gutenberg Galaxy: the Making of Typographic Man*. Toronto: Toronto University Press.

Nachum, L. and Keeble, D. (2000) 'Foreign and indigenous firms in the media cluster of Central London'. Working Paper no. 154, Cambridge University, Centre for Business Research.

Nonaka, I. and Reinmöller, P. (1998) 'Toward endogenous knowledge creation for Asian economic development', *in Wissenschaftszentrum Berlin Jahrbuch*. Berlin: WZB.

Pavlik, J. (1999) 'Content and economics in the multimedia industry: the case of New York's Silicon Alley', in H. Braczyk, G. Fuchs and H. Wolf (eds), *Multimedia and Regional Economic Restructuring*. London: Routledge.

Porter, M. (1998) *On Competition*. Cambridge, MA: Harvard Business School Press.

Putnam, R. (1993) *Making Democracy Work*. Princeton: Princeton University Press.

Rallet, A. and Torre, A. (1998) 'On geography and technology: proximity relations in localized innovation networks', in M. Steiner (ed.), *Clusters and Regional Specialization*. London: Pion.

Rogers, E. and Larsen, J. (1984) *Silicon Valley Fever*. New York: Basic.

Russ, A. (1998) 'Multimedia: a new industry in a global city'. Unpublished MSc thesis, Department of Geography, King's College, London.

Safer, S. (2000) 'Get 'em while they're young: America's teens may be leading the handheld revolution', *Red Herring*, 78: 290.

Saxenian, A. (1994) *Regional Advantage: Culture and Competition in Silicon Valley and Route 128*. Cambridge and London: Harvard University Press.

Schitag, Ernst & Young (1998) *Germany's Biotechnology Takes Off in 1998*. Stuttgart: Schitag, Ernst & Young.

Schmitz, H. and Nadvi, K. (1999) 'Clustering and industrialization: introduction to the special issue', *World Development*, 27: 1503–14.

Scott, A. (1998) 'From Silicon Valley to Hollywood: growth and development of the multimedia industry in California', in H. Braczyk, P. Cooke and M. Heidenreich (eds), *Regional Innovation Systems*. London: UCL Press.

Scott, A. (1999) 'Patterns of employment in southern California's multimedia and digital visual effects industry: the form and logic of an emerging labour market', in H. Braczyk, G. Fuchs and H. Wolf (eds), *Multimedia and Regional Economic Restructuring*. London: Routledge.

Tödtling, F. and Sedlacek, S. (1997) 'Regional economic transformation and the innovation system of Styria', *European Planning Studies*, 5: 43–64.

Von Hippel, E. (1988) *The Sources of Innovation*. Oxford: Oxford University Press.

Wolff, A. (1998) *Burn Rate*. London: Orion.

18

Globalization and the Structure of New Media Industries

TERRY FLEW
and
STEPHEN McELHINNEY

TERRY FLEW
and
STEPHEN McELHINNEY

GLOBALIZATION AND THE MEDIA

Globalization is a term used to describe, and make sense of, a series of interrelated processes including:

- internationalization of production, trade and finance, with the rise of multinational corporations, reductions in cross-border tariffs upon flows of goods and services, the deregulation of financial markets, and the rise of Internet-based electronic commerce;
- international movements of people (as immigrants, guest workers, refugees, tourists, students and expert advisers), the development of diasporic and emigrant communities, and the increasingly multicultural nature of national societies;
- international communications flows, delivered through telecommunications, information and media technologies such as broadband cable, satellite and the Internet, which facilitate transnational circulation of cultural commodities, texts, images and artifacts;
- global circulation of ideas, ideologies and 'keywords', such as the so-called export of 'Western values', democratic aspirations or environmental consciousness;
- establishment of international regimes in intellectual property which entrench the enforceability of ownership of knowledge and information;
- emergence of local resistance to globalization for domestic political and cultural objectives, by both nationalist movements of the political right, and progressive and anti-colonialist movements of the left;
- the development of international organizations, including regional trading blocs such as the European Union (EU), the North American Free Trade Agreement (NAFTA), the Association of South East Asian Nations (ASEAN) and the Asia–Pacific Economic Cooperation grouping (APEC);
- cultural, professional and standards bodies such as UNESCO, the World Trade Organization, the World Intellectual Property Organization, the European Broadcasting Union, the Asian Broadcasting Union and the International Telecommunication Union;
- the increasingly significant role played by global non-government organizations (NGOs), such as Amnesty International, Greenpeace, Médecins sans Frontières and the Red Cross in domestic and international politics;
- the growing significance of international law to national policies, such as the United Nations Convention on Human Rights, the 'Millennium Round' of the World Trade Organization and the Kyoto Convention on greenhouse gas emissions.

Developments in communications media have an important role in all of these processes of globalization. The technological forms that are used to communicate messages influence the communicative practice of individuals and institutions, and this in turn influences societies and cultures. Developments in communications media are important in all processes of globalization. There are three dimensions to this centrality of media to globalization. First, media constitute the technologies and service delivery platforms through which international flows are transacted. Second, the media industries are leaders in the push towards global expansion and integration. Finally, the media provide informational content and images of the world through which people seek to make sense of events in distant places.

Manuel Castells (1996; 2000) has provided an important contribution by placing communications media at the centre of the changes that are driving globalization. Castells argues that the period since the late 1970s has seen discontinuous historical and structural change in the economy, society and culture, driven by advances in information and communications technologies (ICTs). Central elements of this information technology paradigm, or *informational society*, include the pervasive effects of ICTs through all forms of social interaction, the networking logic of systems and social relationships and the flexibility of these networks, and the convergence of specific technologies into a highly integrated system. As a result, economies have become globally interdependent, with effects felt through entire societies as information and communications establish new forms of relationships 'between economy, state and society in a system of variable geometry' (1996: 1). While there has been an integrated capitalist world economy since the sixteenth century, the current configuration is, for the first time, a global economy 'with the capacity to work as a unit in real time on a planetary scale' (1996: 92). While both globalization and ICTs have a 'fetish' element to them, in that both are utilized as ideological rationales for political change centred around neoliberal projects to deregulate national economies (Sussman, 1997), Castells cautions that 'the prophetic hype and ideological manipulation characterizing most discourses on the information technology revolution should not mislead us into underestimating its truly fundamental significance' (1996: 30).

The role played by communications media in overcoming barriers of space and time should not be seen as being without historical precedent, although the scale, pace and pervasiveness of change are historically unique. James Carey (1992a) has drawn attention to the profound significance of the development of the telegraph in the 1840s, which enabled the rise of the modern, multidivisional corporate enterprise, monopolistic markets and futures exchanges. The telegraph was at the centre of the development of the electrical goods industries; and it restructured everyday language through its impacts on popular journalism, as it required a new economy of writing style and made the concept of objectivity central to reportage. Most importantly, it meant that the movement of messages was separated from the movement of physical objects, and hence communication separated from transportation, and this 'freed communication from the constraints of geography' (1992a: 204). Associated with this, it changed the way in which communication was thought about, and provided a new model – the transmission model – for conceiving of communication as a social practice. Carey points out that, in this sense, 'the telegraph was not only a new tool of commerce but also a thing to think with, an agency for the alteration of ideas' (1992a: 204).

Media have been given a particularly significant role in globalization debates, because of the particular part that global media are seen as playing in the cultural weakening of the bonds which tie people to nation-states. Drawing upon Ernest Gellner's (1983) observation that culture provides the 'political roof' that links a nation to its people, and Benedict Anderson's (1991) account of the historical role of popular print media in enabling the development of the modern nation as an 'imagined community', some have seen the rise of global broadcast media as leading to an uncoupling between polity and culture within the nation, which is analogous to the uncoupling of polity and economy associated with the rise of multinational corporations and global financial markets. Utilizing the work of Canadian communications historian Harold Innis (1951), Joshua Meyrowitz (1985) and James Carey (1992b) have observed that while print culture was associated with the rise of nationalism, as it promoted continuity over time, decentralization and regional differentiation, broadcast media were space binding, promoting centralization of production, decentralization of dissemination, and international distribution. Drawing upon Anthony Giddens' (1997) interpretation of globalization as a 'consequence of modernity' that involves a 'disembedding' of social relations from local contexts, Chris Barker has described television as simultaneously 'globalized because it is an institution of capitalist modernity' and as 'contributing to the globalization of modernity through the world-wide circulation of images and discourses' (1997: 13). In other words, global media, and global broadcast media in particular, are globalizing in their form as well as their content, and are controlled by corporate interests keen to expand their global market reach. Arjun Appadurai has referred to global mediascapes as one of the five 'landscapes' of global cultural flow – the others being ethnoscapes, technoscapes, financescapes and ideoscapes – which have generated 'fundamental disjunctures between economy, culture and politics' (1990: 296) in all societies over the last 20–30 years.

These views represent conventional starting points for conceptualizing globalization of the media. However, they also reflect perceptions that are rooted in the study of North American or European media discourses. There is equal merit in recognizing that media industries are regulated by national governments, and the markets for information and entertainment are national as well as international. Most nations continue to impose restrictions on ownership and control over electronic media industries and often use quotas or censorship to inhibit the importation of content (OECD, 1999: 133–4). Moreover, media companies with ambitions to build global or multinational markets for services or products often face market hurdles including linguistic differences, preferences for local content and collapsing economic conditions. Even new media technologies like the Internet face regulation, although the traditional mechanisms used by governments have much less effect than on traditional broadcasting and related industries. Access to computers, reliable telecommunications infrastructure and capacities to afford services are market factors inhibiting globalization. Furthermore, linguistic and cultural factors ensure that only the educated and largely English-speaking elites can use global services, while inequalities of access mean that only about 2–3 per cent of the world's population have accessed the Internet, with 84 per cent of Internet users being in 15 countries, and 40 per cent of Internet users being in North America (Cyberatlas, 2000). Similar levels of disparity are evident in the infrastructure of the new global information economy, including the secure servers with encryption technologies sufficient to support contemporary e-commerce and other forms of online business services and government operation. The OECD (2000a) reported that 95 per cent of the 74,000 secure servers in the world were located in member countries whilst 52,000 were located in the US alone.

THE POLITICAL ECONOMY OF GLOBALIZATION: 'STRONG GLOBALIZATION' THEORIES AND THEIR CRITICS

Any listing of the trends and developments associated with globalization raises the issue of whether, as Castells proposes, such developments point to a *qualitative* shift in the pattern of economic, social, political and cultural relations within and between states and societies, or whether they are extensions and intensifications of more long-standing trends, i.e. part of a *quantitative* change. There are also important questions of the relationship between local forms of agency and external structural imperatives. Should globalization be seen as an external force imposing changes upon local and national laws, institutions and policies, or as a set of developments induced primarily by these institutions? While communications technologies such as broadband cable, satellite and the Internet are often presented as forcing nation-states to become more

open to globalizing influences, others, such as Linda Weiss in her analysis of the role of the state in East Asian industrialization, have argued that 'globalization must be seen as a politically rather than a technologically induced phenomenon' (1997: 23).

Globalization theories have been developed in the fields of economics, sociology and politics, as well as in media, communications and cultural studies. So-called *strong globalization* theories argue that these developments mark out such a qualitative shift in societies that the analytical and normative categories that guided social analysis in the nineteenth and twentieth centuries, such as the nation-state, society, national economies and national cultures, will be less and less applicable. In arguing that globalization is a factor in the 'end of organized capitalism', John Urry presents a 'strong globalization' case in these terms:

> There has been a 'globalisation' of economic, social and political relationships which has undermined the coherence, wholeness and unity of individual societies. Such developments include the growth of multinational corporations whose annual turnover dwarfs the national income of many individual nation states; the spectacular development of electronically transmitted information which enables geographically distant units to be organizationally unified; the fragile growth of international state organisations which constrain the autonomy of individual nation states; the growth of means of mass communication which can simultaneously link 20–30 per cent of the world's population in a shared cultural experience; the possibility of technological disasters that know no national boundaries … There has been a 'globalisation' of economic and social relationships and a greatly heightened awareness of the 'simultaneity' of events and experiences occurring in geographically distant locations. (1989: 97–8)

In economic terms, globalization has been defined by the International Monetary Fund as 'the rapid integration of economies worldwide through trade, financial flows, technology spillovers, information networks, and cross-cultural currents' (1997: 1). An extreme interpretation of the impact of economic globalization was developed by Robert Reich, former Secretary of Labour in the Clinton Administration, who argued that the erosion of national economic sovereignty since the early 1970s had proceeded to the point where it was no longer possible to claim that 'citizens are in the same large boat, called the national economy … bound together … by a common economic fate', and that, in the United States context, 'as almost every factor of production – money, technology, factories and equipment – moves effortlessly across borders, the very idea of an American economy is becoming meaningless, as are the notions of an American corporation, American capital, American products, and American technology' (1992: 7, 8).

Economists have always recognized the international nature of economic transactions and, at least in the mainstream traditions, have seen international trade and investment as largely positive activities. Yet globalization is perceived as a challenge to mainstream economic theory, since, from Adam Smith and David Ricardo to John Maynard Keynes and modern macroeconomic theory, the working premise has been that of an inter*national* economy, or a world economy where transactions take place between sovereign nations and economic agents with an identifiable national economic base. The only major economic theorist not to have started from this working premise was Karl Marx, who argued with Freidrich Engels in *The Communist Manifesto* in 1848 that capitalism possessed a structural tendency towards globalization, as 'the need for a constantly expanding market for its products chases the bourgeoisie over the whole surface of the globe ... [and] the bourgeoisie has through its exploitation of the world market given a cosmopolitan character to production and consumption in every country' (Marx and Engels, 1969: 83).

Economists have cast serious doubts on the empirical and intellectual foundations of 'strong globalization' arguments. Paul Krugman (1997) accuses writers such as Robert Reich of peddling a form of 'pop internationalism' that distorts international trade theory by treating nations as competing entities, analogous to capital and labour. Political economists such as David Gordon (1988) have argued that the statistical evidence presented as proof of economic globalization is misleading, and that capital is considerably less globally 'footloose' and independent of the actions of nation-states than is apparent from many of the absolute figures that are used as evidence. A particularly misleading aspect of how evidence is used in globalization debates, noted by Andrew Glyn and Bob Sutcliffe (1998), is their focus upon trends in the manufacturing sector, which are then taken as indicative of the economy as a whole; the inclusion of services would reduce overall globalization trends, since services are considerably less internationally traded (and, in the case of many government services, less internationally tradeable) than manufactured goods.

In the most extensive critique of economic globalization theories, Paul Hirst and Grahame Thompson (1996) have argued that, while there has been an increase in international economic integration since the 1970s, this is not unique in international economic history since the overall level of international trade and investment in the period from 1890 to 1914 is equal to that of the late 1990s. Further, while there has been an increase in international direct investment by major corporations, most remain multinational corporations, operating in a number of countries but with a clearly defined national base, rather than transnational corporations, whose activities are largely outside a national base. Rather than leading to the demise of the nation-state, Hirst and Thompson propose that economic internationalization has been marked by parallel political processes, where supranational and regional organizations of government such as the European Union, NAFTA and APEC are developed and strengthened, but where the nation-state 'as the source and the respecter of binding rules remains central to an internationalized economy and society' (1996: 194). Like Gordon, and Glyn and Sutcliffe, Hirst and Thompson critique globalization theory on the basis of their belief that it presents an overly pessimistic view of the capacity of nation-states to control the activities of corporations, working from the 'race to the bottom' scenario, where the increasingly 'footloose' nature of capital is seen as generating a situation whereby 'capital will be increasingly able to play workers, communities, and nations off against one another as they demand tax, regulation, and wage concessions while threatening to move ... increased mobility of MNCs (multinational corporations) benefits capital while workers and communities lose' (Crotty et al., 1998: 118). By contrast, these theorists believe that new forms of economic internationalization can be responded to with 'the development of new forms of economic governance at the national and international levels' (Hirst and Thompson, 1996: 4).

Analogous debates about globalization have taken place in sociology and cultural studies. Robertson (1991), Waters (1995) and Shaw (1997) have posed the question of whether a global society has replaced or is superseding discrete national societies as the dominant structuring principle of social relations, with major implications for the methods of sociological analysis. Anthony Smith has expressed concern that such arguments are premised upon an overly rationalistic conception of culture as being in some sense determined by technoeconomic structures, and ignoring the 'obstinate fact' that 'national cultures, like all cultures before the modern epoch, are particular, time-bound and expressive ... [and] specific, historical cultures possessing strong emotional connotations for those who share in them' (1991: 178). Stuart Hall (1993) has expressed a similar concern that 'global cosmopolitanism', and a certain blindness to continuities of national cultural experience, are indicative of a certain 'wish-list' element of theories such as liberalism and Marxism, that see nationalism as essentially a transitory and political phenomenon, likely to decline over time as societies become more secular, rational and cosmopolitan. As a result, for Hall, these approaches 'expect, not the revival but the gradual disappearance of the nationalist passion [since] attachments to nation, like those of tribe, region, place, religion, were thought to be archaic particularisms which capitalist modernity would, gradually or violently, dissolve or supersede' (1993: 353).

Hall points out the one-sided nature of this account with reference to the re-emergence of 'small' or suppressed nationalisms in Europe, as the relative weakening of nation-states by global economic and supranational political entities opens up, paradoxically, new spaces for revised forms of 'local' culture and identity. While John Tomlinson (1997) accepts the argument that, in contrast to strong globalization theories, most people remain tied to particular places and territories, he believes that there is nonetheless a significant cultural deterritorialization which occurs less through the physical movements of people from one place to another than through a complex transformation of everyday experience – what he terms 'mundane cosmopolitanism' – and the transformation of localities themselves arising from complex global economic, political and cultural flows. Morley and Robins develop a similar argument in their analysis of European audiovisual culture, observing that while one of the implications of media globalization is that 'audiovisual geographies are … becoming detached from the symbolic spaces of national culture' (1995: 11), one of the consequences of this is a renewed concern with developing strategies to 'reterritorialize' the media and to link them to local territories and communities, even if these communities are increasingly 'imagined' and identity based rather than the common cultures of long-established nation-states.

MEDIA GLOBALIZATION: 'GLOBAL VILLAGE' OR 'CULTURAL IMPERIALISM'?

Two approaches to media globalization have been dominant. Mainstream economists and liberal communications theorists have emphasized the relationship between new technologies and markets, and argued that media globalization promotes new opportunities for shared information, borderless communication and global commerce. Further, they believe that global media encourage the spread of liberal democratic ideas and empower citizens worldwide against unjust forms of local authority, by allowing the 'whole world to watch' and witness such injustices. In *The Death of Distance*, Frances Cairncross concludes that: 'Free to explore different points of view, on the Internet or on the thousands of television and radio channels that will eventually become available, people will become less susceptible to propaganda from politicians who seek to stir up conflicts. Bonded together by the invisible strands of global communications, humanity may find that peace and prosperity are fostered by the death of distance' (1998: 279). Not surprisingly, such arguments find favour with the heads of the giant media corporations. Rupert Murdoch (1993) once famously argued that cable and satellite

broadcasting had not only 'been a key factor in the spread of freedom' worldwide, but would also 'liberate people from the once-powerful media barons'. This echoes the comments by Ted Turner when launching the 24-hour cable global news service CNN. 'We're gonna take the news and put it on the satellite,' said Turner, 'and then we're gonna beam it down into Russia, and we're gonna bring world peace, and we're gonna get rich in the process! Thank you very much! Good luck!' (quoted in Wark, 1994: 36).

For critics of global media, such as political economists and critical communications theorists, these trends have pointed to *cultural imperialism* or *media imperialism*. The political economy tradition has long drawn attention to the adverse political and cultural implications of the unequal distribution of international communications power and resources, and how they intersect with broader structures of dominance and Western hegemony in the international political economy. The cultural domination approach, associated in particular with North American political economists such as Herbert Schiller (e.g. 1969; 1976; 1989; Nordenstreng and Schiller, 1993) and Edward Herman and Noam Chomsky (1988), as well as theorists of the new world information and communication order such as Kaarle Nordenstreng and Cees Hamelink, has stressed the importance of the internationalization and commercialization of global communications to the status of the United States as the world's dominant capitalist economy. In *Mass Communications and American Empire*, the founding text of this tradition, Herbert Schiller argued that 'Nothing less than the viability of the American industrial economy itself is involved in the movement towards international commercialization of broadcasting' (1969: 95). Linking the study of communications dominance to theories of economic imperialism such as world systems and dependency theories, Schiller defined cultural imperialism in *Communications and Cultural Domination* as 'the sum of processes by which a society is brought into the modern world system and how its dominating stratum is attracted, pressured, forced, and sometimes bribed into shaping social institutions to correspond to, or even promote, the values and structures of the dominating centre of the system' (1976: 9).

Anxieties about the influence of global media on culture and values, as well as their direct political and economic power, were expressed at an international level through the new world information and communication order (NWICO) debate. This debate, which occurred through the United Nations Educational, Scientific and Cultural Organization (UNESCO) from the early 1970s and was led by 'Third World' or so-called 'non-aligned' nations, sought to use UNESCO and other international forums to call for a redistribution of global communications resources to redress international inequalities and enable the development of stronger national and regional communications systems in the developing world. The NWICO debate peaked with the submission of the MacBride Report, *Many Voices, One World*, to the 1980 UNESCO general conference in Belgrade, but declined in the face of hostility from the United States and Britain in particular, who withdrew their funding from UNESCO in 1985 (Gerbner et al.,1994).

In a major recent contribution to this literature, Edward Herman and Robert McChesney (1997) have outlined in great detail the rise of global media corporations such as News Corporation, Disney and Time Warner, and shown how their global expansion in the 1980s and 1990s was facilitated by national policies of trade liberalization, deregulation of media markets, telecommunications privatization, and the winding-back of funding to national public broadcasters and other non-commercial media and cultural forms. They argue that this expansion has not been primarily the result of technological change or market competition, but is indicative of the extent of transnational corporate influence over national policy-makers and the hegemonic role that has been played by global media in the international dissemination of ideas. For Herman and McChesney, the global media are the 'new missionaries of global capitalism', and their adverse consequences include the spread of individualistic values, displacement of the public sphere, the strengthening of conservative political forces worldwide, and the erosion of local cultures.

Oliver Boyd-Barrett (1998) distinguishes the cultural domination models, based upon neo-Marxist world systems theory, from approaches more directly rooted in Marxist political economy and the Gramscian model of cultural hegemony (see Brewer, 1980 for a discussion of these distinctions). The latter approaches have been critical of the reductive nature of the 'cultural dominance' model and its inadequate treatment of 'local' conditions, lived experience, and the diversity of forms taken by what Annabelle Sreberny-Mohammadi terms 'the many ordinary, everyday ways that life in the South has been affected by the social structures of imperialism' (1997: 51). In particular, the focus upon conflicts and inequalities between nations in a global state system, and the 'diplomatic' solutions proposed by the NWICO framework, were seen as having the danger of downplaying structures of domination and resistance within nation-states, where the rhetoric of cultural nationalism could be used to promote a conservative and highly regressive national cultural politics (Mattelart et al., 1984).

Two other changes in the dynamics of media globalization were seen as challenging the assumptions of the cultural domination model. First, the process of globalization, and the centrality of communications technologies to this process, meant that models of dependency which assumed direct conflicts with a politically and geographically defined power, and the capacity of the nation-building state to represent mass popular aspirations for 'independence', were becoming less adequate as a way of mapping the relations between economic, political and cultural flows in the world system and their local and national impacts (Canclini, 1986; Martin-Barbero, 1993). Second, the pattern of global media flows has become more complex, as new patterns of audiovisual flow emerged around geolinguistic regions, particularly among Spanish-speaking and Portuguese-speaking communities, and Indian, Chinese and Arabic communities worldwide (Sinclair et al., 1996).

An issue of particular relevance to all critical theories of global media is the relationship between United States hegemony in the global system and the 'soft power' deriving from US media and cultural exports and their impacts upon the culture and values of importing societies. Joseph S. Nye Jr, Assistant Secretary of Defense for international affairs in the Clinton administration, succinctly defined 'soft power' as the 'ability to achieve desired outcomes in international affairs through attraction rather than coercion. It works by convincing others to follow, or getting them to agree to, norms and institutions that produce the desired behaviour. Soft power can rest upon the appeal of one's ideas or the ability to set the agenda in ways that shape the preferences of others' (quoted in Thussu, 1998: 66–7). Jesus Martin-Barbero has observed that, in assessing the relationship between global media and cultural hegemony in Latin America, 'Much more than the many percent of programmes imported from the United States (including programme formats), what will really affect us will be importing the US model of television' (1988: 457). Sinclair et al. make a similar observation in critiquing the cultural imperialism theory which, they argue, 'failed to see that, more fundamental than its supposed ideological influence, the legacy of the USA in world television development was in the implantation of its systemic model for television as a medium – the exploitation of entertainment content so as to attract audiences which could then be sold to advertisers' (1996: 9).

CASE STUDIES IN MEDIA GLOBALIZATION: DISNEY AND NEWS CORPORATION

Disney

The Disney Corporation was founded in the late 1920s as a family company, and stands as an emblematic symbol of media globalization on the basis of near universal recognition of its children's film and television characters, most famously Mickey Mouse, and its famous theme parks and resorts. Its status as a leading global media corporation, rather than an American media corporation that exports cultural product, can be linked to the successful restructuring of the organization in the mid 1980s, led by Michael Eisner. The 1990s have been referred to as the 'Disney decade', as the company shifted its focus to films and, particularly with its $19 billion takeover of Capital Cities/ABC in 1995, television. Disney's ascendancy in marketing media products to children has been strengthened by the capacity to profitably spin off home video sales, merchandise and other consumer products from successful animated films such as *The Little Mermaid, The Lion King, Aladdin, Beauty and the Beast, 101 Dalmatians* and *Pocahontas*. At the same time, Disney subsidiaries such as Touchstone and Miramax have successfully distributed such decidedly 'un-Disney' films as *Pulp Fiction, Scream* and *Armageddon*, while Disney's control of the ESPN sports network, acquired with the ABC takeover, has given it, in the words of one Disney executive, 'two horses to ride in foreign markets, not just one' (quoted in Herman and McChesney, 1997: 83).

While Disney has always embodied themes that are today associated with globalization, such as the famous 'It's a small world' song that concluded *Wonderful World of Disney* television programmes and remains a core Disney philosophy, the Disney corporation is an archetypal American corporation that has internationalized its operations. Janet Wasko (2001) quotes *Fortune* magazine's 1989 description of Disney as 'the archetypal American corporation for the 1990s: a creative company that can move with agility to exploit international opportunities in industries where the US has a competitive advantage'. Its internationalization strategies have occasionally struck problems, most famously in the case of EuroDisney (now Disneyland Paris) when it opened in 1992, when eggs were thrown at Disney executives in outrage at cultural imperialism and over generous subsidies from the French government, but criticism of the 'Disney universe' as constructed through its texts, labour relations strategies and approach to consumers is as strong inside the United States as it is in the rest of the world (2001: Chapters 5, 8). It will always be a magnet for critiques of cultural imperialism, in part (and paradoxically) because of its centrality to American popular culture. Wasko discusses this in relation to negotiations between Disney and the University of Oregon about their shared ownership of a duck as a mascot, where Disney could negotiate a contract that had minimal detail about licensing and use of the mascot because, in the words of Matt Dyste, Director of Merchandise Marketing and Licensing at the University of Oregon, 'They assume that their culture is so seeped into you, that you know what that means' (quoted in Wasko, 2001).

News Corporation

In contrast to Disney, News Corporation is perhaps the most truly 'global' of major media corporations. While it is a company incorporated in Australia, and Australia is the place of birth of its CEO, Rupert Murdoch, News Corporation in 1999 acquired 74 per cent of its revenue from the United States, 17 per cent from the United Kingdom and Europe, and 9 per cent from 'Australasia', incorporating interests in Australia, Asia and the South Pacific. News Corporation is, as Herman and McChesney observe, 'the archetype of the twenty-first century global media firm ... and is the best case study for understanding global media firm behaviour' (1997: 70). This is partly due to its phenomenal global reach, operating across different media – books, newspapers, magazines, broadcast TV, cable and satellite TV, films, music and the Internet – and across six continents, making it 'the first vertically integrated entertainment-and-communications company of truly global reach' (Shawcross, 1997: 399). It also indicates the influence of the 'Murdoch style' over other media conglomerates, which has involved identifiable leadership, a corporate strategy of global expansion and risk-taking, a strong orientation towards popular culture and sports as globally tradable cultural commodities, and a capacity to exercise political influence through control over popular media.

The latter two elements have been the most controversial. Murdoch-owned media have been accused of 'dumbing down' the populations of the United States and Britain. Fox Television, which Murdoch established as a fourth broadcast TV network with Barry Diller in 1987, was criticized for its new style of programmes, including 'reality TV' formats such as 'Cops' and 'America's Most Wanted', as well as 'dysfunctional family' comedies such as 'The Simpsons' and 'Married ... with Children'. In Britain, the relentlessly tabloid style of newspapers such as *The Sun* and *News of the World* attracted considerable criticism, as did Murdoch's heavy-handed approach to editors who failed to 'toe the company line', most famously Harold Evans, whom he hired and then fired as editor of *The Times*, when he took Britain's most prestigious newspaper over in 1981 (Evans, 1984). Perhaps more significantly, Rupert Murdoch was strongly identified in the 1980s with the conservative Reagan and Thatcher governments in the US and Britain. In Britain, Murdoch-owned newspapers such as *The Sun* are infamous for the 'Gotcha!' headline to report the sinking of the Argentine *Belgrano* battleship during the 1982 Falklands War; their partisan approach to the 1984–5 coal miners' strike; the sacking of journalists and printers associated with unions newspaper production moved to Wapping in 1986; and the *Sun* headline that accompanied the surprise re-election of the Conservative government headed by John Major in 1992, 'It was *The Sun* wot won it.' In the United States, journals such as the *Columbia Journalism Review* would condemn Murdoch as a 'sinister force' (quoted in Kiernan, 1986); in Britain, the enmity reached far deeper, and was perhaps best epitomized by the late TV scriptwriter Dennis Potter christening his cancer 'Rupert' and promising to 'kill Rupert Murdoch' as a last act before he died.

Of all the major media organizations, News Corporation has been the most active in the Asia–Pacific region. As a consequence in part of Rupert Murdoch's belief that the twenty-first century would be dominated by the economies of the Asia–Pacific region – including the United States – News Corporation purchased the Hong-Kong-based pan-Asian satellite TV broadcaster in July 1993. At the time, Murdoch confidently predicted that advances in communications and information technologies 'have proved an unambiguous threat to totalitarian regimes everywhere', as faxes, satellite broadcasting and cable-based communications 'make it possible for information-hungry residents of many closed societies to by-pass state controlled television channels' (quoted in Weber, 1995: 51). By 1995, however, such rhetoric had disappeared, as Star TV fashioned localized programming formats for its various Asian markets, partly in recognition of the importance of cultural and linguistic difference to audience viewing patterns, but also to be allowed broadcast rights in countries such as China and Malaysia. Governments in these countries, as well as Singapore, were able to restrict access to satellite TV channels delivering content they believed to be 'inappropriate'; indeed, to be able to broadcast into China, Star TV removed the BBC World Service Television channel from its service (Atkins, 1995).

Two points are apparent from the experience of Star TV in Asia. First, it disproves the claim that global media corporations are irrevocably undermining the capacity of national governments to control information flows, and that the extent to which such global media corporations can effectively operate in national territories is primarily determined by political rather than technological factors. As Will Atkins observes, in the Asian context:

> The state is not withering away in the area of electronic information control: instead, elements of the state are forming links with accommodating private sector partners in order to preserve elements of the broadcasting system most essential to power. (1995: 62)

Second, the experience of cross-border broadcasters such as Star TV, as well as Disney, MTV and CNN, has been that a significant degree of regionalization and localization of such services has been the condition for establishing commercially as well as politically viable transnational broadcasting services. In the words of a News Corporation executive, 'There's no money to be made in cultural imperialism' (Sinclair, 1997: 144). John Sinclair concludes from the experience of global media organizations choosing to 'go local' in the Asian region, as well as Latin America, that:

> The business of international broadcasting is driven by commercial considerations, not any desire for ideological domination as such, and the revival of the rhetorical critique of cultural imperialism has more to do with attempts by national governments to legitimize their positions in the era of global broadcasting, rather than with any actual cultural influence. (1997: 152)

MEDIA GLOBALIZATION AND THE ROLE OF TELECOMMUNICATIONS

Transformation of telecommunications over the last decades of the twentieth century by a combination of technological, regulatory and industrial change must be recognized as the key factor underpinning media globalization and the rise of new media industries and services such as the Internet and increasingly interactive broadcasting platforms. From the outset, the liberalization and privatization programmes begun in the UK during the late 1980s and steadily undertaken throughout Europe, Latin America, Southern Africa and the Asia–Pacific during the 1990s transformed telecommunications systems from relatively static national utilities charged with the supply of telephone and often postal services to become a dynamic engine of the global economy and communications infrastructure (OECD, 1999).

Liberalization and privatization drew a vast amount of investment capital to the sector for a variety of reasons. First, there was recognition that telecommunications infrastructures would underpin the new economy as distribution and transmission platforms. Second, telecommunications had become an almost ubiquitous utility (primarily in developed economies) via long-standing universal service programmes that had required national telephone utilities to build infrastructures reaching almost every household and business. Third, these infrastructures had been increasingly upgraded to provide digital or high-speed data capability to support wireless, Internet or cable connections. Finally, a new generation of personal communications technologies, including mobile telecommunications (e.g. Bluetooth, Symbian and WAP), was increasingly capable of carrying information and entertainment services that were central to the emerging information economy and associated practices that can be described under the emerging descriptive lexicon of 'e-commerce', 'e-health', 'e-government', 'e-business' and so on (see OECD, 1999; ITU, 2000).

The scale of the growth in telecommunications and the size of the leading corporations illustrate the sector's power in the global economy and relevance to the expansion of services provided by media industries. According to the ITU, investment and turnover generated by these reforms to telecommunications during the 1990s are staggering, with the market capitalization of some of the larger global corporations being larger than the gross domestic product in many developing countries (ITU, 2000). Another indicator of the importance of telecommunications as a driver of the new economy can be derived from uptake of mobile telephony including that geared toward the sophisticated interactive information and entertainment services. In a comprehensive survey of mobile communications, the International Telecommunication Union (ITU, 1999) illustrated the growth in the sector with subscribers rising from 11m in 1990 to more than 500m globally in 2000, and with more than 250,000 people connecting to new services each day. Likewise, the growth of telecommunications spawned innovative suppliers of new communications technologies that provide the human interface with new media. Increasingly, globalized suppliers including Nokia, Motorola and Ericsson have created the technologies which have placed new media in our pockets instead of desktops, lounge rooms and offices (see ITU, 2000).

Deutsche Telekom

While telecommunications has not generated the same level of scrutiny as global media industries, it is worth presenting a case study of Deutsche Telekom, which is one of the largest providers of communications services in the world. Deutsche Telekom (DT) began its development through the split and partial privatization of Deutsche Bundespost into separate telecommunications and postal operations in 1989 during the tumultuous events associated with the reunification of Germany. The reform programme, like those undertaken in most countries, involved the separation of service provision from the regulatory and policy functions that had previously been combined within national utilities. DT began its global expansion through the initial step of revamping the telecommunications services in the former Eastern Germany. While the German government maintained regulatory monopolies for some of the services provided by DT, the corporation faced competition for value-added services, data transmission used by business and the emerging mobile market. As liberalization was sweeping across

European telecommunications markets, DT quickly began building alliances or acquiring stakes in regional communications, broadcasting and media companies to capture developing markets in Eastern Europe (e.g. Russia, Ukraine, Hungary, Czech Republic, Croatia, Poland and Slovakia), before expanding globally to provide services in 65 countries (Deutsche Telekom, 2000). Recognizing the challenges from increasingly global competitors, DT formed a joint venture alliance in 1994 with France Télécom and US carrier Sprint to establish Global One which came to operate voice, data and Internet services involving more than 1400 network access points in 65 countries and maintained the furthest-reaching ATM-based network to support financial transactions (Global One, 2000).

Illustrating the ITU's contention that telecommunications is an inherently unstable industry, DT, which by the late 1990s ranked behind AT&T and Japan's NTE as the third largest supplier of telecommunications globally (OECD, 1999), withdrew from Global One and established a joint venture with One-2-One (a former business unit of Cable & Wireless) to concentrate on growing its European presence (Deutsche Telekom, 2000). Like these other conglomerates which increasingly seek to reach global markets, DT remains deeply embedded in its 'home' market through provision of Internet services to 5.3m customers through T-Online, supports 7m online banking accounts (primarily in Germany) and delivers cable television services to 18m households (Deutsche Telekom, 2000). Thus DT, alongside Disney, News Corporation and the other giant global communications corporations (e.g. the UK's BT, Cable & Wireless and Vodafone; US entities AT&T, US West, GTE, Air Touch; Japan's IDC; and even Australia's Telstra), illustrates how telecommunications has been the third pillar underpinning globalization of new media through investment in networks, Internet and data services and development of consumer, business and government markets. Further, connection between telecommunications and computing conglomerates (e.g. AT&T and Phillips; US-owned but European-based ITT and France's Alcatel; Siemens and GEC, among others) illustrates the global financial, business and market shaping forces being generated by the effort for position in the new media and communications economy.

GLOBAL MEDIA AND NATIONAL POLICIES: INFLUENCES AND INTERSECTIONS

There are two important elements that act as regulators of the impact of global media in particular local and national cultures. The first is that of *audiences*. Interpretive approaches, drawing on cultural studies methodologies, have challenged assumptions that global media flows can be identified through measurement of the economic interests of participants. Proponents of these interpretive approaches have pointed to the need to come to terms with the *cultural* meanings that are derived from flows of content and the adoption of media practices, particularly by assessing the relationships with local societies and contexts. Ien Ang has drawn attention to the extent to which 'global media do affect, but cannot control local meanings'; as a result, 'the construction of a "global culture"... should not be conceived as a process of straightforward homogenization', but rather 'local cultures everywhere tend to reproduce themselves ... through the appropriation of global flows of mass-mediated forms and technologies' (1996: 153).

At a more empirical level, Michael Tracey (1988) has argued that globalization rhetoric disguises the extent to which US TV product tends to be less popular than local product in almost every country where both are readily available, as well as the degree to which the presence of US imports acts as a trigger to the development of local programming to meet the cultural needs and expectations of local audiences. These findings are supported by Straubhaar (1997), whose empirical analysis of the balance between local and imported programming in various Asian, Latin American, Middle East and Caribbean nations finds that levels of national television programming have been increasing in the majority of these countries in the period from the 1960s to the 1990s. Lent (1993) also identified a trend for substitution of imports from the US with local content in Thailand.

The issue of 'reterritorialization' has become increasingly possible with new media such as the Internet and the creative use of household information technology and entertainment equipment. One of the fundamental characteristics of the twentieth century was the mass migration of people across the globe. Many of these diasporic communities have sought to remain connected with originating cultures by maintaining links through use of media and communications systems. Cunningham and Sinclair (2000) illustrate the point with research on the ways that Thai, Vietnamese and Filipino migrants have built communities and remain engaged with home societies with a mixture of old and new media. A variety of mechanisms maintaining videotape libraries, programmes on community radio and television services, websites, and commercial pay-TV services (Cunningham and Sinclair, 2000). Such global media flows are illustrative of media globalization, but not of cultural imperialism.

Such trends are a reminder of the second major element regulating media globalization, which is *public policy*, and the role it plays in regulating the relationships between global flows and their local impacts within the nation-state. Philip Schlesinger has proposed that national media and cultural policies can be seen as exercises in 'communicative boundary maintenance', out of which emerge distinctive national media cultures, and particular configurations of local and imported media content and styles (1991: 162). This is particularly apparent in broadcasting, where national public broadcasters, national regulatory systems and audience preferences for locally produced material have intersected with economic and technological forces that promote imported programming, and political, cultural and linguistic factors which make particular countries more or less open to imported English-language content from the United States. Countries such as Australia, Brazil, Canada and Mexico, which have always been highly exposed to globalizing cultural influences, have developed 'hybrid' programme forms that negotiate local, national and international cultural markets. Sustained exposure to overseas television programming has been in these instances the trigger for strengthening national production systems, through protectionist cultural policies of *lé défi américain* (Schlesinger, 1991), cosmopolitan programme formats which 'play at being American' (Caughie, 1990), or the fashioning of 'national champions' which can compete in definable global audiovisual markets, such as 'soaps' and *telenovellas* (Sinclair et al., 1996; Moran, 1998).

While national media and communications policies can set limits to the impact of media globalization on national media cultures, such policies can also act as catalysts for globalization. Media policies such as liberalization of media and communications markets are fundamentally shaped by the interaction of domestic politics with global structures and flows, out of which frequently emerge opportunities that become available to local industries. Although corporations based in Europe and North America are most often cited as driving globalization, it is the partnerships and opportunities they offer domestic businesses which often hold the key to market entry. The partnership between the US computer software giant Microsoft and powerful Australian media conglomerate Publishing & Broadcasting Ltd in Australia in building a web portal called NineMSN, that draws viewers from a range of existing television, print and software businesses to the new media, illustrates this trend (Barr, 2000). The Indian satellite broadcasting system provides another key to conceptualizing media globalization. As a vast and multicultural country, India has attracted foreign investors seeking to establish media and telecommunications businesses. Yet successful entry to the market was not possible until privatization allowed local media and telecommunications interests to develop joint ventures (Mehta, 1998; Thussu, 1999). These commercialized and privatized services could also improve the capacity to reach the various language markets within the country and address political and cultural considerations (Thomas, 1996).

Understanding new media globalization also requires the unpacking of content from the infrastructure that supports production, distribution and exhibition. Establishment of satellite broadcasting systems and telecommunications networks that support the seamless distribution of content is actively supporting the globalization of new media. These mechanisms are being used by local, regional and global businesses to build markets. Several Sino-Thai entrepreneurs have grasped the opportunity to provide the Thai market and regional countries with an alternative to imported programming from either Western countries or Japan. The Thaksin Shinawatra controlled Thaicom satellite carries telecommunications services, Internet services and television broadcasts from the five free-to-air Thai-language stations as well as the pay-TV services featuring CNN, BBC World and Nickelodeon to more than 70 million people in Thailand, Laos, Burma, Cambodia and Vietnam (Anon, 1997: 179–93; Thaicom, 2000).

Transnational corporations have long been associated with globalization. Communications and new media systems have supported the expansion of business beyond national markets to a system whereby components are developed, manufactured, assembled and sold far from where corporations exercise control over these activities. Communications technologies and new media are both enabling mechanisms for these practices and businesses in their own right that support the deterritorialization of industrial practices. Some transnational corporations provide communications infrastructures and software that support the activities of other businesses which may also be transnational in nature. More recently, the Internet has provided the platform for businesses to reach consumers or to provide services to other businesses. It has been argued that such arrangements lead to the *disintermediation* of traditional approaches to production, distribution and supply of goods and services. The Internet has allowed consumers to communicate directly with producers of certain types of goods (e.g. books, music and software) and services (e.g. banking, finance, government transactions and information) without the need to use existing channels including retailers. While these trends became increasingly prevalent in the late 1990s, business models remained in flux as these 'convergent service industries' models are tested by traditional and new media, communications and other service industries.

Intellectual property and copyright have become increasingly important factors in the globalization of media and related communications industries. Bettig (1996) notes copyright provides the means for controlling information and entertainment products and ensuring that they can be exclusively exploited in a particular national market. He also argues that the bulk of the information and entertainment products traded globally are controlled by a handful of corporations based in North America, Europe and Japan. Copyright allows content to be packaged and exploited in different ways across old and new media. For instance, a television programme can be packaged for free-to-air, pay-TV and cable systems. It can be modified and placed on other services and with digital technology reversioned through inclusion of different sound tracks for multiple markets. At all stages, the copyright owner is able to determine how the content is used and can generate a different pricing schedule for each use. With the establishment of global media markets, copyright has been an increasingly important issue in trade negotiations and international relations. US and European software and media industries, in particular, have lobbied for stronger international regimes that require governments to enact laws to protect intellectual property ownership rights that permit the commercial exploitation of content. As trade in intellectual property becomes an increasingly important sector in the US and European economies, with the growth of new media and related software industries, industry groups including the Business Software Alliance, the Motion Picture Distributors Association of America and the Recording Industry Association of America have sought to launch retaliatory trade actions against countries that do not adequately protect copyright, through organizations such as the World Trade Organization (WTO) and the World Intellectual Property Organization (WIPO) (US Trade Representative, 2000).

The capacity of new media to support the collection, use and storage of vast amounts of personal information by business and governments has underpinned debates on the need to build mechanisms which protect the privacy of individuals using the Internet and other technologies (Garfinkel, 2000; Whitaker, 1999). Use of technologies including cookies and web bugs to track behaviour across the web, and the increasing capacity to profile consumers using data gathered from purchases and page accesses, have encouraged the development of international agreements, including the Safe Harbor arrangement between the European Union and United States (see Federal Trade Commission, 2000), to manage the use of and trade in personal information (see Garfinkel, 2000). Both Simon Garfinkel (2000) and Reg Whitaker (1999) also argue that traditional notions of privacy have been curtailed by the development and application of new technologies to the collection and monitoring of personal information by both commercial interests and governments. The Internet and interactive media permit business and government to track and monitor individual behaviour, in ways that would have been previously impossible for even the most authoritarian regime, through the establishment of databases, data-mining techniques, and the application of e-mail monitoring and interception technologies including the 'Carnivore' system utilized by US security agencies. Equally, governments and businesses have sought to adopt technological and procedural measures including web seals and encryption to protect information they have collected from unauthorized access and use. This sensitivity has been argued to be a factor retarding uptake of e-commerce and other online services promoted by government and business including electronic health, banking and other records (OECD, 2000b).

To address the privacy implications of the Internet and other new media, the US government, member states of the European Union, Australia, Canada, Hong Kong, New Zealand and other nations have begun to develop legislative regimes to regulate the collection and use of personal information (OECD, 2000b).

GLOBALIZATION AND POLICY DISCOURSE:
FROM DEVELOPMENT COMMUNICATIONS
TO THE GLOBAL INFORMATION SOCIETY

One of the ways in which media globalization has influenced national media policies is at the level of dominant policy discourse. Theories of cultural and media imperialism had an analogy with the approach of development communication that emerged from countries in Asia and Africa in the mid 1970s. The approach of *development communication* was popularized as a means for governments in economically developing countries and post-colonial societies to determine which technologies and approaches they would take to improve the lot of their citizens. The approach encouraged governments to introduce policies that limited foreign control over local industries, emphasized the primacy of the domestic development task, encouraged cultural and information autonomy, valued democratic institutions and offered support for other countries following similar trajectories. Governments of developing countries often placed provision for basic needs above expenditure on advanced communications and media systems, in the belief that raising capital to pay for these infrastructures would drain national budgets, increase levels of foreign debt and require adoption of technologies that were not proven in local conditions. Moreover, there was recognition that skills to build and operate these systems would not be locally available or could be used for tasks that were more important. Other concerns related to the likelihood that foreign investors would only be interested in providing technologies to profitable customers concentrated in cities, earnings would be repatriated, and governments would lose the capacity to intervene directly in the provision of services.

From the late 1970s, development communication approaches were progressively abandoned as the technological transformation in media and communications industries increased the sophistication and interconnection of media and communications industries. Further, neoliberal economic theories became increasingly influential over national policy formation in both developed and developing countries. In the media and communications sectors, the neoliberal policy agenda could most readily be identified with the trend for countries to privatize national telecommunications monopolies, and to allow the private sector to introduce new television services such as pay-TV, cable and satellite broadcasting. The demise of the new world information and communication order (NWICO) agenda in multilateral forums such as UNESCO in the 1980s marked the symbolic end of development communications as a core element of international media and communications policies. By the early 1990s, incorporation of telecommunications and audiovisual policies into the disciplines of the General Agreement on Trade in Services (GATS), with its expectations of progressive trade liberalization and the elimination of differential treatment of domestic and foreign investors, constituted the dominant discursive and policy landscape informing communications policies worldwide.

A globalized, neoliberal policy agenda was given further impetus by the proposals of the Clinton administration for the establishment of a global information infrastructure (GII). US Vice-President Al Gore announced the core principles of the GII, which overlapped with both the GATS and the United States' own national information infrastructure (NII) initiative announced in 1993. These core principles included: promoting private investment; service development driven by free markets and competition; flexible regulatory systems; non-discriminatory access to foreign investors; and the more traditional policy objectives of universal access and universal service. The principles of the global information infrastructure and the global information society (GII-GIS) have been endorsed by the OECD, which looks toward 'the development of high-speed communication networks, and a set of core services and applications in digital format, into global integrated networks capable of seamless delivery' (OECD, 1997: 8). Through such initiatives, champions of the GII such as Al Gore believe that the GII will 'promote robust and sustainable economic progress, strengthen democracies, facilitate better solutions to global environmental challenges, improve health care and, ultimately, create a greater sense of shared stewardship of our small planet' (White House Press Release, 1995).

The concept of 'citizenship', with its political connotations of egalitarianism and nation building being central to most national media policies, was increasingly displaced by the idea that individual interests could be more readily encapsulated in a privately operated, liberalized and market-driven media and communications environment by applying the discourse of 'consumer sovereignty' (Golding and Murdock, 1989; Mosco, 1998). Such arguments appear, at first glance, to readily fit the new media environment of global communications networks, transborder delivery infrastructures, and technologies such as the Internet and digital broadcasting. Sir Alan Peacock has argued that consumer empowerment is the only sustainable policy option, since 'we have entered an age in which governments will have to accept that the thrust of technology and the growing experience of viewers and listeners of its benefits to them will make it well nigh impossible to exercise firm control over the broadcasting market' (1997: 302).

By contrast, William Melody has argued that much of the literature on the information society 'is either unsupported "blue sky" speculation about future technological and service possibilities, or promotional "hype" by the industries trying to sell the new technologies and potential future services' (1996: 243). Melody sees a critical role for public policy in shaping the development of national information societies, in the context of an emerging global information infrastructure, arguing that 'there will be as many "information societies" as there are societies [and] all countries should not try to charge down a single path emulating the perceived leaders in technological development at any moment in time' (1996: 244). Melody makes the critical point that much discussion about information society policies is focused upon developing the technical infrastructure through which to supply new media and communications services, with considerably less attention paid to developing a society of users of new ICTs, and the sorts of infrastructures that support universal low-cost access to basic information services.

Diane Northfield (1999) has undertaken a critical evaluation of national policies towards the new ICTs, and argues that while many countries have faced a similar range of issues, industry players and local interests, they have responded to these trends in distinctive ways. The effects of globalization in opening national markets to competition between local and foreign interests forced the establishment of policies to accommodate the 'information economy' in recognition that it would underpin other industrial activities as well as be an important sector in its own right. Confronted by the inadequacy of existing media and communications policies to deal with new business models and stakeholder demands, governments began to formally enunciate national policies for the 'information economy'.

From the mid 1990s, these countries began large-scale programmes to support the transition to the 'information society', often setting up agencies to coordinate activities between governments, the private sector and other relevant stakeholders. While general goals of building advanced telecommunications networks capable of broadband or high-speed Internet were raised and the concept of universal service for all consumers was promoted, national responses naturally varied depending on domestic circumstances. Some countries, including Australia, utilized the promise of liberalization and competition combined with government coordination and effort to make services available online to drive the information economy. Canada's 'information highway' policies had a similarly market-driven approach, although they emphasized questions of local content, access and cultural sovereignty. Other national approaches that were more state-led and *dirigiste* included the Singaporean 'intelligent island' model that relied on strong government intervention to create a networked society, Malaysia's multimedia super corridor (MSC) development that enticed foreign capital through development of a massive enterprise zone under different forms of governance, and South Korea's 'informatization' policy that sought to balance corporate sector demands and competing bureaucratic agendas (Northfield, 1999: 87–9; cf. Mathews, 2000). The effect of the globalization of capital has not only created difficulties for national governments in fostering growth of the information economy. The stagnation of traditional industries has forced many local and state governments to develop policies to attract investment in new media and communications sectors. Vincent Mosco provides a particularly ironic example of this trend, with analysis of how the state and municipal governments of the iconic twentieth-century industrial city New York have been forced to compete with other locations to attract new media companies to replace industries that have been able to shift to lower-cost locations by the combination of effective global communications systems and implementation of national information economy policies (1999: 103–16).

Conclusion

Globalization is a central trend of the late twentieth and early twenty-first centuries. Media and communications technologies, corporations and services have been central features of globalization both by being part of its structural formation and by transmitting its social, cultural and political consequences across geographic, linguistic and national boundaries. Rather than leading to the demise of nation-states or the homogenization of national cultures, it has involved the dual processes of synchronization of economic and technological infrastructures and the re-emphasis of valued cultural and social differences for domestic political purposes. In practical terms national governments have responded to global policy discourses promoted by the GATS and the GII by opening national markets to investment and trade across a range of media and communications properties while retaining ownership and control mechanisms that prevent foreign takeover of key industries. In recent years national governments, sensitive to domestic political and economic pressures, have sought to establish new media industries that enable local business to compete with transnational enterprises in local and global markets. Although governments have traditionally intervened in media and communications industries through direct investment, the market liberalization associated with economic globalization has forced sophisticated national regulatory responses. The new media industries have played a central role in these trends, but their capacity to exercise influence independently of supportive arrangements through the negotiating strategies of major economic powers such as the United States, the rules and norms established by multilateral agencies such as the World Trade Organization, and the support of particular national governments, is limited. The 'global information economy' is an unequal one, and one where transnational corporate power is certainly significant and perhaps hegemonic, but its basic contours have similarities with the distribution of power and resources in earlier economic regimes.

REFERENCES

Anderson, Benedict (1991) *Imagined Communities: Reflections on the Origin and Spread of Nationalism.* London: Verso.

Ang Ien (1996) 'Global media/local meaning', in *Living Room Wars: Rethinking Media Audiences for a Postmodern World.* London: Routledge. pp. 50–61.

Anon (1997) 'Thailand', in Alan Baskerville (ed.), *Asian Terrestrial Television.* Thousand Oaks, CA: Baskerville Communications Corporation.

Appadurai, Arjun (1990) 'Disjuncture and difference in the global cultural economy', in Mike Featherstone (ed.), *Global Culture: Nationalism, Globalization and Modernity.* London: Sage. pp. 295–310.

Atkins, Will (1995) '"Friendly and useful": Rupert Murdoch and the politics of television in South-East Asia, 1993–95', *Media International Australia*, 75: 54–64.

Barker, Chris (1997) *Global Television: an Introduction.* Oxford: Basil Blackwell.

Barr, Trevor (2000) *newmedia.com.au: The Changing Face of Australia's Media and Communications.* Australia: Allen & Unwin. pp. 20–39.

Bettig, R.V. (1996) *Copyrighting Culture.* Boulder, CO: Westview.

Boyd-Barrett, Oliver (1998) 'Media imperialism reformulated', in *Electronic Empires: Global Media and Local Resistance.* London: Arnold. pp. 157–76.

Brewer, Anthony (1980) *Marxist Theories of Imperialism.* London: Routledge & Kegan Paul.

Cairncross, Frances (1998) *The Death of Distance: How the Communications Revolution Will Change Our Lives.* London: Orion Business.

Canclini, Nestor Garcia (1986) 'Culture and power: the state of research', *Media, Culture & Society*, 10 (4): 467–98.

Carey, James (1992a) 'Space, time and communication', in *Communications as Culture.* New York: Routledge. pp. 142–72.

Carey, James (1992b) 'Technology and ideology: the case of the telegraph', in *Communications as Culture.* New York: Routledge. pp. 201–30.

Castells, Manuel (1996) *The Rise of the Network Society.* Oxford: Blackwell.

Castells, Manuel (2000) 'Information technology and global capitalism', in Will Hutton and Anthony Giddens (eds), *On the Edge: Living with Global Capitalism.* London: Cape.

Caughie, John (1990) 'Playing at being American: games and tactics', in Patricia Mellencamp (ed.), *Logics of Television.* Bloomington, IN: Indiana University Press. pp. 44–58.

Crotty, James, Epstein, Gerald and Kelly, Patricia (1998) 'Multinational corporations in the neo-liberal regime', in Dean Baker, Gerald Epstein and Robert Pollin (eds), *Globalization and Progressive Economic Policy.* Cambridge: Cambridge University Press. pp. 117–43.

Cunningham, Stuart and Sinclair, John (eds) (2000) *Floating Lives: the Media and Asian Diasporas.* Brisbane, Australia: University of Queensland Press.

Cyberatlas (2000) 'The world's online populations'. URL: http://cyberatlas.internet.com/big_picture/geographics/, accessed 22 July 2000.

Deutsche Telekom (2000) *The Company.* URL: http://telekom.de/dtag, accessed 3 October 2000.

Evans, Harold (1983) *Good Times, Bad Times.* London: Weidenfeld & Nicolson.

Federal Trade Commission (2000) 'Safe Harbor arrangements'. URL: http/:www.FTC.gov/privacy/safeharbor/slip.html, accessed 10 October 2000.

Garfinkel, Simon (2000) *Database Nation: the Death of Privacy in the 21st Century.* Cambridge, MA: O'Reilly and Associates.

Gellner, Ernest (1983) *Nations and Nationalism.* Oxford: Basil Blackwell.

Gerbner, George, Mowlana, Hamid and Nordenstreng, Kaarle (eds) (1994) *The Global Media Debate: its Rise, Fall, and Renewal.* Norwood, NJ: Ablex.

Giddens, Anthony (1997) 'The globalizing of modernity', in Annabelle Sreberny-Mohammadi, Dwayne Winseck, Jim McKenna and Oliver Boyd-Barrett (eds), *Media in Global Context: a Reader.* London: Arnold. pp. 19–26.

Global One (2000) 'Company history'. URL: http://www.global-one.net, accessed 2 October 2000.

Glyn, Andrew and Sutcliffe, Bob (1998) 'Still underwhelmed: indicators of globalization and their misinterpretation', *Review of Radical Political Economics*, 31 (1): 111–32.

Golding, Peter and Murdock, Graham (1989) 'Information poverty and political inequality: citizenship in the age of privatized communications', *Journal of Communications*, 39 (3): 180–95.

Gordon, David (1988) 'The global economy: new edifice or crumbling foundations?', *New Left Review*, 168: 24–65.

Hall, Stuart (1993) 'Culture, community, nation', *Cultural Studies*, 7 (3): 349–63.

Herman, Edward S. and Chomsky Noam (1988) *Manufacturing Consent: the Political Economy of Mass Media*. New York: Pantheon.

Herman, Edward S. and McChesney, Robert W. (1997) *The Global Media: the New Missionaries of Global Capitalism*. London: Cassell.

Hirst, Paul and Thompson, Grahame (1996) *Globalization in Question*. Cambridge: Polity.

Innis, Harold A. (1951) *The Bias of Communication*. Toronto: University of Toronto Press.

International Monetary Fund (1997) *World Economic Outlook*. Paris: IMF.

ITU (1999) *World Telecommunication Development Report 1999: Mobile Cellular/World Telecommunications Indicators*. International Telecommunication Union, October.

ITU (2000) *Mergers and Alliances 1995–1999: Merger Mania as Telecoms go Multimedia*. International Telecommunication Union. URL: www.itu.org, accessed 2 October 2000.

Kiernan, Thomas (1986) *Citizen Murdoch*. New York: Dodd, Mead.

Krugman, Paul (1997) *Pop Internationalism*. Cambridge, MA: MIT Press.

Lent, John (1993) 'Four conundrums of Third World communication', in K. Nordenstreng and H.I. Schiller (eds), *Beyond National Sovereignty: International Communications in the 1990s*. Norwood, NJ: Ablex.

MacBride, Sean (1980) *Many Voices, One World*. Paris: UNESCO.

Martin-Barbero, Jesus (1988) 'Communications from culture: the crisis of the national and the emergence of the popular', *Media, Culture & Society*, 10 (4): 447–66.

Martin-Barbero, Jesus (1993) *Communications, Culture and Hegemony: from the Media to Mediations*, trans. E. Fox and R.A. White. London: Sage.

Marx, Karl and Engels, Friedrich (1969) *The Communist Manifesto* (1848), with introduction by A.J.P. Taylor. Harmondsworth: Penguin.

Mathews, John (2000) 'Innovation: does Australia have anything to learn from Asia?' Paper presented to Brisbane Institute, 23 February. URL: http://www.brisinst.org.au/papers/matthews_Asia.html, accessed 22 July 2000.

Mattelart, Armand, Delcourt, Xavier and Mattelart, Michele (1984) *International Image Markets*. London: Comedia.

Mehta, A. (1998) 'Media regulation in India', *Media Asia*, 25 (2).

Melody, William (1996) 'Towards a framework for designing information society policies', *Telecommunications Policy*, 20 (4): 243–59.

Meyrowitz, Joshua (1985) *No Sense of Place: the Impact of Electronic Media on Social Behaviour*. New York: Oxford University Press.

Moran, Albert (1998) *Copycat TV: Globalization, Program Formats and Cultural Identity*. Luton: University of Luton Press.

Morley, David and Robins, Kevin (1995) *Spaces of Identity: Global Media, Electronic Landscapes and Cultural Boundaries*. London: Routledge.

Mosco, Vincent (1998) 'Political economy, communication, and labor', in G. Sussman and J.A. Lent (eds), *Global Productions: Labor in the Making of the 'Information Society'*. Cresskill, NJ: Hampton.

Mosco, Vincent (1999) 'New York.com: a political economy of the "informational' city", *Journal of Media Economics*, 12 (2): 103–16.

Murdoch, Rupert (1993) Address given at the launch of New World Communications, London, September.

Nordenstreng, Kaarle and Schiller, Herbert I. (eds) (1993) *Beyond National Sovereignty: International Communications in the 1990s*. Norwood, NJ: Ablex.

Northfield, Dianne (1999) *The Information Policy Maze: Global Challenges – National Responses*. Melbourne: Centre for International Research into Communications and Information Technologies (CIRCIT).

OECD (1997) *Towards a Global Information Society. Global Information Infrastructure/Global Information Society: Policy Requirements*. Paris: Organization for Economic Cooperation and Development.

OECD (1999) *Communications Outlook 1999*. Paris: Organization for Economic Cooperation and Development.

OECD (2000a) *Internet and Electronic Commerce Indicators Uptake*. URL: http://www.oecd.org/dsti/sti/it/cm/stats/newindicators.htm, accessed 29 September 2000.

OECD (2000b) *OECD Privacy Guidelines*. URL: http://www.cs3-hq.oecd.org/scripts/pwv3/pwhome/htm, accessed 10 October 2000.

Peacock, Alan (1997) *The Political Economy of Economic Freedom*. Cheltenham: Elgar.

Reich, Robert (1992) *The Work of Nations*. New York: Vintage.

Robertson, Roland (1991) 'Mapping the global condition: globalization as the central concept', in Mike Featherstone (ed.), *Global Culture: Nationalism, Globalization and Modernity*. London: Sage. pp. 15–30.

Schiller, Herbert I. (1969) *Mass Communications and American Empire*. New York: Kelley.

Schiller, Herbert I. (1976) *Communications and Cultural Domination*. New York: International Arts and Science Press.

Schiller, Herbert I. (1989) 'Not yet the post-imperialist era', *Critical Studies in Mass Communication*, 8: 13–28.

Schlesinger, Philip (1991) 'On national identity. I: Cultural politics and the mediologists', in *Media, State and Nation: Political Violence and Collective Identities*. London: Sage. pp. 139–51.

Shaw, Martin (1997) 'The theoretical challenge of global society', in Annabelle Sreberny-Mohammadi, Dwayne Winseck, Jim McKenna and Oliver Boyd-Barrett (eds), *Media in Global Context: a Reader*. London: Arnold. pp. 27–36.

Shawcross, William (1997) *Murdoch: the Making of a Media Empire*. New York: Touchstone.

Sinclair, John (1997) 'The business of international broadcasting: cultural bridges and barriers', *Asian Journal of Communication*. 7 (1): 137–55.

Sinclair, John, Jacka, Elizabeth and Cunningham, Stuart (1996) 'Peripheral vision', in John Sinclair, Elizabeth Jacka and Stuart Cunningham (eds), *New Patterns in Global Television: Peripheral Vision*. Oxford: Oxford University Press.

Smith, Anthony D. (1991) 'Towards a global culture?', in Mike Featherstone (ed.), *Global Culture: Nationalism, Globalization and Modernity*. London: Sage. pp. 171–92.

Sreberny-Mohammadi, Annabelle (1997) 'The many cultural faces of imperialism', in *Beyond Cultural Imperialism: Globalization, Communication and the New International Order*. London: Sage. pp. 49–68.

Strauubhaar, Joseph D. (1997) 'Distinguishing the global, regional and national levels of world television', in Annabelle Sreberny-Mohammadi, Dwayne Winseck, Jim McKenna and Oliver Boyd-Barrett (eds), *Media in Global Context: a Reader*. London: Arnold. pp. 284–98.

Sussman, G. (1997) *Communication, Technology, and Politics in the Information Age*. Thousand Oaks, CA: Sage.

Thaicom (2000) 'Satellite services'. URL: www.thaicom.net, accessed 1 August 2000.

Thomas, Amos Owen (1996) 'Global-diasporic and subnational-ethnic: audiences for satellite television in South Asia', *Journal of International Communication*, 3 (2).

Thussu, Daya Kishan (1998) 'Infotainment international: a view from the South', in *Electronic Empires: Global Media and Local Resistance*. London: Arnold. pp. 63–82.

Thussu, Daya Kishan (1999) 'Privatising the airwaves: the impact of globalisation on broadcasting in India', *Media, Culture & Society*, 21.

Tomlinson, John (1997) *Globalization and Culture*. Cambridge: Polity.

Tracey, Michael (1988) 'Popular culture and the economics of global television', *Intermedia*, 16 (2): 9–24.

Urry, John (1989) 'The end of organised capitalism', in Stuart Hall and Martin Jacques (eds), *New Times: The Changing Face of Politics in the 1990s*. London: Lawrence & Wishart. pp. 94–102.

US Trade Representative (2000) Special 301 Report. URL: www.ustr.gov, accessed 31 July 2000.

Wark, McKenzie (1994) *Virtual Geography: Living with Global Media Events*. Bloomington, IN: Indiana University Press.

Wasko, Janet (2001) *Understanding Disney: the Manufacture of Fantasy*. London: Routledge.

Waters, Malcolm (1995) *Globalization*. London: Routledge.

Weber, Ian G. (1995) 'The moral market: social vision and corporate strategy in Murdoch's rhetoric', *Media International Australia*, 77: 45–53.

Weiss, Linda (1997) 'Globalization and the myth of the powerless state', *New Left Review*, 225: 3–27.

Whitaker, Reg (1999) *The End of Privacy*. New York: New Press.

White House Press Release (1995) 'Remarks by Vice President Al Gore to G-7 Ministers Meeting on the Global Information Initiative'. Brussels, Belgium, 28 February.

19

Information Society and Trade and Industry Policy

ANDERS HENTEN and KNUD ERIK SKOUBY

This chapter is concerned with trade and industry policy aspects of information society concepts and policies. Two sets of concepts are thus the focus of attention, 'information society' and 'trade and industry policy'. Whereas information society questions are widely discussed in this *Handbook* and will not be subject to any extensive deliberation here, it should be noted that the information society concepts are seldom defined or explicitly discussed, and that this applies not only to information society visions of governments, companies, etc., but also to more academic expositions.[1] Although this is regrettable, we will not here venture into a definition exercise regarding the information society concept but use the term in the same manner as it is mostly used, as a framework or template for discussions regarding the changes in society that are related to the increasing production and usage of information and communication technologies and services.

With respect to the other concept, 'trade and industry policy', the delimitation of the area corresponds to what, for instance, the Department of Trade and Industry in the UK and the Department of Commerce in the US deals with, namely the establishment and development of favourable framework conditions for business development in both the production and distribution fields. Trade does not necessarily denote international relations. However, in our exposé, we pay special attention to the international aspects of trade and industry policy developments as the internationalization (or globalization) of the economy increasingly is related to the opportunities offered by information and communication technologies.

Elsewhere in the *Handbook*, other aspects of information society developments are dealt with, including implications for the development of democratic procedures, access to information, etc. Some of these subjects are more or less related to the issue of trade and industry policy. They have a bearing on trade and industry developments, and trade and industry policy cannot be isolated from other policy areas. This is often reflected in information society visions of governments where trade and industry policy initiatives are seen as part of a more encompassing strategy comprising both 'harder' matters concerning economic development and 'softer' issues regarding democracy, education, universal access, etc. In this chapter, however, we seek to concentrate on matters that are at the core of trade and industry policy questions, and other matters will only be dealt with if closely related to this subject.

The chapter first discusses more thoroughly the subject matter of the trade and industry policy aspects of information society concepts and policies. After that, the academic origins of the debates on information society developments are briefly traced. This is followed by a review of trends in economics and other social science research that have keenly affected information society discussions in the political establishment. We then concentrate on the information and communication equipment and service producing sectors themselves, and deal with internationalization aspects. A presentation is given of the main trends in the information society visions and plans that have cropped up since the beginning of the 1990s, and is followed by the summary and conclusion.

The idea and aim of the chapter are thus to review important academic trends and sources in the area of trade and industry policy aspects of information society discussions, and to relate these to the host of information society visions and policy declarations that have been issued by governments and other public authorities since the beginning of the 1990s.

A somewhat reassuring conclusion for the world of academia is that academic analyses seem to have had a visible impact on discussions among political decision-makers in this area. There is not a large gulf between academic analyses and the discussions taking place on the political scene. However, this may be an expression of a lack of sophistication on the part of the academic analyses of the societal changes related to the developments that have been dubbed 'information society', 'knowledge society' and 'network society'.

The main issue of the chapter is to examine the continued need for and existence of national trade and industry policies in the present information society settings characterized by fast technological developments in the information and communication technology fields, internationalization of the economy and a prominent position for liberal policies and ideology.

In trade and industry policies these developments have resulted in a turn away from direct forms of state interventionism towards more indirect forms of framework regulation. But they have not resulted in abolition of the need for or existence of national trade and industry policies as such. Where formerly trade and industry policies were concentrated on regulating more closed national markets, the policies of today focus on situating the national economies as advantageously as possible in the international economy.

This development is reflected in the great number of information society visions and plans that public authorities all over the world have been issuing during the past decade. Although it would seem to be a paradox that a liberalization of the national economies is followed by so much state planning, the reason is exactly the increasing internationalization of the economy that sets the need for new national trade and industry policies. However, these trade and industry policies are often not very specific but consist of broader vision statements, a fundamental belief that market forces will ultimately realize the visions, and an external framework regulation of the markets.

Trade and industry policies all over the world have much that is similar, but there are, of course, also many differences: policies in Europe, for instance, to a greater extent than US policies, are stretched between wealth and welfare policies. In spite of such differences, the chapter mainly deals with policy developments in Europe as these clearly illustrate the general trend from state interventionism to external regulation.

SUBJECT MATTER

In general terms, at present, the two most important areas of interest in the discussions of information societies are information and communication technologies and services, and internationalization – according not only to the information society visions and plans of public authorities but also to more theoretical analyses. ICTs and internationalization are the recurrent themes in most discussions of the matter.

Internationalization is the subject of a separate section in this chapter, where different approaches to the analysis of the internationalization of the economy are put forward, as well as different attitudes to the desirability of this development. There are, however, analysts who claim that the importance ascribed to internationalization (or globalization) is exaggerated and not based on well-documented facts. This applies, for instance, to Paul Krugman (1997) who has argued sharply against tendencies to pay too much attention to the importance of internationalization for the US economy. It also applies, for example, to Paul Bairoch (1996) who has analysed indicators of the degree of internationalization over a long period stretching back to the late nineteenth century, and who shows that internationalization was as developed at the beginning of the twentieth century as it was at the beginning of the 1990s. It furthermore applies to Paul Hirst and Grahame Thompson in their book *Globalization in Question* (1996). But apart from such 'dissenting' views, there is an overwhelming focus on internationalization as an important trend in trade and industry developments today.

ICTs are, obviously, of central importance, and there are (at least) two sides to this importance. One side is related to the production of information and communication technologies and services. The other side has to do with the implications of the usage of these technologies and services in other societal connections – where the usage in other business areas is the other half of the issue in this chapter.

In a way, the focus of attention with respect to ICTs has changed, moving to and fro during the past 40 years or so. In the first period, in the 1960s and 1970s, there was a strong interest in the usage of information technologies for the purpose of automating industrial production. However, as we shall see in the following section on the origins of the discussions on information societies, there was, at the same time, an interest in information-processing occupations. In the following period, the focus of attention shifted more to the production of information and communication technologies and services. This was clearly the case in the European Community where big research programmes were launched, with first and foremost the Research in

Advanced Communications in Europe (RACE) programme in the telecommunications field, demonstrating the interest in promoting the ICT sector in Europe by way of joint research initiatives.

Although this interest in promoting ICT production is still important, research interest gradually shifted back to the usage side during the 1990s. In the European Union, this shift is partly reflected in the changing focus of the telecommunications-oriented research programmes, from Advanced Communication Technologies and Services (ACTS) to Information Society Technologies (IST) today, where the title in itself illustrates both the central importance that the European Community attaches to information and communication technologies in the building of information societies, and the preferred framework and direction of information technology developments, namely their ability to support information society developments. But it is even more clearly reflected in the many information and network society vision statements by EU institutions or public authorities in individual member states.

However, lately one could claim that the centre of attention is returning to the production of information and communication products – however, this time with an emphasis on the production of services and content. There is a rising discussion concerning a new network economy or simply 'the new economy', which in some presentations of the theme also encompasses 'old physical' production areas if they adopt the new ways of trading and interacting electronically, but mostly deals with the production of information or knowledge content and goods and services that are related to networked technologies and services.[2]

Of course, this kind of overall characterization of research and discussion themes risks suppressing other important development trends. All along there have been analyses and debates regarding both the development of information and communication technologies and services and their implications for other production fields. However, the shifts in focus between the production of ICTs and the usage of ICTs still illustrate important development trends in the discussions, especially with respect to the shift in emphasis from the production side in the 1980s towards the implication side in the 1990s. This is very clear, at present, as the implication side is very much where the discussion is today.

There are, however, two important themes to be added to the issues of internationalization and ICTs in the characterization of central questions concerning trade and industry policy aspects of information society developments. The first one is services and their increasingly dominant position in the economy. Services constitute around 60–70 per cent of national GDP and occupations in developed economies. In developing countries, the picture is more mixed. However, services in developing countries also constitute the largest share of registered production.

It is, however, far from all services that are of interest in relation to the information society theme. Most services are 'old-fashioned' person-to-person services or services dealing with physical goods as, for instance, many repair services. However, information- and knowledge-intensive services constitute a growing share of services in total, and these services can, to different degrees, be entered on electronic media and transported on communication networks. There is, therefore, a special synergy between ICTs and information-intensive services, and services do play a special role in the development of information societies. This should be and often is reflected in trade and industry policy developments.

The second theme is liberalization. Since the beginning of the 1980s, a wave of liberalization has dominated politics and ideology, not only in the US, Europe and Japan but in almost every region of the world. It has strongly affected the communication areas as the societal organization of both telecommunications and broadcasting has been changed considerably. But it has also more generally affected the whole manner in which trade and industry policies are conducted. Liberalization and its many consequences with respect to new regulatory provisions were during the 1990s an important part of information society programmes. Liberalization of telecommunications and broadcasting are perhaps the most important results of the whole surge towards 'information societies'.

ORIGINS

Although debates on information, knowledge or network societies are most often seen as something new, they actually go back almost 40 years and even further if, for instance, some of the discussions on the importance of knowledge and the growth of services are included. We will, however, confine ourselves to the contributions that are directly linked to the present understanding of information society developments with a bearing on trade and industry policy.

The 'information society' concept itself can be traced back to the first half of the 1960s. A group of researchers from Napier University in Scotland have done a thorough investigation in this field, discussing the different possible origins of the concept and concluding that 'the lion's share of the credit for inventing the "information society"' must be assigned to the editorial staff of the Japanese journal *Haso Asahi* which ran a number of articles with titles including the words 'information society' from 1964 onwards (Duff et al., 1996: 119).

In the US, the term 'information society' was not used until 1970 where it first appeared in the discussions of the American Society for Information Science (1996: 118). However, the origins on the content side rather than the actual words are most often ascribed to the American economist Fritz Machlup, whose work *The Production and Distribution of Knowledge in the United States* was published in 1962. But as pointed out by Duff et al. (1996: 118), Machlup's book is concerned with the 'knowledge industry', not with the 'information society'.

Nevertheless, seen from our perspective in this chapter, Machlup's book constitutes an important starting point for the development of the conception and understanding of the trade and industry implications of the development of knowledge/information societies. He developed a foundation for analyses of the 'information economy' and documented the importance of knowledge production and distribution in a society that, at that time, was conceived as an industrial society.

Later, when this development had moved much further, Machlup's work was followed by a great many other 'measurements' of the information economy. The work led by Marc Uri Porat and resulting in the publication *The Information Economy: Definition and Measurement* (1977) was the most prominent example. While Machlup operated with a definition of knowledge production that centred on sectors producing what he saw as knowledge products, the team led by Porat included two information sectors, the primary and the secondary, where the primary sector comprises companies that produce information goods and services and the secondary includes all information services for internal use in public institutions and private companies. On this basis, it was concluded that, in 1967, 53 per cent of all labour income in the US could be ascribed to information work of different kinds (1977, vol. I: 8).

Another often-cited originator of information society analyses is Daniel Bell, who published *The Coming of Post-Industrial Society* in 1973. Although the term 'post-industrial society' cannot unequivocally be equated with the term 'information society', this book has since been seen as the foundation for subsequent theories concerning the information society concept – even though Bell was not too confident about the concept 'information society' himself (see, for instance, Duff, 1998). In his book, Bell analyses different aspects of what is now often summarized by the term 'information society': the composition of the workforce, the importance of information and knowledge in society, and the development of computer and communication technologies – all of which are issues that are still central to the discussions on information society developments.

The last origin to be dealt with here, even though many others might deserve mentioning, is the book by Peter Drucker, *The Age of Discontinuity* (1969). Even in 1969 Drucker was writing about the new 'knowledge technologies'. He also analysed what he called the development 'from international to world economy' (Drucker, 1994: 77–168) – a theme that is today vital in many analyses of the changing world economic conditions under the headline of 'globalization'. Last but not least, he stated that the economy could best be described as a 'knowledge economy', thus preceding the many subsequent claims for a knowledge economy by a couple of decades.

THEORIES OF INDUSTRIAL CHANGE

This section reviews trends in the theories of industrial and economic change that clearly have affected thinking on trade and industry policy among political and administrative decision-makers. It is, of course, conceivable that more popular writings, as for instance the works of Alvin Toffler (1980), John Naisbitt (1982) or Nicholas Negroponte (1995), have had a greater and more direct impact on decision-makers. However, here we concentrate on the more academic contributions.

The theoretical contributions that we have chosen are the so-called regulation school, theories on flexible specialization, and theories on changes in the technoeconomic paradigms. There are many common threads in these theories. They all focus on industrial and economic change and they all have a kind of holistic approach[3] to change, integrating different aspects of the societal complex – not just the economic aspect.

It could be argued, and with good reason, that by far the most influential trend in trade and industrial policy in the past 20 years has been liberalism and, with respect to economic theory, a return to neoclassical economics. This trend has had a strong impact both on theoretical thinking and on practical policies. However, we have in this section chosen to look at theories that take alternative approaches although they do not exclude the trend of liberalism (discussed later). Liberal thoughts can be incorporated and are often part of the theoretical complexes.

The *regulation school* clearly has – in its intention at any rate – a focus on the totality of societal formation. It is interested in the relationship between production, consumption and political intervention and it also examines the social struggles that lie behind the actual organization of the economy and the political sphere. The two most important concepts are 'accumulation regime' and 'mode of regulation' – where the first denotes conditions in the production sphere with an emphasis on the relations between capital and labour and capital growth, and the second deals with political organization and intervention. The interesting thing is to study how these two spheres relate to one another.

The regulation school is often called the French school of regulation, as some of the more prominent proponents are French: Michel Aglietta (1979), Alain Lipietz (1987) and Robert Boyer (1990). The regulation school clearly had its roots in a Marxist discourse on production relations, but has contributed to a much broader trend trying to explain the reasons for the economic (and political) crisis that began in the 1970s and the subsequent changes in the economic and political system. The emphasis has been on explaining how the accumulation regime and the mode of regulation were constructed in the post-World War II period, why and how this system has been breaking down, and in what direction the economic and political system is developing today.

The period from the end of World War II to the beginning of the 1970s is seen as a relatively stable period with steady economic growth. The period is called the Fordist period,[4] after Henry Ford as the paradigmatic representative of both mass production and relative welfare for workers. The Ford Corporation, when it really took off, paid higher wages to its employees than the average production site. This created a more stable labour force and also allowed for higher consumption by the employees. The paradigmatic system is thus based on a relationship and adaptation between mass production and mass consumption. The question is how such a system is created and what holds it together.

Part of the answer is that it is created in and by the social struggles between the classes and that it is held together, among other things, by the political governance of the state. There is a strong focus on the role of the state in the theories of the regulation school – which is obvious from its name. Markets are not seen as functioning independently of the political governance system. Markets are, to a large extent, politically constructed or, at least, held together by political regulation or intervention, and the founding economic theories of the Fordist period were much inspired by the writings of John Maynard Keynes who had, *inter alia*, emphasized the importance of stabilizing demand in order to avoid the worst fluctuations of the market.

However, this system gradually broke down during the 1970s and 1980s, triggered by the so-called oil crises of the 1970s. The period that followed was called the post-Fordist epoch by the regulation school, and the main questions being what caused this dissolution and what are the bases of a new period of economic growth.

The main reason for the dissolution of the Fordist period dealt with by the theories of post-Fordism is the increasing globalization of economic, political and ideological conditions. Another important reason is that there are limits to the positive relationship between production and consumption. Higher wages do facilitate more consumption and, therefore, increased production. But higher wages also cut down on the profits of investment, and consequently means were developed to undercut the strongholds of labour, comprising direct attacks on trade unions and changes in the organization of production.

Regarding globalization, the reason that these processes are so important to the regulation school is that production (and consumption) in the Fordist system, basically, is nationally oriented. With increasing globalization, national relations between production and consumption fall apart, there is increased international competition putting pressure on social contracts between capital and labour, and the role of the state is changed. This last point has, in the general debate, often been interpreted as a diminishing role for the state. However, proponents of the regulation school have been more inclined to see it as a new role for the nation-state. In the increasingly global marketplaces, nations tend to compete for production to be located in their country, competing on establishing the most favourable conditions for investment. But this does not necessarily mean bad conditions for employees and people in general. A new role for the nation-state is to develop conditions with highly qualified labour power, efficient infrastructures, etc. This line of thought has, for instance, been taken by Robert Boyer and Daniel Drache (1996).

But what is the relevance of all this to trade and industry policy in an information society context? There is not much emphasis on the role of information or of information and communication technologies in the regulation school. However, the reason that it is interesting is the description of the post-Fordist epoch with its new, more flexible production structures, its more global production structures, and its emphasis on new roles for the nation-state: all of these issues are central in today's information society discussion.

The *flexible specialization* theory, which is the second theoretical trend to be presented here, can be interpreted as a variation of the theory of post-Fordism, which, as described, also underlines the importance of flexible work processes in the new era. However, the strength of the flexible specialization theoretical branch is that it sheds light and concentrates specifically on production structures, whereas the regulation school is more concerned with the relations between production and political regulation.

The primary proponents of the theory of flexible specialization are Michael Piore and Charles Sabel with their book *The Second Industrial Divide* (1984). But many others have followed, and there is a whole branch of analyses based on the concept of flexible specialization.

Piore and Sabel (1984) explicitly reject the explanation for the economic crises of the 1970s which proposes that state regulation limits the initiatives of entrepreneurs. They also reject the idea that the oil crises have any significant importance. None of these rejections, however, is directed against proponents of the school of regulation, as they do not see the oil crises as anything else than triggering events, and as they have focused not on the limitations that national states might have put on private initiative, but on the changing role that the national state has had to adopt in the face of globalization. However, these rejections show that Piore and Sabel's theory of flexible specialization is focused on the inner working of production and that the reasons for the breakdown of the former system must be found in the structures of production themselves.

Piore and Sabel point at cycles of production where new uses of labour and machines are followed by periods of expansion, but which culminate in crises signalling the limits of these arrangements (1984: 4). According to the authors, there are two kinds of crises: one where the existing match between production and consumption falls apart, and the other where the type of technology chosen and the production structures around it reach their limits of expansion (1984: 4–5).

This second kind of crisis is the one that interests Piore and Sabel the most. They describe situations in which different technology paths are possible as 'industrial divides'. The first great industrial divide took place at the beginning of the nineteenth century, when the dominant mode of production chosen was mass production instead of flexible craft production. Today, we face a second industrial divide, as the mass production system has entered crisis and it is once again possible to choose a new path where craft-based flexible production methods constitute a feasible possibility.

The words 'choose/chosen' are well considered by Piore and Sabel, as they believe that there is no one 'natural' path of production structures but that production structures are social constructs. The authors propose that a structure of flexible specialization is the best 'choice' in the present situation.

The relevance of this theory for our discussion of trade and industry policy with regard to information society developments is once again the emphasis on new production structures and the possibilities in these more flexible systems. One would think that ICTs would have a prominent place in such systems as they allow for a better coordination of, for instance, networks of companies. And computer technology is also dealt with in the book, representing new and more flexible work tools instead of special-purpose machines used in the production of standardized mass production items. However, ICT is seen not as *the* vital technology in the development of flexible production structures, but as one important element among others (1984: 262).

The third and last of the theories that will be presented in this section is the so-called theory of *technoeconomic paradigms*. The most outstanding representatives of this theoretical trend are Christopher Freeman and Luc Soete (1982) and Giovanni Dosi (1984). Many of the thoughts in this theoretical trend are similar to those presented in the paragraphs on the regulation school and on flexible specialization. However, the theory of technoeconomic paradigms is characterized by a keener concentration on technology – especially technological innovation. It is, therefore, also often subsumed under the broader term 'innovation economics'.[5]

Technology has often not played any central role in economic theory, although there are some prominent exceptions: Adam Smith (partly), Karl Marx and Joseph Schumpeter. Mostly technology has been seen as an exogenous factor not to be dealt with more extensively. But in the theory of technoeconomic paradigms, technology is assigned a central role and is made the object of thorough analysis.

Four different kinds of innovation are depicted: (1) incremental innovations, which are the day-to-day improvements in existing production and marketing activities; (2) radical innovations, which are the results of more committed research and development activities which may result in wholly new products, but normally are confined to individual production sectors; (3) innovations of technological systems that are more fundamental innovations affecting a number of sectors; (4) changes in the technoeconomic paradigm, which affect the whole production system and constitute the basis for new production paradigms.

The understanding of the term 'paradigm' is borrowed from the philosopher Thomas Kuhn, whose book *The Structure of Scientific Revolutions* (1962) analysed the developments in science as structured by paradigmatic ideas changing over time. In the theory of technoeconomic paradigms this understanding is transferred to the field of production where succeeding technoeconomic paradigms are seen as based on different technologies and associated organizations of production.

The first paradigm or wave in the industrial era from 1780 to 1840 was the time of the industrial revolution. The key products were textiles and the energy systems were based on waterpower. A second paradigm revolved around iron and coal production and energy systems built on steam power, etc. Since the late twentieth century, a new technoeconomic paradigm has been under way, based on microelectronics and computer networks. ICTs are thus the central technologies in this new wave, illustrated by the fact that ICTs are used in practically all production areas. ICTs are the pervasive and generic technologies of our time.

Such thoughts are not entirely new as they are based on the works of Joseph Schumpeter, especially his book *Business Cycles* (1939), and before him Kondratieff (1925) and his theory of long waves in economic life. However, the proponents of the theory of technoeconomic paradigms have combined the thoughts of Schumpeter with Kuhn's theory of successive paradigms and have used these theoretical tools to examine the vital importance of ICTs today, and the many implications that these developments have on economic and social developments. There is no doubt that these thoughts have had a significant impact on the understanding of information society developments among political and administrative decision-makers.

THE ICT SECTOR

The sector comprising information, communication and telecommunication activities, the ICT sector, has emerged as one of the most dynamic conglomerates of economic activities among industrialized countries and increasingly also among developing countries. The use of computing and communication technologies is transforming the way we produce, consume and accumulate wealth. It is generally acknowledged that a thorough restructuring is evolving and this is often described under the headings of convergence or 'new economy', indicating that economics rooted in the ICT sector is based on new relations, rules and models of accumulation. However, it is not clear to what extent something is new from a theoretical point of view. This has partly to do with the fact that ICT is a troublesome area for the analyst. The activities of the sector unfold in three distinctly different areas or dimensions:

1 as a generic technology that is applied in most economic activities;
2 as an industry producing the equipment and software support for the generic technology;
3 as a broad and fast-growing service industry using the technology, equipment and software support mentioned above.

It is the combined effects of the three areas that give the ICT sector its vast potential. The background is that computing was 'just' part of the array of new technologies that resulted from the war effort and formed the material basis for the Fordist boom, first in the US and then gradually in the rest of the Western world. After four shifts of generation in computing, the fifth generation unexpectedly took the form of a rapid integration of computing and communications in the 1980s (Eliasson, 1998). This again was based on two developments. One is the introduction of personal computers. The other is the breakup of the Bell/AT&T system.

During the 1980s, personal computers were steadily adopted by businesses. By 1990, they began to enter the home and the microprocessor became embedded in tools, products for the home, cars, etc. By 2000, the power of computer chips was still being doubled roughly every 18 months (Moore's law), and increasingly pervasive computing is a reality as almost everything comes with a small, cheap chip. But it is in the combination with telecommunications, related to the Internet and mobile services, that the biggest potentials are emerging.

The trajectory of telecommunications parallels the computing development but is, to a large extent, rooted in organizational/institutional developments. The breakup of AT&T initiated in 1982 resulted immediately in heavy entrepreneurial activity in the US as companies like MCI and Sprint raced to build nationwide fibre-optic networks. But it also initiated a global liberalization drive propelled in Europe by the European Commission from 1987 onwards. The call for liberalization in Europe was really articulated by the issue of the Green Book of 1987 that aimed to make the European telecommunication market become one market like its rivals in the US and Japan. Further, the ambition was to create a competitive market with its alleged virtues of lower prices and faster service and technology development. By 1 January 1998, telecommunication markets including infrastructure provision and telephony had opened up for competition in the majority of countries in the European Union and the European Economic Area. Telecommunication markets were liberalized.

Now, competition as an organizing principle may mean very different things. The most important dimension of the discussion concerns the differences between proponents of pure competition in the form of *laissez-faire*, where the market is just liberalized without any further regulation (advocated by incumbent operators), and types of regulated competition where an asymmetric regulation is established in order to open the market for new providers.

The pure competitive situation presupposes non-violation of the traditional full competition assumptions: no dominant supplier, no barriers to entry, transparent pricing, etc. None of these assumptions was initially or is today fulfilled on the telecommunication markets, with incumbent operators still having a dominant market share and controlling the delivery channels – the networks. These severe market failures call for forceful regulation to ensure, for example, non-discriminatory access to networks, transparent pricing, etc. Hardly anyone disputes that this type of regulation is needed, and the liberalization that has been under development in the EU for the last 15 years has been liberalization in the sense that regulations aim at advancing competition. Such a liberalization of markets does not, however, in itself lead to a situation where new competitors can obtain considerable market shares and compete with the incumbent operators on an equal footing. The former national monopolies have far too dominant positions in existing markets for this to develop.[6]

Even if it seems that the liberalization of telecommunication markets has not led to anything resembling a fully competitive market, and instead of legal monopolies we now have the old incumbents as quasi-monopolies with competition at the fringes, the liberalization of telecommunications has, nevertheless, played a dominating role in ICT developments. What began as fringes open for competition outside the focus of the traditional operators have developed into some of the most dynamic areas: the Internet, international communication, mobile and value added.

The symbiotic relationship that developed between the computer and telecommunication technology sectors led to major economic growth, first in the US from the beginning of the 1990s, and a few years later in Europe as well. Generally attributed to the explosive growth of the Internet, there have been traditional economic growth effects as direct job creation, and traditional side effects as exponential growth in hardware and infrastructure companies. Building the new information infrastructure is one of the great global businesses. But the most dynamic immediate economic impact is related to the third part of the converging ICT sector, the content-producing communication and mass communication industry. The ICT-related media industry is growing very fast to be ready to take advantage of the network's capabilities such as interactivity and individual customization (e.g. video on demand). The Internet is expected to develop into the main medium and the old television networks are engaged in a struggle with newcomers such as Disney and Microsoft for the dominance of digital TV. The empirical evidence of this is unfolding as mergers, fights for future markets, etc., but the field of convergence is still new as an academic discipline and the related social science research is still in its infancy. As a tendency, two points of view can be seen. One is the conventional view on convergence, in the sense that this is seen as an important driver for technological and economic development (Baldwin et al., 1996). Another point of view is more critical towards these possibilities in convergence owing to, for example, inherent differences among the traditional sectors involved with respect to technologies, organization and other structures (Garnham, 1996).

One effect of the emerging convergence, the liberalization and internationalization in the ICT areas, is that standards developments increasingly become an important issue. In a network, environment standards and interoperability are crucial. In the old regime with monopoly operators, standardization was dealt with in official or semi-official institutions such as the ITU with its subcommittees.

In a market-driven environment this is no longer sufficient, and as a result standardization research is a fast-growing area that is acquiring great importance. Compatibility is a central theme and has been elaborated, for example, by Paul Allen (1995) and Stanley Besen (1995).

Statistically, the development of the ICT sector can be illustrated in different ways. As mentioned above, the sector is one of the most dynamic ones as the growth contribution of the sector is far greater than its share of GDP. Following the discussion above, the direct growth contribution from the US ICT sector during the 1990s has been estimated at about 15 per cent (OECD, 1999), whereas the total growth contribution of the sector has been estimated at 25–30 per cent (US Department of Commerce, 1999). This compares with a sector share of GDP of 8 per cent (US Department of Commerce, 1999). Furthermore, the development of the ICT sector in the emerging network economy has led to increasing productivity and competition and lower inflation. These effects are so far distinguishable especially in the US,[7] but are increasingly felt in Europe and even in developing countries. One of the strongest indirect economic effects is seen in the service industries where ICTs create the possibilities for new divisions of labour and new tendencies in internationalization. Traditionally, most services have to be consumed where and when they are produced, as they cannot be transported. Once information-intensive services are detached from human beings and stored on electronic media, they can be transferred on telecommunication lines and traded across borders. Other services also experience an increased tradability when the acts of contacting and contracting become easier with new ICTs.

The emergence of ICTs as the pervasive and generic technologies in the global economy makes it difficult today to see these technologies just 'as one important element among others' (Piore and Sabel, 1984: 262). The convergence of computing, telecommunications and mass media as a phenomenon associated with the development of ICTs has introduced 'placelessness' in production, i.e. geographical localization is becoming less important. That placelessness is gaining importance especially in the production of services has been argued from a theoretical point of view (UN, 1994) and can be observed in, for example, the development of Bangalore, where a region in a developing country has emerged as a vital partner in the international production of software. This is, however, no longer a unique example. Increasingly, there is evidence that ICTs enable the participation of developing countries in the international division of labour at an advanced level. During the last few years a small but growing indigenous software industry directed towards both the home market and the international market has emerged in West Africa and is increasingly seen as a possible avenue for participation in the global information society (Wayo Seini et al., 1998).

Alongside the development of ICTs, internationalization is often depicted as the most important fundamental feature of information society developments. But why is this, and how does the importance of internationalization manifest itself? These questions are briefly dealt with at the beginning of this section, after which the discussion concentrates on developments in theories of internationalization with special interest for trade and industry policies.

The overall importance of internationalization is related to the implications that it has for the productive structures in different countries, based on competition from producers from other countries (import and settlement), and to the new possibilities for expansion (export and settlement) and political governance: compare the discussions of the above-mentioned regulation school. This applies broadly to all industries (but not to the same extent), including the sectors that produce information and communication goods and services. On the other hand, ICTs have strong implications for the possibilities for trading and producing internationally because ICTs improve communications both between trading partners and inside transnational corporations. There is thus an affinity between questions of internationalization and questions of trade and industry policies in an information society context.

At the beginning of the chapter, the extent of the importance of internationalization was briefly discussed. Paul Krugman, Paul Bairoch, and Paul Hirst and Grahame Thompson were mentioned as examples of researchers who have advanced the view that too much emphasis can be attached to the phenomenon of internationalization. The reason for this view may be that in some expositions, if not all, far too many developments are attributed to internationalization.[8] After a good number of years spent attracting attention to the questions of internationalization,[9] it may seem to some economists that everything in public debates, apparently, can be explained by reference to the developments of internationalization and that this requires some measure of correction. Examples of writings that either favour or condemn internationalization, i.e. see it as either a great advantage or a threat, are K. Ohmae's *The Borderless World* (1990) (advantage) and H.-P. Martin and H. Schumann's *Die Globaliserungsfalle* (1996) (threat). However, in spite of such differences in view, there is general agreement that internationalization is extremely important and has vast implications, not only for trade and industry development but also for society at large.

Theories of internationalization deal with many subjects, and it is impossible to do them justice in such a short space. However, the theme can be subdivided into two categories, namely trade and foreign establishment (settlement). Most often, these two subjects are treated separately, and in this section we concentrate on the discussions that take trade as their point of departure, not because foreign establishment is uninteresting – quite the contrary – but because trade discussions constitute the classical point of departure in theories of internationalization and because most of the themes that are interesting in an information society trade and policy discussion context can be approached via the trade debates.

Classical trade theory builds on David Ricardo's *The Principles of Political Economy and Taxation* (1817) where the theory of comparative advantages was first expounded. In fact, Adam Smith in his book *The Wealth of Nations* (1776) had already paved the way for a theory of absolute advantages. These two trends in the theoretical work regarding trade have continued to exist ever since. They do not necessarily exclude each other, but they emphasize different aspects of the determinants of trade. The theory of comparative advantages focuses on the determinants of international specialization, while the theory of absolute advantages focuses on economic power relations between countries. The theory of comparative advantages has had a dominant position ever since Ricardo, but for the last 20–30 years criticism has become stronger and theories of, for instance, 'strategic trade policies' and even theories of absolute advantages have gained strength.

The theory of comparative advantages clearly has some explanatory power in relation to trade between countries with different endowments. But the strongest reason for the persistence of the dominant position of this theory in international economic relations is probably that it supports the normative claim for the advantages of free trade. However, the numerous problems in this theory have increasingly become clear with the changes in international economic relations. The assumptions on which the theory builds are not only very strict but in many ways highly unrealistic.[10]

In relation to our discussion, we will only mention three assumptions that are clearly unrealistic: that both product markets and factor markets are assumed to be perfectly competitive; that all factors of production are perfectly mobile within countries but immobile between countries; and that different countries enjoy equal access to the same body of technological knowledge. The first assumption applies generally in traditional neoclassical economics, but is no more realistic in international relations than in national circumstances. One of the implications is that there are production areas where economic rents (extra profit and/or extra high wages) are appropriated, and not only on a short-term basis. The second assumption regarding immobility of production factors is notoriously not true: international investment is gaining increasing importance. The third assumption concerning technical knowledge cannot be subscribed to either: this is one of the differences between countries that has a growing importance today.

The second assumption is the one that has attracted most attention in broader public discussions on international economic relations. Where internationalization formerly, to a larger extent, consisted of trade between countries, international investment and settlement in foreign countries is gaining increasing importance. The extent to which this is true can be discussed and is discussed, but international investments are important and have a growing importance. On a world political level, this is reflected in the negotiations in the World Trade Organization (WTO) where not only traditional trade questions are raised, and in the attempt by the Organization for Economic Cooperation and Development (OECD) to establish a multilateral agreement on investment (MAI). It is also reflected in the increasing internationalization of services, where modes of internationalization other than traditional trade are of central importance.

Such developments and observations have led to a discussion of whether the term 'globalization' is more appropriate than the term 'internationalization', as the word 'internationalization' in itself denotes relations between (inter) nations while globalization, ostensibly, better expresses a situation where national borders are becoming less important in economic activities. We see the advantages of the term 'globalization' if internationalization is understood as describing merely traditional trade relations between countries. However, in both trade relations and international investment, there are still large national interests and one should not underestimate the importance of nation-state initiatives. As we shall see in the following, an increasing role for the nation-state in international trade and industry policies can even be envisioned and defended.

The first and third assumptions regarding the theory of comparative advantages have been widely discussed in academic work. The question is whether, or to what extent, the theory of comparative advantages is the best way to analyse the positions of strengths and weaknesses of countries in different production areas and whether, or to what extent, the proposition of free trade advantages for all can be supported. The obvious fact is that different countries have different possibilities for access to technological knowledge and technologies. Furthermore, there are clearly production areas where rent is appropriated and where, for instance,

higher wages cannot be explained by labour power with higher competencies.

These facts have been analysed and crystallized in theories regarding strategic trade policies (see e.g. Paul Krugman, 1986), competitive advantages (e.g. Michael Porter, 1990) and even absolute advantages (e.g. Giovanni Dosi et al., 1990). The argument in 'strategic trade policies' is that, as some sectors produce higher rents and as technological innovations play an important role in the differences between companies and countries, one cannot rely on some automatic comparative advantage to create the best of all economic worlds. Strategic policy moves can be appropriate. The term 'competitive advantages' points in the same direction. Instead of more static comparative advantages, based on, for example, natural endowments, more dynamic competitive advantages are the foundations of the distribution of production. And, in the theory of absolute advantages, this argument is taken even further, claiming that some countries may have an overall advantage, covering almost all sectors, and that they will not move all their production into the sectors where their advantages are the best because this is not realistic, and because they are also highly competitive in the sectors where their advantages are the smallest. With ICTs, this situation is very feasible as ICTs are used in all sectors and, therefore, affect the competitiveness of all sectors in the countries that are advanced in the use of these technologies.

In essence, this situation does not contradict the theory of comparative advantages. However, in reality it leaves very little room for countries with lower absolute advantages. In continuation of this, it should also be stated that the above-mentioned theories do not entirely discard the existence of comparative advantages. But the role assigned for comparative advantages is relatively insignificant.

The conclusion of all this, in our case dealing with trade and industry policies, is that national and/or regional trade and industry policies are not becoming less relevant than they were in less internationalized phases. In a world where comparative advantages are the dominant mechanisms of distribution of production, there is not a great need for policy intervention, as wealth will automatically be optimized in all countries. However, if strategic moves are necessary and if competitive and even absolute advantages can be created, this calls for appropriate policies to be applied. However, as we shall see in the following section, it also calls for very much the same policies in all countries as they respond to similar mechanisms and priorities.

An open question in continuation of this is whether all countries really face similar situations. Do the poorer countries face issues similar to those faced by the richer countries? The degree of internationalization is, for instance, much lower in poor countries compared with rich countries. By far the largest share of international trade and international investments take place between the US, Europe and the richer countries in Asia. The whole African continent seems practically exempt from international economic relations if one examines international trade and investment on an overall scale, for example, the percentage of international trade in which African countries are involved. However, seen from the perspective of these national economies, international economic relations play an important role and most of the policy discussions follow the same lines as in the richer countries. This partly reflects a policy import from richer countries but also reflects the fact that many of the questions that poorer countries face are not fundamentally different from those faced by richer countries.

POLICY VISIONS

Following the arguments in the sections above, there is general agreement that technological, economic and political developments together constitute the drivers in an increasing internationalization of the economic system. In this relation it is, however, also interesting to analyse to what extent it is possible to conduct national/regional policies. The question is multifaceted and has been dealt with in research during the 1990s (e.g. Hirst and Zeitlin, 1992). As an immediate empirical observation, a surprising global coordination and timing of plans and visions for the information society can be seen. In 1993 the US government published *The National Information Infrastructure: Agenda Action*; the same year, the European Commission published its White Paper, *Growth, Competitiveness and Employment*; and in 1994 the Japanese government released *Reforms toward the Intellectual Creative Society of the 21st Century*. These were followed during 1994 and 1995 by plans and strategies issued by many countries in Europe. This applies, for example, to the UK and France and to the Netherlands, Sweden and Denmark. In other parts of the world, Singapore, South Korea, Canada and Australia published national plans during these years. And so did some developing countries in Asia, such as Malaysia, Thailand and the Philippines. Additionally, a G7 meeting in Brussels addressed the question in February 1995, and a Global Information Infrastructure Commission has been set up on the basis of a private initiative.

It is remarkable that so many countries and international institutions, at the same time, elaborate plans and programmes for the exploitation of the potentials of the emerging new information and communication technologies. Not since the construction of the railway system has a similar common international interest and enthusiasm for a technology and its possibilities been shown. Another analogy to this development comes easily to mind. As in the case of the railways, the electronic communication systems are only really useful when they are connected and developed more or less on the same level. It may be possible for a large country like the US to make some progress in ICTs alone. However, for smaller European countries, the advancement of one country very heavily depends on the advancement of other countries. The simultaneous drawing up of information society plans might be seen as an implicit understanding of this and, to a great extent, all of these strategy statements and plans build on the ideas and thoughts in the theoretical literature described earlier.

However, a closer analysis clearly reveals that these first-generation plans/visions hardly represent social planning in a strict sense, owing to two sets of assumptions. The basic problems in planning for a national information society are simply assumed away in the plans presented. The general assumptions are that the information society is emerging as a matter of fact, and attention can then be turned to the support of existing economic-political interests and problems. The second set of underlying assumptions is in reality that the market is taking care of the development of new services, technologies and structures. What seemed to be a global planning exercise was in reality a demonstration of the general acceptance of the neoliberal policy vision.

Following the major reorganization of the telecommunication sector in most EU countries, the EU Commission and the member countries have, since the mid 1990s, been engaged in a second wave of information society plans. Where the first wave of plans emphasized liberalization of telecommunications and information technology development, the second wave has focused more on social aspects of information society developments.[11] This understanding is, to a large extent, well founded – especially if the first wave is seen as being represented by the Bangemann Report and the Action Plan of 1994 (European Commission, 1994). However, the shift has to be seen against a changed socioeconomic setting.

The first initiative of the European Commission in its information society planning of the 1990s was the White Paper *Growth, Competitiveness and Employment* of 1993. This was prepared by the Commission under the chairmanship of the former French Socialist Minister of Finance, Jacques Delors, and clearly bears the hallmark of a social democratic concern for job creation and equal opportunity combined with a focus on Europe's competitiveness in an increasingly internationalizing world economy. This broadly focused White Paper was followed by the Bangemann Report in 1994 on the basis of an initiative by the Council. Martin Bangemann is a former German FDP (liberal) minister, and the emphasis in the report, and the Action Plan that built on it, is much more on the issues of liberalization of telecommunications and the primacy of the private sector in the development of an information society.

In 1995, the European Commission initiated a high-level expert group (HLEG), and an Information Society Forum (ISF) was established to analyse 'the social aspects of the information society', as the HLEG (1997) puts it in its final policy report. As a justification for this focus, the HLEG wrote: 'Until that time, the debate on the emerging information society had been dominated by issues relating to the technological and infrastructure challenges and the regulatory economic environment' (1997: 14). There was, therefore, a perceived need for refocusing on the social dimensions of the 'European model' in line with the White Paper (HLEG, 1997: 17).

The development in EU information society policy can thus be seen as having changed from a technology- and market-oriented focus to a broader social concern. One of the reasons for this priority is clearly that the development of the basic infrastructure through the liberalization of telecommunication has developed in a satisfactory way – seen from the point of view of the Commission. But even if other issues in other contexts may be given priority, the second-generation visions clearly cover a broader area than the first-generation visions. This has not, however, changed the clear neoliberal basis for the visions – a feature that is almost universal even in the present emerging plans/visions from former planned economies in developing countries, where Ghana's vision 'Ghana 2020' can be mentioned as a specific example.

SUMMARY AND CONCLUSION

The most conspicuous developments that have taken place through the last two to three decades with respect to trade and industry policy trends in an information society context can be summarized in the following way. On the technological side, information and communication technologies and services have developed and expanded vastly, and the processes of digitalization have allowed for new technological possibilities to be explored, among them a beginning convergence between formerly separate information and communication sectors. On the economic side, economies have internationalized to an increasing degree, and especially the growing internationalization of production processes (epitomized in the term 'globalization') and the beginning internationalization of services is seen as important. On the political (and ideological) side, liberalism has changed the political climate considerably and has had a clear impact on the societal organization of, for example, electronic communication areas. And other important development trends and features could be mentioned, such as the ever increasing importance of services in the economies, the growth in information processing occupations, the role of information and knowledge in society, new and more flexible work processes and organizations, and changes in the role of national states.

These developments are reflected in economic and social science research and have greatly impacted on the trade and industrial policies implemented by public authorities. With respect to economic and social science theories with influence on information society visions of public authorities, at least four different trends (or areas of research) deserve mentioning here.

The first is concerned with the liberalization of the different communication sectors. Two of these sectors, telecommunications and broadcasting, were formerly in state monopoly or very strictly regulated. However, over the past 20 years this has changed, which clearly has been reflected in economic and social science research where a great deal of work has been done regarding the implications of liberalization.

The second research area is concerned with trends in the internationalization/globalization processes in the economic (and other) sphere(s). This area of research can hardly be drawn together in just one or a few trends. Many different processes are examined, though there is a dominant interest in international investment and the globalization of production structures.

The third deals with evolutionary (and revolutionary) developments in the economy and the importance of technological change. The theories examined in this chapter, to a large extent, are part of these areas of interest – although they also touch upon internationalization and state regulation. It is a broad category encompassing research interested in the technology side of production (innovation economics) and the evolutionary processes in the economy (evolutionary economics).

The fourth theoretical trend is interested in institutional aspects of the economy. This trend has not explicitly been dealt with in this chapter, but plays an important role in the discussions concerning flexible production and the importance and implications of electronic communications in production and distribution.

The influence of these theoretical trends on the discussions and decisions taken at a broader societal level, e.g. among decision-makers on the political scene, has been discussed in the course of this chapter and the evaluation expressed has been that there clearly is a connection between the academic world and the world of economic and political decisions in this area. However, a modification of this evaluation could be made. As much as it is a question of academic research influencing political discussions, one could claim that both 'worlds' have been under the influence of the significant changes that have taken place during the past two to three decades. Still, the overall evaluation is that discussions and concepts that have been crystallized in academic research have had a relatively strong influence on broader political debates and decisions in this area.

In a sense, it is strange that, since the beginning of the 1990s, there has been a surge of information and network society visions and plans issued by public authorities. Often, one of the common understandings is that with the many changes in the economic and political systems, state planning is *passé*. However, there has probably never been so much political planning as has been witnessed in relation to all the information society vision statements in the last decade.

But the content of these plans has changed considerably compared with former political interventions. This change has often been described as a turn away from direct state interventionism towards an emphasis on the creation of framework conditions for economic activity. This development can, for instance, be seen in telecommunications where direct control via ownership of operators is relinquished and indirect regulation is implemented.

The background for this development is multifaceted. However, the development towards framework regulation fits in well with the increasing internationalization where public authorities aim at creating the best possible framework conditions for businesses in an international competitive environment; note, for example, the discussions of the regulation school on the changes in the role of the state.

Analyses show that the trade and industry policies relevant to the information society, implemented in the different countries, are to a large extent similar. The reason is partly that policy directions in one country inspire other countries – and for the poorer countries also there is external pressure from transnational corporations, richer countries and international organizations. However, it is also a result of the competition to become a prime site for production of different kinds in the international divisions of labour. Dynamic competitive advantages are increasingly important compared with more static comparative advantages. This has led to internationalization not only of production but also of trade and industry policies.

There are, nevertheless, differences in the policies. This applies, to some extent, to the priority given to the combination of 'harder' trade and industry policy measures and 'softer' areas like culture, education, etc., although most information/network society visions today include such areas. But more fundamentally, it applies to the perspective in which trade and industry policies are seen. In Europe, there is a tendency to consider the creation of wealth and welfare as two aspects that should not be separated. In the US, there is a focus on wealth creation, and welfare is considered a byproduct. This is, of course, partly a reflection of the fact that social democratic governments dominate the European Union at present. But it is also a more basic difference, based on the differences in positions of strength of the social classes in the various areas.

Notes

1 However, in this volume Frank Webster's contribution discusses the information society concepts, which are more comprehensively examined in Webster (1995).

2 Shapiro and Varian (1999) can be seen as an example of such an emphasis on information and knowledge content and networked communication goods and services.

3 This is the expression used by Webster (1995) when examining the regulation school.

4 With inspiration from the writings of Antonio Gramsci (1971).

5 Basic works in the tradition of innovation economics are Rosenberg (1982) and Nelson and Winter (1982).

6 A vast amount of research has been done in the field of telecommunication liberalization and regulation. For a comprehensive overview, see Melody (1997).

7 The US Department of Commerce (1999) has estimated a general lowering of the rate of inflation of 0.7 per cent in the 1990s.

8 This is the line of argumentation in, for example, Krugman (1997).

9 In the case of Krugman, see, for instance, Krugman (1986; 1990).

10 For a discussion of the assumptions underlying the theory of comparative advantages, see e.g. Grimwade (1989).

11 This is, for instance, the understanding of the Commission itself: see European Commission (1996), which is presented as 'an updated and revised Action Plan in order to launch a second phase of the EU information society strategy'.

References

Aglietta, Michel (1979) A *Theory of Capitalist Regulation*. London: New Left Books.

Allen, Paul (1995) 'Standardization policies for network technologies', in Richard Hawkins et al. (eds), *Standards, Innovation and Competitiveness*. Cheltenham: Elgar.

Bairoch, Paul (1996) 'Globalization myths and realities', in Robert Boyer and Daniel Drache (eds), *States against Markets*. London: Routledge. pp. 173–92.

Baldwin, Thomas, McVoy, Stevens and Steinfield, Charles (1996) *Convergence: Integrating Media, Information and Communication Systems*. London: Sage.

Bell, Daniel (1973) *The Coming of Post-Industrial Society*. New York: Basic.

Besen, Stanley (1995) 'The standard processes in telecommunication and information technology', in Richard Hawkins et al. (eds), *Standards, Innovation and Competitiveness*. Cheltenham: Elgar.

Boyer, Robert (1990) *The Regulation School: a Critical Introduction*. New York: Columbia University Press.

Boyer, Robert and Drache, Daniel (eds) (1996) *States against Markets*. London: Routledge.

Dosi, Giovanni (1984) *Technical Change and Industrial Transformation*. London: Macmillan.

Dosi, Giovanni, Pavitt, Keith and Soete, Luc (1990) *The Economics of Technical Change and International Trade*. Brighton: Harvester Wheatsheaf.

Drucker, Peter (1994) *The Age of Discontinuity* (1969). New Brunswick, NJ: Transaction.

Duff, Alistair (1998) 'Daniel Bell's theory of the information society', *Journal of Information Science*, 24 (6): 373–93.

Duff, Alistair, Craig, David and McNeill, David (1996) 'A note on the origins of the "information society"', *Journal of Information Science*, 22 (2): 117–22.

Eliasson, G. (1998) *The Macroeconomic Effects of the Computer and Communications Technology*. Stockholm: KTH.

European Commission (1994) *Europe's Way to the Information Society: an Action Plan*. COM(94)347. Brussels: EC.

European Commission (1996) *Europe at the Forefront of the Global Information Society: Rolling Action Plan*. COM(96)607. Brussels: EC.

Freeman, Christopher and Soete, Luc (1982) *The Economics of Industrial Innovation*. London: Pinter.

Garnham, Nicholas (1996) 'Constraints on multimedia convergence', in William Dutton (ed.), *Information and Communication Technologies: Visions and Realities*. Oxford: Oxford University Press. pp. 103–19.

Gramsci, Antonio (1971) 'Americanism and Fordism', in *Selections from the Prison Notebooks*. London: Lawrence & Wishart.

Grimwade, Nigel (1989) *International Trade: New Patterns of Trade*. London: Routledge.

Hirst, Paul and Thompson, Grahame (1996) *Globalization in Question*. Cambridge: Polity.

Hirst, Paul and Zeitlin, Jonathan (1992) 'The problem of "globalisation"', *Economy and Society*, 21 (4): 357–96.

HLEG (1997) *Building the European Information Society for Us All*. DG V. Brussels: European Commission.

Kondratieff, N. (1925) 'The long wave in economic life', *Review of Economic Statistics*, 17: 105–15.

Krugman, Paul (ed.) (1986) *Strategic Trade Policy and the New Internnational Economics*. Cambridge, MA: MIT Press.

Krugman, Paul (1990) *Rethinking International Trade*. Cambridge, MA: MIT Press.

Krugman, Paul (1997) *Pop lnternationalism*. Cambridge, MA: MIT Press.

Kuhn, Thomas (1962) *The Structure of Scientific Revolutions*. Chicago: Chicago University Press.

Lipietz, Alain (1987) *Mirages and Miracles: the Crisis of Global Fordism*. London: Verso.

Machlup, Fritz (1962) *The Production and Distribution of Knowledge in the United States*. Princeton, NJ: Princeton University Press.

Martin, H.-P. and Schumann, H. (1996) *Die Globaliserungsfalle: Der Angriff auf Demokratie und Wohlstand*. Reinbek: Rowohlt.

Melody, William (1997) *Telecom Reform: Principles, Policies and Regulatory Practices*. Lyngby: Technical University of Denmark.

Naisbitt, John (1982) *Megatrends: Ten New Directions Transforming Our Lives*. New York: Warner.

Negroponte, Nicholas (1995) *Being Digital*. New York: Knopf.

Nelson, R.R. and Winter, S.G. (1982) *An Evolutionary Theory of Economic Change*. Cambridge, MA: Harvard University Press.

OECD (1999) *The Economic and Social Impact of Electronic Commerce*. Paris: Organization for Economic Cooperation and Development.

Ohmae, K. (1990) *The Borderless World*. New York: Harper.

Piore, Michael and Sabel, Charles (1984) *The Second Industrial Divide: Possibilities for Prosperity*. New York: Basic.

Porat, Marc Uri (1977) *The Information Economy: Definition and Measurement*. Washington, DC: US Department of Commerce.

Porter, Michael (1990) *Competitive Advantages of Nations*. London: Macmillan.

Ricardo, David (1947) *The Principles of Political Economy and Taxation* (1817). London: Dent.

Rosenberg, Nathan (1982) *Inside the Black Box: Technology and Economy*. Cambridge: Cambridge University Press.

Schumpeter, Joseph (1939) *Business Cycles: a Theoretical, Historical and Statistical Analysis of the Capitalist Process*. New York: McGraw-Hill.

Shapiro, Carl and Varian, Hal (1999) *Information Rules: a Strategic Guide to the Network Economy*. Cambridge, MA: Harvard Business School Press.

Smith, Adam (1947) *The Wealth of Nations* (1776). London: Dent.

Toffler, Alvin (1980) *The Third Wave*. London: Collins.

UN (1994) *The Tradability of Banking Services*. ST/CTC/168. Geneva: United Nations.

US Department of Commerce (1999) *The Emerging Digital Economy*. Washington, DC: USDC.

Wayo Seini, A., Abdulai, M.-S. and Kwadwo Asenso-Okyere, W. (1998) *Telematics Usage for Ghana's Development*. A report prepared for the Ghana National Committee for Internet Connectivity (GNCIC). http://www.bellanet.org/partners/aisi/nici/ghana/ghanaa.

Webster, Frank (1995) *Theories of the Information Society*. London: Routledge.

20

The Economics of Information and Industrial Change

DON LAMBERTON

The economics of information is not a tidy, separate small part of economics for some reason of special interest in media matters. The information perspective is a significant challenge to the whole corpus of economics, with destructive implications for mainstream economic theory and its analytical and policy outcomes, yet holding great potential for new theory, new approaches to organization, and new solutions to decision and policy problems. Information, which includes knowledge or 'information of indefinite tenure' (Machlup, 1982: 9), is multifaceted: a resource, a commodity, a perception of pattern, a constitutive force in society (Braman, 1989). It is central to the making of decisions by consumers, business and governments and so plays a key role in the way the economic system works.

For the most part, the economy is envisaged or modelled as predominantly a market system in which business and households are the basic sectors.[1] The business sector employs workers and makes the decisions to invest in plant and equipment that enable the production of goods and services. Purchasing power flows from business to households in the form of wages, rent, interest and dividends that fund household spending. More reality is achieved in the model by adding government, financial institutions and the rest of the world. Business subdivides into industries, each of which produces some widely identified good or service: wheat, beer, motor cars, food, chemicals, computers, software, media. These goods and services are purchased by households, governments and other firms or by the rest of the world. Such market systems function within a wider social framework and require elaborate, durable and costly institutions.

What do the words 'industrial change' cover? A complete catalogue would be very lengthy; major items would be new products and services, new technologies, new forms of organization, new policy initiatives including regulatory changes, new institutions, new standards, innovation, substitution of new for old, demand shifts, cost reductions and cost increases, outsourcing, downsizing, restructuring, mergers, takeovers, alliances, new images, new theories. It is important to appreciate that from an industrial change perspective, media and multimedia have some special characteristics but share basic involvement in information activities with industry at large. Much recent debate has focused on what has been regarded as special, whereas this chapter seeks to restore the balance. A recent review (Wildman, 1998) of media and multimedia listed the following research matters: advances in IT, revised regulatory philosophy, economies of scope and scale, programme choice, the public good character of media content, advertising, multimedia as integration for delivery by a single medium of different types of content, despecialization of transmission technologies, and integrated packages of media and telecommunications services. It is hoped that this chapter will provide a framework for analysis of the role of information in industrial change that extends beyond the media context.

AN INFORMATION PERSPECTIVE

The economics of information looks through the economist's lens at the information activities in all parts and all processes of the economy. It would be easy to assume that an economics of information is now being created in response to recent changes: computerization, satellites, mobile phones, ATMs and the like (Shapiro and Varian, 1999). These developments have spawned a naming flurry with a surfeit of adjectives: new, information, knowledge-based, digital, online, Internet, attention (because information consumes the scarce resource of attention), administrative, nude (transparent and exposed), Cisco (in the image of the giant networking equipment firm). Each in its own way attempts to highlight the feature perceived as central to the contemporary economy; and each runs the risk of overemphasizing some part of the new at the expense of the old. Consider, for example, the online version which sees online business activity as a separate *economy* and makes comparison with national economies. Online activity is not a separate economy, nor are NASDAQ businesses as a group. They are part of a larger whole, using and building upon the labour force, the knowledge base, public assets, the legal framework, other institutions, and the entire social capital of the society.

Nor is the information economy new. A perceptive 1960 paper by Richard Meier speculated about 'probably the most significant category of developments in natural science, engineering and psychology over the last decade. *Information theory* and *information technology* are', he said, 'bringing about striking changes in the organization of production and, through their influences upon institutions and professions, have been adding to our understanding of the properties of economic growth' (1960: 98). The following year, Stigler saw information as still in 'a slum dwelling in the town of economics' but with prospects of moving to a better location (1961: 61); and only one year later Fritz Machlup's (1962) major empirical effort delineated in rich detail for the first time the dimensions of the US knowledge-based economy in which knowledge production and distribution accounted for 29 per cent of GNP.

A reviewer of Machlup's book judged it to contain enough dynamite to blast traditional economics into orbit (Boulding, 1963: 36). His judgement was correct but – changing the metaphor – economists rolled with the punches, took on board some of the questions and some of the jargon, and evaded the need to get down to the fundamentals. With the millennium approaching, a leading practitioner of the economics of information could state that 'standard economic theory has little to say about the efficiency of the knowledge based economy' (Stiglitz, 1999: 19, n. 14).[2]

It is important to consider why the economics discipline has been unable or unwilling to change. Of course, the pressure can be seen either as a problem in keeping up with industrial change – the change from economies dominated by steel, manufacturing, chemicals, textiles and shipping to a world in which the most important firms are in telecommunications, computers, software, education and tourism; from the days of US Steel and DuPont to the emergence of global firms like Microsoft and Cisco – or an internal matter of obsolescence of the discipline. Economics Nobel winner Kenneth Arrow (1974) has mounted a good case for all successful organizations being subject to organizational obsolescence or lock-in. This is inherent, he argues, in the economic characteristics of information: 'the combination of uncertainty, indivisibility, and capital intensity associated with information channels and their use imply (a) that the actual structure and behavior of an organization may depend heavily upon random events, in other words on history, and (b) the very pursuit of efficiency may lead to rigidity and unresponsiveness to further change' (1974: 49). If the economics discipline itself is viewed as an organization, rigidity and unresponsiveness are only to be expected.

This critique is strengthened by the likelihood of distorted images. Cost considerations plus management practices leave the analyst dependent upon incomplete, inappropriate and outdated statistics collected by national and international agencies. Even if the data did not suffer from these deficiencies, it is likely the analyst is wearing faulty lenses. Having studied two provincial towns, one in South East Asia and one in North Africa, every now and again over four decades, anthropologist Clifford Geertz (1995) posed the question of how the goings-on in those towns had changed. He had telling words about what actually takes place in this attempt to provide answers and the implications for objectivity and science.

> Floundering through mere happenings and then concocting accounts of how they hang together is what knowledge and illusion alike consist in. The accounts are concocted out of available notions, cultural equipment ready to hand. But like any equipment it is brought to the task; value added, not extracted. If objectivity, rightness, and science are to be had it is not by pretending they run free of the exertions which make or unmake them. (1995: 3)

These cautions have special application to attempts to make sense of industrial change in the information economy. Uncertainty is the complement of knowledge; information activities constitute the major claim on resources; and the limitations of the information and information handling capabilities of each individual create social interdependence.

MARKET AND TECHNOLOGY BIASES

Two elements of bias have to be emphasized. First, there is the tyranny of the market. Economics has been reluctant to become involved in the study of what happens inside organizations (Simon, 1991); it did not take an active interest in either psychology or organization science and it tried to keep aloof from management and marketing. This situation is changing; and while there is some deliberate and systematic crossing of borders (Dow and Earl, 1999; Droege, 1997; Hodgson, 1999; Lamberton, 1996a; Lazaric and Lorenz, 1998; Macdonald, 1998; Macdonald and Nightingale, 1999), there are still major deficiencies in theoretical and empirical research and official statistical collections. There were major consequences for economic theory because it had taken 'on a character belonging to the manipulable, calculable, external world of things, not the world of the conscious mind in its eternal stations on the edge of the void of time, the conscious mind whose being consists precisely in the endless gaining of knowledge' (Shackle, 1972: 3).

'Things' could easily include plant and machinery and buildings but could not cope with intangible assets. An important consequence is that an economic statistic that is crucial for the economic modelling and storytelling, investment, excludes the very things that are thought to be of increasing importance in the information economy. The old questions such as 'What is investment?', 'What is capital?' have come to the surface again. Should expenditure on information be treated as investment? Is information capital? Like other forms of capital, information is structured (Lamberton, 1999); its parts complement each other, imposing sequences or lags, and there are interactions with other 'assets'. For example, a reputation for consistent behaviour can reduce information costs. It is now recognized that significant elements of investment – education, R&D, computers, software, organizational capital, institution building – ought to be included on a systematic basis (Kirova and Lipsey, 1998; Webster 1999).

Because 'things' were easier to handle, the second bias – a sharp focus on technology in a hardware sense – shaped efforts to make sense of the information revolution by focusing on information and communication technologies (ICT) rather than information. Machlup's (1962) pioneering work and later research had adopted a wide coverage and, by capturing both the information activities that happened in markets and those that happened inside organizations, had sought to deal in a comprehensive way with the role of information. This led to the development of concepts of both a primary information sector for goods and services sold on established markets, and a secondary information sector to record the value added of information activities used in producing non-information goods and services. Some influential reports adopted a different approach. For example, Miles et al. (1990) emphasized the convergence of computing and communications. Some process was leading to the convergence and, to the extent computers and telecommunications had been transformed by that process, they were said to be the core of IT. Because that process was facilitating transformations in the whole economy – the information economy – they believed the interesting issue was the extent to which products and services were ICT intensive. As a final step, the factor promoting convergence was identified: the microelectronics revolution.

The process of informatization was, from this perspective, to be seen as the progressive application of information and communication technologies. Official documents acquired an ITEC (Information Technology, Electronics and Communications) label. A United Kingdom Green Paper (Hawkins et al., 1997), for example, was given a quite specific title: *Mapping and Measuring the ITEC Sector in the United Kingdom*. There was scant recognition of the profound role of information as explored, on an interdisciplinary basis, in a major conference in the 1980s (Machlup and Mansfield, 1983). Historical research could, of course, exercise a corrective influence. Is it reasonable to assume that the information economy began with microelectronics? Organizational development is reported to have been the main form of technological progress during the eighteenth century (Groenewegen, 1977). Changes that led to the growth of clerical occupations to such an extent that they became the dominant occupational group (Schement and Curtis, 1995: 71–101) suggest an earlier date for the onset of the information revolution. What of a future in which it is conceivable that electronics might merge with or be supplanted by biotechnology?

What lies behind this promotion of ITEC primacy which was accorded priority status in growth and development plans and has a great deal to do with the observed patterns of industrial change? Governments and those responsible for policy rhetoric have had a key role. But as Mathias warned, 'Some present day governments … like some economic historians and contemporary tourists, have been too impressed by dramatic instances of the latest technology when making judgments about the sources of productivity' (1983: 18). A cursory study of economic history shows how these iconic industries rise and fall, for example, steel, textiles, motor vehicles, aerospace and, recently, the more general 'hi-tech' category. Of course, some new industries may prove longlasting because they reach to fundamental aspects of the human experience. The genome project may be a good illustration. The decoding and dissemination of the human genome fits into 'a vastly larger landscape of legal, ethical and political issues', is 'certainly part of the information economy', and 'probably has more far-reaching implications for the human species than any other aspect of the "information revolution"' (Tyler, 1999: 518).

As implied earlier, the tyranny of the market has complemented the technological determinism. A strong case can be made (Simon, 1991) for viewing the economy, not as a market system, but as an organizational economy, with market relations amongst organizations. Those promoting the ITEC view seem unwilling to recognize that the market is 'the largest and most effective information system in existence' (Machlup, 1979: 113). It seems a reasonable approach to say that when bureaucracy, both private and public, is combined with the market the resulting aggregate is the information economy. The primary and secondary information sector concepts emerged from attempts, working with very limited statistical data, to show that such an economy functioned through the combined roles of market and administrative decision. Analysis of the linkages within and between industry sectors and between information and non-information sectors involved a great deal more than the information component that Miles et al. conceded had been a feature of all societies. A solution to these difficulties is to treat bureaucracy or organization generally as technology.[3]

The notion that markets can always, in principle, deliver better outcomes than states and the law, i.e. neoliberal economic rationalism, as a basis for economic policy with respect to industrial change, has distinct weaknesses. First, as mentioned earlier, mainstream economics of the non-information economics variety has little to say about the efficiency of the information economy. Second, the private enterprise component makes rather simplistic assumptions about administrative efficiency, responsiveness and innovativeness (Nelson, 1981: 60). These assumptions are in effect judgements about information processes which have been subjected to research. While that research (Macdonald, 1996; 1998; Macdonald and Nightingale, 1999) has not managed to provide simple models of industrial change, it has established the complexity involved and effectively undermined the sweeping claims of the privatization approach.[4] This is an important stage in the development of ideas about industrial development because it challenges the strong presumption that has held sway ever since Adam Smith's *Wealth of Nations*, that the industrialist knows best how to conduct his own business.

ECONOMIC CHARACTERISTICS OF INFORMATION

Asking questions about efficiency in the modern information economy raises issues, not just about IT and telecommunications, but about capabilities (Loasby, 1998), information stocks, organizational capital and learning. This is a far cry from the old economics with its firms that were given units of coordinating ability, reading best practice resource combinations from a recipe book (see Lamberton, 1965), and it points to the policy vacuum that has been created by the information revolution. For example, should policy address not only education

in school but also education of industrialists (Pandit et al., 1997)? And if the effectiveness of such 'messages' depends upon the state of readiness of the recipients, is monitoring of learning and performance desirable? Some will respond by invoking the economic rationalist market view but there are quite fundamental difficulties. Information can be a commodity, as is readily apparent from the wide range of information industries, but only to a limited extent (Arrow, 1984: 142). Therefore, it is not permissible to simply treat information as the $n+1$th commodity and then proceed with the analysis as if nothing else had changed. A market system with information elements cannot lead to the traditional efficient allocation of resources. First, information is indivisible in use: the same information is not bought twice in ordinary circumstances; and 'how to' information about production is independent of the scale of production. Therefore, it pays a business planning large-scale operations to buy better information than a small firm. A consequence is that information creates economies of scale throughout the economy and this causes a departure from what is expected of the competitive economy. It seems reasonable to think that the more information intensive the economy as a whole, the greater the likelihood that this is a significant departure.

Second, information is inappropriable. The possessor does not lose information when it is transmitted. Also, the cost of transmitting information is normally much lower than the initial cost of production. Add to this the facts that information has the characteristics of a public good[5] and that intellectual property rights cannot give absolute security of benefits. The consequence of this combination of circumstances is that investment in uncertain activities like R&D will be less than optimal from a social point of view.

This general viewpoint, shaped by Arrow's classic 1962 paper, was welcomed by vested interests because it justified subsidization of those activities. Politically, it was welcomed in a Cold War setting. Industry stood to benefit, as did both universities and research centres and their employees. Thinking based on this modelling of the process of R&D, innovation and development has remained a powerful influence. There are, however, several flaws in the modelling.

The Arrovian analysis tends to be somewhat supply based. For example, looking to the demand side, it is apparent that there is often no public ready and eager to utilize information. This emerges on closer scrutiny of the characteristics of information. Arrow, in his original analysis, was aware of this (Lamberton, 1999) and he acknowledged:

- Difficulties arose in defining an item of information and differentiating it from other items.
- Information purchases were often made largely in ignorance of their value.

- Some generators of information had advantages of special knowledge and skills.
- Intellectual property rights could never provide complete protection.
- Information items in use are interdependent.

These qualifications to the reasoning seem to have slipped out of sight in subsequent debate and policy formulations. It is therefore necessary to resurrect the complexity of information structures and the continuous nature of information processes. Two comments serve this purpose. First, 'Knowledge is not a pile of homogeneous material, but a complex structure of heterogeneous thoughts, each available at zero marginal cost but usable only together with resources available only at positive and often very high cost' (Machlup, 1982: 10). Second, there is need for modelling of the economy, or of its parts, 'in which information is continuously being collected and processed and in which decisions, based on that information, are continuously being made' (Stiglitz, 1985: 23).

Considerations of structure and flow provide scope for strategic behaviour and modify conclusions about divisibility and appropriability. The scope of indivisibilities may be extended and appropriability may be enhanced. There may then be opportunities for organizational experiment, e.g. alliances. The scope of competition may well be diminished. From an analytical perspective, there is a shift from modelling of optimizing to study of historical processes. Sequences of experiment, learning, decision and innovation become important. This shift has major implications for management, innovation and policy and the industrial change they generate. Information in its diverse combinations of characteristics, structured forms and sequences contrasts sharply with information as an all-purpose lubricant in the economic system.

RESEARCH

The scope of research in the economics of information is so wide that this context permits only a highly selective coverage under each of the topics selected. A short summary is given along with appropriate and up-to-date references to permit fuller exploration.

Property Rights

Intellectual property 'is a broad term that is used to describe the wide range of rights that are conferred by the legal system in relation to discrete items of information that have resulted from some form of human intellectual activity' (Ricketson, 1992: 54), such as inventions, scientific discoveries, literary and artistic works, trademarks, industrial designs.

Traditional categories devised centuries ago have been found inadequate. 'Patents' and 'copyright' became overloaded but provision had to be made for items as diverse as integrated circuits, software, plant varieties, genetic materials, personal images, cultural works and surgical techniques. This has been achieved through wider interpretations of the old categories or through new, specific pieces of legislation, e.g. for plant varieties.

The importance of economic considerations has been widely acknowledged (Drahos, 1998; 2000; Lamberton, 1994). However, the definition quoted above is a lawyer's definition and it ignores the impossibility of items of information being discrete. Their complementarity is what gives them meaning and economic significance; and those complementarities build sequences and create lags that affect choices. There are legal disputes over property rights where, for example, it has been argued that a sculpture might have been created as a 'response' to a photograph. This points to wide-ranging possibilities of complex learning and response in the production and dissemination of information.

Industrial change in a knowledge-based economy is leading to growing tension between the system of legal relations and economic determinants. Continuation of this trend seems highly probable if economic activity becomes even more information intensive. 'Information is the basis of production, production is carried on in discrete legal entities, and yet information is a fugitive resource, with limited property rights' (Arrow, 1996: 651). Several consequences are already apparent. First, legal activity is increased. A good illustration is the use of meta-tags, one of the associational tools essential to the operation of the World Wide Web. Their function as indices of websites which search engines read and rely upon in looking for appropriate content in response to queries submitted to them has generated controversies as meta-tag use impacts on the property rights of website owners (Ramiscal, 2000). Second, costs are raised in the settling and anticipation of legal conflicts. Markets for protective strategies and technologies are fostered, both domestically and internationally; and impetus is given to attempts to further develop protective technologies. Other consequences will include: internal efforts by firms to improve their assessment of the value of information assets; business efforts to cope with intellectual property problems by forming alliances; and calls for an expanded role on the part of governments and international organizations.

A related element in the industrial change process is the establishment of standards amongst those having an economic incentive to be concerned with the technical basis of product network. Where the numbers involved are large, there are coordination problems. Some become locked into their alternative; and knowledge of alternatives may be imperfect. Diversity may undermine very real long-run opportunities for better systems. A firm's business strategy often aims to have its alternative adopted as the industry standard – and such dominance is a regulatory matter. Various outcomes for innovation emerge: on the one hand, there can be encouragement of R&D and improvement of goods and services, or, on the other hand, the activities can be made more rigid and hinder innovation. The outcomes in particular circumstances will depend upon 'the market structure, chance historical events, and the costs of technical alternatives' (Greenstein, 1992). As in the case of intellectual property rights, better understanding of these alternative outcomes might come from adoption of an information perspective with special attention to learning.

Market Structure

Industrial economics and industrial organization research has adopted market structure as a major focus of analysis. Sutton (1998) synthesizes the two major approaches in terms of (1) industry characteristics and (2) evolution of the size distribution of firms in a 'typical' industry. He provides systematic statistical evidence and detailed case studies; gives attention to both the telecommunications and computer industries; and treats the issues and analysis so comprehensively as to be an effective antidote to the excessive hype and wild projections of the development of information-related industries of recent times.

For decades, market structure research has been dominated by the seemingly simple notion of barriers to new competition. Sutton explains that 'a proper understanding of market structure requires a meshing of two ideas: strategic interaction between groups of close substitute products and (approximate) independence across clusters of such products' (1998: 495). His analysis builds on the old idea of a gap in the chain of substitutes using three principles: first, firms do not pursue loss-making strategies; second, if a profitable opportunity exists, some firm will take it; and, third, in markets consisting of independent submarkets, a 'symmetry' principle excludes the possibility that a firm enjoy some advantage over its rivals in entering a submarket by virtue of earlier experience in other submarkets. His objective is to limit the number of outcomes that could be expected to show up in empirical data. He acknowledges real-world complexity: 'Any adequate story of why, within the limits set by these few constraints, structure takes this form or that, must come to grips with the influence of history. If we track down, industry by industry, the events that caused things to go one way or another, we rapidly find ourselves immersed in the historian's domain of accident and personality' (1998: xv).

The choice is posed as between richer theory and statistical regularity.

Has there been some major omission in this approach? The information perspective would seem to be a candidate. Each of Sutton's principles turns on what assumptions are made about what firms know. The first two imply knowledge of future losses and profits; and the symmetry principle denies the role of the informational asymmetries flowing from prior experience. In the knowledge-based economy, information costs loom large in the costs structures of firms (Eliasson et al., 1990). Should not these information mechanisms somehow be made part of the central analysis rather than be tucked away in the residual 'domain of accident and personality'? Information is a resource, albeit intangible; and changes in information costs and information technology shape organizational forms and the expectations of decision-makers. Of course, this change would have other consequences. It would require an even more complicated picture of the market, theory that is only now beginning to be built, and propositions that do not fit easily with conventional industry data.

The information perspective must be integral to industrial change. Just as it has been recognized that there is no catalogue of alternative technologies, so too there is awareness that firms find or create their profitable opportunities. They are obliged to learn and to seek comparative advantage through learning. Those processes seem so important in the knowledge-based economy that they ought to be part of the search for statistical regularity and not treated as exceptions.

The firm as the unit would seem to warrant further consideration. Some industries, especially information-intensive ones, show a marked tendency to resort to alliances, e.g. telecommunications, basic research and airlines. The alliances development lacks good theory. In this context, it seems clear that the firm is not a clearly defined entity and changes in organizational form have implications for the modelling of market structure.

Demand Studies

The major concern about demand studies relevant to the information economy is that they relate to demand for IT, access, advertising but only indirectly to information itself. Telecommunications has received a good deal of attention. Here the classic work is Taylor's *Telecommunications Demand in Theory and Practice* (1994), complemented by *Information Economics and Policy* (1989) and more recently by Loomis and Taylor's *The Future of the Telecommunications Industry: Forecasting and Demand Analysis* (1999). These studies suffer from the limitation that they are very largely based on North American data and there is need for similar studies in other economic and social conditions, with different patterns of consumption, different income levels, different regulatory arrangements, and generally different stages of technological development (e.g. Das and Srinivasan, 1999; Karikari and Gyimah-Brempong, 1999).

Topics that have been clarified include residential access, business demand, price and income elasticities, cross-price elasticities between services, and demand for custom-calling features. Externalities had been seen as important for toll-to-local subsidy reasons but now attention has been given to the ways in which calls 'give rise to further calls, quite independently of price and income' in a process labelled 'the dynamics of information exchange' (Taylor, 1994: 259). This marks an all-too-rare event when the narrower 'telecom economics' is brought into an analytical partnership with the wider economics of information.

Research priorities were: business demand, residential cross-price elasticities, the relationship between telecommunications and other goods and services in household budgets, the dynamics of information exchange, and firm-specific elasticities (as monopoly suppliers have been replaced by duopoly or oligopoly). As Taylor saw the research agenda:

> The challenge for demand analysis in the telephone companies ... is to forge links with marketing departments and to become integrated into company budgeting and forecasting processes. Applied demand analysis has a strategic role to play in a competitive environment, ranging from the conventional types of elasticity estimation in traditional markets to the identification of new markets. The possibilities are vast. It only requires imagination, hard work – and some humility – on the part of economists and demand analysts. (1994: 270)

Such research has been hampered by the deregulation and restructuring of telecommunications, and reflects both a high degree of specialization and business interests. The most productive research might prove to be on the dynamics of information exchange theme. For example, how do communities of interest form (1994: 268, n. 19)? Worthwhile questions include: How do such communities cohere and disintegrate? How are new information goods and services adopted? How do calls create need for further calls? How are business (and more generally organizational) needs for information shaped and managed? Findings from such research might throw some light upon a wide range of phenomena and processes: e.g. changing urban patterns of cooperation and conflict; intercountry relationships; and the formation of regional patterns (Madden, 1999).

Two further topics serve to illustrate the potential of demand studies. First, a recent RAND report addresses the question, 'What are the opportunities for and the obstacles to increased use of the Internet and electronic mail to facilitate communication between government agencies and the citizen clients?' (Neu et al., 1999: iii). The communication envisaged is citizen–government personal communication rather than the downloading of forms. Surveys indicated that such usage had barely begun. Security issues loomed large. Trends were reported as 'not encouraging ... [and] many gaps in the availability of a computer at home were major in both [1993 and 1997] and had *widened* in the four-year interval' (1999: xxi). Operational concerns were acknowledged but the Internet was nevertheless judged appropriate for the purpose, allowing improved service. The conclusion was an expression of faith: 'Citizens will eventually insist on communication with government agencies by e-mail' (1999: xxiii).

It may seem reasonable to ask why, if large numbers of interactive transactions are taking place on the Internet, there is no demand for citizen–government communication. However, nearly half the US population does not have the necessary access, and operation of a dual system would add to cost. Even if security problems are all solved, the nature of the communication involved may present major difficulties. The full costs have not been assessed, especially in respect of legal aspects, and citizens may well want and feel entitled to time to reflect. At the heart of the report's optimism is a failure to appreciate that homogeneous goods account for the bulk of trade on the Internet. Even lowering of cost and provision of facilities may not offset the consequences of intermittent communication about diverse, specific matters. Not even the hoped-for extension of agent technology (Vulkan, 1999) will present an immediate solution to these content difficulties.

A second topic points to the barriers to demand for information in a developing country context, where 'downloading' proves inappropriate (Stiglitz, 1999: 4). This is a major issue for development policy and programmes.

> Logic dictates that information is an essential resource for the social and economic development of Third World countries, but how can this be demonstrated? How tangible is the linkage between information investments and the achievement of specific development goals? The limited status accorded to information in most developing countries suggests that its potential value is not self-evident. (Menou, 1993: ix)

It is a valid response by those accountable for policies and decisions, when faced with reports of growing numbers of computers, telephone lines and databases, to ask, 'So what?'

A research programme of the International Development Research Centre (IRDC) in Canada (McConnell, 1995; Menou, 1993) has pursued case studies of the impact of *information* in different geographical and information environments (e.g. Africa, Asia, the Caribbean and Latin America).

There are lessons to be learned here as a similar approach is needed in many other situations. The real issues arise from the limitations of the resources and capabilities available and the perceptions of the value of information; and these issues cannot be addressed if the focus is on IT in a narrow sense. A wide range of outcomes between the extremes of stagnation and information cascades[6] (Geroski, 2000) is possible.

The IT Productivity Paradox

The IT productivity paradox has been debated for a long time and is not resolved: the ubiquitous computer is seen as a source of great productivity gains and profits, bringing a golden age of growth, and yet it remains difficult to detect the impact. Some observers highlight technical support, new software and retraining, concluding there are substantial hidden costs. Others point to such indicators as the massive outlays on new IT, stock market booms in new technology stocks, business and policy hype, and IT skill shortages in developed and undeveloped countries alike. They offer various explanations: e.g. the measurements are defective; the payoff is still in the pipeline. Care has to be taken to sort out the elements of truth in both sides of the argument.

Is there an authoritative evaluation? US research by leading productivity analysts reports that

> computer-related gains, large returns to the production and use of computers, and network effects are fundamentally changing the US economy. However, they are not ushering in a period of faster growth of output and total factor productivity. Rather, returns to investment in IT equipment have been successfully internalized by computer producers and computer users. These economic agents are reaping extraordinary rewards for mobilizing investment resources and restructuring economic activities. The rewards are large because of the swift pace of technical change and the rapid deployment of IT equipment through substitution, not because of spillovers to third parties standing on the sidelines of the computer revolution. (Jorgenson and Stiroh, 1999: 114)

A companion study puts this into historical perspective:

> Much of what we are seeing now is 'second order', for example the VCR which combines TV and movies but does not have the fundamental impact of either, and much of the use of the internet which substitutes one form of entertainment for another. Enthusiasts might note that the computer has not created the paperless office, but rather a duplication of electronic activities, all of which generate paper. (Gordon, 1999: 127)

Much in these debates has to be discounted heavily. Stock market valuations of new technology stock are notoriously optimistic and, like the business 'strategies' that inspire them, overly influenced by technological possibilities that take little account of social and economic conditions that affect outcomes.

The Jorgenson and Stiroh analysis emphasizes substitution of IT for other types of capital and labour: 'the massive substitution towards computers in both business and household sectors as the price of computers fell dramatically in the 1980s and 1990s' (1999: 109). The technical change residual in their analysis is the growth spillover after allowing for the growth of all other inputs, including IT equipment – also labelled the growth of total factor productivity. Contrary to the expectations of what they call a Computer Cargo Cult among economists and economic historians, there has been no flood of spillovers after the deployment of IT equipment: 'the story of the computer revolution is one of relatively swift price declines, huge investment in IT equipment, and rapid substitution of this equipment for other inputs' (1999: 110).

Some parts of this analysis can be challenged. The knowledge-based economy calls for a wider definition of measured investment. Education and learning are not to be measured only in terms of schools and universities, as business, official agencies and households are engaged in a continuous process of learning. Knowledge production should take in both R&D and other expenditures that achieve the same ends. Surely software qualifies for inclusion? What of organizational capital and institution building? In separating out expenditure on computers, it seems desirable to take account of the pervasive nature of computers. Jorgenson and Stiroh concede they

> have substantially understated the impact of IT equipment, since we have focused specifically on computers and do not include closely related high-technology products. For example, much telecommunications gear is indistinguishable from IT equipment. Also, computers and semiconductors are now routinely embedded in automobiles and machinery, but we exclude these intermediate inputs from the aggregate production function. (1999: 113)

But just as computers find their way to distant places through processes of change, so too do changes in knowledge, organizational form, new behaviour patterns, new languages and new capabilities. How do these figure in the measured growth of inputs and TFP calculations (Lee et al., 2000; Preissl, 1997; Shin, 2000)?

There is a view that the modern human capacity emerged with *H. sapiens* and that the crucial innovation may have been the invention of language.

> For language is not simply the medium by which we express our ideas and experiences to each other. Rather it is fundamental to the thought process itself. It involves

categorizing and naming objects and sensations in the outer and inner worlds and making associations between resulting mental symbols. It is, in effect, impossible for us to conceive of thought (as we are familiar with it) in the absence of language, and it is the ability to form mental symbols that is the fount of our creativity, for only once we create such symbols can we recombine them and ask such questions as 'What if ...?'
(Tattersall and Matternes, 2000: 44)

Suppose 'computerization' as it progresses involves a change equally fundamental. What might be the social and economic manifestations?

Two matters would seem to be related to this query. The first is coordination – a concept not by any means fully explored in economics but one that has loomed larger since the development of the economics of information. In many applications, IT effects coordination and this leads to substitution of equipment for labour. As the perceived cost of coordination declines, more coordination is put into use. Given more time, potential for infrastructure changes in not only equipment but also organization is detected, and internal reorganization and industry restructuring take place in ways deemed appropriate to the coordination capabilities. Perhaps there is a case for asking whether some of the technological change is demand induced. It would be necessary to include abstract improvements such as organizational and attitudinal changes under the technological change heading.

These thoughts can be brought to bear on the impact of new media. Dudley (1999) asks the question: what has been the relationship, if any, between Europe's communications technology and its rate of economic growth over the past millennium? In the tradition of Innis, his analysis is framed in terms of relative changes in decoding, transmission and storage information costs. This permits a plausible account of history through changes in technology and capabilities – an account that makes use of the characteristics of languages and changes in relative component costs. It points to the possibility that the productivity failure reported by Jorgenson and Stiroh has occurred to date because the new technologies are not yet sufficiently cost-effective to displace those whose positions of strength were established in the previous cycle of cost changes. If so, the Computer Cargo Cult adherents can take heart.

Information and Organization

Organizational change issues have been raised under other headings. One topic, already mentioned, will expose some of the issues involved. The firm, no longer a mathematical point as it was in classical economic theory, is now an imperfect network of information flows. The information it requires comes from outside sources as well as being generated internally. Just as the firm's product was made a variable by the development of monopolistic and imperfect competition theory, so the organization has been made a variable through the development of the economics of information.

This has opened up a great new territory for management, for those seeking to provide management services and for disciplines like management studies and organization science. Much of the literature reflects preoccupation with the new technologies and their possibilities. The prime purpose of obtaining information remains control, but a great deal of management effort in the new economy assumes that there are known ways of collating information and achieving control. Information can be identified, obtained, put to use, and stored away until the next time it is needed. This is an industrial model of information utilization, e.g. data warehousing, but for the most part lacking in cost analysis. Psuedo-measurement has generated strange units and calculations. One encounters references to 'shelf-kilometres' of documents; and, in a strange mix of ingenuity and ingenuousness, one study of the productivity of space telescopes conjures up the number of research papers using observations from a particular station per square metre of telescope lens (Trimble, 1996: 237–46)! Tacit knowledge is defined as what cannot be articulated, but this has not prevented plans to create electronic databases of tacit knowledge. While all this reflects some sense of the value and importance of information, there is a failure to address the real management issues. What information is needed? Is it obtainable within the organization? What are the likely external sources? Do internal and external flows mix easily? What costs are involved? What skills are required? If organizational obsolescence is taken to be a normal experience because of the economic characteristics of information, are there remedies?

A belief that the needed information can be obtained and applied seems often to serve as a barrier to good management.

> [A]dvocates of change ... encourage change as they acknowledge information, as something contained within a system ... This is change which is sufficiently ordered to be studied, to be modeled, to be learnt and taught, to fit into existing policy and strategy ... This is the change of mission statements and vision statements. (Macdonald, 1998: 283)

The simple, inescapable truth is that managers do not face 'an endless examination in arithmetic', nor is there 'an algebra of business which only needs to be supplied with a sufficiency of information to guarantee success' (Shackle, 1968: 3). New technology can do much to create, store and make available information but it cannot ensure such a sufficiency. The new managerialism that focuses on control and performance is responding to the inappropriateness of time worked as a measure but has confidence that the relevant activities can be measured. 'There is little consideration for the intangible, the unmeasurable, the indirect, the long term; flexibility is sacrificed to technical efficiency. Rather than reconciling themselves with living with uncertainty, managers are provided with the comfortable delusion that method will eliminate uncertainty' (Macdonald, forthcoming).

Space does not permit exploration of the entire management empire, but one industrial change can illustrate the relevance of the economics of information. Alliances between firms have become more prominent, e.g. in telecommunications, airlines and media. In the case of telecommunications, by the 1990s, well over 50 per cent of all international phone calls were handled by the four major alliances. Globalization has created pressures to expand, but why has this been done through alliances rather than by mergers and takeovers? To date there are no adequate theories of alliances and there has been an inclination to attribute their growth to deregulation, including a more permissive antitrust policy towards interfirm collaboration, e.g. in respect to basic research. If, however, alliances are entered into both to fill the gaps left by deregulation and to effect information sharing and coordination, then this latter influence obviously falls within the economics of information. In so far as a new organizational form is involved, this is to be shared with organization science and management (Engelbrecht, 1997: 19–42; Noam and Singhal, 1996).

Some sense of the complexity of administrative and institutional processes emerges from an examination of the potentially productive but sadly neglected role of the subversive, not the machine-breaking Luddite, dobber or whistleblower, but the thinking person who persists in asking 'Why?' and challenges orthodoxy, whether it be in the boardroom, on the factory floor, in interdepartmental meetings, or in the community at large. In contrast to most of the other resources that have to be used with information, the services of the subversive may well be low cost but highly productive.

A market element in the provision of additional information precludes genuine dissent. Life is easier and the pay better in a climate of consensus. The consequence is that there is failure to address the unwillingness or inability of executives to consider what they deem irrelevant – or threatening – once their organizations have become obsolete or are victims of lock-in. The economical use of information supposedly effected by the market system may not really be a virtue; executives may be using as much information as they are capable of or willing to use, in which case there is little to be gained from pressing upon them the services of more and more knowledge officers, gatekeepers, mentors, part-time board members and consultants. What is needed are 'reality instructors' – an invention of novelist Saul

Bellow – and some way of ensuring that their message is heard and understood. Meantime, a company float with dissent as its chief or only product would not be looked upon with favour in the stock market. Can new organizational design influence the demand side and achieve optimum use of information? Possibly, but it will require keeping clear of technological fundamentalism, plus both thoroughgoing innovation in organizational design and the backing of new social sanctions.

Economics of Language

If language is fundamental to the thought process itself, there ought to be an economics of language in the knowledge-based economy (Lamberton, 1998; Snow, 1998: 159–72). It seems a logical extension of concern with information. One of the pioneering papers expressed the belief that inquiring into language and communication systems was dealing with 'the essential stuff of economics' and hoped there would be 'a future economics of the most developed and most fully studied system of communication within human organizations: the language, spoken or written' (Marschak, 1965: 523).

As noted in discussing the IT productivity paradox, machine languages may play a similar role to that of natural languages. Researchers should be alive to the potential for machine languages to affect and effect mental symbols and influence organization (Pelikan, 1969: 625–31; Ryan, 1993).

Economic Development

The great bulk of literature dealing with communications and development focuses on telecommunications and IT equipment. This technological infrastructure has had attributed to it almost magical powers. But does telecommunications and equipment investment promote economic development, or does economic development create the demand for more telecommunications services? A strong case can be made (see 'Demand studies' earlier) for approaching this question from a different perspective and asking what is the role of information in the development process. Information capabilities are such that a telecommunications infrastructure is not an information infrastructure (Lamberton, 1996b: 31–8).

Attention should focus on the perceptions, aspirations and policies of industries and governments in their choice of technologies and patterns of socioeconomic development. What factors shape the perceptions of prospects? First, there are cost expectations – e.g. specific costs of modernization of old networks and provision of new networks; costs of infrastructure to make the system as a whole work – and these can be interpreted narrowly as information infrastructure, or much more widely, recognizing that the demand for telecommunications is very largely a derived demand and so a function of the entire process of economic growth. Second, there are some quite deep-seated notions. The causality notion may be the most important. Is telecommunications the linchpin – the 'driver' that leads development? Another notion is globalization; and here it may be that there has been global thinking to excess and too little heard about regionalization (Madden, 1999). Convergence is a third notion. Many studies fail to define this basic concept and list so many paradigms that convergence lacks useful meaning as all these elements are said to be fusing together. For example, communications, information, entertainment, publishing, retailing, financial services, information and Internet paradigms have been proclaimed (Adler, 1995). Then there is coordination, which raises the question whether the market can provide all that is needed. So the building of the infrastructure that is needed for an effective information economy requires organization and institutions as well as markets and technology.

Telephone lines without conversations and data flows do little to generate development. Investment, growth of income and cultural change may do much more, creating, in due course, greater demand for communications. In this way the potential of information as 'a powerful and reusable resource for development' (McConnell, 1995: 2) may be realized.

Policy

Why is it that standard economic theory has little to say about the efficiency of the knowledge-based economy? (See the introduction paragraphs to this chapter.) This can be answered on several levels. If all decision-makers are well informed and new information flow can be ignored, efficient outcomes can be defined. But once the insufficiency of information is admitted, there are problems. As Fritz Machlup suggested, the aim can be 'to act intelligently, with full consideration of the pertinent knowledge at hand and of the pertinent knowledge available at reasonable cost'. This is not the same as seeking 'optimization in making use of the totality of knowledge' and 'requires little argumentation'. Taking cost-effective action falls short of being Pareto efficient. The latter, however, 'invites speculations that may again widen the focus to include choices among alternative actions on different fronts, actions for which different batches of knowledge are used; in this case, we may easily slip again into the sea of undecidability' (1982: 10).

The traditional justifications for intervention in market outcomes are externalities, informational asymmetry and increasing returns. Information phenomena are the trouble spots in economics so it is not altogether unexpected that each of these justifications proves to have informational aspects. It has long been argued that information is very largely a public good. The second justification needs no comment. As for increasing returns, as Samuelson reasoned long ago, they are 'the prime case of deviations from perfect competition … Universal constant returns to scale (in everything, including effective acquisition and communication of knowledge) is practically certain to convert *laissez-faire* or free enterprise into perfect competition' (1967: 117). These hopes are dashed in the knowledge-based economy where the importance of information ensures there are pervasive economies of scale.

Taken together, these considerations are a powerful critique of policy approaches based on mainstream economics. However, awareness of these difficulties has yet to be reflected in policy action – and, for that matter, in much of the modelling and analysis of both researchers and consultants. Both new policy initiatives and modification of existing policies are needed. For example, the focus should shift from short-term allocative efficiency to 'a set of long-term policies aimed at enhancing the knowledge base … through increased investment in the knowledge infrastructure, the knowledge distribution system, and the human knowledge component (human resources, education, training and organisational change)' (Soete, 1996: 387). An excellent illustration of the need for modification arises in the regulatory area. Given the characteristics of information and the new technological capabilities, the knowledge-based economy affords 'greater scope for the suppression of competition' (Stiglitz, 1999: 8). A consistent approach needs to be developed in intellectual property systems where administrative simplicity has hampered efforts to 'fine tune' the term and strength of the rights by taking account of the diversity of inventions and innovations.

In summary, the knowledge-based economy offers opportunity for an enhanced public role in the provision of information, 'invention' of new institutions, establishment of systems of remuneration more appropriate to 'information work', and many ways of effecting greater coordination. This last is a matter for macro- as well as microeconomic policy (Earl, 1998: 331–42).

Distorted Images

There is perennial complaint that official statistics provide distorted images of what is happening in the economy. Costs, administrative inertia and outdated lenses result in a failure to catch up with the industrial and social change that is taking place. The most familiar problem is highlighted by 'shadow' economy studies showing that a quite large part of conventionally defined activity is not captured in official statistics and suggesting that their scope should be extended to take in some elements of non-market activity.

Decisions have to be made about what is important in understanding events in the economy. The emerging focus on the role of knowledge is creating major problems for those responsible for official collections. How is knowledge to be measured? Must all knowledge be measured or just new knowledge? Is new knowledge to be captured in R&D or are there other components that are also important? What should be included in investment – both in knowledge itself and in effecting change (Kirova and Lipsey, 1998)?

A new social accounting is needed, with 'a new paradigm: new models, new variables. This will mean new measures … New approaches, perhaps grounded in other disciplines [than economics], must be developed to quantify knowledge variables like firm learning, know-how, adaptation' (Carter, 1996: 67). All this flows from recognition not just that economic theory, research and policy have to catch up with contemporary conditions but that the failure of the discipline to devise a central role for knowledge has always been a fundamental flaw.

WHAT IS NOT KNOWN

Perhaps Geertz-style narratives will always need to be rewritten; perhaps Shackle's 'endless gaining of knowledge' implies that the tenure of all knowledge expires because the lenses being used are changed as new conceptual frameworks are imagined. This may be an uncomfortable thought for those dominating present academic gatherings, just as contemplating the demise of dominant firms or governments in office makes business leaders and ministers uneasy. Such contemplations link to the unwillingness of governments and industry to support the more challenging social science research.

In terms of research, there is a need to ask what 'not known' implies. Does not listing items in this category imply some knowledge about them? It might be useful here to invoke two categories. First, there are questions sufficiently well defined to be outlined in research funding proposals and acceptable to research councils because they fall within the current paradigms, fads and fashions.[5] The researchers became the prey of endorsed questions. Second, there are confessions of ignorance and expressions of hope and willingness to search for central questions that challenge orthodoxy; to search for new lenses through which to view the economy. Fritz Machlup did so with his 1962 book *The Production and Distribution of Knowledge in the United States*, and it has been widely acknowledged that the impact has been profound even if somewhat less than Kenneth Boulding had hoped.

This overview of the contribution that the economics of information is making to the study of industrial change has been cast in terms of two 'econ' tribes: mainstream economics and the economics of information. A more comprehensive effort to cope with the complexity of the real-world processes of change must acknowledge the many other tribes and disciplines and will require multi-tribal and interdisciplinary work. The shaping of an information science or information studies needs to take guidance from the existing limited understanding of the relationships between the economy in the mainstream sense and the meshing of conventions, knowledge, culture and institutions that makes up society. Hopefully, the joint ventures, alliances and possible mergers amongst the econ tribes would reflect similar senses of direction in multidisciplinary research, so yielding questions for the second, challenging category. This chapter ends with some speculations about some such potential lines of inquiry.

It has been argued that 'there is a *prima facie* case for regarding the evolution of economic systems as an entropic phenomenon but with information rather than energy providing the main propagating role' (Clark, 1991: 102). Hodgson responded, stressing the difficulty: 'Although tantalising, this suggestion must overcome the difficult problem of the definition of "information" and the distinction between different types of information or knowledge' (1993: 300, n. 8). The primary information and secondary information sector approach was an attempt to structure the complex information activities and was modified so that it fits into an input–output framework (Stäglin, 1989). The next stage might be to shift the focus to the demand side; to seek out the mix of characteristics that underlies the demands depicted in such modelling and their relationships with the capabilities and resources of the information users and the constraints on their decisions. For example, attention is now said to be one of the scarce resources. It is not enough to recognize that information is multifaceted; a richer taxonomy is needed (Lamberton, 1999).

The recent focus on telepistemology, the study of knowledge acquired at a distance by means of e.g. the telephone, television and now the Internet, hints at the potential but also shows the difficulties involved. Leo Marx comments on a recent book: 'As the electronic revolution gains momentum, the boundary between humanity's manufactured and its flesh-and-blood bodily experience is rapidly shifting … All the contributors recognize its extent and its import, but most of them … reject the popular delusion that the boundary is about to be erased' (Goldberg, 2000: blurb). Economists studying the demand for Internet services, management experts trying to devise optimal business organizations and all those concerned, especially policy-makers, about the messy philosophical and social problems should pay heed.

Given such awareness, study of the ongoing processes of information provision, learning, decision, organizational change and growth – in short, industrial change – has potential for collaboration. Can, for example, current initiatives in the economics of information (Lamberton, 1998) come together with related efforts in organizational science (Brousseau, 2000; Ciborra, 2000; Macdonald, 1998; Nonaka et al., 1998; Oniki, 1999), evolutionary economics (Eliasson and Taymaz, 2000), cognitive economics (Paquet, 1999) and endogeneous growth theory (Adams, 2000; Engelbrecht, 1999; Romer, 1986)? The complexities become even greater if the spatial dimension is accorded the importance it probably deserves (Droege, 1997; Gaspar and Glaeser, 1998; Wilson and Corey, 2000). But where is the funding organization to provide the support for what could be a momentous occasion?

The potential outcomes have major implications for policy (*The Economist*, 2000). Increasingly in the knowledge-based economy, conventional thought about efficient choices is proving inadequate to the task. There is reason to reject the policy of 'trust the market' on knowledge issues. This may initiate, on the one hand, the pendulum swing back towards intervention; and on the other, a return to mercantilistic initiatives and reliance upon 'trickle-down' to the key issue, poverty. The information revolution has not and will not in some miraculous way eliminate the scarcities and inequities that characterize society and its industrial organization.

NOTES

This chapter builds on and extends Lamberton (1971; 1984; 1996a; 1997). See also Macdonald and Nightingale (1999). Perhaps an explanatory note on 'economics' is permissible. In the context of media and communication literature, one meets frequently the claim that information has been commoditized. Those making this claim should ponder carefully the extent to which major contributors have, as has been done in this chapter, laid stress on the fact that information can be a commodity but only to a limited extent. Similarly, there is an almost standard claim that information for the economist, perhaps defined as what reduces uncertainty, is devoid of content. This is more or less true of the Shannon treatment but that was an engineering approach. Utility and even profit can be interpreted to include not only money gains but also other satisfactions: consumption, power, bequests or interesting challenges. Therefore, the criticism holds for 'information as oil' but it loses its force when the richer concepts of information as structured capital, as resource, as commodity, as perception of pattern and as a constitutive force in

society are adopted. Finally, it should be added that economics does not speak with one voice: it is 'made up of a variety of subfield specialists, different generations with different kinds of training, persons of greatly varying ideological preferences, individuals with markedly different perceptions regarding appropriate methodological choices, and a lot of Indians and a lot of would-be chiefs ... what interests one segment of the profession bores another' (Perlman, 1981: 4).

1 'The concept of a more or less freely functioning market system has been central to economic theory during the last three hundred years of its development' (Vickers, 1995: v). This defines and limits mainstream economics which appears as 'trust the market', 'small government' and economic rationalism. It emphasizes production rather than consumption, judges progress in terms of economic growth, and avoids matters of both institutions and internal organization. The counterview in terms of the tyranny of the market has come increasingly to base its critique on the mostly implicit assumptions about the role of information (Lamberton, 1996a; Middleton, 1998; North, 1990; Stiglitz, 1994; Thurow, 1983; Vickers, 1995; Vines and Stevenson, 1991).

2 An allocation of resources is (Pareto) efficient if no one can be made better off without someone else being made worse off.

3 Schement and Curtis advocate such an approach: 'bureaucracy ... is itself an information technology' (1995: 230).

4 For a new, disaggregated approach to the effects of liberalization on the composition of R&D activity, see e.g. Calderini and Garrone (2001).

5 A public good is characterized by non-rivalrous consumption (the marginal costs of providing it to an additional person are zero) and non-excludability (the costs of excluding an individual from consumption are prohibitively high).

6 For literature on these as economic phenomena see Bikchandani et al. (1998) and Anderson and Holt (1997).

REFERENCES

Adams, J.D. (2000) 'Endogenous R&D spillovers and industrial research productivity'. Working Paper 7484, National Bureau of Economic Research, New York.

Adler, R.P. (1995) 'Introduction', in Institute for Information Studies, *Crossroads on the Information Highway: Convergence and Diversity in Communications Technologies*. Queenstown, MD: Institute for Information Studies.

Anderson, L.R. and Holt, C.A. (1997) 'Information cascades in the laboratory', *American Economic Review*, 87 (2): 847–62.

Arrow, K.J. (1962) 'Economic welfare and the allocation of resources for invention', reprinted in D.M. Lamberton (ed.) (1996), *The Economics of Communication and Information*. Cheltenham: Elgar. pp. 227–43.

Arrow, K.J. (1974) *The Limits of Organization*. New York: Norton.

Arrow, K.J. (1984) *Collected Papers of Kenneth J. Arrow*. Vol. 4: *The Economics of Information*. Oxford: Blackwell.

Arrow, K.J. (1996) 'Technical information and industrial structure', *Industrial and Corporate Change*, 5: 645–52.

Bikchandani, S., Hirshleifer, D. and Welch, I. (1998) 'Learning from behavior of others: conformity, fads, and informational cascades', *Journal of Economic Perspectives*, 12 (3): 151–70.

Boulding, K.E. (1963) 'The knowledge industry. Review of Fritz Machlup, *The Production and Distribution of Knowledge in the United States*', *Challenge*, 11 (8): 36–8.

Braman, S. (1989) 'Defining information: an approach for policymakers', reprinted in D.M. Lamberton (ed.) (1996), *The Economics of Communication and Information*. Cheltenham: Elgar. pp. 3–12.

Brousseau, E. (2000) 'What institutions to organize electronic commerce? Private institutions and the organization of markets', *Economics of Innovation and New Technology*, 9 (3): 245–73.

Calderini, M. and Garrone, P. (2001) 'Liberalisation, industry turmoil and the balance of R&D activities', *Information Economics and Policy*, 13 (2): 199–230.

Carter, A.P. (1996) 'Measuring the performance of a knowledge-based economy', in OECD Documents, *Employment and Growth in the Knowledge-Based Economy*. Paris: OECD. pp. 61–8.

Ciborra, C.U. and associates (2000) *From Control to Drift: the Dynamics of Corporate Information Infrastructures*. Oxford: Oxford University Press.

Clark, N.G. (1991) 'Organisation and information in the evolution of information systems', in P.P. Saviotti and J.S. Metcalfe (eds), *Evolutionary Theories of Economic and Technological Change: Present States and Future Prospects*. Reading, MA: Harwood. pp. 88–107.

Das, P. and Srinivasan, S.J. (1999) 'Demand for telephone usage in India', *Information Economics and Policy*, 11 (2): 177–94.

Dow, S.C. and Earl, P.E. (eds) (1999) *Economic Organization and Economic Knowledge: Essays in Honour of Brian J. Loasby*. Cheltenham: Elgar.

Drahos, P. (ed.) (1998) 'Trade and intellectual property', *Prometheus*, 16 (3) (special issue).

Drahos, P. (ed.) (2000) *Intellectual Property*. Aldershot: Ashgate.

Droege, P. (ed.) (1997) *Intelligent Environments: Spatial Aspects of the Information Revolution*. Amsterdam: North-Holland.

Dudley, L. (1999) 'Communications and economic growth', *European Economic Review*, 43: 595–619.

Earl, P.E. (1998) 'Information, coordination and macroeconomics', *Information Economics and Policy*, 10 (3): 331–42.

Eliasson, G. and Taymaz, E. (2000) 'Institutions, entrepreneurship, economic flexibility and growth: experiments on an evolutionary micro-to-macro model', in U. Canter, H. Hanusch and S. Klepper (eds), *Economic Evolution, Learning, and Complexity*. Heidelberg: Physica. pp. 265–86.

Eliasson, G., Folster, S., Lindberg, T., Pousette, T. and Taymaz, E. (1990) *The Knowledge Based Economy*. Stockholm: Industrial Institute for Economic and Social Research.

Engelbrecht, H.-J. (1997) 'The international economy: knowledge flows and information activities', in D.M. Lamberton (ed.), *The New Research Frontiers of Communications Policy*. Amsterdam: North-Holland. pp. 19–42.

Engelbrecht, H.-J. (1999) 'International knowledge spillovers, absorptive capacity and productivity in OECD countries', in S. Macdonald and J. Nightingale (eds), *Information and Organization: a Tribute to the Work of Don Lamberton*. Amsterdam: North-Holland. pp. 46–85.

Gaspar, J. and Glaeser, E.L. (1998) 'Information technology and the future of cities', *Journal of Urban Economics*, 43: 136–56.

Geertz, C. (1995) *After the Fact: Two Countries, Four Decades. One Anthropologist*. Cambridge, MA: Harvard University Press.

Geroski, P.A. (2000) 'Models of technology diffusion', *Research Policy*, 29 (4–5): 603–25.

Goldberg, K. (ed.) (2000) *The Robot in the Garden: Telerobotics and Telepistemology in the Age of the Internet*. Cambridge, MA: MIT Press.

Gordon, R.J. (1999) 'US economic growth since 1870: one big wave?', *American Economic Review*, 89 (2): 123–8.

Greenstein, S.M. (1992) 'Invisible hands and visible advisors: an economic interpretation of standardization', *Journal of the American Society for Information Science*, 43 (8): 538–49.

Groenewegen, P.D. (1977) 'Adam Smith and the division of labour', *Australian Economic Papers*, 16: 161–74.

Hawkins, R.W., Mansell, R.E. and Steinmueller, W.E. (1997) *Mapping and Measuring the Information Technology, Electronics and Communications Sector in the United Kingdom*. Brighton: SPRU, University of Sussex.

Hodgson, G.M. (1993) *Economics and Evolution: Bringing Life Back into Economics*. Cambridge: Polity.

Hodgson, G.M. (1999) *Economics and Utopia: Why the Learning Economy Is Not the End of History*. London: Routledge.

Jorgenson, D.W. and Stiroh, K.J. (1999) 'Information technology and growth', *American Economic Review*, 89 (2): 109–15.

Karikari, J.A. and Gyimah-Brempomg, K. (1999) 'Demand for international telephone services between US and Africa', *Information Economics and Policy*, 11 (4): 407–35.

Kirova, M. and Lipsey, R. (1998) 'Measuring real investment: trends in the United States and international comparisons'. Working Paper 6404, National Bureau of Economic Research, New York.

Lamberton, D.M. (1965) *The Theory of Profit*. Oxford: Blackwell.

Lamberton, D.M. (ed.) (1971) *The Economics of Information and Knowledge*. Harmondsworth: Penguin.

Lamberton, D.M. (1984) 'The economics of information and organization', in M.E. Williams (ed.), *Annual Review of Information Science and Technology (ARIST)*, vol. 19. Knowledge Industries Publications for American Society for Information Science. pp. 3–30.

Lamberton, D.M. (1994) 'Intellectual property and innovation', in M. Dodgson and R. Rothwell (eds), *Handbook of Industrial Innovation*. Aldershot: Elgar. pp. 301–10.

Lamberton, D.M. (ed.) (1996a) *The Economics of Communication and Information*. Cheltenham: Elgar.

Lamberton, D.M. (1996b) 'A telecommunications infrastructure is not an information infrastructure', *Prometheus*, 14 (1): 31–8.

Lamberton, D.M. (ed.) (1997) *The New Research Frontiers of Communications Policy*. Amsterdam: North-Holland.

Lamberton, D.M. (1998) 'Language and critical mass'. Paper presented at the 12th Biennial International Telecommunications Society Conference, Stockholm.

Lamberton, D.M. (1999) 'Information: pieces, batches or flows?', in S.C. Dow and P.E. Earl (eds), *Economic Organization and Economic Knowledge: Essays in Humour of Brian J. Loasby*. Cheltenham: Elgar. pp. 209–24.

Lazaric, N. and Lorenz, E. (eds) (1998) *Trust and Economic Learning*. Cheltenham: Elgar.

Lee, C.-H. Sophie, Barua, A. and Whinston, A.B. (2000) 'The complementarity of mass customization and electronic commerce', *Economics of Innovation and New Technology*, 9 (2): 81–109.

Loasby, B.J. (1998) 'The organization of capabilities', *Journal of Economic Behavior & Organisation*, 35: 139–60.

Loomis, D.G. and Taylor, L.D. (eds) (1999) *The Future of the Telecommunications Industry: Forecasting and Demand Analysis*. Dordrecht: Kluwer.

Macdonald, S. (ed.) (1996) 'Informal information flow', *International Journal of Technology Management*, 11 (1–2) (special issue).

Macdonald, S. (1998) *Information for Innovation: Managing Change from an Information Perspective*. Oxford: Oxford University Press.

Macdonald, S. (forthcoming) 'Managing with method: information in policy and strategy for innovation', in D.M. Lamberton (ed.), *Managing the Global: Globalization, Employment and Quality of Life*. London: Tauris.

Macdonald, S. and Nightingale, J. (eds) (1999) *Information and Organization: a Tribute to the Work of Don Lamberton*. Amsterdam: North-Holland.

Machlup, F. (1962) *The Production and Distribution of Knowledge in the United States*. Princeton, NJ: Princeton University Press.

Machlup, F. (1979) 'An economist's reflections on an Institute for the Advanced Study of Information Science', *Journal of the American Society for Information Science*, 30 (2): 111–13.

Machlup, F. (1982) 'Optimum utilization of knowledge', *Society, Knowledge, Information, and Decisions*, 20 (1): 8–10.

Machlup, F. and Mansfield, U. (eds) (1983) *The Study of Information: Interdisciplinary Messages*. New York: Wiley.

Madden, G. (1999) 'Asia–Pacific information flows and trade', in S. Macdonald and J. Nightingale (eds), *Information and Organization: a Tribute to the work of Don Lamberton*. Amsterdam: North-Holland. pp. 393–406.

Marschak, J. (1965), 'Economics of language', reprinted in D.M. Lamberton (ed.) (1971), *Economics of Information and Knowledge*. Harmondsworth: Penguin. pp. 37–58.

Mathias, P. (1983) 'The machine: icon of economic growth', in S. Macdonald, D.M. Lamberton and T. Mandeville (eds), *The Trouble with Technology: Explorations in the Process of Technological Change*. London: Pinter.

McConnell, P. (ed.) (1995) *Making a Difference: Measuring the Impact of Information on Development*. Ottawa: International Development Research Centre.

Meier, R.L. (1960) 'Information, resource use and economic growth', in J.J. Spengler (ed.), *Natural Resources and Economic Growth*. Ann Arbor, MI: Resources for the Future, Inc. and Social Sciences Research Council.

Menou, M. (ed.) (1993) *The Impact of Information on Development*. Ottawa: International Development Research Centre.

Middleton, R. (1998) *Charlatans or Saviours? Economists and the British Economy from Marshall to Meade*. Cheltenham: Elgar.

Miles, I. and associates (1990) *Mapping and Measuring the Information Economy*. London: British Library Board.

Nelson, R.R. (1981) 'Assessing private enterprise: an exegesis of tangled doctrine', reprinted in D.M. Lamberton (ed.) (1996), *The Economics of Communication and Information*. Cheltenham: Elgar. pp. 59–77.

Neu, C.R., Anderson, R.H. and Bikson, T.K. (1999) *Sending Your Government a Message: E-mail Communication between Citizens and Government*. Santa Monica, CA: RAND Science and Technology.

Noam, E. and Singhal, A. (1996) 'Supra-national regulation for supra-national telecommunications carriers?' *Telecommunications Policy*, 20 (10): 769–87.

Nonaka, I., Ray, T. and Umemoto, K. (1998) 'Japanese organizational knowledge creation in Anglo-American environments', *Prometheus*, 16 (4): 421–39.

North, D.C. (1990) *Institutions, Institutional Change and Economic Performance*. New York: Cambridge University Press.

Oniki, H. (1999) 'On the informational structure and functioning of Japanese organisations: a comparison with Western organisations', in S. Macdonald and J. Nightingale (eds), *Information and Organization: a*

Tribute to the Work of Don Lamberton. Amsterdam: North-Holland. pp. 197–214.

Pandit, N., Swann, G.M.P. and Watts, T. (1997) 'HTSF marketing and customer education: a role for a technology awareness programme?', *Prometheus*, 15 (3), 293–308.

Paquet, G. (1999) 'Lamberton's road to cognitive economics', in S. Macdonald and J. Nightingale (eds), *Information and Organization: a Tribute to the Work of Don Lamberton*. Amsterdam: North-Holland. pp. 63–79.

Pelikan, P. (1969) 'Language for a limiting factor for centralization', *American Economic Review*, 59 (4): 625–31.

Perlman, M. (1981) 'Editor's note', *Journal of Economic Literature*, 19 (1): 1–4.

Preissl, B. (1997) 'Information technology: a critical perspective on its economic effects', *Prometheus*, 15 (1): 5–25.

Ramiscal, N.G. (2000) 'The nature and functions of metatags: covert infringement of trademarks and other issues', *Prometheus*, 18 (1): 39–57.

Ricketson, S. (1992) 'New wine into old bottles: technological change and intellectual property rights', *Prometheus*, 10 (1): 53–82.

Romer, P.M. (1986) 'Increasing returns and long-run growth', *Journal of Political Economy*, 94 (5): 1002–37.

Ryan, J.P. (1993) 'Machine translation: matching reality to expectations', in S. Nirenburg (ed.), *Progress in Machine Translation*. Amsterdam: IOS.

Samuelson, P.A. (1967) 'The monopolistic competition revolution', in R.E. Kuenne (ed.), *Monopolistic Competition Theory: Essays in Honor of Edward H. Chamberlin*. New York: Wiley. pp. 105–38.

Schement, J.R. and Curtis, T. (1995) *Tendencies and Tensions in the Information Age: the Production and Distribution of Information in the United States*. New Brunswick, NJ: Transaction.

Shackle, G.L.S. (1968) 'Policy, poetry, and success', in G.L.S. Shackle (ed.), *On the Nature of Business Success*. Liverpool: Liverpool University Press. pp. 3–18.

Shackle, G.L.S. (1972), *Epistemics and Economics: a Critique of Economic Doctrines*. Cambridge: Cambridge University Press.

Shapiro, C. and Varian, H.R. (1999) *Information Rules: a Strategic Guide to the Network Economy*. Boston: Harvard Business School Press.

Shin, I. (2000) 'Use of informational network and organizational productivity: firm-level evidence in Korea', *Economics of Innovation and New Technology*, 9 (5): 447–63.

Simon, H.A. (1991) 'Organization and markets', *Journal of Economic Perspectives*, 5 (2): 25–44.

Snow, M.S. (1998) 'Economic, statistical, and linguistic factors affecting success on the test of English as a foreign language (TOEFL)', *Information Economics and Policy*, 10 (2): 159–72.

Soete, L. (1996) 'Globalisation, employment and the knowledge-based economy', in OECD Documents, *Employment and Growth in the Knowledge-Based Economy*. Paris: OECD. pp. 383–7.

Stäglin, R. (1989) 'Towards an input–output subsystem for the information sector', reprinted in D.M. Lamberton (ed.) (1996), *The Economics of Communication and Information*. Cheltenham: Elgar. pp. 114–27.

Stigler, G.J. (1961) 'The economics of information', reprinted in D.M. Lamberton (ed.) (1971), *The Economics of Information and Knowledge*. Cheltenham: Elgar. pp. 61–82.

Stiglitz, J.E. (1985) 'Information and economic analysis: a perspective', *Economic Journal*, supplement, 95: 21–41.

Stiglitz, J.E. (1994) *Whither Socialism?* Cambridge, MA: MIT Press.

Stiglitz, J.E. (1999) 'Public policy for a knowledge economy' (speeches). Available at: www.worldbank.org.

Sutton, J. (1998) *Technology and Market Structure: Theory and History*. Cambridge, MA: MIT Press.

Tattersall, I. and Matternes, J.H. (2000) 'Once we were not alone', *Scientific American*, 282 (1): 38–44.

Taylor, L.D. (ed.) (1989) 'Telecommunications demand modeling', *Information Economics and Policy*, 3 (4) (special issue).

Taylor, L.D. (1994) *Telecommunications Demand in Theory and Practice*. Dordrecht: Kluwer.

The Economist (2000) 'A survey of the new economy', 23 September: 1–40.

Thurow, L.C. (1983) *Dangerous Current: the State of Economics*. New York: Oxford University Press.

Trimble, V. (1996) 'Productivity and impact of large optical telescopes', *Scientometrics*, 36 (2): 237–46.

Tyler, M. (1999) 'Review of Lamberton (ed.), *Communication and Trade'*, *Telecommunications Policy*, 23: 717–18.

Vickers, D. (1995) *The Tyranny of the Market: a Critique of Theoretical Foundations*. Ann Arbor, MI: University of Michigan Press.

Vines, D. and Stevenson, A. (1991) *Information, Strategy and Public Policy*. Oxford: Blackwell.

Vulkan, N. (1999) 'Economic implications of agent technology and e-commerce', *Economic Journal*, 109: F67–90.

Webster, E. (1999) *The Economics of Intangible Investment*. Cheltenham: Elgar.

Wildman, S.S. (1998) 'Media and multimedia: the challenge for policy and economic analysis', *Information Economics and Policy*, 10 (1): 1–7.

Wilson, M.I. and Corey, E. (eds) (2000) *Information Tectonics: Space, Place and Technology in an Electronic Age*. New York: Wiley.

21

The New Economy: Internet Telecommunications and Electronic Commerce?

PETER LOVELOCK and JOHN URE

During the year when this chapter was written, the first phase, or lurch, of the Internet economy had played itself out with the bursting of the dot.com bubble. Claims, hardly theories, of a 'new economy' backed by a 'new economics' or 'silicon economics' came thick and fast during this first phase, driven in the popular imagination by the very 'new media' that were part and parcel of the phenomenon. It was also promoted for all it was worth by the IT companies and telecom equipment manufacturers who stood to gain the most from the boom. Suddenly the Internet was fashionable, even in the literal sense as IT business people started 'dressing down' to more closely resemble their web-culture counterparts. A whole new vocabulary started up. We learned that Internet startups were faced with 'burn rate' problems owing to 'customer acquisition costs', and that industries no longer 'transform', let alone 'change': they 'morph'. Peals of laughter would greet any banker who had the temerity to ask a dot.com startup when the black ink would appear on the balance sheet, an attitude brilliantly captured time and again in *the* textbook of the Internet, the cartoons of Doonesbury. There really seems to have been little more substance to the decision-making processes inside many of these companies than to the characters brought to life by Gary Trudeau.

Yet something important survives – something that is a new permanent feature of the political economy landscape. Whether it constitutes a 'new paradigm' or just an evolving feature of the rapid developments in communications, computers and the media content sector – all of which in fact have a longer history than the commercialization of the Internet – is subject to debate. (See the discussion

of the Internet as a general-purpose technology below.) What does seem to be obvious is that a larger absolute number of people are more mobile across boundaries – geography, skill, language, industry and so on – than ever before, that new (IT) skills are in high demand, that the idea of lifetime employment with one organization is dying out, and that this economic and demographic flux advantages and disadvantages different sets of people and communities. But in principle all of this has happened before. Perhaps the pace and scope – without getting into the globalization debate – of change are new, and the factors that have explanatory power clearly include the Internet and the rise of the 'new media' industries as part of a structural shift within economies.

The term 'new media', which has displaced 'multimedia', has no universally accepted meaning, but at least has the advantage of focusing attention on what constitutes 'new' as opposed to 'multi', where examples can be traced back to early cinema, if not earlier. The Internet, and its association with the World Wide Web, are the most in-your-face examples of the 'new', but of course they rest upon precedent developments in telecommunications and computer networking, as well as the media. We would emphasize that these precedent developments include policy, regulatory and market developments as well as technological ones. Forthcoming from the technological synergies and business convergence of these sectors is electronic commerce, and this is the climacteric, the critical turning point for the apostles of the new economy viewpoint.

It raises many interesting questions. Does the rapid diffusion of the Internet give overwhelming advantages to the first mover, the United States, in areas such as electronic business, or is it a potential equalizer, offering small and medium enterprises (SMEs) in developing economies an equal chance to enter the world market? Will early American dominance of the web homogenize American English as the world's *lingua franca*, or will non-English-language websites and voice-activated and translation software have other effects? Will the spread of the Internet exacerbate or alleviate the digital divide between those with affordable universal access and those without? These questions are important for social and political as well as economic and cultural reasons, but they are raised here only to underscore the unknown. In this chapter we are more narrowly focused on what in the classical tradition would be called issues of political economy. Our aim is to review how the growth and development of the Internet and the closely related developments in telecommunications and electronic commerce, which are both underpinnings to and part of the new media industries, are being researched by scholars and industry specialists. This means that when considering the types of questions raised above we are, in the first instance, more interested in how, methodologically, such questions are being approached than in the questions or answers as such. This implies that if a question raises that much methodological interest, it is probably an interesting question to scholarship, and the converse may also be true.

Before we leave our biases as social scientists, we may add that in our view all materially grounded science early in its development, or early in a new line of inquiry, relies upon empirical data, a process of collection, classification, measurement, etc. These processes themselves are theoretically informed, for example the collection process often involves a selection process; the classification system is not arbitrary; and the choice of metrics and the role assigned to measurement and to the subsequent use of quantitative techniques is quite critical. It is worth making these short points because in the early emergence of studies of the Internet, telecommunications and electronic commerce, the gap between systematic scholarly research and what is often termed 'analysis' in the multitude of public and private media now available can be substantial.

A number of factors can be presented to explain this, including the commercialization of large swathes of higher education, giving rise to one of the foremost components of the new 'knowledge-based' economy, the education industry. But we also would point out that the pace of development and radical change in the areas of the Internet, telecommunications and electronic commerce has been rapid and recent, leaving scholars breathless to catch up. As a consequence, many scholars, for example in the field of economics, are inclined at first to regard these developments as outgrowths of existing industries or commercial practices which can be accommodated within existing theory even if the models have to be tweaked a bit. The 'others' are economists who wish to view the new developments as new in the sense of setting a foundation for a 'new economy' with 'new economics' based upon rather old principles of 'network economics' and 'increasing returns'. Both approaches have something to offer in the sense that healthy scepticism is the basis of good science, but so also is a willingness to recognize a shift of parameters. Our point is simply that the phenomenon under scrutiny is in its formative stages, reliable time series and panel data are often not available, and scholars who must feel their way in the dark will look for any source of enlightenment they can find.

In this chapter we first examine the concept of a new economy, and its relation to 'new media', the Internet and computer networking. We then consider in greater detail the research issues around the Internet, telecommunications networking and electronic commerce, using a political economy perspective throughout.

A NEW ECONOMY?

Despite the lack of any clear definitions of the new economy, its main attributes, according to the OECD in *A New Economy? The Changing Role of Innovation and Information Technology in Growth* (2000), are (1) higher rates of non-inflationary growth, (2) lower rates of unemployment associated with business cycles, and (3) new sources of growth, including areas of increasing returns to scale, network effects and externalities. Among these new sources of growth are several observed factors, popularly labelled 'laws'.

Moore's Law, Metcalfe's Law and Gilder's Law

Moore's law is the observation first made by Gordon Moore, then chairman of Intel, that every 18 months it is possible to double the number of transistor circuits etched on a computer chip.[1] This 'law' has prevailed for the past 40 years.[2] Moore's law implies a tenfold increase in memory and processing power every five years, a hundredfold every ten years, a thousandfold every 15. This is one of the most dramatic rates of sustained technical progress in history.

As extraordinary as Moore's law has proven, of even greater impact has been Metcalfe's law. Bob Metcalfe, inventor of Ethernet, observed that the value of a network is proportional to the square of the number of people using it. Thus, Metcalfe's law, which is a modern version of the old law of increasing returns, says that the value of a network increases in direct proportion to the square of the number of machines that are on it. This is also known as the 'network effect'. The value to any one individual of a telephone or fax machine, for instance, is proportional to the number of friends and associates who have phones or faxes. Double the number of participants, therefore, and the value to each participant is doubled, and the total value of the network is multiplied fourfold.[3]

This advance has pulled through extraordinary rates of associated innovation, and has led to communications capacity exploding at a rate that now dwarfs even Moore's law. The result has become known as 'Gilder's law', named after the high-tech futurologist George Gilder (1997), and forecasts that total bandwidth will triple every year for the next 25 years. Improvements in data compression, amplification and multiplexing now permit a single fibre-optic strand to carry 25 terabits of information per second, that is 25 times more information than the average traffic load of the entire world's communications networks put together.

Network Economics and a New Economy?

But does the power of these technological and business forces bring into being a new economy driven by a new economics? Two converts to the idea that the 'acceleration of productivity growth, driven by information technology, is the most remarkable feature of the US growth resurgence' of the late 1990s are Jorgenson and Stiroh (2000). But they firmly focus on the price–performance indicators of the computer industry itself and the diffusion of these gains to sectors that have undergone a restructuring by substituting lower-cost capital services to take advantage of information technology. They see 'little support for the "new economy" picture of spillovers cascading from information technology producers onto users of this technology' (2000: 4).[4] On the contrary, others such as Besnahan (1999) have taken the view that the networking aspect of computers is becoming decisive in raising productivity through its effects on restructuring bureaucracies and organizations, substituting for many moderate skill white-collar jobs and combining higher levels of managerial, professional and technical skills.

An early collection of papers was Kahin and Keller's *Public Access to the Internet* (1995), which surveyed a range of issues from macro information policy to networked community issues to the microeconomics of the Internet. *Internet Economics* (McKnight and Bailey, 1997) followed, but again the economic focus is micro, on how the economics of the Internet works out, for example how to price for Internet services. This quasi-business approach

also runs through the other major output of the period, Shapiro and Varian's *Information Rules: a Strategic Guide to the Network Economy* (1999), a book with references but without footnotes. Here the thesis 'is that durable economic principles can guide you in today's frenetic business environment' (1999: 1). We may assume that some less frenzied business people have had time to read their mistakes since the dot.com mania came to an end; if not, they had an alternative in Kevin Kelly's *New Rules for the New Economy* (1999). This is the 'you ain't seen nothing yet' school of new economics, and its first sentence begins: 'No one can escape the transforming fire of machines.' There is an inexorability about this version of the new economics, yet Kelly does also raise a crucial issue: uncertainty. Nothing is for certain when technology changes so rapidly, and business models based upon one generation of technology are forced to give way to others based on untried and untested marketing strategies.

For Kelly, founding father of *Wired*, the magazine which epitomized, if not the new economy thinking, certainly the new economy *lifestyle* of the 1990s, the foundation of the new economics is the phenomenon of increasing returns to scale, particularly as propounded in the works of Stanford University professor Brian Arthur (1994). This version of the new economics was regarded as the consequence of Metcalfe's law. As Kelly explained it, 'The prime law of networking is known as the law of increasing returns. Value explodes with membership ... The law of increasing returns is far more than the textbook notion of economies of scale ... industrial economies of scale increase value linearly, while the prime law increases value exponentially – the difference between a piggybank and compound interest' (www.wired.com/archive/5.09/ netrules.html, 1997). For more, see Kelly (1998).

Despite these claims for the networked economy, for a time there was a conspicuous lack of evidence of productivity in the figures.[5] Yet there was a lot of evidence that the new economy gave businesses much greater flexibility in labour markets, including substituting information technology for labour, employing more workers on flexible hours and wage rates, and outsourcing to companies who did likewise.[6] Professional economists like Krugman (1997) refuted the new economy on just these grounds, suggesting that an old-fashioned wage squeeze rather than a new-fashioned economics was at work. More specifically, Krugman took issue with the proposition that increasing returns were becoming a *defining characteristic* of the new economy: 'Against Metcalfe's Law must be set DeLong's Law (after Berkeley's Brad DeLong): in building a network, you tend to do the most valuable connections first. Is the net effect increasing or diminishing returns? It can go either way' ('Networks and increasing returns: a cautionary tale', http://web.mit.edu/krugman/www/metcalfe.htm).

While the debate has identified problems with popular economic prognostications ungrounded in rigorous theory, there remain serious questions as to how 'network economics' plays out in practice, although Shapiro and Varian (1999:182) emphasize the 'double whammy' effects on both the supply and demand sides of the economy. Are the effects of networking principally on the structure of the economy as could be read into the sort of discussion above? Structural shifts do reallocate resources from low- to high-productivity sectors as well as shift resources from labour to capital. How far are they also endogenous, simultaneously raising productivity across the board? How far are the effects instrumental on the velocity of circulation of money and capital,[7] and how do these effects play through the demand and supply sides of the economy?

THE INTERNET

Understanding the Internet's *morphology* provides a basis from which to begin examining the implications of its development and diffusion for industries such as telecommunications, as well as for public policy. This is the approach taken by Denton et al. (2000) in a study for the Asia–Pacific Economic Council (APEC) of international charging arrangements for internet services (ICAIS).[8] According to Denton et al., the frequent description of the Internet as 'a network of networks' simply 'confuses more than it clarifies'. The point is that the Internet is not so much a 'thing' or 'collection of things' (networks, computers, access devices) as a means of global communications (or 'global information system' – see below) using a protocol, or a set of compatible protocols, principally transmission control protocol (TCP) and Internet protocol (IP), otherwise shortened to TCP/IP. This permits computers of all kinds, independent of their internal architectures, to talk to each other across any suitably digitalized connected networks, private or public, wireline or wireless, by transmitting traffic in packets of byte-sized 'bits' of information. Each packet has a header or an address that is intelligible to the routers on the networks that function like the switches on the circuits traditionally used by telephone companies. Because of the lack of any one-to-one circuit connectivity in a packet-switched system it is technically referred to as 'connectionless'.

Denton et al. helpfully cite the resolution of the US Federal Networking Council, an authoritative body of Internet architects, announced on 24 October 1995:[9]

Resolution: The Federal Networking Council (FNC) agrees that the following language reflects our definition of the term 'Internet'.

'Internet' refers to the global information system that

(i) is logically linked together by a globally unique address space based on the Internet Protocol (IP) or its subsequent extensions/follow-ons;

(ii) is able to support communications using the Transmission Control Protocol/Internet Protocol (TCP/IP) suite or its subsequent extensions/follow-ons, and/or other IP-compatible protocols; and

(iii) provides, uses or makes accessible, either publicly or privately, high-level services layered on the communications and related infrastructure described herein.

It is useful to consider the distinction between a 'means of global communications' and a 'global information system'. First, the term 'information' is being used here in an engineering sense, without implications as to its veracity or use, rather like the scientific use of the term 'event' to describe any discrete or measurable occurrence, observation or happening. Second, a means of communications implies an accessible mode of protocol conversion (such as analogue to digital) and traffic transmission, such as a telecommunications system, whereas the term 'information system' as adopted by the FNC implies specifically the role of content on (the web) or over the Internet. This is indicated by the reference to various communications layers in point (iii) of the resolution.

A seven-layered network protocol architecture, known as the open systems interconnection (OSI) reference model, was formalized in 1977 by the International Standards Organization. This model is reproduced in Table 21.1. Each layer in the stack constitutes the 'client' of the layer below it and the 'server' to the layer above it.

Layers provide agreements among people – and the machines that they build and program – as to who will do what, and when. As such, layers are standards. Knowledge of the existence of layers is therefore fundamental to understanding how the Internet works, and why it works differently from previous signal transport media. While the Internet uses a layered signal architecture, the founders of the Internet decided not to conform to the ISO seven-layer model. Rather, TCP/IP takes the top three layers, five through seven, and combines them into one – the application layer.[10]

The result is that the Internet is an open system where new protocols may be added by a process of consensus within the industry. The effect of these protocols can be to change how the system of signal transmission works. Protocols can be introduced without any money being spent on changing any physical object within the signal transmission

Table 21.1   *The OSI reference model*

Layer	Name	Function	Information transferred	TCP/IP protocols
7	Application layer	Program-to-program communication	Application messages	FTTP, HTTP,
6	Presentation layer	Manages data representation conversions[a]	Encrypted data, compressed data	SNMP,
5	Session layer	Establishes and maintains communications channels[b]	Session messages	DNS
4	Transport layer	Responsible for end-to-end integrity of data transmission	Multiple packets	TCP, UDP
3	Network layer	Routes data from one node to another	Packets	IP, ARP
2	Data link layer	Responsible for physical passing of data from one node to another	Frames	Ethernet, PPP
1	Physical layer	Manages data on and off the network media	Bits	Physical wiring

[a] For example, the presentation layer would be responsible for converting from EBCDIC to ASCII.
[b] In practice, this layer is often combined with the transport layer.

system. Thus, to understand why the Internet is driving technological and business change so effectively, one needs to understand the function of layers.

The Internet as a GPT?

The Internet has proved all-pervasive and this has naturally led scholars of the process of innovation to identify the Internet as a general-purpose technology after Besnahan and Trajtenberg (1992).[11] Lipsey et al. (1998) define a GPT as having three characteristics: pervasiveness, technological dynamism and innovational complementarities, where the last is associated with research and development and economic growth connected with a series of complementary goods and services. In the same volume, Harris (1998) focuses on the Internet as a GPT which can bring benefit to small regional economies through the externalities associated with 'network economics', although there are losers in his analysis: unskilled workers unable to adjust.

The advantage of treating the Internet as a 'radical innovation', a 'macro-invention' or a GPT, is to open ways to explore its impact on industrial restructuring, productivity and economic growth of complementary sectors in light of the discussion above.[12] In this regard, the facilitation of electronic commerce and related data transfers may be the key to the productivity question. Certainly the impact on the demand for greater investment in telecommunications bandwidth alone has been remarkable.

A related but separate issue of research concerns the diffusion process, the ways in which the rate of adoption of the Internet is driven and how it is in turn driving the networked economy. Diffusion studies are the subject of a vast

literature, but if one reference is to be made it is worth mentioning the compilation edited by Stoneman (1995), if only to refer to Karshenas and Stoneman (1995) who provide valuable insights into analytical research methods and results. Of particular relevance is their stress on the need for methodologies that do not necessarily privilege endogenous factors in the diffusion process. Their own analytical preference is for discrete choice models which render tidy equilibrium outcomes, so in looking at the diffusion process they distinguish between the 'desire to acquire' and the 'decision to acquire'. The former may be influenced by learning, peer pressure, and so forth (leaving the process open to epidemic models and continuous logistic curve analysis) but the latter is an either/or decision based upon objective criteria, such as price and disposal income (open to the use of cost–benefit, probit and discrete choice models). Here perhaps is an opportunity for the economics and anthropology, sociology, psychology and cultural studies professions to work more closely together in future research agenda.

TELECOMMUNICATIONS

The National Information Infrastructure

The 'information superhighway', rather like the Internet, has a Platonic quality about it: once named it exists in the collective mind and popular imagination of society. The national information infrastructure (NII) gained currency when entered into the initial draft of the High Performance Computing Act (HPCA) of 1991 by Al Gore, then a US senator, with metaphorical reference to the interstate superhighway programme of the 1950s authored and championed by Senator Albert Gore Sr (Gore, 1991; HPCCI, 1994).[13] It went on to become a central plank of the Clinton–Gore administration's platform for the US in late 1993 (Clinton and Gore, 1993). As with the Internet itself, the concept's robustness came from its embrace of a meshing of disparate public and private transmission and switching systems – the highways, junctions and toll booths – and access points and devices – the local loop telephone networks, telephones, computers, cable TVs, cell phones, VSATs (very small aperture terminals) – as well as content.

The goals of the NII were laid out in detail in *The National Information Infrastructure: Agenda for Action* by the 1993 commission established by Vice-President Gore (Executive Office of the President, 1993). Part of its appeal was the appearance of a radical departure in national policy initiative towards information and communications technologies, but one entirely grounded on incremental development. The NII was about promoting integration through interconnection, *not* about building anew or reallocating resources,[14] and its strategic thrust was about international competitiveness: 'The NII will enable US firms to compete and win in the global economy, generating good jobs for the American people and economic growth for the nation.' While it did contain a positive commitment to social objectives,[15] notably to broaden the concept of 'universal service' to bring affordable Internet access to schools and rural communities, its central mantra was: 'The private sector will lead the development of the NII.' The NII was envisioned as a catalyst to innovation, research and development, where federal funds would focus on research left untouched by private investment, as well as providing matching funds for private sector R&D, and the Clinton–Gore vehicle for this was the High Performance Computing and Communications Program (HPCCP) born of the 1991 Act.

The Global Information Infrastructure

The reason why it is important to recount the founding history of the NII and recent United States telecommunications policy is because of their global impact. But this has to be put into perspective. During the second half of the twentieth century the trajectory of telecommunications policy has been roughly similar in developed and developing economies. State-run or private monopolies gave way to a measure of deregulation, which included the separation of posts from telephony functions and their corporatization (Petrazzini, 1995; ITU, 1998a; Lovelock, 1998a) which went some way to removing investment and financial issues from the constraints of national

budgets. It also opened the way for the start of privatization programmes and public listings, and the early liberalization of some markets, usually starting with so-called 'value added' services. The term 'value-added' was in reality, as Cowhey and Aronson (1988) pointed out, not so much a technological or economic one as a regulatory means of distinguishing what would and would not be open to competitive entry. In truth, a basic real-time analogue telephone call is 'value added' as it transforms voice into electromagnetic pulses.

But the timing and scale of the reforms in the US and the size of the information and communications technology sector were bound to be agenda-setting for the rest of the world, not least through global initiatives such as the General Agreement on Trade in Services (GATS) of the GATT, the establishment of the World Trade Organization (WTO) and the achievement of the first WTO services agreement, the Basic Agreement on Telecommunications (BAT) in February 1998. Very much part of the agenda-setting process was Vice-President Gore's 1994 proposal to the International Telecommunication Union (ITU) meeting in Buenos Aires for a global information infrastructure (GII), a 'planetary information network' which, alongside social, educational, health and cultural advantages, would help create a 'global information marketplace' (Macgregor Wise, 1997).[16]

The response of many developing economies, especially those experiencing the economic boom in Asia, was a judicious renaming of existing projects lending them a renewed sense of purpose. These Asian economies were already embarked, in their own ways, on developing information infrastructures. Asian states in the 1990s were encouraging a vigorous outward expansion of their own national companies, meeting the Western and Japanese multinationals at the regional level. Despite the setback of the Asian economic crisis after 1997, no Asian country today wants to proceed slowly in developing its own version of the information superhighway (Langdale, 1997; Noam et al., 1994; Petrazzini, 1995; Ure, 1993; 1995; 1997; Singh, 1999). Malaysia's multimedia supercorridor just to the south of the capital Kuala Lumpur is one example; Singapore's intelligent island project IT2000 is another; the South Korean KII, the Japanese JNII, mainland China's CNII and Taiwan's NII, which is to support an ambition to become a regional operating centre for telecoms and information services, are other examples (Hukill, 2000; Lovelock, 1998b).

The Changing Industrial Structure of Telecommunications

The telecommunications infrastructure is the taproot of the NII, and as such was an important part of the policy agenda of the 1993 commission's report. The subsequent Telecommunications Act 1996 was really the culmination of several decades of legal judgements and Federal Communications Commission (FCC) rulings, during which time wireless operators were recognized as legitimate public and private service providers in long-distance markets; and, through the rulings Computer 1, Computer 2 and Computer 3 (see Bruce et al., 1988; 1994), computer-based data communications and information service providers were likewise legitimated. The 1996 Act took the further step of recognizing the public interest in having cable TV and telecommunications services converge, clearing the last regulatory roadblocks to the seamless information superhighway. For an exegesis of the Act, see Huber et al. (1996). For a more recent critical economic assessment of its impact, see Kahn et al. (1999).

In terms of its wider, global impact on policy-making, the 1996 Act should be compared to the 1982 Supreme Court's Modification of Final Judgment (MFJ) to divest AT&T of its regional Bell operating companies. Similar ground-breaking events in Britain and Japan echoed the judgement.[17] The coincidence of these events – for a critical contemporary assessment see Hills (1986) – in the world's three largest telecommunications markets marked the decisive global turning point of telecommunications from public utility status to commercial commodity status, a shift that resonated with the growing strategic importance of telecommunications within the world of commerce and industry, multinational manufacturing and trading, and especially in the 1980s within the world of global finance.

On the demand side, the growing use of computers in the 1980s, notably minicomputers and personal computers, the growing abundance of satellite communications, and the first commercially marketed mobile cell phones were complementary developments spurring on the use of both data and voice transmissions. Equally dramatic were developments on the supply side. Digital switching and transmission began replacing analogue, and the operations of Moore's law in terms of falling microchip prices and a phenomenal increase in processing power of computers that were used for switching shifted the underlying economics of telecommunications and, with it, the entire structure of the industry.

Huber (1987) imaginatively captured this in a progress report on the divestiture of AT&T for the Department of Justice. Huber noted that the differential effect of the fall in switching costs relative to transmission costs was driving the migration of small-scale switches along the lines of transmission to public, and increasingly private, network nodes or exchange points. In the process the pyramid architecture of the traditional telecommunications network was compressed into a topology more typical of an IT network of distributed nodes:

> When switching is expensive and transmission is cheap, the efficient network looks like a pyramid. One hundred million telephones converge into twenty thousand end-office switches, which converge into a thousand tandem switches, and so on up to a handful of regional master switches at the apex. The system has comparatively few switches; it has many lines. By contrast, when switching is cheap and transmission expensive, the efficient network is a ring. The nodes (switches or computers) are connected along a 'geodesic' – a path of minimum length. (1987: 1.3)

Huber et al. (1993) followed up with an equally challenging second progress report. In it they conclude that economies of scale in the then new technology of optical fibre cable reinforced an element of natural monopoly in long–distance traffic haulage, while the other innovative technology of the period, the civilian use of cellular mobile telephony, was allowing new levels of competitive entry in the local loop.

> By 1982, the lawyers and economists had fully grasped the importance of microwave technology in the long-distance market. But they ignored fiber optics. By 1982, the lawyers and economists thought they understood the wire in the local exchange. But they ignored radio. The result was a divestiture decree that was obsolete almost from the day it went into effect. (1993: 1.42)

In other words, the Consent Decree divesting AT&T of its regional Bell operating companies, leaving them as effective monopolies over vast swathes of state territory, and opening AT&T's long-distance markets to competitive entry, was in logic, and with hindsight, exactly 180 degrees the wrong way about. The point is laboured here to underscore an important aspect in the recent history of policy and regulatory reform. On the one hand, the 1984 divestiture, and the privatization and liberalization moves in Britain and Japan, set precedents and an agenda for most other nations, developing as well as developed, despite the diversity of local circumstances. This is well reflected in a series of World Bank and International Finance Corporation papers: for example, see Ambrose et al. (1990) for the IFC, and Wellenius et al. (1989) and Smith and Staple (1994) for the World Bank.[18]

On the other hand, the work of Huber and many, many others raised a far greater general awareness of the importance of critical and well-grounded thinking for the *design* of policy and regulation, and issues such as information asymmetry within the industry, the dangers of regulatory 'capture', interconnection issues, paying for universal service obligations, and so forth. The volume edited by Brock (1995) captures the mood. Policy liberalization and new market entry also necessitated new or reformed regulatory structures – quasi-independent regulators who could draw upon industry expertise and the professional assistance of accountants, economists and lawyers. Bruce et al. (1988; 1994) and Crandall and Waverman (1995) provide reviews of the policy and regulatory structures and economic debates that serve as benchmarks for subsequent changes.

Leading exponents of liberalization, such as Beesley and Littlechild (1989), devised forms of 'incentive regulation' such as price capping, designed to encourage dominant carriers to act in efficient market-like ways until such time as new entry could establish genuinely competitive markets. Wenders (1987), Mitchell and Vogelsang (1991) and Einhorn (1991) among numerous others provide useful guides and reference to these schemes and debates, many of which first appeared in the *Bell Journal of Economics and Management Science*, later the *Bell Journal of Economics* and more recently the *RAND Journal of Economics*. Debates and analysis among economists appear in most of the leading journals and overlap with legal perspectives in journals such as the *Columbia Law Review*, the *Harvard Law Review* and the *Yale Journal on Regulation*. Specialist technical journals, such as the International Telecommunications Society's *Information Economics and Policy* and policy journals like *Telecommunications Policy*, *Prometheus* and more recently *Info*, are regular sources of analysis and informed discussion. For a review of earlier research literature, see Snow (1986) and for a more recent review of reform issues see Melody (1997).

The highly technical nature of the telecommunications business has always meant that engineers and engineering data have been crucial information sources for analysis by economists and lawyers alike, and from the legendary Bell Labs downwards (or outwards) telephone companies and equipment manufacturers have supplied their own research findings. The London-based Institution of Electrical Engineers (IEE) has been an especially influential source of analysis, commissioning as early as Morgan's *Telecommunications Economics* (1958), followed by *Elements of Telecommunications Economics* Littlechild (1979) and most recently *World Telecommunications Economics* by Wheatley (1999).

In preparing its defence in the late 1970s AT&T employed the skills of leading economists, notably Professor William Baumol (see Sharkey, 1982), to explore economic and social inefficiencies associated with the potential loss of economies of scale and scope. From the work of Baumol et al. (e.g. 1988) came contestability theory which posited that just the threat of competitive entry could induce a monopolist to simulate competitive levels of pricing and output. But equally the prospect remained that the entry of discrete stand-alone telecommunications operators serving selective profitable markets could render the monopoly, and the associated economies of scale and scope, unsustainable.[19] These arguments survived the breakup of AT&T in the form of the efficient component pricing rule (ECPR), advocated strongly by Baumol and Sidak (1994) but vigorously opposed on practical grounds by Albon (1994) and, along with stand-alone cost arguments, on theoretical grounds by Kahn (1998), whose two-volume *Economics of Regulation* (Kahn, 1970–1) remains the seminal work on public sector regulation.

Sidak and Spulber (1998) perhaps represent the dying shots of the argument, maintaining that incumbents should be fully compensated for the unforeseen consequences of regulatory-led liberalization. In his review of their position Trebling (2000) argues, with an eye to the mergers and amalgamations and alliances being formed across the converging sectors of 'new media', that there is no clear-cut evidence that the post-regulated monopoly era will end up as anything other than a market of competitive oligopolies.

Telecommunications Trade in Services, Growth and Development

The argument is not quite dead in many developing countries where concerns over cross-subsidies and universal service, or at least service to the key political constituents within the country, has always been important. The traditional argument for monopolies, or rather *of* monopolies, has been the ability to transfer price according to policy requirements, which can include social objectives such as serving rural communities. The sad twofold fact is that first, in the case of many of the poorest countries the objectives have shown little signs of being met under the state or private monopoly model (ITU, 1984), and second, the traditional source of subsidy, namely long-distance and international traffic, is inexorably disappearing. Everything from callback to Internet telephony, and from refile to international simple resale, operates to bypass the high-priced routes. Bypass proved so irresistible and unstoppable that incumbent carriers increasingly adopted these same means just to keep their business, but two developments swung the arguments beyond dispute by the turn of the century. The first was the global spread of the Internet and the World Wide Web, and the second was the spread of broadband technologies. They challenge the fundamentals of monthly rentals, call charges and value-added service charges, the traditional bread-and-butter telecommunications service revenues (Ure, 2000).

Much of the work on the relationship between telecommunications and development has been done under the auspices of either the International Telecommunication Union (ITU) or the World Bank. These include ITU (1986; 1988a; 1988b).

For helpful reviews of the literature see Saunders et al. (1983; 1994) for the World Bank.

Numerous case studies attempted to measure the economic benefits to rural and agricultural communities of access to telephony, but the benefits already suppose a significant level of integration into a market economy which in turn presupposes a value to be imputed to market information. Where anything beyond simple commodity production exists, markets exist and a value for telecommunications can be derived. This raises interesting possibilities of ways to give local communities and entrepreneurs means to foster local or regional networks at rates of return which would be unacceptable to corporate capital. This is an important area of research still to be developed. The point here also is that the social aim to provide universal service – or universal access, which is not quite the same thing (ITU, 1998b)[20] – sometimes needs to be justified on grounds other than economic development, and this has implications for the ways and means of funding such a commitment. For example, a national network of communications can serve the political aspirations of nation-state builders, can have the effect of opening remote tribal areas and rainforests to stronger outside influences, can aid in disaster relief work, can bring educational or medical benefits to a wider population, and so forth. It cuts many different ways, not all of which are necessarily developmental.

Throughout the 1980s the ITU produced a steady stream of studies on development indicators and by the mid 1990s was still producing charts arguably showing a strong correlation between GDP per capita growth and the number of telephone lines per 100 of the population, known as the teledensity. The statistical analysis often represented no more than an averaging process,[21] and was certainly incapable of supporting an argument for causation (ITU, 1993). Indeed in some cases, for example Indonesia, it could be argued that few of the staple occupations were hindered by the lack of telecommunications, and few would have been significantly enhanced by access to telecommunications, with one or two notable exceptions, such as the hotel and tourism trade. Under these conditions, economic growth was more likely to be cause than consequence.[22]

Jipp (1963), who proposed a simple regression of teledensity (mainlines per head of population) on domestic per capita income, may be rightly considered the pioneer of the econometrics that underlay much of this work. Others followed, but the econometric studies also ran into methodological problems as Roller and Waverman (1996)[23] have pointed out. The first is the problem of simultaneity: that is, the supply of telecommunications (or other public infrastructure) services can cause economic growth but simultaneously economic growth can cause the increase in demand for telecommunications services. So which is the chicken and which the egg? Second, the cause of economic growth may be the cumulative effect of fixed assets, for example in R&D, to which telecommunications investment is closely correlated. When these factors are accounted for, most of the income growth effects from telecommunications investment in previous studies disappears.

Roller and Waverman explicitly tackle these two issues, and then, most interestingly, test for the effects of 'network externalities' on some level of critical mass of network connections. First, following the postulates of new growth theory that looks to model endogenous sources of growth, they internalize the role of telecommunications investment by building a micro-model for its supply and demand. They then estimate the micro-model simultaneously with a macro-model of the relationship between GDP growth and telecommunications using data from across 21 OECD countries and 14 developing countries for 1970–90. They control for country-specific 'fixed effects' by adopting each country's intercept separately, and then test for network externalities by regressing not only on each country's penetration rate (the ITU's 'teledensity') but also on the penetration rate squared, thereby introducing an indicator of network scale. Finding coefficients of < 0 on the former, and > 0 on the latter, they thereby find evidence suggestive of network externalities, and go on to estimate for the OECD as a whole. The OECD average teledensity was 30 (that is, 30 mainlines per 100 population),[24] and from a 10 per cent increase in teledensity they found a GDP growth effect of 2.8 per cent – that is, an elasticity of 0.28. For the US, with a teledensity of 40, they found a growth effect of 7.8 per cent, and for Germany, with a teledensity of 32, a growth effect of 3.7 per cent.

It is too early to conclude the case for network effects proven, although it has intuitive appeal, but then so did the idea that telecommunications investment was a cause of higher economic growth when the most that could be safely assumed was that an efficient telecommunications infrastructure was an enabler, its existence the absence of a constraint. Roller and Waverman's work does seem to imply a serious challenge to the long-held and cherished beliefs of the ITU and the World Bank that investment in traditional telecommunications in developing countries brings economic returns far beyond the financial returns enjoyed by commercial investors, and this is clearly an area that will attract more careful research study. To complicate matters, the growing importance of trade in services, many of which directly or indirectly rely upon telecommunications, will have to be considered in the growth factors. And finally, if network effects are supported by further research, this will also have a bearing on debates about the new or networked economy.

The Broadband Age

The shift from the analogue to the digital to the Internet era is all about a shift from low to higher degrees of uncertainty (see Ure, 2000) and nothing illustrates it better than the emerging age of broadband. Broadband was until the late 1990s a backbone technology for aggregating traffic, but the Internet age opens the demand for broadband in the access networks. End users almost always require more downstream than upstream capacity, so numerous asymmetric subscriber digital line (ASDL) technologies, including wireline, third-generation wireless, fixed wireless, laser beams, cable hybrid fibre coaxial systems and so forth, are competing as modes of access. The interesting underlying business issue is: what will access networks sell? Unlike predominantly voice systems, where the demand for the network arose from the nature of the network's service and connectivity, the demand for 'always-on' broadband access networks is essentially a derived demand for the services, content and applications of Internet providers. Will customers pay for plain old telephone services in the future? 'Always-on' seems to preclude simple metering models, and Internet telephony seems to preclude any form of separate charging for voice traffic. What then is the future of the telephone company? In an era of uncertainty the restructuring of the industry will remain a major topic of research interest.

E-COMMERCE

The earliest forms of computer-based electronic commerce date from the late 1960s. In those days, they served a variety of distinct purposes, such as: time-sharing of mainframe computing CPU cycles; packet-switched express mail delivery; data transfer delivery; and business-to-business facsimile transmission. Businesses acquired early e-commerce services by leasing the value-added networking services of international telephone companies, or by acquiring leased computer time and network access offered by the large in-house shops of GE, IBM, McDonnell Douglas and EDS (Kimberley, 1991; Wigand and Benjamin, 1995).

Through the 1970s and 1980s, businesses began extending their networks to reach out to customers and business partners by electronically sending and receiving purchase orders, invoices and shipping notifications. The result was a proliferation of electronic data (or document) interchange (EDI) transmitted over value-added networks (VANs). In the 1980s, vendors such as McDonnell Douglas and General Motors introduced computer-aided design (CAD), engineering and manufacturing over these communications networks, which allowed managers to collaborate on design and production.

The consequences of such *laissez-faire* development were felt throughout the 1970s and 1980s. Bewildering arrays of proprietary networks, computer architectures and clumsy text-based computer interfaces of proprietary software were haphazardly grouped together with vendor hardware, making e-commerce and computing both labour and capital intensive. None of this came cheaply and all but the largest firms were locked out of e-commerce technologies by their sheer cost and scale. In response, services bureaus grew out of the internal corporate computing operations of larger firms. They used their already substantial economies of scale to offer network and computing services of greater reliability and lower cost than even large firms could develop internally.

Retrospectively – see Clark and Westland (1999) and Kalakota and Whinston (1996) – we can see that the market for e-commerce services over the three decades *up to 1990* could be encapsulated in five broad divisions:

1 Electronic mail, providing store-and-forward services for the business-to-business exchange of information. Mailbox services transferred information directly from the sender to the receiver; gateway services transferred information only as far as a corporate server.
2 Enhanced fax, providing point-to-point delivery of documents encoded as fax rather than e-mail, which usually implied that there was non-text information that needed to be encoded.
3 Electronic data interchange, providing computer-to-computer exchange of information using standardized transaction formats. These transactions typically involved purchase or sales functions.
4 Transaction processing, supporting credit, claims, payment authorization and settlement of transactions. Transaction processing services often involved collaboration between an info mation transport service and an authorization provider, such as a bank.
5 Groupware, employed within a secure, managed environment, which supported e-mail, calendaring, scheduling, real-time conferencing, information sharing and workflow management.

Internet e-commerce took off with the arrival of the Mosaic browser and the World Wide Web in the early 1990s, helped on its way by the liberalization process in telecommunications (see above) and a range of technical and networking innovations. In retrospect, the late 1990s can be seen as the initial phase of a process of long – and potentially profound – transition. Just like traditional commerce, electronic commercial activities involve four basic levels: a *communications* infrastructure, carrying messages about prices, quantities, service or product characteristics; a *marketplace*, the market coordination environment in which buyers meet sellers and negotiate (this, of course, encompasses *intermediaries*, allowing sellers to transact business with buyers); *transaction* mechanisms to send, execute and settle orders (including payments); and *deliverables*, the service or merchandise being exchanged (see Bar and Murasse, 1999; Pico et al., 1999).

What is meant by e-commerce? Part of the problem in coming to terms with e-commerce – and, indeed, one of the problems in *measuring* e-commerce – is the fuzziness of the concept. Sterret and Shah, for example, describe it as 'a broad, somewhat vague term, that essentially represents any transaction handled electronically… it includes, but is not limited to, transactions on the Internet' (1998: 43). Part of the problem is that early attempts to define the concept were provided by those who had very specific, and at times relatively narrow, research agendas. In the introductory paper inaugurating a new *business* journal devoted to e-commerce, Zwass (1996) defined electronic commerce as 'the sharing of business information, maintaining business relationships, and conducting business transactions by means of telecommunications networks' – thereby reflecting the business school bent of the readership. Somewhat similarly, Applegate et al. (1996) reflect their MIS perspective when they define electronic commerce as the use of network communications technology to engage in a wide range of activities up and down the value-added chain both within and outside the organization.

In an effort to reflect the wider economic and societal impact of electronic commerce, the OECD (1997) defined e-commerce as generally referring 'to all forms of transactions relating to commercial activities, including both organizations and individuals, that are based upon the processing and transmission of digitized data, including text, sound, and visual images'. And in attempting to incorporate the broader social impact, the European Commission (1997) went even further in scope:

> Electronic commerce is about doing business electronically. It is based on the electronic processing and transmission of data, including, text, sound, and video. It encompasses many diverse activities including electronic trading of goods and services, online delivery of digital content, electronic funds transfers, electronic share trading, electronic bills of lading, commercial auctions, collaborative design and engineering, online sourcing, public procurement, direct consumer marketing, and after sales service. It involves both products (e.g. consumer goods, specialized medical equipment) and services (e.g. information services, financial and legal services); traditional activities (e.g. healthcare, education) and new activities (virtual malls).

What we are seeing then is that doing business electronically will eventually encompass the same areas as 'traditional' business. Organizations are still exchanging information, marketing their products and services, buying and selling, recruiting new employees, gathering research, and providing customer service; but now, to a greater extent, paper-based and face-to-face transactions are being augmented, if not actually being replaced, by electronic means. So, while it is increasingly accepted that the Internet will transform business transactions and consumer life, the question becomes: how do we measure it?

In 1995, the American Electronics Association estimated that electronic commerce over the Internet totalled around US$200 million. By 1997, Nielsen Media was suggesting Internet-based sales had reached US$21 billion, and that 10 per cent of US companies were already offering products online. The WTO (1998), on the other hand, estimated the figure for e-commerce worldwide to be a more realistic, although still impressive, US$8 billion by 1998. If these figures seem disparate, they pale in comparison to the forecasts that followed. In 1999, the US Department of Commerce (1999) predicted that by 2002 the Internet would be used for more than US$300 billion worth of commerce between businesses alone. By 2000 they were estimating that the amount of business conducted directly on the Internet had increased in revenue to $171.4 billion from $99.8 billion a year earlier, as traditional brick-and-mortar retailers embraced Internet sales and companies began buying their supplies online. These estimates for e-commerce have varied for a variety of reasons, but mostly the differences are attributable to the definitional problems flagged above. Some estimates calculate only online transactions, while others include web-initiated transactions.

Nevertheless, five broad themes can be discerned in the emergence of electronic commerce. The first is the *relative* importance of time. Many of the routines that help define the 'look and feel' of an economy and society are a function of time: mass production is the fastest way of producing at the lowest cost; one's community tends to be geographically determined because time is a determinant of proximity. And while 'Internet time' became a catchcry of the new economy, implying an increased importance on timeliness, electronic commerce also *reduced* the importance of time by speeding up production cycles, and enabling around-the-clock transactions.

The second theme is the disappearance of geographic (and economic) boundaries. The ability to communicate and transact business anywhere, any time, changes not merely *how* business is done but *where* it is done and the extent of the potential market, through the erosion of economic and geographic boundaries.

The third theme is disintermediation.[25] Traditional intermediary functions are being redefined and even replaced. In some cases this is leading to new and far closer relationships between business and consumers. In others it is leading to opportunities for new intermediaries to emerge and provide market coordination.

The fourth theme is open source. The widespread adoption of the Internet as a platform for business is due to its non-proprietary standards and open nature as well as to the huge industry that has evolved to support it. Openness has also emerged as a business strategy. This has led to a shift in the role of consumers; an expectation of openness is building on the part of consumers/citizens, which will cause transformations, for better (e.g. increased transparency, competition) or for worse (e.g. potential invasion of privacy), in the economy and society.

The fifth and final theme is a catalytic effect. Electronic commerce is serving to accelerate, and diffuse more widely, the changes that are already under way in the economy, such as the reform of regulations, the establishment of electronic links between businesses (EDI), the globalization of economic activity and the demand for higher-skilled workers. Likewise, many sectoral trends already under way, such as electronic banking, direct booking of travel and one-to-one marketing, are being accelerated because of e-commerce. This is changing the organization of work structures, increasing interactivity and the number of channels for knowledge diffusion in the workplace.

E-Commerce Models

Broadly speaking, Internet-based electronic commerce can be broken down into three broad categories: business-to-consumer (B2C), business-to-business (B2B), and business-to-government sectors. Taxonomies of emerging e-commerce models are beginning to appear (see, for example, Harrington and Reed, 1996; Kalakota and Whinston, 1996; Sawhney and Kaplan 1999; Timmers, 1998). However, as we noted above in trying to assess the size and the scope of the market, the emerging nature of the market itself makes it difficult to define. As a result, existing taxonomies tend to blur the line between B2B e-commerce and B2C e-commerce. Given that the lines between these two fields are vague, it would be surprising if this were not the case.

Business-to-Consumer (B2C)

Many of the advantages of e-commerce were first exploited by retail 'e-businesses' such as Amazon.com, eTrade and Auto-by-tel that were created as Internet versions of traditional bookstores, brokerage firms and auto dealerships. But in most parts of the world outside the United States,

online consumer-oriented activity is still mostly informational rather than transactional, and although electronic payment systems have now appeared in most countries, traditional means of payment still dominate commercial transactions. Establishing a significant e-commerce presence remains costly, potentially risky, and therefore a barrier for companies – particularly small and medium enterprises (SMEs). This distinction between those that can afford to play the web globally and those that cannot may become an increasingly important issue, and may yet put paid to the concept of the Internet as the great leveller of opportunity.

Business-to-consumer electronic commerce can be broadly classified into two categories: the retailing of tangible and intangible goods. In the initial phase of e-commerce development, the goods retailed online were specific niche products such as computer software (US Department of Commerce, 1998). Intangible products and services sold and distributed online included software, music, magazine articles, news broadcasts, securities brokerage, airline tickets and insurance policies. However, the advent of the Internet has revolutionized the way transactions are conducted in industries from entertainment to banking, travel and insurance by commoditizing information (see Shapiro and Varian, 1999). Where this had its biggest early impact, though, was in the business-to-business or, perhaps, computer-to-computer arena.

Business-to-Business (B2B)

As we have seen, B2B e-commerce, defined here as restricted to computer-to-computer commerce, actually began in the mid 1960s with EDI inspiring a rash of predictions about the advent of the paperless office. By the 1970s, EDI allowed businesses to exchange documentation remotely and securely. It was foreseen – correctly – that this would speed up transaction time and minimize transaction costs.

In the first wave of Internet e-commerce most of the attention focused upon the high-profile vendor examples such as Amazon.com, CDNow or eBay. And, even when attention began focusing on the B2B realm, it was on prominent, well-established firms such as Cisco and Dell that eliminated 'old economy' middlemen and sold directly to business consumers. But the real impact of B2B e-commerce has been taking place on a broader scale.

B2B e-commerce is transforming from simple buy-side and sell-side solutions to a world of electronic markets that enable companies to streamline their commercial processes and reduce operational costs by linking multiple buyers and sellers via the Internet. There are a growing number of electronic exchanges that serve specific industry communities. These online exchanges, or marketspaces, provide access to information about products from a variety of vendors, along with objective industry information (industry forms, research papers, newspaper and trade journal reviews, etc.). The rise of these collaborative online communities is fuelling the growth of online procurement and selling systems, as companies move to get on board with their particular industry site. The integration of online auctions to these sites will further increase the attractiveness of such communities.

The Role of Government

Governments have increasingly come to realize that they, too, have a major role to play in the development of e-commerce, by placing their own procurement procedures and government services online, thereby helping to increase adoption and dissemination. But to achieve even this level of e-commerce promotion and facilitation, governments have to rethink the way they are organized and the manner in which they respond to the economic and social needs of the community. The first reaction of policy-makers to the growth of the Internet was, in essence, to do nothing. The lagging development of new laws or 'cyberlaw' for cyberspace, however, merely exacerbated the problem, and the inability to keep pace with technological developments led to uncertainty and in many instances conflict.

As a result, there has been increasing pressure on governmental agencies, industry bodies, administration agencies, standards organizations and professional and public interest groups to come together to form uniform, universal standards that provide businesses and individuals with better guidance on what they should and should not do on the Internet; and provide a framework for dispute resolution and, eventually, security and redress. It is these areas of public policy and technical standards that present the greatest challenge for the adoption and implementation of electronic commerce on a global basis.[26] Research is emerging which identifies many such issues related to global electronic commerce (GEC). These include: the impact on traditional business (Applegate et al., 1996), electronic payments solutions and security issues (Farhoomand et al., 1998), universal communications protocols and security concerns (Rietveld and Janssen, 1990), linguistics (Barnett and Choi, 1995), taxation laws and currency exchange (Deans and Kane, 1992), intellectual property and intrafirm transborder data flows (Rayport and Sviokla, 1994), shifting legal and social standards (Holbrook, 1997), and data security, privacy, technical security, and legal security, and the imposition of certain rules and obligations to allow business to function (Angelides, 1997).

Some of these challenges to e-commerce have already begun to be addressed by the public sector. The United States, the European Union, Japan and the OECD (1999) agree in their global e-commerce framework proposals on a number of the major policy challenges to be dealt with. These include the legal framework for Internet transactions (e.g. commercial code, intellectual property/copyright and trademarks, domain names, privacy and security); the financial framework (e.g. customs, taxation, electronic payments); and market access and trade logistics (e.g. market access to the Internet, access for suppliers over the Internet, content, shipping of goods, etc.).

The United States government in particular, in recognizing the need to address such issues, has actively sought to prepare a strategy which will accelerate the growth of GEC, and more particularly the Internet. In *A Framework for Global Electronic Commerce* (White House, 1997), an Interagency Working Group on Electronic Commerce under the guidance of US Vice-President Gore (see earlier), established a set of five principles to guide policy development. The framework suggested that: (1) the private sector should lead; (2) governments should avoid undue restrictions on electronic commerce; (3) where governmental involvement is needed, its aim should be to support and enforce a predictable, minimalist, consistent and simple legal environment for commerce; (4) governments should recognize the unique qualities of the Internet; and (5) electronic commerce on the Internet should be facilitated on a global basis.

It also made recommendations in respect of the following: tariffs and taxation, advocating that the Internet should be a tariff-free environment; electronic payment systems, and the need for flexibility in terms of any regulations imposed; the development of a universal commercial code for electronic commerce, which permits parties to be able to do business with each other under the terms and conditions they agree on; intellectual property protection, and associated protection and authentication of products purchased and sold using electronic commerce; privacy, to ensure that people are comfortable doing business across this new medium; security and reliability of the telecommunications infrastructure; and information technology, as relates to content, and technical standards.

The following points summarize the issues and areas for government concern.

Legal Framework

One major effort has been the establishment of the Model Law on Electronic Commerce by the United Nations Commission on International Trade Law (UNCITRAL), which was established to provide national governments with a framework to eliminate legal barriers to e-commerce. Its intention is to make electronic documents, such as those using EDI and e-mail, as official as paper-signed documents. In addition, international efforts in the area of authentication and certification technologies are continuing.

Financial Framework

On the question of customs, it has been agreed by the major developed nations that, as far as possible, zero tariffs should be maintained for goods and services delivered over electronic means. However, existing tariffs would apply for physically delivered goods, even though they were purchased over the Internet. On taxation an uneasy consensus has emerged between the US and Europe that a moratorium on electronic transactions should be adopted. Enforcing taxation once such a moratorium breaks down raises a host of jurisdictional dilemmas.

Social Implications

Electronic commerce is being shaped by, and increasingly will help to shape, modern society as a whole, especially in the areas of education, health and government services. Societal factors will merit attention from a public policy standpoint, two of which are first, access and its determinants (e.g. income) and constraints (e.g. time) (see Hudson in this volume for a discussion of universal access), and second, confidence and trust.

Technology Policy

One of the key features of electronic commerce is the potential system-wide gains in efficiency to be reaped when firms are linked across industries. This suggests the need to widen the notion of 'innovation' from a focus on high technology in manufacturing to include consumer goods and services and to adopt a more systemic perspective. (See also the emphasis that Lamberton in this volume places on the organizational effects of information in the process of industrial change.)

Trade Policy

Electronic commerce will increase international trade, particularly in electronically delivered products, many of which are services which have not yet been exposed to significant international trade but have been 'traded' through foreign direct investment or have operated on a global level only for large corporate clients. This change may come as a shock to sectors that have been sheltered by logistical or regulatory barriers. In addition, it will generate pressures to reduce differences in regulatory standards – accreditation, licensing, restrictions on activity – for newly tradable products.

Competition Policy

Many electronic commerce products benefit from non-rivalry (one person's consumption does not limit or reduce the value of the product to other consumers), network externalities (each additional user of a product increases its value to other users), and increasing returns to scale (unit costs decrease as sales increases). These factors create an environment where producers may engage in practices designed to establish themselves as the *de facto* standard. This can hinder innovation and competition. Another form of anti-competitive strategy is an attempt to restrict access to services through technological gateways. For example, throughout the 1990s cable and direct-to-home satellite television companies vied with each other to control what is termed within the industry 'conditional access' to the customer.[27]

Regulatory Reform

Electronic commerce calls into question the applicability of retail regulations designed for a 'bricks-and-mortar' world, such as restrictions on the size of stores and opening hours, limitations on pricing and promotions, granting of monopolies for the sale of certain products (e.g. liquor) and permit and licensing requirements. In addition, regulations governing the cost and availability of non-discriminatory access to information and communications technologies (ICTs) are required if e-commerce is to flourish.

Government

Conventional economic theory would suggest that governments should only subsidize basic research into ICT technologies. However, the experience of the past three decades shows that most of the major ICT innovations (e.g. time-sharing, networking, routers, workstations, optic fibres, semiconductors (RISC, VLSI), parallel computing), many of which are more applied or developmental in nature, are the result of government-funded research or government programmes. The other area is government going online. Online government procurement is widely regarded as a catalyst for promoting electronic commerce, while government providing services online to citizens not only can educate and promote e-commerce in society, but offers the potential to make government itself more accessible and open.

CONCLUSION: PRODUCTIVITY AND GROWTH

A key economic impact of electronic commerce today is the reducing of firms' production costs, and this is identified as a factor that will spur the spread of e-commerce within and between businesses. By the very nature of the technologies that enable electronic commerce to take place, many of these businesses will be in the heartland of the 'new media' industries.

Although there are measurement problems associated with capturing the quality changes inherent in many of these activities, it is assumed that e-commerce will result in productivity gains (see earlier). Given that e-commerce is more a way of doing business than a sector, these gains could be distributed widely across OECD economies – including in the services sector, which has not enjoyed significant, measurable productivity gains in the past – and could help to enable long-term growth. And if this growth is widely distributed across the global economy, the 'new economy' will have acquired a sustainable material base.

As e-commerce evolves, it is likely to follow the 'reverse product cycle', in which process efficiency gains are followed by quality improvements to existing products and then the creation of new products. (Many of these will be part of the 'new media' sector: see Cooke in this volume.) Typically, it is in this final stage that significant economic growth occurs. E-commerce has the potential to be a platform from which significant new products emerge, many of which will be digital and delivered online. New products have a tendency to beget more new products and processes in a virtuous spiral, just as Edison's electric lamp led to the development of power generation and delivery, which led to other electrical products. From a political economy perspective, the ultimate research question arising from the convergence of the technologies and commercial activities behind new media is whether the results will be as socially transformative as agriculture and manufacturing, or whether the new economy stops at the high street shop.

Notes

1 In 1965 Moore actually projected that the density of transistors on a silicon chip would double every 12 months. He was somewhat overoptimistic in his initial pronouncements, and the accepted timespan has become 18 months.

2 Gordon Moore has been unwilling to extend his 'law' beyond 2010, because that is when current technologies will hit limits dictated by the size of the electron and the nature of silicon. After a certain microprocessor gate size – around one micron, or a billionth of an inch – you can't get any more speed, so you reach a ceiling and Moore's law ceases to have any effect. See Moore (1996).

3 The term 'Metcalfe's law' was coined by George Gilder (1993) (www.discovery.org/gilder), who was seemingly oblivious to its heritage in the telecoms world. For example, Littlechild, when discussing whether network unit costs rose or stabilized with network buildouts, put forward the proposition that 'the number of possible connections between subscribers increases with the square of the number of subscribers', but added the remark, 'the fact that not all subscribers wish to use their telephones at the same time makes possible certain economies' (1979: 47).

4 However, Jorgenson and Stiroh do concede that, contrary to Gordon (1999), they find evidence of total factor productivity growth in non-IT sectors in the late 1990s: 'If these productivity gains do indeed reflect spillovers from the IT into the non-IT industries, this would provide some missing evidence for the new economy side' (2000: 24). The alternative hypothesis is that technological progress in the non-IT industries is autonomous. Jorgenson and Stiroh also cite several sources with similar findings for computer price–production effects, including Oliner and Sichel (2000) who reach different conclusions on computer usage effects.

5 Robert Gordon found US adjusted productivity growth 1979–96 to have been lower than the average for the period since 1870: 'I believe that the inventions of the late nineteenth century and early twentieth century were more fundamental creators of productivity than the electronic/internet era of today' (1999: 127).

6 Jorgenson and Stiroh (1999) repeat Solow's distinction between technical change resulting in the substitution of computers for other factors of production, and technical change resulting in increased production for a given level of inputs. Computers, they argue, contributed just about 0.16 per cent to the 2.4 per cent recorded productivity growth in the US 1990–9, so 'they are not ushering in a period of faster growth of output or total factor productivity. Rather, returns to investment in IT equipment have been successfully internalized by computer producers and computer users' (1999: 114).

7 In terms of Marx's political economy, how far is the money circuit of capital M–C–M speeded up? And in terms of e-commerce, how far is the commodity circulation of capital C–M–C, speeded up? In so far as they are, and the value of labour power is diminished in the new economy, the general rate of profit would rise.

8 Denton, Savage and Frieden were engaged as consultants by the APEC Tel Working Group 1999–2000 to review international charging arrangements for Internet services (ICAIS) across the Asia–Pacific. See www.apii. or.kr/telwg/ICAIS/icais.html.

9 See www.fnc.gov/Internet_res.html.

10 It is also useful to realize that the physical and data link layers have nothing to do with TCP/IP, but TCP/IP must have these layers below it in order to work. The signal must transport across something, even the air.

11 A GPT may be compared with what Mokyr (1990) distinguishes as a 'macro-invention' as opposed to a 'micro-invention' and what Freeman (1987; 1994) would call a 'radical' as opposed to an 'incremental' technology.

12 The *problem* with seeing the Internet in this way is how to make a clear distinction between what is a GPT and what is a complementary innovation. What is the World Wide Web? Another GPT? Or perhaps the *real* GPT, leaving the Internet as an innovation complementary to the telephone and computer networks? Or is the web

best treated as a complementary innovation designed to enhance the productivity of the Internet?

13 The first use of the term 'electronic highway' seems to appear in Ralph Smith's *The Wired Nation* (1972), where he argues for a 'national commitment for an electronic highway system to facilitate the exchange of information and ideas' (quoted in Altschiller, 1995: 7).

14 'The NII will integrate and interconnect these physical components in a technologically neutral manner so that no one industry will be favored over any other' (Altschiller, 1995: 13).

15 The sentence continues: 'It can ameliorate the constraints of geography and economic status, and give all Americans a fair opportunity to go as far as their talents and ambitions will take them' (Altschiller, 1995: 28).

16 A network of agenda-setting bodies has emerged during the period; for example in Asia these include APEC (Asia–Pacific Economic Council), PECC (Pacific Economic Cooperation Council), PBAC (Pacific Business Advisory Council), GIIC (Global Information Infrastructure Commission). Saga (1999) explains how the concept of an Asia–Pacific information infrastructure (APII) has been used within APEC economies to promote numerous agendas, including liberalization and market opening.

17 In Britain, the Cable & Wireless company, nationalized by the post-war Labour government, was chosen by the Conservative government of Prime Minister Margaret Thatcher to kick-start a programme of privatization, the largest chunk of which was British Telecom (or just BT), in 1984. See Harper (1997) for context and assessment. In turn, during the 1990s, Britain's increasingly deregulated and open telecommunications market became a bridgehead for liberalization across the European Union, which effectively began with the publication of the European Commission's Green Paper on Telecommunications in 1987. See Preston (1995). In 1986 the slow privatization process began of Japan's giant domestic carrier, Nippon Telegraph and Telephone (NTT). See Takano (1992) and *Telecommunications Policy* (1997).

18 For subsequent views on the privatization and competition processes in Asia, East Europe and Latin America, see Petrazzini (1995) and Ryan (1997).

19 On stand-alone costing principles, see Faulhaber (1975).

20 Universal service normally implies service on demand, usually at a uniform tariff. Universal access is used here to mean availability, for example connectivity to a village. A further consideration is the widespread use of teledensity as a measure of development. Both universal service and access imply units of measurement at a level more aggregated than the individual, for example the household or the village.

21 For example, the ITU (1993) *Asia–Pacific Telecommunications Indicators* breaks countries into three groupings, low, middle and upper middle income, and plots the teledensity within each grouping against per capita GDPs, but this least-squares method achieves no more than averaging the differences among subgroups of similar cases.

22 Top-down macro-analysis seems less likely to produce convincing evidence of causation than bottom-up micro-analysis which frequently supports the intuition of causation.

23 The original version of Roller and Waverman's paper was presented to a conference in Ottawa, Canada in March 1995 and appears, with a comment by David Aschaker in P. Howitt (ed.) (1996) *The Implications of Knowledge-Based Growth for Micro-Economic Policies.* Calgary: University of Calgary Press. pp. 363–90.

24 The result is 30 and not 30 per cent because teledensity already implies telephone mainlines per 100 population. Telephone mainlines per household might be a more useful measure, especially for developing countries defining universal service targets, but ITU and OECD present per capita data. On the other hand, per capita measures may have more relevance with the spread of cell phones and other forms of personal communications devices.

25 While e-commerce can dramatically reduce some production costs, it does not really offer a 'friction-free' environment. Rather, owing to new costs associated with establishing trust and reducing the risks inherent in this type of activity, it requires new intermediaries. Widespread 'disintermediation' (producers selling directly to consumers without the aid of intermediaries) is unlikely to be any more pronounced than what has already occurred through direct mail, telephone, newspapers, TV and radio. A potentially larger impact involves the ease of access to information that to date has been possessed by intermediaries such as travel agents, insurance agents, stockbrokers and real estate agents. Rather than eliminating intermediaries, it is more likely that their role will be restructured and redefined.

26 The problem is not new. Commerce is global. Law, for the most part, is not. That has been true for hundreds of years. However, the emergence of borderless e-commerce has exacerbated the situation by crystallizing a basic question: how can business be borderless when the law is not? To reap the benefits of e-commerce, it is increasingly recognized that an acceptable level of legal certainty and uniformity must be present. Individual consumers and businesses all require an infrastructure on which they can rely in the event of dispute.

27 In the USA, where the largest markets are, the initiative to open cable networks to competing service providers came not from the national telecommunications and cable industry regulator, the Federal Communications Commission (FCC), but from the consumer protection body, the Federal Trade Commission (FTC). This raises an interesting question for the future role of consumer organizations, as opposed to industry associations, in a world dominated by the Internet.

REFERENCES

Albon, R. (1994) 'Interconnection pricing: an analysis of the efficient component pricing rule', *Telecommunications Policy*, 18 (5): 414–20.

Altschiller, D. (ed.) (1995) *The Information Revolution.* New York and Dublin: Wilson.

Ambrose, W.W., Hennemeyer, P.R. and Chapon, J.-P. (1990) *Privatizing Telecommunications Systems: Business Opportunities in Developing Countries.* Washington, DC: International Finance Corporation.

Angelides, M.C. (1997) 'Implementing the Internet for business: a global marketing opportunity', *International Journal of Information Management*, 17 (6): 405–19.

Applegate, L.M., Holsapple, C.W., Kalakota, R., Radermacher, F.J. and Whinston, A.B. (1996) 'Electronic commerce: building blocks of new business opportunity', *Journal of Organizational Computing and Electronic Commerce*, 6 (1): 1–10.

Arthur, W.B. (1994) *Increasing Returns and Path Dependence in the Economy.* Ann Arbor, MI: University of Michigan Press.

Bar, F. and Murasse, E.M. (1999) 'Charting cyberspace: a US–European–Japanese blueprint for electronic commerce', in R. Steinberg and B. Stokes (eds), *Transatlantic Trade Cooperation in Asia: Sectors, Issues and Modalities.* Lanham, MD: Rowman & Littlefield.

Barnett, G.A. and Choi, Y. (1995) 'Physical distance and language as determinants of the international telecommunications network', *International Political Science Review*, 16: 249–65.

Baumol, W. and Sidak, J.G. (1994) *Toward Competition in Local Telephony.* Cambridge, MA: MIT Press and the American Enterprise Institute for Public Policy Research.

Baumol, W., Panzar, J. and Willig, R. (1988) *Contestable Markets and the Theory of Industry Structure.* Cambridge: Cambridge University Press.

Beesley, M. and Littlechild, S. (1989) 'The regulation of privatized monopolies in the UK', *Rand Journal of Economics*, 20 (3): 454–72.

Besnahan, T.F. (1999) 'Computerisation and wage dispersion: an analytical reinterpretation', *The Economic Journal*, 109 (June): 390–415.

Besnahan, T.F. and Trajtenberg, M. (1992) 'General purpose technologies: engines of growth?' NBER Working Paper 4148; and *Journal of Econometrics*, 65: 83–108.

Blanchard, C. (1994) 'Telecommunications regulation in New Zealand: the Court of Appeal's decision in *Clear Communications v. Telecom Corporation*', *Telecommunications Policy*, 18 (9): 725–33.

Blanchard, C. (1995) 'Telecommunications regulation in New Zealand: light-handed regulation and the Privy Council's judgement', *Telecommunications Policy*, 19 (6): 465–75.

Brock, G.W. (ed.) (1995) *Toward a Competitive Telecommunication Industry: Selected Papers from the 1994 Telecommunications Policy Research Conference.* Hillsdale, NJ: Erlbaum.

Bruce, R., Cunard, J. and Director, M. (1994) *The Telecom Mosaic: Assembling the New International Structure.* London: Butterworths for the International Institute of Communications.

Clark, T.H.K. and Westland, J.C. (1999) *Global Electronic Commerce: Theory and Case Studies.* Cambridge, MA: MIT Press.

Clinton, President William J. and Gore, Vice-President Albert Jr (1993) 'Technology for America's economic growth: a new direction to build economic strength'. Washington, DC: US Government Printing Office, 22 February.

Cowhey, P. and Aronson, J. (1988) *When Countries Talk: International Trade in Telecommunications Services.* Lexington, MA: Ballinger.

Crandall, R.W. and Waverman, L. (1995) *Talk is Cheap: the Promise of Regulatory Reform in North American Telecommunications.* Washington, DC: Brookings Institution.

Deans, P.C. and Kane, M.J. (1992) *International Dimensions of Information Systems and Technology.* Boston: PWS-Kent.

Einhorn, M.A. (ed.) (1991) *Price Caps and Incentive Regulation in Telecommunications.* Boston: Kluwer.

European Commission (1997) *A European Initiative in Electronic Commerce: Communication from the Commission to the Council, the European Parliament, the Economic and Social Committee and the Committee of the Regions.* URL: www.cordis.lu/ esprit/src/ecom-com0.htm.

Executive Office of the President (1993) *The National Information Infrastructure: Agenda for Action.* Washington, DC: EOP.

Farhoomand, A.F., Tuunainen, V.K. and Yee, L.W. (1998) 'Barriers to global electronic commerce: a cross-country study of Hong Kong and Finland', *Journal of Organizational Computing and Electronic Commerce*, 10 (1): 23–48.

Faulhaber, G.R. (1975) 'Cross-subsidization: pricing in public enterprises', *The American Economic Review*, 65: 966–77.

Freeman, C. (1987) 'Information technology and change in techno-economic paradigms', in C. Freeman and L. Soete (eds), *Technical Change and Full Employment.* Oxford: Basil Blackwell.

Freeman, C. (1994) 'Critical survey: the economics of technical change', *Cambridge Journal of Economics*, 18: 1–50.

Gates, W.H. (1996) *The Road Ahead.* Harmondsworth: Penguin.

Gilder, G. (1993) 'Metcalfe's law and legacy', *Forbes ASAP*, September.

Gilder, G. (1997) 'Fiber keeps its promise', *Forbes ASAP*, February.

Gordon, R.J. (1999) 'US economic growth since 1870: one big wave?', *American Economic Review, Papers and Proceedings*, 89 (2): 123–8.

Gore, Albert Jr (1991) 'Information superhighway: the next information revolution', *Futurist*, 25 (1): 21–3.

Harper, J. (1997) *Monopoly and Competition in British Telecommunications: the Past, the Present and the Future.* London: Pinter.

Harrington, L. and Reed, G. (1996) 'Electronic commerce (finally) comes of age', *The McKinsey Quarterly* (2): 68–77.

Harris, R. (1998) 'The Internet as GPT', in E. Helpman (ed.), *General Purpose Technologies and Economic Growth.* Cambridge, MA: MIT Press.

Hills, J. (1986) *Deregulating Telecoms: Competition and Control in the United States, Japan and Britain.* London: Pinter.

Holbrook, M.B. (1997) 'Borders, creativity, and the state of the art at the leading edge', *Journal of Macromarketing,* 17 (Fall): 96–112.

HPCCI (High Performance Computing and Communications Institute) (1994) *High Performance Computing and Communications: Toward a National Information Infrastructure.* Washington, DC: Federal Coordinating Council for Science, Engineering, and Technology.

Huber, P.W. (1987) *The Geodesic Network: 1987 Report on Competition in the Telephone Industry.* Washington, DC: US Department of Justice, Anti-Trust Division.

Huber, P.W., Kellogg, M.K. and Thorne, J. (1993) *The Geodesic Network 11: 1993 Report on Competition in the Telephone Industry.* Washington, DC: Geodesic Company.

Huber, P.W., Kellogg, M.K. and Thorne, J. (1996) *The Telecommunications Act of 1996: Special Report.* New York: Little, Brown.

Hukill, M., Ono, R. and Vallath, C. (eds) (2000) *Electronic Communication Convergence: Policy Changes in Asia.* New Delhi: Sage Publications.

ITU (1984) *The Missing Link: Report of the Independent Commission for Worldwide Telecommunications Development.* Maitland Commission. Geneva: International Telecommunication Union.

ITU (1986) *Information Telecommunications Development.* Geneva: International Telecommunication Union.

ITU (1988a) *Contribution of Telecommunications to the Earnings/Savings of Foreign Exchange in Developing Countries.* Geneva: International Telecommunication Union.

ITU (1988b) *Telecommunications and the National Economy.* Geneva: International Telecommunication Union.

ITU (1993) *Asia–Pacific Telecommunications Indicators,* Geneva: International Telecommunication Union.

ITU (1998a) *General Trends in Telecommunication Restructuring,* 6 vols. Geneva: International Telecommunication Union.

ITU (1998b) *World Telecommunication Development Report 98: Universal Access.* Geneva: International Telecommunication Union.

Jipp, A. (1963) 'Wealth of nations and telephone density', *Telecommunications Journal,* July.

Jorgenson, D.W. and Stiroh, K.J. (1999) 'Productivity growth: current recovery and longer-term trends', *American Economic Review, Papers and Proceedings,* 89 (2): 109–15.

Jorgenson, D.W. and Stiroh, K.J. (2000) *Raising the Speed Limit: US Economic Growth in the Information Age.* New York: Federal Reserve Bank of New York.

Kahin, B. and Keller, J. (eds) (1995) *Public Access to the Internet.* Cambridge, MA: MIT Press.

Kahn, A.E. (1970–1) *The Economics of Regulation,* 2 vols. Cambridge, MA: MIT Press.

Kahn, A.E. (1998) *Letting Go: Deregulating the Process of Deregulation.* East Lansing, MI: Institute of Public Utilities and Network Industries, Michigan State University.

Kahn, A.E., Tardiff, T.J. and Weisman, D.L. (1999) 'The Telecommunications Act at three years: an economic evaluation of its implementation by the Federal Communications Commission', *Information Economics and Policy,* 11 (4): 319–65.

Kalakota, R. and Whinston, A.B. (1996) *Frontiers of Electronic Commerce.* Reading, MA: Addison-Wesley.

Karshenas, M. and Stoneman, P. (1995) 'Technological diffusion', in P. Stoneman (ed.), *Handbook of the Economics of Innovation and Technological Change.* Oxford: Blackwell.

Kelly, K. (1999) *New Rules for the New Economy: 10 Radical Strategies for a Connected World.* Harmondsworth: Penguin.

Kimberley, P. (1991) *Electronic Data Interchange.* Englewood Cliffs, NJ: McGraw-Hill.

Krugman, P. (1997) 'Requiem for the new economy', *Fortune,* 10 November.

Langdale, J.V. (1997) 'International competitiveness in East Asia: broadband telecommunications and interactive media', *Telecommunications Policy,* 21 (3): 235–49.

Lipsey, R., Bekar C. and Carlaw, K. (1998) 'What requires explanation?', in E. Helpman (ed.) (1998) *General Purpose Technologies and Economic Growth.* Cambridge, MA: MIT Press.

Littlechild, S.C. (1979) *Elements of Telecommunications Economics.* Stevenage: Institution of Electrical Engineers, Peter Peregrinus.

Lovelock, P. (1998a) 'Global telecommunication development trends', in *The Emerging Telecommunication Environment.* Geneva: ITU.

Lovelock, P. (1998b) 'Is there an Asian model of information infrastructure development?', *Pacific Review,* 11 (1): 79–106.

Macgregor Wise, J. (1997) *Exploring Technology and Social Space.* London: Sage.

McKnight, L.W. and Bailey, J.P. (eds) (1997) *Internet Economics.* Cambridge, MA: MIT Press.

Melody, William H. (ed.) (1997) *Telecom Reform Principles, Policies and Regulatory Practices.* Den Private Ingeniøfond, Technical University of Denmark.

Mitchell, B.M. and Vogelsang, I. (1991) *Telecommunications Pricing: Theory and Practice.* Cambridge: Cambridge University Press.

Mokyr, J. (1990) *The Lever of Riches: Technological Creativity and Economic Progress.* Oxford: Oxford University Press.

Moore, G. (1996) 'Nanometers and gigabucks: Moore on Moore's law'. University Video Communications (UVC) Distinguished Lecture.

Morgan, T.J. (1958) *Telecommunications Economics. MacDonald* (2nd edn, 1976, Stonehouse, Gloucestershire: Technicopy Ltd).

Noam, E., Komatsuzaki, S. and Conn, D.A. (eds) (1994) *Telecommunications in the Pacific Basin: an Evolutionary Approach.* New York: Oxford University Press.

OECD (1997) *Policy Brief no. 1 on Electronic Commerce*, November. Paris: OECD. URL: www.oecd.org/publications/Pol_brief/9701_Pol.htm.

OECD (1999) *The Economic and Social Impacts of Electronic Commerce: Preliminary Findings and Research Agenda*. Paris: OECD. URL: www.oecd.org/dsti/sti/it/ec/index.htm.

OECD (2000) *A New Economy? The Changing Role of Innovation and Information Technology in Growth*. Paris: OECD. URL: http://electrade.gfi.fr.

Oliner, S.D. and Sichel, D.E. (2000) *The Resurgence of Growth in the Late 1990s: Is Information Technology the Story?* Washington, DC: Federal Reserve Board.

Petrazzini, B. (1995) *The Political Economy of Telecommunications Reform in Developing Countries*. Westport, CT: Praeger.

Pico, A., Bortenlanget, C. and Rohrl, H. (1999) 'Organization of electronic markets: contributions from the new institutional economics', *The Information Society*, 13: 107–23.

Preston, P. (1995) 'Competition and telecommunications in the peripheral regions and smaller economies of Europe', special issue, *Telecommunications Policy*, 19 (4): 253–71.

Rayport, J.F. and Sviokla, J.H. (1994) 'Managing in the marketspace', *Harvard Business Review*, November–December: 141–50.

Rietveld, P. and Janssen, L. (1990) 'Telephone calls and communication barriers: the case of The Netherlands', *The Annals of Regional Science*, 24: 307–18.

Ryan, D.J. (ed.) (1997) *Privatization and Competition in Telecommunications: International Developments*. Westport, CT: Praeger.

Saga, K. (1999) 'APEC: steps to harmonising regional telecom policy', *Telecommunications Policy*, 23 (3/4): 335–44.

Saunders, R.J., Warford, J.J. and Wellenius, B. (1994) *Telecommunications and Economic Development*. Baltimore, MD: Johns Hopkins University Press for the World Bank.

Sawhney, M. and Kaplan, S. (1999) 'The B-to-B boom: let's get vertical', *Business 2.0*, September. URL: http://www.business2.com/articles/1999/09/content/models.html.

Shapiro, C. and Varian, H. (1999) *Information Rules: a Strategic Guide to the Network Economy*. Boston: Harvard University Press.

Sharkey, W. (1982) *The Theory of Natural Monopoly*. Cambridge: Cambridge University Press.

Sidak, J.G. and Spulber, D.F. (1998) *Deregulatory Takings and the Regulatory Contract*. Cambridge: Cambridge University Press.

Singh, J.P. (1999) *Leapfrogging Development? The Political Economy of Telecommunications Restructuring*. New York: State University of New York Press.

Smith, P.L. and Staple, G. (1994) *Telecommunications Sector Reform in Asia: Toward a New Pragmatism*. Washington, DC: World Bank.

Snow, M. (1986) 'Telecommunications literature: a critical review of the economic, technological and public policy issues', *Telecommunications Policy*, 10 (3): 153–83.

Sterret, C. and Shah, A. (1998) 'Going global on the information highway', *Advanced Management Journal*, 63 (3): 42–68.

Stoneman, P. (ed.) (1995) *Handbook of the Economics of Innovation and Technological Change*. Oxford: Blackwell.

Takano, Y. (1992) *Nippon Telegraph and Telephone Privatization Study: Experience of Japan and Lessons for Developing Countries*. Washington, DC: World Bank.

Taylor, L.D. (1994) *Telecommunications Demand in Theory and Practice*. Dordrecht: Kluwer.

Telecommunications Policy (1997) 'Restructuring Japanese telecommunications', special issue, 21 (2).

Timmers, P. (1998) *Strategies and Models for Business-to-Business Trading*. New York: Wiley.

Trebling, H. (2000) 'Review article: deregulatory takings and the regulatory contract', *Telecommunications Policy*, 24 (2): 161–73.

Ure, J. (1993) 'Corporatization and privatization of telecommunications in ASEAN countries', *Pacific Telecommunications Review*, 15 (1): 3–13.

Ure, J. ed. (1997) *Telecommunications in Asia: Policy, Planning and Development*. Hong Kong: Hong Kong University Press.

Ure, J. (2000) 'The era of international simple resale: not waving but drowning?', *Telecommunications Policy*, 23 (2): 9–30.

US Department of Commerce (1998) *Falling through the Net II: New Data on the Digital Divide*. Washington, DC: National Telecommunications and Information Administration (NTIA). URL: www.ntia.doc.gov/ntiahome/net2.

US Department of Commerce (1999) *Falling through the Net: Defining the Digital Divide*. Washington, DC: National Telecommunications and Information Administration (NTIA). URL: www.ntia.doc.gov/ntiahome/fttn99.

Wellenius, B., Stern, P., Nulty, T.E. and Stern, R.D. (eds) (1989) *Restructuring and Managing the Telecommunications Sector*. Washington, DC: World Bank.

Wenders, J.T. (1987) *The Economics of Telecommunications*. Cambridge, MA: Ballinger.

Wheatley, J.J. (1999) *World Telecommunications Economics*. Stevenage: Institution of Electronic Engineers.

White House (1997) *A Framework for Global Electronic Commerce*, 1 July. URL: www.ecommerce.gov/framework.htm.

Wigand, R.T. and Benjamin, R.I. (1995) 'Electronic commerce: effects on electronic markets', *Journal of Computer-Mediated Communication*, 1 (3). URL: http://www.ascusc.org/jcmc/vol1/issue3/wigand.html.

WTO (1998) *Electronic Commerce and the Role of the WTO*. Geneva: World Trade Organization. URL: www.wto.org/.

Zwass, V. (1996) 'Electronic commerce: structures and issues', *International Journal of Electronic Commerce*, 1 (1): 3–23.

22

Universal Access to the New Information Infrastructure

HEATHER E. HUDSON

Technological innovation and the transition to a global digital economy have focused new attention on the importance of access for all to telecommunications facilities and services. 'Universal service', meaning access to basic telephone service for all, remains the primary objective. However, the emergence of the Internet is forcing policy-makers to rethink this concept, in terms of both what services should be universally available, and whether 'access' is a more appropriate goal for so-called 'advanced services'. This chapter examines the availability of telecommunications and information services access in industrialized and developing countries, the changing goals and definitions of universal service, and the strategies being implemented to extend access to various levels of service, particularly in rural and disadvantaged areas.

OVERVIEW

Background

The term 'universal service' originated not as a public policy goal, but as an industrial strategy. Theodore Vail, the early visionary head of AT&T, coined the term to mean the delivery of all telephone services through one network, the Bell system (Mueller, 1997). Vail was later willing to submit to government regulation to achieve his goal: a single, unified carrier providing both local and long-distance service throughout the country. However, by 1920, only 35 per cent of American households had a telephone (Crandall and Waverman, 2000). The Communications Act of 1934, which established the Federal Communications Commission, made no specific reference to universal service, although it did invoke 'the public interest' and stated that its purpose was 'to make available, so far as possible to all people of the United States, a rapid, efficient, nationwide ... communications service with adequate facilities at reasonable charges'. Over the next 40 years, various methods were adopted to apportion the costs of providing telephone service among various elements in the network, which generally resulted in keeping local service prices low through cross-subsidies from long-distance and other services.

The term 'universal service' was reintroduced in 1975 in testimony by AT&T consultant (and former adviser to President Lyndon Johnson) Eugene Rostow, who sought to ward off competition from MCI and other new long-distance competitors, and to resist the efforts of the Department of Justice to break up AT&T: 'In this struggle, the concept of universal service was redefined in a way that linked it to the practices of regulated monopoly' (Mueller, 1997). While AT&T eventually lost the argument that the way to keep local rates low and affordable was to prevent competition, a system of access charges was implemented so that all carriers would contribute to the costs of providing universal service.

Changing Concepts of Universal Service

The concept of universal service today is 'virtually synonymous with government policies designed to promote the affordability of telephone service and access to the network' (Mueller, 1997). In the US, targeted subsidies to ensure affordable access to a basic telephone service are available for low-income households, regardless of where they are located, as well as for telephone companies providing service in high-cost rural and remote areas, with the result that the price of service is lowered for all households, regardless of income. The Telecommunications Act of 1996 adds two new categories: identifying (but not defining) 'advanced services' that should be universally available; and specifying institutions (namely schools, libraries and rural health centres) rather than households as the means through which these services should be made accessible.

Many other countries have some form of universal service policy, which aims to ensure access to at least basic telephone service throughout the society, including low-income, isolated and disadvantaged residents.[1] In developing countries, such policies are generally formulated as goals to extend access to unserved populations or regions.

THE CURRENT CONTEXT

The concept of universal access must be viewed in a context of changing economic, technological and policy environments. Three major trends driving these changes are the rapid introduction of new technologies and services; the restructuring of the telecommunications sector; and globalization of economies and of communications. Together these developments are changing not only the world of telecommunications, but the ways people work, learn and interact. As noted elsewhere in this volume (see Chapter 20), economic activity is becoming increasingly information intensive, as the costs of information processing and transmission decline. Producers and consumers are becoming part of a globalized economy where national boundaries and time zones are becoming irrelevant. This transition to a so-called 'new economy' is being driven largely by the exploitation of the Internet, which in turn is made possible by changes in technology and communications policies.

Key technological trends that are driving the proliferation of new information and telecommunications services include:

- *Digitization* Telecommunications networks are becoming totally digital, so that any type of information, including voice and video, may be sent as a stream of bits. Digital compression allows more efficient use of bandwidth so that customers may have more choices (such as compressed satellite television channels) and/or lower costs, such as use of compressed video for distance education and compressed voice for Internet telephony.
- *Capacity* New technologies such as optical fibre have enormous capacity to carry information, and can be used for services ranging from

entertainment and distance education to transmission of highly detailed images for remote medical diagnosis. Satellites and some terrestrial wireless technologies also offer a tremendous increase in availability of bandwidth.

- *Convergence* The convergence of telecommunications, data processing and imaging technologies is ushering in the era of multimedia, in which voice, data and images may be combined according to the needs of users, and distinctions between the traditional sectors of telecommunications, information processing and broadcasting are increasingly arbitrary and perhaps irrelevant.
- *Ubiquity* Advances in wireless technology such as cellular networks, personal communications systems (PCS) and rural radio subscriber systems offer affordable means of reaching rural customers and urban areas without infrastructure in developing countries. Low-cost wireless services may also replace wireline in industrialized countries as the primary means of personal access.

The policy environment is also changing dramatically, with increasing emphasis on private sector ownership and market-driven competition. Major models of ownership and structure in the telecommunications sector include the following.

Ownership

- *Government-owned and operated utilities* In most countries (with the notable exceptions of the United States and much of Canada), telephone service was initially established as an offshoot of the postal service, through a government-owned entity often known as the PTT (post, telephone and telegraph). Typically, revenues from telecommunications services may be used to subsidize the postal service, or to contribute to the national treasury. Many countries also have separately managed military telecommunications networks; in China, the army as well as other government departments operate public telecommunications networks.
- *Autonomous public sector corporations* For countries with government-owned telecommunications operators, the first step for creating incentives to improve efficiency and innovation in the telecommunications sector is to create an autonomous organization operated on business principles. This is often seen as an intermediate step between a PTT structure and some form of privatization.
- *Privatized corporations* Privatization models range from minor investments by private companies, to joint ventures between private carriers and governments, to full privatization without any government stake or with a small government 'golden share'. Telecommunications carriers in industrialized countries are generally now partially or fully privatized.

Structure

- *Monopoly* Most countries began with a national monopoly model, which has gradually been opened to competition. Many maintain some level of monopoly, for example in the local loop, but alternative providers using wireless and fibre are also beginning to challenge the assumption of natural monopoly in the local loop.
- *Open entry for unserved areas* An intermediate step between national monopoly and competition is a policy of open entry for unserved areas. For example, in the US, Finland, Hungary and Poland, small companies or cooperatives were formed to provide services in areas ignored by the national monopoly carrier.
- *Competition* Competition can range from terminal equipment (now commonly competitive almost everywhere) to new services such as cellular telephony, to value-added services such as Internet access, to full competition in all network services. Hong Kong has perhaps the most competitive environment, with full local competition; many other countries such as the United Kingdom, the United States, Canada, Australia and Japan have authorized local competition, but have little actual competition at the local level.
- *Consolidation* Industrialized countries are now witnessing consolidation among competitors that seek economies of scale or scope, by buying either similar companies (such as the acquisitions by SBC of Pacific Bell and Ameritech, and by Bell Atlantic of NYNEX) or companies that provide new means of accessing customers, such as wireless networks and cable television systems. US examples include AT&T's acquisition of McCaw Wireless and TCI cable television, and Verizon (formed by the merger of Bell Atlantic with GTE).

The ownership and structure of telecommunications networks may influence goals and strategies for universal service. For example, government-owned monopolies may heavily cross-subsidize local and domestic services to extend access; in a competitive environment, dominant carriers (which are likely to be at least partially government owned) may have a special obligation to provide service in areas deemed to be unprofitable. In a fully competitive environment, efforts to ensure universal service must be based on competitively neutral policies such as incentives available to all carriers or explicitly targeted subsidies (see below).

THE IMPORTANCE OF ACCESS TO INFORMATION

The theoretical underpinning of research on the impact of information and communications technologies in general is that information is critical to the social and economic activities that comprise the development process. Much of the research to date on the socioeconomic effects of new communication technologies has examined the role of information networking through telecommunications. Access to information is critical to development; thus information and communication technologies (ICTs) as a means of sharing information are not simply a connection between people, but a link in the chain of the development process itself. Information is obviously central to activities that have come to be known as the 'information sector' including education and research, media and publishing, information equipment and software, and information-intensive services such as financial services, consulting and trade. But information is also critical to other economic activities ranging from manufacturing to agriculture and resource extraction, for management, logistics, marketing and other functions. Information is also important to the delivery of health care and public services (Hudson, 1984; 1995; Saunders et al., 1994).

For individuals, access to information can have personal, social and economic functions, often accomplished using the same devices. An individual can summon help in an emergency via telephone; she may stay in touch with friends and family members and arrange appointments by telephone or e-mail; and she may find the Internet a more efficient means of tracking down consumer information on products and services than the mass media. Entrepreneurial sole proprietors, ranging from programmers and consultants to small farmers and craftspeople, can set up global storefronts on the Internet.

In general, the ability to access and share information can contribute to the development process by improving:

- *efficiency*, or the ratio of output to cost (for example, through use of just-in-time manufacturing and inventory systems, through use of information on weather and soil content to improve agricultural yields);
- *effectiveness*, or the quality of products and services (such as improving health care through telemedicine);
- *reach*, or the ability to contact new customers or clients (for example, craftspeople reaching global markets on the Internet; educators reaching students at work or at home);
- *equity*, or the distribution of development benefits throughout the society (such as to rural and remote areas, to minorities and disabled populations) (Hudson, 1997a).

It is the importance of communication to socioeconomic development and equity that has been the foundation of the 'public interest' concerns in telecommunications, and the concept of universal service as a means of providing accessible and affordable communications throughout the society.

INFORMATION GAPS

In industrialized countries and other high-income countries, telephone service is almost universally available through fixed lines and increasingly through wireless networks. Ownership of computers is widespread, and use of the Internet is increasing dramatically. In the US, about 94 per cent of households have telephones, while 42.1 per cent have personal computers and 26.2 per cent have Internet access (McConnaughey et al., 1999). However, despite growth in access overall, there is a widening gap between high- and low-income households. Urban households with incomes of $75,000 and higher are more than 20 times as likely to have access to the Internet than rural households at the lowest income levels, and more than nine times as likely to have a computer at home (McConnaughey et al., 1999). Blacks, Hispanics and native American populations now lag further behind whites and Asian Americans in computer ownership and online access (see Winseck, and Gandy, in this volume).

In the rural US, there has been significant progress in access to basic telecommunications. Distance no longer accounts for difference in household access to a telephone; income levels are now a better predictor. Yet the gap in access to the Internet persists. Regardless of income level, Americans living in rural areas are lagging behind in Internet access; at the lowest income levels, those in urban areas are more than twice as likely to have Internet access as rural Americans with similar incomes.[2] Those who are connected typically pay more than their urban counterparts for Internet access. Disparities in Internet access are found in the Canadian north and the Australian outback, and in rural and disadvantaged parts of Europe.

However, this so-called 'digital divide' is much more pronounced in developing countries, where access to information and communications technologies (ICTs) remains much more limited. In its *Statement on Universal Access to Basic Communication and Information Services* of April 1997, the United Nations Administrative Committee on Coordination noted:

The information and technology gap and related inequities between industrialized and developing nations are widening: a new type of poverty – information poverty – looms. Most developing countries, especially the Least Developed Countries (LDCs), are not sharing in the communications revolution, since they lack:

- affordable access to core information resources, cutting-edge technology and to sophisticated telecommunications systems and infrastructure;

- the capacity to build, operate, manage and service the technologies involved;
- policies that promote equitable public participation in the information society as both producers and consumers of information and knowledge; and
- a work force trained to develop, maintain and provide the value-added products and services required by the information economy. (ITU, 1998: 10)

Table 22.1 shows the gap in Internet access between the industrialized and developing worlds. More than 85 per cent of the world's Internet users are in developed countries, which account for only about 22 per cent of the world's population.[3] Of course, Internet access requires both communications links and information technologies, particularly personal computers or networked computer terminals. While there is still much less access to telecommunications in developing countries than in industrialized countries, at present, the gap in access to computers is much greater than the gap in access to telephone lines or telephones. High-income countries had 22 times as many telephone lines per 100 population as low-income countries, but 96 times as many computers (Table 22.2). However, as prices for computers continue to decline, access may become more related to perceived value than to price.

Typically, a high percentage of developing country residents live in rural areas (as much as 80 per cent of the population in the least developed countries), where access to communication networks is much more limited than in urban areas (Table 22.3). It should be noted that Table 22.3 overestimates rural access because the 'rest of country' includes everything except the largest city. Also, facilities are not likely to be evenly distributed throughout the country, so that in poorer nations there may be many rural settlements without any communications infrastructure.

ACCESS PARAMETERS

Access versus Service

The terms 'universal access' and 'universal service' are sometimes used interchangeably, although access is becoming the more common term. The distinction is between services that are delivered to all users, and access to a variety of services that may be provided to individual users, households, community facilities, institutions and workplaces, etc. However, it is also necessary to consider access to the technologies connected to these networks that make possible information access and processing, particularly when considering access to the Internet. Typically, end-user equipment would include personal computers with sufficient speed and capacity to process data from the World Wide Web (or

Table 22.1 *Internet access by region, June 1999*

Region	People connected (millions)	% of global people connected	% of global population
Canada and US	97.0	56.6	5.1
Europe	40.1	23.4	13.7
Asia/Pacific	27.0	15.8	56.2
Latin America	5.3	3.1	8.4
Africa	1.1	0.6	12.9
Middle East	0.9	0.5	3.6

Source: Derived from Henry et al., 1999

Table 22.2 *Access indicators*

Country income classification	Tel. lines per 100	PCs per 100	Internet hosts per 10,000	Internet users per 10,000
High	54.1	22.3	28.1	92.0
Upper middle	13.4	2.9	8.4	55.9
Lower middle	9.7	1.3	1.9	19.0
Low	2.5	0.2	0.1	0.9

Source: Derived from ITU, 1998

Table 22.3 *Access to telecommunications*

Country income classification	Teledensity (telephone lines per 100)		
	National	Urban	Rest of country
High	46.0	52.9	43.8
Upper middle	13.7	25.7	11.5
Lower middle	9.7	22.1	7.2
Low	2.5	6.5	2.3

Source: Derived from ITU, 1998

networked terminals with central access to sufficient capacity), and access to value-added services such as Internet service providers (ISPs).

Access is thus a broader concept than service, and involves the following components:

- *Infrastructure* Reach of networks and services, for example to rural areas, low-income populations in inner cities; available bandwidth (such as broadband capacity for high-speed Internet access).
- *Range of services* For example, basic voice service (plain old telephone service or 'POTS'), value-added services such as ISPs.
- *Affordability* Pricing of installation, monthly service, usage by time or volume, etc.
- *Reliability* Quality of service, as shown by extent of outages, breakdowns, circuit blockage, circuits degraded by noise or echoes, etc.

Another important component of access is specification of the entitities to whom telecommunications services should be accessible. Users may be considered in several categories:

- *Public* Geographic, i.e. urban/rural, regional; demographic, i.e. disadvantaged people such as low-income groups, the disabled, ethnic or other minorities.
- *Commercial enterprises* Large and small businesses, entrepreneurs; critical sectors, i.e. agriculture, transportation, manufacturing, tourism, etc.
- *Public services* Health care, education, other government/public services, etc.; non-profit and non-governmental organizations (NGOs).

Universal Access: a Moving Target

Universal access should be considered a dynamic concept with a set of moving targets. Rapid technological change dictates that the definitions of basic and 'advanced' or 'enhanced' services will change over time, while the unit of analysis for accessibility may be the household, the municipality, or even institutions such as schools and health centres. Thus, for example, a multi-tiered definition of access could be proposed, identifying requirements within households, within communities and for education and social service providers. For example:

- *Level one* Community access, for example through kiosks, libraries, post offices, community centres, telecentres.
- *Level two* Institutional access through schools, hospitals, clinics.
- *Level three* Household access.

Economic and demographic diversity in inner cities, impoverished rural areas, and developing countries will require a variety of goals for information infrastructure. In North America and Europe, the goal has been to provide basic telephone service to every household, with the assumption that businesses and organizations could all afford access to at least this grade of service. However, for Internet access, the US is applying community and institutional access models. As noted above, the US Telecommunications Act of 1996 specifies that 'advanced services' should be provided at a discount to schools, libraries and rural health centres. 'Advanced services' are currently interpreted as Internet access. In the future, it is likely that advanced services will be redefined, perhaps to include access to new generations of services available through the Internet or its successors. It should also be noted that industrialized countries such as the US and Canada have extended the concept of basic service beyond quality adequate for voice to include single-party service, and circuits capable of supporting the capacity of current modems, with the assumption that people will want to communicate electronically from their homes.[4] These criteria are also likely to be revised over time to keep pace with the demands of the information economy.

Developing countries generally use community access criteria: China, India, Mexico, Nepal and Thailand, for example, aim for at least one telephone per village or settlement. Other developing countries set targets of public telephones within a radius of a few kilometres in rural areas (ITU, 1998: 69). The ITU's Maitland Commission called for a telephone within an hour's walk throughout the developing world.

The Danger of Electronic Islands and Ghettos

National goals of interoperability and open standards are needed to ensure that users are not left on 'electronic islands' because their service provider is not interconnected with other networks. An analogy would be the early stages of commercial e-mail, when each e-mail service was autonomous, so that communication between subscribers to different services was impossible or at least very cumbersome.

There is still a danger of creating electronic ghettos – low-profit regions such as inner cities and rural areas – that carriers and service providers may

have little incentive to serve or upgrade. For example, large US telephone companies have been reluctant to upgrade their networks in rural areas by adding technologies such as signalling system 7 (SS7), integrated services digital network (ISDN) and digital subscriber line (DSL). Ironically, customers of some rural telephone companies that have invested in new facilities may gain little benefit if the connecting long-distance carriers do not offer similar services.

TECHNOLOGICAL TRENDS

Demand for Internet access has created a market for higher-speed communication than is typically available over a dialup telephone line. The least-cost solution in areas with communications infrastructure is to upgrade these facilities, for example to offer DSL over existing telephone lines or cable modems for access over cable television networks. Where population density is high and funds are available, optical fibre is being provided to the end user (for example, in Singapore and in new subdivisions in industrialized countries). However, high-capacity wireless networks may offer a lower-cost solution than optical fibre to provide high-speed networking.

In the past, there have been few incentives for carriers to provide access to low-income customers such as disadvantaged minorities and inner-city residents who are presumed to have limited demand for new services, and rural and remote regions where the cost of extending or upgrading facilities and services is assumed to be higher than expected revenues. However, technological innovations, many of which were initially designed for other applications, are now creating opportunities to reduce costs and/or increase revenues among these populations. As noted above, high-capacity wireless may be a less expensive means of providing or upgrading access in urban areas. Wireless also has enormous potential in rural areas where the cost of installing cable or fibre is much higher. Satellite systems may also be used in rural areas for basic telephony (generally through a local network connected to a community satellite terminal) or for Internet access (which could also be through an individual VSAT – a very small aperture terminal). More information on these technologies and their implications for improving access is provided in the Appendix to this chapter (pp. 379–81).

There are several significant implications of these technological trends, particularly for rural and developing regions:

- *Distance is no longer a barrier to accessing information* Technologies are available that can provide interactive voice, data and multimedia services virtually anywhere.

- *Costs of providing services are declining* Satellite transmission costs are independent of distance; transmission costs using other technologies have also declined dramatically. Thus communications services can be priced not according to distance, which penalizes rural and remote users, but per unit of information (message, bit) or unit of time.
- *The potential for competition is increasing* Lower costs make rural/remote areas more attractive. New competitors can offer multiple technological solutions, including wireless, satellite, copper, cable and others described above.

In addition, it is no longer technically or economically necessary to set rural benchmarks lower than urban benchmarks for access – both to basic telecommunications and to the Internet. The US Telecommunications Act of 1996 requires that rural services and prices are to be *reasonably comparable* to those in urban areas. This standard rejects the assumption that 'something is better than nothing' in rural areas because minimal service was all that was either technically feasible or economically justifiable. However, as noted above, advances in technologies such as terrestrial wireless and satellite systems can now provide higher quality at lower cost in rural areas. The implications of these changes in policy and technology are particularly critical in enabling rural residents to participate in the digital economy.

While the US and other industrialized countries must upgrade outdated wireline networks and analogue exchanges in rural areas, developing countries can leapfrog old technologies and install fully digital wireless networks. Thus developing country regulators can also adopt rural comparability standards to avoid penalizing rural services and businesses in access to information services. For example, in the Philippines, after extensive discussion, both government and industry representatives agreed on rural benchmarks including digital switching, single-party service, and line quality sufficient for facsimile and data communications.[5]

UNDERSTANDING DEMAND FOR COMMUNICATION SERVICES

Lack of understanding of demand for telecommunications services (i.e. need for the service and ability to pay) creates problems in designing universal service policy. For example, 'low-income' households in industrialized countries may be able to pay for the cost of monthly telephone service subscriptions, which are likely to cost less than other utilities and than entertainment, including cable television (Crandall and Waverman, 2000). Thus,

it may not be necessary to provide a subsidy for service to most low-income households. However, utilization of the network (for long-distance or measured rate calls) which subscribers need to maintain contact for family or work may be much more expensive. Some consumer representatives have advocated a policy of providing a live telephone connection in all dwellings which could be used for emergencies. Other possibilities include blocks on the line to prevent unauthorized use for other than local calls, and prepaid service in the form of a rechargeable account or smart card that allows calling only up to the limit of funds on the card or in the account.

Communications service providers may also be reluctant to extend services to poorer populations who are assumed to have insufficient demand to cover the cost of providing the services and necessary infrastructure. Certainly, household income may be the best indicator of both willingness and ability to pay for communication services. Typically higher-income populations are better educated, and are thus likely to have not only the money but also the skills to use new technologies and services.

However, indicators other than population and household income may be better predictors of demand for communication services. One study estimates that rural users in developing countries are able collectively to pay 1 to 1.5 per cent of their gross *community* income for telecommunications services (Kayani and Dymond, 1997: xviii). The ITU uses an estimate of 5 per cent of *household* income as an affordability threshold. To generate revenues to cover capital and operating costs of the network, the average household income required would be $2060; for a more efficiently run network, it would be $1340 (ITU, 1998: 35). Using the higher estimate, 20 per cent of households in low-income countries could afford a telephone; in lower-middle-income countries the range could be from 40 to 80 per cent; while in upper-middle-income countries such as Eastern Europe, more than 80 per cent of households could afford telephone service (1998: 37).[6]

Just as income may not fully explain demand for information technologies and services, lack of access to telephone service cannot necessarily be attributed to lack of demand or purchasing power. For example, in many developing countries, television sets are much more prevalent than telephones. In industrialized countries, both TV sets and telephone lines are almost universally available. However, in middle-income countries there are twice as many TV sets as telephone lines, while in low-income countries there are more than five times as many TV sets as telephone lines (see Table 22.4). It appears that where television is available, a significant percentage of families will find the money to buy TV sets. Thus, even in the

Table 22.4   *Teledensity versus TV density*

Country income classification	Tel. lines per 100	TV sets per 100	Ratio TV sets/tel. lines
High	54.1	61.9	1.1
Upper middle	13.4	26.3	2.0
Lower middle	9.7	22.7	2.3
Low	2.5	13.1	5.2

Source: Derived from ITU, 1998

poorest countries, there may be much more disposable income available than per capita GDP data would indicate, and there may be significant demand for other information services.

Other approaches may also be used to gauge demand for information services. For example, the presence of video shops indicates significant disposable income available for television sets, video cassette players and cassette rentals. Telephone service resellers (such as in Indonesia, Senegal and Bangladesh), local cable television operators (common in India) and small satellite dishes on rural homesteads and urban flats (common in Eastern Europe and many Asian countries) also signal demand and ability to pay for information services.

A conclusion that can be drawn from the above analysis is that changing the policy environment to create incentives to serve previously ignored populations may significantly increase access among these groups. Incentives are some of the innovative strategies that have been adopted to provide community access to telecommunications, and more recently to the Internet, which are summarized in the next section.

POLICIES AND STRATEGIES TO INCREASE ACCESS

Community Access Requirements

Some countries such as Chile and Mexico have mandated requirements for operators to install payphones in rural communities; South Africa has also required its wireless operators to install fixed rural payphones. Franchised payphones have been introduced in Indonesia, India, Bangladesh and other countries in order to involve entrepreneurs where the operator is still government owned. Indonesia's franchised call offices, known as wartels (*warung telekomunikasi*), operated by small entrepreneurs, generate more than $9000 per line, about ten times more than Telkom's average revenue per line (ITU, 1998: 77). Franchised telephone booths operate in several francophone African countries; in Senegal, phone shops known locally as telecentres average four times the revenue of those operated by the

national carrier (1998: 77–8). In Bangladesh, Grameen Phone has rented cell phones to rural women who provide portable payphone service to their communities. Such examples of simple resale can create incentives to meet pent-up demand even if network competition has not yet been introduced.

Telecentres and other public facilities can provide access to e-mail, which is much faster than the postal service and cheaper than facsimile transmission. For example, a message of 2000 words takes 10 minutes to read over a telephone; 2 minutes to send by fax; and about 4 seconds to transmit via a 28.8 kbps modem (M. Hegener, quoted in ITU, 1998: 80). Such services can be valuable even for illiterates. For example, a Member of Parliament from Uganda stated that his father sent many telegrams during his lifetime, but could neither read nor write. Local scribes wrote down his messages. Similarly, 'information brokers' ranging from librarians to cybercafé staff can help people with limited education to send and access electronic information.

Virtually every major city in the developing world now has cybercafés or privately operated telecentres equipped with personal computers linked to the Internet. The African Communications Group plans wireless kiosks for Internet access, with web pages enabling artisans, farmers and other small entrepreneurs to set up shop in the global marketplace (Petzinger, 1998: B1). Initiatives to provide public Internet access through community telecentres are being supported by several development agencies including the International Telecommunication Union (ITU), UNESCO, United Nations Development Programme (UNDP), Canada's International Development Research Centre (IDRC), and the US Agency for International Development (USAID). South Africa is also supporting the installation of telecentres equipped with phone lines, facsimile and computers with Internet access through a universal service fund; South Africa now plans to provide Internet access to government information and electronic commerce services through post offices. Many other countries are extending public access to the Internet through telecentres, libraries, post offices and kiosks.

Access to telephones through booths, kiosks and telecentres can be coupled with electronic messaging to provide 'virtual telephone service'. TeleBahia in north-eastern Brazil offers a virtual service for small businesses without individual telephones. These customers rent a voice mailbox for a monthly fee and check their messages from a payphone, providing a means for clients to contact them. African Communications Group is setting up wireless public payphones and providing voice mail accounts and pagers that announce incoming messages. The recipient calls back or leaves a voice mail message using a phone card; the service is priced for people making $200 per month (Petzinger, 1998: B1).[7] Similar systems are used for migrant farm workers in California to enable them to stay in touch with their families, and in homeless shelters to enable job seekers to be contacted by employers.

Service Obligations

Many countries include a universal service obligation (USO) as a condition of the licence. The cost of USOs may vary depending on geography and population density. British Telecom's universal service obligation costs just 1 per cent of its total revenue base (Oftel, 1994; quoted in Kayani and Dymond, 1997: 53). Latin American countries with USOs include Argentina, Chile, Mexico, Peru and Venezuela. In Mexico, the privatized monopoly operator TelMex was to provide service to all communities with at least 500 population by the year 2000. In the Philippines, local exchange obligations are bundled with cellular and international gateway licences; licensees were required to install up to 300,000 access lines in previously unserved areas within three years (Hudson, 1997b).

Some countries use a 'carrier of last resort' model which has the obligation to provide service if no other carrier has done so. Typically, the dominant carrier bears this obligation and is entitled to a subsidy to provide the service. However, this approach can be flawed if it provides no incentive for the carrier with the USO to use the most appropriate and inexpensive technology and to operate efficiently. It can also serve as a justification for the dominant carrier to be protected from competition because it has additional costs and obligations not required of new competitors.

However, rather than designating a single carrier of last resort, some countries are introducing bidding schemes for rural subsidies. In Chile, a development fund was established in 1994 to increase access for the approximately 10 per cent of the population in communities without telephone access. The regulator estimated the required subsidies, distinguishing between commercially viable and commercially unviable, and put them out to competitive tender. There were 62 bids for 42 of the 46 projects. Surprisingly, 16 projects were awarded to bids of zero subsidy; as a result of preparing for the bidding process, operators were able to document demand and willingness to pay in many communities. Once completed, these projects will provide service to about 460,000 people, about one-third of the Chilean population without access (ITU, 1998: 79). Peru is introducing a similar programme.

Subsidies

A variety of schemes can be used to subsidize carriers that serve regions where revenues would apparently not cover costs. Subsidies may be paired with USOs to compensate the carrier with the obligation to serve. The traditional means of ensuring provision of service to unprofitable areas or customers has been through cross-subsidies, such as from international or interexchange to local services. However, technological changes and the liberalization of the telecommunications sector now make it impracticable to rely on internal cross-subsidies. For example, customers may bypass high-priced services using so-called 'callback'[8] services or Internet telephony.

In a competitive environment, cross-subsidies cannot be maintained. Carriers that have relied on revenues from one service to subsidize another now face competitors who can underprice them on individual services. Also, new entrants cannot survive if their competitors are subsidized. Therefore, if subsidies are required, they must be made explicit and targeted at specific classes of customers or locations such as:

- *High-cost areas* Carriers may be subsidized to serve locations that are isolated and/or have very low population density so that they are significantly more expensive to serve than other locations. This approach is used in the US and has recently been mandated in Canada.
- *Disadvantaged areas or customers* Subsidies may target economically disadvantaged areas or groups that could not afford typical prices for installation and usage, or where demand for service is significantly lower than average. Some carriers may offer interest-free loans or extended payment periods to assist new subscribers to connect to the network. In the US, the Lifeline programme subsidizes basic monthly service charges for low-income subscribers. The subsidy funds come from a combination of carrier contributions and surcharges on subscriber bills. Some 4.4 million households receive Lifeline assistance. Also in the US, the Linkup programme subsidizes connection to the network for low-income households.
- *Route averaging* Some countries including Australia, Canada, the United Kingdom and the United States require that rates be averaged so

that all customers pay uniform distance charges, regardless of location. Thus, for example, the rate per minute between Sydney and Melbourne would be the same as the rate over an equal distance in the Australian outback, where costs are much higher. Such policies can bridge the digital divide by reducing rural access costs.

Funding Universal Service

Funds for subsidies may be generated from several sources such as contributions required from all carriers: for example, a percentage of revenues, a tax on revenues or a surcharge on customer bills. Subsidies may also come from general tax revenues or other government sources.

- *Transfers among carriers* Some countries with many carriers rely on settlement and repayment pooling schemes among operators to transfer payments to carriers with high operating costs. For example, the US Universal Service Fund is mandated by the Federal Communications Commission (FCC) but administered by the carriers through the National Exchange Carriers Association (NECA), and transfers funds to subsidize access lines to carriers whose costs are above 115 per cent of the national average.[9]
- *Government-financed funds* In Poland, over 7885 localities were connected between 1992 and 1996 with funding of US$20 million from the state budget (ITU, 1998: 78). In 1994, Peru established a rural telecommunications investment fund, FITEL (Fondo de Inversion de Telecomunicaciones), which is financed by a 1 per cent tax on revenues of all telecommunications providers, ranging from the country's newly privatized monopoly operator Telefonica/ENTEL to cable TV operators. Since established, it has generated an average of US$450,000 per month, growing by US$12 million annually (1998: 79). Private sector operators may apply to FITEL for financing (Kayani and Dymond, 1999: 63–4).

Licensing Rural Operators

Some countries grant monopoly franchises to rural operators. For example, Bangladesh has licensed two rural monopoly operators; they are allowed to prioritize the most financially attractive customers and charge a substantial up-front subscriber connection fee. The Bangladesh Rural Telecommunications Authority (BRTA) is profitable, even though it has to provide at least one public call office (PCO) in each village that requests one (Kayani and Dymond, 1997: 18).

However, other countries are opening up rural areas to competition as part of national liberalization policies. Argentina allows rural operators to compete with the two privatized monopolies, Telecom and Telefonica. Some 135 rural cooperatives have been formed to provide telecommunications services in communities with fewer than 300 people (1997: 18). Finland's association of telephone companies has created several jointly owned entities that provide a range of rural, local and long-distance services in their concession areas, in competition with the national operator (1997: 19). In Alaska, a second carrier, GCI, competes with AT&T Alascom to provide long-distance services in rural and remote areas. This competition has benefited Alaskan schools in gaining access to the Internet. GCI has assisted school districts in applying for E-rate subsidies for Internet access, apparently viewing this initiative as a win–win opportunity for both schools and the telephone company.

Although in most countries a single carrier provides both local and long-distance services, it is also possible to delineate territories that can be served by local entities. In the US, the model of rural cooperatives fostered through the Rural Utilities Service (formerly Rural Electrification Administration) has been used to bring telephone service to areas ignored by the large carriers. As noted above, wireless technologies could change the economics of providing rural services, making rural franchises much more attractive to investors. As a result of availability of funds from the RUS for upgrading networks, rural cooperatives in the US typically provide more modern facilities and better Internet access than provided by large telephone companies serving rural areas.

Third parties may also be permitted to lease capacity in bulk and resell it in units of bandwidth and/or time appropriate for business customers and other major users. This approach may be suitable where some excess network capacity exists (e.g. between major cities or on domestic or regional satellites). Resale is one of the simplest ways to introduce some competition and lower rates for users, but is not legal in many developing countries, even where some excess capacity exists in backbone networks.

CURRENT AND FUTURE TRENDS

Understanding Trends in Access

Research is needed to determine which underlying factors are the best explanations of variations in access. For example, in the US, attention is frequently focused on ethnicity and rurality, e.g. access by blacks, Hispanics and native Americans, and on disparities between urban and rural residents. However, other factors such as income and education (often highly correlated) may influence access. Similar analysis in other countries may reveal underlying factors that form barriers to access. As definitions of access change to include computers and Internet connectivity as well as telephone service, we could expect that education would be an increasingly important predictor of access, since better educated people would tend to have better technical skills and greater perceived need for use of computers and online services.

Other industrialized countries show trends broadly similar to those in the US, with access greater among those with higher incomes and more education, and somewhat greater in urban than in rural areas. However, the percentage of the population with Internet access at home or at work is more than twice as high in the US, Canada, the Nordic countries and Australia as in the United Kingdom, and more than three times higher than in Germany, Japan and France (ITU, 1999a: 22). It would be useful to learn what enabling or inhibiting factors are contributing to these disparities.

Studies of outliers and anomalies could also improve our understanding of trends in access to new services and their implications. For example, why are the Scandinavian countries (Finland, Sweden, Norway, Denmark) in the top ten countries in Internet hosts per 1000 population, and what impact is this high level of Internet access likely to have on their economies? Does the fact that Israel, Ireland and Taiwan have more Internet hosts per 1000 population than France and Japan indicate future trends in economic growth, or is it a short-term artifact of national policies? Are middle-income countries such as Egypt and Jordan, which have better Internet access than other economically similar countries, likely to reap greater economic benefits than countries with below-average access such as Tunisia and Algeria? Among the 'Asian tigers', does the greater Internet access of Singapore, Hong Kong and Taiwan give them an advantage over South Korea, Malaysia and Thailand (1999a: 22, 38)?

From Access to Use

Beyond access, it will be important to understand what factors influence use of information services once they are accessible, either through individual ownership and connectivity or via public sites such as schools and libraries. Are there other factors such as computer use at school that are likely to encourage access? Are there strategies such as community access or training that could increase utilization? Among youth, are there specific factors such as exposure at an early age that appear preconditions for later use? Among adults, are there information-seeking behaviours or social norms that may influence use of ICTs? For example, in some cultures,

women may be discouraged from using technology; also, older or less educated people may feel more comfortable using an 'information broker' such as a librarian, social worker or extension agent to find information they need or to contact others electronically.[10] Anecdotal evidence from projects such as SeniorNet in the US and telecentres in developing countries indicates that such resource people can be very important as facilitators, especially at early stages in using the Internet among some populations such as senior citizens and women. For example, at telecentres with local facilitators in Mali, Uganda and Mozambique, from 30 to 45 per cent of the users are women, despite the fact that women typically have less education and exposure to technology than men in these societies.[11]

CONCLUSION

The concept of universal service continues to evolve, both in terms of services that should be universally included and in our understanding of access – meaning that the services are available, affordable and reliable. This chapter has shown how innovative technologies, strategies and policies can help to increase access to communication services. However, it is important to note that more than access will likely be necessary to achieve significant benefits. A workforce with sufficient general education and specialized training as well as an institutional environment that fosters innovation and productivity are likely to be critical factors. Effective applications of these facilities may require training, mentoring and, in some cases, facilitation through intermediaries. Sustainability will continue to be a concern, particularly in maintaining non-commercial forms of access such as through schools and libraries, and non-profit community access centres.

APPENDIX: TECHNOLOGIES AND SERVICES FOR EXTENDING ACCESS

The following are key technologies that offer new or lower-cost access to information and telecommunication services:

Wireline

Digital Subscriber Line (DSL)

This technology offers increased capacity, suitable for Internet access, over existing copper wire, making it an attractive option for upgrading Internet access in urban areas where telephone lines are already installed (its range is too limited for rural areas). However, it should be noted that copper wire is prone to theft in some countries: Telkom South Africa reported more than 4000 incidents of cable theft in 1996, at an estimated cost of R230 million (about US$50 million) (ITU, 1998: 60).

Interactive Cable Systems

Coaxial cable installed to deliver cable television can also be upgraded to provide telephony and Internet access. Cable modems provide faster transmission than DSL; however, older cable systems are not optimally configured for interactivity, and quality of service may be inferior to that provided by telephone companies.

Hybrid Fibre/Coax (HFC)

A combination of optical fibre and coaxial cable can provide broadband services such as TV and high-speed Internet access as well as telephony; this combination is cheaper than installing fibre all the way to the customer premises. Unlike most cable systems, HFC allows two-way communication. The fibre runs from a central switch to a neighbourhood node; coax links the node to the end user such as the subscriber's home or business. HFC is found in many industrialized countries; developing countries with HFC projects include Chile, China, India, South Korea and Malaysia (1998: 57).

Optical Fibre

Optical fibre is commonly found in links between switches, terrestrial backbone networks and submarine cables. Fibre is being installed in new towns and subdivisions in industrialized countries, but the cost of upgrading existing local loops to fibre is very high. However, Singapore has provided fibre to end users, and Japan is committed to upgrading local loops to optical fibre throughout the country.

Terrestrial Wireless

Cellular

Cellular technology, originally designed for mobile services (such as communication from vehicles), is now being introduced for personal communications using small portable handsets. Wireless personal communications are almost ubiquitous in Scandinavia, Japan and Hong Kong, and are proliferating very rapidly in other industrialized and emerging economies. In developing countries without sufficient wireline infrastructure, wireless personal networks can provide a primary service. In China, there are more than 70 million wireless customers; other developing countries where wireless is used as a primary service include Colombia, Lebanon, Malaysia, the Philippines, Sri Lanka,

South Africa, Uganda, Venezuela and Thailand (ITU, 1998: 49).

Wireless Local Loop (WLL)

Wireless local loop systems can be used to extend local telephone services to rural customers without laying cable or stringing copper wire. WLL costs have declined, making it competitive with copper; wireless allows faster rollout to customers than extending wire or cable, so that revenue can be generated more quickly; it also has a lower ratio of fixed to incremental costs than copper, making it easy to add more customers and serve transient populations. Wireless is also less vulnerable than copper wire or cable to accidental damage or vandalism. Examples of countries with WLL projects include Bolivia, Czech Republic, Hungary, Indonesia and Sri Lanka (ITU, 1998: 53).

Cordless

Short-range cordless extensions can provide the link from wireless outstations to subscriber premises; the DECT (digital European cordless telephone) technology standard will also allow the base station to act as a wireless PBX (Kayani and Dymond, 1997: 48). For example, DECT has been used in South Africa for the link to rural subscribers.[12]

Wireless Payphones

Cellular installations can be used to provide fixed public payphones. For example, new cellular operators in South Africa were required to install 30,000 wireless payphones within five years as a condition of the licence. By March 1997, almost 15,000 wireless payphones had been installed (ITU, 1998: 50). Alternatively, a cellular subscriber may resell access. Entrepreneurs in Bangladesh offer payphone service using cell phones leased from Grameen Phone, which they carry by bicycle to various neighbourhoods.

Multi-Access Radio

Time division multiple access (TDMA) radio systems are a means of providing wireless rural telephony. They typically have 30–60 trunks and can accommodate 500–1000 subscribers. Their range can be extended using multiple repeaters (Kayani and Dymond, 1999: 27).

Satellite Technologies

Very Small Aperture Terminals (VSATs)

Small satellite earth stations operating with geosynchronous earth orbiting (GEO) satellites can be used for interactive voice and data, as well as for broadcasting of data, audio and video. Remote villages in Alaska and the Canadian Arctic use satellites for telephone service, Internet access and broadcast reception. VSATs may also offer affordable access for business networks: banks in remote areas of Brazil are linked via VSATs; the National Stock Exchange of India links brokers with rooftop VSATs.

Demand Assignment Multiple Access (DAMA)

In GEO satellite systems, instead of assigning dedicated circuits to each location, DAMA allows the terminal to access the satellite only on demand and eliminates double hops between rural locations served by the same system. The system is very cost-effective because satellite transponder expense is reduced to a fraction of that associated with a fixed-assigned system for the same amount of traffic. Also, digital DAMA systems provide higher-bandwidth capabilities at much lower cost than analogue. DAMA is used to reduce costs of village telephone service in Alaska, and is now used in other satellite dialup networks.

Global Mobile Personal Communications Systems (GMPCS)

Using low earth orbiting (LEO) satellites, these systems – such as Globalstar, Iridium and ICO – can provide voice and low-speed (typically 2400 to 9600 kbps) data virtually anywhere, using handheld transceivers. However, the price per minute for these services may be much higher than national terrestrial services, and the first generation of LEOs has very limited bandwidth.

Internet via Satellite

Internet gateways can be accessed via geostationary satellites. For example, MagicNet (an ISP in Mongolia) and some African ISPs access the Internet in the US via PanAmSat, and residents of the Canadian Arctic use the Anik satellite system, while Alaskan villagers use US domestic satellites. However, these systems are not optimized for Internet use, and may therefore be quite expensive. Several improvements in using GEOs are becoming available:

- *Optimized interactive access via VSAT* Several companies are developing protocols for fully interactive Internet access via satellite, that should be much more efficient than current systems.[13]
- *Hybrid systems* This approach uses a VSAT as a downlink from the ISP, but provides upstream connectivity over existing telephone lines. Some rural schools in the US are using hybrids for Internet access.

- *High-bandwidth LEOs* Future LEO systems are being planned to provide bandwidth on demand. Constellations of LEO satellites such as Teledesic, Cyberstar or Skybridge may provide another means of Internet access via satellite (Hudson, 1998a).
- *Data broadcasting* Satellites designed for digital audio broadcasting (such as Worldspace) can also be used to broadcast web pages to small receivers. Users would not have fully interactive service, but could receive regular downloads of specified pages addressed to their receivers.

Digital Services

Compressed Voice

Compression algorithms can be used to 'compress' digital voice signals, so that eight or more conversations can be carried on a single 64 kbps voice channel, thus significantly reducing transmission costs.

Internet Telephony (Voice over IP)

Some carriers are beginning to offer dialup access to Internet telephony. The advantage of using Internet protocols for voice as well as data is that transmission costs are much lower than over circuit-switched telephony networks.

Compressed Video

Compressed digital video can be used to transmit motion video over as few as two telephone lines (128 kbps), offering the possibility of low-cost video conferencing for distance education and training. Interactive low-resolution video can also now be delivered over the Internet.

Smart Cards

Prepaid phone cards, widely available in Europe and Japan, have been introduced in developing countries to eliminate the need for coin phones (which require coin collection and may be subject to pilferage and vandalism). Cellular operators have now extended this concept to offer prepaid cellular service using rechargeable smart cards, so that telephone service is now available to customers without credit histories or even bank accounts. In South Africa, Vodacom sold more than 300,000 prepaid starter packs and one million recharge vouchers for cellular use in 1997 (ITU, 1998: 44). In Uganda, within one year of licensing a second cellular operator, aggressive marketing of prepaid service and attractive pricing have resulted in there being more cellular customers than fixed lines in the country. For most of the new subscribers, their cell phone is their first and only telephone.[14]

NOTES

1 For a comparison of universal service in the United States, Canada and the United Kingdom, see Crandall and Waverman (2000).

2 Fact sheet: 'Rural areas magnify "digital divide"', www.ntia.doc.gov/ntiahome/digitaldivide/factsheets/rural.htm.

3 It should be noted that Japan and Australia are included in the Asia/Pacific in Table 22.1; the estimate in the text includes them with industrialized countries of Europe and North America.

4 See www.crtc.gc.ca.

5 Meeting at Department of Transport and Communicatons attended by the author, Manila, January 1998.

6 It should be noted that this calculation appears to assume even distribution of income throughout the society at higher income levels, which is not necessarily true.

7 Africa Communications Group is to be known as Adesemi Communications International.

8 The simplest form of callback involves a caller in an area where tariffs are high asking the other party to call back using cheaper rates from their location. Simple examples include a traveller using a hotel's payphone to call home and asking family members to call back to her room, rather than paying the hotel's high charges. Now callers in high-cost areas (typically developing countries) can set up an account with a callback company and then call a special number, hang up and wait for the return call from the cheaper jurisdiction. The company can identify the caller without even answering the call, and can set up the call between the two parties using its own software.

9 See www.neca.org, and information on the Universal Service Fund on the FCC's website, www.fcc.gov.

10 For example, peasant farmers in Ecuador found out how to eliminate a pest that was destroying their potato crop through the assistance of a fieldworker who posted their question on several Internet newsgroups (personal communication, October 1999).

11 Heather E. Hudson, field research and unpublished reports, 1999.

12 It should be noted that a disadvantage of all these wireless technologies is limited bandwidth. While they can be used for e-mail, they do not provide sufficient capacity for accessing the World Wide Web at present. However, a new protocol known as WAP (wireless application protocol) being developed to enable cell phone users to access the web may also make it possible to access text on the web using very limited bandwidth.

13 See www.alohanet.com; also *The Red Herring*, 29 September 1998, www.redherring.com/mag/issue59/limit/html.

14 Personal interview, Uganda Communications Commission, Kampala, November 1999.

REFERENCES

Anderson, Robert H. et al. (1995) *Universal Access to E-Mail: Feasibility and Social Implications.* Washington, DC: RAND.

Aufderheide, Patricia (1987) 'A universal service: telephone policy in the public interest', *Journal of Communication*, 37 (1): 81–96.

Aufderheide, Patricia (1999) *Communications Policy and the Public Interest: the Telecommunications Act of 1996.* New York: Guilford.

Crandall, Robert W. and Waverman, Leonard (2000) *Who Pays for Universal Service?* Washington, DC: Brookings Institution.

Cronin, Francis J., Colleran, Elisabeth K., Herbert, Paul L. and Lewitzky, Steven (1993a) 'Telecommunications and growth: the contribution of telecommunications infrastructure investment to aggregate and sectoral productivity', *Telecommunications Policy*, 17 (9): 677–90.

Cronin, Francis J., Parker, Edwin B., Colleran, Elisabeth K. and Gold, Mark A. (1993b) 'Telecommunications infrastructure and economic development', *Telecommunications Policy*, 17 (6): 415–30.

Duestenberg, Thomas J. and Gordon, Kenneth (1997) *Competition and deregulation in telecommunications: the case for a new paradigm.* Hudson Institute, Indianapolis.

European Union (1993) *Communication on Developing the Universal Service for Telecommunications in a Competitive Environment.* COM 93/543. Brussels, 15 November.

European Union (1996) *Communication on Universal Service for Telecommunications in the Perspective of a Fully-Liberalised Environment.* COM 96/73 final. Brussels, 13 March.

Hardy, Andrew P. (1980) 'The role of the telephone in economic development', *Telecommunications Policy*, 4 (4): 278–86.

Henry, David et al. (1999) *The Emerging Digital Economy II.* Washington, DC: US Department of Commerce.

Hobbs, Vicki M. and Blodgett, John (1999) 'The rural differential: an analysis of population demographics in areas served by rural telephone companies'. Paper presented at the Telecommunications Policy Research Conference, September. See also www.rupri.org.

Hudson, Heather E. (1990) *Communication Satellites: their Development and Impact.* New York: Free Press.

Hudson, Heather E. (1995) *Economic and Social Benefits of Rural Telecommunications: A Report to the World Bank.* Washington, DC: World Bank.

Hudson, Heather E. (1997a) *Global Connections: International Telecommunications Infrastructure and Policy.* New York: Wiley.

Hudson, Heather E. (1997b) 'Converging technologies and changing realities: toward universal access to telecommunications in the developing world', in

Telecom Reform: Principles, Policies, and Regulatory Practices. Lyngby: Technical University of Denmark.

Hudson, Heather E. (1998a) 'The significance of telecommunications for Canadian rural development'. Testimony on behalf of the Public Interest Advocacy Centre and others, Canadian Radio, Television and Telecommunications Commission Hearing on Telecom Public Notice CRTC 97-42, Service to High-Cost Serving Areas.

Hundt, Reed E. (2000) *You Say You Want a Revolution: a Story of Information Age Politics*. New Haven, CT: Yale University Press.

ITU (1998) *World Telecommunication Development Report 1998*. Geneva: International Telecommunication Union.

ITU (1999a) *Challenges to the Network: Internet for Development*. Geneva: International Telecommunication Union, October.

ITU (1999b) *World Telecommunication Development Report 1999*. Geneva: International Telecommunication Union.

Kayani, Rogati and Dymond, Andrew (1997) *Options for Rural Telecommunications Development*. Washington, DC: World Bank.

Maitland Commission (1984) *The Missing Link*. International Commission for Worldwide Telecommunications Development. Geneva: International Telecommunication Union, December.

Margherio, Lynn et al. (1998) *The Emerging Digital Economy*. Washington, DC: US Department of Commerce.

McConnaughey, James W. and Lader, Wendy (1997) *Falling through the Net II: New Data on the Digital Divide*. Washington, DC: National Telecommunications and Information Administration.

McConnaughey, James W. et al. (1999) *Falling through the Net: Defining the Digital Divide*. Washington, DC: National Telecommunications and Information Administration.

Mueller, Milton (1997) *Universal Service: Competition, Interconnection, and Monopoly in the Making of the American Telephone System*. Cambridge, MA: MIT Press.

Mueller, Milton and Schement, Jorge Reina (1996) 'A universal service from the ground up: a study of telephone penetration in Camden, New Jersey', *The Information Society*, 12: 273–92.

National Telecommunications and Information Administration (1994) *20/20 Visions*. Washington, DC: US Department of Commerce.

National Telecommunications and Information Administration (1997) *Falling through the Net: Defining the Digital Divide*. Washington, DC: US Department of Commerce.

OFTEL (1994) *A Framework for Effective Competition*. London: Office of Telecommunications.

O'Siochru, Sean (1996) *Telecommunications and Universal Service: International Experience in the Context of South African Telecommunications Reform*. Ottawa: International Development Research Centre.

Parker, Edwin B. and Hudson, Heather E. (1995) *Electronic Byways: State Policies for Rural Development through Telecommunications*, 2nd edn. Washington, DC: Aspen Institute.

Parker, Edwin B., Hudson, Heather E., Dillman, Don A. and Roscoe, Andrew D. (1989) *Rural America in the Information Age: Telecommunications Policy for Rural Development*. Lanham, MD: University Press of America.

Petzinger, Thomas Jr (1998) 'Monique Maddy uses wireless payphones to battle poverty', *Wall Street Journal*, 25 September: B1.

Saunders, Robert, Warford, Jeremy and Wellenius, Bjorn (1994) *Telecommunications and Economic Development*, 2nd edn. Baltimore, MD: Johns Hopkins University Press.

Schement, Jorge Reina (1995) 'Beyond universal service: characteristics of Americans without telephones', *Telecommunications Policy*, 19: 477–85.

Telecommunications Act of 1996 (1996) United States Congress. Public Law 104-104, 8 February.

World Information Technology and Services Alliance (1998) *Digital Planet: the Global Information Economy*. Washington, DC: WITSA.

Websites

Alaska Public Utilities Commission: www.state.ak.us/local/akpages/COMMERCE/apuc.htm.

Aloha Networks: www.alohanet.com.

Canadian Radio Television and Telecommunications Commission (CRTC): www.crtc.gc.ca.

Department of Commerce: www.ecommerce.gov/ece/.

Federal Communications Commission: www.fcc.gov.

General Communications Inc. (GCI): www.gci.com.

National Computer Board of Singapore: www.ncb.gov.sg.

National Exchange Carriers Association: www.neca.org.

National Telecommunications and Information Administration: www.ntia.doc.gov.

Rural Utilities Service: *The Red Herring*: www.redherring.com.

Vitacom, Inc.: www.vitacom.com.

PART FIVE: POLICY AND REGULATION

Introduction: The Governance of Media Markets

BELLA MODY, HARRY M. TREBING
and
LAURA STEIN

In *Telecommunications Politics* (1995), Mody and collaborators wrote about the forces and factors that influenced the deregulation and privatization of telecommunication in developing countries, home to two-thirds of the world's population. We focused on the role of intergovernmental organizations like the World Bank, foreign capital, the nation-state and domestic capital. We traced the influences of these forces through national case studies. We warned that privatization alone would not achieve competition, and we urged that state–market relations be conceptualized as adaptive rather than opposed. The real question should be the nature of state intervention rather than how much.

Market-opening telecommunication deregulation has been championed on a global and national scale by growth-oriented industry and governments of the US and the UK since the 1980s. At the beginning of the twenty-first century, after two decades of promoting deregulation for competition, the tendency seems to be towards an industry characterized by tight oligopoly (defined as four leading firms together controlling 60–100 per cent of the market). The US formula for competition for global prosperity included three essential steps: (1) mandatory unbundling of local networks; (2) establishment of prices for network access and interconnection that do not inhibit competition, and (3) auctioning the frequency spectrum to promote wireless communication

that can compete with wireline networks. Although there has been successful action in some of these areas in some nations, highly competitive networks have not emerged across the board, and industry concentration and/or tight oligopoly are becoming more and more evident on a national and global basis. Strictly economy-focused governance of liberalization that ignores social formations and political constituencies is rootless and insensitive to local conditions. We need a new architecture for the governance of new media markets that is based on consensus building, freely chosen international collaborations, and respect for the unique conditions in individual societies. In a world increasingly connected by the media, new and old, we cannot do media analysis that is single disciplinary, sectoral or technological or economic alone.

Five economic factors alone raise serious questions about the type of deregulated market structures that are evolving. First, there are substantial network economies inherent in the provision of telecommunications services. These lead to high concentration (to wit, the AOL–Time Warner merger), which, in turn, creates a potential for exercising market and political power that can negate the effects of selective entry through open access. This is especially important when coupled with vertical integration into downstream markets and common ownership of wireline and wireless plant.

Second, unbundling network components for new entrants will not overcome the obstacles confronting such entrants when dealing with an incumbent network providing widespread rebundled retail services. If the new entrant cannot match the wide range of offerings by the incumbent, then it will be confined to niche markets. Niche market rivalry is not a surrogate for workable competition, nor is niche market competition a sufficient constraint on the profits or pricing practices of the incumbent. Where the new entrant is large and has substantial market power, as in the case of new entry by the regional Bell holding companies into long-distance telecommunications markets, there will be a strong incentive for the inter-exchange carrier and the entrant to engage in bilateral oligopoly negotiations that will jeopardize neither the profits nor the discretionary behaviour of either player.

Third, the scope and capital intensity of comprehensive networks create a strong pressure to assure a stream of revenues sufficient to support a capital structure that is heavily weighted by debt capital. This financial burden creates incentives for market differentiation, price leadership and interdependent action. This serves as a further inducement for oligopoly behaviour.

Fourth, the prospects for developing generally accepted 'neutral' pricing guidelines for access appear to be remote. Incumbent telephone companies want high access charges covering profits foregone from not serving retail markets, a contribution to overhead costs, and the incremental cost of interconnection. Entrants want low access charges covering little more than bare-bones incremental costs. The outlook for a swift and straightforward reconciliation by national regulators is far from promising.

Fifth, successful rationing of the frequency spectrum to promote competition depends on the market structure in which auctioning takes place. In a tight oligopoly, the firm has an incentive to buy and withhold the spectrum in anticipation of high prices and profits at a later date, especially if this is necessary to secure a place in a market where future success is dependent on being a major full service provider capable of offering bundled wireline and wireless services. With few restrictions on licensees, oligopolists would be free to exploit such strategies to maximize advantage.

Why worry about oligopoly in telecommunication? Is it not superior to regulated private monopoly or to inefficient public monopolies? The rhetoric promoting market openings did not include the adverse consequences of tight oligopolies that are not amenable to light regulation through price caps, incentive allowances and open access. The first adverse consequence is the strong incentive for oligopolies to engage in an aggressive programme of mergers, acquisitions and various forms of collaborative behaviour such as alliances and joint ventures. Examples include the AT&T–British Telecom Concert project and the Verizon–Vodafone collaborative effort to offer nationwide wireless service in the US. Concert plans to invest $11 billion in a global broadband network capable of supplying international digital Internet service. The Verizon–Vodafone joint venture involves Verizon (a product of the Bell Atlantic–GTE merger) and Vodafone–Air Touch. The goal of this programme is to create a wireless system capable of serving 25 million US customers. Second, prices will no longer track costs. There will be strong incentives to engage in price discrimination and cross-subsidization between markets, to grant price concessions to large buyers, and to resort to patterns of price leadership to stabilize revenues wherever possible. Third, cost savings will not be distributed to final customer classes in a manner that is commensurate with their role in making such savings possible. Fourth, profit levels will be higher over time than those that would be expected to prevail under effective competition. This has been demonstrated in economies like New Zealand where privatization/ deregulation programmes have been put in place. Fifth, network technology will be driven by the requirements of the largest users (multinational corporations) at the expense of a universal network designed to serve all classes. Finally, network denigration and service deterioration are distinct possibilities under tight oligopoly and light regulation. The firm will have a strong incentive to redeploy assets based on profitability expectations. This can result in an incentive to underprovide quality service in many residual markets. The rhetoric for competition has not resulted in competitive market structures, and advances in technology liberated by market openings have not provided suitable solutions to these problems.[1] The implementation of competition policies has required regulatory extension and complexity.[2] A reform of the regulatory process is needed to deal with tight oligopoly through a system of monitoring corporate concentration, together with new innovative programmes that negate the adverse consequences of oligopoly in pricing, investment and marketing. We should expect nothing less from regulatory agencies who are supposed to be custodians of the public interest.

Disappointment with the nation-state as the supposedly public interested service provider, and the availability of eager, willing and able foreign firms looking for new markets has led to intergovernmental agreements on equal treatment of all carriers and sources of capital. Service providers are protecting themselves from competition through mergers and alliances, layoffs (Yoo and Mody, 2000), the introduction of new technologies, and diversification into content provision. Firms are seeking to differentiate themselves on the features of their products and services rather than on price.

What is the status of telecommunication policy and regulation around the world? Government regulators who monitored computing, broadcasting, print and telecommunication have merged in a few countries, but continue to be in conflict in others. The lack of symmetry in regulation between content provision and carriage is being questioned as technological development blurs market boundaries. With broadband technology and increased use of data, mobile and leased lines over voice services, pricing regulation and rebalancing local and long-distance rates is now an issue. Some combinations of regulatory assurance of interconnectivity and determination of rates with industry-based access undertakings have emerged in many countries. Some nations have no explicit policies to promote innovation in the information and communication service industries while many others have used government procurement incentives, research and development programmes and taxation incentives. The Internet as innovation came from innovators free from network control; some worry that the AOL–Time Warner merger will allow cable to control broadband access and compromise the promise of the Internet. National market stimulation policies have been limited to expanding the use of existing technologies through education and public access via telecentres, schools and libraries. Novel applications to meet unmet citizen needs are few and far between, e.g. graphic interfaces for illiterate users interested in information on employment opportunities for unskilled workers. National universal service policies have been premised on social equity more often than on human rights and economic development issues. New policy and regulatory approaches are needed to balance efficiency, distribution and fairness goals. National policy, regulatory measures and their impacts reflect the distinct social and economic conditions in which telecommunication infrastructure is embedded. These range from application of general competition, trade practices law and consumer protection across sectors, to the creation of an industry-specific regulator, to regulation separated from service provision, to maintenance of the traditional organization of service provision and regulation within the same government agency. Competition in the Danish telecommunication market has come further than competition in the EU countries in general partly because of sector-specific regulation. The Finnish conception of economic and electronic equity differs from that of the US; thus Finland has the world's highest PC penetration and Internet usage rates. For 80 per cent of the world's population who live on 20 per cent of the world's income, (about 4.8 million people) arguably, e-equity should be at least as important as e-commerce.

REGULATION AND REGULABILITY OF NEW MEDIA

Whether government regulation of new media is desirable or possible is a point of contention in both popular and academic discourse.[3] Many view these media as natural agents of economic, cultural and political progress. This viewpoint, described variously as technological determinism, technological utopianism or technological optimism, holds that new technologies possess inherent characteristics which naturally tend toward beneficial outcomes. While some view these characteristics as so dominant as to override attempts at regulation altogether, others argue simply that new technologies should be allowed, whenever possible, to develop free from government or market regulation.[4] With regards to computer networks, examples of such thinking can be found in the work of Cate (1995) and Labunski (1997), who argue that the openness of computer networks, the presence of multiple Internet service providers (ISPs), and the capacity of these networks to carry large amounts of data, guarantee that individual rights are well protected in the absence of government regulation. Similarly, Johnson and Post (1997) hold that the ability of global communication systems to traverse national borders undermines the ability of nations to regulate the medium and negates the benefits of global commerce for those countries who attempt to do so. Others, such as Samorski et al. (1997: 155–6) and Froomkin (1997), hold that the decentralized nature of the Internet, the volume of data it carries, and the ability of users to communicate anonymously, render government regulation of the network too costly and inefficient. These scholars draw a causal connection between the ostensible characteristics of new technologies and political, economic and social betterment.

Sceptics of network regulability also point out that government regulation can be circumvented in a number of ways. Users can configure their network connections to appear to reside somewhere else or make use of remailers which allow anonymous and untraceable communication (Johnson and Post, 1997: 9). In 1993, Canadian citizens used an anonymous remailer to establish a Usenet group that carried foreign news coverage of an ongoing high-profile criminal trial which by Canadian law could not be covered by the national press (Froomkin, 1997: 146–7). Government regulation can also be thwarted by the existence of countries, such as Anguilla, Bermuda and the aspiring 'Sealand', willing to act as data havens for the transmission and storage of communication that other countries designate as illegal (Garfinkel, 2000: 232; Gellman, 1997: 267; Mayer-Schönberger and Foster, 1997: 241). Finally, network users in regions that enforce significant content restrictions, such as China, the Middle East and North Africa, can access Internet service providers in foreign countries (Human Rights Watch, 1999: 27; Taubman, 1998: 266), or use proxy servers which act as gateways into otherwise censored websites (Human Rights Watch, 1999: 27).

Others reject the characterization of computer networks as inherently unregulable and uniformly beneficial. They argue for a more nuanced view of the relationship between technology and social outcomes, one which evaluates technology within the context of larger political, economic and social forces, and which acknowledges the malleability of allegedly inherent characteristics. For example, scholars working in the tradition of critical political economy, such as Bettig (1997: 138), McChesney (1996: 99), Mosco (1989: 25) and Schiller (1999: 37), argue that computer networks are tools for the extension of a global market system which seeks to commodify and control information and its uses. From this perspective, new technologies are more likely to facilitate repressive political and economic relations than to transform them. In this view, the potential for computer networks to further positive values, like political participation and equality, can only be achieved by protecting public principles and practices that are not served by the marketplace. Markets should be servants, not masters.

In addition, several historians and theorists of technology highlight the socially constructed nature of technology and its uses. These scholars argue that technology is not an independent artifact, with an inherent or instrumental logic, that inevitably will be developed and deployed in socially efficient and rational ways (Fischer, 1992: 12; Slack, 1984: 59). Rather, technology embodies and reflects the complex social systems within which it is produced and developed. Individual technologies may favour certain uses, but the uses to which technologies ultimately are put cannot be surmised solely by examining their characteristics. For example, Sassen (1998) maintains that the relationship between computer networks and global economic and social processes can be best observed by examining the concrete sites in which that relationship materializes. For Sassen, this site is the information infrastructures implemented in global cities, such as New York, London, Tokyo, Paris, Frankfurt, Zurich, Amsterdam, Sydney, Hong Kong, Buenos Aires, Taipei, Bombay and Mexico City, among others.

Further, the presumption that communication technology alone can bring about political or social change is communicentric and technocentric (Slack, 1984: 144). The development and use of specific technologies are the result not of the artifact itself, but of social struggles and negotiations among numerous parties, including investors, competitors, customers and government agents (Castells, 1996: 5; Fischer, 1992: 18; McOmber,

1999). While it may be somewhat reductive, for the purpose of theoretical differentiation, we will call those who reject the position that technology has an inevitable trajectory apart from larger social forces 'technological constructivists'.

From a technological constructivist perspective, what appear to be the technological *characteristics* of a medium at any given moment are actually a subset of that medium's technological *capabilities*. Thus, within certain parameters, computer networks can be structured to serve different interests and values, to enable or disrupt various political, economic and cultural practices, and to permit different degrees of regulation. The particular set of capabilities that come to the fore in any given technology is an outcome of a complex interplay between the technology and the political, economic and social context in which the capabilities are embedded. This argument is well developed by Lessig (1999: 89), who points out that all computer code, or the human-made software and hardware that structure the environment of computer networks, necessarily constrains or enables different behaviours. Code formalizes such choices as whether data are collected, whether anonymity is possible, who is granted access, and what speech can be heard (1999: 217). Government intervention can shape code by mandating that certain choices be made in the deployment of computer networks. Code can also be shaped and conditioned by private commercial interests who seek to control and exploit information and communication.

Lessig attributes the current freedom of the Internet to its open and non-proprietary protocols that do not condition access on the personal identification of users. He notes, however, that closed, private networks can be layered on top of this otherwise open architecture. These private networks can control access by demanding that all users be authorized, by conditioning access to data on users' credentials, and by monitoring the nature of the data being transmitted. Numerous tools for verifying the identity of Internet users are already in use, including passwords, cookie files placed on users' hard disks by browsers, and digital signatures or certificates that authenticate information about users or their machines (1999: 34–5). Both government and commerce have strong incentives to design more control into the system, and the malleability of the technology makes it possible for them to do so.[5] Lessig (1999: 57) further notes that a second-generation Internet, with an architecture even more conducive to regulation, would allow governments and commerce effective control over users, even if some opportunities for regulatory circumvention prevent absolute control.

Technological constructivism suggests that technology and its uses can be shaped by human agents. Since technology has no inevitable outcomes, citizens and their governments are not consigned to the role of passive observers of technological development. Moreover, while technological determinism rejects the notion that public policy might help determine the social uses of new technologies, technological constructivism posits an affirmative role for communication policies which are based on empirical investigations into the social contexts surrounding specific technologies (Carey, 1988; Fischer, 1992; Slack, 1984). From this perspective, public policy is a necessary and desirable response to the social choices that inevitably accompany the introduction of new technologies. Once we accept the notion that technology is inscribed with social choices and values, the question of whether technology can or will be regulated is rendered irrelevant. The real question is, rather, which values and interests will technology be designed to serve, and whether those values will be publicly or privately, nationally or globally defined.

New global media are the impetus for a reconsideration of law and policy across many areas of information and communication practice. Nations around the world must decide how to respond to the social conflicts engendered by these media, whether that response is to let market forces resolve these issues or to reassert the role of government in defining and enforcing public service values. As Castells (1996: 7) points out, governments can either frustrate the development of technologies or accelerate their development and change the pace of national modernization and economic development. We are at a formative moment in the development of new global media. As many scholars note, policy decisions that are taken now can help shape the long-term infrastructures, institutions, goals, values and outcomes of global information and communication technologies (Carey, 1998: 34; Klopfenstein, 1998: 35; McChesney, 1996: 100; Melody, 1990: 31, 33; Neuman et al., 1993: 77–8).

While governments may have an important role to play in the development of national policies that determine the trajectory of the growth and development of ICT, there is considerable disagreement among scholars about what determines the ability of states to effectively formulate national policies. Typically, studies of national policy-making have been conducted at one of three major analytical levels: at the level of the international system, at the level of the state itself and at the level of civil society (Krasner 1976; Singer, 1961; Waltz, 1979). These levels are differentiated in terms of the assumptions about the influence of factors operating at the domestic and/or international level on state behaviour (Cafruny, 1995).

For 'internationalist' approaches, the state is considered to act more or less independently of domestic social forces. The explanation is sought primarily at the international systemic level and in terms of the imperatives of a given configuration of the international system (Bousquet, 1980;

Chase-Dunn, 1998; Frank, 1969; Gilpin, 1987; Krasner, 1991; Wallerstein, 1980). National communication policies are considered outcomes of, at one extreme, the 'globalization' of new media and interactive communication technologies and, on the other, the manifestations of new forms of cultural imperialism and economic domination by a handful of developed economies. For 'civil society' approaches the state is conceptualized as subordinate to the dominant economic forces in societies, and the struggle among competing economic forces and interest groups is the primary causal variable that explains state actions and behaviour (Jessop, 1989; Miliband, 1968; Poulantzas, 1969; 1973; 1976; 1978). Here national communication policies represent the interests of dominant economic formations, typically manifested in the growing concentration of media ownership and content in capitalist economies (Herman and Chomsky, 1988; Schiller, 1985). In contrast to the internationalist and civil society approaches, state-centred theorists argue that the state is a collection of institutions with a unique centrality in both national and international formations (Evans et al., 1985; Mann, 1983; Nordlinger, 1981; Skocpol, 1977). The state is a force in its own right and does not simply reflect the dynamics of either civil society or the international system. National communication policies, from this perspective, are to be considered as exemplars of state action to promote and protect national goals and objectives (Hamelink, 1983; Katz, 1988; Noll, 1986; Petrazzini, 1993; Sinha, 1995; Tehranian et al., 1977).

More recently, a number of scholars have offered theoretical and empirical accounts of national policy-making that identify the continuities between social forces and the changing nature of the state and global relations. These scholars reject the assumption of the causal primacy of the international system and the corollary assumption of the analytical separation of state and society (Almond, 1988; Cafruny, 1995; Cox, 1986; Palan, 1992; Schmitter, 1985). From this perspective, national communication policies are the outcome of the complex interplay of forces operating within the international arena, the state and civil society (McAnany and Wilkinson, 1996; McDowell, 1994; Sinclair, 1996; Sinha, 1994; 1998). This type of analytical approach may be the most promising for examining issues relating to national policy-making in new media and interactive communication technologies.

We know a lot about *market* fundamentals. The International Labour Organization advocates also looking at the fundamentals in *people's lives*. Economic and social policies are not dichotomous. Telecommunication policies are made by men and women; they can be changed to go beyond the theoretical fundamentalism of foreign dictates and be integrated with a nation's need to eradicate poverty and social exclusion, and to create jobs. First and foremost, we must establish national and international principles to ensure that information and communication technologies are designed to serve collectively defined political, economic and social goals.

The policy and regulation part of this *Handbook* begins with Dwayne Winseck on the new forms of global governance of telecommunication and the new media. He starts with the historical context of transnational corporations of the 1860s to 1890s and brings us to the World Trade Organization of the twenty-first century. Laura Stein and Nikhil Sinha describe the challenges that computer networks present to national policy-makers. They address the legal and policy debates related to intellectual property, privacy and freedom of expression on computer networks. Stefaan Verhulst suggests that the digitalization of content in the new media is leading to a paradigm shift in content regulation. Oscar Gandy focuses on the real divide associated with these new digital media: the distinction between consumers and citizens. While the consumer has been given primacy in market-oriented policy discourses, attention to the needs of citizens is central to public policy and the public sphere. Gwen Urey reviews issues related to regulating labour in the context of employment trends around the world, competing theories of increasing inequality in employment and wage structures, and the organization of work. The authors, women and men, cover the globe in terms of their presentations and their nations of origin: they range across Belgium, Canada, India and the US.

NOTES

1 The Telecommunications Act of 1996 has not been able to establish a structure of access fees that would reconcile the two conflicting goals of the incumbent local exchange carriers (ILECs) and the long-distance carriers. To this problem has been added the question of the adequacy of open access as cable technology and digital subscriber line (DSL) technology change rapidly. AT&T is currently conducting experiments to determine whether Internet service providers can be permitted to use their upgraded cable systems. AT&T also argues that existing contracts prevent open access until the year 2002. The ILECs are promoting DSL as a substitute for achieving access to broadband services, but the ILECs still control approximately 75 per cent of the DSL capacity, thereby maintaining a position of dominance. There is much talk about the need for ensuring that rivals and new entrants have access to both upgraded cable and DSL, but it remains to be seen whether these goals can be achieved in a deregulated environment. In each case the incumbent supplier may choose to make capacity available only under narrow conditions that foreclose the creation of

broadly competitive networks. One can argue that the conflict between upgraded cable and DSL demonstrates the vulnerability of tight oligopoly to rapid technological change. Actual experience indicates that vulnerability arises more from poor management decision-making than from creative waves of competitive Schumpeterian change. Much of AT&T's problem results from its inability to estimate the cost of achieving an upgraded cable network for both its properties and those of other cable systems. Perhaps the best thing that can be said for tight oligopoly is that it introduces a much stronger incentive to reduce internal operating costs than would have prevailed under traditional regulation. The offset is that these cost reductions may culminate in denigrated service.

2 There is growing dissatisfaction with the results of the Telecommunications Act of 1996. The original assumption was that competition would be promoted at all telecommunications levels, resulting in lower prices, greater choice and improved service. However, by the end of 2000 the ILECs continued to control 97–8 per cent of the local exchange market, while prices for local service and complaints about deteriorating service have increased. The largest long-distance exchange carriers (AT&T and WorldCom) appear to have abandoned any significant effort to reach all final customers and provide one-stop shopping and bundled service for all classes of customers. AT&T and WorldCom promoted an aggressive programme of acquisitions which carried AT&T into approximately 50 per cent of the cable television market, while WorldCom built up its system culminating in the capture of MCI. Both carriers have been plagued by diminished earnings, the burden of high debt capital, and a collapse in their stock prices. As a result AT&T will undergo a voluntary restructuring that will disaggregate the system into four entities: business services, customer services, broadband cable (TCI and Media One), and AT&T wireless. WorldCom will spin off MCI through a tracking stock, ultimately culminating in divestiture. At the same time that the long-distance carriers appear to be beset by major problems, the ILECs are moving, as fast as the FCC will permit, to offer a full line of services including local, long-distance, wireless, Internet and video data services. It has become evident that it is far more difficult for the long-distance carrier to incorporate local service than for the local carrier to enter long-distance markets.

3 We use the term 'regulation' to refer generally to rules that govern, control or direct behaviour to desired ends. Agents of regulation may include governments, the marketplace, the self and others. The term 'government regulation' refers more specifically to government action designed in theory to control or direct behaviour in order to achieve goals deemed socially desirable (Rogerson and Thomas, 1998: 430). 'Regulability' refers to the capability of certain behaviours or practices to be regulated (Lessig, 1999: 14).

4 De Sola Pool (1983: 5) terms those who believe that government and other institutional forces can alter the otherwise benevolent course of technology 'soft technological determinists'.

5 Governments could use identification tools to verify attributes about computer users, such as age or place of residence, and determine whether their laws apply to that user. Different government jurisdictions would have an incentive to cooperate with one another to ensure that their laws are applied to their citizens when they engage in activities outside their jurisdiction (Lessig, 1999: 55–6). Commerce, for its part, favours user identification in order to engage in secure and safe transactions (1999: 39).

REFERENCES

Almond, G. (1988) 'The return to the state', *American Political Science Review*, 82 (3): 853–74.

Bettig, Ronald V. (1997) 'The enclosure of cyberspace', *Critical Studies in Mass Communication*, 14: 138–57.

Bousquet, N. (1980) 'From hegemony to competition: cycles of the core', in Terence Hopkins and Immanuel Wallerstein (eds), *Processes of the World System: Political Economy of the World System Annuals*. Beverly Hills: Sage. pp. 46–83.

Cafruny, A. (1995) 'Class, state, and world systems: the transformation of international maritime relations', *Review of International Political Economy*, 2 (2): 283–314.

Carey, James W. (1988) *Communication as Culture: Essays on Media and Society*. Boston: Unwin Hyman.

Carey, James W. (1998) 'The Internet and the end of the national communication system: uncertain predictions of an uncertain future', *Journalism and Mass Communication Quarterly*, 75 (1): 23–34.

Castells, Manuel (1996) *The Rise of the Network Society*. Malden, MA: Blackwell.

Cate, Fred H. (1995) 'The First Amendment and the national information infrastructure', *Wake Forest Law Review*, 30 (1): 1–50.

Chase-Dunn, Christopher (1998) *Global Formation: Structures of the World Economy*. Oxford: Blackwell.

Cox, R.W. (1986) 'Social forces, states and world orders: beyond international relations theory', in Robert Keohane (ed.), *Neorealism and its Critics*. New York: Columbia University Press. pp. 204–54.

Evans, P., Rueschmayer, D. and Skocpol, T. (eds) (1985) *Bringing the State Back in*. Cambridge: Cambridge University Press.

Fischer, Claude S. (1992) *America Calling: a Social History of the Telephone to 1940*. Berkeley, CA: University of California Press.

Frank, Andre Gundar (1969) *The Development of Underdevelopment*. New York: Monthly Review Press.

Froomkin, A. Michael (1997) 'The Internet as a source of regulatory arbitrage', in Brian Kahin and Charles Nesson (eds), *Borders in Cyberspace: Information Policy and the Global Information Infrastructure*. Cambridge, MA: MIT Press. pp. 129–63.

Garfinkel, Simson (2000) 'Welcome to Sealand. Now bugger off', 8(7), July: *Wired*, 230–9.

Gellman, Robert (1997) 'Conflict and overlap in privacy regulation: national, international, and private', in Brian Kahin and Charles Nesson (eds), *Borders in Cyberspace: Information Policy and the Global Information Infrastructure*. Cambridge, MA: MIT Press. pp. 255–82.

Gilpin, R. (1987) *The Political Economy of International Relations*. Princeton, NJ: Princeton University Press.

Hamelink, Cees (1983) *Cultural Autonomy in Global Communications: Planning National Information Policy*. New York: Longman.

Herman, Edward S. and Chomsky, Noam (1988) *Manufacturing Consent*. New York: Pantheon.

Human Rights Watch (1999) *The Internet in the Mideast and North Africa: Free Expression and Censorship*. New York: Human Rights Watch.

Jessop, P. (1989) 'Capitalism, nation-states and surveillance', in David Held and John Thompson (eds), *Social Theory of Modern Societies: Anthony Giddens and his Critics*. Cambridge: Cambridge University Press. pp. 103–28.

Johnson, David R. and Post, David G. (1997) 'The rise of law on the global network', in Brian Kahin and Charles Nesson (eds), *Borders in Cyberspace: Information Policy and the Global Information Infrastructure*. Cambridge, MA: MIT Press. pp. 3–47.

Katz, R. (1988) *The Information Society: an International Perspective*. Cambridge, MA: Harvard University Press.

Klopfenstein, Bruce C. (1998) 'Internet economics: an annotated bibliography', *Journal of Media Economics*, 11 (1): 3–48.

Krasner, S. (1976) 'State power and the structure of international trade', *World Politics*, 28: 317–47.

Krasner, S. (1991) 'Global communications and national power: life on the Pareto frontier', *World Politics*, 47 (3), April: 336–66.

Labunski, Richard (1997) 'The First Amendment at the crossroads: free expression and new media technology', *Communication Law and Policy*, 2 (2): 165–212.

Lessig, Lawrence (1999) *Code and Other Laws of Cyberspace*. New York: Basic.

Mann, M. (1983) 'The autonomous power of the state', *Archives européenes de sociologie*, 25 (2): 185–213.

Mayer-Schönberger, Viktor and Foster, Teree E. (1997) 'A regulatory web: free speech and the global information infrastructure', in Brian Kahin and Charles Nesson (eds), *Borders in Cyberspace: Information Policy and the Global Information Infrastructure*. Cambridge, MA: MIT Press. pp. 235–54.

McAnany, Emile and Wilkinson, Karin (eds) (1996) *Mass Media and Free Trade: NAFTA and the Cultural Industries*. Austin, TX: University of Texas Press.

McChesney, Robert W. (1996) 'The Internet and U.S. communication policy-making in historical and critical perspective', *Journal of Communication*, 46 (1): 98–124.

McDowell, S. (1994) 'India, the LDCs and GATT negotiations on trade and investment services', in R. Stubbs and G. Underhill (eds), *Political Economy and the Changing Global Order*. New York: St Martin's Press. pp. 497–510.

McOmber, James B. (1999) 'Technological autonomy and three definitions of technology', *Journal of Communication*, 49 (3): 137–53.

Melody, William H. (1990) 'Communication policy in the global information economy: whither the public interest?', in Marjorie Ferguson (ed.), *Public Communication: the New Imperatives*. Newbury Park, CA: Sage. pp. 16–39.

Miliband, R. (1968) *The State in Capitalist Society*. London: Weidenfeld & Nicolson.

Mody, Bella, Bauer, Johannes, M. and Straubhaar, Joseph D. (eds) (1995) *Telecommunications Politics: Ownership and Control of the Information Highway in Developing Countries*. Mahwah, NJ: Erlbaum.

Mosco, Vincent (1989) *The Pay-per Society: Computers and Communication in the Information Age*. Norwood, NJ: Ablex.

Neuman, W. Russell, McKnight, Lee and Solomon, Richard Jay (1993) 'The politics of a paradigm shift: telecommunications regulation and the communication revolution', *Political Communication*, 10 (1): 77–94.

Noll, R. (1986) 'The political and institutional context of communications policy', in M. Snow (ed.), *Marketplace for Telecommunications*. New York: Longman. pp. 42–65.

Nordlinger, E. (1981) *On the Autonomy of the Democratic State*. New Haven, CT: Yale University Press.

Palan, R. (1992) 'The second structuralist theories of international relations: a research note', *International Studies Notes*, 17 (3): 32–56.

Petrazzini, B. (1993) 'The politics of telecommunications reform in developing countries', *Pacific Telecommunications Review*, March: 4–23.

Pool, Ithiel de Sola (1983) *Technologies of Freedom*. Cambridge, MA: Harvard University Press.

Poulantzas, N. (1969) 'The problem of the capitalist state', *New Left Review*, 58: 67–78.

Poulantzas, N. (1973) *Political Power and Social Classes*. London: New Left Books.

Poulantzas, N. (1976) *Crisis of the Dictatorships*. London: New Left Review.

Poulantzas, N. (1978) *State, Power, Socialism*. London: New Left Books.

Rogerson, Kenneth S. and Thomas, G. Dale (1998) 'Internet regulation process model: the effect of societies, communities, and governments', *Political Communication*, 15 (4): 427–44.

Samorski, Jan H., Huffman, John L. and Trauth, Denise M. (1997) 'The v-chip and cyber cops: technology vs. regulation', *Communication Law and Policy*, 2 (1): 143–64.

Sassen, Saskia (1998) *Globalization and Its Discontents*. New York: New Press.

Schiller, Dan (1999) *Digital Capitalism: Networking the Global Market System*. Cambridge, MA: MIT Press.

Schiller, Herbert, I. (1985) *Information and the Crisis Economy*. Norwood, NJ: Ablex.

Schmitter, P. (1985) 'Neo corporatism and the state', in Wyn Grant (ed.), *The Political Economy of Corporatism*. New York: St Martin's Press. pp. 32–62.

Sinclair, John (1996) 'Culture and trade: some theoretical and practical considerations', in Emile McAnany and Karin Wilkinson (eds), *Mass Media and Free Trade: NAFTA and the Cultural Industries*. Austin, TX: University of Texas Press. pp. 30–60.

Singer, J. (1961) 'The level of analysis problem in international relations', in K. Knorr and S. Verba (eds), *The International System: Theoretical Essays*. Princeton, NJ: Princeton University Press. pp. 77–92.

Sinha, Nikhil (1994) 'Information technology, economic development and technological unemployment in developing countries', *Revue Tiers Monde*, April–June: 411–24.

Sinha, Nikhil (1995) 'Telecommunications regulatory reform in the Third World: an institutional perspective', in Bella Mody, Joseph Straubhaar and Johannes Bauer (eds), *Telecommunications Politics: Ownership and Control of the Information Highway in Developing Countries*. New York: Erlbaum. pp. 297–308.

Sinha, Nikhil (1998) 'Telecommunications reforms and the changing role of the state in India'. Paper presented at the 48th Annual Conference of the International Communication Association, Jerusalem, 20–24 July.

Skocpol, T. (1977) 'Wallerstein's world capitalist system: a theoretical and historical critique', *American Journal of Sociology*, 82: 1075–89.

Slack, Jennifer D. (1984) *Communication Technologies and Society: Conceptions of Causality and the Politics of Technological Intervention*. Norwood, NJ: Ablex.

Taubman, Geoffrey (1998) 'A not-so World Wide Web: the Internet, China, and the challenges to nondemocratic rule', *Political Communication*, 15 (2): 255–72.

Tehranian, Majid, Hakimzadeh, Farhad and Vidale, Marcello (1977) *Communications Policy for National Development: a Comparative Perspective*. London: Routledge & Kegan Paul.

Wallerstein, Immanuel (1980) *The Modern World System*. New York: Academic.

Waltz, K. (1979) *Theory of International Politics*. Reading, MA: Addison-Wesley.

Yoo, H. and Mody, B. (2000) 'Predictors of downsizing in the US local telephone industry', *The Information Society*, 16 (1): 23–33.

23

Wired Cities and Transnational Communications: New Forms of Governance for Telecommunications and the New Media

DWAYNE WINSECK

This chapter places the global media in historical context and then analyses efforts to reinvent the contours of global communication since the 1990s. In contrast to the view that recent developments are driven by deregulation and new technologies, I argue that telecommunications and new media are being shaped and governed by three vital features of the emerging mediascape: new domestic regulators, new systems of private authority, and the World Trade Organization (WTO).

I argue that several WTO agreements adopted in the 1990s are the cornerstones of this emerging governance regime. These agreements extend markets for telecommunications and online information services mainly in North America, Europe and Japan but also in some key urban business districts scattered across the 'Third World'. Based on these observations, I suggest that the lines of inclusion and exclusion in cyberspace do not directly map onto the divide between developed and developing countries, and that the 'information revolution' is often as much a part of the experience for some people living in, say, Bangkok, Shanghai and São Paulo as it is for citizens in North America, Japan and Europe. For all others, talk of a global information society remains fantastic. Given these patterns I refer to the existence of a transnational communication system and wired cities in contrast to the more idealistic vision of an all-embracing global media system.

The chapter also considers the rise of private sector transnational policy alliances and their growing influence in the OECD, the WTO and ITU. I also consider how self-regulatory standards and the design of communication technologies are affecting privacy policy, Internet content regulation, and the overall evolution of telecommunications networks and new media. Returning to the WTO, I argue that the agency could actually expand media freedoms by preventing governments from regulating any information and media service, including the Internet, delivered over telecommunications networks. However, such prospects are unlikely on the grounds that the WTO is a vehicle for expanding free trade rather than free speech and because the agreements have been used more to limit *any* attempts to establish new policies that do not further commercial interests.

Lastly, I argue that the WTO is integral to efforts to create a global order based on limited democracy, where governance is about managing the technical and legal infrastructure of the global economy rather than promoting democracy. This is evident in the absence of normative issues from the WTO's telecommunications policy regime and by the chasm between this framework and the most vital human rights documents of our times, i.e. the Universal Declaration of Human Rights (1948) and the International Covenant on Civil and Political Liberties (1966). The fact that many of the governments that signed the WTO's telecommunications agreements have not signed basic human rights documents leads me to conclude that the real problem with globalization is that it has not gone far enough, in terms of providing better access to new means of communication, addressing key communication issues, or fostering a culture of democracy on a global scale.

A SHORT HISTORY OF THE GLOBAL MEDIA

The 'global media system' is far less encompassing than commonly assumed and deeper historically than often acknowledged. In fact, any discussion of the 'global media' should begin from the late nineteenth century, when a worldwide web of cable communication firms and news agencies emerged as the pre-eminent transnational corporations of their times.

By the late nineteenth century, both Britain and the US had embraced a 'free trade in cables' policy and aggressively used such policies to expand access to foreign markets for firms such as All American Cables, the Anglo American Telegraph Company, the Eastern Extension Telegraph Company and Western Union, among others (Shreiner, 1924: 44–6). These policies were also used to buttress cable cartels and leverage access to domestic markets as a means of obtaining reciprocal privileges for American and British communication firms abroad. As one lawyer for All American Cables summarized this state of affairs, 'the British and American lines … get what they can for themselves and, where it is possible, break up the monopolies of the rivals, and so far the British Foreign Office has actively assisted the British lines and the American State Department has actively assisted the American lines' (quoted in Shreiner, 1924: 80). As a result, British and American cable companies gained monopoly concessions for up to 60 years throughout Latin America. In fact, from 1870 to 1920, Latin America was divided up among a small handful of companies and similar conditions prevailed on the rest of the world's main communication routes (1924: 80; Pike and Winseck, 2001).

Oliver Boyd-Barrett (1999) has identified similar arrangements among the global news agencies: Reuters, Havas, Wolf and Associated Press. By the 1860s, these news agencies had worldwide operations linked to the press in numerous countries, and within a decade or two such alliances included the cable companies. Yet, this nascent system of global communication was nowhere near universal. Networks connected major cities and were used by business, the press and governments, not the public (Pike and Winseck, 2001).

After World War I, there was a hiatus in the 'global media' and research in the field was largely reduced to studies on propaganda and people's (in)ability to comprehend foreign news. The idea of the 'global media' was also eclipsed as international agreements consigned each successive new media technology – radio, television, satellite broadcasting and so on – to operations mainly *within* national boundaries. This state of affairs only changed in the 1970s and 1980s as developing countries called on UNESCO and the ITU to establish policies that would further a more equitable allocation of communication resources. This push for a new world information and communication order (NWICO) sought greater access to new and old media, more diverse information flows within and among *all* countries, and distributive justice. In response, UNESCO and the ITU undertook major studies by the MacBride Commission and the Maitland Commission, respectively, and as a result implemented concrete initiatives that, for example, strove to achieve a 'free and balanced flow of information', to expand developing countries' participation in both organizations, to allocate more equitably resources held in common (e.g. radio spectrum and orbital locations for geostationary satellites), and to augment communication infrastructures through the creation of the International Program for Development Communication and the supply of technical and financial support to regional news and broadcasting agencies. Of course, the aims of NWICO were only partially realized, but these efforts did go some way toward creating a global media system that better reflected the needs of all countries rather than slavishly buttressing the dominance of Europe, Japan and North America.

NWICO soon met its nemesis among those countries which chafed at the idea of creating a new world communication order based on equity and the redistribution of power and resources. By the mid 1980s NWICO and its supporting agencies were eclipsed, as the United States, Britain and Singapore abandoned UNESCO and threatened the same fate for the ITU if it refused to embrace sweeping internal reforms, competition and privatization, as well as a greater role for the General Agreement on Tariffs and Trade (GATT) (later the WTO) in telecommunications and information services (Cowhey, 1990: 181; United States, 1996: 17). As a result, 'free trade in communications' was revived from its prolonged slumber, the authority of UNESCO and the ITU was redefined and reduced, and debates over NWICO were emasculated. Moreover, UNESCO re-embraced the 'free flow of information' doctrine in its efforts to woo back Britain, Singapore and the United States, and the WTO made the doctrine a cornerstone of the nascent global communication policy regime by requiring all its members to permit the 'unrestricted movement of information within and across borders' (WTO, 1994b: Article 5(c)(e)).

In the wake of NWICO's demise, a new regime was created, one anchored in the WTO, new domestic regulators, and an augmented role for the private sector in the ITU, OECD and the WTO as well as through a plethora of self-regulatory initiatives. As the following sections show, these agencies, as well as UNESCO, adopted several new roles to assist the creation of new communication markets and policy frameworks: (1) *research* covering main trends and access to communication resources in various regions of the world and in support of privatization, competition and the development of new regulatory frameworks in specific countries; (2) a *supplemental role* supporting, for example, the development of telecentres as community resources providing people in developing countries with greater access to telecommunication services; and, finally, (3) the provision of *financial assistance* to support regulatory and policy-making capacities in developing countries (rather than networks and information services, which were now the exclusive domain of the market).

THE TRANSFORMATION AND PRIVATIZATION OF GLOBAL COMMUNICATIONS POLICY

Several other events recast the governance regime for telecommunications and new media on a worldwide basis. The most significant was the breakup of AT&T in 1984. After divestiture, AT&T entered global markets and the newly created Regional Bell Operating Companies (RBOCs) did the same to experiment with broadcasting, cable television and information services, something they were prohibited from doing in the United States. The impact of these developments was amplified by the privatization of BT and Cable & Wireless, respectively, and the onset of telecommunications competition between 1984 and 1991 in Britain. The scope of privatization and liberalization steadily widened thereafter as Australia, Canada, Japan, New Zealand and the European Union embraced competition in telecommunications between 1990 and 1998 (Cowhey, 1990; OECD, 1999: 47; United States, 1996). The debt crisis, the World Bank's structural adjustment policies, and neoliberal ideology also accelerated privatization and, to a lesser degree, competition. By the late 1990s, Chile, China, the Congo, Madagascar, Mexico, the Philippines and Uganda had embraced competition, while Argentina, Bolivia, Brazil, Costa Rica, Eritrea, Kenya, Kuwait, Nigeria, Peru, Sudan and Venezuela announced plans to do the same by 2001 (ITU, 1997: 32; 1999).

In the face of these changes and threats of withdrawal by the US and Britain, the ITU adopted internal reforms and acceded to an enlarged policy remit for the WTO, OECD, ICANN and so on. It also became a staunch advocate of privatization, competition and regulatory reform. Through internal reforms, ITU membership grew beyond national

governments and telecommunication monopolies to include equipment manufacturers, information service providers and computer systems vendors. This altered context reduced the ITU's focus on telecommunications companies' needs and enlarged the influence of new players on the evolution of new networks and the ever greater range of services delivered over them – e.g. virtual private networks, electronic data interchange, e-mail, the Internet, and so on. This helped foster more open network designs that gave users greater flexibility, allowed new services to flourish, and prevented new media such as the Internet from becoming mere appendages to extant telecommunication monopolies (Abbate, 1999: 152–65). Simultaneously, however, these changes disconnected new services from the ITU's previous emphasis on public service and development principles.

The ITU's internal reforms reflected the subordination of conventional communication policy issues to the market in other ways as well, as members of the private sector were endowed with new voting privileges alongside national governments and as private members came to outnumber governments by 450 to 187 by the early 1990s. The private sector also amassed new power as the ITU adopted privately funded annual colloquia on telecommunications policy and as it created new entities, such as the World Telecommunications Advisory Council, through which private sector members gained greater access to technical standards committees and the Secretary-General. In stark contrast, efforts to elevate the status of public interest groups in global communication policy were rebuffed by the private sector members now driving the policy agenda at the ITU (Kleinwachter, 1999: 10; Tarjanne, 1999: 60).

By the early 1990s the ITU had redesigned itself as an architect of expanded markets. However, this did not mean deregulation, as commonly assumed. Instead, one of the new roles of the ITU, in conjunction with the World Bank, the International Monetary Fund and even the United Nations Development Programme, is to advise governments on how to introduce privatization and competition, remove barriers to media convergence and promote electronic commerce (ITU, 1999; UNDP, 2000; Wallsten, 1999; Wellenius and Stern, 1994). A consensus has emerged that new markets need to be cultivated and that this requires government intervention under the wise tutelage of the ITU, World Bank and IMF. As such, markets do not emerge naturally, but are actively constituted through the agencies at the core of the new governance regime. Reflecting this, one of the biggest ironies of 'deregulation' was the *massive expansion* in the number of communications regulators worldwide, from ten at the outset of the 1990s to nearly 90 by the decade's end. In fact, designing markets and regulatory regimes became a burgeoning industry, with specialists being sent to the four corners of the earth by the FCC, CRTC, OFTEL, the US-based Telecommunications Training Institute and the World Bank, and as countries such as Brazil, Kenya and Zambia imported Western policy regimes wholesale. In fact, more aid money now goes to creating governance regimes than to developing the communication networks and services that people will actually use (Hills, 1998: 462; ITU, 1999: 5–6; OECD, 1999: 237).

THE WTO AND NEW POLICIES
FOR TELECOMMUNICATIONS AND NEW MEDIA

It is within this context that several WTO agreements covering telecommunications and information services were adopted. While these agreements are often seen as the pillars of a radically new governance regime, they mainly consolidated the status quo among the 72 countries that signed them, with the crucial proviso that WTO oversight ensures that countries cannot reverse course and that the future of competition and privatization will proceed according to WTO rules (Drake and Noam, 1997). There are four cornerstones to the WTO's nascent governance regime for telecommunications and new media: the 1994 agreement on enhanced services; the 1996 Singapore Agreement eliminating taxes on information technologies; the 1997 Basic Telecommunications Agreement; and the creation of a Global Electronic Commerce Task Force in 1998 and the ensuing moratorium on the taxation of cyberspace. The remainder of this chapter focuses on these agreements in relation to the following areas: (1) privatization, (2) regulated competition and (3) the adoption of new policies for new media.

The WTO and Privatization

Between 1984 and 1999, 110 telecommunications companies were privatized. Some of these were full privatizations, such as British Telecom, while others were partial, such as Malaysia Telecom, Singapore Telecom and many others. Beyond sheer numbers, the key questions are why this spate of privatizations occurred at this time, and what impact the WTO had on these trends.

In fact, the privatization of telecommunications operators was very uneven and took on a myriad of forms that reflected economic conditions, historical experience and political cultures. For example, in the 1980s the debt crisis hit Latin American countries the hardest and this translated into a wave of privatizations across the continent. The link between the debt crisis and privatization was highlighted as several foreign banks became part owners in newly privatized PTOs in return for debt cancellation. In contrast, robust markets and strong states in Asia meant that privatization was pursued less, while greater reliance was placed on the selective introduction of competition. In Africa, privatizations were fewer and limited in scope, owing to the colonial overtones of returning state-owned PTOs to foreign operators, especially since they had only been brought under domestic control after independence was gained from the 1960s onwards. Thus, broader political, economic and historical considerations had a much greater impact on telecommunications privatizations than did the WTO, well into the 1990s.

While some commentators dismissed concerns about neocolonialism out of hand, the pattern of acquisition of privatized PTOs by European and American operators does follow colonial lines – as indicated in Table 23.1.

Yet, many countries did embrace privatization and the WTO as a means of attracting the foreign investment needed to build the telecommunication infrastructures that would catapult them into the 'global information age'. The need for investment was obvious as 60 per cent of all telephone lines remained located in the OECD countries, two-thirds of all households worldwide lacked access to telephone service, 43 countries had less than one telephone per 100 people, and the length of waiting lists was often measured in years rather than days (ITU, 1998a: 13–15, A8–A10). Similar figures for the Internet are even more stark. By the end of 1999, only 3 per cent of the world's population had access to the Internet. In 23 countries there was no connection to the Internet whatsoever and another 58 countries each had fewer than 1000 Internet users (Netwizards, 1999). In stark contrast, 45 per cent of all Internet users resided in North America, another 35 per cent in Europe and 11 per cent in Japan. Indeed, just 20 countries accounted for nine out of ten Internet users worldwide. The global distribution of Internet users is shown in Figure 23.1.

The promise of greater access to basic telephone service and the Internet depends on a great deal of investment. Analysts estimated that over $7 billion was needed in Africa alone to achieve just one telephone line per 100 people, while others claimed that $200 billion was needed in the late 1990s to achieve modest levels of access to telecommunications services in Africa, Asia, Latin America and Central Europe (Wellenius and Stern, 1994). Promoters of the WTO claimed that it would address these needs by reducing foreign ownership limits, that is, bolstering privatization, advancing investment in new services, and creating a 'less politicized … regulatory environment' (Tarjanne, 1999: 56; Thompson, 1999: 1).

Nonetheless, the WTO agreements did not compel countries to undertake privatization or permit foreign ownership. Although there was great pressure to adopt such commitments, many countries did not, much to the consternation of the United

Table 23.1   *Top ten beneficiaries of developing countries' telecommunications privatizations* (1984–98)

Acquiring telecoms provider	Acquired company and country	Amount (US$ millions)
France Télécom	Côte d'Ivoire	660
	Sonatel (Senegal)	212
	Telecom Vanuatu	5.5
	Telecom Argentina	3,867
	CTE (El Salvador)	275
	TelMex	16,032.3
	MobilNet (Egypt)	360
		21,411.8
Telefonica	CRT (Brazil)	1,151
	CTC (Chile)	115
	Intel (El Salvador)	70
	Telefonica Peru	5,693
		7,029
GTE	Compania Telefonos (Venezuela)	**6,905**
STET (Italy)	Telecom Srbija	525
	Telecom Argentina	3,867
	Entel Bolivia	610
	Entel (Chile)	293
	Empresa de Telecom (Cuba)	366
		5,661
SBC/Ameritech	Telekom South Africa	777.5
	Matav (Hungary)	2,491.5
		3,269
MCI	Embratel (Brazil)	**2,784**
Deutsche Telekom	Matav (Hungary)	**2,491.5**
Telecom Netherlands	PT Telekomunikasi Selular (Indonesia)	392
	SPT Telecom (Czech)	1,902.5
		2,294.5
Cable & Wireless	Telecom Vanuatu	5.5
	Barbados External Telecom	483
	Barbados Telco	
	C&W Jamaica	349
	C&W Panama	1,225
	TSTT (Trinidad & Tobago)	147
		2,209.5
Swiss Télécom PTT	SPT Telecom (Czech)	**1,902.5**

Source: World Bank, 2000

States. Consistent with existing trends, Latin American countries took the greatest steps to eliminate foreign ownership restrictions. Asian and African countries marginally raised permissible levels of foreign ownership in incumbent PTOs while allowing more investment in new services (GIIC, 1997: 88–95; ITU, 1998b: 10).

This less than enthusiastic embrace of privatization through the WTO reflects the fact that privatization has not been an unequivocal success. Privatization has often simply substituted a privately owned monopoly for a state-owned one, and private monopolies are little better than state-owned ones at improving access to telecommunications services (ITU, 1998a: 55, A8–A10; Melody, 1999: 14). As a result, a new consensus has emerged that improved access to services depends on well-designed regulatory regimes that establish clear goals that new

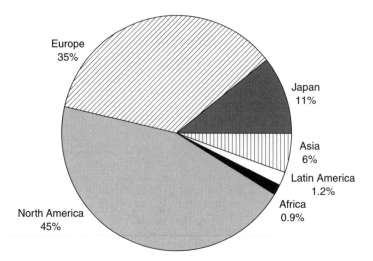

Figure 23.1   *Global distribution of Internet users, July 1999 (Netwizards, 1999)*

telecommunications operators must meet within specific time frames. Thus, in Argentina, Côte d'Ivoire, Ghana, Mexico and South Africa, among others, privatized PTOs were required to establish between 225,000 and 2.5 million new subscriber lines within five years (ITU, 1998a: 71). These approaches, coupled with the expansion of regulatory architectures referred to above, underlined the transition from the dogma of deregulation in the 1980s and early 1990s to the idea that adequate governance regimes are vital pillars of telecommunications policy reform.

The WTO embraced the 'new governance paradigm' through its *Regulatory Reference Paper*, a document signed by 55 countries that were committed to creating a regulatory architecture rooted in several key principles: transparency, interconnection, autonomy and the fair allocation of scarce resources (WTO, 1997b). The *Reference Paper* was also an exercise in the technocratic management of telecommunications politics. There were no provisions for public interventions in the regulatory arena and there was a dearth of normative principles usually associated with communication policy, such as privacy, freedom of expression, access and diversity. This was not an oversight. It reflected the persistent opposition to privatization among labour unions, citizens and others, opposition that had halted or postponed privatization in Brazil, Costa Rica, India and elsewhere (Petrazinni, 1997). The WTO played a key role in this context, as the ITU noted, by providing '[h]igh level government officials with the opportunity to rely on its negotiations to dismantle domestic political opposition and to move forward with new market strategies that would have otherwise been impossible to implement' (ITU, 1997: 12). In essence, the WTO limited democracy in order to help expand telecommunications and information services markets.

These limits impede the democratization of global communication policy. They are reminiscent of communication policy in the United States and Canada prior to the late 1960s and mid 1970s when the FCC and CRTC only permitted those with a *material interest* to attend regulatory proceedings before courts (the *United Church of Christ* case in the United States in 1966) and changing political conditions forced them to sanction greater citizen and public interest group participation in the communication regulatory process. Elevating a similar process of *political liberalization* to the ITU and WTO could offer a step toward progressive global communication policy reform.

The WTO, Competition and Wired Cities on the Global Information Infrastructure

Similar observations can be made with respect to the WTO's impact on competition in telecommunications. As with privatization, the promise was that the WTO would further competition and improve access to telecommunications services. The WTO's case was bolstered by studies by academics, the OECD and ITU demonstrating that developing countries that introduced competition were more effective than those that had retained monopolies at increasing people's access to basic telephone service as well as to new services such as cellular telephony and the Internet.[1] Moreover, the same studies also indicated that competition had not diminished access in Britain, Canada and the United States, although it was noted that most people now paid higher rates for basic telephone service (ITU, 1999: 7–8; OECD, 1995; Petrazinni, 1997; UNCTAD, 2000: 86–96).

Backed by such studies, the 1997 Basic Telecommunications Agreement sought to expand the number of countries formally committed to competition in telecommunications. This was not to be. The agreement mainly reinforced the status quo among the 72 countries that signed it, and only a few countries expanded their embrace of competition (Drake and Noam, 1997). One of the biggest ironies was that several countries used the occasion to lock in monopolies for lengthy periods, as in Jamaica, for example, where the privately owned affiliate of Cable & Wireless now has the advantage of a national monopoly until 2013 backed by the force of international law (GIIC, 1997: 88–95).

Nonetheless, the promotion of competition by the WTO did spur on a huge increase in investment – as promised. The key questions, though, are by whom and where?

The Basic Telecommunications Agreement and regulatory liberalization triggered a rush to wire up cities and the globe on an unprecedented scale (FCC, 2000: 6–8; OECD, 1999: 61–5; Staple, 2000: Figure 1). In the OECD countries as well as developing countries, much of this new investment has been by new competitors, and in developing countries the investment between 1995 and 1998 was triple that over the entire previous decade (OECD, 1999: 61–5; World Bank, 2000).

As a result, the global telecommunications system grew from half a billion telephone subscribers in 1989 to an estimated 2 billion in 2000 (Staple, 2000: Figure 1). Moreover, in a remarkably short span of time, the Internet grew from a couple of million users to about 190 million by the turn of the century. The number of countries connected to the Internet also rose from 90 to 200 during the decade. Consequently, the gap between developed and developing countries' access to telecommunications services narrowed appreciably, although stark divisions between the 'information rich' and 'information poor' persisted, and in some cases were magnified, along urban and rural lines, relative to new ICTs, and between regions of the world connected to the thickening web of local and global networks and those for whom all such developments are remote from daily experience. Indeed, while there were some improvements in access to telecommunications services throughout Africa, Asia and Latin America during the 1990s, only a handful of countries – Argentina, Brazil, China, Columbia, Korea, Singapore and South Africa – accounted for the vast majority of new telephone subscribers and three-quarters of all new Internet users in these regions (ITU, 1998a: 13–15; Netwizards, 1999; UNDP, 1999: 25–37).[2]

Much of the new investment in telecommunications has occurred in the laying of fibre-optic cables across the Atlantic between Europe and North America and across the Pacific between the US, Japan, China, Hong Kong and Singapore.[3] While these cables span the globe, they terminate in local networks concentrated in 150 to 200 cities worldwide and mainly serve corporate users, governments and 1–10 per cent of the population living in these wired cities (AT&T, 2000; BT, 2000a; France Télécom, 1999). In the three years since the Basic Telecommunications Agreement, the capacity of fibre cables linking the globe increased a hundredfold. The agreement contributed to this by advancing competition in international telecommunications services in 55 countries and permitting competitors to establish their own networks in 44 others (FCC, 1999a: 5; ITU, 1997: 65).

Despite unprecedented competition in telecommunications, only a handful of consortia are creating a global information infrastructure. The cartel-like consortia building these global systems revolve around a combination of new and incumbent telecommunications operators – the Fibre Link Around the Globe (FLAG),[4] the Japan–US Cable Network[5] and the China–US Cable Network,[6] on the one hand, and an array of new competitors, cable companies and Microsoft, on the other (FCC, 1999a; 1999b). With respect to the latter, Global Crossing has emerged as a major force in global cable communications and as a provider of broadband networks in dozens of cities. Global Crossing is also backed by Microsoft, Softbank (Japan) and the Canadian Imperial Bank of Commerce. Through Microsoft's stakes in numerous telecommunications and cable systems, Global Crossing is also tied to several new companies wiring up cities around the world, such as Pan European Networks, NTL, Telewest, Rogers, Hong Kong Telecom, Globo Cabo and Qwest (Global Crossing, 1999; Microsoft, 1999a; 1999b; 1999c).

The most intense efforts to hardwire cities into the global communications grid are taking place in Europe and North America. Incumbent PTOs have been joined by new providers in Europe such as Qwest / KPN, Level 3/Colt, Global Crossing / Racal, Global Telesystems and Viatel, among others, in an effort to build fibre-optic networks within and between Antwerp, Berlin, Brussels, Frankfurt, London, Munich, Paris and another ten or so cities in Europe. These processes are furthered by WorldCom's and AT&T's acquisition of competitive local companies, such as Brooks, MFS, MetroNet, Teleport as well as the Internet-based networks of CompuServe, IBM and Uunet, among others (AT&T, 2000; BT, 2000a; FCC, 2000: 7–8; WorldCom, 1999). AT&T has aggressively pursued this course of action, by acquiring two of the largest US cable systems – TCI and Media One – and by signing exclusive covenants with AOL–Time Warner and Comcast to cross-market AT&T's telephone services as well as their jointly provided high-speed Internet service. For AT&T,

this tangled web of connections helps to further its aim of delivering a bundle of telephone, Internet and video services over broadband networks in just ten US cities and local telephone service in 83 others (AT&T, 2000; Time Warner, 1999).

The plans of AT&T, AOL–Time Warner and so on to wire up cities one at a time depart dramatically from the vision of universal information highways prominent during the mid 1990s. In central Canada, ADSL and high-speed cable access are being implemented only in a dozen or so urban centres and to just two-thirds of the population in these cities. Similar patterns are visible in the US, where USWest, Bell South, Bell Atlantic and SBC are providing ADSL to one-quarter of their subscribers living in 30 to 40 cities. In fact, most US telecommunications companies have abandoned their efforts to deliver video over broadband networks to people's homes altogether (AT&T, 2000; FCC, 2001; Time Warner, 1999). As WorldCom's chairman Bernard Ebbers concedes, 'Not AT&T, MFS [WorldCom's local arm], or anyone else, is going to build local telephone facilities to residential customers. Nobody ever will' (quoted in Huber, 1997: iii). In the face of this scaled-down approach, a process of 'electronic redlining' is occurring as low-income districts in cities and rural areas are bypassed and broadband networks and multimedia services are provided exclusively to areas where there is sufficient demand and ability to pay for them. Even optimistic reports anticipate that fewer than 15 per cent of North American homes will have broadband Internet access between 2005 and 2010 (Bar et al., 1999: 14–15; Staple, 2000: 6).

The global information infrastructure dissects urban spaces on an even finer basis, tying districts within cities, and even specific buildings, into the global grid. Thus, FLAG's transatlantic cable, for example, links *downtown Manhattan* with Brittany, France and Cornwall, Britain (FLAG, 2000). These spaces are parsed even further as specific buildings – about 40,000 to 60,000 worldwide according to WorldCom and AT&T – are hardwired into fibre-optic networks and information flows traversing the planet at the speed of light (AT&T, 2000; BT, 2000a; WorldCom, 1999).

As major cities, corporate offices and residential suburbs in Europe and North America are wired up, entire swathes of the globe are being virtually eliminated from cyberspace. This is most observable with respect to Africa, where many countries have fewer than 0.5 telephone lines per 100 people, only 100,000 Internet accounts exist for a population of 750 million (outside South Africa), and projects announced in the early 1990s as part of the GII languish. Indeed, a major pillar of the GII – AT&T's Africa One proposal to lay a fibre-optic cable around the continent – has been transferred to Global Crossing and deferred until at least 2002

(UNCTAD, 2000: 88–92). Connections to and within Africa are so sparse that there is not even enough bandwidth to accommodate what little Internet traffic there is and information flows between African countries are routinely routed through former colonial metropoles. This reinforces the paths of colonial communication laid down in the late nineteenth century, as does the enormous price of Internet access in Africa – ranging from $150 per year in Botswana to $1700 per year in Angola and Kenya (UNCTAD, 2000: 94–103; ITU, 1999b: 6).

Africa's near complete excommunication from the 'global information society' is not representative of conditions in the 'Third World' as a whole, though. Indeed, as mentioned above, access to basic telephone service and the Internet grew impressively in a few countries throughout the 1990s. Moreover, many of the advanced networks and ICTs deployed in the transnational core are also being implemented in the business districts and affluent suburbs of Latin America, Asia and, to a lesser extent, Africa (BT, 2000a; FCC, 2000: 7; WorldCom, 1999).

AT&T, for instance, gained millions of cable system subscribers in Latin America and Asia through its acquisition of TCI (AT&T, 2000: 47–50). Microsoft has also done the same through alliances and ownership stakes in Globo Cabo, Brazil's largest multimedia conglomerate, Global Crossing and Hong Kong Telecom (Microsoft, 1999a; 1999b; 1999c). These arrangements exemplify the growing web of alliances between the 'global media' and regional players as well as the thrust to bring the 'information revolution' to 'Third World' elites. As Microsoft and Globo Cabo note, they are striving to 'accelerate the deployment of advanced broadband and Internet services to millions of Brazilians' (Microsoft, 1999b: 2), although their efforts only apply to 10 per cent of the elite residing in just three cities: São Paulo, Rio de Janeiro and Belo Horizonte. For the rest of Brazil's citizens, access to basic telephone services, computers and the Internet remains far out of reach (ITU, 1998a: A7, A78; Netwizards, 1999).

Beyond Brazil, Microsoft has joined with Global Crossing to create a network that not only links Europe, North America and Japan, but also connects up with Global Crossing's local networks in the major business centres of Asia. Thus, as the companies note, Global Crossing is creating

an advanced fiber optic communications network connecting *business centers* in the East Asian Region to Global Crossing's worldwide fiber optic network. The network … will *connect cities* in Taiwan, Singapore, Hong Kong, Malaysia, China, Korea and the Philippines, giving the region unprecedented access to a seamless broadband network for a variety of services, including

Table 23.2   *Wired cities and disconnected countries in the global information society*

	% of people in largest city with Internet access, 2000	% of people in country with Internet access, 1999	Teledensity in largest city, 1996	Rest of country teledensity, 1996
Brazil	21	0.65	16.5	8.7
Mexico	28	0.8	N/A	9.5
China	12	0.5	19	4.3
Malaysia	23	2.5	22.4	14.2
Thailand	22	0.42	33.1	7
OECD (average)		13.5		49

Source: Netwizards, 1999; Angus Reid Research 2000; ITU, 1998: A28–A30; OECD, 1999: 74, 86

Web hosting, electronic commerce and low-cost, high quality telephony. (Microsoft, 1999c, emphasis added)

The focus on wiring up business centres and urban districts also maps onto the contours of inclusion and exclusion in cyberspace. Although 80 per cent of all Internet users live in just ten countries (Netwizards, 1999),[7] a recent study indicates that Internet use is as much, and sometimes even more, a part of daily life for people in São Paulo, Mexico City, Beijing, Shanghai, Kuala Lumpur and Bangkok, for example, as it is for citizens in the OECD countries (Angus Reid Research, 2000).[8] The study, however, did not reveal the stark divide between these 'wired cities' and Internet access in these countries as a whole, something that can be done by drawing on additional sources – as shown in Table 23.2.

Thus, the nodal points on the global communications grid are places such as São Paulo, Hong Kong, Shanghai, Singapore, Johannesburg, Toronto, New York, London, Brussels, Paris, Amsterdam and so on; and, as WorldCom and AT&T note, the 40,000 to 60,000 buildings worldwide that house the affluent and specialized users of the new GII. These patterns of inclusion and exclusion challenge our visions about the geography and political economy of communication. We can no longer adequately refer to First and Third Worlds, North and South, and so on, but must recognize regions that are hardwired to networks and information flows and thus 'switched on', and the vast disconnected or 'switched off' regions of the world (Castells, 1996). Or, as Saskia Sassen (1999) states, we need to think about the dialectical relationship between integration and centralization on the one hand, and marginalization on the other. Sassen conveys the essence of this way of thinking as follows:

Economic globalization and the new information technologies ... create new spaces *for* centrality ... The most powerful of these new geographies of centrality at the inter-urban level binds the major international financial and business centres: New York, London, Tokyo, Paris, Frankfurt, Zurich, Amsterdam, Los Angeles, Sydney, and Hong Kong, among others. But this geography now also includes cities such as São

Paulo and Mexico City ... But also within global cities we see a geography of centrality and one of marginality. For instance, New York City has the largest concentration of fiber optic cable-served buildings in the world, but they are mostly in the center of the city, while Harlem, a low-income African-American community a mere two miles north of Manhattan's center, has one such building ... This does not *have* to be so. (1999: 181–2)

These observations illustrate that rather than witnessing the emergence of all-inclusive communicative spaces, the boundaries of cyberspace are mapped by differences between those using available technologies to produce and receive flows of communication, and the rest of the populations cut off from such means and thus rooted in more local forms of culture. In the nascent transnational communication system there is simultaneously a homogenization of a deterritorialized core of wired places and affluent users *and* a heterogeneity of cultural experience in the dispersed peripheries.

Of course, it could be objected that conclusions about the 'global media' cannot be drawn from an analysis of the Internet and broadband networks alone. However, the same relationship between spaces of centrality and places of marginality also applies to the 'old media'. Despite talk of a global media system, the linchpins of this system – AOL–Time Warner, AT&T, BT, Bertelsmann, Disney/ABC, Microsoft, Viacom and so on – only receive 20–30 per cent of their revenues from foreign markets and, even then, three-quarters is from just five countries beyond North America: Britain, France, Germany, Japan and Italy (AT&T, 2000; Disney, 2000: 34; Time Warner, 1999: 27; Viacom, 1999). Furthermore, even though global channels such as CNN, BBC World, ESPN and MTV are available in 130 or more countries, only a few households outside North America subscribe to them. In Asia, for example, only 1.4 per cent of households receive CNN, 1 per cent the BBC and 0.9 per cent ESPN (Maherzi, 1997: 187).

In the end, the vision of a global media system should be discarded in favour of the idea of a transnational communication system. This transnational communication system integrates particular places and classes and transforms the 'information revolution' into reality for some, namely those living in North America, Japan and Europe as well as an elite class of users living in a few cities scattered throughout the 'Third World'. For the rest of the world, the idea of a global information society remains fantastic, indeed.

The WTO and New Policies for New Media: Universal Service, Regulating the Internet and Media Convergence

The fragmented geography of the transnational communications systems clashes with the vision of the GII promoted in the 1990s, a vision that gave as much weight to universal service as to private investment, competition and flexible regulation (Group of 7, 1995). Many of these principles are contained in the WTO's telecommunications agreements, as we have seen, but did the agreements cover universal service? The short answer is yes. On the one hand, the Basic Telecommunications Agreement allows '[a]ny member ... to define the kind of universal service obligation it wishes to maintain ... provided they are administered in a transparent, nondiscriminatory, and competitively neutral manner and are not more burdensome than necessary' (WTO, 1997b: Section 3). On the other hand, however, the WTO does not contemplate universal service policies for an expansive array of 'luxury services', but as a narrowly tailored approach to telephone service (McLarty, 1998: 56).

In fact, the Annex on Telecommunications specifically *prevents* the adoption of universal service policies for enhanced services,[9] such as electronic databases, the Internet and so on (WTO, 1994b: Article 5). The NAFTA, upon which the telecommunications annex is modelled, also makes this point, declaring that governments cannot require an enhanced service provider to '(a) provide ... services to the public generally; (b) cost justify its rates; (c) file a tariff; (d) interconnect its networks with any particular customer or network; or (e) conform to any ... standard or technical regulation for interconnection other than for interconnection to a public telecommunications ... network' (NAFTA, 1992, Article 1303(2)). In the face of these restrictions, it is not surprising that there have been no attempts to update universal service in light of the Internet, broadband networks and other new media, except for narrowly tailored programmes to connect schools, public libraries, hospitals and so on to the Internet. This reflects not only the increasing faith in markets, but also the constraints contained in the WTO agreements that prevent universal service policies from being expanded commensurate with the availability of new ICTs as well as citizens' needs in an 'information society' (Winseck, 1998: 225–7).

At the same time that the distinction between basic and enhanced services and the narrow definition of universal service constrains governments, such constraints could possibly be used to enlarge the scope of media freedoms. As is well known, many countries have tried to regulate Internet content. Although some of these efforts have been thwarted by the courts, as in the US and France, or rejected as a barrier to the growth of the Internet, as in Canada, efforts to regulate the Internet persist. China requires users to register with police and prohibits people from spreading 'state secrets', Singapore limits the number of ISPs and requires them to block a proscribed list of URLs, and numerous other countries curtail freedom of expression on the Internet in a myriad of ways. While the Internet is often considered to be immune to these efforts, ongoing attempts to license ISPs, restrict access to 'objectionable content', and censor information published online likely have a chilling effect on freedom of expression (GILC, 1998: 3).

The Annex on Telecommunications is interesting in this respect in so far as it prevents the regulation of enhanced services and permits the free 'movement of information within and across borders' (WTO, 1994b: Article 5(c)(e)). In doing so, the WTO codifies the free flow of information principle, which could be used to curtail governments' attempts to regulate information flowing through telecommunications networks, thus helping to expand electronic media freedoms where they are weak or to strengthen them where they are challenged.[10] For this reason, Human Rights Watch (1999), for instance, lauds China's entry into the WTO, not only as a means of opening its telecommunications system to competition and foreign investment, but as a means of allowing Chinese citizens access to information beyond the reach of government control and censorship.

At the same time, however, the aim of the WTO is to promote global markets, not human rights. This point was illustrated during interviews with the Broadcasting Authority of Singapore in 1996, at which time it was acknowledged that Singapore's commitments to the Annex on Telecommunications could restrict its efforts to regulate Internet content. However, this was seen as unlikely because trade ministers would be reluctant to pursue a 'free speech' agenda through the WTO. Attempts to pursue freedom of expression through the WTO could also be limited by provisions that allow countries to adopt measures 'necessary to protect public morals or to maintain public order', although this exemption can only be invoked 'where a ... serious threat is posed to one of the fundamental interests of society' (WTO, 1994a: Article XIV).

While the Annex on Telecommunications might restrict governments' attempts to regulate Internet content, the same cannot be said with respect to private systems of censorship. Major commercial

Internet providers, governments and some multi-lateral organizations, such as UNESCO, are advocating rating systems and content filtering software as a key pillar of the nascent governance regime for telecommunications and new media and as an alternative to government regulation. This is occurring mainly in response to concerns that the Internet has made it too easy for children to access pornography, hate literature, violent content and so on. The most notable measure in this respect is the 'voluntary' international rating system – the Internet Content Rating Association (ICRA) – being adopted by members of the GBDCE: AOL–Time Warner, Disney/ABC, Bertelsmann, Microsoft, IBM, British Telecom, Bell Canada, among others (Bertelsmann, 1999; GBDCE, 1999; ICRA, 1999).

While the aim of protecting children and the voluntary status of these measures are deserving, rating systems and filtering software possess several troublesome features. Filters using the ICRA standard, for instance, block not only 'objectionable' content, but *all unrated sites*. Out of the several million websites available in 1999, just over 100,000 had adopted this standard (ICRA, 1999: 3), meaning that vast regions of cyberspace were eliminated solely on the grounds that they were unrated. In addition, the sites of the mainstream multimedia companies – precisely the ones that are members of the GBDCE – are more likely to be rated, and thus accessible to users.

Content filters are being adopted by ISPs and in other segments of the Internet further upstream without users' knowledge. The fact that sponsors of the ICRA-based standards are also major suppliers of browsers, such as Netscape (AOL–Time Warner) and Explorer (Microsoft), and Internet access providers, allows them to assume a pivotal role as online gatekeepers, erecting a worldwide system of content regulation that shapes who gains access to the desktops of users and who does not. In tandem with the consolidation of ISPs and portals around a phalanx of companies associated with the GBDCE – AOL–Time Warner, Bertelsmann, BT, Disney/ABC, France Télécom, WorldCom, Microsoft, Telefonica, Vivendi and so on – rating systems extend these companies' control over the evolution of the Internet (Bertelsmann, 1999; ICRA, 1999; Lessig, 1999).

As censorship capabilities are embedded deeper into the architecture of the Internet, it will become easier for governments to compel their use, further turning the ICRA schemes into a state-backed system of private censorship. The fact that this has already been the case in Australia and has been discussed within the US, as well as embraced by the CRTC in Canada as an alternative to government regulation, and advocated by France and UNESCO as a form of coregulation, underlines these concerns (GILC, 1999; Lessig, 1999).

THE WTO, MEDIA CONVERGENCE AND COMMUNICATION POLICY IN AN ONLINE WORLD

The idea that the telecommunications agreements have a bearing on universal service and Internet content regulation suggests that the WTO has more influence on communication and cultural policy issues than commonly thought. While the relevance of the WTO to such issues appears to be minimal because broadcasting and cable media are excluded from the agreements (WTO, 1994b: Article 2(b)), the impact of the WTO is greater than is often assumed. For one, the WTO agreements *do not* contain a cultural exemption clause and countries *can* include film and television programming as goods and services covered by the WTO. Indeed, 19 countries have done so with respect to television programming and another 25 made commitments covering global news agencies (WTO, 1998: 7). In addition, there is intense pressure to include the 'cultural industries', although some countries want the WTO to adopt a 'special instrument' that would identify measures that could be used to promote the cultural industries (Canada's position) while others want to continue excluding the cultural industries from the WTO altogether – France's position (Canada, 1999).

Regardless of the outcomes of these debates, the distinctions drawn by the WTO between basic and enhanced services as well as between those services formally covered by the agreement – telecommunications and information services – and those that are not, i.e. the 'cultural industries', are dissolving in the face of media convergence and as all information is translated into digital form and sent across the same networks. These processes are also furthered as governments relax restrictions on cross-ownership and eliminate policies that prevented telecommunications companies from influencing content flowing through their networks (ITU, 1999a: 6–7; Winseck, 1998). Media convergence is also being propelled by ownership changes that have created enormous transnational multimedia conglomerates, as with, for example, the AOL–Time Warner merger, AT&T's emergence as a dominant cable system operator and provider of high-speed Internet services through its acquisitions of TCI and Media One, Microsoft's stakes in telecommunications and cable systems, set-top boxes, web TV and online services, as well as telecommunications companies' advent as dominant Internet access providers (OECD, 1999: 49). As these companies distribute telecommunications, video, computer and Internet services over the same broadband infrastructure, how can narrow distinctions drawn by the WTO between telecommunications and cultural industries, and between basic and enhanced services, be maintained?

The absorption of all new media into the catch-all category of 'enhanced services' could restrict the application of *any* communication policies to the new media. Canada, for instance, has extended cultural policies to video on demand (VOD) by defining it as a broadcasting service. As such, these services are required to contribute to content production funds and to ensure the availability of specified amounts of Canadian programming (CRTC, 1994a: 47; 1994b). The CRTC has even held out the prospect of doing the same for the Internet once it is widely used for the distribution of broadcast programming (CRTC, 1999b). Putting questions regarding the Internet aside for a moment, even within Canada some telecommunications operators argue that since VOD is delivered to users over telecommunications networks on a point-to-point basis, these are not broadcasting but enhanced services. As such, they argue, VOD should be exempt from the cultural policy aims of the Broadcasting Act 1991 (Cohen, 1993). While these challenges to the extension of cultural policies to new media in Canada failed, similar ventures pursued through the WTO are likely to be more successful. As the United States International Trade Commission notes,

> the *Annex on the Negotiations on Basic Telecommunications* permits the provision of audiovisual services over telecommunications networks ... This, in combination with technological advances, global networking, and the deregulation of information networks, may limit the applicability of audiovisual restrictions on US service suppliers. (1996: 602)

Although such issues were set aside during negotiations to avoid a confrontation that might scuttle the Basic Telecommunications Agreement, the US made it clear that programming delivered over telecommunications networks will be treated as enhanced services (GIIC, 1997: 9, 33). The WTO's evolving framework for electronic commerce will likely further erode distinctions between areas of the electronic media covered by the WTO and those beyond its reach, erasing any lines between data, commerce and culture. In the end, the emerging expansive definition of e-commerce, broadcast programming on the Internet, and fibre-optic cables capable of carrying 100 hours of video a second to and from the numerous 'wired cities' connected to the transnational communications grid, means that cultural policy could be rendered redundant altogether or, perversely, maintained only for the disenfranchised masses living on the margins of the 'global information society'.

Rather than celebrating or lamenting the future of cultural policy, however, it needs to be recognized that such prospects are somewhat speculative and only apply to a third of the world's countries that have assented to the WTO's emerging governance regime for telecommunications and new media. In addition, there *is* a need for new policies that reinforce open media systems and advance communicative rights and freedoms – a point I will return to presently. Finally, the idea that convergence will dissolve the foundations of cultural and communications policy for the new media will likely only be drawn on selectively to prevent the adoption of *any* policies that threaten commercial interests but ignored with respect to measures that further ends jointly sought by the communication industries and governments, such as industry-defined, government-supported approaches to Internet rating and filtering systems.

This latter point was recently illustrated by an EC proposal to establish new policies with respect to technical standards for networks and service providers, online advertising, market power, privacy and universal service (EC, 1996). Although some aspects of the proposal were troublesome, the focus on structural issues and the 'lightest regulatory framework possible' did suggest a worthwhile effort. But, as the EU Committee of the American Chamber of Commerce, the International Communications Roundtable[11] and European publishers made clear, they opposed any new policies for 'the Internet, online networks, video services and other sources of information' (EU Committee of the American Chamber of Commerce, 1996: 4). As Time Warner's Manuel Kohnstamm emphasized, 'electronic services should not be subject to either broadcast or telecoms rules' (quoted in Schenker, 1996: 3).

In contrast to the pleadings of the GBDEC and others, I want to conclude this last section of the chapter by arguing that, at the least, new policies are needed to ensure that new media platforms remain open.[12] Threats to the evolution of open media systems are coming as much from the communication industries as from governments, if not more. As even the ITU notes, 'the Internet ... is not immune from the tendencies towards oligopoly that exist in all industries' (1999b: 17). Indeed, nearly three-quarters of Internet backbone bandwidth is controlled by just three companies – Uunet (WorldCom), Sprint and BBN (GTE). The dominant position of PTOs as Internet access providers as well as the consolidation of ownership and control over broadband cable access in North America among a few multimedia conglomerates – AOL–Time Warner, AT&T, Comcast, Rogers and Shaw – display similar tendencies (Bar et al., 1999: 10–12; OECD, 1999: 49).

Just as important as questions of ownership is how control over network architectures is being used to bias the evolution of cyberspace towards a closed media model. In contrast to the model of open network access typically associated with the Internet, it is clear that telecommunications and cable companies' forays onto the Internet have been followed by efforts to privilege their own Internet access providers and content over unaffiliated ISPs and content sources. In fact, the dominant high-speed Internet service in North America – @Home[13] – limits the amount of information subscribers can send over the Internet as well as the amount of video they can download from non-affiliated sources (Bar et al., 1999: 18–20). These attempts to transform the Internet into a closed media system have erupted into several regulatory skirmishes. Thus far, local courts in the United States have supported open access mandates that have been imposed on AT&T by some cities, such as Portland, Oregon, despite opposition from AT&T and the FCC (FCC, 1999c; USDC, 1999). In Canada, in contrast, the CRTC (1999a) has forced cable and telecommunications companies to open their networks, despite protestations from groups.

Questions about open media access are playing out in more than just the policy arena. Indeed, the future of the Internet is being determined at the level of technological design, in the technical codes that constitute its architecture, as Lawrence Lessig (1999) puts it. Cable and telecommunications companies' attempts to use network design to augment their control over the evolution of new media are revealed in a recent paper by Cisco Systems (1999), a leading provider of broadband Internet-protocol-based networks. Cisco's network designs give cable system operators the ability to prioritize content from their own or affiliated sources, while assigning lower priority and less bandwidth, or restricting access altogether, to unaffiliated content sources.

This ability to manage access to and use of networks is facilitated by features that permit cable system operators to 'isolate traffic by the type of application, even down to specific brands, by the interface used, by the user type and individual user identification, or by the site address' (Cisco, 1999: 3). This fine-grained management of information flows gives cable system operators unprecedented knowledge about users, a feature that raises many questions about privacy but one which, more to the point, allows operators to narrowly segment audiences and target 'express services to premium customers ready to pay for superior network performance' (1999: 8). These network design decisions thus further the commercialization of the Internet and overlay the model of the 'old media' atop the new, superimposing yet another layer of online gatekeepers that can restrict incoming content 'as well as subscribers' outgoing access to information' (1999: 5). The aim, as Cisco makes clear, is to allow a cable system operator to 'offer [its] own or a partner's services with full-speed features to encourage the adoption of your services' while restricting access to services and content provided by others (1999: 5). Thus, rather than enhancing the open, non-hierarchical and democratic qualities of

the Internet, networks are already being designed as systems of control that further the commercialization of cyberspace and discrimination between content sources, service quality, and the kind of network environment allocated to different classes of users (Bar et al., 1999: 26–30).

In the face of such efforts, policies are needed to prevent the creation of closed access to *networks* (Cisco's network design features; AT&T's, AOL–Time Warner's, etc., efforts to prevent ISP access to high-speed networks), *operating systems* (Microsoft versus US Department of Justice) and *content* (technology-based rights management systems, rating systems and network designs that allow discrimination amongst content sources). Indeed, maintaining openness at each of these levels should be the focus of all new policies for new media. Decisions taken now will decide whether the Internet evolves as an 'open network', as many argue it should and as decisions by the CRTC in Canada support, or as a 'closed network', as in the approach adopted in the US (Bar et al., 1999; CRTC, 1999a; Mansell, 1999).

The transnational reach of AT&T, AOL–Time Warner, Cisco and Microsoft, among others, means that current North American debates about open systems design are also relevant to the politics of cyberspace in other countries. However, the stress of the WTO's telecommunications policy regime on expanding markets and its almost complete lack of attention to the unique qualities of communication networks provide few tools to address these issues. In fact, its weak principles regarding market power and prohibitions against regulating enhanced services limit prospects that such policies will be developed to counteract the advent of closed media systems at the global level. Other multilateral agencies, such as the OECD (1997: 30–9), have displayed a similar disregard for these issues, arguing that open access should be *encouraged*, not mandated, and that any methods adopted should not interfere with property rights and investment incentives.

This is the same logic that has governed the FCC's refusal to enforce open access in the US, a policy presented as a 'hands-off' approach to the Internet, but one that François Bar and his colleagues (1999) argue misinterprets 30 years of regulatory history in the US and confuses the principle of 'doing no harm' with 'doing nothing'. The same point applies with equal force to the emerging policy regime for telecommunications and new media at the global level.

CONCLUSION

Analysing the governance of telecommunications and new media is complicated by the fact that old explanatory frameworks rooted in debates over the NWICO and free flow of information, and their various theoretical props (modernization, dependency or cultural imperialism), no longer offer sturdy guideposts. This is not because there are no parallels between the past and the present. There are – and three or four stand out in particular.

The potential for all electronic media to form a global communications system since the mid nineteenth century comes quickly to mind, as do parallels between the monopolies granted to the global cable operators of that time throughout Latin America, Africa and Asia and the exclusive concessions granted to France Télécom, Cable & Wireless, Telefonica, SBC and so on during the recent privatization of PTOs in the same regions. One can also point to affinities between the cartel-like organizations among cable companies, global news agencies and the domestic press in the late nineteenth century and the 'strategic alliances' today between, for instance, Global Crossing, Microsoft, AT&T and regional media conglomerates. Lastly, the subordination of communicative values and human rights to 'free trade' and mercantilist state policies designed to create global champions and to hastily usher in the newest modes of electronic media are also common features of the 'global media' in the late nineteenth and on the cusp of the twenty-first century.

Yet, there are crucial differences as well. This chapter analysed some of these, including the proliferation of regulatory regimes, the reality of a transnational communications system versus a global one, and how control over networks and technological design is shaping the evolution of cyberspace. There are several other issues that should guide analysis of telecommunications and new media in a global context today.

First, it needs to be recognized that privatization and competition have been neither as disastrous as many critics anticipated nor as beneficial as their defenders claim. Second, privatization and competition have done little to curb monopolization strategies designed to control the evolution of telecommunications and new media. Third, the idea of a GII, or the more ambitious notion of a 'global information society', has been eclipsed by a system of transnational communications and wired cities that serve the few rather than the many. The idea of a global media system is hardly a plausible one when 97 per cent of the world's population has no access to the Internet and nearly two-thirds do not even have access to a 120-year-old technology, the telephone. Once again, it is not yet the age of the global media.

Lastly, telecommunications reform has involved a technocratic approach to governance. In fact, a defining feature of each of the three pillars of the nascent governance regime – new domestic regulators, self-regulation and the WTO – is the exclusion of citizens from the policy process, the *a priori* exclusion of new media from the reach of universal service and cultural policies, as well as their dissociation from communicative and human rights. This point is vital because information and communication have always been associated with media freedoms and democracy. However, the new governance regime, and the WTO in particular, erase such conceptions in many ways. The WTO contains no references to freedom of expression, privacy, diversity and so on; consequently, it conceptually strips information and communication of their unique qualities in order to force them into a 'free trade' framework. The conceptual disassociation is further highlighted by the fact that many countries which signed the telecommunications agreements have not signed the Universal Declaration of Human Rights (1948) or the International Covenant on Civil and Political Liberties (1966).[14]

In this context, the WTO needs to address the unique qualities of communication and to reconcile the globalization of trade with the globalization of human rights. This can be accomplished by drawing a closer alliance between the WTO and the broader body of UN-based human rights law as well as by requiring all who sign the telecommunications agreements to adopt basic human rights documents. From this point of view, the problem with globalization is that it has not gone far enough!

NOTES

1 There were, however, numerous exceptions to these generalizations, such as China, Costa Rica and Iran, to name just a few, although the forces of neoliberalism ignored these counter-examples as far as possible.

2 Internet users in Africa, Asia and Latin America rose from 2.2 million in 1996 to 15.3 million in 1999.

3 The importance of cable communications is underscored by the fact that '80 per cent of all international telecommunications traffic originating in the US is carried by undersea cables' (FCC, 1999a: 5).

4 FLAG is 37 per cent owned by Bell Atlantic and includes AT&T, Dallah Al Baraka (Saudi Arabia), General Electric, Marubeni Corporation (Japan), Telecom Holding Company (Thailand), Asian Infrastructure Fund (Hong Kong) (FLAG, 2000).

5 Consortium includes: AT&T, PSINet, Com Tech, Frontier, GTE HTI, GTE INS, IXnet, Level 3, PRIMUS, Qwest, RSL, SBC, Teleglobe, Viatel, WorldCom, PGE, PCI, Sprint, BT, C&W, CHT-I, DDI, Global One, IDC, JT, KDD, KPN, NTT, SingTel, TM, Telstra and VSNL (FCC, 1999a).

6 Consortium includes: AT&T, China Telecom, Chunghwa Telecom, Hongkong Telecom, KDD, Korea Telecom, WorldCom, NTT, SingTel, Sprint, Teleglobe, Telekom Malaysia and Telstra (FCC, 1999b).

7 The ten countries are: the US (70.5m users); Japan (19.6m); Britain (11.9m); Germany (10.6m); Canada (10.2m); Australia (6.5m); France (4.9m); Finland (4.3m); Netherlands (4.8m); Taiwan (4m).

8 The study focused on entire countries when looking at Internet use in Europe, North America and Japan but, inexplicably, only looked at major cities when focusing on Brazil, China, Mexico, Thailand, etc.

9 Enhanced services are 'services offered over common carrier transmission facilities ... which employ computer processing applications that: (i) act on the format, content code, protocol or similar aspects of the subscriber's transmitted information; or (ii) provide the subscriber additional, different, or restructured information; or (iii) involve subscriber interaction with stored information' (US Schedule of Commitments to the Annex on Telecommunications, 1994, quoted in McLarty, 1998: 9; this definition is replicated in NAFTA, 1992: Chapter 13, Article 1310). This definition is so broad as to bring any service delivered over telecommunications networks within its scope, a point returned to below.

10 This applies in particular to countries which have signed the telecommunications agreements, but which regularly censor the Internet and/or inadequately guarantee freedom of expression: Antigua-Barbuda, Argentina, Bangladesh, Brazil, Colombia, Côte d'Ivoire, Ecuador, El Salvador, Ghana, Guatemala, India, Indonesia, Malaysia, Mexico, Morocco, Nicaragua, Pakistan, Peru, Senegal, Singapore, Sri Lanka, Venezuela. The imminent prospect of China joining the WTO means that it too could be added to this list.

11 This organization is the precursor to the GBDEC.

12 There is also a need for the adoption of policies regarding a more expansive conception of universal service, privacy and the creation of 'electronic public spaces' and which better balance the rights of copyright owners and users, although there is insufficient space here to address these issues.

13 @Home is offered by all of the dominant North American cable system operators, such as AT&T, Comcast, Rogers, Shaw and so on.

14 These include Antigua and Barbuda, Bangladesh, Brunei, Ghana, Indonesia, Malaysia, Pakistan, Papua New Guinea, Turkey and, if it is ultimately included, which now appears to be almost certain, China (UNDP, 1999: 2442–5).

References

Abbate, J. (1999) *Inventing the Internet*. Boston, MA: MIT Press.

Angus Reid Research (2000) *Faces of the Web*. Available at: www.angusreid.com.

AT&T (2000) *Annual Report 1999*. Available at: www.att.com/ir/pdf/99my.pdf.

Bar, F., Cohen, S., Cowhey, P., DeLong, B., Kleeman, M. and Zysman, J. (1999) 'Defending the Internet revolution in the broadband era'. Berkeley Roundtable on the International Economy (BRIE), E-conomy Working Paper 12.

Bertelsmann (1999) *Self Regulation of Internet Content*. Available at: www.stiftung.bertelsmann.de/internet-content/english/frameset_home.htm.

Boyd-Barrett, O. (1999) 'Global news agencies', in O. Boyd-Barrett and T. Rantanen (eds), *The Globalization of News*. London: Sage. pp. 19–34.

BT (1999) *World Communications Report*. Available at: www.bt.com.

BT (2000) *Annual Report 1999*. Available at: www.bt.com.

Canada (1999) *Canadian Culture in a Global World*. Available at: www.infoexport.gc.ca/trade-culture.

Castells, M. (1996) *The Information Age*, vol. 1. Malden, MA: Blackwell.

Cisco Systems (1999) *Controlling your Network: a Must for Cable Operators*. San Jose, CA: Cisco Systems.

Cohen, A. (1993) Correspondence with J.C. Meldrum, Vice President and Corporate Counsel, SaskTel. Unpublished letter 8 October on file with author.

Cowhey, P. (1990) 'The international telecommunications regime', *International Organization*, 44 (2): 169–99.

Cox, R. (1992) 'Global perestroika', in R. Miliband and L. Panitch (eds), *New World Order?* New York: New Left Review. pp. 30–43.

CRTC (1994a) *Review of Regulatory Framework (Dec. 94–19)*. Canadian Radio-television and Telecommunications Commission. Ottawa: Ministry of Supply and Services.

CRTC (1994b) *Exemption Order Respecting Experimental Video on Demand Programming Undertakings (Dec. 94–118)*. Canadian Radio-television and Telecommunications Commission. Ottawa: Ministry of Supply and Services.

CRTC (1999a) *Application Concerning Access by Internet Service Providers to Incumbent Cable Carriers' Telecommunications Facilities (Dec. 99–11)*. Canadian Radio-television and Telecommunications Commission. Ottawa: Ministry of Supply and Services.

CRTC (1999b) *New Media*. Canadian Radio-television and Telecommunications Commission. Ottawa: Ministry of Supply and Services.

Disney (1999) *Annual Report*. Available at: www.disney.com.

Drake, W.J. and Noam, E. (1997) 'The WTO deal on basic telecommunications', *Telecommunications Policy*, 21 (9/10): 799–818.

EC (1996) 'Proposal for a European Parliament and Council Directive on a common framework for general authorisations and individual licences in the field of telecommunications services'. European Commission. *Official Journal of the European Communities*, C. 90/5, 27 March.

EU Committee of the American Chamber of Commerce (1996) 'Proposal for a directive on a common framework for general authorizations and individual licenses in the field of telecommunication services'. Unpublished paper submitted to EC. Brussels: EU CACC.

FCC (1999a) 'Cable landing license'. Federal Communications Commission Available at: www.fcc. gov.org.

FCC (1999b) 'Undersea cables public forum'. Federal Communications Commission Available at: www.fcc. gov.org.

FCC (1999c) 'Amicus Curiae brief of the Federal Communications Commission in *AT&T et al. v. City of Portland and Multnomah County*. In the United States Court of Appeals, Ninth District' Available at: http://natoa.org.

FCC (2000) *Report on International Telecommunications Markets*. Federal Communications Commission Available at: www.fcc.gov.org.

FCC (2001) *Competition in the Market for the Delivery of Video Programming (7th Annual Report)*. Washington, DC: Federal Communications Commission.

FLAG (1999) 'Organizational structure'. Available at: www.flagltd.com.

France Télécom (1999) *1998 Annual Report*. Available at: www.francetelecom.fr.

Gill, S. (1997) 'Global structural change and multilateralism', in S. Gill (ed.), *Globalization, Democratization and Multilateralism*. New York: St Martin's Press. pp. 1–17.

Global Business Dialogue on Electronic Commerce (1998) 'Suggestions for discussion by the participants in the Round Table: Globalisation and the Information Society'. Available at: www.gbde.org/structure/printsugg.html.

Global Business Dialogue on Electronic Commerce (1999) 'Organizational structure'. Available at: www.gbde.org/structure/bsc.html.

Global Crossing (1999) 'Global Crossing, Softbank and Microsoft establish joint venture to build telecom network providing advanced services throughout Asia'. Available at: www.globalcrossing.bm.

GIIC (1997) *The WTO Telecoms Agreement*. Global Information Infrastructure Commission. Washington, DC: Centre for Strategic and International Studies.

GILC (1998) *Regardless of Frontiers*. Global Internet Liberty Campaign. Available at: www.gilc.org.

GILC (1999) 'GILC statement on international ratings and filters submitted to the Internet content summit'. Global Internet Liberty Campaign. Available at: www.eff. org/pub/Censorship/Ratin…990907_gilc_intl_rating. statement.html.

Group of 7 (1995) *G7 Ministerial Conference on the Global Information Society*. Brussels: Group of 7.

Hills, J. (1998) 'Liberalization, regulation and development', *Gazette*, 60 (6): 459–76.

Huber, P. (1997) *Local Exchange Competition under the 1996 Telecom Act*. Available at: www.phuber.com/.

Human Rights Watch (1999) 'Human Rights Watch envisions possible press freedom gains in wake of WTO deal'. Available at: www.ifex.org.

ICRA (1999) 'An invitation to membership'. Internet Content Ratings Association. Available at: www. icra.org.

ITU (1997) *World Telecommunications Development Report*. Geneva: International Telecommunication Union.

ITU (1998a) *World Telecommunications Development Report*. Geneva: International Telecommunication Union.

ITU (1998b) *General Trends in Telecommunication Reform, 1998: World*, vol. 1. Geneva: International Telecommunication Union.

ITU (1999a) *Trends in Telecommunication Reform 1999*. International Telecommunication Union. Available at: www.itu.org.

ITU (1999b) *Challenges to the Network*. International Telecommunication Union. Available at: www. itu.org.

Kleinwachter, W. (1999) 'Transnational management of TAP projects and new challenges to the international regulatory framework'. Paper prepared for the European Commission's Telematics Applications Programme.

Lessig, L. (1999) *Code and Other Laws of Cyberspace*. New York: Basic.

Maherzi, L. (1997) *World Communication Report*. Paris: UNESCO.

Mansell, R. (1999) 'New media competion and access', *New Media & Society*, 1 (2): 155–82.

McLarty, T. (1998) 'Liberalized telecommunications trade in the WTO', *Federal Communications Law Journal*, 51 (1): 1–59.

Melody, W. (1999) 'Telecom reform', *Telecommunications Policy*, 25: 7–34.

Microsoft (1999a) *Annual Report 1999*. Available at: www.microsoft.com.

Microsoft (1999b) 'Globo and Microsoft announce strategic agreements and investments to develop new Internet services in Brazil'. Available at: www. microsoft.com.

Microsoft (1999c) 'Microsoft partners with Softbank and Global Crossing to increase broadband connectivity in Asia'. Available at: www.microsoft.com.

Netwizards (1999) 'Internet user survey, July 1999'. Available at: www.netwizards.org.

NewsCorp (1999) *Annual Report 1999*. Available at: www.newscorp.com/report99/.

OECD (1995) *Telecommunications Infrastructure*. Paris: Organization for Economic Cooperation and Development.

OECD (1999) *Communications Outlook*. Paris: Organization for Economic Cooperation and Development.

Petrazzini, B. (1997) 'Regulating communication services in developing countries', in W. Melody (ed.), *Telecoms Reform*. Lyngby: Technical University of Denmark.

Pike, R. and Winseck, D. (2001) 'Monopoly's first moment in global electronic communication', *Journal of the Canadian Historical Association*, February.

Sassen, S. (1999) *Globalization and its Discontents*. New York: New Press.

Schenker, J. (1996) 'On-line providers protest European license scheme', *Communications Weekly International*, 5 February: 1, 30.

Shreiner (1924) *Cable & Wireless and their Role in the Foreign Relations of the United States*. Boston: Arno.

Staple, G. (2000) 'The soft network'. Available at: www.telegeography.com/Publications/tg00_intro.

Tarjanne, P. (1999) 'Preparing for the next revolution in telecommunications', *Telecommunications Policy*, 25: 51–63.

Thompson, B. (1999) 'Investing in the global information infrastructure'. Speech presented to the Global Information Infrastructure Commission Conference, Geneva, 11 October. Available at: www.giic.org/events/991011HBT.html.

Time Warner (1999) *Annual Report 1998*. Available at: www.timewarner.com.

UNCTAD (2000) *Building Confidence*. United Nations Conference on Trade and Development. Geneva: United Nations.

UNESCO (1995) *UNESCO and an Information Society for All*. United Nations Educational, Scientific and Cultural Organization. Available at: www.unesco.org/.

United States (1996) *Future of International Telecommunications Trade Issues*. Washington, DC: US Government Printing Office.

United States International Trade Commission (1996) *General Agreement on Trade in Services (GATS)*. Investigation no. 332–358. Lexis Nexis Database.

USDC (1999) *AT&T et al. v. City of Portland and Multnomah County*. United States District Court for the District of Oregon, cv 99-65-PA.

Viacom (1999) *Annual Report 1998*. Available at: www.viacom.com.

Wallsten, S.J. (1999) *An Empirical Analysis of Competition, Privatization and Regulation in Africa and Latin America*. Washington, DC: World Bank.

Wellenius, B. and Stern, P. (1994) *Implementing Reforms in the Telecommunications Sector*. Washington, DC: World Bank.

Winseck, D. (1998) *Reconvergence*. Cresskill, NJ: Hampton.

World Bank (2000) 'Telecom projects with private participation (1984–1998) (PPI Database)'. Washington, DC: World Bank.

WorldCom (1999) *1999 WorldCom Annual Report*. Available at: www.wcom.com.

WTO (1994a) *General Agreement on Trade in Services*. World Trade Organization. Available at: www.wto.org.

WTO (1994b) *Annex on Telecommunications*. World Trade Organization. Available at: www.wto.org.

WTO (1997a) *Fourth Protocol to the General Agreement on Trade in Services*. World Trade Organization. Available at: www.wto.org.

WTO (1997b) *Regulatory Reference Paper*. World Trade Organization. Available at: www.wto.org.

WTO (1998) *Audiovisual Services*, s/c/w/40. Geneva: World Trade Organization.

24

New Global Media and Communication Policy: the Role of the State in the Twenty-First Century

LAURA STEIN and NIKHIL SINHA

Global information and communication technologies (ICTs) could precipitate extraordinary political, cultural and economic transformations over the twenty-first century. Carey (1998: 28) predicts that global communication systems such as the Internet will alter physical and symbolic environments worldwide just as the telegraph, telephones and railroads altered national and international landscapes throughout the nineteenth and early twentieth centuries. While most scholars agree that global media can effect change on a global scale, they differ sharply over the nature of these changes. Will these new media facilitate freedom of expression and access to knowledge and information, or will they deepen and intensify the control and commodification of information on a national and transnational scale? What values and principles will global communication systems serve and what role can or should national governments play in determining the structure and use of these media?

Indeed, regulation of information and communication systems is critical to nation-states for several reasons. First, communication systems are central to political processes. Democracies and non-democracies alike recognize the role of communication systems in conveying information to their citizens. In addition, democracies depend on communication systems to generate the social knowledge necessary to collective decision-making processes (Barber, 1984: 197; Dewey, 1954: 155; Entman, 1989; Enzensberger, 1974; Rucinski, 1991) and to ensure citizens' communication rights (Melody, 1990: 19; Zhao, 2000: 43). At the same time, global media and other global phenomena have worldwide effects that are in the interests of all nations to regulate. Yet, the mechanisms for representing, discussing, evaluating and collectively responding to these phenomena among affected populations are insufficient or lacking altogether. In this sense, global ICTs, as well as globalization generally, create a crisis of representation for political institutions and processes worldwide (Carey, 1998: 34). Second, ICTs are enmeshed in the social and cultural fabric of nations. Information and communication are part of the shared national symbolic environment, as well as the environment of other social or communal formations (Babe, 1995: 40). Consequently, many nations are concerned with how ICTs may impact their social and cultural life. For example, many nations fear that the availability of obscene, racist or blasphemous speech on the Internet will have a corrupting influence on their societies. A third and related reason why effective regulation of global media has relevance to nation-states is the ultimate inseparability of real and virtual spaces. Although global ICTs host virtual transborder activities, virtual activities are experienced by real citizens rooted in real places. As such, nation-states have an interest in regulating these activities (Lessig, 1999: 190). Research which insists that virtual activities exist in 'cyberspace', rather than in real space, reifies network activity and prematurely dismisses the power and jurisdiction of nation-states to regulate them.[1]

This chapter addresses some of the challenges faced by nation-states in devising communication policies for the new global ICTs. Since a comprehensive discussion of global ICT policy would be too vast and unwieldy, we focus exclusively on computer networks, a prominent and growing sector of ICTs that have a potentially global reach. Computer networks are sets of computers that are linked at physical and logical levels (Schiller, 1999: xv). Computer networks, including the Internet, constitute new media in that they enable the convergence of formerly separate media forms onto a common delivery platform (Melody, 1990: 16; Schiller, 1999: 74). Drawing on aspects of other media, including print, audio, video and voice-based communications, computer networks allow for the creation of new media forms with new characteristics. These networks, along with the practices and policies that surround them, are a good observation point from which to view the challenges new media pose to national regulators.

We begin by examining three key areas of legal and policy conflict over computer networks; namely, intellectual property, privacy and freedom of expression. Legal and regulatory trends and developments in these areas reveal how new technologies are destabilizing existing policy regimes and demanding a rethinking of communication policy on the part of national governments. The chapter concludes by examining some policy principles and new models of regulation proposed by scholars to adapt national governance mechanisms for the effective regulation of global media. The discussion will be structured by the recognition that national policies are the outcome of a complex interplay of domestic and international forces. The nature and character of the state, the strengths of its institutional framework and its relationship to domestic and international forces will largely determine the form and content of such policies.

THREE AREAS OF POLICY DEVELOPMENT:
INTELLECTUAL PROPERTY, PRIVACY
AND FREEDOM OF EXPRESSION

Global computer networks raise challenging questions for law and policy on intellectual property, privacy and freedom of expression. A comprehensive analysis of these questions is beyond the scope of this chapter. Nevertheless, a broad sketch of central policy dilemmas in each of these areas, as well as the options open to national regulators, can situate otherwise abstract policy discussions in concrete social conflicts and choices currently facing many nations. Not only are many social conflicts around computer networks clustered around these key areas of policy development, but perhaps more importantly law and policy in these areas shape the contours of the public use and exchange of information and communication. Though law and policy in

each of these areas is in a state of flux worldwide, it is possible to discern patterns and trends that constitute the roots of policy dilemmas which are likely to play themselves out over the next couple of decades.

As they currently exist, computer networks possess a number of features that represent uncharted territory for governments wishing to implement and enforce policy and regulation. These features include the ability of computer networks to collect, store, process and retrieve vast quantities of information (Branscomb, 1994: 3; *The Economist*, 1999: 21; Johnson, 1994; OECD, 1997: 13; Peterson, 1995: 164); to copy information quickly and easily (Alleyne, 1995: 140; Halbert, 1999: 26); to allow direct and interactive communication between individuals and small groups (Morris and Ogan, 1996: 44); to bypass governmental and non-governmental media gatekeepers (Human Rights Watch, 1999: 12; Taubman, 1998: 261); to send information along decentralized and unpredictable pathways (Froomkin, 1997: 131; Lessig, 1999: 166); to allow network users to communicate anonymously (Froomkin, 1997: 129; Lessig, 1999: 14); and to permit interactions between persons located in different legal and political jurisdictions (Kahin and Nesson, 1997: x; Lessig, 1999: 192; Reidenberg, 1997: 86; Robinson, 1989: 44). These features have considerable impact on the abilities of governments to regulate and enforce policies applying to computer networks.

Conflicts in the areas of intellectual property and privacy have arisen largely because of the increasing commodification of information. Information has become a valuable asset, and the ability of governments, organizations and individuals to monitor, control and trade information requires laws and policies that clearly delineate the property rights of all actors in the information exchange process. In the absence of supranational property rights regimes, the role of defining property rights within networked environments necessarily falls upon national governments. In the case of freedom of expression, tensions have arisen because governments themselves have implemented laws or policies designed to protect national political and normative goals, often to the detriment of the speech rights of their own citizenry. The next three sections examine these conflicts, the ways governments are attempting to address them, and the options available for them to do so.

Intellectual Property

Computer networks intensify the conflict, ever present in intellectual property law, between expression as a commodity and as a collective good. Intellectual property law grants copyright holders exclusive rights to control copying and other uses of creative works *for a limited period of time*. In this sense, intellectual property is not analogous to material property. Intellectual property law presumes that creativity is encouraged when copyright holders can benefit financially from their labour, but that the exclusive control of these works eventually becomes a detriment to society (Bettig, 1992: 149). Ultimately, the collective good requires that information, knowledge and creative expression become freely and widely accessible to all. The collective good aspect of intellectual property is also captured in the notion of fair use. Fair use permits non-copyright holders to copy works for the purpose of comment, criticism and other activities which are understood to further the advancement of knowledge. By creating new opportunities both to control information and expression and to evade that control, computer networks invite challenges to both the copyright holder's right to control their work and the public's right to access this work.

Computer network technology can facilitate the extension of copyright controls or the free exchange of information and communication. Scholars are split on whether computer networks will underprotect or overprotect intellectual property. Many scholars note that computer networks enable non-copyright holders to engage in the widespread duplication and dissemination of copyrighted material. The ease with which computer networks permit such activities works to undermine copyright holders' control over intellectual property products (Thurow, 1997: 98–9). This underprotection of property rights results in a loss of domestic and international profits; a decline in the research, development and creation of new products; and a reluctance to engage in global trade among nations that export information-based products and services (Alleyne, 1995: 140; Jussawalla, 1992: 3, 43–4). Those who worry that new technology will underprotect copyrights focus on the need to develop law, policy and new technologies which promote the rights of intellectual property holders on computer networks (Thurow, 1997).

Others argue that computer technology may increase copyright holder control over intellectual property and override collective fair use principles for the sake of private profits (Halbert, 1999; Hunter and Herbeck, 1999; Lessig, 1999: 127). Copyright holders can use software to track and control the uses of a creative work, including how many times a work is viewed and how it can be altered or manipulated. Such software effectively allows copyright holders to disaggregate and charge for every aspect of information use (Halbert, 1999: 128; Lessig, 1999: 136). Copyright holders can also make access to creative works contingent upon private contracts, such as click-wrap or shrink-wrap agreements, which consumers tacitly accept when they view online information or open a software product package. These 'agreements' specify the terms and conditions of access and often demand that consumers relinquish their

rights to fair use and collective good protections associated with intellectual property law (Feemster, 2000; Halbert, 1999: 62; Lessig, 1999: 135). In addition, copyright holders can limit the circulation of creative works online to trusted systems that agree to abide by their terms and conditions and that interact exclusively with other systems that agree to do so (Lessig, 1999: 129). Those who believe that computer technology will overprotect copyright argue that new developments in intellectual property law or practice must maintain the public's rights to access products and ideas.

Global computer networks, and the growing global trade in intellectual property goods, are also sites of tension between developed and developing countries. While there are no 'international copyrights' that enable individuals to protect work throughout the world, most countries are members of the Berne Union for the Protection of Literary and Artistic Property (Berne Convention) and the Universal Copyright Convention, which allow producers of intellectual property to protect their works in countries of which they are not a citizen or national.[2] Fearing information piracy on a global scale, developed nations argue that strong enforcement of intellectual property rights and internationally harmonized legal regimes are necessary to facilitate a global trade in information products (Burk, 1997: 221; Jussawalla, 1992: 4; OECD, 1997: 11–12; White House, 1997: 12). Nations with strong intellectual property regimes have exerted political and economic pressure, often in the form of international treaties and agreements, on countries that fail to enforce copyright (Alleyne, 1995: 34, 133; Bettig, 1997: 150; Boyle, 1997: 121–3; Burk, 1997: 221; Halbert, 1999: 77). For example, bilateral trade agreements have enabled the US to enact copyright laws in Singapore, Malaysia, Indonesia and South Korea (Jussawalla, 1992: 67). The international intellectual property rights regime has been strengthened through the World Intellectual Property Organization (May, 1998: 256) and the US succeeded in pushing through strong protections for intellectual property in the Trade Related Intellectual Property (TRIPS) agreement under the auspices of the World Trade Organization (Goldstein, 1994: 195; May, 1998: 256; Sell, 1995). The TRIPS agreement requires member states to comply with certain standards of protection for copyright, trademarks, industrial designs, patents, etc. (Jackson, 1998: 473).

Yet many developing countries are reluctant to uphold intellectual property laws or agreements that make access to information more costly, impede technology transfer and increase the monopoly power of multinational corporations (Alleyne, 1995: 133; Jussawalla, 1992: 39–40, 58). Countries who view intellectual creativity as a collective rather than an individual creation, who themselves hold few copyrights, or who seek to further national and economic development through the cheap and widespread dissemination of intellectual products, see little reason to enforce restrictive copyright laws (Alleyne, 1995: 124; Burk, 1997: 213; Halbert, 1999: 78). However, many developing countries find themselves in a dilemma. While less stringent enforcement of international intellectual property regimes may provide developing countries with greater access to information resources from the more advanced industrial economies, the same rules may allow multinational corporations to extract and exploit economic and commercial information about national industrial and agricultural resources within developing counties. As Thurow (1997: 100, 103) notes, rather than conform to the intellectual property regimes of developed countries, developing countries should ensure that any copyright regime they adopt addresses their particular needs.

As we have earlier stated, computer networks can be used to alter the balance that different countries have achieved between information as a commodity and as a social good. Tensions over intellectual property law both within and between countries revolve largely around where to draw the line between information control and the free flow of information. As trade in online information, products and services grows, copyright holders seek out ways to charge for every use of information, to prevent unauthorized uses, and to assert and extend their ownership over information, ideas and artifacts (Bettig, 1997: 140, 147; Halbert, 1999: 49; Mosco, 1989). Such behaviour is in keeping with the logic of the marketplace and constitutes a modern enclosure movement (similar to that of the enclosure of public lands in England during the first half of the nineteenth century) in which ideas and information are being converted from common goods into private property (Bettig, 1992: 138; 1997: 138; Thurow, 1997: 101). The more cultural artifacts and assets are privately controlled and monopolized, the fewer opportunities the public has to participate in the iterative creation and re-creation of social and cultural life (Bettig, 1992: 152; Halbert, 1999: 147). While the commercialization of computer networks and information may be inevitable, as Abrahamson (1998: 14) argues, many fear that unchecked commercialization and commodification will impede information's widespread distribution and the social benefits that come from sharing information (Besser, 1999; Halbert, 1999; Thurow, 1997: 101). From this perspective, too much control over information discourages creativity, commentary and criticism. On an international level, excessive control over intellectual property inhibits the free flow of information between developed and developing countries and leads to a loss in social and economic welfare (Jussawalla, 1992: 86, 110–11). As private parties reach to extend copyright protections locally and globally, societies must ask themselves at what point information control and ownership exceed adequate incentives and rewards for the creation and trade of intellectual artifacts and begin to harm the collective good.

Precisely where to strike this balance is a matter of both law and policy. Governments must decide the extent to which copyright will be protected on computer networks and which rights will be upheld against the technology's ability to negate them. Many nations have been quick to devise laws and legislation that bolster intellectual property protections for copyright holders and strengthen the global trade in information (Bettig, 1997: 150; Halbert, 1999: 37, 43–4). Law and policy will also decide the extent to which private computer code and practices will be allowed to override the collective good aspects of intellectual property law, and what Lessig (1999: 126–7) calls the copy duties of copyright holders. Governments must also consider whether, and under what conditions, information and knowledge should be publicly available and accessible (Branscomb, 1994: 3; Demac, 1994: 63; Lessig, 1999; Thurow, 1997: 103) and to what extent they will adhere to international agreements, like the TRIPS, in their struggle to access and disseminate global information while protecting potentially valuable local intellectual and information resources. The ability of governments to effectively address these issues varies widely and, as we shall discuss later, is dependent on a variety of international and domestic factors not all of which are subject to governmental control.

Privacy

The ability of computers to collect, search and exchange data feeds a growing market for personal information and harbours the potential to erode personal privacy. Personal information can be collected any time someone writes a cheque, uses a credit or debit card, engages in a financial transaction, views World Wide Web pages, or does anything else that generates a data trail (*The Economist*, 1999; Peterson, 1995: 167), and it includes names, telephone numbers, marital status, education level, job history, credit history, medical records, and any other information that can be linked to specific persons or data subjects (Branscomb, 1994: 4). Often, individuals have little choice but to reveal this information, which is collected without their consent or knowledge, or is a byproduct of a sale or service transaction (1994: 4; Gandy, 1993: 78, 82; Peterson, 1995: 164). Furthermore, personal information can become the basis for decisions made about an individual by others, such as whether someone is offered a job, targeted for government surveillance or eligible for medical insurance (Branscomb, 1994: 4). As Gandy (1993: 83–4) notes, personal information derives its market value from the signals it gives organizations about the desirability of forming relationships with individuals as consumers, employees or political agents.

The growing trade in personal information has many nations concerned about the privacy rights of their citizens. Though conceptions of privacy vary from country to country, privacy is frequently linked to the rights of individuals to enjoy autonomy, to be left alone, and to determine whether and how information about one's self is revealed to others (Branscomb, 1994: 28; Johnson, 1994: 225; Peterson, 1995: 171; Westin, 1967: 7). A useful definition of privacy is provided by Westin: 'privacy is the claim of individuals, groups and institutions to determine for themselves, when, how and to what extent information about them is communicated to others' (1967: 158). A central privacy concern of many nations, and one which we will focus on here, involves the ability of individuals to access and control how their personal information is used by others (Gellman, 1997: 278; Global Internet Liberty Campaign, 1998: 1; Peterson, 1995: 164). As computer networks provoke more and more privacy conflicts between information subjects and information users, the question of who controls personal information takes on increasing importance. Surveillance of individuals by businesses and governments, the dissemination of personal data across national borders, and the use of information for purposes other than that for which it was originally collected, as well as other uses and abuses of personal information, are prodding many governments to rethink their privacy policies. Governments must determine whether privacy policies are necessary to limit the collection and use of personal information by both governmental and private parties, and, if such policies are necessary, how best to formulate them.

Opponents of government regulation of privacy argue that privacy rights are bad for commerce, technologically unenforceable, and antithetical to free speech. This view, typified by an issue of *The Economist* (1999) focusing on privacy, holds that privacy rights impede the free flow of information by putting constraints on the trafficking of personal information and that the inability to control technology makes the decline of privacy as a value inevitable. The ability of privacy rights to inhibit unfettered trade in personal information is also seen as interfering with free speech, though Peterson (1995: 173) points out that the equation of free trade with free speech comes primarily from businesses who sell personal information and marketing firms who use it to sell products. For many opponents of government privacy regulations, voluntary self-regulation on the part of industries and organizations who control personal information is the best means of addressing privacy concerns. From this perspective, personal information belongs to those who collect it (Branscomb, 1994: 13), and ownership confers the right to determine how it is used. On this view, the only way for governments to balance privacy concerns against free speech and the free flow of information is to allow private companies to self-regulate (Cochran, 1996).

Proponents of government privacy regulation argue that privacy is a social value that governments must affirmatively protect. In their view, personal information is a type of asset or property that is rightly controlled by the person who generates it, rather than those who collect it (Branscomb, 1994; Gandy, 1993; Lessig, 1999: 156; Westin, 1967). Indeed, those who collect this information surreptitiously or without fair compensation can be seen as engaging in a type of theft (Gandy, 1993: 82). According to Peterson (1995: 186) and Branscomb (1994: 30), the taking of this asset warrants some form of compensation. However, while Branscomb (1994: 28) believes that responsible companies could offer consumers sufficient incentives to release their personal information, Gandy (1993: 91) maintains that fair or equitable compensation is impossible because individuals have no way of estimating the true value of their information. From this perspective, industry self-regulation is an inadequate means of protecting privacy rights. Self-regulation generates conflicting and complex rules among different industries and sectors which increase the costs of business compliance and which undermine consumer confidence (Green et al., 2000). Government regulation, on the other hand, allows for consistent privacy policies which facilitate the flow of legitimately traded information, bolster electronic commerce and protect human rights (Araki, 1989: 193; Global Internet Liberty Campaign, 1998; Green et al., 2000; OECD, 1997: 15, 18).

The privacy policies of the United States and the European Union (EU) draw on the two approaches to privacy rights outlined above and illustrate two contrasting ways in which governments can respond to privacy concerns. In its 1995 Data Protection Directive, the EU explicitly affirms the right to privacy of EU citizens, and defines a comprehensive set of principles and provisions that adhere to that right. The Directive accords specific rights and responsibilities to data subjects and data processors, protects data subjects' rights to control the collection and use of personal information by both governments and private companies, and harmonizes data protection rules among member countries. Among its many provisions, the Directive requires that companies or agencies wanting to process personal information first gain the unambiguous consent of the data subject.[3] Since data subjects must 'opt into' personal data transactions by granting their free and informed consent, the burden of initiating this process falls on the would-be information processor and non-consenting data subjects are spared the task of tracking and halting objectionable uses of their information (Peterson, 1995: 180). Another provision, perhaps the most controversial in the Directive, prevents personal data from being exported to countries that do not provide comparable levels of protection. Some view this rule as an impediment to the development of electronic commerce in EU countries and to trade with outside countries, such as the United States, which lack significant privacy protections (*The Economist*, 1999: 23; Mitchener, 2000: 32). At the very least, the Directive creates pressure on countries who want to trade with European Union members to develop comparable data protection rules (Global Internet Liberty Campaign, 1998).

Unlike the European Union's comprehensive approach to data protection, the United States' approach is characterized by fragmentation. No comprehensive federal privacy policy exists. Instead, the US employs a mixture of narrowly targeted federal legislation, state law and industry self-regulation to address privacy concerns. Federal legislation has focused on specific problems related to particular industries, technologies or types of data. Furthermore, while federal legislation places restraints on how the government can use or process information, these rules do not apply to private organizations who collect information (Branscomb, 1994: 17).[4] Several state constitutions protect information privacy, but these provisions also apply only to the public sector (Peterson, 1995: 165). For the most part, the US administration advocates private sector self-regulation and marketplace solutions as the best means to address concerns over personal information (White House, 1997: 19). Among US businesses, the preferred method of privacy protection is to permit consumers to exercise an 'opt-out option', under which personal information may be collected and processed unless consumers request otherwise. Under the US position, the burden of protecting privacy and personal information falls upon the individual, and the corporations and organizations collecting the information have wide latitude in the use and dissemination of information.[5] Tensions between the conflicting privacy approaches of the US and the European Union have resulted in a Safe Harbor agreement, finalized in the spring of 2000, which allows US-based companies to choose between formal oversight by EU regulators or qualifying self-regulatory regimes enforced by the US Federal Trade Commission.[6]

Governments around the world have started to tackle the difficult issue of devising laws and policies to protect the data privacy of their citizens. These positions range from the strong protections offered by the EU to the self-regulation model adopted by the US. However, this remains a constantly shifting legal and policy terrain, and most national positions are still in a state of flux. Instead of describing the state of national policies as they relate to specific countries, we offer a broad schema that allows for the assessment and analysis of national policies and, consequently, the condition of privacy protections offered by national policies. Broadly, governmental attempts to regulate data privacy can be assessed according to the degree of protection offered to citizens in four general categories: consent, disclosure, security and accuracy, and enforcement. *Consent* deals with the right of individuals to decide when, how and what kinds of information about them is collected over a computer network. It also includes the activities for which that information is collected and the clarity with which an individual is made aware that consent is required and being asked for. *Disclosure* deals with the terms, conditions and circumstances under which an agency collecting information is permitted to disclose that information to other agencies, including the kinds of organizations and activities for which disclosure may be permissible. *Security* and *accuracy* involve the obligation of information collecting agencies to ensure that the collected information is securely stored and accurately maintained. The obligation to maintain accurate information contains the implicit right of individuals to have access to the information about themselves to ensure its accuracy and demand correction in case of errors. Finally, the effectiveness of privacy and data protection laws depends on their mechanisms for *enforcement*.

Persistent questions about who should control personal information suggest that governments will eventually have to clarify ownership rights and responsibilities. Information has become a major asset and commodity, necessitating the protection and definition of ownership rights (Branscomb, 1994: 1). Property rights in information, like property rights in traditional and tangible property, must ultimately be defined through law and legislation (Mensch, 1990: 13, 23; Michelman, 1987: 1319, 1335–6; Streeter, 1996: 207). Streeter (1996: 207) and Boyle (1997: 27) point out that all property rights and entitlements are socially constructed artifacts of governments who must allocate specific legal powers to some and withhold them from others. In the case of information assets, this allocation of rights is by no means straightforward. As Gandy (1993: 75) argues, personal information is created when someone observes the behaviour of another, and property rights in that information are highly debatable. Whether personal information belongs to those who generate it or those who collect it, and whether anyone has the right to traffic in this information, are political questions that must be determined through the development and application of legislative, policy and regulatory mechanisms.

Freedom of Expression

Freedom of expression is a value that numerous nations endorse as a political or social right. While countries, such as India, the US, Canada and others, protect speech rights in their national constitutions, many others acknowledge this right in international human rights agreements. For instance, both the International Covenant on Civil and Political Rights (1966) and the Universal Declaration of Human Rights (1948) guarantee people 'freedom to seek, receive and impart information and ideas' in all media regardless of geographical frontiers. While it may be true that many nations support freedom of expression in theory rather than practice (Human Rights Watch, 1999: 3), speech rights nevertheless remain an expressed value and goal of many nations.

Computer networks open up new and significant opportunities to engage in expression. Computer networks allow groups within civil society to forge direct connections with one another through electronic mail, web pages, file transfers, real-time messaging, and online newsletters and discussion groups. In this sense, computer networks fill a communicative gap between interpersonal media, like telephones, and mass media, like television (Human Rights Watch, 1999: 14; Kavanaugh, 1998). These networks also enable communication which bypasses media gatekeepers and resists government controls on speech. People around the world can utilize these networks to circulate political and cultural content that is censored or suppressed offline, such as sexually explicit works, politically dissident information and ideologies, hate speech, banned texts, and other materials deemed subversive. Computer networks make it possible, as Taubman (1998: 261) argues, to establish social networks outside official government channels. One reason they can do so is that current computer network technology makes government control of speech in this medium a complex proposition (Froomkin, 1997: 129; Lessig, 1999: 166). The ability to communicate anonymously, to encrypt messages so that only specified senders and receivers can read them, and to distribute data over decentralized routes all make computer network communication difficult to monitor or block. For those with access to them, these networks enable a range of practices conducive to freedom of expression.[7]

The ability to circulate what some governments deem objectionable content has provoked social conflict, and in some cases swift policy responses, in numerous countries. Both the United States and Australia have made bids, successfully in the case of the latter and unsuccessfully in that of the former, to criminalize the distribution of sexually explicit material on the Internet on the grounds that it could be available to children (Murphy, 1999).[8] In China, the government requires Internet service providers (ISPs) to block objectionable pornographic or political sites. Included among these sites are those carrying American news media, news and commentary from Taiwan, appeals to free Tibet, and other content which threatens to disrupt 'public order' (Froomkin, 1997: 145; McCarthy, 2000: 22; Rosenthal, 2000: A1; Smith, 2000: C2; Taubman, 1998: 264–5). In Kuwait, Israel and Saudi Arabia, the Internet has been perceived as a threat to local religious and moral sensibilities (Human Rights Watch, 1999: 21, 24; Wheeler, 1998: 362, 365). Scholars have suggested that government regulation of content may occur for political and ideological reasons or as a response to societal pressures to repress 'immoral' or 'unethical' communication (Rogerson and Thomas, 1998; Taubman, 1998). Although each country has a different definition of what constitutes objectionable content, these definitions are grounded in the cultural values, political beliefs and historical circumstances of each.

Government attempts to control political and cultural content on computer networks raise questions of how speech rights will be configured in these forums and what content government can legitimately regulate. While some scholars would prefer that computer networks be free from any government regulation which affects content (Cate, 1995: 1; Labunski, 1997: 191–2), others find it unrealistic to expect governments to refrain from content regulation (Mayer-Schönberger and Foster, 1997). For many countries, content regulation is an extension of social and cultural norms and standards. Rules that apply offline, such as restricting access to pornography or discouraging speech that insults or degrades racial, ethnic or other social groups, become applicable online. As Wheeler (1998) argues, the cultural values and frameworks of a nation will affect the practices and policies surrounding computer networks.

Scholarship on speech rights and computer networks focuses on three primary concerns that relate to the conditions prohibiting or promoting freedom of expression. First, analysts identify potential methods of government control of information. Although scholars unanimously acknowledge that total control is difficult to achieve, they nevertheless catalogue numerous methods whereby governments can effectively (if not completely) control speech. Second, scholars examine the efforts of authoritarian or non-democratic governments to control political speech. This research scrutinizes the popular assumption that computer networks are inherently democratic and able to deflect government control. Third, scholars examine the jurisdictional questions raised when the social and cultural restrictions on speech in one country clash with those of another. The ability of citizens to access materials that are banned or restricted in their own countries raises the question of whether international cooperation and agreement will be necessary to enforce content regulations or whether such regulations will become increasingly untenable.

The openness of computer network architecture has not prevented governments from pursuing numerous strategies to control or contain access to objectionable content within their borders. As Mayer-Schönberger and Foster (1997: 235) note, national restrictions on freedom of expression are common around the world. Although specific content regulations may change from year to year, most regulations exhibit commonalities that are likely to persist over time. Regulatory restrictions and content containment strategies can be divided into those that attempt to control gateways to content and those that attempt to control the users themselves. Governments have multiple means of controlling or creating content gateways. Many governments require ISPs to filter or block objectionable content on their systems. By limiting the number of ISPs available, licensing them, or managing them outright, governments can keep a close watch on ISP activities. Governments can also establish proxy servers that act as gateways through which users must pass to gain access to global networks. Both ISPs and proxy servers can utilize software that filters content based on criteria such as the e-mail addresses of senders and recipients, Internet protocol addresses which identify message origins or destinations, or characters that appear in the body of a message (Human Rights Watch, 1999: 36; Kavanaugh, 1998: 37). Kuwait, Saudi Arabia, Yemen, the United Arab Emirates, Tunisia, Algeria and China are among the countries who have used these methods to constrain access (Human Rights Watch, 1999: 24; Kavanaugh, 1998: 82, 84; McCarthy, 2000: 21–2; Taubman, 1998: 265; Wheeler, 1998: 362–3). In China, Singapore and the United Arab Emirates, governments also mandate the blocking of some of the more well-known anonymous remailer sites which could help citizens circumvent content regulation (Human Rights Watch, 1999: 39). Measures like these counteract the decentralized architecture of computer networks by utilizing or creating centralized access points that are amenable to control. Governments may also monitor or restrict user access to the network. For example, in Jordan the government restricts user access by keeping the price of Internet service artificially high (Human Rights Watch, 1999), while in Myanmar only those who are close to the ruling party are authorized to use e-mail (Barron, 2000). Other nations, such as Iraq, Libya, Syria and Saudi Arabia, have chosen to deny their citizens access altogether (Human Rights Watch, 1999: 27; Schneider, 2000: A1). Finally, Chinese Internet users and publishers risk criminal penalties if they fail to register with the government (Taubman, 1998: 264).

Several studies, including Human Rights Watch's (1999) study on the Middle East and North Africa, Kavanaugh's (1998) study on North Africa, and Taubman's (1998) study on China, suggest that non-democratic governments can project their political and cultural will onto computer networks. These studies collectively argue that non-democratic governments are able to increase access to the medium while simultaneously militating against the potential unintended effects of exposing citizens to what Taubman (1998: 257–8) terms 'ideational pluralism'. Ideational pluralism, or multiple sources of ideas and information, threatens the ability of non-democratic governments to maintain hegemony over information and ideology within their borders. It also offers politically discontent groups access to viewpoints and perspectives that could help foment opposition movements. Cognizant of the threats to centralized power posed by computer networks, many non-democratic governments attempt to strike a balance between the control of information and the diffusion of technology seen as promoting economic and social advancement. While these strategies help to maintain the primacy of state-controlled information in the short term, whether they will be able to successfully control content in the long run remains to be seen. Nevertheless, all of these studies presume that network technology will be the Trojan horse that foils government control of content. There is already some evidence of the successful use of the Internet to 'subvert' the political control governments have sought to exercise over dissenting movements. During the Tiananmen Square uprising in 1989 and the attempted coup in the Soviet Union in 1990, phone, fax and computer networks provided alternative sources of information to the outside world (Fredrick, 1993, 293; Quarterman, 1990: xxiii–xxiv). In Mexico, a representative for the Zapatista movement, Subcommandante Marcos, was able to use the Internet to communicate with his supporters and the rest of the world (Ford and Gil, 2001). Similarly, during the Kosovo war, the dissident radio station B92 was able to continue broadcasting by using the Internet even after the station was closed down by Serbian police (Hibbert, 1999: 401).

Diverse and contradictory content regulations also raise questions about whether a nation's rules have jurisdiction over content that originates elsewhere. Examples of jurisdictional conflict over content include a 1995 attempt by the German government to force the global access provider CompuServe to block German users' access to 200 sexually explicit computer discussion groups and a subsequent effort on the part of the French government to pressure the search engine Yahoo! into preventing French citizens from viewing Nazi memorabilia on its English-language auction sites (Associated Press, 2000; Delaney, 2000: B10; Rogerson and Thomas, 1998: 247). Both cases raised, but have yet to answer, the question of exactly whose laws should apply to communication that regularly crosses national borders. At present, global computer networks are governed by contradictory national laws (Mayer-Schönberger and Foster, 1997). Such laws are a concern of companies who worry about their liability for data that regularly travel through multiple countries with diverse policies (White House, 1997). Contradictory laws and unclear jurisdictions are also a concern of countries who seek to protect national norms and values.

Unlike the dilemmas new technologies have precipitated in intellectual property and privacy policies, tensions over political and cultural content are the result not of conflicts over information ownership but over the social, cultural and political environment of different countries. Ultimately, these conflicts beg the question of whether governments can or should regulate content over computer networks in order to protect national values, given the political and cultural diversity both among and within nations. For many countries, the ability of citizens to communicate over computer networks destabilizes existing balances between the free flow of information and information control. While some analysts argue that computer networks are ultimately incompatible with government controls and authoritarian rule (Froomkin, 1997: 141; Wriston, 1994), others are less certain that governments will fail to assert control over these networks (Kavanaugh, 1998: xiii). Research in this area must continue to ask whether and under what conditions regulations affecting freedom of expression are appropriate and sustainable, and whether the current openness of computer networks engenders freedom of expression, or whether social and cultural practices and values will instead reshape the architecture of computer networks.

POLICY PRINCIPLES AND MODELS OF GLOBAL MEDIA REGULATION

Computer networks have already precipitated serious social conflicts in the areas of intellectual property, privacy and speech rights. Although computer technology and services are constantly evolving, many of the conflicts they engender will persist through successive incarnations of the technology. For this reason, governments must define the purposes, principles and values that should animate their communication systems. Making these social choices now will allow these decisions to be incorporated into technology and industry as they develop, rather than forcing costly and inefficient changes later. Thoughtful policy choices should also ensure that valued rights are respected and protected throughout this period of technological innovation and change brought on by global computer

networks. This section explores models of regulation and policy principles that can be applied to computer networks. Several policy models exist for managing and resolving conflicts over computer networks, including marketplace and private sector regulation, national government regulation, and international or multinational regulatory regimes. None of these options are mutually exclusive; they can be used in combination to supplement and counterbalance each other's protections. Nevertheless, we will discuss these models separately in order to highlight the distinctions between them and to examine their respective advantages and disadvantages. After reviewing these models, we go on to consider the principles and guidelines that might successfully steer future developments in intellectual property, privacy, and speech rights law and policy.

Given that computer networks can and will be regulated, nation-states must determine what methods of regulation to employ, whether these are public or market-oriented, based on national laws and normative systems, or subject to international agreements and covenants. To be effective, regulations must be enforceable and achieve collectively desired outcomes. Yet, global communication systems challenge the ability of nation-states to effectively regulate and to exercise their sovereignty. Sovereignty refers to a ruling body's power to make and enforce policies that affect people or territories within its jurisdiction. One challenge comes from market institutions that increasingly assert their claim to privately regulate transactions over these networks. Another comes from the ability of communication and information to regularly cross national borders, thereby calling the jurisdictional limits of nation-states into question. Furthermore, the increasing ability of individuals and organizations to communicate globally begs the question of whether international instruments would be more effective agents of regulation than nation-states. These factors put pressure on nation-states to redefine their role in formulating and enforcing communication policy.

Whether future communication policies are market-driven or the product of national or international regulatory regimes, scholarship suggests that these policies require a socially agreed set of principles at their core. Principles are general rules or propositions on which subsequent actions can be based. In addition, they are a jargon-free way of expressing policy goals (Proceedings of the Annenberg Washington Program Panel Two, 1995: 84–5). Defining the core principles of national and international communication policy has several advantages. First, principles can underscore the values that nations wish to privilege with regards to privacy, intellectual property, speech rights and other policy areas. Principles can help nations protect access to communication systems and content, set minimum standards of conduct among data processors and collectors, and delineate spheres of public knowledge and information. Defining principles at the outset of technological development allows governments to shape communication systems before special interests become entrenched and change becomes more difficult (Kirby, 1983: 13). Principles also provide a firm foundation on which to build coordinated and comprehensive legislation. For Branscomb (1994: 84), principles are a superior basis for legislation to their alternative – narrowly conceived laws formulated in response to narrowly framed problems. Principles can also foster the linkages necessary to coordinate between national and international policy, law and technological development. Socially sanctioned principles can facilitate the harmonization of domestic laws among nations (OECD, 1997: 11), treaty negotiations among countries (Kirby, 1983: 14), and the overall development of global communication systems (OECD, 1997: 4). Finally, nations that have an express commitment to communication policy principles possess clearer benchmarks for assessing whether specific regulations achieve their desired goals.[9] Without larger principles or goals in mind, any policy becomes its own end.

Principles are a critical step towards setting national and international policy goals. Yet, they are only the first step. Once principles are determined, nations must decide how to apply them. Principles must be incorporated into national and international law and legislation if they are to have any force or effect. Meshing international and other guidelines, which do not have the force of law, with legal traditions and practices in individual countries will be challenging (Kirby, 1983: 17–18). Nations will also have to decide the domains in which to apply these principles. For example, while EU privacy principles apply across all information processing, marketplace policies focus on specific industries, technologies and other sectoral divisions. In the area of speech rights, scholars disagree over whether access principles should be applied according to the specific technology involved (Cate, 1995; Labunski, 1997), the functions of the medium (Melody, 1990; Plotkin, 1996: 238), or the classification of an entity as a content provider or transmission facility (OECD, 1997: 4). Despite these difficulties, the process of harmonizing and coordinating national and international policy cannot succeed without attention to the fundamental principles that will guide these policies and shape global communication systems.

Market-Based Regulation

Marketplace regulation of computer networks, through code and contracts, threatens to significantly narrow the sovereign powers of many nations. The use of competitive markets to allocate communication resources is favoured by many scholars and policy-makers. According to supporters of marketplace regulation, markets are responsive to fluctuating demands for products and services, can measure the value individuals assign to various communication services, and 'depoliticize' decision-making by allowing private actors within the marketplace to determine resource allocation (de Sola Pool, 1983; Kahn, 1988: Preface). The primary goal of market systems is economic efficiency, and the ability of economic efficiency to maximize the wealth of nations is equated with the overall public interest and beneficial social outcomes (Office of Technology Assessment, 1990: 21–2). From this perspective, marketplace regulation is preferred to government regulation which is seen as hindering the efficient allocation of resources, as well as improvements in products and services (Hilton, 1972; Kahn, 1988; MacAvoy, 1979).

Market regulation, also referred to as private sector or self-regulation, allows private actors operating within competitive markets to settle social conflicts over communication (Mosco, 1988). Under a market model, businesses can develop their own rules, standards and practices (Glickman and Carney, 2000: 196), and consumers are free to patronize those businesses whose rules and practices they favour. The legitimacy of this model rests on the assumption that consumers can choose at any time to 'exit' a relationship that involves one set of rules in order to form a new relationship under another rule set (Johnson and Post, 1997: 32). In this model, the role of government is limited to establishing a legal framework that facilitates commerce, provides industries with incentives to regulate themselves, and maintains marketplace competition and consumer choice. Extending the argument to the international arena, market theorists maintain that an international market economy, institutionalized in international economic regimes characterized by self-regulating norms and rules, would constitute a public good for all nations in the system because it would ensure the greatest economic benefit for the greatest number (Gilpin, 1987; Kindleberger, 1978; Krasner, 1991; Waltz 1979). This is the preferred model of the US, which would like the private sector to build and control computer networks (Bettig, 1997: 146; White House, 1997: 18–19).

Johnson and Post (1997), Reidenberg (1997: 100) and others argue that computer networks are good candidates for private sector self-regulation. In their view, computer networks constitute distinct spaces, clearly demarcated from the real world, with their own unique problems. They argue that computer network providers and infrastructure organizations can take on their own sovereign powers by creating their own borders and rules of order. Network users and system operators could devise their own rules for controlling behaviour in these spaces, and system operators could ban users who didn't follow their rules. Banned or discontented users would be able to establish new relationships with other system operators, presumably under better conditions and terms of service. Johnson and Post suggest that, excepting cases where network activities affect the vital interests of nation-states, national governments could defer their authority over behaviour in these spaces to network self-regulation. While Reidenberg (1997: 96) believes that governments must continue to protect the public interest over computer networks, he also suggests that they reallocate some of their authority to the virtual world. On a similar note, Louveaux et al. (1999) suggest that 'cyber-tribunals' or 'virtual magistrates' be set up online to provide non-judicial dispute resolution for conflicts that occur over computer networks.

Private sector regulations may be implemented through voluntary standards and codes, contracts between service or access providers and consumers, and the conscious design of network architecture. While private sector regulations allow businesses to determine the methods and values behind network regulation, they risk short-changing the public good aspects of communication law and policy. Voluntary standards and codes allow businesses maximum flexibility in regulating their own behaviour over computer networks. However, voluntary rules can easily result in overlapping and conflicting guidelines, especially since these rules can apply variously to individual companies, industry sectors, particular corporate functions, professional associations or the technology itself (Gellman, 1997: 256, 260). Poorly structured private sector regulations can also leave significant gaps in the areas and practices they cover. Furthermore, since there are no penalties for failing to enforce voluntary rules, incentives to adhere to them may be weak.

Regulation of behaviour over computer networks can also be achieved through the use of private contracts. Access or service providers can subject network users to contractual arrangements as part of their terms of service (Bing et al., 1983: 114; Proceedings of the Annenberg Washington Program Panel One, 1995: 26). These contracts effectively establish private law and policy on computer networks. For example, those who control intellectual property increasingly employ contracts to lay out conditions and terms of service. These contracts may specify acceptable uses of their products and require consumers to waive their rights under intellectual property law, such as the right of fair use or first sale (Lessig, 1999: 135). Thus, while contracts can be used to resolve conflicts surrounding information flows over computer networks, they can also be used to displace or circumvent rights established under public law.

Finally, the private sector can use technology to solve problems associated with intellectual property, privacy and freedom of expression. Lessig (1999: 7) argues that, without government intervention, computer networks will be regulated by code, or the software and hardware that makes up these systems. There are many examples of regulation through network technology. Technological means, such as filtering or age verification systems, can be used to control access to objectionable expression over computer networks (1999: 175–6; White House, 1997: 25). Software programs can be used to protect privacy by determining a user's privacy preferences and alerting the user when computer sites don't meet their standards (Global Internet Liberty Campaign, 1998; Green et al., 2000: 94; Lessig, 1999: 160). Technology can also be used to extend the control of copyright holders over intellectual property by tracking and controlling copies of materials or by designing technology in a way that limits its potential uses. For example, digital audiotape (DAT) is designed to degrade in quality with successive copies, even though DAT is technically capable of producing an infinite number of perfect copies (Lessig, 1999: 128). While technology can solve problems brought on by computer networks, it will solve these problems according to who has power in the marketplace and who controls or owns the technology (Lessig, 1999: 7). In some cases, consumers may be able to use technology to protect their rights and preferences. Privacy software or filtering programs implemented by the end user exhibit this capability. Conversely, technology may be used to strip consumers and citizens of rights they hold under public law, as in the case of some intellectual property technologies or content filters imposed by companies, service providers or governments. In the case of content filters, network users may be unaware that regulations are being applied and, therefore, be incapable of challenging them. Given the potential of technology to override public values, many analysts believe that governments must have a role in monitoring and penalizing network practices which fail to conform to accepted rights and standards (Global Internet Liberty Campaign, 1998; Green et al., 2000: 94; Lessig, 1999: 160).

Critics of marketplace regulation argue that allowing businesses to determine the social purposes of computer networks results in the erosion of public service values traditionally maintained by governments (Lessig, 1999: 59; Schiller, 1999: 59, 87). By defining economic efficiency as the end goal of communication systems, market regimes reduce information and communication to mere commodities, and fail to recognize the other roles they play within political, social and cultural life (Babe, 1995: 18). Regulating behaviour on computer networks through contract and code takes areas of regulation, including privacy, intellectual property and speech rights, out of the domain of public political processes and into that of private organizations. Rights that exist in the public realm of government will not necessarily find protection in the private realm of commerce. Governments' role in regulating media is dramatically transformed. Whereas a public service model of government regulation expects governments to ensure access to and availability of services and technology, affordable prices for essential services, and the rights of media owners and users (Office of Technology Assessment, 1990: 23), the market model views governments as enforcers of market rules and requirements, such as property rights, contracts and information flows. Citizens who are dissatisfied with the terms of service can seek out another service provider, but they do not have the opportunity to change those terms by having a 'voice' in those systems (Hirschman, 1986: 77: Lessig, 1999: 201). Lessig (1999: 199) argues that governments which allow market regulation to control the architecture of the Internet will undoubtedly experience a loss of sovereignty.

Private sector regulation of computer networks is problematic in a number of other regards. As articulated by Johnson and Post (1997), network self-regulation presumes that online behaviour takes place in a unique space that is detached from the real world. This line of reasoning reifies computer networks and the activities that take place over them. In fact, as scholars such as Lessig (1999: 190) and Mayer-Schönberger and Foster (1997: 238) point out, these networks are not extraterritorial. Behaviour that takes place in online space simultaneously occurs in real geographic space. Consequently, both spaces have a degree of control over network actors. The marketplace model also characterizes network actors as consumers who are free to change rule sets whenever they become dissatisfied with conditions under a particular network service, access or content provider. Yet, for many network users, the label of consumer falls short of accurately characterizing their relationship to online spaces. As Lessig (1999: 201-3) points out, people become members of online communities; they spend time there, build relationships and establish social capital. Given these circumstances, moving to another rule set can constitute a significant burden, and human dignity may demand that people have some opportunity to shape these spaces (1999: 217). Finally, private sector regulation has certain disadvantages compared with government regulation. Unlike government regulations which are transparent in the sense that they are publicly known and scrutinized, private sector regulations are often non-transparent. Private regulators can be less forthcoming and less accountable than their public counterparts (1999: 178-1). Private sector regulations are also less likely to achieve the kind of

coordinated and predictable network environment many business users seek. While these regulations may resolve some conflicts over information and communication, they may also work to achieve private goals, like the extension of control over information, that disregard public values. Even with private sector regulations in play, governments must be called on to resolve disputes that arise and to ensure that public values associated with law on intellectual property, privacy and speech rights are preserved.

National Government Regulation

National government regulation of communication policy can be set through national laws, legislation and rule-making bodies. Policy may be written into government constitutions, as is the case with speech rights protections in many countries. Newer constitutions may even include rights associated with data protection, such as the right to access and control personal information found in the constitutions of Hungary and South Africa. National legislation allows countries to systematically consider different policy options and to collectively choose the values animating their communication systems. National judiciaries can adjudicate conflicts that arise according to the legal traditions and customs of a given country.

National regulation allows for political choices to be made on a scale commensurate with citizen participation and with government accountability. National governments possess the tools to devise and enact policies that protect public values and interests (Reidenberg, 1997: 96). For example, as research on data protection shows, comprehensive national regulation is key to controlling abuses of information privacy (Lessig, 1999: 163; Peterson, 1995: 164; Reidenberg, 1997: 95). Governments also define the rules that govern communication markets and act as a line of defence against private actors who use contracts, technology or other methods to erode public rights in favour of private interests. Hence, Lessig (1999: 197-9) argues that governments must ultimately decide the degree of protection to give to values that are called into question by new technologies, as well as the appropriate balance between the rights and responsibilities of network users and network owners.

Notwithstanding the importance of the role governments can and in many cases should play in the governance of new communication technologies, of significant concern is their very ability to devise and enforce effective regulations. The main dilemma being faced by governments is how to respond to the growing technological and economic pressures brought about by global computer networks, while safeguarding important social and political goals and objectives. While there is no correct blueprint for what makes government oversight successful, there are certain themes and characteristics that will determine the effectiveness and credibility of national regulation. First, it is important to recognize that the development of national policies toward communication technologies is a political process, and the nature of the political system and the dominant political ideology will be key factors in determining the nature and substance of the policy process. Second, the strength of the legal system, including the nature of contractual laws and the property rights regime within a country, will be critical for providing stability and enforceability of national policies. Finally, the nature and effectiveness of safeguarding institutions like the judiciary and the regulatory agencies and instruments developed to oversee computer networks will be crucial to determining the effectiveness of the management of these new technologies. Many countries lack the institutional framework required to effectively develop and implement national policies and regulations.

Another challenge to national sovereignty stems from the ability of computer networks to facilitate interactions between people and organizations residing in different legal jurisdictions. Legal differences between jurisdictions cut across multiple areas of law, including privacy, freedom of expression and intellectual property, and are often related to the different culture, history and attitudes of specific countries (Kirby, 1983: 11–12). When communication crosses many jurisdictions and has effects in many places, including outside its country of origin, the authority of any one territorial sovereign to apply laws becomes questionable. The ability of computer network communication to regularly cross national borders makes it difficult for governments to determine whether an activity or actor falls within their jurisdiction (Rogerson and Thomas, 1998: 430). In addition, the architecture of global computer networks, with its possibilities of anonymity and decentralized communication, can frustrate governments' attempts to identify and locate people engaged in illegal behaviour (Lessig, 1999: 19). In effect, these features of global communication systems weaken the relationship between sovereignty and geographical territory (Gellman, 1997: 271; Kirby, 1983: 12; Reidenberg, 1977: 85). Sovereign power has traditionally depended on the ability to regulate behaviour within a particular geographic territory and on the implicit or explicit consent of those governed (Johnson and Post, 1997: 5–6; Perritt, 1997). These aspects of sovereignty do not readily translate into a context in which behaviour involves multiple jurisdictions.

Such behaviour is increasingly being seen as part of the emergence of a global or transnational civil society (Braman and Sreberny-Mohammadi, 1996; Calabrese, 1999; Frederick, 1993; Hamelink, 1991). Defining civil society as that part of collective social life that is free from both the power of the state and the market, these scholars document the impact of computer networks on growing transborder cooperation between various types of citizens groups especially in the areas of human rights, consumer protection, peace, gender equality, racial justice, environmental activism, consumer protection and workers' rights (Frederick, 1993: 285). These new social movements, non-governmental organizations (NGOs) and citizen advocacy groups have taken advantage of networks such as the Association for Progressive Communications (a network connecting dozens of smaller networks such as Econet, PeaceNet, ConflictNet, and WorkNet) to provide alternative mechanisms for citizens to support and participate in a variety of global activities. A number of scholars have documented the use of communication technologies in general and computer networks in particular to foster transnational progressive, alternative and radical social movements (Calabrese, 1999; Downing, 2001; Ford and Gil, 2001; Waterman, 1998). Though there is no doubt that computer networks have increased the scope for global civic engagement by citizens often in opposition to the positions taken by their own national governments, the long-term impact of both new technologies and new social movements on the overwhelming power of states and markets is as yet undetermined. It is important to note that though legal and jurisdictional conflicts may weaken the ability of nations to regulate, they do not render national regulation altogether ineffective. Nations can still assert control over network users, operators and infrastructures within their jurisdictions (Reidenberg, 1997: 99). For example, data havens, or countries which apply few or no rules to computer network communication, may not be able to shield computer network communication from the jurisdictional claims of other countries. Other nations may succeed in claiming jurisdiction over the network equipment and facilities which allow data havens to achieve connectivity outside their territory, or over the network users and operators who maintain citizenship outside the data haven (Garfinkel, 2000: 238–9).

While national government regulation is both unavoidable and, in many cases, desirable, it also has significant weak points. If not kept in check by a strong conception of public rights, governments may go beyond maintaining the structures which protect rights and instead become a prime violator of these rights. As we have noted, authoritarian regimes continue to limit the range of information and ideas that they want circulating within their civil societies and view computer networks as real threats to their ability to control the nature and flow of information within their societies. Further, for governments who fail to set national policy in a comprehensive or coordinated way, conflicting rules can hinder electronic commerce and create uncertainty for network users (Gellman, 1997: 256–7). Finally, national regulation alone cannot solve problems that arise when communication crosses numerous jurisdictions with conflicting policies. Such cases call for international and multilateral policy responses. Nevertheless, the authority of nations to regulate across jurisdictions remains precarious, and national rules will be harder to assert over global computer networks absent an amenable network architecture and international cooperation.

International and Multinational Regimes

Effective regulation of global computer networks may require the development or refinement of international instruments and institutions for communication policy-making. Many scholars point out the growing links between national and international policy. Domestic policies in one country can easily have effects on other countries (Michalski, 1989: 15; OECD, 1995: 4). Transnational laws, such as the European Union Privacy Directive, have ramifications for countries both inside and outside their jurisdiction (Kirby, 1983: 52; OECD, 1995: 5). And global transactions raise transnational problems whose solutions require international cooperation and coordination (Kirby, 1989: 167; Lessig, 1999: 205–6; Mayer-Schönberger and Foster, 1997: 243; OECD, 1997: 5). Proponents of the global marketplace argue that international organizations should be used to harmonize conflicting commercial regulations and set the rules of the global market game (Bitterman, 1989: 308; Cate, 1994; Glickman and Carney, 2000). From this perspective, international ICT policy is necessary to rationalize and refine global competition. From another angle, Lessig (1999: 205) argues that global ICTs open up new communicative spaces in which citizens from around the world can participate. As activity in such spaces increases, more questions are raised about our legal status there (1999: 226). For Lessig, clarification of the rights and responsibilities that adhere to international spaces and international life is essential for the fair and humane treatment of all network users and participants.

Conflicting legal rules have created pressures to harmonize regulation across countries or to find some method of coordinating or cooperating among multiple jurisdictions (Glickman and Carney, 2000: 195; Hudson, 1994: 141; Lessig, 1999: 192). In other words, nations must accept laws that apply across multiple jurisdictions or agree on a way to determine, in cases of conflict, whose laws apply. International cooperation could come in many forms. Countries could mandate the regulability of network architecture, and mutually agree to enforce one another's laws by instituting mandatory

electronic identification and zoning (Lessig, 1999: 207). Nations could cede some of their sovereign powers to third parties, such as international regulatory agencies, arbitrators or courts (Johnson and Post, 1997) – though, in this case, national legal systems would be necessary to implement, enforce or interpret third-party decisions (Perritt, 1997). Whichever mechanisms or methods are chosen, cooperation and coordination will require the establishment of international policy principles which serve as a common denominator between countries and/or which indicate the circumstances in which sovereignty should be deferred. Establishing these principles requires that nations come to some agreement on the political and economic goals of international society and international life (Alleyne, 1995: 17).

Global information flows, along with the jurisdictional limitations of nation-states, necessitate the development of transnational regimes for communication law and policy. The majority of communication and legal scholars support the idea that the protection of legitimate rights and interests on global communication systems requires international cooperation (Bitterman, 1989: 308; Blumenthal, 1999: 550; Cate, 1994; Glickman and Carney, 2000; Kirby, 1989: 167; Lessig, 1999: 205–6; Mayer-Schönberger and Foster, 1997: 243; OECD, 1997: 14; Thurow, 1997: 100; White House, 1997: 12). What these scholars disagree on, as our earlier discussions on speech rights, intellectual property and privacy suggest, are the normative goals of international cooperation and how these goals are best achieved. Since these perspectives have already been covered at length in earlier sections, our purpose here will be to briefly survey the current landscape of transnational treaties, agreements and organizations, along with the promises and pitfalls they hold for global media regulation.

Transnational communication regimes are nearly as old as the earliest global media, the mails and the telegraph. In 1849, multinational agreements were forged to rationalize the transnational use of the telegraph, and in 1865 20 countries signed a multilateral treaty that created the International Telegraph Union (ITU), an organization designed to set the rules for international telegraphy. Later renamed the International Telecommunication Union and incorporated into the United Nations, the ITU makes binding decisions regarding the technical regulation of telecommunications, including the protocols used for modems. In the case of the mails, the formation of an organization in 1874 that would eventually become the Universal Postal Union (UPU) heralded the beginning of a multinational postal regime. The UPU today encourages worldwide international cooperation and standardization of postal services (Bing et al., 1983: 133). Intellectual property law has been subject to multilateral copyright agreements since 1886 when several countries, including Japan, Germany, France and the United Kingdom, adopted the Berne Convention for the Protection of Literary and Artistic Works. The Berne Convention sought to establish international norms for intellectual property protection by requiring member states to accord the same intellectual property protections to nationals from other member states as exist for their own citizens, a concept known as the national treatment standard (Berne Convention, 1886; Braunstein, 1989; Goldstein, 1994: 183–4). To date, international rule-makings and organizations have centred largely on the areas of mails, telecommunications and intellectual property (Alleyne, 1995: 21).

The preponderance of international intellectual property agreements and organizations is due largely to the desire of intellectual property holding countries to protect their goods against piracy and fraud. International agreements generally aim to establish international intellectual property principles and to harmonize intellectual property laws (Bing et al., 1983: 134; Jussawalla, 1992, 4). In addition to the Berne Convention, intellectual property protections have been part of numerous bilateral and multilateral agreements, including the Universal Copyright Convention (UCC), the World Trade Organization (WTO), the North American Free Trade Agreement (NAFTA), the US–Canada Free Trade Agreement, and many others. Since 1967, the Berne Convention has been administered by the World Intellectual Property Organization (WIPO).[10] Another prominent international intellectual property agreement, the Universal Copyright Convention (UCC), was created in 1952 to impose minimum intellectual property requirements on the US, Latin America, Europe, Asia and Africa. Administered by the United Nations Educational, Scientific and Cultural Organization (UNESCO), the UCC acts as the smallest common denominator for intellectual property law at the international level (Bing et al., 1983: 79). In 1996, the Berne Convention was updated to include the WIPO Copyright Treaty and the WIPO Performances and Phonograms Treaty. These two treaties sought to strengthen intellectual property rules in relation to digital communication and to encourage online commerce (White House, 1997: 13). Another international intellectual property organization, the Internet Corporation for Assigned Names and Numbers (ICANN), was established in the late 1990s in order to administer Internet domain names and intellectual property addresses. Unlike all of the aforementioned organizations which are publicly funded and maintained, ICANN is a private, non-profit group.

Countries have been slower to forge transnational agreements on privacy issues and speech rights. Two transnational organizations, the Organization for Economic Cooperation and Development (OECD) and the Council of Europe, have devised privacy guidelines for transnational information flows based on fair information practices (Gellman, 1997: 265). OECD and Council of Europe guidelines have become the foundation for numerous countries' privacy policies. In addition, the European Union leads the world in promoting international cooperation and harmonization of privacy policies. The EU Privacy Directive, like other EU Directives, formulates centralized policy objectives and standards at the European level and asks EU member states to implement these in their respective nations. Although Directives do not create transnational rights that citizens can draw on directly, they do allow member countries to implement uniform rules in such areas as data protection and intellectual property (Reidenberg, 1997: 94–5). In the case of the Privacy Directive, the EU has been able to coordinate information policy among its member nations and to pressure many nations outside the EU to conform to higher privacy standards. Finally, several international rights covenants exist which include speech rights clauses, convenants such as the Universal Declaration of Human Rights, the International Covenant on Civil and Political Rights, and the (European) Convention for the Protection of Human Rights (Cate, 1994: 470). These agreements declare the intentions of their signatories to uphold the values of freedom of expression and information.

International and multinational agreements and organizations exist in various states of development in countries across the world, with intellectual property rights regimes tending to be more developed, speech rights less so, and privacy rights somewhere in between. While these efforts represent necessary first steps in ensuring global communication rights regimes that can keep pace with global communication processes, they also highlight several issues that will need to be addressed if nations are to pursue more equitable international policies. These issues include how such regimes will affect included and excluded countries, how representative they are of the world's citizens and countries, and how their rules will be coordinated, monitored and enforced. First, multinational regimes are prone to inclusion and exclusion problems. As we saw with the EU data protection rules and some intellectual property rules, excluded countries that did not ascribe to an agreement's norms and standards felt pressured to conform nevertheless. This issue is particularly pronounced for developing countries who are pressured to adhere to restrictive intellectual property rights that do little to promote the growth of knowledge and information in their home countries. Conversely, countries that are party to these agreements have difficulty protecting their rights in outside territories. Protecting rights globally may require some uniform standards that all countries can agree to, but which leave room for flexibility and experimentation. As Burk (1997: 226, 231) suggests, international agreements should create minimum standards of protection which at the same time permit innovation and variation. One example of such flexibility is the inclusion of a global 'fair use' clause in the Berne Convention and UCC. Supported by African, Asian and Latin American countries, this clause allows for the circulation of copyrighted works for the purposes of teaching, scholarship or research if member countries obtain licences and provide reasonable remuneration (Goldstein, 1994: 187–9).

A second issue, and one to which less attention has been paid, concerns the representative aspects of international regimes. Ideally, international regimes should allow participating countries to coordinate law and policy so as to further the common good for all involved and should be representative of, and accountable to, those who fall under their regulations. In practice, these regimes may be unduly affected by differentials in political and economic power so that the stronger powers dominate the rule-making and policy processes (Alleyne, 1995: 152). Representation may also turn out to be a problematic aspect of private, non-profit regulatory bodies, such as ICANN. ICANN is responsible for assigning name and address spaces on the Internet, essentially delegating property rights to specific individuals. While Glickman and Carney (2000: 196) laud ICANN as a new model of international regulation, Mueller (1999: 517, 519) argues that ICANN's private status allowed it to avoid public input and scrutiny during its formation and led ultimately to public demands for procedural safeguards like those applying to government organizations. For Mueller (1999), the rhetoric of private regulation simply masks a policy process in which valuable rights and assets are allocated without adequate public representation and accountability. Lastly, international regimes may need to be consolidated, clarified or made more effective. At present, there are numerous organizations, treaties and agreements regulating various aspects of intellectual property, privacy and speech rights law. For example, in the area of intellectual property, Kirby (1983: 49) notes that there are a number of pre-existing organizations capable of dealing with intellectual property issues, and Jussawalla (1992: 56) sees a need to specify relations between TRIPS, WIPO and the UCC. In addition, regimes can only be effective to the extent that they monitor and enforce the principles and rules they set forth. Yet, the link between some regimes and mechanisms for monitoring or enforcing policy is weak. For example, while many international rights covenants protect speech rights, none sponsors organizations which monitor speech rights violations or enforce speech rights protections.

INTERNATIONAL POLICY PRINCIPLES

Arriving at internationally accepted principles will be a formidable task. One method might be for nations to examine the principles contained in existing policy agreements. Yet, while Bing et al. (1983: 81) review contemporary policy instruments for indications of global communications principles, they also suggest that relying on established principles is insufficient. Global communication systems raise new and unanswered questions. In some cases decision-makers may be able to apply old principles in a new context, but in others new principles will have to be developed in accord with social, cultural and political values. In this section, we briefly lay out some suggested policy principles for intellectual property, privacy and speech rights.

In the area of intellectual property, nations must determine what principles will define the public use and availability of information and knowledge. Will fair use and first-sale principles be extended into global communication systems, or will these principles be swept away by technological design, legal means or industry practices? What length of time should copyright holders enjoy monopoly rights over intellectual property, and at what point does this monopoly become a detriment to society? Scholars suggest that principles must protect the fundamental philosophical aim of intellectual property law, the promotion and dissemination of knowledge and creativity throughout society (Halbert, 1999; Lessig, 1999; Thurow, 1997). Halbert (1999: 158) argues that intellectual property rules should strike a balance between the public good and private gain; intellectual property holders should be able to profit from their work, but not at the expense of the greater common good. Lessig (1999: 141) and Thurow (1997: 102) maintain that intellectual property principles should effectively demarcate public from private knowledge and establish a public domain or intellectual commons in which knowledge and information are broadly accessible. This public domain might include basic scientific knowledge (Thurow, 1997: 102), computer software code which enacts basic functions or processes (Jussawalla, 1992: 112), and cultural symbols that have already duly profited their intellectual property holders (Halbert, 1999).

Privacy principles, defining the values associated with the collection and use of personal information, have already been developed in numerous countries. Many of these countries have data protection or information privacy laws which are based on guidelines set forth by the OECD and the Council of Europe and on general principles of fair information practices (Council of Europe, 1981; Gandy, 1993: 7; Gellman, 1997: 265; Global Internet Liberty Campaign, 1998; OECD, 1981). These principles generally favour the values of openness and transparency in information collection and processing. Among the principles set forth on privacy are that individuals should have the right to control their own data, to have data about them collected fairly and lawfully, to opt into (rather than out of) data processing and sharing, to access and correct inaccurate data about themselves, and to limit secondary uses of personal data (Branscomb, 1994: 24; Global Internet Liberty Campaign, 1998; Hausman, 1994: 138; Lessig, 1999: 156; Maxeiner, 1995: 99; OECD, 1997: 14; Peterson, 1995: 184). In addition, countries should require data collectors to disclose their information and privacy practices, impose penalties on those who fail to comply with privacy rules, and assign a government agency the task of monitoring and enforcing privacy policy (EU Data Protection Directive, 1995; Green et al., 2000: 84; OECD, 1981).

Speech rights principles cover access to communication systems, resources and content. Some scholars, such as Hudson (1994: 137) and Melody (1990: 30), argue that universal access must be a core principle of communication policy. Melody (1990) favours the application of universal service principles to all communication systems that constitute essential facilities. The concept of universal service mandates non-discriminatory access to, and pricing of, communication systems and services. This concept is also favoured by Human Rights Watch (1999: 5, 7) as a means of preventing system gatekeepers and owners from charging monopoly prices for their services, giving special treatment to favoured content and service providers, or discriminating among those who wish to interconnect with their systems. Analysts also suggest that centralized content censorship should be eschewed. For speech rights absolutists, the government is never justified in regulating speech. For others, such as the OECD (1997: 15), governments must promote the free flow of information in a way that respects both speech and privacy rights. One principle which seeks to contain unwelcome government content censorship, put forth by Samorski et al. (1997: 163) and Human Rights Watch (1999: 4), holds that control over content should, whenever possible, be delegated to end users. Receiver-based software allows individual users to set their own parameters for filtering unwanted content and could reduce pressures on service providers to act as content gatekeepers. Human Rights Watch (1999: 6) further suggests that government surveillance be subject to due process and judicial supervision so that it doesn't unduly infringe on individuals' privacy or civil rights. Additional speech rights principles have been set out in UNESCO's new world information and communication order (NWICO) initiative, which advocates a plurality of information sources, freedom and responsibility of communication workers, and the rights of all citizens to participate

in international information exchanges and communication processes (Alleyne, 1995: 123).

CONCLUSION

New media, and the practices and institutions surrounding them, pose significant challenges to regulatory regimes around the world. National control over communication systems is complicated by technologies whose reach and effect extends beyond the jurisdictional boundaries of nation-states. Many governments fear the loss of political and economic sovereignty, others the loss of cultural identity. New media highlight a gap that now exists between life and governance; people can interact in supranational or global arenas that as of yet have no definitive mode of governance. Global networks offer a vast array of options to people, corporations and organizations for the pursuit of political, economic and cultural activities. Nations who wish to determine the goals and values that animate global media systems must pursue effective legal and legislative frameworks both nationally and internationally. In addition to transgressing jurisdictional boundaries, new media also test the conceptual and definitional boundaries of policy regimes affecting intellectual property, privacy and speech rights. Social conflicts in each of these areas demand policy responses that demarcate public rights, set behavioural standards and curtail abusive practices. New global media raise fundamental questions and concerns about who will control communication systems and the terms and conditions of access to them. These questions and concerns cannot be addressed simply by turning to legal precedent or technological solutions. Rather, nations must declare the principles that will define or re-define the social values and purposes of media systems in today's world.

Communication and legal scholars have been charting and surveying shifts in the regulatory landscape, assessing these shifts in normative terms, and seeking workable models of global media regulation. This scholarship tracks the tremors that occur as technologies, processes of commodification or private sector regulation collide with national norms, values and practices. Communication scholars identify the characteristics and practices accompanying new technologies, examine their social and political effects, and look for indications of whether these technologies will aid or abate social control. Legal scholars observe the conflicts new technologies are already creating in national and international life and explore various tools and mechanisms that might reconcile national policy goals with jurisdictional concerns.

Monitoring and assessing the changing landscape of communication systems is a critical task in this era of rapid technological and industrial change. Only by doing so can we determine how these systems interact with global political economic processes, how their structures are being configured and developed, and how national and international policy-makers can intervene to protect socially determined goals. Global media systems like the Internet raise a classic problem of political organization. As the effects and consequences of global technology extend beyond the mechanisms for governing them, we must investigate the terms under which national and international governance mechanisms can claim to legitimately represent the world's nations and citizenry. Scholars of political communication and the philosophy of communication should investigate the institutional and communicative resources and requirements necessary for global governance. Scholars must also examine the real practices and effects of existing national and international policy instruments and institutions. Closer study of these areas will fill the gaps that currently exist in our knowledge of how new media are affecting the regulatory landscape and help point the way towards sensible, humane and representative global communications policy.

NOTES

1 An example of such research can be found in Johnson and Post (1997), who argue that global networks constitute their own spaces with their own sovereignty. These authors underplay the fact that those who communicate over ICTs are already subject to real-world sovereigns who have an obligation to protect their citizens.

2 Under these treaties, the following works may be protected: (1) both unpublished and published works of an author who is a national or resident of a country that is a member of these treaties; or (2) published works, with permission, of an author who is not a national or resident of a country that is a member of these treaties.

3 For more details on the Directive, see the Directive on the Protection of Individuals with Regard to the Processing of Personal Data and on the Free Movement of Such Data. For a concise summary of the Directive's provisions, see Rosenoer (1997: 156–60).

4 For example, the Privacy Act of 1974 (5 U.S.C. § 552a) mandates limited privacy protections for government-maintained databases, including the right of individuals to review and correct personal information stored in government records. The rules do not apply to privately held databases.

5 Although the US continues to advocate self-regulation and narrow sectoral rules, numerous analysts have deemed the US approach a failure (Branscomb, 1994; Gellman, 1997; Global Internet Liberty Campaign, 1998; Green et al., 2000; *The Economist*, 1999). US privacy protections are a patchwork of inconsistent, weak and inadequately enforced rules which leave US citizens with no substantive protections for personal information. No federal agency oversees or enforces data protection in the US, and support for such rules among the business community is weak (Gellman, 1997: 267, 274; Mitchener, 2000).

6 Under the agreement, any organization must offer individuals the opportunity to choose (opt out) whether and how personal information they provide is used or disclosed to third parties. For sensitive information (i.e. personal information about medical or health conditions, racial or ethnic origin, political opinions, religious or philosophical beliefs, trade union membership or information specifying the sex life of the individual) they must be given affirmative or explicit (opt in) choice if the information is to be used for a purpose other than those for which it was originally collected. Organizations are required to take reasonable precautions to protect information from loss, misuse and unauthorized access, disclosure, alteration and destruction and to take reasonable steps to ensure individuals have access to personal information about them and are able to correct, amend or delete that information where it is inaccurate.

7 This section focuses on speech rights restrictions posed by national governments. Freedom of expression and access to communication resources can also be restricted by non-governmental actors, such as system operators or network infrastructure owners (Office of Technology Assessment, 1990: 169). While this type of censorship is rare and ineffective at present owing to the competitive market for network access and services and the current open network architecture, it may figure more prominently in the future (Lessig, 1999: 167). Although not our focus here, we believe that any private sector developments which threaten freedom of expression should be closely examined by policy-makers and corrected when necessary.

8 Although the US rules were struck down in a resulting Supreme Court case, the US Congress continues to pursue legislation that will restrict the availability of pornography on the Internet. For details on the Supreme Court case, see Reno (1997).

9 For example, while markets systems have as their primary goal the efficient allocation of resources, efficiency is only one value among many that most countries would apply to communication systems. Markets and other models of regulation must be evaluated against the range of goals which countries aim to achieve, including those related to privacy, access and speech rights.

10 WIPO also helps countries create and reform intellectual property rules, comply with international intellectual property treaties, and encourage more specialists to enter the intellectual property field (Alleyne, 1995: 30). In the 1990s, WIPO took on the additional role of investigating Internet domain name trademark conflicts, making recommendations on how to resolve top-level domain disputes, and otherwise managing the international domain name trademark regime (Mueller, 1999: 505–6).

REFERENCES

Abrahamson, David (1998) 'The visible hand: money, markets, and media evolution', *Journalism and Mass Communication Quarterly*, 75 (1): 14–18.

Alleyne, Mark D. (1995) *International Power and International Communication*. New York: St Martin's Press.

Araki, Toshihiro (1989) 'Information technology and legal issues', in Meheroo Jussawalla, Tadayuki Okuma and Toshihiro Araki (eds), *Information Technology and Global Interdependence*. New York: Greenwood. pp. 193–6.

Associated Press (2000) 'French court says Yahoo! broke racial law', *New York Times*, 23 May (online).

Babe, Robert E. (1995) *Communication and the Transformation of Economics: Essays in Information, Public Policy, and Political Economy*. Boulder, CO: Westview.

Barber, Benjamin R. (1984) *Strong Democracy: Participatory Politics for a New Age*. Berkeley, CA: University of California Press.

Barron, Sandy (2000) 'Myanmar works hard to keep the Internet out', *New York Times*, 14 July (online).

Berne Convention (1886) Berne Convention for the Protection of Literary and Artistic Works, 9 September 1886, 828 U.N.T.S. 221 (1972).

Besser, Howard (1999) 'Will copyright protect the public interest?', *Peace Review*, 11 (1): 25–31.

Bettig, Ronald V. (1992) 'Critical perspectives on the history and philosophy of copyright', *Critical Studies in Mass Communication*, 9 (2): 131–55.

Bettig, Ronald V. (1997) 'The enclosure of cyberspace', *Critical Studies in Mass Communication*, 14 (2): 138–57.

Bing, J., Forsberg, P. and Nygaard, E. (1983) 'Legal problems related to transborder data flows', in Organization for Economic Cooperation and Development (ed.), *An Exploration of Legal Issues in Information and Communication Technologies*, 8. Paris: OECD. pp. 59–135.

Bitterman, Mary G.F. (1989) 'Conclusions from TIDE II', in Meheroo Jussawalla, Tadayuki Okuma and Toshihiro Araki (eds), *Information Technology and Global Interdependence*. New York: Greenwood. pp. 307–8.

Blumenthal, Marjory S. (1999) 'The politics and policies of enhancing trustworthiness for information systems', *Communication Law and Policy*, 4 (4): 513–55.

Boyle, James (1997) *Shamans, Software, and Spleens: Law and the Construction of the Information Society*. Cambridge, MA: Harvard University Press.

Braman, Sandra and Sreberny-Mohammadi, Annebelle (1996) *Communication and Transnational Civil Society*. Creskill, NJ: Hampton.

Branscomb, Anne Wells (1994) *Who Owns Information? From Privacy to Public Access*. New York: Basic.

Braunstein, Yale M. (1989) 'Economics on intellectual property rights in the international arena', in Meheroo Jussawalla, Tadayuki Okuma and Toshihiro Araki (eds),

Information Technology and Global Interdependence. New York: Greenwood. pp. 183–92.

Burk, Dan L. (1997) 'The market for digital piracy', in Brian Kahin and Charles Nesson (eds), *Borders in Cyberspace: Information Policy and the Global Information Infrastructure*. Cambridge, MA: MIT Press. pp. 205–34.

Calabrese, Andrew (1999) 'Communication and the end of sovereignty', *Info*, 1 (4): 313–26.

Carey, James W. (1998) 'The Internet and the end of the national communication system: uncertain predictions of an uncertain future', *Journalism and Mass Communication Quarterly*, 75 (1): 23–34.

Cate, Fred H. (1994) 'Global information policymaking and domestic law', *Indiana Journal of Global Legal Studies*, 1 (2): 467–87.

Cate, Fred H. (1995) 'The First Amendment and the national information infrastructure', *Wake Forest Law Review*, 30 (1): 1–50.

Cochran, Wendell (1996) 'Computers, privacy, and journalists: a suggested code of information practices', *Journal of Mass Media Ethics*, 11 (4): 210–22.

Council of Europe (1981) Convention for the Protection of Individuals with Regard to the Automatic Processing of Personal Data, ETS No. 108, Strasburg.

Delaney, Kevin J. (2000) 'Yahoo! returns to French court to address Nazi paraphernalia', *Wall Street Journal*, 11 August: B10.

Demac, Donna A. (1994) 'Multimedia and intellectual property rights', *Media Studies Journal*, 8 (1): 59–63.

Dewey, John (1954) *The Public and its Problems* (1927). Athens, OH: Ohio University Press.

Downing, John D.H. (2001) *Radical Media: Rebellious Communication and Social Movements*. Thousand Oaks, CA: Sage.

Entman, Robert (1989) *Democracy without Citizens*. New York: Oxford University Press.

Enzensberger, Hans Magnus (1974) *The Consciousness Industry*. New York: Seabury.

EU Data Protection Directive (1995) Directive 95/46/EC of the European Parliament and of the Council of 24 October 1995 on the Protection of Individuals with Regard to the Processing of Personal Data and the Free Movement of Such Data. Available at: http://www.privacy.org/pi/intl_orgs/ec/final_EU_Data_Protection.html.

Feemster, Ron (2000) 'When libraries faced the future', *University Business*, February. Available at: http://www.universitybusiness.com/0002/library.html.

Ford, Tamara V. and Gil, Genève (2001) 'Radical Internet use', in John D.H. Downing (ed.), *Radical Media: Rebellious Communication and Social Movements*. Thousand Oaks, CA: Sage. pp. 201–34.

Frederick, Howard (1993) 'Networks and emergence of global civil society', in Linda M. Harasim (ed.), *Global Networks: Computers and International Communication*. Cambridge, MA: MIT Press. pp. 283–95.

Froomkin, A. Michael (1997) 'The Internet as a source of regulatory arbitrage', in Brian Kahin and Charles Nesson (eds), *Borders in Cyberspace: Information*

Policy and the Global Information Infrastructure. Cambridge, MA: MIT Press. pp. 129–63.

Gandy, Oscar H. (1993) 'Toward a political economy of personal information', *Critical Studies in Mass Communication*, 10: 70–97.

Garfinkel, Simson (2000) 'Welcome to Sealand. Now bugger off', *Wired*, July: 230–9.

Gellman, Robert (1997) 'Conflict and overlap in privacy regulation: national, international, and private', in Brian Kahin and Charles Nesson (eds), *Borders in Cyberspace: Information Policy and the Global Information Infrastructure.* Cambridge, MA: MIT Press. pp. 255–82.

Gilpin, Robert (1987) *The Political Economy of International Relations.* Princeton, NJ: Princeton University Press.

Glickman, Howard and Carney, Dan (2000) 'Watching over the World Wide Web', *Business Week*, 28 August: 195–6.

Global Internet Liberty Campaign (1998) *Privacy and Human Rights: an International Survey of Privacy Laws and Practice.* Available at: http://www.gilc.org/privacy/survey/intro.html.

Goldstein, Paul (1994) *Copyright's Highway: the Law and Lore of Copyright from Gutenberg to the Celestial Jukebox.* New York: Hill & Wang.

Green, H., France, M., Stepanek, M. and Borrus, A. (2000) 'Online privacy: it's time for rules in Wonderland', *Business Week*, 20 March: 83–8, 92.

Halbert, Debora J. (1999) *Intellectual Property in the Information Age.* Westport, CT: Quorum.

Hamelink, Cees (1991) *Communication: the Most Violated Human Right.* Stockholm: Inter Press Service Dispatch.

Hausman, Carl (1994) 'Information age ethics: privacy ground rules for navigating in cyberspace', *Journal of Mass Media Ethics*, 9 (3): 135–44.

Hibbert, Bill (1999) 'Regulation of electronic publishing and commerce', *Info*, 1 (5): 393–404.

Hilton, George W. (1972) 'The basic behavior of regulatory commissions', *American Economic Review*, 62 (2): 47–54.

Hirschman, Albert O. (1986) *Rival Views of Market Society and Other Recent Essays.* New York: Viking.

Hudson, Heather (1994) 'Toward universal access to information', *Media Studies Journal*, 8 (1): 137–42.

Human Rights Watch (1999) *The Internet in the Mideast and North Africa: Free Expression and Censorship.* New York: Human Rights Watch.

Hunter, Christopher D. and Herbeck, Dale (1999) 'From LaMacchia to the No Electronic Theft Act: criminal copyright infringement and the freedom of expression'. Paper presented at the Annual Meeting of the International Communication Association, San Francisco, CA.

International Covenant on Civil and Political Rights (1966), G.A. Res. 2200, U.N. GAOR, 21st Sess., Supp. No. 16, at 52, U.N. Doc. A/6316, art. 19.

Jackson, Margaret (1998) 'Keeping secrets: international developments to protect undisclosed business information and trade secrets', *Information, Communication & Society*, 1 (4): 467–87.

Johnson, David R. and Post, David G. (1997) 'The rise of law on the global network', in Brian Kahin and Charles Nesson (eds), *Borders in Cyberspace: Information Policy and the Global Information Infrastructure.* Cambridge, MA: MIT Press. pp. 3–47.

Johnson, J.T. (1994) 'The private I, you, they', *Journal of Mass Media Ethics*, 9 (4): 223–8.

Jussawalla, Meheroo (1992) *The Economics of Intellectual Property in a World without Frontiers.* New York: Greenwood.

Kahin, Brian and Nesson, Charles (1997) 'Preface', in Brian Kahin and Charles Nesson (eds), *Borders in Cyberspace: Information Policy and the Global Information Infrastructure.* Cambridge, MA: MIT Press. pp. vii–xi.

Kahn, Alfred E. (1988) *The Economics of Regulation: Principles and Institutions.* Cambridge, MA: MIT Press.

Kavanaugh, Andrea L. (1998) *The Social Control of Technology in North Africa.* Westport, CT: Praeger.

Kindleberger, Charles P. (1978) *International Economics*, 6th edn (1st edn 1958). Homewood, IL: Irwin.

Kirby, Michael D. (1983) 'Legal aspects of information technology', in Organization for Economic Cooperation and Development (ed.), *An Exploration of Legal Issues in Information and Communication Technologies*, 8. Paris: OECD. pp. 9–57.

Kirby, Michael D. (1989) 'Informatics and democratic society: beyond the Tokyo Summit', in Meheroo Jussawalla, Tadayuki Okuma and Toshihiro Araki (eds), *Information Technology and Global Interdependence.* New York: Greenwood. pp. 157–71.

Krasner, Stephen D. (1991) 'Global communications and national power: life on the Pareto optimal curve', *World Politics*, 43 (3): 336–66.

Labunski, Richard (1997) 'The First Amendment at the crossroads: free expression and new media technology', *Communication Law and Policy*, 2 (2): 165–212.

Lessig, Lawrence (1999) *Code and Other Laws of Cyberspace.* New York: Basic.

Louveaux, S., Salaün, A. and Poullet, Y. (1999) 'User protection in cyberspace', *Info*, 1 (6): 521–37.

MacAvoy, Paul W. (1979) *The Regulated Industries and the Economy.* New York: Norton.

Maxeiner, James R. (1995) 'Freedom of information and the EU Data Protection Directive', *Federal Communications Law Journal*, 48 (1): 93–104.

May, Christopher (1998) 'Capital, knowledge and ownership', *Information, Communication & Society*, 1 (3): 246–69.

Mayer-Schönberger, Viktor and Foster, Teree E. (1997) 'A regulatory web: free speech and the global information infrastructure', in Brian Kahin and Charles Nesson (eds), *Borders in Cyberspace: Information Policy and the Global Information Infrastructure.* Cambridge, MA: MIT Press. pp. 235–54.

McCarthy, Terry (2000) 'China dot now', *Time*, 28 February: 16–23.

Melody, William H. (1990) 'Communication policy in the global information economy: whither the public interest?', in Marjorie Ferguson (ed.), *Public Communication: the New Imperatives*. Newbury Park, CA: Sage. pp. 16–39.

Mensch, Elizabeth (1990) 'The history of mainstream legal thought', in David Kairys (ed.), *The Politics of Law: a Progressive Critique*. New York: Pantheon. pp. 13–37.

Michalski, Wolfgang (1989) 'Advanced information technologies: challenges and opportunities', in Meheroo Jussawalla, Tadayuki Okuma and Toshihiro Araki (eds), *Information Technology and Global Interdependence*. New York: Greenwood. pp. 9–18.

Michelman, Frank I. (1987) 'Possession vs. distribution in the constitutional idea of property', *Iowa Law Review*, 72: 1319–50.

Mitchener, Brandon (2000) 'EU privacy rules carry a cost', *Wall Street Journal*, 14–15 April: 29, 32.

Morris, Merrill and Ogan, Christine (1996) 'The Internet as mass medium', *Journal of Communication*, 46 (1): 39–50.

Mosco, Vincent (1988) 'Toward a theory of the state and telecommunications policy', *Journal of Communication*, 38: 107–25.

Mosco, Vincent (1989) *The Pay-per Society: Computers and Communication in the Information Age*. Norwood, NJ: Ablex.

Mueller, Milton (1999) 'ICANN and Internet governance: sorting through the debris of "self-regulation"', *Info*, 1 (6): 497–520.

Murphy, Jamie (1999) 'Australia passes law on limiting the Internet', *New York Times*, 1 July (online).

Office of Technology Assessment (1990) *Critical Connections: Communications for the Future*. Washington, DC: US Government Printing Office.

OECD (1981) *Guidelines Governing the Protection of Privacy and Transborder Data Flows of Personal Data*. Paris: Organization for Economic Cooperation and Development.

OECD (1995) *Information Technology Policies: Organizational Structure in Member Countries*, 3 (43). Paris: Organization for Economic Cooperation and Development.

OECD (1997) *Global Information Infrastructure – Global Information Society (GII–GIS): Policy Recommendations for Action*, 81 (5). Paris: Organization for Economic Cooperation and Development.

Perritt, Henry H., Jr (1997) 'Jurisdiction in cyberspace: the role of intermediaries', in Brian Kahin and Charles Nesson (eds), *Borders in Cyberspace: Information Policy and the Global Information Infrastructure*. Cambridge, MA: MIT Press. pp. 164–202.

Peterson, Sandra Byrd (1995) 'Your life as an open book: has technology rendered personal privacy virtually obsolete?', *Federal Communications Law Journal*, 48 (1): 163–86.

Plotkin, Adam S. (1996) 'The First Amendment and democracy: the challenge of new technology', *Journal of Mass Media Ethics*, 11 (4): 236–45.

Pool, Ithiel de Sola (1983) *Technologies of Freedom*. Cambridge, MA: Harvard University Press.

Privacy Act (1974) 5 U.S.C. § 552a.

Proceedings of the Annenberg Washington Program Panel One (1995) 'Information issues: intellectual property, privacy, integrity, interoperability, and the economics of information', *Federal Communications Law Journal*, 48 (1): 5–55.

Proceedings of the Annenberg Washington Program Panel Two (1995) 'Information policy making', *Federal Communications Law Journal*, 48 (1): 57–91.

Quaterman, John S. (1990) *The Matrix: Computer Networks and Conferencing Systems Worldwide*. Bedford, MA: Digital.

Reidenberg, Joel R. (1997) 'Governing networks and rule-making in cyberspace', in Brian Kahin and Charles Nesson (eds), *Borders in Cyberspace: Information Policy and the Global Information Infrastructure*. Cambridge, MA: MIT Press. pp. 84–105.

Reno (1997) *Reno, Attorney General of the United States, et al. v. American Civil Liberties Union et al.*, 521 U.S. 844.

Robinson, Peter (1989) 'Information technology and the relationship among OECD countries', in Meheroo Jussawalla, Tadayuki Okuma and Toshihiro Araki (eds), *Information Technology and Global Interdependence*. New York: Greenwood. pp. 40–6.

Rogerson, Kenneth S. and Thomas, G. Dale (1998) 'Internet regulation process model: the effect of societies, communities, and governments', *Political Communication*, 15 (4): 427–44.

Rosenoer, Jonathan (1997) *CyberLaw: the Law of the Internet*. New York: Springer.

Rosenthal, Elizabeth (2000) 'China issues rules to limit e-mail and web content', *New York Times*, 27 January: A1.

Rucinski, Dianne (1991) 'The centrality of reciprocity to communication and democracy', *Critical Studies in Mass Communication*, 9 (2): 184–94.

Samorski, Jan H., Huffman, John L. and Trauth, Denise M. (1997) 'The V-chip and cyber cops: technology vs. regulation', *Communication Law and Policy*, 2 (1): 143–64.

Schiller, Dan (1999) *Digital Capitalism: Networking the Global Market System*. Cambridge, MA: MIT Press.

Schneider, Howard (2000) 'Syria advances cautiously into the online age', *Washington Post*, 27 April: A1.

Sell, Susan K. (1995) 'The origins of a trade-based approach to intellectual protection: the role of industry organizations', *Science Communication*, 17 (2): 163–85.

Smith, Craig (2000) 'Tough new rules don't faze Chinese Internet start-ups', *New York Times*, 4 October: C2.

Streeter, Thomas (1996) *Selling the Air: a Critique of the Policy of Commercial Broadcasting in the United States*. Chicago: University of Chicago Press.

Taubman, Geoffrey (1998) 'A not-so World Wide Web: the Internet, China, and the challenges to nondemocratic rule', *Political Communication*, 15 (2): 255–72.

The Economist (1999) 'The end of privacy', *The Economist*, 1 May: 15, 21–3.

Thurow, Lester C. (1997) 'Needed: a new system of intellectual property rights', *Harvard Business Review*, September–October: 95–103.

Universal Declaration of Human Rights (1948) G.A. Res. 217 (III), U.N. Doc. A/810, art. 19.

Waltz, K. (1979) *Theory of International Politics*. Reading, MA: Addison-Wesley.

Waterman, Peter (1998) *Globalization, Social Movements and the New Internationalism*. London: Mansell.

Westin, Alan F. (1967) *Privacy and Freedom*. New York: Atheneum.

Wheeler, Deborah L. (1998) 'Global culture or culture clash: new information technologies in the Islamic world – a view from Kuwait', *Communication Research*, 25 (4): 359–76.

White House (1997) 'A framework for global electronic commerce'. 1 July.

Wriston, Walter B. (1994) 'The inevitable global conversation', *Media Studies Journal*, 8 (1): 17–25.

Zhao, Yuezhi (2000) 'Caught in the web: the public interest and the battle for control of China's information superhighway', *Info*, 2 (1): 41–66.

25

About Scarcities and Intermediaries: the Regulatory Paradigm Shift of Digital Content Reviewed

STEFAAN G. VERHULST

Much discussion about the digitalization of content and the consequent convergence of broadcasting, telecommunications and IT suggests that digitalization challenges existing communications regulation (Gillett and Vogelsang, 1999; Verhulst and Marsden, 1999; Verhulst et al., 1999). Familiar and traditional regulatory models are suddenly questioned and brought into conflict (Hitchens, 1997). This chapter starts from the assumption that the search for appropriate regulatory and policy responses necessary as a result of the policy vacuum created by new technologies is leading to a 'paradigm shift', in Thomas Kuhn's traditional sense of the word.[1] Kuhn describes the uncertainty and chaotic process of changing from one world view to another that occurs during a paradigm shift. In his definition, as the new paradigm emerges, it subsumes the previous paradigm and replaces it with one that answers more questions and encompasses more of the consensus of the community.[2] This chapter demonstrates the paradigm shift in content regulation and observes that the existing laws that serve as the regulatory framework to control content are coming under increasing scrutiny.

In response to this scrutiny, scholars, governments and industry worldwide have been searching for a new regulatory paradigm (Longstaff, 2000). The European Commission released its Green Paper on the regulatory implications of convergence as early as December 1997, consultations were finalized late 1999 and consequent Directives were drafted in 2000. In March 1998, the Organization for Economic Cooperation and Development (OECD) hosted a Roundtable on Communications Convergence. The United Kingdom Green Paper on convergence followed in July 1998 and a White Paper was released at the end of 2000. During the same period a number of other European countries, the USA, Canada and Australia conducted reviews and consultations on the most appropriate regulatory regime for the introduction of digital television. Japan announced a review of the impact of convergence on communication regulations and the Productivity Commission in Australia published the results of its review of broadcasting regulation in early 2000.

All these efforts indicate first that, despite the ongoing debate about the diminishing role of regulation in a converged world, the proposed new paradigm is more one of reregulation and self-regulation than deregulation (Prosser, 1997: Chapter 10). Second, the paradigm shift is expected to be evolutionary. Television services will merge further with online services when telecommunication networks are sufficiently advanced.[3] Uncertainty over the speed of change makes it difficult for governments and policy-makers to determine the priority that should be given to reform. Doing nothing may retard market developments. Moving too soon may mean that decisions are made with too little information.

Third, there remain strong geographical differences in thinking about regulation. Commercial television regulation in Europe and the US is historically divergent and as a result the debate about a possible paradigm shift is different. In Europe, the overriding political importance ascribed to the medium resulted in strict prior regulation of both content and structure. In the US, First Amendment protection of free speech has led to an artificial obsession with exclusively structural controls, though government has contrived to ensure similar outcomes to those in Europe.

Finally, as a result of the evolutionary character, there are two distinct service categories and regulatory responses within the new communications platforms. The first are TV-type services that require live full motion video (high bandwidth) delivered to the home. The second are online Internet-type services that require interactivity and medium bandwidth delivered to the home. Differences between the TV-type approach and the online interactive Internet-type approach can be noticed in the functions of the applications such as entertainment and shopping versus communication and information, the target users such as consumers at home and interest groups, and data types such as audio/video versus text/programmes. Differences can also be noticed in the terminal devices, such as the differences between low-resolution TV sets and PC/NC, in the geographic scope such as between national, regional and global, and between distribution that is terrestrial, over cable or over the telephone.

Access ethics that determine whether the system will be closed, open or universal, economic orientation that governs whether information is shared or sold, and the rollout schedule that shows the maturity level of the situation, also illustrate differences between the TV-type approaches and the online Internet-type approaches (Press, 1994). The differences are slowly disappearing as convergence is becoming more and more real. However, they remain important for policy-makers – not least because the divergent policy and regulatory perspectives (not to mention rivalry) which the broadcasting and telecommunications regulatory bodies bring to the task make choosing or designing regulatory tools suitable for convergence extremely difficult.

Within those parameters, this chapter aims to outline the so-called paradigm shift in traditional means of controlling content, often labelled 'negative regulation'[4] (Waverman, 2000). Digitalization clearly affects all areas of communications policy, and all sectoral regulations involved, yet this chapter will mainly focus on audiovisual content as the area where content policies and regulations are most heavily concentrated (Jassem, 1999: 31–49). It considers the assumption of loss of scarcity and of intermediaries as convergence takes place. It reviews the role self-regulation can play as an alternative paradigm to government or command-and-control regulation within that context. And finally, the chapter concludes by evaluating the assumptions that are associated with the new paradigm.

One theoretical reflection should be made at the outset of this chapter. There is an assumption implicit in the notion of a paradigm shift called 'technological determinism' that concerns the causal relationship between technological developments and social impact or change. This technological determinism is of course not new.[5] Indeed, within several theories of social evolution, technological innovations are regarded as the most important determinants of societal change (Kahn and Wiener, 1967; Bell, 1973; Kerr, 1983). Yet, causal theories vary in the degree of determinism they reflect, although those expounding them seldom make this explicit. Critics have sometimes made a distinction between 'hard' and 'soft' technological determinism, the latter allowing somewhat more scope for human control and cultural variation (Chandler, 1995).

In their definitions, strong or hard technological determinism is the extreme stance that a particular communication technology is either a sufficient condition (sole cause) or at least a necessary condition (requiring additional preconditions) for determining social organization and development. Either way, certain consequences are seen as inevitable or at least highly probable.

Weak or soft technological determinism, more widely accepted by scholars, claims that the presence of a particular communication technology is an enabling or facilitating factor leading to potential opportunities which may or may not be taken up in particular societies or periods. Its absence may also be a constraint to development. Within that context, Ithiel de Sola Pool declared that 'Technology shapes the structure of the battle but not every outcome' (Finnegan et al., 1987: 32). Other 'factors' are also involved, and 'technoeconomic determinism' is sometimes associated with this stance. The 'weak case' is less tidy and less generic than the 'strong case' but it is more in accord with the available evidence. This chapter adopts an intermediate position in this debate of technological determinism versus social choice, acknowledging the importance of technological innovation but without ignoring the impact of other political, economic, legal and cultural variables.

THE UNDERPINNINGS OF THE PARADIGM SHIFT

Digitalization and Convergence

At the heart of the paradigm shift lies digitalization, whereby all forms of data such as alphanumeric text, graphics, still and moving pictures, and sounds are translated into 0s and 1s or digital bits.[6] This then enables controlled storage in large volume, easy manipulation and display of these data, and quick transmission without loss of quality in an integrated bit stream on a common channel (Garnham, 1994: 10). This common digital environment is driving the convergence that is taking place at all levels of the value chain (Verhulst et al., 1996: 4–6).

Convergence of the content of media or of media forms allows for the integration of the different kinds of information. The strict demarcation between different media becomes blurred (Cable and Distler, 1995: 2). Negroponte describes this state as 'mediumlessness' (1995: 71). Different content that had previously been carried by different physical media might be carried by a single medium like a CD-ROM. On the other hand, content that had previously been carried by a single medium may be distributed through several different physical media such as electronic newspapers (Institute for Information Studies, 1995: xiii).

As a result of digitalization of content, almost every message can be transported from point A to any point B in any physical way. The movement from a single-purpose network or transmission mode towards multipurpose networks is the result (Ducey, 1995: 3). This is called convergence of delivery channels.

Digital content requires a display terminal (desktop) and a decoder (set-top) (Garnham, 1994: 10). As stated in the World Telecommunication Development Report in 1995, there are essentially three user devices for accessing new communications services: the mobile telephone, the personal computer and the television (International Telecommunication Union, 1995). The concept of either PCTV (a PC with the ability to receive television signals) or a television with microprocessor technology for receiving digitally encoded data via phone lines has prompted the idea of a combined interactive platform designed to suit all needs (Dataquest, 1995). This idea is called convergence of customer interfaces. Besides this battle for the desktop, there is also a much more significant battle for the so-called middleware such as the set-top box or conditional access decoder, application programme interface and electronic programme guides. Electronic programme guides are a key issue in the regulatory questions discussed below.

Digitalization has led to the convergence of industries and markets, the creation of a new media consumption environment and hence a fundamentally different regulatory context.

Regulatory Context

Shift in Scarcities and Intermediaries

Digitalization and convergence drastically change the foundation upon which the traditional regulatory broadcasting regime is based. The analogue model was characterized by scarcity of frequencies and few intermediaries, a one-to-many flow of

information, distinctive industry sectors, linear programming, a mediated consumption environment and national boundaries. All this created the shared perception that broadcasting was pervasive and invasive in society and that television content needed to be controlled in a structural and restrictive or negative manner to ensure that public policy goals such as quality, diversity, impartiality and fairness were met.[7] The rise of digital television and the Internet has confounded these traditional understandings of 'television' and broadcasting regulation (Owen, 1999). Table 25.1 outlines the foundation behind regulation for the analogue and digital models.

As shown in Table 25.1 the debate about digital content is based on the assumption that there is abundance, as opposed to scarcity in the analogue model, and that there are new and different mediation processes in the digital environment that are not present in the analogue environment. As part of the latter assumption, disintermediation and individual involvement cause traditional mediators to become obsolete.

Information flow and the number of channels available have steadily grown as digitalization and cheaper content production have made more data publicly available. Three related technological/ commercial 'laws' have heavily influenced these and other assumptions about content and network abundance: Moore's law, Metcalfe's law and the more recent Gilder's law.

Moore's law is based on the observation that the maximum processing power of a microchip, at a given price, doubles roughly every 18 months.[8] That means computer power increases at an explosive rate, and conversely the price of a given level of computing power decreases at the same dramatic rate.

Metcalfe's law, on the other hand, describes a technological and economic force that pushes the growth of the Internet. As a network grows, the utility of being connected to that network grows even more. Thus Metcalfe's law says that the value of a network is equivalent to the square of the number of nodes.[9]

Gilder's law, finally, says that bandwidth will rise at a rate three times the rate at which processing power is increasing, or three times the rate of Moore's law (Gilder, 2000). In other words, with processing power doubling every 18 months, bandwidth will double every six months.

These three 'laws' drive the 'abundance' determinism associated with digital technology; yet the question remains, which we will address further, whether these 'laws' can also be applied to content. In addition, so-called 'disintermediation' is the development of new content producers, the ability of users to link to information without any indirect barrier or mediation, and the ability to obtain non-linear access to programming that ranges from on demand

Table 25.1 *Regulatory context*

Analogue model	Digital model
• Scarcity and few players (duopoly)	• Abundant players (branding)
• One-to-many	• Many-to-many
• Distinctive sectors	• Convergence of sectors
• Linear programming	• Non-linear programming (on demand)
• Mediated consumption environment	• Disintermediation and individual consumption environment
• National boundaries	• Transnational and global

to interactivity.[10] It is assumed that within this new digital setting, the locus of power has shifted from the service or content provider to the user, creating a many-to-many communications environment (Berman and Weitzner, 1995). The significance of the 'old intermediaries', who mediated the flow of information from the top to the bottom, has decreased and the new digital services are global, recognizing no national boundaries.

In addressing the new regulatory paradigm, governments do not have the comfort of being able to consider the issues simply within the confines of their territorial four walls. Not only do those concerned have to contend with the impact of these technological developments, but they also have to recognize that these technological advances will not respect traditional jurisdictional boundaries. As a result of these features, it is claimed that scarcity, and hence the pervasiveness of content, disappear as the basis for regulation.[11]

Shift in Information Flows

Another way of representing the paradigm shift of content structures has been suggested by Bordewijk and van Kaam (1982), who developed a framework to identify the main forms of 'information traffic'. According to them, the two main features of communication flows are: (1) storage and access to information and (2) use of information in the context of control of time and choice. Cross-tabulating both according to whether they are central or individual depicts a set of four categories of content flow. Table 25.2 demonstrates this cross-tabulation. The four categories in the table can be explained as follows:

- *Allocution* is the simultaneous transmission of a centrally constituted 'offer' of information intended for immediate attention, according to a centrally determined time scheme such as in traditional broadcasting.
- *Conversation* is an exchange between individuals of content already available to them, according to a mutually convenient time scheme such as over the telephone.
- *Consultation* is the selective consultation by individual participants of a central store of information at times determined by each individual such as when individuals use the library or newspapers.
- *Registration* is the collection of information available to, or about, individual participants, according to a centrally determined choice of subject and time in a central storage area or 'store'. This is a long-established element in many organizations for record-keeping, control, and surveillance.

The difference between a central and an individual information store is also analogous to that between a mass media organization and a single audience member. It can correspond to the difference between information-rich individuals and those who are information poor. The difference between central and individual control of access also relates to that between constraint and freedom and between low and high communication potential. One other use of the scheme, according to van Dijk (1994: 119), is to note that the top row entries, allocation and registration, are associated with a need for government regulation, and the bottom row, conversation and consultation, with absence of interference.

In brief, the earlier paradigm governing content regulation was based upon an allocution model. In contrast, digital content allows for an increase in the possibilities for consultation such as in interactive TV, for conversation such as over e-mail, and for registration such as through subscription-based content. This suggests a shift from allocution to the other cells of the model. It also indicates a general empowerment of the individual to gain information and a reduction in the dominance of centralized public sources or intermediaries, as indicated above.[12] It is possible for individual information stores to develop so that much more extensive 'conversation' patterns could reduce dependence on and hence influence central information stores (McQuail, 1986).

Andrew Shapiro makes a similar observation with regard to the Internet in his book *The Control Revolution* (1999). He convincingly shows how the Internet purports to radically expand control over personal connections with the world. According to Shapiro, the Internet drastically increases our individual ability to make and affect choices about how

Table 25.2   *Information flows*

	Central information store	Individual information store
Central control of time and subject	Allocution	Registration
Individual control of time and subject	Consultation	Conversation

we take in news and other information, how we engage each other in social interactions, education, work and political life, and how we make decisions about allocating collective resources.[13] As such, the shift challenges the invasiveness, publicness and influence that have been attributed to traditional broadcasting and which will be discussed at length below.

THE REGULATORY PARADIGM SHIFT

Rationales Behind Content Regulation

The starting point for every regulatory intervention and reform must be the policy objective, not the means of achievement. In other words, the need and rationale for the changes in rules and techniques must be identified before all other considerations. Justifications for intervention often arise from an alleged inability of the marketplace to deal with particular structural problems. Among the concerns listed by Hoffman-Riem (1996) are 'pluralism, diversity, fairness, and impartiality; social responsibility; maintenance of high quality programming and of cultural and linguistic identity; coverage of important events; protection against abuse of market power; strengthening national and regional industries; protection of consumers; and maintenance of standards in matters of violence, sex, taste and decency'. Other rationales are often brought up in political debate over media and content regulation and the details of a programme frequently only reflect political force.[14]

In the prior paradigm, where there was a scarcity of channels that were viewed mainly by families or in semi-public settings, it was justified for democratically accountable public institutions to intervene and regulate what was seen. The rationale for intervention hinged on liberal democratic notions of the particular importance of media and notions of market failure and harm to individuals, particularly children. Former European Commissioner for Audiovisual Policy, Marcelino Oreja (1999), summarized these notions and rationales from a European perspective.

The starting point is, of course, to recognize the crucial role that media play in our society. The role of the media goes much further than simply providing information about events and issues; media also play a formative role in society. That is, they are largely responsible for forming the concepts, belief systems and even the languages – visual and symbolic as well as verbal – which citizens use to make sense of, and to interpret the world in which they live ... There are a certain number of public interest objectives which should be preserved in our societies, and which have a European dimension. In my opinion, these could be summarized as follows: ensuring plurality of ownership; ensuring fair and effective competition; ensuring diversity of content; protecting individual rights to privacy, free speech, etc.; protecting intellectual property rights; maximizing individual consumer choice and access to information; and, very importantly, ensuring a high level of protection of minors and human dignity.

In addition, content regulation of broadcasting was seen as justified because of the particular features of broadcast content, which distinguish it from other media such as telephones and the press. These include pervasiveness, invasiveness, publicness and influence (Tambini and Verhulst, 2000).

- *Pervasiveness* Because terrestrial transmitters can carry only a limited number of channels, and the broadcasting spectrum provides only a limited space for programming, each programme has been perceived as pervasive. It has therefore been imperative from the outset to ensure that terrestrial broadcasting channels reflect the opinions, taste and culture of as many different people as possible, often through a public broadcasting system or public service obligations.[15] In addition, in the 1980s, media policies were developed to ensure that political, ethnic and other minorities had more presence on television. These policies were justified because of the pervasiveness of the medium of TV, and of the scarce range of available channels.

- *Invasiveness* Content is more invasive if users do not know what content they are about to receive or do not actively choose it. As opposed to traditional broadcasting, content accessed in books and via the Internet is more likely to be deliberately chosen. The lack of control over the products offered by broadcast media has justified setting up a legal regime specific to them in order to protect the listener or viewer (Poulet and Lamouline, 1995: 36). When content is invasive, central negative content controls may apply. New forms of delivery, such as encrypted narrowcasting, where adult users have a high degree of choice and control, are generally subject to less regulation than free-to-air television (Department of Culture, Media and Sport, 1999: 1.14).

- *Publicness* All societies have taboos that are crucial for monitoring social cohesion and individuals' sense of trust and community. Taboos exclude certain topics from 'public' communication and, conversely, public communication is reserved for topics and content that are considered part of the public domain and of a specific value. Broadcast media are considered one of the key places where societies think about and discuss crucial issues about survival and purpose. The contents they carry constitute a large part of what individuals have in common and provide key reference points in broader political and cultural debates.

- *Influence* Broadcasts have sometimes been accredited with the ability to directly influence revolutions and bring down governments but can also have a subtler agenda-setting influence as they determine the focus of public political debate each day. The high degree of influence of broadcast content warrants close public regulation of potential abuses and makes it imperative to develop the means to ensure that content is not used in a manipulative way. Where there are very few dominant sources of information, or just a handful of television channels, their influence can be of paramount importance in forming public opinion. It is justified to ensure that such content is neither harmful nor undemocratic, and that it promotes publicly shared values, rather than those of a powerful minority.

Digitalization challenges these justifications. As a result of convergence, it is claimed that the pervasiveness, invasiveness, publicness and influence of content decrease or even disappear. To a certain extent, the European Green Paper on Convergence demonstrated a different perspective on this issue:

> The fundamental objectives underpinning regulation in the Member States are not undermined by convergence ... Nevertheless the nature and characteristics of convergence as well as the perceived need of industry actors for regulatory intervention to be limited and closely targeted, should lead public authorities at both a national and a European level to re-examine the role and weight of regulation in a converging marketplace. (European Commission, 1997)

Public interest objectives do not become irrelevant or invalid as a result of technological change. Where the listed features of pervasiveness, invasiveness, publicness and influence remain, content regulations may continue to apply. The regulatory challenge in content regulation in a digital setting is thus to find appropriate legislative and other mechanisms to safeguard these policy objectives. It is suggested that a functional approach is needed, one which does not depend solely on technology or forms of delivery, but which recognizes the nature of the content and the character of the audience receiving it. All this led to the call for and shift towards self-regulatory approaches within the new regulatory paradigm.

Shift in Regulatory Mechanism

Because analogue television was considered as more pervasive, invasive and influential within society than any other medium, the call for and development of stronger government regulation were justified. Broadcasting regulation was and is based upon a licensing system with guidelines restricting what kinds of content and advertisements can be broadcast, specific programme schedules or watershed policies, classification of programmes developed by a single institution, and consequent acoustic or visual announcement of programmes.

Broadcasters, as a rule, took their responsibility toward programming content very seriously, and have been keenly aware of the expectations of their audiences, who could complain to statutory bodies in case of offence. Moreover, analogue television was controlled nationally and audiovisual policies were in many cases nationalistic. Finally, access rules and mechanisms ranging across ownership rules, must-carry rules, listed events and even public service broadcasting monopolies all helped to ensure that broadcasters fulfilled the envisioned roles.

Clearly, these approaches, originally established for terrestrially based mass audience channels, have become much more difficult to maintain as the sources of programming have multiplied and new technologies have made the prospect of regulation far more unmanageable. Because of converging technologies, it is also increasingly difficult to differentiate between 'telecommunications' and 'broadcasting'. New mechanisms and paradigms appropriate for a changing multichannel, digital and online environment need to be considered. Table 25.3 provides a review of the traditional methods used to control broadcasting content compared with the new methods now being developed for controlling content in the online converged environment.

Self-regulation plays an overarching role in this search for adequate solutions. It involves many regulatory subjects such as domain names, standard setting of conditional access systems, open access and e-commerce. However, most of the public concern and debate concerning self-regulation has focused on illegal and harmful content, the scope of this chapter. This concern has prompted substantial and public industrial response. However, given the

Table 25.3   *Regulatory mechanism*

Traditional means of content control	Paradigm shift: digital ecology

1 Government regulation through:
  • licensing systems (programme code)
  • programme scheduling (watershed)
  • physical bottlenecks (broadcasting responsibility)
  • statutory complaints mechanism
	1 Self-regulation through:
	  • codes of conduct
	  • green/red listing (pool)
	  • technical bottlenecks (parent empowerment)
	  • hotlines

2 Single institutional approach (monopoly)	2 Plural/competing approaches
3 Sector-specific rules	3 Content/convey distinction
4 Media ownership rules (diversity/pluralism)	4 Access and bottleneck regulation

complexity of the new services (different platforms with different communications capacities) no single approach, relying on one form or one set of actors, can provide a solution to content concerns in the changing and shifting environment that is the Internet. The development of a self-regulatory regime for digital services will comprise multiple complementary actions, tools and mechanisms. At least four main strands have been suggested and recommended:[16]

• First, codes of conduct should be adopted to ensure that Internet content and service providers act in accord with the law and with principles of social responsibility.
• Second, there should be comprehensive use of rating/filtering technology and green/red lists.
• Third, content response and complaints systems such as hotlines must be made available to users.
• Fourth, success requires awareness among users of the means to filter and block content, their power to redress complaints, and the level of conduct that is promised by the industry.

It has been argued that the most distinct of these means for enhancing protection and free speech is the use of filtering and blocking mechanisms, using plural and often competing rating systems. This is not to say that legal controls or codes of conduct are unimportant, but rather that the shift from 'hard law to software' can clearly be considered as an empowerment and improvement of users' choice. Hence the major response to the call for self-regulation involves processes that promote filtering and rating systems.

Shift from Law to Technology

Lawrence Lessig in his book *Code and Other Laws of Cyberspace* (1999) has also made an analysis of the paradigm shift from 'hard law to software'. He challenges the myth that cyberspace is incapable of regulation, and argues that our notions of liberty and rules are undergoing a transformation as we are forced to make value choices not previously confronted in constitutional theory. According to

Lessig, social order is created by human activity in four realms – technology, economy, civic institutions and the polity. Table 25.4 outlines these realms. Social order emerges because human activity is routinized or regulated in each of these realms. Lessig defines the 'modalities of regulation' in each realm – architecture, the market, norms and laws – by the nature and timing of constraints and the enforcement agents (1999: 235–7). Sociologically, many other aspects of social order can be added in each realm. Central in the discussion below are the institutions through which activity is channelled and the nature of relationships, identity and participation in each.

Using the terminology in Table 25.4, Lessig suggests that the very architecture of cyberspace allows profound control of information flows. Technical rules and protocols are themselves critical regulators of cyberspace. In these terms, the 'code' becomes the constitution for cyberspace. At the same time, Lessig points out that 'code' is not the sole regulator of behaviour in cyberspace. Social norms form an important aspect of control in cyberspace, whether those norms are formed locally or remotely. Similarly, market regulation (such as pricing and terms of service) has a powerful and central constraining effect on behaviour in cyberspace. Finally, Lessig indicates that law is still present in the equation. Indeed, he argues that law may regulate the architecture itself, or change behavioural norms.

Lessig's discussion of modalities of regulation is not simply descriptive, but proscriptive. First, he argues that open code, as opposed to proprietary code, reduces the capacity of government to impose requirements on citizens. At the same time, while open code might make it harder for government to control the myriad of software developers around the world, open code can also facilitate the capability of government to impose particular software modules for products sold in its territory. Second, as the Internet moves into a commercial phase, the emerging paradigm requires urgent measures to preserve the Internet's openness. Lessig's concern in the discussion of cyberspace is that in the face of a powerful technology, there is a tendency to

Table 25.4 *Paradigm of society*

Characteristics of social interaction	Realms of social order			
	Technology	Economy	Civic institutions	Polity
Modalities of regulation	Architecture	Market	Norm	Law
Enforcement agent	None	Seller/buyer	Peers	Police/courts
Timing of constraint	Before	During	Before/after	After
Nature of constraint	Physical	Money	Opprobrium	Sanction
Basis of relationships	Structure/flow	Production	Experience	Power
Basis of participation	Inhabitant	Producer/consumer	Member	Citizen
Primary institutions	Place/space	Enterprise	Family/	State
	Internet	Union	Church	Media

passively accept the technological edicts of the code writers, rather than assert control over the definitions and development of society.

> We will treat code-based environmental disasters – like Y2K, like the loss of privacy, like the censorship of filters, like the disappearance of an intellectual commons – as if they were produced by gods, not by Man. We will watch as important aspects of privacy and free speech are erased by the emerging architecture of the panopticon, and we will speak, like modern Jeffersons, about nature making it so – forgetting that here, we are nature. We will in many domains of our social life come to see the Net as the product of something alien – something we cannot direct because we cannot direct anything. Something instead that we must simply accept, as it invades and transforms our lives. (1999: 233)

Lessig goes on to issue a call to arms (1999: 58–9). The animus for the call is a fear that the dictates of the code writers, driven by commercial interests, will be corrosive of fundamental values in our society such as justice, equality and democracy (1999: 15, 206, 209). He stresses the need to act to preserve key values and policy objectives on the Internet.

These legal, market and technological analyses suggest that there is a close nexus between technology and the economic and legal structure and that these spheres are driving changes through the remainder of society. As Manuel Castells argues in his book *The Rise of the Network Society* (1996), technology deployment, economic activity, social interaction and political institutions, within broad limits, can be directed toward specific goals.

> Yet, if society does not determine technology, it can, mainly through the state, suffocate its development. Or alternatively, again mainly by state intervention, it can embark on an accelerated process of technological modernization able to change the fate of economies, military power, and social well being in a few years. Indeed, the ability or inability of societies to master technology, and particularly technologies that are

strategically decisive in each historical period, largely shapes their destiny, to the point where we could say that while technology *per se* does not determine historical evolution and social change, technology (or the lack of it) embodies the capacity of societies to transform themselves, as well as the uses to which societies, always in a conflictive process, decide to put their technological potential. (1996: 7)

These concerns involve values that are very much at the heart of the debate over the role the government should take in a self-regulatory environment, the subject of the next section.

THE PARADIGM SHIFT REVIEWED

The Concept and Definition of Self-Regulation

The initial problem inherent in every approach to self-regulation lies with definition. There is no single definition for self-regulation that is entirely satisfactory, nor should there be. Self-regulation on the Internet evolves as the nature of the Internet alters. Different profiles of self-regulation emerge that adjust to the varying regulated aspects of the Internet. Self-regulation has and will continue to have different meanings from sector to sector and from state to state. Furthermore, whatever its implications or suggestions, self-regulation is almost always a misnomer. It hardly ever exists without some relationship to the state – a relationship that itself varies greatly. The meaning of self-regulation shifts depending upon the extent of government coercion or involvement and upon accurate public perceptions of the relationship of private sector and state.

Despite these and similar complexities, governments, industries and users employ the term 'self-regulation' frequently, almost indiscriminately. It is assumed to have a predetermined meaning when it does not. A study of self-regulation in the media sector and European Community law noted that 'the term "self-regulation" is often used as a matter of course, as if it were (1) a specific and defined term, and (2) an equally specific and defined regulatory practice. Yet in general, this is not the case' (Ukrow, 1999: 11). From the outset, then, in order to manage social concerns connected to the new technology there needs to be an exploration of self-regulation's variety of meanings and the implications of each meaning.

> Larry Irving, former US Assistant Secretary of Commerce, observed: At one end of the spectrum, the term is used quite narrowly, to refer only to those instances where the government has formally delegated the power to regulate, as in the delegation of securities industry oversight to the stock exchanges. At the other end of the spectrum, the term is used when the private sector perceives the need to regulate itself for whatever reason – to respond to consumer demand, to carry out its ethical beliefs, to enhance industry reputations, or to level the market playing field – and does so.[17]

Even here, the range of variable meanings emerges. Because 'self-regulation' is thought to exist when private entities have been commanded to act or become the delegates of state power, the intertwining of state and private industry is implicitly recognized, although the 'governmental nature of self-regulation' may differ across sectors (Baldwin and Cave, 1999: 125). Questions remain over the propriety and clarity of delegation, the circumstances under which state functions can or ought to be carried out by private groups, and the division of power and responsibility between the state and private groups.

On the other hand, as Secretary Irving suggests, the private sector 'perceives the need to regulate itself'. The source of that need is often the threat of public regulation, a societal demand for increased responsibility by the private sector, or economic factors. Other variables may include the extent of the role played by self-regulators, the degree of binding legal force attached to self-regulatory rules, and their coverage of an industrial sector (1999: 126). These areas of indeterminacy are grounds for a statement in a recent bibliography on self-regulation on the Internet prepared for the OECD: 'While there is broad consensus that self-regulation of the Internet is critical to its future growth, there is little consensus about how to achieve or implement a self-regulatory regime' (Gidari, 1998).

The 'Self' of Internet Self-Regulation

In addition to the confusion over how to define self-regulation, determining what ought to be included in the 'self' of self-regulation in the context of digital content is also a complex question. A cornucopia of institutions partakes of self-regulatory characteristics. Voluntary institutions generated by the Internet and not by government are the very backbone of efforts to deal with harmful content.[18] In many discussions, governments have failed to recognize that the Internet industry is not monolithic and that there is no single 'industry' that speaks for the whole of the Internet (Gidari, 1998). Moreover, the fact that the Internet is relatively young and still in a rapid growth stage also means that in many cases effective cooperative action such as the creation of industry associations is also in its early stages. One interesting example of such cooperation is the pan-European Association of the Internet Service Providers' Associations (EuroISPA) of some EU member states.[19]

The definition of 'self' cannot be divided between different sectors of the industry that form cohesive communities either. Indeed, it has been suggested that self-regulation operates more effectively when it involves interrelated levels of the industry, which often do not form one coherent body. For example, Boddewyn's (1989) study of the advertising industry found that self-regulatory systems were strengthened when they included distribution systems such as television networks. Many of the Internet self-regulatory bodies contain representatives from different sectors of the industry. For example, in Australia, Internet Industry Association Australia (IIA) has a membership that includes telecom carriers, content creators and hardware developers.[20] In contrast, the self-regulatory organizations in the United Kingdom tend to have a narrower membership, with the Internet Service Providers' Association (ISPA) and the London Internet Exchange (LINX) the two leading ISP groups, whose memberships are restricted to providers.[21]

There is also an increasing social demand for breadth in the definition of 'self' for self-regulation on the Internet. If the function of self-regulation is to minimize harmful and illegal conduct on the Internet, particularly as it affects young people, then it must become more, rather than less, extensive. Albert Gidari (1998), Executive Director of the Internet Law and Policy Forum, has stated that often the 'self' in self-regulation too narrowly focuses only on the business sector. A narrow conception of self-regulation places too much of the burden on industry to solve the legal and policy issues when other participants such as stakeholders and administrators could contribute to the overall self-regulatory regime.

Because of the multisectoral nature of online content, a wide variety of self-regulating communities or mediating institutions is likely to come into existence. Moreover, competing self-regulatory regimes may emerge within any given sector. Resulting patterns and institutions of self-regulation will differ geographically. Each state has different social demands, different constitutional structures, and different traditions of industry–government cooperation in the fields of media and speech. One study of self-regulation and self-generation of standards that compared the experiences in Canada and the United States demonstrated marked differences in the scope of cooperation with the government, shared standards, and the notion of self-regulation as a social and collaborative act (McDowell and Maitland, 1998).

When it comes to content regulation, differences in self-regulation, state to state, will also turn on the speech traditions in each society and the way that each conceptualizes the Internet and digital content. Where the Internet is perceived as derived or related to telephony, self-regulatory practices and standards that have emerged in telecommunications may predominate. In the United States, partly because of the First Amendment tradition, self-regulation is distinctively a form of avoidance of, confrontation with, and studied separation from government. However, a comparative overview of self-regulatory systems in the media in all EU member states identified clear differences in meaning and structure of the self-regulatory systems (Brohmer and Ukrow, 1999).

Costs and Benefits of Self-Regulation

It is generally suggested that the professed advantages of self-regulation over governmental regulation include efficiency, increased flexibility, increased incentives for compliance, reduced cost, and minimized government intrusion in the speech field (Price and Verhulst, 2000). However, when considering these self-regulatory attempts as an effective alternative to government regulation, several considerations must be weighed.

First, self-regulation ought to be perceived as a paradigm different from deregulation or non-regulation. Deregulation directly aims at removing any regulation perceived to be excessive and hindering market forces. Self-regulation, as an ideology or approach to management, does not aim primarily to dismantle or dispense with a framework for private activity.

Second, self-regulation involves a dialogue between government and a business association. The form of the dialogue depends on the situation of each party at the beginning of discourse. This may differ across sectors, across countries and in time. As a result, self-regulation has and will continue to have different meanings in different contexts. It is clear, then, that whatever its implication or suggestion, self-regulation is almost always a misnomer. Self-regulation rarely exists without some relationship to the state, which is a relationship that varies greatly.

Third, it is naive to suggest, as is done continually, that self-regulation does not itself involve

significant regulatory costs. For any system, regulatory or self-regulatory, costs are determined by a combination of the policy goals they envisage and the structures and dynamics of the economic and social activities they regulate. Monitoring and evaluative costs otherwise assumed by governments may be incurred directly by individual companies or indirectly by industry associations that will also generate significant amounts of third-party costs associated with governmental compliance procedures.

Fourth, self-regulation can quickly become moribund without strong and committed support for its development, implementation and enforcement. The very nature of a voluntary system potentially creates a 'free-rider problem', where some actors expend significant resources on the development, monitoring and implementation of codes and standards while others ignore their existence. To be a living and working instrument, a code of conduct or its equivalent must, in practice, be implemented with the agreement of the industry sector to which it is applied.

Fifth, effective self-regulation requires active consumer and citizen consultation based upon shared responsibility at all stages of development and implementation. Without user involvement, a self-regulatory mechanism will not accurately reflect user needs, will not be effective in delivering the standards it promotes, and will not create confidence. Table 25.5 demonstrates these five considerations.

Self-Regulatory Mechanism

In addition to the considerations regarding the concept of self-regulation, there are also several challenges in the suggested self-regulatory mechanism.

Codes of Conduct

Codes of practice or good conduct embody, at times, mutual obligations by competing actors, for example, in the form of agreements, that require each of them to take certain actions to restrict content that would give any one of them a temporary competitive advantage. Codes provide an indication of the nature of the self-regulatory authority, including whether or not it will impose sanctions for breaches of the code, and upon whom. Codes are often the instrument for the generation or refinement of norms. In the Internet setting, norms negotiated between the industry and government authority are codified to produce the rules.

There are a number of industry initiatives under way directed at developing codes of conduct, and a number of national governments specifically endorse codes as a front-line mechanism for addressing content issues (Blinderman et al., 2000).

Table 25.5   *Self-regulation*

Advantages of self-regulation over governmental regulation	Considerations and challenges for self-regulation
• Increased efficiency • Increased flexibility • Increased incentives for compliance • Transnational scope • Increased expertise • Reduced cost • Minimized government intrusion in the speech field	• It is almost always a misnomer and government involvement usually continues • The paradigm is different from deregulation or non-regulation • It involves significant regulatory costs • Self-regulation requires active consumer and citizen consultation (corporatist) • Strong and committed support or social responsibility from all parties is necessary; free-riders should be considered • A balance between the carrot and the stick may improve effectiveness

However, a level of compliance needs to be ensured. Users, both industry and consumers, need guidance with regard to the content of these codes and an impartial arbiter needs to have an appropriate redress mechanism – variables often absent in current initiatives.

Rating and Filtering

As indicated above, rating and filtering techniques may offer the best solution to empower parents in controlling the content they deem to be suitable or unsuitable. Developing rating systems is always difficult. However, within an Internet and converged communications setting the following additional challenges can be observed:

• How can sufficient coverage of websites be reached to encourage the use of rating and blocking software?
• How can varieties of rating software be made available to all who want to use them?
• How can the cultural bias (many are US-centric) of existing rating systems be overcome?
• How can an internationally acceptable system be developed that allows national differences?
• How can such systems be made easy to use for content providers and for parents alike?
• How can accuracy, objectivity and consistency of ratings be ensured?

Many initiatives have been developed in response to these questions. Internet Content Rating for Europe (INCORE) and the EU Internet Action Plan have examined guidelines for developing self-rating systems that are appropriate for European cultural and linguistic specifics and are also suitable for global requirements. At the national level, Germany, via the Secorvo Jugendshutz study, and the UK, through the Internet Watch Foundation, have considered the adaptation of US ratings systems to their specific value systems.

Several US-based awareness campaigns such as GetNetWise and NetParents have developed with the goal of highlighting the functioning of filter systems. Since most websites are not currently rated, most software provides users with the option of blocking sites that do not contain Platform for Internet Content Selection (PICS) ratings. However, this choice may be appropriate for some, but it severely restricts the available options. By blocking most of the web (including possibly some sites designed for younger users), this approach presents children with a severely restricted view of the world.

Zoning

Zoning, or the development of green and red lists, is often considered a more effective manner for creating a 'safe playground'. There are, however, several problems with filtering based on lists of sites to be blocked.

First, both green and red lists are always under-inclusive and incomplete. Owing to the decentralized nature of the Internet, it is practically impossible to search all Internet sites for 'objectionable' or 'acceptable' material. Furthermore, since new websites are constantly appearing, even regular updates from the software vendor will not block out all adult websites. Each updated list will be obsolete as soon as it is released, as any site that appears after the update will not be on the list, and will not be blocked.

The volatility of individual sites is yet another potential cause of trouble. Adult material might be added to or removed from a site soon after the site is added to or removed from a list of blocked sites.

There is a general lack of transparency concerning the criteria used by list developers. This obscurity is compounded by practices used to protect lists of blocked sites. Vendors often consider these lists to be proprietary intellectual property, which they protect through encryption. Encryption renders the lists incomprehensible to end users. Companies such as Cyberpatrol have vigorously fought organizations that published Cyberpatrol's

Table 25.6   *Self-regulator mechanisms for a digital age*

Ideal	Reality: key challenges
Codes of conduct 'Reflects industry morality'	• Level of compliance/awareness • User guidance • Impartiality of arbiter • Appropriate redress
Rating and filtering 'Golden fleece of parental empowerment'	• Volume of content • Different transmission paths • Objectivity and plurality • Ease to use/access for all parties • Awareness and literacy
Zoning 'Safe playground'	• Underinclusive/overrestrictive • Transparency • Property rights and access
Hotlines 'Concern response system'	• Awareness • Transparency • Expertise • Public/private partnership

lists of blocked sites and programs that would break the encryption. Peacefire.org was one such organization that posted a program that enabled users to access the list developed by CyberPatrol. CyberPatrol challenged the posting in court, claiming copyright violation.[22]

Hotlines

Finally, hotlines have been suggested as an appropriate content concern response system for a decentralized and global environment such as the Internet. However, as Burkert (2000) has indicated, the quality, rules, procedures and organizational contexts of these hotlines play an important role in the acceptance, functioning and effectiveness of content concern response systems. Hotlines need to establish efficient communications systems, with availability, reliability and transparency as the main qualitative requirements.

Table 25.6 outlines the challenges in instituting codes of conduct, rating and filtering, zoning, and hotlines as effective self-regulatory mechanisms. This is juxtaposed with the ideal of each mechanism, to summarize this section.

CONCLUDING REMARKS: NEW SCARCITIES AND NEW INTERMEDIARIES

The current regulatory paradigm shift for digital content, as outlined and reviewed above, is based upon assumptions of disintermediation and loss of scarcity, which in themselves decrease the pervasiveness, invasiveness, publicness and influence of content. Yet a critical analysis may indicate that some of these assumptions are incomplete, and are based upon limited notions of access, scarcity and mediation. Indeed, a subtler phenomenon of reintermediation is emerging, and in many ways it creates new (artificial) scarcities (Mansell, 1999: 155–81).

The process of reintermediation is initiated by several elements. One of the dilemmas posed by the increasing flow of information is that too much information paralyses and enervates. The abundance of content has led to a call for and the creation of new types of mediation and hence new intermediaries that can:

• search and navigate in the wealth of information for the right match of information needed;
• warn or even filter and block information that is unwanted or considered harmful;
• contextualize or give information about information through so-called metadata;
• integrate and decode different streams of information;
• customize the reception and consumption of services and information; and
• verify or authenticate the source, the user, and whether payment has been received (Firestone, 1994–5).

These requirements have caused the emergence of new intermediaries in the form of electronic programme guides, portals, search engines, walled gardens, filters, push technology, billing software and intelligent agents. It is predicted that many of these components will be combined within new

Table 25.7 *New challenges*

Regulatory paradigm	New challenges
Disintermediation	Reintermediation
Abundance	New scarcities
User empowerment	Sender power
Open access	Closed offering
Civic sphere	Commercial sphere

middleware such as the Multimedia Home Platform to be developed by the Digital Video Broadcasting Group.[23] Table 25.7 delineates the new challenges in the Internet environment against the previous assumptions about that environment.

These new communications network intermediaries do not work, however, in a user-neutral way. The selection, evaluation and functions are to a large extent determined by the creators of the gateway (Hargittai, 2000: 233–53). They decide how much information there will be, what form it will take, in what package or bundle, at what price, and whether there will be choice and access at all. Ultimately, content producers and distributors are not interested only in providing full and free access for users; they are interested in attracting an audience for their portals, packages and developed services, linked with advertising or subscription revenue.

Moreover, there are many ways that intermediaries can influence users' communication patterns. Representation and placement of the information or programming that 'match' the need allow for promotion of or discrimination against some services. The design of the navigation device by intermediaries can influence choice and access (Introna and Nissenbaum, 2000: 1–17). Stand-alone filter systems limit users to decisions made by the software vendor. Moreover, to customize the service, intermediaries also collect valuable information about users and their communication patterns, with risks of privacy intrusions. The danger here is that new and artificial scarcities are created: access to information will vary according to the portal and gateway that are used and whether the user can afford specific subscription fees. As such, information exiles may result if no regulatory paradigm is reconsidered soon – perhaps an even much bigger challenge and priority for policy-makers.

Notes

The author is grateful to the Markle Foundation for a visiting scholarship in the autumn of 2000 at their New York headquarters that enabled further review of the paradigm shift. The chapter reflects also the content of two seminars held at the Markle Foundation.

1 In his groundbreaking book, Kuhn (1970) argued that 'paradigms', or conceptual world views, that consist of formal theories, classic experiments and trusted methods, define scientific research and thought. Scientists typically accept a prevailing paradigm and try to extend its scope by refining theories, explaining puzzling data, and establishing more precise measures of standards and phenomena. Eventually, however, their efforts may generate insoluble theoretical problems or experimental anomalies that expose a paradigm's inadequacies or contradict it altogether. This accumulation of difficulties triggers a crisis that can only be resolved by an intellectual revolution that replaces an old paradigm with a new one. Kuhn's book revolutionized the history and philosophy of science, and his concept of paradigm shifts was extended to such disciplines as political science, economics, sociology and even law.

2 A more recent and perhaps more 'business management' version of the paradigm concept is offered by Joel Barker (1993). It states that 'a paradigm is a set of rules and regulations that: (i) defines boundaries; and (ii) tells you what to do to be successful within those boundaries' (1993: 14).

3 This is expected to be evolutionary since all parts of the value chain (content, packaging, distribution and customer interface) cannot easily develop simultaneously; the technology required for advanced networks is either not fully developed or remains too expensive to be commercially viable; most of the interactive TV services that a switched broadband network would support are very similar to existing and developing broadcast services. Thus a huge incremental expense would have to be supported by a relatively small range of new services; evolutionary development is more appropriate to the expected nature of consumer demand. For a further discussion see Jamieson (1995: 11).

4 As opposed to 'positive regulation' which includes universal service provisions, state aid, etc.

5 The American sociologist and economist Thorstein Veblen (1857–1929) apparently coined the term 'technological determinism' (Ellul, 1990).

6 In addition to digitalization, there are some other common key technological advances such as compression, optical fibre and extended switching (Negroponte, 1995: 12).

7 These public policy goals are generally based upon the view that broadcasting is a means of communicative self-development and important to the functioning of a democratic society. For a detailed analysis of the rationales behind broadcasting regulation see Hoffman-Riem (1996: 297).

8 For a critical analysis of the value of Moore's law for other technologies see Coffman and Odlyzko (2001).

9 The 'law' postulates that if n people are in a network, the value of the overall network is n^2, given the myriad new connections that can be made to the nth participant. A simple example is that of a fax machine that becomes more useful the more people are connected to it.

10 Disintermediation may also be achieved by the removal of intermediaries from the industry value chain (Moore, 1996).

11 Charles Firestone (1993) has also indicated that at each level of the communications process, production, distribution and reception, there have been two paradigmatic stages of regulation, one of scarcity and one of apparent abundance and competition. At the scarcity stage, usually obtained after an initial period of skirmishing among pioneers for position, the regulation has taken the general form of governmental intervention in order to promote the broader public interest. At the abundant or competitive stage, which overlaps the earlier stage, there has been a reversal, a deregulation to promote greater efficiency. In each case, the paradigm is a regulatory religion, at times demanding faith on the part of the believers.

12 However, what is available for consultation in central stores can still be centrally determined and much will depend on how diverse the central stores are in content and management. Furthermore, in other interpretations the 'registration' pattern may significantly increase the potential for central control through surveillance of information and information-related activities, which may often be politically sensitive.

13 Paradoxically, however, the Internet often becomes a tool to segregate us hermetically from unwanted but sometimes invaluable experiences.

14 For a US account see Corn-Revere (1997). For a more European and UK-oriented discussion see Feintuck (forthcoming).

15 This was particularly pronounced in the US by the famous case *Red Lion Broadcasting Co. v. FCC* (1969), in which the Supreme Court upheld the FCC's 'fairness doctrine', which required licensees to cover controversial issues of public importance and provide a reasonable opportunity for the presentation of opposing points of view. The Court explained that in order to avoid interference on the airwaves, a government agency must limit the number of broadcast speakers. Because only a lucky few can be licensed to broadcast, the government can require those few to act as trustees or fiduciaries on behalf of the larger excluded community, and obligate them to present views, representative of the community, that otherwise would have no broadcasting outlet.

16 The European Internet Action Plan lists these ways as crucial to create a 'safer' Internet environment. See Decision no. 276/1999/EC of the European Parliament and of the Council of 25 January 1999 adopting a Multiannual Community Action Plan promoting safer use of the Internet by combating illegal and harmful content on global networks.

17 Quote by Larry Irving obtained when he was introducing a collection of papers analysing the prospects of self-regulation for protecting privacy (National Telecommunications Information Administration, 1997).

18 However, the history of a voluntary association such as the Internet Corporation for Assigned Names and Numbers (ICANN) indicates how seeming autonomy begins with government encouragement. See http://www.icann.org (17 February 2000).

19 To learn more about EuroISPA see http://www.euroispa.org/index.html (19 February 2000).

20 For information about Internet Access Australia see http://www.iia.net.au (19 February 2000).

21 For information about ISPA UK see http://www.ispa.org.uk (20 February 2000), and for the London Internet Exchange Ltd see http://www.linx.net (19 February 2000).

22 After the case was initially lost, a federal appeals court in the US allowed the American Civil Liberties Union (ACLU) to recommend that peacefire.org along with two other clients exercise their First Amendment rights and continue to post the lists. In addition, the recent copyright law regulations passed by the Library of Congress in October 2000 exempt ' "reverse engineering" of or unauthorized access to filtering software in order to expose the list of blocked sites' from the law. For further information about the case see ACLU press releases entitled: 'Censorware copyright controversy leaves clients, consumers in the dark, ACLU says', Tuesday 28 March 2000, and 'ACLU gives clients green light to post blocking software code', Tuesday 31 October 2000. They are available at http://www.aclu.org/news/2000/n032800b.html and http://www.aclu.org/news/2000/n103100.html, respectively (viewed 3 January 2001). Even in light of these events, the considerations behind protecting their lists remain substantial for the companies developing them.

23 See http://www.dvb.ch.

REFERENCES

Baldwin, R. and Cave, M. (1999) *Understanding Regulation*. Oxford: Oxford University Press.

Barker, J.A. (1993) *Discovering the Future: the Business of Paradigms*. New York: Harper Business.

Bell, D. (1973) *The Coming of Post-Industrial Society: a Venture in Social Forecasting*, reprinted 1976. London: Heinemann Educational.

Berman, J. and Weitzner, D.J. (1995) 'Abundance and user control: renewing the democractic heart of the First Amendment in the age of interactive media', *The Yale Law Journal*, 104 (7): 1619–31.

Blinderman, E., Price, M. and Verhulst, S. (2000) *Codes of Conduct and Other Self-Regulatory Documents: Emerging Patterns of Norm Formulation and Enforcement on the Internet*. Gutersloh: Bertelsmann Foundation.

Boddewyn, J.J. (1989) *Advertising Self-Regulation and Outside Participation: a Multinational Comparison*. New York: Quorum.

Bordewijk, J.L. and van Kaam, B. (1982) *Allocutie: Enkele gedachten over communicatievrijheid in een bekabeld land*. Baarn: Bosch & Keunig.

Brohmer, J. and Ukrow, J. (1999) *Die Selbstkontrolle in Medienberich in Europa: Eine Rechtsvengleichende Untersuchung* (on file).

Burkert, H. (2000) 'The issue of hotlines', in J. Waltermann and M. Machill (eds), *Protecting Our*

Children on the Internet: Towards a New Culture of Responsibility. Gutersloh: Bertelsmann Foundation.

Cable, V. and Distler, C. (1995) *Global Superhighways: the Future of International Telecommunications Policy*. London: Royal Institute of International Affairs.

Castells, M. (1996) *The Rise of the Network Society*. Oxford: Blackwell.

Chandler, D. (1995) 'Technological or media determinism'. At the Media and Communications Studies site: http://www.aber.ac.uk/media/Documents/tecdet/tecdet.html (viewed 3 January 2001).

Coffman, K.G. and Odlyzko, A.M. (2001) 'Internet growth: is there a "Moore's law" for data traffic?', in J. Abello, P.M. Pardalos and M.G.C. Resende (eds), *Handbook of Massive Data Sets*. The Hague: Kluwer.

Corn-Revere, R. (ed.) (1997) *Rationales and Rationalizations: Regulating the Electronic Media*. Washington, DC: Media Institute.

Dataquest (1995) *The War for the Interactive Platform of the Future: TV versus PC*. Report. Available at: http://www.dataquest.com/.

Department of Culture, Media and Sport (1999) *Regulating Communications: the Way Ahead. Results of Consultation Paper*. London: Department of Culture, Media and Sport.

Ducey, R.V. (1995) *A New Digital Marketplace in Information and Entertainment Services: Organizing around Connectivity and Interoperability*. Washington, DC: National Association of Broadcasters.

Ellul, J. (1990) *The Technological Bluff*. Grand Rapids, MI: Eerdmans.

European Commission (1997) *Green Paper on the Convergence of the Telecommunications, Media and Information Technology Sectors and the Implications for Regulation: Towards an Information Society Approach*. Com (97) 623.

Feintuck M. (forthcoming) *Media Regulation, the Public Interest and the Law*. Edinburgh: Edinburgh University Press.

Finnegan, R. Salaman, G. and Thompson, K. (eds) (1987) *Information Technology: Social Issues*. London: Hodder & Stoughton/Open University.

Firestone, C. (1993) 'The search for the holy paradigm: regulating the information infrastructure'. Presented at the Conference on the Changing Nature of Information Infrastructure, Washington, DC, 12 October.

Firestone, C. (1994–5) 'Digital culture and civil society: a new role for intermediaries?', *Intermedia*, 22 (6).

Garnham, N. (1994) 'What is multimedia?', in *Legal Aspects of Multimedia and GIS*. Lisbon 27/28 Legal Advisory Board Conference (DG XIII), October.

Gidari, A. (1998) 'Observations on the state of self-regulation of the Internet'. The Ministerial Conference of the OCED, 'A borderless World: realizing the potential for global electronic commerce'. Ottawa, Canada: Internet Law and Policy Forum.

Gilder, G. (2000) *Telecosm: How Infinite Bandwidth Will Revolutionize Our World*. New York: Free Press.

Gillett, S.E. and Vogelsang, I. (eds) (1999) *Competition, Regulation and Convergence*. Hillsdale, NJ: Erlbaum.

Hargittai, E. (2000) 'Open portals or closed gates? Channeling content on the World Wide Web', *Poetic*, 27 (4): 233–53.

Hitchens, L. (1997) 'Introduction to the special feature on Communications Regulation – New Patterns and Problems', *Journal of Information, Law and Technology (JILT)*, 3. Available at: http://elj.warwick.ac.uk/jilt/issue/1997_3/hitchen.htm.

Hoffman-Riem, W. (1996) *Regulating Media: the Licensing and Supervision of Broadcasting in Six Countries*. New York: Guilford.

Institute for Information Studies (1995) 'Crossroads on the information highway: convergence and diversity in communications technologies', *Annual Review of the Institute for Information Studies*. Washington, DC: The Aspen Institute.

International Telecommunication Union (1995) *World Telecommunication Development Report 1995*. Geneva: ITU. Available at: http://www.itu.int/ti/wtdr95/ (viewed 3 January 2001).

Introna, L. and Nissenbaum, H. (2000) 'Shaping the web: why the politics of search engines matters', *The Information Society*, 16 (3): 169–85.

Jamieson, J. (1995) *Convergence and the New Media: a Roadmap*. London: Institute for Public Policy Research.

Jassem, H. (1999) 'Different strokes for different folks: the intersection of regulatory principles and technology', in S.J. Drucker and G. Gumpert (eds), *Real Law @ Virtual Space: Regulation in Cyberspace*. New Jersey: Hampton.

Kahn, H. and Wiener, A.J. (1967) *The Year 2000*. New York: Macmillan.

Kerr, C. (1983) *The Future of Industrial Societies: Convergence or Continuing Diversity?* Cambridge, MA: Harvard University Press.

Kuhn, T. (1970) *The Structure of Scientific Revolutions*, 2nd edn. Chicago: University of Chicago Press.

Lessig, L. (1999) *Code and Other Laws of Cyberspace*. New York: Basic.

Longstaff, P.H. (2000) *New Ways to Think about the Visions Called 'Convergence': A Guide for Business and Public Policy*. Program on Information Resources Policy, Harvard, July.

Mansell, R. (1999) 'New media competition and access: the scarcity–abundance dialectic', *New Media & Society*, 1 (2): 155–82.

McDowell, S.D. and Maitland, C. (1998) 'Developing television ratings in Canada and the United States: the perils and promises of self-regulation', in M.E. Price (ed.), *The V-Chip Debate*. New York: Erlbaum.

McQuail, D. (1986) 'Is media theory adequate to the challenge of new communications technologies?', in M. Ferguson (ed.), *New Communication Technologies and the Public Interest*. London: Sage. pp. 1–18.

Moore, C. (1996) 'Disintermediation: communications technologies are having some impact', in *Dataquest Interactive: Ask the Analyst*, 19 March.

National Telecommunications and Information Administration (1997) 'Privacy and Self-Regulation in the Information Age', Introduction. http://www.ntia. doc.gov/reports/privacy_rpt.htm.

Negroponte, N. (1995) *Being Digital*. London: Hodder & Stoughton.

Oreja, M. (1999) Seminar on 'Self-regulation in the media'. Jointly organized by the German Presidency of the European Union and the European Commission.

Owen, B. (1999) *The Internet Challenge to Television*. Cambridge, MA: Harvard University Press.

Poulet, Y. and Lamouline, C. (1995) *From Information Superhighways to 'Electronic Democracy': the Impact of Information and Communication Technology on Individual Liberties*. Strasburg: Council of Europe, 4 December.

Press, L. (1994) 'Two cultures, the Internet and interactive TV'. Les Autoroutes électroniques: usages, droit et promesses, 13 May. Available at: http://www.droit. umontreal.ca/CDRP/Conferences/AE/index_fr.html.

Price, M. and Verhulst, S. (2000) 'The concept of self-regulation and the Internet', in J. Waltermann and M. Machill (eds), *Protecting Our Children on the Internet: Towards a New Culture of Responsibility*. Gutersloh: Bertelsmann Foundation.

Prosser, T. (1997) *Law and the Regulators*. Oxford: Clarendon.

Shapiro, A.L. (1999) *The Control Revolution: How the Internet is Putting Individuals in Charge and Changing the World We Know*. New York: PublicAffairs.

Tambini, D. and Verhulst, S. (2000) 'The transition to digital and content regulation', in D. Tambini (ed.), *Communications Reform*. London: Institute for Puplic Policy Research.

Ukrow, J. (1999) *Self-Regulation in the Media Sector and European Community Law*. Saarbrücken: EMR.

Van Dijk, J. (1994) *De netwerkmaatschappij: Sociale aspecten van nieuwe media*. Houten/Zaventem: Bohn Stafleu Vam Loghum.

Verhulst, S. and Marsden, C. (1999) *Convergence in Digital Television Regulation*. London: Blackstone.

Verhulst, S., Goldberg, D. and Prosser, T. (1996) *The Impact of New Communications Technologies on Concentration and Pluralism*. Strasburg: Council of Europe.

Verhulst, S., Goldberg, D. and Prosser, T. (1999) *Regulating the Changing Media*. Oxford: Clarendon.

Waverman, L. (2000) *Broadcasting Policy Hits the Internet*, 22 May. Available at the Global Internet Project: http://www.gip.org/ under 'publications' and category 'governance'.

26

The Real Digital Divide:
Citizens versus Consumers

OSCAR H. GANDY, JR

The study of new media can be approached from a variety of perspectives. One useful approach frames the new media from within a set of distinct perspectives on the users or audiences for these media. Webster and Phalen (1997) describe three prominent constructions that dominate much contemporary writing about audiences. We are familiar with the somewhat critical notion of the audience as a commodity. This perspective suggests that audiences are 'produced' by the media system for sale to advertisers or sponsors of persuasive appeals. A somewhat different construction recognizes that audiences may be consumers of the information and entertainment that media provide. The third perspective, which constructs audiences as 'victims' in need of protection, is explored as a focus of attention common to academics and regulators who are concerned about the harms which might be caused by exposure to certain types of content, such as the increasingly explicit sex and violence on television.

What Webster and Phalen seem to have ignored in their review of the dominant perspectives within audience studies is the somewhat faded construction of the audience as citizen who participates actively in the public sphere. This is an audience thought to have been served historically by non-commercial public broadcasters who once provided high-quality public affairs programming as an alternative to commercial fare. This is the same audience that was served to a lesser extent by segments of the commercial press that were governed more by a concern for the public interest than for the bottom line.

The disregard of the needs of the audience as citizen in favour of the desires of the audience as consumer is likely to widen in what we have come to describe as the new media environment. While mainstream discourse tends to describe the new media in terms of digital convergence, I see the new media as widening the distinction between the citizen and the consumer, and for me, this is the 'real digital divide'.

A Brief History of The Real Digital Divide

The distinction between citizen and consumer is fundamental, although it is often confused or glossed over through an unsatisfactory merger within popular and academic discursive reference to the citizen/consumer. Toby Miller suggests that the citizen is a 'wizened figure from the past and the consumer is a naive phenomenon, essentially a creature of the nineteenth century' (1999: 282). Even though he suggests that both are related as shadows are to the figures that walk the earth, it is the consumer who has been given primacy in contemporary policy discourse.

At the heart of the emergent distinctions between citizens and consumers is a continuing debate about the role of the government and the nature of its responsibility for ensuring that the public interest and the public welfare of citizens are well served. The policies and institutions developed during the heyday of the welfare state were explicitly charged with guaranteeing that the public as a whole, as well as the poor and disadvantaged in particular, would have access to the basic requirements of existence.

At the present time, when the assumptions underlying the identification of basic human needs essential to citizenship have been challenged, we are no longer certain that access to information will be included in that set. We have been warned that 'to argue that one or another type of communication activity is necessary to secure competent citizenship, one would have to appeal to other elements of reason than scientific ones' (Calabrese and Borchert, 1996: 264), and by all signs, most of those elements have been declared ineligible.

The distinctions between the citizen and the consumer are drawn most sharply in the contemporary debates about the nature and function of the public sphere in comparison with the nature and function of the 'free market' (Sunstein, 1997). Contemporary thinking about the public sphere has been influenced substantially by contributions from Jürgen Habermas (1989). This discursive environment is valued for its role in the development of public will and its expression as public opinion. The idealized public sphere is thought to be a fundamental resource for the evolution and growth of democracy (Baker, 2001; Curran, 2000).

The interests of the sovereign consumer have come to replace the interests of citizens as a basis for evaluating the performance of a variety of social systems (Kuttner, 1999). Kuttner credits essays published by liberal economists Arthur Okun and Charles Schultz in the mid 1970s with starting the intellectual swing back towards a fundamentalist *laissez-faire* conception of the ideal. Even though the economists associated with Ronald Reagan's administration are credited with initiating the dismantling of the welfare state, Kuttner (1999: 37) suggests that the door had been opened quite wide by the liberals who had come before him.

Neoliberal political philosophy has found a comfortable berth in an intellectual stream of postmodern thought that denies the possibility of an institutionalized representation of common or collective interests. This is also a view that is pessimistic regarding the possibility of arriving at a democratic consensus (Villa, 1992). Ironically, despite the obvious inequalities we observe within the marketplace, the market is praised as being more responsive than political systems to individual interests (Pauwels, 1999).

Michael Tracey characterizes this recent shift in the ideological ground as having been nothing short of revolutionary:

> Once these intellectual constructs had taken hold, sanctified by the election of numerous right-wing governments, then on the political dais could be placed the individual-as-consumer and the needs and interests of 'the corporation'. And buried deep beneath the rubble of the old order were such concepts as public good, public interest, community, public culture, citizenship, governance, and, increasingly, the nation-state. (1998: 52)

At the core of this shift was the emergence of the 'public choice' school of political economy which made use of sophisticated models to demonstrate the 'impossibility' of democratic governance. On the basis of this assumption, public choice theorists argued against attempting to govern in any part of the social realm in which markets might perform at least as well as government. It is clear that the market was usually given the benefit of the doubt in the absence of compelling evidence to the contrary (Reder, 1999).

Classical works in this area include Anthony Downs' *Economic Theory of Democracy* and Mancur Olson's *The Logic of Collective Action*. While it may be overreaching to claim that these scholars actively identified with and argued on behalf of those with the most power and resources in society, it seems clear that the *laissez-faire* policies that reflect this discursive thread ultimately serve those interests. Indeed, as Kuttner argues, 'much of the degradation of political democracy is the result precisely of market forms and norms taking over the political process' (1999: 348).

A Technological Wedge

The real digital divide is not the product of an autonomous shift in political philosophy. Instead, it is the product of a complex interaction between forces emerging from dynamically shifting spheres, of which the sphere of technology is of central importance (Best and Kellner, 1991; Webster, 1995). Carlotta Perez (1985) invites us to place historic changes in technical systems within the scope of Joseph Schumpeter's interpretation of Kondratieff's long waves of economic expansion and contraction. Among a variety of economic theories that seek to explain the business cycle, long-wave theory is concerned with interpreting the relationships between cycles of economic growth and social and political change (Beniger, 1986; Gordon, 1986; Hall and Preston, 1988).

Perez calls our attention to the relationships between what she identifies as a technoeconomic sphere and a socioinstitutional framework that either facilitates or constrains the emergence of new technical systems (Webster, 1995). Knox and Agnew (1994: 12) illustrate the relationships between long waves and the shorter Kuznet cycles of infrastructural investment. These systems are examined in relation to changes in the nature of capitalist production relations, as well as to critical changes in the relations between the market and the state. It is by examining the complex relations between these systems that we can begin to understand the ways in which new media technology, including the Internet, has been enabled by a process of liberalization and deregulation that has been accompanied by the canonization of the market and its logic (Werbach, 1997). It is this process that has inserted a powerful epistemological wedge between the domains of citizens and consumers.

Schumpeter's characterization of the waves of technological innovation has been described in terms of the waves of 'creative destruction' that they set in motion. Calabrese (1999) cautions us not to assume that the outcomes of such transformations are not always progressive. From his perspective, changes we discuss in terms of globalization are the result of improvements in the position of transnational corporations in relation to those of individual governments. Globalization as a process is dependent upon the spread of telecommunications systems and institutions.

Changes in technical systems are accompanied by changes in social relations. Along these lines, Calabrese identifies the emergence of a new form of 'global citizenship' that reserves the traditional benefits of citizenship for 'the wealthiest members of global society, particularly the corporate-legal person' (1999: 263). While he takes due note of the role of social movements for global democracy, such as the call for a new world information and communication order (NWICO) and its institutionalization within the McBride Commission of UNESCO, Calabrese is ambivalent about the contributions of this movement at the grassroots level of organization. He concludes that 'the effort to develop a progressive global cultural agenda poses little threat to the "trade and investment" orientation of global policymaking in media and communication' (1999: 272).

As Don Lamberton (in this volume) discusses with regard to the economics of information, the movement into what we refer to as an information age has also been shaped in large part by the transformation of information into a commodity. This a fundamental process that heightens the distinction between what economists refer to as public and private goods. Public goods are characterized by several things, the most important of which is the fact that the use of the good 'by one person does not prevent or diminish its use by others' (Noll, 1993–4: 29–30). Private goods, on the other hand, are marked by the ability of persons to limit or otherwise control access to and use of those goods. Information is, by its essence, primarily a public good, and it is only by means of technology and aggressive regulatory control that its private nature can be made dominant.

Vincent Mosco (1989) has captured the essence of this process in terms of the 'pay-per society' that he sees as emerging in its wake. Access to information in the information age would be determined by ability and willingness to pay, rather than by some determination of need or right associated with one's status as citizen or 'member' of a given society. The ability of computer-based systems to manage distinct transactions in smaller and smaller units helps to facilitate the spread of this logic into more and more areas of social life (Robins and Webster, 1999). Increasingly, social interactions become market transactions: 'The growth of our ability to use communications and information systems to measure and monitor market activity with logical exactitude, supports those who contend that market rules should replace, as fully as possible, any government or other public intervention' (Mosco, 1989: 35). It is here that the division between the realm governed by citizens or members of society and the realms governed by consumers in markets is widened by the wedge of information technology.

A Marketplace Logic

Marketization is a term that has been used to characterize the shift in public policy that supports the establishment of a dominant role for private corporations in the management of public culture (Murdock and Golding, 1999). Marketization evolved rapidly along with the adoption of a 'marketplace standard' for the regulation of media in the 'public interest, convenience and necessity' (Polic and Gandy, 1991). Prior to the development of marketization, the dominant regulatory model in the United States was one of public trusteeship, a system through which private firms would be granted the opportunity to operate what was usually a quite profitable broadcast enterprise as long as that operation was determined to be in the public interest.

The spread of marketization has been hastened by the use of auctions as an 'efficient' means of allocating basic communications resources, such as control of segments of the electromagnetic spectrum. The role for citizens in the determination of which provider might gain a 'licence' or a franchise to operate a communication service in the public interest was never great. It has virtually disappeared under the current wave of marketization.

The development of marketization has also been accompanied by a much revised approach toward market concentration. Not only have the number of mergers within the media industries increased, but limits on the extent of ownership within markets have been reduced almost to insignificance (McChesney, 1999). The assumption that oligopoly is an efficient level of organization for communications has been accompanied by acceptance of the view that it is not actual competition, but the *possibility* of competitive entry into a market that will serve to discipline service providers (McNamara, 1991). As supporters of marketization have presented the idea of digital convergence as a marker of technological progress, they suggest that any 'artificial' barriers to entry into the communications market would represent a cost to society (Murdock and Golding, 1999).

Supporters of marketization suggest that government intervention in media markets can only be justified when it appears necessary to force markets to do what they would ordinarily do without interference. It should be clear, however, that there never were any markets that were truly self-regulating. The market for information is no different. The rational management of information markets depends upon a complex network of codes and modes of regulatory intervention that are required to manage the massive externalities, rent-seeking and opportunistic actions that are commonplace rather than exceptional (Mansell, 1993). The introduction of information technology and new media systems only increases the need for governance.

New Media and Convergence

The new media may be defined in comparison with earlier versions of communications technology (Bolter and Grusin, 2000). The new media are, for the most part, old media that have been transformed through their reconfiguration into devices capable of managing digital signals. Of special significance is the extent to which these signals can be combined or multiplexed, so that they can be distributed by means of a single cable, wire or waveguide, for storage or display by different devices within a household (Midwinter, 1995). The new media can be highly specialized or optimized for a particular function, or they can be highly flexible, like the multimedia computer that is capable of reproducing high-fidelity sound and brilliant colour images as well as alphanumeric text.

New media systems continue to be added to the mix. They are distinguished primarily by the extent to which they enable greater fidelity, realism, reliability and ease of operation. Of particular importance in the ways in which the new media have developed is the degree of miniaturization that has been enabled by the development of the transistor and the printed circuit, and their incorporation into the microchip. Miniaturization not only enables portability, but more fundamentally supports the *privatization* of media consumption. The development of the 'Walkman' by Sony marked a critical moment in the development of individualized, personal media. The expansion of channels afforded by advances in digital signal processing also contributes to individualized, private consumption of media. The emergence of an endless supply of 'my' media for the 'me' generation is the logical consequence of a technological move toward the expansion of options through the compression and integration of signals.

The convergence of forms that is enabled by digital signal processing also has implications for a convergence of functions in terms of the times and places where media content will be acquired and consumed. The notion of a 'seamless web of interconnectivity' that has emerged as an ideal state for convergent media includes the expectation that devices would be able to 'tap into' the global information network by a variety of means, almost without regard to location, and without fear of encountering incompatible technical standards.

Douglas Kellner (1999) reminds us that new communications technologies are more than 'information technologies'. They are 'also technologies of entertainment, communication and play, encompassing and restructuring both labor and leisure' (1999: 243). Kellner's point is that the new media have emerged to serve new functions within a transformed capitalism, and the new economy seems poised to incorporate work and recreation into the same media systems to an extent more common than in the past.

Kellner suggests that we are 'too early in the beginnings of this adventure to determine its structure, social relations, cultural forms and effects' although it is clear enough to him that 'a technological revolution is going on, that it will have massive effects' (1999: 253). His is an invitation to develop theories that will support intervention into the stream of development to ensure that the democratic possibilities of the new media are not foreclosed.

Household Demand for New Media

As we are reminded by Robins and Webster (1999), however, changes in technology are not independent of other changes in the environments into which they are introduced, and from which they emerge. The nature of demand for information resources changes as the nature of the organization of social and family life changes. Jorge Schement (1995) invites us to think about information as a resource that is consumed within households, but the nature of households has changed dramatically.

Schement describes a steady decline in the average size of the American household, which began around 1840. This decline reflects a substantial increase in the number of single-person households. Individualization in media technology has therefore been accompanied by individualization in households – a proportion that reached 25 per cent by 1990. The fact that people who live alone also happen to be high users of media should not surprise us.

Schement's analysis of the rates of penetration of different media in American households identifies several facts worthy of our attention. The availability of radios, televisions and increasingly computers in several rooms of the house enables both an expansion of the time spent with media and an increase in the amount of time spent consuming those media in isolation from others. The decline in movie attendance (Austin, 1989) and other public entertainment also 'reflects the decline of public life and the dominance of the private sphere' (Schement, 1995: 149).

This is not without consequence. As people have turned away from the newspaper toward television and radio, they have abandoned a medium characterized by 'depth for sources of more simplistic information' (Schement, 1995: 148). In order to manage an increase in the amount and variety of information available to them, people have had to either become more active in filtering this information or, as increasingly appears to be the case, delegate to other 'trusted agents' the responsibility for serving this function. As a result of the aura of personalization that surrounds these new media, individuals may actually feel better about knowing less and less about the world around them.

We have traditionally understood media use within the home as serving as a 'window on the world' that exists beyond our own direct personal experience. The 'uses and gratifications' perspective (Blumler and Katz, 1974) also emphasized the ways in which media are used to provide refuge or escape from the pressures and demands of the outside world. In addition, reliance on advertising as the primary means of financing media consumed in the home has firmly established a link between the home and the marketplace. The ease with which market transactions can be completed through the Internet has only strengthened this link.

Schement (1995) also suggests that new media have increased the amount of work that will be performed at home by telecommuters and others who are continually 'accessible' through a variety of networked connections to the home. Schement suggests that as a result of these changes, 'the themes that once formed the old boundaries – between work and home, between public and private life, between labor and leisure – no longer appear so clear or so fixed' (1995: 156).

As the functions served by media in the home become integrated and blurred, it becomes difficult to determine the best way to evaluate the performance of those media. From a market perspective, continually increasing demand works well enough. From a public interest perspective, only a few seem concerned enough to ask.

Media Performance and the Public Interest

Denis McQuail (1992) has organized the most comprehensive review of the ways in which the performance of mass media has been evaluated through the lens of a public interest standard. Although McQuail suggests that the meaning of the public interest is difficult to pin down, one would usually find an emphasis on the distinction between the public and the private aspects of communication. He suggests that we use, at least provisionally, 'the term "public interest" to refer to the complex of supposed informational, cultural and social benefits to the wider society which go beyond the immediate, particular and individual interests of those who participate in public communication, whether as senders or receivers' (1992: 3).

Because of differences in the definition of the public interest, as well as in the evaluation of the means thought most likely to ensure it, there is no simple way to evaluate the performance of individual media, or the media system as a whole. Because of conflicting ideas about the nature of the public interest, it is impossible even to predict that an increase in source and content diversity would result in a net contribution to the public interest. McChesney (1999) describes this as a massive paradox. There has been an increase in the supply of media, and a subsequent increase in the amount of time devoted to its consumption by individuals. At the same time, an examination of numerous measures of civic well-being in the United States suggest an overall decline. Robert Putnam (1995) has described this in terms of a decline in 'social capital' that he sees as a consequence of reduced interaction between people. This reduced interaction is believed to reflect declining interpersonal trust.

McChesney (1999) explains this 'rich media, poor democracy' paradox in terms of a decline in the extent to which public service is a principle governing the operation of media. Others emphasize the shift away from engagement with serious topics toward an emphasis on sensationalism and escapist fare. Some of the criticism of mainstream television fare is that it demands little from its audiences, whereas public broadcasting fare has traditionally been more demanding. Indeed, at one point in the history of public broadcasting, the pursuit of qualitative measures of the audience was an attempt to articulate and then quantify the levels of engagement assumed to be beneficial to an active and informed public (Frank and Greenberg, 1982).

There is no longer a well-established and legitimate basis for regulation and control of media. McQuail suggests that 'in an "information society", the "public interest", however defined, is more to lie in securing the benefits of information and communication than in preventing harm from communication' (1992: 307). At the same time, this reluctance to control the distribution of media considered by some to be harmful is nearly matched by a lack of concern about subsidizing or ensuring broader access to media and information on 'public interest' grounds.

McQuail suggests that it is critical to examine not only what is available within the market, but also what actually reaches the public and with what consequences for public welfare. Although his analysis is a bit limited by its engagement with the audience at an aggregate level, Philip Napoli's (1997) approach to the reassessment of programme diversity seems responsive to McQuail's concern. Diversity in output needs to be considered in light of diversity of exposure or consumption. Other critics suggest that an increase in the diversity of supply of media may actually be disruptive of the social whole if people tend to become more narrowly specialized in their exposure to this material (Katz, 1996). Whereas Putnam (1995) largely assumed that media exposure led to withdrawal from society, McQuail's suggestions invite an analysis of the extent to which the consumption of more hours of less diverse, less challenging, and less socially relevant content produces more or less engagement with others in the public sphere.

Evaluating Commercial Media Performance

Part of the concern with the public interest is the extent to which the presumed needs of the citizen for news and public affairs could be expected to be supplied by commercial media. John McManus (1994) provides one of the more detailed explications of the distinction between what a market-driven and a more traditional, socially responsible press would provide. McManus observes a tendency among commercial news media to rely on sensationalism, rather than analysis, because fast-moving action is entertaining rather than challenging to the audience.

Of course, it is important to recognize the contribution that a steady diet of sensationalist, personalized news coverage might make to the development of the tastes and preferences of the next generation of audiences for the news. Contrary to the assumptions of mainstream economists, tastes and preferences are learned over time, and to the extent that competitive pressures lead the producers of news to lower the bar, then we should expect the level of audience expectations to move in the same direction.

In a sense, we can understand this transformation in public expectation and demand as a kind of *deskilling*. We have traditionally thought about deskilling in relation to the introduction of new technologies that made it unreasonable for people to invest in learning skills that were no longer required. To the extent that people come to depend upon pre-digested news, they can no longer be expected to invest in the development of the analytical skills needed to make sense of more complex arguments and evidence. Some observers suggest that many of 'the younger generation, with access to an incredible array of entertainment, appear to have given up even the pretense that "being informed" is useful and necessary. US. journalism itself sometimes seems to be giving up the effort to

do anything but tell stories and provide spectacle' for this population (Bird, 2000: 225–6).

A concern with the general decline in the quality of the mass press toward what is characterized as 'tabloid journalism' has been explored by a number of authors in a recent collection (Sparks and Tulloch, 2000). Colin Sparks (2000) frames the debates about 'tabloidization' as a non-specific concern about a decline in American journalistic standards. Acccording to the critics he reviews, the performance of the mainstream press is seen to suffer from imitation, or from adoption of the standards of this less respectable medium, or as a result of its pursuit of stories that had their origins in the tabloid press. Tracey sees this as part of a 'dumbing down' which is to be understood through 'a sense of the corrosive influence of the main currents of popular culture: linguistic poverty and therefore a mental and moral poverty ... the trivialization of public discourse, and evangelism of the ephemeral, the celebration of the insignificant, and the marginalization of the important, [by] cults of empty celebrity' (1998: 264).

Calabrese (2000) reminds us that, at least within the television mainstream in the United States, concerns about commercial viability have always played a role in the production and distribution of news. Still, it is also clear that in a more recent history of commercial broadcasting, mainstream news organizations have found themselves in more direct competition with so-called tabloid news programmes. Calabrese associates this move toward the bottom with the changes in the definition of the public responsibilities of commercial broadcasters, and the more general move to the market as the arbiter of the public interest. He cites the assessment in 1982 by FCC Commissioner Mark Fowler that the public interest was whatever the public was most interested in, as the key indicator of this conceptual shift. He argues further that the application of audience ratings to the evaluation of news programmes is the primary indicator of the 'dictatorship of the market' (2000: 46).

The Public Interest and Public Service Media

The tensions between the interests that may be most closely identified with those of consumers, which we would expect to be served by the private market, and the interests that we would identify more closely with those of citizens, which would be served by organs of the public sphere, have often been played out in the struggles to shape public or government-supported media systems (Raboy, 1990).

Michael Tracey underscores the differences between commercial and public service broadcasting quite succinctly: 'In a public system, television producers acquire money to make programmes. In a commercial system they make programmes to acquire money' (1998: 18).

The concerns expressed by William Hoynes (1999) are also quite clear: 'In an increasingly commercialized media world, the past decade's expansion in television channel capacity and the explosion of the world wide web, paradoxically, only reinforce the need for the kind of citizen-oriented, non-commercial media that public broadcasting can be.' Hoynes suggests that the mission of public broadcasting included a commitment to provide for public exposure to contemporary issues and perspectives that would not gain access to the commercial networks. Unfortunately, of course, it was precisely this kind of content that brought unwanted political pressure to bear on the flow of funding to the public broadcasting system in the United States.

One argument used against funding of public broadcasts is the claim that their function has been absorbed by commercial media. Public broadcasters are no longer a source of alternative fare. By focusing on the programmes classified as culture, civic discourse, education and information more generally, Noam (1998) identified several cable networks that were devoted almost entirely to the production and distribution of these sorts of programmes. On the basis of his assessment of the distribution of these programmes by cable networks and some independent stations, Noam concluded that the amount of public interest programming available to the general public has actually increased substantially. In Noam's view, the amount of total programme hours 'increased phenomenally' at an 'annual compound growth rate of 10%' (1998: 38). The amount of what he termed 'public interest programming' increased some 365 per cent between 1969 and 1997.

While Noam's analysis of commercial programme supply was focused on rather broadly defined content categories, important criticism of both commercial and non-commercial broadcast performance emphasizes differences *within* categories. William Hoynes (1999) provided an analysis of what he describes as 'the most widely-circulating public affairs programs' available through the Public Broadcasting Service (PBS) in 1998. This sample of 75 programmes included a large number of business reports, in addition to weekly reviews of the news. In addition to a characterization of the different stories, Hoynes took note of the occupational status of those who 'are granted access to the public airwaves' through PBS programmes. Not surprisingly, these programmes present a rather narrow range of 'elite' voices. Although Hoynes acknowledged the journalistic tradition of reliance on such sources, he suggests that if the public broadcasting service is truly an alternative service, then we should expect a departure from tradition. Not surprisingly, Hoynes found that news about the economy was 'almost entirely

refracted through the views of business people, investors, and reporters who explain what corporate leaders and investors are currently thinking ... In sum, the economic coverage is so narrow that the views and the activities of most citizens become irrelevant.'

Hoynes' conclusion from his analysis of public affairs on PBS (1999; Croteau et al., 1996) is that 'the public-as-citizens approach is taking a back seat to the public-as-market model at the "new PBS"'. He suggests that

> instead of wide-ranging discussions and debates, the kinds that might engage viewers as citizens, not simply as audiences, public television provides programs that are populated by the standard set of elite news sources ... and a similar brand of insider discourse, that is featured regularly on commercial television. This insider orientation makes it hard to define what, outside of the one-hour length of the evening news and the documentary format, defines public television as innovative, independent, or alternative.

Ironically, Hoynes would seem to agree with Noam's conclusion that there is very little that the public broadcasting system in the United States provides that is not already widely available from commercial sources.

B.J. Bullert (1997) argues that both 'journalistic standards' and a fear of controversy that might threaten relationships between public broadcasters have served to limit the contribution that social documentaries might make.

> The issue is not simply that the views of minority and marginalized groups are worthy of public attention, but that the quality of our political life depends on all of us knowing more about the life experiences of each of us, especially those whose lives are underrepresented in the mass media. The struggle for representation and access to the public television airwaves is a political struggle for legitimacy in the public forum.

Caution in the selection and support of independent production means that 'public television's promise as a vital forum in our democracy will remain unrealized' (1997: 191).

Willard Rowland (1998) identified some of the contradictions faced by the public broadcasters in the United States that he felt were unlike those experienced by other public broadcasters around the globe. But all public broadcasters appear to have been forced to struggle with the need to be different at the same time they were expected to be popular. Rowland suggests that with few exceptions 'the debate in the US. has never been able to address the linkages among entertainment, popularity and quality so well developed abroad. The notion that there could be a public-service mandate to bring quality into the popular and thereby improve the tenor of a wide range of television, and that to do so would require the establishment of a large-scale, exceedingly well funded noncommercial programming institution, has never been widely understood in the US.' Tracey suggests that for the BBC at least, it was agreed that 'the essence of public service broadcasting is to make popular programmes good, and good programmes popular' (1998: 21).

Other reviews of the continually evolving public broadcasting system are similarly mixed. At one level, Blumler's (1998) assessment of the status of the commitment by European public broadcasters to meeting the special needs of children was largely positive. In fact, survey data indicated that there had been a marked expansion in the amount of programming designed specifically for children. At the same time, this expansion in the amount of programming was accompanied by a paradoxical reduction in its diversity, reflecting increased reliance upon imported material. A substantial part of that material was animation from the United States. The influence of commercial standards is suggested in the fact that those public broadcasters with higher amounts of commercial income also tended to programme more imported animation. Rather than increasing diversity, as these broadcasters have responded to the market, 'the range of its children's programming has narrowed' (1998: 348).

What we now observe is a belief that there is no special authority, and no automatic assumption that public agencies are any more likely to supply essential cultural materials than any other suppliers. Indeed, in the view of some observers, 'public interest objectives appear as barriers to the free play of these [market] forces rather than as essential guarantors of access to the communicative and cultural resources required to underwrite citizenship rights' (Murdock and Golding, 1999: 127). Murdock and Golding find a clear sign in British telecommunications policy reports that references to citizens, and the interests of citizens, have been deleted in favour of references to the interests of consumers.

New Media and the Public Sphere

We are reminded by Nancy Fraser (1993: 2) that the public sphere, in the sense that Habermas (1989; 1996) describes it, is a place in which political participation occurs through discourse. That is, the public sphere is 'not an arena of market relations but rather one of discursive relations'. The fact that historically there were probably competing public spheres does not eliminate the more basic distinction between these political spheres and that of the market. The fact that there may be 'subaltern counterpublics', where differences in power, interests and needs may be reflected in identity terms, ought not invite confusion about whether such distinctions justify differential treatment (Baker, 1997).

Although the public interest 'burden' of broadcasters has been lessened quite substantially of late, the introduction of each new technical system provides an opportunity for advocates of explicit guarantees of public benefit to argue their importance. The authorization of digital broadcasting in the United States is among the most recent (Firestone and Garmer, 1998), although much of the discussion has been focused on the status of rationales for regulation, rather than a reconsideration of what sorts of guarantees serve the public interest.

Sara Bentivegna (1998) asks whether it is even possible to use the concept of the public sphere in the age of the Internet. Because of the nature of the Internet and the ways in which it facilitates access to information and communication, it seems to some observers that the Internet environment might be an ideal 'electronic public square'. Bentivegna and others note that substantial limitations in access have been discussed under the rubric of a digital divide, but they remind us that even the idealized bourgeois public sphere had been marked by numerous divides and exclusions.

Bentivegna suggests that Internet newsgroups come quite close to meeting the requirements of the Athenian *agora* in that in the best of these groups there is equality among members. In addition, participation involves reference to personal experience, and discussions involve the reformulation and interpretation of information provided by traditional mainstream media. Her analysis of four Italian newsgroups devoted to political discussion in 1997 indicated that there was a high level of active discursive engagement. She also observed a high level of interaction from different individuals that was enabled in part by the absence of participants attempting to monopolize discussion by sending a large number of messages.

While much of the popular media's attention to newsgroups has been focused on the absence of civility in these discussions, Bentivegna suggests that the 'prevailing tone of discussion seems to be based on the respect for the speaker – who is only rarely insulted or even attacked – and upon the desire to participate in the discussion, asking and offering information or soliciting opinions' (1998: 7). Her conclusions regarding the potential for political discourse within virtual communities were actually quite favourable. Because the interaction within newsgroups is akin to conversation, where people both produce and consume information, 'the asymmetry of the communicative relations activated by the traditional media is, in this case, entirely nullified'. Bentivegna recognizes some of the limitations of her research, including the impossibility of knowing the number of inactive participants (lurkers, who only read, but never contribute to the discussion), or of knowing what kinds of barriers keep other potential participants out of the interaction.

The perspective of Benjamin Barber (1998) is far less sanguine. First, he takes issue with the meaningfulness of virtual communities. He suggests that 'there may be some new form of community developing among the myriad solitaries perched in front of their screens and connected only by their fingertips to the new web defined by the Internet. But the politics of that "community" has yet to be invented, and it is hardly likely to be as democratic as a result of market imperatives' (1998: 83). While he grants the existence of sites of the sort Bentivegna examines, he believes that they are in a distinct and declining minority. Barber agrees that technologies can help democracy, 'but only if they are programmed to do so, and then, only in terms of the paradigms and political theories that inform the program. Left to the market it is likely only to reproduce the vices of politics as usual' (1998: 91).

Barber's assessment of the potential of the Internet is based on a survey of the World Wide Web (Barber et al., 1997). Like Bentivegna, Barber and his colleagues sought to include websites that addressed political issues, including those which encouraged civic and political participation. If he had merely sought out the most popular sites on the web, very few sites devoted to political discourse would have been identified. Very few political sites have made it into the lists of 'top 100 sites', and Barber et al. suggest that 'the internet is at present predominantly commercial and is becoming more so by the day, coming to resemble a realm of shopping, play, entertainment, and little else' (1997: 38).

Barber's (1984) preference for what he refers to as 'strong democracy' led him to seek out sites that were explicitly concerned with 'engaging citizens in public decision-making'. Although the range of websites included in Barber's analysis was quite broad, the overwhelming majority appeared to be rather traditional one-way sources of information. 'Numerous sites that were supposedly dedicated to leading people into a process of civic and political participation merely posted essays or catalogued organizations to contact for further information – an obvious and severe underutilization of the internet's capacities' (Barber et al., 1997: 33). Because web page designers tend to provide numerous links to other sites, Barber and his colleagues suggested that the 'World Wide Web is truly a *web*, in which users are caught and sometimes trapped' rather than aided in their search for engagement in the democratic process.

The Markle Foundation funded a number of experiments designed to evaluate the utility of new media as a resource for public discourse (Murray, 1998). However, even when the experiments were conducted within a community of sophisticated elites, it was difficult to sustain interest. This was especially true when there were problems with the technology, or with the quality of the content.

Murray suggests that in order for these 'hyperforums' to succeed, it will be important to determine who is likely to be in the community of participants, and what their motivations and expectations of the experience are. In the past, this sort of planning has proven to be troublesome even in an experimental context. It seems far from likely that it would be sustainable as a voluntary community service activity.

Calabrese and Borchert (1996) suggest that here, too, the difference between a 'consumer' model, and a 'civic' model, of network activity will ultimately determine the contribution of the Internet to 'post-industrial democracy'. They suggest that the network environment will be stratified and segmented, and that a 'new class of technical and professional intelligentsia' will be engaged in activities that will be 'exclusionary, both by default and by design' (1996: 252). Interestingly, they suggest that the civic activities of this new class will be financed primarily by the revenue generated by the lower social strata who will be involved in the network primarily as consumers, rather than as participants, or sources of argument and analysis.

Although these issues are pursued to some degree by Bentivegna (in this volume), it is also important to consider some of the challenges that the 'borderless' character of the Internet poses for notions of citizenship (Kahin and Nesson, 1997). David Johnson and David Post (1998) discuss the problems occasioned by the failure of 'geographically based governance mechanisms' to manage the systems of relations that the Internet has made commonplace. Unlike postmodernists who deny the possibility of governability, Johnson and Post have been evaluating a variety of different ways of identifying or dividing up 'patches' of territory defined in part by the nature of the interactions or transactions that take place. A similar perspective is explored by Jerry Kang (2000), who suggests that different rules governing racial identification may be established as a function of the nature of the transactions that define the appropriate 'zoning' regulations for different 'cyberspaces'.

Problems of establishing the rights and responsibilities of membership are quite different from those associated with geographically defined domains. Johnson and Post (1998: 46–7) seem to prefer the sorts of constructed identities that are more compatible with markets, rather than polities. Individuals who are dissatisfied with the rules established by system operators (sysops), or by volunteers, are expected to 'vote with their modems', relying on *exit* rather than *voice*. They recognize, however, that this market-oriented form of governance will 'play havoc with our notions of the virtues of equality'. They fail to recognize that there will also be important differences in the ability of 'netizens' to recognize and respond to threats and opportunities in a dynamic network environment.

DIFFERENCE AND INEQUALITY

The most common references to the digital divide have been those which emphasize the varying gaps in access between social groups defined by race, gender and ethnicity. These varying gaps have been discussed in the context of public policies designed to ensure universal access to information services. The idea of universal service had initially been identified with the development of a regulated monopoly that would ensure that basic telephone service would be available to all at a reasonable cost, and without regard to the substantial differences in the actual cost of supplying that service in low-density rural areas (Wilson, 2000). Universal service in telecommunications had come to be equated with an entitlement, a right to goods and services that have been argued to be essential for participation in society. While a high degree of success may be claimed for the efforts to achieve universal access, the issue remains on the public agenda (Sparks, 2001).

Depending upon how access is defined and measured, differences in access have been characterized as reflecting a digital divide, that over time has narrowed with regard to gender, while widening with regard to race and ethnicity in the United States (Anderson et al., 1995; Benton Foundation, 1998; Garmer, 1998; Hoffman et al., 1998; National Telecommunications and Information Administration, 1998; Neu et al., 1999). Similar disparities have been identified in other nations, and between nations (Dutton, 1999).

Susan Hadden (1991) examined the ways in which different technological systems diffused as a function of the extent to which they were dependent upon the existence of a particular infrastructural base. Technical systems that made use of already existing systems in the home diffused far more rapidly than systems that depended upon the creation of a network. The diffusion of cable television is a prime example in that it has taken far longer than broadcast television to diffuse throughout the population. She argued further that the ways in which a networked interactive technology become woven into the social fabric of a society makes some degree of public decision-making unavoidable. Here she made reference both to network economies and to the fact that the use of public space and resources makes it impossible for the adoption of some technologies to depend solely upon individual decisions.

Telecommunications networks are fundamentally social technologies, and, as a result, it is appropriate to consider the extent to which universal access is both necessary and beneficial for the society as a whole. The extent to which networks are defined by their connectivity and interactivity helps to define their social character. From this perspective, Hadden (1991) argued that universal access means more than availability, but includes widespread use of the technology. Her examination of the substantial inequality in access to basic telephone service led to the conclusion that 'the seemingly natural and inevitable forces of diffusion' are not sufficient to ensure that genuinely universal service would be achieved (1991: 68–9).

By focusing on functions, rather than technologies, Hadden suggested that there was a need to establish universal access to 'essential information'. This is a view that was echoed by Nicholas Garnham (1999) from the perspective of Amartya Sen's capabilities approach to the evaluation of welfare systems. Sen's approach to the determination of needs in relation to the quality of life that a social system might be expected to provide takes into account a recognition that people differ in their natural endowments. As a result, they will require different sorts of enhancements to achieve a requisite level of functional capability. Sen's argument is that there is far less variation in capacities between people, and, as a result, there is a greater possibility of arriving at interpersonal comparisons as the basis for evaluating social policy than of using the notions of utility that have troubled economists for so long.

Garnham and Hadden agree that access is not sufficient as a goal of universalism. Functional utility must be specified as that goal. Garnham argues that the 'capabilities approach moves us away from the metrics of both money and pleasure toward the ways of being and doing enabled by communication and toward an analysis of the barriers that stand in the way' (1994: 124).

Eric Fredin's (2001) discussions regarding the nature of hypertext and the expanded capacity for personalization in the new computer-based media underscore the importance of our recognizing that diversity of exposure will characterize our use of media. He suggests that in order for hypermedia to work, people will continually make choices within rather than merely between news stories. Fredin describes a variety of hypertext formats that seem likely to emerge to help structure the choices that audiences for news might make. It is in the nature of the medium that substantial differences will emerge between individuals in terms of the skill and creativity that navigation through a maze of potential links will invite and reward. Fredin's futuristic look at the relations between information users and information providers describes a way in which the public interest is served by means of a highly individualized rather than a commonly shared framework of understanding.

Given the shift in philosophy that subordinates interests associated with citizenship to those associated with culture and individualistic consumption, it is not surprising that the existence of a digital divide has come to be understood in terms of a market failure that is expected to decline in importance over time (Garmer, 1998). The fact that specialized content is focused on the upscale consumer can be taken as an explanation for the fact that the digital divide is almost non-existent at higher levels of income (Neu et al., 1999). The absence of content of interest to those from underclass backgrounds, those with low levels of literacy in English, and those with interests in local politics and culture explains the reluctance of such persons to invest in acquiring computers and network services, or even spending much time using Internet-based resources in libraries and community centres (Children's Partnership, 2000).

WHAT IS TO BE DONE?

Tracey (1998: 263) suggests that diversity and the differences among us are indeed social constructions, but he argues further that the particular construction of these differences is shaped in large part by the new systems of communication that have emerged in the past 20 years. The social trajectory enabled by the new media 'profoundly individualistic and definitely not collective, public, shared, or coherent'. The real digital divide appears likely to widen.

Most critical observers of this unfolding process agree that it is concerted action, rather than some natural self-correcting tendency within complex systems, that will re-establish a balance between the roles, spheres and media of exchange and coordination that Habermas (White, 1988), Perez and others (Webster, 1995) have identified for us.

Robert Kuttner is clear in his recommendations for the future:

> If markets are not perfectly correcting, then the only check on their excesses must be extra-market institutions. These reside in values other than market values, and in affiliations that transcend mere hedonism and profit maximization. To temper the market, one must reclaim civil society and government, and make clear that government and civic vitality are allies, not adversaries. That enterprise, in turn, requires a more effective politics, both as the emblem of a free democratic people and as the necessary counterweight to the inflated claims about markets. If we are to balance markets with other social goals, that requires an engaged and informed electorate, as well as healthy, legitimate political institutions. (1999: 362)

The real digital divide has not been produced by some irreversible geological process. Each of the underlying systems that have been involved in shifting our fields of view are still responsive to collective action. The new media can be used to mobilize a social collective in defence of cherished values, including those associated with individual and collective identity. Despite the objections of postmodernists and entrepreneurs as well, a renewed citizens' movement is likely to emerge to ensure that 'the people' will not become extinct, nor will they live out their lives in special preserves or sanctuaries. Instead they will come together to build a new global public sphere. As to when this will occur, only time will tell.

REFERENCES

Anderson, R., Bikson, T., Law, S. and Mitchell, B. (1995) *Universal Access to E-mail: Feasibility and Societal Implications*. Santa Monica, CA: RAND Corporation.

Austin, B. (1989) *Immediate Seating: a Look at Movie Audiences*. Belmont, CA: Wadsworth.

Baker, C.E. (1997) 'Giving the audience what it wants', *Ohio State Law Journal*, 58 (2): 311–417.

Baker, C.E. (2001) 'Implications of rival visions of electoral campaigns', in W. Bennett and R. Entman (eds), *Mediated Politics: Communication in the Future of Democracy*. New York: Cambridge University Press. pp. 342–60.

Barber, B. (1984) *Strong Democracy*. Berkeley, CA: University of California Press.

Barber, B. (1998) 'The new telecommunications technology: endless frontier or the end of democracy?', in M. Price, R. Nole and L. Morrisett (eds), *A Communications Cornucopia: Markle Foundation Essays on Information Policy*. Washington, DC: Brookings Institution. pp. 72–98.

Barber, B., Matteson, K. and Peterson, J. (1997) 'The state of "electronically enhanced democracy": a survey of the internet'. Walt Whitman Center for the Culture and Politics of Democracy, Rutgers University, New Brunswick, NJ.

Beniger, J. (1986) *The Control Revolution: Technical and Economic Origins of the Information Society*. Cambridge, MA: Harvard University Press.

Bentivegna, S. (1998) 'Talking politics on the net'. Joan Shorenstein Center, Harvard University, Cambridge, MA.

Benton Foundation (1998) *Losing Ground Bit by Bit: Low Income Communities in the Information Age*. Washington, DC: Benton Foundation.

Best, S. and Kellner, D. (1991) *Postmodern Theory: Critical Interrogations*. New York: Guilford.

Bird, S.E. (2000) 'Audience demands in a murderous market', in C. Sparks and J. Tulloch (eds), *Tabloid Tales: Global Debates over Media Standards*. Lanham, MD: Rowman & Littlefield. pp. 213–28.

Blumler, J. (1998) 'Children's television in European public broadcasting', in R. Noll and M. Price (eds), *A Communications Cornucopia: Markle Foundation Essays on Information Policy*. Washington, DC: Brookings Institution. pp. 337–49.

Blumler, J. and Katz, E. (eds) (1974) *The Uses of Mass Communications: Current Perspectives on Gratifications Research*. Beverly Hills, CA: Sage.

Bolter, J. and Grusin, R. (2000) *Remediation: Understanding New Media*. Cambridge, MA: MIT Press.

Bullert, B.J. (1997) *Public Television: Politics and the Battle over Documentary Film*. New Brunswick, NJ: Rutgers University Press.

Calabrese, A. (1999) 'The welfare state, the information society, and the ambivalence of social movements', in A. Calabrese and J.-C. Burgelman (eds), *Communication, Citizenship, and Social Policy*. Lanham, MD: Rowman & Littlefield. pp. 259–77.

Calabrese, A. (2000) 'Political space and the trade in television news', in C. Sparks and J. Tulloch (eds), *Tabloid Tales: International Studies on the Tabloidization of Newspapers and Television*. Lanham, MD: Rowman & Littlefield. pp. 43–62.

Calabrese, A. and Borchert, M. (1996) 'Prospects for electronic democracy in the United States: rethinking communication and social policy', *Media, Culture & Society*, 18: 249–68.

Children's Partnership (2000) *Online Content for Low-Income and Underserved Americans: the Digital Divide's New Frontier*. Santa Monica, CA: Children's Partnership.

Croteau, D., Hoynes, W. et al. (1996) *The Political Diversity of Public Television: Polysemy, the Public Sphere, and the Conservative Critique of PBS*. Journalism and Mass Communications Monographs 157.

Curran, J. (2000) 'Rethinking media and democracy', in J. Curran and M. Gurevitch (eds), *Mass Media and Society*, 3rd edn. London: Arnold. pp. 120–54.

Downs, A. (1957) *An Economic Theory of Democracy*. New York: Harper.

Dutton, W. (ed.) (1999) *Society on the Line: Information Politics in the Digital Age*. Oxford: Oxford University Press.

Firestone, C. and Garmer, A. (eds) (1998) *Digital Broadcasting and the Public Interest*. Reports and papers of the Aspen Institute Communications and Society Program. Washington, DC: Aspen Institute.

Frank, R. and Greenberg, M. (1982) *Audiences for Public Television*. Beverly Hills, CA: Sage.

Fraser, N. (1993) 'Rethinking the public sphere: a contribution to the critique of actually existing democracy', in B. Robbins (ed.), *The Phantom Public Sphere*. Minneapolis, MN: University of Minnesota Press. pp. 1–32.

Fredin, E. (2001) 'Frame breaking and creativity in hypermedia news stories', in S. Reese, O. Gandy and A. Grant (eds), *Framing Public Life*. Hillsdale, NJ: Erlbaum.

Garmer, A. (1998) *Investing in Diversity*. Washington, DC: Aspen Institute.

Garnham, N. (1999) 'Amartya Sen's "capabilities" approach to the evaluation of welfare: its application to communications', in A. Calabrese and J.-C. Burgelman (eds), *Communication, Citizenship, and Social Policy*. Lanham, MD: Rowman & Littlefield. pp. 113–24.

Gordon, R. (ed.) (1986) *The American Business Cycle*. Chicago: University of Chicago Press.

Habermas, J. (1989) *The Structural Transformation of the Public Sphere: an Inquiry into a Category of Bourgeois Society*. Cambridge, MA: MIT Press.

Habermas, J. (1996) *Between Facts and Norms: Contributions to a Discourse Theory of Law and Democracy*. Cambridge, MA: MIT Press.

Hadden, S. (1991) 'Technologies of universal service', in *Universal Telephone Services: Ready for the 21st Century?* Queenstown, MD: Institute for Information Studies.

Hall, P. and Preston, P. (1988) *The Carrier Wave: New Information and the Geography of Innovation, 1846–2003*. London: Unwin Hyman.

Hoffman, D., Novak, T. and Venkatash, A. (1998) 'Diversity on the Internet: the relationship of race to access and usage', in A. Garmer (ed.), *Investing in Diversity: Advancing Opportunities for Minorities and the Media*. Washington, DC: Aspen Institute. pp. 125–93.

Hoynes, W. (1999) 'The cost of survival: political discourse and the "new PBS"', *FAIR*, http://www.fair.org/reports/pbs-study-1999.html.

Inglehart, R. (1997) *Modernization and Postmodernization: Cultural, Economic and Political Change in 43 Societies*. Princeton, NJ: Princeton University Press.

Johnson, D. and Post, D. (1998) 'The new "civic virtue" of the Internet', in *The Emerging Internet*. Queenstown, MD: Institute for Information Studies. pp. 23–57.

Kahin, B. and Nesson, C. (eds) (1997) *Borders in Cyberspace: Information Policy and the Global Information Infrastructure*. Cambridge, MA: MIT Press.

Kang, J. (2000) 'Cyber-race', *Harvard Law Review*, 113 (5): 1130–208.

Katz, E. (1996) 'And deliver us from segmentation', *The Annals of the American Academy of Political and Social Science*, 546 (July): 22–33.

Kellner, D. (1999) 'Technologies, welfare state, and prospects for democratization', in A. Calabrese and J.-C. Burgelman (eds), *Communication, Citizenship, and Social Policy*. Lanham, MD: Rowman & Littlefield. pp. 239–56.

Knox, P. and Agnew, J. (1994) *The Geography of the World Economy: an Introduction to Economic Geography*. New York: Arnold.

Kuttner, R. (1999) *Everything for Sale: the Virtues and Limits of Markets*. Chicago: University of Chicago Press.

Mansell, R. (1993) *The New Telecommunications: a Political Economy of Network Evolution*. Thousand Oaks, CA: Sage.

McChesney, R. (1999) *Rich Media, Poor Democracy*. Urbana, IL: University of Illinois Press.

McManus, J. (1994) *Market-Driven Journalism: Let the Citizen Beware?* Thousand Oaks, CA: Sage.

McNamara, J. (1991) *The Economics of Innovation in the Telecommunications Industry*. New York: Quorum.

McQuail, D. (1992) *Media Performance: Mass Communications and the Public Interest*. Newbury Park, CA: Sage.

Midwinter, J. (1995) 'Convergence of telecommunications, cable, and computers in the 21st century: a personal view of the technology', in *Crossroads on the Information Highway: Convergence and Diversity in Communications Technologies*. Queenstown, MD: Institute for Information Studies. pp. 19–66.

Miller, T. (1999) 'Television and citizenship: a new international division of cultural labor', in A. Calabrese and J.-C. Burgelman (eds), *Communication, Citizenship, and Social Policy*. Lanham, MD: Rowman & Littlefield. pp. 279–92.

Mosco, V. (1989) *The Pay-per Society: Computers and Information in the Information Age*. Norwood, NJ: Ablex.

Murdock, G. and Golding, P. (1999) 'Common markets: corporate ambitions and communication trends in the UK and Europe', *The Journal of Media Economics*, 12 (2): 117–32.

Murray, B. (1998) 'Promoting deliberative discourse on the web', in R. Noll, M. Price and L. Morrisett (eds), *A Communications Cornucopia: Markle Foundation Essays on Information Policy*. Washington, DC: Brookings Institution. pp. 243–78.

Napoli, P. (1997) 'Rethinking program diversity assessment: an audience-centered approach', *The Journal of Media Economics*, 10 (4): 59–74.

National Telecommunications and Information Administration (1998) *Falling through the Net II: New Data on the Digital Divide*. Washington, DC: US Department of Commerce.

Neu, C.R., Anderson, R. and Bikson, T. (1999) *Sending your Government a Message: E-mail Communication between Citizens and Government*. Washington, DC: RAND Corporation.

Noam, E. (1998) 'Public interest programming by American commercial television'. Paper presented at a conference on the Future of Public Broadcasting, Columbia University, New York, March.

Noll, R. (1993–4) 'The economics of information: a user's guide', in *The Knowledge Economy: the Nature of Information in the 21st Century*. Queenstown, MD: Institute for Information Studies. pp. 25–52.

Olson, M. (1971) *The Logic of Collective Action: Public Goods and the Theory of Groups*. Cambridge, MA: Harvard University Press.

Pauwels, C. (1999) 'From citizenship to consumer sovereignty: the paradigm shift in European audiovisual policy', in A. Calabrese and J.-C. Bergelman (eds), *Communication, Citizenship, and Social Policy*. Lanham, MD: Rowman & Littlefield. pp. 65–76.

Perez, C. (1985) 'Microelectronics, long waves and world structural change: new perspectives for developing countries', *World Development*, 13 (3): 441–63.

Polic, J. and Gandy, O. (1991) 'The emergence of the marketplace standard', *Media Law & Practice*, 55–64.

Putnam, R. (1995) 'Bowling alone', *Journal of Democracy*, 6: 77.

Raboy, M. (1990) *Missed Opportunities: the Story of Canada's Broadcasting Policy*. Montreal: McGill–Queen's University Press.

Reder, M. (1999) *Economics: the Culture of a Controversial Science*. Chicago: University of Chicago Press.

Robins, K. and Webster, F. (1999) *Times of the Technoculture*. New York: Routledge.

Rowland, W. (1998) 'The institution of public broadcasting'. Paper presented at a Conference on the Future of Public Broadcasting, Columbia University, New York, March.

Schement, J.R. (1995) 'Divergence and convergence: the evolving information environment of the home', in *Crossroads on the Information Highway. Convergence and Diversity in Communications Technologies*. Queenstown, MD: Institute for Information Studies. pp. 135–60.

Sparks, C. (2000) 'Introduction', in C. Sparks and J. Tulloch (eds), *Tabloid Tales: Global Debates Over Media Standards*. Lanham, MD: Rowman & Littlefield. pp. 1–42.

Sparks, C. (2001) 'The Internet and the global public sphere', in W. Bennett and R. Entman (eds), *Mediated Politics: Communication in the Future of Democracy*. Cambridge: Cambridge University Press. pp. 75–95.

Sparks, C. and Tulloch, J. (eds) (2000) *Tabloid Tales: Global Debates over Media Standards*. Lanham, MD: Rowman & Littlefield.

Sunstein, C. (ed.) (1997) *Free Markets and Social Justice*. New York: Oxford University Press.

Tracey, M. (1998) *The Decline and Fall of Public Service Broadcasting*. New York: Oxford University Press.

Villa, D. (1992) 'Postmodernism and the public sphere', *American Political Science Review*, 86 (3): 712–21.

Webster, F. (1995) *Theories of the Information Society*. London: Routledge.

Webster, J. and Phalen, P. (1997) *The Mass Audience: Rediscovering the Dominant Model*. Mahwah, NJ: Erlbaum.

Werbach, K. (1997) *Digital Tornado: the Internet and Telecommunications Policy*. Washington, DC: Federal Communications Commission, Office of Plans and Policy.

White, S. (1988) *The Recent Work of Jurgen Habermas: Reason, Justice and Modernity*. New York: Cambridge University Press.

Wilson, K. (2000) *Deregulating Telecommunications*. New York: Rowman & Littlefield.

27

Labour and New Media

GWEN UREY

This chapter examines how technological changes, especially those involving the new media of computing and advanced communications (new media technology, NMT), relate to labour. Labour can be thought of in terms of competitive free markets, in which employers and workers freely exchange labour and wages. Alternatively, workers and employers can be assumed to exist in a contentious relationship. In any case, employers do need to hire workers who can effectively complete today's tasks with the tools at hand, and technological change always occurs in the context of a capitalist mode of production.

The first section reviews employment trends to provide empirical context for issues pertinent to labour. The second section presents competing theories about why employment and wage structures are becoming increasingly unequal. The third section looks briefly at the organization of work, and the fourth section reviews issues related to regulating labour.

EMPLOYMENT TRENDS

The driving forces behind employment growth in industrialized countries are population growth and increasing rates of participation among women (Godbout, 1993). During the last four decades, the US and Canada together added roughly 2 million jobs per year; Japan together with Europe's largest economies – France, Germany, Italy, Sweden and the UK – added another 850,000 jobs per year until the 1990s. As Figure 27.1 shows, job growth has been 'bumpier' throughout in the US and Canada, but Europe and Japan have seen little growth at all during the 1990s: the average trend since 1991 has been an annual loss of 50,000 jobs for that group of

countries. Most Western European countries have experienced an average annual increase of 0.2 per cent in unemployment during the last three decades, resulting in persistently high rates in the 1990s, especially in Italy and France, where unemployment exceeded 11 per cent every year since 1993 and 1994, respectively (US Bureau of Labor Statistics, 1999).

Sectoral Change around the World

The sectoral composition of employment in industrialized countries is increasingly dominated by services, and also exhibits convergence across countries. For industrialized countries, Figure 27.2 shows the convergence in the growing share of service employment (US Bureau of Labor Statistics, 1999). Trends in manufacturing's share are more diverse from region to region, with the regions having the most low-skilled workers – Africa and Asia – increasing the proportions of their workforce in manufacturing every decade from 1950 to 2000. In Central and South America, the proportion of workers engaged in manufacturing increased until the 1980s, and in Europe until the 1970s. Differences in how things are measured and the accuracy of measurement make comparing employment statistics across countries difficult, especially when comparing labour forces of industrialized economies with those in developing and transitional economies (see Turvey, 1990).

Change in Some NMT Industries in the US

Sectoral changes provide the background on which are painted employment shifts occurring across

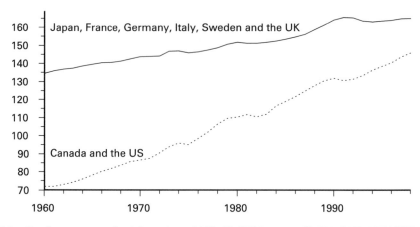

Figure 27.1   *Employment growth, eight nations, 1959–98 (US Bureau of Labor Statistics, 1999)*

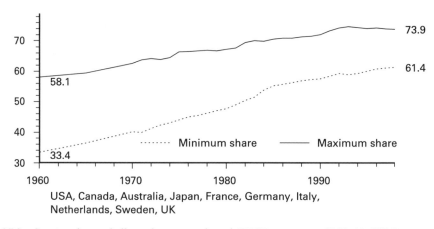

Figure 27.2   *Service share of all employment, selected OECD countries, 1960–98 (US Bureau of Labor Statistics, 1999). For each year, the minimum and maximum shares of service employment from among the ten countries are plotted. So, for example, in 1960 service employment represented at least 33.4 per cent and at most 58.1 per cent of all employment in these countries*

industries. US goods-producing sectors employed 25.1 and 25.3 million workers in 1988 and 1998, respectively, and are projected to comprise a similar number of jobs, 25.7 million, in 2008, for projected annual rates of change of 0.1 in both ten-year periods. In 1988, US civilian non-farm employment stood at 125.8 million workers. By 2008, it is projected that almost that many – 119.6 million – will be employed in service-producing industries (Thomson, 1999: 34). With the exception of the federal government, employment growth is anticipated for every service-producing sector, for an annual growth rate of 1.8 per cent overall.

Employment is measured both by industrial sector, such as manufacturing, and by occupation, such as engineer or cashier. Two- and three-digit industrial classifications describe each industry. For example, within two closely related two-digit subsectors of durable goods manufacturing (SICs 35 and 36), there is employment growth in some industries at the three-digit classification level and employment decline in others: US employment in communications equipment manufacturing (SIC 366) is projected to increase 0.7 per cent annually until 2008, whereas employment in computer and office equipment (SIC 357) is projected to decrease 0.3 per cent annually (1999: Table 4).

Table 27.1 shows projected employment growth in key NMT-related industries. The two-digit business services subsector includes the three-digit

Table 27.1   *Employment in selected NMT-related service industries*

Industry		1988 employment	1998 employment	Projected 2008 employment	Annual rate of change 1988–98	Projected annual rate of change 1998–2008
Service producing sectors		80,598	100,502	119,591	2.2	1.8
Services		26,019	37,548	49,302	3.7	2.8
(73)	Business	4,638	8,584	13,146	6.3	4.4
(737)	Computer and data processing	673	1,599	3,472	9.0	8.1
(78)	Motion pictures	341	573	636	5.3	1.0
(87, 89)	Engineering and management	2,263	3,237	4,328	3.6	2.9
Communications services		1,280	1,470	1,768	1.4	1.9
(481, 482, 489)	Telephone and telegraph communications	942	1,042	1285	1.0	2.1
(484)	Cable and pay television	111	181	230	5.0	2.4

Source: Thomson, 1999: Tables 1 and 4

industry with the highest growth projection, 'computer and data processing services', in which employment is projected to increase 8.1 per cent annually, after increasing 9.0 per cent annually between 1988 and 1998.

Looking at Occupations

The shift towards a more skilled workforce has increasingly left unskilled workers among the unemployed or the working poor (Kapstein, 1996). In some cases the automation of tasks is apparent, but only detailed employment data can verify speculation about the destruction of particular jobs. For example, the ATM automates banking transactions, and we might assume that the ATM thus 'destroys' bank teller jobs (Morisi, 1996), but between 1990 and 1995 there were net increases of 23,500 establishments and 36,000 jobs in the depository institution industry, despite the dramatic increase in the role of ATMs. During the same period, the number of ATMs increased by half, and their use grew from almost 6 million transactions in 1990 to almost 10 million in 1995 (US Bureau of Census, 1998: Tables 793 and 825).

Any industry requires workers in a variety of occupations: the computer and data processing services industry, for example, will need computer programmers but also will need accountants. Factors contributing to job churning in NMT-related sectors include employer preferences for new workers with skills specific to producing goods and services with short life cycles, and outsourcing of projects by firms in many sectors (Cooke, 2000: 44–5). Seven of the 30 'fastest-growing

occupations' relate directly to the development and skilled use of computer and communications technologies. As Table 27.2 shows, analysts predict that the numbers of workers in these occupations will nearly double from 1.8 million in 1998 to almost 3.5 million in 2008. These seven categories represented 1.3 per cent of all jobs in 1998, but are forecast to account for 2.2 per cent of all jobs in 2008. Although not among the 30 fastest-growing occupations, computer programmers are among the 30 occupations with the largest absolute growth forecast, with 191,000 jobs to be added by 2008. Computer programmers, together with the occupations in Table 27.2, will account for 8.9 per cent of net employment growth by 2008. Using Machlup's (1963) taxonomy of information work, Martin (1999) documents a steady loss of US jobs between 1970 and 1997 in the three lower categories, in which work is about 'acting on' information (Machlup's transporters, transformers and processors) and a steady increase in the three upper categories, in which work is about 'acting with' information (Machlup's interpreters, analysers and creators).

Tables 27.3 and 27.4 show the results of cross-tabulating 1998 US data for 23 NMT-intensive occupations across 13 NMT-intensive industries. Table 27.3 shows how many workers were employed in each industry and occupation in 1998. Marginal percentages on the left show the proportion of employment within each occupation that is accounted for by the 13 industries. For example, these industries employed 86,390 writers and editors, who comprised 65 per cent of their overall employment. Marginal percentages along the bottom show the proportion of employment within an

Table 27.2 *Employment in selected NMT-related occupations, from Bureau of Labor Statistics list of 30 fastest-growing civilian occupations*

Rank	Occupation	Employment 1998	Projected 2008 empl.	Projected job growth 1998–2008	Projected % growth 1998–2008	Education and training needed
1	Computer engineers	299,000	622,000	323,000	108	Bachelor's degree
2	Computer support specialists	429,000	869,000	440,000	102	Associate degree
3	Systems analysts	617,000	1,194,000	577,000	94	Bachelor's degree
4	Database administrators	87,000	155,000	68,000	77	Bachelor's degree
8	Desktop publishing specialists	30,000	53,000	23,000	74	Long-term on-the-job training
11	Data processing equipment repairers	79,000	117,000	38,000	47	Post-secondary vocational training
26	Engineering, natural science, and computer and info. systems managers	326,000	468,000	142,000	43	Work experience plus bachelor's or higher degree

Source: Braddock, 1999: Table 3

industry accounted for by these occupations, with the maximum being the computer programming and data processing industry. Table 27.4 shows the distribution of median wages. In many of the occupations, including a third of the communications professional occupations, the median among these industries is less than the overall median across all industries for the occupation. The highest median wages for five of the nine communications professionals lie in the service industries sector, led by the motion picture distribution industry. In contrast, with only one exception, non-service industries provided the highest median wage for occupations in other groups. A single industry – telephone telecommunications – provided the highest median wage for five of the 23 occupations. Manufacturing industries provide the top median wages for four occupations, including two in the communications professions – $25.67 per hour for technical writers and $31.22 for PR specialists in computer and office equipment manufacturing.

NEW MEDIA ARE PRODUCTION TOOLS

Technology was the 'prime driver of productivity gains' throughout the second half of the twentieth century (Blinder, 2000). Investment in new tools was an established business practice long before NMTs became important tools during the 1980s and 1990s. With an improved tool, the same worker in the same time can produce a good or service in greater quantity or of greater quality. NMTs also may enhance productivity indirectly, by facilitating more efficient organization of work or the intensification of work. Employers may also adopt new technologies simply to gain control over workers.

The diffusion of computing technologies during the last quarter of the twentieth century contributed to and accompanied important changes in production in most industries. Finland, Sweden and Canada lead OECD countries in the share of employees using computers (OECD, 1998). Whereas 40.2 per cent of Europeans used computers at work in 1998 (INRA, 1999), by 1997 half of US workers used computers on the job (US Bureau of Census, 2000: Table 696). In a 1999 survey of 656 US CEOs by the Conference Board, 25 per cent ranked 'changing technology' among their top three marketplace concerns, comparing closely with the 23 per cent who put 'shortage of key skills' (Berman, 1999: 53). But, in what economists dubbed the 'productivity paradox', accelerated productivity growth was not a consequence of widespread computer adoption. Between 1973 and 1999, the average annual rate of productivity growth in the US was only 1.41 per cent, less than half what it had been between 1959 and 1973 (Blinder, 2000). Computer-facilitated change resulted in neither sharper increases in productivity growth for the economy nor greater rates of profit at the firm level (Strassman, 1999).

Between 1996 and 1999, the rate of change in productivity in the US rebounded to 2.7 per cent per year, almost equalling the 1959–73 rate of 2.94. If this rate continues, the 'productivity paradox' may disappear.

Worker Knowledge and Skill

Workers also use their skills to produce goods and services, but they have a different relation to their skills than to their tools – as skills are embodied in the worker and belong to the worker. On average, skilled workers command higher wages than

Table 27.3 Employment in 23 NMT-related occupations in 13 NMT-related industries, 1988

| | | Manufacturing | | | | | Communications services | | | | | Services | | |
Proportion of employment represented by selected industries	Sum of employment in selected industries (table row sum)	Newspapers publishing, or publishing and printing	Periodicals publishing, or publishing and printing	Books publishing, or publishing and printing	Computer and office equipment	Communications equipment	Telephone communications	Radio and television broadcasting stations	Cable and other pay television services	Communications services, not elsewhere classified	Advertising	Computer programming, data processing, and other computer-related services	Motion picture production and allied services	Motion picture distribution and allied services
Engineers														
35%	324,360													
Computer engineers														
60%	181,860	100			27,560	9,720	9,600	370	490	660	210	133,150		
Electr. engineers														
25%	82,250	30			25,720	18,120	15,330	2,160	870	610	90	18,640	680	
Electr. eng. techs														
20%	60,250	200			10,310	10,780	12,520	1,900	2,290	1,440		19,940	870	
Computer programming professionals														
39%	715,100													
Computer programmers														
50%	284,550	1,530	1,040	800	14,020	2,770	17,120	280	300	350	1,340	245,790	1,670	310
Syst. analysts, EDP														
33%	182,930	1,620	1,120	1,110	6,320	3,160	17,590	160	490	990	2,140	148,260	310	50
Comp. supt specialists														
36%	164,640	1,720	870	920	14,760	3,680	7,250	470	990	410	2,140	130,700	1,170	80
All other comp. scis														
37%	36,430	440	280	260	660	350	360	140	40		290	30,070	210	140
Database administrators														
27%	24,590	510	460	270	500	160	2,100	40	340	40	370	19,120	350	40
Comp. progr. aides														
33%	21,960	290	70	100	220		1,710		50		180	18,960	180	
Communications professionals														
62%	277,670													
Writers and editors														
65%	86,390	36,340	17,590	8,690	330	310	390	6,040	860	90	8,450	4,840	2,400	60
Reporters and corresps														
93%	48,970	35,580	1,260	50				11,320	310	70	290	160	370	
Announcers, radio and TV														
96%	47,100	50						46,100	380	620	130		4,980	780
Broadcast technicians														
90%	33,360	80			1,680	1,110	130	22,990	3,660		120			
Tech. writers and editors														
44%	21,780	1,330	1,120	640	280		920	2,560	420	40	870	15,030		
PR specialists														
14%	13,410	880	360	650				6,900	1,320		4,930	2,290		80
Camera operators														
94%	10,970							3,380	360	30			2,750	
Film editors														
96%	9,820	60						5,600	170	40	60		5,780	210
Broadcast news analysts														
96%	5,870													
Machine operators														
20%	129,760													
Data entry, not composing														
11%	45,240	1,190	860	930	260	980	1,920	590	320	90	860	36,820	400	110
Computer operators														
17%	33,610	1,280	270	240	1,360	280	2,950	680	600		700	24,600	560	
Directory asst operators														
97%	25,450						22,420					3,030		
Central office operators														
95%	18,940						18,720	50	70	100				
Data entry composing														
37%	6,520	2,920	940	250							340	2,070		
All selected occupations														
42%	1,446,890	86,150	26,240	14,910	103,980	51,420	131,030	111,730	14,330	5,580	23,510	853,470	22,680	1,860
Total employment in industry														
	5,054,730	441,150	138,160	123,940	379,730	276,870	1,027,650	245,980	191,920	24,560	267,040	1,662,750	257,550	17,430
Selected occupations as a proportion of each industry's total employment														
28.6%		19.5%	19.0%	12.0%	27.4%	18.6%	12.8%	45.4%	7.5%	22.7%	8.8%	51.3%	8.8%	10.7%

Table 27.4   Median lowly wages ($) in 23 NMT-related occupations in 13 NMT-related industries, 1998

					Manufacturing					Communications service				Services			
	Median (all industries)	Lowest median (these industries)	Median of the median wages (these industries)	Highest median (these industries)	Newspapers publishing, or publishing and printing	Periodicals publishing, or publishing and printing	Books publishing, or publishing and printing	Computer and office equipment	Communications equipment	Telephone communications	Radio and television broadcasting stations	Cable and other pay television services	Communications services, not elsewhere classified	Advertising	Computer programming, data processing, and other computer-related services	Motion picture production and allied services	Motion picture distribution and allied services
Engineers																	
Electr. engineers	29.93	*20.37*	29.39	**32.39**	32.29			**32.39**	29.50	29.27	*20.37*	23.78	29.04	26.12	30.97	31.01	25.25
Computer engineers	29.77	*20.49*	29.49	**32.41**	31.70			32.19	27.86	29.30	*20.49*	31.82	**32.41**	25.77	29.49		
Electr. eng. techs	17.30	*14.95*	16.45	**20.97**	18.04			16.45	15.59	20.91	*14.95*	15.60	**20.97**	16.40	16.40	16.65	17.93
Computer programming professionals																	
Syst analysts, EDP	25.09	*22.74*	25.39	**30.33**	24.50	26.06	23.58	28.18	25.17	30.15	28.08	*22.74*	28.31	23.51	25.39	**30.33**	25.25
Computer programmers	23.83	*15.60*	24.02	**28.84**	23.21	21.16	21.90	27.97		24.00	*15.60*	24.03	24.12	19.81	25.04	25.27	**28.84**
Database administrators	23.07	*17.93*	22.12	**28.10**	21.60	22.12	21.78	24.24	22.71	**28.10**	23.58	21.91	19.15	22.58	25.01	21.72	*17.93*
All other computer scientists	22.44	*17.26*	23.52	**29.06**	*17.26*	23.52	19.45	24.45	**29.06**	24.36	18.09	21.66	18.86	23.88	23.90	18.33	22.44
Computer support specialists	17.85	*17.51*	18.55	**20.36**	*17.51*	18.95	18.05	19.12	18.22	20.15	18.55	18.55	18.86	**20.36**	18.32	18.89	17.79
Computer programmer aides	14.20	*13.46*	14.39	**17.32**	14.35	15.48	14.27	14.80	14.39	**17.32**	15.06	*13.46*		14.52	13.89	13.61	
Communications professionals																	
Technical writers and editors	19.75	*14.62*	19.78	**25.67**	*14.62*	15.66	16.26	**25.67**	21.35	17.20		15.93	18.20	19.78	20.22		
Writers and editors	16.62	*12.92*	17.34	**21.76**	14.98	17.95	16.24	21.14	19.02	22.25	13.92	18.32	20.65	18.51	17.34	**21.76**	*12.92*
PR specialists	16.61	*12.76*	17.90	**31.22**	14.84	17.90	16.21	**31.22**			*12.76*	15.79	15.95	16.71	18.62		16.80
Film editors	18.64	*13.33*	13.84	**22.19**	12.53						14.13			*13.33*		**22.19**	16.70
Broadcast news analysts	15.18	*12.44*		**18.92**	11.96		13.83				15.14	**18.92**	*12.44*	11.09	*10.07*		
Reporters and correspondents	12.52	*10.07*	11.96	**16.37**	10.42	**16.37**					12.47	11.91	13.29	12.14	*10.07*		
Broadcast technicians	12.14	*10.42*	13.14	**18.28**						18.16	10.70	12.98				17.10	**18.28**
Camera operators	10.35	*8.90*	11.79	**13.98**							*8.90*	11.79				**13.98**	
Announcers, radio and TV	8.63	*8.51*	9.79	**21.71**	9.95						*8.51*	11.03	9.63	8.56		**21.71**	
Machine operators																	
Computer operators	12.03	*10.94*	13.43	**15.61**	13.39	14.75	13.46	12.84	13.95	**15.61**	*10.94*	12.73	11.75	15.21	11.96	14.33	
Directory asst operators	14.68	*8.36*	11.66	**14.95**						**14.95**	*8.36*	12.26	9.51		8.36		
Central office operators	12.61	*8.36*	10.89	**12.86**						**12.86**		10.32					
Data entry, except composing	9.22	*8.67*	9.89	**11.41**	9.66	9.77	10.46	10.01	**11.41**	10.71	10.09			9.63	*8.67*	9.77	
Data entry composing	9.39	*8.97*	10.09	**11.21**	9.55	10.23	**11.21**							10.09	*8.97*		9.56

Note: For each occupation, the median wage is shown in *italics* if it is the lowest median for that occupation, in a box if it is the highest median for that occupation.

Table 27.5 *Median earnings, 1997 and computer usage*
(a) Occupations, earnings and computer usage

	% using computers	Applications index[a]	Year-round full-time indexed to median earnings	
			Female	Male
Executive, administrators and managerial	77.5	4	1.32	1.49
Professional speciality	71.7	9	1.42	1.50
Technical and related support	75.1	12	1.10	1.12
Sales	54.8	17	0.86	1.06
Admin. support, inc. clerical	77.6	22	0.90	0.87
Precision production, craft and repair	25.0	26	0.87	0.94
Machine operators, assemblers, and inspectors	17.3	32	0.71	0.80
Service workers	16.4	30	0.64	0.66
Farming, forestry and fishing	9.3	20	0.69	0.52

[a] Derived by ranking each occupation as to the proportion of its workers using computers who use spreadsheets for analysis, communications (e-mail and bulletin boards) and database software.
Source: United States Bureau of Census, 2000: Tables 696 and 703

(b) Regression coefficients

	All workers		Year-round full time	
	Female	Male	Female	Male
% using computers	0.62	0.59	0.65	0.62
Application score	0.54	0.63	0.78	0.66

unskilled workers within the same industry, and differences between skilled and unskilled wages and levels of unemployment have been growing since the early 1970s.

Of the 20.3 million jobs forecast to be added between 1998 and 2008 in the US, 40.2 per cent will require an associate degree or higher. Thus, while that much education was required for 25.5 per cent of jobs in 1998, it will be required of 27.3 per cent by 2008. Figure 27.3 shows trends in the 'college premium' in the wages of men and women between 1975 and 1997 in the US. The premium measures the mean wage of workers with a high school education as a proportion of the mean wage of workers with a college education. It declined in the late 1970s, but grew throughout the 1980s and remained high in the 1990s. Skills may be acquired through experience as well as education, but as Figure 27.4 shows, when the experience (age) premium for workers *without* college educations levels off, their average annual earnings ($28,855 for those aged 34–39) nearly coincide with mean earnings for the youngest workers with college degrees ($27,194 for those aged 18–24 with BAs).

Psacharopoulos (1994) conducts periodic surveys of the public and private return to investment in education. His 1994 survey provides evidence that all education, including higher education, yields a healthy rate of return, especially in private terms. Worldwide, he calculated a 20.3 per cent private rate of return for higher education.

Technology and Inequality in Employment and Wages

For the last two decades, rapid diffusion of NMT has coincided with widening of the wage and employment inequality between skilled and unskilled workers. Some argue that the diffusion of NMTs represents a fundamental shift in demand for high-skilled workers – a skill-biased technological change (SBTC) (Autor et al., 1997; Berman et al., 1998; Bound and Johnson, 1992). Others argue that trade and outsourcing of low-skill tasks to lower-wage countries influence the ratio of demand for skilled versus unskilled labour, as industrialized countries specialize in high-skilled exports and import low-skill content goods from developing countries (Castells, 1998; Wood, 1994). Some straddle the fence between SBTC and a more geographic explanation, arguing that technology and globalization are so intertwined in the reorganization of labour that it is absurd to try to measure their influences separately (Feenstra and Hanson, 1996; ILO, 1998). A third theory treats the biased distribution of sophisticated NMTs in the world's workplaces as a *consequence* rather than a cause of increased inequality in employment and wages.

Skill-Biased Technological Change

Those who study SBTC as a cause of rising inequality work in a competitive market framework.

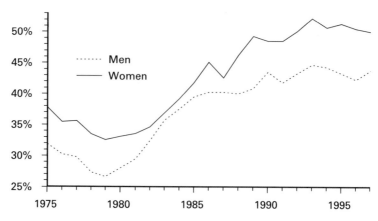

Figure 27.3   *Wage premium for college degrees in the United States, 1975–97 (Economic Policy Institute publication of CPS data)*

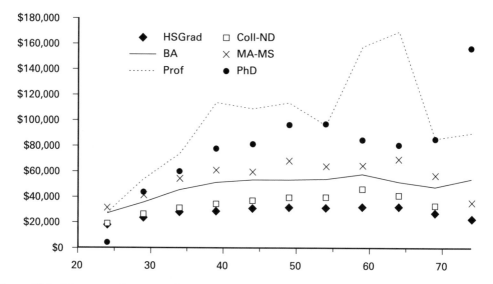

Figure 27.4   *Mean annual earnings by education achievement and age in the United States, 1995 (US Bureau of Census, 1998)*

and assume that skilled workers will be able to command a higher wage than unskilled workers to the extent that their skills cost less than a technology that could substitute. The task of empirical research has been to demonstrate how NMTs relate to the specific skills needed by employers. Using existing national-level statistical series, researchers have demonstrated SBTC only crudely.

SBTC pervaded specific industries throughout OECD economies between 1970 and 1990. In the US, SBTC accounted for 70 per cent of the drop in manufacturing employment between 1979 and 1987 and trade accounted for 9 per cent. Three industries – machinery and computers, electronic machinery, and publishing – accounted for

40 per cent of the increased demand for higher skills within industries. As evidence that the skill demand is specifically computer related, researchers point to case studies (Berman et al., 1998). The rate of change in demand for higher-skilled workers in several manufacturing industries in OECD countries accelerated between 1970 and 1995 compared with the 1940–70 period. Overall, increased utilization of computing skills and computer technology accounted for 30 to 50 per cent of the relative shift in demand for high-skilled workers (Autor et al., 1997: 32).

Firms invest in computing and communications technology and demand is increasing for high-skilled relative to low-skilled workers. The desire to increase productivity motivates firms to invest in technology (Siegel and Griliches, 1991), but technology alone does not necessarily create productivity gains. Rather, both the technology and its implementation into organized work processes count. Training, workforce skill upgrading, and other investments in human capital are key factors in generating productivity increases from new technologies (Berman et al., 1998; Black and Lynch, 1997; Coleccia and Papaconstantinou, 1996).

US and German workers who use computers on their jobs earn 10 to 15 per cent higher wages (DiNardo and Pischke, 1997; Krueger, 1993). French workers enjoy a 15–20 per cent wage premium and are shielded from layoffs, but it is higher-paid workers who are selected to use computers (Entorf et al., 1999). However, German workers who used calculators, telephones, pens or pencils, or who sat down to work also earned the premium, thus casting some doubt on the literal interpretation of the computer use wage differential (DiNardo and Pischke, 1997).

SBTC researchers explore the dynamics of trends in skill-related inequality, and also examine the ability of labour markets to adjust to SBTC. Many European labour markets are seen as rigid, especially in contrast to the US labour market (Krueger and Pischke, 1997; Card et al., 1996 on France and Canada). But SBTC researchers rarely tend to explore messy human variables, such as what those workers do with those computers, what skills they employ along the way, and what other differences arise in their conditions of work.

In their review of SBTC literature, Luker and Lyons (1997: 22) found support for reversing the direction of causality. Rather than new technologies creating demand for skilled workers, skilled workers create the conditions for the introduction of new technologies.

Geography and Trade

Wood (1994) stresses increased trade between the North and the South and argues that SBTC in the North itself may be induced largely by increased trade with the South. Also, he notes that the SBTC research is far from complete, and 'skilled as well as unskilled workers have been replaced by microprocessors … [and there is] evidence that skill differentials have widened less in countries where the microprocessor revolution seems most advanced' (1994: 288–9).

Galbraith (1998) cautions against basing a theory about inequality on an assumption of competitive markets. Instead, he sees anti-competitive influences as a more probable cause of rising inequality in employment and wages. Through monopolistic practices, such as charging prices well above the marginal cost of production (the price assumed

under competitive market conditions), technology companies 'will emerge in the dominant position in an unstable world' (1998: 49). Technology companies are able to do this, Galbraith argues, because of economic instability. In addition to advocating a theory of monopoly practices by technology companies, Galbraith argues against the notion that SBTC *causes* inequality (1998: Chapter 2). Galbraith points out that although computers may be pervasive tools in the workplace, the notion of a relationship between skill and using them is counter-intuitive, and has not been adequately addressed by SBTC research:

> Computer skills are easy to learn. Millions do it at home. Small children work on computers … Computers don't make things hard; they make things easy … To the extent they do so, computers therefore reduce, rather than enhance, the aggregate skill level required for the performance of certain tasks. (1998: 32–3)

Institutional and spatial factors contribute to earnings inequality. Between 1974 and 1997, the share of income going to the top 20 per cent of the US population grew steadily from 40.6 to 47.2 per cent, while the share accruing to the lowest quintile fell from 12 to 9.9 per cent (Mishel et al., 1999). Mishel et al. found that 'the falling real value of the minimum wage along with continuing deunionization – can explain one-third of the growing wage inequality among prime-age workers' in the US (1999: 19). In a review of studies, Freeman found consistent evidence that 'declining unionization … accounted for about one fifth of the increase in US earnings inequality [1975–95]. In addition, half to two thirds of the greater earnings inequality in the US compared to the rest of the OECD can be explained by unionization and other forms of collective bargaining (Freeman, cited in Bradbury et al., 1996: 6–7).

The argument that powerful people create inequality is more compelling than an argument based on technological determinism. The case of Microsoft, which had a profit rate of 31 per cent of revenues in 1998 (*Fortune*, 2000), supports Galbraith's position. The US Supreme Court ruled against Microsoft's labour practices, including discrimination against long-term 'orange badge' employees denied the same retirement benefits, including stock options, enjoyed by 'blue badge' employees. The latter are on the Microsoft payroll, whereas the former, many in skilled positions such as software testers, editors, technical writers, programmers and graphic designers, get their pay cheques from one of twenty temporary agencies or outside contractors. In Silicon Valley, 42 per cent of workers are employed through temporary agencies (Cohen, 2000; Holmes, 2000). Workers hired through temporary agencies know that high-tech firms can seek workers from the equivalent of such agencies around the world.

Relocating the Argument

While questions remain about computer skill as a particular and remunerable form of human capital, the 'undisputable and universal positive correlation between education and earnings' is much better understood (Psacharopoulos, 1994: 1330). Given on the one hand the well-understood contribution of education to wages, and on the other hand the many unknowns about how computer skills in particular influence wages, there is, not surprisingly, great debate about whether or not computer training should be aggressively integrated into school curricula at every level. Is computer training what elementary, secondary or higher education pupils need to prepare them for future employment in the information society? Or, as Carnoy (1998) and others argue, should curriculum reform focus on preparing graduates to work in environments undergoing organizational change as an indirect result of NMT technologies? In the US, about half of workers in the Heldrich Center (2000) work trends survey responded that 'computer skills are very important'. Over 80 per cent responded that communications skills, basic literacy, and critical thinking skills were very important. Similarly, a Canadian study found that employers believed that most post-secondary graduates are technically competent, but often lack 'essential skills (e.g. communications and teamwork) and management skills (e.g. cost control and budgeting)' (Canada, Advisory Council on Science and Technology, 2000). In a market framework, learning computer skills in school should translate into future earnings. In a dialectical framework, enhancing students' abilities to constantly create new knowledge will empower them *vis-à-vis* the tendency of technological changes to make a worker's knowledge redundant.

Braverman criticizes earlier claims that average skill levels required of workers were rising, by pointing out that perhaps that was not an interesting average. A more interesting question was

> whether the scientific and educated content of labor tends toward *averaging* or, on the contrary, toward *polarization*. If the latter is the case, to then say that the 'average skill has been raised' is to adopt the logic of the statistician who, with one foot in the fire and the other in ice water, will tell you that 'on average,' he is perfectly comfortable. The mass of workers gain nothing from the fact that the decline in their command over the labor process is more than compensated for by the increasing command on the part of managers and engineers. (1974: 425)

Very general statistics about the uses to which US workers put computers certainly suggests that the trend is toward polarization. Table 27.5a relates median earnings in occupational classifications to two measures of computer usage: proportion of workers in an industry using computers and an application score. Braverman would notice that we can tell nothing about inequality within occupations by looking at Table 27.5a, but we can see the significant disparity across occupations, with the median earnings in the top two classifications at one-and-a-half the overall median, while the median earner in the bottom classifications gets less than two-thirds of the overall median. In Table 27.5a, there is noticeable correspondence between the earnings indices and the computer variables. This is shown more precisely in Table 27.5b. In fact, for year-round full-time female workers, the use of sophisticated applications (spreadsheets for analysis, communications and database software) can explain 78 per cent of the earnings difference.

THE ORGANIZATION AND RELATIONS OF PRODUCTION

In addition to their places in changing production processes, NMTs facilitate change in how production is organized, especially the globalization of production. Corporate capacity to tap labour markets heretofore unavailable reflects capital's ability to influence both regulatory regimes and technological trajectories. Many credit information and communications technologies help with reducing time and distance as obstacles to corporate capacity to extend globally and penetrate deeply. But the desire of capitalists to extend and to penetrate have largely driven the research and development agendas of those who produce these very technologies – especially the capitalists at the helm of technology companies (Urey, 1995). As we look at major trends in the organization of production, the division of labour, and how workers fare *vis-à-vis* those trends, we should remain sceptical of technological determinism.

NMTs facilitate the coordination of multiple tasks, even if they occur at different times or in different places. The resulting fragmentation of work may reduce a worker's sense of the whole process and his or her awareness of and ability to be in solidarity with others involved in the process. The work itself may be very similar, but the fact of disparate times or locations allows employers to maintain very different conditions of work. Indians working in Silicon Valley as software programmers or systems analysts, for example, earn ten times more than Indians in the same occupations working for the same Silicon Valley firms but in Bangalore (Saxenian, 1999: 66). Average salaries for software programmers in India in 1996 were estimated by Mitter and Sen (1999) at 16 per cent of US salaries (up from 9 per cent in 1994). Technology does not create salary differences; rather technology facilitates corporate ability to tap global labour markets and integrate geographically dispersed production processes.

Flexible Production

Piore and Sabel's (1984) analysis of industrial change informed many industrial policy discussions during the 1980s and 1990s. As governments and firms struggled to recover from the oil shocks of the 1970s, they reorganized production into systems of flexible specialization, based on principles of craft production, technological sophistication and dynamism. The resulting 'second industrial divide' separated the economies that adapted more successfully from those that did not.

Piore and Sabel compare the modes of mass production in Germany, Japan, France and Italy prior to the crises. Differences in the relationship of management to workers carried through during the adoption of flexible specialization. In France, labour had lost its once significant power, whereas in Japan, workers were in a stronger position. In Germany and Italy, worker–management relations were unstable at the moment of crisis, with labour in a state of losing ground. In Japan and Italy, workers retained extensive craft knowledge, but industrial reorganization in France had destroyed the basis for an appreciation of craft principles among workers. In Germany, workers possessed craft knowledge despite a management strategy of undermining the value of craft principles (1984: Chapter 6). In Germany, Italy and Japan, the persistence of craft knowledge 'lit the way' to the evolution of flexible specialization. It took different forms in each country owing to the local specificity of crafts, and also to the social and political contexts in which the crafts were embedded. Thus, in Italy, flexible specialist firms depended upon 'familialism and the artisan-category exemption ... mercantile traditions and local government intervention' (1984: 228). In Germany, large firms decentralized their operations to 'return to the workshop as the basic unit of production' (1984: 232).

Flexible specialization evolved broadly from existing roots in Japan, Germany and Italy, while manifesting more as an anomaly in France and the US. But it held promise as an alternative to mass production in some industries and inspired policy-makers to articulate strategies for creating conditions to enable industries, including many NMT-related industries, to grow based on a flexible specialization model. Innovation is key to the competitive capacity of flexible specialization, and one of the two major obstacles to innovation is 'characteristic problems in coordinating innovative activity' (1984: 264).

Piore and Sabel look as much at the relations among stakeholders as at the role of technology in enabling innovation. Their work influenced scholars who focused on how workers in specific sectors produced innovation and achieved competitiveness. Saxenian's (1996) study comparing California's Silicon Valley and Massachusetts' Route 128 corridor in the early 1990s stressed the importance of social networks of technology workers as an underlying factor in the growth of Silicon Valley industries.

More recently, Saxenian studied such networks among immigrant communities in Silicon Valley. Indian and Chinese employers 'in the most technologically dynamic and globally competitive sectors of the Silicon Valley economy' (1999: 22) rely on ethnically defined social and professional networks for access to engineers and other skilled workers in operations located domestically and in the home countries:

> Silicon Valley's new immigrant entrepreneurs ... are increasingly building professional and social networks that span national boundaries and facilitate flows of capital, skill, and technology. In so doing, they are creating transnational communities that provide the shared information, contacts, and trust that allow local producers to participate in an increasingly global economy. (1999: 54)

In the US and elsewhere, the software industry has grown up as a flexible specialist industry. With the exceptions of Electronic Data Systems and Microsoft, software companies – unlike other companies in other major high-tech industries – have not grown into giants. At numbers 235 and 284, respectively, the two exceptions are the only software companies on *Fortune*'s 1999 Global 500 list. In contrast, 9 companies represent computers and office equipment, 25 represent electronics and other electrical equipment and 20 represent telecommunications (*Fortune*, 2000).

Division of Labour

Piore and Sabel's work also informed discussions about how more traditional industries could become more flexible and innovative. Reform to achieve either objective was seen, in part, as a function of the capacity of workers and managers to collaborate. Many such reforms employ NMTs to integrate activities and intensify the knowledge and information content of day-to-day operations. But Walker (1989) cautions against technological determinism, putting as much importance on the role of social relations in determining the nature and conditions of work. Truly collaborative divisions of labour remain the exception in the US as well as in Europe, even when they have a demonstrable effect on profitability (Benders et al., 2000). Popular theories too quickly assumed that computer systems that integrate activities across departments will create more collaborative interaction among the staffs of those departments and result in jobs that are more intellectually gratifying. There is limited evidence to support claims that such technological changes *cause* post-Taylorist divisions of labour to evolve (Alsene, 1994).

Mansell discusses behaviours of firms seeking to 'construct, manage and use rapidly expanding global electronic networks' (1996: 103). Their ability to succeed in these efforts depends heavily on the performance of workers acting *with* information, in the Machlupian sense. Mansell studied seven firms spanning three industries in three countries. To achieve strategic global electronic network goals, firms needed network designers and users who could engage in 'a continuous process of learning and experimentation' (1996: 124). Workers involved in implementing these strategies not only need competence in 'acting with' information, but also need sound judgement about the consequences of their day-to-day technical decisions for safeguarding their firms' information assets.

Kelley surveyed 1015 plants in the US, and classifies management approaches to implementing programmable automation (defined as 'the use of computers to direct and control the operation of machines' technologies) into three types: 'scientific management [Taylorist], technocentric participative, or worker-centered participative' (1989: 233–6). She found worker organization to be a stronger predictor than technical conditions of the division of labour: 'Faced with a union, US management is more likely to adopt a Taylorist approach to work organization and less likely to choose a worker-centered control approach' (1989: 245–6).

This subsection has explored the relationship of NMTs to changes in the division of labour for a broad variety of skilled workers in technology-based occupations. In a much more narrowly defined study of highly skilled new media workers in New York City, Batt et al. sought to 'know more about Internet oriented work and about the challenges facing people who do that work' (2000: 4). Most of the workers they surveyed will not show up in US Bureau of Labor Statistics employment data: many are self-employed independent contractors, and even those who sign on as 'regular employees'change employers two or three times per year (2000: 7). Batt et al. found that:

> Some of this mobility is a consequence of the nature of work in the industry, much of which is organized around short term projects such as developing a website, an advertisement, or the special effects for a film. But it is also a consequence of opportunity, ethos, and career paths organized around the acquisition of a marketable portfolio of specialized skills and prestige projects rather than long term tenure with one employer. (2000: 7)

Thus, highly skilled NM workers guard their 'marketable portfolios' as personal monopolies. Indeed, these workers spent just under half their time working on NM projects, and spent the rest of their average 53.5 hour per week work time on 'looking for

work, client relations, and administrative tasks', *in addition to* an average of 13.5 hours per week on obtaining new skills (2000: 5–6).

Implications for Industrial and Labour Policy

Relationships among research and training institutions, firms in which innovations are applied, and government bodies that create and enforce policies comprise a nation's system of innovation, which helps shape the opportunity structures of workers as well as firms (Freeman and Soete, 1997; Lundvall, 1992; Nelson, 1993). Especially important for workers are the opportunities for education (OECD, 1999; US Congress, 1999; US Economics and Statistics Administration, 2000).

The European Community's 'Information Society' project attempts to facilitate the evolution of a European system of innovation promoting capacity in information-technology-related industries and occupations (Commission of the European Communities, 2000a). *Strategies for Jobs in the Information Society* urges support for programmes at all levels of schooling, job training, public service provision and firms. Through 'national action plans', countries will develop specific strategies to achieve targets established in the EC's strategy: member states should measurably 'increase capacity and uptake in 3rd level education, maintaining gender balance and matching industry requirements' by the end of 2003 (2000a: 17). Also, Europe's social partners should 'set up framework conditions and practical arrangements to enable telework to take place on a wide scale' by the end of 2000. Austria's trade unions provide an example of 'best practice' in meeting the recommendation with the issue of standardized contracts for teleworkers and collective bargaining agreements for telework in several sectors (2000a: 18).

Strategies does not promise better conditions of work or higher wages. It acknowledges that 'employment has become on average less stable and less certain than in the past and more dependent on high skills and adaptability' (2000a: 13). The strategy's underlying agenda is more about creating 'a world of greater access to work for all' (2000a: 14) (or greater access to workers for all employers) and strengthening the competitive position of Europe by presenting a united front in competing with the US. The press release for *Strategies* claims it will help 'to overcome the gap that has opened up with the US on access to the internet and use of information and communication technology' (Commission of the European Communities, 2000b). *Strategies* is an ambitious attempt to knit together and bring coherence to differing and sometimes competing initiatives that have been occurring at local and national levels.

Place-based strategies of governments and corporations attempt to enhance local production potential in order to achieve a variety of specific goals – profit, tax revenue, employment, etc. To the extent that these strategies involve workers, it may be to provide training or to facilitate job markets, but it is rarely to enhance worker power *vis-à-vis* employers. As production demands more flexible labour, workers face more uncertainty and risk, especially in NMT industries.

How is Labour Faring, and What Can Labour Do?

More people are working. Demand for skilled workers is rising, but outside the NMT-specific industries it is more the generic skills that count, including literacy, communication and having 'the right attitudes and behaviors'. Technologies have matured; a generally skilled person can be expected to learn how to use a computer application related to his or her job, so outside the NMT industries specialization need not be tied to a particular technology. But having the 'right' attitudes and behaviours often means being obedient to the boss, especially in the US, where employers have greater discretion about how to treat their workers (Freeman and Rogers, 1999).

For many, the conditions of work are worsening. Only 22 per cent of young US workers have jobs that include health benefits, compared with 30 per cent 10 years ago (Quinn and Schoen, 2000). Even among the highly skilled NMT workers surveyed by Batt et al. (2000: 6), only 11 per cent of those working as independent contractors had health coverage from an employer. Only one-third of female workers in the US feel that they are receiving equal compensation (Granville, 1999).

Increasingly, jobs involve use of NMTs embedded in a division of labour that does not enhance the power of the worker. Freeman and Rogers (1999) surveyed US workers about workplace decisions. Related to NMTs, 52 per cent thought 'it is very important to have a lot of influence' on 'deciding how to work with new equipment or software', but only 28 per cent said they had 'a lot of direct influence' in that area. Citing a variety of organizational changes facilitated by management information systems, Yates (1999) observes that 'so careful have the capitalists' calculations become that workers in modern automobile factories work as much as 57 seconds of every minute, often for ten to twelve hours per day'. Workers subject to volatile work hours – i.e. hours that are more flexible for the employer – are most likely to be non-white, female, unmarried, part-timers, private sector, non-union, or employed in less skilled occupations. Conversely, those who are white, male, married, in unions, more educated, or in skilled occupations are more likely to have access to flexible daily work schedules. Twenty-eight per cent of US workers had access to flexible schedules in 1997, compared with 15 per cent in 1991 (Golden, 2000).

Labour has been less nimble than capital at organizing its activities to transcend time or space. The International Labour Office found that the proportion of workers who are unionized fell by over 20 per cent in 35 out of 66 countries for which they had comparable data; declines were particularly steep in Argentina, Costa Rica, Mexico, Venezuela, the US, Australia, New Zealand, Israel, France and Portugal (ILO, 1998: 7). Attacks on unions from corporate America and even the federal government contributed to an erosion of support and credibility (Harrison and Bluestone, 1988; Walker, 1999) that labour in the US may only recently have begun to reverse. As Walker (1999) points out,

> Working people sorely need the protection and the wage gains that unionization makes possible. … And they need to support international labor organizing and sanctions against egregious forms of exploitation like child labor. They also need government industrial policy that softens the blow of restructuring and retiring old capital stock. The good news is that the American labor movement is beginning to stir again.

In the US, union stirrings include reinvigoration of traditional unions, such as the United Auto Workers (UAW) and the Communications Workers of America (CWA), often organizing on new turf. The UAW has been active in organizing graduate students working as teaching assistants, and the Washington Alliance of Technology Workers, formed by Microsoft orange-badge writers and testers, affiliated with the CWA (Cohen, 2000). New collaborative projects help create shared visions among established unions and associations of workers in the 'new economy', including NMT workers. These place-based local projects, such as Silicon Valley @work, created by Working Partnerships USA and the South Bay AFL-CIO, unite around issues of justice and grassroots empowerment.

Informal associations of NMT workers also seek to shape the identity of the industry through institutionalization of worker-oriented organizations such as Webgrrls. With chapters around the world, Webgrrls facilitates interaction among workers in local job markets through its websites and face-to-face meeting opportunities. The organization's mission is to provide:

> a forum for women in or interested in new media and technology to network, exchange job and business leads, form strategic alliances, mentor and teach, intern and learn the skills to help women succeed in an increasingly technical workplace and world. (Webgrrls, 2000)

Webgrrls has grown rapidly and achieved prominence within a genre of NMT worker-based groups organized around job-related issues, making use of web technologies for much interaction, and sometimes also having some identification with place and face-to-face interaction at events in those places. A related genre is the identity-based group that facilitates job-related networking and development (Hyde, 1999).

In some cases, alliances between new and traditional occupations may evolve more readily. The graphic artists' union represents 'illustrators, designers, web creators, production artists, surface designers and other creatives who have come together to pursue common goals, share their experience, raise industry standards, and improve the ability of visual creators to achieve satisfying and rewarding careers' (Graphic Arts Guild, 2000). Graphic artists unionized by creating the Graphic Arts Guild in 1967, and affiliated with the UAW in 1999.

Unions and union-based organizations such as the Economic Policy Institute and the New Economy Information Service have helped articulate new strategies that take on globalization with internationalization and that make effective use of the Internet and other media (Mishel et al., 1999; Jessup, 2000). The interaction of 'old guard' unionists and new labour activists at demonstrations surrounding the World Trade Organization meetings in 1999 and 2000 heralds a stronger future for the union movement in the US in the coming decade.

The dialectic between workers and employers manifests itself overtly in the struggle to create the identity of the specifically 'new media industry'. On the one hand are workers handling multiple positions and working out strategies of guarding their own 'marketable portfolios'; on the other hand are employers complaining that 'There's no loyalty in this business. They want more money ... or they're out the door' (cited in PriceWaterhouse-Coopers, 2000: 33). In their study of the industry for the New York New Media Association (NYNMA), PriceWaterhouseCoopers found that labour costs comprised 40 per cent of new media companies' expenses. According to their study, while the number of employees increased from 71,500 full-time equivalent positions in 1995 to 249,639 in 1999, or 37 per cent per year, payroll increased from $1.4 billion to $8.31 billion – 56 per cent annually. On a per capita (FTE) basis, that means the average real annual earnings for these workers went from about $22,000 in 1995 to about $33,000 (both in 1999 dollars) during the period, a 34 per cent increase in real earnings – but $33,000 is still a very modest salary.

'New media associations' on the model of the NYNMA have sprung up elsewhere, especially in the northeast US. The mission statement of the Philadelphia Area NMA is typical and promises to 'host networking and educational gatherings,

provide services for our members, lobby for favorable business conditions at the local, state, and national levels, and generally seek to increase awareness of the industry and its importance to the region' (PANMA, 2000). NMAs provide markets in which employers and workers can interact: job listings and résumé banks are typical. While seeking 'partnerships' with worker organizations that can facilitate their access to skilled workers, employers nonetheless have not welcomed unionization (see, for example, Rizzo, 1997).

Benner (2000) examines three types of organizations that function as intermediaries between workers and firms in Silicon Valley, including worker-based associations such as unions, private sector entities aimed at facilitating the labour market, and public sector entities such as employment divisions of state and local government. Workers measure the extent to which any organization assists them in developing their own 'human capital' or knowledge assets; extending personal networks leading to good jobs or knowledge-enhancing opportunities; or augmenting their power *vis-à-vis* employers. Furthermore, 'in the current context, the ability to wield this power in the labor market, rather than in direct relationship with a single employer, is most important' (2000: 57).

This chapter has reviewed trends in employment and in the organization of labour, and has looked at how workers in NMT fields fit into that larger picture. To the degree that the economy of the future will be different because it is a 'knowledge' economy, NMT workers are leading the way by building a social infrastructure of formal and informal organizations that help them enhance and maintain control over their knowledge assets. To the degree that the economy of the future will be the same because corporations have more money and clout, NMT companies have done less to demonstrate that they are illuminating a new road. While skilled workers have 'given up' the job security of employment trends of the past, their employers don't want to give up anything. While enjoying the benefits of workers' abilities to learn in their own time and develop networks that extend beyond the company, corporations still want to monopolize knowledge gained by workers within company boundaries. Laws such as the Trade Secrets Act can restrict workers' employment options by preventing them from working for firms that would benefit from knowledge that the worker gained while working for a competitor (Hyde, 1999). Clearly, in NMT production, workers and employers exist in a contentious relationship. Employers bring residual power over compensation and conditions of work to this relationship, but NMT workers are creating new forms of power by organizing and forming around diverse interests, including work-related knowledge, but also around dimensions that transcend their roles as workers, such as place and identity.

At regional, national and state levels, governments struggle to transform educational infrastructures to create a more 'information-literate' workforce. Local economies compete to generate business environments that will nurture NMT-sector industries. Transformed educational infrastructures and strong industries should be good for workers as well as companies. But workers also may need more from their governments, given broad changes in the nature of employment that go beyond the NMT sectors. Like other workers faced with employment arrangements that are less likely to include benefits or job security, NMT workers need the help of governments to ensure access to health insurance, disability insurance, pensions, etc. These issues unite NMT workers with diverse professional and non-professional workers in the 'new economy'. Governments need to take a stronger role in creating benefits structures that are meaningful for workers and for which employers pay their fair share, whether directly into such programmes or indirectly through taxation.

REFERENCES

Alsene, Eric (1994) 'Computer integration and the organization of work', *International Labour Review*, 133 (5–6): 657–76.

Autor, David H., Katz, Lawrence F. and Krueger, Alan B. (1997) 'Computing inequality: have computers changed the labor market?' Working Paper no. 5956, National Bureau of Economic Research, Cambridge, MA.

Batt, Rosemary, Christopherson, Susan, Rightor, Ned and van Jaarsveld, Danielle (2000) *Net Working: Work Patterns and Workforce Policies for the New Media Industry*. Washington, DC: Economic Policy Institute.

Benders, Jos, Huijgen, Fred, Pekruhl, Ulrich and O'Kelly, Kevin P. (2000) 'Useful but unused – the fate of group work in Europe'. Available at: europa.eu.int/comm/employment_social/news/group_en.htm.

Benner, Christopher Chatham (2000) 'Navigating flexibility: labor markets and intermediaries in Silicon Valley'. Dissertation, University of California, Berkeley, Department of City and Regional Planning.

Berman, Eli, Bound, John and Machin, Stephen (1998) 'Implications of skill-biased technological change: international evidence', *Quarterly Journal of Economics*, 113 (4): 1245–79.

Berman, Melissa (1999) 'Boss issues', *Across the Board*, (July/August): 53–4.

Black, Sandra E. and Lynch, Lisa M. (1997) 'How to compete: the impact of workplace practices and information technology on productivity'. Working Paper no. 6120, National Bureau of Economic Research, Cambridge, MA.

Blinder, Alan S. (2000) 'The internet and the new economy'. Brookings Institution Policy Brief no. 60. Available at: www.brookings.edu/comm/PolicyBriefs/pb060/pb60.htm.

Bound, John and Johnson, George (1992) 'Changes in the structure of wages in the 1980s: an evaluation of alternative explanations', *American Economic Review*, 82 (3): 371–92.

Bradbury, Katharine L., Kodrzycki, Yoland K. and Mayer, Christopher J. (1996) 'Spatial and labor market contributions to earnings inequality: an overview', *New England Economic Review* (May/June): 1–10.

Braddock, Douglas (1999) 'Occupational employment projections to 2008', *Monthly Labor Review,* 122 (11): 51–77.

Braverman, Harry (1974) *Labor and Monopoly Capital: the Degradation of Work in the Twentieth Century.* New York: Monthly Review Press.

Canada, Advisory Council on Science and Technology (2000) *Stepping up: Skills and Opportunities in the Knowledge Economy. Report of the Expert Panel on Skills*. Ottawa: Her Majesty the Queen in Right of Canada (Industry Canada).

Card, David, Kramarz, Francis and Lemieux, Thomas (1996) 'Changes in the relative structure of wages and employment: a comparison of the United States, Canada, and France'. Working Paper no. 5487, National Bureau of Economic Research, Cambridge, MA.

Carnoy, Martin (1998) 'The changing world of work in the information age', *New Political Economy*, 3 (1): 123–8.

Castells, Manuel (1998) *End of Millennium*. Oxford: Blackwell.

Cohen, Larry (2000) Remarks in 'Organizing unions in the new economy discussion'. Available at: www.newecon.org/labor/organizing/.

Colecchia, A. and Papaconstantinou, George (1996) *The Evolution of Skills in OECD Countries and the Role of Technology*. Paris: OECD, Directorate for Science, Technology and Industry.

Commission of the European Communities (2000a) *Strategies for Jobs in the Information Society*. Brussels: European Commission.

Commission of the European Communities (2000b) 'Europe's net generation: catching up with the US?', press release for *Strategies*. Brussels: European Commission.

Cooke, Sandra (2000) 'The information technology workforce', in *Digital Economy 2000*. Washington, DC: US Department of Commerce, Economics and Statistics Administration, Office of Policy Development. pp. 43–52.

DiNardo, John E. and Pischke, Jorn-Steffen (1997) 'The returns to computer use revisited: have pencils changed the wage structure too?', *Quarterly Journal of Economics*, 112 (1): 291–303.

Entorf, Horst, Gollac, Michel and Kramarz, Francis (1999) 'New technologies, wages, and worker selection', *Journal of Labor Economics*, 17 (3): 464–91.

Feenstra, Robert C. and Hanson, Gordon H. (1996) 'Globalization, outsourcing, and wage inequality'. Working Paper no. 5424, National Bureau of Economic Research, Cambridge, MA.

Fortune (2000) 'Fortune Global 500', *Fortune Magazine*, 141 (4). Available at: www.fortune.com/fortune/global 500/intro2.html.

Freeman, Christopher and Soete, Luc (1997) *The Economics of Industrial Innovation*. Cambridge, MA: MIT Press.

Freeman, Richard B. and Rogers, Joel (1999) *What Workers Want*. Ithaca, NY: Cornell University Press.

Galbraith, James K. (1998) *Created Unequal: the Crisis in American Pay*. New York: Free Press.

Godbout, Todd M. (1993) 'Employment change and sectoral distribution in 10 countries, 1970–90', *Monthly Labor Review*, 116 (10): 3–20.

Golden, Lonnie (2000) 'The time bandit: what US workers surrender to get greater flexibility in work schedules'. Issue Brief no. 146, Economic Policy Institute.

Granville, Suzanne (1999) 'Women workers and the new economy'. Remarks delivered at a Conference on American Labor and the New Economy – a Day of Dialogue, Washington, DC, 22 January.

Graphic Arts Guild (2000) Graphic Arts Guild web page: www.gag.org.

Harrison, Bennett and Bluestone, Barry (1988) *The Great U-Turn: Corporate Restructuring and the Polarizing of America*. New York: Basic.

Heldrich Center (2000) *Making the Grade? What American Workers Think Should Be Done to Improve Education*. John J. Heldrich Center for Workforce Development.

Holmes, Stanley (2000) 'Microsoft policy may jolt temp industry', *Los Angeles Times*, 1 July: C1+.

Hyde, Alan (1999) 'What do "equal employment" and "loyalty" mean if internal labor markets die? The emerging employment law of Silicon Valley's high-velocity labor market'. Speech delivered to the New York University 52nd Conference on Labor, 20 May. Available at: Andromeda.rutgers.edu/~hyde.

ILO (1998) *World Labour Report 1997–98: Industrial Relations, Democracy and Social Stability*. Geneva: International Labour Organization.

INRA (1999) *Measuring Information Society (Eurobarometer 50.1)*. Brussels: DG XIII, European Commission.

Jessup, David (2000) Remarks in 'Organizing unions in the new economy: discussion'. Available at: newecon.org/labor/organizing/.

Kapstein, Ethan (1996) 'Workers and the world economy', *Foreign Affairs*, 75 (3): 16–37.

Katz, Lawrence F. and Krueger, Alan B. (1991) 'Changes in the structure of wages in the public and private sectors'. Working Paper no. 3667, National Bureau of Economic Research, Cambridge, MA.

Kelley, Maryellen R. (1989) 'Alternative forms of work organization under programmable automation', in Stephen Wood, (ed.), *The Transformation of Work*. London: Unwin Hyman. pp. 235–46.

Krueger, Alan B. (1993) 'How computers have changed the wage structure: evidence from Microdata, 1984–89', *Quarterly Journal of Economics*, 108 (1): 33–60.

Krueger, Alan B. and Pischke, Jorn-Steffen (1997) 'Observations and conjectures on the U.S. employment miracle'. Working Paper no. 6146, National Bureau of Economic Research, Cambridge, MA.

Luker, William, Jr and Lyons, Donald (1997) 'Employment shifts in high-technology industries, 1988–96', *Monthly Labor Review*, 120 (6): 12–25.

Lundvall, Bengt-Ake (ed.) (1992) *National Systems of Innovation: Towards a Theory of Innovation and Interactive Learning*. New York: St Martin's Press.

Machlup, Fritz (1963) *The Production and Distribution of Knowledge in the United States*. Princeton, NJ: Princeton University Press.

Mansell, Robin (1966) 'Designing electronic commerce', in Robin Mansell and Roger Silverstone (eds), *Communication by Design: the Politics of Information and Communication Technologies*. Oxford: Oxford University Press. pp. 103–28.

Martin, Stana B. (1999) 'Employment in the information age: information technology and information work', *Journal of Policy, Regulation and Strategy for Telecommunications Information and Media*, 1 (3): 272–83.

Mishel, Lawrence, Bernstein, Jared and Schmitt, John (1999) *State of Working America, 1998–99*. Ithaca, NY: Cornell University Press.

Mitter, Swasti and Sen, Asish (1999) 'Case study on Kolkata (Calcutta): can the Bangalore phenomenon be replicated in Kolkata?' Paper presented at the Workshop on Telework, Teletrade and Sustainable Development: Indian Experience in a Global Context, NCST and UNU/INTECH, Mumbai, 15–16 November.

Morisi, Teresa L. (1996) 'Commercial banking transformed by computer technology', *Monthly Labor Review*, 119 (8): 30–6.

Nelson, Richard (ed.) (1993) *National Innovation Systems: a Comparative Analysis*. New York: Oxford University Press.

OECD (1998) *Use of Information and Communication Technologies at Work*. Directorate for Science, Technology and Industry, Committee for Information, Computers and Communications Policy, Working Party on the Information Economy. Paris: Organization for Economic Cooperation and Development.

OECD (1999) *Workshops on the Economics of the Information Society: a Synthesis of Policy Implications*. Directorate for Science, Technology and Industry, Committee for Information, Computers and Communications Policy, Working Party on the Information Economy. Paris: Organization for Economic Cooperation and Development.

PANMA (2000) Philadelphia Area New Media Association website: www.panma.org/mission/index.htm.

Piore, Michael J. and Sabel, Charles F. (1984) *The Second Industrial Divide: Possibilities for Prosperity*. New York: Basic.

PriceWaterhouseCoopers (2000) *3rd New York New Media Industry Survey*. New York: New York New Media Association and PriceWaterhouseCoopers.

Psacharopoulos, George (1994) 'Rates of return to education', *World Development*, 22 (9): 1325–43.

Quinn, Kevin and Schoen, Cathy (2000) 'On their own: young adults living without health insurance'. Report no. 391, Commonwealth Fund, Boston.

Rizzo, John (1997) 'Temp terrors! Hire the right tech temp and avoid a horror story', *ComputerUser.com*, 28 October, www.computeruser.com/magazine/national/1521/covr1521.html.

Saxenian, AnnaLee (1996) *Regional Advantage: Culture and Competition in Silicon Valley and Route 128*. San Francisco: Public Policy Institute of California.

Saxenian, AnnaLee (1999) *Silicon Valley's New Immigrant Entrepreneurs*. Cambridge, MA: Harvard University Press.

Siegel, Donald and Griliches, Zvi (1991) 'Purchased services, outsourcing, computers, and productivity in manufacturing'. Working Paper no. 3678, National Bureau of Economic Research, Cambridge, MA.

Strassman, Paul A. (1999) 'Paradox revisited', *Computerworld*, 6 September, www.computerworld. com/cwi/story/0,1199,NAV47-74-213-225-951_STO36885, 00.html.

Thomson, Allison (1999) 'Industry output and employment projections to 2008', *Monthly Labor Review*, 122 (11): 33–50.

Turvey, Ralph (ed.) (1990) *Developments in International Labor Statistics*. New York: Pinter.

Urey, Gwendolyn Hume (1995) 'The political economy of new investment in telephone systems in developing countries'. PhD dissertation, Cornell University.

US Bureau of Census (2000) *Statistical Abstract of the United States: 1999*. Washington, DC: US Department of Commerce.

US Bureau of Census (1998) 'Pin C-09: occupation of longest job by industry of longest job in 1997 – persons 15 years old and over'. Washington, DC: US Department of Commerce.

US Bureau of Labor Statistics (1999) 'Comparative civilian labor force statistics, ten countries, 1960–98'. Washington, DC: Department of Labor, 13 April.

US Congress (1999) *American Worker Project*. Committee on Education and the Workforce. Available at: www.house.gov/ed_workforce/oversight/awp/awp. htm.

US Economics and Statistics Administration (2000) *Digital Economy 2000*. Washington, DC: US Department of Commerce.

Walker, Richard (1989) 'Machinery, labour and location', in Stephen Wood (ed.), *The Transformation of Work*. London: Unwin Hyman. pp. 59–90.

Walker, Richard (1999) 'Putting capital in its place: globalization and the prospects for labor'. Working Paper, Department of Geography, University of California, Berkeley, March.

Webgrrls (2000) Webgrrls website: www.webgrrls.com.

Wood, Adrian (1994) *North–South Trade, Employment and Inequality: Changing Fortunes in a Skill-Driven World*. Oxford: Clarendon.

Yates, Michael (1999) 'Braverman and the class struggle', *Monthly Review*, 50 (8). Available: www.monthlyreview.org/ 199yates.htm.

PART SIX: CULTURE AND NEW MEDIA

Introduction

MARK POSTER

Culture has become a problem for everyone. What was once a safe ground of inquiry has shifted as if by some earthquake whose effects long went unmeasured on academic Richter scales. Culture is now an unstable terrain marked by the scars of two decades of discursive rumbles. Where you stand on the culture question immediately places you, a bit too precisely for the comfort of many, on the map of scholarly and even political dispute. The humanities, the arts and the social sciences are now fractured into contentious subgroupings that run across disciplinary boundaries, all by dint of that little word 'culture'. Everyone wants to claim the term as their own, yet when they do so 'culture' receives new, unexpected meanings. Historians now practise empirical cultural history but find themselves slammed in the face by literary criticism and theory. Sociologists want to quantify culture, only to provoke the complaints of humanists who set in opposition number and subtlety, magnitude and meaning. Aestheticians decry the application of the term to popular culture. Anthropologists deconstruct culture and practise ethnography in the 'advanced' societies. Adepts of cultural studies wonder if their discourse can survive departmentalization.

Minorities and subcultures of great variety raise the banner of culture and insist on recognition. Conservatives defend what they see as culture as if it were under attack by communism, terrorism and Arab fundamentalism. National cultures collapse into multiplicity. Avant-garde cultures are considered modern and therefore paradoxically retrograde.

Youth cultures are not simply rebellious but trickle up the social ladder, so to speak, to influence adult styles and habits. Genders are not biological but cultural, multiplying with the preferences and styles of their claimants. The most unstable groupings lay their claims to privileged cultural status: border cultures (Anzaldua, 1987) and even refugee camp cultures (Malkki, 1995) become models for the rest.

Culture has lost its boundary. The high and the low are mixed together. The finest creative sensibilities design packaging for commodities. The separation of culture from nature is in question. Scientists create animals in the laboratory. The air, the water and the skies are polluted by the social activities of high-tech nations. Nothing stands outside the cultivatable and so culture itself must be regarded as constructed rather than as given, historically contingent rather than timeless and certain. So sceptics ask if everything is constructed, then perhaps nothing is constructed. If everything emerges from a cultural process, the word has lost its specificity and coherence.

Despite this conflicted cacophony the term 'culture' remains useful, even essential, for studying new media. The paradox is this: without a concept of culture, the study of new media incorporates by default the culture of the dominant institutions in society. The state wishes to perfect its system of control over the population so as to secure its territorial boundaries. Corporations and entrepreneurs want nothing more than to glean greater profits.

These are the cultures of the state and the economy, these are their characteristic gestures and motivations. Imposing these aims upon new media, the state and the economy regard them as tools for a more convenient implementation. In short, they colonize new media with the culture of instrumentality or performativity. In their approach to the Internet, the state and the economy frame it as something that is useful to them, something that may improve their pre-existing practices, make things go faster or more smoothly. Or not. These institutions are also concerned that the Internet might disrupt or hamper their ongoing activities: the state might be threatened by terrorists using the net,[1] or banks and other financial institutions might be vulnerable to hackers. In either case, the question for them is instrumental: how will the net benefit or harm their existing goals? Even when the state and the corporations look to the Internet for new ways of doing things, they do not put into question their foundations.

As long as we remain within an instrumental framework we cannot question it, define its limits, look to new media in relation to how they might generate new cultures. In this way, the culture of instrumentality obstructs research on the Internet, research that might open up the question of culture, of possible new cultural formations, of postmodern cultures.

The state and the economy are not the only institutions or groups which approach the net in terms of their own culture: some of the democratizing political tendencies within the academy often exhibit similar impulses. The problem in this case is not exactly the culture of instrumentality, although at times it may be: it is rather the question of the subject, the self. In a collaborative volume on 'race, class and gender on the Internet', the editor Bosah Ebo frames the work with the following question: 'Will the Internet create a cybertopia or will it exacerbate class divisions by creating a cyberghetto?' (1998: 9). If the state and the corporations look to the Internet to perpetuate their positions of domination, scholars like Ebo look to it for signs of change among groups in positions of subordination. He asks if groups determined by race, class and gender will, as a consequence of the Internet, improve their standing or recede further from positions of power. Here again the Internet serves as a tool for determining the fate of groups *as they are currently constituted*. Although this question is certainly legitimate, it is not critical of current cultural forms. Ebo and the authors in his book do not ask, in this regard, another question: how may the Internet mediate the transformation of existing cultural figures, or how may new cultural forms emerge which do not necessarily improve the position of existing groups as they are currently constituted but change them in unforeseeable ways? The question of culture in relation to the Internet involves a risk,

a step into the unfamiliar precisely with respect to the figure of the self. If this question is foreclosed, one cannot examine critically the political culture of new media. One can merely put forward existing cultural figures of the self – race, class and gender, or citizen, manager and worker – to test the role of new media in furthering their positions as they see themselves and as they are. Such a framework is instrumental and overlooks systematically the constitutive character of media not in some form of technological determinism but as a space which encourages practices and which, in turn, serves to construct new types of subjects.

There is a perhaps more subtle way in which critical studies refuses the cultural question of the Internet. In this case scholars do not so much presuppose existing forms of race, class and gender. The uniqueness of the Internet is here fully recognized. But it is configured as a threat, not to specific groups but to general types of practice that are characterized as 'human'. Margaret Morse, for instance, argues 'there is a basic human need for reciprocity and the reversibility of "I" and "you" in discourse – seeing and being seen, recognizing others and being recognized, speaking, listening and being listened to'. And again: 'there is a human need for and pleasure in being recognized as a partner in discourse, even when the relation is based on a simulation that is mediated by or exchanged with machines' (1998: 10, 14). The virtual quality of the Internet, Morse continues, undermines these human needs by its machinic mediation. She continues the lament noted above that the Internet promotes patriarchy and capitalism but she especially is concerned that it erodes the 'sociality' of 'a well-functioning society' (1998: 35). For this cultural critic the Internet destabilizes community and undermines the felicity of face-to-face relations. As an aside one must ask why, if humans are so needful of bodily presence, they so regularly turn away from each other and bury their heads in books and newspapers, stare vacantly at television, move catatonically with portable music players blaring in their ears, or gaze with fascination at a networked computer screen. If one assumes, as a cultural critic, that whatever intercedes between relations of presence detracts from the human condition, then one cannot investigate potentials for rendering cyberspace inhabitable, one cannot ask the *political* question of what to do about the Internet. Cultural critics are better served by acknowledging the innovation of the Internet and examining how democratic groups might explore it and act politically so as to ensure its most beneficent configuration (McRobbie, 1994).

To approach the cultural question of the Internet is no easy task. Computer-mediated communication fundamentally shifts the registers of human experience as we have known them in modern society and even as they have been known through the ages.

Time and space, body and mind, subject and object, human and machine are each drastically transformed by practices carried out on networked computers. Even if one is aware of this and consciously acts in cyberspace as one does in territorial space, reproducing the motivations of the world of bodily presence, the effects of machinic mediation work just as surely to alter the human experience. What then can be the culture or cultures of cyberspace?

It is important not to pose this question in too stark terms. Cyberspace is surely no total departure from all previous history. Historians are right to remind us that the Internet does not mark the first reshuffling of the basic conditions of cultural formation as enumerated in the couplets above. From cave painting and smoke signals to writing and the alphabet, decisive shifts in the system of signification have accompanied humans throughout the past. In *Information Ages: Literacy, Numeracy, and the Computer Revolution* (1998), Michael Hobart and Zachary Schiffman point out the long heritage of computer-generated information. What occurs with networked computing, they argue, began at least as far back as writing: the commutation of signification into information. 'Information', they contend, 'is … wedded to writing insofar as writing gives stability to the mental objects abstracted from the flow of experience, such that one can access them readily and repeatedly' (1998: 30). Writing thus changes the time and space of signification, making it endure and shifting it from resonating air to papyrus or paper. It changes the relation of signification to the body and mind, abstracting it from living beings and securing it in bound volumes. It alters the relation of subject and object, confirming signification as a practice of the subject but also affirming that signification subsists in the world of objects. Finally, writing has shifted the relation of human to machine since the onset of printing: signification would now require elaborate crafts, masses of capital and collective labour.

If Hobart and Schiffman are wise to connect the Internet to earlier practices of signification, their insights need not deter us from formulating a problematic of the cultural novelty of cyberspace. We must turn to history for guidance in this project so as to acknowledge the constructedness of the Internet and to recognize its relations with earlier forms. Historical understanding alone enables the scholar to estimate the contours of the object under investigation as contingent and unfounded. But we must also turn to those deviant and most controversial historians of culture, Friedrich Nietzsche and Michel Foucault, who corrected a surreptitious reintroduction of foundationalism when historians see only the continuity of the present object with the past. The problem Nietzsche and Foucault raise for historians is to connect the present with the past in a way that undercuts the unreflective legitimacy of the present, that acknowledges lineage while

allowing for innovation, that traces the links of rationalities while holding open the emergence of the unexpected.

The study of the culture of the Internet then must seek in the analytics of man/machine, subject/object, body/mind, time/space a new configuration of the construction of the subject. In the chapters in this part, this is what the authors have sought by reviewing the current literature on the subject and attempting to further in a preliminary way the formulation of the most apposite questions. But more needs first to be said about the question of the subject. For it must not be assumed that this term is automatically useful in examining the Internet cultures.

We need to distinguish between the terms 'individual', 'self', 'identity' and 'subject'. The 'individual' may be taken as an empirical given, an empty term that requires elaboration to specify its parameters in a given time and place. Similarly the term 'self' refers in an undefined way to the mind, personality, soul, psyche of the individual. By contrast, the terms 'identity' and 'subject' are currently deployed in cultural analysis laden with much heavier meaning, much more theoretical and political weight than the former terms. 'Subject' is used as the modern configuration of the self, best expressed in Descartes as ontological separateness from material objects, as the profound centre of the individual, affording a distance from the world that enables the exercise of reason, reason that may grasp reality as certain truth. The figure of such an individual provides the legitimacy for most modern institutions – representative democracy, law, capitalist economics, science, education. Only if there is a prior and general sense that such a figure of the individual is viable does any argument make sense for citizenship, the rational economic man, systematic and discursive investigations of nature, long years of education in reading and writing. Of course all of this is determined in discourse at the ideological level. The 'subject' then is the cultural basis for modern society.

'Identity' comes into discursive play when the coherence of the individual as a cultural figure begins to collapse. Identity was used seriously as an analytic term first in the 1950s by Erik Erikson (1968) precisely to step back from the Freudian subject and take an easier attitude toward the self, one that gave importance to questions of ego maintenance, continuity and stability, features of the psyche that Freud may be said to have assumed. Instead of an autonomous agent who might control his or her destiny, instead of the subject of the progressive, humanist vision, Erikson presents an individual who is deeply confused about who he/she is (Gleason, 1996: 470). Erikson's self, far from being a heroic bourgeois subject, experiences life as a series of crises, forming an ego that has a tentative stability, always under threat of difusion or even disintegration. This continually negotiated, fragile ego is what Erikson means by the term 'identity'. Identity then is a renegotiated figure of the subject that accounts for the failure of modernity to realize the metanarrative of progress. We need to keep in mind this massive cultural shift when we examine identity in relation to new media. The term 'identity' is the recognition of the failure of Western culture, a failure inscribed in the massive disasters of the twentieth century. It is an ideological compromise that saves and masks traditional individualism, adjusts it to changes in culture such as the disappearance of the proletariat, the emergence of consumer culture, the diffusion of electronic media, the demise of Europe from world hegemony, the end of the West as a basis for universality. When the term is carried over into the new social movements of women, minorities, sexual preference and post-colonialism, it carries with it the burdens of its past. Individuals defined as their identity are hardly agents in the sense of the figure of the subject.

The difference between the individual as subject and the individual as identity becomes exigent in relation to new media. Individuals are constituted as subjects or identities (as cultural selves) in linguistic practices. In repeated enunciations, individuals become interpellated and recognized as coherent selves who function in a social world. Increasingly the process of interpellation occurs through mediations of information machines in addition to face-to-face interactions. First printed pages, then broadcast media and now networked computing shift the scene in which the individual becomes and continues to practise selfhood. I use the term 'postmodernity', however contested it has become, to designate the shift in incidence from a combination of face-to-face and print arenas of interpellation to one that includes to an important degree broadcast media and networked computing.

The term 'postmodern' designated for Lyotard (1984) the collapse of modern culture's metanarrative of progress and for Jameson (1991) a change in the culture of capitalism. In both instances postmodernity registered not an institutional transformation or an alteration of practices so much as a new figure of the self. Postmodernity for them certainly referred to social phenomena like the collapse of the distinction between high and low culture, or even to a more general blurring of boundaries in all areas of everyday life. But the weight of the category bore most heavily on the process of subjectivation or the constitution of the self. For Lyotard the self was disengaged from historicity and for Jameson in addition it was fragmented, dispersed, low in affect and one-dimensional. These theorists discerned a new figure of the self only through the backdrop of the older modern subject, the heroic bourgeois/proletarian agent. In both cases the trope for the change was tragedy, a fall from a higher place. In the essays on the culture of new media that follow, the reader needs to keep this theoretical

heritage in mind but also to recognize the importance of framing the change to postmodernity in a way that opens the analysis to political possibilities, rather than closes the discussion with a large sigh of regret.

Those who would further the critical cultural study of the media have begun to recognize the need for a deployment of the term 'postmodern' in a manner that makes it suitable for analysis without either a celebratory fanfare or sarcastic smirks. In the study of broadcast media, for instance, Lynne Joyrich (1996: 63) argues persuasively that television brings consumer desires to the individual with an immediacy that undermines the separation of subject and object, the basic condition for the constitution of the self as subject. If this is the case, the cultural study of new media has no choice but to register this transformation with the use of some term. Like Joyrich, I suggest the term 'postmodernity' for this purpose.

The danger of the term, as she recognizes, is that it illicitly incorporates a certain universalism. Lyotard and Jameson certainly suffer from this tendency. Since the category of the subject was discursively inscribed as universal, even though it betrayed its conditions of birth in white, Western male culture, the suggestion that it has collapsed incorporated the same universalist gesture. The problem rests not with the aspiration for the universal as such but rather with the fact that the universal can only escape clandestine hierarchical resonances if it is enunciated universally, a condition that has never been possible in human history. Lacking such a condition, the universal must be approached with great caution. Until the enunciative conditions exist for the articulation of the universal we must always stress the contingent quality of discursive claims, the situatedness of knowledge, as Donna Haraway (1991) says. The issue is not really who speaks but how they speak, how they recognize themselves and inscribe themselves in their discourse in relation to the Western pattern of the all-knowing, unconditioned subject. As a corrective to the universalist inscription of the term 'postmodern' I suggest a focus on the specificity of the media in the process of self-construction.

Joyrich deploys the category of gender to very much the same end. Gender operates to render specific and contingent the epistemological position of enunciation. But gender – along with race, class, sexual preference and age – is not enough to deflect enunciation from the tendency to reinscribe foundational identity. We can escape better, if never completely, this danger if we include the machinic and the space/time configuration specific to the mediated scene of interpellation. If we are to study the culture of new media we need to take into account the information machines that increasingly mediate our symbolic practices. And these machines (be they print, broadcast or networked computing) extract us from territorial spaces and phenomenological time, repositioning us in strange new ways. These media of course are not themselves born innocent but arise from existing patterns of hierarchy in relation to class, race and gender. But they enable practices that fit badly with earlier complexes of domination, putting them into question and thereby opening the field – if we are not too defensive about and beholden to these older patterns – to new spaces of politics. This part of the *Handbook* will look at some of these spaces – ethnicity, the nation-state, democracy, capitalism – keeping these prospects in mind.

Joyrich recognizes the destabilizing effects of the multiple, fragmented self of postmodernity. She proposes a most promising stance toward the phenomenon: 'I am trying neither to celebrate nor to lament postmodern fragmentation. Instead I hope to reveal the ways in which the sexed and cyborg body have been linked in both the televised and the critical imagination' (1996: 132). In her analysis she applauds television shows like 'Peewee's Playhouse', 'Max Headroom' and 'Moonlighting' for their transgressive potential, although she reminds readers of their commercial and discursive limitations, even of their recuperating closures. What she pays less attention to however is the machinic level, that is, television as an information machine of the broadcast model that sets into play practices of self-constitution whose specificity and difference from other such devices, in particular books and networked computing, require elaboration. If television, like consumption, is associated in critical writing with the feminine, as she argues, those discourses also deal poorly with the machinic quality of this visual medium, either ignoring it or instrumentalizing it. It is to this crucial mediation, with particular reference to new media, that the essays in this part turn.

Jennifer Daryl Slack and J. Macgregor Wise, in their chapter 'Cultural studies and technology', introduce this part on culture and new media with a broad examination of the relation of technology to culture, in particular with reference to the discourse of cultural studies. The question of the relation of technology to culture is a vexed one, with many pitfalls along the path to productive analysis. Slack and Wise review many of these problems, in particular the notorious issue of technological determinism, but also questions of causality and progress that are commonplace in discussions of media technology. In much of the humanities and social sciences, the mere mention of media as an important ingredient in social and cultural analysis is enough to raise the red flag of determinism. Our authors explore this issue with subtlety, going on to open the other side of the issue, that of culture and cultural analysis. In some detail Slack and Wise discuss the traditions of cultural studies in relation to media, but expand beyond this to positions like those of Deleuze and Foucault. They review the literature on the relation of technology to culture in terms of four central issues: agency, genealogy, identity and inequality, and social space and the body. These more focused topics allow them to thread their way through the vast and dense thicket of the media technology question. Their conclusion is that while many important studies have been accomplished, much remains to be done in developing analytics of technology from a cultural studies point of view.

Michael Curry's chapter, 'Discursive displacement and the seminal ambiguity of space and place', explores, with great historical range and conceptual complexity, the relation of space to technology. Curry leads the reader to the current context of new media and space by an analysis of the relation of place, space and region to various technologies and to an associated sequence of categories, topography, chorography and geography. We learn from Curry the enormous difficulty of understanding the relation of technology to space because of the continuous, apparently unavoidable, 'discursive displacement' and ambiguity of the terms we use in this regard. And when we add the category of culture into the mix, Curry shows us how much more difficult our task becomes. The new media of cyberspace, itself incorporating a spatial term, opens the question of territory, of nation, of specificity of place and abstraction of mapping in productive but puzzling ways.

Timothy Luke's piece, entitled 'Power and political culture', examines the scholarship on new media and politics. This most controversial issue, Luke argues, is flawed by some persistent tendencies, especially those that instrumentalize the question, treating new media as a neutral tool to further or to impede the prospects of pre-existing political institutions, groups and movements, and those that project a utopia emerging from the development of the Internet. Luke wisely insists upon the specificity of new media in generating new forms of political association, force relations and domination. Luke's chapter is organized into three sections: the relation of politics to culture in the online world in the context of national governments and other power structures; the emergence of new identities in power relations specific to new media; and the literature on the questions of the relation of netizenship to citizenship. His comprehensive review of the literature on the politics of cyberspace rigorously assesses the state of the study and points to many new directions for further research and theorizing.

The concluding chapter by Don Slater, 'Social relationships and identity online and offline', reviews with subtlety and in depth the scholarship concerning the relation of online to offline communication. Slater characterizes Internet studies of the 1990s as flawed by a tendency to regard online communication either as a space apart from 'real life' with its own culture, or as purely instrumental and subordinate to the culture of real life. Slater deconstructs the online/offline distinction by discussing four characteristics attributed to life online: virtuality, spatiality, disembedding and disembodiment. Slater argues, against those who attribute a specific culture to online experience as well as those who view it as purely a tool, that online communication is something enacted by people. He contends for instance that cyberculture, as it is described in the scholarship of the 1990s, derives in part from games culture that antedated the Internet, such as dungeons and dragons, as well as from the counterculture of the 1960s. Consequently what we are given as cyberculture is not unique to it but a mixture of many elements only some of which are particular to new media. Slater argues deftly that the culture of new media is not an attribute of the media themselves but a result of social practices: that people make the culture of cyberspace. Citing his own study of Internet use in Trinidad he suggests that the online/offline dichotomy is erased in use as people simply integrate their experience of cyberspace into their pre-existing lives. He goes on to point out various methodological problems in studying new media, problems that plague ethnography in particular, in relation to online and offline identities. Slater concludes that advancing Internet usage might well result in the integration of online and offline cultures.

The salient issue that emerges from this part of the *Handbook* is that of the need for comparative media studies. It has become clear that numerous dangers confront the study of the culture of the Internet if it is not set in the context of earlier and contemporary media. Even if one regards media as integrated into social practice, as Slater contends, one must nonetheless be able to discriminate between the cultures that emerge in different mediated practices. This research agenda requires the collaboration of scholars from many disciplines, the humanities and social sciences but also the arts and computer science. As we see in this part of the *Handbook*, contributions range from history (myself) through political science (Luke), geography/philosophy (Curry) and anthropology (Slater) to sociology (Slack and Wise). Such a requirement for interdisciplinarity in the study of the Internet elicits a new culture among researchers, even if some of them might gainsay the cultural novelty of new media.

NOTE

1 *Wired News* reports that 20 nations attempt to keep the Internet out of their borders, that 45 nations seriously censor it, and that this is an improvement in Internet 'freedom' over the recent past (McCabe, 1999).

REFERENCES

Anzaldua, G. (1987) *Borderlands/La Frontera: the New Mestiza*. San Francisco: Aunt Lute.

Ebo, B. (ed.) (1998) *Cyberghetto or Cybertopia? Race, Class, and Gender on the Internet*. Westport, CT: Praeger.

Erikson, E. (1968) *Identity: Youth and Crisis*. New York: Norton.

Gleason, P. (1996) 'Identifying identity: a semantic history', in W. Sollors (ed.), *Theories of Ethnicity: a Classical Reader*. New York: New York University Press. pp. 460–87.

Haraway, D. (1991) *Simians, Cyborgs and Women: the Re-Invention of Nature*. New York: Routledge.

Hobart, M. and Schiffman, Z. (1998) *Information Ages: Literacy, Numeracy, and the Computer Revolution*. Baltimore, MD: Johns Hopkins University Press.

Jameson, F. (1991) *Postmodernism, or, the Cultural Logic of Late Capitalism*. Durham, NC: Duke University Press.

Joyrich, L. (1996) *Re-Viewing Reception: Television, Gender, and Postmodern Culture*. Bloomington, IN: Indiana University Press.

Lyotard, J.-F. (1984) *The Postmodern Condition*. Minneapolis: University of Minnesota Press.

Malkki, L. (1995) *Purity and Exile: Violence, Memory, and National Cosmology among Hutu Refugees in Tanzania*. Chicago: University of Chicago Press.

McCabe, H. (1999) 'The net: enemy of the state?', *Wired News*.

McRobbie, A. (1994) *Postmodernism and Popular Culture*. New York: Routledge.

Morse, M. (1998) *Virtualities: Television, Media Art, and Cyberculture*. Bloomington, IN: Indiana University Press.

28

Cultural Studies and Technology

JENNIFER DARYL SLACK
and J. MACGREGOR WISE

Relating technology to culture – an admirable, if elusive, pursuit – has a long and rich history. For decades, at least, scholars and policy-makers have argued against approaches to technology that posit it as a mere technical tool and for approaches that acknowledge technology in relation to culture – 'in context' as it is often put. The difficulty is of course that the relationship between culture and technology is every bit as much a theoretical problem as it is a task of description, and technological practitioners are often unaware of the work performed by their own theoretical assumptions.[1] A particularly pervasive tendency when discussing new technologies (including new communication and information technologies such as satellite, cable, digital broadcast and narrowcast, the Internet, the World Wide Web) is to treat them as if they were completely revolutionary, capable of (*sui generis* as it were) changing everything and likely to do so. Cultural studies is especially suited to revealing and critiquing the work of tendencies such as this and to positing an alternative way of understanding and shaping the relationship between technologies and culture.

Cultural studies' emphasis on the radical contextuality of phenomena under study and its use of articulation as both analytic tool and model of practice put it in a position to critique the assumptions embedded in technological practice and to contribute to the ongoing development of a more dynamic approach to new media technology. In this chapter, we sketch the most salient components of a developing cultural studies approach to technology and culture. In doing so we draw as much as possible on work on new media that, as we clarify below, 'counts' as cultural studies. But because explicit cultural studies treatments of technology are few, we focus as much on the implications for thinking about new media from a cultural studies perspective. Our treatment of the issue, then, folds in several purposes: first, to utilize a cultural studies perspective to show how contemporary issues involving new media are embedded within (and against) a long genealogy of issues and debates; second, to characterize an emerging cultural studies approach to technology; third, to draw attention to scholarship that contributes specifically to a cultural studies approach to new media; fourth, to consider problems that a cultural studies of new media faces; and finally, to speculate on directions for further research.

WHAT COUNTS AS CULTURAL STUDIES

Cultural studies is not and never has been one thing, but that does not mean that it is anything and everything (Hall, 1990: 11). It is, rather, like an ongoing conversation: a series of regroupings and revisionings, issues considered, questions asked, responses offered, topics explored, risks taken and directions tried. Because the conversation takes place within changing historical moments, the shape of the conversation is connected to historical events, political realities, institutional situations and theoretical and intellectual influences. The longer and/ or more intensely a participant has engaged in the conversation, the more likely they have become part of it and the more likely they are to understand its nuances. Cultural studies is thus more like art than science. In the same way that an artistic movement is shaped loosely by the goals, concerns, challenges and interests of the participating artists and evolves along with the changes they instantiate, so too is cultural studies shaped loosely by the participants in the conversation, evolving as the conversation changes. In the same way that questions designed to clarify what constitutes belonging to a particular artistic movement are most difficult at the 'edges' of what seem to be (conjuncturally) central to definitions of the movement ('is this piece cubist or surrealist?'), so too is it difficult to discern at the edges exactly what is or is not cultural studies.

That having been said, there are a number of worthwhile positions explaining what cultural studies has been. As long as one understands that these positions are themselves only a part of the conversation, they are instructive. They can help us envision what 'counts' as a cultural studies approach to technology generally and to new media technology specifically. Nelson et al.'s (1992) Introduction to *Cultural Studies* is one of the more helpful as it offers an excellent bibliography to the definitional task (pre-1992), is widely read, and remains historically close to crucial dynamics of the ongoing conversation. Nelson et al. point to the following:

> Cultural studies is an interdisciplinary, transdisciplinary, and sometimes counter disciplinary field. (1992: 4)

> Cultural studies is ... committed to the study of the entire range of a society's arts, beliefs, institutions, and communicative practices. (1992: 4)

> Culture is understood *both* as a way of life – encompassing ideas, attitudes, languages, practices, institutions, and structure of power – and as a whole range of cultural practices: artistic forms, texts, canons, architecture, mass-produced commodities, and so forth. (1992: 5)

> Its practitioners see cultural studies not simply as a chronicle of cultural change but as an intervention in it, and see themselves not simply as scholars providing an account but as politically engaged participants. (1992: 5)

> [An] emphasis on contingencies is central to contemporary cultural studies, to a theory of articulation, and to models for carrying out conjunctural analysis – analysis, that is, which is embedded, descriptive, and historically and contextually specific. (1992: 8)

The last requires additional explanation. An emphasis on contingency suggests that cultural theorists understand what something 'is' as constituted in a particular historical conjuncture. Thus, as opposed to having an essential, independent identity, what something 'is' is contingent on a particular configuration of relationships. This 'radical contextuality' insists that a context is not something 'out there', independent, into which other independent things move, are inserted or removed. Context and phenomena are, rather, mutually constitutive. The analysis of any phenomenon is precisely the act of contextualizing it. This mode of analysis is termed 'articulation', which points to the double-pincered work of describing the connection (following Deleuze and Guattari, 1987, we refer to this as

'tracing') as well as the act of drawing or making the connection (again following Deleuze and Guattari, we refer to this as 'mapping').

The distinction between tracing and mapping is a crucial one, because radical contextuality and articulation theory recognize that theories, methods and practices are always embedded in, reflective of and limited by their historical circumstances. Theories, methods and practices are seen as particular ways of engaging and giving shape to these circumstances. The act of theorizing is not therefore a case of getting something right or wrong, and cultural studies does not purport to advance one correct theory (or even the idea that there can be one correct theory), or one correct methodology, or even one correct political practice. However, this is not a theoretical, methodological or political relativism; one theory, practice or method is not just as good as any other. Instead, cultural studies works to understand the embedded contexts of theories, methods and practices and their institutional and disciplinary specificity, at the same time that it undertakes analysis of the specific phenomenon under investigation. Cultural studies thus demands the ongoing work of theorizing in relation to the ongoing analysis of changing historical conjunctures. This makes cultural studies work tremendously difficult when done rigorously.

Drawing on these broad parameters, we can say that the analysis of culture necessitates at some point an analysis of technology, since technology in some form will always be part of the context of everyday life. Historically, understanding the role of technology in culture seems particularly pressing as: (1) new media technology plays a central role in changing global political economic configurations, (2) new media technology contributes to defining a new organization of knowledge, the information age, and (3) new media technology plays a conspicuous role in popular culture.

Theoretically, cultural studies works with and against a series of problematics that have shaped understanding of, and debate about, the relationship between technology and culture. The problematics that have most dominated work on culture and technology are as follows:

- *The question of causality* Does technology drive cultural change (technological determinism)? Or is technology a neutral tool, its effects and politics determined solely by its uses ('guns don't kill people, people kill people')? At the heart of this issue is not only the direction of causality (culture versus technology), but the nature of that causality (absolute determinism, relative determinism, expressive causality, etc.).
- *The question of technological dependence* Have we become so dependent on our tools that we have created a *de facto* technological determinism? Have we become slaves to our own machines?

- *The question of progress* What is the relationship between technology and progress? Technology has become central to discourses on progress and development. The pervasive sense is that technology is instrumental in moving cultures inevitably and inexorably toward a state of perfection. By this logic, more technology equals progress equals a better life.

To say that these problematics are 'worked with and is to mitigate against simply dismissing them as 'wrong', worthy only of being discarded. Instead, in 'working with' these problematics, cultural studies recognizes and critiques their power in shaping a role for technology. In 'working against' these problematics, cultural studies recognizes that the role of technology can change – in part – by changing the terms of the debate. To put this very concretely, we (those of us who study culture and technology) have long since accepted that technology is not neutral, that technology does not cause cultural change (or vice versa) in any simple way, that the relationship between technology and culture is contingent not determined, that neither we nor technology are slave to the other, and that technological development is not necessarily progress. Okay, so what then? Where do we go after that? There is a pressing need in this techno-fetishistic culture to cultivate an understanding of technology that insists on theories that challenge current practices, that give us somewhere to go and provide us with direction. Work in the cultural studies of technology is finding its way there.

These problematics, then, as the discussion below illustrates, are being transformed by what we take to be four major problematics of cultural studies: agency; genealogy; identity, politics and power; and social space and corporeality. Each of these has important applications and implications for understanding the relationship between culture and new media technology.[2]

In the process of discussing the work that makes these advances, we acknowledge that we have chosen to see and represent that work as an emerging cultural studies approach to technology. In this way we add not only to the discussion of new media technology and culture but to the discussion of what – theoretically – constitutes cultural studies. Readers may note that from time to time we draw on figures (such as Bruno Latour and Langdon Winner) from the social studies of technology (SST) or science, technology and society (STS) approaches prevalent in many of the other contributions to this collection. The commonality of these works points to articulations between sociological and cultural approaches to the study of technology. However, in citing them here we often rearticulate their theories and case studies, drawing them into the context of cultural studies. Differentiating a cultural studies approach to technology from an SST or STS approach entails more than the observation that one focuses on culture and the other on society. Indeed, the distinctions between what constitutes 'culture' and what constitutes 'society' have always been a source of contention, if not significant overlap. Rather, what differentiates the cultural studies approach to technology from the SST or STS approaches is the radical nature of the contextuality that cultural studies foregrounds and the deep commitment to theory as an essential part of the analysis, as we have outlined above.

FROM CAUSALITY TO AGENCY

Questions of causality – in many guises – have haunted the study of technology throughout history. Although the questions have been formulated in many different ways, the underlying problematic has been 'what causes what'. Perhaps the oldest formulation assuming that technology has effects – Plato's exploration of the effects of writing technology – dates this concern at least as far back as the fourth century BC. The delineation of effects (and side effects) has occupied much contemporary work on new media technology, in studies by the Office of Technology Assessment for example. The delineation of kinds of side effects has been taken almost to the level of absurdity by Edward Tenner in *Why Things Bite Back* (1996). Conversely, the position that technology is a neutral tool that merely responds to (is an effect of) the needs and desires of the culture permeates treatments of technology. There have been many ways to characterize the causal possibilities, all of which tend to suggest the operation of a binary distinction: autonomous versus non-autonomous technology (Winner, 1977); mechanistic versus non-mechanistic causality (Slack, 1984); substantive versus instrumental theory (Borgmann, 1984; Feenberg, 1991); and technological versus social determinism (Wise, 1997).

The binary distinctions fail on two counts. First, the binary cannot adequately explain the complexity of either everyday discourse about, or mobilization of, technology. What is, perhaps, most interesting about the theoretically rigorous attempt at making binary distinctions is the fact that in everyday life we tend to rely on atheoretical, opportunistic combinations of claims about causality as the circumstances demand: technology is treated as both a neutral instrument *and* a powerful cause of cultural change. Second, the binary is inadequate to the task of explaining the theoretically acknowledged complex imbrication of technology and culture. The history of debates in technology studies, philosophy of technology, SST and STS points to the fact that the causal relationship between technology and culture is neither one way nor the other. The fundamental mistake seems to be the fact that the binary assumes that technology and culture are separate phenomena. The theoretical problem is, rather, to find a way to understand the role of technology, acknowledging that technology is always already a part of culture, not a cause or an effect of it. At the same time the challenge remains to distinguish the ways in which technology is effective, for it clearly does make a difference which technologies we use.

Both of these failings have been recognized by virtually all contemporary critical and cultural theorists studying technology. In place of the constricting binary, theorists have developed a variety of figures designed to comprehend technology as effective, but as irreducible to either cause or effect. Raymond Williams, in his pivotal book, *Television: Technology and Cultural Form* (1975), introduces the notion of a 'community of selected emphasis and intention' (1975: 18) in order to argue that new media technologies (television in this case) emerge within a configuration of emphasis, interests and intentions, as part of that configuration. The configuration, or complex, that contextualizes the emergence of television for Williams is 'mobile privatization', in which the technology serves 'an at once mobile and home-centered way of living' (1975: 26). Interestingly, Williams' model for understanding the emergence of new media technologies never really generated studies in its image. In part, this may be because it took far longer for cultural studies to accept widely the importance of studying media technology (as opposed to media content). Further, when cultural studies finally directed its attention to technology, it moved beyond Williams' expressive causal commitments (Slack, 1984: 73–8).

The new direction is paved, instead, by Winner's (1986) idea of technology as forms of life; Slack's notion of technology as articulation (1989); Latour's (1988; 1996; Callon and Latour, 1981) and Haraway's (1992) conceptions of technological agency; and Wise's (1997) technology as assemblage. Each of these figures resists the commonsense equation of technology with 'things', with the comforting sense that the boundaries of what any particular technology is can be clearly delimited. For example, cultural theorists resist studying the computer as if it was simply the hardware, the software and the networks that connect the computer to other computers and other media. Rather, they are drawn to understanding the technology to be a form of life, an articulation, an apparatus or an assemblage within which agency flows.

One way to characterize the shift is to see it as a change from focusing on 'what causes what' to attending to 'how things happen'. The shift blurs the vision of the 'whats': technology, culture, effects. Instead the mechanisms of stasis, resistance and change, not categories of identity, become the objects of study. Langdon Winner's 'forms of life', though never widely adopted, was an early formulation of this shift. He argued that as the devices, techniques and systems that we commonly understand to be technology 'become woven into the texture of everyday existence', they 'shed their tool-like qualities to become part of our very humanity'. They become '[d]eeply insinuated into people's perceptions, thoughts, and behaviour'. They become, in short, 'an indelible part of modern culture' (Winner, 1986: 12). It becomes impossible to talk about the effect of one on the other, since earlier innovations are both reflections of culture and the conditions of further cultural development. Drawing on the Marxist conception that the forms within which we live our lives define who we are, Winner focuses on how technologies embody ways of engaging the world: of making it, reproducing it, changing it. Indeed, Winner points out the danger of separating technology from the culture and society: it allows one to be easily swayed by the rhetoric of revolution that accompanies new media technologies (a belief he terms 'mythinformation', 1986: 105) and allows for serious misconceptions about the possibilities for democracy with new technologies such as the computer. Rather, he argues, new technologies tend to reinforce the overall power structure, not overthrow it. Winner, however, does not offer a theoretical approach, model or method sufficiently developed to go much beyond acknowledging that technologies *are* forms of life and that they *do* tend to reinforce existing structures of power. Also, persistent in Winner's formulation is a tendency to characterize technologies as 'things'. Winner's work illustrates how difficult it is to move beyond our cultural habit of understanding technologies as things, even in the act of arguing against it.

Following Stuart Hall (1986), who formulated one of the earliest and most influential accounts of the concept of articulation, Jennifer Daryl Slack argues that technology can be understood as an articulation, as 'a nonnecessary connection of different elements that, when connected in a particular way, form a specific unity' (1989: 331). If technology (she uses the example of the personal computer) is itself an articulation of elements (hardware, software, network, etc.) that can be connected in different ways with other elements (economics, ideology, politics, policy, gender, etc.), then technology as a generic term and any specific common-sense technology (such as the computer) are contingent rather than determined, dispersed rather than discrete. The question of the relationship between technology and culture is thus reframed to foreground the connections that constitute technology.

A still more dramatic shift away from the problematic of causality occurs when the idea of agency is taken up and radically transformed. Those most responsible for developing this concept in relation to technology are Bruno Latour, Donna Haraway and J. Macgregor Wise. Latour begins to transform the idea of agency by revisioning what it means to be an actor. An actor for Latour is not limited to humans as agents, but is 'any element which bends space around itself, makes other elements dependent upon itself and translates their will into a language of its own' (Callon and Latour, 1981: 286). The resulting aggregate of elements is an 'actor network'. Agency, it follows, is the ability to achieve effects either through physical contact or through non-corporeal means (Wise, 1997: xv). Agency structures movement; it distributes and organizes entities (human and other than human), spaces and places. Latour was particularly influential in introducing the notion that, in this sense, technology is an actor or agent that exercises agency (Latour, 1988; 1993; 1996). Technology can bend space around itself, render other elements dependent on it, and translate the will of others into a language of its own. Technology structures movement; it distributes and organizes entities, spaces and places. A dramatic example is the electric eye door opener, which allows people to move from one place to another. If a person is too short, the electric eye will not sense them, the door will not open, and the short person's movement in space will be restricted (a form of discrimination). If the electricity is shut off, the door will indiscriminately prohibit movement through that particular space (see Latour, 1988, for a parallel example of an automatic door closer, which we will return to below). Latour goes so far as to give technology a voice: in *Aramis, or the Love of Technology* (1996), Aramis, a failed new transportation technology, speaks of the reasons for its own death.

Donna Haraway, influenced by Latour's actor-network theory, links the notion of actors with the concept of articulation. She writes that actors 'take provisional, never-finished shape in articulatory practices' and observes that 'humans and unhumans' (technology, for example) 'articulate … in a social relationship' (1992: 313). Rapidly receding here are the once comfortable notions that technology is an identity with identifiable boundaries, that there is a clear-cut distinction between technology and humans, and that only humans exercise agency. Consequently the binary problematic of determination (what causes what) begins to recede. Not entirely, however, for the 'thingness' of actors sneaks back in the guise of the construction that *actors exercise agency*. For example, Haraway works with constructions such as 'jaguars, among other actors' (1992: 313) and Latour works with statements such as 'Humans and nonhumans take on form by redistributing the competencies and performance of the multitude of actors that they hold on to and that hold on to them' (1996: 225). This return to 'actors exercising agency' seems always to reintroduce the seductive and familiar distinction between things (technologies) and culture, and hence the causal problematic.

The cultural studies conception of technology does finally move dramatically away from the ultimately binary conception of 'thingness' under the influence of the work of Gilles Deleuze and Félix Guattari. Lawrence Grossberg (1996), drawing on the work of Deleuze and Guattari, asserts that agency is not a property of an identity, an agent. Rather, agency is a flow that circulates through and produces a sense of agents. Grossberg puts it this way: 'Agency is the product of diagrams of mobility and placement which define or map the possibilities of where and how specific vectors of influence can stop and be placed' (1996: 102). It is the work of agency that lets abstract identities stand as identities: human; animal; technology in general; specific technologies, etc. Each abstraction is produced in relations of agency.

J. Macgregor Wise (1997) develops this Deleuzoguattarian sense of agency in *Exploring Technology and Social Space*. He argues that 'machinic assemblages' (in lieu of technology) are articulations of physiochemical, organic and enunciative strata. Likewise, 'assemblages of enunciation' (in lieu of language) are also articulations of physiochemical, organic and enunciative strata. These assemblages articulate (taking the form of a double articulation) to 'mark the territory', that is, they delineate 'how things happen' as well as 'what does not happen' (1997: 57–80). Agency in this conception 'is not a given, but is distributed, differentiated, and territorialized. The resultant actor-network can thus be understood and critiqued without falling back on the problematic notion of a rational network builder' (1997: 70). Agency, in this sense, works to avoid the conundrum of the binary that adheres to the problematic of identity. From this Deleuzoguattarian perspective, technologies – particular artifacts or services – are seen as 'habits … contractions of action, substance, and thought, a condensation of technology and language' (1997: 71). While grasped as wholes (what Deleuze and Guattari term 'molarities'), they are in fact abstract, differentiated assemblages.

The language of Deleuze and Guattari used by Wise and others (for example, Elmer, 1999) is difficult to be sure – and therefore a decided disadvantage if the goal is to develop a broad-based cultural studies approach to new technology. But it is hardly surprising that a challenge to the tenacious articulation of technology as 'thing' existing in a binary relationship with culture would be a difficult link to sever and that it would take radical language and thought to challenge it. Jonathan Sterne (1999b) has pointed directly to the difficulty of applying such an approach to specific new media technology such as the Internet. The difficulty, as illustrated for Sterne in Wise's work, is that one 'focuses more on discourses about and around the Internet than on attempting a description of the Internet itself' (1999b: 275). However, the real challenge for culture theorists, as illustrated in Sterne's own complaint, is a deep-seated loyalty to 'the Internet [or any new media technology] *itself*' (emphasis added). As if there were such a thing.

FROM THE INEVITABILITY OF PROGRESS TO GENEALOGY

Cultural studies' conception of technology deeply undercuts the common-sense cultural commitment to the equation of progress with the development of new technology. Just as attention to articulation moves the understanding of technology from causal terms to a conception of agency, so too does it displace conceptions of inevitability and progress. Inevitability is supplanted by contingency; progress with genealogy; and idealist conceptions of freedom with an understanding of responsibility as defined and distributed within differentially structured terrains.

It has long been the case that Western (and now increasingly global) culture has equated the development of new technology with progress. The progress 'narrative', as described by Nisbet (1980), holds that the human species – by nature – is developing steadily toward increasing perfection here on earth. And technology has long been seen as a marker of that progress – as its (causal) agent (see Smith and Marx, 1994). For example, international development projects beginning in the 1940s have often used new media technologies as indicators of degrees of 'civilization' (Lerner, 1958). So deeply held is the assumption that new technology and progress are linked that David Noble (1982) once claimed that it was 'heretical' to even ask the question: is it so?

The concept of technological progress depends on a unidirectional, evolutionary model of change (Berland, 2000), a teleologically driven conception of history where origins are decidable and origins determine endings. But cultural studies is in some sense predicated on the idea that origins do not determine endings (Carey, 1975/1989), that there are no 'guarantees' (Hall, 1983), and that connections, outcomes, effects are always 'contingent' rather than determined. Hall, in his widely quoted interview on articulation, emphasizes the role of contingency:

> An articulation is thus the form of the connection that *can* make a unity of two different elements, under certain conditions. It is a linkage which is not necessary, determined, absolute and essential for all time. You have to ask, under what circumstances *can* a connection be forged or made? So the so-called 'unity' of a discourse [or any abstract identity, such as technology or progress] is really the articulation of different, distinct elements which can be rearticulated in different ways because they have no necessary 'belongingness'. (1986: 53)

Indeed, the interventionist commitments of cultural theorists of the new media technology lead them, on the one hand, to trace significant articulations and, on the other hand, to unhinge them, so to speak, to map or rearticulate them. For example, Charles Acland, in tracing the articulations of IMAX (large-format cinema technology) in Canada, insists that it must be seen 'as a multiple articulation of technological system, corporate entity and cinema practice invested in the notion of expanded cinema, or what Andre Bazin ... called the myth of total cinema' (1998: 431). For Acland, this particular configuration is a symptom of a general shift in patterns of leisure toward the re-introduction of a technologically mediated form of the tourist gaze, about which he is obviously critical. Although Acland does not map explicit directions for change, one cannot read his argument without considering what might make it possible to rearticulate this configuration.

Often, cultural studies of new media technology are timid in exposing the intent of their work as mapping the need (if not the direction) for rearticulating the terrain. It is sometimes a frustrating weakness of these studies that superficially they profess only to describe (trace) a developing historical conjuncture when, theoretically, they really are mapping strategies. It is almost as though cultural theory has developed in powerful ways a bit beyond our ability to exploit it. Our work is often – perhaps merely (though not insignificantly) for local political reasons – tamed. Dare we be explicit about the fact that not all technological development is progress? The terrain of study of new media technology is rife with criticism of those who suggest too much that might be taken as negative. Jill J. McMillan and Michael J. Hyde's (2000) case study of the pressure to adopt a technological progress narrative at Wake Forest University illustrates the difficulties of challenging particular technological developments, and even of posing questions that might be considered critical of technology. This is the conjuncture, after all, where appropriate political rhetoric includes positions taken by President William Clinton in his 1996 State of the Union Address announcing 'America's Technological Literacy Campaign', where the goal is 'to make every young person technologically literate', the assumption being that this will 'provide all our children with a greater opportunity to learn the skills they need to thrive into the next century' (America's Technology Literacy Challenge, 1996). The 'politically correct' position to take with regard to technology in this conjuncture is, 'yes, it is inevitable; yes, it is the way forward; we just need to be smart enough to use it for good not ill'. As if the effects of technologies were only about the use of things – after the fact.

Methodologically, cultural studies has an affinity with the practice of genealogy, as it has come down to us from Nietzsche, via Foucault. Genealogy is explicitly opposed to the progress narrative. It does not assume a single, evolutionary direction; it does not assume that ideas or practices retain their logic. It looks instead to the way in which multitudes of elements career, crash, invade, struggle, plunder and play, such that complex and changing arrangements characterize an apparatus (for Deleuze and Guattari, an assemblage) within which we would understand technology to be disbursed. The task of genealogy is, as Foucault puts it, to record the singularity of events outside any monotonous finality; it must seek them in the

> most unpromising places, in what we tend to feel is without history – in sentiments, love, conscience, instincts; it must be sensitive to their recurrence, not in order to trace the gradual curve of their evolution, but to isolate the different scenes where they engaged in different roles. Finally, genealogy must define even those instances where they are absent, the moment when they remained unrealized. (1977b: 139–40)

A genealogical method thus displaces the 'object' of study away from an analysis of things (such as a particular new media technology) and toward a patient tracking of the apparatus within which things take on particular meanings and play particular roles. Thomas Tierney's *The Value of Convenience* (1993) provides an example of this method. This is not a book about particular technologies; it is about the context within which particular kinds of technologies are produced and consumed. It is about the emergence of a notion of a need for convenience (a need to overcome the bodily limits of time and space) and the way that particular kinds of technologies are sought after, used to fill that need, and contribute to it. Tierney does not depict a linear, evolutionary path to explain technologies in any reductionist or essentialist way. Instead, this is a book about conceptions of privacy, the economic work of consumption practices, the settlement of the American West, changing modes of transportation, the devolution of Protestantism, the development of the idea of labour as a calling, the 'death' of God, the fear of death, etc. But yes, it tells us an enormous amount about why, for example, we simply have to have cell phones or faster computers, and why we have to teach our children certain kinds of literacy skills as though those were *the* skills that ensured their survival into the twenty-first century. There are things in Tierney's account, but interestingly they are not the point.

Genealogy is hard and frustrating work: never complete, and always open to revision and contestation. It is not about objects that stand still for scrutiny. It is, like cultural studies generally, a conversation, a mapping project, in which the exploration of possibilities for rearticulation is the point.

IDENTITY, POLITICS AND POWER

The issue of identity has always been central to cultural studies work, from its disputes with Marxism's class determination of identity to the importance of the idea of identity to culture (and culture to identity). Marxist positions suggest that the individual is determined by class position, but it has been cultural studies' argument that such relations are non-necessary, that is, they are articulated. The connections between class, culture and identity are the result of struggle; they are not natural but can be rearticulated with work. This, again, is not a relativism. Individuals and groups construct their identity within and against unequal structures of power. As Marx once wrote in the *Eighteenth Brumaire of Louis Bonaparte*: 'Men make history, but they do not make it just as they please' (quoted in Feuer, 1959: 321).

Cultural studies also argues against essentialist positions on identity. Rather identity is the product of social relations and experience. Following Williams (1958/1989) in 'Culture is ordinary', identity is formed in the relations among traditions and heritage and a whole way of life, that is, in the living of that heritage and the negotiation of the challenges that experience raises to that heritage. From this we can identify two problematics of cultural studies work. The first is the question of identity: how is identity created? The second is the question of reproduction: how are social relations – and especially social inequalities – reproduced? What is the role of cultural practices in the reproduction of social relations?

Technology interjects its role in these problematics in three ways. (1) How is technology a constituent of identity? (2) How is technology a cultural practice (part of the broader theme of this essay)? (3) How do technologies reproduce social inequalities; in other words, how are technologies political and how do they factor in issues of power? Though we can identify work on gender, race and class bias of technologies, little work has been done within a cultural studies approach to technology and identity apart from the more Foucauldian notion of technologies of the self (though this work is important) (Foucault, 1988; Probyn, 1993).

When talking about the politics of technology, at least two things can be meant. One is the more generally circulated argument around the political *uses* of technology. Often these debates rely on a neutral view of technology, that a technology's politics are determined by its uses. However, Winner (1986) has persuasively argued that we should consider that the technological arrangement itself, prior to its specific use, not only reflects but imposes a social order. His examples are by now well known: the bridges on Long Island were designed by Robert Moses to be too low for buses to be let through, thus cutting off access to the island to the poor and minorities who were more likely to use public transport; campuses were designed (and redesigned) to make it difficult for students to organize after the student protests of the 1960s; expensive industrial machines were installed in Cyrus McCormick's reaper manufacturing plant in order to replace workers and force out the unions (the machines were taken out after the unions were defeated); the mechanical tomato harvester developed by University of California researchers favoured large farms over smaller farms and had a significant impact on farm labour in California and also on the types of tomatoes grown; buildings are designed that discriminate against the disabled; and so on. Technologies, Winner argues, are ways of building order into the world, and design decisions can affect populations for generations. In addition, he argues that some technologies are by their very nature political in that they tend to favour centralization or decentralization, egalitarian organization or non-egalitarian organization, or tend to be repressive or liberating. His example here is nuclear energy, which by the truly dangerous nature of its material demands security, elite control and centralization. Winner acknowledges that the level of determination varies on a case-by-case basis. Some technologies require certain social conditions and arrangements to work (for example, a ship at sea in a storm cannot be run via participatory democracy), and some technologies are more or less compatible with different social systems (for example, solar energy is potentially more democratic than nuclear energy). Iain Boal argues that all technologies have a 'value slope', that is, 'they conduce to certain forms of life and of consciousness, and against others' (1995: 12).

In writing about communication technology, Harold Innis (1951) introduced the idea of the 'bias' of a technology: bias towards centralization or decentralization of power. For example, Eric Michaels (1989), in an essay on the Aboriginal Australian use of television, notes that broadcast television is by its nature highly centralized (one-to-many broadcasting) and prone to elite control. It is also prone to homogenization and the imposition of values from one location on a broader area. 'The bias of mass broadcasting is concentration and unification; the bias of Aboriginal culture is diversity and autonomy' (1989: 13). Aboriginal culture, which values time, locality and kinship, runs at odds with the standard broadcast model that threatens Aboriginal culture.

When we discuss bias we mean tendency; these are not absolute determinations. It is very possible to have democratic television (for example, public access, low-power local stations, as the Aboriginal Warlpiri developed) or radio (for example, pirate radio stations which often cover only a few blocks), but such uses are discouraged (and are often illegal).

When we talk about the bias of electronic communication technologies we should, of course, immediately think of new media such as the Internet and World Wide Web. These technologies are biased towards decentralization, though as Andrew Shapiro (1999) points out, democracy on the Internet – despite its bias – is not a sure thing. We hear from proponents of these technologies many of the same promises for democracy, equality and world peace which were proposed for the telegraph, telephone, radio, television, etc. Indeed, cyberspace itself has its roots in the nineteenth century. Jon Stratton (1997) argues that its origins can be found in attempts to speed up the circulation of commodities. Drawing on Carey's (1983/1989) germinal work on the cultural and social impact of the telegraph (especially on markets), Stratton places the origins of cyberspace within capital's processes of deterritorialization and reterritorialization. Electronic communication technologies are fundamentally associated with industrial and finance capital's attempts at control (cf. Beniger, 1986). Public space, that of either the imagined community, the public sphere or the mass audience, is structured to ensure general passivity on the part of the public (the public is represented by others and therefore becomes a spectator to democracy as well as television). Stratton writes that the fragmentation of the mass media through new technologies of cable, satellite and video, plus the global flows of people, technologies, ideas and so on (described by Appadurai, 1996), plus the increase in interactivity, result in a 'qualitative shift' which works to undermine the old mass media (and political) model of centre and periphery. This shift is being countered, and the democratizing potentials constrained, by the rearticulation of the Internet into the information superhighway in which the Internet becomes another mass media delivery vehicle (with portals such as Yahoo! replacing networks). In addition, Stratton writes that frequent appeals to the trope of community in relation to the Internet hark back to a narrowly ideological and culturally specific view of what constitutes a community. The lesson to draw from Stratton is not that these technologies are inherently one way or the other, but that the Internet is the site of political struggle among (at least) information technology's value slope, capitalistic institutions, and the cultures through which it is developed and disseminated.

The political biases of technology have frequently been addressed through the lens of gender. The work on gender and technology is fairly extensive, including work on new media (for example, Balsamo, 1996; Cherny and Weise, 1996; Haraway, 1985; Miller, 1995; Rakow, 1988; Stone, 1995). That technologies have a gender bias is evident from Ruth Schwartz Cowan's work, *More Work for Mother* (1983). This classic study found that so-called labour-saving household appliances actually increased the amount of time that women were required to do housework and reinforced the social roles of women in the household and men out at work. Laura Miller's (1995) influential essay, 'Women and children first: gender and the settling of the electronic frontier', illustrates that technological gender bias has political uses. She argues, for example, that the depiction of cyberspace as a realm biased against, if not overtly hostile to, women serves the political function of increasing broad regulation and control over the Internet.

Beyond questions of gender bias and its political uses, cultural theorists have raised questions of gender identity as well. MUDs, MOOs, IRCs and other text-only media do not display a user's gender, thus allowing for passing or gender-bending online, about which great numbers of both academic and popular essays have been written (for example, see Spender, 1996; essays in Cherny and Weise, 1996; and essays in Jones, 1998). The ability to elide or bend gender has the potential to be politically empowering by evening the playing field. For example, the usual gendered tactics of dominating a conversation can be lessened, and ideas can be more readily evaluated on the basis of their merit rather than on the appearance of the speaker. Online gender-bending throws into question the nature of gendered identity and enters into debates over essentialist versus anti-essentialist frameworks for understanding gender. Basically, the questions become: *can* a person mask their gender effectively online? Can a man successfully masquerade as a woman, and vice versa? Or will gender always out? Dale Spender (1996), for example, drawing on decades of research on language, believes that a user's gender will eventually make itself known. This argument tends to fall back into an essentialist position, but not necessarily. It could be seen as recognizing the point that one cannot so easily shrug off years of socialization. For Miller, these arguments lead her to question how 'adequate those [gender] roles are to the task of describing real human beings' anyway (1995: 57).

Similar issues arise in relation to race and online environments. Though works on the racial bias of new media are not as extensive as those on gender, these issues are being addressed under the phrase 'the digital divide', a phrase taken up by the Clinton administration in the spring of 2000 to discuss the wiring of inner-city schools, native American reservations, and other 'have nots'. Issues of racial identity online have been addressed only recently (Kolko et al., 2000; Nakamura, 1995). The starting point of these discussions is the alleged erasure of race in cyberspace (accompanying erasures of gender, class, ability and so forth). An MCI advertisement entitled 'Anthem' (discussed in Kolko et al., 2000: 15, 134, 180) sets out the utopian scenario: 'There is no race. There is no gender. There is no age. There are no infirmities. There are only minds. Utopia? No, Internet.' Though we may wish for a utopian society where, to echo Martin Luther King, Jr, we judge people at last by the content of their character and not the colour of their skin, a world where prejudice does not play any role in our reactions, interactions and exchanges, the reality is something different. When the trope of 'no race in cyberspace' is not only established in discourses about the Internet but also built into the architecture of the system itself (there often isn't even a command in virtual environments to indicate race), the elision of race only serves to support the culturally unspoken dominant: whiteness. When one's race is not mentioned, the default assumption is that one is white. Tara McPherson (2000) labels this a version of 'covert' racism where race is simply ignored, but segregation nonetheless ensues. This reinforces the point that cyberspace exists not in a vacuum but in a particular social and cultural conjuncture. As Kolko et al. write:

> You may be able to go online and not have anyone know your race or gender – you may even be able to take cyberspace's potential for anonymity a step further and masquerade as a race or gender that doesn't reflect the real, offline you – but neither the invisibility nor the mutability of online identity makes it possible for you to escape your 'real world' identity completely. Consequently, race matters in cyberspace precisely because all of us who spend time online are already shaped by the ways in which race matters offline, and we can't help but bring our own knowledge, experiences, and values with us when we log on. (2000: 4–5)

One limitation to approaching technology in terms of the bias or value slope of a technology is that, careful as they are, these accounts are still haunted by the spectre of technological determinism, in that social problems tend to be seen as technology's 'fault'. What is needed is an approach which exorcizes this ghost. For this, cultural theorists of technology turn to Latour. Latour's work explains how effectivity occurs in the parallel processes of delegation and prescription. Delegation occurs when a task is assigned to someone or something. Latour offers the example of a door. For a door to work effectively, that is, to keep undesired things out and to permit desired passage through, it needs to be consistently shut after it has been opened (or else why have a door?). The task of shutting a door can be delegated to humans: either hire someone to stand there and open or close the door, or train people to shut the door behind them. Neither option is completely foolproof (one may hire a fool or have foolish people pass through one's door, leaving it standing open). One could delegate the task to a machine: an automatic door closer (or groom) which does the task quietly, efficiently and consistently. In this way we delegate tasks to non-humans (stoplights instead of traffic cops, etc.). Technologies are our lieutenants; they stand in place of (in lieu of) our own actions.

However, we cannot consider the process of delegation alone. To do so would be to fall into a naive social constructionism, as though technologies merely embodied social desire. This is naive because once technologies are in place, they prescribe behaviours back on us. The door closer will work in a certain way (too fast, too slow, too stiff) and we must adjust to the properties of this particular machine (just as we know which copying machine to use and which jams more frequently, or which elevator is faster). One must be able to push on a door with a certain amount of force and then hold it from slamming back. Further, technology prescribes behaviour back on *all* those who encounter it, not just those who initially delegate the task (for example, designers, city planners, engineers and so on). Those who delegate and those who are impinged upon can be (and often are) quite disparate groups of people (Star, 1991). In this way Latour argues that technologies are moral. They impose 'correct' behaviour and foster 'good' habits. 'In spite of the constant weeping of moralists, no human is as relentlessly moral as a machine, especially if it is (she is, he is, they are) as "user friendly" as my computer' (Latour, 1988: 301). In addition, the technology may be discriminatory, making it difficult for small children, the elderly, or the physically challenged to move through the door.

The impact of information and communication technologies (ICTs) on the nature of the labour market as a whole is enormous (Aronowitz and DiFazio, 1994; Dyer-Witheford, 1999). No one feels the prescription of new ICTs more than those who are forced to work with them every day and whose livelihoods depend on them. Data-intensive work can lead easily to physical effects, such as carpal tunnel syndrome, eye strain and so on. New ICTs provide myriad opportunities for surveillance, such as the counting of key strokes. The emphasis on speed is a means of extending management control over the workforce. As Andrew Ross has put it, 'let's not forget that for every one of us who wants our PCs and software to go faster, there are fifty others who want them to go slower' (1998: 20).

But the process of prescription should not be taken on its own either. This leads straight to technological determinism, because it only considers how technology affects society. Rather, Latour emphasizes that we must grasp both processes. The politics of technology goes in both directions: what is delegated and what is prescribed. This is not to suggest that the equation of power balances out. Rather it is to suggest that the same care that has been taken when examining the ideology, politics and power of cultural *texts* needs to be extended to cover technologies as well. But to do so we need to develop a subtle enough language which can adequately describe these processes.

SOCIAL SPACE AND CORPOREALITY

A more recent concern of cultural studies has been that of social space (Grossberg, 1993). When this problematic is applied to technology it means more than saying that technology is social or that the impact on society is socially determined. The social in this approach is inherently and predominantly spatial; the spatial dimensions of technology are social. Historically, arguments along these lines have fallen into a technological determinism. For example, Elizabeth Eisenstein (1979) argued that the printing press changed the shape of European society. But a spatial approach is not necessarily deterministic. Cultural studies approaches technology as a contingent social agent in everyday life.

One approach to this view of technology has been through the nexus of time–space orality and literacy. Drawing on the work of Carey (for example, 1989), Eric Havelock (for example, 1982), Innis (for example, 1951), Marshall McLuhan (for example, 1964) and Walter Ong (for example, 1982), this general approach examines how the characteristics of communication technologies shape the experience of the users and even mould society itself. For example, Innis has argued that communication technologies have a 'bias' not only towards either centralization or decentralization, but more crucially towards space or time. Carving on stone is a more permanent medium and serves to maintain a society longitudinally through time. Papyrus, though less permanent, is lighter and much more portable, and therefore has a bias toward space. The choice of medium, then, has consequences for the political shape of that society. Time-bias media focus on maintenance of community in time: space-bias media focus on control over space, and therefore promote empire. Yet, space-bias media also hold forth the possibility of the democratization of society. More recent scholars, such as Berland (1992) and Carey (1989), have argued that modern electronic technologies are space-biased and therefore fundamentally concerned with control. From the promises of global connectivity of the telephone companies to the 'World' in the World Wide Web, new media discourses emphasize space over time. This control of space is perhaps both exacerbated and foiled by the electronic language of new media that, as Mark Poster (1990) points out, can no longer be located in space and time. With its 'time–space coordinates undermined', electronic language 'is everywhere and nowhere, always and never. It is truly material/immaterial' (1990: 85).

The characteristics of a medium may have psychodynamic effects as well as social effects. For example, Ong (1982) discusses the physical characteristics of sound and sound reception and how these characteristics shape an orally based culture. Likewise, with limited extrasomatic resources, an oral society is dependent on mnemonics, repetition and ritualized questioning to create and pass along knowledge. The invention of writing and the printing press allowed for deeper, more unique thoughts and ideas to be expressed, though these also emphasized linear thought (McLuhan and Fiore, 1967). Recent cultural studies work has followed through on this thread, noting that social space is not just a visual space, but an aural and oral space as well (Sterne, 1999a).

Social space, in this cultural tradition following Innis, is both a sphere of politics (community versus control) and a phenomenological space (living in an oral, or print, or electronic world). Contemporary cultural studies has begun to address issues of technology and social space in terms of agency and corporeality in an attempt to avoid the latent determinism of the earlier tradition. Following Deleuze and Guattari, Wise (1997: 57–82) has identified two types of agency, corporeal and incorporeal; the first is termed technology, and the second language. Key to understanding these concepts is the relation between them. Technology and language are articulated and presuppose each other. Human social space is the result of this articulation and is always made up of both language and technology and a particular, contingent relation between them. For example, discourse on new media, especially in the United States, tends to emphasize linguistic agency over the technological. This is the foundation of democracy, the ability of the free citizen to instigate change through non-corporeal means: the vote. Indeed, trends in new media emphasize the democratic possibilities of the new technologies. With the power of language, we control machines that might otherwise overpower us. It is often made to seem as if new technologies are themselves incorporeal: the mere bits of cyberspace (for example, Mitchell, 1995; Negroponte, 1995). However, to the extent that social space is increasingly permeated by technologies (especially those of communication), we need to realize that these technologies also operate in the realm of corporeal agency, despite the seeming ephemerality of the digital.

Approaching technology in terms of corporeality involves considering the materiality of the technology itself, the system itself, the linkages and connections of the physical infrastructure. For example, if we consider virtual communities, non-corporeal agency involves the exchange of ideas, and the notion that these communities involve only the meeting of minds. But virtual communities are more than this; they are organizations and networks which have materiality. A virtual community is a network of corporeal procedures. We need to consider the effects of that corporeality on the communication within, the actions of, and the shaping of the network itself. Harrison and Stephen (1999) write that technologies, especially virtual communities, are *embodiments* of ideas. It is not just the

ideas themselves which shape virtual communities, but how they are embodied in technologies which impinge back on the user and system, making corporeal demands of their own.

One of the key sites of corporeal agency, and a focus of postmodern treatments of technology, is the body itself. As Slack wrote a decade ago, one question cultural studies of technology might/must ask is how technology articulates in/with postmodern culture:

> What is the pleasure of using a PC? Are the techniques pleasurable (for example, the techniques of writing or bookkeeping)? Is the pleasure tactile, aural, visual? How does the body challenge/engage/disengage/control/master/command the PC? What is the nature of that interaction? Does the body become superfluous? (1989: 343)

Affect, we are arguing, is a corporeal aspect of new technologies. Affect is often cited in discourses around new technologies (especially work on virtual communities, for example, Rheingold, 1993) as a certain intensity of purpose behind new technologies. As Rheingold has written, virtual communities need to be more than simply virtual if they are to be more than merely ersatz communities (1993: 23). This means not just adding in physical meetings (picnics, get-togethers) to the composition of a virtual community, but considering affective responses to online activity as an embodied response.

Anne Balsamo's *Technologies of the Gendered Body* (1996) is an exemplar of a contemporary cultural studies approach to issues of the body. Though the book does spend time analysing the representations of body and how bodies signify (aspects of incorporeal agency), it also examines non-signifying aspects of the technocorporeal articulation. Balsamo asks, 'how is the body, as a "thing of nature", transformed into a "sign of culture"?' (1996: 3). The body is both a product of social forces and a process of identity creation. Her book concerns a range of new technologies from body-building to cosmetic surgery, pregnancy to the plugged-in cyberpunk.

Information technology is accelerating us, Mark Dery argues, to an escape velocity. In *Escape Velocity* (1996) he describes subcultures caught up in the techno-transcendentalist movement that pushes the body to its limits, ultimately attempting to abandon the body in the pure space of cyberspace. Examples are numerous in writings on cyberculture where material structures (especially the body) are abandoned and subjects are left to play in 'the city of bits' (Mitchell, 1995; Moravec, 1988; Negroponte, 1995).

Decorporealization has its dangers, however, and it definitely has its blind spots. It ignores many of the effects of power and politics outlined in the previous section. For example, Brook and Boal have written:

The wish to leave body, time, and place behind in search of electronic emulation of community does not accidentally intensify at a time when the space and time of everyday life have become so uncertain, unpleasant, and dangerous for so many – even if it is the people best insulated from risk who show the greatest fear … But the flight into cyberspace is motivated by some of the same fears and longings as the flight to the suburbs: it is another 'white flight'. (1995: ix)

The focus on corporeal agency has other implications. Much of the work on technology, and not only in cultural studies, focuses on representation and the processes of signification: what technology means; how it is represented; what it represents; and so on. These questions are meant to get at the cultural aspects of technology. But a version of culture that deals only with representation and signification is a limited version of culture indeed. Culture is much more than simply signifying practices. Lefebvre (1991) argues, using a model of social space, that there are non-signifying aspects to space and culture.

In *The Production of Space*, Lefebvre presents three ways of thinking about space: spatial practice, representations of space, and representational space (or, more briefly, space as it is perceived, conceived and lived.) Spatial practice 'embraces production and reproduction, and the particular locations and spatial sets characteristic of each social formation. Spatial practice ensures continuity and some degree of cohesion. In terms of social space, this cohesion implies a guaranteed level of competence and a specific level of performance' (1991: 33). Representations of space are abstract, conceptualized space, a plane of concepts (for example, modern social space is constructed around concepts of efficiency, newness/revolution, technicism and so on). Representational space (or, better and more literally, spaces of representation) is 'space as directly lived through its associated images and symbols, and hence the space of inhabitants and "users"' (1991: 39).

In terms of technology, then, we need to consider technology as a spatial practice, and technology's effect on spatial practices. We could consider the rearrangement of the work environment, even the dissolution of the work environment, into a virtual office. We could also consider the way devices such as personal stereos, pagers and ankle trackers articulate space. Changes in representations of space are particularly evident with new media, with new data-mapping technologies on the one hand and new geographies of cyberspace on the other (Elmer, 1999). Finally, spaces of representation present new media technologies as a new frontier (cf. Rheingold, 1993), a neighbourhood mall, a salon or café, and so on (see also discussions in Jones, 1997; 1998).

One of the more recent and, we believe, important articulations or discourses around the idea of social space comes from recent work in urban geography which brings together the spatial disciplines of geography (for example Massey, 1994) and the more corporeal/material approach of urban studies that considers urban space. An exemplary work in this area is the book *Telecommunications and the City* (1996) by Stephen Graham and Simon Marvin, which looks at the idea of city space from a variety of perspectives, taking into account the telecommunications infrastructure (that is, in this case, the telephone system), the changing nature of the urban landscape, urban planning and economics, and Latourian notions of agency, plus how such things contribute to the construction of space, the construction of private and public through new media technologies (see also Droege, 1997).

Approaches to technology and social space overlap approaches to technology, politics and power in the issue of surveillance. Graham and Marvin write, 'telecommunications, combined with computers and media technologies, are at the most fundamental level control and surveillance technologies' (1996: 213). Such control technologies 'have allowed large and complex industrial societies to develop' (1996: 214). While acknowledging the dystopian spin that is often placed on issues of surveillance and control, Graham and Marvin rightly point out that surveillance is not one singular thing but occurs in a variety of contexts, and the diverse means of surveillance are not yet centralized.

Deriving from the work of Foucault (especially 1977a), the principle of surveillance has been used to talk about a number of issues, for example how architecture (including streets, schools, prisons and so on) can be structured under the idea of the gaze. This is a visual model of surveillance. Demanding consideration is work that puts surveillance in a historical context, as Foucault did, but which is sometimes forgotten, with the effect that surveillance is used as a more universalist principle. Some of the last writing of Deleuze (1995) was on new forms of surveillance and control, outlining a regime of control that differs from the more institutionally based disciplinary society of the nineteenth century which Foucault delineated. It is also important to note non-visual aspects of surveillance, especially the management of personal data and new organizations of, and linkages between, previously disparate databases of information to create superprofiles. The idea of consumer surveillance, for example, has most prominently been discussed from a political economy standpoint (Gandy, 1993). But there have been other attempts to discuss both the social effects of surveillance (Lyon, 1994; Poster, 1990) and the cultural effects of surveillance (Bogard, 1996; Staples, 1997).

In terms of Lefebvre's notion of social space, we can see surveillance as articulating a spatial practice (the construction of public/private space), the changing nature of representations of space (the wavering line between public and private) and representations of space. Surveillance is a practice that creates a physical setup (arena, panopticon, practice) that assesses representations of space (video monitors of a public square) according to ideologically loaded presumptions of criminality and identity. Surveillance has moved from watching and then catching after the fact to predicting, then watching, then catching *before* the fact. This applies to visually oriented notions of surveillance as well as to other forms of data surveillance, including marketing (Gandy, 1993). What is established is a crucial linkage between surveillance and simulation (Bogard, 1996; see also Graham's, 1998, response to Bogard).

The question to ask here is, what would a more explicitly cultural studies approach to surveillance look like? Following from our analysis in this chapter, we suggest examining the articulations and stratifications of discourse and technology, what technologies are purported to represent or mean and how they fit in within broader discourses of society. But we also need to think through how surveillance becomes part of culture, how notions of privacy and control articulate to *practices* of surveillance and the materiality of shaped social space.

In addition to issues of corporeality and surveillance, contemporary cultural studies work on social space also addresses dimensions of everyday life and globalization. The work on everyday life derives jointly from cultural studies' ethnographic tradition (for example, Hall and Jefferson, 1976; Willis, 1977) and more recently from the works of Lefebvre (1991) and Michel de Certeau (1984). Yet except for studies of technology in the home (particularly television, see Silverstone and Hirsch, 1992; for IT in the home, see Noble, 1999), technology remains absent. Perhaps a cultural studies of everyday life inflected via Latour's notion of technology as social actors might prove generative in future studies. If nothing else, the Y2K computer issue (the so-called millennium bug) pointed out the ubiquity of technology in the daily lives of industrialized countries, as people worried about their toasters not working after New Year's Day 2000.

Most work on globalization focuses on political economy, though more studies are addressing the cultural aspects of the process (Bird et al., 1993; Tomlinson, 1999; Waters, 1995). Few, however, have addressed globalization in terms of both culture and technology. Stratton (1997) is an exception, though his essay ends up being more political economy than culturally oriented. Most discourses of globalization fail to engage issues of culture and technology despite the fact that most accounts of globalization do not fail to note that globalization is dependent upon new media, communication and information technologies

connecting financial markets, factories and so on. The area demands further work.

CONCLUSION

To undertake cultural studies of new media technology is neither exact nor scientific. It is always provisional. This makes the question of responsibility decidedly tricky. If we do not conceive of easily identifiable agents who (or that) exercise agency in any easily identifiable way, how can we hold anyone or anything responsible in any way? The risk of disbursing agency (especially across both humans and non-humans) is that it becomes possible to so disburse responsibility as to create either paralysis or the total denial of any responsibility. However, even though the self and subjectivity are in a sense abstractions, different conceptions of self and subjectivity enable and constrain possibilities with potentially enormous consequences in relations of power. As Grossberg explains:

> Obviously, within cultural studies, the question of agency involves more than a simple question of whether or how people control their own actions through some act of will. In classical modern terms, the issue of agency raises questions of the freedom of the will, or of how people can be responsible for their determined actions. But in broader cultural terms, questions of agency involve the possibilities of action as interventions into the processes by which reality is continually being transformed and power enacted. (1996: 99)

There is a pressing need in cultural studies to link these theoretical insights to practical decision-making, with, for example, decisions regarding the new media technology. There is a need to consider dimensions of agency, politics and space in the design, implementation and use of new media.

It is always easy to make these suggestions or critiques of other people in other places (designers, policy-makers, the public), but if we are to hold on to the conjunctural aspect of cultural studies we must also address our own practices which most often are within the context of higher education. As it has aptly been put by Calvin O. Schrag, 'A university that does not respond to the technological developments of the current age can be said to be both nonresponsive and irresponsible in the moral sense' (quoted in McMillan and Hyde, 2000). We are commanded to respond responsibly in ways that cultural studies has not yet determined how to do. Sterne, like other cultural theorists, is characteristic in claiming that 'Cultural studies' usefulness to Internet research should … be measured by the degree to which it can get its readers to think beyond the technophilic–technophobic dichotomy, beyond the rhetoric of millennial [now in 2001, we can substitute revolutionary] transformation' (1999b: 282). Okay, but what then do we do? And what sense do we make of the construction 'we do'?

A cultural studies that 'lets us off the hook' is antithetical to the impulses that still articulate to the motivations of most of its practitioners. Yet, quite honestly, because cultural studies (in North America at least) is so firmly ensconced within technophilic and corporatizing universities, it is difficult to find a theoretical and practical path that does not result in the identification of the cultural theorist as technophilic, technophobic or opportunistic. There clearly is work yet to be undertaken.

NOTES

1 For example, see Carol Cohn (1989) for an analysis of the gendered ways that defence intellectuals characterize their technologies and practices; see Richard Coyne (1995) on the philosophical assumptions of information technology designers.

2 We are aware of, and uncomfortable with, the inadequacy of our occasional use of the construction 'the relationship between culture and technology', which gives the impression that culture is one thing and technology is another. While cultural studies works actively against such a construction, the phrase is so widely used in the discourse on technology that it is difficult to find a replacement that does not sound ridiculously theoreticist. Likewise we are aware of, and uncomfortable with, the almost inevitable slides in the meaning of technology as, on the one hand, an object of analysis in the abstract sense (as in technology and culture) and, on the other hand, an object of analysis in the more concrete sense of a particular technology or technological apparatus.

REFERENCES

Acland, Charles (1998) 'IMAX technology and the tourist gaze', *Cultural Studies*, 12 (3): 429–45.

America's Technology Literacy Challenge (1996) 15 February, www.whitehouse.gov/WH/New/edtech/2pager.html.

Appadurai, Arjun (1996) *Modernity at Large: Cultural Dimensions of Globalization*. Minneapolis: University of Minnesota Press.

Aronowitz, Stanley and DiFazio, William (1994) *The Jobless Future: Sci-Tech and the Dogmas of Work*. Minneapolis: University of Minnesota Press.

Balsamo, Anne (1996) *Technologies of the Gendered Body: Reading Cyborg Women*. Durham, NC: Duke University Press.

Beniger, James (1986) *The Control Revolution: Technological and Economic Origins of the Information Society*. Cambridge, MA: Harvard University Press.

Berland, Jody (1992) 'Angels dancing: cultural technologies and the production of space', in Lawrence Grossberg, Cary Nelson and Paula A. Treichler (eds), *Cultural Studies*. New York: Routledge. pp. 38–51.

Berland, Jody (2000) 'Cultural technologies and the "evolution" of technological cultures', in Andrew Herman and Thomas Swiss (eds), *The World Wide Web and Contemporary Cultural Theory: Magic, Metaphor, Power*. New York: Routledge.

Bird, Jon, Curtis, Barry, Putnam, Tim, Robertson, George and Tickner, Lisa (eds) (1993) *Mapping the Futures: Local Cultures, Global Change*. New York: Routledge.

Boal, Iain (1995) 'A flow of monsters: Luddism and virtual technologies', in James Brook and Iain Boal (eds), *Resisting the Virtual Life: the Culture and Politics of Information*. San Francisco: City Lights. pp. 3–15.

Bogard, William (1996) *The Simulation of Surveillance: Hypercontrol in Telematic Societies*. Cambridge: Cambridge University Press.

Borgmann, Albert (1984) *Technology and the Character of Contemporary Life: a Philosophical Inquiry*. Chicago: University of Chicago Press.

Brook, James and Boal, Iain A. (eds) (1995) *Resisting the Virtual Life: the Culture and Politics of Information*. San Francisco: City Lights.

Callon, Michel and Latour, Bruno (1981) 'Unscrewing the big leviathan: how actors macro-structure reality and how sociologists help them do so', in K. Knorr-Cetina and A. Cicourel (eds), *Advances in Social Theory and Methodology: toward an Integration of Micro- and Macro-Sociologies*. Boston: Routledge & Kegan Paul. pp. 277–303.

Carey, James W. (1975/1989) 'A cultural approach to communication', reprinted in *Communication as Culture: Essays on Media and Society*. Boston: Unwin Hyman. pp. 13–36.

Carey, James W. (1983/1989) 'Technology and ideology: the case of the telegraph', reprinted in *Communication as Culture: Essays on Media and Society*. Boston: Unwin Hyman. pp. 201–30.

Carey, James W. (1989) 'Space, time, and communications: a tribute to Harold Innis', in *Communication as Culture: Essays on Media and Society*. Boston: Unwin Hyman. pp. 142–72.

Cherny, Lynn and Weise, Elizabeth Reba (1996) *Wired_Women: Gender and New Realities in Cyberspace*. Seattle: Seal.

Cohn, Carol (1989) 'Sex and death in the rational world of defense intellectuals', in Micheline R. Malson, Jean F. O'Barr, Sarah Westphal-Wihl and Mary Wyler (eds), *Feminist Theory in Practice and Process*. Chicago: University of Chicago Press. pp. 107–38.

Cowan, Ruth Schwartz (1983) *More Work for Mother: the Ironies of Household Technology from the Open Hearth to the Microwave*. New York: Basic.

Coyne, Richard (1995) *Designing Information Technology in the Postmodern Age: from Method to Metaphor*. Cambridge, MA: MIT Press.

de Certeau, Michel (1984) *The Practice of Everyday Life*, trans. Steven Rendall. Berkeley, CA: University of California Press.

Deleuze, Gilles (1995) *Negotiations: 1972–1990*, trans. Martin Joughin. New York: Columbia University Press.

Deleuze, Gilles and Guattari, Félix (1987) *A Thousand Plateaus: Capitalism and Schizophrenia*, trans. Brian Massumi. Minneapolis: University of Minnesota Press.

Dery, Mark (1996) *Escape Velocity: Cyberculture and the End of the Century*. New York: Grove.

Droege, Peter (ed.) (1997) *Intelligent Environments: Spatial Aspects of the Information Revolution*. New York: Elsevier.

Dyer-Witheford, Nick (1999) *Cyber-Marx: Cycles and Circuits of Struggle in High-Technology Capitalism*. Urbana, IL: University of Illinois Press.

Eisenstein, Elizabeth (1979) *The Printing Press as an Agent of Change: Communications and Cultural Transformations in Early Modern Europe*. New York: Cambridge University Press.

Elmer, Greg (1999) 'Diagrams, maps and markets: the technological matrix of geographical information systems', *Space and Culture*, 3: 41–60.

Feenberg, Andrew (1991) *Critical Theory of Technology*. New York: Oxford University Press.

Feuer, Lewis S. (ed.) (1959) *Marx and Engels: Basic Writings on Politics and Philosophy*. Garden City, NY: Anchor.

Foucault, Michel (1977a) *Discipline and Punish: the Birth of the Prison*, trans. Alan Sheridan. Harmondsworth: Penguin.

Foucault, Michel (1977b) 'Nietzsche, genealogy, history', in *Language, Counter-Memory, Practice: Selected Essays and Interviews*, trans. D.F. Bouchard and S. Simon. Ithaca, NY: Cornell University Press.

Foucault, Michel (1988) *Technologies of the Self: a Seminar with Michel Foucault*, edited by Luther H. Martin, Huck Gutman and Patrick H. Hutton. Amherst, MA: University of Massachusetts Press.

Gandy, Oscar H., Jr (1993) *The Panoptic Sort: a Political Economy of Personal Information*. Boulder, CO: Westview.

Graham, Stephen (1998) 'Spaces of surveillant simulation: new technologies, digital representations, and material geographies', *Environment and Planning D: Society and Space*, 16: 483–504.

Graham, Stephen and Marvin, Simon (1996) *Telecommunications and the City: Electronic Spaces, Urban Places*. New York: Routledge.

Grossberg, Lawrence (1993) 'Cultural studies and/in new worlds', *Critical Studies in Mass Communication*, 10 (1): 1–22.

Grossberg, Lawrence (1996) 'Identity and cultural studies: is that all there is?', in Stuart Hall and Paul DuGay (eds), *Questions of Cultural Identity*. London: Sage. pp. 87–107.

Hall, Stuart (1983) 'The problem of ideology – Marxism without guarantees', in Betty Matthews (ed.), *Marx*

100 Years on. London: Lawrence & Wishart. pp. 57–84.

Hall, Stuart (1986) 'On postmodernism and articulation: an interview with Stuart Hall', by Lawrence Grossberg, *Journal of Communication Inquiry*, 10 (2): 45–60.

Hall, Stuart (1990) 'The emergence of cultural studies and the crisis of the humanities', *October*, 53: 11–23.

Hall, Stuart and Jefferson, Tony (eds) (1976) *Resistance though Rituals: Youth Subcultures in Post-War Britain*. London: Unwin Hyman.

Haraway, Donna (1985) 'A cyborg manifesto: science, technology and socialist-feminism in the 1980s', *Socialist Review*, 80: 65–108.

Haraway, Donna (1992) 'The promises of monsters: a regenerative politics for inappropriate/d others', in Lawrence Grossberg, Cary Nelson and Paula A. Treichler (eds), *Cultural Studies*. New York: Routledge. pp. 295–337.

Harrison, Teresa M. and Stephen, Timothy (1999) 'Researching and creating community networks', in Steve Jones (ed.), *Doing Internet Research: Critical Issues and Methods for Examining the Net*. Thousand Oaks, CA: Sage.

Havelock, Eric (1982) *The Literate Revolution in Greece and its Cultural Consequences*. Princeton, NJ: Princeton University Press.

Innis, Harold Adams (1951) *The Bias of Communication*. Toronto: University of Toronto Press.

Jones, Steve (1997) *Virtual Culture: Identity and Communication in Cybersociety*. Thousand Oaks, CA: Sage.

Jones, Steve (ed.) (1998) *Cybersociety 2.0: Revisiting Computer-Mediated Communication and Community*. Thousand Oaks, CA: Sage.

Kolko, Beth E., Nakamura, Lisa and Rodman, Gilbert B. (2000) *Race in Cyberspace*. New York: Routledge.

Latour, Bruno (alias Jim Johnson) (1988) 'Mixing humans and nonhumans together: the sociology of a door-closer', *Social Problems*, 35 (3): 298–310.

Latour, Bruno (1993) *We Have Never Been Modern*, trans. C. Porter. Cambridge, MA: Harvard University Press.

Latour, Bruno (1996) *Aramis, or the Love of Technology*, trans. C. Porter. Cambridge, MA: Harvard University Press.

Lefebvre, Henri (1991) *The Production of Space*, trans. D. Nicholson-Smith. Cambridge, MA: Blackwell.

Lerner, Daniel (1958) *The Passing of Traditional Society: Modernizing the Middle East*. Glencoe, IL: Free Press.

Lyon, David (1994) *The Electronic Eye: the Rise of Surveillance Society*. Minneapolis: University of Minnesota Press.

Massey, Doreen (1994) *Space, Place, and Gender*. Minneapolis: University of Minnesota Press.

McLuhan, Marshall (1964) *Understanding Media: the Extensions of Man*. New York: Signet.

McLuhan, Marshall and Fiore, Quentin (1967) *The Medium is the Message: an Inventory of Effects*. New York: Bantam.

McMillan, Jill J. and Hyde, Michael J. (2000) 'Technological innovation and change: a case study in the formation of organizational conscience', *Quarterly Journal of Speech*, 86 (1): 19–47.

McPherson, Tara (2000) 'I'll take my stand in Dixie-net: white guys, the South, and cyberspace', in Beth E. Kolko, Lisa Nakamura and Gilbert B. Rodman (eds), *Race in Cyberspace*. New York: Routledge. pp. 117–31.

Michaels, Eric (1989) *For a Cultural Future: Francis Jupurrurla Makes TV at Yuendumu*. Sydney: Art and Text.

Miller, Laura (1995) 'Women and children first: gender and the settling of the electronic frontier', in James Brook and Iain A. Boal (eds), *Resisting the Virtual Life: the Culture and Politics of Information*. San Francisco: City Lights. pp. 49–57.

Mitchell, William J. (1995) *City of Bits: Space, Place and the Infobahn*. Cambridge, MA: MIT Press.

Moravec, Hans (1988) *Mind Children: the Future of Robot and Human Intelligence*. Cambridge, MA: Harvard University Press.

Nakamura, Lisa (1995) 'Race in/for cyberspace: identity tourism and racial passing on the internet', *Works and Days*, 13 (1–2): 181–93.

Negroponte, Nicholas (1995) *Being Digital*. New York: Knopf.

Nelson, Cary, Treichler, Paula A. and Grossberg, Lawrence (1992) 'Cultural studies: an introduction', in Lawrence Grossberg, Cary Nelson and Paula A. Treichler (eds), *Cultural Studies*. New York and London: Routledge. pp. 1–16.

Nisbet, Robert (1980) *History of the Idea of Progress*. New York: Basic.

Noble, David (1982) 'Introduction', in M. Cooley, *Architect or Bee? The Human/Technology Relationship*. Boston: South End.

Noble, Greg (1999) 'Domesticating technology: learning to live with your computer', *Australian Journal of Communication*, 26 (2): 59–76.

Ong, Walter (1982) *Orality and Literacy: the Technologizing of the Word*. London and New York: Routledge.

Plato (1952) *Phaedrus*, trans. R. Hackforth. Cambridge: Cambridge University Press.

Poster, Mark (1990) *The Mode of Information: Poststructuralism and Social Control*. Chicago: University of Chicago Press.

Probyn, Elspeth (1993) *Sexing the Self: Gendered Positions in Cultural Studies*. London and New York: Routledge.

Rakow, Lana F. (1988) 'Gendered technology, gendered practice', *Critical Studies in Mass Communication*, 5 (1): 57–70.

Rheingold, Howard (1993) *The Virtual Community: Homesteading on the Electronic Frontier*. New York: HarperCollins.

Ross, Andrew (1998) *Real Love: in Pursuit of Cultural Justice*. New York: New York University Press.

Shapiro, Andrew L. (1999) 'The net that binds: using cyberspace to create real communities', *The Nation*, 21 June: 11–15.

Silverstone, Roger and Hirsch, Eric (eds) (1992) *Consuming Technologies: Media and Information in Domestic Spaces*. New York: Routledge.

Slack, Jennifer Daryl (1984) *Communication Technologies and Society: Conceptions of Causality and the Politics of Technological Intervention*. Norwood, NJ: Ablex.

Slack, Jennifer Daryl (1989) 'Contextualizing technology', in Brenda Dervin, Lawrence Grossberg, Barbara J. O'Keefe and Ellen Wartella (eds), *Rethinking Communication*. Vol. 2: *Paradigm Exemplars*. Newbury Park, CA: Sage.

Smith, Merritt Roe and Marx, Leo (eds) (1994) *Does Technology Drive History? The Dilemma of Technological Determinism*. Cambridge, MA: MIT Press.

Spender, Dale (1996) *Nattering on the Net: Women, Power and Cyberspace*. Melbourne: Spinifex.

Staples, William G. (1997) *The Culture of Surveillance: Discipline and Social Control in the United States*. New York: St Martin's Press.

Star, Susan Leigh (1991) 'Power, technology and the phenomenology of conventions: on being allergic to onions', in J. Law (ed.), *A Sociology of Monsters? Power, Technology, and the Modern World*. Oxford: Blackwell. pp. 27–57.

Sterne, Jonathan (1999a) 'The Audible Past: Modernity, Technology and the Cultural History of Sound'. Unpublished doctoral dissertation, University of Illinois, Urbana-Champaign.

Sterne, Jonathan (1999b) 'Thinking the Internet: cultural studies versus the millennium', in Steve Jones (ed.), *Doing Internet Research: Critical Issues and Methods for Examining the Net*. Thousand Oaks, CA: Sage. pp. 257–87.

Stone, Allucquère Rosanne (1995) *The War of Desire and Technology at the Close of the Mechanical Age*. Cambridge, MA: MIT Press.

Stratton, Jon (1997) 'Cyberspace and the globalization of culture', in D. Porter (ed.), *Internet Culture*. New York: Routledge. pp. 253–75.

Tenner, Edward (1996) *Why Things Bite Back: Technology and the Revenge of Unintended Consequences*. New York: Vintage.

Tierney, Thomas F. (1993) *The Value of Convenience: a Genealogy of Technical Culture*. Albany, NY: State University of New York Press.

Tomlinson, John (1999) *Globalization and Culture*. Chicago: University of Chicago Press.

Waters, Malcolm (1995) *Globalization*. New York: Routledge.

Williams, Raymond (1958/1989) 'Culture is ordinary', reprinted in Robin Gable (ed.), *Resources of Hope: Culture, Democracy, Socialism*. New York: Verso. pp. 3–18.

Williams, Raymond (1975) *Television: Technology and Cultural Form*. New York: Schocken.

Willis, Paul E. (1977) *Learning to Labor: How Working Class Kids Get Working Class Jobs*. Farnborough: Saxon House.

Winner, Langdon (1977) *Autonomous Technology: Technics-out-of-Control as a Theme in Political Thought*. Cambridge, MA: MIT Press.

Winner, Langdon (1986) 'Technologies as forms of life', in *The Whale and the Reactor: a Search for Limits in an Age of High Technology*. Chicago: University of Chicago Press. pp. 3–18.

Wise, J. Macgregor (1997) *Exploring Technology and Social Space*. Thousand Oaks, CA: Sage.

29

Discursive Displacement and the Seminal Ambiguity of Space and Place

MICHAEL R. CURRY

The last few years have seen a dramatic increase in interest in a series of questions like the following: is the world somehow getting smaller? Is the world becoming more homogeneous? Are unique places disappearing? And more technically: how does one think about borders in an era in which information can move so freely? What can we expect to happen to the nation-state? Will national identity come to be redefined, or cease to exist? And finally: what has been the role of technology in the various changes that have occurred?

If these questions have been in the air for many years, there can be little doubt that they have become more frequent since the development of the Internet, and that they are now posed with a greater sense of urgency. Might not there be a true declaration of independence for cyberspace? How can we be sure of the dangers lurking there? What kind of world will we live in when e-commerce sites replace the corner store? And, who am I, really, when so many of my interactions with others are technologically mediated? These are all questions, in the end, about places and about interactions in space. For that reason, in order to formulate reasonable answers to these questions one needs an understanding of the concepts of space and of place.

It may at first glance seem that the matter is simple – the world is a world of places within a larger space. Yet if this simple answer works passably when one is trying to decide how to organize a closet, it runs out of explanatory power well before one attempts to mobilize it in answering the questions raised above. When one turns to concrete questions, about the source of territorial disputes, and the possibility of their resolution; or about the

extent of and connections among markets; or about the appropriate ways to draw a map of the world, one immediately finds sets of beliefs so contradictory and yet so firmly held that this simple 'location in space' understanding of places emerges as quite useless. Something better is needed.

Here I would suggest that if one wishes to deal with these more complex questions one needs to see that in every era there has been a close interconnection between the technologies available for communication and representation and the ways in which people have conceptualized space and place. Indeed, in a particular era one cannot really make sense of those technologies without having an understanding of the ways in which space and place are conceptualized, just as one cannot understand those conceptualizations without having an understanding of the available technologies.

What follows will be in four sections. First, I shall lay out three traditional ways of thinking about space – as place, region and space. I shall show that each of those conceptions can only be understood against the background of the technologies available for the storage of knowledge, and for the representation and communication of that knowledge.

Second, I shall turn to the modern era. I shall show the ways in which elements of each of these earlier conceptions of space and place were in the seventeenth and eighteenth centuries fashioned into versions of what is now taken to be common sense. This new common sense set the stage for the development of a wide range of modern intellectual enterprises – from physics to political theory – but has at the same time functioned to obscure and devalue certain still important elements of the traditional experience and understanding of space and place.

Third, I shall point to one very important reason why this process of obscuring has itself remained obscure: certain features of the concepts of space and place allow and even encourage a kind of discursive displacement. Through this process a group of authors, or even a single author, find themselves using terms like space and place in multiple ways; and it can easily appear that a rich and inclusive concept is being invoked, where the richness is in fact only apparent.

And finally, I shall turn to some current concerns about the relationship between technology and society. I shall show that these concerns are typically couched in terms of one or more of the spatial conceptions that I have described. It turns out that this contemporary discourse is very much subject to discursive displacement, and we often find that people who appear to be presenting opposing viewpoints are simply talking about different matters. Yet here, as is so often the case, this displacement has a positive side; it is part of the sometimes conscious process by which language changes, and through which the relationships among disparate phenomena come to be understood.

TOPOGRAPHY, CHOROGRAPHY AND GEOGRAPHY

The concern with the nature of places on the face of the earth and with the spatial organization of those places – and of human activity more generally – has long been the vocation of geographers. But in fact, the term 'geography' today encompasses what were previously thought of as three rather separate forms of inquiry. And although the three had in a sense been stitched together by the time of Ptolemy (born about AD 100), the fact that they once were separate is indicative of their pointing to three very different ways of conceptualizing space and place, three different ways of gaining knowledge of them, and three different ways of representing that knowledge.

The three forms of inquiry are topography, chorography and geography. Putting the matter most simply, topography was traditionally the art of writing about places; chorography the art of writing about regions; and geography the art of writing about the earth as a whole. This would seem to suggest that each form of inquiry or activity appeals to a different scale, from small to large, that of the *topos*, the *choros* or the *geos*. But to put the matter in this way is to risk giving away the game, by seeing these inquiries from a decidedly contemporary perspective. For to see the differences as in a sense merely of degree is to miss the true distinctiveness of each concept.

On Topography

The concepts of *choros* and *topos* raise immediate problems, just because over a period of several hundred years the two terms traded meanings. As E.V. Walter has noted (1988: 120–1), *choros*, the older of the two, originally appealed to subjective meanings, to the emotional cast associated with a place, as well as to the more 'objective' features of location; in contrast, the newer *topos*, which appeared for the first time in Aeschylus in about 470 BC, was typically used to refer to this more objective sense of the term 'place'. But by the third century *topos* had begun to be used in the expression for holy places, while *choros* had begun to be used to refer to what we would now think of as regions, to administrative districts, and in the process had begun to lose its emotional tinge.

By the time of Ptolemy it appears to have come to be accepted that there existed a topographic tradition and a chorographic one, where the topographic appeared to require skill in drawing, and the chorographic dealt 'for the most part, with the nature rather than the size of the lands' and with 'qualitative matters' (Ptolemy, 1948: 163). Yet this way of rendering the distinction, laid out in the second century AD, misses something essential.

We can begin to get at that something if we note rather a different way of characterizing the topographical tradition. As Fred Lukermann suggested, in classical geography

> 'Topography' was defined as the order of discrete units one to another. 'Topographical location' was referent solely to the contiguity of places. (1961: 194)

Now, this notion of a topographical description as referring to the 'order of discrete units' may seem perplexing, unless we note an essential feature of topographical accounts. While it would seem odd to devote oneself to constructing a simple list of the order of places (one would have the equivalent of a railroad timetable, without the time), if that list is in the form of a chronology or narrative of what was seen as one went from place to place the project seems far more comprehensible.

Indeed, we find just such topographical descriptions in Homer, where

> We reached the Aeolian island next, the home of Aeolus,
> Hippotas' son, beloved by the gods who never die –
> a great floating island it was, and round it all
> huge ramparts rise of indestructible bronze
> and sheer rock cliffs shoot up from sea to sky.
> (Homer, 1996: x, 1–5)

Here the reference to Homer points to a central feature of the topographic account of a place – that such accounts developed within cultures that did not use writing. They were originally oral accounts, ordered in narrative and therefore temporal terms. They were accounts of places in terms of the things that a traveller saw, or would see, along a certain route.

Well known among topographical descriptions have been what are termed *periploi*, accounts of 'sailing around' some place. In one of the most famous of these, the *periplus* of Hanno (apparently from the first half of the fifth century), we read that

> We quickly sailed out and passed a land full of fire and incense … Frightened, we quickly sailed away from there also, and sailing on for four days we saw by night the land full of fire…
>
> [W]e came to a gulf called Horn of the South.
>
> In the gulf there was an island, like the first, and containing a lake. On the lake was another island full of wild men. By far the majority of them were women with hairy bodies. The interpreters called them Gorillas … We captured three women … who bit and scratched those who led them and did not want to follow. (Ramin, 1976: 120)

Today, of course, any account of the *periploi* includes a map, but as Dilke (1985) points out, it is unlikely that the originals contained maps: they were simply narrative in form.

If we follow the suggestion of authors like Havelock (1986) and Ong (1982), this narrative form should come as no surprise, since in a pre-literate society the use of narrative is an excellent mnemonic strategy. But if narrative is one such strategy, when we turn to other early authors we find a second. In Hesiod, for example, we find the admonitions

> When the Pleiades born of Atlas rise before the sun, begin the reaping; the ploughing, when they set. (1988: 48)
>
> When the carryhouse [snail] climbs up the plants to escape the Pleiades, then digging of vines is past, it is time to sharpen sickles and wake up the labourers. Avoid shady seats and sleeping till sunrise at harvest time. (1988: 54)

Here the narrative is interspersed with symbols, which as in Homer fill the function of ordering the world and rendering it memorable.

Indeed, these early topographic accounts describe a world awash in symbols. It is a world in which the snail can be a sign of the season for work, but where the snail is connected with the heavens, with the place of the Pleiades, and where both are connected to what one sees on the earth – the labour of farmers. Here, in an important sense the snail, the heavens and the farmer are all elements of a larger web of symbols, where the elements that make up the world are all and always actively significatory. This is not a world captured in maps, or lists, or other written descriptions; neither is it a

world in which one is actively searching for some simplifying world picture. Rather, it is a world in which people inhabit places, where the relationships between those places and others are represented just in terms of narrative and symbol.

If within the topographic tradition places are represented through narrative accounts, we can see the places themselves as constituted through the practices that are the subject matter of those accounts. In constructing those accounts their authors describe what is acceptable and what is not; they define places as constituted of sets of possibilities and constraints. Places are defined in terms of those things that are in place and those that are out of place, those that belong and those that do not.

It may seem as though today we are far indeed from the primary oral cultures within which topography emerged. But this way of experiencing and representing places is in fact alive and well. We see the experience in the everyday activity of judging that something – dirt, pollution, or a suspected criminal – is 'out of place' (Wood and Beck, 1994). We use topographic representations in the everyday practices of giving directions (Denis et al., 1999). And this appeal to landmarks and narratives was right at the centre of the landscape studies of influential planners like Kevin Lynch (Appleyard et al., 1964; Lynch, 1960). In each case we create or appeal to accounts that are in an important sense the work of insiders, of people whose knowledge of places both emerges from and is represented in terms of the experiences that they have had while passing through a place. Primordially oral and narrative in form, topographic accounts have made the transition to later technologies of representation and communication, though not, as we shall see, without certain difficulties.

On Chorography

If the topographic tradition provided a model for representing everyday places, and a model that was equally at ease in oral cultures and in later textual cultures, it in fact existed alongside a second mode of thinking about and representing places and space, the chorographic. Here chorography seems to occupy a kind of middle ground, between the generalities of geography and the particularities of topography.

It may seem odd that I say that the chorographic existed alongside the topographic, given my earlier comment about the difficulty in the absence of writing of maintaining a store of knowledge about locations and their interrelations. But there has always existed a text adequate for the storage of certain kinds of geographical information, and that text is in the heavens. In fact, chorography began its formal existence as a branch of astrology, and it was not until the middle of the seventeenth century that a clean break between the two was effected in the later work of the first truly modern geographer, Bernhardus Varenius (1650; Lukermann, 1963; see, more generally, Barton, 1994).

This appeal to the heavens was not, of course, new. Recall Hesiod's dictum that 'When the Pleiades born of Atlas rise before the sun, begin the reaping; the ploughing, when they set' (1988: 48). Here the obvious interpretation is that the heavens are being used as a kind of calendar. But at the same time, they are providing a means for distinguishing among the places on the surface of the earth itself. There is a sense here in which one can map from the stars onto the earth, and use the pattern of the stars as a means for discerning a pattern on the earth.

The origin of this view is controversial. It appears to have reached a level of some sophistication in Babylon by 1000 BC, and to have been put in written form there in about 700 BC. In Greece the matter is more complex. Writing in about 7 BC, Strabo (1917) claimed that by the fourth century Eudoxus had developed a systematic ordering of the earth, based on the heavens. But others believe the first systematic understanding was developed by Eratosthenes, who died in 196 BC (Honigmann, 1929), or by Hipparchus, who died about 120 BC (Bunbury, 1959).

In any event, by the beginning of the Christian era a system had been developed that divided the surface of the earth into a number (five, six or seven) of horizontal bands, or *klimata*, each with a different character. From the heavens one could tell whether one was in the torrid, temperate or frigid zone, and within each existed a different way of life (actually, it was at first believed that nothing could live within the torrid zone, between what later came to be termed the Tropics of Cancer and Capricorn). Each zone was, that is, a separate and identifiable region.

Writing in the second century, Ptolemy described the aim of chorography in this way; it is

the description of the individual parts, as if one were to draw merely an ear or an eye ... chorography deals, for the most part, with the nature rather than with the size of the lands. (1948: 163)

And in his *Tetrabiblos*, he expanded upon the idea of such regions.

Thrace, Macedonia, Illyria, Hellas, Achaia, Crete and likewise the Cyclades, and the coastal regions of Asia Minor and Cyprus ... have in addition familiarity with the south-east triangle, Taurus, Virgo, and Capricornus, and its co-rulers, Venus, Saturn, and Mercury. As a result the inhabitants of these countries are brought into conformity with these planets and both in body and soul are of a more mingled constitution. They too have qualities of leadership and are noble and independent, because of Mars; they are liberty-loving and self-governing, democratic framers of law, through Jupiter;

lovers of music and of learning, fond of contests and clean livers, through Venus. (Ptolemy, 1940: 137)

Contemporary readers typically find statements such as this unnerving; the apparently uncritical acceptance of the causal role of Mars and Venus does not sit easily with the modern temperament. But I would suggest that two points need to be kept in mind here. First, if we strip away the references to the heavens, we are left with a series of characterizations of regional cultures that may seem simplistic, but that nonetheless have an air of familiarity. They are not, in the end, that different from the characterizations that one hears today about Chinese, Finns or Californians.

Second, in the period between Hesiod and Ptolemy the nature of discourse concerning causation began to change. If in Hesiod's period the world consisted of places rich in signs, there did not exist a means for ordering the various types and functions of signs. And so, it was common to elide what we would take to be the clear distinction between the name of something, its causal powers, the material of which it was made, and the events with which it was associated. It was not, in fact, until the fourth century BC that Aristotle developed the famous typology of causes, or explanations, within which these signs come to be seen as clearly distinguishable:

In one sense, then, (1) that out of which a thing comes to be and which persists, is called 'cause' ...

In another sense (2) the form or the archetype, i.e. the statement of the essence, and its genera, are called 'causes' ...

Again (3) the primary source of the change or coming to rest; e.g. the man who gave advice is a cause, the father is cause of the child, and generally what makes of what is made and what causes change of what is changed.

Again (4) in the sense of end or 'that for the sake of which' a thing is done, e.g. health is the cause of walking about. ('Why is he walking about?' we say. 'To be healthy', and, having said that, we think we have assigned the cause.) (1941: 194b 23–35)

By the time of Ptolemy the discourse about the relations between the heavens and regions on the earth had begun to fall into line with the terminology used by Aristotle. But even in cases where an author seems explicitly to be using the concept of cause, it is risky for the reader to assume that the concept is as clearly delineated as it was in Aristotle; a closer reading often reveals a world in which the boundary between cause and sign is not at all clearly demarcated. Indeed, we see this repeatedly in works on the relationship between people and the environment, where it is often difficult to determine whether the author is speaking of cause, or of sign (see the medical works of Hippocrates, 1950; see also Glacken, 1976).

From Chorography to Geography

There was a third way in which in the period between Hesiod and Ptolemy the discourse about places underwent a subtle but dramatic set of changes. Recall that within the topographic tradition a description of places did not involve a clear distinction between the question 'What is next to this?' and 'What did we come to next?'; distance and extension were in a certain way equivalent to time and sequence. The connection between any two places was characterized in terms of just such a relationship, and that relationship was imagined to be *the* relationship, and not merely some vernacular version of a more precise and accurate representation.

But by the fourth century BC – and here once again Aristotle was a key player – the conceptualization of space and place had undergone a substantial formalization. For Aristotle, empirical observation showed that the world tends toward stasis. Objects move until they stop. And the critical issue, and the absolutely central issue here, is why they stop: they stop because they have reached the place where they belong. They have reached their natural place. In the *Physics* this view was laid out in terms of the basic elements, air, earth, fire and water. Light things made of air and fire rise, while heavy things of water and earth fall. Each moves until it reaches its natural place, and once there stays, absent disturbing, unnatural motions. As Aristotle put it,

> All place admits of the distinction of up and down, and each of the bodies is naturally carried to its appropriate place and rests there, and this makes the place either up or down. (1941: 211a 3–5)

So in one way Aristotle's work is based on a conceptualization within which place is absolutely central, and in which an adequate account of the world needs to be couched in terms of the question of what goes where. In an important sense, Aristotle has developed a physics that is grounded within a world of places, and their relationships one to another.

At the same time though – and in the same work – he has developed a very different way of thinking about space and place. There he argues that 'Place is what contains that of which it is the place … [and] place can be left behind by the thing and is separable' (1941: 211a 1–3). Here he has laid out an alternative vision, wherein what is important will turn out to be space, and not place, and where space will come to be conceptualized as an inert container.

This, in Ptolemy, comes to be the model at play in conceptualizing the geographic. For Ptolemy, the geographic

> is concerned with quantitative rather than with qualitative matters, since it has regard in every case for the correct proportions of distances, but only in the case of the more general features does it concern itself with securing a likeness, and then only with respect to configuration … while chorography does not require the mathematical method, in geography this method plays the chief part. (1948: 163–4)

When Ptolemy turns away from the chorographical to the geographical the concern turns to the representation of the entire surface of the earth; and his *Geography* relies upon mathematics as a means for 'securing a likeness' of the earth. Here the observer becomes strictly a visual observer, and the place of that observer is defined in those same visual terms. The observer, in Ptolemy's attempt to project the round earth onto a flat surface, is always an outside observer, and the view is always a view from above.

On the face of it this mathematics-based representation looks very much like that which we see in Ptolemy's astrological work, and might be imagined in that way to resemble chorographical representations. But there is a fundamental difference between the division of the world into *klimata* and the development of a representation of the world in which a grid of lines of latitude and longitude is laid over a representation of the world. For in the former case the lines establish regions of difference, while in the latter case the lines may (though they need not) merely be markers on a surface of infinite variation.

The Rise of Space

It may seem a luxury to have discussed at such length these three traditions – the topographical, the chorographical and the geographical – and the more so just because the first two seem almost to have vanished. The term 'topographical' is used today to refer to maps, and in a sense rather different from the one in which it was used two millennia ago; and few but geographers have even heard of the chorographic. In a sense, they have been swallowed up by the geographical.

But in fact, in the topographical and the geographical we can see rather clearly the issues that arise in contemporary conceptualizations of space and place. And in the effacement (and reconstruction) of the topographic and the chorographic we see at play certain social and technological forces that remain important today.

So, for example, in Ptolemy's geography the earth is imagined to be a globe that has some objective existence, such that in principle any person should be able to determine the location of every object and event on that surface. Here space is imagined to be absolute and pre-existing, while location is always a matter to be defined in terms of that absolute space. The location of any particular object is a contingent matter; things do not belong in one place or another, and space is not hierarchical.

Here the arrangement of objects on the face of the earth can be characterized through the use of a mathematical system – in this case a grid – that is independent of the features on the earth. Rather, that grid is imposed upon the surface by a viewer. Further, the viewer is imagined to be capable of imaginatively stepping outside the earth, and viewing it as if from above. And it is possible to take advantage of that vantage point to create representations of the earth's surface.

This conception of space is in fact very much like the one propounded in Newton's *Principia* (1686).

> Absolute space, in its own nature, without relation to anything external, remains always similar and immovable…
>
> Place is a part of space which a body takes up, and is according to the space, either absolute or relative… Positions properly have no quantity, nor are they so much the places themselves, as the properties of places. (1934: 6–7)

And as it happens, it was Newton who produced the illustrations for Varenius' *Geographia generalis* (1650), seen by many as the founding work of modern geography.

So it seems fair to say that by the eighteenth century this conception – of what is conventionally termed 'absolute' space – had entered into the mainstream. It has since become the accepted way of imagining and conceptualizing space and the objects characterized as being within it, and has come to be seen as foundational for discourse about the workings of the world, at an everyday as well as a conceptual level.

In doing so it has effected the rejection of Aristotle's view of the universe as a universe of places. Newton can thus be seen as having been a significant player in the formulation of a view of the world in which places are of no importance, and, in fact, one finds little theoretical discussion of the concept of place for the next 300 years.

Still, and in spite of its widespread acceptance, the view of space as absolute has faced opposition on several fronts, and the positions taken by those opponents have remained important alternatives. One of those alternatives was articulated in a series of letters between Leibniz and Newton's proxy, Samuel Clarke. There Leibniz noted how people come to believe in space, through the concept of motion.

> They consider that many things exist at once and they observe in them a certain order of co-existence, according to which the relation of one thing to another is more or less simple … When it happens that one of those co-existent things changes its relation to a multitude of

others, which do not change their relation among themselves … we then say, it is come into the place of the former; and this change we call a motion in that body. (Alexander, 1956: fifth paper, § 47)

The way in which we understand motion leads to the belief in the existence of absolute space.

> And supposing, or feigning, that among those co-existents, there is a sufficient number of them, which have undergone no change; then we may say, that those which have such a relation to those fixed existents, as others had to them before, have now the *same place* which those others had. And that which comprehends all those places, is called *space*. (Fifth paper, § 47)

Yet, Leibniz argues, to go along with Newton and move from this perception to the conclusion there is something called 'absolute space' is to move from the realm of science to that of metaphysics. Rather, we need to understand that space is nothing more than 'something merely relative, as time is; … I hold it to be an order of coexistences, as time is an order of successions' (third paper, § 4). Space, that is, is purely relational; it consists just in those relations, and nothing else.

Nonetheless, if Leibniz is rejecting much about Newton's view, he is also accepting much. Both, in the end, are abstract and formal. So both involve the rejection of views of space or place that give a central role to the actions of everyday life. In Newton this is a rejection of the relational in favour of the absolute; in Leibniz there is an embracing of the relational, and a rejection of the absolute. But in both the relations of contiguity that before were temporalized, and described in narrative terms, are reinscribed in the quantitative terms appropriate to modernism.

If one avenue for appealing to a more concrete conception of space was cut off in the Leibnizian, relational model, another was soon thereafter cut off in the epistemological move now associated with Kant. In his 'pre-critical' inaugural essay Kant (1929) had formulated an argument in support of the view that space must be seen as absolute. We see that this must be the case, he argued, when we attend to the simplest of matters. Consider, he said, a pair of gloves. If we look at the relationships among the parts, at their angles and lengths, we find that a right-handed glove and a left-handed glove are in fact identical. So if space is indeed just a matter of relations, the two are identical. But just try putting a left-handed glove on your right hand!

But in a sense, this argument is merely of scholarly interest, just because Kant is now remembered for having laid out in his later *Critique of Pure Reason* (1965), a very different and more influential view. The argument there is subject to a range of interpretations, but it was – and is – widely seen as meaning that space is not something that is 'out there', but rather is believed to exist as a result of a sort of mental structuring of the world. Indeed, in the nineteenth and twentieth centuries this view, that people mentally structure their worlds, has come itself to be seen as a kind of common sense, and this view has provided an intellectual foundation for a wide range of forms of inquiry, from cultural anthropology to social psychology, and means of understanding differences, of race, gender and ethnicity.

So we might well see Kant's inaugural dissertation as far more important than it is usually seen to be, just because it is the swan song for the view that in theorizing about space one needs to begin from the embodied individual. After the *Critique of Pure Reason* it became possible to see space as a purely human invention, something that could not possibly have causal efficacy, but must instead be caused, that must be a part not of the substructure but of the mental superstructure of the world.

The Reinvention of the Region

Thus, by the end of the eighteenth century the concept of 'place' had lost its status as a theoretical concept, and so too had 'space'. This is not, of course, to suggest that the topographic and the geographic had simply disappeared. In a rather less theorized form the topographic tradition retained a place. Indeed, in its barest form, and with the clearest connection to its oral roots, it has persisted, as in the practices of giving directions, describing travels, and the like. Is there, after all, all that much difference between Pausanias' second-century AD 'Further along the road you come to the SPLIT as they call it; on this road Oedipus murdered his father' (1987: 49) and this by Lévi-Strauss?

> At Dakar we had said goodbye to the Old World and, without sighting the Cape Verde Islands, had reached the fateful latitude seven degrees north, where in 1498, during his third voyage, Columbus, who was heading in the right direction for the discovery of Brazil, changed course towards the north-west, and so managed, by some miracle, to arrive two weeks later at Trinidad and the coast of Venezuela. (1977: 67)

In both there is an elision of the boundary between space and time, as movement is narrativized. In both there is an appeal to the symbolic, as a means of ordering the landscape. In both the relationships among places are characterized in relational, rather than absolute, terms. And in both is the author at the centre of the account.

And of course, the geographic tradition remained important, the more so because of the practical – and especially economic – aspects of the age of exploration (Sobel and Andrewes, 1998; Andrewes et al., 1996). But in a fundamental sense, the nineteenth century was a time of the invention of the region, and the revivification of the chorographic

(Kimble, 1951). In fact, it was only then that it became possible to see the landscape in the way that Paul Vidal de la Blache described it, in his *The Personality of France* (1928):

> A geographical individuality does not result simply from geological and climatic conditions. It is not something delivered complete from the hand of Nature ... [A] country is a storehouse of dormant energies, laid up in germ by Nature but depending for employment upon man. It is man who reveals a country's individuality by moulding it to his own use. He establishes a connection between unrelated features, substituting for the random effects of local circumstances a systematic co-operation of forces. Only then does a country acquire a specific character differentiating it from others, till at length it becomes, as it were, a medal struck in the likeness of a people. (1928: 14)

Here we see echoes of the places developed within a strictly oral tradition, and in one sense, of course, this is no surprise, since the peasants of whom Vidal spoke were largely illiterate. And here at the regional scale we see in operation one of the fundamental means of the construction of places, the carrying out of habitual activities, or practices. As Vidal put it,

> Man is an animal of habits even more than initiative ... he digs in willingly, if he is not shaken by some shock from outside, into the way of life in which he was born. (1911: 304)

But if the inhabitants of these regions were largely illiterate, it is important to see that the modern region, whether the agricultural region of France or the nation-state, was in important ways a product of new technologies, and especially the printing press. Nowhere is this laid out more clearly than in Benedict Anderson's celebrated *Imagined Communities* (1991). In that work Anderson describes various elements of the rise of the nation-state, but pays particular attention to the development of printing. Printed language, he suggests, at once creates a unified field for communication and exchange; gives a fixity to language; and creates a language of singular authority (Anderson, 1991: 44–5).

Anderson in fact suggests that there is something inauthentic about the nation-state, that it is only 'imagined', and is to be contrasted with those places that are 'real'. It is to be contrasted, perhaps, with the region that Kimble described, wherein people have 'real' relationships one with another, or, more generally, to be contrasted with the places of the lost – or, in fact obscured – topographic tradition.

It seems to me, though, that with respect to the possibility of creating the modern region a number of other technologies need to be considered, as do other features of print technology. One of those, certainly, is the use of print for the dissemination of documents containing data about individuals. In the sixteenth century, not long after the development of the printing press, there were moves – in France, for example – to create registers of populations. But such systems were gradually replaced, beginning in the seventeenth century, when the development of what was termed 'political arithmetic' seemed to provide tools useful to the nation-state, both for social control and for political and ideological purposes (Hacking, 1975; Rusnock, 1995).

By the beginning of the nineteenth century political arithmetic had been replaced, at least in France and Great Britain, by statistics. Ted Porter suggests,

Implicitly, at least, statistics tended to equalize subjects. It makes no sense to count people if their common personhood is not seen as somehow more significant than their differences. (1986: 25)

As Horkheimer and Adorno had earlier put the matter, this view derived from a deeper belief, that

Bourgeois society is ruled by equivalence. It makes the dissimilar comparable by reducing it to abstract quantities. To the Enlightenment, that which does not reduce to numbers, and ultimately to the one, becomes illusion; modern positivism writes it off as literature. (1972: 7)

And so, as statistics replaced political arithmetic, there developed what Ian Hacking has termed 'an avalanche of numbers' (1982). Noting that between 1820 and 1840 'the rate of increase in the printing of numbers appears to be exponential whereas the rate of increase in the printing of words was linear' (1982: 282), he argues that in France

After 1820 ministry [annual] reports were still supposed to have limited circulation, but the sheer fact of multiple printings put them in the public domain. They were ready to be reproduced or condensed in the mass circulation police gazettes and the like … Disease, madness, and the state of the threatening underworld, *les misérables*, created a morbid and fearful fascination for numbers upon which the bureaucracies fed. (1982: 286–7)

Growing bureaucracies, then, created the categories by which people were categorized, managed the enumeration and statistical analysis, and maintained themselves even in the absence of evidence that their products were of any real utility.

If Anderson's 'imagined communities' can be thought of as new, so too can the regions defined through these technologies. For here we have a region – or place – that is not defined in terms of people's everyday interactions and in terms of sets of narratives told about those interactions, as in the case of places developed among people who communicate only orally. But neither is this a region grounded simply in the written word. It is not just

defined in terms of lists of characteristics, or chronicles of events, each connected with its author and the circumstances in which it was written. The particularity of the lists of individuals, maintained in a church or government office, has been replaced by the census, where individuals are of interest only in so far as they can be treated as members of a particular class. Indeed, here the individual exists only as a set of characteristics, attached to a neutral self.

So here the modern nation-state is a region that – in part I hasten to emphasize – is created through the production and circulation of works whose explicit aim is to characterize that place in a thoroughgoing way (Giddens, 1981; 1991). Its inhabitants take on an existence as members of broad and fluid sets of categories, some of which may have no apparent meaning to them. They are, in an important sense, virtual individuals. But they are virtual individuals who exist in a place that is very real, a place that in part obtains its reality through the process of creation of that virtuality.

Discursive Displacement

Apart from the development of print media and of statistics, there was of course a range of factors at work in the creation of regions such as the reified nation-state of which Anderson speaks. Technological developments such as the railroad (Borchert, 1967), the telegraph (Thompson, 1947), the photograph (Trachtenberg, 1989) and standardized time (Bartky, 1989) worked alongside political and economic changes to promote the view that we live in a world that can properly be thought of as a world of regions.

As in the earlier cases of place and space, this development did not go untheorized; the late nineteenth and early twentieth centuries saw a spate of works, many focusing on geopolitics, that attempted to make sense of this world of regions (Mackinder, 1904; 1919; Ratzel, 1899; see also Innis, 1950; and more recently Godlewska and Smith, 1994; and Livingstone, 1992).

But here, as in the earlier cases of place and space, there came to be at work a process that I term 'discursive displacement'. (Note that I use the term here in a somewhat different way than do authors such as Gayatri Spivak.) Indeed, this process of displacement has consistently characterized the discourse about space, place and the region. And the place where this displacement is most evident is not in the topographic or the geographic, but in the chorographic. There, one is inclined to say, there has been a dual process of displacement, toward the topographic and toward the geographic, that has persistently undercut attempts to treat it as real.

In his *The Betweenness of Place* (1991), Nicholas Entrikin argued that the discourse concerning places suffers from a tension, wherein it is at once pulled toward the particular and toward the universal. I would suggest, though, that here this tension can better be seen not in the arena of places, but in that of the region, in the chorographic. And it seems to me the key to understanding that tension is technology.

Recall that in its earliest form chorography appealed to the heavens as a means of characterizing regions; a region could be defined in terms of its position under a certain constellation. Now, unambiguous as this may seem, this means of definition right at the outset established a tension, and enabled the process of displacement. That is because if the heavens provided a means of definition, they were able to do so only to the extent that people were able to keep track of *them*. And that was typically done by the symbolic reidentification of patterns in the heavens with objects on earth – the ram, etc. – and by the construction of narratives about the characteristics of those symbolized patterns. So while the stars functioned as a kind of *ur* text, they at once invited the viewer to think about their referent – the places on the earth – in terms derivative of the oral.

At the same time, descriptions of regions very often take those regions to have just the sorts of characteristics, of symbolic and narrative interconnection, that we typically associate with places. Nations, for example, typically have founding myths, and the date of the founding of a nation-state is the most celebrated of holidays. Indeed, narratives underlie almost all holidays, and those narratives are one important means by which nations establish and maintain their identities (Zerubavel, 2000).

So too are narratives of inclusion and exclusion strongly associated with the definition and maintenance of borders. One maintains a border through joint narratives of its legitimacy and of the means by which it is maintained. In the United States, for example, the stories of barbed wire, surveillance cameras and sensors, and armed INS agents are surely as effective at maintaining the border as those agents and objects themselves.

So on the one hand, there is a kind of displacement in the case of the chorographic that involves accounts of regions taking on the characteristics of the most traditional, oral topographical accounts. The accounts take on a narrative form; they appeal more to various sorts of symbols; their authors personalize the accounts; and they define the region in relational terms.

But on the other hand, there is another form of displacement, as the discourse of the regional is pulled into the geographical. In the most obvious way this happens as it comes to be accepted that any region can be given borders and plotted on a map, given geographical coordinates. If this seems an obvious thing, reflection will show that it has only been very recently that this view of the region has come to be accepted. For example, if we look at the means that were used by Europeans during the sixteenth and seventeenth centuries to establish sovereignty over non-European lands, we find the following:

> Cutting trees and boughs, and digging or making, if there be an opportunity, some small building, which should be in a part where there is some marked hill or a large tree, and you shall say how many leagues it is from the sea, a little more or less, and in which part, and what signs it has, and you shall make a gallows there, and have somebody bring a complaint before you, and as our captain and judge you shall pronounce upon and determine it, so that, in all, you shall take said possession. (Keller et al., 1938: 40)

Nowhere is there mention of the establishment of a border; rather, what is described is much more in keeping with traditional topographical methods of place-making and description.

But if, as Bernard Heise has shown, through the seventeenth and into the eighteenth centuries there was little sense of the world as being divisible into regions that had natural boundaries, there was an emerging sense of something else:

> baroque writers saw [geographies] as historical-political entities constituted through the various negotiations pursued by Europe's ruling Houses and governments. John Speed's *The Theater of the Empire of Great Britain* (1611), for instance, constructed his geography quite literally as a political body. (1998: 157)

So in contrast to earlier works, Speed's intention was instead to

> Take a view as well of the outward Body and Lineaments of the now flourishing British Monarchy ... which shall be the content of our first or *Chorographical Tome*. (quoted in Heise, 1998: 157)

The chorographic, in this way, begins to become a subset of the geographic, as it comes to be seen as possible to place the 'outward Body and Lineaments' on a map.

Still, it is not really until the nineteenth century that the map attains a sort of primacy. For until the institutionalization of the methods of land surveying used in, for example, Jefferson's official US land survey system, where a grid was laid out on the surface of the earth, the typical way of marking out boundaries was in fact topographic in form; it involved walking and following a set of directions, in what is in the US referred to as the 'metes and bounds' system. Even if a piece of property was mapped, the map had no legal reality; it was merely a representation of a route to be taken, and that route defined the border.

But with the development of systems like the one introduced by Jefferson, the map began to take on a more important role, as a true representation of what existed. Here the farm, village or county became disembodied, as each took on a new relationship with the map, one in which the region was merely an area circumscribed by a line (Thrower, 1966).

At the same time, in this way the chorographic began to give primacy to what had previously been a matter of the geographic, the view from above. And this view became increasingly important through the eighteenth and nineteenth centuries as nation-states began increasingly to develop historical atlases, that appealed to topographical narratives, but at the same time attempted ideologically to support the state through images 'from above' of the extent of the state and its location in relation to others (Black, 1997).

I have laid out several ways in which there is what I term a displacement in discourse about space and place. The topographical moves toward the chorographic; the geographic moves toward the chorographic; and the chorographic moves toward both the geographic and the topographic. Or, places come to be treated like regions; space gets turned into region; and regions come to be treated like places, and like spaces. Or, relationally defined places become absolute spaces, while spaces come to be seen in relational terms, while in the case of regions, both may happen, and at once.

How does this happen? Consider a person whose only means of communication is oral involved in a discussion about a place, with a person who is also able to write, draw maps and so on. The first person talks about events that happened at a particular place, placing them in narrative terms, always talking about one place in relationship with another. The second person listens to the first, but is prepared to construct a map of the travels described, to annotate the map with lists of items and people mentioned, and so on. Even so, this second person is able to engage in a discussion that the first finds comprehensible, to which she finds herself able to respond. In one sense the two are engaged in a discourse about places. But in another, the two are doing very different things. And we can see this even more clearly when the second person engages in a written exchange with a third. The third begins sketching out the precise location of the events and locations described by the first, and then continues by calculating distances, areas, intersections of activities, the location of the sun in relationship to the stars during the day of the discussion.

At this stage the discourse has moved beyond the point at which the first person is able to find it comprehensible. And this begins to point to the differences in the discourses being carried out by the first and second. In effect, as Wittgenstein (1968) put it, each is playing a different language game. Each is saying (or writing) things comprehensible in one context and not in another. And the discursive displacement occurs when people use what appear to be the same words and sentences, but where on reflection each person may see those words as 'going with' rather a different set of others.

In fact, the words 'space' and 'place' are seminally ambiguous, just because each has from early in its history been capable of being used within the three different discourses of the topographic, the chorographic and the geographic. And as I have suggested, this ambiguity has been supported by the development and use of a series of technologies, of writing, surveying and mapping, and then of transportation and communication, just because it seems possible to build a mutually comprehensible discourse about space and place around each technology.

This long-standing technological support for the intuition that I can at once be at a location that is a unique 'here' and at a location that can be precisely characterized in terms of a larger space has been an important element in the promotion of this discursive displacement and the support of the ambiguity of place and space. And it seems to make sense to argue that it is the lack of such technological support that has stood in the way of the development of such an ambiguity in the case of concepts that are in some ways like the concept of place, such as community, culture and society. While it is possible to imagine community at a range of scales, from the very small to the global, what is lacking in the discourse that surrounds the concept is this displacement, this tendency to move into discourses more proper to cognate concepts.

SPACE AND PLACE TODAY

By the twentieth century the notion that we live in a world of regions had become very much a part of common sense. The region had come to be taken as a natural unit, whether at the scale of the neighbourhood, the town, the state, the nation or the continent. In each case it was imagined to be possible to circumscribe an area, to draw a line around it in a way that would define an inside and an outside. Indeed, if in various cases it was possible to imagine that what constituted a region might change, or might historically have been different, there was little disagreement on one fact: The region, the chorographic, existed.

At the same time, one essential element of the common-sense discourse about regions was the belief that all of these regions could be arrayed within some absolute space. The chorographic existed against the background of the geographic; any region could be displayed on a map, on the globe. And finally, places were conceptualized as locations-within-space; the topographic had shrunk to a point.

In a very important sense, accounts by theorists and historians of those regions accepted those views. Granted, we find in their accounts a more sophisticated understanding of the ways in which regions are constructed, as of the means by which geographical space is measured and represented. But the acceptance of these two prongs of thinking about space – that the region is a natural object and that there is some absolute space – was almost universal. Indeed, we can see its universality if we look only as far as the blank reactions to claims by physicists at the turn of the twentieth century that space is relative; non-physicists seemed to find it impossible to imagine alternatives to the chorographic/geographic orthodoxy, and certainly were unable to see that such alternatives were all around them.

One part of this failure arose from the ways in which those interested in what have come to be termed the social sciences represented regions. Their research, often deriving from fieldwork, and from extensive interactions with inhabitants of the regions being studied, was typically reported in the form of representations from which those individuals had been excised. In a recapitulation of the move from the early to the later Kant, the body had disappeared. And in the process, those individual and local practices through which regions are constructed had also disappeared, leaving, for many, the region to exist merely as a mental construction, as a set of beliefs. This was, in fact, the state of thinking – both vernacular and theoretical – about space and place within the first half of the twentieth century. We see it in a wide range of areas, from the most mundane to the most notorious (as in the Nazi thinking about region and space: Herf, 1990).

The World as Picture

But in the latter part of the twentieth century there developed two opposing intellectual movements, one deconstructive and one constructive, that gave rise to a recasting of these ways of thinking. And these intellectual movements have, in turn, fed into a more popular sentiment that has proclaimed the death of the region.

The first of these, the deconstructive, is perhaps most clearly seen in the work of Heidegger, and particularly his celebrated essay on 'The age of the world picture' (1977). There Heidegger pointed to the modern era as the source of the idea that it is possible to step back from the world and see it as though it is a picture, one comprehensively visible to the individual gaze. This idea, in turn, leads to the idea that we can see the earth, in its entirety, as a laboratory, as the site of a set of controlled experiments. In the end, the idea of the world as picture leads to the idea that everything in the world can and should be an object of empirical enquiry.

Continued in several of Heidegger's other works (1993a; 1993b), this deconstructive approach might perhaps best be seen as involving the recognition of the historical contingency of the geographical, which now comes to be seen as emerging from within a social and technological complex. At the same time, it begins a repudiation of the long-standing view that vision is a natural process that needs no explication (Jay, 1993).

More or less contemporaneous with Heidegger's work was another body of work that in rather a different way took a deconstructive tack toward the concept of space. This was the later work of Wittgenstein. In his early work (1961), Wittgenstein had laid out a theory of language that was strikingly geographical. There he argued that language could be seen as 'mapping' onto the world, so that a linguistic statement had the same logical structure as some state of affairs in the world. But in his later work, and especially in his *Philosophical Investigations* (1968), he took that early work to task for having been taken in by a set of spatial terms that were in fact merely seductive metaphors. In the end, he suggested, it is all too easy to be taken in by terms like 'space' and 'map', to imagine that these terms are capable of doing conceptual 'work'. But in fact, they very often are simply images, that turn our attention away from the fact that words only have meanings within the contexts of the individuals and groups that use them, in particular situations and particular places (Curry, 2000b).

Both Heidegger and Wittgenstein, then, took a deconstructive turn. Both called into question the modernist orthodoxy that had viewed the world as an object with a given form of spatiality, the map and visual image as capable of grasping that spatiality, and language itself as a spatially structured entity capable of mediating between a spatial world and an internal, mental space.

The New Topography

This deconstructive turn was soon followed by a constructive move, by a series of works that re-inserted an emplaced body into the world. One element of this turn was the reintroduction into theoretical discourse of the concept of place.

Certainly one interesting – and telling – feature of this reintroduction has been the way in which the discourse around space and place has moved from one in which the concept of place did not exist to one in which the concept is almost ubiquitous – yet its past invisibility is itself unnoticed. It is as though the ubiquity of the word 'place' in everyday discourse has misled theorists into imagining that it must always have been there. But as we have seen, there was an almost 200-year hiatus in which the term was virtually unused. And this is more than a mere historical gripe, since the lack of historical continuity, and especially through what can only be described as one of the major eras of change in human society, has rendered it more difficult to make sense of the relationship between technological and social changes on the one hand, and changes in the nature and experience of places on the other.

In fact, it was only in the 1960s that the concept of place began to re-emerge in academic discourse. It seems fair to say that that emergence was largely mediated through popular culture. So, for example, reacting against modernist urban planning, Jane Jacobs' *The Death and Life of Great American Cities* (1961) placed into popular discourse the notion that in planning one needs both to look at the everyday activities of people who live and work in urban neighbourhoods, and to attend to neighbourhoods not simply as districts or regions, but rather as places constructed through those everyday activities. And responding to the popular image of the ugly American, Edward T. Hall's *The Silent Language* (1959) pointed to the ways in which people interact with one another when in close proximity, within places such as offices and cafés. (Neither, I should add, uses the term 'place' systematically.) This newly popularized discourse moved in part into the social sciences, where it became formalized in environmental psychology (Proshansky et al., 1970) and proxemics (Sommer, 1969).

But at the same time, there occurred a very different move, toward what might be termed a new topography. Here the aim was very different; it was to explore 'place' as an ontological category. The claim, that is, was that we need to recognize that we live in a world of places, and that those places are real. Introduced into academic work by authors like Bachelard (1969), Relph (1976) and Tuan (1974), this approach resuscitated the topographic tradition by rejecting – as work in environmental psychology and proxemics did not – the ontological priority of absolute space. Rather, it took concepts like 'absolute space' and 'region' to be human inventions, albeit inventions that have come to be embedded in the everyday architecture and institutions of the world (Tuan, 1974; 1980).

One element of this interest in the ontological status of places was a desire to rethink the role of people in the construction of places, as well as other social formations (Lefebvre, 1991). In *Discipline and Punish* (1977), for example, Foucault attacked the traditional view that power operates in a top-down manner, and pointed to ways in which individuals engage in actions that in turn place limitations on what they can do. He thereby suggested that the means by which places are constructed are far more complex than they had seemed when those places were viewed simply as homogeneous regions, produced through actions defined by the rule of law.

So by the 1970s there had emerged a body of literature that saw places as real entities, and that viewed the construction of places, like the much earlier representation of places within the topographic tradition, as a complex matter – of naming, classifying and narrating, as well as of the physical organization of the landscape and of sets of institutions that operate within it (Augé, 1995; Nora, 1984).

At the same time, there emerged a set of intellectual developments that supported the new concern with places. Here ethnicity, race, gender and age came to be seen as 'real' categories, expressive of real differences (Morley and Robins, 1995). This literature undercut the traditional way of thinking of places in chorographic terms, simply as small regions but fundamentally homogeneous regions. It suggested instead that in almost any place there will be divisions based on a wide range of characteristics. And at the same time it suggested that any place is fundamentally complex, its existence less a matter of a sharing of attitudes, beliefs and practices than of the existence of beliefs and practices that are different but often intersecting and interdependent.

Together these two developments, of an interest in places as real entities and of an interest in the diversity of identity, have led to a third feature of the new topography, and that is a concern with reflexivity. The view that a place may be seen as having a real, *sui generis* existence has seemed to suggest that there can be no single, privileged place from which to have access to all of the others; in that way it has suggested that knowledge generated in the laboratory or university ought not to be seen as simply for that reason needing to be accorded special respect (Bourdieu and Wacquant, 1992; Pickering, 1986). Similarly, the recognition of the complexity of forms and bases of identity has made clearer the extent to which the typical giving of added credence to the account of a person simply because of that person's ethnicity or gender was a mistake.

In both cases, of place and identity, many have gone further, to suggest not only that one ought to be suspicious of claims to epistemological privilege, but also that there can be no knowledge claims that are other than local. On this postmodern view, to accept the differences among places is to be led down a slippery slope, to the conclusion that every difference makes a difference (Dear, 1988; Soja, 1989; 1996).

Topography, Chorography and Geography Revisited

The re-emergence over the last 25 years of place as an important category has been a striking phenomenon, as has been the more recent development of interest in space and spatiality. Today, we might say that there are three broad approaches to the concepts of space and place. On one end of a scale we might place works that, as I have here, attempt to draw on historical distinctions, such as the distinction among the topographic, the chorographic and the geographic, or between absolute and relational models of space. In various ways those approaches focus on the distinction between the universal and the particular (Entrikin, 1991; Tuan, 1996), look to broader historical connections between those concepts and other philosophical issues (Casey, 1993; 1997), address particular issues such as resistance (Certeau, 1984), or attend to the relationship between those concepts and the technological regimes within which they have operated (Curry 1996; 1998; 2000a).

At the other extreme, many works operate within what might be termed the high-modern tradition. They accept as given the view that there is some encompassing absolute space, and that places are simply locations within space. Here the geographic becomes the substrate, and the chorographic and the topographic refer to the region and the location. Widely accepted throughout the social sciences, this view is right at the root of much of the discourse today based within maps, geographic information systems, and other geographic information technologies such as remote sensing and global positioning systems.

Between those two extremes lies the largest body of theory about and using the concepts of space and place. And in this middle ground we see the largest number of works whose goal is to understand the nature of new technologies. Here, as we shall see, the attempt to develop theoretical accounts of these technologies has both taken advantage of and fallen victim to the process of discursive displacement, as the concepts of place, region and space, the topographical, the chorographical and the geographical, have undergone a continuous process of reshuffling.

In the last half century the development of new technologies for communication and representation has seemed to demand a reconceptualization of the spatial organization of the world. One very common way of thinking about these changes has been in terms of a family of concepts, of time–space compression, of the collapse of space and time, and of the global village (Abler et al., 1971; Brunn and Leinbach, 1991; Janelle, 1969; McLuhan and Powers, 1989). Here the suggestion is that more rapid means of communication and transportation are in a sense shrinking the world. In doing so they are bringing people closer together. This is at once causing the destruction of what has long counted as the local, and the construction of new forms of the local. Motivated by two powerful metaphors, of the process of time–space compression and of the consequent global village, this image has been widely accepted.

A second, and in some ways related model, has been advanced in the wake of the development of the Internet and the World Wide Web. On this model, the Internet (or the web) constitutes a fundamentally different form of social existence, and hence geographical existence. It is a new kind of place, and ought for that reason to exist outside traditional, place-based legal structures (Barlow, 1996; Johnson and Post, 1996; Lessig, 1996). As Lessig put the matter:

> Cyberspace is a place. People live there. They experience all the sorts of things that they experience in real space, there. For some, they experience more. They experience this not as isolated individuals, playing some high tech computer game; they experience it in groups, in communities, among strangers, among people they come to know, and sometimes like. (1996: 1403)

And third, there is an increasingly large literature that attempts to integrate these developments into a comprehensive model, one that sees the world as in some important way driven by economics, and that believes it possible to integrate the economic with the political, technological and cultural – and in doing so, to make sense of what appears to be a new, or at least an altered, form of spatial organization. Here a central issue has been the way in which an economy based upon flows, of capital and information, can at the same time engender the creation of a certain geographical fixity, which in turn provides the basis for those flows (Brenner, 1998; Castells, 1977; 1991; 1997; Lefebvre, 1991; Smith, 1996). And there has been some agreement that an adequate answer needs to rethink the ways in which scholars have conceptualized the scale of geographical elements in the world, from the body through the household, to the urban, regional, national and global.

There are a number of things to be said about this literature, but I would like to focus on only one, the commitment to various sorts of conceptions of space and place involved there. Explicitly, there is a rejection of what is often termed the 'container' view of space as an absolute. There is at the same time an implicit – and sometimes explicit – appeal to the relational conception of space advocated by Leibniz. And third, there is an attempt to problematize the regional. Here new regions may emerge at smaller scales, at the scale of the local for example, in the context of economic and technological changes.

At the same time, in each case, of the global village, the web and the new geography of scale, there is a consistent appeal to a particular form of spatial imagery. In the case of the global village, a community created through sets of relations is treated metaphorically as a village, as the sort of community that traditionally was spatially encompassed. Much the same is true of the web, viewed as cyberspace, a new form of place that is 'out there', but that is spoken of as an object. And in the new geographies of scale the focus is inevitably on the 'superimposition and interpenetration of social spaces' (Brenner, 1998: 478) where spaces are spoken of, again, as objects. In each case, in the process of attempting to problematize conventionally conceived regions the authors allow the image of the *region* to re-emerge. And again, in each case, the rejection of absolute space in favour of relational space is undercut, just in the ways that discourse about the objects in question – the global village, the web or the world economy – is carried on in spatialized terms, terms that suggest that those objects themselves must somehow be in some larger, encompassing space.

I make these comments not to suggest that the authors in question have somehow failed in their analyses. Indeed, quite to the contrary, I wish to suggest that these ways of conceptualizing space and place, this discursive displacement, is very much an inevitable element of the project in which each is engaged. As we have seen, it is quite possible to envision forms of discourse that do not appeal to the image of the region as a container, or that do not imagine the possibility of an abstracted relational space, or that cannot conceive of a non-narrativized place. But the long accretion of sets of practices and institutions that have envisioned space first in modernist, absolute terms and then in regional terms, and that recast the world in those terms, has rendered it difficult indeed to envision the world in other terms, or more accurately, to recognize those many instances in which the world is envisioned in those terms.

If in Hesiod's time the world was rife with symbols, such that the snail could be seen as a sign of a sort of work to be done, and the place of the Pleiades a sign of another, it is now difficult to discuss such signs without slipping into a discourse of calendars and cardinal directions. And this is just the problem faced by the student of new technologies, and particularly those imagined to be as revolutionary as some that are abroad today: whereas those technologies may indeed be associated with a refiguring of the relationships among place, region and space, the ease of slipping from one form of discourse to another makes understanding the potential forms of such change all the more difficult.

REFERENCES

Abler, Ronald, Adams, John S. and Gould, Peter (1971) *Spatial Organization: the Geographer's View of the World*. Englewood Cliffs, NJ: Prentice-Hall.

Alexander, H.G. (1956) *The Leibniz–Clarke Correspondence, together with Extracts from Newton's Principia and Opticks*. New York: Barnes & Noble Imports.

Anderson, Benedict (1991) *Imagined Communities: Reflections on the Origin and Spread of Nationalism*. London: Verso.

Andrewes, William J.H., Harvard University Collection of Historical Scientific Instruments and National Association of Watch and Clock Collectors (1996) *The Quest for Longitude: the Proceedings of the Longitude Symposium, Harvard University, Cambridge, Massachusetts, November 4–6, 1993*. Cambridge, MA: Collection of Historical Scientific Instruments, Harvard University.

Appleyard, Donald, Myer, John Randolph and Lynch, Kevin (1964) *The View from the Road*. Cambridge, MA: published for the Joint Center for Urban Studies of the Massachusetts Institute of Technology and Harvard University by the MIT Press.

Aristotle (1941) 'Physica', in Richard McKeon (ed.), *The Basic Works of Aristotle*, trans. R.P. Hardie and R.K. Gaye. New York: Random House. pp. 218–397.

Augé, Marc (1995) *Non-Places: Introduction to an Anthropology of Supermodernity*. London: Verso.

Bachelard, Gaston (1969) *The Poetics of Space*, trans. Maria Jolas. Boston: Beacon.

Barlow, John Perry (1996) 'A cyberspace independence declaration', http://www.eff.org/pub/Publications/John_Perry_Barlow/barlow_0296.declaration.

Bartky, Ian R. (1989) 'The adoption of standard time', *Technology and Culture*, 30 (1): 25–56.

Barton, Tamsyn (1994) *Ancient Astrology*. London: Routledge.

Black, Jeremy (1997) *Maps and History*. New Haven, CT: Yale University Press.

Borchert, John (1967) 'American metropolitan evolution', *Geographical Review*, 57: 301–32.

Bourdieu, Pierre and Wacquant, Loïc J.D. (1992) *An Invitation to Reflexive Sociology*. Chicago: University of Chicago Press.

Brenner, Neil (1998) 'Between fixity and motion: accumulation, territorial organization and the historical geography of spatial scales', *Environment and Planning D*, 16 (4): 459–81.

Brunn, Stanley and Leinbach, Thomas (eds) (1991) *Collapsing Space and Time: Geographic Aspects of Communications and Information*. London: Harper.

Bunbury, E.H. (1959) *A History of Ancient Geography*. New York: Dover.

Casey, Edward S. (1993) *Getting Back into Place: toward a Renewed Understanding of the Place-World*. Bloomington, IN: Indiana University Press.

Casey, Edward S. (1997) *The Fate of Place: a Philosophical History*. Berkeley, CA: University of California Press.

Castells, Manuel (1977) *The Urban Question*, trans. Alan Sheridan. London: Arnold.

Castells, Manuel (1991) *The Informational City: Information Technology, Economic Restructuring, and the Urban–Regional Process*. London: Blackwell.

Castells, Manuel (1997) *The Power of Identity*. London: Blackwell.

Certeau, Michel de (1984) *The Practice of Everyday Life*. Berkeley, CA: University of California Press.

Curry, Michael R. (1996) *The Work in the World: Geographical Practice and the Written Word.* Minneapolis: University of Minnesota Press.

Curry, Michael R. (1998) *Digital Places: Living with Geographic Information Technologies.* London: Routledge.

Curry, Michael R. (2000a) 'The power to be silent: testimony, identity, and the place of place', *Historical Geography*, 28: 13–24.

Curry, Michael R. (2000b) 'Wittgenstein and the fabric of everyday life', in Nigel Thrift and Mike Crang (eds), *Thinking Space*. London: Routledge.

Dear, Michael J. (1988) 'The postmodern challenge: reconstructing human geography', *Transactions, Institute of British Geographers*, NS 13: 262–74.

Denis, M., Pazzaglia, F., Cornoldi, C. and Bertolo, L. (1999) 'Spatial discourse and navigation: an analysis of route directions in the city of Venice', *Applied Cognitive Psychology*, 13 (2): 145–74.

Dilke, O.A.W. (1985) *Greek and Roman Maps*. Ithaca, NY: Cornell University Press.

Entrikin, J. Nicholas (1991) *The Betweenness of Place*. Basingstoke: Macmillan.

Foucault, Michel (1977) *Discipline and Punish: the Birth of the Prison*, trans. Alan Sheridan. New York: Vintage.

Giddens, Anthony (1981) *Power, Property and the State*. Berkeley, CA: University of California Press.

Giddens, Anthony (1991) *Modernity and Self-Identity: Self and Society in the Late Modern Age*. Cambridge: Polity.

Glacken, Clarence J. (1976) *Traces on the Rhodian Shore: Nature and Culture in Western Thought from Ancient Times to the End of the Eighteenth Century*. Berkeley, CA: University of California Press.

Godlewska, Anne and Smith, Neil (1994) *Geography and Empire*. Oxford: Blackwell.

Hacking, Ian (1975) *The Emergence of Probability*. Cambridge: Cambridge University Press.

Hacking, Ian (1982) 'Biopower and the avalanche of printed numbers', *Humanities in Society*, 5: 279–95.

Hall, Edward T. (1959) *The Silent Language*. New York: Doubleday.

Havelock, Eric A. (1986) *The Muse Learns to Write: Reflections on Orality and Literacy from Antiquity to the Present*. New Haven, CT: Yale University Press.

Heidegger, Martin (1977) 'The age of the world picture', in *The Question Concerning Technology and other Essays*, trans. William Lovitt. New York: Garland. pp. 115–54.

Heidegger, Martin (1993a) 'The question concerning technology', in David Farrell Krell (ed.), *Basic Writings*. New York: HarperCollins. pp. 307–42.

Heidegger, Martin (1993b) 'Building dwelling thinking' (1951), in David Farrell Krell (ed.), *Basic Writings*. New York: HarperCollins. pp. 343–63.

Heise, Bernard W. (1998) 'Visions of the world: geography and maps during the baroque age, 1550–1750'. Unpublished dissertation, Cornell University, Ithaca, NY.

Herf, Jeffrey (1990) *Reactionary Modernism: Technology, Culture and Politics in Weimar and the Third Reich*. Cambridge: Cambridge University Press.

Hesiod (1988) 'Works and days', in M.L. West (ed. and trans.), *Theogony and Works and Days*. Oxford: Oxford University Press. pp. 35–61.

Hippocrates (1950) 'Airs, waters, places', in *The Medical Works of Hippocrates*, trans. John Chadwick and W.N. Mann. Oxford: Blackwell. pp. 90–111.

Homer (1996) *The Odyssey*, trans. Robert Fagles. New York: Penguin.

Honigmann, Ernst (1929) *Die sieben Klimata und die Poleis episimoi: eine Untersuchung zur Geschichte der Geographie und Astrologie im Altertum und Mittelalter*. Heidelberg: Winter.

Horkheimer, Max and Adorno, Theodor W. (1972) *Dialectic of Enlightenment*, trans. John Cumming. New York: Seabury.

Innis, Harold Adams (1950) *Empire and Communications*. Oxford: Clarendon.

Jacobs, Jane (1961) *The Death and Life of Great American Cities*. New York: Random House.

Janelle, Donald (1969) 'Spatial reorganization: a model and a concept', *Annals of the Association of American Geographers*, 59: 348–64.

Jay, Martin (1993) *Downcast Eyes: the Denigration of Vision in Twentieth-Century French Thought*. Berkeley, CA: University of California Press.

Johnson, David R. and Post, David (1996) 'Symposium: surveying law and borders – the rise of law in cyberspace', *Stanford Law Review*, 48: 1367.

Kant, Immanuel (1929) 'On the first ground of the distinction of regions in space', in *Kant's Inaugural Dissertation and Early Writings on Space*, trans. John Handyside. Chicago: Open Court.

Kant, Immanuel (1965) *The Critique of Pure Reason*, trans. Norman Kemp Smith. New York: St Martin's Press.

Keller, Arthur S., Lissitzyn, Oliver J. and Mann, Frederick J. (1938) *Creation of Rights of Sovereignty through Symbolic Acts*. New York: Columbia University Press.

Kimble, George H.T. (1951) 'The inadequacy of the regional concept', in L.D. Stampp and S.W. Wooldridge (eds), *London Essays in Geography*. London: Longman. pp. 151–74.

Lefebvre, Henri (1991) *The Production of Space*, trans. David Nicholson-Smith. New York: Basil Blackwell.

Lessig, Lawrence (1996) 'Symposium: surveying law and borders – the rise of law in cyberspacee', *Stanford Law Review*, 48: 1403.

Lévi-Strauss, Claude (1977) *Tristes tropiques*, trans. John Weightman and Doreen Weightman. New York: Pocket.

Livingstone, David N. (1992) *The Geographical Tradition*. Oxford: Blackwell.

Lukermann, Fred (1961) 'The concept of location in classical geography', *Annals of the Association of American Geographers*, 51: 194–210.

Lukermann, Fred (1963) 'The intimate relation of chronology, geography and astrology according to Bernhardus Varenius'. Paper presented at the Annual Meeting of the Association of American Geographers.

Lynch, Kevin (1960) *The Image of the City*. Cambridge, MA: Technology Press.

Mackinder, Halford John (1904) *The Geographical Pivot of History*. No publisher.

Mackinder, Halford John (1919) *Democratic Ideals and Reality: a Study in the Politics of Reconstruction*. New York: Holt.

McLuhan, Marshall and Powers, Bruce R. (1989) *The Global Village: Transformations in World Life and Media in the 21st Century*. New York: Oxford University Press.

Morley, David and Robins, Kevin (1995) *Spaces of Identity: Global Media, Electronic Landscapes, and Cultural Boundaries*. London: Routledge.

Newton, Isaac (1934) *Sir Isaac Newton's Mathematical Principles of Natural Philosophy and his System of the World*, trans. Andrew Motte and Florian Cajori. Berkeley, CA: University of California Press.

Nora, Pierre (1984) *Les Lieux de mémoire*. Paris: Gallimard.

Ong, Walter J. (1982) *Orality and Literacy: the Technologizing of the Word*. London: Routledge.

Pausanias (1987) 'Guide to Greece', in Paul Fussell (ed.), *The Norton Book of Travel*. New York: Norton. pp. 48–58.

Pickering, Andrew (1986) *Constructing Quarks: a Sociological History of Particle Physics*. Chicago: University of Chicago Press.

Porter, Theodore M. (1986) *The Rise of Statistical Thinking, 1820–1900*. Princeton, NJ: Princeton University Press.

Proshansky, Harold M., Ittelson, William H. and Rivlin, Leanne G. (eds) (1970) *Environmental Psychology: Man and his Physical Setting*. New York: Holt, Rinehart & Winston.

Ptolemy (1940) *Tetrabiblos*, trans. F.E. Robbins. London: Heinemann.

Ptolemy (1948) 'The elements of geography', in Morris Raphael Cohen (ed.), *A Source Book in Greek Science*. Cambridge, MA: Harvard University Press. pp. 162–81.

Ramin, Jacques (1976) *Le Périple d'Hannon (The Periplus of Hanno)*. Oxford: British Archaeological Reports.

Ratzel, Friedrich (1899) *Anthropogeographie*. Stuttgart: Engelhorn.

Relph, Edward (1976) *Place and Placelessness*. London: Pion.

Rusnock, Andrea (1995) 'Quantification, precision, and accuracy: determinations of population in the *ancien régime*', in M. Norton Wise (ed.), *The Values of Precision*. Princeton, NJ: Princeton University Press. pp. 17–38.

Smith, N. (1996) 'Spaces of vulnerability: the space of flows and the politics of scale', *Critique of Anthropology*, 16 (1): 63–77.

Sobel, Dava and Andrewes, William J.H. (1998) *The Illustrated Longitude*. New York: Walker.

Soja, Edward W. (1989) *Postmodern Geographies: the Reassertion of Space in Critical Social Theory*. London: Verso.

Soja, Edward W. (1996) *Thirdspace: Journeys to Los Angeles and Other Real-and-Imagined Places*. Cambridge, MA: Blackwell.

Sommer, Robert (1969) *Personal Space: the Behavioral Basis of Design*. Englewood Cliffs, NJ: Prentice-Hall.

Strabo (1917) *The Geography of Strabo*, trans. H.L. Jones. London: Heinemann.

Thompson, Robert L. (1947) *Wiring a Continent: the History of the Telegraph Industry in the United States, 1832–66*. Princeton, NJ: Princeton University Press.

Thrower, Norman (1966) *Original Survey and Land Subdivision: a Comparative Study of the Form and Effect of Contrasting Cadastral Systems*. Chicago: Rand McNally.

Trachtenberg, Alan (1989) *Reading American Photographs: Images as History, Mathew Brady to Walker Evans*. Noonday, NY: Hill & Wang.

Tuan, Yi-Fu (1974) *Topophilia: a Study of Environmental Perception, Attitudes, and Values*. Englewood Cliffs, NJ: Prentice-Hall.

Tuan, Yi-Fu (1980) 'Rootedness versus sense of place', *Landscape*, 24 (1): 3–8.

Tuan, Yi-Fu (1996) *Cosmos and Hearth: a Cosmopolite's Viewpoint*. Minneapolis: University of Minnesota Press.

Varenius, Bernhardus (1650) *Geographia generalis, in qua affectiones generales telluris explicantur*. Amstelodami: L. Elzevirium.

Vidal de la Blache, Paul (1911) 'Les genres de vie dans la géographie humaine', *Annales de Géographie*, 20: 193–212, 289–304.

Vidal de la Blache, Paul (1928) *The Personality of France*, trans. H.C. Brentnall. London: Knopf.

Walter, Eugene Victor (1988) *Placeways: a Theory of the Human Environment*. Chapel Hill, NC: University of North Carolina Press.

Wittgenstein, Ludwig (1961) *Tractatus logico-philosophicus*, trans. D.F. Pears and Brian F. McGuinness. London: Routledge & Kegan Paul.

Wittgenstein, Ludwig (1968) *Philosophical Investigations*, trans. G.E.M. Anscombe. New York: Macmillan.

Wood, Denis and Beck, Robert J. (1994) *Home Rules*. Baltimore, MD: Johns Hopkins University Press.

Zerubavel, Eviator (2000) 'The social construction of historical discontinuity'. Paper presented at the Department of Sociology, University of California: Los Angeles.

30

Power and Political Culture

TIMOTHY W. LUKE

This chapter rethinks the remediations of political culture and power, which are unfolding on what is called 'the Internet', or the ever changing network of networks that are knit together out of information and communication technologies (ICTs). Rapid change in the digital domains of the Internet is widely acknowledged, so to write about the net effects of new media emerging on the Internet is a hazardous enterprise. In that respect, this analysis is not much different from many others, which either precede, or now parallel, its examination of politics and the Internet. In other ways, however, this chapter is different in as much as it explores the power effects of computer networks, digital discourses and online organizations on political culture and institutions by re-examining what is technologically new as well as what is socially new.

For better or worse, many fields of human agency – both individual and collective – and of social structure – on all levels of aggregation – are being repolarized, because computer-mediated communication (CMC) 'rewraps', as Poster (1990) argues, who dominates whom, where, when and how. Few questions are either as interesting or as significant as this one at this historical juncture, because the *modi operandi* of most social practices are being reshaped out of bits for bits and with bits by the new media of ICTs. At another turn in history, one could ask to see a foundational text, which had been accepted as the definitive articulation of order. As Walker (1993: 26–49) maintains, there were once princes, principalities and *The Prince* interoperating in triangular constellations of energy, form, intelligence, matter and will to decode the emergent (dis)order of sovereignty, nationality and economy in modernity. The royal 'we' of action imposed its conditions for thought and practice, even as it erased its own autonomous authority with jurisdictive myths, constitutional mechanisms and violent manhandlings. Similar changes are afoot today, but digitalization appears to be re(con)textualizing all those foundations into ones and zeros so thoroughly that one cannot find 'the programmer'. This analysis, then, seeks to understand how political culture today, in large part, ultimately can circulate online (Poster, 1995; Bukatman, 1993). In this environment, systemcraft can be soulcraft, and the crafted soul acquires digital forms of being from the system (Rushkoff, 1994). Nonetheless, the technology itself guarantees that much of what is said in this volume will be partly outmoded after the presses roll simply because of rapid changes at the interface.

Historically, the Internet was the creation of the United States of America – the 'hyperpower' allegedly at the heart of post Cold War world order (Abbate, 1999). Yet, the legal authority, managerial acumen and administrative effectiveness of various national and international bodies now nominally in charge of the net, like the Internet Architecture Board (IAB), the Internet Engineering Task Force (IETF), the International Corporation for Assigned Names and Numbers (ICANN), or the Internet Society (ISOC) itself, are quite uncertain. As a 1997 FCC policy brief observed:

> Most of the underlying architecture of the Internet was developed under the auspices, directly or indirectly, of the United States Government. The government has not, however, defined whether it retains authority over Internet management functions, or whether these responsibilities have been delegated to the private sector. The degree to which any existing body can lay claim to representing 'the Internet community' is also unclear. (Cited in Abbate, 1999: 208)

In this power vacuum, which has been created and maintained by state and non-state interests, new groups are reimagining human community (Anderson, 1991), pushing their own ideologies and interests in pursuit of neoliberal utopias and non-liberal resistances (Luke, 1989). In an ironic twist to Engels' famous characterization of socialism, the ICTs associated with the Internet are moving societies from the government of people to the administration of things, which, in turn, remediates new modes of control into governance over people and things (van der Pjil, 1998; Kroker and Weinstein, 1994).

Out on the networks, people who are not of the same race, gender, class, nationality or locality are interacting in cyberspace through operational interfaces that reduce their identities to strings of text, synthesized speech or stylized graphics (de Kerckhove, 1998). Once on the net, they seek to leverage cyberspace to serve various offline agendas (Gibson, 1984). Their efforts to operate together and alone in the digital domain, however, are also creating cultural commonalities, or conventional understandings manifest in act and artifact that characterize their shared forms of life, which are pitched against their offline interests. Face-to-face interactions between persons become online events with digital beings; material systems with well-proven redundancies, proven safeguards and fixed practices are supplanted by unstable clusters of code in fragile telematic networks; locatable sites in real space under identifiable, albeit perhaps not effective, governmental control are displaced by cyberspatial addresses under very little or no governmental oversight (Grisham, 1999; Slouka, 1995). Yet, all of this expresses a new kind of productive power (Foucault, 1980) articulated as ones and zeros.

The net also provides social forces with alternative modes of action and types of artifacts to organize their cultural interactions, institutionalize political movements, and advance economic demands on a deterritorialized metanational basis in 24 × 7 time frames (Anderson, 1991; Hauben, 1997). The networks are operational venues whose assignment, sale and use generate a new governance challenge: how to create, border, police and use virtual spaces (Slevin, 2000). Some net-ready interests realize that these spaces, and hence the legal jurisdictions, strategic alliances, cultural norms and communal rituals which will prevail in them are up for grabs (Everard, 2000). Cyberspace, as both its emerging 'hacktivist' and 'netizenship' practices indicate (Hauben, 1997), will be contested space in so far as the operational effects of informatics can be simultaneously experienced everywhere and nowhere. One recent study found the United States to be the most common domain source of Usenet messages, for example, in the 1990s, but 'anonymous', or no territorial region of origin, was the 15th most common source in Usenet messages (Smith and Kollock, 1999: 197) of the nearly 200 states and government entities with top-level domains. If the governmentality problematic is, as Foucault claims, the challenge of conveniently arranging things and people to organize the conduct of conduct, then the web poses tremendous new transnational challenges for governance, especially who governs whom, where, when and how (Jordan, 1999; Luke 1995).

Individuals and groups can become fully enmeshed within the tactics and strategies of complex forms of normalizing power, which can be political regimes or technical regimens, whose institutions, procedures, analyses and techniques loosely organize mass populations and their material environments in different highly politicized symbolic material economies (Ihde, 1990; Poster, 1990). It provides an inexact set of bearings, but Foucault asserts:

> it is the tactics of government which make possible the continual definition and redefinition of what is within the competence of the state and what is not, the public versus the private, and so on; thus the state can only be understood in its survival and its limits on the basis of the general tactics of governmentality. (1991: 103)

Because governmentalizing practices are always at the centre of political struggle, the online interactions of populations in highly organized economies now compel state regimes to redefine continually what is within their administrative competence throughout the informationalizing process (Beck, 1997; Luke, 1994).

The devotees of digitalization among the digerati, like Nicholas Negroponte, overrate the positive aspects of telematic life, while they underplay how most negative social and political tendencies will continue in cyberspace like they are offline. For Negroponte, 'the change from atoms to bits is irrevocable and unstoppable' (1995: 4), and digitalization ultimately means dematerialization. To mark this turning point in human history, he asserts 'computing is not about computers any more. It is about living' (1995: 6). His claim in all too many ways is true. Here is the political and ethical problematic of 'the polis' – living how, living where, living for whom, and by whose leave – only now while online.

Much of the literature on ICTs misses the Internet's governmentality to the degree it presumes the existence of positive affinities rooted in artifacts (Adas, 1989). Stefnik, for example, asserts that the net is redrawing the edges of groups and individuals, and this power is the source of its transformative power as well as the contra-transformative pushbacks against it:

> New technologies bring change. When they are fundamental to transportation and communication they affect

more than just the mechanics of how we work and live. Because of them, we find ourselves interacting with people from different cultures who hold different values, people who used to be very far away. We learn to operate in a global space – experiencing cultural clashes and making cultural accommodations. Technological changes lead to cultural changes – especially changes in the social and legal institutions that are now coevolving with the technology of the Internet. (1999: 1)

Consequently, Stefnik maintains that new edges get fixed in this process of technological change:

Groups can have edge just as individuals have edges. In a group, confusion at the edge usually shows up as lack of agreement about the right course of action. Members may express contradictory and shifting views. Over time the people in a group may align themselves to make a change, then back off, only to try again later ... This is why the edge for technologies of connection is open to conflict between global and local values. Such a conflict can evoke resistance, a push-back, as people seek stability and attempt to preserve the status quo. The pushback thus acts to preserve cultural diversity. (1999: 2, 3)

As one of the Xerox Corporation's leading in-house scientists, Stefnik can propound this sense of the network society, and get an audience. Yet his vision is tremendously self-serving. People and organizations like Stefnik and Xerox bring change, not 'technologies'. The 'we' whose work and life are being affected is not large, not cohesive, and not an agent as such, but Stefnik turns to technology to create an artifactual affinity. And this 'we' then becomes conscious and cohesive, and copes with a cultural give-and-take along the edges of an apparently open, free-flowing and consensual search for stability. Some – both inside and outside the group – resist and push back, but others go along with the new connections. At one level, this account is not entirely false, but on many other levels it is almost untrue (Feenberg, 1999).

Only Deibert's sophisticated analysis of the social epistemologies and political technics of media as environments begins to approach the complexity of networked economies and societies with real insight. Deibert's *Parchment, Printing, and Hypermedia: Communication in World Order Transformation* (1997) rearranges the connections of different historical periods, ranging from the medieval to the modern and the postmodern, into distinctive communicative technics, represented as parchment manuscripts, printed literature and electronic hypermedia. A change is identified in the relations between the informers and the informed. While this might not represent a new mode of information, as Poster claims, the workings of post-modern decentredness and electronic hypermedia are altered as a result of the fit 'between this social

epistemology and the emerging hypermedia environment' (1997: 200).

The culture of network society owes a lot to new companies, institutions and organizations that create new digital media, and then exploit their capabilities to redefine and then satisfy new human needs. Thus, the Internet becomes the focus of everyday life. 'The net is not a separate environment that individuals can choose or not choose to utilize'. Instead, as Martin asserts,

In an Internet worked world, networks will be the back-bone of social and economic life. Just as governments help organize society, and just as cities help organize the daily activities of individuals, networks will increasingly become the primary tool for organizing information. The choice not to participate automatically removes these groups or individuals from the mainstream. (1997: 211)

To not go online then is to choose antiquation, anachronism and anti-progressiveness (Tapscott, 1997).

Like all previous technological generations of new practices, whether the telephone, automobile, radio, aeroplane or television, the nets are producing the politics and culture of a 'new generation' (Tapscott, 1997). According to Martin, 'This is a generation united under the banner of interactivity, which thrives on making connections. This group of online, interactive, digital individuals are the consumers in the Digital Estate' (1997: 211). Tapscott, Martin and Negroponte all regard these interactive generation populations, 'I-Generation' individuals, as the vanguard of universal virtuality. They have that special knowledge the members of any vanguard require: 'They know it will not be long before interactivity is taken for granted and that memories of pre-internetworking will be tantamount to realizing the days before machines could fly. After critical-mass, everyone will already belong' (Martin, 1997: 211). The intrinsic value to adding more nodes to the net turns its new media into a concrete normativity that assumes, or assures, everyone will belong (Hassan, 1977).

In most respects, informatics are only the latest wrinkle in 'modernity' (Harvey, 1989; Mumford, 1963). Once again, a fresh set of cultural transformations, resting in a destructively productive new technics with its own unformed social mores, appears as the source and goal of yet another universalizing moral order, uniform vision of nature, and univocalized economic model (Mumford, 1970). Bits, like most modern things defined by commodified commercial operations, are privileged objects, which can go from anywhere to anywhere at anytime for anybody (Slouka, 1995). Yet this potential omnipresence, first, mostly glosses over how much 'anywhere' actually remains (in world systems terms) as a set of very limited venues, or truly 'manywheres', albeit often widely distributed geographically; second, ignores how most movements go from somebody at one privileged site to somebody, or actually 'manybodies', at another special place; and third, discounts how speeds in anytime are arrayed in 'manytimes' as a function of willingness to pay, salience of authority, or quality of connectivity (Luke, 1997: 121–44).

POLITICS AND CULTURE IN CYBERSPACE

The fractalizing power of cyberspace as a political culture construct can be tracked out into several philosophical patches and theoretical thickets (Grusin and Bolter, 1999; Kelly, 1998; Levy, 1997; Miller, 1996). Perhaps we never have been modern (Latour, 1993), but one promising perspective leads into the critiques of postmodernity. These writings puzzle through the emergence of transnational space by reconsidering the relationships of territory to the earth, and their deterritorializing remediations in contemporary thought and practice.

On one level, following Lyotard, the concept of postmodernity might mark the decline of modernity's grand narratives, which have until quite recently embedded Western capitalist humanity's and society's economic, political and social-technological practices in some deeper metaphysical substance. These metanarratives, or the fables of reason and freedom, see science and technology bring gradual, but inevitable, progress to individuals and societies through the unfolding of history. Lyotard, however, saw this historical period closing during the 1960s and 1970s with the transition to post-industrialism. His analysis is based

upon the perception of the existence of a modern era that dates from the time of the Enlightenment and that now has run its course: and this modern era was predicated on the notion of progress in knowledge, in the arts, in technology, and in human freedom as well, all of which was thought of as leading to a truly emancipated society: a society emancipated from poverty, despotism and ignorance. But all of us can see that the development continues to take place without leading to the realization of any of these dreams of emancipation. (1984: 39)

With this rising distrust in any metanarratives of truth, enlightenment or progress, Lyotard sees science and technology falling under the sway of 'another language game, in which the goal is no longer truth, but performativity – that is, the best possible input/output equation' (1984: 46).

On another level, following Jameson, the mediations of performativity are found in 'a new social system beyond classical capitalism', proliferating across 'the world space of multinational capital' (1992: 59, 54). More specifically, as Harvey argues, this new regime for multinational capital

began by disintegrating the Fordist regime of industrial production, capital accumulation and state intervention patched together on a national basis during the 1930s through the 1970s by welfare states. In its place, new arrangements for flexible accumulation, productive specialization and public deregulation have surfaced within many loosely coupled transnational alliances since the 1970s. As Harvey observes, 'flexible accumulation typically exploits a wide range of seemingly contingent geographical circumstances, and reconstitutes them as structured internal elements of its own encompassing logic ... the result has been the production of fragmentation, insecurity, and ephemeral uneven development within a highly unified global space economy of capital flows' (1989: 294, 296). On the horizon drawn by flexible accumulation, Lyotard's cultural vision of performativity is what anchors 'the new world order' of the 1990s and 2000s, as most spatial barriers and all time zones collapse in the cultural compression caused by transnational businesses' acceleration of production and consumption. Today, 'the State and/or company must abandon the idealist and humanist narratives of legitimation in order to justify the new goal: in the discourse of today's financial backers of research, the only credible goal is power. Scientists, technicians, and instruments are purchased not to find truth, but to augment power' (Lyotard, 1984: 46).

Corporate enthusiasts, such as Cairncross (1997), see this development as 'the death of distance'. In this vein, Jameson argues, 'we are back in the spatial itself', and critical analysis

infers a certain supplement of spatiality in the contemporary period and suggests that there is a way in which, even though other modes of production ... are distinctively spatial, ours has been spatialized in a unique sense, such that space is for us an existential and cultural dominant, a thematized or foregrounded feature or structural principle standing in striking contrast to its relatively subordinate and secondary ... role in earlier modes of production. (1992: 365)

Even though this new world spatiality might be an existential and social dominant, its networked qualities remain fairly vague (Castells, 1996–8). Indeed, this phenomenon lacks much permanence, closure or primordialism. Jameson reaches for common household technological referents, like channel surfing on cable TV with a remote control, to substantiate his sense of this new consciousness. His discussion lacks theoretical heft, because he also ignores and underplays cyberspace, when it, in fact, seems to be a much richer instantiation of 'the new space that thereby emerges [and which] involves the suppression of distance (in the sense of Benjamin's aura) and the relentless saturation of any remaining voids and empty places, to the point where the postmodern body ... is now exposed to a perceptual barrage of immediacy from which all sheltering layers and intervening mediations have been removed' (1992: 412–13).

Out in the digital domain, one slips into spaces of suppressed distance shorn of sheltering mediations and brimming with buckets of immediacy. This is what saturates the final remaining hidden zones of world markets. While he does not state it in these terms, Jameson captures many of the qualities found in the telematic environments of the net. Out online, the peculiar spatial quality of cyberspace as a cultural domain for dispersion, decentring and discontinuity comes into its own. Hence 'we', the networked subjects enveloped in the world spaces of transnational capital, and then remediated in connected clusters of code, 'turn out to be whatever we are in, confront, inhabit, or habitually move through, provided it is understood that under current conditions we are obliged to renegotiate all those spaces or channels back and forth in a single Joycean day' (1992: 373). Cyberspace contains layer upon layer of multiple interrelating, and diversely channelled, ephemeral constructs which everyone moves through, inhabits and confronts on every single day of their Joycean existences (Shenk, 1997; Poster, 1995; Kelly, 1994). The browser histories from such online odysseys will mark these renegotiations all too well as a 'multidimensional set of radically discontinuous realities' which replicates itself online throughout every last void and empty place of the world from the poorest rural household up to the richest global marketplace. Jameson misconstrues these changes as an 'unimaginable decentering of global capital itself' (1992: 413), when, in fact, it is the radical recentring of the imagination behind valorizing exchange that now occurs 24 × 7 in the digital domain.

The analysis of concrete power arrangements for the net ranges from the new idealism of the digital digerati, such as Kelly (1994) or Negroponte (1995), to the more sophisticated materialist perspectives of analysts such as Deibert (1997) or Mattelart (2000). Communications media are a perfect illustration of the normalizing mediations of proactive power put forward by Foucault. To paraphrase McLuhan, who saw all technologies as media providing 'extensions of man' psychically and physically (1964: 19–67), men and women online become psychic and physical peripheral plug-ins for other central processing units, leaving men and women to impersonate 'being digital' as variable extensions of digital technologies. Connectivity as a mechanism of power depends upon the cultivation of the body as well as the mind, and getting online anywhere all the time allows businesses to extract time, energy and labour from a new culture of production and consumption as ones and zeros. The material functionalities of connectivity can be liberating, but only in the very peculiar fashions permitted by the mode of information. Big businesses do not want to maintain

today's digital divides between those online with access and those offline without access (Martin and Schumann, 1997). In fact, it is only by granting new commodified freedoms to more people in the digital domain that global businesses can constantly 'increase subjected forces' and 'improve force and efficacy of that which subjects them' (Foucault, 1980: 104) in the rapid circulation of commodified goods and services. The digital divides in world society between white, Hispanic, black or Asian computer use are destined to close. Until bits can command many more atoms of all classes, creeds and colours, digital being will remain incomplete.

ICTs do not operate autonomously or discretely (Hobart and Schiffman, 1998). Rather, contemporary informatics, as they intermesh with the circuits of commodity production and consumption, permit one to see how fully metanationalized cyberspace can amalgamate online with both: '(1) Technologies of production, which permit us to produce, transform, or manipulate things', and, '(2) technologies of the self, which permit individuals to effect by their own means or with the help of others a certain number of operations on their own bodies and souls, thought, conduct, and way of being, so as to transform themselves in order to attain a certain state of happiness, purity, wisdom, perfection, or immortality' (Foucault, 1988: 18). These coaligned technologies of production and the self fuse in virtual environments. And, it is the transnational spaces of the net that are promoting 'the ultimate realization of the private individual as a productive force. The system of needs must wring liberty and pleasure from him as so many functional elements of the reproduction of the system of production and the relations of power that sanction it' (Baudrillard, 1981: 85).

NETWORKS: GOVERNING WITH OR THROUGH TECHNOLOGY

To rethink the cultural limits and political possibilities of exercising power over the Internet, one must gauge the social, political and economic changes being caused by this new technological system (Nye, 1990; Rutsky, 2000). Too many approaches to the technology and culture of the net are plagued by a mindset of naive instrumentalism. That is, the net is simply a tool like any other, and it is being used consciously and rationally by autonomous human agents to serve effectively the instrumental ends of its users. According to these views, democracies online basically will be just like democracies offline except that their officials and constituents will use e-mail and/or have webchat (Rash, 1997; Rheingold, 1993). Even though we know democracies with newspapers, televisions and telephones are not entirely like those without them because a new mediated technoculture of mass communications (Deibert, 1997) reshapes their operations, the naive instrumentalism of too many political analyses of the net rehashes reality in this unproductive fashion. On one level, a political reading of the Internet can focus upon 'governing with technology'. This approach sees the net as a tool to rationalize and redirect many processes of government. On a second level, one also can examine how the net constitutes a regime of 'governance through technology'. By rethinking how technologies have 'anonymous histories' (Giedion, 1948) that shape space, temper time and package performance apart from the conscious intention of their users, this approach to politics – as it is conducted through computer-mediated communications over information networks – would re-examine the practices and values of how political subjectivity would change in digital environments in many fundamental ways (Heim, 1998). Digital networks can be used by existing governments to govern, but they also can create new operational domains with their own cultural discourses and practices beyond the scope of today's territorial sovereignty as it works now (Adams, 1998; Mattelart, 1994; Ohmae, 1990). In this manner, 'netizenship' is potentially far more than 'citizenship', because the net is much more expansive than any city, polis or state.

Most importantly, the current commercialization of cyberspace is transforming the political realities of online life (Virilio, 1995). The initial interface of disembodied subjectivity, distributed community and cybernetic play celebrated in the early days of the net is rapidly being eclipsed by newer interface values tied to reimagining cyberspace as hyperreal estate, virtual markets and online e-commerce (Brin, 1998; Gates, 1999; Grossman, 1997). Negroponte is not entirely mistaken when he puffs up the potentialities of 'being digital' (1995: 11–20) as the latest grand transition of modernization. In his digital materialism, the economies and societies still organized around making and moving matter, or 'atoms', will be slipsliding away into a new domain focused upon inventing and integrating information, or 'bits'. Space will be occupied by reworked atoms, but this occupation will also be filled by the flow of continuously upgraded bits (Bukatman, 1993). Without saying so, Negroponte essentially recasts digital technics as a nascent form of nanotechnology with which bits reach out and reshape atoms at will as part and parcel of digital being.

This recognition acquires articulation in Bill Gates' views on personal computing. He outlines another style of being digital in elaborate tales about his, and allegedly 'everyone' else's, experiences of 'growing up' since the 1970s with computers:

In the minds of a lot of people at school we became linked with the computer, and it with us ... In doing so, we caused a kind of revolution – peaceful, mainly – and now the computer has taken up residence in our offices and homes ... Inexpensive computer chips now show up in engines, watches, antilock brakes, facsimile machines, elevators, gasoline pumps, cameras, thermostats, treadmills, vending machines, burglar alarms, and even talking greeting cards ... Now that computing is astoundingly inexpensive and computers inhabit every part of our lives, we stand on the brink of another revolution. This one will involve unprecedentedly inexpensive communication; all the computers will join together to communicate with us and for us. (1996: 2–5)

For Gates and Microsoft, computers are just what will remake built environments for the betterment of all. Like it or not, digital being on this hyperreal estate is the place where human beings find computers are linked to us, computers tie us into networks, and computers colonize other artifacts to communicate with each other and, of course, us (Mitchell, 1995). Hence, governance through technology is inescapable.

Unlike the public projects underpinning the polis, this odd remembrance by Gates belies larger corporate agendas for private profit and power to sustain an informatic 'subpolis'. What is more, the financial, professional and technical development networks behind this subpolis leave its possibilities for collective action and imagination caught somewhere between the traditional vision of politics and non-politics. This idea snags something quite significant out of the bitstream. As Beck suspects, big technological systems, like cybernetic networks, telecommunications grids or computer applications, are becoming

a third entity, acquiring the precarious hybrid status of a *sub-politics*, in which the scope of social changes precipitated varies inversely with their legitimation ... The direction of development and results of technological transformation become fit for discourse and subject to legitimation. Thus business and technoscientific action acquire a *new political and moral dimension* that had previously seemed alien to technoeconomic activity ... now the potential for structuring society migrates from the political system into the subpolitical system of scientific, technological, and economic modernization. *The political becomes non-political and the non-political political* ... A revolution under the cloak of normality occurs, which escapes from possibilities of intervention, but must all the same be justified and enforced against a public becoming critical ... The political institutions become the administrators of a development they neither have planned for nor are able to structure, but must nevertheless somehow justify ... Lacking a place to appear, the decisions that change society become tongue-tied and anonymous ... What we *do not* see and *do not want* is changing the world more and more obviously and threateningly. (1992: 186–7)

In the name of digital materialism, Gates and thousands of other far more anonymous and usually more tongue-tied computer geeks like him are mounting a revolution from their desktops by designing, building and owning new subpolitical spaces (Roszak, 1994). Digitalization generated out on the WWW, from within the Wintel operating system, or with ASCII code, all too often is neither seen nor wanted. Nevertheless, the collective decisions taken through these codes and systems by technicians and tradesmen to structure the economy and society around such 'sub-political systems of scientific, technological, and economic modernization' (Beck, 1992: 186) are changing the world without much, if any, state regulation, political planning structure or civic legitimation.

Thus, corporate campaigns for the expanded ownership and control of public goods, like cyberspace, are frequently dressed out in a new pluralism of open-ended popular decisions. Because hackers, debuggers and other users are always running an ongoing open review of past design decisions, Microsoft and other vendors design feedback from their customers and their users. Either way, the net work of networkers out on the nets builds and then maintains the multilayered complexities of this digital domain as a computer-mediated subpolis. Network connectivity, then, is 'your passport' into 'a new, mediated way of life' (Gates, 1996: 5). More than an object, not quite yet a subject, online connectivity can provide a pass, a port and a presence for entering into a new way of life.

George Gilder's celebration of 'the new age of intelligent machines' (1989: 381) sees this coming e-formation of our world of matter-centred manufacture attaining absolute immanence in societies under the sway of information-denominated 'Mind'. Conflating the Cold War with cyberwar in 1989, Gilder asserts:

> The overthrow of matter in business will reverberate through geopolitics and exalt the nations in command of creative minds over the nations in command of land and resources. Military power will accrue more and more to the masters of information technology. Finally, the overthrow of matter will stultify all materialist philosophy and open vistas of human imagination and moral revival. (1989: 18)

This effusion of humans and machines in a progressive pact of transcendent unity ten years later, however, is leading more toward MP3 downloads, $8 online stock trades on Ameritrade, 24 × 7 swap meets on eBay, and cyberporn on demand, than it is to an opening of communal concord between all humans. Oddly enough, Gilder fails to show how the old materialist philosophy has been stultified. Instead it returns in the discursive discipline of an informatic materialism in which silicon, fibre and code will reknit humans and their machines into new subpolitical collectives of economic

development. This utopian talk is no different from that made by other technological determinists who attributed these same powers over the past century to rayon, radio and railroads and it raises the question of how to govern with technology (Nye, 1996).

The wide open spaces of the Internet are administered loosely by the Internet Society (ISOC), which also is the home of the Internet Engineering Task Force (IETF) and the Internet Architecture Board (IAB). Drawing together people from transnational telecoms, big software houses, national scientific agencies, professional-technical groups and media companies, ISOC is a major force in the management of the informatic subpolis. Its programmes, however, are metanational in as much as its members seek to maintain the net's uniquely metanational qualities by safeguarding 'the viability and global scaling of the Internet' in ways that 'assure the open development, evolution, and use of the Internet for the benefit of all people throughout the world' (http://www.isoc.org/mission).

Another interpretation of this dynamic partnership between people and intelligent machines finds its voice in singing the praises of 'friction-free capitalism' out on the net (Gates, 1999). Its reflexive epistemology also sees the wired world's digital exchanges in global terms (Lewis, 1997). As Bill Gates observes:

> The global information market will be huge and will combine all the various ways human goods, services and ideas are exchanged. On a practical level, this will give you broader choices about most things, including how you earn and invest, what you buy and how much you pay for it, who your friends are and how you spend your time with them, and where and how securely you and your family live. Your workplace and your idea of what it means to be 'educated' will be transformed, perhaps almost beyond recognition. Your identity, of who you are and where you belong, may open up considerably. In short, just about everything will be done differently. (1996: 6–7)

Opening up the norms of identity – who you are and where you belong – here becomes a credo for reconfiguring the entire globe into a vast internal market for transnational exchange: this perhaps is the essence of digital being. In the network society, we are becoming bits, everything is becoming bits, and globalization is just being digital (Castells, 1996–8).

This development is not 'friction-free'. Instead, as Lyotard suggests, 'economic powers have reached the point of imperiling the stability of the State through new forms of the circulation of capital that go by the generic name of *multinational corporations*', and these new modes of revalorizing exchange 'imply that investment decisions have, at least in part, passed beyond the control of the nation-states' (1984: 5). Even though it probably was not what Hayles (1999) envisioned when she cast posthumanism as that condition in which no organism can be entirely differentiated from its environment, no self is separate from society, and no agency lacks structure, corporate powers are growing so pervasive online that bits are becoming almost monetized. Emergent knowledges framed as bits begin

> circulating along the same lines as money, instead of for its 'educational' value or political (administrative, diplomatic, military) importance; the pertinent distinction would no longer be between knowledge and ignorance, but rather, as is the case with money, between 'payment knowledge' and 'investment knowledge' – in other words, between units of knowledge exchange in a daily maintenance framework (the reconstitution of the work force, 'survival') versus funds of knowledge dedicated to optimizing the performance of a project. (Lyotard, 1984: 6)

Online, bits can meld payment and investment knowledge into a single performative flow that pays out by drawing new investments, and draws new investments as its payoff.

By fabricating digital domains, and then continually struggling to master their telemetrical terrain, posthumans also fulfil Lyotard's prophecies about 'the postmodern condition'. That is, 'knowledge in the form of an informational commodity indispensable to productive power is already, and will continue to be, a major – perhaps *the* major – stake in the worldwide competition for power'; in fact, the struggle over cyberspace intranationally and transnationally illustrates how fully the residents of nation-states must fight for 'control of information, just as they battled in the past for control over territory, and afterwards for control of access to and exploitation of raw materials and cheap labor' (1984: 5). Online mediations of digital being work through data / information / knowledge in accord with familiar liberal humanist goals. Online and offline, information 'is and will be produced in order to be sold, it is and will be consumed in order to be valorized in a new production: in both cases, the goal is exchange' (1984: 4). In these spaces, everything in society, the marketplace and culture

> is made conditional on performativity. The redefinition of the norms of life consists in enhancing the system's competence for power. That this is the case is particularly evident in the introduction of telematic technology: the technocrats see in telematics a promise of liberalization and enrichment in the interactions between interlocutors; but what makes this process attractive for them is that it will result in new tensions in the system, and these will lead to an improvement in its performativity. (1984: 64)

Once again, the system is the solution, and solutions come from accepting the systems.

Still, as this transnational informatic subpolis and neoliberal marketplace grow, the role and stature of the traditional polis – whatever this might be – in many nation-states could well decline. Even though everyone currently remains captured as bodies within some type of face-to-face political system, their civic abilities to exercise certain practices of rule-making, rule-applying and rule adjudication offline do not map over to the subpolitical domains of online technics. Democracy offline may become the engine of collective inaction or, worse, the audience for endless spectacles of quasi-theatrical scandal. In turn, new decisive revolutions will be made metanationally, as Beck maintains, *'under the cloak of normality'* (1992: 186) thanks to telematic global powers such as Microsoft and Bill Gates or AOL and Steve Case. 'In contemporary discussions', as Beck suggests, 'the "alternative society" is no longer expected to come from parliamentary debates on new laws, but rather from the application of microelectronics, genetic technology, and information media' (1992: 223).

Other openly transnationalist organizations, like the Electronic Frontier Foundation (EFF), espouse the principles of offline human rights for the online settlement and improvement of cyberspace as an e-public domain. While EFF seeks to leverage offline state authorities to protect online freedoms, its image of the 'electronic frontier' is essentially metanational. Indeed, it wants 'to make [the electronic frontier] truly useful and beneficial not just to a technical elite, but to everyone' (http://www.eff.org/EFF docs/). Similarly the Global Internet Liberty Campaign (GILC) also pushes metanational ideas, claiming 'there are no borders in cyberspace' and joining together its multinational membership 'to protect and promote fundamental human rights such as freedom of speech and the right of privacy on the Net for users everywhere' (http://www.gilc.org/about/members.html).

One of the most significant effects of the net, then, is the tendency for connectivity to disintegrate, or at least disrupt, those long-standing forms of institutional action in markets, governments or cultures that have presumed fixed built environments and face-to-face human engagement. Such operations relied upon physical sites of political power (agency offices, election booths, service bureaucracies), economic production (corporate headquarters, sales offices, managerial suites), personal consumption (brokerage offices, new bookstores, car dealerships) and cultural reproduction (public libraries, civic centres, graduate schools), but these venues can easily be morphed into online sites in a fashion that reduces costs, cuts employment, enhances service and raises consumer satisfaction. Physical collocation and geographic contiguity continue to be important on many levels, but online 'electronic proximity' (Dertouzos, 1997: 229) is cross-cutting many institutional practices that have evolved in the real time, real life, real space of what William Gibson (1984) calls 'the meatworld'. In these cross-cuts, the shapeshifting outlines of 'e-proximate' interactions surface out of every e-commerce transaction, e-media page download, e-schooling lesson and e-governance contact made with ICTs.

Dertouzos envisions the networks as 'the information marketplace'. Open 24 × 7, these electronic sites, or I-marts, are an 'e-proximate' space in which 'people and computers buy, sell, and freely exchange information and information services' in round-the-clock transactions that 'involve the processing and communication of information under the same economic motives that drive today's traditional marketplace for goods and services' (1997: 9–10). As Marx warns us, the ever growing socialization of production is coupled with the increasing privatization of ownership and control behind such digital domains (Shapiro, 1999). This tendency does not trouble Dertouzos. Instead, he opines that 'the profit motive' drives today's traditional markets, so there is no reason for it not to persist in cyberspace. The information marketplace exists in order to amplify and extend its existence by collecting consumers, satisfying their needs with need satisfactions, and reselling the information about all or any of these individual and collective choices (Lyon, 1994). Whose service, who serves, who is served, what kind of service, when service works, how service happens in such I-marts, however, would all depend upon economic, political and social decisions, not technical choices *per se*. Yet these realities are painted over in the colours of a constructive interaction that can occur only in/of/for/by the informatic tools of such infostructures. Technics completely occludes the essentially hyperpolitical nature of the I-Mart.

Cultural scripts, sites and structures hammered out over decades or centuries by human beings, as physically collocated or institutionally mediated agents, cannot easily adapt to many online environments (Anderson, 1991). Consequently, new virtual forms of organization, or 'e-formations', are thrown together to match the surging flows of bits, both into and out of the e-proximities of online environments. The quasi-anarchic practices of the nets before 1994, which emphasized user autonomy, individuality, mutual aid, creativity and collective chaos, are still preferred by some, but state regulators, corporate salespersons, religious authorities and economic planners are all struggling to impose more familiar forms of bureaucratic regulation, self-interested profit seeking, and conventional morality upon cyberspace without much success.

Most of their new first-generation adaptations to the time and space compression of the net also are uncomfortably, but perhaps all too predictably, privileging the corporate practices and freewheeling markets of transnational enterprise, which is already running roughshod over most of the world's territorial jurisdictions (Kelly, 1994). Business-to-business

(B2B) commerce will be around $400 billion in 2000, but it is predicted to rise to $7.4 trillion in 2004 (Schneider, 2000: G1). And many of the 'inefficiencies' it is removing from 'the supply chain' or 'enterprise transactions' are people's jobs, national industries and regional ties.

The regimen of e-commerce, despite the pronouncements by dot.com utopians pushed every day on CNBC or CNNfn, is not yet fully defined or finally sealed with respect to its specific operations (Rochlin, 1997). It is instead ironically imagined now in the very collectivist terms of global business: personal connectivity determines social utility, intrusive smartness colonizes the objects of everyday life, data mining of everyone's net work accelerates the surveillance of services, and general productivity depends upon individual e-lancing labour. Even though Bill Gates (1996; 1999) pretends 'the road ahead' is a friction-free path to greater economic liberty, most of the goods and services defining this freedom presume that those who experience e-proximity must endure tremendous levels of unrelenting psychodemographic monitoring – both online and offline. In retail e-commerce as well as B2B trade, the networks produce power that can rerationalize energy production, resource extraction, materials processing, service delivery and capital accumulation as system-supportive performativity.

NETIZENS AND NETIZENSHIP

To survive in the fast capitalist world of the twenty-first century, it is not enough for territorial states or political entities to maintain offline legal jurisdiction over their allegedly sovereign territories and/or constituent members. The net is a governmentality engine, whose subpolitical assemblies of informatic artifacts create new collective subjectivities and collections of subjects beyond the territorial polis in the flows of transnational exchange (Saco, 2000). In online governmentality, the disciplinary articulations of software packages and hardware functionalities also centre upon enforcing 'the right disposition of things' between humans conducting their conduct in cybernetic environments as e-publics (Foucault, 1991).

Many agencies of subnational, national and transnational governmentality now must preoccupy themselves with the conduct of conduct by tracking digital e-haviors on informatic networks. Until the late 1990s, it was the offline involvements of people with family, community and nation – as public interests – that mostly guided civic conduct; at this juncture, however, growing Internet economies and societies seek to be accepted as another ethical e-public ground for normalizing any individual's behaviour. Cybernetic domains are spaces under a special kind of subnational self-policing supervision fulfilled in the free flight of packet switching. The prospects for an informatic prosperity, which are looming ahead on a global scale, will not be possible without some manner of governmentality to guide 'the controlled insertion of bodies into the machinery of production and the adjustment of the phenomena of population to economic processes' (Foucault, 1980: 141).

Living in societies organized out of telematic networks will require a broad facility for coping with many different language games nested in new technocultures. Many decision-makers strive, however, to reduce such heterogeneous social, political and cultural elements to fit the logics of techno-economic performativity. That is, they struggle to manage

> these clouds of sociality according to input/output matrices, following a logic which implies that their elements are commensurable and that the whole is determinable. They allocate our lives for the growth of power. In matters of social justice and of scientific truth alike, the legitimation of that power is based on its optimizing the system's performance efficiency. The application of this criterion to all of our games necessarily entails a certain level of terror, whether soft or hard: be operational (that is, commensurable) or disappear. (Lyotard, 1984: xxiv)

Such decision rules acquire paramount importance for everyone in the telematic economies and societies of the current world system. The politics of networked places, connectivity spaces and digital domains, as Lyotard suggests, frequently revolve around one question: 'who decides what knowledge is and who knows what needs to be decided? In the computer age, the question of knowledge is now more than ever a question of government' (1984: 9). Whether the governed will be citizens or netizens is an intriguing question. The pervasiveness of today's neoliberal market capitalist ideologies is rooted in a quest for focused efficiency; and, in turn, these basic cultural conditions of production are shaping the productive conditions of digitalization as much, or even more, than the boxes and wires themselves are remaking collective infrastructure.

Consequently, one finds that the online *bourgeois* of digital sites appears to have interests, capabilities and goals which appear as antithetical to those commonly shared by the offline *citoyen* of material cities. This flexible geometry of indefinite boundaries, open architectures and unfixed locations online in the 'netropolis' of 'virtual life' constantly contradicts the fixed geometries of definite boundaries, closed communities and inflexible locations offline in the 'polis' still out there in 'the meat world' in 'real life'. Without a re-examination of new technology as lifeworld, we cannot assess the impact of new technologies on our existing lifeworlds (Ihde, 1990).

Netizenship as political culture can unfold within the containment vessels of the polis as digital democracy, electronic voting or online organizing, which would mark the net reshaping the polis to support e-citizenship, e-governance and e-management inside existing territorial jurisdictions (Bryan et al., 1998). Graeme Browning's 'how-to' manual, for example, *Electronic Democracy: Using the Internet to Influence American Politics* (1996), is written to apply the net to this task. This 'cyberage book' has been urging readers since 1996 to use the net 'to reach decision makers at all levels of government, research political issues, and effectively promote your causes' in the ever accelerating effort 'to become a successful online activist'. Yet, the Great Seal of the United States of America on a PC's VDT, and the unfurled Stars and Stripes under the keyboard, as they are photographed on the cover of Browning's manual for e-citizens, are only the first, and most obvious, application of this book's cybernetic remediation of citizens within the polis. Saco's *Cybering Democracy* (2000) addresses many of these concerns quite effectively. The net can also generate innumerable post-national, non-statal, territorial collectives of people in which any given polis is essentially accidental to the wiredness of some new netropolis (Hauben, 1997). The interests of identity and community articulated at www.islamicity.com, for example, are not necessarily the same as those at www.whitehouse.gov, www.senate.gov or www.house.gov. Indeed, the 'actually transnational' qualities of the net starkly contradict the 'nominally national' identities of their users (Reich, 1991).

Nevertheless, such a vision of netizenship is essentially the naive instrumentalist one that imagines ICT connectivity as such creates strong common interests, shared goals or communal values. Everyone on the net allegedly wants unconstrained and free connectivity to something, but sharing access to, and the use of, a set of telematic tools may not automatically create a free and equal fraternity of metanationals. In fact, there are many different varieties of netizens and netizenship, and they are still entangled in the technical dictates of the online interface and the consumerist expectations of offline use. The net is not one system with a single set of functionalities; it is instead a machinic collective of many things, diverse sites and varying capabilities resting upon multiple metanational links between both online and offline communities. And, as a result, many people in most nations end up 'falling through the Net' (National Telecommunications and Information Administration, 1995; 1998; 1999). A shared sense of common goals and interests still is in many ways incomplete, because the typical sources of its definition – a common economic life within shared markets or a common political life under a single sovereign authority that together might realize material security and physical safety – are not yet fully in place (Solomon, 1997). When, however, one's financial life is mostly nested with something like eTrade, one's commercial survival is tied to eBay, one's mass media consumption is dependent upon Yahoo!, one's family ties are maintained through AOL, and one's business affairs are conducted through Commerce One.com, then a transnational basis emerges for discrete, diverse and divided groups to develop a united opposition to offline political interests as well as to other online political forces (Lewis, 1997).

This tendency to normalize the net and its political impact upon society is also found in Wayne Rash Jn.'s *Politics on the Nets: Wiring the Political Process* (1997). His celebration of the Internet highlights its ability to accelerate communication, open up multipoint communication to more audiences, and short-circuit the 'filtering processes' found in the mass media. While all of this is true, these positions tend to ignore other rapid forms of communication, downplay the problems of open multipoint communication, and suggest that the net is not somehow filtered in its workings.

Similarly, Rash apparently believes that the net will be accessible essentially all of the time to just about everyone. Waving off the negative impact of the net on politics, he argues that the democratic base of politics is broadened with the Internet as 'a direct effect of opening electronic communications for the delivery of services and for the reception of interest and opinion' (1997: 152). Because of this alleged openness, 'outside of repressive societies politics and the nets will become one, and as a result it will look a lot like society because it will be a part of society' (1997: 167). This might open up the political process to more political parties and groups, but it is unlikely to open up all domains of the net, or even most key decision-making centres on the net, to everyone simply because technology can drop 'the price of entry onto the National stage to a level that nearly anyone can afford' (1997: 169).

One increasingly may doubt, for example, the status and role of the territorialized national, or 'the citizen' born to subjectivity in a polis, or political structure, while revelling in the statuses and roles of a deterritorialized consumer/producer or 'buyer and seller' fulfilling the subjectivity of the agora or marketplace. As a consumer, it is an easy transition to adopt the status and role of a telematic node, or 'the netizen' whose subjectivity opens in the net. Caught up within many more complex language games, like other nodal points in a network, any individual can be a sender, a receiver and/or a referent in the relays routing informational flows. States with the technoeconomic ability to mount national information infrastructure initiatives, like the United States or Singapore, may do so, and thereby recast the spaces filled by their territorialized nationality to suit telematic nodality. Many regimes, however, lack the industry, initiative and/or infrastructure to transmogrify their constituents' agency or state structures along such nationally informationalized lines. Consequently, other information infrastructure initiatives pursued by hardware makers, transnational telco alliances or dot.com entrepreneurs infiltrate most nations with performative protocols that suit the world's most dominant businesses and great powers.

Some (Ohmae, 1990) celebrate this 'borderless world', others see it as a creative chaos (Kelly, 1994), and still others fear its inhumane/unfair/anti-egalitarian qualities (Virilio, 1997). Most importantly, the older embedded identities of territorial nationality at physical sites are being tested by newer user identities tied to telematic nodes generated for, by and of digital cites (Luke, 1996: 320–39). Where the informational world system has occupied much of the psychosocial space left for the traditional lifeworld, multiculturalist politics remediate the push and pull of nodal social forces (Beck, 1997). A nodal identity permits one to be located practically anywhere, because the net is almost everywhere. The 'Other' is just another 'self', and each self merely another other, always out there everywhere online and offline, so it pays to accept all other identities, communities, platforms and systems in the valorization of bits and commodities (Hillis, 1999). As long as basic connections can be maintained for sending and receiving the discursive core of any multiculturalized identity and community, the foundational referents of such metanational collectivities can easily flow anywhere in national spaces that their carriers' personal and professional lives take them (Everard, 2000; Luke, 1998; Lyotard, 1984).

Furthermore, the disconnection of networked telematic ties from grounded organic traditions could enable new discursive formations beyond those of any nation's kith and kin to reshape human identities in new cybernetic consumption communities formed around shared consumer goods, common mass media, mutual machine uses, coincident aesthetic preferences or parallel market niches (Jones, 1995). Spending one's limited supplies of time online screen-to-screen means not engaging one's attention and energy in the collective life of one's face-to-face coresidents and contemporaries offline. Instead, compatriots in the shared territorial space of a metropolis often can be ignored as more and more e-migrate into cyberspace (Gilster, 1997). In this e-migration, new quarters of the netropolis begin to take shape:

> Thousands of users spend many hours each week 'living' in virtual communities, each with its own residents and laws and even politics. In these virtual communities, users interact with others whom they know only in their online personas, which may be quite different from

who they are in their offline hours; thus the 'residents' of virtual communities are more welcoming – and even more real – than the world with which they spend the rest of their time. (Carter, 1998: 195–6)

Quasi-cultures with some real solidity, therefore, begin to reproduce themselves on a global basis around the e-havior of e-lancing, e-commerce, e-voting, e-governance, and e-learning. Turkle's musings about 'life on the screen' easily support such visions of e-migration out on to the cyberscapes of online environments (Johnson, 1997). In cyberspace, society and community become composite materials concocted out of the various codes, discourses and games composing the bitstream (Horn, 1998). New e-figurations for online collaboration 'blur the boundaries between self and game, self and rule, self and simulation' such that as one player observes, '"you are what you pretend to be ... you are what you play." But people don't just become who they play, they play who they are or who they want to be or who they don't want to be' (Turkle, 1997: 192).

The WYSIWYG aesthetics of a graphic user interface in multitasked, window-driven, cross-platform connectivity out on the nets essentially become 'a powerful new metaphor for thinking about the self as a multiple, distributed system ... The experience of this parallelism encourages treating on-screen and off-screen lives with a surprising degree of equality' (1997: 21). No one single screen necessarily has primacy, and all of them operate in parallel according to the contingent configurations most appropriate at that time for the individuals and groups choosing to collaborate in this or that fashion (Luke, 1989). These tendencies, as Turkle suggests, point to netizens 'taking things at their interface value', or a political culture in which 'people are increasingly comfortable with substituting representations of reality for the real' (1997: 23). Jerry Everard takes on these issues of sovereignty in cyberspace in *Virtual States: the Internet and the Boundaries of the Nation-State* (2000). He quite correctly sees the state persisting into the era of networked economies and societies for quite solid material reasons: state domains, anchor economies and stage wars – all of these practices will continue in cyberspace. So Turkle might be right, but perhaps only within specific parameters.

In reviewing the contradictions of citizenship and netizenship, any analysis must consider newly emergent tendencies and unfolding possibilities. Despite what many would-be netizens claim, the net is still a comparatively small realm of user domains with relatively few hard and fast rules. Virtual life along with e-commerce, e-schooling, and e-governance are quite promising, but from a global perspective only a very privileged few now enjoy such online services. As Markham (1998) notes, real experience in virtual space can be very different from real life offline. Most people remain in the corporeal, material, substantial tracks of a life offline, and nationality

for them continues to be a major determinant of their life chances. Today's rhetorics of universal netizenship, then, must be examined carefully. On one level, these literatures may only be the latest expression for very modern forms of technified utopianism, which embed an enthusiasm for universal access to a new technology at the base of new designs for social transformation. The PC touts in *Wired* only recapitulate the now long-past millenarian dreams spun over the years by railroaders, aviators, radiomen, motorists, rocketeers and TV people in *Popular Mechanics* or *Popular Science*, who have imagined their new technics would remake humanity anew and for the better. On another level, however, successful would-be netizens also seem to be laying the foundations for cyber-secessionist movements from face-to-face markets, urban life, banks, public affairs, schools and social institutions, which only will accentuate and aggravate the already deep splits (Martin and Schumann, 1997; Reich, 1991) between the informationally competent classes (labelled by some as 'symbolic analysts' or 'the successful fifth') and the informationally obsolescent and superfluous classes (recognized by others as the deindustrialized underemployed or even underclass making up the unsuccessful remaining four-fifths of society).

CONCLUSIONS

On the net, one finds points of coincidence, cooperation and cofiguration condensing into new modes of transnational cohabitation – separate and apart from existing maps of familiar behaviours. As online identity and community are turned into normative ideals by information rhetorics and cybertechnics, they will begin to normalize the behaviour of individuals and populations as the behaviour of online game players, Napster users and Usenet regulars all suggest. Consequently, the accumulation of all the net's operational components now constitutes a vast incorporeal engine of agency and structure in virtual realities (Kelly, 1998; Mattelart, 1994). Yet, these online cooperant possibilities are also finding other very concrete means for power to gain actualization, incarnation and effectuation offline in physical bodies and social groups. Being digital online is also digitalizing concrete modes of becoming offline in many remarkable ways. Therefore, the various ethical personae which are made in cyberspace as forms of digital being need to be tracked far more closely.

For three decades, the Internet, or the network of networks that this regrettably singular term still denotes, has evolved, first, in accord with military-bureaucratic plans and then, later, in concord with technical-corporate agendas. In both instances, the net's techno-economic action remains shielded from the demands of democratic legitimation by its own constitution. At the same time, however, it loses its non-political character. It is *neither politics nor non-politics*, but a third entity: economically guided action in pursuit of interests. (Beck, 1992: 222)

On the net, many varieties of economically guided action are pursuing national, corporate and personal monetary interests as performativity, just as Lyotard suggested. These dynamics, in which virtually everything in cyberspace becomes an I-mart, ironically and simultaneously also shield the networks from democratic legitimation, rob them of their non-political character, give them subpolitical powers, and lock their users into performativity games (Mattelart and Mattelart, 1992).

On one level, networks are simply rhetorical representations of various ideological projects, like Michael Dertouzos' 'information marketplace', Bill Gates' 'friction-free capitalism', and Nicholas Negroponte's 'being digital', that dress out cybernetic goods and services in the semantic costumes of more traditional activities. On a second level, networks are a new global infrastructure of material systems – chips and cables, routines and routers, modems and machines all stacked up upon themselves. Such physical assets cannot be discounted entirely from cyberspace, because without these components nothing would operate. And, on a third level, networks are institutionalized entities whose code-carried infostructure coevolves hand-in-hand with its machine-made infrastructure. Control over specific segments of capital, labour, knowledge and communication, however, turns such big informatic systems into public spheres with their own virtual and material assets to serve, protect and defend (Habermas, 1989). Here bits reach out, touch someone, organize something, and then reconstitute both human acts and non-human artifacts into subpolitical clusters of operational performativity. Politics, or who dominates whom, from both the inside and the outside of which systems, becomes the most significant question for any system's designers, owners and users as well as for the citizens of those nations that these networked systems criss-cross.

To explore these questions, this chapter has performed three tasks. First, it re-examined the politics and culture of an online economy and society in the lifeworld made by ICTs where national state structures, corporate market strategies and complex technoscience systems are all promoting highly individualized modes of life. Second, it reconsidered how governing with, and governance through, digital technics create new technically mediated identities and communities tied to online commerce, education and faith out of new media. Third, it reconsidered how existing literatures treat netizenship in contrast to citizenship and it looked at current visions of digital democracy. In many ways, they are imagined only as more flexible, specialized articulations of the televisual consumerist modes of political participation that have developed in the US since the 1950s, or as a much more aterritorial/nonstatal netropolitan life that might lead to forms of netizenship based upon a government by netizens, of the netizenry, and for netizenship in the workings of the net itself (Saco, 2000; Hauben, 1997).

This chapter also approached the question of political culture online by moving past the current literatures, in which governing with cybernetic technologies, by such means as online voting, digital citizenship and cybernetic party building, typically are celebrated. Instead of seeing netizenship as more of the same, only with computers, this discussion sought to problematize the performative sites and operational practices of citizenship by examining how intertwined they are with certain technics, built environments and machinic systems. Digital political behaviours are being imagined in today's cybernetic writings to be just like embodied civic behaviours, but they are not. This recognition must lead us to a more critical exploration of the imbricate coevolution of human subjects and non-human objects in which, first, citizens cannot be easily separated from cities and, second, netizens ought not to be thought about apart from networks. Likewise, such developments in political culture should not be examined apart from the ongoing processes of modernization in which new informational technologies are integrated as part and parcel of new forms of personal agency being valorized by e-commerce and e-government.

REFERENCES

Abbate, Janet (1999) *Inventing the Internet*. Cambridge, MA: MIT Press.

Adams, James (1998) *The Next World War: Computers Are the Weapons and the Frontline is Everywhere*. New York: Simon & Schuster.

Adas, Michael (1989) *Machines as the Measure of Men: Science, Technology, and Ideologies of Western Dominance*. Ithaca, NY: Cornell University Press.

Anderson, Benedict (1991) *Imagined Communities*, rev. edn. London: Verso.

Baudrillard, Jean (1981) *For a Critique of the Political Economy of the Sign*. St Louis: Telos.

Baudrillard, Jean (1993) *The Transparency of Evil: Essays on Extreme Phenomena*. London: Verso.

Beck, Ulrich (1992) *The Risk Society*. London: Sage.

Beck, Ulrich (1997) *The Reinvention of Politics*. Oxford: Polity.

Brin, David (1998) *The Transparent Society*. Reading, MA: Addison-Wesley.

Browning, Graeme (1996) *Electronic Democracy: Using the Internet to Influence American Politics*. Wilson, CT: Pemberton.

Bryan, Cathy, Tsagarousianou, Roza and Tambini, Damian (1998) 'Electronic democracy and the civic networking movement in context', in Roza Tsagarousianou, Damian

Tambini and Cathy Bryan (eds), *Cyberdemocracy: Technology, Cities, and Civic Networks*. London: Routledge.

Bukatman, Scott (1993) *Terminal Identity*. Durham, NC: Duke University Press.

Businessweek (2000) 21 February: 41.

Cairncross, Frances (1997) *The Death of Distance: How the Communications Revolution Will Change Our Lives*. Boston: Harvard Business School Press.

Carter, Stephen (1998) *Civility: Manners, Morals, and the Etiquette of Democracy*. New York: Basic.

Castells, Manuel (1996–8) *The Information Age*, vols I–III. Oxford: Blackwell.

Deibert, Ronald J. (1997) *Parchment, Printing, and Hypermedia: Communication in World Order Transformation*. New York: Columbia University Press.

De Kerckhove, Derrick (1998) *Connected Intelligence: the Arrival of the Web Society*. Toronto: Somerville.

Dertouzos, Michael (1997) *What Will Be: How the New World of Information Will Change Our Lives*. New York: HarperCollins.

Everard, Jerry (2000) *Virtual States: the Internet and the Boundaries of the Nation-State*. London: Routledge.

Feenberg, Andrew (1999) *Questioning Technology*. New York: Routledge.

Foucault, Michel (1980) *History of Sexuality*, vol. I. New York: Vintage.

Foucault, Michel (1988) *Technologies of the Self*. Amherst, MA: University of Massachusetts Press.

Foucault, Michel (1991) *The Foucault Effect: Studies in Governmentality*, edited by Graham Burchell, Colin Gordon and Peter Miller. Chicago: University of Chicago Press.

Gates, Bill (1999) *Business @ the Speed of Thought: Using a Digital Nervous System*. New York: Warner.

Gates, Bill with Norman Myhrvold and Peter Rinearson (1996) *The Road Ahead*. New York: Viking.

Gergen, Kenneth (1991) *The Saturated Self: Dilemmas of Identity in Contemporary Life*. New York: Basic.

Gibson, William (1984) *Neuromancer*. New York: Ace.

Giedion, Siegfried (1948) *Mechanization Takes Command: A Contribution to Anonymous History*. New York: Norton.

Gilder, George (1989) *Microcosm*. New York: Simon & Schuster.

Gilster, Paul (1997) *Digital Literacy*. New York: Wiley.

Grisham, Gordon (1999) *The Internet: a Philosophical Inquiry*. London: Routledge.

Grossman, Wendy (1997) *net.wars*. New York: New York University Press.

Grusin, R. and Bolter, J. (1999) *Remediation: Understanding New Media*. Cambridge, MA: MIT Press.

Habermas, Juergen (1989) *The Structural Transformation of the Public Sphere*. Cambridge, MA: MIT Press.

Harvey, David (1989) *The Condition of Postmodernity*. Oxford: Blackwell.

Hassan, Ihab (1977) 'Prometheus as performer: towards a posthumanist culture', in Michael Benamou and Charles Caramella (eds), *Performance in Modern Change*. Madison, WI: Coda.

Hauben, Michael (1997) *Netizens: on the History and Impact of USENet and the Internet*. Los Alamitos, CA: IEEE Computer Society Press.

Hayles, N. Katherine (1999) *How We Became Posthuman: Virtual Bodies in Cybernetics, Literature, and Informatics*. Chicago: University of Chicago Press.

Heim, Michael (1998) *Virtual Realism*. Oxford: Oxford University Press.

Hillis, Ken (1999) *Digital Sensations: Space, Identity and Experient in Virtual Reality*. Minneapolis: University of Minnesota Press.

Hobart, M. and Schiffman, Z. (1998) *Information Ages*. Baltimore, MD: Johns Hopkins University Press.

Horn, Stacey (1998) *Cyberville*. New York: Warner.

Ihde, Don (1990) *Technology and the Lifeworld: from Garden to Earth*. Bloomington, IN: Indiana University Press.

Jameson, Fredric (1992) *Postmodernism, or the Cultural Logic of Late Capitalism*. Durham, NC: Duke University Press.

Johnson, Steven (1997) *Interface Culture*. San Francisco: Harper Edge.

Jones, Stephen G. (ed.) (1995) *Cybersociety: Computer-Mediated Communication and Community*, 2nd edn. London: Sage.

Jordan, Tim (1999) *Cyberpower: the Culture and Politics of Cyberspace and the Internet*. New York: Routledge.

Kelly, Kevin (1994) *Out of Control: the Rise of Neo-Biological Civilization*. Reading, MA: Addison-Wesley.

Kelly, Kevin (1998) *New Rules for the New Economy*. New York: Viking.

Kroker, A. and Weinstein, M. (1994) *Data Trash: the Theory of the Virtual Class*. New York: St Martin's Press.

Latour, Bruno (1993) *We Have Never Been Modern*. London: Harvester Wheatsheaf.

Levy, Pierre (1997) *Becoming Virtual*. New York: Plenum.

Lewis, T.G. (1997) *The Friction-Free Economy: Marketing Strategies for a Wired World*. New York: Harper Business.

Luke, Timothy W. (1989) *Screens of Power: Ideology, Domination, and Resistance in Informational Society*. Urbana, IL: University of Illinois Press.

Luke, Timothy W. (1994) 'Placing powers/siting spaces: the politics of global and local in the new world order', *Environment and Planning D: Society and Space*, 12: 613–28.

Luke, Timothy W. (1995) 'New world order or neo-world orders: power, politics and ideology in informationalizing glocalities', in Mike Featherstone, Scott Lash and Roland Robertson (eds), *Global Modernities*. London: Sage. pp. 91–107.

Luke, Timothy W. (1996) 'Identity, meaning and globalization: space–time compression and the political economy of everyday life', in Scott Lash, Paul Heelas and Paul Morris (eds), *Detraditionalization: Critical Reflections on Authority and Identity*. Oxford: Blackwell. pp. 109–33.

Luke, Timothy W. (1997) 'The politics of digital inequality: access, capabilities, and distribution in cyberspace', *New Political Science*, 41–2 (Fall): 121–44.

Luke, Timothy W. (1998) 'Running flat out on the road ahead: nationality, sovereignty, and territoriality in the world of the information superhighway', in Gearóid Ó Tuathail and Simon Dalby (eds), *Rethinking Geopolitics*. London: Routledge. pp. 274–94.

Lyon, David (1994) *The Electronic Eye: the Rise of Surveillance Society*. Minneapolis: University of Minnesota Press.

Lyotard, Jean-François (1984) *The Postmodern Condition: a Report on Knowledge*. Minneapolis: University of Minnesota Press.

Markham, Annette (1998) *Life Online: Researching Real Experience in Virtual Space*. Walnut Creek, CA: Altamira.

Martin, Chuck (1997) *The Digital Estate: Strategies for Competing, Surviving and Thriving in an Internet Worked World*. New York: McGraw-Hill.

Martin, Hans-Peter and Schumann, Harald (1997) *The Global Trap: Globalization and the Assault on Democracy and Prosperity*. London: Zed.

Mattelart, Armand (1994) *Mapping World Communication: War, Progress, Culture*. Minneapolis: University of Minnesota Press.

Mattelart, Armand (2000) *Networking the World, 1794–2000*. Minneapolis: University of Minnesota Press.

Mattelart, Armand and Mattelart, Michele (1992) *Rethinking Media Theory*. Minneapolis: University of Minnesota Press.

McLuhan, Marshall (1964) *Understanding Media: the Extensions of Man*. New York: Signet.

Miller, Steven E. (1996) *Civilizing Cyberspace*. New York: ACM Press.

Mitchell, William J. (1995) *City of Bits*. Cambridge, MA: MIT Press.

Mumford, Lewis (1963) *Technics and Civilization*. New York: Harcourt Brace Jovanovich.

Mumford, Lewis (1970) *The Pentagon of Power*. New York: Harcourt Brace.

National Telecommunications and Information Administration (1995) *Falling through the Net: a Survey of 'Have Nots' in Rural and Urban America*. Washington, DC: US Department of Commerce. Available at: http://www.ntia.doc.gov/ntiahome/fallingthru.html.

National Telecommunications and Information Administration (1998) *Falling through the Net II: New Data on the Digital Divide*. Washington, DC: US Department of Commerce. Available at: http://www.ntia.doc.gov/ntiahome/net2/.

National Telecommunications and Information Administration (1999) *Americans in the Information Age: Falling through the Net*. Washington, DC: US Department of Commerce. Available at: http://ntia.doc.gov./ntiahome/digitaldivide/.

Negroponte, Nicholas (1995) *Being Digital*. New York: Knopf.

Nye, David E. (1990) *Electrifying America: Social Meanings of a New Technology*. Cambridge, MA: MIT Press.

Nye, David E. (1996) *The Technological Sublime*. Cambridge, MA: MIT Press.

Ohmae, Kenichi (1990) *The Borderless World: Power and Strategy in the Interlinked Economy*. New York: Harper & Row.

Poster, Mark (1990) *The Mode of Information*. Chicago: University of Chicago Press.

Poster, Mark (1995) *The Second Media Age*. Chicago: University of Chicago Press.

Rash, Wayne Jr (1997) *Politics on the Nets: Wiring the Political Process*. New York: Freeman.

Reich, Robert (1991) *The Work of Nations: Preparing Ourselves for 21st Century Capitalism*. New York: Knopf.

Rheingold, Howard (1993) *The Virtual Community*. Reading, MA: Addison-Wesley.

Rochlin, Gene (1997) *Trapped in the Net: the Unanticipated Consequences of Computerization*. Princeton, NJ: Princeton University Press.

Roszak, Theodore (1994) *The Cult of Information*, 2nd edn. Berkeley, CA: University of California Press.

Rushkoff, Douglas (1994) *Cyberia: Life in the Trenches of Hyperspace*. San Francisco: HarperCollins.

Rutsky, R.L. (2000) *High Techuê: Art and Technology from the Machine Assistance to the Postman*. Minneapolis: University of Minnesota Press.

Saco, Diana (2000) *Cybering Democracy*. Minneapolis: University of Minnesota Press.

Schneider, Greg (2000) 'Net firms get down to business', *Washington Post*, 5 April: 61, 16.

Shapiro, Andrew (1999) *The Control Revolution*. New York: Public Affairs Press.

Shenk, David (1997) *Data Smog*. San Francisco: Harper Edge.

Slevin, James (2000) *The Internet and Society*. Oxford: Polity.

Slouka, Mark (1995) *War of the Worlds: Cyberspace and the High-Tech Assault on Reality*. New York: Basic.

Smith, Gary and Kollock, Peter (1999) *Communities in Cyberspace*. New York: Routledge.

Solomon, Elinore Harris (1997) *Virtual Money: Understanding the Power and Risks of Money's High-Speed Journey into Electronic Space*. Oxford: Oxford University Press.

Stefnik, Mark (1999) *The Internet Edge: Social, Technical, and Legal Challenges for a Networked World*. Cambridge, MA: MIT Press.

Tapscott, Don (1996) *The Digital Economy: Promise and Peril in an Age of Networked Intelligence*. New York: McGraw-Hill.

Tapscott, Don (1997) *Growing up Digital: the Rise of the Net Generation*. New York: McGraw-Hill.

Turkle, Sherry (1997) *Life on the Screen: Identity in the Age of the Internet*. New York: Touchstone.

Van der Pjil, Kees (1998) *Transnational Classes and International Relations*. London: Routledge.

Virilio, Paul (1995) *The Art of the Motor*. Minneapolis: University of Minnesota Press.

Virilio, Paul (1997) *Open Sky*. London: Verso.

Walker, R.B.J. (1993) *Inside/Outside: International Relations as Political Theory*. Cambridge: Cambridge University Press.

31

Social Relationships and Identity Online and Offline

DON SLATER

The very idea of approaching the new media in terms of a sharp distinction between the online and the offline has given research in this area a peculiar profile. In contrast to the typically panicked reception of older new media technologies (telephone, television), fearful of their ill effects on social relationships and identities, the Internet has posed the possibility of entirely new relationships and identities, constituted within new media, and in competition with ostensibly non-mediated, older forms of relationship. In this respect, the new media have been studied less as media that are used within existing social relations and practices, and more as a new social space which constitutes relations and practices of its own. The research agenda from this point of view focuses not on the characteristics and uses of these media as means of communication but rather on the kinds of social life and cultures that they are capable of sustaining, and how these specifically online socialities relate to the 'offline world'. Even more broadly, the 'online' side of this distinction has often been understood not simply in terms of what its 'inhabitants' do but as something like a unified 'cyberculture' with patterns of sociality that seem automatically to flow from the nature of the technology itself.

This kind of language characterized the early literature on the Internet, to a greater or lesser extent, up to the late 1990s, though it is now in decline. As a result, the burden of this chapter is not so much to present what has been 'discovered' about the difference between online and offline, or their impact on each other. Rather, it needs to show how and why that distinction has coloured the new media research agenda, and how and why it is being deconstructed. That is to say, the distinction has not

been sustained, and is probably more symptomatic of an historical period than fruitful as a methodological presumption. Moreover, it is possible that the reasons the distinction has not been sustained have as much to do with actual changes in the nature and social place of the new media as they have to do with analytical weaknesses in the distinction itself.

DISTINGUISHING LIFE ONLINE

Christine Hine (2000) distinguishes between regarding the Internet as a culture and as a cultural artifact. The latter perspective, as developed through the sociology of science and technology, involves investigating the co-configuration of objects and social contexts, and hence considering how a technology may be interpreted as to its social and technical potentials. In this case, one is looking at how a means of communication is used within an offline social world. On the other hand, to study the Internet as culture means regarding it as a social space in its own right, rather than as a complex object used within other, contextualizing spaces. It means looking at the forms of communication, sociality and identity that are produced within this social space, and how they are sustained using the resources available within the online setting. Mark Poster (1995a; 1995b) has made a related distinction between the Internet as a tool, and hence part of a modernist orientation to the new media as something used instrumentally within wider social projects; and the Internet as a postmodern space of transformation, in which the subject of communication is transformed within the process of communicating. Poster usefully contrasts different uses and media within the Internet (e-mail used at the office is not likely to have the same identity implications as intense involvement in a MUD [multi-user dungeon]), but his distinction, like Hine's, implies that both analysts and participants can orient themselves to what might otherwise be just another medium as if it were a meaningful social space or cyberspace. There is a strong argument that, although past media have also seemed to constitute new forms and spaces of sociality, even virtualities (McLuhan, 1974; Standage, 1999), they have quickly been absorbed into everyday practices as utilities, or that they lacked some qualities that render the new media more capable of sustaining complex social spaces. Certainly, it is this feature of the Internet – mythologized as 'cyberspace' – that has been considered unique and revolutionary to new media, and therefore its key characteristic to be investigated. It is not a medium but a place to be or to dwell.

Ironically, early studies of computer-mediated communications emphasized how their apparent lack of online cues as to offline settings and identities resulted in an impoverished and anarchic asociality, reflected in poor social order and group efforts (see, for example, Baym in this volume; Hine, 2000; Jones, 1995). The irony is that this detachment from offline context is precisely what grounded the greatest claims for online sociality as both a vehicle for liberating social order and facilitating group effort. The latter is exemplified not just by mundane intranets, but also by the kind of shareware and open source software efforts that led a Microsoft employee to acknowledge that Linux could mobilize the 'combined IQ of the Internet' to solve its technical problems.

The claim that the new media sustain online social spaces that can be inhabited and investigated relatively independently of offline social relations has been advanced on quite various grounds, and from the earliest days of the Internet. We can summarize them in terms of four properties: virtuality, spatiality, disembedding and disembodiment. Each of these emphasizes a radical disjuncture between online and offline relationships and identities. However, we need to be clear from the outset that each of these dimensions has often been put forward as a characterization of the new media: they are generally stated as if they were intrinsic properties of the media themselves, and hence ways of investigating their specificity as new mediations of social life. The problem, as we will discuss later, is that they attempt to specify the properties of the new media independently of the particular social uses and networks in which they are embedded, as things in themselves from which particular uses (or effects) naturally flow. Two obvious fallacies arise from this. The first is a technological determinism. The second is an assumption that the Internet is a unified

phenomenon, whereas it is in fact quite a diversity of software and hardware technologies which can be used differently and in different combinations. Quite simply: the use of ICQ or other chat systems by Indonesian parents as opposed to American teenagers is likely to be determined by more than simply the technology; while the same American teenagers or Indonesian parents may regard ICQ as opposed to websites completely differently with respect to virtuality, spatiality and so on.

Virtuality

First, the ideas of virtuality and simulation evoke the construction of a space of representation that can be related to 'as if' it were real, and therefore effects a separation from, or even replacement of, the 'really real'. It therefore contrasts with several terms that might characterize the offline world: 'real', 'actual' and 'material' being the central ones (Shields, 2000). The extreme point of virtuality, which exercised much of the early literature, is the idea of 'virtual reality': a space of representations in which all one's senses are exposed to coordinated representations such that the experience is completely immersive (though not mistaken for a 'real' one) and the participant can respond to stimuli as if to a real world that behaves consistently, in a rule-governed, non-arbitrary manner. Paradoxically, this literal notion of virtual reality as immersive multimedia (for example, Springer, 1991) was contemporary with an Internet whose virtuality was almost entirely textual, immersive not because of its sensory but rather because of its social and intellectual character: cybersex, for example, was a virtual reality not because it literally simulated sexual experiences but because it allowed for absorbing interactive narratives based on the quasi-presence of the other and their participation in constructing a text. Moreover, this sense of the online as a virtual space was largely exemplified by MUDs and MOOs which in fact descended very directly from offline role-playing fantasy games in which a limited number of rules could constitute a bounded, shared world and generate an unpredictable infinity of behaviours which nonetheless made sense as part of a consistent shared reality (Fine, 1983). We might also compare the notion of virtuality with theories of film realism, which also focus on the textual generation of internally consistent and hence absorbing worlds (Kuhn, 1982; MacCabe, 1985).

Hence, the focus moved from the virtual as simulation to the virtual as a coherent social space, and one in which new rules and ways of being and relating could emerge precisely because of the separation from the constraints of the 'really real'. We can flesh this out through the remaining three terms: spatiality, disembedding and disembodiment.

Spatiality

Closely related to virtuality was the apparent ability of the new media to constitute a place, or places. 'Cyberspace' captures the sense of a social setting that exists purely within a space of representation and communication – software, the network – and therefore does not map clearly onto offline spaces. At the same time, cyberspace itself can, and indeed must, be mapped.

Virtuality is a spatially ambiguous experience. *Where* is cyberspace? It exists entirely within a computer space, distributed across increasingly complex and fluid networks. An experience of early Internet users was the difficulty of understanding that clicking on a hypertext link could take you to a file anywhere in the world – it could be on your own computer or in another hemisphere – and it did not matter: a new and integrated space was being encountered whose coordinates related to a different physics. Indeed, the spatiality of cyberspace largely resides in the connections which make up the network. However, the boundaries of the network are themselves ambiguous and converge with other technologies, relations and information. Hence, some of the literature (Imken, 1999) prefers to talk of the 'matrix' to indicate an extended electronic and informational space that is considerably wider than the Internet, and one less easily split into offline and online. The spatial qualities of the online are in any case highly variable and contradictory (Crang, 1997). For example, on the one hand there is a stress on its complexity, its seemingly inexhaustible range and speed of movement, its unmappability (Dodge and Kitchen, 2000), which seem to render it a space to explore or discover but never comprehend. This enhances metaphors of the online as a truly new domain. On the other hand, the representations through which the virtual is constructed and experienced are famously domestic and simplifying. Far from the abstract data representations which inhabited Gibson's (1984) original vision of cyberspace, the real virtual is talked about in terms of rooms, places, sites; and accessed through browsers and portals intended to make the space coherent in terms of individual and largely consumerist interests.

Finally, the network organization of new media itself implies a new kind of spatiality which might be separate from yet transformative of offline social organization. Based on point-to-point communication rather than broadcast models, the new media appear both as non-hierarchical and as evading offline hierarchies. There appears to be an inexorable technological push in the direction of horizontal connections which are uncontrollable: for example, there is the rise of peer-to-peer networking (e.g. Gnutella) in which connections are entirely distributed to individual users, thereby bypassing any central organizing technical or social institution and hence any physical, real-world location that can be held accountable.

Disembedding and Community

The most obvious feature of computer-mediated communications is that it allows communications between people who are spatially dispersed. The important factor in a chat room is not where in the world you are, but how you are using the communicative facilities at your disposal. The irrelevance of geographical position to Internet communication is often referred to as 'disembedding'. For example, in using a MUD or a chat facility such as ICQ one is effectively removed or separated from one's immediate locale ('disembedded'), which becomes irrelevant to the ongoing interaction. At the same time, the MUD or ICQ channel constitutes a new context of communication. It is inhabited by people who may be widely dispersed, but they share a context, rules and often a history of communication, and can properly treat their interactions as real, as having consequences (at least within the Internet context) and as valued.

The notion of 'disembedding' arose prior to and outside new media debates as a characterization of central features of modernity. In the work of Giddens (1990) and Thompson (see also Slevin, 2000), in particular, it is related to two communications-related developments: time–space compression, whereby increasing speed of interconnection (whether by penny post or electronic instant messaging) shortens the effective social distance between any connected points; and time–space distanciation, in which local times and spaces are melded into increasingly homogeneous global units of measurement which coordinate highly dispersed activities to a unified beat (attempts to establish a single 'Internet time' are a very literal version of this, characteristically the initiative of a private watch-making corporation, Swatch). In fact, it could be argued that the most prestigious model for understanding the Internet in these terms long predated it: Marshall McLuhan's (1974) idea of 'the global village'. McLuhan argued that electronic media (radio and television in his time) created a sense of simultaneity: an event portrayed on TV was happening in every living room where a TV was turned on, at the same time. This, along with the properties of the specific media, produced new forms of involvement and participation in which, as in the village, everyone could be present at the same event at the same time. Time was obliterated and spatial separation no longer had any impact on communication. The Internet added to the simultaneous reception of television the interactivity of online social relations (Kitchen, 1998: 15). The apparent annihilation of space online promotes a sense of co-presence, that people can be present to each other in a way that corresponds to face-to-face interaction. To the extent that this co-presence is a function of the technology, it makes sense that it is socially enacted through media-specific communicative conventions, for example, flaming, smilies or 'netiquette' (e.g., Danet, 1998).

The notion of disembedding gave rise to one of the largest sets of claims about life online: that new media could sustain communities whose existence was largely or entirely virtual. Rheingold (1993), for example, argued that cyberspace was capable of constituting all the diversity of offline interaction and exchange:

> There is no such thing as a single, monolithic, online subculture; it's more like an ecosystem of subcultures, some frivolous, others serious. The cutting edge of scientific discourse is migrating to virtual communities, where you can read the electronic pre-preprinted reports of molecular biologists and cognitive scientists. At the same time, activists and educational reformers are using the same medium as a political tool. You can use virtual communities to find a date, sell a lawn-mower, publish a novel, conduct a meeting.

This disembedding could be seen as highly positive in many respects. Above all, the process of disembedding could be interpreted as freeing one from the confines of one's immediate location, empowering participants to connect with anyone from anywhere in the world on the basis of common interests or pleasures. A specifically post-modern politics and sociality was enacted in these elective communities, mobile sociality or neotribes (Bauman, 1990; Maffesoli, 1996). This capacity for online community could be variously framed: as transcending and overcoming the fragmented and anomic character of contemporary offline life through the postmodern equivalent of utopian communities; as reinvigorating qualities such as democracy, debate and self-organization in offline life (e.g. the use of the Internet to foster political participation, knowledge and accountability); as vying with offline life by claiming greater reality or value; or, negatively, as contributing to processes that drain offline sociality of its remaining communality (by replacing, disembodying, mediating, increasing fragmentation).

Disembodiment and Identity

Just as going online seemed to detach one from place, it also seemed to detach one from the body. 'Disembodiment' signifies that a person's online identity is apparently separate from their physical presence, a condition associated with two features: textuality and anonymity. Although new channels of communication such as voice over IP and video conferencing are becoming available on the Internet, most communication between people has thus far been textual, at most complemented by some graphics. In a chat channel a person is only known to others through what they type and their claims about themselves cannot be verified or contradicted by their body and its expressions. Indeed, the phrase 'you are what you type' summed up the sense that a person's online performance of identity had to be taken at face value, if only because there is no other information to go on. This conspicuously includes such visible markers of sex, 'race' and age which, in offline interactions, fix identities in bodies. At the same time, online presence is apparently disembodied in the broader sense that it can be detached from other ways in which offline presences are held stable and accountable: names, addresses, one's past relationships and biography as they are fixed through e.g. law, credentials, memberships (including marriages). Simply, online identities are potentially anonymous with respect to one's offline identity, to which it might be very difficult to trace one's online performance.

Hence, much experience and discussion of online relationships is framed by the simple issue of deception and authenticity: on what basis should one believe that anyone online is who they claim to be; and can relationships that are plagued by this degree of doubt (or gullibility) be treated as serious and 'real' relationships? The alternative position, which characterizes the 'cyberlibertarianism' that dominated much of the early experience of new media disembodiment, is to treat it as an occasion to deconstruct the entire notion of authenticity, particularly in so far as it involves fixing the reality of identities through their embodiment (a manoeuvre that is fundamental to essentialisms such as racism and sexism). In this reading, the new media provide a space for four kinds of separation and liberation from prior identities and relationships: first, one can perform whatever identity one chooses (I can be a man, a woman or an extraterrestrial toad); second, one can create entirely new identities that are impossible or inconceivable in offline worlds constrained by social and bodily physics (famously, I can be one of seven different sexes on Lambda-MOO); third, because all presences online are textual they are also self-evidently *performances*, and therefore one can be liberated from the concept of authenticity itself, and enter a different ethics and politics, that of performance; and, finally, this ethics and politics, in its most prevalent version, is carried out by 'cyborg' or 'hybrid' identities: they are defined not by a fixed and monadic individualization but rather by fluidity and interconnection. Cyberspace appeared as the site of a sociology of the future, in which identities are mobile, fluid and openly experienced as performative rather than authentic.

This programme is incomprehensible if not related to poststructuralist traditions, particularly in their conjunction with feminism. That is to say, new media spaces appeared as locations in which to practise and observe operations of deconstruction and performativity that long predated them, as will be discussed below.

INVESTING IN LIFE ONLINE

All of these claims need careful critique and qualification, as we will argue. However, it is also crucial to recognize that the online/offline distinction that they underwrite is not simply an academic one: it also has a powerful cultural and political status. A wide range of constituencies have had a considerable investment in establishing the alterity and newness of the new media as a social space. The very notion of 'cyberspace' was a screen onto which were projected many potent fears and hopes.

First, historical accounts of early Internet users reveal a strange counter-cultural world that comprised remnants and echoes of 1960s libertarian counter-culture; the emergent nerd culture of university engineering and computer science departments; and an unusually wide range of youth subcultures (including games subcultures) (Kitchen, 1998; Turkle, 1984). This very characterization of the origins of 'cyberculture' should cast doubt on the online/offline distinction. Cyberculture did not spring out of the intrinsic characteristics of new media, but arose from possibilities in virtuality that were recognized by games-playing cultures (e.g. 'Doom' and 'Quake', but also pre-Internet, BBS experiences of online poker; and before that 'Dungeons and Dragons'); science fiction and fantasy (cyberpunk); fashions in subcultural music and dress such as techno, rave, postpunk grunge and feminist music (e.g. riotgrrrls); new decentralized models of political organization; and many more. 'Cyberculture' was never a unified online culture but a highly diverse amalgam of cultural conjunctures, not all of which originated in the new media.

What these loose strands of cyberculture certainly converged around was an ethos that focused on a wide range of (often incompatible) freedoms. Net libertarianism involved a claim to total freedom in two senses: the civic sense of the right to any kind of speech, interaction and association, and an opposition to all censorship (which, unlike in offline life, seemed to be technologically guaranteed under the notion that the net treats censorship as 'noise' and routes itself around it, rendering itself invulnerable to offline sources of regulation and prohibition); and the sense of the free circulation of things, without conventional property rights or *prices* (Ross, 1998; Slater, 2000b). The latter was exemplified in such notions as the Internet as a 'gift economy' (an inexorable wave of the future that would engulf the older offline economy e.g.,

Barbrook, 1999), and in a disregard for intellectual property rights in favour of shareware and open systems. As in any libertarianism, the net version could bring together populisms of the far right and left in an agreed opposition to any form of hierarchy, governmental or corporate. There could be no clearer or wilder invocations of the online world as a place of freedom and alterity than John Perry Barlow's famous Declaration of Independence of Cyberspace or the fight against the Communications Decency Act. It is no surprise that this libertarianism, like so many previous ones (Brown, 1997; Ross, 1998), saw itself as inhabiting a new frontier territory or Wild West, embracing a claim to defend a new *space* (Rheingold, 1993, subtitled his book *Homesteading on the Electronic Frontier*). It was both ungoverned (or self-governed) and in principle ungovernable by any but its own inhabitants.

Second, cyberspace as different converged with another agenda: new economy and the dematerialization of economic relations and flows. Again, it is ironic that postmoderns and business consultants alike, and odd figures in between such as *Wired*'s Kevin Kelly or Demos's Geoff Mulgan, could all assert that the new media constituted a vanguard socioeconomic space in which the principles of the future could be discerned: connectivity (or 'connexity', as Mulgan (1998) put it), networking, disintermediation, dematerialization, etc. Online would come to engulf and overtake the offline.

Third, as indicated above, the online/offline distinction offers the space for a practical exploration or even realization of an intellectual trajectory that draws on poststructuralism, postmodernism and (post)feminism. The agenda is to deconstruct the notion of real and authentic identities (particularly notions which anchor them in nature, reason or the body) in favour of a model of identity as performance. As a corollary it has generally involved an embrace of decentring or fragmentation: if a depth model of real identities generated by a core reality is rejected as oppressive and false, then an embrace of fluid identities defined by shifting associations, connections and boundaries constitutes both a politico-ethical strategy and a new kind of truth. For example, both Butler (1990; 1993) and Haraway (1990) are centrally concerned with the critique of conventional politics of representation which presumes 'real' identities ('woman', 'black', 'gay') that can be more or less truthfully represented (in politics or discourses). New media point to other forms of representation and corresponding organization in which people identify themselves through performances structured by their interaction with constantly changing, and not necessarily human (machines, networks, objects), others. Haraway's 'cyborg' has wide currency as the hero of new media politics: an ever monstrous structure because it challenges the authenticity of all identities by existing, fluidly, at the borders between them. A further step, exemplified by Sadie

Plant's (1995; 1996; 1997) work, has been to identify this performative and connective model of identity, and its privileged enactment online, as an essentially feminine modality, and hence interpret the Internet as a fundamentally feminine space, a femininity evoked and discerned through metaphors of weaving, networking and diffusion. Indeed, Plant's imagery was largely a rendering of Irigaray's brand of psychoanalytic feminism, transferred from the act of writing to the interactivity of the new media. In all these versions, new media appear as a space apart from offline life from which can be launched both critiques of the conventional world and explorations of alternative ways of being, acting and relating.

This political-intellectual investment in a separable cyberspace is highly paradoxical, particularly in respect to the issue of bodies and identities. Amidst much celebration of a deconstruction or liberation from identities fixed in bodies, often traced to modern materialism and scientism, cyberlibertarianism nonetheless also seems to proclaim the technical realization of the Enlightenment dream of mind/body dualism, and a liberation of mind from body (Lupton, 1995), a separation which is experienced as both pleasure and terror (Hayles, 1999). Moreover, in consonance with the same Enlightenment relation to the world, cyberspace seems to promise a technical mastery, or transcendence, of mind over body, in which you can really be whatever you conjure up or type; the limits of offline physicality are escaped and remade by mind and desire. Several authors have interpreted this extravagant fantasy as a compensatory and escapist response to experiences of fragmentation and loss of control within people's broader social life. Robins (1995: 136), for example, argues that in much cyberutopian and cyborg literature, cyberspace appears as a place untouched by 'the social and political turbulence of our time', to which its inhabitants respond either by conjuring up a 'unified subjectivity', fusion and unmediated community, or alternatively by celebrating the dissolution of all unities as an occasion for pleasure, play and fantasies of creative mastery and total gratification.

This paradoxical relationship of online transcendence to offline fragmentation seems somewhat confirmed by the widespread observation that much, if not most, online behaviour does not conform to cyberlibertarian expectations. That is to say, it may well be that poststructuralist deconstructions and postmodern diagnoses of bodies and identities are completely correct, as are the hopes they place in practices which alter the terms of identity performance, but this does not mean that actual new media users are in fact engaged in anything like this. Springer (1996) and Bassett (1997) both offer an analysis in which the experience of disembodiment not only does not produce experimental identities but actually results in hypergendered performances. In the MUD self-descriptions

analysed by Bassett, although participants were offered a wide choice of genders (far more than two) they almost invariably described themselves in hypermasculine or hyperfeminine terms. If anything, the lack of constraint on online performance provided an occasion to realize, in fantasy, the most conventional offline gender aspirations. Slater's (Rival et al., 1998; Slater, 1998; 2000a and b) work replicates this finding of conventionality: the concern of participants in an apparently unconstrained social scene for sexually explicit fantasies and representations was overwhelming the maintenance of a conventional normativity which included both ethical conservatism and sexual boundaries drawn from the conventions of offline pornography (homophobic, woman as sexually insatiable); moreover, even where there was creative exploration of sexuality it was highly regulated and strategically wedded to issues of authenticity (performance was treated as untruth). Claudia Springer analyses the hypergendering of identities not only in cyberspace but also in popular culture generally as a reaction to the problematization of the body and sexuality that is completely opposite to that expected by cyberutopians: it is precisely because the production of unambiguously sexed and heterosexual bodies is at the centre of social identities (not just sexual but national, racial and so on) that any problematization of the body will provoke fear and retrenchment. The body is indeed becoming more problematic as the essential ground of identity: it really is becoming more cyborg and merged with technology, revealed as performance, reconstructed through feminism and new sexualities. It is precisely *because* various new technologies such as the Internet make the body problematic that people exaggerate, rather than abandon, gender. The response is not an embrace of new possibilities but an attempt to act out these threatened identities on an intensified scale through a renewed assertion of mind over body. None of this should be surprising on the basis of a more reasonable reading of Butler (and Haraway) than is typical of much of the more utopian literature. Butler's work, after all, stresses the regulation of performance through discourses and powers such as compulsory heterosexuality, which bolt the entire normativity of sexuality–gender–sex in place, and might be expected to do so ever more urgently as this regulatory structure is technologically challenged.

VIRTUALITY AS PRACTICE

Much discussion of online social relations and identities seems to seek a highly generalized answer, and therefore tends to technological determinism: the impression is that by virtue of going online one is automatically involved in new social processes. It can be quite difficult to avoid this kind of logic. For example, Baym, in this volume, argues against the early research assumption that media characteristics will have determining effects on interaction, asserting that 'there are many other contributors to online interpersonal dynamics'. This apparently uncontroversial statement unfortunately entirely misses the problem about arguing from media characteristics: how can we possibly identify the properties of a medium independently from how people use and understand these facilities? (The case of short text messaging on mobile phones will surely count as the classic case: this 'medium characteristic' simply *did not exist* – for the phone designers, telecoms companies, industry analysts and government regulators – until it was 'discovered' apparently spontaneously by hordes of teenagers.) Reducing 'media characteristics' to one 'variable' amongst others simply underwrites, rather than deconstructs, the crude positivism of such approaches. How can 'media characteristics' be counted as one variable lined up alongside 'contexts, users and the choices those users make' when I, for one, cannot identify the former except as it emerges through the latter? Baym instead treats 'users' perceptions of CMC and their 'desires' as just another variable (however 'central') rather than as a core analytical issue. Moreover, Baym treats the move from the earlier assumption to current research as if it were a move from simplistic thinking to an appreciation of diversity, which also misses the point. The problem was not that the earlier approaches were simplistic, and that complexifying them by throwing in more 'variables' would solve anything. Rather, what we need are more rich and integrated accounts of the social relations which generate and might make sense of these 'variables'. Such integrated accounts will only emerge from deep ethnographic studies of particular social groups with real histories, and cannot emerge from abstract, mechanistic and culturally impoverished social psychological typologies of 'group differences'.

What is really required, therefore, is a move from asking about 'the nature of online relationships and identities', to asking the entirely different question: 'What do people do online?': the former already presumes a difference and a specificity (it presumes 'media characteristics'), the latter is an open-ended investigation. Above all, it leaves open the possibility that the relationship between online and offline social processes is an issue *for participants* or users and that they may come up with quite different responses to it. Hence, concepts like 'virtuality' or 'cyberspace' can be treated as (one possible) result of people's practices.

The classic example of this approach is also one of the earliest: Sherry Turkle's (1995) *Life on the Screen* gives a view of fairly extreme involvement in simulated environments – MUDs and MOOs – which are bounded and contained but allow for intense attachment to constructed identities, both of self and other. At the limit point, 'real life' (RL) is simply one 'window' on the screen, equal in investment and validity to any of the virtual lives going on in other (mudding) windows. What is interesting about Turkle's work is that, largely by virtue of her psychological orientation and interview-based material, she focuses less on presumed intrinsic features of the media and much more on how (and indeed why) participants construct and invest in these online lives. She construes these involvements as a developmental or therapeutic stage in the overall development of a participant's identity and social capacities. The value of immersive online participation to the participant is linked to the notion of a 'moratorium': a time, and in this case space, in which actions are protected from the realities of consequences, commitments and accountability (at least to outside agents: there is clearly an often intense ethics internal to the scene). Participants in her account may not be aware of the therapeutic or strategic function of their involvement: it's simply an absorbing game, played with gusto. On the other hand, interviews consistently raise a sense of liberation from the confines of real-world identities which are often self-characterized as inadequate – shy, geeky, unattractive, unassertive, etc. The projective space of online life is a relief.

Turkle is therefore observing how participants are using certain communicative potentials and constructing social spaces according to the need for a strategic separation from real life. Her work has a clearly normative dimension: identification with online life has a therapeutic potential but this is entirely compromised when participants confuse online experimentation with real life and as it were refuse to re-emerge. In contrast to much cyberculture which refuses to give greater ontological, ethical or social status to 'real life', Turkle is clear that the distinction is essential to mental health.

From Turkle's book one can build up a very simple and common-sense view of a normative relation between online and offline experiences and their valuation by participants: immersive experiences, in which identity and sociality are treated with deep seriousness, give way to, for example, more instrumental uses of the Internet, clearly integrated into everyday life (Poster, 1995a); or playful uses of virtual spaces but with greater irony, less involvement or seriousness.

In this approach, virtuality is not a premise or assumed feature of the Internet; on the contrary, it is a social accomplishment – something that participants may or may not choose to do or to value, and which they need to accomplish through highly reflexive skills in using the communicative potentials of the various Internet media. The important questions then become: why and when do participants choose to construct 'cyberspaces' as separate from other spheres of social action, and to what extent; how do they accomplish this; and how do they understand the ensuing relationships?

We might contrast the world Turkle investigates with Miller and Slater's (2000) ethnography of Internet use in relation to Trinidad. By starting from people's practice, rather than presumptions about media characteristics such as virtuality, it became clear that the online/offline distinction played little if any role in people's use or experience of the Internet: people integrated the various Internet media into existing social practices and identities. For example, rather than using the Internet as a vehicle of disembedding from local context and Trinidadian identity, they consistently used it as a means of enacting and furthering their 'Trinidadian-ness'; indeed, it was the site for a considerable intensification of their awareness of themselves as 'Trini'. Entirely online relationships were often treated as being in the same plane as offline rela-tionships, and were integrated with them; or rela-tionships (e.g. amongst schoolchildren) were pursued seamlessly from offline to online and back again. On the other hand, we were able to interpret the Trinidadian use of the Internet as part of a desire to overcome the virtuality of Trinidad *prior* to the Internet. As a highly diasporic country, as well as one forged through dislocations of slavery, inden-tured labour and economic and political migration, it was always an identity that had to be constructed virtually, over distance, as an idea or 'imagined community' (Anderson, 1986). The Internet was widely experienced as a highly mundane tool for sustaining Trinidadian relationships and identities in very concrete ways: a family dispersed across several continents could use e-mail to keep a con-stant, everyday contact and hence sense of a 'house-hold' that was previously impossible; Trinidadians living 'away' could perform key aspects of their culture in chat rooms (the verbal banter of 'ole talk'; the fluid sociality of 'liming'). Hence, far from being virtual, Trinidadian use of the Internet aimed at realizing concretely a *previously* virtual identity (Slater, in press 2002).

The minimal place of the online/offline distinc-tion in Trinidad is not an argument against this dis-tinction as such (any more than the cyber literature can sustain an argument for it). Rather it is an argument that virtuality is one possible, but not neces-sary, emergent feature of people's assimilation of a new medium, and has to be established empirically in any given case. It is also crucial to recognize that the question of virtuality and the status of online identities and relationships are frequently a matter of extensive, articulate and reflexive discussion amongst participants in particular Internet settings. For example, Slater (1998; 2000a and b) looked at complex understandings and negotiations over the meaning and value of online relationships and 'objects'. One of the most vivid case studies of

reflexive understandings of the ambiguity of online realities is Julian Dibbell's (1994; 1998) 'rape in cyberspace' article. The female-presenting avatar of a long-term female participant in a MUD is textu-ally 'raped' by a male-presenting character. The woman involved is extremely upset and at the same time feels distinctly odd about being upset over a virtual event, something occurring in a purely tex-tual space with no bodily or offline consequences. She is absolutely clear that this was not a real rape, and should not be treated as such; she is equally clear that as a virtual event it has serious conse-quences for herself and for the online social order in which she and others have made significant per-sonal and social investments. This involvement in the virtual is socially new and unexplored: its mean-ing has to be framed both in its own right (much of the discussion is about how the MUD responded as an online community) and in relation to other reali-ties. Finally, Dibbell's article posed the issue of the textuality of online life. Libertarian arguments are frequently based on a radical separation between what one says/portrays and what one physically does (e.g. pornography as textual space of fantasy is something other than an act of rape). Investment in virtuality seriously clouds this issue in that the con-stituted reality of the place arises from texts as shared actions: they do not represent something else, but constitute something new. The question Dibbell's article raised is about the ambiguous status of that something. (For a further discussion of the framing of online 'rape' in relation to different brands of online feminism, see Ward, 2000.)

METHODOLOGIES

The lines are drawn between the online and the offline as much by methodology as by theory, poli-tics and culture. As previously indicated, the ques-tion originally addressed to the new media was, ironically, whether or not they were so situationally impoverished as to render them unfit for sociality; and comparison with face-to-face interaction, as if it were a normative standard ('pure', 'unmediated'), persists. Hence, methodological tools for investigat-ing the means for achieving sustained interaction and understanding have been crucial. As it became apparent that interaction not only was sustained but evinced a seemingly unique and emergent culture specific to these media as social spaces, the research agenda became extremely skewed towards phenomena that were, by definition, internal to online relationships and identities. Some of this research has focused on analysis of the textuality of interaction (e.g. Danet, 2001, looks at the playful use of signs, graphics, timing, indexical references and staging in what she treats literally as theatrical performance). There has been a great interest in phenomena such as smilies and netiquette which attempt to, respectively, compensate for absent physical cues and regulate interaction in situationally appropriate ways. The conversational and contextually detached character of chat has also been ripe for ethnomethodological treatment, though less than one might expect.

However, the overwhelmingly dominant approach has been loosely ethnographic or participant observation in character. This has significantly been in part a result of the fact that the literature was generated by both academics and non-academics who were themselves learning the new media by exploring them and therefore could not (or would not) detach their analysis from the participation that generated it. More than this, however, the claim that CMC settings can sustain rich, durable and new forms of sociality invites the claims to community we have already investigated and, following closely on their heels, the correlate claim that ethnography is the way to study community. Ethnography carries with it assumptions about community and bounded social spaces that both seemed appropriate to the Internet and at the same time framed it in a very particular way, as a social space that could be examined in its own right, as internally meaningful and understandable in its own terms. The invocations to both community and ethnography arose very early indeed and arose in similar spaces (examples might include: Reid, 1991; Bruckman and Resnick, 1993; Jones, 1995; Reid, 1995; Baym, 1996; Hamman, 1995; Kling, 1996; Agre and Schuler, 1997; Borden and Harvey, 1998; van Dijk, 1998; Markham, 1998; Cherny, 1999; Smith and Kollock, 1999): MUDs, virtual communities such as the WELL and crossovers such as LambdaMOO. Ethnography meant participation in online communities, often supported by online interviews, with a view to learning online ways of being and doing: just as with a bounded face-to-face community, one could understand the history, language, rules and values of a newsgroup or MUD by participating in it. This version of online ethnography took literally the extrapolation of 'community' to 'cyberspace', and therefore made two assumptions that rested on a radical separation between online and offline: that online sociality really had this kind of cultural coherence; and that either describing or accounting for it entirely in its own terms was a valid and fruitful enterprise. The first assumption seemed to presume what had to be established (cultural coherence), and the second accepted a very limited notion of explanation.

It is well to point out that just as claims to community invited ethnography, so too the choice of ethnography could *presume* the existence of online community. Ethnography as a methodological tradition of hermeneutic engagement with lived cultures is always already wedded to the notion of a bounded community in which such cultures are grounded. There are interesting ironies here: in the early literature, ethnography was closely linked to the claim that online life could be investigated as an integral culture or social order in its own right; later uses of the term have pointed in exactly the opposite direction, to the need to contextualize online within offline (Hakken, 1999; Miller and Slater, 2000; 2002). The relation between ethnography and the online/offline distinction was further complicated by the deconstruction within anthropology of the very notion of a community that could be treated as bounded and 'other' to the observer (Clifford and George 1986; Clifford, 1988). In so far as the idea of virtual community either draws on romantic notions of a bounded community, or is contrasted with it (virtual communities replace or displace real organic face-to-face community), it adopts a version of community that is no longer current in the study of offline ones. The objects of contemporary ethnography are not bounded communities inhabited by people who are quite separate from 'us'. Rather they are distributed, multi-sited cultures, which are already highly mediated (rather than organic, face-to-face) and in profound contact with 'others' rather than bounded and pristine. This also means that both online and offline the relation between culture and place is not something that can be assumed (here's a culture: now study it); rather the complex construction of relations between culture and place are central to what an ethnography has to study. How does its object come to be defined in the first place?

These critiques have a two-pronged implication for ethnographies of online life. On the one hand, they cut the ground from under the assumption that Internet communities exist in any unproblematic sense or that we can know in advance what one is and then study it. On the other hand, they open up the field to notions of ethnography that are far more appropriate to the Internet as an object. A clear and sophisticated example is Christine Hine's *Virtual Ethnography* (2000), which tries to investigate the formation of an online network of participants in a political issue (the Louise Woodward affair) as an emergent and fluid property of social practices. For example, she highlights what could be termed a dialectical relationship between Internet as culture and as cultural artifact. Hine describes the various Internet media (newsgroups, WWW) as 'potentially diverse but locally stabilized' (2000: 12). The stability of these media as cultural artifacts is partly bound up with the fact that participants regard them as a social space in which they reflexively monitor their own and others' performances. One's sense of what a good website or newsgroup communication is depends on monitoring what other people are doing *online* as well as on the place of these technologies in one's offline life. Her study looks at how:

The Internet has routinely been employed by its users to monitor their own interpretations in the light of other users' interpretations. It has been treated as a performative space in which users need to act appropriately. Through this, the technology is stabilized by users themselves. The social relations which form on the Internet stabilize the technology and encourage its users to understand it in particular ways. (2000: 12)

Nonetheless, the question of whether a purely online ethnography is methodologically defensible is fraught. On the one hand, the grounds for rejecting it are often seriously wrong-headed. For example, they often rest on misguided and romantic comparison with face-to-face interaction. This has a long history within ethnography: the authenticity and even heroic encounter of the ethnographer with the Other is treated as a direct and unmediated relationship with their brute reality. Yet it is obvious that physical presence is no guarantee of truth, nor is mediated presence necessarily untrue – especially if that is what one is actually studying. This connects with a second issue, the veracity and verification of claims made online: informants may lie about various aspects of their identity, undetectably. This is obviously a more serious problem in a context which is famous for identity play, in which distortion of identity has little negative consequence for participants. In fact, however, it is entirely unclear and unproven that this is a good characterization of cyberspace in general: it is precisely what needs to be studied, not presumed (see Baym, Chapter 4). So long as it is presumed by critics of any online study, it can mean applying far higher standards of reliability to investigating this object as opposed to others. One could question every returned form in a mailed survey as to whether the respondent really was a man, or a teenager, etc. The common-sense assumption would be that doubt only arises where there is some reason to lie or pretend. In the case of cyber ethnographies, similarly, questions arise where there might be some point in lying about one's gender, and where the truth or falsity of that claim has some bearing. A simple example: if one is studying how a particular discursive space is organized in cyberspace, the gendering of the performed identities might be crucial, but not their offline identities. On the other hand, if one were trying to understand *why* certain performances arose, then actual genders might be crucial. And the fact that it is crucial to the researcher is still to be distinguished from the question of whether it is salient to the participants and therefore might give grounds for doubt. The point here is not to argue for or against giving anyone the benefit of the doubt but simply to say that – as in any research situation – the researcher has to make judgements and rules on the basis of situation-specific knowledge and thinking.

The crucial methodological question about the online/offline relationship, however, lies at another level: questions about the adequacy of descriptions and explanations. Do we need offline information in order to make sense of so-called online sociality? And the answer is: it depends on the question. An investigation into the question of 'How are cyberspaces sustained?' is obviously capable of widely different constructions. Rather like the distinction between macro- and micro-sociology, at one extreme, it might take in the political economy of access, differential IT skills and the kinds of material and symbolic power that enable only some people to participate, under particular social conditions, hence structuring the kinds of communication and sociality that go on there. At the other extreme, we can legitimately bracket these questions in order to describe (rather than explain) the mechanisms by which those who are able to participate sustain an internally coherent sociality, following them outwards to other media, or offline, as this seems ethnographically relevant. The relationship between online and offline is therefore methodologically negotiable in terms of criteria of relevance and levels of analysis.

Finally, it is worth pointing out that ethnographically the distinction between offline and online does not clearly map onto the distinction between actual and virtual (as discussed further, below). Participants may treat some of their online activity as virtual, some as real. For example, it is a commonplace of using the new media that in one window one may be telling someone about what is happening in another window; the former is accorded a reality status from which the participant can comment on the 'virtual' action going on in the latter. Rather than a single online/offline or virtual/real distinction, what we are dealing with is more in line with Goffman's (1986) frame analysis.

DECONSTRUCTION AND CONVERGENCE OF ONLINE AND OFFLINE

The issue for this chapter has not been the 'effects' of the online on the offline or vice versa. Rather, the issue is how the distinction between the two has been constitutive of so many understandings of the Internet and its sociological significance and social innovation. What has been interesting is that both proponents and critics of the Internet have largely encountered it as something which stands outside offline realities. This focus has had good and bad points. On the one hand, it focuses attention on the media-specific and is a way of unearthing the radical potentials of the new technology (shall we become posthuman?); on the other hand, these very gains have also been losses in trying to understand and explain how the new potentials are actually used, for that requires attention to the continuities between the offline and online: a focus on the conditions and contexts of Internet use.

The implication of this discussion is that virtuality should be investigated not as a property of new media (indeed, any media) but rather as a possible social accomplishment of people using these media. The important questions are *whether* new media users make a distinction between online and offline, and if they do, *when* and *why* do they do it, and *how* they accomplish it practically. It is the making of the distinction that needs studying, rather than assuming it exists and then studying its consequences. An obvious corollary of regarding virtuality as practice is that any boundary drawn between online and offline will always be contingent, variable and unstable. This is true both historically and within specific interactions. We will take up this contingency under three different aspects: first, connections between communicative channels; second, the relation between medium and context; and third, changing social structures.

Use of the online/offline distinction often assumes, bizarrely, an opposition between CMC on the one hand and face-to-face, embodied interaction on the other. At the same time, there is an assumption that 'virtuality' maps onto the former, 'reality' onto the latter. This is obviously far too simple: conversations and MUDs hardly exhaust the communicative contexts of modernity. In fact, new media exist within a far wider mediascape that already blurs the online/offline distinction in diverse ways. For example, in Slater's sexpics research, informants who engaged in cybersex relationships often also engaged in phone sex. This could mean that virtuality is not restricted to being online, but can embrace, and even link, several media (the same point is made by those who cannot see any difference between penpals and cyber-relationships). Conversely, people moving from Internet chat to phone sex could regard this as a move from the virtual to the real. The move to telephone was seen as rendering the relationship more embodied and 'real': the 'grain of the voice' gave an authenticity to the other's presence, but also allowed verification of some identity claims (yes, she really is a woman, doesn't seem to be American, sounds like she could be twenty-something). Finally, different media within 'the Internet' might be integrated with other media in different ways in different relations to the online/offline distinction: erotic use of IRC was compatible with entirely non-sexual use of e-mail and ICQ (or, more often, people set up separate accounts, channels, lists, etc. for different activities).

That is to say, first, virtuality does not adequately capture the variety of online/offline contexts, and does not map onto them in a stable way. Second, even the term 'online' might not map consistently onto a single media technology. The telephone could legitimately be seen as part of the online experience in some circumstances, and that experience might or might not be regarded as a virtual one. This complexity is obviously compounded both by technical change and by users' increasingly sophisticated assimilation of new media into everyday life. For example, the merging of the PDA and the mobile phone, or of Internet and television, or of telephone and computer through voice over IP, might make it impossible to use the term 'online' meaningfully in the sense that was employed by the first generation of Internet research. These real potentials for convergence might be argued *either* to broaden what we mean by online, or – quite the opposite – to reduce any sense of 'the online' by integrating new media into a broader mediascape. This blurring of the online/offline distinction by producers reconfiguring technologies is complemented by users' often unpredictable ways of relating technologies to everyday life (as well as there own re-programming of technologies).

To move to the second aspect, we can also put this in broader methodological terms. The relationship between online and offline is sometimes interpreted as the relationship between phenomenon and context. Hence putting the Internet in context might mean placing the online into the offline (e.g. Hakken, 1999). This can be quite reductive: the offline is treated as that which makes sense of, or explains, the online. Again, this would seem to travesty both ethnography and most contemporary science studies (e.g., Bijker and Law, 1992; Latour, 1999; Silverstone and Hirsch, 1992; see Miller and Slater, 2002). Putting the online into the offline reifies both: it assumes a thing called the Internet and a thing called society, or community, or social relations, and at best investigates how one affects the other. The point developed above is to break down the dualism and see how each configures the other. We might take as an example a place that looks like a self-evident context in which the offline meets the online: the cybercafé. And yet the cybercafé is not a simple context in which the new media are used; it is in fact a diverse social field which reconfigures the Internet in different ways and is in turn reconfigured by it. For example, Wakeford (1999) examines the production of different Internets in terms of the different socialities enacted by different kinds of cybercafés, in particular in relation to gender. We can compare this with Miller and Slater (2002), in which two different cybercafés involved the construction of quite different relations between the online and offline. In the first, the Internet was largely regarded as a tool of community development and skilling which prioritized offline projects and relationships and focused on the instrumental use of websites, multimedia software and e-mail. In the second, the focus was on extensive sociality through chat systems: online and offline relationships seemed to exist on one seamless plane.

Different contexts, different Internets; but also, different Internets, different contexts.

Finally, while various forms of convergence and interpenetration of media and contexts destabilize the online/offline distinction, there are also powerful regulatory forces operating on it. For example, many of the central political measures which are currently reformulating Internet use are being implemented specifically *in order* to remove the distinction between online and offline identities and social relations. Commercial and political use of the Internet requires that online participants are established as legal subjects with rights and responsibilities. Their unity as legal subjects needs to be verified through such things as electronic signatures and encryption; secure means of payment and financial verification (e.g. credit card transactions); definition and enforcement of copyright, taxation and the honouring of contracts. In contrast to cyberlibertarian discourses, it seems clear that the potential to establish multiple, mobile, fragmented identities, and to treat them as real, is in fact decided by offline regulatory regimes and generally in the direction of legal fixity. That is to say, the general tendency is to to assimilate online to offline and erase the distinction. The reality status of an on-line relationship is therefore complex in any particular instance and subject to broader institutional/ legal arrangements. Offering your credit card number and clicking 'submit' makes for a legally binding transaction, as 'real' as if it were face to face. On the other hand, it would be hard to imagine law courts awarding palimony to an online sexual partner after the relationship ended. Or not just now; there is a widely shared prophetic assumption, which might be self-fulfilling, that relationships which are treated as virtual today will become increasingly accepted and end up being regarded as real and binding. This may be true, but we need to understand the particular social grounds upon which ontological, legal or ethical status is accorded to such relationships.

Business organization, taking up the possibilities of e-commerce, also seems to move in the direction of integrating online and offline. The term 'clicks and mortar' – denoting a company that has both online and offline presence, both websites and shops – indicates that firms are having to rethink their relationship rather than assume their separation. Some companies are concerned to translate their offline symbolic and material capital (brand name and stock) into a significant online presence; others move in the opposite direction, capitalizing on web-based reputation and turnover. As in general, virtuality is a matter of social practices, and in the case of e-commerce the existence of an online/offline distinction may well be the result of marketing strategy: for example, there are new online banks that erase visible connection to the well-established offline banks that own them, in order to attract a different clientele. Similarly, the buzzword of 'disintermediation' is about using web-based facilities to bring consumers directly into the management systems of the firm: querying inventory, order tracking, customer services and so on. Although this invokes the rhetoric of a frictionless, dematerialized economy and virtual relationships, it is a very material knitting of the consumer into communications systems, which happen to cut out the 'middlemen' and hence massively reduce transaction costs. On the other hand, the fact that much political and commercial regulation moves in the direction of integrating online and offline does not mean that it simply reduces the online to *pre-existing* offline relations and identities.

CONCLUSION

The line of argument advanced here is certainly not specific to Internet studies: radio, television and telephone have equally to be understood through their particular appropriations. Television watched by an isolated Euro-American couch potato is arguably rather more virtual, for example, than a television in the communal setting of a Mexican taverna or a student common room. Further, as noted above, there is some evidence that new forms of mediation are historically first experienced as 'virtual' in that they seem to replace or mediate other forms of mediation which have historically been established as 'real'. Why *do* people seem to think that telephones are more real than internet chats? At the same time, the enormous social salience of notions of virtuality and cyberspace in relation to the Internet indeed seems to point to something media specific. Not media-specific characteristics, but rather (as noted earlier) a historically and geographically locatable convergence of politics with an investment in defining the Internet as a 'space apart'.

It seems perfectly valid to treat the online/ offline distinction as part of a transitional phase for both users and researchers. It was a way for both to think through the communicative potentials and specificities of a range of new media in the process of seeing how to assimilate them into a wide range of social practices and institutions. It is more than likely that the online/offline distinction will be regarded as rather quaint and not quite comprehensible inside ten years. Users and researchers are already well advanced in the process of disaggregating 'the Internet' into its diversity of technologies and uses, generating a media landscape in which virtuality is clearly not a feature of the media but one social practice of media use amongst many others.

Moreover, as we have stressed throughout, the shift away from 'virtuality' is not merely a matter of research agendas, but also of the evolving practices of users as well as of commercial and legal regulatory structures. Real social diversity and change in the shaping of the online/offline distinction means that there is a desperate need, firstly, for ethnographic research that is attentive both to rich particularity and 'holistic' understanding of social relationships; and, secondly, for comparative and historical ethnography. It is fairly pointless to look abstractly for correlations between the variables of media 'characteristics' and communicative practices when participants are busily redefining both across times and places.

REFERENCES

Agre, P.E. and Schuler, D. (eds) (1997) *Reinventing Technology, Rediscovering Community: Critical Studies in Computing as a Social Practice*: Ablex.

Anderson, B. (1986) *Imagined Communities*. London: Verso.

Barbrook, R. (1999) *The hi-tech Gift economy* http://www.firstmonday.dk/issus/issue3 12/barbrook/index.html

Bassett, C. (1997) 'Virtually gendered: life in an online world', in K. Gelder and S. Thornton (eds), *The Subcultures Reader*. London: Routledge.

Bauman, Z. (1990) *Thinking Sociologically*. Oxford: Basil Blackwell.

Baym, N. K. (1996) 'The Emergence of Community in Computer-Mediated Communication', in R. Shields (ed.), *Cultures of Internet: Virtual Spaces, Real Histories, Living Bodies*, London: Sage: 138–163.

Bijker, W. E. and Law, J. (eds) (1992) *Shaping technology/building society: Studies in Sociotechnical change*. Cambridge, MA: MIT Press.

Borden, D. L. and Harvey, K. (eds) (1998) *The Electronic Grapevine: Rumor, Reputation and Reporting in the New On-Line Environment*. Mahwah, NJ: L Erlbaum Associates.

Brown, S.L. (1997) 'The free market as salvation from government: the anarcho-capitalist view', in J.G. Carrier (ed.), *Meanings of the Market: the Free Market in Western Culture*. Oxford: Berg.

Bruckman, A. and Resnick, M. (1993) *Virtual professional community: Results from MediaMoo*. ftp media.mit.edu in pub/MediaMoo/Papers/Media Moo3 cyberconf.

Butler, J. (1990) *Gender Trouble: Feminism and the Subversion of Identity*. London: Routledge.

Butler, J. (1993) *Bodies That Matter*. London: Routledge.

Castells, M. (1996) *The Rise of Network Society*. Oxford: Blackwell.

Cherny, L. (1999) *Conversation and community: Chat in a virtual world*, Stanford, CA: CSLI Publications.

Clifford, J. (1988) *The Predicament of Culture: Twentieth Century Ethnography, Literature and Art*. London: Harvard University Press.

Clifford, J.M. and George, E. (eds) (1986) *Writing Culture: the Poetics and Politics of Ethnography*. London: University of California Press.

Crang, P. (1997) 'Introduction: cultural turns and the (re)constitution of economic geography', in R. Lee and J. Wills (eds), *Geographies of Economies*. London: Arnold.

Danet, B. (1998) 'Text as Mask: Gender, Play and Performance on the Internet', in S.G. Jones (ed.), *Cybersociety 2.0: Revisiting Computer-Mediated Communication and Technology*. London: Sage.

Danet, B. (2001) *Cyberpl@y: Communicating Online*. Oxford: Berg.

Dibbell, J. (1994) 'A rape in cyberspace; or, how an evil clow, a Haitian trickster spirit, two wizards, and a cast of dozens turned a database into a society', in M. Dery (ed.), *Flame Wars: the Discourse of Cyberculture*. London: Duke University Press.

Dibbell, J. (1998) *My Tiny Life: Crime and Passion in a Virtual World*. New York: Henry Holt.

Dijk, J. V. (1998) 'The reality of virtual communities', *Trends in Communication* 1(1): 39–63.

Dodge, M. and Kitchen, R. (2000) *Mapping Cyberspace*. London: Routledge.

Fine, G. A. (1983) *Shared Fantasy: Role-Playing Games as Social Worlds,* Chicago: University of Chicago Press.

Gibson, W. (1984) *Necromancer*. London: Gollanz.

Giddens, A. (1990) *The Consequences of Modernity*. Cambridge: Polity.

Goffman, E. (1986) *Frame Analysis*: Northeastern University Press.

Hakken, D. (1999) *Cyborgs@Cyberspace*. New York: Routledge.

Hamman, R. (1996) *Cyborpasms: Cybersex Amongst Multiple-Selves and Cyborgs in the Narrow-Bandwidth Space of America Online Chat Rooms*, University of Essex.

Haraway, D. (1990) 'A manifesto for cyborgs: science, technology and socialist feminism in the 1980s', in L. Nicholson (ed.), *Feminism/Postmodernism*. London: Routledge.

Hayles, N.K. (1999) *How We Became Posthuman: Virtual Bodies in Cybernetics, Literature, and Informatics*. Chicago: University of Chicago Press.

Hine, C. (2000) *Virtual Ethnography*. London: Sage.

Imken, O. (1999) 'The convergence of virtual and actual in the Global Matrix', in M. Crang, P. Crang and J. May (eds), *Virtual Geographies: Bodies and Spaces, Relations*. London: Routledge.

Jones, S.G. (ed.) (1995) *CyberSociety: Computer-Mediated Communication and Community*. London: Sage.

Kitchen, R. (1998) *Cyberspace: the World in the Wires*. Chichester: Wiley.

Kling, R. (1996) 'Social Relationships in Electronic Forums. Hangouts, Salons, Workplaces and Communities', *CMC Magazine*, 3(7).

Kuhn, A. (1982) *Women's Pictures: Feminism and Cinema*. London: Routledge & Kegan Paul.

Latour, B. (1999) *Pandora's Hope*. Cambridge: Harvard University Press.

Lupton, D. (1995) 'The embodied computer/user', in M. Featherstone and R. Burrows (eds), *Cyberspace, Cyberbodies, Cyberpunk: Cultures of Technological Embodiment*. London: Routledge.

MacCabe, C. (1985) 'Realism and the cinema: notes on some Brechtian themes', in T. Bennett, S. Boyd-Bowman, C. Mercer and J. Woollacott (eds), *Popular Television and Film*. London: BFI.

Maffesoli, M. (1996) *The Time of the Tribes*. London: Sage.

Markham, A. (1998) *Life Online: Researching Real Experience in Virtual Space*. London: Sage.

Marvin, C. (1988) *When Old Technologies Were New*. New York: Oxford University Press.

McLuhan, M. (1974) *Understanding Media*. London: Abacus.

Miller, D. and Slater, D. (2000) *The Internet: an Ethnographic Approach*. London: Berg.

Miller, D. and Slater, D. (2002) 'Cybercafés', in M. Johnson (ed.), *Internet Ethnographies*. Oxford: Berg.

Mulgan, G. (1998) *Connexity: Responsibility, Freedom, Business and Power in the New Century*. London: Vintage.

Plant, S. (1995) 'The future looms: weaving women and cybernetics', in M. Featherstone and R. Burrows (eds), *Cyberspace, Cyberbodies, Cyberpunk: Cultures of Technological Embodiment*. London: Routledge.

Plant, S. (1996) 'On the matrix: cyberfeminist solutions', in R. Shields (ed.), *Cultures of Internet: Virtual Spaces, Real Histories, Living Bodies*. London: Sage.

Plant, S. (1997) *Zeros and Ones: Digital Women and the New Technoculture*. London: Fourth Estate.

Poster, M. (1995a) *CyberDemocracy: Internet and the Public Sphere*. Available at: http://www.hnet.uci.edu/mposter/writings/democ.html.

Poster, M. (1995b) 'Postmodern virtualities', in M. Featherstone and R. Burrows (eds), *Cyberspace, Cyberbodies, Cyberpunk: Cultures of Technological Embodiment*. London: Routledge.

Reid, E. (1991) *Electropolis: Communication and Community of Internet Relay Chat*.

Reid, E. (1995) 'Virtual worlds: culture and imagination', in S. G. Jones (ed.), *Cybersociety: Computer-Mediated Communication and Community*. London: Sage.

Rheingold, H. (1993) *The Virtual Community: Homesteading on the Electronic Frontier*. Reading, MA: Addison-Wesley.

Rival, L., Slater, D. and Miller, D. (1998) 'Sex and sociality: comparative ethnography of sexual objectification', *Theory, Culture and Society*, 15 (3–4): 295–322.

Robins, K. (1995) 'Cyberspace and the world we live in', in M. Featherstone and R. Burrows (eds), *Cyberspace,*

Cyberbodies, Cyberpunk: Cultures of Technological Embodiment. London: Routledge.

Ross, A. (1998) *Real Love: in Pursuit of Cultural Justice*. New York: New York University Press.

Shields, R. (2000) 'Performing virtualities: virtual spaces?', *Space and Culture* 4 (5).

Slater, D.R. (1998) 'Trading sexpics on IRC: embodiment and authenticity on the internet', *Body and Society*, 4 (4): 91–117.

Slater, D.R. (2000a) 'Consumption without scarcity: exchange and normativity in an internet setting', in P. Jackson, M. Lowe, D. Miller and F. Mort (eds), *Commercial Cultures: Economies, Practices, Spaces*. London: Berg. pp. 123–42.

Slater, D.R. (2000b) 'Political discourse and the politics of need: discourses on the good life in cyberspace', in L. Bennett and R. Entman (eds), *Mediated Politics*. Cambridge: Cambridge University Press.

Slater, D. R. (in press 200la) 'Making things real: ethics and order on the Internet', *Theory, Culture and Society* Special issue: Sociality/Materiality.

Slater, D. R. (in press 2002) 'Modernity under construction: building the Internet in Trinidad', in P. Brey, T. Misa and A. Rip (eds), *Modernity and Technology: The Empirical Turn*, Boston: MIT Press.

Slevin, J. (2000) *The Internet and Society*. Cambridge: Polity.

Smith, M. and Kollock, P. (eds) (1999) *Communities in Cyberspace*. London: Routledge.

Springer, C. (1991) 'The pleasure of the interface', *Screen*, 32 (3).

Springer, C. (1996) *Electronic Eros: Bodies and Desire in the Postindustrial Age*. Austin, Tx: University of Texas Press.

Standage, T. (1999) *The Victorian Internet: the Remarkable Story of the Telegraph and the Nineteenth Century's On-line Pioneers*. London: Penguin.

Thompson, J.B. (1995) *The Media and Modernity: A Social Theory of the Media*. Cambridge: Polity.

Turkle, S. (1984) *The Second Self: Computers and the Human Spirit*. London: Grafton.

Turkle, S. (1995) *Life on the Screen: Identity in the Age of the Internet*. New York: Simon & Schuster.

Wakeford, N. (1999) 'Gender and the landscapes of computing in an Internet cafe', in M. Crang, P. Crang and J. May (eds), *Virtual Geographies: Bodies and Spaces, Relations*. London: Routledge.

Ward, K. (2000) 'The emergence of the hybrid community: rethinking the physical/virtual dichotomy', *Space and Culture* 4/5.

Index